DECISION GUIDES

Graduate School

Graduate Schools in the U.S. 2003

THOMSON
PETERSON'S™
Australia • Canada • Mexico • Singapore • Spain • United Kingdom • United States

THOMSON
PETERSON'S

About The Thomson Corporation and Peterson's

With revenues approaching US$6 billion, The Thomson Corporation (www.thomson.com) is a leading global provider of integrated information solutions for business, education, and professional customers. Its Learning businesses and brands (www.thomsonlearning.com) serve the needs of individuals, learning institutions, and corporations with products and services for both traditional and distributed learning.

Peterson's, part of The Thomson Corporation, is one of the nation's most respected providers of lifelong learning online resources, software, reference guides, and books. The Education Supersite[SM] at www.petersons.com—the Internet's most heavily traveled education resource—has searchable databases and interactive tools for contacting U.S.-accredited institutions and programs. In addition, Peterson's serves more than 105 million education consumers annually.

For more information, contact Peterson's, 2000 Lenox Drive, Lawrenceville, NJ 08648; 800-338-3282; or find us on the World Wide Web at www.petersons.com/about.

ISSN 1528-5901
ISBN 0-7689-0937-6

Printed in Canada

10 9 8 7 6 5 4 3 2 1 04 03 02

Contents

How to Use This Book

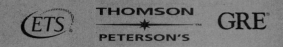

The 2003 edition of the *Decision Guides* marks the beginning of collaborative efforts between Peterson's and Educational Testing Service (ETS) and the Graduate Record Examinations (GRE) Board. This collaboration builds upon Peterson's survey research and publication capabilities and the GRE Program's long-term relationship with the graduate education community, including administration of the Graduate Record Examinations. This collaboration will enable a greater range of potential graduate students to access comprehensive information as they make decisions about pursuing graduate education. At the same time, it enables institutions to achieve greater promotion and awareness of their graduate offerings.

How to Use This Book

The graduate and professional programs in this *Decision Guide* are offered by colleges and universities in the United States and U.S. territories. They are accredited by U.S. accrediting bodies recognized by the Department of Education or the Council on Higher Education Accreditation. Each institution qualifies as a doctorate/research– or master's–level institution according to the *Carnegie Classification of Institutions of Higher Education*, and most are regionally accredited.

Information in this *Decision Guide* is presented in profile form. Each profile provides basic information about an institution. The format of the profiles is constant, making it easy to compare one institution with another and one program with another. Any item that does not apply to or was not provided by a graduate unit is omitted from its listing. Information about the overall institution comes first. Information about autonomous graduate units follows with lists of the specific graduate degree programs offered. For complex institutions that combine their graduate studies under a unified administrative structure, degrees may be listed under divisional subheadings.

Institution Information. The institution's name, city, and Web address make up the heading. The following paragraph begins with information about the institution's control, gender makeup of the student body, and category of institutional structure. The total figure for graduate, professional, and undergraduate student enrollment follows, including figures for full-time and part-time graduate students. Next comes the number of full-time and part-time faculty members. Information about the institution's computer services and library facilities follows. Graduate tuition and fee information for full-time and part-time students follows. (Please be aware that tuition can be different, and frequently higher, in specific graduate programs. You should always check with the particular program if a tuition difference will be a factor in your selection.) A general graduate program application contact and telephone number ends this first paragraph.

Graduate Units. The name of the unit is followed by the name and title of the head of the unit. Institutions have varying levels of discreteness in defining administrative units, and these are presented according to the information that the institution has provided to Peterson's. Each degree-program field of study offered by the unit is listed with abbreviations for all postbaccalaureate degrees awarded.

For Further Information

For many programs there is more in-depth narrative style information that can be located at www.petersons.com/graduate. There is a notation of the availability of this information at the end of the relevant profiles.

How This Information Was Gathered

The information published in this book was collected through *Peterson's Annual Survey of Graduate and Professional Institutions.* Each spring and summer, this survey is sent to more than 1,700 institutions offering postbaccalaureate degree programs, including accredited institutions in the United States and U.S. territories. (See article entitled Accreditation and Accrediting Agencies.) Deans and other administrators provide information on specific programs as well as overall institutional information. Peterson's editorial staff then goes over each returned survey carefully and verifies or revises responses after further research and discussion with administrators at the institutions. Extensive files on past responses are kept from year to year.

While every effort is made to ensure the accuracy and completeness of the data, information is sometimes unavailable or changes occur after publication deadlines. The omission of any particular item from a directory or profile signifies either that the item is not applicable to the institution or program or that information was not available. If no usable information was submitted by an institution, its name, address, and program name are still included in order to indicate the existence of graduate work.

The Admissions Process

Generalizations about graduate admissions practices are not always helpful because each institution has its own set of guidelines and procedures. Nevertheless, some broad statements can be made about the admissions process that may help you plan your strategy.

General Requirements

All graduate schools and departments have some requirements that applicants for admission must meet. Typically, these requirements include undergraduate transcripts (which provide information about undergraduate grade point average and course work applied toward a major), admission test scores, and letters of recommendation. In some fields, such as art and music, portfolios or auditions may be required in addition to other evidence of talent. Some institutions require that the applicant have an undergraduate degree in the same subject as the intended graduate major.

Most institutions evaluate each applicant on the basis of the applicant's total record, and the weight accorded any given factor varies widely from institution to institution and from program to program.

Admission Tests

Two major testing programs are used in graduate admissions: the Graduate Record Examinations (GRE) testing program, sponsored by the GRE Board and administered by Educational Testing Service, Princeton, New Jersey, and the Miller Analogies Test, produced by The Psychological Corporation, San Antonio, Texas.

The Graduate Record Examinations testing program consists of a General Test, eight Subject Tests, and a Writing Assessment. The General Test measures verbal, quantitative, and analytical reasoning skills. The test consists of three sections: a 30-minute verbal section, a 45-minute quantitative section, and a 60-minute analytical section. In addition, an unidentified verbal, quantitative, or analytical section that doesn't count toward a score may be included, and an identified research section that is not scored may also be included. The General Test is available on computer at convenient times throughout the year at test centers around the world.

The Subject Tests measure achievement and assume undergraduate majors or extensive background in the following eight disciplines:

- Biochemistry, Cell and Molecular Biology
- Biology
- Chemistry
- Computer Science
- Literature in English
- Mathematics
- Physics
- Psychology

Testing time is approximately 2 hours and 50 minutes. The Subject Tests are available at regularly scheduled paper-based administrations at test centers around the world.

The Writing Assessment measures proficiency in critical thinking and analytical writing ability. The test consists of two analytical writing tasks: a 45-minute "Present Your Perspective on an Issue" task and a 30-minute "Analyze an Argument" task. The Writing Assessment is available on computer at convenient times throughout the year at test centers around the world.

As of October 1, 2002, the General Test will be composed of verbal and quantitative sections and an analytical writing section. The verbal and quantitative sections will be unchanged from their present content. The analytical writing section will be identical to the Writing Assessment. The analytical measure will no longer be part of the General Test.

You can obtain more information about the GRE tests by consulting the *GRE Information and Registration Bulletin* or visiting the GRE Web site at www.gre.org. The *Bulletin* can be obtained at many undergraduate colleges. You can also download it from the GRE Web site or obtain it by contacting Graduate Record Examinations, Educational Testing Service, Princeton, NJ 08541-6000, telephone 1-609-771-7670.

If you expect to apply for admission to a program that requires any of the GRE tests, you should select a test date well in advance of the application deadline. Score reporting for the computer-based tests takes approximately ten to fifteen days. Score reporting for the paper-based tests takes approximately six weeks.

The Miller Analogies Test is administered at more than 600 licensed testing centers in the United States and Canada. Testing time is 50 minutes. The test consists entirely of analogies. You can obtain a list of test centers and a Bulletin of Information, which contains instructions for taking the test, by writing to The Psychological Corporation, Controlled Test Center, 555 Academic Court, San Antonio, Texas 78204.

Factors Involved in Selecting a Graduate School or Program

Selecting a graduate school and a specific program of study is a complex matter. Program and course offerings; the nature, size, and location of the institution; admission requirements; cost; and the availability of financial assistance are among the many factors that affect one's choice of institution. Other considerations are the quality of the faculty, the job placement and achievements of the program's graduates, and the institution's resources, such as libraries, laboratories, and computer facilities. If you are to make the best possible choice, you need to learn as much as you can about the schools and programs you are considering before you apply.

The following steps may help you narrow your choices.

- Talk to alumni of the programs or institutions you are considering to get their impressions of how well they were prepared for work in their fields of study.
- Remember that graduate school requirements change, so be sure to get the most up-to-date information possible.
- Talk to department faculty and the graduate adviser at your undergraduate institution. They often have information about programs of study at other institutions.
- Visit the Web sites of the graduate schools in which you are interested to request a graduate catalog. Contact the department chair in your chosen field of study for additional information about the department and the field.
- Visit as many campuses as possible. Call ahead for an appointment with the graduate adviser in your field of interest and be sure to check out the facilities and talk to students.

When and How to Apply

You should begin the application process at least one year before you expect to begin your graduate study. Find out the application deadline for each institution (many are provided in the profile section of this volume). Go to the institution Web site and find out if you can apply online. If not, request a paper application form. Fill out this form thoroughly and neatly. Assume that the school needs all the information it is requesting and that the admissions officer will be sensitive to the neatness and overall quality of what you submit. Do not supply more information than the school requires.

The institution may ask at least one question that will require a three- or four-paragraph answer. Compose your response on the assumption that the admissions officer is interested in both what you think and how you express yourself. Keep your statement brief and to the point, but, at the same time, include all pertinent information about your past experiences and your educational goals. Individual statements vary greatly in style and content, which helps admissions officers to differentiate among applicants. Many graduate departments give considerable weight to the statement in making their admissions decisions, so be sure to take the time to prepare a thoughtful and concise statement.

If recommendations are a part of the admissions requirements, choose carefully the individuals you ask to write them. It is generally best to ask current or former professors to write the recommendations, provided they are able to attest to your intellectual ability and motivation for doing the work required of a graduate student. It is advisable to provide stamped, preaddressed envelopes to people being asked to submit recommendations on your behalf.

Completed applications, including references and transcripts and admission test scores, should be received at the institution by the specified date.

Be advised that institutions do not usually make admissions decisions until all materials have been received. Enclose a self-addressed postcard with your application, requesting confirmation of receipt. Allow at least 10 days for the return of the postcard before making further inquiries.

If you plan to apply for financial support, it is imperative that you file your application early. See the Financial Support article, beginning on page 7.

How Admission Decisions Are Made

The program you apply to is directly involved in the admissions process. Although the final decision is usually made by the graduate dean (or an associate) or by the faculty admissions committee, recommendations from faculty members in your intended field are important. At some institutions, an interview is incorporated into the decision process.

A Special Note for International Students

In addition to the steps already described, there are some special considerations for international students who intend to apply for graduate study in the United States. All graduate schools require an indication of competence in English. The purpose of the Test of English as a Foreign Language (TOEFL) is to evaluate the English proficiency of people who are nonnative speakers of English and want to study at colleges and universities where English is the language of instruction. The TOEFL is administered by Educational Testing Service (ETS) under the general direction of a policy board established by the College Board and the Graduate Record Examinations Board.

The TOEFL is administered as a computer-based test throughout most of the world and is available year-round by appointment only. It is not necessary to have previous computer experience to take the test. The test consists of three sections—listening, reading, and writing. Total testing time is approximately 4 hours. The fee for the computer-based TOEFL is $110, which must be paid in U.S. dollars. The *Information Bulletin for Computer-Based Testing* contains information about the new testing format, registration procedures, and testing sites.

TOEFL will be offered in the paper-based format in the People's Republic of China and in low-volume testing areas. The paper-based TOEFL consists of three sections—listening comprehension, structure and written expression, and reading comprehension. Testing time is approximately 3 hours. The Test of Written English (TWE) is also given. TWE is a 30-minute essay that measures the examinee's ability to compose in English. Examinees receive a TWE score separate from their TOEFL score. The fee for the paper-based TOEFL is $110, which must be paid in U.S. dollars. There is no additional charge for TWE. The *Information Bulletin* contains information on local fees and registration procedures.

Additional information and registration materials are available from the TOEFL Program Office, P.O. Box 6151, Princeton, New Jersey 08541-6151. Telephone: 609-771-7100. E-mail:

toefl@ets.org. World Wide Web: http://www.toefl.org.

International students should apply especially early because of the time lags associated with overseas mail. Furthermore, many United States graduate schools have a limited number of spaces for international students, and many more students apply than the schools can accommodate.

Most graduate schools in the United States require international applicants to submit a certification of support, which is a statement attesting to the applicant's financial resources for the period of graduate study. International students may find financial assistance from institutions so limited that students must be essentially self-supporting during graduate study.

Financial Support

The range of financial support at the graduate level is very broad. The following generalized descriptions will give you an idea of what you might expect and what will be expected of you as a financial support recipient.

Fellowships, Scholarships, and Grants

These are usually outright awards of a few hundred to many thousands of dollars with no service to the institution required in return. Fellowships and scholarships are usually awarded on the basis of merit and are highly competitive. Grants are made on the basis of financial need or special talent in a field of study. Many grants not only cover tuition, fees, and supplies but also include stipends for living expenses with allowances for dependents. However, the terms of each grant should be examined because some do not permit recipients to supplement their income with outside work. Fellowships, scholarships, and grants may vary in the number of years for which they are awarded.

Assistantships and Internships

Teaching Assistantships

These usually provide a salary and full or partial tuition remission, and they may also provide health benefits. Unlike fellowships, scholarships, and grants, which require no service to the institution, teaching assistantships require recipients to provide the institution with a specific amount of undergraduate teaching, ideally related to the student's field of study. Some teaching assistants are limited to grading papers, compiling bibliographies, or monitoring laboratories. At some graduate schools, teaching assistants must carry lighter course loads than regular full-time students.

Research Assistantships

These are very similar to teaching assistantships in the manner in which financial assistance is provided. The difference is that recipients are given basic research assignments in their disciplines rather than teaching responsibilities. The work required is normally related to the student's field of study; in most instances, the assistantship supports the student's thesis or dissertation research.

Administrative Internships

These are similar to assistantships in application of financial assistance funds, but the student is given an assignment on a part-time basis, usually as a special assistant to one of the university's administrative officers. The assignment may not necessarily be directly related to the recipient's discipline.

Dormitory and Counseling Assistantships

These are frequently assigned to graduate students in psychology, counseling, and social work. Duties can vary from being available in a dean's office for a specific number of hours for consultation with undergraduates to living in campus residences and being responsible for both counseling and administrative tasks or advising student activity groups. Dormitory assistantships sometimes include room and board in addition to tuition and stipends.

The GI Bill

This provides financial assistance for students who are veterans of the United States armed forces. If you are a veteran, contact your local Veterans Administration office to determine your eligibility and to get full details about benefits.

Loans

Most graduate students, except those pursuing Ph.D.'s in certain fields, borrow to finance their graduate programs. There are basically two sources of student loans—the federal government and private loan programs. You should read and understand the terms of these loan programs before submitting your loan application.

Federal Loans

Federal Stafford Loans. The Federal Stafford Loan Program offers government-sponsored, low-interest loans to students through a private lender such as a bank, credit union, or savings and loan association.

There are two components of the Federal Stafford Loan program. Under the *subsidized* component of the program, the federal government pays the interest accruing on the loan while you are enrolled in graduate school on at least a half-time basis. Under the *unsubsidized* component of the program, you pay the interest on the loan from the day proceeds are issued. Eligibility for the federal subsidy is based on demonstrated financial need as determined by the financial aid office from the information you provide on the Free Application for Federal Student Aid (FAFSA). (See "Applying for Need-Based Financial Aid," below, for more information on the FAFSA.) A cosigner is not required, since the loan is not based on creditworthiness.

Although Unsubsidized Federal Stafford Loans may not be as desirable as Subsidized Federal Stafford Loans from the consumer's perspective, they are a useful source of support for those who may not qualify for the subsidized loans or who need additional financial assistance.

Graduate students may borrow up to $18,500 per year through the Stafford Loan Program, up to a maximum of $138,500, including undergraduate borrowing. This may include up to $8500 in Subsidized Stafford Loans, depending on eligibility, up to a maximum of $65,000, including undergraduate borrowing. The amount of the loan borrowed through the Unsubsidized Stafford Program equals the total amount of the loan (as much $18,500) minus your eligibility for a Subsidized Stafford Loan (as much as $8500). You may borrow up to the cost of the school in which you are enrolled or will attend, minus estimated financial assistance from other federal, state, and private sources, up to a maximum of $18,500.

The interest rate for the Federal Stafford Loans varies annually and is set every July. The rate during in-school, grace, and deferment periods is based on the 91-Day U.S. Treasury Bill rate plus 1.7 percent, capped at 8.25 percent. The rate during repayment is based on the 91-Day U.S. Treasury Bill rate plus 2.3 percent, capped at 8.25 percent. The 2001–02 rate was 6.39 percent.

Two fees may be deducted from the loan proceeds upon disbursement: a guarantee fee of up to 1 percent, which is deposited in an insurance pool to ensure repayment to the lender if the borrower defaults, and a federally mandated 3 percent origination fee, which is used to offset the administrative cost of the Federal Stafford Loan Program.

Under the *subsidized* Federal Stafford Loan Program, repayment begins six months after your last enrollment on at least a half-time basis. Under the *unsubsidized* program, repayment of interest begins within thirty days from disbursement of the loan proceeds, and repayment of the principal begins six months after your last enrollment on at least a half-time basis. Some lenders may require that some payments be made even while you are in school, although most lenders will allow you to defer payments and will add the accrued interest to the loan balance. Under both components of the program repayment may extend over a maximum of ten years with no prepayment penalty.

Federal Direct Loans. Some schools participate in the Department of Education's Direct Lending Program instead of offering Federal Stafford Loans. The two programs are essentially the same except that with the Direct Loans, schools themselves generate the loans with funds provided from the federal government. Terms and interest rates are virtually the same except that there are a few more repayment options with Federal Direct Loans.

Federal Perkins Loans. The Federal Perkins Loan is a long-term loan available to students demonstrating financial need and is administered directly by the school. Not all schools have these funds, and some may award them to undergraduates only. Eligibility is determined from the information you provide on the FAFSA. The school will notify you of your eligibility.

Eligible graduate students may borrow up to $6000 per year, up to a maximum of $40,000, including undergraduate borrowing (even if your previous Perkins Loans have been repaid). The interest rate for Federal Perkins Loans is 5 percent, and no interest accrues while you remain in school at least half-time. There are no guarantee, loan, or disbursement fees. Repayment begins nine months after your last enrollment on at least a half-time basis and may extend over a maximum of ten years with no prepayment penalty.

Deferring Your Federal Loan Repayments. If you borrowed under the Federal Stafford Loan Program or the Federal Perkins Loan Program for previous undergraduate or graduate study, some of your repayments may be deferred (i.e., suspended) when you return to graduate school, depending on when you borrowed and under which program.

There are other deferment options available if you are temporarily unable to repay your loan. Information about these deferments is provided at your entrance and exit interviews. If you believe you are eligible for a deferment of your loan repayments, you must contact your lender to complete a deferment form. The deferment must be filed prior to the time your repayment is due, and it must be refiled when it expires if you remain eligible for deferment at that time.

Supplemental Loans

Many lending institutions offer supplemental loan programs and other financing plans, such as the ones described below, to students seeking assistance in meeting their expected contribution toward educational expenses.

If you are considering borrowing through a supplemental loan program, you should carefully consider the terms of the program and be sure to "read the fine print." Check with the program sponsor for the most current terms that will be applicable to the amounts you intend to borrow for graduate study. Most supplemental loan programs for graduate study offer unsubsidized, credit-based loans. In general, a credit-ready borrower is one who has a satisfactory credit history or no credit history at all. A creditworthy borrower generally must pass a credit test to be eligible to borrow or act as a cosigner for the loan funds.

Many supplemental loan programs have a minimum annual loan limit and a maximum annual loan limit. Some offer amounts equal to the cost of attendance minus any other aid you will receive for graduate study. If you are planning to borrow for several years of graduate study, consider whether there is a cumulative or aggregate limit on the amount you may borrow. Often this cumulative or aggregate limit will include any amounts you borrowed and have not repaid for undergraduate or previous graduate study.

The combination of the annual interest rate, loan fees, and the repayment terms you choose will determine how much you will repay over time. Compare these features in combination before you decide which loan program to use. Some loans offer interest rates that are adjusted monthly, some quarterly, some annually. Some offer interest rates that are lower during the in-school, grace, and deferment periods, and then increase when you begin repayment. Most programs include a loan "origination" fee, which is usually deducted from the principal amount you receive when the loan is disbursed, and must be repaid along with the interest and other principal when you graduate, withdraw from school, or drop below half-time study. Sometimes the loan fees are reduced if you borrow with a qualified cosigner. Some programs allow you to defer interest and/or principal payments while you are enrolled in graduate school. Many programs allow you to capitalize your interest payments; the interest due on your loan is added to the outstanding balance of your loan, so you don't have to repay immediately, but this increases the amount you owe. Other programs allow you to pay the interest as you go, which will reduce the amount you later have to repay.

Federal Work-Study Program (FWS)

Employment is another way some students finance their graduate studies. The federally funded Federal Work-Study Program provides eligible students with employment opportunities, usually in public and private nonprofit organizations. Federal funds pay up to 75 percent of the wages, with the remainder paid by the employing agency. FWS is available to graduate students who demonstrate financial need. Not all schools have these funds, and some only award them to undergraduates. Each school sets its application deadline and work-study earnings limits. Wages vary and are related to the type of work done.

Private Student Loans

In addition to the federal loan programs, there are many private loan programs that can help graduate students. Most private loan programs disburse funds based on creditworthiness rather than financial need. Some loan programs target all types of graduate students; others are designed specifically for business, law, or medical students. In addition, you can use other types of private loans not specifically designed for education to help finance your graduate degree.

CitiAssist Loans. Offered by Citibank, these no-fee loans help graduate students fill the gap between the financial aid they receive and the money they need for school. Visit www.studentloan.com for more loan information from Citibank.

EXCEL Loan. This program, sponsored by Nellie Mae, is designed for students who are not ready to borrow on their own and wish to borrow with a creditworthy cosigner. Visit www.nelliemae.com for more information.

Key Alternative Loan. This loan can bridge the gap between education costs and traditional funding. Visit www.keybank.com for more information.

Graduate Access Loan. Sponsored by the Access Group, this is for graduate students enrolled at least half-time. The Web site is www.accessgroup.com.

Signature Student Loan. A loan program for students who are enrolled at least half-time, this is sponsored by Sallie Mae. Visit www.salliemae.com for more information.

Remember that these are generalized statements about financial assistance at the graduate level. Because each institution allots its aid differently, you should communicate directly with the school and the specific department of interest to you. It is not unusual, for example, to find that an endowment vested within a specific department supports one or more fellowships. You may fit its requirements and specifications precisely.

Applying for Need-Based Financial Aid

Schools that award federal and institutional financial assistance based on need will require you to complete the FAFSA and, in some cases, an institutional financial aid application.

If you are applying for federal student assistance, you **must** complete the FAFSA. A service of the U.S. Department of Education, it is free to all applicants. You must send the FAFSA to the address listed in the FAFSA instructions or you can apply online at http://www.fafsa.ed.gov.

After your FAFSA information has been processed, you will receive a Student Aid Report (SAR). If you are an entering student, you may want to make copies of the SAR and send them to the school(s) to which you are applying. If you are a continuing student, you should make a copy of the SAR and forward the original document to the school you are attending.

Follow the instructions on the FAFSA if your situation changes and you need to correct information reported on your original application.

If you would like more information on federal student financial aid, visit the FAFSA Web site or request *The Student Guide 2002–2003* from the following address: Federal Student Aid Information Center, P.O. Box 84, Washington, DC 20044.

The U.S. Department of Education also has a toll-free number for questions concerning federal student aid programs. The number is 1-800-4-FED AID (1-800-433-3243). If you are hearing impaired, call toll-free, 1-800-730-8913.

Accreditation and Accrediting Agencies

Colleges and universities in the United States, and their individual academic and professional programs, are accredited by nongovernmental agencies concerned with monitoring the quality of education in this country. Agencies with both regional and national jurisdictions grant accreditation to institutions as a whole, while specialized bodies acting on a nationwide basis—often national professional associations—grant accreditation to departments and programs in specific fields.

Institutional and specialized accrediting agencies share the same basic concerns: the purpose an academic unit—whether university or program—has set for itself and how well it fulfills that purpose, the adequacy of its financial and other resources, the quality of its academic offerings, and the level of services it provides. Agencies that grant institutional accreditation take a broader view, of course, and examine university-wide or college-wide services that a specialized agency may not concern itself with.

Both types of agencies follow the same general procedures when considering an application for accreditation. The academic unit prepares a self-evaluation, which focuses on the concerns mentioned above and includes an assessment of both its strengths and weaknesses; a team of representatives of the accrediting body reviews this evaluation, visits the campus, and makes its own report; and finally, the accrediting body makes a decision on the application. Often, even when accreditation is granted, the agency makes a recommendation regarding how the institution or program can improve. All institutions and programs are reviewed every few years to determine whether they continue to meet established standards; if they do not, they may lose their accreditation.

Accrediting agencies themselves are reviewed and evaluated periodically by the U.S. Department of Education and the Council for Higher Education Accreditation (CHEA). Agencies recognized adhere to certain standards and practices, and their authority in matters of accreditation is widely accepted in the educational community.

This does not mean, however, that accreditation is a simple matter, either for schools wishing to become accredited or for students deciding where to apply. Indeed, in certain fields the very meaning and methods of accreditation are the subject of a good deal of debate. **Those who are applying to graduate school should be aware of the safeguards provided by regional accreditation, especially in terms of degree acceptance and institutional longevity. Indeed, many institutions that offer graduate study will accept only those applicants whose undergraduate degree is from a regionally accredited institution.** (NOTE: Most institutions profiled in the *Decision Guides* are regionally accredited.) Beyond this, applicants should understand the role that specialized accreditation plays in their field, as this varies considerably from one discipline to another. In certain professional fields, it is necessary to have graduated from a program that is accredited in order to be eligible for a license to practice, and, in some fields, the federal government also makes this a hiring requirement.

Institutions and programs that present themselves for accreditation are sometimes granted the status of candidate for accreditation, or what is known as "preaccreditation." This may happen, for example, when an academic unit is too new to have met all the requirements for accreditation. Such status signifies initial recognition and indicates that the school or program in question is working to fulfill all requirements; it does not, however, guarantee that accreditation will be granted.

Readers are advised to contact agencies directly for answers to their questions about accreditation. The names and addresses of all agencies recognized by the U.S. Department of Education and the Council for Higher Education Accreditation are listed below.

Institutional Accrediting Agencies—Regional

MIDDLE STATES ASSOCIATION OF COLLEGES AND SCHOOLS

Accredits institutions in Delaware, District of Columbia, Maryland, New Jersey, New York, Pennsylvania, Puerto Rico, and the Virgin Islands.

Jean Avnet Morse, Executive Director
Commission on Higher Education
3624 Market Street
Philadelphia, Pennsylvania 19104-2680
Telephone: 215-662-5606
Fax: 215-662-5501
E-mail: jamorse@msache.org
World Wide Web: http://www.msache.org

NEW ENGLAND ASSOCIATION OF SCHOOLS AND COLLEGES

Accredits institutions in Connecticut, Maine, Massachusetts, New Hampshire, Rhode Island, and Vermont.

Charles M. Cook, Director
Commission on Institutions of Higher Education
209 Burlington Road
Bedford, Massachusetts 01730-1433
Telephone: 781-271-0022
Fax: 781-271-0950
E-mail: ccook@neasc.org
World Wide Web: http://www.neasc.org

NORTH CENTRAL ASSOCIATION OF COLLEGES AND SCHOOLS

Accredits institutions in Arizona, Arkansas, Colorado, Illinois, Indiana, Iowa, Kansas, Michigan, Minnesota, Missouri, Nebraska, New Mexico, North Dakota, Ohio, Oklahoma, South Dakota, West Virginia, Wisconsin, and Wyoming.

Steven D. Crow, Executive Director
The Higher Learning Commission
30 North LaSalle, Suite 2400
Chicago, Illinois 60602-2504
Telephone: 312-263-0456
Fax: 312-263-7462
E-mail: scrow@hlcommission.org
World Wide Web: http://www.ncahigherlearningcommission.org

NORTHWEST ASSOCIATION OF SCHOOLS AND COLLEGES

Accredits institutions in Alaska, Idaho, Montana, Nevada, Oregon, Utah, and Washington.

Sandra E. Elman, Executive Director
Commission on Colleges
11130 Northeast 33rd Place, Suite 120
Bellevue, Washington 98004
Telephone: 425-827-2005
Fax: 425-827-3395
E-mail: pjarnold@cocnasc.org
World Wide Web: http://www.cocnasc.org

SOUTHERN ASSOCIATION OF COLLEGES AND SCHOOLS

Accredits institutions in Alabama, Florida, Georgia, Kentucky, Louisiana, Mississippi, North Carolina, South Carolina, Tennessee, Texas, and Virginia.

James T. Rogers, Executive Director
Commission on Colleges
1866 Southern Lane
Decatur, Georgia 30033
Telephone: 404-679-4500
Fax: 404-679-4558
E-mail: jrogers@sacscoc.org
World Wide Web: http://www.sacscoc.org

WESTERN ASSOCIATION OF SCHOOLS AND COLLEGES

Accredits institutions in California, Guam, and Hawaii.

Ralph A. Wolff, Executive Director
The Senior College Commission
985 Atlantic Avenue, Suite 100
Alameda, California 94501
Telephone: 510-748-9001
Fax: 510-748-9797
E-mail: wascsr@wascsenior.org
World Wide Web: http://www.wascweb.org

Institutional Accrediting Agencies—Other

ACCREDITING COUNCIL FOR INDEPENDENT COLLEGES AND SCHOOLS

Dr. Steven A. Eggland, Executive Director
750 First Street, NE, Suite 980
Washington, D.C. 20002-4241
Telephone: 202-336-6780
Fax: 202-842-2593
E-mail: steve@acics.org
World Wide Web: http://www.acics.org

DISTANCE EDUCATION AND TRAINING COUNCIL
Michael P. Lambert, Executive Secretary
1601 Eighteenth Street, NW
Washington, D.C. 20009-2529
Telephone: 202-234-5100
Fax: 202-332-1386
E-mail: detc@detc.org
World Wide Web: http://www.detc.org

Specialized Accrediting Agencies

ACUPUNCTURE
Dort S. Bigg, Executive Director
Accreditation Commission for Acupuncture and Oriental Medicine
7501 Greenway Center Drive, Suite 820
Greenbelt, Maryland 20770
Telephone: 301-313-0855
Fax: 301-313-0913
E-mail: 73352.2467@compuserve.com
World Wide Web: http://www.ccaom.org

ART AND DESIGN
Samuel Hope, Executive Director
National Association of Schools of Art and Design
11250 Roger Bacon Drive, Suite 21
Reston, Virginia 20190
Telephone: 703-437-0700
Fax: 703-437-6312
E-mail: info@arts-accredit.org
World Wide Web: http://www.arts-accredit.org

CHIROPRACTIC
Paul D. Walker, Executive Vice President
The Council on Chiropractic Education
8049 North 85th Way
Scottsdale, Arizona 85258-4321
Telephone: 480-443-8877
Fax: 480-483-7333
E-mail: cce@adata.com
World Wide Web: http://www.cce-usa.org

CLINICAL LABORATORY SCIENCE
Olive M. Kimball, Executive Director
National Accrediting Agency for Clinical Laboratory Sciences
8410 West Bryn Mawr Avenue, Suite 670
Chicago, Illinois 60631-3415
Telephone: 773-714-8880
Fax: 773-714-8886
E-mail: info@naacls.org
World Wide Web: http://www.naacls.org

DANCE
Samuel Hope, Executive Director
National Association of Schools of Dance
11250 Roger Bacon Drive, Suite 21
Reston, Virginia 20190
Telephone: 703-437-0700
Fax: 703-437-6312
E-mail: info@arts-accredit.org
World Wide Web: http://www.arts-accredit.org

DENTISTRY
Laura M. Neumann, D.D.S., M.P.H., Associate Executive Director, Education
American Dental Association
211 East Chicago Avenue, 18th Floor
Chicago, Illinois 60611
Telephone: 312-440-2500
Fax: 312-440-2915
E-mail: neumannl@ada.org
World Wide Web: http://www.ada.org

EDUCATION
Arthur Wise, President
National Council for Accreditation of Teacher Education
2010 Massachusetts Avenue, NW
Washington, D.C. 20036-1023
Telephone: 202-466-7496
Fax: 202-296-6620
E-mail: ncate@ncate.org
World Wide Web: http://www.ncate.org

ENGINEERING
George D. Peterson, Executive Director
Accreditation Board for Engineering and Technology, Inc.
111 Market Place, Suite 1050
Baltimore, Maryland 21202-4102
Telephone: 410-347-7700
Fax: 410-625-2238
E-mail: accreditation@abet.org
World Wide Web: http://www.abet.org

ENVIRONMENT
National Environmental Health Science and Protection Accreditation Council
720 South Colorado Boulevard, Suite 970-S
Denver, Colorado 80246-1925
Telephone: 303-756-9090
Fax: 303-691-9490
E-mail: staff@neha.org
World Wide Web: http://www.neha.org/AccredCouncil.html

FORESTRY
Michele Harvey, Director, Science and Education
Committee on Education

Society of American Foresters
5400 Grosvenor Lane
Bethesda, Maryland 20814
Telephone: 301-897-8720 Ext. 119
Fax: 301-897-3690
E-mail: harveym@safnet.org
World Wide Web: http://www.safnet.org

HEALTH SERVICES ADMINISTRATION

Accrediting Commission on Education for Health Services Administration
730 11th Street, NW, Fourth Floor
Washington, DC 20001-4510
Telephone: 202-638-5131
Fax: 202-638-3429
E-mail: accredcom@aol.com
World Wide Web: http://monkey.hmi.missouri.edu/acehsa/

INTERIOR DESIGN

Kayem Dunn, Director
Foundation for Interior Design Education Research
146 Monroe Center, NW, Suite 1318
Grand Rapids, Michigan 49503-2822
Telephone: 616-458-0400
Fax: 616-458-0460
E-mail: fider@fider.org
World Wide Web: http://www.fider.org

JOURNALISM AND MASS COMMUNICATIONS

Susanne Shaw, Executive Director
Accrediting Council on Education in Journalism and Mass Communications
School of Journalism
Stauffer-Flint Hall
University of Kansas
Lawrence, Kansas 66045
Telephone: 785-864-3986
Fax: 785-864-5225
E-mail: sshaw@ukans.edu
World Wide Web: http://www.ukans.edu/~acejmc

LANDSCAPE ARCHITECTURE

Ronald C. Leighton, Accreditation Manager
Landscape Architectural Accreditation Board
American Society of Landscape Architects
636 Eye Street, NW
Washington, D.C. 20001-3736
Telephone: 202-898-2444
Fax: 202-898-1185
E-mail: rleighton@asla.org
World Wide Web: http://www.asla.org

LAW

Carl Monk, Executive Vice President and Executive Director
Accreditation Committee
Association of American Law Schools
1201 Connecticut Avenue, NW, Suite 800
Washington, D.C. 20036-2605
Telephone: 202-296-8851
Fax: 202-296-8869
E-mail: cmonk@aals.org
World Wide Web: http://www.aals.org

John A. Sebert, Consultant on Legal Education
American Bar Association
750 North Lake Shore Drive
Chicago, Illinois 60611
Telephone: 312-988-6738
Fax: 312-988-5681
E-mail: sebertj@staff.abanet.org
World Wide Web: http://www.abanet.org/legaled

LIBRARY

Ann L. O'Neill, Director
Office for Accreditation
American Library Association
50 East Huron Street
Chicago, Illinois 60611
Telephone: 800-545-2433
Fax: 312-440-9374
E-mail: aoneill@ala.org
World Wide Web: http://www.ala.org

MARRIAGE AND FAMILY THERAPY

Donald B. Kaveny, Director
American Association for Marriage and Family Therapy
1133 15th Street, NW, Suite 300
Washington, D.C. 20005-2710
Telephone: 202-452-0109
Fax: 202-223-2329
E-mail: dkaveny@aamft.org
World Wide Web: http://www.aamft.org

MEDICAL ILLUSTRATION

Alice Katz, Chair
Accreditation Review Committee for the Medical Illustrator
St. Luke's Hospital
Instructional Resources
232 South Woods Mill Road
Chesterfield, Missouri 63017
Telephone: 314-205-6158
Fax: 314-205-6144
World Wide Web: http://www.caahep.org/accreditation/ mi/mi_accreditation.htm

MEDICINE

Liaison Committee on Medical Education

The LCME is administered in even-numbered years, beginning each July 1, by:

David P. Stevens, M.D., Secretary
Association of American Medical Colleges
2450 N Street, NW
Washington, D.C. 20037
Telephone: 202-828-0596
Fax: 202-828-1125
E-mail: dstevens@amc.org
World Wide Web: http://www.lcme.org

The LCME is administered in odd-numbered years, beginning each July 1, by:

Frank Simon, M.D., Secretary
American Medical Association
515 North State Street
Chicago, Illinois 60610
Telephone: 312-464-4657
Fax: 312-464-5830
E-mail: frank_simon@assn.org
World Wide Web: http://www.ama-assn.org

MUSIC

Samuel Hope, Executive Director
National Association of Schools of Music
11250 Roger Bacon Drive, Suite 21
Reston, Virginia 20190
Telephone: 703-437-0700
Fax: 703-437-6312
E-mail: info@arts-accredit.org
World Wide Web: http://www.arts-accredit.org

NATUROPATHIC MEDICINE

Robert Lofft, Executive Director
Council on Naturopathic Medical Education
P.O. Box 11426
Eugene, Oregon 97440-3626
Telephone: 541-484-6028
E-mail: dir@cnme.org
World Wide Web: http://www.cnme.org

NURSE ANESTHESIA

Betty J. Horton, Director of Accreditation
Council on Accreditation of Nurse Anesthesia Educational Programs
222 South Prospect Avenue, Suite 304
Park Ridge, Illinois 60068-4010
Telephone: 847-692-7050
Fax: 847-693-7137
E-mail: bhorton@aana.com
World Wide Web: http://www.aana.com

NURSE MIDWIFERY

Betty Watts Carrington, Chair
Division of Accreditation
American College of Nurse-Midwives
818 Connecticut Avenue, NW, Suite 900
Washington, D.C. 20006
Telephone: 202-728-9860
Fax: 202-728-9897
E-mail: info@acnm.org
World Wide Web: http://www.midwife.org/educ

NURSING

Geraldene Felton, Executive Director
National League for Nursing
61 Broadway, 33rd Floor
New York, New York 10006
Telephone: 800-669-1656
Fax: 212-812-0393
E-mail: gfelton@nlnac.org
World Wide Web: http://www.nln.org

OCCUPATIONAL THERAPY

Doris Gordon, Director of Accreditation
American Occupational Therapy Association
4720 Montgomery Lane
P.O. Box 31220
Bethesda, Maryland 20824-1220
Telephone: 301-652-2682
TDD: 800-377-8555
Fax: 301-652-7711
E-mail: accred@aota.org
World Wide Web: http://www.aota.org

OPTOMETRY

Joyce Urbeck, Administrative Director
Council on Optometric Education
American Optometric Association
243 North Lindbergh Boulevard
St. Louis, Missouri 63141
Telephone: 314-991-4100
Fax: 314-991-4101
E-mail: urbeckcoe@aol.com
World Wide Web: http://www.aoanet.org

OSTEOPATHIC MEDICINE

John B. Crosby, Executive Director
American Osteopathic Association
142 East Ontario Street
Chicago, Illinois 60611
Telephone: 800-621-1773
Fax: 312-202-8200
E-mail: info@aoa-net.org
World Wide Web: http://www.aoa-net.org

PASTORAL EDUCATION

Gregory Stoddard, Chair
Accreditation Commission
Association for Clinical Pastoral Education, Inc.
1549 Clairmont Road, Suite 103
Decatur, Georgia 30033-4611

Telephone: 404-320-1472
Fax: 404-320-0849
E-mail: acpe@acpe.edu
World Wide Web: http://www.acpe.edu

PHARMACY

Peter H. Vlasses, Executive Director
American Council on Pharmaceutical Education
311 West Superior Street
Chicago, Illinois 60610
Telephone: 312-664-3575
Fax: 312-664-4652
E-mail: acpe@compuserve.com
World Wide Web: http://www.acpe-accredit.org

PHYSICAL THERAPY

Mary Jane Harris, Director
Department of Accreditation
American Physical Therapy Association
1111 North Fairfax Street
Alexandria, Virginia 22314-1488
Telephone: 800-999-2782/703-684-2782
TDD: 703-683-6748
Fax: 703-684-7343
E-mail: accreditation@apta.org
World Wide Web: http://www.apta.org

PLANNING

Beatrice Clupper, Director
American Institute of Certified Planners/Association of Collegiate Schools of Planning
Merle Hay Tower, Suite 302
3800 Merle Hay Road
Des Moines, Iowa 50310
Telephone: 515-252-0729
Fax: 515-252-7404
E-mail: fi_pab@netins.net
World Wide Web: http://netins.net/web/pab_fi66

PODIATRIC MEDICINE

Alan R. Tinkleman, Director
Council on Podiatric Medical Education
American Podiatric Medical Association
9312 Old Georgetown Road
Bethesda, Maryland 20814-2752
Telephone: 301-571-9200
Fax: 301-581-9299
E-mail: artinkleman@apma.org
World Wide Web: http://www.apma.org

PSYCHOLOGY AND COUNSELING

Susan F. Zlotlow, Director
Office of Program Consultation and Accreditation
American Psychological Association
750 First Street, NE
Washington, DC 20002
Telephone: 202-336-5979
Fax: 202-336-5978
E-mail: apaaccred@apa.org
World Wide Web: http://www.apa.org/ed/accred.html

Carol L. Bobby, Executive Director
Council for Accreditation of Counseling and Related Educational Programs
American Counseling Association
5999 Stevenson Avenue
Alexandria, Virginia 22304
Telephone: 703-823-9800
Fax: 703-823-0252
E-mail: cacrep@aol.com
World Wide Web: http://www.counseling.org/CACREP

PUBLIC AFFAIRS AND ADMINISTRATION

Michael A. Brintnall, Executive Director
Commission on Peer Review and Accreditation
National Association of Schools of Public Affairs and Administration
1120 G Street, NW, Suite 730
Washington, DC 20005
Telephone: 202-628-8965
Fax: 202-626-4978
E-mail: naspaa@naspaa.org
World Wide Web: http://www.naspaa.org

PUBLIC HEALTH

Patricia Evans, Executive Director
Council on Education for Public Health
800 Eye Street, NW, Suite 202
Washington, DC 20001-3710
Telephone: 202-789-1050
Fax: 202-789-1895
E-mail: patevans@ceph.org
World Wide Web: http://www.ceph.org

RABBINICAL AND TALMUDIC EDUCATION

Bernard Fryshman, Executive Vice President
Association of Advanced Rabbinical and Talmudic Schools
175 Fifth Avenue, Suite 711
New York, New York 10010
Telephone: 212-477-0950
Fax: 212-533-5335

REHABILITATION EDUCATION

Jeanne Patterson, Executive Director
Council on Rehabilitation Education
Commission on Standards and Accreditation
1835 Rohlwing Road, Suite E
Rolling Meadows, Illinois 60008

Telephone: 847-394-1785
Fax: 847-394-2108
E-mail: patters@polaris.net
World Wide Web: http://www.core-rehab.org

SOCIAL WORK
Nancy Randolph, Director
Division of Standards and Accreditation
Council on Social Work Education
1725 Duke Street, Suite 500
Alexandria, Virginia 22314-3457
Telephone: 703-683-8080
Fax: 703-683-8099
E-mail: info@cswe.org
World Wide Web: http://www.cswe.org

SPEECH-LANGUAGE PATHOLOGY AND AUDIOLOGY
Sharon Goldsmith, Director
American Speech-Language-Hearing Association
10801 Rockville Pike
Rockville, Maryland 20852
Telephone: 800-638-8255
Fax: 301-571-0457
E-mail: accreditation@asha.org
World Wide Web: http://www.asha.org/

THEATER
Samuel Hope, Executive Director
National Association of Schools of Theatre
11250 Roger Bacon Drive, Suite 21
Reston, Virginia 20190
Telephone: 703-437-0700
Fax: 703-437-6312
E-mail: info@arts-accredit.org
World Wide Web: http://www.arts-accredit.org/nast

THEOLOGY
Daniel O. Aleshire, Executive Director
Association of Theological Schools in the United States and Canada
10 Summit Park Drive
Pittsburgh, Pennsylvania 15275-1103
Telephone: 412-788-6505
Fax: 412-788-6510
E-mail: aleshire@ats.edu
World Wide Web: http://www.ats.edu

VETERINARY MEDICINE
Donald G. Simmons, Director of Education and Research Division
American Veterinary Medical Association
1931 North Meacham Road, Suite 100
Schaumburg, Illinois 60173
Telephone: 847-925-8070
Fax: 847-925-1329
E-mail: dsimmons@avma.org
World Wide Web: http://www.avma.org

Directory of Graduate and Professional Programs by Field

■ ACCOUNTING

Abilene Christian University M
Alabama State University M
American University M
Angelo State University M
Appalachian State University M
Arizona State University M,D
Auburn University M
Baldwin-Wallace College M
Ball State University M
Bayamón Central University M
Baylor University M
Bentley College M,O
Bernard M. Baruch College of the City University of New York M,D
Bloomsburg University of Pennsylvania M
Boise State University M
Boston University M,D,O
Bowling Green State University M
Bradley University M
Brenau University M
Bridgewater State College M
Brigham Young University M
Brooklyn College of the City University of New York M
California State University, Chico M
California State University, Fullerton M
California State University, Hayward M
California State University, Los Angeles M
California State University, Sacramento M
Canisius College M
Carnegie Mellon University D
Case Western Reserve University M,D
The Catholic University of America M
Central Michigan University M
Charleston Southern University M
City University M,O
Clark University M
Clemson University M
Cleveland State University M
The College of Saint Rose M
The College of William and Mary M
Colorado State University M
Columbia University M,D
Cornell University D
Dallas Baptist University M
Delta State University M
DePaul University M
Dominican University M
Drexel University M,D,O
Eastern College M
Eastern Connecticut State University M
Eastern Michigan University M
East Tennessee State University M
Edinboro University of Pennsylvania O
Fairfield University M,O
Fairleigh Dickinson University, Florham-Madison Campus M
Fairleigh Dickinson University, Teaneck–Hackensack Campus M
Florida Agricultural and Mechanical University M
Florida Atlantic University M
Florida Gulf Coast University M
Florida Institute of Technology M
Florida International University M
Florida State University M,D
Fordham University M
Fort Hays State University M
Gannon University O
The George Washington University M,D
Georgia Southern University M
Georgia State University M,D
Gonzaga University M
Governors State University M
Hawaii Pacific University M
Hofstra University M
Houston Baptist University M
Illinois State University M
Indiana University Bloomington M,D
Indiana University Northwest M,O
Indiana University South Bend M
Inter American University of Puerto Rico, Metropolitan Campus M
Inter American University of Puerto Rico, San Germán Campus M
Iowa State University of Science and Technology M
Jackson State University M
James Madison University M
Johnson & Wales University M
Kansas State University M
Kennesaw State University M
Kent State University M,D
King's College M
Lamar University M
Lehigh University M,D
Lehman College of the City University of New York M
Long Island University, Brooklyn Campus M
Long Island University, C.W. Post Campus M
Louisiana State University and Agricultural and Mechanical College M,D
Louisiana Tech University M,D
Loyola University Chicago M
Marquette University M
Maryville University of Saint Louis M,O
Miami University M
Michigan State University M,D
Middle Tennessee State University M
Mississippi College M
Mississippi State University M
Monmouth University M,O
Montana State University–Bozeman M
Montclair State University M
National University M
New Jersey City University M
New Mexico State University M
New York Institute of Technology M,O
New York University M,D,O
North Carolina State University M
Northeastern Illinois University M
Northeastern University M,O
Northern Illinois University M
Northern Kentucky University M
Northwestern University D
Northwest Missouri State University M
Nova Southeastern University M
Oakland University M,O
The Ohio State University M,D
Oklahoma City University M
Oklahoma State University M,D
Old Dominion University M
Oral Roberts University M
Pace University, New York City Campus M
Pace University, White Plains Campus M
The Pennsylvania State University University Park Campus M,D
Philadelphia University M
Pittsburg State University M
Pontifical Catholic University of Puerto Rico M,D
Purdue University M,D
Purdue University Calumet M
Queens College of the City University of New York M
Quinnipiac University M
Regis University M,O
Rider University M
Robert Morris College M
Rochester Institute of Technology M
Roosevelt University M
Rutgers, The State University of New Jersey, Newark M,D
St. Ambrose University M
St. Bonaventure University M,O
St. Cloud State University M
St. Edward's University M,O
St. John's University (NY) M,O
Saint Joseph's University M
Saint Louis University M,D
Saint Peter's College M,O
St. Thomas University M,O
San Diego State University M
San Jose State University M
Seattle University M
Seton Hall University M,O
Slippery Rock University of Pennsylvania M
Southeastern University M
Southern Illinois University Carbondale M,D
Southern Illinois University Edwardsville M
Southern University and Agricultural and Mechanical College M
Southern Utah University M
Southwest Baptist University M
Southwest Missouri State University M
Southwest Texas State University M
State University of New York at Albany M
State University of New York at Binghamton M,D
State University of New York at New Paltz M
State University of New York Institute of Technology at Utica/Rome M
State University of West Georgia M
Stephen F. Austin State University M
Stetson University M
Strayer University M
Suffolk University M,O

Syracuse University	M,D
Temple University	M,D
Texas A&M International University	M
Texas A&M University	M,D
Texas A&M University–Corpus Christi	M
Texas Christian University	M
Texas Tech University	M,D
Trinity University	M
Troy State University Dothan	M
Truman State University	M
Universidad del Turabo	M
Universidad Metropolitana	M
University at Buffalo, The State University of New York	M,D
The University of Akron	M
The University of Alabama	M,D
The University of Alabama in Huntsville	M
The University of Arizona	M
University of Arkansas	M
University of Baltimore	M
University of California, Berkeley	D
University of Central Florida	M
University of Chicago	M,D
University of Cincinnati	M,D
University of Colorado at Boulder	M
University of Colorado at Colorado Springs	M
University of Colorado at Denver	M
University of Connecticut	M,D
University of Delaware	M
University of Denver	M
University of Florida	M,D
University of Georgia	M
University of Hartford	M
University of Hawaii at Manoa	M
University of Houston	M,D
University of Houston–Clear Lake	M
University of Idaho	M
University of Illinois at Chicago	M
University of Illinois at Springfield	M
University of Illinois at Urbana–Champaign	M,D
University of Indianapolis	M
The University of Iowa	M,D
University of Kansas	M,D
University of Kentucky	M
University of La Verne	M
The University of Memphis	M,D
University of Miami	M
University of Minnesota, Twin Cities Campus	M,D
University of Mississippi	M,D
University of Missouri–Columbia	M,D
University of Missouri–Kansas City	M
University of Missouri–St. Louis	M,O
The University of Montana–Missoula	M
University of Nebraska at Omaha	M
University of Nebraska–Lincoln	M,D
University of Nevada, Las Vegas	M
University of Nevada, Reno	M
University of New Hampshire	M
University of New Haven	M
University of New Mexico	M
University of New Orleans	M
The University of North Carolina at Chapel Hill	M,D
The University of North Carolina at Charlotte	M
The University of North Carolina at Greensboro	M
The University of North Carolina at Wilmington	M
University of North Florida	M
University of North Texas	M,D
University of Notre Dame	M
University of Oklahoma	M
University of Oregon	M,D
University of Pennsylvania	M,D
University of Rhode Island	M
University of St. Thomas (MN)	M,O
The University of Scranton	M
University of South Alabama	M
University of South Carolina	M
University of South Dakota	M
University of Southern California	M
University of Southern Indiana	M
University of Southern Maine	M
University of Southern Mississippi	M
University of South Florida	M
The University of Tennessee	M,D
The University of Tennessee at Chattanooga	M
The University of Tennessee at Martin	M
The University of Texas at Arlington	M,D
The University of Texas at Austin	M,D
The University of Texas at Dallas	M
The University of Texas at El Paso	M
The University of Texas at San Antonio	M
The University of Texas of the Permian Basin	M
University of Toledo	M
University of Tulsa	M
University of Utah	M,D
University of Virginia	M
University of West Florida	M
University of Wisconsin–Madison	M,D
University of Wisconsin–Whitewater	M
University of Wyoming	M
Utah State University	M
Villanova University	M
Virginia Commonwealth University	M,D
Virginia Polytechnic Institute and State University	M,D
Wake Forest University	M
Washington State University	M
Weber State University	M
Western Carolina University	M
Western Connecticut State University	M
Western Illinois University	M
Western Michigan University	M
Western New England College	M
West Texas A&M University	M
West Virginia University	M
Wheeling Jesuit University	M
Wichita State University	M
Widener University	M
Wilkes University	M
William Woods University	M
Wright State University	M
Yale University	D
York College of Pennsylvania	M
Youngstown State University	M

■ ACOUSTICS

The Catholic University of America	M,D
The Pennsylvania State University University Park Campus	M,D

■ ACTUARIAL SCIENCE

Ball State University	M
Boston University	M
Central Connecticut State University	M
Georgia State University	M
Roosevelt University	M
Temple University	M
The University of Iowa	M,D
University of Nebraska–Lincoln	M
University of Wisconsin–Madison	M,D

■ ACUPUNCTURE AND ORIENTAL MEDICINE

Mercy College	M
Santa Barbara College of Oriental Medicine	M
University of Bridgeport	M

■ ADDICTIONS/SUBSTANCE ABUSE COUNSELING

Antioch New England Graduate School	M
The College of New Jersey	O
The College of William and Mary	M,D
Francis Marion University	M
Governors State University	M
Johns Hopkins University	M,D,O
Kean University	M,O
Loyola College in Maryland	M,O
Monmouth University	M,O
National-Louis University	M,O
New York University	M,D,O
Notre Dame de Namur University	M
Pace University, White Plains Campus	M
Sage Graduate School	M
St. Mary's University of San Antonio	M,D,O
Slippery Rock University of Pennsylvania	M
Springfield College	M,O
University of Alaska Anchorage	O
University of Detroit Mercy	O
University of Great Falls	M
University of Illinois at Springfield	M
University of Louisiana at Monroe	M
University of North Florida	M,O
Wayne State University	O

■ ADULT EDUCATION

Antioch University McGregor	M
Auburn University	M,D,O
Ball State University	M,D
California State University, Los Angeles	M
Central Missouri State University	M,O
Cheyney University of Pennsylvania	M
Cleveland State University	M
Coppin State College	M
Cornell University	M,D
Drake University	M,D,O
East Carolina University	M,O
Eastern Washington University	M
Florida Agricultural and Mechanical University	M,D
Florida Atlantic University	M,D,O
Florida International University	M,D
Florida State University	M,D,O
Fordham University	M,D,O
Grand Valley State University	M
Harvard University	M,D,O
Indiana University of Pennsylvania	M
Kansas State University	M,D
Marshall University	M
Michigan State University	M,D,O
Morehead State University	M,O
National-Louis University	M,D,O
Newman University	M
North Carolina Agricultural and Technical State University	M
North Carolina State University	M,D
Northern Illinois University	M,D
Nova Southeastern University	D
Oregon State University	M
The Pennsylvania State University Harrisburg Campus of the Capital College	D

The Pennsylvania State University University Park Campus	M,D
Portland State University	D
Regis University	M,O
Rutgers, The State University of New Jersey, New Brunswick	M,D
Saint Joseph's University	M
Saint Michael's College	M,O
San Francisco State University	M,O
Seattle University	M,O
State University of New York College at Buffalo	M
Suffolk University	M,O
Teachers College, Columbia University	M,D
Texas A&M University–Kingsville	M
Troy State University Montgomery	M
Tusculum College	M
University of Alaska Anchorage	M
University of Arkansas	M,D,O
University of Arkansas at Little Rock	M
University of Central Oklahoma	M
University of Connecticut	M,D
University of Denver	M,D,O
University of Georgia	M,D,O
University of Idaho	M,D
The University of Memphis	M,D,O
University of Michigan–Dearborn	M
University of Minnesota, Twin Cities Campus	M,D,O
University of Missouri–Columbia	M,D,O
University of Missouri–St. Louis	M,D
University of New Hampshire	M,D,O
University of Oklahoma	M,D
University of Rhode Island	M
University of Southern Maine	M,O
University of Southern Mississippi	M,D,O
University of South Florida	M,D,O
The University of Tennessee	M
University of the Incarnate Word	M
The University of West Alabama	M
University of Wisconsin–Madison	M,D
University of Wisconsin–Platteville	M
University of Wyoming	M,D,O
Valdosta State University	M,D,O
Virginia Commonwealth University	M
Virginia Polytechnic Institute and State University	M,D,O
Western Washington University	M
Widener University	M,D
Wright State University	O

■ ADVANCED PRACTICE NURSING

Barry University	M
Baylor University	M
Bowie State University	M
Brenau University	M
California State University, Fresno	M
Carlow College	M,O
Case Western Reserve University	M
The Catholic University of America	M,D
College of Mount Saint Vincent	M,O
Columbia University	M,O
Concordia University Wisconsin	M
Coppin State College	M
DePaul University	M
DeSales University	M
Duke University	M,O
Duquesne University	M
Eastern Kentucky University	M
East Tennessee State University	M,O
Edinboro University of Pennsylvania	M
Emory University	M
Fairfield University	M,O
Florida Atlantic University	M,O
Florida State University	M
Gannon University	M,O
George Mason University	M,D
Georgia Southern University	M,O
Georgia State University	M,D
Grambling State University	M
Gwynedd-Mercy College	M
Hardin-Simmons University	M
Hawaii Pacific University	M
Holy Names College	M
Houston Baptist University	M
Howard University	M,O
Hunter College of the City University of New York	M,O
Husson College	M
Indiana University–Purdue University Indianapolis	M
Indiana University South Bend	M
Johns Hopkins University	M,O
Kennesaw State University	M
La Roche College	M
La Salle University	M,O
Long Island University, Brooklyn Campus	M,O
Long Island University, C.W. Post Campus	M,O
Loyola University Chicago	M
Loyola University New Orleans	M
Madonna University	M
Marquette University	M,O
Marymount University	M,O
Midwestern State University	M
Minnesota State University, Mankato	M
Molloy College	M,O
Monmouth University	M,O
Mount Saint Mary College	M
New York University	M,O
Niagara University	M
Northeastern University	M,O
North Georgia College & State University	M
Oakland University	M,O
Pacific Lutheran University	M
Quinnipiac University	M
Rutgers, The State University of New Jersey, Newark	M,D
Sacred Heart University	M
Sage Graduate School	M
Saginaw Valley State University	M
St. John Fisher College	M,O
Saint Joseph College	M,O
Saint Xavier University	M,O
San Francisco State University	M
San Jose State University	M
Seattle Pacific University	O
Seton Hall University	M
Simmons College	M,O
Sonoma State University	M
Southern Illinois University Edwardsville	M
Spalding University	M
State University of New York College at Brockport	M,O
State University of New York Institute of Technology at Utica/Rome	M,O
Stony Brook University, State University of New York	M,O
Texas Woman's University	M,D
University at Buffalo, The State University of New York	M,D,O
University of Cincinnati	M,D
University of Colorado at Colorado Springs	M
University of Delaware	M,O
University of Hawaii at Manoa	M,D,O
University of Mary	M
University of Miami	M,D
University of Michigan	M
University of Minnesota, Twin Cities Campus	M
University of Missouri–Kansas City	M,D
University of Nevada, Las Vegas	M
University of New Mexico	M,O
University of Northern Colorado	M
University of North Florida	M
University of Pennsylvania	M,O
University of Pittsburgh	M
University of Portland	M,O
University of San Diego	M,D,O
University of San Francisco	M
The University of Scranton	M
University of South Carolina	O
University of Southern Maine	M,O
University of Southern Mississippi	M,D
The University of Tampa	M
The University of Tennessee at Chattanooga	M
The University of Texas at Arlington	M
The University of Texas at El Paso	M
The University of Texas–Pan American	M
University of Wisconsin–Oshkosh	M
Vanderbilt University	M,D
Villanova University	M,O
Virginia Commonwealth University	O
Wagner College	O
Wayne State University	M
Western Connecticut State University	M
Wilmington College	M
Wright State University	M

■ ADVERTISING AND PUBLIC RELATIONS

Austin Peay State University	M
Ball State University	M
Boston University	M
California State University, Fullerton	M
Carnegie Mellon University	M
Colorado State University	M
Emerson College	M
Loyola University Chicago	M
Marquette University	M
Michigan State University	M,D
Monmouth University	M,O
Morehead State University	M
Northwestern University	M
Rowan University	M
San Diego State University	M
Syracuse University	M
Towson University	O
The University of Alabama	M
University of Denver	M
University of Florida	M,D
University of Houston	M
University of Illinois at Urbana–Champaign	M
University of Maryland, College Park	M,D
University of Miami	M,D
University of New Haven	M
University of Oklahoma	M
University of St. Thomas (MN)	M,O
University of Southern California	M
University of Southern Mississippi	M,D
The University of Tennessee	M,D
The University of Texas at Austin	M,D
University of the Sacred Heart	M
University of Wisconsin–Stevens Point	M
Virginia Commonwealth University	M
Wayne State University	M,D

■ AEROSPACE/AERONAUTICAL ENGINEERING

Arizona State University	M,D
Auburn University	M,D
Boston University	M,D
Brown University	M,D
California Institute of Technology	M,D,O

California Polytechnic State University, San Luis Obispo	M
California State University, Long Beach	M
California State University, Northridge	M
Case Western Reserve University	M,D
Cornell University	M,D
Embry-Riddle Aeronautical University	M
Embry-Riddle Aeronautical University, Extended Campus	M
Florida Institute of Technology	M,D
The George Washington University	M,D,O
Georgia Institute of Technology	M,D
Howard University	M,D
Illinois Institute of Technology	M,D
Iowa State University of Science and Technology	M,D
Massachusetts Institute of Technology	M,D,O
Middle Tennessee State University	M
Mississippi State University	M
North Carolina State University	M,D
The Ohio State University	M,D
Old Dominion University	M,D
The Pennsylvania State University University Park Campus	M,D
Polytechnic University, Brooklyn Campus	M
Princeton University	M,D
Purdue University	M,D
Rensselaer Polytechnic Institute	M,D
Rutgers, The State University of New Jersey, New Brunswick	M,D
Saint Louis University	M
San Diego State University	M,D
San Jose State University	M
Stanford University	M,D,O
Syracuse University	M,D
Texas A&M University	M,D
University at Buffalo, The State University of New York	M,D
The University of Alabama	M,D
The University of Arizona	M,D
University of California, Davis	M,D,O
University of California, Irvine	M,D
University of California, Los Angeles	M,D
University of California, San Diego	M,D
University of Central Florida	M
University of Cincinnati	M,D
University of Colorado at Boulder	M,D
University of Colorado at Colorado Springs	M
University of Connecticut	M,D
University of Dayton	M,D
University of Florida	M,D,O
University of Houston	M,D
University of Illinois at Urbana–Champaign	M,D
University of Kansas	M,D
University of Maryland, College Park	M,D
University of Michigan	M,D,O
University of Minnesota, Twin Cities Campus	M,D
University of Missouri–Columbia	M,D
University of Missouri–Rolla	M,D
University of Notre Dame	M,D
University of Oklahoma	M,D
University of Southern California	M,D,O
The University of Tennessee	M,D
The University of Texas at Arlington	M,D
The University of Texas at Austin	M,D
University of Virginia	M,D
University of Washington	M,D
Utah State University	M,D
Virginia Polytechnic Institute and State University	M,D
Webster University	M
West Virginia University	M,D
Wichita State University	M,D

■ AFRICAN-AMERICAN STUDIES

Boston University	M
Clark Atlanta University	M,D
Columbia University	M
Cornell University	M
Indiana University Bloomington	M
Morgan State University	M,D
North Carolina Agricultural and Technical State University	M
The Ohio State University	M
Princeton University	D
State University of New York at Albany	M
Temple University	M,D
University of California, Berkeley	D
University of California, Los Angeles	M
The University of Iowa	M
University of Massachusetts Amherst	M,D
University of Wisconsin–Madison	M
West Virginia University	M,D
Yale University	M,D

■ AFRICAN STUDIES

Boston University	M,O
Columbia University	O
Cornell University	M
Florida International University	M
Howard University	M,D
Johns Hopkins University	M,D,O
New York University	M
Northwestern University	O
The Ohio State University	M
Ohio University	M
St. John's University (NY)	M,O
State University of New York at Albany	M
University of California, Los Angeles	M
University of Connecticut	M
University of Florida	O
University of Illinois at Urbana–Champaign	M
University of Wisconsin–Madison	M,D
West Virginia University	M,D
Yale University	M

■ AGRICULTURAL ECONOMICS AND AGRIBUSINESS

Alabama Agricultural and Mechanical University	M
Alcorn State University	M
Auburn University	M,D
California Polytechnic State University, San Luis Obispo	M
Clemson University	M
Colorado State University	M,D
Cornell University	M,D
Illinois State University	M
Iowa State University of Science and Technology	M,D
Kansas State University	M,D
Louisiana State University and Agricultural and Mechanical College	M,D
Michigan State University	M,D
Mississippi State University	M,D
Montana State University–Bozeman	M
New Mexico State University	M
North Carolina Agricultural and Technical State University	M
North Carolina State University	M,D
North Dakota State University	M
Northwest Missouri State University	M
The Ohio State University	M,D
Oklahoma State University	M,D
Oregon State University	M,D
The Pennsylvania State University University Park Campus	M,D
Prairie View A&M University	M
Purdue University	M,D
Rutgers, The State University of New Jersey, New Brunswick	M
Sam Houston State University	M
Santa Clara University	M
South Carolina State University	M
Southern Illinois University Carbondale	M
Texas A&M University	M,D
Texas A&M University–Kingsville	M
Texas Tech University	M,D
Tuskegee University	M
The University of Arizona	M
University of Arkansas	M
University of California, Berkeley	D
University of California, Davis	M,D
University of Connecticut	M,D
University of Delaware	M
University of Florida	M,D
University of Georgia	M,D
University of Hawaii at Manoa	M,D
University of Idaho	M
University of Illinois at Urbana–Champaign	M,D
University of Kentucky	M,D
University of Maine	M
University of Maryland, College Park	M,D
University of Massachusetts Amherst	M,D
University of Minnesota, Twin Cities Campus	M,D
University of Missouri–Columbia	M,D
University of Nebraska–Lincoln	M,D
University of Nevada, Reno	M
University of Puerto Rico, Mayagüez Campus	M
University of Rhode Island	M,D
The University of Tennessee	M
University of Vermont	M
University of Wisconsin–Madison	M,D
University of Wyoming	M
Virginia Polytechnic Institute and State University	M,D
Washington State University	M,D
West Texas A&M University	M
West Virginia University	M

■ AGRICULTURAL EDUCATION

Alcorn State University	M,O
Arkansas State University	M,O
Clemson University	M
Cornell University	M,D
Eastern Kentucky University	M
Florida Agricultural and Mechanical University	M
Iowa State University of Science and Technology	M,D
Louisiana State University and Agricultural and Mechanical College	M,D
Michigan State University	M,D
Mississippi State University	M,D,O
New Mexico State University	M
North Carolina Agricultural and Technical State University	M
North Carolina State University	M,D,O
North Dakota State University	M
Northwest Missouri State University	M
The Ohio State University	M,D
Oklahoma State University	M,D
Oregon State University	M
The Pennsylvania State University University Park Campus	M,D

Purdue University	M,D,O
Sam Houston State University	M
Southwest Texas State University	M
Stephen F. Austin State University	M
Texas A&M University	M,D
Texas A&M University–Commerce	M
Texas A&M University–Kingsville	M
Texas Tech University	M
The University of Arizona	M
University of Arkansas	M
University of Florida	M,D
University of Georgia	M,D,O
University of Idaho	M
University of Illinois at Urbana–Champaign	M
University of Maryland Eastern Shore	M
University of Minnesota, Twin Cities Campus	M,D
University of Nebraska–Lincoln	M
University of Puerto Rico, Mayagüez Campus	M
The University of Tennessee	M
University of Wisconsin–River Falls	M
Utah State University	M
West Virginia University	M

■ AGRICULTURAL ENGINEERING

Clemson University	M,D
Colorado State University	M,D
Cornell University	M,D
Iowa State University of Science and Technology	M,D
Kansas State University	M,D
Louisiana State University and Agricultural and Mechanical College	M,D
Michigan State University	M,D
North Carolina Agricultural and Technical State University	M
North Carolina State University	M,D
North Dakota State University	M
The Ohio State University	M,D
Oklahoma State University	M,D
The Pennsylvania State University University Park Campus	M,D
Purdue University	M,D
Rutgers, The State University of New Jersey, New Brunswick	M
South Dakota State University	M,D
Texas A&M University	M,D
The University of Arizona	M,D
University of Arkansas	M,D
University of California, Davis	M,D
University of Dayton	M
University of Florida	M,D,O
University of Georgia	M,D
University of Hawaii at Manoa	M
University of Idaho	M,D
University of Illinois at Urbana–Champaign	M,D
University of Kentucky	M,D
University of Maine	M
University of Maryland, College Park	M,D
University of Minnesota, Twin Cities Campus	M,D
University of Missouri–Columbia	M,D
University of Nebraska–Lincoln	M,D
The University of Tennessee	M,D
University of Wisconsin–Madison	M,D
Utah State University	M,D
Virginia Polytechnic Institute and State University	M,D

■ AGRICULTURAL SCIENCES—GENERAL

Alabama Agricultural and Mechanical University	M,D
Alcorn State University	M
Arkansas State University	M,O
Auburn University	M,D
Brigham Young University	M,D
California Polytechnic State University, San Luis Obispo	M
California State Polytechnic University, Pomona	M
California State University, Chico	M
California State University, Fresno	M
Central Missouri State University	M
Clemson University	M,D
Colorado State University	M,D
Illinois State University	M
Iowa State University of Science and Technology	M,D
Kansas State University	M,D
Louisiana State University and Agricultural and Mechanical College	M,D
Michigan State University	M,D
Mississippi State University	M,D,O
Montana State University–Bozeman	M,D
Murray State University	M
New Mexico State University	M,D
North Carolina Agricultural and Technical State University	M
North Carolina State University	M,D
North Dakota State University	M,D
Northwest Missouri State University	M
The Ohio State University	M,D
Oklahoma State University	M,D
Oregon State University	M,D
The Pennsylvania State University University Park Campus	M,D
Prairie View A&M University	M
Purdue University	M,D
Sam Houston State University	M
South Dakota State University	M,D
Southern Illinois University Carbondale	M
Southern University and Agricultural and Mechanical College	M
Southwest Missouri State University	M
Tarleton State University	M
Tennessee State University	M
Texas A&M University	M,D
Texas A&M University–Commerce	M
Texas A&M University–Kingsville	M,D
Texas Tech University	M,D
Tuskegee University	M
The University of Arizona	M,D
University of Arkansas	M,D
University of California, Davis	M
University of Connecticut	M,D
University of Delaware	M,D
University of Florida	M,D
University of Georgia	M,D
University of Hawaii at Manoa	M,D
University of Idaho	M,D
University of Illinois at Urbana–Champaign	M,D
University of Kentucky	M,D
University of Maine	M,D
University of Maryland, College Park	P,M,D
University of Maryland Eastern Shore	M
University of Minnesota, Twin Cities Campus	M,D
University of Missouri–Columbia	M,D
University of Nebraska–Lincoln	M,D
University of Nevada, Reno	M,D
University of New Hampshire	M,D
University of Puerto Rico, Mayagüez Campus	M
The University of Tennessee	M,D
University of Vermont	M,D
University of Wisconsin–Madison	M,D
University of Wisconsin–River Falls	M
University of Wyoming	M,D
Utah State University	M,D
Virginia Polytechnic Institute and State University	M,D
Washington State University	M,D
Western Kentucky University	M
West Texas A&M University	M
West Virginia University	M,D

■ AGRONOMY AND SOIL SCIENCES

Alabama Agricultural and Mechanical University	M,D
Alcorn State University	M
Auburn University	M,D
Brigham Young University	M
Colorado State University	M,D
Cornell University	M,D
Iowa State University of Science and Technology	M,D
Kansas State University	M,D
Louisiana State University and Agricultural and Mechanical College	M,D
Michigan State University	M,D
Mississippi State University	M,D
Montana State University–Bozeman	M
New Mexico State University	M,D
North Carolina State University	M,D
North Dakota State University	M,D
The Ohio State University	M,D
Oklahoma State University	M,D
Oregon State University	M,D
The Pennsylvania State University University Park Campus	M,D
Prairie View A&M University	M
Purdue University	M,D
South Dakota State University	M,D
Southern Illinois University Carbondale	M
Southwest Missouri State University	M
Texas A&M University	M,D
Texas A&M University–Kingsville	M
Texas Tech University	M,D
Tuskegee University	M
The University of Arizona	M,D
University of Arkansas	M,D
University of California, Davis	M,D
University of California, Riverside	M,D
University of Connecticut	M,D
University of Delaware	M,D
University of Florida	M,D
University of Georgia	M,D
University of Hawaii at Manoa	M,D
University of Idaho	M,D
University of Illinois at Urbana–Champaign	M,D
University of Kentucky	M,D
University of Maine	M,D
University of Maryland, College Park	M,D
University of Massachusetts Amherst	M,D
University of Minnesota, Twin Cities Campus	M,D
University of Missouri–Columbia	M,D
University of Nebraska–Lincoln	M,D
University of New Hampshire	M,D
University of Puerto Rico, Mayagüez Campus	M
The University of Tennessee	M,D
University of Vermont	M,D
University of Wisconsin–Madison	M,D

University of Wyoming	M,D
Utah State University	M,D
Virginia Polytechnic Institute and State University	M,D
Washington State University	M,D
West Virginia University	M,D

■ ALLIED HEALTH—GENERAL

Andrews University	M
Baylor University	M
Belmont University	M,D
Boston University	M,D,O
College of Mount Saint Vincent	M,O
Creighton University	P,M,D
Duquesne University	M
East Carolina University	M,D
Eastern Kentucky University	M
East Tennessee State University	M,O
Emory University	M
Florida Gulf Coast University	M
Georgia Southern University	M,O
Georgia State University	M,D
Governors State University	M
Grand Valley State University	M
Idaho State University	M,D,O
Indiana University–Purdue University Indianapolis	M
Ithaca College	M
Jackson State University	M
Loma Linda University	M,D
Long Island University, C.W. Post Campus	M,O
Marymount University	M,O
Maryville University of Saint Louis	M
MCP Hahnemann University	M,D,O
Minnesota State University, Mankato	M,O
Northern Arizona University	M
Northern Michigan University	M
Nova Southeastern University	M,D
Oakland University	M,O
The Ohio State University	M
Old Dominion University	M,D,O
Quinnipiac University	M
Regis University	M,D
Saint Louis University	M
Seton Hall University	M,D
Southwest Texas State University	M
Temple University	M,D
Tennessee State University	M
Texas Woman's University	M,D
Towson University	M
University at Buffalo, The State University of New York	M,D
The University of Alabama at Birmingham	M,D,O
University of Connecticut	M
University of Detroit Mercy	M
University of Florida	M,D
University of Illinois at Chicago	M,D
University of Kansas	M,D
University of Kentucky	M
University of Louisiana at Monroe	M
University of Louisville	M
University of Massachusetts Lowell	M,D
University of New Mexico	P,M,D,O
The University of North Carolina at Chapel Hill	M,D
University of North Florida	M,O
University of South Alabama	M,D
University of South Dakota	M
University of Southern California	M,D,O
The University of Texas at El Paso	M
University of Vermont	M
University of Wisconsin–Eau Claire	M
University of Wisconsin–Milwaukee	M
Virginia Commonwealth University	M,D,O
Washington University in St. Louis	M,D,O
Wayne State University	M,O
Wichita State University	M

■ ALLOPATHIC MEDICINE

Boston University	P
Brown University	P
Case Western Reserve University	P
Columbia University	P
Creighton University	P
Dartmouth College	P
Duke University	P
East Carolina University	P
East Tennessee State University	P
Emory University	P
Georgetown University	P
The George Washington University	P
Harvard University	P
Howard University	P,D
Indiana University–Purdue University Indianapolis	P
Johns Hopkins University	P
Loma Linda University	P
Loyola University Chicago	P
Marshall University	P
MCP Hahnemann University	P
Mercer University	P,M
Michigan State University	P
New York University	P
Northwestern University	P
The Ohio State University	P
Saint Louis University	P
Southern Illinois University Carbondale	P
Stanford University	P
Stony Brook University, State University of New York	P
Temple University	P
Tufts University	P
Tulane University	P
University at Buffalo, The State University of New York	P
The University of Alabama at Birmingham	P,M,D
The University of Arizona	P
University of California, Davis	P
University of California, Irvine	P
University of California, Los Angeles	P
University of California, San Diego	P
University of California, San Francisco	P
University of Chicago	P
University of Cincinnati	P
University of Florida	P
University of Hawaii at Manoa	P
University of Illinois at Chicago	P
University of Illinois at Urbana–Champaign	
The University of Iowa	P
University of Kansas	P
University of Kentucky	P
University of Louisville	P
University of Maryland	P
University of Miami	P
University of Michigan	P
University of Minnesota, Duluth	P
University of Minnesota, Twin Cities Campus	P
University of Missouri–Columbia	P
University of Missouri–Kansas City	P
University of Nevada, Reno	P
University of New Mexico	P
The University of North Carolina at Chapel Hill	P
University of North Dakota	P
University of Pennsylvania	P
University of Pittsburgh	P
University of Rochester	P
University of South Alabama	P
University of South Carolina	P
University of South Dakota	P
University of Southern California	P
University of South Florida	P
University of Utah	P
University of Vermont	P
University of Virginia	P,M
University of Washington	P
University of Wisconsin–Madison	P
Vanderbilt University	P,M,D
Virginia Commonwealth University	P
Wake Forest University	P
Washington University in St. Louis	P
Wayne State University	P
West Virginia University	P
Wright State University	P
Yale University	P
Yeshiva University	P

■ AMERICAN STUDIES

Appalachian State University	M
Baylor University	M
Boston University	M,D
Bowling Green State University	M,D
Brandeis University	M,D
Brigham Young University	M
Brown University	M,D
California State University, Fullerton	M
California State University, Long Beach	M,O
Case Western Reserve University	M,D
Claremont Graduate University	M,D
The College of William and Mary	M,D
Columbia University	M
East Carolina University	M
Eastern Michigan University	M
Fairfield University	M
Florida State University	M
The George Washington University	M,D
Harvard University	D
Indiana University Bloomington	D
Michigan State University	M,D
Montana State University–Bozeman	M
New Mexico Highlands University	M
New York University	M,D
Northeastern State University	M
The Pennsylvania State University Harrisburg Campus of the Capital College	M
Pepperdine University	M
Purdue University	M,D
Saint Louis University	M,D
State University of New York College at Cortland	O
Stony Brook University, State University of New York	M,O
University at Buffalo, The State University of New York	M,D
The University of Alabama	M
The University of Arizona	M
University of California, Davis	M,D
University of California, Los Angeles	M
University of Central Oklahoma	M
University of Delaware	M,D
University of Hawaii at Manoa	M,D
The University of Iowa	M,D
University of Kansas	M,D
University of Louisiana at Lafayette	D
University of Maryland, College Park	M,D
University of Massachusetts Boston	M
University of Michigan	M,D
University of Michigan–Flint	M
University of Minnesota, Twin Cities Campus	D
University of Mississippi	M
University of New Mexico	M,D
University of Pennsylvania	M,D

University of Southern Maine	M
University of South Florida	M
The University of Texas at Austin	M,D
University of Wyoming	M
Utah State University	M
Washington State University	M,D
Western Carolina University	M
West Virginia University	M,D
Yale University	M,D

■ ANALYTICAL CHEMISTRY

Boston College	M,D
Brigham Young University	M,D
California State University, Fullerton	M
California State University, Los Angeles	M
Case Western Reserve University	M,D
Clarkson University	M,D
Cleveland State University	M,D
Cornell University	D
Florida State University	M,D
Georgetown University	M,D
The George Washington University	M,D
Governors State University	M
Howard University	M,D
Illinois Institute of Technology	M,D
Indiana University Bloomington	M,D
Kansas State University	M,D
Kent State University	M,D
Marquette University	M,D
Miami University	M,D
Michigan State University	M,D
Northeastern University	M,D
Old Dominion University	M
Oregon State University	M,D
Purdue University	M,D
Rensselaer Polytechnic Institute	M,D
Rutgers, The State University of New Jersey, Newark	M,D
Rutgers, The State University of New Jersey, New Brunswick	M,D
San Jose State University	M
Seton Hall University	M,D
South Dakota State University	M,D
Southern University and Agricultural and Mechanical College	M
State University of New York at Binghamton	M,D
Stevens Institute of Technology	M,D,O
Tufts University	M,D
The University of Akron	M,D
University of Cincinnati	M,D
University of Georgia	M,D
University of Louisville	M,D
University of Maryland, College Park	M,D
University of Michigan	D
University of Missouri–Columbia	M,D
University of Missouri–Kansas City	M,D
University of Nebraska–Lincoln	M,D
University of Nevada, Las Vegas	M
University of Southern Mississippi	M,D
University of South Florida	M,D
The University of Tennessee	M,D
The University of Texas at Austin	M,D
University of Toledo	M,D
Wake Forest University	M,D
Washington State University	M,D
West Virginia University	M,D

■ ANATOMY

Auburn University	M
Boston University	M,D
Case Western Reserve University	M,D
Colorado State University	M,D
Columbia University	M,D
Duke University	D
East Carolina University	D
East Tennessee State University	M,D
Howard University	M,D
Indiana University Bloomington	M,D
Indiana University–Purdue University Indianapolis	M,D
Iowa State University of Science and Technology	M,D
Johns Hopkins University	D
Kansas State University	M,D
Loma Linda University	M,D
Loyola University Chicago	M,D
Michigan State University	M,D
The Ohio State University	M,D
Purdue University	M,D
Saint Louis University	M,D
Stony Brook University, State University of New York	D
Temple University	D
Texas A&M University	M,D
University at Buffalo, The State University of New York	M,D
The University of Arizona	D
University of California, Irvine	M,D
University of California, Los Angeles	D
University of California, San Francisco	D
University of Chicago	D
University of Cincinnati	D
University of Florida	D
University of Georgia	M
University of Illinois at Chicago	M,D
The University of Iowa	D
University of Kansas	M,D
University of Kentucky	D
University of Louisville	M,D
University of Maryland	M,D
University of Minnesota, Duluth	M,D
University of North Dakota	M,D
University of Rochester	M,D
University of Southern California	M,D
University of South Florida	D
The University of Tennessee	M,D
University of Utah	M,D
University of Vermont	D
University of Wisconsin–Madison	M,D
Virginia Commonwealth University	M,D,O
Wake Forest University	D
Wayne State University	M,D
West Virginia University	M,D
Wright State University	M
Yeshiva University	D

■ ANIMAL BEHAVIOR

Arizona State University	M,D
University of California, Davis	M,D
University of Colorado at Boulder	M,D
University of Minnesota, Twin Cities Campus	M,D
University of Missouri–St. Louis	M,D,O
The University of Montana–Missoula	D
The University of Tennessee	M,D
The University of Texas at Austin	M,D

■ ANIMAL SCIENCES

Alabama Agricultural and Mechanical University	M,D
Alcorn State University	M
Angelo State University	M
Arkansas Tech University	M
Auburn University	M,D
Brigham Young University	M
California State Polytechnic University, Pomona	M
California State University, Fresno	M
Clemson University	M
Colorado State University	M,D
Cornell University	M,D
Iowa State University of Science and Technology	M,D
Kansas State University	M,D
Louisiana State University and Agricultural and Mechanical College	M,D
Michigan State University	M,D
Mississippi State University	M
Montana State University–Bozeman	M
New Mexico State University	M,D
North Carolina State University	M,D
North Dakota State University	M,D
Oklahoma State University	M,D
Oregon State University	M,D
The Pennsylvania State University University Park Campus	M,D
Prairie View A&M University	M
Purdue University	M,D
Rutgers, The State University of New Jersey, New Brunswick	M,D
South Dakota State University	M,D
Southern Illinois University Carbondale	M
Sul Ross State University	M
Texas A&M University	M,D
Texas A&M University–Kingsville	M
Texas Tech University	M,D
Tuskegee University	M
The University of Arizona	M,D
University of Arkansas	M,D
University of California, Davis	M
University of Connecticut	M,D
University of Florida	M,D
University of Georgia	M,D
University of Hawaii at Manoa	M
University of Idaho	M,D
University of Illinois at Urbana–Champaign	M,D
University of Kentucky	M,D
University of Maine	M
University of Maryland, College Park	M,D
University of Massachusetts Amherst	M,D
University of Minnesota, Twin Cities Campus	M,D
University of Missouri–Columbia	M,D
University of Nebraska–Lincoln	M,D
University of Nevada, Reno	M
University of New Hampshire	M,D
University of Puerto Rico, Mayagüez Campus	M
University of Rhode Island	M
The University of Tennessee	M,D
University of Vermont	M,D
University of Wisconsin–Madison	M,D
University of Wyoming	M,D
Utah State University	M,D
Virginia Polytechnic Institute and State University	M,D
Washington State University	M,D
West Texas A&M University	M
West Virginia University	M,D

■ ANTHROPOLOGY

American University	M,D
Arizona State University	M,D
Ball State University	M
Bethel College (MN)	M
Boston University	M,D
Brandeis University	M,D
Brigham Young University	M
Brown University	M,D
California State University, Bakersfield	M
California State University, Fullerton	M
California State University, Hayward	M
California State University, Long Beach	M

California State University, Los Angeles	M
California State University, Northridge	M
California State University, Sacramento	M
Case Western Reserve University	M,D
The Catholic University of America	M,D
City College of the City University of New York	M
The College of William and Mary	M,D
Colorado State University	M
Columbia University	M,D
Cornell University	D
Duke University	D
East Carolina University	M
Eastern New Mexico University	M
Emory University	D
Florida Atlantic University	M
Florida State University	M,D
The George Washington University	M
Georgia State University	M
Harvard University	M,D
Hunter College of the City University of New York	M
Idaho State University	M
Indiana University Bloomington	M,D
Iowa State University of Science and Technology	M
Johns Hopkins University	D
Kent State University	M,D
Lehigh University	M
Louisiana State University and Agricultural and Mechanical College	M,D
Marshall University	M
Michigan State University	M,D
Minnesota State University, Mankato	M
Montclair State University	M
New Mexico Highlands University	M
New Mexico State University	M
New School University	M,D
New York University	M,D
Northern Arizona University	M
Northern Illinois University	M
Northwestern University	D
The Ohio State University	M,D
Oregon State University	M
The Pennsylvania State University University Park Campus	M,D
Portland State University	M,D
Princeton University	D
Purdue University	M,D
Rice University	M,D
Rutgers, The State University of New Jersey, New Brunswick	M,D
San Diego State University	M
San Francisco State University	M
Southern Illinois University Carbondale	M,D
Southern Methodist University	M,D
Stanford University	M,D
State University of New York at Albany	M,D
State University of New York at Binghamton	M,D
Stony Brook University, State University of New York	M,D
Syracuse University	M,D
Teachers College, Columbia University	M,D
Temple University	M,D
Texas A&M University	M,D
Texas Tech University	M
Tulane University	M,D
University at Buffalo, The State University of New York	M,D
The University of Alabama	M
The University of Alabama at Birmingham	M
University of Alaska Fairbanks	M,D
The University of Arizona	M,D
University of Arkansas	M,D
University of California, Berkeley	D
University of California, Davis	M,D
University of California, Irvine	M,D
University of California, Los Angeles	M,D
University of California, Riverside	M,D
University of California, San Diego	D
University of California, San Francisco	D
University of California, Santa Barbara	M,D
University of California, Santa Cruz	M,D
University of Chicago	M,D
University of Cincinnati	M
University of Colorado at Boulder	M,D
University of Colorado at Denver	M
University of Connecticut	M,D
University of Denver	M
University of Florida	M,D
University of Georgia	M,D
University of Hawaii at Manoa	M,D
University of Houston	M
University of Idaho	M
University of Illinois at Chicago	M,D
University of Illinois at Urbana–Champaign	M,D
The University of Iowa	M,D
University of Kansas	M,D
University of Kentucky	M,D
University of Maryland, College Park	M
University of Massachusetts Amherst	M,D
The University of Memphis	M
University of Michigan	M,D
University of Minnesota, Duluth	M
University of Minnesota, Twin Cities Campus	M,D
University of Mississippi	M
University of Missouri–Columbia	M,D
The University of Montana–Missoula	M
University of Nebraska–Lincoln	M
University of Nevada, Las Vegas	M,D
University of Nevada, Reno	M,D
University of New Mexico	M,D
University of Oklahoma	M,D
University of Oregon	M,D
University of Pennsylvania	M,D
University of Pittsburgh	M,D
University of South Carolina	M
University of Southern California	M,D
University of Southern Mississippi	M
University of South Florida	M,D
The University of Tennessee	M,D
The University of Texas at Arlington	M
The University of Texas at Austin	M,D
The University of Texas at San Antonio	M
University of Toledo	M
University of Tulsa	M
University of Utah	M,D
University of Virginia	M,D
University of Washington	M,D
University of Wisconsin–Madison	M,D
University of Wisconsin–Milwaukee	M,D
University of Wyoming	M
Vanderbilt University	M,D
Washington State University	M,D
Washington University in St. Louis	M,D
Wayne State University	M,D
West Chester University of Pennsylvania	M,O
Western Michigan University	M
Western Washington University	M
West Virginia University	M
Wichita State University	M
Yale University	M,D

■ APPLIED ARTS AND DESIGN—GENERAL

Alfred University	M
Arizona State University	M
California State University, Fresno	M
California State University, Fullerton	M,O
California State University, Los Angeles	M
Cardinal Stritch University	M
Carnegie Mellon University	M,D
Drexel University	M
The George Washington University	M
Howard University	M
Illinois Institute of Technology	M,D
Indiana University Bloomington	M
Iowa State University of Science and Technology	M
Lamar University	M
Louisiana State University and Agricultural and Mechanical College	M
Louisiana Tech University	M
New School University	M
New York University	M
North Carolina State University	M,D
Pratt Institute	M
Purdue University	M
Rochester Institute of Technology	M
Rutgers, The State University of New Jersey, New Brunswick	M
San Diego State University	M
San Jose State University	M
Southern Illinois University Carbondale	M
Stephen F. Austin State University	M
Suffolk University	M
Sul Ross State University	M
Syracuse University	M
University of California, Berkeley	M
University of California, Los Angeles	M
University of Central Oklahoma	M
University of Cincinnati	M
University of Illinois at Urbana–Champaign	M,D
University of Kansas	M
University of Massachusetts Dartmouth	M
University of Michigan	M
University of Minnesota, Twin Cities Campus	M,D
University of Notre Dame	M
University of Wisconsin–Madison	M,D
Virginia Commonwealth University	M
Virginia Polytechnic Institute and State University	M,D
Wayne State University	M
Western Michigan University	M
Yale University	M

■ APPLIED MATHEMATICS

American University	M
Arizona State University	M,D
Auburn University	M,D
Brown University	M,D
California Institute of Technology	M,D
California State Polytechnic University, Pomona	M
California State University, Fullerton	M
California State University, Long Beach	M
California State University, Los Angeles	M
Case Western Reserve University	M,D
Central Missouri State University	M
Claremont Graduate University	M,D
Clark Atlanta University	M
Clemson University	M,D

Cleveland State University	M
Columbia University	M,D
Cornell University	M,D
East Carolina University	M
Florida Institute of Technology	M,D
Florida State University	M,D
The George Washington University	M
Georgia Institute of Technology	M,D
Hampton University	M
Harvard University	M,D
Hofstra University	M
Howard University	M,D
Hunter College of the City University of New York	M
Indiana University Bloomington	M,D
Indiana University of Pennsylvania	M
Indiana University–Purdue University Fort Wayne	M
Indiana University–Purdue University Indianapolis	M,D
Iowa State University of Science and Technology	M,D
Johns Hopkins University	M,D
Kent State University	M,D
Lehigh University	M,D
Long Island University, C.W. Post Campus	M
Michigan State University	M,D
Montclair State University	M,O
New Jersey Institute of Technology	M,D
Nicholls State University	M
North Carolina State University	M,D
North Dakota State University	M,D
Northwestern University	M,D
Oakland University	M
Oklahoma State University	M,D
The Pennsylvania State University University Park Campus	M,D
Princeton University	M,D
Rensselaer Polytechnic Institute	M
Rice University	M,D
Rochester Institute of Technology	M
Rutgers, The State University of New Jersey, New Brunswick	M,D
St. John's University (NY)	M
San Diego State University	M
Santa Clara University	M
Southern Methodist University	M,D
Stevens Institute of Technology	M,D
Stony Brook University, State University of New York	M,D
Temple University	M,D
Towson University	M
Tulane University	M,D
The University of Akron	M,D
The University of Alabama	M,D
The University of Alabama at Birmingham	M,D
The University of Alabama in Huntsville	M,D
The University of Arizona	M,D,O
University of Arkansas at Little Rock	M
University of California, Berkeley	D
University of California, Davis	M,D
University of California, San Diego	M,D
University of California, Santa Barbara	M
University of California, Santa Cruz	M,D
University of Central Oklahoma	M
University of Chicago	M,D
University of Cincinnati	M,D
University of Colorado at Boulder	M,D
University of Colorado at Colorado Springs	M
University of Colorado at Denver	M,D
University of Dayton	M
University of Delaware	M,D
University of Denver	M,D
University of Florida	M,D
University of Georgia	M,D
University of Houston	M,D
University of Illinois at Chicago	M,D
University of Illinois at Urbana–Champaign	M,D
The University of Iowa	D
University of Kansas	M,D
University of Maryland, Baltimore County	M,D
University of Maryland, College Park	M,D
University of Massachusetts Amherst	M
University of Massachusetts Lowell	M,D
The University of Memphis	M,D
University of Michigan–Dearborn	M
University of Minnesota, Duluth	M
University of Missouri–Columbia	M
University of Missouri–Rolla	M
University of Missouri–St. Louis	M,D,O
University of Nevada, Las Vegas	M
University of New Hampshire	M,D
The University of North Carolina at Charlotte	M,D
University of Pittsburgh	M
University of Puerto Rico, Mayagüez Campus	M
University of Rhode Island	M,D
University of Southern California	M,D
University of South Florida	M,D
The University of Tennessee	M,D
The University of Texas at Austin	M,D
The University of Texas at Dallas	M,D
University of Toledo	M,D
University of Washington	M,D
Virginia Commonwealth University	M
Virginia Polytechnic Institute and State University	M,D
Wayne State University	M,D
Western Michigan University	M
West Virginia University	M,D
Wichita State University	M,D
Worcester Polytechnic Institute	M,D,O
Wright State University	M
Yale University	M,D

■ APPLIED PHYSICS

Alabama Agricultural and Mechanical University	M,D
Appalachian State University	M
Brooklyn College of the City University of New York	M,D
California Institute of Technology	M,D
Carnegie Mellon University	M,D
Columbia University	M,D
Cornell University	M,D
DePaul University	M
George Mason University	M
Georgia Institute of Technology	M,D
Harvard University	M,D
New Jersey Institute of Technology	M,D
Northern Arizona University	M
Pittsburg State University	M
Princeton University	M,D
Rensselaer Polytechnic Institute	M,D
Rice University	M,D
Rutgers, The State University of New Jersey, Newark	M,D
Stanford University	M,D
State University of New York at Binghamton	M
Texas Tech University	M,D
University of Arkansas	M
University of California, San Diego	M,D
University of Central Oklahoma	M
University of Louisiana at Lafayette	M
University of Maryland, Baltimore County	M,D
University of Massachusetts Boston	M
University of Massachusetts Lowell	M,D
University of Michigan	D
University of Missouri–St. Louis	M,D
University of New Orleans	M
The University of North Carolina at Charlotte	M
University of Puerto Rico, Río Piedras	M,D
University of South Florida	M,D
University of Washington	M,D
Virginia Commonwealth University	M
Virginia Polytechnic Institute and State University	M,D
West Virginia University	M,D
Yale University	M,D

■ APPLIED SCIENCE AND TECHNOLOGY

The College of William and Mary	M,D
Harvard University	M,O
James Madison University	M
New Jersey Institute of Technology	M
Oklahoma State University	M
Rensselaer Polytechnic Institute	M
Southern Methodist University	M,D
Southwest Missouri State University	M
University of Arkansas at Little Rock	M,D
University of California, Berkeley	D
University of California, Davis	M,D

■ AQUACULTURE

Auburn University	M,D
Clemson University	M,D
Kentucky State University	M
Purdue University	M,D
University of Florida	M,D
University of Rhode Island	M
Virginia Polytechnic Institute and State University	M,D

■ ARCHAEOLOGY

Boston University	M,D
Brown University	M,D
Columbia University	M,D
Cornell University	M,D
Florida State University	M,D
George Mason University	M
Harvard University	M,D
Michigan Technological University	M
New York University	M,D
Northern Arizona University	M
Princeton University	D
Southern Methodist University	M,D
Tufts University	M
University of California, Berkeley	M,D
University of California, Los Angeles	M,D
University of Chicago	M,D
University of Massachusetts Boston	M
The University of Memphis	M
University of Michigan	D
University of Minnesota, Twin Cities Campus	M,D
University of Missouri–Columbia	M,D
The University of North Carolina at Chapel Hill	M,D
University of Pennsylvania	M,D
The University of Tennessee	M,D
The University of Texas at Austin	M,D
University of Virginia	M,D
Washington University in St. Louis	M,D
Yale University	M

■ ARCHITECTURAL ENGINEERING

Illinois Institute of Technology	M,D
Kansas State University	M

North Carolina Agricultural and Technical State University	M
Oklahoma State University	M
The Pennsylvania State University University Park Campus	M,D
Rensselaer Polytechnic Institute	M
University of Colorado at Boulder	M,D
University of Kansas	M
The University of Memphis	M
University of Miami	M,D
The University of Texas at Austin	M

■ ARCHITECTURAL HISTORY

Arizona State University	D
Cornell University	M,D
Texas A&M University	M,D
University of California, Berkeley	M,D
University of Pittsburgh	M,D
University of Virginia	M,D

■ ARCHITECTURE

Arizona State University	M
Ball State University	M
California Polytechnic State University, San Luis Obispo	M
California State Polytechnic University, Pomona	M
Carnegie Mellon University	M,D
The Catholic University of America	M
City College of the City University of New York	M,O
Clemson University	M
Columbia College Chicago	M
Columbia University	M,D
Cornell University	M,D
Florida Agricultural and Mechanical University	M
Florida International University	M
Georgia Institute of Technology	M,D
Harvard University	M,D
Howard University	M
Illinois Institute of Technology	M,D
Iowa State University of Science and Technology	M
Kansas State University	M
Kent State University	M
Lawrence Technological University	M
Louisiana State University and Agricultural and Mechanical College	M
Massachusetts Institute of Technology	M,D
Miami University	M
Mississippi State University	M
Montana State University–Bozeman	M
Morgan State University	M
New Jersey Institute of Technology	M
New School University	M
New York Institute of Technology	M
North Carolina State University	M
The Ohio State University	M
Oklahoma State University	M
The Pennsylvania State University University Park Campus	M
Pratt Institute	M
Princeton University	M,D
Rensselaer Polytechnic Institute	M
Rice University	M,D
Syracuse University	M
Texas A&M University	M,D
Texas Tech University	M
Tulane University	M
University at Buffalo, The State University of New York	M
The University of Arizona	M
University of California, Berkeley	M,D
University of California, Los Angeles	M,D
University of Cincinnati	M
University of Colorado at Denver	M,D
University of Florida	M,D
University of Hawaii at Manoa	D
University of Houston	M
University of Idaho	M
University of Illinois at Chicago	M
University of Illinois at Urbana–Champaign	M
University of Kansas	M
University of Kentucky	M
University of Maryland, College Park	M
University of Miami	M
University of Michigan	M,D
University of Minnesota, Twin Cities Campus	M
University of Nebraska–Lincoln	M
University of Nevada, Las Vegas	M
University of New Mexico	M
The University of North Carolina at Charlotte	M
University of Notre Dame	M
University of Oklahoma	M
University of Oregon	M
University of Pennsylvania	M,D,O
University of Puerto Rico, Río Piedras	M
University of Southern California	M
University of South Florida	M
The University of Tennessee	M
The University of Texas at Arlington	M
The University of Texas at Austin	M,D
The University of Texas at San Antonio	M
University of Utah	M
University of Virginia	M
University of Washington	M,O
University of Wisconsin–Milwaukee	M,D
Virginia Polytechnic Institute and State University	M
Washington State University	M
Washington University in St. Louis	M
Yale University	M

■ ART/FINE ARTS

Adams State College	M
Adelphi University	M
Alfred University	M
American University	M
Antioch University McGregor	M
Arizona State University	M
Arkansas State University	M
Arkansas Tech University	M
Ball State University	M
Barry University	M
Bloomsburg University of Pennsylvania	M
Boise State University	M
Boston University	M
Bowling Green State University	M
Bradley University	M
Brandeis University	O
Brigham Young University	M
Brooklyn College of the City University of New York	M,D
California State University, Chico	M
California State University, Fresno	M
California State University, Fullerton	M,O
California State University, Long Beach	M
California State University, Los Angeles	M
California State University, Northridge	M
California State University, Sacramento	M
Carnegie Mellon University	M
Central Michigan University	M
Central Missouri State University	M
Central Washington University	M
City College of the City University of New York	M
Claremont Graduate University	M
Clemson University	M
The College of New Rochelle	M
Colorado State University	M
Columbia University	M
Cornell University	M
East Carolina University	M
Eastern Illinois University	M
Eastern Michigan University	M
East Tennessee State University	M
Edinboro University of Pennsylvania	M
Florida Atlantic University	M
Florida International University	M
Florida State University	M
Fontbonne College	M
Fort Hays State University	M
The George Washington University	M
Georgia Southern University	M
Georgia State University	M
Governors State University	M
Howard University	M
Hunter College of the City University of New York	M
Idaho State University	M
Illinois State University	M
Indiana State University	M
Indiana University Bloomington	M
Indiana University of Pennsylvania	M
Inter American University of Puerto Rico, San Germán Campus	M
James Madison University	M
John F. Kennedy University	M
Johnson State College	M
Kansas State University	M
Kent State University	M
Lamar University	M
Lehman College of the City University of New York	M
Long Island University, C.W. Post Campus	M
Louisiana State University and Agricultural and Mechanical College	M
Louisiana Tech University	M
Maharishi University of Management	M
Mansfield University of Pennsylvania	M
Marshall University	M
Marywood University	M
Miami University	M
Michigan State University	M
Minnesota State University, Mankato	M
Mississippi College	M
Mississippi State University	M
Montana State University–Bozeman	M
Montclair State University	M
Morehead State University	M
New Jersey City University	M
New Mexico State University	M
New School University	M
New York University	M,D
Norfolk State University	M
Northern Illinois University	M
Northwestern State University of Louisiana	M
Northwestern University	M
Norwich University	M,O
The Ohio State University	M
Ohio University	M
Oklahoma City University	M
Old Dominion University	M
The Pennsylvania State University University Park Campus	M
Pittsburg State University	M
Portland State University	M
Pratt Institute	M

Purchase College, State University of New York M
Purdue University M
Queens College M
Queens College of the City University of New York M
Radford University M
Rensselaer Polytechnic Institute M
Rhode Island College M
Rochester Institute of Technology M
Rutgers, The State University of New Jersey, New Brunswick M
St. Cloud State University M
Sam Houston State University M
San Diego State University M
San Francisco State University M
San Jose State University M
Southern Illinois University Carbondale M
Southern Illinois University Edwardsville M
Southern Methodist University M
Stanford University M,D
State University of New York at Albany M
State University of New York at New Paltz M
State University of New York at Oswego M
State University of New York College at Brockport M
Stephen F. Austin State University M
Stony Brook University, State University of New York M
Sul Ross State University M
Syracuse University M
Temple University M
Texas A&M University–Commerce M
Texas A&M University–Kingsville M
Texas Christian University M
Texas Tech University M,D
Texas Woman's University M
Towson University M
Tufts University M
Tulane University M
University at Buffalo, The State University of New York M
The University of Alabama M
University of Alaska Fairbanks M
The University of Arizona M
University of Arkansas M
University of Arkansas at Little Rock M
University of California, Berkeley M
University of California, Davis M
University of California, Irvine M
University of California, Los Angeles M
University of California, San Diego M
University of California, Santa Barbara M
University of Chicago M,D
University of Cincinnati M
University of Colorado at Boulder M
University of Connecticut M
University of Delaware M
University of Denver M
University of Florida M
University of Georgia M,D
University of Guam M
University of Hartford M
University of Hawaii at Manoa M
University of Houston M
University of Idaho M
University of Illinois at Chicago M
University of Indianapolis M
The University of Iowa M
University of Kansas M
University of Kentucky M
University of Louisville M
University of Maryland, Baltimore County M
University of Maryland, College Park M
University of Massachusetts Amherst M
University of Massachusetts Dartmouth M
The University of Memphis M
University of Miami M
University of Michigan M
University of Minnesota, Duluth M
University of Minnesota, Twin Cities Campus M
University of Mississippi M
University of Missouri–Columbia M
University of Missouri–Kansas City M
The University of Montana–Missoula M
University of Nebraska–Lincoln M
University of Nevada, Las Vegas M
University of New Hampshire M
University of New Mexico M
University of New Orleans M
The University of North Carolina at Chapel Hill M
The University of North Carolina at Greensboro M
University of North Dakota M
University of Northern Colorado M
University of Northern Iowa M
University of North Texas M,D
University of Notre Dame M
University of Oklahoma M
University of Oregon M
University of Pennsylvania M
University of Rochester M,D
University of Saint Francis (IN) M
University of South Carolina M
University of South Dakota M
University of Southern California M
University of South Florida M
The University of Tennessee M
The University of Texas at Austin M
The University of Texas at El Paso M
The University of Texas at San Antonio M
The University of Texas at Tyler M
The University of Texas–Pan American M
University of Tulsa M
University of Utah M
University of Washington M
University of Wisconsin–Madison M
University of Wisconsin–Milwaukee M
University of Wisconsin–Superior M
Utah State University M
Vanderbilt University M
Virginia Commonwealth University M
Washington State University M
Washington University in St. Louis M
Wayne State University M
Webster University M
Western Carolina University M
Western Connecticut State University M
Western Washington University M
West Texas A&M University M
West Virginia University M
Wichita State University M
William Paterson University of New Jersey M
Winthrop University M
Yale University M

■ ART EDUCATION

Alfred University M
Arcadia University M,O
Ball State University M
Boise State University M
Boston University M
Bridgewater State College M
Brigham Young University M
Brooklyn College of the City University of New York M
California State University, Long Beach M
California State University, Los Angeles M
Carlow College M
Carthage College M,O
Case Western Reserve University M
Central Connecticut State University M
Central Missouri State University M
College of Mount St. Joseph M
The College of New Rochelle M
The College of Saint Rose M
Columbus State University M
Eastern Kentucky University M
Eastern Michigan University M
Eastern Washington University M
Fitchburg State College M
Florida Atlantic University M
Florida International University M
Florida State University M,D,O
Georgia Southern University M,O
Georgia State University M,D,O
Harvard University M,D,O
Henderson State University M
Hofstra University M
Indiana University Bloomington M,D,O
Indiana University–Purdue University Indianapolis M
Jacksonville University M
James Madison University M
Kean University M
Kent State University M
Kutztown University of Pennsylvania M,O
Lesley University M,O
Long Island University, C.W. Post Campus M
Manhattanville College M
Maryville University of Saint Louis M
Marywood University M
Miami University M
Michigan State University M
Millersville University of Pennsylvania M
Minnesota State University, Mankato M
Mississippi College M
Montclair State University M
Morehead State University M
Nazareth College of Rochester M
New Jersey City University M
New York University M,D
North Carolina Agricultural and Technical State University M
North Georgia College & State University M,O
Notre Dame de Namur University M,O
The Ohio State University M,D
Ohio University M
The Pennsylvania State University University Park Campus M,D
Pittsburg State University M
Pratt Institute M
Purdue University M,D,O
Queens College of the City University of New York M,O
Radford University M
Rhode Island College M
Rochester Institute of Technology M
Rockford College M
Rowan University M
Saint Michael's College M,O
Sam Houston State University M
San Jose State University M
Southeast Missouri State University M
Southern Connecticut State University M
Southwestern Oklahoma State University M

Stanford University M,D
State University of New York at New Paltz M
State University of New York at Oswego M
State University of New York College at Buffalo M
State University of West Georgia M
Stony Brook University, State University of New York M,O
Sul Ross State University M
Syracuse University M,O
Teachers College, Columbia University M,D
Temple University M
Texas Tech University M,D,O
Texas Woman's University M
Towson University M
The University of Alabama at Birmingham M
The University of Arizona M
University of Arkansas at Little Rock M
University of Central Florida M
University of Cincinnati M
University of Dayton M
University of Florida M
University of Georgia M,D,O
University of Houston M,D
University of Idaho M
University of Illinois at Urbana–Champaign M,D
University of Indianapolis M
The University of Iowa M,D
University of Kansas M
University of Kentucky M
University of Louisville M
University of Massachusetts Amherst M
University of Massachusetts Dartmouth M
University of Minnesota, Twin Cities Campus M,D
University of Mississippi M
University of Nebraska at Kearney M
University of New Mexico M
The University of North Carolina at Greensboro M
The University of North Carolina at Pembroke M
University of Northern Iowa M
University of North Texas M,D
University of Rio Grande M
University of South Alabama M
University of South Carolina M
University of Southern Mississippi M
University of South Florida M
The University of Tennessee M,D,O
The University of Texas at Austin M
The University of Texas at Tyler M
University of Toledo M
University of Wisconsin–Madison M,D
University of Wisconsin–Milwaukee M
University of Wisconsin–Superior M
Valdosta State University M
Virginia Commonwealth University M
Wayne State College M
Western Carolina University M
Western Kentucky University M
West Virginia University M
Wichita State University M
William Carey College M
Winthrop University M
Xavier University M

■ ART HISTORY

American University M
Bloomsburg University of Pennsylvania M
Boston University M,D,O
Bowling Green State University M
Brigham Young University M
Brooklyn College of the City University of New York M
Brown University M,D
California State University, Fullerton M,O
California State University, Long Beach M
California State University, Los Angeles M
California State University, Northridge M
Case Western Reserve University M,D
City College of the City University of New York M
Cleveland State University M
Columbia University M,D
Cornell University D
Duke University D
Emory University D
Florida State University M,D,O
The George Washington University M
Georgia State University M
Harvard University D
Howard University M
Hunter College of the City University of New York M
Illinois State University M
Indiana State University M
Indiana University Bloomington M,D
James Madison University M
Johns Hopkins University M,D
Lamar University M
Louisiana State University and Agricultural and Mechanical College M
Michigan State University M
Montclair State University M
New York University M,D
Northwestern University D
The Ohio State University M,D
Ohio University M
The Pennsylvania State University University Park Campus M,D
Pratt Institute M
Purchase College, State University of New York M
Queens College of the City University of New York M
Rutgers, The State University of New Jersey, New Brunswick M,D
San Diego State University M
San Francisco State University M
San Jose State University M
Southern Methodist University M
State University of New York at Binghamton M,D
Stony Brook University, State University of New York M,D
Sul Ross State University M
Syracuse University M
Temple University M,D
Texas A&M University–Commerce M
Texas Christian University M
Texas Woman's University M
Tufts University M
Tulane University M
University at Buffalo, The State University of New York M
The University of Alabama M
The University of Alabama at Birmingham M
The University of Arizona M
University of Arkansas at Little Rock M
University of California, Berkeley D
University of California, Davis M
University of California, Irvine D
University of California, Los Angeles M,D
University of California, Riverside M
University of California, Santa Barbara M,D
University of Chicago M,D
University of Cincinnati M
University of Colorado at Boulder M
University of Connecticut M
University of Delaware M,D
University of Denver M
University of Florida M
University of Georgia M
University of Hawaii at Manoa M
University of Illinois at Chicago M,D
University of Illinois at Urbana–Champaign M,D
The University of Iowa M,D
University of Kansas M,D
University of Kentucky M
University of Louisville M,D
University of Maryland, College Park M,D
University of Massachusetts Amherst M
The University of Memphis M
University of Miami M
University of Michigan D
University of Minnesota, Twin Cities Campus M,D
University of Mississippi M
University of Missouri–Columbia M,D
University of Missouri–Kansas City M,D
University of Nebraska–Lincoln M
University of New Mexico M,D
The University of North Carolina at Chapel Hill M,D
University of North Texas M,D
University of Notre Dame M
University of Oklahoma M
University of Oregon M,D
University of Pennsylvania M,D
University of Pittsburgh M,D
University of Rochester M,D
University of St. Thomas (MN) M
University of South Carolina M
University of Southern California M,D,O
University of South Florida M
The University of Texas at Austin M,D
The University of Texas at San Antonio M
University of Utah M
University of Virginia M,D
University of Washington M,D
University of Wisconsin–Madison M,D
University of Wisconsin–Milwaukee M,O
University of Wisconsin–Superior M
Virginia Commonwealth University M,D
Washington University in St. Louis M,D
Wayne State University M
West Virginia University M
Yale University D

■ ARTIFICIAL INTELLIGENCE/ ROBOTICS

Carnegie Mellon University M,D
The Catholic University of America M,D
Cornell University M,D
Howard University M,D
Ohio University D
San Jose State University M
University of California, San Diego M,D
University of Georgia M
University of Southern California M
The University of Tennessee M,D

■ ARTS ADMINISTRATION

American University M,O
Boston University M
Carnegie Mellon University M
Columbia College Chicago M
Drexel University M
Eastern Michigan University M

Florida State University	M,D
Indiana University Bloomington	M
New York University	M
The Ohio State University	M
Oklahoma City University	M
Pratt Institute	M
Saint Mary's University of Minnesota	M
Seton Hall University	M
Shenandoah University	M,D,O
Southern Methodist University	
State University of New York at Binghamton	M
Teachers College, Columbia University	M
Temple University	M,D
Texas Tech University	M,D
The University of Akron	M
University of Cincinnati	M
University of Illinois at Springfield	M
University of New Orleans	M
University of Oregon	M
University of Southern California	M
University of Wisconsin–Madison	M
Virginia Polytechnic Institute and State University	M
Webster University	M

■ ART THERAPY

California State University, Los Angeles	M
The College of New Rochelle	M
Emporia State University	M
The George Washington University	M
Hofstra University	M
Lesley University	M,O
Long Island University, C.W. Post Campus	M
Marylhurst University	M
Marywood University	M
MCP Hahnemann University	M
Mount Mary College	M
National University	M,O
Nazareth College of Rochester	M
New York University	M
Norwich University	M,O
Notre Dame de Namur University	M
Pratt Institute	M
Sage Graduate School	M
Southern Illinois University Edwardsville	M
Springfield College	M,O
University of Illinois at Chicago	M
University of Louisville	M
University of Wisconsin–Superior	M
Ursuline College	M

■ ASIAN LANGUAGES

Brigham Young University	M
Columbia University	M,D
Cornell University	M,D
Harvard University	M,D
Indiana University Bloomington	M,D
Monterey Institute of International Studies	M
The Ohio State University	M,D
San Francisco State University	M
Stanford University	M,D
University of California, Berkeley	M,D
University of California, Irvine	M,D
University of California, Los Angeles	M,D
University of Chicago	M,D
University of Colorado at Boulder	M
University of Hawaii at Manoa	M,D
University of Illinois at Urbana–Champaign	M,D
University of Kansas	M
University of Massachusetts Amherst	M
University of Michigan	M,D
University of Oregon	M,D
University of Southern California	M,D
The University of Texas at Austin	M,D
University of Washington	M,D
University of Wisconsin–Madison	M,D
Washington University in St. Louis	M,D
Yale University	D

■ ASIAN STUDIES

Brigham Young University	M
California State University, Long Beach	M,O
Columbia University	M,D,O
Cornell University	M,D
Duke University	M,O
Florida State University	M
The George Washington University	M
Harvard University	M,D
Indiana University Bloomington	M,D
Johns Hopkins University	M,D,O
Ohio University	M
Princeton University	D
St. John's University (NY)	M,O
San Diego State University	M
Seton Hall University	M
Stanford University	M
The University of Arizona	M,D
University of California, Berkeley	M,D
University of California, Irvine	M,D
University of California, Los Angeles	M,D
University of California, Santa Barbara	M
University of Chicago	M,D
University of Hawaii at Manoa	M
University of Illinois at Urbana–Champaign	M,D
The University of Iowa	M
University of Kansas	M
University of Michigan	M,D
University of Minnesota, Twin Cities Campus	M
University of Oregon	M
University of Pennsylvania	M,D
University of Pittsburgh	M
University of San Francisco	M
University of Southern California	M,D
The University of Texas at Austin	M,D
University of Virginia	M
University of Washington	M
University of Wisconsin–Madison	M,D
Washington University in St. Louis	M,D
West Virginia University	M,D
Yale University	M

■ ASTRONOMY

Arizona State University	M,D
Boston University	M,D
Bowling Green State University	M
Brigham Young University	M,D
California Institute of Technology	D
Case Western Reserve University	M,D
Clemson University	M,D
Columbia University	M,D
Cornell University	D
Dartmouth College	M,D
Georgia State University	D
Harvard University	M,D
Indiana University Bloomington	M,D
Iowa State University of Science and Technology	M,D
Johns Hopkins University	D
Louisiana State University and Agricultural and Mechanical College	M,D
Michigan State University	M,D
Minnesota State University, Mankato	M
New Mexico State University	M,D
Northwestern University	M,D
The Ohio State University	M,D
The Pennsylvania State University University Park Campus	M,D
Rice University	M,D
San Diego State University	M
The University of Arizona	M,D
University of California, Los Angeles	M,D
University of California, Santa Cruz	D
University of Chicago	M,D
University of Delaware	M,D
University of Florida	M,D
University of Georgia	M,D
University of Hawaii at Manoa	M,D
University of Illinois at Urbana–Champaign	M,D
The University of Iowa	M
University of Kansas	M,D
University of Kentucky	M,D
University of Maryland, College Park	M,D
University of Massachusetts Amherst	M,D
University of Michigan	M,D
University of Minnesota, Twin Cities Campus	M,D
University of Nebraska–Lincoln	M,D
The University of North Carolina at Chapel Hill	M,D
University of Pittsburgh	M,D
University of Rochester	M,D
University of South Carolina	M,D
University of Southern Mississippi	M
The University of Texas at Austin	M,D
University of Virginia	M,D
University of Washington	M,D
University of Wisconsin–Madison	D
Vanderbilt University	M
West Chester University of Pennsylvania	M
Yale University	M,D

■ ASTROPHYSICS

Clemson University	M,D
Cornell University	D
Harvard University	M,D
Indiana University Bloomington	D
Louisiana State University and Agricultural and Mechanical College	M,D
Michigan State University	M,D
New Mexico Institute of Mining and Technology	M,D
Northwestern University	M,D
The Pennsylvania State University University Park Campus	M,D
Princeton University	D
Rensselaer Polytechnic Institute	M,D
San Francisco State University	M
University of Alaska Fairbanks	M,D
University of California, Berkeley	D
University of California, Los Angeles	M,D
University of California, Santa Cruz	D
University of Chicago	M,D
University of Colorado at Boulder	M,D
University of Minnesota, Twin Cities Campus	M,D
University of Missouri–St. Louis	M,D
The University of North Carolina at Chapel Hill	M,D
University of Oklahoma	M,D
University of Pennsylvania	D

■ ATMOSPHERIC SCIENCES

City College of the City University of New York	M,D
Clemson University	M,D

Colorado State University	M,D
Columbia University	M,D
Cornell University	M,D
Creighton University	M
Drexel University	M,D
Georgia Institute of Technology	M,D
Howard University	M,D
Massachusetts Institute of Technology	M,D
New Mexico Institute of Mining and Technology	M,D
North Carolina State University	M,D
The Ohio State University	M,D
Oregon State University	M,D
Princeton University	D
Purdue University	M,D
Saint Louis University	M,D
South Dakota State University	D
State University of New York at Albany	M,D
Stony Brook University, State University of New York	M,D
Texas Tech University	M,D
The University of Alabama in Huntsville	M,D
University of Alaska Fairbanks	M,D
The University of Arizona	M,D
University of California, Davis	M,D
University of California, Los Angeles	M,D
University of Chicago	M,D
University of Colorado at Boulder	M,D
University of Delaware	D
University of Illinois at Urbana–Champaign	M,D
University of Maryland, Baltimore County	M,D
University of Miami	M,D
University of Michigan	M,D
University of Missouri–Columbia	M,D
University of Nevada, Reno	M,D
University of New Hampshire	
The University of North Carolina at Chapel Hill	M,D
University of North Dakota	M
University of Washington	M,D
University of Wisconsin–Madison	M,D
University of Wyoming	M,D

■ AUTOMOTIVE ENGINEERING

Colorado State University	M,D
Lawrence Technological University	M
University of Detroit Mercy	M,D
University of Michigan	M
University of Michigan–Dearborn	M

■ AVIATION

Central Missouri State University	M
University of New Haven	M
University of North Dakota	M
The University of Tennessee	M

■ AVIATION MANAGEMENT

Delta State University	M
Dowling College	M,O
Embry-Riddle Aeronautical University	M
Embry-Riddle Aeronautical University, Extended Campus	M
University of Dubuque	M

■ BACTERIOLOGY

Purdue University	M,D
The University of Iowa	M,D
University of Virginia	
University of Wisconsin–Madison	M
West Virginia University	M,D

■ BIOCHEMICAL ENGINEERING

California Polytechnic State University, San Luis Obispo	M
Cornell University	M,D
Dartmouth College	M,D
Drexel University	M
Rutgers, The State University of New Jersey, New Brunswick	M,D
University of California, Irvine	M,D
The University of Iowa	M,D
University of Maryland, Baltimore County	M,D

■ BIOCHEMISTRY

Arizona State University	M,D
Boston College	M,D
Boston University	M,D
Brandeis University	M,D
Brigham Young University	M,D
Brown University	M,D
California Institute of Technology	M,D
California State University, Fullerton	M
California State University, Hayward	M
California State University, Long Beach	M
California State University, Los Angeles	M
Carnegie Mellon University	M,D
Case Western Reserve University	M,D
City College of the City University of New York	M,D
Clemson University	M,D
Colorado State University	M,D
Columbia University	M,D
Cornell University	D
Dartmouth College	D
DePaul University	M
Duke University	D,O
Duquesne University	M,D
East Carolina University	D
East Tennessee State University	M,D
Emory University	D
Florida Atlantic University	M,D
Florida State University	M,D
Georgetown University	M,D
The George Washington University	M,D
Georgia Institute of Technology	M,D
Georgia State University	M,D
Harvard University	M,D
Howard University	M,D
Hunter College of the City University of New York	M
Illinois Institute of Technology	M,D
Indiana University Bloomington	M,D
Indiana University–Purdue University Indianapolis	M,D
Iowa State University of Science and Technology	M,D
Johns Hopkins University	M,D
Kansas State University	M,D
Kent State University	M,D
Lehigh University	D
Loma Linda University	M,D
Louisiana State University and Agricultural and Mechanical College	M,D
Loyola University Chicago	M,D
Massachusetts Institute of Technology	D
Mayo Graduate School	D
MCP Hahnemann University	M,D
Miami University	M,D
Michigan State University	M,D
Mississippi State University	M,D
Montana State University–Bozeman	M,D
New Mexico Institute of Mining and Technology	M,D
New Mexico State University	M,D
New York University	M,D
North Carolina State University	M,D
North Dakota State University	M,D
Northern Illinois University	M,D
Northwestern University	D
The Ohio State University	M,D
Ohio University	M,D
Oklahoma State University	M,D
Old Dominion University	M
Oregon State University	M,D
The Pennsylvania State University University Park Campus	M,D
Purdue University	M,D
Queens College of the City University of New York	M
Rensselaer Polytechnic Institute	M,D
Rice University	M,D
Rutgers, The State University of New Jersey, Newark	M,D
Rutgers, The State University of New Jersey, New Brunswick	M,D
Saint Louis University	D
San Jose State University	M
Seton Hall University	M,D
South Dakota State University	M,D
Southern Illinois University Carbondale	M,D
Southern University and Agricultural and Mechanical College	M
Southwest Texas State University	M
Stanford University	D
State University of New York at Albany	M,D
Stevens Institute of Technology	M,D,O
Stony Brook University, State University of New York	D
Syracuse University	D
Temple University	M,D
Texas A&M University	M,D
Tufts University	D
Tulane University	M,D
University at Buffalo, The State University of New York	M,D
The University of Alabama at Birmingham	D
University of Alaska Fairbanks	M,D
The University of Arizona	M,D
University of California, Berkeley	D
University of California, Davis	M,D
University of California, Irvine	D
University of California, Los Angeles	M,D
University of California, Riverside	M,D
University of California, San Diego	M,D
University of California, San Francisco	D
University of California, Santa Barbara	D
University of Chicago	D
University of Cincinnati	M,D
University of Colorado at Boulder	M,D
University of Connecticut	M,D
University of Delaware	M,D
University of Detroit Mercy	M,D
University of Florida	D
University of Georgia	M,D
University of Hawaii at Manoa	M,D
University of Houston	M,D
University of Idaho	M,D
University of Illinois at Chicago	M,D
University of Illinois at Urbana–Champaign	M,D
The University of Iowa	M,D
University of Kansas	M,D
University of Kentucky	D
University of Louisville	M,D
University of Maine	M,D
University of Maryland	D

University of Maryland, Baltimore County	D
University of Maryland, College Park	M,D
University of Massachusetts Amherst	M,D
University of Massachusetts Lowell	M,D
University of Miami	D
University of Michigan	D
University of Minnesota, Duluth	M,D
University of Minnesota, Twin Cities Campus	D
University of Missouri–Columbia	M,D
University of Missouri–Kansas City	D
University of Missouri–St. Louis	M,D,O
The University of Montana–Missoula	M,D
University of Nebraska–Lincoln	M,D
University of Nevada, Reno	M,D
University of New Hampshire	M,D
University of New Mexico	M,D
The University of North Carolina at Chapel Hill	M,D
University of North Dakota	M,D
University of North Texas	M,D
University of Notre Dame	M,D
University of Oklahoma	M,D
University of Oregon	M,D
University of Pennsylvania	D
University of Pittsburgh	M,D
University of Rhode Island	M,D
University of Rochester	M,D
The University of Scranton	M
University of South Alabama	D
University of South Carolina	M,D
University of Southern California	M,D
University of Southern Mississippi	M,D
University of South Florida	M,D
The University of Tennessee	M,D
The University of Texas at Austin	M,D
University of the Pacific	M,D
University of Toledo	M,D
University of Utah	M,D
University of Vermont	M,D
University of Virginia	D
University of Washington	D
University of Wisconsin–Madison	M,D
Utah State University	M,D
Vanderbilt University	M,D
Virginia Commonwealth University	M,D,O
Virginia Polytechnic Institute and State University	M,D
Wake Forest University	D
Washington State University	M,D
Washington University in St. Louis	D
Wayne State University	M,D
West Virginia University	M,D
Worcester Polytechnic Institute	M,D
Wright State University	M
Yale University	M,D
Yeshiva University	D

■ BIOENGINEERING

Alfred University	M,D
Arizona State University	M,D
Auburn University	M,D
California Polytechnic State University, San Luis Obispo	M
Carnegie Mellon University	M,D
Case Western Reserve University	M,D
Clemson University	M,D
Colorado State University	M,D
Cornell University	M,D
Georgia Institute of Technology	M,D,O
Kansas State University	M,D
Louisiana State University and Agricultural and Mechanical College	M,D
Massachusetts Institute of Technology	M,D
Mississippi State University	M,D
North Carolina State University	M,D
The Ohio State University	M,D
Oklahoma State University	M,D
Oregon State University	M,D
The Pennsylvania State University University Park Campus	M,D
Purdue University	M,D
Rice University	M,D
Rutgers, The State University of New Jersey, New Brunswick	M
Syracuse University	M
Tufts University	O
University of Arkansas	M,D
University of California, Berkeley	D
University of California, Davis	M,D
University of California, San Diego	M,D
University of California, San Francisco	D
University of Connecticut	M,D
University of Florida	M,D,O
University of Georgia	M,D
University of Hawaii at Manoa	M
University of Illinois at Chicago	M,D
University of Illinois at Urbana–Champaign	
University of Maryland, College Park	M,D
University of Missouri–Columbia	M,D
University of Nebraska–Lincoln	M,D
University of Notre Dame	M,D
University of Pennsylvania	M,D
University of Pittsburgh	M,D
University of Toledo	M,D
University of Utah	M,D
University of Washington	M,D
Virginia Polytechnic Institute and State University	M,D

■ BIOETHICS

Case Western Reserve University	M
Duquesne University	M,D
Loma Linda University	M
Saint Louis University	D
University of Maryland	M
University of Pennsylvania	
University of Pittsburgh	M
The University of Tennessee	M,D
University of Virginia	M

■ BIOINFORMATICS

George Mason University	M
Indiana University Bloomington	M
Iowa State University of Science and Technology	M,D
New Jersey Institute of Technology	M,D
North Carolina State University	M,D
Rensselaer Polytechnic Institute	M
Rice University	M,D
University of California, Riverside	D
University of California, San Diego	D
University of Washington	M

■ BIOLOGICAL AND BIOMEDICAL SCIENCES—GENERAL

Adelphi University	M
Alabama Agricultural and Mechanical University	M
Alabama State University	M,O
Alcorn State University	M
American University	M
Andrews University	M
Angelo State University	M
Anna Maria College	M
Appalachian State University	M
Arizona State University	M,D
Arkansas State University	M,D,O
Auburn University	M,D
Austin Peay State University	M
Ball State University	M,D
Barry University	M
Baylor University	M,D
Bemidji State University	M
Bloomsburg University of Pennsylvania	M
Boise State University	M
Boston College	M,D
Boston University	M,D
Bowling Green State University	M,D,O
Bradley University	M
Brandeis University	M,D,O
Brigham Young University	M,D
Brooklyn College of the City University of New York	M,D
Brown University	M,D
California Institute of Technology	D
California Polytechnic State University, San Luis Obispo	M
California State Polytechnic University, Pomona	M
California State University, Chico	M
California State University, Dominguez Hills	M,O
California State University, Fresno	M
California State University, Fullerton	M
California State University, Hayward	M
California State University, Long Beach	M
California State University, Los Angeles	M
California State University, Northridge	M
California State University, Sacramento	M
California State University, San Bernardino	M
California State University, San Marcos	M
California University of Pennsylvania	M
Carnegie Mellon University	M,D
Case Western Reserve University	M,D
The Catholic University of America	M,D
Central Connecticut State University	M,O
Central Michigan University	M
Central Missouri State University	M
Central Washington University	M
Chicago State University	M
City College of the City University of New York	M,D
Clarion University of Pennsylvania	M
Clark Atlanta University	M,D
Clark University	M,D
Clemson University	M,D
Cleveland State University	M,D
College of Staten Island of the City University of New York	M
The College of William and Mary	M
Colorado State University	M,D
Columbia University	M,D
Creighton University	M,D
Dartmouth College	D
Delaware State University	M
Delta State University	M
DePaul University	M
Drexel University	M,D
Duke University	D
Duquesne University	M
East Carolina University	M,D
Eastern Illinois University	M
Eastern Kentucky University	M
Eastern Michigan University	M
Eastern New Mexico University	M
Eastern Washington University	M
East Stroudsburg University of Pennsylvania	M
East Tennessee State University	M,D
Edinboro University of Pennsylvania	M
Emory University	D
Emporia State University	M

Fairleigh Dickinson University, Florham-Madison Campus M
Fairleigh Dickinson University, Teaneck–Hackensack Campus M
Fayetteville State University M
Florida Agricultural and Mechanical University M
Florida Atlantic University M
Florida Institute of Technology M,D
Florida International University M,D
Florida State University M,D
Fordham University M,D
Fort Hays State University M
Frostburg State University M
George Mason University M
Georgetown University M,D
The George Washington University M,D
Georgia College and State University M
Georgia Institute of Technology M,D
Georgian Court College M
Georgia Southern University M
Georgia State University M,D
Hampton University M
Harvard University M,D,O
Hofstra University M
Hood College M
Howard University M,D
Humboldt State University M
Hunter College of the City University of New York M,D
Idaho State University M,D
Illinois Institute of Technology M,D
Illinois State University M,D
Indiana State University M,D
Indiana University Bloomington M,D
Indiana University of Pennsylvania M
Indiana University–Purdue University Fort Wayne M
Indiana University–Purdue University Indianapolis M,D
Jackson State University M,D
Jacksonville State University M
James Madison University M
John Carroll University M
Johns Hopkins University M,D
Kansas State University M,D
Kent State University M,D
Lamar University M
Lehigh University D
Lehman College of the City University of New York M,D
Loma Linda University M,D
Long Island University, Brooklyn Campus M
Long Island University, C.W. Post Campus M
Louisiana State University and Agricultural and Mechanical College M,D
Louisiana Tech University M
Loyola University Chicago M
Marquette University M,D
Marshall University M,D
Massachusetts Institute of Technology P,D
Mayo Graduate School D
McNeese State University M
MCP Hahnemann University M,D,O
Miami University M,D
Michigan State University M,D
Michigan Technological University M,D
Middle Tennessee State University M
Midwestern State University M
Millersville University of Pennsylvania M
Minnesota State University, Mankato M
Mississippi College M
Mississippi State University M,D
Montana State University–Bozeman M,D
Montclair State University M,O
Morehead State University M
Morgan State University M,D
Murray State University M,D
New Jersey Institute of Technology M,D
New Mexico Highlands University M
New Mexico Institute of Mining and Technology M
New Mexico State University M,D
New York University M,D
North Carolina Agricultural and Technical State University M
North Carolina Central University M
North Carolina State University M,D
Northeastern Illinois University M
Northeastern University M,D
Northern Arizona University M,D
Northern Illinois University M,D
Northern Michigan University M
Northwestern University D
Northwest Missouri State University M
Nova Southeastern University M
Oakland University M
The Ohio State University M,D
Ohio University M,D
Old Dominion University M,D
The Pennsylvania State University University Park Campus M,D
Pittsburg State University M
Portland State University M,D
Prairie View A&M University M
Princeton University D
Purdue University M,D
Purdue University Calumet M
Queens College of the City University of New York M
Quinnipiac University M
Rensselaer Polytechnic Institute M,D
Rhode Island College M
The Rockefeller University D
Rutgers, The State University of New Jersey, Camden M
Rutgers, The State University of New Jersey, Newark M,D
St. Cloud State University M
Saint Francis University M
St. John's University (NY) M,D
Saint Joseph College M
Saint Joseph's University M
Saint Louis University M,D
Salem International University M
Sam Houston State University M
San Diego State University M,D
San Francisco State University M
San Jose State University M
Seton Hall University M
Shippensburg University of Pennsylvania M
Sonoma State University M
South Dakota State University M,D
Southeastern Louisiana University M
Southeast Missouri State University M
Southern Connecticut State University M
Southern Illinois University Carbondale M,D
Southern Illinois University Edwardsville M
Southern Methodist University M,D
Southern University and Agricultural and Mechanical College M
Southwest Missouri State University M
Southwest Texas State University M
Stanford University M,D
State University of New York at Albany M,D
State University of New York at Binghamton M,D
State University of New York at New Paltz M
State University of New York College at Brockport M
State University of New York College at Buffalo M
State University of New York College at Cortland M
State University of New York College at Fredonia M
State University of New York College at Oneonta M
State University of West Georgia M
Stephen F. Austin State University M
Stony Brook University, State University of New York D
Sul Ross State University M
Syracuse University M,D
Tarleton State University M
Temple University M,D
Tennessee State University M,D
Tennessee Technological University M
Texas A&M University M,D
Texas A&M University–Commerce M
Texas A&M University–Corpus Christi M
Texas A&M University–Kingsville M
Texas Christian University M
Texas Southern University M
Texas Tech University M,D
Texas Woman's University M,D
Touro College M
Towson University M
Truman State University M
Tufts University M,D,O
Tulane University M,D,O
Tuskegee University M
University at Buffalo, The State University of New York M,D
The University of Akron M
The University of Alabama M,D
The University of Alabama at Birmingham M,D
The University of Alabama in Huntsville M
University of Alaska Anchorage M
University of Alaska Fairbanks M,D
The University of Arizona M,D
University of Arkansas M,D
University of California, Berkeley D
University of California, Irvine M,D
University of California, Los Angeles M,D
University of California, Riverside M,D
University of California, San Diego M,D
University of California, San Francisco D
University of California, Santa Cruz D
University of Central Arkansas M
University of Central Florida M,O
University of Central Oklahoma M
University of Chicago M,D
University of Cincinnati M,D
University of Colorado at Denver M
University of Connecticut M,D
University of Dayton M,D
University of Delaware M,D
University of Denver M,D
University of Detroit Mercy M
University of Florida M,D
University of Guam M
University of Hartford M
University of Hawaii at Manoa M,D
University of Houston M,D
University of Houston–Clear Lake M
University of Idaho M,D
University of Illinois at Chicago M,D
University of Illinois at Springfield M
University of Illinois at Urbana–Champaign M,D

University of Indianapolis	M
The University of Iowa	M,D
University of Kansas	M,D
University of Kentucky	M,D
University of Louisiana at Lafayette	M,D
University of Louisiana at Monroe	M
University of Louisville	M,D
University of Maine	D
University of Maryland	M,D
University of Maryland, Baltimore County	M,D
University of Maryland, College Park	M,D
University of Massachusetts Amherst	M,D
University of Massachusetts Boston	M
University of Massachusetts Dartmouth	M
University of Massachusetts Lowell	M,D
The University of Memphis	M,D
University of Miami	M,D
University of Michigan	M,D
University of Minnesota, Duluth	M
University of Minnesota, Twin Cities Campus	M,D
University of Mississippi	M,D
University of Missouri–Columbia	M,D
University of Missouri–Kansas City	M,D
University of Missouri–St. Louis	M,D,O
The University of Montana–Missoula	M,D
University of Nebraska at Kearney	M
University of Nebraska at Omaha	M
University of Nebraska–Lincoln	M,D
University of Nevada, Las Vegas	M,D
University of Nevada, Reno	M,D
University of New Hampshire	M,D
University of New Mexico	M,D
University of New Orleans	M,D
The University of North Carolina at Chapel Hill	M,D
The University of North Carolina at Charlotte	M,D
The University of North Carolina at Greensboro	M
The University of North Carolina at Wilmington	M
University of North Dakota	M,D
University of Northern Colorado	M,D
University of Northern Iowa	M
University of North Texas	M,D
University of Notre Dame	M,D
University of Oregon	M,D
University of Pennsylvania	M,D
University of Pittsburgh	M,D
University of Puerto Rico, Mayagüez Campus	M
University of Puerto Rico, Río Piedras	M,D
University of Richmond	M
University of Rochester	M,D,O
University of San Francisco	M
University of South Alabama	M,D
University of South Carolina	M,D
University of South Dakota	M,D
University of Southern California	M,D
University of Southern Mississippi	M,D
University of South Florida	M,D
The University of Tennessee	M,D
The University of Texas at Arlington	M,D
The University of Texas at Austin	M,D
The University of Texas at Brownsville	M
The University of Texas at El Paso	M,D
The University of Texas at San Antonio	M,D
The University of Texas at Tyler	M
The University of Texas of the Permian Basin	M
The University of Texas–Pan American	M
University of the Incarnate Word	M
University of the Pacific	M
University of Toledo	M,D
University of Tulsa	M,D
University of Utah	M,D
University of Vermont	M,D
University of Virginia	M,D
University of Washington	M,D
University of West Florida	M
University of Wisconsin–Eau Claire	M
University of Wisconsin–La Crosse	M
University of Wisconsin–Madison	M,D
University of Wisconsin–Milwaukee	M,D
University of Wisconsin–Oshkosh	M
Utah State University	M,D
Vanderbilt University	M,D
Villanova University	M
Virginia Commonwealth University	M,D,O
Virginia Polytechnic Institute and State University	M,D
Virginia State University	M
Wagner College	M
Wake Forest University	M,D
Walla Walla College	M
Washington State University	M,D
Washington University in St. Louis	D
Wayne State University	M,D,O
West Chester University of Pennsylvania	M
Western Carolina University	M
Western Connecticut State University	M
Western Illinois University	M,O
Western Kentucky University	M
Western Michigan University	M,D
Western Washington University	M
West Texas A&M University	M
West Virginia University	M,D
Wichita State University	M
William Paterson University of New Jersey	M
Winthrop University	M
Worcester Polytechnic Institute	M,D
Wright State University	M,D
Yale University	D
Yeshiva University	D
Youngstown State University	M

■ BIOMEDICAL ENGINEERING

Arizona State University	M,D
Boston University	M,D
Brown University	M,D
California Polytechnic State University, San Luis Obispo	M
California State University, Northridge	M
Carnegie Mellon University	M,D
Case Western Reserve University	M,D
The Catholic University of America	M,D
Clemson University	M,D
Cleveland State University	D
Colorado State University	M,D
Columbia University	M,D
Cornell University	M,D
Dartmouth College	M,D
Drexel University	M,D
Duke University	M,D
Florida International University	M
Georgia Institute of Technology	M,D,O
Harvard University	M,D
Illinois Institute of Technology	D
Indiana University–Purdue University Indianapolis	M,D
Johns Hopkins University	M,D
Louisiana Tech University	M,D
Marquette University	M,D
Massachusetts Institute of Technology	D
Mayo Graduate School	D
Mercer University	M
Mississippi State University	M,D
New Jersey Institute of Technology	M
Northwestern University	M,D
The Ohio State University	M,D
The Pennsylvania State University University Park Campus	M,D
Purdue University	M,D
Rensselaer Polytechnic Institute	M,D
Rice University	M,D
Rutgers, The State University of New Jersey, New Brunswick	M,D
Stanford University	M
Stony Brook University, State University of New York	M,D,O
Syracuse University	M
Texas A&M University	M,D
Tulane University	M,D
The University of Akron	M
The University of Alabama at Birmingham	M,D
University of California, Berkeley	D
University of California, Davis	M,D
University of California, Irvine	M,D
University of California, Los Angeles	M,D
University of California, San Diego	M,D
University of California, San Francisco	D
University of Connecticut	M,D
University of Florida	M,D,O
University of Houston	M,D
University of Illinois at Chicago	M,D
University of Illinois at Urbana–Champaign	
The University of Iowa	M,D
University of Kentucky	M,D
The University of Memphis	M,D
University of Miami	M,D
University of Michigan	M,D
University of Minnesota, Twin Cities Campus	M,D
University of Nevada, Reno	M,D
The University of North Carolina at Chapel Hill	M,D
University of Pennsylvania	M,D
University of Pittsburgh	M,D
University of Rochester	M,D
University of Southern California	M,D
The University of Tennessee	M,D
The University of Texas at Arlington	M,D
The University of Texas at Austin	M,D
University of Utah	M,D
University of Vermont	M
University of Virginia	M,D
University of Washington	M,D
Vanderbilt University	M,D
Virginia Commonwealth University	M,D
Virginia Polytechnic Institute and State University	
Wake Forest University	D
Washington University in St. Louis	M,D
Wayne State University	M,D
Worcester Polytechnic Institute	M,D,O
Wright State University	M

■ BIOMETRICS

Cornell University	M,D
North Carolina State University	M,D
Oregon State University	M,D
State University of New York at Albany	M,D
The University of Alabama at Birmingham	M,D
University of California, Los Angeles	M,D
University of Nebraska–Lincoln	M
University of Southern California	M
University of Wisconsin–Madison	M

■ BIOPHYSICS

Boston University	M,D
Brandeis University	D

California Institute of Technology	D
Carnegie Mellon University	M,D
Case Western Reserve University	M,D
Clemson University	M,D
Columbia University	M,D
Cornell University	D
Duke University	O
East Carolina University	M,D
East Tennessee State University	M,D
Emory University	D
Florida State University	D
Georgetown University	M,D
Harvard University	D
Howard University	D
Indiana University–Purdue University Indianapolis	M,D
Iowa State University of Science and Technology	M,D
Johns Hopkins University	M,D
Massachusetts Institute of Technology	D
Northwestern University	D
The Ohio State University	M,D
Oregon State University	M,D
Princeton University	D
Purdue University	D
Rensselaer Polytechnic Institute	M,D
Stanford University	D
Stony Brook University, State University of New York	D
Syracuse University	M,D
Texas A&M University	M,D
University at Buffalo, The State University of New York	M,D
The University of Alabama at Birmingham	D
University of California, Berkeley	M,D
University of California, Davis	M,D
University of California, Irvine	D
University of California, San Diego	M,D
University of California, San Francisco	D
University of Cincinnati	M,D
University of Connecticut	M,D
University of Hawaii at Manoa	M,D
University of Illinois at Chicago	M,D
University of Illinois at Urbana–Champaign	D
The University of Iowa	M,D
University of Kansas	M,D
University of Louisville	M,D
University of Miami	D
University of Michigan	D
University of Minnesota, Twin Cities Campus	M,D
University of Missouri–Kansas City	D
The University of North Carolina at Chapel Hill	M,D
University of Pennsylvania	D
University of Pittsburgh	D
University of Rochester	M,D
University of Southern California	M,D
University of South Florida	D
University of Vermont	M,D
University of Virginia	D
University of Washington	D
University of Wisconsin–Madison	D
Vanderbilt University	D
Virginia Commonwealth University	M,D,O
Washington State University	M,D
Washington University in St. Louis	D
Wright State University	M
Yale University	M,D
Yeshiva University	D

■ BIOPSYCHOLOGY

American University	M
Boston University	M
Carnegie Mellon University	D
Columbia University	M,D
Cornell University	D
Drexel University	M,D
Duke University	D
Emory University	D
Harvard University	M,D
Howard University	M,D
Hunter College of the City University of New York	M
Louisiana State University and Agricultural and Mechanical College	M,D
Mayo Graduate School	D
Northwestern University	D
The Ohio State University	D
The Pennsylvania State University University Park Campus	M,D
Rutgers, The State University of New Jersey, Newark	D
Rutgers, The State University of New Jersey, New Brunswick	D
State University of New York at Albany	M,D
State University of New York at Binghamton	M,D
Stony Brook University, State University of New York	D
University of Colorado at Boulder	M,D
University of Connecticut	M,D
University of Delaware	D
University of Illinois at Urbana–Champaign	M,D
University of Michigan	D
University of Minnesota, Twin Cities Campus	D
University of New Orleans	M,D
University of Oregon	M,D
University of Wisconsin–Madison	D

■ BIOSTATISTICS

Arizona State University	M,D
Boston University	M,D
Brown University	M,D
Case Western Reserve University	M,D
Columbia University	M,D
Drexel University	M,D
Emory University	M,D
Georgetown University	M
The George Washington University	M,D
Harvard University	M,D
Iowa State University of Science and Technology	M,D
Johns Hopkins University	M,D
Loma Linda University	M
The Ohio State University	D
Rice University	M,D
San Diego State University	M,D
Tulane University	M,D
The University of Alabama at Birmingham	M,D
University of California, Berkeley	M,D
University of California, Los Angeles	M,D
University of Cincinnati	M,D
University of Illinois at Chicago	M,D
The University of Iowa	M,D
University of Michigan	M,D
University of Minnesota, Twin Cities Campus	M,D
The University of North Carolina at Chapel Hill	M,D
University of Pennsylvania	M,D
University of Pittsburgh	M,D
University of Rochester	M,D
University of South Carolina	M,D
University of Southern California	M,D
University of South Florida	M,D
University of Utah	M
University of Vermont	M
University of Washington	M,D
Virginia Commonwealth University	M,D
Western Michigan University	M
Yale University	M,D

■ BIOTECHNOLOGY

Brown University	M,D
Dartmouth College	M,D
East Carolina University	M
Florida Institute of Technology	M,D
Howard University	M,D
Illinois Institute of Technology	M,D
Illinois State University	M
Kean University	
Manhattan College	M
National University	M
North Carolina State University	M
Northwestern University	M,D
The Pennsylvania State University University Park Campus	M
Salem International University	M
Stephen F. Austin State University	M
Texas A&M University	M
Tufts University	O
University of Connecticut	M,D
University of Delaware	M,D
University of Massachusetts Boston	M
University of Massachusetts Lowell	M,D
University of Minnesota, Twin Cities Campus	M
University of Missouri–St. Louis	M,D,O
University of Pennsylvania	M
The University of Texas at San Antonio	M
University of Virginia	D
University of Washington	D
University of Wisconsin–Madison	
William Paterson University of New Jersey	M
Worcester Polytechnic Institute	M,D
Worcester State College	M

■ BOTANY AND PLANT SCIENCES

Alabama Agricultural and Mechanical University	M,D
Arizona State University	M,D
Auburn University	M,D
Brigham Young University	M,D
California State University, Chico	M
California State University, Fresno	M
California State University, Fullerton	M
Claremont Graduate University	M,D
Clemson University	M
Colorado State University	M,D
Cornell University	M,D
Eastern Illinois University	M
Emporia State University	M
Florida State University	M,D
Illinois State University	M,D
Indiana University Bloomington	M,D
Iowa State University of Science and Technology	M,D
Kent State University	M,D
Lehman College of the City University of New York	D
Louisiana State University and Agricultural and Mechanical College	M,D
Miami University	M,D
Michigan State University	M,D
Mississippi State University	M,D
Montana State University–Bozeman	M,D
North Carolina Agricultural and Technical State University	M
North Carolina State University	M,D

North Dakota State University	M,D
The Ohio State University	M,D
Ohio University	M,D
Oklahoma State University	M,D
Oregon State University	M,D
Purdue University	M,D
Rensselaer Polytechnic Institute	M,D
Rutgers, The State University of New Jersey, New Brunswick	M,D
South Dakota State University	M,D
Southern Illinois University Carbondale	M,D
Southwest Missouri State University	M
Texas A&M University	M,D
Texas A&M University–Kingsville	M
Texas Tech University	M,D
University of Alaska Fairbanks	M,D
The University of Arizona	M,D
University of Arkansas	D
University of California, Berkeley	D
University of California, Davis	M,D
University of California, Riverside	M,D
University of California, San Diego	D
University of Colorado at Boulder	M,D
University of Connecticut	M,D
University of Delaware	M,D
University of Florida	M,D
University of Georgia	M,D
University of Hawaii at Manoa	M,D
University of Idaho	M,D
University of Illinois at Chicago	M,D
University of Illinois at Urbana–Champaign	M,D
The University of Iowa	M,D
University of Kentucky	M
University of Maine	M,D
University of Maryland, College Park	M,D
University of Massachusetts Amherst	M,D
University of Michigan	M,D
University of Minnesota, Twin Cities Campus	M,D
University of Missouri–St. Louis	M,D,O
University of New Hampshire	M,D
The University of North Carolina at Chapel Hill	M,D
University of North Dakota	M,D
University of Oklahoma	M,D
University of Pennsylvania	D
University of Rhode Island	M,D
University of South Florida	M
The University of Tennessee	M,D
The University of Texas at Austin	M,D
University of Vermont	M,D
University of Washington	M,D
University of Wisconsin–Madison	M,D
University of Wisconsin–Oshkosh	M
University of Wyoming	M,D
Utah State University	M,D
Virginia Polytechnic Institute and State University	M,D
Washington State University	M,D
Washington University in St. Louis	D
West Texas A&M University	M
West Virginia University	M,D
Yale University	D

■ BUILDING SCIENCE

Arizona State University	M
Auburn University	M
Carnegie Mellon University	M,D
Rensselaer Polytechnic Institute	M
University of California, Berkeley	M,D
University of Florida	M
University of Southern California	M

■ BUSINESS ADMINISTRATION AND MANAGEMENT—GENERAL

Adelphi University	M,O
Alabama Agricultural and Mechanical University	M
Alabama State University	M
Alaska Pacific University	M
Albany State University	M
Alcorn State University	M
Alfred University	M
Alliant International University	M,D
American International College	M
American University	M
Andrews University	M
Angelo State University	M
Anna Maria College	M,O
Antioch New England Graduate School	M
Antioch University Los Angeles	M
Antioch University McGregor	M
Antioch University Seattle	M
Appalachian State University	M
Aquinas College	M
Argosy University-Sarasota	M,D
Arizona State University	M,D
Arizona State University West	M
Arkansas State University	M,O
Ashland University	M
Assumption College	M,O
Auburn University	M,D
Auburn University Montgomery	M
Augsburg College	M
Augusta State University	M
Aurora University	M
Averett University	M
Avila College	M
Azusa Pacific University	M
Baker University	M
Baldwin-Wallace College	M
Ball State University	M
Barry University	M
Bayamón Central University	M
Baylor University	M
Bellarmine University	M
Bellevue University	M
Belmont University	M
Benedictine College	M
Benedictine University	M
Bentley College	M,O
Bernard M. Baruch College of the City University of New York	M,D,O
Biola University	M
Bloomsburg University of Pennsylvania	M
Boise State University	M
Boston College	M
Boston University	M,D,O
Bowie State University	M
Bowling Green State University	M
Bradley University	M
Brandeis University	M
Brenau University	M
Bridgewater State College	M
Brigham Young University	M
Butler University	M
California Baptist University	M
California Lutheran University	M
California Polytechnic State University, San Luis Obispo	M
California State Polytechnic University, Pomona	M
California State University, Bakersfield	M
California State University, Chico	M
California State University, Dominguez Hills	M
California State University, Fresno	M
California State University, Fullerton	M
California State University, Hayward	M
California State University, Long Beach	M
California State University, Los Angeles	M
California State University, Northridge	M
California State University, Sacramento	M
California State University, San Bernardino	M
California State University, San Marcos	M
California State University, Stanislaus	M
California University of Pennsylvania	M
Cameron University	M
Campbellsville University	M
Campbell University	M
Canisius College	M
Capital University	M
Cardinal Stritch University	M
Carnegie Mellon University	M,D
Case Western Reserve University	M,D,O
The Catholic University of America	M
Centenary College of Louisiana	M
Central Connecticut State University	M
Central Michigan University	M
Central Missouri State University	M
Chadron State College	M
Chaminade University of Honolulu	M
Chapman University	M
Charleston Southern University	M
Christian Brothers University	M
The Citadel, The Military College of South Carolina	M
City University	M,O
Claremont Graduate University	M,D,O
Clarion University of Pennsylvania	M
Clark Atlanta University	M
Clarkson University	M
Clark University	M
Clemson University	M,D
Cleveland State University	M,D
College of Notre Dame of Maryland	M
The College of Saint Rose	M
The College of St. Scholastica	M
College of Santa Fe	M
The College of William and Mary	M
Colorado State University	M
Colorado Technical University	M,D
Columbia University	M,D
Columbus State University	M
Concordia University (CA)	M
Concordia University Wisconsin	M
Cornell University	M,D
Creighton University	M
Cumberland University	M
Dallas Baptist University	M
Dartmouth College	M
Delaware State University	M
Delta State University	M
DePaul University	M
DeSales University	M
Doane College	M
Dominican University	M
Dominican University of California	M
Dowling College	M,O
Drake University	M
Drexel University	M,D,O
Drury University	M
Duke University	M,D
Duquesne University	M
East Carolina University	M
Eastern College	M
Eastern Illinois University	M
Eastern Kentucky University	M
Eastern Michigan University	M
Eastern New Mexico University	M
Eastern Washington University	M
East Tennessee State University	M,O

Edgewood College	M
Elon University	M
Embry-Riddle Aeronautical University	M
Emmanuel College	M
Emory University	M
Emporia State University	M
Fairfield University	M,O
Fairleigh Dickinson University, Florham-Madison Campus	M
Fairleigh Dickinson University, Teaneck–Hackensack Campus	M
Fayetteville State University	M
Ferris State University	M
Fitchburg State College	M
Florida Agricultural and Mechanical University	M
Florida Atlantic University	M,D
Florida Gulf Coast University	M
Florida Institute of Technology	M
Florida International University	M,D
Florida Metropolitan University–Brandon Campus	M
Florida Metropolitan University–North Orlando Campus	M
Florida Metropolitan University–Pinellas Campus	M
Florida Metropolitan University–Tampa Campus	M
Florida State University	M,D
Fontbonne College	M
Fordham University	M
Fort Hays State University	M
Framingham State College	M
Franciscan University of Steubenville	M
Francis Marion University	M
Fresno Pacific University	M
Friends University	M
Frostburg State University	M
Gannon University	M,O
Gardner-Webb University	M
Geneva College	M
George Fox University	M
George Mason University	M
Georgetown University	M
The George Washington University	M,D
Georgia College and State University	M
Georgia Institute of Technology	M,D
Georgian Court College	M
Georgia Southern University	M
Georgia Southwestern State University	M
Georgia State University	M,D
Gonzaga University	M
Governors State University	M
Grand Canyon University	M
Grand Valley State University	M
Hamline University	M
Hampton University	M
Harding University	M
Hardin-Simmons University	M
Harvard University	M,D,O
Hawaii Pacific University	M
Heidelberg College	M
Henderson State University	M
Hofstra University	M
Holy Family College	M
Holy Names College	M
Hood College	M
Hope International University	M
Houston Baptist University	M
Howard University	M
Humboldt State University	M
Husson College	M
Idaho State University	M
Illinois Institute of Technology	M,D
Illinois State University	M
Indiana State University	M,D,O
Indiana University Bloomington	M,D
Indiana University Northwest	M,O
Indiana University of Pennsylvania	M
Indiana University–Purdue University Fort Wayne	M
Indiana University–Purdue University Indianapolis	M
Indiana University South Bend	M
Indiana Wesleyan University	M
Inter American University of Puerto Rico, Metropolitan Campus	M,D
Inter American University of Puerto Rico, San Germán Campus	M,D
Iona College	M,O
Iowa State University of Science and Technology	M
Ithaca College	M
Jackson State University	M,D
Jacksonville State University	M
Jacksonville University	M
James Madison University	M
John Carroll University	M
John F. Kennedy University	M,O
Johns Hopkins University	M,O
Johnson & Wales University	M
Kansas State University	M
Kennesaw State University	M
Kent State University	M
King's College	M
Kutztown University of Pennsylvania	M
Lake Erie College	M
Lamar University	M
La Salle University	M,O
La Sierra University	M,O
Lawrence Technological University	M
Lebanon Valley College	M
Lehigh University	M
Le Moyne College	M
Lesley University	M
LeTourneau University	M
Lewis University	M
Liberty University	M
Lincoln Memorial University	M
Lincoln University (MO)	M
Lindenwood University	M
Lipscomb University	M
Long Island University, Brooklyn Campus	M
Long Island University, C.W. Post Campus	M,O
Louisiana State University and Agricultural and Mechanical College	M,D
Louisiana State University in Shreveport	M
Louisiana Tech University	M,D
Loyola College in Maryland	M
Loyola Marymount University	M
Loyola University Chicago	M
Loyola University New Orleans	M
Lynchburg College	M
Lynn University	M
Madonna University	M
Maharishi University of Management	M,D
Malone College	M
Marian College of Fond du Lac	M
Marist College	M,O
Marquette University	M
Marshall University	M
Marylhurst University	M
Marymount University	M,O
Maryville University of Saint Louis	M,O
Marywood University	M
Massachusetts Institute of Technology	M,D
McNeese State University	M
Mercer University	M
Mercy College	M
Meredith College	M
Metropolitan State University	M
Miami University	M
Michigan State University	M,D
Michigan Technological University	M
MidAmerica Nazarene University	M
Middle Tennessee State University	M
Midwestern State University	M
Minot State University	M
Mississippi College	M
Mississippi State University	M,D
Monmouth University	M,O
Montclair State University	M
Monterey Institute of International Studies	M
Morgan State University	M,D
Mount Saint Mary College	M
Mount Saint Mary's College and Seminary	M
Murray State University	M
National-Louis University	M
National University	M
Nazareth College of Rochester	M
New Mexico Highlands University	M
New Mexico State University	M,D
New School University	M,D,O
New York Institute of Technology	M,O
New York University	M,D,O
Niagara University	M
Nicholls State University	M
North Carolina Central University	M
North Carolina State University	M
North Central College	M
North Dakota State University	M
Northeastern Illinois University	M
Northeastern State University	M
Northeastern University	M,O
Northern Arizona University	M
Northern Illinois University	M
Northern Kentucky University	M
North Park University	M
Northwestern University	M
Northwest Missouri State University	M
Northwest Nazarene University	M
Norwich University	M
Notre Dame de Namur University	M
Nova Southeastern University	M,D
Oakland City University	M
Oakland University	M,O
The Ohio State University	M,D
Ohio University	M
Oklahoma City University	M
Oklahoma State University	M,D
Old Dominion University	M,D
Olivet Nazarene University	M
Oral Roberts University	M
Oregon State University	M,O
Our Lady of the Lake University of San Antonio	M
Pace University, New York City Campus	M,D,O
Pace University, White Plains Campus	M,O
Pacific Lutheran University	M
Palm Beach Atlantic College	M
Park University	M
The Pennsylvania State University at Erie, The Behrend College	M
The Pennsylvania State University Harrisburg Campus of the Capital College	M
The Pennsylvania State University University Park Campus	M,D
Pepperdine University	M
Pfeiffer University	M
Philadelphia University	M
Piedmont College	M
Pittsburg State University	M
Plymouth State College	M

Point Loma Nazarene University M
Point Park College M
Polytechnic University, Brooklyn Campus M
Polytechnic University, Westchester Graduate Center M
Pontifical Catholic University of Puerto Rico M,D
Portland State University M,D
Prairie View A&M University M
Providence College M
Purdue University M,D
Purdue University Calumet M
Queens College M
Quincy University M
Quinnipiac University M
Radford University M
Regent University M
Regis College (MA) M
Regis University M,O
Rensselaer Polytechnic Institute M,D
Rice University M
Rider University M
Rivier College M
Robert Morris College M
Roberts Wesleyan College M
Rochester Institute of Technology M
Rockford College M
Rockhurst University M
Rollins College M
Roosevelt University M
Rowan University M
Rutgers, The State University of New Jersey, Camden M
Rutgers, The State University of New Jersey, Newark M,D
Sacred Heart University M
Sage Graduate School M
Saginaw Valley State University M
St. Ambrose University M,D
St. Bonaventure University M,O
St. Cloud State University M
St. Edward's University M,O
Saint Francis University M
St. John Fisher College M
St. John's University (NY) M,O
Saint Joseph's University M
Saint Leo University M
Saint Louis University M,D
Saint Martin's College M
Saint Mary College M
Saint Mary's College of California M
Saint Mary's University of Minnesota M
St. Mary's University of San Antonio M
Saint Michael's College M,O
Saint Peter's College M
St. Thomas Aquinas College M
St. Thomas University M,O
Saint Xavier University M,O
Salem State College M
Salisbury State University M
Salve Regina University M
Samford University M
Sam Houston State University M
San Diego State University M
San Francisco State University M
San Jose State University M
Santa Clara University M
School for International Training M,O
Seattle Pacific University M
Seattle University M,O
Seton Hall University M,O
Shenandoah University M,O
Silver Lake College M
Simmons College M
Slippery Rock University of Pennsylvania M
Sonoma State University M
South Carolina State University M
Southeastern Louisiana University M
Southeastern Oklahoma State University M
Southeastern University M
Southeast Missouri State University M
Southern Connecticut State University M
Southern Illinois University Carbondale M,D
Southern Illinois University Edwardsville M
Southern Methodist University M
Southern Nazarene University M
Southern Oregon University M
Southern University and Agricultural and Mechanical College M
Southern Utah University M
Southern Wesleyan University M
Southwest Baptist University M
Southwestern Oklahoma State University M
Southwest Missouri State University M
Southwest Texas State University M
Spring Arbor University M
Spring Hill College M
Stanford University M,D
State University of New York at Albany M,D
State University of New York at Binghamton M,D
State University of New York at New Paltz M
State University of New York at Oswego M
State University of New York College at Oneonta M
State University of New York Empire State College M
State University of New York Institute of Technology at Utica/Rome M
State University of West Georgia M
Stephen F. Austin State University M
Stetson University M
Stevens Institute of Technology M,D,O
Stony Brook University, State University of New York M,O
Strayer University M
Suffolk University M,O
Sul Ross State University M
Syracuse University M,D
Tarleton State University M
Temple University M,D
Tennessee State University M
Tennessee Technological University M
Texas A&M International University M
Texas A&M University M,D
Texas A&M University–Commerce M
Texas A&M University–Corpus Christi M
Texas A&M University–Kingsville M
Texas A&M University–Texarkana M
Texas Christian University M
Texas Southern University M
Texas Tech University M,D,O
Texas Wesleyan University M
Texas Woman's University M
Thomas Edison State College M
Trevecca Nazarene University M
Trinity College (DC) M
Troy State University M
Troy State University Dothan M
Troy State University Montgomery M
Tulane University M,D
Tusculum College M
Union University M
Universidad del Turabo M
Universidad Metropolitana M
University at Buffalo, The State University of New York M,D
The University of Akron M
The University of Alabama M,D
The University of Alabama at Birmingham M,D
The University of Alabama in Huntsville M
University of Alaska Anchorage M
University of Alaska Fairbanks M
The University of Arizona M,D
University of Arkansas M,D
University of Arkansas at Little Rock M
University of Baltimore M
University of Bridgeport M
University of California, Berkeley P,M,D,O
University of California, Davis M
University of California, Irvine M,D
University of California, Los Angeles M,D
University of California, Riverside M
University of Central Arkansas M
University of Central Florida M,D
University of Central Oklahoma M
University of Chicago M,D
University of Cincinnati M,D
University of Colorado at Boulder M,D
University of Colorado at Colorado Springs M
University of Colorado at Denver M
University of Connecticut M,D
University of Dayton M
University of Delaware M
University of Denver M
University of Detroit Mercy M
University of Dubuque M
The University of Findlay M
University of Florida M,D
University of Georgia M,D
University of Guam M
University of Hartford M
University of Hawaii at Manoa M
University of Houston M,D
University of Houston–Clear Lake M
University of Houston–Victoria M
University of Idaho M
University of Illinois at Chicago M,D
University of Illinois at Springfield M
University of Illinois at Urbana–Champaign M,D
University of Indianapolis M
The University of Iowa M,D
University of Kansas M
University of Kentucky M,D
University of La Verne M
University of Louisiana at Lafayette M
University of Louisiana at Monroe M
University of Louisville M
University of Maine M
University of Mary M
University of Mary Hardin-Baylor M
University of Maryland, College Park M,D
University of Maryland University College M
University of Massachusetts Amherst M,D
University of Massachusetts Boston M
University of Massachusetts Dartmouth M
University of Massachusetts Lowell M
The University of Memphis M,D
University of Miami M,D
University of Michigan M,D
University of Michigan–Dearborn M
University of Michigan–Flint M
University of Minnesota, Duluth M
University of Minnesota, Twin Cities Campus M,D
University of Mississippi M,D
University of Missouri–Columbia M,D

University of Missouri–Kansas City	M
University of Missouri–St. Louis	M,O
University of Mobile	M
The University of Montana–Missoula	M
University of Nebraska at Kearney	M
University of Nebraska at Omaha	M
University of Nebraska–Lincoln	M,D
University of Nevada, Las Vegas	M
University of Nevada, Reno	M
University of New Hampshire	M
University of New Haven	M
University of New Mexico	M
University of New Orleans	M
University of North Alabama	M
The University of North Carolina at Chapel Hill	M,D
The University of North Carolina at Charlotte	M
The University of North Carolina at Greensboro	M,O
The University of North Carolina at Pembroke	M
The University of North Carolina at Wilmington	M
University of North Dakota	M
University of Northern Iowa	M
University of North Florida	M
University of North Texas	M,D
University of Notre Dame	M
University of Oklahoma	M,D
University of Oregon	M,D
University of Pennsylvania	M,D
University of Pittsburgh	M,D
University of Portland	M
University of Puerto Rico, Mayagüez Campus	M
University of Puerto Rico, Río Piedras	M,D
University of Redlands	M
University of Rhode Island	M,D
University of Richmond	M
University of Rochester	M,D
University of St. Francis (IL)	M
University of Saint Francis (IN)	M
University of St. Thomas (MN)	M,O
University of St. Thomas (TX)	M
University of San Diego	M
University of San Francisco	M
The University of Scranton	M
University of Sioux Falls	M
University of South Alabama	M
University of South Carolina	M,D
University of South Dakota	M
University of Southern California	M,D
University of Southern Colorado	M
University of Southern Indiana	M
University of Southern Maine	M
University of Southern Mississippi	M
University of South Florida	M,D
The University of Tampa	M
The University of Tennessee	M,D
The University of Tennessee at Chattanooga	M
The University of Tennessee at Martin	M
The University of Texas at Arlington	M,D
The University of Texas at Austin	M,D
The University of Texas at Brownsville	M
The University of Texas at Dallas	M,D
The University of Texas at El Paso	M
The University of Texas at San Antonio	M
The University of Texas at Tyler	M
The University of Texas of the Permian Basin	M
The University of Texas–Pan American	M,D
University of the District of Columbia	M
University of the Incarnate Word	M,D
University of the Pacific	M
University of the Sacred Heart	M
University of the Virgin Islands	M
University of Toledo	M
University of Tulsa	M
University of Utah	M,D
University of Vermont	M
University of Virginia	M,D
University of Washington	M,D
University of West Florida	M
University of Wisconsin–Eau Claire	M
University of Wisconsin–Green Bay	M
University of Wisconsin–La Crosse	M
University of Wisconsin–Madison	M,D
University of Wisconsin–Milwaukee	M,D
University of Wisconsin–Oshkosh	M
University of Wisconsin–Parkside	M
University of Wisconsin–Stevens Point	M
University of Wisconsin–Whitewater	M
University of Wyoming	M
Utah State University	M
Valdosta State University	M
Vanderbilt University	M,D
Villanova University	M
Virginia Commonwealth University	M,D,O
Virginia Polytechnic Institute and State University	M,D
Virginia State University	M
Wagner College	M
Wake Forest University	M
Walden University	D
Walsh University	M
Washburn University of Topeka	M
Washington State University	M,D
Washington University in St. Louis	M,D
Wayland Baptist University	M
Waynesburg College	M
Wayne State College	M
Wayne State University	M
Weber State University	M
Webster University	M,D
West Chester University of Pennsylvania	M
Western Carolina University	M
Western Connecticut State University	M
Western Illinois University	M
Western International University	M
Western Kentucky University	M
Western Michigan University	M
Western New England College	M
Western New Mexico University	M
Western Washington University	M
Westminster College (UT)	M,O
West Texas A&M University	M
West Virginia University	M
Wheeling Jesuit University	M
Whitworth College	M
Wichita State University	M
Widener University	M
Wilkes University	M
William Carey College	M
William Paterson University of New Jersey	M
William Woods University	M
Wilmington College	M
Winthrop University	M
Woodbury University	M
Worcester Polytechnic Institute	M,O
Wright State University	M
Xavier University	M
Yale University	M,D
York College of Pennsylvania	M
Youngstown State University	M

■ BUSINESS EDUCATION

Albany State University	M
Alfred University	M
Arkansas State University	M,O
Armstrong Atlantic State University	M
Ashland University	M
Auburn University	M,D,O
Ball State University	M
Bloomsburg University of Pennsylvania	M
Bowling Green State University	M,O
California State University, Northridge	M
Central Connecticut State University	M
Central Michigan University	M
Central Washington University	M
Chadron State College	M,O
College of Mount St. Joseph	M
Eastern Kentucky University	M
Eastern Michigan University	M
Emporia State University	M
Florida Agricultural and Mechanical University	M
Georgia Southern University	M
Georgia Southwestern State University	M,O
Hofstra University	M
Inter American University of Puerto Rico, Metropolitan Campus	M
Inter American University of Puerto Rico, San Germán Campus	M
Iona College	M
Jackson State University	M
Johnson & Wales University	M
Lehman College of the City University of New York	M
Louisiana State University and Agricultural and Mechanical College	M,D
Louisiana Tech University	M,D,O
Maryville University of Saint Louis	M,O
McNeese State University	M
Middle Tennessee State University	M
Mississippi College	M
Montclair State University	M
Nazareth College of Rochester	M
New York University	M,D,O
Northwestern State University of Louisiana	M,O
Old Dominion University	M,O
Rider University	O
Robert Morris College	M
Shenandoah University	M,D,O
South Carolina State University	M
Southeast Missouri State University	M
State University of New York College at Buffalo	M
State University of West Georgia	M,O
Texas Southern University	M
Troy State University Dothan	M
University of Central Arkansas	M
University of Central Florida	M
University of Georgia	M,D,O
University of Idaho	M
University of Louisville	M
University of Minnesota, Twin Cities Campus	M,D
University of South Alabama	M
University of South Florida	M
University of Toledo	M,D,O
University of Wisconsin–Whitewater	M
Utah State University	M,D
Valdosta State University	M,D,O
Wayne State College	M
Western Kentucky University	M
Wright State University	M

■ CANADIAN STUDIES

Johns Hopkins University	M,D,O

■ CARDIOVASCULAR SCIENCES

Long Island University, C.W. Post Campus	M,O

Northeastern University	M
University of South Dakota	M,D
University of Virginia	

■ CELL BIOLOGY

Arizona State University	M,D
Boston University	M,D
Brandeis University	M,D
Brown University	M,D
California Institute of Technology	D
Carnegie Mellon University	M,D
Case Western Reserve University	M,D
The Catholic University of America	M,D
Central Connecticut State University	M,O
Colorado State University	M,D
Columbia University	M,D
Cornell University	D
Dartmouth College	D
Duke University	D,O
East Carolina University	D
Emory University	D
Emporia State University	M
Florida Institute of Technology	M
Florida State University	M,D
Fordham University	M,D
George Mason University	M
Georgetown University	D
Georgia State University	M,D
Harvard University	D
Illinois Institute of Technology	M,D
Indiana University Bloomington	M,D
Indiana University–Purdue University Indianapolis	M,D
Iowa State University of Science and Technology	M,D
Johns Hopkins University	D
Kansas State University	M,D
Kent State University	M,D
Loyola University Chicago	M,D
Maharishi University of Management	M,D
Marquette University	M,D
Massachusetts Institute of Technology	D
MCP Hahnemann University	M,D
Michigan State University	D
New York University	M,D
North Carolina State University	M,D
North Dakota State University	D
Northwestern University	D
Oakland University	M
The Ohio State University	M,D
Ohio University	M,D
Oregon State University	D
The Pennsylvania State University University Park Campus	M,D
Princeton University	D
Purdue University	D
Quinnipiac University	M
Rensselaer Polytechnic Institute	M,D
Rice University	M,D
Rutgers, The State University of New Jersey, New Brunswick	M,D
Saint Joseph College	M
Saint Louis University	D
San Diego State University	M,D
San Francisco State University	M
Southwest Missouri State University	M
State University of New York at Albany	M,D
Stony Brook University, State University of New York	M,D
Temple University	D
Texas A&M University	D
Tufts University	D
Tulane University	M,D
University at Buffalo, The State University of New York	D
The University of Alabama at Birmingham	D
The University of Arizona	M,D
University of Arkansas	M,D
University of California, Berkeley	D
University of California, Davis	D
University of California, Irvine	M,D
University of California, Los Angeles	M,D
University of California, Riverside	M,D
University of California, San Diego	D
University of California, San Francisco	D
University of California, Santa Barbara	M,D
University of California, Santa Cruz	D
University of Chicago	D
University of Cincinnati	D
University of Colorado at Boulder	M,D
University of Connecticut	M,D
University of Delaware	M,D
University of Florida	M,D
University of Georgia	M,D
University of Hawaii at Manoa	M,D
University of Illinois at Chicago	M,D
University of Illinois at Urbana–Champaign	D
The University of Iowa	D
University of Kansas	M,D
University of Maryland	D
University of Maryland, Baltimore County	D
University of Maryland, College Park	M,D
University of Massachusetts Amherst	D
The University of Memphis	M,D
University of Miami	D
University of Michigan	M,D
University of Minnesota, Duluth	M,D
University of Minnesota, Twin Cities Campus	M,D
University of Missouri–Kansas City	M,D
University of Missouri–St. Louis	M,D,O
University of Nevada, Reno	M,D
University of New Haven	M
University of New Mexico	M,D
The University of North Carolina at Chapel Hill	M,D
University of Notre Dame	M,D
University of Pennsylvania	D
University of Pittsburgh	M,D
University of Rochester	M,D
University of South Alabama	D
University of South Carolina	M,D
University of South Dakota	M,D
University of Southern California	M,D
University of South Florida	D
The University of Texas at Austin	D
The University of Texas at Dallas	M,D
University of Utah	D
University of Vermont	M,D
University of Virginia	D
University of Washington	D
University of Wisconsin–Madison	M,D
Vanderbilt University	M,D
Virginia Polytechnic Institute and State University	M,D
Washington State University	M,D
Washington University in St. Louis	D
Wayne State University	M,D
West Virginia University	M,D
Yale University	D
Yeshiva University	D

■ CELTIC LANGUAGES

Harvard University	M,D

■ CERAMIC SCIENCES AND ENGINEERING

Alfred University	M,D
Case Western Reserve University	M,D
Clemson University	M,D
Georgia Institute of Technology	M,D
The Pennsylvania State University University Park Campus	M,D
Rensselaer Polytechnic Institute	M,D
Rutgers, The State University of New Jersey, New Brunswick	M,D
University of California, Berkeley	M,D
University of California, Los Angeles	M,D
University of Cincinnati	M,D
University of Florida	M,D,O
University of Missouri–Rolla	M,D

■ CHEMICAL ENGINEERING

Arizona State University	M,D
Auburn University	M,D
Brigham Young University	M,D
Brown University	M,D
California Institute of Technology	M,D
Carnegie Mellon University	M,D
Case Western Reserve University	M,D
City College of the City University of New York	M,D
Clarkson University	M,D
Clemson University	M,D
Cleveland State University	M,D
Colorado State University	M,D
Columbia University	M,D,O
Cornell University	M,D
Drexel University	M,D
Florida Agricultural and Mechanical University	M,D
Florida Institute of Technology	M,D
Florida State University	M,D
Georgia Institute of Technology	M,D,O
Howard University	M
Illinois Institute of Technology	M,D
Iowa State University of Science and Technology	M,D
Johns Hopkins University	M,D
Kansas State University	M,D
Lamar University	M,D
Lehigh University	M,D
Louisiana State University and Agricultural and Mechanical College	M,D
Louisiana Tech University	M,D
Manhattan College	M
Massachusetts Institute of Technology	M,D
McNeese State University	M
Michigan State University	M,D
Michigan Technological University	M,D
Mississippi State University	M
Montana State University–Bozeman	M,D
New Jersey Institute of Technology	M,D,O
New Mexico State University	M,D
North Carolina Agricultural and Technical State University	M
North Carolina State University	M,D
Northeastern University	M,D
Northwestern University	M,D
The Ohio State University	M,D
Ohio University	M,D
Oklahoma State University	M,D
Oregon State University	M,D
The Pennsylvania State University University Park Campus	M,D
Polytechnic University, Brooklyn Campus	M,D
Polytechnic University, Westchester Graduate Center	M
Princeton University	M,D
Purdue University	M,D
Rensselaer Polytechnic Institute	M,D
Rice University	M,D

Rutgers, The State University of New Jersey, New Brunswick	M,D
San Jose State University	M
Stanford University	M,D,O
Stevens Institute of Technology	M,D,O
Syracuse University	M,D
Tennessee Technological University	M,D
Texas A&M University	M,D
Texas A&M University–Kingsville	M
Texas Tech University	M,D
Tufts University	M,D
Tulane University	M,D
University at Buffalo, The State University of New York	M,D
The University of Akron	M,D
The University of Alabama	M,D
The University of Alabama in Huntsville	M
The University of Arizona	M,D
University of Arkansas	M,D
University of California, Berkeley	M,D
University of California, Davis	M,D,O
University of California, Irvine	M,D
University of California, Los Angeles	M,D
University of California, Riverside	M,D
University of California, San Diego	M,D
University of California, Santa Barbara	M,D
University of Cincinnati	M,D
University of Colorado at Boulder	M,D
University of Connecticut	M,D
University of Dayton	M
University of Delaware	M,D
University of Detroit Mercy	M,D
University of Florida	M,D,O
University of Houston	M,D
University of Idaho	M,D
University of Illinois at Chicago	M,D
University of Illinois at Urbana–Champaign	M,D
The University of Iowa	M,D
University of Kansas	M,D
University of Kentucky	M,D
University of Louisiana at Lafayette	M
University of Louisville	M,D
University of Maine	M,D
University of Maryland, Baltimore County	M,D
University of Maryland, College Park	M,D
University of Massachusetts Amherst	M,D
University of Massachusetts Lowell	M
University of Michigan	M,D,O
University of Minnesota, Twin Cities Campus	M,D
University of Missouri–Columbia	M,D
University of Missouri–Rolla	M,D
University of Nebraska–Lincoln	M,D
University of Nevada, Reno	M,D
University of New Hampshire	M,D
University of New Mexico	M,D
University of North Dakota	M
University of Notre Dame	M,D
University of Oklahoma	M,D
University of Pennsylvania	M,D
University of Pittsburgh	M,D
University of Puerto Rico, Mayagüez Campus	M
University of Rhode Island	M,D
University of Rochester	M,D
University of South Alabama	M
University of South Carolina	M,D
University of Southern California	M,D,O
University of South Florida	M,D
The University of Tennessee	M,D
The University of Texas at Austin	M,D
University of Toledo	M,D
University of Tulsa	M,D
University of Utah	M,D
University of Virginia	M,D
University of Washington	M,D
University of Wisconsin–Madison	M,D
University of Wyoming	M,D
Vanderbilt University	M,D
Villanova University	M
Virginia Polytechnic Institute and State University	M,D
Washington State University	M,D
Washington University in St. Louis	M,D
Wayne State University	M,D
Western Michigan University	M
West Virginia University	M,D
Widener University	M
Worcester Polytechnic Institute	M,D
Yale University	M,D
Youngstown State University	M

■ CHEMISTRY

American University	M,D
Arizona State University	M,D
Arkansas State University	M,O
Auburn University	M,D
Ball State University	M
Baylor University	M,D
Boston College	M,D
Boston University	M,D
Bowling Green State University	M,D
Bradley University	M
Brandeis University	M,D
Brigham Young University	M,D
Brooklyn College of the City University of New York	M,D
Brown University	M,D
California Institute of Technology	D
California State Polytechnic University, Pomona	M
California State University, Fresno	M
California State University, Fullerton	M
California State University, Hayward	M
California State University, Long Beach	M
California State University, Los Angeles	M
California State University, Northridge	M
California State University, Sacramento	M
Carnegie Mellon University	M,D
Case Western Reserve University	M,D
The Catholic University of America	M,D
Central Connecticut State University	M
Central Michigan University	M
Central Washington University	M
City College of the City University of New York	M,D
Clark Atlanta University	M,D
Clarkson University	M,D
Clark University	M,D
Clemson University	M,D
Cleveland State University	M,D
College of Staten Island of the City University of New York	D
The College of William and Mary	M
Colorado State University	M,D
Columbia University	M,D
Cornell University	D
Dartmouth College	D
Delaware State University	M
DePaul University	M
Drexel University	M,D
Duke University	D
Duquesne University	M,D
East Carolina University	M
Eastern Illinois University	M
Eastern Kentucky University	M
Eastern Michigan University	M
Eastern New Mexico University	M
East Tennessee State University	M
Emory University	D
Emporia State University	M
Fairleigh Dickinson University, Florham-Madison Campus	M
Florida Agricultural and Mechanical University	M
Florida Atlantic University	M,D
Florida Institute of Technology	M,D
Florida International University	M,D
Florida State University	M,D
George Mason University	M
Georgetown University	M,D
The George Washington University	M,D
Georgia Institute of Technology	M,D
Georgia State University	M,D
Hampton University	M
Harvard University	M,D
Howard University	M,D
Hunter College of the City University of New York	M
Idaho State University	M
Illinois Institute of Technology	M,D
Illinois State University	M
Indiana State University	M
Indiana University Bloomington	M,D
Indiana University of Pennsylvania	M
Indiana University–Purdue University Fort Wayne	M
Indiana University–Purdue University Indianapolis	M,D
Iowa State University of Science and Technology	M,D
Jackson State University	M,D
John Carroll University	M
Johns Hopkins University	M,D
Kansas State University	M,D
Kent State University	M,D
Lamar University	M
Lehigh University	M,D
Long Island University, Brooklyn Campus	M
Louisiana State University and Agricultural and Mechanical College	M,D
Louisiana Tech University	M
Loyola University Chicago	M,D
Marquette University	M,D
Marshall University	M
Massachusetts Institute of Technology	D
McNeese State University	M
Miami University	M,D
Michigan State University	M,D
Michigan Technological University	M,D
Middle Tennessee State University	M,D
Minnesota State University, Mankato	M
Mississippi College	M
Mississippi State University	M,D
Montana State University–Bozeman	M,D
Montclair State University	M
Morgan State University	M
Murray State University	M
New Jersey Institute of Technology	M,D
New Mexico Highlands University	M
New Mexico Institute of Mining and Technology	M,D
New Mexico State University	M,D
New York University	M,D
North Carolina Agricultural and Technical State University	M
North Carolina Central University	M
North Carolina State University	M,D
North Dakota State University	M,D
Northeastern Illinois University	M
Northeastern University	M,D
Northern Arizona University	M
Northern Illinois University	M,D
Northern Michigan University	M

Northwestern University	D
Oakland University	M,D
The Ohio State University	M,D
Oklahoma State University	M,D
Old Dominion University	M
Oregon State University	M,D
The Pennsylvania State University University Park Campus	M,D
Pittsburg State University	M
Polytechnic University, Brooklyn Campus	M,D
Polytechnic University, Westchester Graduate Center	M
Pontifical Catholic University of Puerto Rico	M
Portland State University	M,D
Prairie View A&M University	M
Princeton University	M,D
Purdue University	M,D
Queens College of the City University of New York	M
Rensselaer Polytechnic Institute	M,D
Rice University	M,D
Rochester Institute of Technology	M
Roosevelt University	M
Rutgers, The State University of New Jersey, Camden	M
Rutgers, The State University of New Jersey, Newark	M,D
Rutgers, The State University of New Jersey, New Brunswick	M,D
Sacred Heart University	M
St. John's University (NY)	M
Saint Joseph College	M
Saint Joseph's University	M
Saint Louis University	M
Sam Houston State University	M
San Diego State University	M,D
San Francisco State University	M
San Jose State University	M
Seton Hall University	M,D
South Dakota State University	M,D
Southeast Missouri State University	M
Southern Connecticut State University	M
Southern Illinois University Carbondale	M,D
Southern Illinois University Edwardsville	M
Southern Methodist University	M
Southern University and Agricultural and Mechanical College	M
Southwest Missouri State University	M
Southwest Texas State University	M
Stanford University	D
State University of New York at Albany	M,D
State University of New York at Binghamton	M,D
State University of New York at New Paltz	M
State University of New York at Oswego	M
State University of New York College at Buffalo	M
State University of New York College at Fredonia	M
State University of New York College of Environmental Science and Forestry	M,D
Stephen F. Austin State University	M
Stevens Institute of Technology	M,D,O
Stony Brook University, State University of New York	M,D
Sul Ross State University	M
Syracuse University	M,D
Temple University	M,D
Tennessee State University	M
Tennessee Technological University	M
Texas A&M University	M,D
Texas A&M University–Commerce	M
Texas A&M University–Kingsville	M
Texas Christian University	M,D
Texas Southern University	M
Texas Tech University	M,D
Texas Woman's University	M
Tufts University	M,D
Tulane University	M,D
Tuskegee University	M
University at Buffalo, The State University of New York	M,D
The University of Akron	M,D
The University of Alabama	M,D
The University of Alabama at Birmingham	M,D
The University of Alabama in Huntsville	M
University of Alaska Fairbanks	M,D
The University of Arizona	M,D
University of Arkansas	M,D
University of Arkansas at Little Rock	M
University of California, Berkeley	M,D
University of California, Davis	M,D
University of California, Irvine	M,D
University of California, Los Angeles	M,D
University of California, Riverside	M,D
University of California, San Diego	M,D
University of California, San Francisco	D
University of California, Santa Barbara	M,D
University of California, Santa Cruz	M,D
University of Central Florida	M
University of Central Oklahoma	M
University of Chicago	M,D
University of Cincinnati	M,D
University of Colorado at Boulder	M,D
University of Colorado at Denver	M
University of Connecticut	M,D
University of Delaware	M,D
University of Denver	M,D
University of Detroit Mercy	M,D
University of Florida	M,D
University of Georgia	M,D
University of Hawaii at Manoa	M,D
University of Houston	M,D
University of Houston–Clear Lake	M
University of Idaho	M,D
University of Illinois at Chicago	M,D
University of Illinois at Urbana–Champaign	M,D
The University of Iowa	M,D
University of Kansas	M,D
University of Kentucky	M,D
University of Louisiana at Monroe	M
University of Louisville	M,D
University of Maine	M,D
University of Maryland, Baltimore County	D
University of Maryland, College Park	M,D
University of Massachusetts Amherst	M,D
University of Massachusetts Boston	M
University of Massachusetts Dartmouth	M
University of Massachusetts Lowell	M,D
The University of Memphis	M,D
University of Miami	M,D
University of Michigan	D
University of Minnesota, Duluth	M
University of Minnesota, Twin Cities Campus	M,D
University of Mississippi	M,D
University of Missouri–Columbia	M,D
University of Missouri–Kansas City	M,D
University of Missouri–Rolla	M,D
University of Missouri–St. Louis	M,D
The University of Montana–Missoula	M,D
University of Nebraska–Lincoln	M,D
University of Nevada, Las Vegas	M
University of Nevada, Reno	M,D
University of New Hampshire	M,D
University of New Mexico	M,D
University of New Orleans	M,D
The University of North Carolina at Chapel Hill	M,D
The University of North Carolina at Charlotte	M
The University of North Carolina at Greensboro	M
The University of North Carolina at Wilmington	M
University of North Dakota	M,D
University of Northern Colorado	M,D
University of Northern Iowa	M
University of North Texas	M,D
University of Notre Dame	M,D
University of Oklahoma	M,D
University of Oregon	M,D
University of Pennsylvania	M,D
University of Pittsburgh	M,D
University of Puerto Rico, Mayagüez Campus	M
University of Puerto Rico, Río Piedras	M,D
University of Rhode Island	M,D
University of Rochester	M,D
University of San Francisco	M
The University of Scranton	M
University of South Carolina	M,D
University of South Dakota	M
University of Southern California	M,D
University of Southern Mississippi	M,D
University of South Florida	M,D
The University of Tennessee	M,D
The University of Texas at Arlington	M,D
The University of Texas at Austin	M,D
The University of Texas at Dallas	M,D
The University of Texas at El Paso	M
The University of Texas at San Antonio	M
The University of Texas at Tyler	M
University of the Pacific	M,D
University of Toledo	M,D
University of Tulsa	M
University of Utah	M,D
University of Vermont	M,D
University of Virginia	M,D
University of Washington	M,D
University of Wisconsin–Madison	M,D
University of Wisconsin–Milwaukee	M,D
University of Wyoming	M,D
Utah State University	M,D
Vanderbilt University	M,D
Villanova University	M
Virginia Commonwealth University	M,D
Virginia Polytechnic Institute and State University	M,D
Wake Forest University	M,D
Washington State University	M,D
Washington University in St. Louis	M,D
Wayne State University	M,D
West Chester University of Pennsylvania	M
Western Carolina University	M
Western Illinois University	M
Western Kentucky University	M
Western Michigan University	M,D
Western Washington University	M
West Texas A&M University	M
West Virginia University	M,D
Wichita State University	M,D
Worcester Polytechnic Institute	M,D
Wright State University	M
Yale University	D
Youngstown State University	M

■ CHILD AND FAMILY STUDIES

Abilene Christian University	M
Arizona State University	D
Auburn University	M,D
Bowling Green State University	M,D
Brandeis University	M
Brigham Young University	M,D
California State University, Los Angeles	M
Central Michigan University	M
Central Washington University	M
College of Mount Saint Vincent	M,O
Colorado State University	M
Concordia University (NE)	M
Concordia University Wisconsin	M
Cornell University	D
East Carolina University	M
Fitchburg State College	M,O
Florida State University	M,D
Harvard University	M,D,O
Indiana State University	M
Iowa State University of Science and Technology	M,D
Kansas State University	M,D
Kent State University	M
Loma Linda University	M,O
Miami University	M
Michigan State University	M,D
Middle Tennessee State University	M
Montclair State University	M
North Dakota State University	M
Northern Illinois University	M
Nova Southeastern University	M,D
The Ohio State University	M,D
Ohio University	M
Oklahoma State University	M,D
Oregon State University	M,D
The Pennsylvania State University University Park Campus	M,D
Purdue University	M,D
Roberts Wesleyan College	M
Sage Graduate School	M
St. Cloud State University	M
Saint Joseph College	M,O
San Jose State University	M
South Carolina State University	M
Southwest Texas State University	M
Stanford University	D
Syracuse University	M,D
Tennessee State University	M
Texas Tech University	M,D
Texas Woman's University	M,D
Tufts University	M,D,O
The University of Akron	M
The University of Alabama	M
The University of Arizona	M,D
University of California, Davis	M
University of Connecticut	M,D
University of Delaware	M,D
University of Denver	M,D,O
University of Georgia	M,D
University of Great Falls	M
University of Illinois at Springfield	M
University of Kentucky	M
University of La Verne	M
University of Maryland, College Park	M
University of Minnesota, Twin Cities Campus	M,D
University of Missouri–Columbia	M,D
University of Nebraska–Lincoln	M,D
University of Nevada, Reno	M
University of New Hampshire	M
University of New Mexico	M,D
The University of North Carolina at Charlotte	M
The University of North Carolina at Greensboro	M,D
University of North Texas	M
University of Pittsburgh	M
University of Rhode Island	M
University of Southern Mississippi	M,D
The University of Tennessee	M,D
The University of Tennessee at Martin	M
The University of Texas at Austin	M,D
The University of Texas at Dallas	M
University of Utah	M
University of Vermont	M
University of Wisconsin–Madison	M,D
Utah State University	M,D
Virginia Polytechnic Institute and State University	M,D
Wayne State University	O
West Virginia University	M
Wheelock College	M,O

■ CHIROPRACTIC

University of Bridgeport	P,M

■ CITY AND REGIONAL PLANNING

Alabama Agricultural and Mechanical University	M
Arizona State University	M
Auburn University	M
Ball State University	M
Boston University	M
California Polytechnic State University, San Luis Obispo	M
California State Polytechnic University, Pomona	M
California State University, Chico	M
The Catholic University of America	M
Clemson University	M
Cleveland State University	M
Columbia University	M,D
Cornell University	M,D
Delta State University	M
DePaul University	M,O
Eastern Kentucky University	M
Eastern Washington University	M
East Tennessee State University	M
Florida Atlantic University	M
Florida State University	M,D
George Mason University	M
Georgia Institute of Technology	M
Harvard University	M,D
Hunter College of the City University of New York	M
Indiana University–Purdue University Indianapolis	M
Iowa State University of Science and Technology	M
Jackson State University	M
Kansas State University	M
Massachusetts Institute of Technology	M,D
Michigan State University	M,D
Morgan State University	M
New York University	M,O
North Park University	M
The Ohio State University	M,D
Old Dominion University	M
The Pennsylvania State University University Park Campus	M
Portland State University	M,D
Pratt Institute	M
Princeton University	M,D
Rutgers, The State University of New Jersey, New Brunswick	M,D
San Diego State University	M
San Jose State University	M
Southwest Missouri State University	M
State University of New York at Albany	M
Texas A&M University	M,D
Texas Southern University	M
Tufts University	M
University at Buffalo, The State University of New York	M
The University of Akron	M
The University of Arizona	M
University of California, Berkeley	M,D
University of California, Davis	M
University of California, Irvine	M,D
University of California, Los Angeles	M,D
University of Cincinnati	M
University of Colorado at Denver	M
University of Florida	M
University of Hawaii at Manoa	M
University of Illinois at Chicago	M,D
University of Illinois at Urbana–Champaign	M,D
The University of Iowa	M
University of Kansas	M
University of Louisville	M
University of Maryland, College Park	M
University of Massachusetts Amherst	M,D
The University of Memphis	M
University of Michigan	M,D,O
University of Minnesota, Twin Cities Campus	M
University of Nebraska–Lincoln	M
University of New Mexico	M
University of New Orleans	M
The University of North Carolina at Chapel Hill	M,D
University of Oklahoma	M
University of Oregon	M
University of Pennsylvania	M,D,O
University of Pittsburgh	M
University of Puerto Rico, Río Piedras	M
University of Rhode Island	M
University of Southern California	M,D
University of Southern Maine	M,O
The University of Tennessee	M
The University of Texas at Arlington	M
The University of Texas at Austin	M,D
University of Toledo	M
University of Virginia	M
University of Washington	M,D
University of Wisconsin–Madison	M,D
University of Wisconsin–Milwaukee	M
Utah State University	M
Valdosta State University	M
Virginia Commonwealth University	M,O
Virginia Polytechnic Institute and State University	M
Washington State University	M
Wayne State University	M
West Chester University of Pennsylvania	M
West Virginia University	M,D

■ CIVIL ENGINEERING

Arizona State University	M,D
Auburn University	M,D
Boise State University	M
Bradley University	M
Brigham Young University	M,D
California Institute of Technology	M,D
California Polytechnic State University, San Luis Obispo	M
California State University, Fresno	M
California State University, Fullerton	M
California State University, Long Beach	M,O
California State University, Los Angeles	M
California State University, Northridge	M
California State University, Sacramento	M
Carnegie Mellon University	M,D
Case Western Reserve University	M,D

The Catholic University of America M,D
City College of the City University of New York M,D
Clarkson University M,D
Clemson University M,D
Cleveland State University M,D
Colorado State University M,D
Columbia University M,D,O
Cornell University M,D
Drexel University M,D
Duke University M,D
Florida Agricultural and Mechanical University M,D
Florida Atlantic University M
Florida Institute of Technology M,D
Florida International University M,D
Florida State University M,D
The George Washington University M,D,O
Georgia Institute of Technology M,D
Howard University M
Illinois Institute of Technology M,D
Iowa State University of Science and Technology M,D
Johns Hopkins University M,D
Kansas State University M,D
Lamar University M,D
Lawrence Technological University M
Lehigh University M,D
Louisiana State University and Agricultural and Mechanical College M,D
Louisiana Tech University M,D
Loyola Marymount University M
Manhattan College M
Marquette University M,D
Massachusetts Institute of Technology M,D,O
McNeese State University M
Michigan State University M,D
Michigan Technological University M,D
Mississippi State University M,D
Montana State University–Bozeman M,D
New Jersey Institute of Technology M,D,O
New Mexico State University M,D
North Carolina Agricultural and Technical State University M
North Carolina State University M,D
North Dakota State University M
Northeastern University M,D
Northwestern University M,D
The Ohio State University M,D
Ohio University M
Oklahoma State University M,D
Old Dominion University M,D
Oregon State University M,D
The Pennsylvania State University University Park Campus M,D
Polytechnic University, Brooklyn Campus M,D
Polytechnic University, Westchester Graduate Center M,D
Portland State University M,D
Princeton University M,D
Purdue University M,D
Rensselaer Polytechnic Institute M,D
Rice University M,D
Rutgers, The State University of New Jersey, New Brunswick M,D
San Diego State University M
San Jose State University M
Santa Clara University M
South Dakota State University M
Southern Illinois University Carbondale M
Southern Illinois University Edwardsville M
Southern Methodist University M,D
Stanford University M,D,O
Stevens Institute of Technology M,D,O
Syracuse University M,D
Temple University M
Tennessee Technological University M,D
Texas A&M University M,D
Texas A&M University–Kingsville M
Texas Tech University M,D
Tufts University M,D
Tulane University M,D
University at Buffalo, The State University of New York M,D
The University of Akron M,D
The University of Alabama M,D
The University of Alabama at Birmingham M,D
The University of Alabama in Huntsville M
University of Alaska Anchorage M
University of Alaska Fairbanks M
The University of Arizona M,D
University of Arkansas M,D
University of California, Berkeley M,D
University of California, Davis M,D,O
University of California, Irvine M,D
University of California, Los Angeles M,D
University of Central Florida M,D,O
University of Cincinnati M,D
University of Colorado at Boulder M,D
University of Colorado at Denver M,D
University of Connecticut M,D
University of Dayton M
University of Delaware M,D
University of Detroit Mercy M,D
University of Florida M,D,O
University of Hawaii at Manoa M,D
University of Houston M,D
University of Idaho M,D
University of Illinois at Chicago M,D
University of Illinois at Urbana–Champaign M,D
The University of Iowa M,D
University of Kansas M,D
University of Kentucky M,D
University of Louisiana at Lafayette M
University of Louisville M,D
University of Maine M,D
University of Maryland, College Park M,D
University of Massachusetts Amherst M,D
University of Massachusetts Lowell M
The University of Memphis M,D
University of Miami M,D
University of Michigan M,D,O
University of Minnesota, Twin Cities Campus M,D
University of Missouri–Columbia M,D
University of Missouri–Rolla M,D
University of Nebraska–Lincoln M,D
University of Nevada, Las Vegas M,D
University of Nevada, Reno M,D
University of New Hampshire M,D
University of New Mexico M,D
University of New Orleans M
The University of North Carolina at Charlotte M
University of North Dakota M
University of Notre Dame M,D
University of Oklahoma M,D
University of Pittsburgh M,D
University of Puerto Rico, Mayagüez Campus M,D
University of Rhode Island M,D
University of South Carolina M,D
University of Southern California M,D,O
University of South Florida M,D
The University of Tennessee M,D
The University of Texas at Arlington M,D
The University of Texas at Austin M,D
The University of Texas at El Paso M
The University of Texas at San Antonio M
University of Toledo M,D
University of Utah M,D
University of Vermont M,D
University of Virginia M,D
University of Washington M,D
University of Wisconsin–Madison M,D
University of Wyoming M,D
Utah State University M,D,O
Vanderbilt University M,D
Villanova University M
Virginia Polytechnic Institute and State University M,D
Washington State University M,D
Washington University in St. Louis M,D
Wayne State University M,D
West Virginia University M,D
Widener University M
Worcester Polytechnic Institute M,D,O
Youngstown State University M

■ CLASSICS

Boston College M
Boston University M,D
Brandeis University M
Brown University M,D
The Catholic University of America M,D
Columbia University M,D
Cornell University D
Duke University D
Florida State University M,D
Fordham University M,D
Harvard University M,D
Hunter College of the City University of New York M
Indiana University Bloomington M,D
Johns Hopkins University M,D
Kent State University M
Loyola University Chicago M,D
New York University M,D
The Ohio State University M,D
Princeton University D
Rutgers, The State University of New Jersey, New Brunswick M,D
San Francisco State University M
Southwest Missouri State University M
Stanford University M,D
State University of New York at Albany M
Syracuse University M
Tufts University M
Tulane University M
University at Buffalo, The State University of New York M,D
The University of Arizona M
University of California, Berkeley M,D
University of California, Irvine M,D
University of California, Los Angeles M,D
University of California, Santa Barbara M,D
University of Chicago M,D
University of Cincinnati M,D
University of Colorado at Boulder M,D
University of Florida M,D
University of Georgia M
University of Hawaii at Manoa M
University of Illinois at Urbana–Champaign M,D
The University of Iowa M,D
University of Kansas M
University of Kentucky M
University of Maryland, College Park M
University of Massachusetts Amherst M
University of Michigan M,D
University of Minnesota, Twin Cities Campus M,D

University of Mississippi	M
University of Missouri–Columbia	M,D
University of Nebraska–Lincoln	M
The University of North Carolina at Chapel Hill	M,D
The University of North Carolina at Greensboro	M
University of Oregon	M
University of Pennsylvania	M,D
University of Pittsburgh	M,D
University of Southern California	M,D
The University of Texas at Austin	M,D
University of Vermont	M
University of Virginia	M,D
University of Washington	M,D
University of Wisconsin–Madison	M,D
University of Wisconsin–Milwaukee	M
Vanderbilt University	M,D
Villanova University	M
Washington University in St. Louis	M
Wayne State University	M
Yale University	D

■ CLINICAL LABORATORY SCIENCES/MEDICAL TECHNOLOGY

California State University, Dominguez Hills	M,O
California State University, Long Beach	M
The Catholic University of America	M,D
Duke University	M
Fairleigh Dickinson University, Teaneck–Hackensack Campus	M
Indiana State University	M,D
Inter American University of Puerto Rico, Metropolitan Campus	M
Inter American University of Puerto Rico, San Germán Campus	O
Johns Hopkins University	M,D
Long Island University, C.W. Post Campus	M,O
Michigan State University	M
Northeastern University	M,D
Northwestern University	M
Quinnipiac University	M
St. John's University (NY)	M
Salve Regina University	M
San Francisco State University	M
University at Buffalo, The State University of New York	M
The University of Alabama at Birmingham	M
University of Florida	M
University of Illinois at Chicago	M
The University of Iowa	M,D
University of Maryland	M
University of Massachusetts Lowell	M
University of Minnesota, Twin Cities Campus	M
University of North Dakota	M
University of Rhode Island	M
University of Southern Mississippi	M
University of the Sacred Heart	O
University of Utah	M
University of Vermont	M
University of Washington	M
University of Wisconsin–Milwaukee	M
Vanderbilt University	M
Virginia Commonwealth University	M
Wayne State University	M
West Virginia University	M

■ CLINICAL PSYCHOLOGY

Abilene Christian University	M
Adelphi University	D,O
Alabama Agricultural and Mechanical University	M,O
Alliant International University	M,D
American International College	M
American University	D
Antioch New England Graduate School	D
Antioch University Los Angeles	M
Appalachian State University	M
Arizona State University	D
Austin Peay State University	M
Azusa Pacific University	M,D
Ball State University	M
Barry University	M,O
Baylor University	M,D
Bowling Green State University	M,D
Brigham Young University	M,D
California Lutheran University	M
California State University, Dominguez Hills	M
California State University, Fullerton	M
California State University, San Bernardino	M
Cardinal Stritch University	M
Case Western Reserve University	D
The Catholic University of America	D
Central Michigan University	D
Chapman University	M
Chestnut Hill College	M,D
City College of the City University of New York	M,D
Clark University	D
Cleveland State University	M
College of St. Joseph	M
The College of William and Mary	D
DePaul University	M,D
Drexel University	M,D
Duke University	D
Duquesne University	M,D
East Carolina University	M
Eastern Illinois University	M
Eastern Kentucky University	M,O
Eastern Michigan University	M
East Tennessee State University	M
Edinboro University of Pennsylvania	M
Emory University	D
Emporia State University	M
Fairleigh Dickinson University, Florham-Madison Campus	M
Fairleigh Dickinson University, Teaneck–Hackensack Campus	M,D
Florida Institute of Technology	D
Florida State University	D
Fordham University	D
Francis Marion University	M
Gallaudet University	D
George Fox University	M,D
George Mason University	D
The George Washington University	D
Hofstra University	M,D,O
Howard University	M,D
Idaho State University	M,D
Illinois Institute of Technology	M,D
Illinois School of Professional Psychology, Chicago Northwest Campus	M,D
Illinois State University	M,D,O
Immaculata College	M,D,O
Indiana State University	M,D
Indiana University of Pennsylvania	D
Indiana University–Purdue University Indianapolis	M,D
Jackson State University	D
Kent State University	M,D
Lamar University	M
La Salle University	M,D
Lesley University	M,O
Loma Linda University	D
Long Island University, Brooklyn Campus	D
Long Island University, C.W. Post Campus	D
Louisiana State University and Agricultural and Mechanical College	M,D
Loyola College in Maryland	M,D,O
Loyola University Chicago	M,D
Madonna University	M
Marquette University	M,D
Marshall University	M
MCP Hahnemann University	M,D
Miami University	D
Millersville University of Pennsylvania	M
Minnesota State University, Mankato	M
Montclair State University	M
Morehead State University	M
Murray State University	M
New College of California	M
New School University	M,D
New York University	M,D,O
Norfolk State University	M
North Dakota State University	M,D
Northwestern State University of Louisiana	M
Northwestern University	D
Nova Southeastern University	D,O
The Ohio State University	D
Ohio University	D
Oklahoma State University	M,D
Old Dominion University	D
Pace University, New York City Campus	M,D
The Pennsylvania State University University Park Campus	M,D
Pontifical Catholic University of Puerto Rico	M
Queens College of the City University of New York	M
Radford University	M,O
Roosevelt University	M,D
Rutgers, The State University of New Jersey, New Brunswick	M,D
St. John's University (NY)	M,D
Saint Louis University	M,D
St. Mary's University of San Antonio	M
Saint Michael's College	M
Sam Houston State University	M
San Diego State University	M,D
San Jose State University	M
Seattle Pacific University	D
Southern Illinois University Carbondale	M,D
Southern Illinois University Edwardsville	M
Southern Methodist University	M
Spalding University	M,D
State University of New York at Albany	M,D
State University of New York at Binghamton	M,D
Stony Brook University, State University of New York	D
Suffolk University	D
Syracuse University	M,D
Teachers College, Columbia University	M,D
Temple University	D
Texas A&M University	M,D
Texas Tech University	M,D
Towson University	M,O
The Union Institute	D
University at Buffalo, The State University of New York	M,D
The University of Alabama	D

The University of Alabama at Birmingham	M,D
University of Alaska Anchorage	M
University of California, San Diego	D
University of California, Santa Barbara	M,D
University of Central Florida	M,D
University of Cincinnati	M,D
University of Connecticut	M,D
University of Dayton	M
University of Delaware	D
University of Denver	D
University of Detroit Mercy	M,D
University of Florida	D
University of Hartford	M,D
University of Hawaii at Manoa	M,D
University of Houston	D
University of Houston–Clear Lake	M
University of Illinois at Springfield	M
University of Illinois at Urbana–Champaign	M,D
University of Kansas	M,D
University of La Verne	D
University of Louisville	D
University of Maine	M,D
University of Maryland, College Park	M,D
University of Massachusetts Amherst	M,D
University of Massachusetts Boston	D
University of Massachusetts Dartmouth	M
The University of Memphis	M,D
University of Miami	M,D
University of Michigan	D
University of Minnesota, Twin Cities Campus	D
University of Mississippi	M,D
University of Missouri–St. Louis	M,D,O
The University of Montana–Missoula	D
University of New Mexico	M,D
The University of North Carolina at Chapel Hill	D
The University of North Carolina at Charlotte	M
The University of North Carolina at Greensboro	M,D
University of North Dakota	D
University of North Texas	M,D
University of Oregon	D
University of Pennsylvania	D
University of Rhode Island	D
University of Rochester	M,D
University of South Carolina	D
University of South Dakota	M,D
University of Southern California	M,D
University of South Florida	D
The University of Tennessee	M,D
The University of Texas at El Paso	M,D
The University of Texas at Tyler	M,O
The University of Texas of the Permian Basin	M
The University of Texas–Pan American	M
University of Toledo	M,D
University of Tulsa	M,D
University of Vermont	D
University of Virginia	D
University of Washington	D
University of Wisconsin–Madison	D
University of Wisconsin–Milwaukee	M,D
Utah State University	M,D
Valdosta State University	M,O
Valparaiso University	M
Virginia Commonwealth University	D
Virginia Polytechnic Institute and State University	M,D
Washburn University of Topeka	M
Washington State University	M,D
Washington University in St. Louis	M,D
Wayne State University	M,D
West Chester University of Pennsylvania	M
Western Carolina University	M
Western Illinois University	M,O
Western Michigan University	M,D,O
Westfield State College	M
West Virginia University	M,D
Wichita State University	M,D
Widener University	D
William Paterson University of New Jersey	M
Wright State University	D
Xavier University	M,D
Yeshiva University	D

■ CLOTHING AND TEXTILES

Auburn University	M
Cornell University	M,D
Florida State University	M,D
Indiana State University	M
Indiana University Bloomington	M
Iowa State University of Science and Technology	M,D
Kansas State University	M,D
Michigan State University	M,D
North Carolina State University	M
The Ohio State University	M,D
Oklahoma State University	M,D
Oregon State University	M,D
Philadelphia University	M
Purdue University	M,D
Syracuse University	M
Texas Woman's University	M,D
The University of Akron	M
The University of Alabama	M
University of California, Davis	M
University of Georgia	M,D
University of Kentucky	M
University of Missouri–Columbia	M
University of Nebraska–Lincoln	M,D
University of North Texas	M
University of Rhode Island	M
The University of Tennessee	M,D
Virginia Polytechnic Institute and State University	M,D
Washington State University	M

■ COGNITIVE SCIENCES

Arizona State University	D
Boston University	M,D
Brandeis University	M,D
Brown University	M,D
Carnegie Mellon University	D
Claremont Graduate University	M,D
Dartmouth College	D
Duke University	D
Emory University	D
Florida State University	D
The George Washington University	D
Georgia Institute of Technology	M
Harvard University	M,D,O
Hunter College of the City University of New York	M
Indiana University Bloomington	D
Iowa State University of Science and Technology	M,D
Johns Hopkins University	D
Louisiana State University and Agricultural and Mechanical College	M,D
Massachusetts Institute of Technology	D
New Mexico Highlands University	M
New York University	M,D,O
Northwestern University	D
The Ohio State University	D
The Pennsylvania State University University Park Campus	M,D
Rutgers, The State University of New Jersey, Newark	D
Rutgers, The State University of New Jersey, New Brunswick	D
State University of New York at Binghamton	M,D
Temple University	D
University at Buffalo, The State University of New York	M,D
The University of Akron	M,D
The University of Alabama	D
University of California, San Diego	D
University of Connecticut	M,D
University of Delaware	D
University of Illinois at Urbana–Champaign	M,D
University of Louisiana at Lafayette	D
University of Maryland	M,D
University of Maryland, Baltimore County	M,D
University of Maryland, College Park	D
University of Minnesota, Twin Cities Campus	D
The University of North Carolina at Greensboro	M,D
University of Notre Dame	D
University of Oregon	M,D
University of Pittsburgh	D
University of Rochester	M,D
The University of Texas at Austin	M,D
The University of Texas at Dallas	M
University of Wisconsin–Madison	D
Wayne State University	M,D

■ COMMUNICATION—GENERAL

Abilene Christian University	M
American University	M
Andrews University	M
Angelo State University	M
Arizona State University	M,D
Arizona State University West	M
Arkansas State University	M
Arkansas Tech University	M
Auburn University	M
Austin Peay State University	M
Ball State University	M
Barry University	M,O
Baylor University	M
Bethel College (MN)	M
Boise State University	M
Boston University	M
Bowling Green State University	M,D
Brigham Young University	M
California State University, Chico	M
California State University, Fullerton	M
California State University, Long Beach	M
California State University, Los Angeles	M
California State University, Northridge	M
California State University, Sacramento	M
California University of Pennsylvania	M
Carnegie Mellon University	M
Central Connecticut State University	M
Central Michigan University	M
Central Missouri State University	M
Clarion University of Pennsylvania	M
Clark University	M
Clemson University	M
Cleveland State University	M
The College of New Rochelle	M,O
College of Notre Dame of Maryland	M
Colorado State University	M
Cornell University	M,D
DePaul University	M
Drexel University	M
Drury University	M

Duquesne University	M,D
Eastern Michigan University	M
Eastern Washington University	M
East Tennessee State University	M
Edinboro University of Pennsylvania	M
Emerson College	M
Fairleigh Dickinson University, Teaneck–Hackensack Campus	M
Fitchburg State College	M
Florida Atlantic University	M
Florida Institute of Technology	M
Florida State University	M,D
Fordham University	M
Fort Hays State University	M
Georgetown University	M
Georgia State University	M,D
Governors State University	M
Grand Valley State University	M
Harvard University	M,O
Hawaii Pacific University	M
Howard University	M,D
Illinois Institute of Technology	M
Illinois State University	M
Indiana State University	M
Indiana University Bloomington	M,D
Indiana University–Purdue University Fort Wayne	M
Iona College	M,O
Ithaca College	M
Kent State University	M,D
Loyola Marymount University	M
Loyola University New Orleans	M
Mansfield University of Pennsylvania	M
Marquette University	M
Marshall University	M
Marywood University	M
Miami University	M
Michigan State University	M,D
Michigan Technological University	M,D
Mississippi College	M
Monmouth University	M,O
Montana State University–Billings	M
Morehead State University	M
New Jersey Institute of Technology	M
New Mexico State University	M
New School University	M
New York Institute of Technology	M
New York University	M,D,O
Norfolk State University	M
North Carolina State University	M
North Dakota State University	M
Northeastern State University	M
Northern Illinois University	M
Northwestern University	M,D
The Ohio State University	M,D
Ohio University	M,D
The Pennsylvania State University University Park Campus	M,D
Pepperdine University	M
Pittsburg State University	M
Point Park College	M
Purdue University	M,D
Purdue University Calumet	M
Quinnipiac University	M
Regent University	M,D
Regis University	M,O
Rensselaer Polytechnic Institute	M,D
Rochester Institute of Technology	M
Roosevelt University	M
Rutgers, The State University of New Jersey, New Brunswick	M,D
Sage Graduate School	M
Saginaw Valley State University	M
Saint Louis University	M
San Diego State University	M
San Jose State University	M
Seton Hall University	M
Shippensburg University of Pennsylvania	M
South Dakota State University	M
Southern Illinois University Carbondale	M,D
Southern Methodist University	M
Southwest Missouri State University	M
Southwest Texas State University	M
Stanford University	M,D
State University of New York at Albany	M,D
State University of New York College at Brockport	M
Stephen F. Austin State University	M
Suffolk University	M
Syracuse University	M,D
Teachers College, Columbia University	M,D
Temple University	M,D
Texas Southern University	M
Texas Tech University	M
Towson University	M,O
Trinity College (DC)	M
University at Buffalo, The State University of New York	M,D
The University of Akron	M
The University of Alabama	M,D,O
The University of Arizona	M,D
University of Arkansas	M
University of Baltimore	D
University of California, San Diego	M,D
University of California, Santa Barbara	D
University of California, Santa Cruz	O
University of Central Florida	M
University of Cincinnati	M
University of Colorado at Boulder	M,D
University of Colorado at Colorado Springs	M
University of Colorado at Denver	M
University of Connecticut	M
University of Dayton	M
University of Delaware	M
University of Denver	M,D
University of Dubuque	M
University of Florida	M,D
University of Georgia	M,D
University of Hartford	M
University of Hawaii at Manoa	M
University of Houston	M
University of Illinois at Chicago	M
University of Illinois at Springfield	M
University of Illinois at Urbana–Champaign	D
The University of Iowa	M,D
University of Kansas	M,D
University of Kentucky	M,D
University of Louisiana at Lafayette	M
University of Louisiana at Monroe	M
University of Maine	M
University of Maryland, Baltimore County	M
University of Maryland, College Park	M,D
University of Massachusetts Amherst	M,D
The University of Memphis	M,D
University of Miami	M,D
University of Missouri–Columbia	M,D
University of Missouri–Kansas City	M
The University of Montana–Missoula	M
University of Nebraska at Omaha	M
University of Nebraska–Lincoln	M,D
University of Nevada, Las Vegas	M
University of New Mexico	M,D
The University of North Carolina at Chapel Hill	M,D
The University of North Carolina at Greensboro	M
University of North Dakota	M
University of Northern Colorado	M
University of Northern Iowa	M
University of North Texas	M
University of Oklahoma	M,D
University of Oregon	M,D
University of Pennsylvania	M,D
University of Pittsburgh	M,D
University of Portland	M
University of South Alabama	M
University of Southern California	M,D,O
University of Southern Mississippi	M,D
University of South Florida	M,D
The University of Tennessee	M,D
The University of Texas at Austin	M,D
The University of Texas at Dallas	D
The University of Texas at El Paso	M
The University of Texas at Tyler	M
The University of Texas–Pan American	M
University of the Incarnate Word	M
University of the Pacific	M
University of the Sacred Heart	M
University of Utah	M,D
University of Vermont	M
University of Washington	M,D
University of West Florida	M
University of Wisconsin–Madison	M,D
University of Wisconsin–Milwaukee	M
University of Wisconsin–Stevens Point	M
University of Wisconsin–Superior	M
University of Wisconsin–Whitewater	M
University of Wyoming	M
Utah State University	M
Wake Forest University	M
Washington State University	M
Wayne State College	M
Wayne State University	M,D
Webster University	M
West Chester University of Pennsylvania	M
Western Illinois University	M
Western Kentucky University	M
Western Michigan University	M
Westminster College (UT)	M
West Texas A&M University	M
West Virginia University	M
Wichita State University	M
William Paterson University of New Jersey	M

■ COMMUNICATION DISORDERS

Abilene Christian University	M
Adelphi University	M,D
Alabama Agricultural and Mechanical University	M
Appalachian State University	M
Arizona State University	M,D
Arkansas State University	M
Armstrong Atlantic State University	M
Auburn University	M
Ball State University	M,D
Baylor University	M
Bloomsburg University of Pennsylvania	M
Boston University	M,D,O
Bowling Green State University	M,D
Brigham Young University	M
Brooklyn College of the City University of New York	M
California State University, Chico	M
California State University, Fresno	M
California State University, Fullerton	M
California State University, Hayward	M
California State University, Long Beach	M
California State University, Los Angeles	M
California State University, Northridge	M
California State University, Sacramento	M
California University of Pennsylvania	M

Case Western Reserve University M,D,O
Central Michigan University M,D
Central Missouri State University M
Clarion University of Pennsylvania M
Cleveland State University M
The College of New Jersey M
The College of New Rochelle M
The College of Saint Rose M
Duquesne University M
East Carolina University M,D
Eastern Illinois University M
Eastern Kentucky University M
Eastern Michigan University M
Eastern New Mexico University M
Eastern Washington University M
East Stroudsburg University of Pennsylvania M
East Tennessee State University M
Edinboro University of Pennsylvania M
Emerson College M
Florida Atlantic University M
Florida International University M
Florida State University M,D
Fontbonne College M
Fort Hays State University M
Gallaudet University M,D
The George Washington University M
Georgia State University M
Governors State University M
Hampton University M
Harvard University D
Hofstra University M
Howard University M,D
Hunter College of the City University of New York M
Idaho State University M
Illinois State University M
Indiana State University M,D,O
Indiana University Bloomington M,D
Indiana University of Pennsylvania M
Ithaca College M
Jackson State University M
James Madison University M
Kean University M
Kent State University M,D
Lamar University M,D
Lehman College of the City University of New York M
Loma Linda University M
Long Island University, Brooklyn Campus M
Long Island University, C.W. Post Campus M
Louisiana State University and Agricultural and Mechanical College M,D
Louisiana Tech University M
Loyola College in Maryland M,O
Marquette University M
Marshall University M
Marywood University M
Massachusetts Institute of Technology D
Miami University M
Michigan State University M,D
Minnesota State University, Mankato M
Minnesota State University Moorhead M
Minot State University M
Mississippi University for Women M
Montclair State University M
Murray State University M
Nazareth College of Rochester M
New Mexico State University M
New York University M,D
North Carolina Central University M
Northeastern State University M
Northeastern University M
Northern Arizona University M
Northern Illinois University M
Northern Michigan University M
Northwestern University M,D
Nova Southeastern University M,D
The Ohio State University M,D
Ohio University M,D
Oklahoma State University M
Old Dominion University M
Our Lady of the Lake University of San Antonio M
The Pennsylvania State University University Park Campus M,D
Plattsburgh State University of New York M
Portland State University M
Purdue University M,D
Queens College of the City University of New York M
Radford University M
Rockhurst University M
St. Cloud State University M
St. John's University (NY) M
Saint Louis University M
Saint Xavier University M
San Diego State University M,D
San Francisco State University M
San Jose State University M
Seton Hall University M,D
South Carolina State University M
Southeastern Louisiana University M
Southeast Missouri State University M
Southern Connecticut State University M
Southern Illinois University Carbondale M
Southern Illinois University Edwardsville M
Southwest Missouri State University M
Southwest Texas State University M
State University of New York at New Paltz M
State University of New York College at Buffalo M
State University of New York College at Fredonia M
State University of New York College at Geneseo M
State University of West Georgia M
Stephen F. Austin State University M
Syracuse University M,D
Teachers College, Columbia University M,D
Temple University M
Texas A&M University–Kingsville M
Texas Christian University M
Texas Woman's University M
Towson University M,D
Truman State University M
University at Buffalo, The State University of New York M,D
The University of Akron M
The University of Alabama M
The University of Arizona M,D
University of Arkansas M
University of California, San Diego D
University of Central Arkansas M
University of Central Florida M
University of Central Oklahoma M
University of Cincinnati M,D
University of Colorado at Boulder M,D
University of Connecticut M,D
University of Florida M,D
University of Georgia M,D,O
University of Hawaii at Manoa M
University of Houston M
University of Illinois at Urbana–Champaign M,D
The University of Iowa M,D
University of Kansas M,D
University of Kentucky M
University of Louisiana at Lafayette M
University of Louisiana at Monroe M
University of Louisville M
University of Maine M
University of Maryland, College Park M,D
University of Massachusetts Amherst M,D
The University of Memphis M,D
University of Minnesota, Duluth M
University of Minnesota, Twin Cities Campus M,D
University of Mississippi M
University of Missouri–Columbia M
University of Montevallo M
University of Nebraska at Kearney M
University of Nebraska at Omaha M
University of Nebraska–Lincoln M
University of Nevada, Reno M,D
University of New Hampshire M
University of New Mexico M
The University of North Carolina at Chapel Hill M,D
The University of North Carolina at Greensboro M
University of North Dakota M,D
University of Northern Colorado M
University of Northern Iowa M
University of North Texas M
University of Oregon M,D
University of Pittsburgh M,D
University of Redlands M
University of Rhode Island M
University of South Alabama M,D
University of South Carolina M,D
University of South Dakota M
University of Southern Mississippi M,D
University of South Florida M
The University of Tennessee M,D,O
The University of Texas at Austin M,D
The University of Texas at Dallas M,D
The University of Texas at El Paso M
The University of Texas–Pan American M
University of the District of Columbia M
University of the Pacific M
University of Toledo M
University of Tulsa M
University of Utah M,D
University of Virginia M
University of Washington M,D
University of Wisconsin–Eau Claire M
University of Wisconsin–Madison M,D
University of Wisconsin–Milwaukee M
University of Wisconsin–Oshkosh M
University of Wisconsin–River Falls M
University of Wisconsin–Stevens Point M
University of Wisconsin–Whitewater M
University of Wyoming M
Utah State University M,O
Valdosta State University M,O
Vanderbilt University M,D
Washington State University M
Washington University in St. Louis M,D
Wayne State University M,D
West Chester University of Pennsylvania M
Western Carolina University M
Western Illinois University M
Western Kentucky University M
Western Michigan University M
Western Washington University M
West Texas A&M University M
West Virginia University M
Wichita State University M,D
William Paterson University of New Jersey M
Worcester State College M

■ COMMUNITY COLLEGE EDUCATION

Eastern Washington University M
Florida International University D
George Mason University D
Michigan State University M,D
North Carolina State University M,D
Northern Arizona University M,D
Old Dominion University M,O
Pittsburg State University O
Princeton University D
University of South Florida M
Western Carolina University M

■ COMMUNITY HEALTH

Brooklyn College of the City University of New York M
Brown University M,D
Columbia University M,D
Emory University M
The George Washington University M
Harvard University M
Johns Hopkins University M,D
Long Island University, Brooklyn Campus M
Minnesota State University, Mankato M
Old Dominion University M,O
Sage Graduate School M
Saint Louis University M
Stony Brook University, State University of New York M,O
Temple University M
Trinity College (DC) M
University at Buffalo, The State University of New York M,D
University of California, Los Angeles M,D
University of Illinois at Chicago M,D
University of Illinois at Urbana–Champaign M,D
University of Minnesota, Twin Cities Campus M
University of Missouri–Columbia M
The University of North Carolina at Greensboro M
University of Northern Colorado M
University of North Florida M,O
University of North Texas M
University of Pittsburgh M
University of South Florida M,D
The University of Tennessee M,D
University of Wisconsin–La Crosse M
University of Wisconsin–Madison M,D
Wayne State University M,O
West Virginia University M

■ COMMUNITY HEALTH NURSING

Augsburg College M
Bellarmine University M
Boston College M,D
Capital University M
Case Western Reserve University M
Georgia Southern University M,O
Hawaii Pacific University M
Holy Names College M
Hunter College of the City University of New York M
Indiana University–Purdue University Indianapolis M
Indiana Wesleyan University M,O
Johns Hopkins University M
La Roche College M
La Salle University M,O
Lewis University M,O
MCP Hahnemann University M
Northeastern University M,O
Rutgers, The State University of New Jersey, Newark M,D
Sage Graduate School M
Saint Xavier University M,O
San José State University M
Southern Illinois University Edwardsville M
Texas Woman's University M,D
University of Cincinnati M,D
University of Hawaii at Manoa M,D,O
University of Illinois at Chicago M
University of Maryland M,D
University of Massachusetts Lowell M
University of Michigan M
University of Minnesota, Twin Cities Campus M
University of New Mexico M,O
The University of North Carolina at Chapel Hill M,D
The University of North Carolina at Charlotte M
University of South Carolina M
University of Southern Mississippi M,D
The University of Texas at Brownsville M
The University of Texas at El Paso M
Valdosta State University M
Wayne State University M
Wright State University M

■ COMPARATIVE AND INTERDISCIPLINARY ARTS

Columbia College Chicago M
Goddard College M
John F. Kennedy University M
Ohio University D
San Francisco State University M

■ COMPARATIVE LITERATURE

American University M
Antioch University McGregor M
Arizona State University M,D
Brigham Young University M
Brown University M,D
California State University, Fullerton M
Carnegie Mellon University M,D
Case Western Reserve University M,D
The Catholic University of America M,D
Columbia University M,D
Cornell University D
Dartmouth College M
Duke University D
Emory University D,O
Fairleigh Dickinson University, Teaneck–Hackensack Campus M
Florida Atlantic University M
Harvard University D
Indiana University Bloomington M,D
Johns Hopkins University D
Long Island University, Brooklyn Campus M
Louisiana State University and Agricultural and Mechanical College M,D
Michigan State University M
New York University M,D
Northwestern University M,D,O
Ohio University M
Oklahoma City University M
The Pennsylvania State University University Park Campus M,D
Princeton University D
Purdue University M,D
Rutgers, The State University of New Jersey, New Brunswick D
San Francisco State University M
Stanford University D
State University of New York at Binghamton M,D
Stony Brook University, State University of New York M,D
University at Buffalo, The State University of New York M,D
The University of Arizona M,D
University of Arkansas M,D
University of California, Berkeley M,D
University of California, Davis D
University of California, Irvine M,D
University of California, Los Angeles M,D
University of California, Riverside M,D
University of California, San Diego M,D
University of California, Santa Barbara M,D
University of California, Santa Cruz M,D
University of Chicago M,D
University of Colorado at Boulder M,D
University of Connecticut M,D
University of Georgia M,D
University of Illinois at Urbana–Champaign M,D
The University of Iowa M,D
University of Maryland, College Park M,D
University of Massachusetts Amherst M,D
University of Michigan D
University of Minnesota, Twin Cities Campus M,D
University of Missouri–Columbia M,D
University of New Hampshire M,D
University of New Mexico M,D
The University of North Carolina at Chapel Hill M,D
University of Oregon M,D
University of Pennsylvania M,D
University of Puerto Rico, Río Piedras M
University of Rochester M
University of Southern California M,D
The University of Texas at Austin M,D
The University of Texas at Dallas M,D
University of Utah M,D
University of Washington M,D
University of Wisconsin–Madison M,D
University of Wisconsin–Milwaukee M,D
Vanderbilt University M,D
Washington University in St. Louis M,D
Wayne State University M
Western Kentucky University M
West Virginia University M
Yale University D

■ COMPUTATIONAL SCIENCES

Arizona State University M,D
California Institute of Technology M,D
Carnegie Mellon University M,D
Clemson University M,D
The College of William and Mary M
Cornell University M,D
George Mason University M,D,O
The George Washington University M
Iowa State University of Science and Technology M,D
Kean University M
Louisiana Tech University M,D
Massachusetts Institute of Technology D
Michigan State University M,D
Michigan Technological University D
Mississippi State University M,D
Princeton University D
Rice University M,D
Stanford University M,D
State University of New York College at Brockport M
Temple University M,D
The University of Iowa D
University of Massachusetts Lowell M,D
University of Michigan–Dearborn M

University of Minnesota, Duluth	M
University of Minnesota, Twin Cities Campus	M,D
University of Puerto Rico, Mayagüez Campus	M
The University of Texas at Austin	M,D
Western Michigan University	M

■ COMPUTER ART AND DESIGN

Alfred University	M
Carnegie Mellon University	M,D
Clemson University	M
Columbia University	M
Cornell University	M,D
Florida Atlantic University	M
Indiana University Bloomington	M
Long Island University, C.W. Post Campus	M
Mississippi State University	M
New Mexico Highlands University	M
New School University	M
Rensselaer Polytechnic Institute	M
Rochester Institute of Technology	M
Syracuse University	M

■ COMPUTER EDUCATION

Arcadia University	M,O
Ashland University	M
California State University, Dominguez Hills	M,O
California State University, Los Angeles	M
California University of Pennsylvania	M
Cardinal Stritch University	M
DeSales University	M
Eastern Washington University	M
Florida Institute of Technology	M,D,O
Fontbonne College	M
Jacksonville University	M
Lesley University	M,D,O
Long Island University, C.W. Post Campus	M
Mississippi College	M
Nazareth College of Rochester	M
New York Institute of Technology	M,O
Northwest Missouri State University	M
Nova Southeastern University	M,D,O
Ohio University	M,D
Oklahoma State University	M,D
Philadelphia University	M
Providence College	M
Saint Martin's College	M
Shenandoah University	M,D,O
Shippensburg University of Pennsylvania	M
Stanford University	M,D
Teachers College, Columbia University	M
University of Bridgeport	M,O
University of Central Oklahoma	M
University of Florida	M,D,O
University of Georgia	M
University of Michigan	M,D
University of North Texas	M
The University of Texas at Tyler	M
Wilkes University	M
Wright State University	M

■ COMPUTER ENGINEERING

Auburn University	M,D
Boise State University	M
Boston University	M,D
California State University, Long Beach	M
California State University, Northridge	M
Carnegie Mellon University	M,D
Case Western Reserve University	M,D
Clarkson University	M,D
Clemson University	M,D
Cleveland State University	M,D
Colorado State University	M,D
Colorado Technical University	M
Cornell University	M,D
Dartmouth College	M,D
Drexel University	M,D
Duke University	M,D
Florida Atlantic University	M,D
Florida Institute of Technology	M,D
Florida International University	M
George Mason University	M,D
The George Washington University	M,D,O
Georgia Institute of Technology	M,D
Illinois Institute of Technology	M,D
Indiana State University	M
Iowa State University of Science and Technology	M,D
Johns Hopkins University	M,D
Kansas State University	M,D
Lehigh University	M
Louisiana State University and Agricultural and Mechanical College	M,D
Manhattan College	M
Marquette University	M,D
Michigan State University	M,D
Mississippi State University	M,D
New Jersey Institute of Technology	M,D,O
New Mexico State University	M,D
New York Institute of Technology	M
North Carolina State University	M,D
North Dakota State University	M
Northeastern University	M,D
Northwestern University	M,D,O
Oakland University	M
Oklahoma State University	M,D
Old Dominion University	M,D
Oregon Institute of Technology	M
Oregon State University	M,D
The Pennsylvania State University University Park Campus	M,D
Polytechnic University, Brooklyn Campus	M
Polytechnic University, Westchester Graduate Center	M
Portland State University	M,D
Princeton University	M,D
Purdue University	M,D
Rensselaer Polytechnic Institute	M,D
Rice University	M,D
Rochester Institute of Technology	M
Rutgers, The State University of New Jersey, New Brunswick	M,D
St. Mary's University of San Antonio	M
San Jose State University	M
Santa Clara University	M,D,O
Southern Methodist University	M,D
State University of New York at New Paltz	M
Stevens Institute of Technology	M,D,O
Stony Brook University, State University of New York	M,D
Syracuse University	M,D,O
Temple University	M
Texas A&M University	M,D
The University of Alabama at Birmingham	M,D
The University of Alabama in Huntsville	M,D
The University of Arizona	M,D
University of Arkansas	M,D
University of Bridgeport	M
University of California, Davis	M,D
University of California, Irvine	M,D
University of California, San Diego	M,D
University of California, Santa Barbara	M,D
University of California, Santa Cruz	M,D
University of Central Florida	M,D,O
University of Cincinnati	M,D
University of Colorado at Boulder	M,D
University of Colorado at Colorado Springs	M,D
University of Dayton	M,D
University of Denver	M,D
University of Florida	M,D,O
University of Houston	M,D
University of Houston–Clear Lake	M
University of Idaho	M
University of Illinois at Chicago	M,D
University of Illinois at Urbana–Champaign	M,D
The University of Iowa	M,D
University of Kansas	M
University of Louisiana at Lafayette	M,D
University of Louisville	D
University of Maine	M,D
University of Maryland, College Park	M,D
University of Massachusetts Amherst	M,D
University of Massachusetts Dartmouth	M,D,O
University of Massachusetts Lowell	M,D
The University of Memphis	M,D
University of Miami	M,D
University of Michigan	M,D
University of Michigan–Dearborn	M
University of Minnesota, Twin Cities Campus	M,D
University of Missouri–Columbia	M,D
University of Missouri–Rolla	M,D
University of Nebraska–Lincoln	M,D
University of Nevada, Las Vegas	M,D
University of Nevada, Reno	M,D
University of New Mexico	M,D
The University of North Carolina at Charlotte	M,D
University of Notre Dame	M,D
University of Oklahoma	M,D
University of Puerto Rico, Mayagüez Campus	M
University of Rhode Island	M,D
University of Rochester	M,D
University of South Carolina	M,D
University of Southern California	M,D
University of South Florida	M,D
The University of Texas at Arlington	M,D
The University of Texas at Austin	M,D
The University of Texas at El Paso	M,D
University of Virginia	M,D
Villanova University	M
Virginia Polytechnic Institute and State University	M,D
Wayne State University	M,D
Western Michigan University	M
West Virginia University	D
Widener University	M
Worcester Polytechnic Institute	M,D,O
Wright State University	M,D

■ COMPUTER SCIENCE

Alabama Agricultural and Mechanical University	M
Alcorn State University	M
American University	M
Appalachian State University	M
Arizona State University	M,D
Arkansas State University	M
Auburn University	M,D
Azusa Pacific University	M,O
Ball State University	M
Baylor University	M
Boise State University	M
Boston University	M,D
Bowie State University	M

Bowling Green State University	M
Bradley University	M
Brandeis University	M,D
Bridgewater State College	M
Brigham Young University	M,D
Brooklyn College of the City University of New York	M,D
Brown University	M,D
California Institute of Technology	M,D
California Polytechnic State University, San Luis Obispo	M
California State Polytechnic University, Pomona	M
California State University, Chico	M
California State University, Fresno	M
California State University, Fullerton	M
California State University, Hayward	M
California State University, Long Beach	M
California State University, Northridge	M
California State University, Sacramento	M
California State University, San Bernardino	M
California State University, San Marcos	M
Carnegie Mellon University	M,D
Case Western Reserve University	M,D
The Catholic University of America	M,D
Central Connecticut State University	M
Central Michigan University	M
Chicago State University	M
City College of the City University of New York	M,D
City University	M,O
Clark Atlanta University	M
Clarkson University	M,D
Clemson University	M,D
The College of Saint Rose	M
College of Staten Island of the City University of New York	M,D
The College of William and Mary	M,D
Colorado State University	M,D
Colorado Technical University	M,D
Columbia University	M,D,O
Columbus State University	M
Cornell University	M,D
Creighton University	M
Dartmouth College	M,D
DePaul University	M,D
Drexel University	M
Duke University	M,D
East Carolina University	M
Eastern Michigan University	M
Eastern Washington University	M
East Stroudsburg University of Pennsylvania	M
East Tennessee State University	M
Edinboro University of Pennsylvania	O
Emory University	M,D
Fairleigh Dickinson University, Teaneck–Hackensack Campus	M
Fitchburg State College	M
Florida Atlantic University	M,D
Florida Gulf Coast University	M
Florida Institute of Technology	M,D
Florida International University	M,D
Florida State University	M,D
Fordham University	M
Frostburg State University	M
George Mason University	M,D
The George Washington University	M,D,O
Georgia Institute of Technology	M,D
Georgia Southwestern State University	M
Georgia State University	M,D
Governors State University	M
Hampton University	M
Harvard University	D
Hofstra University	M
Hood College	M
Howard University	M
Hunter College of the City University of New York	D
Illinois Institute of Technology	M,D
Illinois State University	M
Indiana University Bloomington	M,D
Indiana University–Purdue University Fort Wayne	M
Indiana University–Purdue University Indianapolis	M
Inter American University of Puerto Rico, Metropolitan Campus	M
Iona College	M
Iowa State University of Science and Technology	M,D
Jackson State University	M
Jacksonville State University	M
James Madison University	M
Johns Hopkins University	M,D
Kansas State University	M,D
Kent State University	M,D
Kutztown University of Pennsylvania	M
Lamar University	M
La Salle University	M
Lawrence Technological University	M
Lehigh University	M,D
Lehman College of the City University of New York	M
Long Island University, Brooklyn Campus	M
Louisiana State University and Agricultural and Mechanical College	M,D
Louisiana Tech University	M
Loyola Marymount University	M
Loyola University Chicago	M
Maharishi University of Management	M
Marist College	M
Marquette University	M,D
Marymount University	M,O
Massachusetts Institute of Technology	M,D,O
McNeese State University	M
Michigan State University	M,D
Michigan Technological University	M
Middle Tennessee State University	M
Midwestern State University	M
Minnesota State University, Mankato	M
Mississippi College	M
Mississippi State University	M,D
Monmouth University	M
Montana State University–Bozeman	M,D
Montclair State University	M,O
New Jersey Institute of Technology	M,D
New Mexico Highlands University	M
New Mexico Institute of Mining and Technology	M,D
New Mexico State University	M,D
New York Institute of Technology	M
New York University	M,D
North Carolina Agricultural and Technical State University	M
North Carolina State University	M,D
North Central College	M
North Dakota State University	M,D
Northeastern Illinois University	M
Northeastern University	M,D
Northern Illinois University	M
Northwestern University	M,D
Northwest Missouri State University	M
Nova Southeastern University	M,D
Oakland University	M
The Ohio State University	M,D
Ohio University	M,D
Oklahoma City University	M
Oklahoma State University	M,D
Old Dominion University	M,D
Oregon State University	M,D
Pace University, New York City Campus	M,D,O
Pace University, White Plains Campus	M,D,O
The Pennsylvania State University Harrisburg Campus of the Capital College	M
The Pennsylvania State University University Park Campus	M,D
Polytechnic University, Brooklyn Campus	M,D
Polytechnic University, Westchester Graduate Center	M,D
Portland State University	M
Princeton University	M,D
Purdue University	M,D
Queens College of the City University of New York	M
Regis University	M,O
Rensselaer Polytechnic Institute	M,D
Rice University	M,D
Rivier College	M
Rochester Institute of Technology	M,O
Roosevelt University	M
Rutgers, The State University of New Jersey, New Brunswick	M,D
Sacred Heart University	M,O
St. Cloud State University	M
St. John's University (NY)	M
Saint Joseph's University	M
Saint Louis University	M,D
St. Mary's University of San Antonio	M
Saint Xavier University	M
Sam Houston State University	M
San Diego State University	M
San Francisco State University	M
San Jose State University	M
Santa Clara University	M,D,O
Shippensburg University of Pennsylvania	M
South Dakota State University	M
Southeastern University	M
Southern Illinois University Carbondale	M
Southern Illinois University Edwardsville	M
Southern Methodist University	M,D
Southern Oregon University	M
Southern University and Agricultural and Mechanical College	M
Southwest Texas State University	M
Stanford University	M,D
State University of New York at Albany	M,D
State University of New York at Binghamton	M,D
State University of New York at New Paltz	M
State University of New York Institute of Technology at Utica/Rome	M
Stephen F. Austin State University	M
Stevens Institute of Technology	M,D,O
Stony Brook University, State University of New York	M,D,O
Suffolk University	M
Syracuse University	M,D
Tarleton State University	M
Temple University	M,D
Texas A&M University	M,D
Texas A&M University–Commerce	M
Texas A&M University–Corpus Christi	M
Texas A&M University–Kingsville	M
Texas Tech University	M,D
Towson University	M
Tufts University	M,D,O
Tulane University	M,D

University at Buffalo, The State University of New York M,D
The University of Akron M
The University of Alabama M,D
The University of Alabama at Birmingham M,D
The University of Alabama in Huntsville M,D
University of Alaska Fairbanks M,D
The University of Arizona M,D
University of Arkansas M,D
University of Arkansas at Little Rock M
University of Bridgeport M
University of California, Berkeley M,D
University of California, Davis M,D
University of California, Irvine M,D
University of California, Los Angeles M,D
University of California, Riverside M,D
University of California, San Diego M,D
University of California, Santa Barbara M,D
University of California, Santa Cruz M,D
University of Central Florida M,D
University of Central Oklahoma M
University of Chicago M,D
University of Cincinnati M,D
University of Colorado at Boulder M,D
University of Colorado at Colorado Springs M,D
University of Colorado at Denver M
University of Connecticut M,D
University of Dayton M
University of Delaware M,D
University of Denver M,D
University of Detroit Mercy M
University of Florida M,D,O
University of Georgia M,D
University of Hawaii at Manoa M,D,O
University of Houston M,D
University of Houston–Clear Lake M
University of Idaho M,D
University of Illinois at Chicago M,D
University of Illinois at Springfield M
University of Illinois at Urbana–Champaign M,D
The University of Iowa M,D
University of Kansas M,D
University of Kentucky M,D
University of Louisiana at Lafayette M,D
University of Louisville M,D
University of Maine M,D
University of Mary Hardin-Baylor M
University of Maryland, Baltimore County M,D
University of Maryland, College Park M,D
University of Maryland Eastern Shore M
University of Massachusetts Amherst M,D
University of Massachusetts Boston M,D
University of Massachusetts Dartmouth M
University of Massachusetts Lowell M,D
The University of Memphis M,D
University of Miami M
University of Michigan M,D
University of Michigan–Dearborn M
University of Minnesota, Duluth M
University of Minnesota, Twin Cities Campus M,D
University of Missouri–Columbia M,D
University of Missouri–Kansas City M,D
University of Missouri–Rolla M,D
University of Missouri–St. Louis M,D,O
The University of Montana–Missoula M
University of Nebraska at Omaha M
University of Nebraska–Lincoln M,D
University of Nevada, Las Vegas M,D
University of Nevada, Reno M
University of New Hampshire M,D
University of New Haven M
University of New Mexico M,D
University of New Orleans M
The University of North Carolina at Chapel Hill M,D
The University of North Carolina at Charlotte M
The University of North Carolina at Greensboro M
University of North Dakota M
University of Northern Iowa M
University of North Florida M
University of North Texas M,D
University of Notre Dame M,D
University of Oklahoma M,D
University of Oregon M,D
University of Pennsylvania M,D
University of Pittsburgh M,D
University of Rhode Island M,D
University of Rochester M,D
University of San Francisco M
University of South Alabama M
University of South Carolina M,D
University of South Dakota M
University of Southern California M,D
University of Southern Maine M
University of Southern Mississippi M,D
University of South Florida M,D
The University of Tennessee M,D
The University of Tennessee at Chattanooga M
The University of Texas at Arlington M,D
The University of Texas at Austin M,D
The University of Texas at Dallas M,D
The University of Texas at El Paso M
The University of Texas at San Antonio M,D
The University of Texas at Tyler M
The University of Texas–Pan American M,D
University of Toledo M,D
University of Tulsa M,D
University of Utah M,D
University of Vermont M
University of Virginia M,D
University of Washington M,D
University of West Florida M
University of Wisconsin–Madison M,D
University of Wisconsin–Milwaukee M,D
University of Wyoming M,D
Utah State University M
Vanderbilt University M,D
Villanova University M
Virginia Commonwealth University M
Virginia Polytechnic Institute and State University M,D
Wake Forest University M
Washington State University M,D
Washington University in St. Louis M,D
Wayne State University M,D
Webster University M,O
West Chester University of Pennsylvania M,O
Western Carolina University M
Western Connecticut State University M
Western Illinois University M
Western Kentucky University M
Western Michigan University M,D
Western Washington University M
West Virginia University M,D
Wichita State University M
Worcester Polytechnic Institute M,D,O
Wright State University M,D
Yale University D

■ CONFLICT RESOLUTION AND MEDIATION/PEACE STUDIES

Alliant International University M
American University M,D,O
Antioch University McGregor M
Arcadia University M
California State University, Dominguez Hills M,O
Chaminade University of Honolulu M
Cornell University M,D
Dallas Baptist University M
Duquesne University M,O
Fresno Pacific University M
George Mason University M,D
John F. Kennedy University O
Johns Hopkins University M,D,O
Kennesaw State University M
Lesley University M,O
Montclair State University M,O
Nova Southeastern University M,D,O
Pepperdine University M
St. Edward's University M,O
St. Mary's University of San Antonio M
University of Baltimore M
University of Massachusetts Boston M,O
University of Missouri–Columbia M
University of Missouri–St. Louis M
University of Notre Dame M
Wayne State University M,O

■ CONSERVATION BIOLOGY

Arizona State University M,D
Central Michigan University M
Columbia University M,D,O
Frostburg State University M
San Francisco State University M
State University of New York at Albany M
University of Arkansas D
University of Central Florida M,O
University of Hawaii at Manoa M,D
University of Maryland, College Park M
University of Minnesota, Twin Cities Campus M,D
University of Missouri–St. Louis M,D,O
University of Nevada, Reno D
University of New Orleans M,D
University of Wisconsin–Madison M
Virginia Polytechnic Institute and State University M,D

■ CONSTRUCTION ENGINEERING AND MANAGEMENT

Arizona State University M
Auburn University M,D
Bradley University M
The Catholic University of America M
Clemson University M
Colorado State University M,D
Florida International University M
Georgia Institute of Technology M,D
Iowa State University of Science and Technology M,D
Marquette University M,D
Michigan State University M
Montana State University–Bozeman M,D
Stevens Institute of Technology M
Texas A&M University M,D
University of California, Berkeley M,D
University of Colorado at Boulder M,D
University of Denver M
University of Florida M
University of Houston M
University of Kansas M
University of Michigan M,D,O
University of Missouri–Rolla M,D
University of Southern California M
University of Washington M,D
Washington University in St. Louis M
Western Michigan University M

■ CONSUMER ECONOMICS

Colorado State University	M
Florida State University	M,D
Iowa State University of Science and Technology	M,D
Michigan State University	M,D
Minnesota State University, Mankato	M
Montclair State University	M
The Ohio State University	M,D
Purdue University	M,D
Syracuse University	M
Texas Tech University	D
The University of Alabama	M
The University of Arizona	M,D
University of Georgia	M,D
University of Illinois at Urbana–Champaign	M,D
The University of Memphis	M
University of Missouri–Columbia	M
University of Nebraska–Lincoln	M,D
The University of Tennessee	M,D
University of Utah	M
University of Vermont	M
University of Wisconsin–Madison	M,D
University of Wyoming	M
Virginia Polytechnic Institute and State University	M,D

■ CORPORATE AND ORGANIZATIONAL COMMUNICATION

Austin Peay State University	M
Barry University	M,O
Bentley College	M,O
Bowie State University	M,O
Canisius College	M
Carnegie Mellon University	M
Central Connecticut State University	M
Central Michigan University	M
Columbia University	M
Concordia University Wisconsin	M
DePaul University	M
Emerson College	M
Fairleigh Dickinson University, Florham-Madison Campus	M
Florida State University	M,D
Fordham University	M
Howard University	M,D
Illinois Institute of Technology	M
John Carroll University	M
La Salle University	M
Lindenwood University	M
Manhattanville College	M
Marquette University	M
Marylhurst University	M
Monmouth University	M,O
Murray State University	M
North Carolina State University	M
Northwestern University	M
Oklahoma City University	M
Queens College	M
Radford University	M
Rollins College	M
Roosevelt University	M
Sage Graduate School	M
Seton Hall University	M
Simmons College	M
Syracuse University	M
Towson University	M
University of Arkansas at Little Rock	M
University of Colorado at Boulder	M,D
University of Connecticut	M,D
University of Denver	M
University of Florida	M,D
University of Portland	M
University of St. Thomas (MN)	M,O
University of Southern California	M,D
University of Wisconsin–Stevens Point	M
University of Wisconsin–Whitewater	M
Wayne State University	M,D
Western Kentucky University	M
Western Michigan University	M
West Virginia University	M

■ COUNSELING PSYCHOLOGY

Abilene Christian University	M
Alabama Agricultural and Mechanical University	M,O
Alaska Pacific University	M
Alliant International University	M,D
Andrews University	D
Angelo State University	M
Anna Maria College	M,O
Antioch New England Graduate School	M
Antioch University McGregor	M
Arcadia University	M
Argosy University-Sarasota	M,D,O
Arizona State University	D
Assumption College	M,O
Auburn University	M,D,O
Avila College	M
Ball State University	M,D
Benedictine University	M
Boston College	M,D
Boston University	M,D
Bowie State University	M
Brigham Young University	M,D
Butler University	M,O
California Baptist University	M
California State University, Bakersfield	M
California State University, Chico	M
California State University, Sacramento	M
California State University, San Bernardino	M
California State University, Stanislaus	M
Central Washington University	M
Chaminade University of Honolulu	M
Chapman University	M
Chestnut Hill College	M,D
City University	M
Cleveland State University	M
College of Mount Saint Vincent	M,O
The College of New Rochelle	M
College of St. Joseph	M
Colorado State University	D
Columbus State University	M,O
Concordia University (IL)	M,O
Dominican University of California	M
Eastern College	M
Eastern Nazarene College	M
Eastern Washington University	M
Fitchburg State College	M,O
Florida State University	D
Fordham University	M,D,O
Fort Valley State University	M
Framingham State College	M
Franciscan University of Steubenville	M
Frostburg State University	M
Gallaudet University	M
Gannon University	M,D
Gardner-Webb University	M
Geneva College	M
George Fox University	M
Georgian Court College	M
Georgia State University	M,D,O
Goddard College	M
Gonzaga University	M
Holy Family College	M
Holy Names College	M,O
Hope International University	M
Houston Baptist University	M
Howard University	M,D,O
Idaho State University	M,O
Illinois School of Professional Psychology, Chicago Northwest Campus	M,D
Illinois State University	M,D,O
Immaculata College	M,D,O
Indiana State University	M,D,O
Iowa State University of Science and Technology	M,D
James Madison University	M,O
John Carroll University	M,O
John F. Kennedy University	M
Kutztown University of Pennsylvania	M
La Salle University	M
Lehigh University	M,D,O
Lesley University	M,O
Lewis University	M
Liberty University	M
Lindenwood University	M
Louisiana Tech University	M,D,O
Loyola College in Maryland	M,O
Loyola Marymount University	M
Loyola University Chicago	D
Marist College	M,O
Marymount University	M,O
Marywood University	M,D
Michigan State University	M,D,O
MidAmerica Nazarene University	M
Mississippi College	M,O
Monmouth University	M,O
Morehead State University	M
Mount St. Mary's College	M
National University	M,O
New Jersey City University	M
New Mexico State University	M,D,O
New York Institute of Technology	M
New York University	M,D,O
Nicholls State University	M,O
Northeastern State University	M
Northeastern University	M,D,O
Northern Arizona University	D
Northwestern University	M
Northwest Missouri State University	M
Notre Dame de Namur University	M
Nova Southeastern University	M
The Ohio State University	D
Our Lady of the Lake University of San Antonio	M,D
Palm Beach Atlantic College	M
The Pennsylvania State University University Park Campus	D
Prescott College	M
Radford University	M,O
Regent University	M,D
Regis University	M,O
Rivier College	M
Rutgers, The State University of New Jersey, New Brunswick	M
St. Edward's University	M,O
Saint Martin's College	M
Saint Mary's University of Minnesota	M
St. Mary's University of San Antonio	M,D,O
St. Thomas University	M
Saint Xavier University	M,O
Salve Regina University	M,O
Sam Houston State University	M,D
San Francisco State University	M
San Jose State University	M
Santa Clara University	M
Seton Hall University	D
Southern Illinois University Carbondale	M,D
Southern Methodist University	M
Southern Nazarene University	M
Springfield College	M,O
Stanford University	D

Institution	Degrees
State University of New York at Albany	M,D,O
State University of New York at Oswego	M,O
Tarleton State University	M
Teachers College, Columbia University	M,D
Temple University	M,D
Tennessee State University	M,D
Texas A&M International University	M
Texas A&M University	D
Texas A&M University–Commerce	M,D
Texas A&M University–Texarkana	M
Texas Tech University	M,D
Texas Woman's University	M,D
Towson University	M,O
Trevecca Nazarene University	M
Trinity College (DC)	M
Truman State University	M
The University of Akron	M,D
University of Baltimore	M,D
University of California, Santa Barbara	M,D
University of Central Arkansas	M
University of Central Oklahoma	M
University of Colorado at Denver	M
University of Connecticut	M,D
University of Denver	M,D,O
University of Georgia	M,D
University of Great Falls	M
University of Houston	M,D
University of Kansas	M,D
University of Kentucky	M,D,O
University of La Verne	M
University of Mary Hardin-Baylor	M
University of Maryland, College Park	M,D,O
The University of Memphis	M,D
University of Miami	D
University of Minnesota, Duluth	M
University of Minnesota, Twin Cities Campus	D
University of Missouri–Columbia	M,D,O
University of Missouri–Kansas City	M,D,O
University of Nevada, Las Vegas	M,D
The University of North Carolina at Greensboro	M,D,O
University of North Dakota	M,D
University of Northern Colorado	M,D
University of North Florida	M
University of North Texas	M,D
University of Notre Dame	D
University of Oklahoma	D
University of Oregon	M,D
University of Pennsylvania	M
University of Rhode Island	M
University of Saint Francis (IN)	M
University of San Francisco	M,D
University of Southern California	M,D,O
The University of Tennessee	M,D,O
The University of Texas at Austin	M,D
University of the Pacific	M,D
University of Wisconsin–Madison	D
Utah State University	M,D
Valdosta State University	M,O
Valparaiso University	M
Virginia Commonwealth University	M,D,O
Walla Walla College	M
Washington State University	M,D
Webster University	M
Western Michigan University	M,D
Western Washington University	M
Westfield State College	M
West Virginia University	M,D
William Carey College	M

■ COUNSELOR EDUCATION

Institution	Degrees
Abilene Christian University	M
Adams State College	M
Alabama Agricultural and Mechanical University	M,O
Alabama State University	M,O
Albany State University	M
Alcorn State University	M,O
Alfred University	M
Angelo State University	M
Appalachian State University	M,O
Argosy University-Sarasota	M,D,O
Arizona State University	M
Arkansas State University	M,O
Auburn University	M,D,O
Auburn University Montgomery	M,O
Augusta State University	M,O
Austin Peay State University	M,O
Barry University	M,D,O
Bayamón Central University	M
Boise State University	M
Boston University	M,O
Bowie State University	M
Bowling Green State University	M
Bradley University	M
Bridgewater State College	M,O
Brigham Young University	M,D
Brooklyn College of the City University of New York	M,O
Butler University	M,O
California Lutheran University	M
California Polytechnic State University, San Luis Obispo	M
California State University, Bakersfield	M
California State University, Dominguez Hills	M
California State University, Fresno	M
California State University, Fullerton	M
California State University, Hayward	M
California State University, Long Beach	M,O
California State University, Los Angeles	M
California State University, Northridge	M,O
California State University, Sacramento	M
California State University, San Bernardino	M
California State University, Stanislaus	M
California University of Pennsylvania	M
Campbell University	M
Canisius College	M,O
Carson-Newman College	M
Carthage College	M,O
The Catholic University of America	M,D
Central Connecticut State University	M
Central Michigan University	M
Central Missouri State University	M,O
Central Washington University	M
Chadron State College	M,O
Chapman University	M
Chicago State University	M
The Citadel, The Military College of South Carolina	M
Clark Atlanta University	M,D
Clemson University	M
Cleveland State University	M,O
The College of New Jersey	M
College of St. Joseph	M
The College of Saint Rose	M
College of Santa Fe	M
College of the Southwest	M
The College of William and Mary	M,D
Columbus State University	M,O
Concordia University (IL)	M,O
Concordia University Wisconsin	M
Creighton University	M
Dallas Baptist University	M
Delta State University	M
DePaul University	M
Doane College	M
Drake University	M
Duquesne University	M,D
East Carolina University	M,O
East Central University	M
Eastern College	M
Eastern Illinois University	M
Eastern Kentucky University	M,O
Eastern Michigan University	M,O
Eastern New Mexico University	M
Eastern Washington University	M
East Tennessee State University	M
Edinboro University of Pennsylvania	M,O
Emporia State University	M
Fairfield University	M,O
Fitchburg State College	M,O
Florida Agricultural and Mechanical University	M,D
Florida Atlantic University	M,O
Florida Gulf Coast University	M
Florida International University	M
Florida State University	M,O
Fordham University	M,D,O
Fort Hays State University	M
Fort Valley State University	M,O
Freed-Hardeman University	M
Fresno Pacific University	M
Frostburg State University	M
Gallaudet University	M
George Mason University	M
The George Washington University	M,D,O
Georgia Southern University	M,O
Georgia State University	M,D,O
Governors State University	M
Gwynedd-Mercy College	M
Hampton University	M
Hardin-Simmons University	M
Heidelberg College	M
Henderson State University	M
Heritage College	M
Hofstra University	M,O
Houston Baptist University	M
Howard University	M,D,O
Hunter College of the City University of New York	M
Idaho State University	M,D,O
Illinois State University	M,D
Immaculata College	M,D,O
Indiana State University	M,D,O
Indiana University Bloomington	M,D,O
Indiana University of Pennsylvania	M
Indiana University–Purdue University Fort Wayne	M
Indiana University–Purdue University Indianapolis	M
Indiana University South Bend	M
Indiana University Southeast	M
Indiana Wesleyan University	M
Inter American University of Puerto Rico, Metropolitan Campus	M
Inter American University of Puerto Rico, San Germán Campus	M
Iona College	M
Iowa State University of Science and Technology	M,D
Jackson State University	M,O
Jacksonville State University	M,O
John Carroll University	M,O
Johns Hopkins University	M,D,O
Johnson State College	M
Kansas State University	M,D
Kean University	M,O
Keene State College	M,O
Kent State University	M,D
Kutztown University of Pennsylvania	M
Lamar University	M,O
La Sierra University	M,O
Lehigh University	M,D,O

Lehman College of the City University of New York	M
Lewis University	M
Liberty University	M,D
Lincoln Memorial University	M,O
Lincoln University (MO)	M
Long Island University, Brooklyn Campus	M,O
Long Island University, C.W. Post Campus	M,O
Longwood College	M
Louisiana State University and Agricultural and Mechanical College	M,D,O
Louisiana Tech University	M,D,O
Loyola College in Maryland	M,O
Loyola Marymount University	M
Loyola University Chicago	M
Loyola University New Orleans	M
Lynchburg College	M
Malone College	M
Manhattan College	M,O
Marshall University	M,O
Marymount University	M,O
Marywood University	M
McNeese State University	M
Michigan State University	M,D,O
Middle Tennessee State University	M,O
Midwestern State University	M
Millersville University of Pennsylvania	M
Minnesota State University, Mankato	M
Minnesota State University Moorhead	M
Mississippi College	M,O
Mississippi State University	M,D,O
Montana State University–Billings	M
Montana State University–Northern	M
Montclair State University	M
Morehead State University	M,O
Murray State University	M,O
National University	M
New Mexico Highlands University	M
New Mexico State University	M,D,O
New York University	M,D,O
Niagara University	M,O
Nicholls State University	M,O
North Carolina Agricultural and Technical State University	M
North Carolina Central University	M
North Carolina State University	M,D,O
North Dakota State University	M
Northeastern Illinois University	M
Northeastern State University	M
Northeastern University	M
Northern Arizona University	M
Northern Illinois University	M,D
Northern State University	M
Northwestern Oklahoma State University	M
Northwestern State University of Louisiana	M,O
Northwest Missouri State University	M
Northwest Nazarene University	M
Oakland University	M,D,O
Ohio University	M,D
Oklahoma State University	M,D
Old Dominion University	M,O
Oregon State University	M,D
Our Lady of the Lake University of San Antonio	M
Palm Beach Atlantic College	M
The Pennsylvania State University University Park Campus	M,D
Pittsburg State University	M
Plattsburgh State University of New York	M,O
Plymouth State College	M
Portland State University	M
Prairie View A&M University	M
Providence College	M
Purdue University	M,D,O
Purdue University Calumet	M
Queens College of the City University of New York	M
Radford University	M
Regent University	M,D
Rhode Island College	M,O
Rider University	M,O
Rivier College	M
Rollins College	M
Roosevelt University	M,D
Sage Graduate School	M,O
St. Bonaventure University	M,O
St. Cloud State University	M
St. John's University (NY)	M,O
Saint Louis University	M,D
Saint Martin's College	M
Saint Mary's College of California	M
St. Thomas University	M,O
Salem State College	M
Sam Houston State University	M,D
San Diego State University	M
San Jose State University	M
Santa Clara University	M
Seattle Pacific University	M
Seattle University	M
Seton Hall University	M
Shippensburg University of Pennsylvania	M
Siena Heights University	M
Slippery Rock University of Pennsylvania	M
Sonoma State University	M
South Carolina State University	M,D,O
South Dakota State University	M
Southeastern Louisiana University	M
Southeastern Oklahoma State University	M
Southeast Missouri State University	M
Southern Arkansas University–Magnolia	M
Southern Connecticut State University	M,O
Southern Illinois University Carbondale	M,D
Southern Oregon University	M
Southern University and Agricultural and Mechanical College	M
Southwestern Oklahoma State University	M
Southwest Missouri State University	M
Southwest Texas State University	M
Spalding University	M
Springfield College	M,O
State University of New York at Albany	M,D,O
State University of New York College at Brockport	M,O
State University of New York College at Oneonta	M,O
State University of West Georgia	M,O
Stephen F. Austin State University	M
Stetson University	M
Suffolk University	M,O
Sul Ross State University	M
Syracuse University	M,D,O
Tarleton State University	M
Tennessee State University	M,D
Texas A&M International University	M
Texas A&M University	M,D
Texas A&M University–Commerce	M,D
Texas A&M University–Corpus Christi	M
Texas A&M University–Kingsville	M
Texas Christian University	M
Texas Southern University	M,D
Texas Tech University	M,D,O
Texas Woman's University	M,D
Trevecca Nazarene University	M
Trinity College (DC)	M
Troy State University	M
Troy State University Dothan	M,O
Troy State University Montgomery	M,O
University at Buffalo, The State University of New York	M,D,O
The University of Akron	M
The University of Alabama	M,D,O
The University of Alabama at Birmingham	M
University of Alaska Anchorage	M
University of Alaska Fairbanks	M,O
University of Arkansas	M,D,O
University of Arkansas at Little Rock	M
University of Central Arkansas	M
University of Central Florida	M
University of Central Oklahoma	M
University of Cincinnati	M,D,O
University of Colorado at Colorado Springs	M
University of Colorado at Denver	M
University of Dayton	M
University of Delaware	M,D
University of Detroit Mercy	M
University of Florida	M,D,O
University of Georgia	M,D
University of Great Falls	M
University of Guam	M
University of Hartford	M,O
University of Hawaii at Manoa	M
University of Houston–Clear Lake	M
University of Idaho	M,D,O
University of Illinois at Urbana–Champaign	M,D,O
The University of Iowa	M,D
University of La Verne	M,O
University of Louisiana at Lafayette	M
University of Louisiana at Monroe	M,O
University of Louisville	M,D,O
University of Maine	M,O
University of Maryland, College Park	M,D,O
University of Maryland Eastern Shore	M
University of Massachusetts Amherst	M,D,O
University of Massachusetts Boston	M,O
The University of Memphis	M,D
University of Miami	M
University of Minnesota, Twin Cities Campus	M,D,O
University of Missouri–Kansas City	M,D,O
University of Missouri–St. Louis	M,D
The University of Montana–Missoula	M,D,O
University of Montevallo	M
University of Nebraska at Kearney	M,O
University of Nebraska at Omaha	M
University of Nevada, Reno	M,D,O
University of New Hampshire	M
University of New Mexico	M,D
University of New Orleans	M,D,O
University of North Alabama	M
The University of North Carolina at Chapel Hill	M
The University of North Carolina at Charlotte	M
The University of North Carolina at Greensboro	M,D,O
The University of North Carolina at Pembroke	M
University of Northern Colorado	M,D
University of Northern Iowa	M,D
University of North Florida	M
University of North Texas	M,D
University of Puerto Rico, Río Piedras	M,D
University of Saint Francis (IN)	M
University of San Diego	M
University of San Francisco	M,D

The University of Scranton	M
University of South Alabama	M,O
University of South Carolina	D,O
University of South Dakota	M,D,O
University of Southern Maine	M,O
University of South Florida	M,O
The University of Tennessee	M,D,O
The University of Tennessee at Chattanooga	M,O
The University of Tennessee at Martin	M
The University of Texas at Austin	M,D
The University of Texas at Brownsville	M
The University of Texas of the Permian Basin	M
The University of Texas–Pan American	M,D
University of the District of Columbia	M
University of the Pacific	M,D
University of Toledo	M,D
University of Vermont	M
University of Virginia	M,D,O
University of Washington	M,D
The University of West Alabama	M
University of Wisconsin–Madison	M
University of Wisconsin–Oshkosh	M
University of Wisconsin–Platteville	M
University of Wisconsin–River Falls	M
University of Wisconsin–Stevens Point	M
University of Wisconsin–Stout	M,O
University of Wisconsin–Superior	M
University of Wisconsin–Whitewater	M
Utah State University	M,D
Valdosta State University	M,O
Vanderbilt University	M
Villanova University	M
Virginia Commonwealth University	M
Virginia Polytechnic Institute and State University	M,D,O
Virginia State University	M
Wake Forest University	M
Walla Walla College	M
Walsh University	M
Wayne State College	M
Wayne State University	M,D,O
West Chester University of Pennsylvania	M
Western Carolina University	M
Western Connecticut State University	M
Western Illinois University	M,O
Western Kentucky University	M,O
Western Michigan University	M,D
Western New Mexico University	M
Western Washington University	M
West Texas A&M University	M
Whitworth College	M
Wichita State University	M,D,O
Widener University	M,D
William Paterson University of New Jersey	M
Wilmington College	M,D
Winona State University	M
Winthrop University	M
Wright State University	M
Xavier University	M
Xavier University of Louisiana	M
Youngstown State University	M

■ CRIMINAL JUSTICE AND CRIMINOLOGY

Albany State University	M
American International College	M
American University	M,D
Anna Maria College	M
Arizona State University West	M
Armstrong Atlantic State University	M
Auburn University Montgomery	M
Boise State University	M
Boston University	M
Bowling Green State University	M,D
California State University, Fresno	M
California State University, Long Beach	M
California State University, Los Angeles	M
California State University, Sacramento	M
California State University, San Bernardino	M
California State University, Stanislaus	M
Central Connecticut State University	M
Central Michigan University	M
Central Missouri State University	M,O
Chaminade University of Honolulu	M
Chapman University	M
Charleston Southern University	M
Chicago State University	M
Clark Atlanta University	M
Coppin State College	M
Delta State University	M
Drury University	M
East Carolina University	M
East Central University	M
Eastern Kentucky University	M
Eastern Michigan University	M
East Tennessee State University	M
Ferris State University	M
Fitchburg State College	M
Florida Atlantic University	M
Florida Gulf Coast University	M
Florida International University	M
Florida Metropolitan University–Brandon Campus	M
Florida Metropolitan University–Pinellas Campus	M
Florida State University	M,D
Fordham University	M,D
The George Washington University	M
Georgia State University	M
Grambling State University	M
Grand Valley State University	M
Illinois State University	M
Indiana State University	M
Indiana University Bloomington	M,D
Indiana University Northwest	M,O
Indiana University of Pennsylvania	M,D
Inter American University of Puerto Rico, Metropolitan Campus	M
Iona College	M
Jackson State University	M
Jacksonville State University	M
Kent State University	M
Lamar University	M
Lewis University	M
Lincoln University (MO)	M
Long Island University, C.W. Post Campus	M
Longwood College	M
Loyola University Chicago	M
Loyola University New Orleans	M
Lynn University	M
Madonna University	M
Marshall University	M
Marywood University	M
Metropolitan State University	M
Michigan State University	M,D
Middle Tennessee State University	M
Minot State University	M
Mississippi College	M
Monmouth University	M,O
Morehead State University	M
National University	M
New Jersey City University	M
New Mexico State University	M
Niagara University	M
North Carolina Central University	M
Northeastern State University	M
Northeastern University	M
Northern Arizona University	M
Oklahoma City University	M
Oklahoma State University	M,D
The Pennsylvania State University University Park Campus	M,D
Pontifical Catholic University of Puerto Rico	M
Portland State University	M,D
Radford University	M
Rutgers, The State University of New Jersey, Newark	M,D
St. Ambrose University	M
St. Cloud State University	M
Saint Joseph's University	M
Saint Mary's University of Minnesota	M
St. Mary's University of San Antonio	M
St. Thomas University	M,O
Salve Regina University	M
Sam Houston State University	M,D
San Diego State University	M
San Jose State University	M
Seton Hall University	M
Shippensburg University of Pennsylvania	M
Southeast Missouri State University	M
Southern Illinois University Carbondale	M
Southwest Texas State University	M
State University of New York at Albany	M,D
State University of New York College at Buffalo	M
Suffolk University	M
Sul Ross State University	M
Tarleton State University	M
Temple University	M,D
Tennessee State University	M
Texas A&M International University	M
Troy State University	M
Universidad del Turabo	M
The University of Alabama	M
The University of Alabama at Birmingham	M
University of Arkansas at Little Rock	M
University of Baltimore	M
University of California, Irvine	M,D
University of Central Florida	M,O
University of Central Oklahoma	M
University of Cincinnati	M,D
University of Colorado at Colorado Springs	M
University of Colorado at Denver	M
University of Delaware	M,D
University of Detroit Mercy	M
University of Great Falls	M
University of Illinois at Chicago	M
University of Louisiana at Monroe	M
University of Louisville	M
University of Maryland, College Park	M,D
University of Massachusetts Lowell	M
The University of Memphis	M
University of Missouri–Kansas City	M
University of Missouri–St. Louis	M,D
The University of Montana–Missoula	M
University of Nebraska at Omaha	M,D
University of Nevada, Las Vegas	M
University of New Haven	M
University of North Alabama	M
The University of North Carolina at Charlotte	M
University of North Florida	M
University of Pittsburgh	M,D
University of South Carolina	M
University of Southern Mississippi	M,D
University of South Florida	M,D
The University of Tennessee	M,D

The University of Tennessee at Chattanooga	M
The University of Texas at Arlington	M
The University of Texas at San Antonio	M
The University of Texas of the Permian Basin	M
The University of Texas–Pan American	M
University of Wisconsin–Milwaukee	M
University of Wisconsin–Platteville	M
Valdosta State University	M
Villanova University	M
Virginia Commonwealth University	M,O
Washington State University	M
Wayne State University	M
Webster University	M
West Chester University of Pennsylvania	M
Western Connecticut State University	M
Western Illinois University	M,O
Western New England College	M
Western Oregon University	M
Westfield State College	M
West Texas A&M University	M
Wichita State University	M
Widener University	M
Wilmington College	M
Wright State University	M
Xavier University	M
Youngstown State University	M

■ CULTURAL STUDIES

Claremont Graduate University	M,D
Cornell University	M,D
George Mason University	D
Simmons College	M
Stony Brook University, State University of New York	M,O
University of California, Davis	M,D
University of Chicago	M,D
University of Minnesota, Twin Cities Campus	M,D
The University of Texas at San Antonio	M,D
University of the Sacred Heart	M

■ CURRICULUM AND INSTRUCTION

Andrews University	M,D,O
Angelo State University	M
Appalachian State University	M
Argosy University-Sarasota	D,O
Arizona State University	M,D
Arkansas State University	M,D,O
Arkansas Tech University	M
Ashland University	M
Auburn University	M,D,O
Aurora University	M,D
Austin Peay State University	M,O
Averett University	M
Azusa Pacific University	M
Ball State University	M,O
Baylor University	M,D,O
Bemidji State University	M
Benedictine University	M
Bloomsburg University of Pennsylvania	M
Boise State University	M,D
Boston College	M,D,O
Boston University	M,D,O
Bowling Green State University	M
Bradley University	M
California Baptist University	M
California Polytechnic State University, San Luis Obispo	M
California State University, Bakersfield	M
California State University, Chico	M
California State University, Dominguez Hills	M
California State University, Fresno	M
California State University, Sacramento	M
California State University, Stanislaus	M
Carson-Newman College	M
Castleton State College	M
The Catholic University of America	M,D
Centenary College of Louisiana	M
Central Missouri State University	M,O
Central Washington University	M
Chapman University	M
City University	M,O
Claremont Graduate University	M,D
Clark Atlanta University	M,O
Clemson University	D
Cleveland State University	M
College Misericordia	M
The College of St. Scholastica	M
College of the Southwest	M
The College of William and Mary	M
Colorado Christian University	M
Concordia University (CA)	M
Concordia University (IL)	M,O
Concordia University (OR)	M
Concordia University Wisconsin	M
Converse College	O
Coppin State College	M
Cornell University	M,D
Delaware State University	M
DePaul University	M,D
Doane College	M
Dominican University	M
Dominican University of California	M
Drexel University	M
Duquesne University	D
Eastern Michigan University	M
Eastern Washington University	M
Emporia State University	M
Fairleigh Dickinson University, Teaneck–Hackensack Campus	M
Ferris State University	M
Florida Atlantic University	M,D,O
Florida Gulf Coast University	M
Florida International University	D,O
Fordham University	M,D,O
Framingham State College	M
Franciscan University of Steubenville	M
Freed-Hardeman University	M
Fresno Pacific University	M
Frostburg State University	M
Gannon University	M
The George Washington University	M,D,O
Georgia Southern University	D
Gonzaga University	M
Grambling State University	M,D
Harvard University	M,D,O
Hood College	M
Houston Baptist University	M
Idaho State University	M,O
Illinois State University	M,D
Indiana State University	M,D,O
Indiana University Bloomington	M,D,O
Indiana University of Pennsylvania	M,D
Indiana Wesleyan University	M
Inter American University of Puerto Rico, San Germán Campus	M
Iowa State University of Science and Technology	M,D
Johns Hopkins University	M
Johnson State College	M
Kansas State University	D
Kean University	M,O
Keene State College	M
Kent State University	M,D,O
Kutztown University of Pennsylvania	M,O
Lander University	M
La Sierra University	M,D,O
Lehigh University	M,D,O
Lesley University	M,D,O
Lincoln Memorial University	M,O
Lock Haven University of Pennsylvania	M
Loras College	M
Louisiana State University and Agricultural and Mechanical College	M,D,O
Louisiana Tech University	M,D,O
Loyola College in Maryland	M,O
Loyola University Chicago	M,D
Lynchburg College	M
Malone College	M
Miami University	M
Michigan State University	M,D,O
MidAmerica Nazarene University	M
Middle Tennessee State University	M,O
Midwestern State University	M
Minnesota State University, Mankato	M,O
Minnesota State University Moorhead	M
Montana State University–Billings	M
Montclair State University	M,D
Morehead State University	O
National-Louis University	M,D,O
New Mexico Highlands University	M
New Mexico State University	M,D,O
Nicholls State University	M
North Carolina State University	M,D
Northeastern University	M
Northern Arizona University	D
Northern Illinois University	M,D
Northwest Nazarene University	M
Notre Dame de Namur University	M,O
Oakland University	M,D,O
Ohio University	M,D
Oklahoma City University	M
Oklahoma State University	M,D
Olivet Nazarene University	M
Oral Roberts University	M,D
Our Lady of the Lake University of San Antonio	M,D
Pace University, New York City Campus	M,O
Pace University, White Plains Campus	M,O
Pacific Lutheran University	M
The Pennsylvania State University Great Valley Campus	M
The Pennsylvania State University Harrisburg Campus of the Capital College	M
The Pennsylvania State University University Park Campus	M,D
Plattsburgh State University of New York	M
Point Park College	M
Pontifical Catholic University of Puerto Rico	M,D
Portland State University	M,D
Prairie View A&M University	M
Purdue University	M,D,O
Purdue University Calumet	M
Radford University	M
Rhode Island College	O
Rider University	M
Rowan University	M
St. Bonaventure University	M
Saint Louis University	M,D
Saint Martin's College	M
Saint Mary College	M
Saint Michael's College	M,O
Saint Peter's College	M,O
Saint Xavier University	M,O
Sam Houston State University	M,D,O
San Diego State University	M
Seattle University	M,O
Siena Heights University	M
Simpson College and Graduate School	M
Sonoma State University	M

South Dakota State University	M
Southeastern Louisiana University	M
Southern Illinois University Carbondale	M,D
Stanford University	M,D
State University of New York at Albany	M,D,O
Syracuse University	M,D,O
Tarleton State University	M
Teachers College, Columbia University	M,D
Tennessee State University	D
Tennessee Technological University	M,O
Texas A&M University	M,D
Texas A&M University–Corpus Christi	M
Texas Southern University	M,D
Texas Tech University	M,D,O
Trevecca Nazarene University	M
Trinity College (DC)	M
Troy State University Dothan	M,O
Universidad Metropolitana	M
The University of Alabama	D
University of Alaska Fairbanks	M,O
University of Arkansas	D
University of California, Davis	D
University of Central Florida	M,D,O
University of Cincinnati	M,D
University of Colorado at Boulder	M,D
University of Colorado at Colorado Springs	M
University of Colorado at Denver	M
University of Connecticut	M,D
University of Delaware	M,D
University of Denver	M,D,O
University of Detroit Mercy	M
University of Great Falls	M
University of Hawaii at Manoa	D
University of Houston	M,D
University of Houston–Clear Lake	M
University of Illinois at Chicago	M,D
University of Illinois at Urbana–Champaign	M,D,O
The University of Iowa	M,D
University of Kansas	M,D
University of Kentucky	M,D
University of Louisiana at Lafayette	M
University of Louisiana at Monroe	D,O
University of Massachusetts Amherst	M,D,O
University of Massachusetts Boston	M
University of Massachusetts Lowell	M,D,O
The University of Memphis	M,D
University of Michigan	M,D
University of Minnesota, Twin Cities Campus	M,D
University of Mississippi	M,D,O
University of Missouri–Columbia	M,D,O
University of Missouri–Kansas City	M,D,O
University of Missouri–St. Louis	M,D
The University of Montana–Missoula	M,D
University of Nebraska at Kearney	M
University of Nebraska–Lincoln	M,D,O
University of Nevada, Las Vegas	M,D,O
University of Nevada, Reno	M,D,O
University of New Orleans	M,D,O
The University of North Carolina at Chapel Hill	M,D
The University of North Carolina at Charlotte	M,D,O
The University of North Carolina at Greensboro	D
University of Northern Iowa	M,D
University of North Texas	D
University of Oklahoma	M,D
University of Puerto Rico, Río Piedras	M,D
University of Redlands	M
University of St. Thomas (MN)	M,D,O
University of San Diego	M,D
University of San Francisco	M,D
University of South Carolina	M,D,O
University of South Dakota	M,D,O
University of Southern California	M,D
University of Southern Mississippi	M,D,O
The University of Tennessee	M,D,O
The University of Tennessee at Chattanooga	M,O
The University of Tennessee at Martin	M
The University of Texas at Arlington	M
The University of Texas at Austin	M,D
The University of Texas at Brownsville	M
The University of Texas at Tyler	M
University of the Pacific	M
University of Toledo	M,D,O
University of Vermont	M
University of Virginia	M,D,O
University of Washington	M,D
University of West Florida	M,D,O
University of Wisconsin–Madison	M,D
University of Wisconsin–Milwaukee	M
University of Wisconsin–Oshkosh	M
University of Wisconsin–Superior	M
University of Wisconsin–Whitewater	M
University of Wyoming	M,D
Utah State University	D
Valparaiso University	M
Vanderbilt University	M,D
Virginia Commonwealth University	M,O
Virginia Polytechnic Institute and State University	M,D,O
Walla Walla College	M
Washburn University of Topeka	M
Washington State University	M,D
Wayne State College	M
Wayne State University	M,D,O
Weber State University	M
Western Connecticut State University	M
Western Illinois University	M,O
West Texas A&M University	M
West Virginia University	M,D
Wichita State University	M
William Woods University	M
Wright State University	O
Xavier University of Louisiana	M

■ DANCE

American University	M
Arizona State University	M
Brigham Young University	M
California State University, Fullerton	M
California State University, Long Beach	M
California State University, Sacramento	M
Case Western Reserve University	M,D
Florida State University	M
George Mason University	M
Indiana University Bloomington	M
New York University	M,D
Northern Illinois University	M
The Ohio State University	M
Purchase College, State University of New York	M
Sam Houston State University	M
San Diego State University	M
Shenandoah University	M,D,O
Southern Methodist University	M
State University of New York College at Brockport	M
Teachers College, Columbia University	M
Temple University	M,D
Texas Christian University	M
Texas Tech University	D
Texas Woman's University	M,D
Tufts University	M,D
University of California, Irvine	M
University of California, Los Angeles	M,D
University of California, Riverside	D
University of Colorado at Boulder	M,D
University of Hawaii at Manoa	M,D
University of Illinois at Urbana–Champaign	M
The University of Iowa	M
University of Maryland, College Park	M
University of Michigan	M
University of Minnesota, Twin Cities Campus	M,D
University of Nebraska–Lincoln	M
University of Nevada, Las Vegas	M
University of New Mexico	M
The University of North Carolina at Greensboro	M
University of Oklahoma	M
University of Oregon	M
University of Utah	M
University of Washington	M
University of Wisconsin–Milwaukee	M

■ DECORATIVE ARTS

New School University	M

■ DEMOGRAPHY AND POPULATION STUDIES

Arizona State University	M,D
Bowling Green State University	M,D
Brown University	D
Cornell University	M,D
Duke University	D
Florida State University	M,O
Fordham University	M,D
Georgetown University	M
Harvard University	M,D
Johns Hopkins University	M
The Pennsylvania State University University Park Campus	M,D
Princeton University	D
State University of New York at Albany	M,D,O
Tulane University	M
University of California, Berkeley	M,D
University of California, Irvine	M
University of Illinois at Urbana–Champaign	M,D
University of Pennsylvania	M,D
University of Southern California	M

■ DENTAL HYGIENE

Boston University	M,D,O
Old Dominion University	M
University of Maryland	M
University of Missouri–Kansas City	M

■ DENTISTRY

Boston University	P
Case Western Reserve University	P
Columbia University	P
Creighton University	P
Harvard University	P
Howard University	P,O
Indiana University–Purdue University Indianapolis	P
Loma Linda University	P
Marquette University	P
New York University	P
Nova Southeastern University	P
The Ohio State University	P
Southern Illinois University Edwardsville	P
Stony Brook University, State University of New York	P,O
Temple University	P
Tufts University	P

University at Buffalo, The State University of New York	P
The University of Alabama at Birmingham	P
University of California, Los Angeles	P,O
University of California, San Francisco	P
University of Detroit Mercy	P,M,O
University of Florida	P,O
University of Illinois at Chicago	P
The University of Iowa	P
University of Kentucky	P,M
University of Louisville	P
University of Maryland	P,D
University of Michigan	P
University of Minnesota, Twin Cities Campus	P
University of Missouri–Kansas City	P
The University of North Carolina at Chapel Hill	P
University of Pennsylvania	P
University of Pittsburgh	P,M,O
University of Southern California	P,O
University of the Pacific	P
University of Washington	P
Virginia Commonwealth University	P
West Virginia University	P

■ DEVELOPMENTAL BIOLOGY

Arizona State University	M,D
Brandeis University	M,D
Brown University	M,D
California Institute of Technology	D
Carnegie Mellon University	M,D
Case Western Reserve University	M,D
Columbia University	M,D
Cornell University	M,D
Emory University	D
Florida State University	M,D
Indiana University Bloomington	D
Iowa State University of Science and Technology	M,D
Johns Hopkins University	D
Kansas State University	M,D
Marquette University	M,D
Massachusetts Institute of Technology	D
Northwestern University	D
The Ohio State University	M,D
The Pennsylvania State University University Park Campus	M,D
Princeton University	D
Purdue University	D
Rensselaer Polytechnic Institute	M,D
Rutgers, The State University of New Jersey, New Brunswick	M,D
Stanford University	D
State University of New York at Albany	M,D
Stony Brook University, State University of New York	D
Tufts University	D
University of California, Davis	D
University of California, Irvine	M,D
University of California, Los Angeles	M,D
University of California, Riverside	M,D
University of California, San Diego	D
University of California, San Francisco	D
University of California, Santa Barbara	M,D
University of Chicago	D
University of Cincinnati	M,D
University of Colorado at Boulder	M,D
University of Connecticut	M,D
University of Illinois at Chicago	M,D
University of Kansas	M,D
University of Massachusetts Amherst	D
University of Miami	D
University of Michigan	M,D
University of Minnesota, Twin Cities Campus	M,D
University of Missouri–St. Louis	M,D,O
The University of North Carolina at Chapel Hill	M,D
University of Pennsylvania	D
University of Pittsburgh	D
University of Rochester	M,D
University of South Carolina	M,D
The University of Texas at Austin	D
University of Wisconsin–Madison	D
Virginia Polytechnic Institute and State University	M,D
Washington University in St. Louis	D
West Virginia University	M,D
Yale University	D
Yeshiva University	D

■ DEVELOPMENTAL EDUCATION

Ferris State University	M
Grambling State University	M,D
National-Louis University	M,O
Rutgers, The State University of New Jersey, New Brunswick	M
Southwest Texas State University	M
University of California, Berkeley	M

■ DEVELOPMENTAL PSYCHOLOGY

Andrews University	M
Arizona State University	D
Boston College	M,D
Bowling Green State University	M,D
Brandeis University	M,D
California State University, San Bernardino	M
Carnegie Mellon University	D
Claremont Graduate University	M,D
Clark University	D
Cornell University	D
Duke University	D
Duquesne University	M,D
Eastern Washington University	M
Emory University	D
Florida International University	M,D
Fordham University	D
Gallaudet University	M,O
George Mason University	M,D
Harvard University	M,D
Howard University	M,D
Illinois State University	M,D,O
Indiana University Bloomington	D
Louisiana State University and Agricultural and Mechanical College	M,D
Loyola University Chicago	D
Michigan State University	M,D
New York University	M,D,O
The Ohio State University	D
The Pennsylvania State University University Park Campus	M,D
Rutgers, The State University of New Jersey, New Brunswick	D
Stanford University	D
Suffolk University	D
Teachers College, Columbia University	M,D
Temple University	D
Tufts University	M,D,O
The University of Alabama at Birmingham	M,D
University of California, Santa Cruz	D
University of Connecticut	M,D
University of Illinois at Urbana–Champaign	M,D
University of Kansas	M,D
University of Maine	M,D
University of Maryland, Baltimore County	D
University of Maryland, College Park	M,D
University of Miami	M,D
University of Michigan	D
The University of Montana–Missoula	D
University of Nebraska at Omaha	M,D,O
University of New Orleans	M,D
The University of North Carolina at Chapel Hill	D
The University of North Carolina at Greensboro	M,D
University of Notre Dame	D
University of Oregon	M,D
University of Pittsburgh	D
University of Rochester	M,D
University of Wisconsin–Madison	D
Virginia Polytechnic Institute and State University	M,D
Wayne State University	M,D
West Virginia University	M,D
Yeshiva University	D

■ DISABILITY STUDIES

Brandeis University	M
Johns Hopkins University	M,D,O
Suffolk University	M,O
University of Illinois at Chicago	M,D

■ DISTANCE EDUCATION DEVELOPMENT

Florida State University	M,D,O
New York Institute of Technology	M,O
Nova Southeastern University	M,D
University of Maryland University College	M
Western Illinois University	M,O

■ EARLY CHILDHOOD EDUCATION

Alabama Agricultural and Mechanical University	M,O
Alabama State University	M,O
Albany State University	M
Anna Maria College	M
Antioch New England Graduate School	M
Appalachian State University	M
Arcadia University	M,O
Arkansas State University	M,O
Ashland University	M
Auburn University	M,D,O
Auburn University Montgomery	M,O
Augusta State University	M,O
Averett University	M
Ball State University	M,D
Barry University	M
Bayamón Central University	M
Bellarmine University	M
Belmont University	M
Bloomsburg University of Pennsylvania	M
Boise State University	M
Boston College	M
Boston University	M,D,O
Brenau University	M,O
Bridgewater State College	M
Brooklyn College of the City University of New York	M
California State University, Fresno	M
California State University, Sacramento	M
Carlow College	M
Central Connecticut State University	M
Central Michigan University	M
Chestnut Hill College	M
Cheyney University of Pennsylvania	O
Chicago State University	M
City College of the City University of New York	M

Cleveland State University	M
College of Mount St. Joseph	M
The College of New Rochelle	M
College of Our Lady of the Elms	M,O
The College of Saint Rose	M
Columbus State University	M,O
Concordia University (IL)	M,D,O
Concordia University (NE)	M
Concordia University Wisconsin	M
Cumberland College	M
Dallas Baptist University	M
Dominican University	M
Drake University	M
Duquesne University	M
Eastern Connecticut State University	M
Eastern Michigan University	M
Eastern Nazarene College	M,O
Eastern Washington University	M
East Tennessee State University	M
Edinboro University of Pennsylvania	M
Emporia State University	M
Fairfield University	M,O
Fitchburg State College	M
Florida Agricultural and Mechanical University	M
Florida Atlantic University	M
Florida International University	M
Florida State University	M,D,O
Fordham University	M,D,O
Fort Valley State University	M
Francis Marion University	M
Gallaudet University	M,D,O
Gannon University	M,O
George Mason University	M
The George Washington University	M
Georgia College and State University	M,O
Georgia Southern University	M,O
Georgia Southwestern State University	M,O
Georgia State University	M,D,O
Golden Gate Baptist Theological Seminary	P,M,D,O
Governors State University	M
Grambling State University	M
Grand Valley State University	M
Henderson State University	M
Heritage College	M
Hofstra University	M
Hood College	M
Howard University	M,O
Hunter College of the City University of New York	M,O
Idaho State University	M,O
Indiana State University	M,D,O
Indiana University of Pennsylvania	M
Indiana University–Purdue University Indianapolis	M
Jackson State University	M,D,O
Jacksonville State University	M,O
Jacksonville University	M,O
James Madison University	M
Johns Hopkins University	M
Kean University	M
Kennesaw State University	M
Kent State University	M
Kutztown University of Pennsylvania	M,O
Lehman College of the City University of New York	M
Lesley University	M,D,O
Long Island University, C.W. Post Campus	M
Loyola College in Maryland	M
Lynchburg College	M
Marshall University	M
Marygrove College	M
Maryville University of Saint Louis	M
Marywood University	M
McNeese State University	M
Mercer University	M,O
Miami University	M
Middle Tennessee State University	M,O
Minnesota State University, Mankato	M
Montana State University–Billings	M
Montclair State University	M
Murray State University	M,O
National-Louis University	M,O
Nazareth College of Rochester	M
New Jersey City University	M
New York University	M,D,O
Norfolk State University	M
North Carolina Agricultural and Technical State University	M
Northeastern State University	M
Northern Arizona University	M
Northern Illinois University	M
North Georgia College & State University	M,O
Northwestern State University of Louisiana	M
Northwest Missouri State University	M
Nova Southeastern University	M,D,O
Oakland University	M,D,O
Oklahoma City University	M
Old Dominion University	M
Oral Roberts University	M,D
Pacific University	M
The Pennsylvania State University University Park Campus	M,D
Piedmont College	M
Pittsburg State University	M
Portland State University	M
Rhode Island College	M
Rivier College	M
Roosevelt University	M,D
Rutgers, The State University of New Jersey, New Brunswick	M,D
Saginaw Valley State University	M
Saint Joseph College	M
Saint Mary's College of California	M
Saint Xavier University	M,O
Salem State College	M
Salisbury State University	M
Samford University	M,D,O
Sam Houston State University	M,O
San Francisco State University	M
Siena Heights University	M
Slippery Rock University of Pennsylvania	M
Sonoma State University	M
South Carolina State University	M
Southern Oregon University	M
Southwestern Oklahoma State University	M
Spring Hill College	M
State University of New York at Binghamton	M
State University of New York at New Paltz	M
State University of New York College at Cortland	M
State University of West Georgia	M,O
Stephen F. Austin State University	M
Syracuse University	M
Teachers College, Columbia University	M,D
Temple University	M,D
Tennessee Technological University	M,O
Texas A&M International University	M
Texas A&M University–Commerce	M,D
Texas A&M University–Kingsville	M
Texas Southern University	M,D
Texas Tech University	M,D,O
Texas Woman's University	M,D
Towson University	M
Trinity College (DC)	M
Troy State University	M,O
Tufts University	M,D,O
Universidad Metropolitana	M
University at Buffalo, The State University of New York	M,D,O
The University of Alabama	M,D,O
The University of Alabama at Birmingham	M,D
University of Alaska Southeast	M
University of Arkansas	M
University of Arkansas at Little Rock	M,O
University of Bridgeport	M,O
University of Central Arkansas	M
University of Central Florida	M,O
University of Central Oklahoma	M
University of Cincinnati	M
University of Colorado at Denver	M
University of Dayton	M
University of Detroit Mercy	M
The University of Findlay	M
University of Florida	M,D,O
University of Georgia	M,D,O
University of Hartford	M
University of Houston	M,D
University of Houston–Clear Lake	M
The University of Iowa	M,D
University of Kansas	M,D
University of Louisville	M
University of Maryland, Baltimore County	M,D
University of Maryland, College Park	M,D,O
University of Massachusetts Amherst	M,D,O
The University of Memphis	M,D
University of Miami	M,O
University of Michigan	M,D
University of Michigan–Flint	M
University of Minnesota, Twin Cities Campus	M
University of Montevallo	M
University of Nebraska at Kearney	M
University of New Hampshire	M
University of North Alabama	M
The University of North Carolina at Chapel Hill	D
The University of North Carolina at Greensboro	M
University of North Dakota	M
University of Northern Colorado	M
University of Northern Iowa	M
University of North Texas	M,D
University of Oklahoma	M,D
University of Pennsylvania	M
University of Pittsburgh	M
University of Portland	M
University of Puerto Rico, Río Piedras	M
The University of Scranton	M
University of South Alabama	M,O
University of South Carolina	M,D,O
University of Southern Mississippi	M,D,O
University of South Florida	M,D,O
The University of Tennessee	M,D,O
The University of Tennessee at Chattanooga	M,O
The University of Texas at Brownsville	M
The University of Texas at Tyler	M
The University of Texas of the Permian Basin	M
The University of Texas–Pan American	M
University of the District of Columbia	M
University of the Incarnate Word	M
University of Toledo	M,D,O
The University of West Alabama	M
University of West Florida	M
University of Wisconsin–Milwaukee	M
University of Wisconsin–Oshkosh	M
University of Wyoming	M,D
Valdosta State University	M,O
Vanderbilt University	M,D

Virginia Commonwealth University	M,O
Washington University in St. Louis	M
Webster University	M
Western Illinois University	M,O
Western Kentucky University	M
Western Michigan University	M
Western Oregon University	M
Westfield State College	M
Wheelock College	M
Widener University	M,D
Worcester State College	M
Wright State University	M
Xavier University	M
Youngstown State University	M

■ EAST EUROPEAN AND RUSSIAN STUDIES

Boston College	M
Columbia University	M,O
Florida State University	M
Georgetown University	M
The George Washington University	M
Harvard University	M
Hunter College of the City University of New York	M
Indiana University Bloomington	M,O
Johns Hopkins University	M,D,O
La Salle University	M
The Ohio State University	M,D,O
Stanford University	M
University of Connecticut	M
University of Illinois at Chicago	M,D
University of Illinois at Urbana–Champaign	M
University of Kansas	M
University of Michigan	M,O
University of Minnesota, Twin Cities Campus	M
The University of North Carolina at Chapel Hill	M
The University of Texas at Austin	M
University of Washington	M
Yale University	M

■ ECOLOGY

Arizona State University	M,D
Brown University	D
Colorado State University	M,D
Columbia University	D,O
Cornell University	D
Duke University	M,D,O
Eastern Kentucky University	M
Emory University	D
Florida Institute of Technology	M
Florida State University	M,D
Fordham University	M,D
Frostburg State University	M
George Mason University	M
Goddard College	M
Illinois State University	M,D
Indiana State University	M,D
Indiana University Bloomington	M,D
Iowa State University of Science and Technology	M,D
Kansas State University	M,D
Kent State University	M,D
Lesley University	M,O
Marquette University	M,D
Michigan State University	M,D
Minnesota State University, Mankato	M
Montana State University–Bozeman	M,D
North Carolina State University	M,D
The Ohio State University	M,D
Oklahoma State University	M,D
Old Dominion University	D
The Pennsylvania State University University Park Campus	M,D
Princeton University	D
Purdue University	M,D
Rice University	M,D
Rutgers, The State University of New Jersey, New Brunswick	M,D
San Diego State University	D
San Francisco State University	M
State University of New York at Albany	M,D
Stony Brook University, State University of New York	D
The University of Arizona	M,D
University of California, Davis	M,D
University of California, Irvine	M,D
University of California, San Diego	D
University of California, Santa Barbara	M,D
University of Chicago	D
University of Colorado at Boulder	M,D
University of Connecticut	M,D
University of Delaware	M,D
University of Florida	M,D
University of Georgia	M,D
University of Hawaii at Manoa	M,D
University of Illinois at Chicago	M,D
University of Illinois at Urbana–Champaign	D
University of Maine	M,D
University of Miami	M,D
University of Michigan	M,D
University of Minnesota, Twin Cities Campus	M,D
University of Missouri–St. Louis	M,D,O
The University of Montana–Missoula	M,D
University of Nevada, Reno	D
The University of North Carolina at Chapel Hill	M,D
University of North Dakota	M,D
University of Notre Dame	M,D
University of Oregon	M,D
University of Pennsylvania	D
University of Pittsburgh	M,D
University of Rochester	M,D
University of South Carolina	M,D
University of South Florida	M,D
The University of Tennessee	M,D
The University of Texas at Austin	M,D
University of Utah	M,D
University of Wisconsin–Madison	M,D
Utah State University	M,D
Virginia Polytechnic Institute and State University	M,D
Washington University in St. Louis	D
William Paterson University of New Jersey	M
Yale University	D

■ ECONOMICS

Alabama Agricultural and Mechanical University	M
Albany State University	M
American University	M,D
Arizona State University	M,D
Auburn University	M,D
Baylor University	M
Bentley College	M,O
Bernard M. Baruch College of the City University of New York	M
Boston College	M,D
Boston University	M,D
Bowling Green State University	M
Brandeis University	M,D
Brooklyn College of the City University of New York	M
Brown University	M,D
California Institute of Technology	D
California State Polytechnic University, Pomona	M
California State University, Fullerton	M
California State University, Hayward	M
California State University, Long Beach	M
California State University, Los Angeles	M
Carnegie Mellon University	M,D
Case Western Reserve University	M
The Catholic University of America	M
Central Michigan University	M
Central Missouri State University	M
City College of the City University of New York	M
Claremont Graduate University	M,D
Clark Atlanta University	M
Clark University	D
Clemson University	M,D
Cleveland State University	M
Colorado State University	M,D
Columbia University	M,D
Converse College	M
Cornell University	D
DePaul University	M
Drexel University	M,D,O
Duke University	M,D
East Carolina University	M
Eastern College	M
Eastern Illinois University	M
Eastern Michigan University	M
East Tennessee State University	M
Emory University	D
Florida Atlantic University	M
Florida International University	M,D
Florida State University	M,D
Fordham University	M,D,O
Fort Hays State University	M
George Mason University	M,D
Georgetown University	D
The George Washington University	M,D
Georgia Institute of Technology	M
Georgia State University	M,D
Harvard University	M,D
Howard University	M,D
Hunter College of the City University of New York	M
Illinois State University	M
Indiana State University	M
Indiana University Bloomington	M,D
Indiana University–Purdue University Indianapolis	M
Iowa State University of Science and Technology	M,D
Johns Hopkins University	M,D,O
Kansas State University	M,D
Kent State University	M
Lehigh University	M,D
Long Island University, Brooklyn Campus	M
Louisiana State University and Agricultural and Mechanical College	M,D
Louisiana Tech University	M,D
Loyola College in Maryland	M
Marquette University	M
Massachusetts Institute of Technology	M,D
Miami University	M
Michigan State University	M,D
Middle Tennessee State University	M,D
Mississippi State University	M,D
Montana State University–Bozeman	M
Montclair State University	M
Morgan State University	M
Murray State University	M
New Mexico State University	M
New School University	M,D

New York University	M,D,O
North Carolina State University	M,D
Northeastern University	M
Northern Illinois University	M,D
Northwestern University	M,D
The Ohio State University	M,D
Ohio University	M
Oklahoma State University	M,D
Old Dominion University	M
Oregon State University	M,D
Pace University, New York City Campus	M
Pace University, White Plains Campus	M
The Pennsylvania State University University Park Campus	M,D
Portland State University	M,D
Princeton University	D
Purdue University	M,D
Quinnipiac University	M
Rensselaer Polytechnic Institute	M
Rice University	M,D
Roosevelt University	M
Rutgers, The State University of New Jersey, Newark	M
Rutgers, The State University of New Jersey, New Brunswick	M,D
St. Cloud State University	M
St. John's University (NY)	M,O
Saint Louis University	M,D
Saint Martin's College	M
St. Mary's University of San Antonio	M
San Diego State University	M
San Francisco State University	M
San Jose State University	M
Seattle Pacific University	M
South Dakota State University	M
Southern Illinois University Carbondale	M,D
Southern Illinois University Edwardsville	M
Southern Methodist University	M,D
Southwest Missouri State University	M
Stanford University	D
State University of New York at Albany	M,D,O
State University of New York at Binghamton	M,D
State University of New York College at Buffalo	M
Stony Brook University, State University of New York	M,D
Suffolk University	M
Syracuse University	M,D
Teachers College, Columbia University	M,D
Temple University	M,D
Texas A&M University	M,D
Texas A&M University–Commerce	M
Texas Christian University	M
Texas Tech University	M,D
Tufts University	M
Tulane University	M,D
University at Buffalo, The State University of New York	M,D,O
The University of Akron	M
The University of Alabama	M,D
University of Alaska Fairbanks	M
The University of Arizona	M,D
University of Arkansas	M,D
University of California, Berkeley	D
University of California, Davis	M,D
University of California, Irvine	M,D
University of California, Los Angeles	M,D
University of California, Riverside	M,D
University of California, San Diego	M,D
University of California, Santa Barbara	M,D
University of California, Santa Cruz	M,D
University of Central Florida	M
University of Chicago	D
University of Cincinnati	M,D
University of Colorado at Boulder	M,D
University of Colorado at Denver	M
University of Connecticut	M,D
University of Delaware	M,D
University of Denver	M
University of Detroit Mercy	M
University of Florida	M,D
University of Georgia	M,D
University of Hawaii at Manoa	M,D
University of Houston	M,D
University of Idaho	M
University of Illinois at Chicago	M,D
University of Illinois at Springfield	M
University of Illinois at Urbana–Champaign	M,D
The University of Iowa	D
University of Kansas	M,D
University of Kentucky	M,D
University of Maine	M
University of Maryland, Baltimore County	M
University of Maryland, College Park	M,D
University of Massachusetts Amherst	M,D
University of Massachusetts Lowell	M
The University of Memphis	M,D
University of Miami	M,D
University of Michigan	M,D
University of Minnesota, Twin Cities Campus	M,D
University of Mississippi	M,D
University of Missouri–Columbia	M,D
University of Missouri–Kansas City	M,D
University of Missouri–St. Louis	M,O
The University of Montana–Missoula	M
University of Nebraska at Omaha	M
University of Nebraska–Lincoln	M,D
University of Nevada, Las Vegas	M
University of Nevada, Reno	M
University of New Hampshire	M,D
University of New Mexico	M,D
University of New Orleans	D
The University of North Carolina at Chapel Hill	M,D
The University of North Carolina at Charlotte	M
The University of North Carolina at Greensboro	M
University of North Texas	M
University of Notre Dame	M,D
University of Oklahoma	M,D
University of Oregon	M,D
University of Pennsylvania	M,D
University of Pittsburgh	M,D
University of Puerto Rico, Río Piedras	M
University of Rhode Island	M,D
University of Rochester	M,D
University of San Francisco	M
University of South Carolina	M,D
University of Southern California	M,D
University of Southern Mississippi	M,D
University of South Florida	M
The University of Tennessee	M,D
The University of Tennessee at Chattanooga	M
The University of Texas at Arlington	M
The University of Texas at Austin	M,D
The University of Texas at Dallas	M,D
The University of Texas at El Paso	M
University of Toledo	M
University of Utah	M,D
University of Virginia	M,D
University of Washington	M,D
University of Wisconsin–Madison	D
University of Wisconsin–Milwaukee	M,D
University of Wyoming	M,D
Utah State University	M,D
Vanderbilt University	M,D
Virginia Commonwealth University	M
Virginia Polytechnic Institute and State University	M,D
Virginia State University	M
Washington State University	M,D,O
Washington University in St. Louis	M,D
Wayne State University	M,D,O
West Chester University of Pennsylvania	M
Western Illinois University	M
Western Michigan University	M,D
West Texas A&M University	M
West Virginia University	M,D
Wichita State University	M
Wright State University	M
Yale University	M,D
Youngstown State University	M

■ EDUCATION—GENERAL

Abilene Christian University	M
Adams State College	M
Adelphi University	M,D,O
Alabama Agricultural and Mechanical University	M,O
Alabama State University	M,O
Alaska Pacific University	M
Albany State University	M,O
Alcorn State University	M,O
Alfred University	M
Alliant International University	M,D
American International College	M,D,O
American University	M,D,O
Andrews University	M,D,O
Angelo State University	M
Anna Maria College	M
Antioch New England Graduate School	M
Antioch University Los Angeles	M
Antioch University McGregor	M
Antioch University Seattle	M
Appalachian State University	M,D,O
Aquinas College	M
Arcadia University	M,O
Argosy University-Sarasota	D,O
Arizona State University	M,D
Arizona State University West	M
Arkansas State University	M,D,O
Arkansas Tech University	M
Armstrong Atlantic State University	M
Ashland University	M,D
Auburn University	M,D,O
Auburn University Montgomery	M,O
Augusta State University	M,O
Aurora University	M,D
Austin Peay State University	M,O
Averett University	M
Avila College	M
Azusa Pacific University	M,D
Baker University	M
Baldwin-Wallace College	M
Ball State University	M,D,O
Barry University	M,D,O
Bayamón Central University	M
Baylor University	M,D,O
Bellarmine University	M
Belmont University	M
Bemidji State University	M
Benedictine University	M
Bethel College (MN)	M
Biola University	M
Bloomsburg University of Pennsylvania	M
Boise State University	M,D
Boston College	M,D,O
Boston University	M,D,O
Bowie State University	M

Bowling Green State University	M,D,O
Bradley University	M
Brenau University	M,O
Bridgewater State College	M,O
Brigham Young University	M,D
Brooklyn College of the City University of New York	M,O
Brown University	M
Butler University	M,O
Cabrini College	M
California Baptist University	M
California Lutheran University	M,O
California Polytechnic State University, San Luis Obispo	M
California State Polytechnic University, Pomona	M
California State University, Bakersfield	M
California State University, Chico	M
California State University, Dominguez Hills	M,O
California State University, Fresno	M,D
California State University, Fullerton	M
California State University, Hayward	M
California State University, Long Beach	M,O
California State University, Los Angeles	M,D
California State University, Northridge	M,O
California State University, Sacramento	M
California State University, San Bernardino	M
California State University, San Marcos	M
California State University, Stanislaus	M
California University of Pennsylvania	M
Cameron University	M
Campbellsville University	M
Campbell University	M
Canisius College	M,O
Cardinal Stritch University	M,D
Carlow College	M
Carnegie Mellon University	M,D
Carson-Newman College	M
Carthage College	M,O
Castleton State College	M,O
The Catholic University of America	M,D
Centenary College of Louisiana	M
Central Connecticut State University	M,O
Central Michigan University	M,D,O
Central Missouri State University	M,D,O
Central Washington University	M
Chadron State College	M,O
Chaminade University of Honolulu	M
Chapman University	M
Charleston Southern University	M
Chestnut Hill College	M
Cheyney University of Pennsylvania	M,O
Chicago State University	M
The Citadel, The Military College of South Carolina	M,O
City College of the City University of New York	M,O
City University	M,O
Claremont Graduate University	M,D
Clarion University of Pennsylvania	M,O
Clark Atlanta University	M,D,O
Clark University	M
Clemson University	M,D,O
Cleveland State University	M,D,O
College Misericordia	M
College of Mount St. Joseph	M
College of Mount Saint Vincent	M,O
The College of New Jersey	M,O
The College of New Rochelle	M,O
College of Notre Dame of Maryland	M
College of Our Lady of the Elms	M,O
College of St. Catherine	M
College of St. Joseph	M
The College of Saint Rose	M,O
The College of St. Scholastica	M
College of Santa Fe	M
College of Staten Island of the City University of New York	M,O
College of the Southwest	M
The College of William and Mary	M,D,O
Colorado Christian University	M
Columbia College Chicago	M
Columbus State University	M,O
Concordia University (CA)	M
Concordia University (IL)	M,O
Concordia University (OR)	M
Concordia University (NE)	M
Concordia University Wisconsin	M
Converse College	M,O
Coppin State College	M
Cornell University	M,D
Creighton University	M
Cumberland College	M,O
Cumberland University	M
Dallas Baptist University	M
Delaware State University	M
Delta State University	M,D,O
DePaul University	M,D
DeSales University	M
Doane College	M
Dominican University	M
Dominican University of California	M,O
Dowling College	M,D,O
Drake University	M,D,O
Drexel University	M
Drury University	M
Duke University	M
Duquesne University	M,D,O
East Carolina University	M,D,O
East Central University	M
Eastern College	M,O
Eastern Connecticut State University	M
Eastern Illinois University	M,O
Eastern Kentucky University	M,O
Eastern Michigan University	M,D,O
Eastern Nazarene College	M,O
Eastern New Mexico University	M
Eastern Oregon University	M
Eastern Washington University	M
East Stroudsburg University of Pennsylvania	M
East Tennessee State University	M,D,O
Edgewood College	M,O
Edinboro University of Pennsylvania	M,O
Elon University	M
Emmanuel College	M
Emory University	M,D,O
Emporia State University	M,O
Fairfield University	M,O
Fairleigh Dickinson University, Teaneck–Hackensack Campus	M
Fayetteville State University	D
Ferris State University	M
Fitchburg State College	M,O
Florida Agricultural and Mechanical University	M,D
Florida Atlantic University	M,D,O
Florida Gulf Coast University	M
Florida International University	M,D,O
Florida State University	M,D,O
Fontbonne College	M
Fordham University	M,D,O
Fort Hays State University	M,O
Franciscan University of Steubenville	M
Francis Marion University	M
Freed-Hardeman University	M
Fresno Pacific University	M
Friends University	M
Frostburg State University	M
Gallaudet University	M,D,O
Gannon University	M,D,O
Gardner-Webb University	M
Geneva College	M
George Fox University	M,D
George Mason University	M,D
The George Washington University	M,D,O
Georgia College and State University	M,O
Georgian Court College	M
Georgia Southern University	M,D,O
Georgia Southwestern State University	M,O
Georgia State University	M,D,O
Goddard College	M
Gonzaga University	M,D
Governors State University	M
Grambling State University	M,D
Grand Canyon University	M
Grand Valley State University	M
Gratz College	M
Gwynedd-Mercy College	M
Hamline University	M,D
Hampton University	M
Harding University	M
Hardin-Simmons University	M
Harvard University	M,D,O
Heidelberg College	M
Henderson State University	M
Heritage College	M
Hofstra University	M,D,O
Holy Family College	M
Holy Names College	M,O
Hood College	M
Hope International University	M
Houston Baptist University	M
Howard University	M,D,O
Hunter College of the City University of New York	M,O
Idaho State University	M,D,O
Illinois State University	M,D
Indiana State University	M,D,O
Indiana University Bloomington	M,D,O
Indiana University Northwest	M
Indiana University of Pennsylvania	M,D,O
Indiana University–Purdue University Fort Wayne	M
Indiana University–Purdue University Indianapolis	M
Indiana University South Bend	M
Indiana University Southeast	M
Indiana Wesleyan University	M
Inter American University of Puerto Rico, Metropolitan Campus	M,D
Inter American University of Puerto Rico, San Germán Campus	M
Iowa State University of Science and Technology	M,D
Jackson State University	M,D,O
Jacksonville State University	M,O
Jacksonville University	M,O
James Madison University	M
John Carroll University	M
John F. Kennedy University	M
Johns Hopkins University	M,D,O
Johnson & Wales University	M
Johnson State College	M
Kansas State University	M,D
Kean University	M,O
Keene State College	M,O
Kennesaw State University	M
Kent State University	M,D,O
Kutztown University of Pennsylvania	M,O
Lake Erie College	M
Lamar University	M,O
Lander University	M
La Salle University	M
La Sierra University	M,D,O
Lawrence Technological University	M
Lehigh University	M,D,O

Lehman College of the City University of New York	M
Le Moyne College	M
LeMoyne-Owen College	M
Lesley University	M,D,O
Lewis University	M,O
Liberty University	M,D
Lincoln Memorial University	M,O
Lincoln University (MO)	M
Lindenwood University	M
Lipscomb University	M
Lock Haven University of Pennsylvania	M
Long Island University, Brooklyn Campus	M,O
Long Island University, C.W. Post Campus	M,O
Longwood College	M
Louisiana State University and Agricultural and Mechanical College	M,D,O
Louisiana State University in Shreveport	M,O
Louisiana Tech University	M,D,O
Loyola College in Maryland	M,O
Loyola Marymount University	M
Loyola University Chicago	M,D
Loyola University New Orleans	M
Lynchburg College	M
Lynn University	M,D
Madonna University	M
Maharishi University of Management	M
Malone College	M
Manhattan College	M,O
Manhattanville College	M
Mansfield University of Pennsylvania	M
Marian College of Fond du Lac	M
Marquette University	M,D,O
Marshall University	M,O
Mary Baldwin College	M
Marygrove College	M
Marymount University	M,O
Maryville University of Saint Louis	M
Marywood University	M
McNeese State University	M,O
Mercer University	M,O
Mercy College	M,O
Meredith College	M
Miami University	M,D,O
Michigan State University	M,D,O
MidAmerica Nazarene University	M
Middle Tennessee State University	M,D,O
Midwestern State University	M
Millersville University of Pennsylvania	M
Milligan College	M
Minnesota State University, Mankato	M,O
Minnesota State University Moorhead	M,O
Mississippi College	M,O
Mississippi State University	M,D,O
Mississippi University for Women	M
Monmouth University	M,O
Montana State University–Billings	M
Montana State University–Bozeman	M,D,O
Montana State University–Northern	M
Montclair State University	M,D
Morehead State University	M,O
Morgan State University	M,D
Mount Mary College	M
Mount Saint Mary College	M
Mount St. Mary's College	M
Mount Saint Mary's College and Seminary	M
Murray State University	M,D,O
National-Louis University	M,D,O
National University	M
Nazareth College of Rochester	M
New Jersey City University	M,O
Newman University	M
New Mexico Highlands University	M
New Mexico State University	M,D,O
New School University	M
New York Institute of Technology	M,O
New York University	M,D,O
Niagara University	M,O
Nicholls State University	M
Norfolk State University	M
North Carolina Agricultural and Technical State University	M
North Carolina Central University	M
North Carolina State University	M,D,O
North Central College	M
North Dakota State University	M,O
Northeastern Illinois University	M
Northeastern State University	M
Northeastern University	M
Northern Arizona University	M,D
Northern Illinois University	M,D,O
Northern Kentucky University	M
Northern Michigan University	M,O
Northern State University	M
North Georgia College & State University	M,O
North Park University	M
Northwestern Oklahoma State University	M
Northwestern State University of Louisiana	M,O
Northwestern University	M,D
Northwest Missouri State University	M,O
Northwest Nazarene University	M
Norwich University	M,O
Notre Dame de Namur University	M,O
Nova Southeastern University	M,D,O
Oakland City University	M
Oakland University	M,D,O
The Ohio State University	M,D,O
Ohio University	M,D
Oklahoma City University	M
Oklahoma State University	M,D,O
Old Dominion University	M,D,O
Olivet Nazarene University	M
Oral Roberts University	M,D
Oregon State University	M,D
Our Lady of the Lake University of San Antonio	M,D
Pace University, New York City Campus	M,O
Pace University, White Plains Campus	M,O
Pacific Lutheran University	M
Pacific University	M
Palm Beach Atlantic College	M
Park University	M
The Pennsylvania State University Great Valley Campus	M
The Pennsylvania State University Harrisburg Campus of the Capital College	M,D
The Pennsylvania State University University Park Campus	M,D
Peru State College	M
Piedmont College	M
Pittsburg State University	M,O
Plattsburgh State University of New York	M,O
Plymouth State College	M
Point Loma Nazarene University	M,O
Point Park College	M
Pontifical Catholic University of Puerto Rico	M,D
Portland State University	M,D
Prairie View A&M University	M
Prescott College	M
Providence College	M
Purdue University	M,D,O
Purdue University Calumet	M
Queens College	M
Queens College of the City University of New York	M,O
Quincy University	M
Quinnipiac University	M
Radford University	M
Regent University	M,D,O
Regis College (MA)	M
Regis University	M,O
Rhode Island College	D
Rice University	M
Rider University	M,O
Rivier College	M
Robert Morris College	M
Roberts Wesleyan College	M,O
Rockford College	M
Rockhurst University	M
Rollins College	M
Roosevelt University	M,D
Rowan University	M,D,O
Rutgers, The State University of New Jersey, New Brunswick	M,D,O
Sacred Heart University	M,O
Sage Graduate School	M,O
Saginaw Valley State University	M,O
St. Bonaventure University	M,O
St. Cloud State University	M,O
Saint Francis University	M
St. John's University (NY)	M,D,O
Saint Joseph College	M,O
Saint Joseph's College (ME)	M
Saint Joseph's University	M,D,O
Saint Leo University	M
Saint Louis University	M,D,O
Saint Martin's College	M
Saint Mary College	M
Saint Mary's College of California	M
Saint Mary's University of Minnesota	M
St. Mary's University of San Antonio	M
Saint Michael's College	M,O
Saint Peter's College	M,O
St. Thomas Aquinas College	M,O
St. Thomas University	M,O
Saint Xavier University	M,O
Salem International University	M
Salem State College	M,O
Salisbury State University	M
Samford University	M,D,O
San Diego State University	M,D
San Francisco State University	M,D,O
San Jose State University	M,O
Santa Clara University	M,O
School for International Training	M
Seattle Pacific University	M,D,O
Seattle University	M,D,O
Seton Hall University	M,D,O
Shenandoah University	M,D,O
Shippensburg University of Pennsylvania	M,O
Siena Heights University	M
Silver Lake College	M
Simmons College	M,O
Slippery Rock University of Pennsylvania	M
Sonoma State University	M
South Carolina State University	M,D,O
South Dakota State University	M
Southeastern Louisiana University	M
Southeastern Oklahoma State University	M
Southern Arkansas University–Magnolia	M
Southern Connecticut State University	M,O
Southern Illinois University Carbondale	M,D
Southern Illinois University Edwardsville	M,O

Southern Nazarene University	M
Southern Oregon University	M
Southern University and Agricultural and Mechanical College	M
Southern Utah University	M
Southwest Baptist University	M
Southwestern Oklahoma State University	M
Southwest Missouri State University	M,O
Southwest Texas State University	M
Spalding University	M,D
Spring Arbor University	M
Springfield College	M
Spring Hill College	M
Stanford University	M,D
State University of New York at Albany	M,D,O
State University of New York at Binghamton	M,D
State University of New York at New Paltz	M,O
State University of New York at Oswego	M,O
State University of New York College at Brockport	M
State University of New York College at Cortland	M,O
State University of New York College at Fredonia	M,O
State University of New York College at Geneseo	M
State University of New York College at Oneonta	M
State University of New York College at Potsdam	M
State University of West Georgia	M,D,O
Stephen F. Austin State University	M,D
Stetson University	M,O
Suffolk University	M,O
Sul Ross State University	M
Syracuse University	M,D,O
Tarleton State University	M,O
Teachers College, Columbia University	M,D
Temple University	M,D
Tennessee State University	M,D
Tennessee Technological University	M,O
Texas A&M International University	M
Texas A&M University	M,D
Texas A&M University–Commerce	M,D
Texas A&M University–Corpus Christi	M,D
Texas A&M University–Kingsville	M,D
Texas A&M University–Texarkana	M
Texas Christian University	M,O
Texas Southern University	M,D
Texas Tech University	M,D,O
Texas Wesleyan University	M
Texas Woman's University	M,D
Towson University	M
Trevecca Nazarene University	M,D
Trinity College (DC)	M
Trinity University	M
Troy State University	M,O
Troy State University Dothan	M,O
Troy State University Montgomery	M,O
Truman State University	M
Tufts University	M,O
Tusculum College	M
Union University	M,O
Universidad del Turabo	M
Universidad Metropolitana	M
University at Buffalo, The State University of New York	M,D,O
The University of Akron	M,D
The University of Alabama	M,D,O
The University of Alabama at Birmingham	M,D,O
University of Alaska Anchorage	M
University of Alaska Fairbanks	M,O
University of Alaska Southeast	M
The University of Arizona	M,D,O
University of Arkansas	M,D,O
University of Arkansas at Little Rock	M,D,O
University of Bridgeport	M,D,O
University of California, Berkeley	M,D,O
University of California, Davis	D
University of California, Irvine	D
University of California, Los Angeles	M,D
University of California, Riverside	M,D
University of California, San Diego	M
University of California, Santa Barbara	M,D
University of California, Santa Cruz	M,O
University of Central Arkansas	M,D
University of Central Florida	M,D,O
University of Central Oklahoma	M
University of Cincinnati	M,D,O
University of Colorado at Boulder	M,D
University of Colorado at Colorado Springs	M
University of Colorado at Denver	M,D,O
University of Connecticut	M,D
University of Dayton	M,D,O
University of Delaware	M,D
University of Denver	M,D,O
University of Detroit Mercy	M,O
University of Evansville	M
The University of Findlay	M
University of Florida	M,D,O
University of Georgia	M,D,O
University of Great Falls	M
University of Guam	M
University of Hartford	M,D,O
University of Hawaii at Manoa	M,D
University of Houston	M,D
University of Houston–Clear Lake	M
University of Houston–Victoria	M
University of Idaho	M,D,O
University of Illinois at Chicago	M,D
University of Illinois at Urbana–Champaign	M,D,O
University of Indianapolis	M
The University of Iowa	M,D,O
University of Kansas	M,D,O
University of Kentucky	M,D,O
University of La Verne	M,O
University of Louisiana at Lafayette	M
University of Louisiana at Monroe	M,D,O
University of Louisville	M,D,O
University of Maine	M,D,O
University of Mary	M
University of Mary Hardin-Baylor	M
University of Maryland, Baltimore County	M,D
University of Maryland, College Park	M,D,O
University of Maryland Eastern Shore	M
University of Massachusetts Amherst	M,D,O
University of Massachusetts Boston	M,D,O
University of Massachusetts Dartmouth	M
University of Massachusetts Lowell	M,D,O
The University of Memphis	M,D,O
University of Miami	M,D,O
University of Michigan	M,D
University of Michigan–Dearborn	M
University of Michigan–Flint	M
University of Minnesota, Twin Cities Campus	M,D,O
University of Mississippi	M,D,O
University of Missouri–Columbia	M,D,O
University of Missouri–Kansas City	M,D,O
University of Missouri–St. Louis	M,D
University of Mobile	M
The University of Montana–Missoula	M,D,O
University of Montevallo	M,O
University of Nebraska at Kearney	M,O
University of Nebraska at Omaha	M,D,O
University of Nebraska–Lincoln	M,D,O
University of Nevada, Las Vegas	M,D,O
University of Nevada, Reno	M,D,O
University of New England	M
University of New Hampshire	M,D,O
University of New Haven	M
University of New Mexico	M,D,O
University of New Orleans	M,D,O
University of North Alabama	M,O
The University of North Carolina at Chapel Hill	M,D
The University of North Carolina at Charlotte	M,D,O
The University of North Carolina at Greensboro	M,D,O
The University of North Carolina at Pembroke	M
The University of North Carolina at Wilmington	M
University of North Dakota	M,D,O
University of Northern Colorado	M,D,O
University of Northern Iowa	M,D,O
University of North Florida	M,D
University of North Texas	M,D,O
University of Notre Dame	M
University of Oklahoma	M,D,O
University of Oregon	M,D
University of Pennsylvania	M,D
University of Pittsburgh	M,D
University of Portland	M
University of Puerto Rico, Río Piedras	M,D
University of Redlands	M
University of Rhode Island	M
University of Rio Grande	M
University of Rochester	M,D
University of St. Francis (IL)	M
University of Saint Francis (IN)	M
University of St. Thomas (MN)	M,D,O
University of St. Thomas (TX)	M
University of San Diego	M,D
University of San Francisco	M,D
The University of Scranton	M
University of Sioux Falls	M
University of South Alabama	M,D,O
University of South Carolina	M,D,O
University of South Dakota	M,D,O
University of Southern California	M,D,O
University of Southern Colorado	M
University of Southern Indiana	M
University of Southern Maine	M,O
University of Southern Mississippi	M,D,O
University of South Florida	M,D,O
The University of Tennessee	M,D,O
The University of Tennessee at Chattanooga	M,O
The University of Tennessee at Martin	M
The University of Texas at Arlington	M
The University of Texas at Austin	M,D
The University of Texas at Brownsville	M
The University of Texas at El Paso	M,D
The University of Texas at San Antonio	M,D
The University of Texas at Tyler	M,O
The University of Texas of the Permian Basin	M
The University of Texas–Pan American	M,D
University of the District of Columbia	M
University of the Incarnate Word	M
University of the Pacific	M,D
University of the Sacred Heart	M
University of the Virgin Islands	M
University of Toledo	M,D,O
University of Tulsa	M
University of Utah	M,D
University of Vermont	M,D
University of Virginia	M,D,O
University of Washington	M,D,O

The University of West Alabama M
University of West Florida M,D,O
University of Wisconsin–Eau Claire M
University of Wisconsin–Green Bay M
University of Wisconsin–La Crosse M
University of Wisconsin–Madison M,D
University of Wisconsin–Milwaukee M,D
University of Wisconsin–Oshkosh M
University of Wisconsin–Parkside M
University of Wisconsin–Platteville M
University of Wisconsin–River Falls M
University of Wisconsin–Stevens Point M
University of Wisconsin–Stout M
University of Wisconsin–Superior M
University of Wisconsin–Whitewater M
University of Wyoming M,D,O
Ursuline College M
Utah State University M,D,O
Valdosta State University M,D,O
Valparaiso University M
Vanderbilt University M,D
Villanova University M
Virginia Commonwealth University M,D,O
Virginia Polytechnic Institute and State University M,D,O
Virginia State University M
Viterbo University M
Wagner College M
Wake Forest University M
Walden University D
Walla Walla College M
Walsh University M
Washburn University of Topeka M
Washington State University M,D
Washington University in St. Louis M,D
Wayland Baptist University M
Wayne State College M,O
Wayne State University M,D,O
Weber State University M
Webster University M
West Chester University of Pennsylvania M,O
Western Carolina University M,D,O
Western Connecticut State University M
Western Illinois University M,O
Western Kentucky University M,O
Western Michigan University M,D,O
Western New Mexico University M
Western Oregon University M
Western Washington University M
Westfield State College M,O
Westminster College (UT) M
West Texas A&M University M
West Virginia University M,D
Wheelock College M,O
Whitworth College M
Wichita State University M,D,O
Widener University M,D
Wilkes University M
William Carey College M
William Paterson University of New Jersey M
William Woods University M
Wilmington College M,D
Winona State University M
Winthrop University M,O
Worcester State College M,O
Wright State University M,O
Xavier University M
Xavier University of Louisiana M
Youngstown State University M,D

■ EDUCATIONAL ADMINISTRATION

Abilene Christian University M
Adelphi University M,O
Alabama Agricultural and Mechanical University M,O
Alabama State University M,O
Albany State University M,O
Alliant International University M,D
American International College M,D,O
American University M
Andrews University M,D,O
Angelo State University M
Antioch New England Graduate School M
Antioch University McGregor M
Appalachian State University M,D
Arcadia University M,O
Argosy University-Sarasota D,O
Arizona State University M,D
Arizona State University West M
Arkansas State University M,D,O
Arkansas Tech University M
Ashland University M,D
Auburn University M,D,O
Auburn University Montgomery M,O
Augusta State University M,O
Aurora University M,D
Austin Peay State University M,O
Azusa Pacific University M,D
Baldwin-Wallace College M
Ball State University M,D,O
Barry University M,D,O
Bayamón Central University M
Baylor University M,D,O
Belmont University M
Bemidji State University M
Benedictine College M
Bernard M. Baruch College of the City University of New York M
Boston College M,D,O
Boston University M,O
Bowie State University M
Bowling Green State University M,D,O
Bradley University M
Bridgewater State College M,O
Brigham Young University M,D
Brooklyn College of the City University of New York O
Butler University M,O
California Baptist University M
California Lutheran University M
California Polytechnic State University, San Luis Obispo M
California State University, Bakersfield M
California State University, Dominguez Hills M
California State University, Fresno M,D
California State University, Fullerton M
California State University, Hayward M
California State University, Long Beach M
California State University, Los Angeles M
California State University, Northridge M
California State University, Sacramento M
California State University, San Bernardino M
California State University, Stanislaus M
California University of Pennsylvania M
Campbell University M
Canisius College M,O
Cardinal Stritch University M,D
Carlow College M
Castleton State College M,O
The Catholic University of America M,D
Centenary College of Louisiana M
Central Connecticut State University O
Central Michigan University M,D,O
Central Missouri State University M,D,O
Central Washington University M
Chadron State College M,O
Chapman University M
Charleston Southern University M
Chestnut Hill College M
Cheyney University of Pennsylvania M,O
Chicago State University M
The Citadel, The Military College of South Carolina M,O
City College of the City University of New York M,O
City University M,O
Claremont Graduate University M,D
Clark Atlanta University M,D,O
Clemson University M,D,O
Cleveland State University M,O
The College of New Jersey M
The College of New Rochelle M,O
College of Notre Dame of Maryland M
College of Our Lady of the Elms M,O
The College of Saint Rose M,O
College of Santa Fe M
College of Staten Island of the City University of New York O
College of the Southwest M
The College of William and Mary M,D
Columbus State University M,O
Concordia University (CA) M
Concordia University (IL) M,D,O
Concordia University (OR) M
Concordia University (NE) M
Concordia University Wisconsin M
Converse College M,O
Creighton University M
Cumberland College O
Dallas Baptist University M
Delta State University M,O
DePaul University M,D
Doane College M
Dominican University M
Dowling College D,O
Drake University M,D,O
Duquesne University M,D
East Carolina University M,D,O
Eastern Illinois University M,O
Eastern Kentucky University M,O
Eastern Michigan University M,D,O
Eastern Nazarene College M,O
Eastern Washington University M
East Tennessee State University M,D,O
Edgewood College M,O
Edinboro University of Pennsylvania M,O
Emmanuel College M
Emporia State University M
Fairleigh Dickinson University, Teaneck–Hackensack Campus M
Fayetteville State University M
Ferris State University M
Fitchburg State College M,O
Florida Agricultural and Mechanical University M,D
Florida Atlantic University M,D,O
Florida Gulf Coast University M
Florida International University M,D,O
Florida State University M,D,O
Fordham University M,D,O
Fort Hays State University M,O
Framingham State College M
Franciscan University of Steubenville M
Fresno Pacific University M
Friends University M
Frostburg State University M
Gallaudet University M,D,O
Gardner-Webb University M
Geneva College M
George Mason University M
The George Washington University M,D,O
Georgia College and State University M,O
Georgian Court College M
Georgia Southern University M,D,O

Georgia State University	M,D,O
Gonzaga University	M,D
Governors State University	M
Grambling State University	M,D
Grand Valley State University	M
Gwynedd-Mercy College	M
Harding University	M
Harvard University	M,D,O
Henderson State University	M
Heritage College	M
Hofstra University	M,D,O
Hood College	M
Houston Baptist University	M
Howard University	M,O
Hunter College of the City University of New York	O
Idaho State University	M,D,O
Illinois State University	M,D
Immaculata College	M,D,O
Indiana State University	M,D,O
Indiana University Bloomington	M,D,O
Indiana University of Pennsylvania	M,D,O
Indiana University–Purdue University Fort Wayne	M
Indiana University–Purdue University Indianapolis	M
Inter American University of Puerto Rico, Metropolitan Campus	M
Inter American University of Puerto Rico, San Germán Campus	M
Iona College	M
Iowa State University of Science and Technology	M,D
Jackson State University	M,D,O
Jacksonville State University	M,O
Jacksonville University	M
James Madison University	M
John Carroll University	M
Johns Hopkins University	M,D,O
Johnson & Wales University	D
Kansas State University	M,D
Kean University	M,O
Keene State College	M,O
Kent State University	M,D,O
Kutztown University of Pennsylvania	M
Lamar University	M,O
La Sierra University	M,D,O
Lehigh University	M,D,O
Lesley University	M,D,O
Lewis University	M,O
Liberty University	M,D
Lincoln Memorial University	M,O
Lincoln University (MO)	M
Long Island University, Brooklyn Campus	M
Long Island University, C.W. Post Campus	M,O
Longwood College	M
Loras College	M
Louisiana State University and Agricultural and Mechanical College	M,D,O
Louisiana Tech University	M,D,O
Loyola College in Maryland	M,O
Loyola Marymount University	M
Loyola University Chicago	M,D
Lynchburg College	M
Lynn University	M,D
Madonna University	M
Manhattan College	M,O
Marian College of Fond du Lac	M
Marshall University	M,O
Marygrove College	M
Maryville University of Saint Louis	M
Marywood University	M
McNeese State University	M,O
Mercy College	M,O
Miami University	M,D
Michigan State University	M,D,O
Middle Tennessee State University	M
Midwestern State University	M
Millersville University of Pennsylvania	M
Minnesota State University, Mankato	M,O
Minnesota State University Moorhead	M,O
Mississippi College	M
Mississippi State University	M,D,O
Monmouth University	M,O
Montclair State University	M
Morehead State University	M,O
Morgan State University	M,D
Mount St. Mary's College	M
Murray State University	M,O
National-Louis University	M,D,O
National University	M
New Jersey City University	M
Newman University	M
New Mexico Highlands University	M
New Mexico State University	M,D,O
New York Institute of Technology	M,O
New York University	M,D,O
Niagara University	M,O
Nicholls State University	M
Norfolk State University	M
North Carolina Agricultural and Technical State University	M
North Carolina Central University	M
North Carolina State University	M,D
North Central College	M
North Dakota State University	M,O
Northeastern Illinois University	M
Northeastern State University	M
Northern Arizona University	M,D
Northern Illinois University	M,D,O
Northern Michigan University	M,O
Northern State University	M
North Georgia College & State University	M,O
Northwestern State University of Louisiana	M,O
Northwestern University	M,D
Northwest Missouri State University	M,O
Northwest Nazarene University	M
Notre Dame de Namur University	M
Nova Southeastern University	M,D,O
Oakland University	M,D,O
The Ohio State University	M,D,O
Ohio University	M,D
Oklahoma State University	M,D,O
Old Dominion University	M,O
Oral Roberts University	M,D
Oregon State University	M
Our Lady of the Lake University of San Antonio	M,D
Pace University, New York City Campus	M,O
Pace University, White Plains Campus	M,O
Pacific Lutheran University	M
The Pennsylvania State University University Park Campus	M,D
Pittsburg State University	M,O
Plattsburgh State University of New York	O
Plymouth State College	M
Portland State University	M,D
Prairie View A&M University	M
Providence College	M
Purdue University	M,D,O
Purdue University Calumet	M
Queens College of the City University of New York	O
Radford University	M
Rhode Island College	M,O
Rider University	M
Rivier College	M
Robert Morris College	M
Roosevelt University	M,D
Rowan University	M,D
Rutgers, The State University of New Jersey, New Brunswick	M,D,O
Sacred Heart University	M,O
Saginaw Valley State University	M,O
St. Bonaventure University	M,O
St. Cloud State University	M,O
Saint Francis University	M
St. John Fisher College	M
St. John's University (NY)	M,D,O
Saint Joseph's University	D
Saint Louis University	M,D,O
Saint Mary's College of California	M
Saint Mary's University of Minnesota	M,D
St. Mary's University of San Antonio	M
Saint Michael's College	M,O
Saint Peter's College	M,O
Saint Xavier University	M,O
Salem State College	M
Salisbury State University	M
Samford University	M,D,O
Sam Houston State University	M,D
San Diego State University	M
San Francisco State University	M,O
San Jose State University	M,O
Santa Clara University	M
Seattle Pacific University	M,D
Seattle University	M,D,O
Seton Hall University	M,D,O
Shenandoah University	M,D,O
Shippensburg University of Pennsylvania	M
Silver Lake College	M
Simmons College	M,O
Sonoma State University	M
South Carolina State University	M,D,O
South Dakota State University	M
Southeastern Louisiana University	M
Southeastern Oklahoma State University	M
Southeast Missouri State University	M,D,O
Southern Arkansas University–Magnolia	M
Southern Connecticut State University	O
Southern Illinois University Carbondale	M,D
Southern Illinois University Edwardsville	M,O
Southern Oregon University	M
Southern University and Agricultural and Mechanical College	M
Southwest Baptist University	M
Southwestern Oklahoma State University	M
Southwest Missouri State University	M,O
Southwest Texas State University	M
Spalding University	M,D
Springfield College	M,O
Stanford University	M,D
State University of New York at Albany	M,D,O
State University of New York at New Paltz	M,O
State University of New York at Oswego	M,O
State University of New York College at Brockport	M,O
State University of New York College at Buffalo	M,O
State University of New York College at Cortland	O
State University of New York College at Fredonia	O
State University of West Georgia	M,O
Stephen F. Austin State University	M,D

Stetson University M,O
Stony Brook University, State University of New York M,O
Suffolk University M,O
Sul Ross State University M
Syracuse University M,D,O
Tarleton State University M,O
Teachers College, Columbia University M,D
Temple University M,D
Tennessee State University M,D
Tennessee Technological University M,O
Texas A&M International University M
Texas A&M University M,D
Texas A&M University–Commerce M,D
Texas A&M University–Corpus Christi M,D
Texas A&M University–Kingsville M,D
Texas Christian University M,O
Texas Southern University M,D
Texas Tech University M,D,O
Texas Woman's University M
Towson University O
Trevecca Nazarene University M
Trinity College (DC) M
Trinity University M
Troy State University M
Troy State University Dothan M,O
Troy State University Montgomery O
Union University M,O
Universidad del Turabo M
Universidad Metropolitana M
University at Buffalo, The State University of New York M,D,O
The University of Akron M,D
The University of Alabama M,D,O
The University of Alabama at Birmingham M,D,O
University of Alaska Anchorage M
University of Alaska Fairbanks M,O
The University of Arizona M,D,O
University of Arkansas M,D,O
University of Arkansas at Little Rock M,D,O
University of Bridgeport D,O
University of California, Berkeley M,D
University of California, Irvine D
University of California, Los Angeles D
University of Central Arkansas M,O
University of Central Florida M,D,O
University of Central Oklahoma M
University of Cincinnati M,D,O
University of Colorado at Colorado Springs M
University of Colorado at Denver M,D,O
University of Connecticut M,D
University of Dayton M,D
University of Delaware M,D
University of Denver M,D,O
University of Detroit Mercy M,O
The University of Findlay M
University of Florida M,D,O
University of Georgia M,D,O
University of Great Falls M
University of Guam M
University of Hartford M,D,O
University of Hawaii at Manoa M,D
University of Houston M,D
University of Houston–Clear Lake M
University of Idaho M,D,O
University of Illinois at Chicago M,D
University of Illinois at Springfield M
University of Illinois at Urbana–Champaign M,D,O
The University of Iowa M,D,O
University of Kansas M,D
University of Kentucky D,O
University of La Verne M,D,O
University of Louisiana at Lafayette M
University of Louisiana at Monroe M,D,O
University of Louisville M,D,O
University of Maine M,D,O
University of Mary M
University of Mary Hardin-Baylor M
University of Maryland, College Park M,D,O
University of Massachusetts Amherst M,D,O
University of Massachusetts Boston M,D,O
University of Massachusetts Lowell M,D,O
The University of Memphis M,D,O
University of Miami M
University of Michigan M,D
University of Minnesota, Twin Cities Campus M,D,O
University of Mississippi M,D,O
University of Missouri–Columbia M,D,O
University of Missouri–Kansas City M,D,O
University of Missouri–St. Louis M,D
The University of Montana–Missoula M,O
University of Montevallo M,O
University of Nebraska at Kearney M,O
University of Nebraska at Omaha M,D,O
University of Nebraska–Lincoln M,D,O
University of Nevada, Las Vegas M,D,O
University of Nevada, Reno M,D,O
University of New Hampshire M,O
University of New Mexico M,D,O
University of New Orleans M,D,O
University of North Alabama M,O
The University of North Carolina at Chapel Hill M,D
The University of North Carolina at Charlotte M,D,O
The University of North Carolina at Greensboro M,D,O
The University of North Carolina at Pembroke M
The University of North Carolina at Wilmington M
University of North Dakota M,D,O
University of Northern Colorado M,D,O
University of Northern Iowa M,D
University of North Florida M,D
University of North Texas M,D
University of Oklahoma M,D
University of Oregon M,D
University of Pennsylvania M,D
University of Pittsburgh M,D
University of Puerto Rico, Río Piedras M,D
University of Redlands M
University of St. Thomas (MN) M,D,O
University of San Diego M,D
University of San Francisco M,D
The University of Scranton M
University of Sioux Falls M
University of South Alabama M,O
University of South Carolina M,D,O
University of South Dakota M,D,O
University of Southern California M,D,O
University of Southern Maine M,O
University of Southern Mississippi M,D,O
University of South Florida M,D,O
The University of Tennessee M,D,O
The University of Tennessee at Chattanooga M,O
The University of Texas at Arlington M
The University of Texas at Austin M,D
The University of Texas at Brownsville M
The University of Texas at El Paso M,D
The University of Texas at Tyler M,O
The University of Texas of the Permian Basin M
The University of Texas–Pan American M
University of the Pacific M,D
University of Toledo M,D,O
University of Utah M,D
University of Vermont M,D
University of Virginia M,D,O
University of Washington M,D,O
The University of West Alabama M
University of West Florida M,O
University of Wisconsin–La Crosse M
University of Wisconsin–Madison M,D
University of Wisconsin–Milwaukee M
University of Wisconsin–Oshkosh M
University of Wisconsin–Stevens Point M
University of Wisconsin–Superior M,O
University of Wisconsin–Whitewater M
Ursuline College M
Valdosta State University M,D,O
Vanderbilt University M,D
Villanova University M
Virginia Commonwealth University M
Virginia Polytechnic Institute and State University M,D,O
Virginia State University M
Walla Walla College M
Washburn University of Topeka M
Washington State University M,D
Wayne State College M,O
Wayne State University M,D,O
Western Carolina University M,D,O
Western Illinois University M,O
Western Kentucky University M,O
Western Michigan University M,D,O
Western New Mexico University M
Western Washington University M
Westfield State College M,O
West Texas A&M University M
West Virginia University M,D
Wheelock College M,O
Whitworth College M
Wichita State University M,D,O
Widener University M,D
Wilkes University M
William Carey College M
William Woods University M
Wilmington College M,D
Winona State University M
Winthrop University M
Worcester State College M
Wright State University M,O
Xavier University M
Xavier University of Louisiana M
Yeshiva University M,D,O
Youngstown State University M,D

■ EDUCATIONAL MEASUREMENT AND EVALUATION

Abilene Christian University M
Angelo State University M
Arkansas State University M,O
Boston College M,D,O
Claremont Graduate University M,D
Cleveland State University M
College of the Southwest M
Florida State University M,D,O
Gallaudet University O
George Mason University M
Georgia State University M,D
Hofstra University M
Houston Baptist University M
Iowa State University of Science and Technology M,D
Kent State University M,D
Louisiana State University and Agricultural and Mechanical College M,D,O
Loyola University Chicago M,D
Michigan State University M,D,O
Mississippi College M
New York University M,D,O
North Carolina State University D
Northwestern Oklahoma State University M

Ohio University M,D
Rutgers, The State University of New Jersey, New Brunswick M
Seattle University O
Southern Connecticut State University M
Southern Illinois University Carbondale M,D
Southwestern Oklahoma State University M
Stanford University M,D
State University of New York at Albany M,D,O
State University of West Georgia D
Sul Ross State University M
Syracuse University M,D,O
Teachers College, Columbia University M,D
Texas A&M University M,D
Texas Christian University M
Texas Southern University M,D
The University of Alabama M,D,O
University of California, Berkeley M,D
University of Colorado at Boulder D
University of Connecticut M,D
University of Delaware M,D
University of Denver M,D,O
University of Florida M,D,O
University of Hawaii at Manoa D
The University of Iowa M,D,O
University of Kansas M,D
University of Kentucky M,D
University of Maryland, College Park M,D
University of Massachusetts Amherst M,D,O
The University of Memphis M,D
University of Miami M,D
University of Michigan M,D
University of Minnesota, Twin Cities Campus M,D,O
University of Missouri–St. Louis M,D
University of Nevada, Las Vegas M,D,O
The University of North Carolina at Greensboro M,D
University of North Dakota D
University of Northern Colorado M,D
University of North Texas D
University of Pennsylvania M,D
University of Pittsburgh M,D
University of Puerto Rico, Río Piedras M
University of South Carolina M,D
University of South Florida M,D,O
The University of Tennessee M,D,O
The University of Texas–Pan American M,D
University of the Incarnate Word M
University of the Pacific M,D
University of Toledo M,D,O
University of Virginia M,D
University of Washington M,D
Utah State University M,D
Vanderbilt University M,D
Virginia Polytechnic Institute and State University D
Washington University in St. Louis D
Wayne State University M,D,O
West Chester University of Pennsylvania M
West Texas A&M University M
Wilkes University M

■ EDUCATIONAL MEDIA/ INSTRUCTIONAL TECHNOLOGY

Adelphi University M,O
Alabama State University M,O
Alliant International University M,D
American University M
Appalachian State University M,O
Arcadia University M,O
Arizona State University M,D
Arkansas Tech University M
Auburn University M,D,O
Azusa Pacific University M
Baldwin-Wallace College M
Barry University M,D,O
Bloomsburg University of Pennsylvania M
Boise State University M
Boston University M,D,O
Bowling Green State University M
Bridgewater State College M
Brigham Young University M,D
California State University, Chico M
California State University, Los Angeles M
California State University, San Bernardino M
California State University, Stanislaus M
Central Connecticut State University M
Central Michigan University M
Central Missouri State University M
Chestnut Hill College M
Chicago State University M
City University M,O
Cleveland State University M
College of Mount Saint Vincent M,O
The College of New Jersey M
The College of Saint Rose M,O
The College of St. Scholastica M
Concordia University (CA) M
Dowling College D,O
Duquesne University M
East Carolina University M,O
Eastern Washington University M
East Tennessee State University M
Emporia State University M
Fairfield University M,O
Ferris State University M
Florida Atlantic University M
Florida Gulf Coast University M
Florida State University M,D,O
Fort Hays State University M
Framingham State College M
Fresno Pacific University M
Frostburg State University M
Gallaudet University O
Gannon University M
George Mason University M
The George Washington University M
Georgia College and State University M,O
Georgian Court College M
Georgia Southern University M,O
Georgia State University M,D,O
Governors State University M
Grand Valley State University M
Harvard University M,D,O
Idaho State University M,D,O
Indiana State University M,D,O
Indiana University Bloomington M,D,O
Indiana University of Pennsylvania M
Indiana University–Purdue University Indianapolis M
Inter American University of Puerto Rico, Metropolitan Campus M
Iona College M,O
Iowa State University of Science and Technology M,D
Jackson State University M,D,O
Jacksonville State University M
Jacksonville University M
Johns Hopkins University M,O
Kent State University M
Lehigh University M,D
Long Island University, Brooklyn Campus M
Long Island University, C.W. Post Campus M,D,O
Longwood College M
Louisiana State University and Agricultural and Mechanical College M,D,O
Loyola College in Maryland M
Malone College M
Marywood University M
McNeese State University M
Michigan State University M,D,O
MidAmerica Nazarene University M
Minnesota State University, Mankato M,O
Mississippi State University M,D,O
Mississippi University for Women M
Montana State University–Billings M
National-Louis University M,O
National University M
New Jersey City University M
New York Institute of Technology M,O
New York University M,D,O
North Carolina Agricultural and Technical State University M
North Carolina Central University M
North Carolina State University D
Northern Arizona University M
Northern Illinois University M,D
Northwestern State University of Louisiana M,O
Northwestern University M,D
Northwest Missouri State University M
Notre Dame de Namur University M,O
Nova Southeastern University M,D,O
Oakland University O
Ohio University M,D
Old Dominion University M
Our Lady of the Lake University of San Antonio M
Pacific Lutheran University M
The Pennsylvania State University Great Valley Campus M
The Pennsylvania State University University Park Campus M,D
Pittsburg State University M,O
Pontifical Catholic University of Puerto Rico M,D
Portland State University M
Purdue University M,D,O
Purdue University Calumet M
Radford University M
Rochester Institute of Technology M
Rowan University M
St. Cloud State University M
Saint Michael's College M,O
Salem State College M
Salisbury State University M
San Diego State University M
San Francisco State University M,O
San Jose State University M,O
Seton Hall University M,O
Simmons College M,O
Southeastern Oklahoma State University M
Southeast Missouri State University M
Southern Connecticut State University M,O
Southern Illinois University Edwardsville M
Southern University and Agricultural and Mechanical College M
State University of New York at Albany M,D,O
State University of New York College at Buffalo M
State University of New York College at Potsdam M
State University of West Georgia M,O
Stony Brook University, State University of New York M,O
Teachers College, Columbia University M,D
Texas A&M University M

Texas A&M University–Commerce M,D
Texas Southern University M
Texas Tech University M,D,O
Towson University M,D
Troy State University Dothan M,O
The University of Alabama M,D
University of Alaska Southeast M
University of Arkansas M
University of Arkansas at Little Rock M
University of Central Arkansas M
University of Central Florida M,D
University of Central Oklahoma M
University of Colorado at Denver M
University of Connecticut M,D
University of Dayton M
The University of Findlay M
University of Florida M,D,O
University of Georgia M,D,O
University of Hartford M
University of Hawaii at Manoa M
University of Houston–Clear Lake M
The University of Iowa M,D,O
University of Maryland, Baltimore County M,D
University of Maryland, College Park M,D,O
University of Massachusetts Amherst M,D,O
The University of Memphis M,D
University of Michigan M,D
University of Nebraska at Kearney M,O
University of Nevada, Las Vegas M,D,O
University of New Mexico M,D,O
The University of North Carolina at Charlotte M,D,O
University of North Dakota M
University of Northern Colorado M
University of Northern Iowa M
University of Oregon M,D
University of St. Thomas (MN) M,D,O
University of San Francisco M,D
University of Sioux Falls M
University of South Alabama M,D
University of South Carolina M
University of South Dakota M,O
University of Southern California M,D
University of South Florida M,D
The University of Tennessee M,D,O
The University of Texas at Brownsville M
University of the Sacred Heart M
University of Toledo M,D,O
University of Washington M,D
The University of West Alabama M
University of Wyoming M,D,O
Utah State University M,D,O
Vanderbilt University M,D
Walden University M
Wayne State College M
Wayne State University M,D,O
Webster University M
West Chester University of Pennsylvania M,O
Western Connecticut State University M
Western Illinois University M,O
Western Kentucky University M
Western Oregon University M
Westfield State College M
West Texas A&M University M
Widener University M,D

■ EDUCATIONAL PSYCHOLOGY

American International College M,D,O
Andrews University M,D
Arcadia University M,O
Arizona State University M,D
Auburn University M,D,O
Austin Peay State University M,O
Ball State University M,D,O
Baylor University M,D,O
Boston College M,D
Brigham Young University M,D
California State University, Long Beach M
California State University, Northridge M,O
The Catholic University of America M,D
Chapman University M
Clark Atlanta University M,D
The College of Saint Rose M
Eastern College M
Eastern Illinois University M
Eastern Michigan University M
Edinboro University of Pennsylvania M
Florida State University M,D,O
Fordham University M,D,O
Georgia State University M,D
Harvard University M,D,O
Howard University M,D,O
Illinois State University M,D,O
Indiana State University M,D,O
Indiana University Bloomington M,D,O
Indiana University of Pennsylvania M,O
John Carroll University M
Kansas State University M,D
Kean University M,O
Kent State University M,D
La Sierra University M,O
Loyola Marymount University M
Loyola University Chicago M,D
Marist College M,O
Miami University M,O
Michigan State University M,D,O
Minot State University O
Mississippi State University M,D,O
Montclair State University M
National-Louis University M,D,O
New Jersey City University M,O
Northeastern University M
Northern Arizona University D
Northern Illinois University M,D
Oklahoma State University M,D
The Pennsylvania State University University Park Campus M,D
Purdue University M,D,O
Rhode Island College M
Rutgers, The State University of New Jersey, New Brunswick M,D
Southern Illinois University Carbondale M,D
Southern Illinois University Edwardsville M
Stanford University D
State University of New York at Albany M,D,O
Teachers College, Columbia University M,D
Temple University M,D
Tennessee Technological University M,O
Texas A&M University M,D
Texas A&M University–Commerce M,D
Texas Tech University M,D,O
University at Buffalo, The State University of New York M,D,O
The University of Alabama M,D,O
The University of Arizona M,D
University of California, Davis D
University of Colorado at Boulder M,D
University of Colorado at Denver M
University of Connecticut M,D
University of Denver M,D,O
University of Florida M,D,O
University of Georgia M,D,O
University of Hawaii at Manoa M,D
University of Houston M,D
University of Illinois at Urbana–Champaign M,D,O
The University of Iowa M,D,O
University of Kansas M,D
University of Kentucky M,D,O
University of Mary Hardin-Baylor M
University of Maryland, College Park M,D,O
The University of Memphis M,D
University of Minnesota, Twin Cities Campus M,D,O
University of Mississippi M,D,O
University of Missouri–Columbia M,D,O
University of Missouri–St. Louis M,D
University of Nebraska at Omaha M,D,O
University of Nebraska–Lincoln M,O
University of Nevada, Las Vegas M
University of Nevada, Reno M,D,O
University of New Mexico M,D
The University of North Carolina at Chapel Hill M,D
University of Northern Colorado M,D
University of Northern Iowa M,O
University of Oklahoma M,D
University of Pittsburgh D
University of South Carolina M,D
University of South Dakota M,D,O
University of Southern California M,D,O
The University of Tennessee M,D,O
The University of Texas at Austin M,D
The University of Texas at El Paso M
The University of Texas–Pan American M,D
University of the Pacific M,D
University of Toledo M,D,O
University of Utah M,D
University of Virginia M,D,O
University of Washington M,D
University of Wisconsin–Madison M,D
University of Wisconsin–Milwaukee M
Wayne State University M,D,O
West Virginia University M,D
Wichita State University M,D,O
Widener University M,D

■ EDUCATION OF THE GIFTED

Arkansas State University M
Arkansas Tech University M
Ashland University M
Barry University M,D,O
Belmont University M
California State University, Los Angeles M,D
California State University, Northridge M
Carthage College M,O
Clark Atlanta University M,O
Cleveland State University M
The College of New Rochelle M,O
The College of William and Mary M
Converse College M
Drury University M
Emporia State University M
Grand Valley State University M
Hardin-Simmons University M
Indiana State University M,D,O
Jacksonville University M,O
Johns Hopkins University M,D,O
Johnson State College M
Kent State University M,D,O
Maryville University of Saint Louis M
Millersville University of Pennsylvania M
Minnesota State University, Mankato M
Mississippi University for Women M
Norfolk State University M
Northeastern Illinois University M
Nova Southeastern University M,O
Ohio University M,D
Purdue University M,D,O
St. Cloud State University M,O
Teachers College, Columbia University M,D
Texas A&M International University M
Texas A&M University M,D
University of Arkansas at Little Rock M

University of Central Arkansas M
University of Connecticut M,D
University of Georgia M,D,O
University of Houston M,D
University of Louisiana at Lafayette M
University of Nebraska at Kearney M
University of Northern Colorado M
University of Northern Iowa M
University of South Alabama M
University of Southern Mississippi M,D,O
University of South Florida M
The University of Texas–Pan American M,D
West Virginia University M,D
Whitworth College M
William Carey College M
Wright State University M
Xavier University M
Youngstown State University M

■ EDUCATION OF THE MULTIPLY HANDICAPPED

Boston College M,O
Cleveland State University M
Fresno Pacific University M
Gallaudet University M,D,O
Georgia State University M
Hunter College of the City University of New York M
Minnesota State University, Mankato M
Minot State University M
Montclair State University M
Norfolk State University M
University of Arkansas at Little Rock M
University of Illinois at Urbana–Champaign M,D,O
University of South Alabama M
Western Oregon University M
West Virginia University M,D
Xavier University M

■ ELECTRICAL ENGINEERING

Alfred University M
Arizona State University M,D
Auburn University M,D
Boise State University M
Boston University M,D
Bradley University M
Brigham Young University M,D
Brown University M,D
California Institute of Technology M,D
California Polytechnic State University, San Luis Obispo M
California State Polytechnic University, Pomona M
California State University, Chico M
California State University, Fresno M
California State University, Fullerton M
California State University, Long Beach M
California State University, Los Angeles M
California State University, Northridge M
California State University, Sacramento M
Carnegie Mellon University M,D
Case Western Reserve University M,D
The Catholic University of America M,D
City College of the City University of New York M,D
Clarkson University M,D
Clemson University M,D
Cleveland State University M,D
Colorado State University M,D
Colorado Technical University M
Columbia University M,D,O
Cornell University M,D
Dartmouth College M,D
Drexel University M,D
Duke University M,D
Fairleigh Dickinson University, Teaneck–Hackensack Campus M
Florida Agricultural and Mechanical University M,D
Florida Atlantic University M,D
Florida Institute of Technology M,D
Florida International University M,D
Florida State University M,D
Gannon University M
George Mason University M,D
The George Washington University M,D,O
Georgia Institute of Technology M,D
Howard University M,D
Illinois Institute of Technology M,D
Indiana University–Purdue University Indianapolis M,D
Iowa State University of Science and Technology M,D
Johns Hopkins University M,D
Kansas State University M,D
Lamar University M,D
Lehigh University M,D
Louisiana State University and Agricultural and Mechanical College M,D
Louisiana Tech University M,D
Loyola Marymount University M
Manhattan College M
Marquette University M,D
Massachusetts Institute of Technology M,D,O
McNeese State University M
Mercer University M
Michigan State University M,D
Michigan Technological University M,D
Minnesota State University, Mankato M
Mississippi State University M,D
Montana State University–Bozeman M,D
New Jersey Institute of Technology M,D,O
New Mexico State University M,D
New York Institute of Technology M
North Carolina Agricultural and Technical State University M,D
North Carolina State University M,D
North Dakota State University M
Northeastern University M,D
Northern Illinois University M
Northwestern University M,D,O
Oakland University M
The Ohio State University M,D
Ohio University M,D
Oklahoma State University M,D
Old Dominion University M,D
Oregon State University M,D
The Pennsylvania State University Harrisburg Campus of the Capital College M
The Pennsylvania State University University Park Campus M,D
Polytechnic University, Brooklyn Campus M,D
Polytechnic University, Westchester Graduate Center M,D
Portland State University M,D
Princeton University M,D
Purdue University M,D
Rensselaer Polytechnic Institute M,D
Rice University M,D
Rochester Institute of Technology M
Rutgers, The State University of New Jersey, New Brunswick M,D
St. Mary's University of San Antonio M
San Diego State University M
San Jose State University M
Santa Clara University M,D,O
South Dakota State University M
Southern Illinois University Carbondale M,D
Southern Illinois University Edwardsville M
Southern Methodist University M,D
Stanford University M,D,O
State University of New York at Binghamton M,D
State University of New York at New Paltz M
Stevens Institute of Technology M,D,O
Stony Brook University, State University of New York M,D
Syracuse University M,D,O
Temple University M
Tennessee Technological University M,D
Texas A&M University M,D
Texas A&M University–Kingsville M
Texas Tech University M,D
Tufts University M,D,O
Tulane University M,D
Tuskegee University M
University at Buffalo, The State University of New York M,D
The University of Akron M,D
The University of Alabama M,D
The University of Alabama at Birmingham M,D
The University of Alabama in Huntsville M,D
University of Alaska Fairbanks M
The University of Arizona M,D
University of Arkansas M,D
University of Bridgeport M
University of California, Berkeley M,D
University of California, Davis M,D
University of California, Irvine M,D
University of California, Los Angeles M,D
University of California, Riverside M,D
University of California, San Diego M,D
University of California, Santa Barbara M,D
University of Central Florida M,D,O
University of Cincinnati M,D
University of Colorado at Boulder M,D
University of Colorado at Colorado Springs M,D
University of Colorado at Denver M
University of Connecticut M,D
University of Dayton M,D
University of Delaware M,D
University of Denver M,D
University of Detroit Mercy M,D
University of Florida M,D,O
University of Hawaii at Manoa M,D
University of Houston M,D
University of Idaho M,D
University of Illinois at Chicago M,D
University of Illinois at Urbana–Champaign M,D
The University of Iowa M,D
University of Kansas M,D
University of Kentucky M,D
University of Louisville M
University of Maine M,D
University of Maryland, Baltimore County M,D
University of Maryland, College Park M,D
University of Massachusetts Amherst M,D
University of Massachusetts Dartmouth M,D,O
University of Massachusetts Lowell M,D
The University of Memphis M,D
University of Miami M,D
University of Michigan M,D
University of Michigan–Dearborn M
University of Minnesota, Twin Cities Campus M,D
University of Missouri–Columbia M,D

University of Missouri–Rolla M,D
University of Nebraska–Lincoln M,D
University of Nevada, Las Vegas M,D
University of Nevada, Reno M,D
University of New Hampshire M,D
University of New Haven M
University of New Mexico M,D
University of New Orleans M
The University of North Carolina at Charlotte M,D
University of North Dakota M
University of Notre Dame M,D
University of Oklahoma M,D
University of Pennsylvania M,D
University of Pittsburgh M,D
University of Puerto Rico, Mayagüez Campus M
University of Rhode Island M,D
University of Rochester M,D
University of South Alabama M
University of South Carolina M,D
University of Southern California M,D,O
University of South Florida M,D
The University of Tennessee M,D
The University of Texas at Arlington M,D
The University of Texas at Austin M,D
The University of Texas at Dallas M,D
The University of Texas at El Paso M,D
The University of Texas at San Antonio M
University of Toledo M,D
University of Tulsa M
University of Utah M,D,O
University of Vermont M,D
University of Virginia M,D
University of Washington M,D
University of Wisconsin–Madison M,D
University of Wyoming M,D
Utah State University M,D,O
Vanderbilt University M,D
Villanova University M
Virginia Polytechnic Institute and State University M,D
Washington State University M,D
Washington University in St. Louis M,D
Wayne State University M,D
Western Michigan University M
Western New England College M
West Virginia University M,D
Wichita State University M,D
Widener University M
Wilkes University M
Worcester Polytechnic Institute M,D,O
Wright State University M
Yale University M,D
Youngstown State University M

■ ELECTRONIC COMMERCE

American University M
Bentley College M,O
Boston University M
California State University, Hayward M
Carnegie Mellon University M
City University M,O
Clemson University M
Creighton University M
DePaul University M
Fairleigh Dickinson University, Teaneck–Hackensack Campus M
Johns Hopkins University M,O
Maryville University of Saint Louis M,O
Mercy College M
Morehead State University M
National University M
New Jersey Institute of Technology M
New York Institute of Technology M,O
Northwestern University M
Notre Dame de Namur University M
Old Dominion University M
Regis University M,O
Rensselaer Polytechnic Institute M,D
Sacred Heart University M,O
St. Edward's University M,O
Southern Illinois University Edwardsville M
Stevens Institute of Technology M,O
Temple University M
University at Buffalo, The State University of New York M,D,O
The University of Akron M
University of Denver M
University of Minnesota, Twin Cities Campus M
University of Missouri–St. Louis M,O
University of St. Thomas (MN) M,O
University of San Diego M
West Chester University of Pennsylvania M
Wright State University M

■ ELECTRONIC MATERIALS

Northwestern University M,D,O
Princeton University M,D
University of Arkansas M,D

■ ELEMENTARY EDUCATION

Abilene Christian University M
Adams State College M
Adelphi University M,O
Alabama Agricultural and Mechanical University M,O
Alabama State University M,O
Alaska Pacific University M
Alcorn State University M,O
Alfred University M
American International College M,D,O
American University M
Andrews University M
Anna Maria College M
Antioch New England Graduate School M
Appalachian State University M
Arcadia University M,O
Arizona State University West M
Arkansas State University M,O
Arkansas Tech University M
Armstrong Atlantic State University M
Auburn University M,D,O
Auburn University Montgomery M,O
Austin Peay State University M,O
Ball State University M,D
Barry University M
Bayamón Central University M
Bellarmine University M
Belmont University M
Benedictine University M
Bloomsburg University of Pennsylvania M
Boston College M
Boston University M
Bowie State University M
Bridgewater State College M
Brigham Young University M,D
Brooklyn College of the City University of New York M
Brown University M
Butler University M,O
California State University, Fullerton M
California State University, Long Beach M
California State University, Los Angeles M
California State University, Northridge M
California State University, San Bernardino M
California State University, Stanislaus M
California University of Pennsylvania M
Campbell University M
Carson-Newman College M
Centenary College of Louisiana M
Central Connecticut State University M,O
Central Michigan University M
Central Missouri State University M,O
Central Washington University M
Chadron State College M,O
Charleston Southern University M
Chestnut Hill College M
Cheyney University of Pennsylvania M
Chicago State University M
City College of the City University of New York M
Clarion University of Pennsylvania M
Clemson University M
Cleveland State University M
The College of New Jersey M
The College of New Rochelle M
College of Our Lady of the Elms M,O
College of St. Joseph M
The College of Saint Rose M
College of Staten Island of the City University of New York M
The College of William and Mary M
Columbia College Chicago M
Concordia University (OR) M
Concordia University (NE) M
Converse College M
Cumberland College M,O
Dallas Baptist University M
Delta State University M,O
DePaul University M
Dowling College M
Drake University M
Drury University M
Duquesne University M
East Carolina University M
Eastern Connecticut State University M
Eastern Illinois University M
Eastern Kentucky University M
Eastern Michigan University M
Eastern Nazarene College M,O
Eastern Oregon University M
Eastern Washington University M
East Stroudsburg University of Pennsylvania M
East Tennessee State University M
Edinboro University of Pennsylvania M
Elon University M
Emmanuel College M
Emporia State University M
Fairfield University M,O
Fayetteville State University M
Ferris State University M
Fitchburg State College M
Florida Agricultural and Mechanical University M
Florida Atlantic University M
Florida Gulf Coast University M
Florida International University M
Florida State University M,D,O
Fordham University M,D,O
Fort Hays State University M
Francis Marion University M
Friends University M
Frostburg State University M
Gallaudet University M,D,O
Gardner-Webb University M
The George Washington University M
Grambling State University M
Grand Canyon University M
Grand Valley State University M
Hampton University M
Harding University M

Harvard University	M,D,O
Henderson State University	M
Hofstra University	M,O
Holy Family College	M
Hood College	M
Houston Baptist University	M
Howard University	M
Hunter College of the City University of New York	M
Immaculata College	M,D,O
Indiana State University	M,D,O
Indiana University Bloomington	M,D,O
Indiana University Northwest	M
Indiana University–Purdue University Fort Wayne	M
Indiana University–Purdue University Indianapolis	M
Indiana University South Bend	M
Indiana University Southeast	M
Inter American University of Puerto Rico, Metropolitan Campus	M
Iona College	M
Iowa State University of Science and Technology	M,D
Jackson State University	M,D,O
Jacksonville State University	M,O
Jacksonville University	M
John Carroll University	M
Johns Hopkins University	M
Kansas State University	M
Kent State University	M
Kutztown University of Pennsylvania	M,O
Lamar University	M,O
Lander University	M
Lehigh University	M,D,O
Lehman College of the City University of New York	M
LeMoyne-Owen College	M
Lesley University	M,D,O
Liberty University	M,D
Lincoln University (MO)	M
Long Island University, Brooklyn Campus	M
Longwood College	M
Louisiana State University and Agricultural and Mechanical College	M,D,O
Loyola Marymount University	M
Loyola University New Orleans	M
Maharishi University of Management	M
Manhattanville College	M
Mansfield University of Pennsylvania	M
Marshall University	M
Mary Baldwin College	M
Marymount University	M
Maryville University of Saint Louis	M
Marywood University	M
McNeese State University	M
Mercy College	M,O
Miami University	M
Middle Tennessee State University	M,O
Midwestern State University	M
Millersville University of Pennsylvania	M
Minnesota State University, Mankato	M,O
Minot State University	M
Mississippi College	M
Mississippi State University	M,D,O
Monmouth University	M
Montana State University–Northern	M
Morehead State University	M
Morgan State University	M
Mount Saint Mary College	M
Mount St. Mary's College	M
Murray State University	M,O
National-Louis University	M
Nazareth College of Rochester	M
Newman University	M
New York Institute of Technology	M,O
New York University	M,D,O
Niagara University	M
North Carolina Agricultural and Technical State University	M
North Carolina Central University	M
Northern Arizona University	M
Northern Illinois University	M,D
Northern Kentucky University	M
Northern Michigan University	M
Northern State University	M
Northwestern Oklahoma State University	M
Northwestern State University of Louisiana	M,O
Northwestern University	M,D
Northwest Missouri State University	M,O
Notre Dame de Namur University	M,O
Nova Southeastern University	M,O
Ohio University	M,D
Oklahoma City University	M
Old Dominion University	M
Olivet Nazarene University	M
Oregon State University	M
Pacific Lutheran University	M
Pacific University	M
Palm Beach Atlantic College	M
The Pennsylvania State University University Park Campus	M,D
Pittsburg State University	M
Plattsburgh State University of New York	M
Plymouth State College	M
Portland State University	M
Purdue University	M,D,O
Purdue University Calumet	M
Queens College	M
Queens College of the City University of New York	M,O
Quinnipiac University	M
Rhode Island College	M
Rider University	O
Rivier College	M
Rockford College	M
Rollins College	M
Roosevelt University	M,D
Rowan University	M
Rutgers, The State University of New Jersey, New Brunswick	M,D
Sacred Heart University	M,O
Sage Graduate School	M
Saginaw Valley State University	M
St. Cloud State University	M
St. John Fisher College	M
St. John's University (NY)	M
Saint Peter's College	M,O
St. Thomas Aquinas College	M
St. Thomas University	M
Saint Xavier University	M,O
Salem International University	M
Salem State College	M
Salisbury State University	M
Samford University	M,D,O
Sam Houston State University	M,D,O
San Diego State University	M
San Francisco State University	M
San Jose State University	M
Seton Hall University	M
Shenandoah University	M,D,O
Shippensburg University of Pennsylvania	M
Siena Heights University	M
Simmons College	M
Slippery Rock University of Pennsylvania	M
South Carolina State University	M
Southeastern Oklahoma State University	M
Southeast Missouri State University	M
Southern Arkansas University–Magnolia	M
Southern Connecticut State University	M,O
Southern Illinois University Edwardsville	M
Southern Oregon University	M
Southern University and Agricultural and Mechanical College	M
Southwestern Oklahoma State University	M
Southwest Missouri State University	M
Southwest Texas State University	M
Spalding University	M
Spring Hill College	M
State University of New York at Binghamton	M
State University of New York at New Paltz	M
State University of New York at Oswego	M
State University of New York College at Brockport	M
State University of New York College at Buffalo	M
State University of New York College at Cortland	M
State University of New York College at Fredonia	M
State University of New York College at Geneseo	M
State University of New York College at Oneonta	M
State University of New York College at Potsdam	M
Stephen F. Austin State University	M
Stetson University	M
Sul Ross State University	M
Syracuse University	M,O
Teachers College, Columbia University	M
Temple University	M,D
Tennessee State University	M,D
Tennessee Technological University	M,O
Texas A&M International University	M
Texas A&M University–Commerce	M,D
Texas A&M University–Corpus Christi	M
Texas A&M University–Kingsville	M
Texas A&M University–Texarkana	M
Texas Christian University	M
Texas Southern University	M,D
Texas Tech University	M,D,O
Texas Woman's University	M,D
Towson University	M
Trevecca Nazarene University	M
Trinity College (DC)	M
Troy State University	M,O
Troy State University Montgomery	M
Tufts University	M,O
University at Buffalo, The State University of New York	M,D,O
The University of Akron	M,D
The University of Alabama	M,D,O
The University of Alabama at Birmingham	M
University of Alaska Southeast	M
The University of Arizona	M,D
University of Arkansas	M,O
University of Bridgeport	M,O
University of Central Arkansas	M
University of Central Florida	M
University of Central Oklahoma	M
University of Cincinnati	M,D
University of Connecticut	M,D
The University of Findlay	M
University of Florida	M,D,O

University of Georgia M,D,O
University of Great Falls M
University of Hartford M
University of Hawaii at Manoa M
University of Houston M,D
University of Idaho M,D,O
University of Illinois at Chicago M,D
University of Indianapolis M
The University of Iowa M,D
University of Louisiana at Monroe M,O
University of Louisville M,O
University of Maine M,O
University of Mary M
University of Maryland, Baltimore County M,D
University of Massachusetts Amherst M,D,O
University of Massachusetts Boston M,D,O
The University of Memphis M,D
University of Miami M,D,O
University of Minnesota, Twin Cities Campus M
University of Missouri–Kansas City M,D,O
University of Missouri–St. Louis M,D
University of Montevallo M
University of Nebraska at Kearney M
University of Nebraska at Omaha M
University of Nevada, Las Vegas M,D,O
University of Nevada, Reno M,D,O
University of New Hampshire M
University of New Mexico M
University of North Alabama M,O
The University of North Carolina at Chapel Hill M
The University of North Carolina at Charlotte M
The University of North Carolina at Pembroke M
The University of North Carolina at Wilmington M
University of North Dakota M,D
University of Northern Colorado M,D
University of North Florida M
University of North Texas M
University of Oklahoma M,D
University of Pennsylvania M
University of Pittsburgh M
University of Rhode Island M
The University of Scranton M
University of South Alabama M,O
University of South Carolina M,D,O
University of South Dakota M
University of Southern Indiana M
University of Southern Mississippi M,D,O
University of South Florida M,D,O
The University of Tennessee M,D,O
The University of Texas at Brownsville M
The University of Texas of the Permian Basin M
The University of Texas–Pan American M
University of the Incarnate Word M
University of Toledo M,D,O
The University of West Alabama M
University of West Florida M
University of Wisconsin–Eau Claire M
University of Wisconsin–La Crosse M
University of Wisconsin–Milwaukee M
University of Wisconsin–Platteville M
University of Wisconsin–River Falls M
University of Wisconsin–Stevens Point M
University of Wyoming M,D
Utah State University M
Vanderbilt University M,D
Villanova University M
Wagner College M
Washington State University M,D
Washington University in St. Louis M
Wayne State College M
Wayne State University M,D,O
West Chester University of Pennsylvania M
Western Carolina University M
Western Illinois University M,O
Western Kentucky University M,O
Western Michigan University M
Western New Mexico University M
Western Washington University M
Westfield State College M
West Texas A&M University M
West Virginia University M
Wheelock College M
Widener University M,D
Wilkes University M
William Carey College M
William Paterson University of New Jersey M
Wilmington College M,D
Winthrop University M
Worcester State College M
Wright State University M
Xavier University M
Youngstown State University M

■ EMERGENCY MEDICAL SERVICES

MCP Hahnemann University M

■ ENERGY AND POWER ENGINEERING

New Jersey Institute of Technology M,D,O
New York Institute of Technology M,O
Rensselaer Polytechnic Institute M,D
Southern Illinois University Carbondale D
University of Massachusetts Lowell M,D
The University of Memphis M,D
University of North Dakota D
Worcester Polytechnic Institute M,D,O

■ ENERGY MANAGEMENT AND POLICY

Boston University M
New York Institute of Technology M,O
University of California, Berkeley M,D

■ ENGINEERING AND APPLIED SCIENCES—GENERAL

Alabama Agricultural and Mechanical University M
Andrews University M
Arizona State University M,D
Auburn University M,D
Boston University M,D
Bradley University M
Brigham Young University M,D
Brown University M,D
California Institute of Technology M,D,O
California Polytechnic State University, San Luis Obispo M
California State Polytechnic University, Pomona M
California State University, Chico M
California State University, Fresno M
California State University, Fullerton M
California State University, Long Beach M,D,O
California State University, Los Angeles M
California State University, Northridge M
California State University, Sacramento M
Carnegie Mellon University M,D
Case Western Reserve University M,D
The Catholic University of America M,D
Central Missouri State University M,D,O
Central Washington University M
Christian Brothers University M
City College of the City University of New York M,D
Clarkson University M,D
Clemson University M,D
Cleveland State University M,D
Colorado State University M,D
Columbia University M,D,O
Cornell University M,D
Dartmouth College M,D
Drexel University M,D
Duke University M,D
East Carolina University M
Eastern Illinois University M
East Tennessee State University M
Fairfield University M
Fairleigh Dickinson University, Teaneck–Hackensack Campus M
Florida Agricultural and Mechanical University M,D
Florida Atlantic University M,D
Florida Institute of Technology M,D
Florida International University M,D
Florida State University M,D
Gannon University M
George Mason University M,D
The George Washington University M,D,O
Georgia Institute of Technology M,D,O
Georgia Southern University M
Grand Valley State University M
Harvard University M,D
Howard University M,D
Idaho State University M,D
Illinois Institute of Technology M,D
Indiana State University M,D
Indiana University–Purdue University Fort Wayne M
Indiana University–Purdue University Indianapolis M,D
Iowa State University of Science and Technology M,D
Johns Hopkins University M,D
Kansas State University M,D
Kent State University M
Lamar University M,D
Lawrence Technological University M
Lehigh University M,D
Louisiana State University and Agricultural and Mechanical College M,D
Louisiana Tech University M,D
Loyola College in Maryland M
Loyola Marymount University M
Manhattan College M
Marquette University M,D
Marshall University M
Massachusetts Institute of Technology M,D,O
McNeese State University M
Mercer University M
Miami University M
Michigan State University M,D
Michigan Technological University M,D
Mississippi State University M,D
Montana State University–Bozeman M,D
Morgan State University M,D
National University M
New Jersey Institute of Technology M,D,O
New Mexico State University M,D
New York Institute of Technology M,O
North Carolina Agricultural and Technical State University M,D
North Carolina State University M,D,O
North Dakota State University M,D
Northeastern University M,D

Northern Arizona University	M
Northern Illinois University	M
Northwestern University	M,D,O
Oakland University	M,D
The Ohio State University	M,D
Ohio University	M,D
Oklahoma State University	M,D
Old Dominion University	M,D
Oregon State University	M,D
The Pennsylvania State University at Erie, The Behrend College	M
The Pennsylvania State University Harrisburg Campus of the Capital College	M
The Pennsylvania State University University Park Campus	M,D
Pittsburg State University	M
Portland State University	M,D
Prairie View A&M University	M
Princeton University	M,D
Purdue University	M,D
Purdue University Calumet	M
Rensselaer Polytechnic Institute	M,D
Rice University	M,D
Rochester Institute of Technology	M,O
Rowan University	M
Rutgers, The State University of New Jersey, New Brunswick	M,D
Saginaw Valley State University	M
St. Cloud State University	M
St. Mary's University of San Antonio	M
San Diego State University	M,D
San Francisco State University	M
San Jose State University	M
Santa Clara University	M,D,O
Seattle University	M
South Dakota State University	M,D
Southern Illinois University Carbondale	M,D
Southern Illinois University Edwardsville	M
Southern Methodist University	M,D
Stanford University	M,D,O
State University of New York at Binghamton	M,D
State University of New York Institute of Technology at Utica/Rome	M
Stevens Institute of Technology	M,D,O
Stony Brook University, State University of New York	M,D,O
Syracuse University	M,D,O
Temple University	M,D
Tennessee State University	M
Tennessee Technological University	M,D
Texas A&M University	M,D
Texas A&M University–Kingsville	M
Texas Tech University	M,D
Tufts University	M,D
Tulane University	M,D
Tuskegee University	M,D
University at Buffalo, The State University of New York	M,D
The University of Akron	M,D
The University of Alabama	M,D
The University of Alabama at Birmingham	M,D
The University of Alabama in Huntsville	M,D
University of Alaska Anchorage	M
The University of Arizona	M,D
University of Arkansas	M,D
University of Bridgeport	M
University of California, Berkeley	M,D
University of California, Davis	M,D,O
University of California, Irvine	M,D
University of California, Los Angeles	M,D
University of California, Riverside	M,D
University of California, Santa Barbara	M,D
University of Central Florida	M,D,O
University of Cincinnati	M,D
University of Colorado at Boulder	M,D
University of Colorado at Colorado Springs	M,D
University of Colorado at Denver	M,D
University of Connecticut	M,D
University of Dayton	M,D
University of Delaware	M,D
University of Denver	M,D
University of Detroit Mercy	M,D
University of Florida	M,D,O
University of Hartford	M
University of Hawaii at Manoa	M,D
University of Houston	M,D
University of Idaho	M,D
University of Illinois at Chicago	M,D
University of Illinois at Urbana–Champaign	M,D
The University of Iowa	M,D
University of Kansas	M,D
University of Kentucky	M,D
University of Louisiana at Lafayette	M,D
University of Louisville	M,D
University of Maine	M,D
University of Maryland, Baltimore County	M,D
University of Maryland, College Park	M,D
University of Massachusetts Amherst	M,D
University of Massachusetts Dartmouth	M,D,O
University of Massachusetts Lowell	M,D
The University of Memphis	M,D
University of Miami	M,D
University of Michigan	M,D,O
University of Michigan–Dearborn	M,D
University of Minnesota, Twin Cities Campus	M,D
University of Mississippi	M,D
University of Missouri–Columbia	M,D
University of Missouri–Rolla	M,D
University of Nebraska–Lincoln	M,D
University of Nevada, Las Vegas	M,D
University of Nevada, Reno	M,D
University of New Haven	M,O
University of New Mexico	M,D
University of New Orleans	M,D,O
The University of North Carolina at Charlotte	M,D
University of North Dakota	M,D
University of North Texas	M
University of Notre Dame	M,D
University of Oklahoma	M,D
University of Pennsylvania	M,D
University of Pittsburgh	M,D,O
University of Portland	M
University of Puerto Rico, Mayagüez Campus	M,D
University of Rhode Island	M,D
University of Rochester	M,D
University of St. Thomas (MN)	M,O
University of South Alabama	M
University of South Carolina	M,D
University of Southern California	M,D,O
University of Southern Colorado	M
University of Southern Indiana	M
University of Southern Mississippi	M
University of South Florida	M,D
The University of Tennessee	M,D
The University of Tennessee at Chattanooga	M
The University of Texas at Arlington	M,D
The University of Texas at Austin	M,D
The University of Texas at Dallas	M,D
The University of Texas at El Paso	M,D
The University of Texas at San Antonio	M
The University of Texas at Tyler	M
University of Toledo	M,D
University of Tulsa	M,D
University of Utah	M,D,O
University of Vermont	M,D
University of Virginia	M,D
University of Washington	M,D
University of Wisconsin–Madison	M,D,O
University of Wisconsin–Milwaukee	M,D
University of Wisconsin–Platteville	M
University of Wyoming	M,D
Utah State University	M,D,O
Vanderbilt University	M,D
Villanova University	M,O
Virginia Commonwealth University	M,D
Virginia Polytechnic Institute and State University	M,D
Washington State University	M,D
Washington University in St. Louis	M,D
Wayne State University	M,D,O
Western Michigan University	M,D
Western New England College	M
West Texas A&M University	M
West Virginia University	M,D
Wichita State University	M,D
Widener University	M
Worcester Polytechnic Institute	M,D,O
Wright State University	M,D
Yale University	M,D
Youngstown State University	M

■ ENGINEERING DESIGN

The Catholic University of America	D
Stanford University	M
University of Central Florida	M,D,O
University of Illinois at Urbana–Champaign	M
University of New Hampshire	D
University of New Haven	M,O

■ ENGINEERING MANAGEMENT

California Polytechnic State University, San Luis Obispo	M
California State University, Northridge	M
The Catholic University of America	M
Clarkson University	M
Colorado State University	M,D
Dallas Baptist University	M
Dartmouth College	M
Drexel University	M,D
Duke University	M
Florida Institute of Technology	M
The George Washington University	M,D,O
Kansas State University	M,D
Lamar University	M
Long Island University, C.W. Post Campus	M
Loyola Marymount University	M
Marquette University	M,D
Massachusetts Institute of Technology	M,O
Mercer University	M
New Jersey Institute of Technology	M
Northeastern University	M,D
Northwestern University	M
Oakland University	M
Ohio University	M,D
Old Dominion University	M,D
The Pennsylvania State University University Park Campus	M
Portland State University	M,D
Rensselaer Polytechnic Institute	M,D
Rochester Institute of Technology	M
Saint Martin's College	M
St. Mary's University of San Antonio	M
Santa Clara University	M
Southern Methodist University	M,D

Stanford University M,D
Syracuse University M
Texas Tech University M,D
Tufts University M
The University of Akron M
University of Alaska Anchorage M
University of Alaska Fairbanks M
University of Central Florida M,D,O
University of Colorado at Boulder M
University of Colorado at Colorado Springs M
University of Dayton M
University of Denver M
University of Detroit Mercy M
University of Florida M,D,O
University of Kansas M
University of Louisiana at Lafayette M
University of Maryland, Baltimore County M
University of Massachusetts Amherst M
University of Michigan–Dearborn M
University of Minnesota, Duluth M
University of Missouri–Rolla M,D
University of New Orleans M,O
The University of North Carolina at Charlotte M
University of Southern California M
University of South Florida M,D
The University of Tennessee M
The University of Tennessee at Chattanooga M
University of Tulsa M
Virginia Polytechnic Institute and State University M
Wayne State University M
Western Michigan University M
Widener University M

■ ENGINEERING PHYSICS

Cornell University M,D
George Mason University M
Polytechnic University, Westchester Graduate Center M
Rensselaer Polytechnic Institute M,D
Stevens Institute of Technology M,D,O
University of California, San Diego M,D
University of Florida M,D,O
University of Maine M
University of Oklahoma M,D
University of South Florida M,D
University of Vermont M
University of Virginia M,D
University of Wisconsin–Madison M,D
Yale University M,D

■ ENGLISH

Abilene Christian University M
Adelphi University M
Andrews University M
Angelo State University M
Antioch University McGregor M
Appalachian State University M
Arcadia University M
Arizona State University M,D
Arkansas State University M,O
Arkansas Tech University M
Auburn University M,D
Austin Peay State University M
Ball State University M,D
Baylor University M,D
Belmont University M
Bemidji State University M
Boise State University M
Boston College M,D,O
Boston University M,D
Bowling Green State University M,D
Bradley University M
Brandeis University M,D
Bridgewater State College M
Brigham Young University M
Brooklyn College of the City University of New York M,D
Brown University M,D
Butler University M
California Polytechnic State University, San Luis Obispo M
California State Polytechnic University, Pomona M
California State University, Bakersfield M
California State University, Chico M
California State University, Dominguez Hills M,O
California State University, Fresno M
California State University, Fullerton M
California State University, Hayward M
California State University, Long Beach M
California State University, Los Angeles M
California State University, Northridge M
California State University, Sacramento M
California State University, San Bernardino M
California State University, San Marcos M
California State University, Stanislaus M
Carnegie Mellon University M,D
Case Western Reserve University M,D
The Catholic University of America M,D
Central Connecticut State University M
Central Michigan University M
Central Missouri State University M
Central Washington University M
Chapman University M
Chicago State University M
The Citadel, The Military College of South Carolina M
City College of the City University of New York M
Claremont Graduate University M,D
Clarion University of Pennsylvania M
Clark Atlanta University M
Clark University M
Clemson University M
Cleveland State University M
The College of New Jersey M
The College of Saint Rose M
College of Staten Island of the City University of New York M
Colorado State University M
Columbia University M,D
Converse College M
Cornell University M,D
DePaul University M
Duke University D
Duquesne University M,D
East Carolina University M
Eastern Illinois University M
Eastern Kentucky University M
Eastern Michigan University M
Eastern New Mexico University M
Eastern Washington University M
East Tennessee State University M
Emory University D
Emporia State University M
Fairleigh Dickinson University, Teaneck–Hackensack Campus M
Fayetteville State University M
Florida Atlantic University M
Florida International University M
Florida State University M,D
Fordham University M,D
Fort Hays State University M
Gannon University M
Gardner-Webb University M
George Mason University M
Georgetown University M
The George Washington University M,D
Georgia College and State University M
Georgia Southern University M
Georgia State University M,D
Governors State University M
Hardin-Simmons University M
Harvard University M,D,O
Henderson State University M
Hofstra University M
Holy Names College M
Howard University M,D
Humboldt State University M
Hunter College of the City University of New York M
Idaho State University M,D
Illinois State University M,D
Indiana State University M,O
Indiana University Bloomington M,D
Indiana University of Pennsylvania M,D
Indiana University–Purdue University Fort Wayne M
Indiana University–Purdue University Indianapolis M
Iona College M
Iowa State University of Science and Technology M,D
Jackson State University M
Jacksonville State University M
James Madison University M
John Carroll University M
Johns Hopkins University D
Kansas State University M
Kent State University M,D
Kutztown University of Pennsylvania M
Lamar University M
La Sierra University M
Lehigh University M,D
Lehman College of the City University of New York M
Long Island University, Brooklyn Campus M
Long Island University, C.W. Post Campus M
Longwood College M
Loras College M
Louisiana State University and Agricultural and Mechanical College M,D
Louisiana Tech University M
Loyola Marymount University M
Loyola University Chicago M,D
Maharishi University of Management M
Marquette University M,D
Marshall University M
Marymount University M
McNeese State University M
Miami University M,D
Michigan State University M,D
Middle Tennessee State University M,D
Midwestern State University M
Millersville University of Pennsylvania M
Minnesota State University, Mankato M
Mississippi College M
Mississippi State University M
Montana State University–Bozeman M
Montclair State University M
Morehead State University M
Morgan State University M
Murray State University M
New Mexico Highlands University M
New Mexico State University M,D
New York University M,D
North Carolina Agricultural and Technical State University M

North Carolina Central University	M
North Carolina State University	M
North Dakota State University	M
Northeastern Illinois University	M
Northeastern University	M,D,O
Northern Arizona University	M
Northern Illinois University	M,D
Northern Michigan University	M
Northwestern State University of Louisiana	M
Northwestern University	M,D
Northwest Missouri State University	M
Notre Dame de Namur University	M
Oakland University	M
The Ohio State University	M,D
Ohio University	M,D
Oklahoma State University	M,D
Old Dominion University	M
Oregon State University	M
Our Lady of the Lake University of San Antonio	M
The Pennsylvania State University University Park Campus	M,D
Pittsburg State University	M
Portland State University	M
Prairie View A&M University	M
Princeton University	D
Purdue University	M,D
Purdue University Calumet	M
Queens College of the City University of New York	M
Radford University	M
Rhode Island College	M
Rice University	M,D
Rivier College	M
Roosevelt University	M
Rutgers, The State University of New Jersey, Camden	M
Rutgers, The State University of New Jersey, Newark	M
Rutgers, The State University of New Jersey, New Brunswick	D
St. Bonaventure University	M
St. Cloud State University	M
St. John's University (NY)	M,D
Saint Louis University	M,D
Saint Xavier University	M,O
Salem State College	M
Salisbury State University	M
Sam Houston State University	M
San Diego State University	M
San Francisco State University	M,O
San Jose State University	M
Seton Hall University	M
Simmons College	M
Slippery Rock University of Pennsylvania	M
Sonoma State University	M
South Dakota State University	M
Southeastern Louisiana University	M
Southeast Missouri State University	M
Southern Connecticut State University	M
Southern Illinois University Carbondale	M,D
Southern Illinois University Edwardsville	M
Southern Methodist University	M
Southern Oregon University	M
Southwest Missouri State University	M
Southwest Texas State University	M
Stanford University	M,D
State University of New York at Albany	M,D
State University of New York at Binghamton	M,D
State University of New York at New Paltz	M
State University of New York at Oswego	M
State University of New York College at Brockport	M
State University of New York College at Buffalo	M
State University of New York College at Cortland	M
State University of New York College at Fredonia	M
State University of New York College at Potsdam	M
State University of West Georgia	M
Stephen F. Austin State University	M
Stetson University	M
Stony Brook University, State University of New York	M,D
Sul Ross State University	M
Syracuse University	M,D
Tarleton State University	M
Temple University	M,D
Tennessee State University	M
Tennessee Technological University	M
Texas A&M International University	M
Texas A&M University	M,D
Texas A&M University–Commerce	M,D
Texas A&M University–Corpus Christi	M
Texas A&M University–Kingsville	M
Texas Christian University	M,D
Texas Southern University	M
Texas Tech University	M,D
Texas Woman's University	M,D
Truman State University	M
Tufts University	M,D
Tulane University	M,D
University at Buffalo, The State University of New York	M,D
The University of Akron	M
The University of Alabama	M,D
The University of Alabama at Birmingham	M
The University of Alabama in Huntsville	M
University of Alaska Anchorage	M
University of Alaska Fairbanks	M
The University of Arizona	M,D
University of Arkansas	M,D
University of California, Berkeley	D
University of California, Davis	M,D
University of California, Irvine	M,D
University of California, Los Angeles	M,D
University of California, Riverside	M,D
University of California, San Diego	M,D
University of California, Santa Barbara	D
University of Central Arkansas	M
University of Central Florida	M,O
University of Central Oklahoma	M
University of Chicago	M,D
University of Cincinnati	M,D
University of Colorado at Boulder	M,D
University of Colorado at Denver	M
University of Connecticut	M,D
University of Dayton	M
University of Delaware	M,D
University of Denver	M,D
University of Florida	M,D
University of Georgia	M,D
University of Hawaii at Manoa	M,D
University of Houston	M,D
University of Houston–Clear Lake	M
University of Idaho	M
University of Illinois at Chicago	M,D
University of Illinois at Springfield	M
University of Illinois at Urbana–Champaign	M,D
University of Indianapolis	M
The University of Iowa	M,D
University of Kansas	M,D
University of Kentucky	M,D
University of Louisiana at Lafayette	M,D
University of Louisiana at Monroe	M
University of Louisville	M,D
University of Maine	M
University of Maryland, College Park	M,D
University of Massachusetts Amherst	M,D
University of Massachusetts Boston	M
The University of Memphis	M,D
University of Miami	M,D
University of Michigan	M,D,O
University of Minnesota, Duluth	M
University of Minnesota, Twin Cities Campus	M,D
University of Mississippi	M,D
University of Missouri–Columbia	M,D
University of Missouri–Kansas City	M,D
University of Missouri–St. Louis	M
The University of Montana–Missoula	M
University of Montevallo	M
University of Nebraska at Kearney	M
University of Nebraska at Omaha	M
University of Nebraska–Lincoln	M,D
University of Nevada, Las Vegas	M,D
University of Nevada, Reno	M,D
University of New Hampshire	M,D
University of New Mexico	M,D
University of New Orleans	M
University of North Alabama	M
The University of North Carolina at Chapel Hill	M,D
The University of North Carolina at Charlotte	M
The University of North Carolina at Greensboro	M,D,O
The University of North Carolina at Wilmington	M
University of North Dakota	M,D
University of Northern Colorado	M
University of Northern Iowa	M
University of North Florida	M
University of North Texas	M,D
University of Notre Dame	M,D
University of Oklahoma	M,D
University of Oregon	M,D
University of Pennsylvania	M,D
University of Pittsburgh	M,D
University of Puerto Rico, Mayagüez Campus	M
University of Puerto Rico, Río Piedras	M
University of Rhode Island	M,D
University of Richmond	M
University of Rochester	M,D
University of St. Thomas (MN)	M
The University of Scranton	M
University of South Alabama	M
University of South Carolina	M,D
University of South Dakota	M,D
University of Southern California	M,D
University of Southern Mississippi	M,D
University of South Florida	M,D
The University of Tennessee	M,D
The University of Tennessee at Chattanooga	M
The University of Texas at Arlington	M,D
The University of Texas at Austin	M,D
The University of Texas at Brownsville	M
The University of Texas at El Paso	M
The University of Texas at San Antonio	M
The University of Texas at Tyler	M
The University of Texas of the Permian Basin	M
The University of Texas–Pan American	M
University of the Incarnate Word	M
University of Toledo	M

University of Tulsa M,D
University of Utah M,D
University of Vermont M
University of Virginia M,D
University of Washington M,D
University of West Florida M
University of Wisconsin–Eau Claire M
University of Wisconsin–Madison M,D
University of Wisconsin–Milwaukee M,D
University of Wisconsin–Oshkosh M
University of Wisconsin–Stevens Point M
University of Wyoming M
Utah State University M
Valdosta State University M
Valparaiso University M
Vanderbilt University M,D
Villanova University M
Virginia Commonwealth University M
Virginia Polytechnic Institute and State University M
Virginia State University M
Wake Forest University M
Washington State University M,D
Washington University in St. Louis M,D
Wayne State University M,D
West Chester University of Pennsylvania M
Western Carolina University M
Western Connecticut State University M
Western Illinois University M
Western Kentucky University M
Western Michigan University M,D
Western Washington University M
Westfield State College M
West Texas A&M University M
West Virginia University M,D
Wichita State University M
William Paterson University of New Jersey M
Winona State University M
Winthrop University M
Wright State University M
Xavier University M
Yale University M,D
Youngstown State University M

■ ENGLISH AS A SECOND LANGUAGE

Adelphi University M,O
Alliant International University M,D
American University M,O
Andrews University M
Arizona State University M
Azusa Pacific University M,O
Ball State University M,D
Biola University M,D,O
Boston University M,O
Bowling Green State University M,D
Brigham Young University M,O
California State University, Dominguez Hills M,O
California State University, Fresno M
California State University, Fullerton M
California State University, Los Angeles M
California State University, Sacramento M
California State University, San Bernardino M
California State University, Stanislaus M
Carson-Newman College M
The Catholic University of America M,D
Central Connecticut State University M
Central Michigan University M
Central Missouri State University M
Central Washington University M
Cleveland State University M
The College of New Jersey M,O
The College of New Rochelle M,O
College of Notre Dame of Maryland M
College of Our Lady of the Elms M,O
Eastern College O
Eastern Michigan University M
Eastern Nazarene College M,O
Emporia State University M
Fairfield University M,O
Florida International University M
Fordham University M,D,O
Framingham State College M
Fresno Pacific University M
George Mason University M
Georgetown University M,D,O
Georgia State University M,O
Gonzaga University M
Grand Canyon University M
Hawaii Pacific University M
Heritage College M
Hofstra University M
Holy Names College O
Hunter College of the City University of New York M
Indiana State University M
Indiana University Bloomington M,D,O
Indiana University of Pennsylvania M,D
Inter American University of Puerto Rico, Metropolitan Campus M
Inter American University of Puerto Rico, San Germán Campus M
Kean University M,O
Lehman College of the City University of New York M
Long Island University, Brooklyn Campus M
Lynn University M,D
Madonna University M
Manhattanville College M
Marymount University M
Mercy College M,O
Michigan State University M,D
Montclair State University M
Monterey Institute of International Studies M
Murray State University M
Nazareth College of Rochester M
New Jersey City University M
Newman University M
New York University M,D,O
Northern Arizona University M,D
Nova Southeastern University M,O
Ohio University M
Oklahoma City University M
Oral Roberts University M,D
The Pennsylvania State University University Park Campus M
Pontifical Catholic University of Puerto Rico M,D
Portland State University M
Prescott College M
Queens College of the City University of New York M
Rhode Island College M
Rutgers, The State University of New Jersey, New Brunswick M,D
St. Cloud State University M
St. John's University (NY) M
Saint Michael's College M,O
Salem State College M
Salisbury State University M
Sam Houston State University M,O
San Francisco State University M
San Jose State University M,O
School for International Training M
Seattle Pacific University M
Seattle University M,O
Seton Hall University M,O
Shenandoah University M,D,O
Simmons College M
Southeast Missouri State University M
Southern Connecticut State University M
Southern Illinois University Carbondale M
Southern Illinois University Edwardsville M
State University of New York at New Paltz M
Stony Brook University, State University of New York M,D
Teachers College, Columbia University M,D
Texas A&M University–Kingsville M
Universidad del Turabo M
University at Buffalo, The State University of New York M,D,O
The University of Alabama M,D
The University of Arizona M,D
University of California, Los Angeles M
University of Central Florida M,O
University of Central Oklahoma M
University of Colorado at Denver M
University of Delaware M,D
The University of Findlay M
University of Florida M,D,O
University of Guam M
University of Hawaii at Manoa M,D
University of Houston M,D
University of Idaho M
University of Illinois at Chicago M
University of Illinois at Urbana–Champaign M
University of Maryland, Baltimore County M
University of Maryland, College Park M,D,O
University of Massachusetts Boston M
University of Miami M,D,O
University of Minnesota, Twin Cities Campus M
University of Nevada, Las Vegas M,D,O
University of Nevada, Reno M,D
University of Northern Iowa M
University of Pennsylvania M,D
University of Pittsburgh M,O
University of Puerto Rico, Río Piedras M
University of San Francisco M,D
University of South Carolina M,D,O
University of Southern California M,D
University of Southern Maine M,O
University of South Florida M
The University of Tennessee M,D,O
The University of Texas at Brownsville M
The University of Texas at San Antonio M,D
The University of Texas–Pan American M
University of Toledo M
University of Washington M,D
Wagner College M
Wayne State College M
West Chester University of Pennsylvania M
Western Kentucky University M
West Virginia University M
Whitworth College M
Wright State University M

■ ENGLISH EDUCATION

Alabama State University M,O
Albany State University M
Alfred University M
Andrews University M
Appalachian State University M
Arcadia University M,O
Arkansas State University M,O
Arkansas Tech University M
Armstrong Atlantic State University M

Auburn University	M,D,O
Austin Peay State University	M
Belmont University	M
Boston College	M
Boston University	M,D,O
Brooklyn College of the City University of New York	M
Brown University	M
California Baptist University	M
California State University, San Bernardino	M
Campbell University	M
Carthage College	M,O
Central Missouri State University	M
Chadron State College	M,O
Chapman University	M
Charleston Southern University	M
Clemson University	M
College of Our Lady of the Elms	M,O
The College of William and Mary	M
Colorado State University	M
Columbia College Chicago	M
Columbus State University	M,O
Delta State University	M
DeSales University	M
Eastern Kentucky University	M
Edinboro University of Pennsylvania	M
Fitchburg State College	M
Florida Atlantic University	M
Florida Gulf Coast University	M
Florida International University	M
Florida State University	M,D,O
Framingham State College	M
Gardner-Webb University	M
Georgia College and State University	M,O
Georgia Southern University	M,O
Georgia State University	M,D,O
Henderson State University	M
Hofstra University	M,O
Hunter College of the City University of New York	M
Indiana University Bloomington	M,D
Indiana University of Pennsylvania	M,D
Indiana University–Purdue University Fort Wayne	M
Indiana University–Purdue University Indianapolis	M
Iona College	M
Jackson State University	M
Jacksonville University	M
Kutztown University of Pennsylvania	M,O
Lehman College of the City University of New York	M
Long Island University, Brooklyn Campus	M
Long Island University, C.W. Post Campus	M
Longwood College	M
Louisiana Tech University	M,D,O
Loyola Marymount University	M
Lynchburg College	M
Manhattanville College	M
McNeese State University	M
Mercer University	M,O
Miami University	M,D
Michigan State University	M,D
Millersville University of Pennsylvania	M
Minnesota State University, Mankato	M
Minot State University	M
Montclair State University	M
National-Louis University	M,O
New York University	M,D,O
North Carolina Agricultural and Technical State University	M
Northeastern Illinois University	M
Northeastern University	M
Northern State University	M
North Georgia College & State University	M,O
Northwestern State University of Louisiana	M
Northwest Missouri State University	M
Notre Dame de Namur University	M,O
Nova Southeastern University	M,O
Oregon State University	M
Plattsburgh State University of New York	M
Plymouth State College	M
Portland State University	M
Purdue University	M,D,O
Queens College of the City University of New York	M,O
Quinnipiac University	M
Rider University	O
Rockford College	M
Rollins College	M
Rutgers, The State University of New Jersey, New Brunswick	M
Sage Graduate School	M
Salem State College	M,O
Salisbury State University	M
San Francisco State University	M,O
South Carolina State University	M
Southern Illinois University Edwardsville	M
Stanford University	M,D
State University of New York at Binghamton	M
State University of New York College at Brockport	M
State University of New York College at Buffalo	M
State University of New York College at Cortland	M
State University of West Georgia	M,O
Stony Brook University, State University of New York	M,O
Syracuse University	M,D,O
Teachers College, Columbia University	M,D
Texas A&M University–Commerce	M,D
Texas Tech University	M,D,O
University at Buffalo, The State University of New York	M,D,O
University of Alaska Fairbanks	M,O
The University of Arizona	M,D
University of California, Berkeley	M,D,O
University of Central Florida	M
University of Colorado at Denver	M
University of Connecticut	M,D
University of Delaware	M,D
University of Florida	M,D,O
University of Georgia	M,D,O
University of Idaho	M
University of Illinois at Chicago	M,D
University of Indianapolis	M
The University of Iowa	M,D
University of Louisiana at Monroe	M,D,O
University of Michigan	M,D
University of Minnesota, Twin Cities Campus	M
The University of Montana–Missoula	M
University of Nevada, Las Vegas	M,D,O
University of Nevada, Reno	M,D
University of New Hampshire	M,D
The University of North Carolina at Chapel Hill	M
The University of North Carolina at Greensboro	M,D,O
The University of North Carolina at Pembroke	M
University of Oklahoma	M,D
University of Pittsburgh	M,D
University of Puerto Rico, Río Piedras	M,D
University of South Carolina	M,D
University of South Florida	M,D
The University of Tennessee	M,D,O
The University of Texas at El Paso	M
The University of Texas at Tyler	M
University of the District of Columbia	M
University of Vermont	M
University of Washington	M,D
The University of West Alabama	M
University of Wisconsin–Eau Claire	M
University of Wisconsin–Madison	M,D
University of Wisconsin–River Falls	M
Vanderbilt University	M,D
Washington State University	M,D
Wayne State College	M
Western Carolina University	M
Western Connecticut State University	M
Western Kentucky University	M
Widener University	M,D
Wilkes University	M
William Carey College	M
Worcester State College	M
Xavier University	M

■ ENTOMOLOGY

Auburn University	M,D
Clemson University	M,D
Colorado State University	M,D
Cornell University	M,D
Iowa State University of Science and Technology	M,D
Kansas State University	M,D
Louisiana State University and Agricultural and Mechanical College	M,D
Michigan State University	M,D
Mississippi State University	M,D
Montana State University–Bozeman	M
New Mexico State University	M
North Carolina State University	M,D
North Dakota State University	M,D
The Ohio State University	M,D
Oklahoma State University	M,D
Oregon State University	M,D
The Pennsylvania State University University Park Campus	M,D
Purdue University	M,D
Rutgers, The State University of New Jersey, New Brunswick	M,D
South Dakota State University	M
Texas A&M University	M,D
Texas Tech University	M,D
The University of Arizona	M,D
University of Arkansas	M,D
University of California, Davis	M,D
University of California, Riverside	M,D
University of Connecticut	M,D
University of Delaware	M,D
University of Florida	M,D
University of Georgia	M,D
University of Hawaii at Manoa	M,D
University of Idaho	M,D
University of Illinois at Urbana–Champaign	M,D
University of Kentucky	M,D
University of Maine	M
University of Maryland, College Park	M,D
University of Massachusetts Amherst	M,D
University of Minnesota, Twin Cities Campus	M,D
University of Missouri–Columbia	M,D
University of Nebraska–Lincoln	M,D
University of North Dakota	M,D
University of Rhode Island	M,D
The University of Tennessee	M
University of Wisconsin–Madison	M,D
University of Wyoming	M,D

Virginia Polytechnic Institute and State University M,D
Washington State University M,D
West Virginia University M,D

■ ENTREPRENEURSHIP

American University M
Bentley College M,O
California Lutheran University M
California State University, Hayward M
Columbia University M
DePaul University M
Fairleigh Dickinson University, Florham-Madison Campus M
Fairleigh Dickinson University, Teaneck–Hackensack Campus M
Georgia State University M,D
Indiana University Bloomington M
Kennesaw State University M
Michigan State University M,D
Rensselaer Polytechnic Institute M,D
Suffolk University M,O
The University of Akron M
University of Colorado at Boulder M,D
University of Houston D
University of Minnesota, Twin Cities Campus M
University of Wisconsin–Madison M

■ ENVIRONMENTAL AND OCCUPATIONAL HEALTH

Anna Maria College M
Boston University M,D
California State University, Fresno M
California State University, Northridge M
Central Missouri State University M,O
Colorado State University M,D
Columbia University M,D
East Carolina University M
East Tennessee State University M
Emory University M
The George Washington University M
Harvard University M,D
Hunter College of the City University of New York M
Illinois State University M
Indiana University of Pennsylvania M
Johns Hopkins University M,D
Loma Linda University M
Montclair State University M,O
Murray State University M
New York University M,D
Northwestern University M,D
Oregon State University M
Polytechnic University, Brooklyn Campus M
Purdue University M,D
San Diego State University M,D
State University of New York at Albany M,D
Stony Brook University, State University of New York M,O
Temple University M
Towson University D
Tufts University M,D
Tulane University M,D
The University of Alabama at Birmingham D
University of California, Berkeley M,D
University of California, Irvine M,D
University of California, Los Angeles M,D
University of Cincinnati M,D
University of Georgia M,D
University of Illinois at Chicago M,D
The University of Iowa M,D
University of Miami M
University of Michigan M,D
University of Minnesota, Twin Cities Campus M,D
University of Nevada, Reno M,D
University of New Haven M
The University of North Carolina at Chapel Hill M,D
University of Oklahoma M,D
University of Pittsburgh M,D
University of South Carolina M,D
University of Southern Mississippi M
University of South Florida M,D
University of the Sacred Heart M
University of Washington M,D
University of Wisconsin–Eau Claire M
Virginia Commonwealth University M
Wayne State University M,O
West Chester University of Pennsylvania M
Western Kentucky University M
Yale University M,D

■ ENVIRONMENTAL BIOLOGY

Antioch New England Graduate School M
Baylor University M,D
Duquesne University M
Eastern Illinois University M
Emporia State University M
Georgia State University M,D
Governors State University M
Hood College M
Montana State University–Bozeman M,D
Morgan State University D
New York University M,D
Ohio University M,D
Rutgers, The State University of New Jersey, New Brunswick M,D
Sonoma State University M
State University of New York College of Environmental Science and Forestry M,D
Tennessee Technological University M
University of California, Berkeley M
University of Colorado at Boulder M,D
University of Louisiana at Lafayette M,D
University of Louisville D
University of Massachusetts Amherst M,D
University of Massachusetts Boston D
University of Nevada, Las Vegas D
University of North Dakota M,D
University of Notre Dame M,D
University of Southern Mississippi M,D
University of Wisconsin–Madison M,D
Washington University in St. Louis D
West Virginia University M,D

■ ENVIRONMENTAL DESIGN

Arizona State University D
Cornell University M
Michigan State University M,D
San Diego State University M
San Jose State University M
Texas Tech University D
University of California, Berkeley M,D
University of California, Irvine M,D
University of Missouri–Columbia M
Virginia Polytechnic Institute and State University D
Yale University M

■ ENVIRONMENTAL EDUCATION

Antioch New England Graduate School M,D
Arcadia University M,O
Brooklyn College of the City University of New York M
California State University, Fullerton M
California State University, San Bernardino M
City College of the City University of New York M
Florida Institute of Technology M,D,O
Gannon University M,O
Indiana University Bloomington M,D,O
Lesley University M,O
Maryville University of Saint Louis M
New York University M
Northern Illinois University M,D
Prescott College M
Rowan University M
Slippery Rock University of Pennsylvania M
Southern Connecticut State University M,O
Southern Oregon University M
State University of New York at New Paltz M
Universidad Metropolitana M
University of New Hampshire M
West Virginia University M

■ ENVIRONMENTAL ENGINEERING

Auburn University M,D
California Institute of Technology M,D
California Polytechnic State University, San Luis Obispo M
Carnegie Mellon University M,D
The Catholic University of America M
Clarkson University M,D
Clemson University M,D
Colorado State University M,D
Columbia University M,D
Cornell University M,D
Dartmouth College M,D
Drexel University M,D
Duke University M,D
Florida Agricultural and Mechanical University M,D
Florida International University M
Florida State University M,D
The George Washington University M,D,O
Georgia Institute of Technology M,D
Harvard University M,D
Howard University M
Idaho State University M,D
Illinois Institute of Technology M,D
Iowa State University of Science and Technology M,D
Johns Hopkins University M,D
Lamar University M
Lehigh University M,D
Louisiana State University and Agricultural and Mechanical College M,D
Manhattan College M
Marquette University M,D
Massachusetts Institute of Technology M,D,O
Michigan State University M,D
Michigan Technological University M,D
Montana State University–Bozeman M,D
New Jersey Institute of Technology M,D
New Mexico Institute of Mining and Technology M
New Mexico State University M,D
New York Institute of Technology M
North Carolina Agricultural and Technical State University M
North Dakota State University M
Northeastern University M,D
Northwestern University M,D
Ohio University M,D
Oklahoma State University M,D

Old Dominion University M,D
Oregon State University M,D
The Pennsylvania State University Harrisburg Campus of the Capital College M
The Pennsylvania State University University Park Campus M,D
Polytechnic University, Brooklyn Campus M
Polytechnic University, Westchester Graduate Center M
Princeton University D
Rensselaer Polytechnic Institute M,D
Rice University M,D
Rutgers, The State University of New Jersey, New Brunswick M,D
South Dakota State University M
Southern Methodist University M,D
Stanford University M,D,O
State University of New York College of Environmental Science and Forestry M,D
Stevens Institute of Technology M,D,O
Syracuse University M,D
Temple University M
Texas A&M University M,D
Texas A&M University–Kingsville M
Texas Tech University M,D
Tufts University M,D
Tulane University M,D
University at Buffalo, The State University of New York M,D
The University of Alabama M
The University of Alabama at Birmingham M,D
The University of Alabama in Huntsville M
University of Alaska Fairbanks M
The University of Arizona M,D
University of Arkansas M
University of California, Berkeley M,D
University of California, Davis M,D,O
University of California, Irvine M,D
University of California, Los Angeles M,D
University of California, Riverside M,D
University of California, Santa Barbara M,D
University of Central Florida M,D,O
University of Cincinnati M,D
University of Colorado at Boulder M,D
University of Connecticut M,D
University of Dayton M
University of Delaware M,D
University of Detroit Mercy M,D
University of Florida M,D,O
University of Houston M,D
University of Idaho M
University of Illinois at Urbana–Champaign M,D
The University of Iowa M,D
University of Kansas M,D
University of Louisville M,D
University of Maine M,D
University of Maryland, College Park M,D
University of Massachusetts Amherst M
University of Massachusetts Lowell M
The University of Memphis M,D
University of Michigan M,D,O
University of Missouri–Columbia M,D
University of Missouri–Rolla M,D
University of Nebraska–Lincoln M,D
University of Nevada, Las Vegas M,D
University of Nevada, Reno M,D
University of New Haven M,O
The University of North Carolina at Chapel Hill M,D
University of Notre Dame M,D
University of Oklahoma M,D
University of Pennsylvania M,D
University of Pittsburgh M,D
University of Rhode Island M,D
University of Southern California M,D
University of South Florida M,D
The University of Tennessee M
The University of Texas at Arlington M,D
The University of Texas at Austin M
The University of Texas at El Paso M,D
University of Utah M,D
University of Virginia M,D
University of Washington M,D
University of Wisconsin–Madison M,D
University of Wyoming M,D
Utah State University M,D,O
Vanderbilt University M,D
Villanova University M
Virginia Polytechnic Institute and State University M,D
Washington State University M
Washington University in St. Louis M,D
Wayne State University M,D
West Virginia University M,D
Worcester Polytechnic Institute M,D,O
Youngstown State University M

■ ENVIRONMENTAL POLICY AND RESOURCE MANAGEMENT

American University M,D,O
Antioch New England Graduate School M,D
Antioch University Seattle M
Baylor University M
Bemidji State University M
Boise State University M
Boston University M,O
Brown University M
California State University, Fullerton M
Central Washington University M
Clark University M
Clemson University M
Colorado State University M,D
Columbia University M
Cornell University M,D
Duke University M,D
Duquesne University M,O
East Carolina University D
Florida Gulf Coast University M
Florida Institute of Technology M,D
Florida International University M
Friends University M
George Mason University M,D
The George Washington University M
Hardin-Simmons University M
Illinois Institute of Technology M
Johns Hopkins University M,D,O
Kansas State University M
Lamar University M
Long Island University, C.W. Post Campus M
Longwood College M
Louisiana State University and Agricultural and Mechanical College M
Michigan State University M,D
Michigan Technological University M
Montana State University–Bozeman M
Montclair State University M,O
Monterey Institute of International Studies M
National University M
New Jersey Institute of Technology M,D
New Mexico Highlands University M
New York Institute of Technology M,O
North Carolina State University M
North Dakota State University M
Northeastern Illinois University M
Ohio University M
Oregon State University M,D
The Pennsylvania State University University Park Campus M
Portland State University M,D
Prescott College M
Princeton University M,D
Purdue University M,D
Rensselaer Polytechnic Institute M,D
Rochester Institute of Technology M
St. Cloud State University M
Saint Joseph's University M
Saint Mary's University of Minnesota M
San Francisco State University M
San Jose State University M
Seton Hall University M,O
Shippensburg University of Pennsylvania M
Slippery Rock University of Pennsylvania M
Southwest Missouri State University M
Southwest Texas State University M
Stanford University M
State University of New York at Albany M
State University of New York College of Environmental Science and Forestry M,D
Texas Tech University D
Troy State University M
Tufts University M,D,O
Universidad del Turabo M
Universidad Metropolitana M
University of Alaska Fairbanks M
The University of Arizona M
University of California, Berkeley M,D
University of California, Irvine M,D
University of California, Santa Barbara M,D
University of California, Santa Cruz D
University of Chicago M,D
University of Connecticut M
University of Delaware M,D
University of Denver M
University of Hawaii at Manoa M
University of Houston–Clear Lake M
University of Idaho M,D
University of Illinois at Springfield M
University of Maine M
University of Maryland University College M
University of Michigan M,D
University of Minnesota, Twin Cities Campus M
University of Missouri–St. Louis M,D,O
The University of Montana–Missoula M
University of Nevada, Reno M
University of New Hampshire M,D
The University of North Carolina at Chapel Hill M,D
University of Oregon M
University of Rhode Island M,D
University of St. Thomas (MN) M,O
University of San Francisco M
University of South Carolina M
University of Southern California M
The University of Tennessee M,D
The University of Texas at Austin M
University of Vermont M,D
University of Washington M,D
University of Wisconsin–Green Bay M
University of Wisconsin–Madison M,D
Virginia Commonwealth University M
Webster University M
West Virginia University M,D
Wright State University M
Yale University M,D

■ ENVIRONMENTAL SCIENCES

Alabama Agricultural and Mechanical University	M,D
Alaska Pacific University	M
American University	M
Antioch New England Graduate School	D
Arkansas State University	M,D,O
California State University, Chico	M
California State University, Fullerton	M
City College of the City University of New York	M,D
Clemson University	M,D
Cleveland State University	M,D
College of Staten Island of the City University of New York	M
Columbus State University	M
Drexel University	M,D
Duke University	M,D
Duquesne University	M,O
Florida Atlantic University	M
Florida Institute of Technology	M,D
Florida International University	M
George Mason University	M,D
Harvard University	M,D
Humboldt State University	M
Idaho State University	M,D
Indiana University Bloomington	M,D
Inter American University of Puerto Rico, San Germán Campus	M
Jackson State University	M,D
Lehigh University	M,D
Long Island University, C.W. Post Campus	M
Louisiana State University and Agricultural and Mechanical College	M,D
Loyola Marymount University	M
Marshall University	M
McNeese State University	M
Miami University	M
Michigan State University	M,D
Minnesota State University, Mankato	M
Montana State University–Bozeman	M,D
Montclair State University	M,O
New Jersey Institute of Technology	M,D
New Mexico Highlands University	M
New Mexico Institute of Mining and Technology	M,D
Northern Arizona University	M
Nova Southeastern University	M,D
Oakland University	M,D
The Ohio State University	M,D
Ohio University	M
Oklahoma State University	M,D
Pace University, White Plains Campus	M
The Pennsylvania State University Harrisburg Campus of the Capital College	M
The Pennsylvania State University University Park Campus	M
Polytechnic University, Brooklyn Campus	M
Portland State University	M,D
Queens College of the City University of New York	M
Rensselaer Polytechnic Institute	M,D
Rice University	M,D
Rutgers, The State University of New Jersey, New Brunswick	M,D
South Dakota State University	D
Southern Illinois University Edwardsville	M
Southern University and Agricultural and Mechanical College	M
Stanford University	M,D,O
State University of New York at Albany	M
State University of New York College of Environmental Science and Forestry	M,D
Stephen F. Austin State University	M
Stony Brook University, State University of New York	M
Tarleton State University	M
Tennessee Technological University	D
Texas A&M University–Corpus Christi	M
Texas Christian University	M
Texas Tech University	M,D
Towson University	M,O
Tufts University	M,D
Tuskegee University	M
The University of Akron	M
The University of Alabama in Huntsville	M,D
University of Alaska Anchorage	M
University of Alaska Fairbanks	M
The University of Arizona	M,D
University of California, Berkeley	M,D
University of California, Davis	M,D
University of California, Los Angeles	D
University of California, Riverside	M,D
University of California, Santa Barbara	M,D
University of Chicago	D
University of Cincinnati	M,D
University of Colorado at Denver	M
University of Guam	M
University of Houston–Clear Lake	M
University of Idaho	M
University of Illinois at Urbana–Champaign	M,D
University of Kansas	M,D
University of Maine	M,D
University of Maryland	M,D
University of Maryland, Baltimore County	M,D
University of Maryland, College Park	M,D
University of Maryland Eastern Shore	M,D
University of Massachusetts Boston	M,D
University of Massachusetts Lowell	M,D
University of Michigan–Dearborn	M
The University of Montana–Missoula	M
University of Nevada, Las Vegas	M
University of Nevada, Reno	M,D
University of New Haven	M
The University of North Carolina at Chapel Hill	M,D
University of Northern Iowa	M
University of North Texas	M,D
University of Oklahoma	M,D
The University of Tennessee at Chattanooga	M
The University of Texas at Arlington	M,D
The University of Texas at El Paso	D
The University of Texas at San Antonio	M
University of Virginia	M,D
University of Wisconsin–Green Bay	M
University of Wisconsin–Madison	M,D
Virginia Commonwealth University	M
Virginia Polytechnic Institute and State University	M,D
Washington State University	M,D
Washington University in St. Louis	M
Western Connecticut State University	M
Western Washington University	M
West Texas A&M University	M
Wichita State University	M
Wright State University	M
Yale University	M,D

■ EPIDEMIOLOGY

Boston University	M,D
Brown University	M,D
California State University, Long Beach	M
Case Western Reserve University	M,D
Columbia University	M,D
Cornell University	M,D
Emory University	M,D
Georgetown University	M
The George Washington University	M,D
Harvard University	M,D
Johns Hopkins University	M,D
Loma Linda University	M,D
Michigan State University	M
North Carolina State University	M,D
Purdue University	M,D
San Diego State University	M,D
Stanford University	M,D
State University of New York at Albany	M,D
Texas A&M University	M,D
Tufts University	M,D
Tulane University	M,D
University at Buffalo, The State University of New York	M,D
The University of Alabama at Birmingham	D
The University of Arizona	M,D
University of California, Berkeley	M,D
University of California, Davis	M,D
University of California, Los Angeles	M,D
University of California, San Diego	D
University of Cincinnati	M,D
University of Hawaii at Manoa	M
University of Illinois at Chicago	M,D
The University of Iowa	M,D
University of Maryland	M,D
University of Maryland, Baltimore County	M
University of Miami	D
University of Michigan	M,D
University of Minnesota, Twin Cities Campus	M,D
The University of North Carolina at Chapel Hill	M,D
University of Pennsylvania	M,D
University of Pittsburgh	M,D
University of South Carolina	M,D
University of Southern California	M,D
University of South Florida	M,D
University of Virginia	M
University of Washington	M,D
Wake Forest University	M
Yale University	M,D

■ ERGONOMICS AND HUMAN FACTORS

Bentley College	M
The Catholic University of America	M
Clemson University	M,D
Cornell University	M
Embry-Riddle Aeronautical University	M
Florida Institute of Technology	M
New York University	M,D
Purdue University	M,D
Rensselaer Polytechnic Institute	M
San Jose State University	M
Tufts University	M,D
University of Central Florida	M,D,O
The University of Iowa	M,D
University of Miami	M,D
Wright State University	M,D

■ ETHICS

Biola University	P,M,D
Claremont Graduate University	M,D
Marquette University	M,D

St. Edward's University	M
University of Baltimore	M
University of Maryland, Baltimore County	M,O
University of Nevada, Las Vegas	M

■ EVOLUTIONARY BIOLOGY

Arizona State University	M,D
Brown University	D
Columbia University	D,O
Cornell University	D
Emory University	D
Florida State University	M,D
George Mason University	M
Harvard University	D
Indiana University Bloomington	M,D
Iowa State University of Science and Technology	M,D
Lehigh University	D
Marquette University	M,D
Michigan State University	M,D
New York University	M,D
Northwestern University	D
The Ohio State University	M,D
The Pennsylvania State University University Park Campus	M,D
Princeton University	D
Purdue University	M,D
Rice University	M,D
Rutgers, The State University of New Jersey, New Brunswick	M,D
State University of New York at Albany	M,D
Stony Brook University, State University of New York	D
The University of Arizona	M,D
University of California, Davis	D
University of California, Irvine	M,D
University of California, Riverside	D
University of California, San Diego	D
University of California, Santa Barbara	M,D
University of Chicago	D
University of Colorado at Boulder	M,D
University of Delaware	M,D
University of Hawaii at Manoa	M,D
University of Illinois at Chicago	M,D
University of Illinois at Urbana–Champaign	D
University of Louisiana at Lafayette	M,D
University of Massachusetts Amherst	M,D
University of Miami	M,D
University of Michigan	M,D
University of Minnesota, Twin Cities Campus	M,D
University of Missouri–St. Louis	M,D,O
University of Nevada, Reno	D
The University of North Carolina at Chapel Hill	M,D
University of Notre Dame	M,D
University of Oregon	M,D
University of Pittsburgh	M,D
University of Rochester	M,D
University of South Carolina	M,D
The University of Tennessee	M,D
The University of Texas at Austin	M,D
University of Utah	M,D
Virginia Polytechnic Institute and State University	M,D
Washington University in St. Louis	D
Yale University	D

■ EXERCISE AND SPORTS SCIENCE

American University	M
Appalachian State University	M
Arizona State University	M,D
Armstrong Atlantic State University	M
Ashland University	M,D
Austin Peay State University	M
Ball State University	D
Barry University	M
Benedictine University	M
Bloomsburg University of Pennsylvania	M
Boise State University	M
Brigham Young University	M,D
Brooklyn College of the City University of New York	M
California Baptist University	M
California State University, Fresno	M
California University of Pennsylvania	M
Case Western Reserve University	M,D
Central Connecticut State University	M
Central Michigan University	M
Central Missouri State University	M
Cleveland State University	M
The College of St. Scholastica	M
Colorado State University	M
East Carolina University	M,D
East Stroudsburg University of Pennsylvania	M
Florida Atlantic University	M
Florida State University	M,D
George Mason University	M
The George Washington University	M
Georgia State University	M,D
Howard University	M
Indiana State University	M
Indiana University Bloomington	M,D,O
Indiana University of Pennsylvania	M
Iowa State University of Science and Technology	M,D
Ithaca College	M
Kent State University	M,D
Long Island University, Brooklyn Campus	M
Marshall University	M
Miami University	M
Michigan State University	M,D
Mississippi State University	M
Montclair State University	M
Morehead State University	M
New Mexico Highlands University	M
Northeastern Illinois University	M
Northeastern University	M
Northern Michigan University	M
Oakland University	M
Ohio University	M
Oregon State University	M,D
Purdue University	M,D
Queens College of the City University of New York	M
St. Cloud State University	M
San Diego State University	M
Seton Hall University	M
Southern Connecticut State University	M
Southern Illinois University Edwardsville	M,O
Springfield College	M,D,O
Syracuse University	M,O
Texas Tech University	M
Texas Woman's University	M
University at Buffalo, The State University of New York	M,D
The University of Akron	M
University of California, Davis	M
University of Connecticut	M,D
University of Dayton	M
University of Delaware	M
University of Florida	M,D
University of Georgia	M,D,O
University of Houston	M,D
University of Houston–Clear Lake	M
The University of Iowa	M,D
University of Louisville	M
University of Massachusetts Amherst	M,D
The University of Memphis	M
University of Miami	M,D
University of Mississippi	M,D
University of Missouri–Columbia	M,D
The University of Montana–Missoula	M
University of Nebraska at Kearney	M
University of Nevada, Las Vegas	M
University of New Orleans	M,O
The University of North Carolina at Chapel Hill	M
The University of North Carolina at Greensboro	M,D
University of North Florida	M,O
University of Oklahoma	M
University of Oregon	M,D
University of Pittsburgh	M
University of South Alabama	M
University of South Carolina	M,D
The University of Tennessee	M,D,O
The University of Texas at El Paso	M
The University of Texas at Tyler	M
University of the Pacific	M
University of Toledo	M
University of Utah	M,D
University of West Florida	M
University of Wisconsin–La Crosse	M
Virginia Polytechnic Institute and State University	M,D
Wake Forest University	M
Wayne State College	M
West Chester University of Pennsylvania	M,O
Western Michigan University	M
West Texas A&M University	M
West Virginia University	M,D
Wichita State University	M

■ EXPERIMENTAL PSYCHOLOGY

American University	M,D
Appalachian State University	M
Bowling Green State University	M,D
Brooklyn College of the City University of New York	M,D
California State University, San Bernardino	M
Case Western Reserve University	D
The Catholic University of America	M,D
Central Michigan University	M,D
Central Washington University	M
City College of the City University of New York	M,D
Cleveland State University	M
The College of William and Mary	M
Colorado State University	D
Columbia University	M,D
Cornell University	D
DePaul University	M,D
Duke University	D
Fairleigh Dickinson University, Florham-Madison Campus	M
George Mason University	M
Harvard University	M,D
Howard University	M,D
Illinois State University	M,D,O
Johns Hopkins University	D
Kent State University	M,D
Lehigh University	D
Long Island University, C.W. Post Campus	M
Miami University	D
Morehead State University	M
Northeastern University	M,D
The Ohio State University	D
Ohio University	D
Oklahoma State University	M,D

St. John's University (NY)	M
Saint Louis University	M,D
Southern Illinois University Carbondale	M,D
State University of New York at Albany	M,D
Stony Brook University, State University of New York	D
Syracuse University	M,D
Temple University	D
Texas Tech University	M,D
Towson University	M,O
University of California, Santa Cruz	D
University of Cincinnati	M,D
University of Connecticut	M,D
University of Dayton	M
University of Hartford	M
University of Louisville	D
University of Maine	M,D
University of Maryland, College Park	M,D
The University of Memphis	M,D
University of Mississippi	M,D
University of Missouri–St. Louis	M,D,O
The University of Montana–Missoula	D
University of Nebraska at Omaha	M,D,O
The University of North Carolina at Chapel Hill	D
University of North Dakota	M,D
University of North Texas	M,D
University of Rhode Island	D
University of South Carolina	M,D
University of South Florida	D
The University of Tennessee	M,D
The University of Tennessee at Chattanooga	M
The University of Texas at Arlington	M,D
The University of Texas at El Paso	M,D
The University of Texas–Pan American	M
University of Toledo	M,D
University of Wisconsin–Oshkosh	M
Washington University in St. Louis	M,D
Western Michigan University	M,D,O
Xavier University	M,D

■ FACILITIES MANAGEMENT

Cornell University	M
Indiana State University	M
Indiana University of Pennsylvania	M
Michigan State University	M,D
Pratt Institute	M
University of North Texas	M,O

■ FILM, TELEVISION, AND VIDEO

American University	M
Antioch University McGregor	M
Boston University	M
Brigham Young University	M
Brooklyn College of the City University of New York	M
California State University, Fullerton	M
Carnegie Mellon University	M
Central Michigan University	M
Chapman University	M
Claremont Graduate University	M
Columbia College Chicago	M
Columbia University	M
Emerson College	M
Florida State University	M
George Mason University	M
Howard University	M
Loyola Marymount University	M
Montana State University–Bozeman	M
New Mexico Highlands University	M
New York University	M
Northwestern University	M,D
Ohio University	M
Rochester Institute of Technology	M
San Diego State University	M
San Francisco State University	M
Stanford University	M,D
Syracuse University	M
Temple University	M
The University of Alabama	M
University of California, Los Angeles	M,D
University of Denver	M
The University of Iowa	M
The University of Memphis	M,D
University of Miami	M,D
University of Michigan	O
The University of Montana–Missoula	M
University of New Orleans	M
The University of North Carolina at Greensboro	M
University of North Texas	M
University of Oklahoma	M
University of Southern California	M
The University of Texas at Austin	M,D
University of Utah	M
University of Wisconsin–Milwaukee	M

■ FINANCE AND BANKING

Adelphi University	M
Alabama Agricultural and Mechanical University	M
Alliant International University	M,D
American University	M,D,O
Arizona State University	M,D
Bentley College	M,O
Bernard M. Baruch College of the City University of New York	M,D
Boston College	M,D
Boston University	P,M,D
Brandeis University	M,D
Bridgewater State College	M
California Lutheran University	M
California State University, Fullerton	M
California State University, Hayward	M
California State University, Los Angeles	M
California State University, Northridge	M
Cardinal Stritch University	M
Carnegie Mellon University	D
Case Western Reserve University	M,D
The Catholic University of America	M
Central Michigan University	M
Charleston Southern University	M
City University	M,O
Claremont Graduate University	M
Clark Atlanta University	M
Clark University	M
Columbia University	M,D
Concordia University Wisconsin	M
Cornell University	D
Dallas Baptist University	M
DePaul University	M,O
Dowling College	M,O
Drexel University	M,D,O
Eastern College	M
Eastern Michigan University	M
East Tennessee State University	M
Fairfield University	M,O
Fairleigh Dickinson University, Florham-Madison Campus	M
Fairleigh Dickinson University, Teaneck–Hackensack Campus	M
Florida Agricultural and Mechanical University	M
Florida International University	M
Fordham University	M
Fort Hays State University	M
Gannon University	O
The George Washington University	M,D
Georgia State University	M,D
Hawaii Pacific University	M
Hofstra University	M
Houston Baptist University	M
Illinois Institute of Technology	P,M
Indiana University Bloomington	M,D
Inter American University of Puerto Rico, Metropolitan Campus	M
Inter American University of Puerto Rico, San Germán Campus	M
Iona College	M,O
Johns Hopkins University	M,O
Kennesaw State University	M
Kent State University	D
King's College	M
Long Island University, C.W. Post Campus	M,O
Louisiana State University and Agricultural and Mechanical College	M,D
Louisiana Tech University	M,D
Loyola College in Maryland	M
Marywood University	M
Mercy College	M
Metropolitan State University	M
Miami University	M
Michigan State University	M,D
Middle Tennessee State University	M,D
Mississippi State University	M
Montclair State University	M
National University	M
New School University	M
New York Institute of Technology	M,O
New York University	M,D,O
Northeastern Illinois University	M
Northeastern University	M
Northwestern University	D
Oklahoma City University	M
Oklahoma State University	M,D
Oral Roberts University	M
Our Lady of the Lake University of San Antonio	M
Pace University, New York City Campus	M
Pace University, White Plains Campus	M
The Pennsylvania State University University Park Campus	M,D
Philadelphia University	M
Pontifical Catholic University of Puerto Rico	M,D
Portland State University	M
Purdue University	M,D
Quinnipiac University	M
Regis University	M,O
Rensselaer Polytechnic Institute	M,D
Robert Morris College	M
Rochester Institute of Technology	M
Rutgers, The State University of New Jersey, Newark	M,D
Sage Graduate School	M
St. Bonaventure University	M,O
St. Cloud State University	M
St. Edward's University	M,O
St. John's University (NY)	M,O
Saint Joseph's University	M
Saint Louis University	M,D
Saint Peter's College	M
St. Thomas Aquinas College	M
Saint Xavier University	M,O
San Diego State University	M
Seattle University	M,O
Seton Hall University	M,O
Southeastern University	M
Southern Illinois University Edwardsville	M
State University of New York at Albany	M

State University of New York at Binghamton M,D
State University of New York at New Paltz M
Suffolk University M,O
Syracuse University M,D
Temple University M,D
Texas A&M International University M
Texas A&M University M,D
Texas Tech University M,D
Troy State University Dothan M
The University of Akron M
The University of Alabama M,D
The University of Arizona M
University of Baltimore M
University of California, Berkeley D
University of Central Florida M,D
University of Cincinnati M,D
University of Colorado at Boulder M,D
University of Colorado at Colorado Springs M
University of Colorado at Denver M
University of Connecticut M,D
University of Denver M
University of Dubuque M
The University of Findlay M
University of Florida M,D
University of Houston M,D
University of Houston–Clear Lake M
University of Illinois at Chicago D
University of Illinois at Urbana–Champaign M,D
The University of Iowa D
University of La Verne M
The University of Memphis M,D
University of Minnesota, Twin Cities Campus M,D
University of Missouri–St. Louis M,O
University of Nebraska–Lincoln M,D
University of New Haven M
University of New Mexico M
The University of North Carolina at Chapel Hill D
University of North Texas M,D
University of Oregon M,D
University of Pennsylvania M,D
University of Rhode Island M,D
University of St. Thomas (MN) M,O
University of San Francisco M
The University of Scranton M
University of Southern California M
The University of Tennessee M,D
The University of Tennessee at Chattanooga M
The University of Texas at Arlington M,D
The University of Texas at Austin D
The University of Texas at San Antonio M
University of Toledo M
University of Tulsa M
University of Utah M,D
University of Wisconsin–Madison M
University of Wyoming M
Vanderbilt University D
Virginia Commonwealth University M
Virginia Polytechnic Institute and State University M,D
Virginia State University M
Wagner College M
Webster University M
West Chester University of Pennsylvania M
Western International University M
Western New England College M
West Texas A&M University M
Wilkes University M
Wright State University M
Yale University D
York College of Pennsylvania M
Youngstown State University M

■ FINANCIAL ENGINEERING

Claremont Graduate University M,D,O
Columbia University M,D,O
Polytechnic University, Brooklyn Campus M
Polytechnic University, Westchester Graduate Center M
Princeton University M,D
University of Michigan M
University of Tulsa M

■ FIRE PROTECTION ENGINEERING

Anna Maria College M
University of Maryland, College Park M
University of New Haven M
Worcester Polytechnic Institute M,D,O

■ FISH, GAME, AND WILDLIFE MANAGEMENT

Arkansas Tech University M
Auburn University M,D
Brigham Young University M,D
Clemson University M,D
Colorado State University M,D
Cornell University M,D
Frostburg State University M
Iowa State University of Science and Technology M,D
Louisiana State University and Agricultural and Mechanical College M,D
Michigan State University M,D
Mississippi State University M
Montana State University–Bozeman M,D
New Mexico State University M
North Carolina State University M
Oregon State University M,D
The Pennsylvania State University University Park Campus M,D
Purdue University M,D
South Dakota State University M,D
Sul Ross State University M
Tennessee Technological University M
Texas A&M University M,D
Texas A&M University–Kingsville M,D
Texas Tech University M,D
University of Alaska Fairbanks M,D
The University of Arizona M,D
University of Florida M,D
University of Idaho M,D
University of Maine M,D
University of Massachusetts Amherst M,D
University of Miami M,D
University of Minnesota, Twin Cities Campus M,D
University of Missouri–Columbia M,D
The University of Montana–Missoula M,D
University of New Hampshire M,D
University of North Dakota M,D
University of Rhode Island M,D
The University of Tennessee M
University of Vermont M
University of Washington M,D
Utah State University M,D
Virginia Polytechnic Institute and State University M,D
West Virginia University M

■ FOLKLORE

The George Washington University M
Indiana University Bloomington M,D
University of California, Berkeley M
University of Louisiana at Lafayette M,D
The University of North Carolina at Chapel Hill M
University of Oregon M
University of Pennsylvania M,D
The University of Texas at Austin M,D
Utah State University M
Western Kentucky University M

■ FOOD SCIENCE AND TECHNOLOGY

Alabama Agricultural and Mechanical University M,D
Auburn University M,D
Brigham Young University M
California State Polytechnic University, Pomona M
California State University, Fresno M
Chapman University M
Clemson University D
Colorado State University M,D
Cornell University M,D
Drexel University M,D
Florida State University M,D
Framingham State College M
Iowa State University of Science and Technology M,D
Kansas State University M,D
Louisiana State University and Agricultural and Mechanical College M,D
Michigan State University M,D
Mississippi State University M,D
North Carolina State University M,D
North Dakota State University M,D
The Ohio State University M,D
Oklahoma State University M,D
Oregon State University M,D
The Pennsylvania State University University Park Campus M,D
Purdue University M,D
Rutgers, The State University of New Jersey, New Brunswick M,D
Texas A&M University M,D
Texas Tech University M,D
Texas Woman's University M,D
Tuskegee University M
The University of Akron M
University of Arkansas M,D
University of California, Davis M,D
University of Delaware M,D
University of Florida M,D
University of Georgia M,D
University of Hawaii at Manoa M
University of Idaho M
University of Illinois at Urbana–Champaign M,D
University of Kentucky M
University of Maine M,D
University of Maryland, College Park M,D
University of Maryland Eastern Shore M
University of Massachusetts Amherst M,D
University of Minnesota, Twin Cities Campus M,D
University of Missouri–Columbia M,D
University of Nebraska–Lincoln M,D
University of Puerto Rico, Mayagüez Campus M
University of Rhode Island M,D
The University of Tennessee M,D
The University of Tennessee at Martin M
University of Wisconsin–Madison M,D
University of Wisconsin–Stout M
University of Wyoming M
Utah State University M,D

Virginia Polytechnic Institute and State University	M,D
Washington State University	M,D
Wayne State University	M,D
West Virginia University	M,D

■ FOREIGN LANGUAGES EDUCATION

Andrews University	M
Auburn University	M,D,O
Boston College	M
Boston University	M
Bowling Green State University	M
Brigham Young University	M
Brooklyn College of the City University of New York	M
California State University, Chico	M
College of Our Lady of the Elms	M,O
The College of William and Mary	M
Eastern Washington University	M
Fairfield University	M,O
Florida Atlantic University	M
Florida International University	M
Georgia Southern University	M
Georgia State University	M,D,O
Hofstra University	M
Hunter College of the City University of New York	M
Indiana University Bloomington	M,D
Iona College	M
Jacksonville University	M
Long Island University, C.W. Post Campus	M
Louisiana Tech University	M,D,O
Manhattanville College	M
Marygrove College	M
Michigan State University	M,D
Middle Tennessee State University	M
Monterey Institute of International Studies	M
New York University	M,D,O
North Georgia College & State University	M,O
Notre Dame de Namur University	M,O
The Pennsylvania State University University Park Campus	M,D
Plattsburgh State University of New York	M
Purdue University	M,D,O
Queens College of the City University of New York	M,O
Quinnipiac University	M
Rhode Island College	M
Rider University	O
Rivier College	M
Rutgers, The State University of New Jersey, New Brunswick	M,D
School for International Training	M
Southwest Texas State University	M
Stanford University	M
State University of New York at Binghamton	M
State University of New York College at Cortland	M
State University of West Georgia	M
Stony Brook University, State University of New York	M,O
Teachers College, Columbia University	M,D
University at Buffalo, The State University of New York	M,D,O
The University of Arizona	M,D
University of California, Irvine	M,D
University of Central Arkansas	M
University of Central Florida	M
University of Connecticut	M,D
University of Delaware	M
University of Florida	M,D,O
University of Georgia	M,D,O
University of Hawaii at Manoa	M,D
University of Idaho	M
University of Illinois at Urbana–Champaign	M,D
The University of Iowa	M,D
University of Louisville	M
University of Maine	M
University of Massachusetts Amherst	M
University of Massachusetts Boston	M
University of Michigan	M,D
University of Minnesota, Twin Cities Campus	M
University of Missouri–Columbia	M,D
University of Nebraska at Kearney	M
The University of North Carolina at Chapel Hill	M
University of Pittsburgh	M,D
University of Puerto Rico, Río Piedras	M,D
University of South Carolina	M
University of Southern Mississippi	M
University of South Florida	M
The University of Tennessee	M,D,O
The University of Texas at Austin	M,D
University of Utah	M
University of Vermont	M
University of Virginia	M,D
University of Wisconsin–Madison	M,D
Vanderbilt University	M,D
West Chester University of Pennsylvania	M
Western Kentucky University	M

■ FORENSIC NURSING

Fitchburg State College	M
Quinnipiac University	M

■ FORENSIC SCIENCES

Castleton State College	M
Fitchburg State College	M,O
Florida International University	M,D
The George Washington University	M
Marshall University	M
Marymount University	M,O
National University	M
Sage Graduate School	M
Sam Houston State University	M,D
The University of Alabama at Birmingham	M
University of Central Florida	M,O
University of Illinois at Chicago	M
University of New Haven	M
Virginia Commonwealth University	M,O

■ FORESTRY

Auburn University	M,D
Clemson University	M,D
Colorado State University	M,D
Cornell University	M,D
Duke University	M,D
Harvard University	M
Iowa State University of Science and Technology	M,D
Louisiana State University and Agricultural and Mechanical College	M,D
Michigan State University	M,D
Michigan Technological University	M,D
Mississippi State University	M,D
North Carolina State University	M,D
Northern Arizona University	M,D
Oklahoma State University	M
Oregon State University	M,D
The Pennsylvania State University University Park Campus	M,D
Purdue University	M,D
Southern Illinois University Carbondale	M
Southern University and Agricultural and Mechanical College	M
State University of New York College of Environmental Science and Forestry	M,D
Stephen F. Austin State University	M,D
Texas A&M University	M,D
The University of Arizona	M,D
University of California, Berkeley	M,D
University of Florida	M,D
University of Georgia	M,D
University of Idaho	M,D
University of Kentucky	M
University of Maine	M,D
University of Massachusetts Amherst	M,D
University of Michigan	M,D,O
University of Minnesota, Twin Cities Campus	M,D
University of Missouri–Columbia	M,D
The University of Montana–Missoula	M,D
University of Nebraska–Lincoln	D
University of New Hampshire	M,D
The University of Tennessee	M
University of Vermont	M
University of Washington	M,D
University of Wisconsin–Madison	M,D
Utah State University	M,D
Virginia Polytechnic Institute and State University	M,D
West Virginia University	M,D
Yale University	M,D

■ FOUNDATIONS AND PHILOSOPHY OF EDUCATION

Antioch New England Graduate School	M
Appalachian State University	M,O
Arizona State University	M
Brigham Young University	M,D
California State University, Long Beach	M
California State University, Los Angeles	M
California State University, Northridge	M
Central Connecticut State University	M
Clemson University	M
College of Mount St. Joseph	M
DePaul University	M
Duquesne University	M
East Carolina University	M
Eastern Michigan University	M
Eastern Washington University	M
Fairfield University	M,O
Florida Atlantic University	M,D,O
Florida State University	M,D,O
The George Washington University	M
Georgia State University	M,D
Harvard University	M,D,O
Hofstra University	M,O
Indiana University Bloomington	M,D,O
Iowa State University of Science and Technology	M,D
Kansas State University	M,D
Kent State University	M,D
Loyola College in Maryland	M,O
Loyola University Chicago	M,D
Maharishi University of Management	M
Millersville University of Pennsylvania	M
New York University	M,D
Niagara University	M
Northern Illinois University	M
The Pennsylvania State University University Park Campus	M,D
Purdue University	M,D,O

Rutgers, The State University of New Jersey, New Brunswick	M,D,O
Saint Louis University	M,D
Southeast Missouri State University	M
Southern Connecticut State University	O
Stanford University	M,D
State University of New York at Binghamton	D
Suffolk University	M,O
Syracuse University	M,D,O
Teachers College, Columbia University	M,D
Texas A&M University	M,D
Texas Christian University	M,O
Troy State University	M
Troy State University Dothan	M,O
University of California, Berkeley	M,D
University of Cincinnati	M,D
University of Connecticut	M,D
University of Florida	M,D,O
University of Georgia	M,D,O
University of Hawaii at Manoa	M,D
University of Houston	M,D
University of Illinois at Urbana–Champaign	M,D,O
The University of Iowa	M,D
University of Kansas	M,D
University of Kentucky	M,D
University of Maryland, College Park	M,D,O
University of Michigan	M,D
University of New Mexico	D
University of New Orleans	M,D,O
University of Oklahoma	M,D
University of Oregon	M,D
University of Pennsylvania	M,D
University of Pittsburgh	M,D
University of South Carolina	D
The University of Tennessee	M,D,O
The University of Texas at El Paso	M,D
University of the Pacific	M,D
University of Toledo	M,D,O
University of Utah	M,D
University of Washington	M,D
The University of West Alabama	M
University of Wisconsin–Madison	M,D
University of Wisconsin–Milwaukee	M
Western Illinois University	M
Widener University	M,D
Youngstown State University	M,D

■ FRENCH

American University	M,O
Arizona State University	M
Auburn University	M
Boston College	M,D
Boston University	M,D
Bowling Green State University	M
Brigham Young University	M
Brown University	M,D
California State University, Fullerton	M
California State University, Long Beach	M
California State University, Los Angeles	M
California State University, Sacramento	M
Case Western Reserve University	M,D
The Catholic University of America	M,D
Central Connecticut State University	M
Colorado State University	M
Columbia University	M,D
Duke University	D
Eastern Michigan University	M
Emory University	D
Florida Atlantic University	M
Florida State University	M,D
Georgia State University	M
Harvard University	M,D
Howard University	M
Hunter College of the City University of New York	M
Illinois State University	M
Indiana State University	M
Indiana University Bloomington	M,D
Johns Hopkins University	M,D
Kansas State University	M
Kent State University	M
Long Island University, C.W. Post Campus	M
Louisiana State University and Agricultural and Mechanical College	M,D
Miami University	M
Michigan State University	M,D
Millersville University of Pennsylvania	M
Minnesota State University, Mankato	M
Montclair State University	M
Monterey Institute of International Studies	M
New York University	M,D,O
Northern Illinois University	M
Northwestern University	D,O
The Ohio State University	M,D
Ohio University	M
The Pennsylvania State University University Park Campus	M,D
Portland State University	M
Princeton University	D
Purdue University	M,D
Queens College of the City University of New York	M
Rhode Island College	M
Rice University	M,D
Rutgers, The State University of New Jersey, New Brunswick	M,D
Saint Louis University	M
San Diego State University	M
San Francisco State University	M
San Jose State University	M
Seton Hall University	M
Southern Connecticut State University	M
Southwest Missouri State University	M
Stanford University	M,D
State University of New York at Albany	M,D
State University of New York at Binghamton	M
Stony Brook University, State University of New York	M,D
Syracuse University	M
Texas Tech University	M
Tufts University	M
Tulane University	M,D
University at Buffalo, The State University of New York	M,D
The University of Alabama	M,D
The University of Arizona	M,D
University of Arkansas	M
University of California, Berkeley	D
University of California, Davis	D
University of California, Irvine	M,D
University of California, Los Angeles	M,D
University of California, San Diego	M,D
University of California, Santa Barbara	M,D
University of Chicago	M,D
University of Cincinnati	M,D
University of Colorado at Boulder	M,D
University of Connecticut	M,D
University of Delaware	M
University of Denver	M
University of Florida	M,D
University of Georgia	M
University of Hawaii at Manoa	M
University of Houston	M,D
University of Idaho	M
University of Illinois at Chicago	M
University of Illinois at Urbana–Champaign	M,D
The University of Iowa	M,D
University of Kansas	M,D
University of Kentucky	M
University of Louisiana at Lafayette	M,D
University of Louisville	M
University of Maine	M
University of Maryland, Baltimore County	M
University of Maryland, College Park	M,D
University of Massachusetts Amherst	M
The University of Memphis	M
University of Miami	D
University of Michigan	D
University of Minnesota, Twin Cities Campus	M,D
University of Mississippi	M
University of Missouri–Columbia	M,D
The University of Montana–Missoula	M
University of Nebraska–Lincoln	M,D
University of Nevada, Las Vegas	M
University of Nevada, Reno	M
University of New Mexico	M,D
The University of North Carolina at Chapel Hill	M,D
The University of North Carolina at Greensboro	M
University of Northern Iowa	M
University of North Texas	M
University of Notre Dame	M
University of Oklahoma	M,D
University of Oregon	M
University of Pennsylvania	M,D
University of Pittsburgh	M,D
University of Rhode Island	M
University of Rochester	M
University of South Carolina	M
University of Southern California	M,D
University of South Florida	M
The University of Tennessee	M,D
The University of Texas at Arlington	M
The University of Texas at Austin	M,D
University of Toledo	M
University of Utah	M
University of Vermont	M
University of Virginia	M,D
University of Washington	M,D
University of Wisconsin–Madison	M,D,O
University of Wisconsin–Milwaukee	M
University of Wyoming	M
Vanderbilt University	M,D
Washington University in St. Louis	M,D
Wayne State University	M
West Chester University of Pennsylvania	M
West Virginia University	M
Yale University	M,D

■ GENETIC COUNSELING

Arcadia University	M
Brandeis University	M
California State University, Northridge	M,O
Case Western Reserve University	M
Johns Hopkins University	M,D
Northwestern University	M
University of California, Berkeley	M
University of California, Irvine	M
University of Cincinnati	M
University of Minnesota, Twin Cities Campus	M,D
The University of North Carolina at Greensboro	M
University of Pittsburgh	M
University of South Carolina	M
Virginia Commonwealth University	M,D,O

■ GENETICS

Arizona State University M,D
Brandeis University M,D
California Institute of Technology D
Carnegie Mellon University M,D
Case Western Reserve University D
Clemson University M,D
Colorado State University M,D
Columbia University M,D
Cornell University D
Dartmouth College D
Duke University D
Emory University D
Florida State University M,D
The George Washington University M,D
Georgia State University M,D
Harvard University D
Howard University M,D
Hunter College of the City University of New York
Illinois State University M,D
Indiana University Bloomington D
Indiana University–Purdue University Indianapolis M,D
Iowa State University of Science and Technology M,D
Johns Hopkins University M,D
Kansas State University M,D
Marquette University M,D
Massachusetts Institute of Technology D
MCP Hahnemann University M,D
Michigan State University D
Mississippi State University M
New York University M,D
North Carolina State University M,D
Northwestern University D
The Ohio State University M,D
Oklahoma State University M,D
Oregon State University M,D
The Pennsylvania State University University Park Campus M,D
Purdue University M,D
Rutgers, The State University of New Jersey, New Brunswick M,D
Stanford University D
State University of New York at Albany M,D
Stony Brook University, State University of New York D
Temple University D
Texas A&M University M,D
Tufts University D
The University of Alabama at Birmingham D
The University of Arizona M,D
University of California, Davis M,D
University of California, Irvine D
University of California, Los Angeles D
University of California, Riverside M,D
University of California, San Diego D
University of California, San Francisco D
University of Chicago D
University of Cincinnati D
University of Colorado at Boulder M,D
University of Connecticut M,D
University of Delaware M,D
University of Florida M,D
University of Georgia M,D
University of Hawaii at Manoa M,D
University of Illinois at Chicago M,D
The University of Iowa M,D
University of Kansas D
University of Maryland, College Park M,D
University of Miami M,D
University of Michigan
University of Minnesota, Twin Cities Campus M,D
University of Missouri–Columbia D
University of Missouri–St. Louis M,D,O
University of New Hampshire M,D
University of New Mexico M,D
The University of North Carolina at Chapel Hill M,D
University of North Dakota M,D
University of Notre Dame M,D
University of Oregon M,D
University of Pennsylvania D
University of Pittsburgh M,D
University of Rhode Island M,D
University of Rochester M,D
The University of Tennessee M,D
The University of Texas at Austin D
University of Utah M,D
University of Vermont M,D
University of Virginia D
University of Washington M,D
University of Wisconsin–Madison M,D
Virginia Commonwealth University M,D,O
Virginia Polytechnic Institute and State University M,D
Wake Forest University M
Washington State University M,D
Washington University in St. Louis D
Wayne State University M,D
West Virginia University M,D
Yale University D
Yeshiva University D

■ GENOMIC SCIENCES

Case Western Reserve University D
North Carolina State University M,D
University of California, Riverside D
University of California, San Francisco D
The University of Tennessee M,D

■ GEOCHEMISTRY

California Institute of Technology M,D
California State University, Fullerton M
Columbia University M,D
Cornell University M,D
The George Washington University M
Georgia Institute of Technology M,D
Indiana University Bloomington M,D
Johns Hopkins University M,D
Massachusetts Institute of Technology M,D,O
New Mexico Institute of Mining and Technology M,D
The Pennsylvania State University University Park Campus M,D
Rensselaer Polytechnic Institute M,D
University of California, Los Angeles M,D
University of Georgia M,D
University of Hawaii at Manoa M,D
University of Illinois at Chicago M,D
University of Illinois at Urbana–Champaign M,D
University of Michigan M,D
University of Missouri–Rolla M,D
University of Nevada, Reno M,D,O
University of New Hampshire M,D
Washington University in St. Louis M,D
Wright State University M
Yale University D

■ GEODETIC SCIENCES

Columbia University M,D
The Ohio State University M,D

■ GEOGRAPHIC INFORMATION SYSTEMS

Boston University M
Clark University M
George Mason University M
Hunter College of the City University of New York M
North Carolina State University M
Saint Mary's University of Minnesota M
Southwest Texas State University M
State University of New York at Albany M,O
University at Buffalo, The State University of New York M,D,O
University of Minnesota, Twin Cities Campus M
The University of Montana–Missoula M
The University of Texas at Dallas M
University of Wisconsin–Madison M,D,O
West Virginia University M,D

■ GEOGRAPHY

Appalachian State University M
Arizona State University M,D
Auburn University M
Boston University M,D
Brigham Young University M
California State University, Chico M
California State University, Fullerton M
California State University, Hayward M
California State University, Long Beach M
California State University, Los Angeles M
California State University, Northridge M
California University of Pennsylvania M
Central Connecticut State University M
Chicago State University M
Clark University D
East Carolina University M
Eastern Michigan University M
Florida Atlantic University M
Florida State University M,D
George Mason University M
The George Washington University M
Georgia State University M
Hunter College of the City University of New York M
Indiana State University M,D
Indiana University Bloomington M,D
Indiana University of Pennsylvania M
Johns Hopkins University M,D
Kansas State University M,D
Kent State University M,D
Louisiana State University and Agricultural and Mechanical College M,D
Marshall University M
Miami University M
Michigan State University M,D
Minnesota State University, Mankato M
New Mexico State University M
Northeastern Illinois University M
Northern Arizona University M
Northern Illinois University M
The Ohio State University M,D
Ohio University M
Oklahoma State University M
Oregon State University M,D
The Pennsylvania State University University Park Campus M,D
Portland State University M,D
Rutgers, The State University of New Jersey, New Brunswick M,D
St. Cloud State University M
Salem State College M
San Diego State University M,D
San Francisco State University M
San Jose State University M
South Dakota State University M

Southern Illinois University Carbondale M,D
Southern Illinois University Edwardsville M
Southwest Texas State University M,D
State University of New York at Albany M,O
State University of New York at Binghamton M
Syracuse University M,D
Temple University M
Texas A&M University M,D
Towson University M
University at Buffalo, The State University of New York M,D,O
The University of Akron M,D
The University of Alabama M
The University of Arizona M,D
University of Arkansas M,D
University of California, Berkeley D
University of California, Davis M,D
University of California, Los Angeles M,D
University of California, Santa Barbara M,D
University of Cincinnati M,D
University of Colorado at Boulder M,D
University of Connecticut M,D
University of Delaware M,D
University of Denver M,D
University of Florida M,D
University of Georgia M,D
University of Hawaii at Manoa M,D
University of Idaho M,D
University of Illinois at Chicago M
University of Illinois at Urbana–Champaign M,D
The University of Iowa M,D
University of Kansas M,D
University of Kentucky M,D
University of Louisiana at Lafayette M
University of Maryland, College Park M,D
University of Massachusetts Amherst M
The University of Memphis M
University of Minnesota, Twin Cities Campus M,D
University of Missouri–Columbia M
The University of Montana–Missoula M
University of Nebraska at Omaha M
University of Nebraska–Lincoln M,D
University of Nevada, Reno M
University of New Mexico M
University of New Orleans M
The University of North Carolina at Chapel Hill M,D
The University of North Carolina at Charlotte M
The University of North Carolina at Greensboro M
University of North Dakota M
University of Northern Iowa M
University of North Texas M
University of Oklahoma M,D
University of Oregon M,D
University of South Carolina M,D
University of Southern California M,D
University of Southern Mississippi M
University of South Florida M
The University of Tennessee M,D
The University of Texas at Austin M,D
University of Toledo M
University of Utah M,D
University of Vermont M
University of Washington M,D
University of Wisconsin–Madison M,D,O
University of Wisconsin–Milwaukee M
University of Wyoming M
Utah State University M
Virginia Polytechnic Institute and State University M
Wayne State University M
West Chester University of Pennsylvania M
Western Illinois University M,O
Western Michigan University M
Western Washington University M
West Virginia University M,D

■ GEOLOGICAL ENGINEERING

Arizona State University M,D
Columbia University M,D
Drexel University M
Michigan State University M,D
Michigan Technological University M,D
The University of Akron M
University of Alaska Fairbanks M,O
The University of Arizona M,D
University of California, Berkeley M,D
University of Idaho M
University of Minnesota, Twin Cities Campus M,D
University of Missouri–Rolla M,D
University of Nevada, Reno M,D,O
University of Oklahoma M,D
University of Utah M,D
University of Wisconsin–Madison M,D

■ GEOLOGY

Auburn University M
Ball State University M
Baylor University M,D
Boise State University M
Boston College M
Bowling Green State University M
Brigham Young University M
Brooklyn College of the City University of New York M,D
California Institute of Technology M,D
California State University, Bakersfield M
California State University, Fresno M
California State University, Fullerton M
California State University, Hayward M
California State University, Long Beach M
California State University, Los Angeles M
California State University, Northridge M
Case Western Reserve University M,D
Central Washington University M
Cleveland State University M,D
Colorado State University M,D
Cornell University M,D
Duke University M,D
East Carolina University M
Eastern Kentucky University M,D
Eastern Washington University M
Florida Atlantic University M
Florida State University M,D
Fort Hays State University M
The George Washington University M,D
Georgia State University M
Idaho State University M
Indiana University Bloomington M,D
Indiana University–Purdue University Indianapolis M
Iowa State University of Science and Technology M,D
Johns Hopkins University M,D
Kansas State University M
Kent State University M,D
Lehigh University M,D
Loma Linda University M
Louisiana State University and Agricultural and Mechanical College M,D
Massachusetts Institute of Technology M,D
Miami University M,D
Michigan State University M,D
Michigan Technological University M,D
New Mexico Institute of Mining and Technology M,D
New Mexico State University M
North Carolina State University M,D
Northern Arizona University M
Northern Illinois University M,D
Northwestern University M,D
The Ohio State University M,D
Ohio University M
Oklahoma State University M
Old Dominion University M
Oregon State University M,D
The Pennsylvania State University University Park Campus M,D
Portland State University M,D
Princeton University D
Queens College of the City University of New York M
Rensselaer Polytechnic Institute M,D
Rutgers, The State University of New Jersey, Newark M
Rutgers, The State University of New Jersey, New Brunswick M,D
San Diego State University M
San Jose State University M
Southern Illinois University Carbondale M,D
Southern Methodist University M,D
State University of New York at Albany M,D
State University of New York at Binghamton M,D
State University of New York at New Paltz M
Stephen F. Austin State University M
Sul Ross State University M
Syracuse University M,D
Temple University M
Texas A&M University M,D
Texas A&M University–Kingsville M
Texas Christian University M
Tulane University M,D
University at Buffalo, The State University of New York M,D
The University of Akron M
The University of Alabama M,D
University of Alaska Fairbanks M,D
University of Arkansas M
University of California, Berkeley M,D
University of California, Davis M,D
University of California, Los Angeles M,D
University of California, Riverside M,D
University of California, San Diego M,D
University of California, Santa Barbara M,D
University of Chicago M,D
University of Cincinnati M,D
University of Colorado at Boulder M,D
University of Connecticut M,D
University of Delaware M,D
University of Florida M,D
University of Hawaii at Manoa M,D
University of Houston M,D
University of Idaho M,D
University of Illinois at Chicago M,D
University of Illinois at Urbana–Champaign M,D
University of Kansas M,D
University of Kentucky M,D
University of Louisiana at Lafayette M
University of Maine M,D
University of Maryland, College Park M,D
University of Massachusetts Amherst M,D
The University of Memphis M,D

University of Miami	M,D
University of Michigan	M,D
University of Minnesota, Duluth	M
University of Minnesota, Twin Cities Campus	M,D
University of Missouri–Columbia	M,D
University of Missouri–Kansas City	M,D
University of Missouri–Rolla	M,D
The University of Montana–Missoula	M,D
University of Nevada, Reno	M,D,O
University of New Hampshire	M,D
University of New Orleans	M
The University of North Carolina at Chapel Hill	M,D
The University of North Carolina at Wilmington	M
University of North Dakota	M,D
University of Oklahoma	M,D
University of Oregon	M,D
University of Pennsylvania	M,D
University of Pittsburgh	M,D
University of Puerto Rico, Mayagüez Campus	M
University of Rhode Island	M
University of South Carolina	M,D
University of Southern Mississippi	M
University of South Florida	M,D,O
The University of Tennessee	M,D
The University of Texas at Arlington	M
The University of Texas at Austin	M,D
The University of Texas at El Paso	M,D
The University of Texas at San Antonio	M
The University of Texas of the Permian Basin	M
University of Toledo	M
University of Tulsa	M
University of Utah	M,D
University of Vermont	M
University of Washington	M,D
University of Wisconsin–Madison	M,D
University of Wisconsin–Milwaukee	M,D
University of Wyoming	M,D
Utah State University	M
Vanderbilt University	M
Virginia Polytechnic Institute and State University	M,D
Washington State University	M,D
Washington University in St. Louis	M,D
Wayne State University	M
West Chester University of Pennsylvania	M
Western Michigan University	M,D
Western Washington University	M
West Virginia University	M,D
Wichita State University	M
Wright State University	M
Yale University	D

■ GEOPHYSICS

Boise State University	M,D
Boston College	M
California Institute of Technology	M,D
Columbia University	M,D
Cornell University	M,D
Florida State University	D
Georgia Institute of Technology	M,D
Idaho State University	M
Indiana University Bloomington	M,D
Johns Hopkins University	M,D
Louisiana State University and Agricultural and Mechanical College	M,D
Massachusetts Institute of Technology	M,D,O
Michigan Technological University	M
New Mexico Institute of Mining and Technology	M,D
North Carolina State University	M,D
Oregon State University	M,D
The Pennsylvania State University University Park Campus	M,D
Princeton University	D
Rensselaer Polytechnic Institute	M,D
Southern Methodist University	M,D
Stanford University	M,D
Texas A&M University	M,D
The University of Akron	M
University of Alaska Fairbanks	M,D
University of California, Berkeley	M,D
University of California, Los Angeles	M,D
University of California, Santa Barbara	M,D
University of Chicago	M,D
University of Colorado at Boulder	M,D
University of Connecticut	M,D
University of Georgia	M,D
University of Hawaii at Manoa	M,D
University of Houston	M,D
University of Idaho	M
University of Illinois at Chicago	M,D
University of Illinois at Urbana–Champaign	M,D
The University of Memphis	M,D
University of Miami	M,D
University of Minnesota, Twin Cities Campus	M,D
University of Missouri–Rolla	M,D
University of Nevada, Reno	M,D,O
University of New Orleans	M
University of Oklahoma	M
The University of Texas at El Paso	M
University of Utah	M,D
University of Washington	M,D
University of Wisconsin–Madison	M,D
University of Wyoming	M,D
Virginia Polytechnic Institute and State University	M,D
Washington University in St. Louis	M,D
West Virginia University	M,D
Wright State University	M
Yale University	D

■ GEOSCIENCES

Ball State University	M
Baylor University	M,D
Boise State University	M
Boston University	M,D
Brown University	M,D
California State University, Chico	M
California University of Pennsylvania	M
Case Western Reserve University	M,D
Central Connecticut State University	M
City College of the City University of New York	M,D
Colorado State University	M,D
Columbia University	M,D
Cornell University	M,D
Dartmouth College	M,D
Emporia State University	M
Florida International University	M,D
Georgia Institute of Technology	M,D
Harvard University	M,D
Indiana State University	M,D
Indiana University Bloomington	M,D
Iowa State University of Science and Technology	M,D
Lehigh University	M,D
Massachusetts Institute of Technology	M,D
Michigan State University	M,D
Mississippi State University	M
Montana State University–Bozeman	M
Montclair State University	M,O
Murray State University	M
New Mexico Institute of Mining and Technology	M,D
North Carolina Central University	M
North Carolina State University	M,D
Northeastern Illinois University	M
Northern Arizona University	M
Northwestern University	M,D
The Pennsylvania State University University Park Campus	M,D
Princeton University	D
Purdue University	M,D
Radford University	M
Rensselaer Polytechnic Institute	M,D
Rice University	M,D
Saint Louis University	M,D
San Francisco State University	M
Southeast Missouri State University	M
Stanford University	M,D,O
State University of New York at Albany	M,D
State University of New York College at Oneonta	M
Stony Brook University, State University of New York	M,D
Texas A&M University–Commerce	M
Texas Tech University	M,D
The University of Akron	M
The University of Arizona	M,D
University of California, Irvine	M,D
University of California, Los Angeles	M,D
University of California, Santa Cruz	M,D
University of Chicago	M,D
University of Florida	M,D
University of Illinois at Chicago	M,D
University of Illinois at Urbana–Champaign	M,D
The University of Iowa	M,D
University of Louisiana at Monroe	M
University of Maine	M,D
University of Massachusetts Amherst	D
The University of Memphis	M,D
University of Michigan	M,D
University of Missouri–Kansas City	M,D
University of Nebraska–Lincoln	M,D
University of Nevada, Las Vegas	M,D
University of New Hampshire	M,D
University of New Mexico	M,D
The University of North Carolina at Charlotte	M
University of Northern Colorado	M
University of Notre Dame	M,D
University of Rochester	M,D
University of San Diego	M,D,O
University of South Carolina	M,D
University of Southern California	M,D
The University of Texas at Austin	M,D
The University of Texas at Dallas	M,D
University of Tulsa	M,D
Washington University in St. Louis	M,D
Western Connecticut State University	M
Western Michigan University	M
Yale University	D

■ GEOTECHNICAL ENGINEERING

Auburn University	M,D
The Catholic University of America	M
Colorado State University	M,D
Cornell University	M,D
Howard University	M
Iowa State University of Science and Technology	M,D
Louisiana State University and Agricultural and Mechanical College	M,D
Marquette University	M,D
Michigan Technological University	D
Northwestern University	M,D
Ohio University	M,D

The Pennsylvania State University University Park Campus	M,D
Rensselaer Polytechnic Institute	M,D
Texas A&M University	M,D
Tufts University	M,D
University of California, Berkeley	M,D
University of California, Los Angeles	M,D
University of Central Florida	M,D,O
University of Colorado at Boulder	M,D
University of Delaware	M,D
University of Illinois at Chicago	D
University of Maine	M,D
University of Missouri–Columbia	M,D
University of Missouri–Rolla	M,D
University of Oklahoma	M,D
University of Rhode Island	M,D
University of Southern California	M
The University of Texas at Austin	M,D
University of Washington	M,D

■ GERMAN

Arizona State University	M
Bowling Green State University	M
Brigham Young University	M
Brown University	M,D
California State University, Fullerton	M
California State University, Long Beach	M
California State University, Sacramento	M
The Catholic University of America	M
Colorado State University	M
Columbia University	M,D
Cornell University	M,D
Duke University	D
Eastern Michigan University	M
Florida Atlantic University	M
Florida State University	M
Georgetown University	M,D
Georgia State University	M
Harvard University	M,D
Illinois State University	M
Indiana University Bloomington	M,D
Johns Hopkins University	D
Kansas State University	M
Kent State University	M
Michigan State University	M,D
Millersville University of Pennsylvania	M
Minnesota State University, Mankato	M
Monterey Institute of International Studies	M
New York University	M,D
Northwestern University	D
The Ohio State University	M,D
The Pennsylvania State University University Park Campus	M,D
Portland State University	M
Princeton University	D
Purdue University	M,D
Rutgers, The State University of New Jersey, New Brunswick	M,D
San Francisco State University	M
Southwest Missouri State University	M
Stanford University	M,D
Stony Brook University, State University of New York	M,D
Texas Tech University	M
Tufts University	M
University at Buffalo, The State University of New York	M
The University of Alabama	M,D
The University of Arizona	M
University of Arkansas	M
University of California, Berkeley	M,D
University of California, Davis	M,D
University of California, Irvine	M,D
University of California, Los Angeles	M,D
University of California, San Diego	M,D
University of California, Santa Barbara	M,D
University of Chicago	M,D
University of Cincinnati	M,D
University of Colorado at Boulder	M
University of Connecticut	M,D
University of Delaware	M
University of Denver	M
University of Florida	M,D
University of Georgia	M
University of Hawaii at Manoa	M
University of Illinois at Chicago	M,D
University of Illinois at Urbana–Champaign	M,D
The University of Iowa	M,D
University of Kansas	M,D
University of Kentucky	M
University of Louisville	M
University of Maryland, Baltimore County	M
University of Maryland, College Park	M,D
University of Massachusetts Amherst	M,D
University of Michigan	M,D
University of Minnesota, Twin Cities Campus	M,D
University of Mississippi	M
University of Missouri–Columbia	M
The University of Montana–Missoula	M
University of Nebraska–Lincoln	M,D
University of Nevada, Reno	M
University of New Mexico	M,D
The University of North Carolina at Chapel Hill	M,D
University of Northern Iowa	M
University of Notre Dame	M
University of Oklahoma	M
University of Oregon	M,D
University of Pennsylvania	M,D
University of Pittsburgh	M,D
University of Rochester	M
University of South Carolina	M
The University of Tennessee	M,D
The University of Texas at Arlington	M
The University of Texas at Austin	M,D
University of Toledo	M
University of Utah	M,D
University of Vermont	M
University of Virginia	M,D
University of Washington	M,D
University of Wisconsin–Madison	M,D
University of Wisconsin–Milwaukee	M
University of Wyoming	M
Vanderbilt University	M,D
Washington University in St. Louis	M,D
Wayne State University	M,D
West Virginia University	M
Yale University	M,D

■ GERONTOLOGICAL NURSING

Arkansas State University	M,O
Boston College	M,D
Case Western Reserve University	M
The Catholic University of America	M,D
College of Mount Saint Vincent	M,O
Columbia University	M,O
Concordia University Wisconsin	M
Duke University	M,O
Emory University	M
Gannon University	M,O
Gwynedd-Mercy College	M
Hunter College of the City University of New York	M
La Roche College	M
Lehman College of the City University of New York	M
Loma Linda University	M
Marquette University	M,O
Nazareth College of Rochester	M
New York University	M,O
Pacific Lutheran University	M
Rutgers, The State University of New Jersey, Newark	M,D
Sage Graduate School	M
San Jose State University	M
Seton Hall University	M
State University of New York at New Paltz	M
Stony Brook University, State University of New York	M
University at Buffalo, The State University of New York	M,D,O
University of Delaware	M,O
University of Maryland	M,D
University of Massachusetts Lowell	M
University of Michigan	M
University of Minnesota, Twin Cities Campus	M
The University of North Carolina at Greensboro	M,O
University of Pennsylvania	M
University of Utah	M,O
Vanderbilt University	M,D
Villanova University	M,O

■ GERONTOLOGY

Abilene Christian University	M
Appalachian State University	M
Arizona State University	O
Ball State University	M
Baylor University	M
California State University, Dominguez Hills	M,O
California State University, Long Beach	M
Case Western Reserve University	M,D,O
Central Missouri State University	M
The College of New Rochelle	M,O
College of Notre Dame of Maryland	M
Concordia University (IL)	M,O
Eastern Illinois University	M
East Tennessee State University	M,O
Florida Atlantic University	M,O
Gannon University	O
George Mason University	M
Hofstra University	M,O
Lindenwood University	M
Long Island University, C.W. Post Campus	M,O
Lynn University	M,O
Marylhurst University	M
Miami University	M
Minnesota State University, Mankato	M
Morehead State University	M
Mount Mary College	M
National-Louis University	M,O
Northeastern Illinois University	M
Notre Dame de Namur University	M
Oregon State University	M
Portland State University	O
Roosevelt University	M
Sage Graduate School	M
St. Cloud State University	M
Saint Joseph College	M
Saint Joseph's University	M
San Francisco State University	M
San Jose State University	M,O
State University of West Georgia	M
Syracuse University	M
Texas A&M University–Kingsville	M
Towson University	M
The University of Arizona	M,O
University of Arkansas at Little Rock	M,O
University of Central Florida	M,O
University of Central Oklahoma	M
University of Illinois at Springfield	M

University of Kansas	M,D
University of Kentucky	D
University of La Verne	M
University of Louisiana at Monroe	M,O
University of Maryland, Baltimore County	M,D,O
University of Massachusetts Boston	D
University of Missouri–St. Louis	M,O
University of Nebraska at Omaha	M,O
University of New Orleans	M,O
The University of North Carolina at Charlotte	M
The University of North Carolina at Greensboro	M
University of Northern Colorado	M
University of North Florida	M,O
University of North Texas	M,O
University of Pittsburgh	M,D,O
University of South Alabama	O
University of South Carolina	O
University of Southern California	M,D,O
University of South Florida	M,D
The University of Tennessee	M
University of Utah	M,O
Virginia Commonwealth University	M,O
Virginia Polytechnic Institute and State University	M,D
Wayne State University	O
Webster University	M
West Chester University of Pennsylvania	M,O
Western Illinois University	M
Western Kentucky University	M
Wichita State University	M
Wilmington College	M

■ GRAPHIC DESIGN

Boston University	M
California State University, Los Angeles	M
Cardinal Stritch University	M
City College of the City University of New York	M
The College of New Rochelle	M
Colorado State University	M
Florida Atlantic University	M
George Mason University	M
Illinois Institute of Technology	M,D
Illinois State University	M
Indiana State University	M
Indiana University Bloomington	M
Iowa State University of Science and Technology	M
Kent State University	M
Louisiana State University and Agricultural and Mechanical College	M
Louisiana Tech University	M
Michigan State University	M
North Carolina State University	M
The Pennsylvania State University University Park Campus	M
Pratt Institute	M
Rochester Institute of Technology	M
San Diego State University	M
San Jose State University	M
Syracuse University	M
Temple University	M
Texas Woman's University	M
University of Baltimore	M
University of Cincinnati	M
University of Guam	M
University of Houston	M
University of Illinois at Chicago	M
University of Illinois at Urbana–Champaign	M
The University of Memphis	M
University of Miami	M
University of Minnesota, Duluth	M
University of New Orleans	M
University of North Texas	M,D
University of Notre Dame	M
The University of Tennessee	M
University of Utah	M
Western Illinois University	M,O
Western Michigan University	M
West Virginia University	M
Yale University	M

■ HAZARDOUS MATERIALS MANAGEMENT

Colorado State University	M,D
Idaho State University	M,D
New Mexico Institute of Mining and Technology	M
Rutgers, The State University of New Jersey, New Brunswick	M,D
Stony Brook University, State University of New York	M,O
University of Central Florida	M,D,O
University of Idaho	M
University of New Mexico	M
University of Oklahoma	M,D
University of South Carolina	M,D
Wayne State University	M,O

■ HEALTH EDUCATION

Adams State College	M
Adelphi University	M,O
Albany State University	M
Alcorn State University	M,O
Arcadia University	M
Auburn University	M,D,O
Austin Peay State University	M
Ball State University	M
Baylor University	M
Boston University	M,O
Brooklyn College of the City University of New York	M
California State University, Long Beach	M
California State University, Los Angeles	M
California State University, Northridge	M
Central Washington University	M
The Citadel, The Military College of South Carolina	M
Cleveland State University	M
The College of New Jersey	M
East Carolina University	M
Eastern College	M
Eastern Kentucky University	M
East Stroudsburg University of Pennsylvania	M
Edinboro University of Pennsylvania	O
Florida Agricultural and Mechanical University	M
Florida International University	M
Florida State University	M,D
Fort Hays State University	M
Frostburg State University	M
Georgia College and State University	M,O
Georgia Southern University	M,O
Georgia Southwestern State University	M,O
Hofstra University	M
Howard University	M
Idaho State University	M
Illinois State University	M
Indiana State University	M
Indiana University of Pennsylvania	M
Indiana University–Purdue University Indianapolis	M
Inter American University of Puerto Rico, Metropolitan Campus	M
Iowa State University of Science and Technology	M,D
Jackson State University	M
Jacksonville State University	M,O
James Madison University	M
John F. Kennedy University	M
Johns Hopkins University	M,D
Kent State University	D
Lehman College of the City University of New York	M
Lesley University	M,O
Loma Linda University	M,D
Long Island University, Brooklyn Campus	M
Louisiana Tech University	M,D,O
Marshall University	M
McNeese State University	M
Michigan State University	M,D
Middle Tennessee State University	M,D
Minnesota State University, Mankato	M
Mississippi State University	M
Mississippi University for Women	M
Montana State University–Bozeman	M
Montclair State University	M
Morehead State University	M
Mount Mary College	M
New Jersey City University	M
New York University	M,D,O
North Carolina Agricultural and Technical State University	M
North Carolina State University	M
Northeastern State University	M
Northern Arizona University	M
Northern State University	M
Northwest Missouri State University	M
Nova Southeastern University	D
Oregon State University	M
The Pennsylvania State University Harrisburg Campus of the Capital College	M
Plymouth State College	M
Portland State University	M
Prairie View A&M University	M
Rhode Island College	M
Rowan University	M
Sage Graduate School	M
Saint Joseph's University	M
Saint Mary's College of California	M
South Dakota State University	M
Southeastern Louisiana University	M
Southern Connecticut State University	M
Southern Illinois University Carbondale	M,D
Southern Illinois University Edwardsville	M,O
Southwestern Oklahoma State University	M
Southwest Texas State University	M
Springfield College	M
State University of New York College at Brockport	M
State University of New York College at Cortland	M
Stephen F. Austin State University	M
Tarleton State University	M,O
Teachers College, Columbia University	M,D
Temple University	M,D
Tennessee State University	M
Tennessee Technological University	M
Texas A&M University	M,D
Texas A&M University–Commerce	M
Texas A&M University–Kingsville	M
Texas Southern University	M
Texas Woman's University	M,D
Tulane University	M

The University of Alabama	M,D
The University of Alabama at Birmingham	M,D
University of Arkansas	M,D
University of Central Arkansas	M
University of Central Oklahoma	M
University of Cincinnati	M
University of Colorado at Denver	D
University of Detroit Mercy	M
University of Florida	M,D
University of Georgia	M,D,O
University of Houston	M,D
University of Illinois at Chicago	M
University of Kansas	M,D
University of Louisiana at Monroe	M
University of Maryland, Baltimore County	M
University of Maryland, College Park	M,D
University of Michigan–Flint	M
The University of Montana–Missoula	M
University of Nebraska at Omaha	M
University of Nebraska–Lincoln	M
University of New Mexico	M,D
University of New Orleans	M,O
The University of North Carolina at Chapel Hill	M,D
University of Northern Iowa	M
University of Pittsburgh	M
University of Rhode Island	M
University of South Alabama	M
University of South Carolina	M,D,O
University of South Dakota	M
University of Southern Mississippi	M
The University of Tennessee	M
The University of Texas at Austin	M,D
The University of Texas at El Paso	M
The University of Texas at Tyler	M
University of Toledo	D
University of Utah	M,D
University of Virginia	M,D
University of West Florida	M
University of Wisconsin–La Crosse	M
University of Wyoming	M
Utah State University	M
Valdosta State University	M
Virginia Polytechnic Institute and State University	M,D,O
Wayne State College	M
Wayne State University	M
West Chester University of Pennsylvania	M
Western Illinois University	M
Western Kentucky University	M
Western Oregon University	M
West Virginia University	M,D
Widener University	M,D
Worcester State College	M
Wright State University	M

■ HEALTH INFORMATICS

The College of St. Scholastica	M
Duke University	M,O
La Salle University	M,O
Loma Linda University	M
New York University	M,O
Touro College	M,O
The University of Alabama at Birmingham	M
University of Central Florida	M,O
University of La Verne	M
University of Minnesota, Twin Cities Campus	M,D
University of Missouri–Columbia	M
University of Virginia	M
University of Washington	M

■ HEALTH PHYSICS/RADIOLOGICAL HEALTH

Colorado State University	M,D
Emory University	M,D
Georgetown University	M
Georgia Institute of Technology	M,D
Illinois Institute of Technology	M,D
Johns Hopkins University	M,D
Massachusetts Institute of Technology	D
MCP Hahnemann University	M,D
Midwestern State University	M
Northwestern University	M,D
Oregon State University	M,D
Purdue University	M,D
San Diego State University	M
Texas A&M University	M
University of Cincinnati	M
University of Florida	M,D,O
University of Illinois at Urbana–Champaign	M,D
University of Kentucky	M
University of Massachusetts Lowell	M,D
University of Michigan	M,D,O
University of Missouri–Columbia	M,D
University of Nevada, Las Vegas	M
University of Pittsburgh	O
Wayne State University	M,D

■ HEALTH PROMOTION

Ball State University	M
Boston University	M
Bridgewater State College	M
Brigham Young University	M,D
California State University, Fresno	M
Central Michigan University	M
Emerson College	M
The George Washington University	M
Georgia State University	M,D
Goddard College	M
Harvard University	M,D
Lehman College of the City University of New York	M
Loma Linda University	M,D
Marymount University	M
Michigan State University	M,D
Northern Arizona University	M
Northwestern State University of Louisiana	M
Portland State University	M
Purdue University	M,D
San Diego State University	M,D
Simmons College	M,O
Southwest Missouri State University	M
Springfield College	M,O
Trinity College (DC)	M
The University of Alabama	D
The University of Alabama at Birmingham	M,D
University of Chicago	M
University of Delaware	M
University of Georgia	M,D,O
University of Kentucky	M,D
University of Massachusetts Lowell	D
The University of Memphis	M
University of Michigan	M,D
The University of Montana–Missoula	M
University of Nevada, Las Vegas	M
The University of North Carolina at Chapel Hill	M,D
The University of North Carolina at Charlotte	M
University of North Texas	M
University of Pittsburgh	M
University of South Carolina	M,D,O
University of Southern California	M
The University of Tennessee	M

University of Utah	M,D
Western Illinois University	M
West Virginia University	M

■ HEALTH PSYCHOLOGY

Appalachian State University	M
Duke University	D
Emporia State University	M
MCP Hahnemann University	D
National-Louis University	M,O
Northern Arizona University	M
Oklahoma State University	M,D
Rutgers, The State University of New Jersey, New Brunswick	D
Santa Clara University	M
Southwest Texas State University	M
Stony Brook University, State University of New York	D
University of California, Irvine	M,D
University of Florida	D
University of Miami	M,D
The University of Montana–Missoula	M
University of North Texas	M,D
Yeshiva University	D

■ HEALTH SERVICES MANAGEMENT AND HOSPITAL ADMINISTRATION

Albany State University	M
Arizona State University	M
Armstrong Atlantic State University	M
Baldwin-Wallace College	M
Barry University	M
Baylor University	M
Bellevue University	M
Bernard M. Baruch College of the City University of New York	M
Boston University	M
Brandeis University	M
Brenau University	M
Brooklyn College of the City University of New York	M
California Lutheran University	M
California State University, Bakersfield	M
California State University, Chico	M
California State University, Fresno	M
California State University, Long Beach	M,O
California State University, Los Angeles	M
California State University, Northridge	M
California State University, San Bernardino	M
Cardinal Stritch University	M
Carlow College	M
Carnegie Mellon University	M
Central Michigan University	M,O
Charleston Southern University	M
Clark University	M
Clemson University	M
Cleveland State University	M,D
College of Mount Saint Vincent	M,O
Colorado Technical University	M,D
Columbia University	M,D
Concordia University (IL)	M,O
Concordia University Wisconsin	M
DePaul University	M
Duke University	M
Duquesne University	M
Eastern Kentucky University	M
East Tennessee State University	M,O
Emory University	M
Fairfield University	M,O
Fairleigh Dickinson University, Florham-Madison Campus	M

Fairleigh Dickinson University, Teaneck–Hackensack Campus	M
Florida Institute of Technology	M
Florida International University	M
Framingham State College	M
Francis Marion University	M
The George Washington University	M,O
Georgia Institute of Technology	M
Georgia Southern University	M
Georgia State University	M,D
Governors State University	M
Harvard University	M,D
Hofstra University	M
Houston Baptist University	M
Howard University	M
Indiana State University	M
Indiana University Northwest	M,O
Indiana University–Purdue University Indianapolis	M
Iona College	M,O
Johns Hopkins University	M,D,O
Kean University	M
King's College	M
Lake Erie College	M
Lesley University	M
LeTourneau University	M
Lindenwood University	M
Loma Linda University	M
Long Island University, Brooklyn Campus	M
Long Island University, C.W. Post Campus	M,O
Loyola University Chicago	M
Lynn University	M,O
Madonna University	M
Marshall University	M
Marymount University	M
Marywood University	M
Mercer University	M
Midwestern State University	M
Mississippi College	M
Monmouth University	M,O
Montana State University–Billings	M
National University	M
New Jersey City University	M
New School University	M,O
New York Institute of Technology	M,O
New York University	M,O
Northeastern University	M
Nova Southeastern University	M
The Ohio State University	M,D
Ohio University	M
Oklahoma City University	M
Old Dominion University	M,D,O
Oregon State University	M
Our Lady of the Lake University of San Antonio	M
Pace University, New York City Campus	M
Pace University, White Plains Campus	M
The Pennsylvania State University Great Valley Campus	M
The Pennsylvania State University Harrisburg Campus of the Capital College	M
The Pennsylvania State University University Park Campus	M,D
Philadelphia University	M
Portland State University	M
Quinnipiac University	M
Rochester Institute of Technology	M,O
Rutgers, The State University of New Jersey, Camden	M
Rutgers, The State University of New Jersey, Newark	M,D
Sacred Heart University	M
Sage Graduate School	M
St. Ambrose University	M
St. John Fisher College	M
Saint Joseph's College (ME)	M
Saint Joseph's University	M
Saint Louis University	M
Saint Mary's College of California	M
Saint Mary's University of Minnesota	M
St. Thomas University	M,O
Saint Xavier University	M,O
Salve Regina University	M
San Diego State University	M,D
San Jose State University	M,O
Seton Hall University	M
Shenandoah University	M,O
Simmons College	M,O
Southeastern University	M
Southwest Baptist University	M
Southwest Missouri State University	M
Southwest Texas State University	M
Springfield College	M
State University of New York at Albany	M
State University of New York at Binghamton	M,D
State University of New York Institute of Technology at Utica/Rome	M
Stony Brook University, State University of New York	M,O
Suffolk University	M,O
Syracuse University	O
Temple University	M,D
Texas Tech University	M,O
Texas Woman's University	M
Touro College	O
Towson University	O
Trinity University	M
Tulane University	M,D
The University of Alabama at Birmingham	M,D
University of Arkansas at Little Rock	M
University of California, Berkeley	M,D
University of California, Los Angeles	M,D
University of Central Florida	M,O
University of Chicago	M,O
University of Cincinnati	M
University of Colorado at Denver	M
University of Connecticut	M,D
University of Denver	M
University of Detroit Mercy	M
University of Florida	M,D
University of Houston–Clear Lake	M
University of Illinois at Chicago	M,D
The University of Iowa	M,D
University of Kansas	M
University of Kentucky	M
University of La Verne	M
University of Louisiana at Lafayette	M
University of Mary Hardin-Baylor	M
University of Maryland, Baltimore County	M
University of Massachusetts Lowell	M
The University of Memphis	M
University of Michigan	M,D
University of Minnesota, Twin Cities Campus	M,D
University of Missouri–Columbia	M
University of Missouri–St. Louis	M,O
University of New Hampshire	M
University of New Haven	M
University of New Orleans	M
The University of North Carolina at Chapel Hill	M,D
The University of North Carolina at Charlotte	M
University of North Florida	M,O
University of North Texas	M,O
University of Pennsylvania	M,D
University of Pittsburgh	M,D,O
University of St. Francis (IL)	M,O
University of St. Thomas (MN)	M,O
University of San Francisco	M
The University of Scranton	M
University of South Carolina	M,D
University of Southern California	M
University of Southern Indiana	M
University of Southern Maine	M,O
University of Southern Mississippi	M
University of South Florida	M,D
The University of Texas at Arlington	M
The University of Texas at Tyler	M
University of Virginia	M
University of Washington	M
University of Wisconsin–Oshkosh	M
Villanova University	M,O
Virginia Commonwealth University	M,D
Walden University	D
Washington State University	M
Washington University in St. Louis	M,D
Webster University	M
West Chester University of Pennsylvania	M
Western Carolina University	M
Western Connecticut State University	M
Western Kentucky University	M
Western New England College	M
Widener University	M
Wilkes University	M
William Woods University	M
Xavier University	M
Yale University	M,D
York College of Pennsylvania	M
Youngstown State University	M

■ HEALTH SERVICES RESEARCH

Arizona State University	M,D
Brown University	M,D
Dartmouth College	M,D
Florida State University	M,D
Indiana University–Purdue University Indianapolis	M
Johns Hopkins University	M,D
Saint Louis University	D
Southwest Texas State University	M
Stanford University	M
Tufts University	M,D
University of Florida	M,D
University of Michigan	M
University of Minnesota, Twin Cities Campus	M,D
University of Rochester	D
University of Southern California	M,D
University of Virginia	M
University of Washington	M,D
Virginia Commonwealth University	D
Wake Forest University	M

■ HIGHER EDUCATION

Antioch University McGregor	M
Appalachian State University	M,O
Arizona State University	M,D
Auburn University	M,D,O
Azusa Pacific University	M
Ball State University	M,D
Barry University	M,D
Bernard M. Baruch College of the City University of New York	M
Boston College	M,D
Bowling Green State University	D
Central Missouri State University	M,D,O
Claremont Graduate University	M,D
Dallas Baptist University	M
DePaul University	M
Eastern Kentucky University	M

Eastern Washington University M
Florida Atlantic University M,D,O
Florida International University D,O
Florida State University M,D,O
Geneva College M
The George Washington University M,D,O
Georgia Southern University M
Georgia State University D
Harvard University M,D,O
Illinois State University M,D
Indiana State University M,D,O
Indiana University Bloomington M,D,O
Indiana University of Pennsylvania M
Indiana University–Purdue University Indianapolis M
Inter American University of Puerto Rico, Metropolitan Campus M
Inter American University of Puerto Rico, San Germán Campus M
Iowa State University of Science and Technology M,D
Johns Hopkins University M,D,O
Kent State University M,D,O
Louisiana State University and Agricultural and Mechanical College M,D,O
Loyola University Chicago D
Minnesota State University, Mankato M,O
Morehead State University M,O
New York University M,D
North Carolina State University M,D
Northeastern State University M
Northwestern University M,D
Nova Southeastern University D
Ohio University M,D
Oklahoma State University M,D,O
Old Dominion University M,O
The Pennsylvania State University University Park Campus M,D
Pittsburg State University M,O
Portland State University D
Purdue University M,D,O
Rowan University M
St. John's University (NY) M,O
Saint Louis University M,D,O
San Jose State University M,O
Seton Hall University D
Southern Illinois University Carbondale M
Spalding University M
Stanford University M,D
Syracuse University M,D,O
Teachers College, Columbia University M,D
Texas A&M University–Commerce M,D
Texas A&M University–Kingsville D
Texas Southern University M,D
Texas Tech University M,D,O
University at Buffalo, The State University of New York M,D,O
The University of Akron M
The University of Alabama M,D,O
The University of Arizona M,D,O
University of Arkansas M,D,O
University of Arkansas at Little Rock D
University of Central Oklahoma M
University of Connecticut M,D
University of Delaware M
University of Denver M,D,O
University of Florida M,D,O
University of Georgia D
University of Houston M,D
University of Illinois at Urbana–Champaign M,D,O
The University of Iowa M,D,O
University of Kansas M,D
University of Kentucky M,D
University of Louisville M,O
University of Maine M,D,O
University of Mary M
University of Maryland, Baltimore County M,D
University of Massachusetts Amherst M,D,O
University of Massachusetts Boston M,D,O
The University of Memphis M,D,O
University of Miami M
University of Michigan M,D
University of Minnesota, Twin Cities Campus M,D
University of Mississippi M
University of Missouri–Columbia M,D,O
University of Nevada, Las Vegas M,D,O
University of New Hampshire M
The University of North Carolina at Greensboro M,D,O
University of North Texas D
University of Oklahoma M,D
University of Oregon M,D
University of Pennsylvania M,D
University of Pittsburgh M,D
University of South Carolina M
University of South Florida M,D,O
The University of Tennessee M
University of Toledo M,D,O
University of Virginia D,O
University of Washington M,D
Vanderbilt University M,D
Wayne State University M,D,O
West Virginia University M,D
Wright State University M,O

■ HISPANIC STUDIES

Brown University M,D
California State University, Los Angeles M
California State University, Northridge M
New Mexico Highlands University M
Pontifical Catholic University of Puerto Rico M
San Jose State University M
University of California, Los Angeles D
University of California, Santa Barbara M,D
University of Illinois at Chicago M,D
University of Pittsburgh M,D
University of Puerto Rico, Mayagüez Campus M
University of Puerto Rico, Río Piedras M,D
University of Washington M

■ HISTORIC PRESERVATION

Ball State University M
Boston University M
Colorado State University M,D
Columbia University M
Cornell University M,D
Eastern Michigan University M
The George Washington University M
Georgia State University M
Middle Tennessee State University M,D
New York University
Rensselaer Polytechnic Institute M
State University of New York College at Buffalo M,O
Texas A&M University M,D
Texas Tech University M
University of California, Riverside M,D
University of Delaware M
University of Georgia M
University of Kentucky M
University of Oregon M
University of Pennsylvania M,O
University of South Carolina M,O
University of Vermont M
University of Washington O
Western Kentucky University M

■ HISTORY

Abilene Christian University M
Alabama State University M
American University M,D
Andrews University M
Angelo State University M
Appalachian State University M
Arizona State University M,D
Arkansas State University M,O
Arkansas Tech University M
Armstrong Atlantic State University M
Auburn University M,D
Ball State University M
Baylor University M
Boise State University M
Boston College M,D
Boston University M,D
Bowling Green State University M,D
Brandeis University M,D
Brigham Young University M
Brooklyn College of the City University of New York M,D
Brown University M,D
Butler University M
California State University, Bakersfield M
California State University, Chico M
California State University, Fresno M
California State University, Fullerton M
California State University, Hayward M
California State University, Long Beach M
California State University, Los Angeles M
California State University, Northridge M
California State University, Stanislaus M
Carnegie Mellon University M,D
Case Western Reserve University M,D
The Catholic University of America M,D
Central Connecticut State University M
Central Michigan University M,D
Central Missouri State University M
Central Washington University M
Chicago State University M
The Citadel, The Military College of South Carolina M
City College of the City University of New York M
Claremont Graduate University M,D
Clark Atlanta University M
Clark University M,D,O
Clemson University M
Cleveland State University M
The College of Saint Rose M
College of Staten Island of the City University of New York M
The College of William and Mary M,D
Colorado State University M
Columbia University M,D
Converse College M
Cornell University M,D
DePaul University M
Duke University D
Duquesne University M
East Carolina University M
Eastern Illinois University M
Eastern Kentucky University M
Eastern Michigan University M
Eastern Washington University M
East Stroudsburg University of Pennsylvania M
East Tennessee State University M
Emory University D
Emporia State University M
Fairleigh Dickinson University, Teaneck–Hackensack Campus M

Fayetteville State University	M
Florida Atlantic University	M
Florida International University	M,D
Florida State University	M,D
Fordham University	M,D
Fort Hays State University	M
George Mason University	M
Georgetown University	M,D
The George Washington University	M,D
Georgia College and State University	M
Georgia Southern University	M
Georgia State University	M,D
Hardin-Simmons University	M
Harvard University	D
Howard University	M,D
Hunter College of the City University of New York	M
Illinois State University	M
Indiana State University	M
Indiana University Bloomington	M,D
Indiana University of Pennsylvania	M
Indiana University–Purdue University Indianapolis	M
Iona College	M
Iowa State University of Science and Technology	M,D
Jackson State University	M
Jacksonville State University	M
James Madison University	M
John Carroll University	M
Johns Hopkins University	D
Kansas State University	M,D
Kent State University	M,D
Lamar University	M
Lehigh University	M,D
Lehman College of the City University of New York	M
Lincoln University (MO)	M
Long Island University, Brooklyn Campus	M,O
Long Island University, C.W. Post Campus	M
Louisiana State University and Agricultural and Mechanical College	M,D
Louisiana Tech University	M
Loyola University Chicago	M,D
Marquette University	M,D
Marshall University	M
Miami University	M
Michigan State University	M,D
Middle Tennessee State University	M,D
Midwestern State University	M
Millersville University of Pennsylvania	M
Minnesota State University, Mankato	M
Mississippi College	M
Mississippi State University	M,D
Monmouth University	M
Montana State University–Bozeman	M
Montclair State University	M
Morgan State University	M,D
Murray State University	M
New Jersey Institute of Technology	M
New Mexico Highlands University	M
New Mexico State University	M
New School University	M,D
New York University	M,D,O
North Carolina Central University	M
North Carolina State University	M
North Dakota State University	M
Northeastern Illinois University	M
Northeastern University	M,D
Northern Arizona University	M,D
Northern Illinois University	M,D
Northwestern State University of Louisiana	M
Northwestern University	D
Northwest Missouri State University	M
Oakland University	M
The Ohio State University	M,D,O
Ohio University	M,D
Oklahoma State University	M,D
Old Dominion University	M
The Pennsylvania State University University Park Campus	M,D
Pepperdine University	M
Pittsburg State University	M
Pontifical Catholic University of Puerto Rico	M
Portland State University	M
Prescott College	M
Princeton University	D
Providence College	M
Purdue University	M,D
Purdue University Calumet	M
Queens College of the City University of New York	M
Rhode Island College	M
Rice University	M,D
Roosevelt University	M
Rutgers, The State University of New Jersey, Camden	M
Rutgers, The State University of New Jersey, Newark	M
Rutgers, The State University of New Jersey, New Brunswick	D
St. Bonaventure University	M
St. Cloud State University	M
St. John's University (NY)	M,D
Saint Louis University	M,D
St. Mary's University of San Antonio	M
Salem State College	M
Salisbury State University	M
Sam Houston State University	M
San Diego State University	M
San Francisco State University	M
San Jose State University	M
Slippery Rock University of Pennsylvania	M
Sonoma State University	M
Southeastern Louisiana University	M
Southeast Missouri State University	M
Southern Connecticut State University	M
Southern Illinois University Carbondale	M,D
Southern Illinois University Edwardsville	M
Southern Methodist University	M,D
Southern University and Agricultural and Mechanical College	M
Southwest Missouri State University	M
Southwest Texas State University	M
Stanford University	M,D
State University of New York at Albany	M,D,O
State University of New York at Binghamton	M,D
State University of New York at Oswego	M
State University of New York College at Brockport	M
State University of New York College at Buffalo	M
State University of New York College at Cortland	M
State University of West Georgia	M
Stephen F. Austin State University	M
Stony Brook University, State University of New York	M,D
Sul Ross State University	M
Syracuse University	M,D
Tarleton State University	M
Temple University	M,D
Texas A&M International University	M
Texas A&M University	M,D
Texas A&M University–Commerce	M
Texas A&M University–Kingsville	M
Texas Christian University	M,D
Texas Southern University	M
Texas Tech University	M,D
Texas Woman's University	M
Troy State University Dothan	M
Truman State University	M
Tufts University	M,D
Tulane University	M,D
University at Buffalo, The State University of New York	M,D
The University of Akron	M,D
The University of Alabama	M,D
The University of Alabama at Birmingham	M
The University of Alabama in Huntsville	M
The University of Arizona	M,D
University of Arkansas	M,D
University of California, Berkeley	M,D,O
University of California, Davis	M,D
University of California, Irvine	M,D
University of California, Los Angeles	M,D
University of California, Riverside	M,D
University of California, San Diego	M,D
University of California, Santa Barbara	M,D
University of California, Santa Cruz	D
University of Central Arkansas	M
University of Central Florida	M
University of Central Oklahoma	M
University of Chicago	M,D
University of Cincinnati	M,D
University of Colorado at Boulder	M,D
University of Colorado at Colorado Springs	M
University of Colorado at Denver	M
University of Connecticut	M,D
University of Delaware	M,D
University of Denver	M
University of Florida	M,D
University of Georgia	M,D
University of Hawaii at Manoa	M,D
University of Houston	M,D
University of Houston–Clear Lake	M
University of Idaho	M,D
University of Illinois at Chicago	M,D
University of Illinois at Urbana–Champaign	M,D
University of Indianapolis	M
The University of Iowa	M,D
University of Kansas	M,D
University of Kentucky	M,D
University of Louisiana at Lafayette	M
University of Louisiana at Monroe	M
University of Louisville	M
University of Maine	M,D
University of Maryland, Baltimore County	M
University of Maryland, College Park	M,D
University of Massachusetts Amherst	M,D
University of Massachusetts Boston	M
The University of Memphis	M,D
University of Miami	M,D
University of Michigan	D,O
University of Minnesota, Twin Cities Campus	M,D
University of Mississippi	M,D
University of Missouri–Columbia	M,D
University of Missouri–Kansas City	M,D
University of Missouri–St. Louis	M,O
The University of Montana–Missoula	M
University of Nebraska at Kearney	M
University of Nebraska at Omaha	M
University of Nebraska–Lincoln	M,D
University of Nevada, Las Vegas	M,D

University of Nevada, Reno	M,D
University of New Hampshire	M,D
University of New Mexico	M,D
University of New Orleans	M
The University of North Carolina at Chapel Hill	M,D
The University of North Carolina at Charlotte	M
The University of North Carolina at Greensboro	M,O
The University of North Carolina at Wilmington	M
University of North Dakota	M,D
University of Northern Colorado	M
University of Northern Iowa	M
University of North Florida	M
University of North Texas	M,D
University of Notre Dame	M,D
University of Oklahoma	M,D
University of Oregon	M,D
University of Pennsylvania	M,D
University of Pittsburgh	M,D
University of Puerto Rico, Río Piedras	M,D
University of Rhode Island	M
University of Richmond	M
University of Rochester	M,D
University of San Diego	M
The University of Scranton	M
University of South Alabama	M
University of South Carolina	M,D,O
University of South Dakota	M
University of Southern California	M,D
University of Southern Mississippi	M,D
University of South Florida	M
The University of Tennessee	M,D
The University of Texas at Arlington	M,D
The University of Texas at Austin	M,D
The University of Texas at Brownsville	M
The University of Texas at El Paso	M,D
The University of Texas at San Antonio	M
The University of Texas at Tyler	M
The University of Texas of the Permian Basin	M
The University of Texas–Pan American	M
University of Toledo	M,D
University of Tulsa	M
University of Utah	M,D
University of Vermont	M
University of Virginia	M,D
University of Washington	M,D
University of West Florida	M
University of Wisconsin–Eau Claire	M
University of Wisconsin–Madison	M,D
University of Wisconsin–Milwaukee	M
University of Wisconsin–Stevens Point	M
University of Wyoming	M
Utah State University	M
Valdosta State University	M
Valparaiso University	M
Vanderbilt University	M,D
Villanova University	M
Virginia Commonwealth University	M
Virginia Polytechnic Institute and State University	M
Virginia State University	M
Wake Forest University	M
Washington State University	M,D
Washington University in St. Louis	M,D
Wayne State University	M,D,O
West Chester University of Pennsylvania	M
Western Carolina University	M
Western Connecticut State University	M
Western Illinois University	M
Western Kentucky University	M
Western Michigan University	M,D
Western Washington University	M
Westfield State College	M
West Texas A&M University	M
West Virginia University	M,D
Wichita State University	M
William Paterson University of New Jersey	M
Winthrop University	M
Wright State University	M
Yale University	M,D
Youngstown State University	M

■ HISTORY OF MEDICINE

Duke University	
New Jersey Institute of Technology	M
Rutgers, The State University of New Jersey, New Brunswick	D
University of Minnesota, Twin Cities Campus	M,D
Yale University	M,D

■ HISTORY OF SCIENCE AND TECHNOLOGY

Arizona State University	M,D
Brown University	M,D
Cornell University	M,D
Georgia Institute of Technology	M,D
Harvard University	M,D
Indiana University Bloomington	M,D
Iowa State University of Science and Technology	M,D
Johns Hopkins University	D
Massachusetts Institute of Technology	D
New Jersey Institute of Technology	M
Polytechnic University, Brooklyn Campus	M
Princeton University	D
Rensselaer Polytechnic Institute	M,D
Rutgers, The State University of New Jersey, New Brunswick	D
University of California, Berkeley	D
University of California, San Diego	M,D
University of California, San Francisco	M,D
University of California, Santa Barbara	D
University of Chicago	M,D
University of Massachusetts Amherst	M,D
University of Minnesota, Twin Cities Campus	M,D
University of Notre Dame	M,D
University of Oklahoma	M,D
University of Pennsylvania	M,D
University of Pittsburgh	M,D
University of Wisconsin–Madison	M,D
Virginia Polytechnic Institute and State University	M,D
West Virginia University	M,D
Yale University	M,D

■ HIV/AIDS NURSING

Columbia University	M,O
Duke University	M,O
University of Delaware	M,O

■ HOLOCAUST STUDIES

Clark University	D

■ HOME ECONOMICS EDUCATION

Brooklyn College of the City University of New York	M
Central Washington University	M
Eastern Kentucky University	M
Florida International University	M
Iowa State University of Science and Technology	M,D
Louisiana State University and Agricultural and Mechanical College	M,D
Michigan State University	M,D
Montclair State University	M
North Dakota State University	M
Northwestern State University of Louisiana	M
The Ohio State University	M
Oregon State University	M
Purdue University	M,D,O
Queens College of the City University of New York	M
South Carolina State University	M
Texas Southern University	M
Texas Tech University	M,D
University of Central Oklahoma	M
University of Georgia	M,D,O
University of Puerto Rico, Río Piedras	M
University of Rhode Island	M
Wayne State College	M
Western Carolina University	M
Western Michigan University	M

■ HORTICULTURE

Auburn University	M,D
Brigham Young University	M
Clemson University	M,D
Colorado State University	M,D
Cornell University	M,D
Iowa State University of Science and Technology	M,D
Kansas State University	M,D
Louisiana State University and Agricultural and Mechanical College	M,D
Michigan State University	M,D
New Mexico State University	M,D
North Carolina State University	M,D
North Dakota State University	M,D
The Ohio State University	M,D
Oklahoma State University	M
Oregon State University	M,D
The Pennsylvania State University University Park Campus	M,D
Purdue University	M,D
Rutgers, The State University of New Jersey, New Brunswick	M,D
Southern Illinois University Carbondale	M
Texas A&M University	M,D
Texas Tech University	M,D
University of Arkansas	M
University of California, Davis	M
University of Delaware	M
University of Florida	M,D
University of Georgia	M,D
University of Hawaii at Manoa	M,D
University of Maine	M
University of Maryland, College Park	M,D
University of Minnesota, Twin Cities Campus	M,D
University of Missouri–Columbia	M,D
University of Nebraska–Lincoln	M,D
University of Puerto Rico, Mayagüez Campus	M
The University of Tennessee	M
University of Washington	M,D
University of Wisconsin–Madison	M,D
Virginia Polytechnic Institute and State University	M,D
Washington State University	M,D
West Virginia University	M,D

■ HOSPICE NURSING

Madonna University	M

■ HOSPITALITY MANAGEMENT

- Central Michigan University M,O
- Cornell University M,D
- Fairleigh Dickinson University, Florham-Madison Campus M
- Fairleigh Dickinson University, Teaneck–Hackensack Campus M
- Florida International University M
- The George Washington University M
- Iowa State University of Science and Technology M,D
- Johnson & Wales University M
- Kansas State University M,D
- Lynn University M
- Michigan State University M
- New York University M,D,O
- The Ohio State University M,D
- Oklahoma State University M,D
- The Pennsylvania State University University Park Campus M,D
- Purdue University M,D
- Rochester Institute of Technology M
- Roosevelt University M
- Temple University M
- Texas Tech University M
- Texas Woman's University M,D
- The University of Alabama M
- University of Denver M
- University of Hawaii at Manoa M
- University of Houston M
- University of Massachusetts Amherst M
- University of Missouri–Columbia M,D
- University of Nevada, Las Vegas M,D
- University of New Haven M
- The University of North Carolina at Greensboro M,D
- University of North Texas M
- University of South Carolina M
- The University of Tennessee M
- University of Wisconsin–Stout M
- Virginia Polytechnic Institute and State University M,D

■ HUMAN-COMPUTER INTERACTION

- Carnegie Mellon University M,D
- DePaul University M
- Georgia Institute of Technology M
- Indiana University Bloomington M
- Tufts University O
- University of Michigan M,D

■ HUMAN DEVELOPMENT

- Arizona State University M,D
- Auburn University M,D
- Boston University M,D,O
- Bowling Green State University M
- Bradley University M
- Brigham Young University M,D
- California State University, San Bernardino M
- The Catholic University of America D
- Central Michigan University M
- Claremont Graduate University M,D
- Colorado State University M
- Cornell University D
- Duke University D
- The George Washington University M
- Harvard University M,D,O
- Howard University M
- Iowa State University of Science and Technology M,D
- Kent State University D
- Marylhurst University M
- Marywood University D
- Montana State University–Bozeman M
- National-Louis University M,D,O
- New York Institute of Technology M
- Northwestern University D
- The Ohio State University M,D
- Oregon State University M,D
- Our Lady of the Lake University of San Antonio M
- The Pennsylvania State University University Park Campus M,D
- Purdue University M,D
- Saint Joseph College M
- Saint Louis University M,D
- Saint Mary's University of Minnesota M
- Southern Illinois University Carbondale M,D
- Texas A&M University M,D
- Texas Southern University M
- Texas Tech University M,D
- Troy State University M
- Troy State University Montgomery M,O
- The University of Alabama M
- The University of Arizona M,D
- University of California, Berkeley M,D
- University of California, Davis D
- University of California, Irvine M,D
- University of Central Oklahoma M
- University of Chicago D
- University of Connecticut M,D
- University of Dayton M
- University of Delaware M,D
- University of Illinois at Chicago M,D
- University of Illinois at Springfield M
- University of Illinois at Urbana–Champaign M,D
- University of Kansas M,D
- University of Maine M
- University of Maryland, College Park M,D,O
- University of Missouri–Columbia M,D
- University of Nevada, Reno M
- The University of North Carolina at Greensboro M,D
- University of North Texas M
- University of Pennsylvania M,D
- University of Pittsburgh M
- The University of Texas at Austin M,D
- The University of Texas at Dallas M,D
- University of Washington M,D
- University of Wisconsin–Madison M,D
- Utah State University M
- Vanderbilt University M,D
- Virginia Polytechnic Institute and State University M,D
- Walsh University M
- Washington State University M
- Wayne State University M

■ HUMAN ECOLOGY-GENERAL

- Alabama Agricultural and Mechanical University M,D
- Appalachian State University M
- Ball State University M
- Bowling Green State University M
- California State University, Fresno M
- California State University, Long Beach M
- California State University, Los Angeles M
- Central Michigan University M
- Central Washington University M
- Cornell University M,D
- East Carolina University M
- Eastern Illinois University M
- Eastern Michigan University M
- Florida State University M,D
- Illinois State University M
- Indiana State University M
- Iowa State University of Science and Technology M,D
- Kansas State University M,D
- Kent State University M
- Lamar University M
- Louisiana State University and Agricultural and Mechanical College M,D
- Louisiana Tech University M
- Marshall University M
- Michigan State University M,D
- Montclair State University M
- New Mexico State University M
- North Carolina Central University M
- The Ohio State University M,D
- Ohio University M
- Oklahoma State University M,D
- Oregon State University M,D
- Prairie View A&M University M
- Purdue University M,D
- Sam Houston State University M
- San Francisco State University M
- South Dakota State University M
- Southeast Missouri State University M
- Southwest Missouri State University M
- Stephen F. Austin State University M
- Texas A&M University–Kingsville M
- Texas Southern University M
- Texas Tech University M,D
- The University of Akron M
- The University of Alabama M,D
- The University of Arizona M,D
- University of Arkansas M
- University of Central Arkansas M
- University of Central Oklahoma M
- University of Georgia M,D
- University of Idaho M
- University of Kentucky M
- University of Louisiana at Lafayette M
- University of Minnesota, Twin Cities Campus M,D
- University of Missouri–Columbia M,D
- University of Nebraska–Lincoln M,D
- The University of North Carolina at Greensboro M,D
- University of North Florida M,O
- University of Southern Mississippi M,D
- The University of Tennessee D
- The University of Tennessee at Martin M
- The University of Texas at Austin M,D
- University of Wisconsin–Madison M,D
- University of Wisconsin–Stevens Point M
- University of Wisconsin–Stout M
- Utah State University M
- Virginia Polytechnic Institute and State University M,D,O

■ HUMAN GENETICS

- Case Western Reserve University D
- Hofstra University M
- Howard University M,D
- Johns Hopkins University D
- MCP Hahnemann University M,D
- Tulane University M,D
- University of California, Los Angeles M,D
- University of Chicago D
- University of Maryland M,D
- University of Michigan M,D
- University of Pittsburgh M,D
- University of Utah M,D
- Virginia Commonwealth University M,D,O
- West Virginia University M,D

■ HUMANITIES

- Antioch University McGregor M
- Arcadia University M

Arizona State University M
Brigham Young University M
California State University, Dominguez Hills M
Central Michigan University M
Clark Atlanta University D
Dominican University of California M
Duke University M
Florida State University M,D
Frostburg State University M
Grambling State University M
Hofstra University M
Indiana State University M
John Carroll University M
Marshall University M
Marymount University M
Michigan State University M
New College of California M
New York University M,O
Old Dominion University M
The Pennsylvania State University Harrisburg Campus of the Capital College M
Prescott College M
Rockhurst University M
Salve Regina University M,D,O
San Francisco State University M
Stanford University M
State University of New York at Albany D
Texas Tech University M
Towson University M
University at Buffalo, The State University of New York M
University of California, Santa Cruz D
University of Chicago M
University of Colorado at Denver M
University of Houston–Clear Lake M
University of Louisville P,M
The University of Texas at Dallas M,D
University of West Florida M
Western Kentucky University M
Wright State University M
Xavier University M

■ HUMAN RESOURCES DEVELOPMENT

Abilene Christian University M
American International College M,O
Antioch University Los Angeles M
Azusa Pacific University M
Barry University M,D
Bowie State University M
California State University, Sacramento M
Carlow College M
Chapman University M
Clemson University M
The College of New Rochelle M,O
Florida International University M
Friends University M
The George Washington University M,D,O
Georgia State University M,D
Heritage College M
Illinois Institute of Technology M,D
Indiana State University M,D
Indiana University Bloomington M
Indiana University of Pennsylvania M
Inter American University of Puerto Rico, Metropolitan Campus M
Inter American University of Puerto Rico, San Germán Campus M
Iowa State University of Science and Technology M,D
John F. Kennedy University M,O
Johns Hopkins University M,O
Kennesaw State University M
Lesley University M
Loyola University Chicago M
Manhattanville College M
Marquette University M
Midwestern State University M
National-Louis University M
New School University M,O
North Carolina Agricultural and Technical State University M
Northeastern Illinois University M
Oakland University M
Palm Beach Atlantic College M
The Pennsylvania State University University Park Campus M
Pittsburg State University M,O
Rochester Institute of Technology M
Rollins College M
St. John Fisher College M
Siena Heights University M
Suffolk University M,O
Texas A&M University M,D
Towson University M
Trinity College (DC) M
Universidad del Turabo M
University of Bridgeport M
University of Georgia M,D,O
University of Illinois at Urbana–Champaign M,D,O
University of Louisville M,D
University of Oregon M
University of Pittsburgh M
University of San Francisco M
The University of Scranton M
The University of Tennessee M,D
The University of Texas at Austin M
University of Wisconsin–Milwaukee M
University of Wisconsin–Stout M
Vanderbilt University M,D
Villanova University M
Virginia Polytechnic Institute and State University M,D
Webster University M
Western Carolina University M
Western New England College M
Xavier University M

■ HUMAN RESOURCES MANAGEMENT

Adelphi University O
Alabama Agricultural and Mechanical University M,O
Albany State University M
American University M
Auburn University M,D
Bernard M. Baruch College of the City University of New York M,D
Boston University M,O
California State University, Hayward M
California State University, Sacramento M
Case Western Reserve University M,D
The Catholic University of America M
Central Michigan University M,O
Chapman University M
City University M,O
Claremont Graduate University M
Clarkson University M
Cleveland State University M
Colorado Technical University M,D
Columbia University M
Concordia University Wisconsin M
Cornell University M,D
Cumberland University M
Dallas Baptist University M
DePaul University M
East Central University M
Eastern Michigan University M
Emmanuel College M
Fairfield University M,O
Fairleigh Dickinson University, Florham-Madison Campus M
Fairleigh Dickinson University, Teaneck–Hackensack Campus M
Florida Institute of Technology M
Florida Metropolitan University–Tampa Campus M
Fordham University M,D,O
Framingham State College M
Gannon University O
George Mason University M
The George Washington University M,D
Georgia State University M,D
Hawaii Pacific University M
Hofstra University M
Holy Family College M
Houston Baptist University M
Indiana University Bloomington M
Inter American University of Puerto Rico, Metropolitan Campus M
Inter American University of Puerto Rico, San Germán Campus M
Iona College M,O
Kennesaw State University M
La Roche College M
Lesley University M,O
Lindenwood University M
Long Island University, Brooklyn Campus M
Long Island University, C.W. Post Campus M,O
Loyola University Chicago M
Lynchburg College M
Manhattanville College M
Marquette University M
Marshall University M
Marygrove College M
Marymount University M,O
Mercy College M
Metropolitan State University M
Michigan State University M,D
National-Louis University M
National University M
New School University M,O
New York Institute of Technology M,O
New York University M,D,O
North Carolina Agricultural and Technical State University M
Nova Southeastern University M
The Ohio State University M,D
Oral Roberts University M
Pontifical Catholic University of Puerto Rico M,D
Purdue University M,D
Regis University M,O
Rivier College M
Rollins College M
Rutgers, The State University of New Jersey, Newark M,D
Rutgers, The State University of New Jersey, New Brunswick M,D
Sage Graduate School M
St. Edward's University M,O
Saint Francis University M
Saint Joseph's University M
St. Thomas University M,O
Salve Regina University M
San Diego State University M
Southeast Missouri State University M
State University of New York at Albany M
Stony Brook University, State University of New York M,O
Suffolk University M,O
Temple University M,D
Trinity College (DC) M
Troy State University M

Troy State University Dothan	M
Troy State University Montgomery	M
Universidad del Turabo	M
The University of Akron	M
University of Connecticut	M,D
The University of Findlay	M
University of Florida	M,D
University of Houston–Clear Lake	M
University of Illinois at Chicago	D
University of Illinois at Urbana–Champaign	M,D
The University of Memphis	M
University of Minnesota, Twin Cities Campus	M,D
University of Missouri–St. Louis	M,O
University of New Haven	M
University of New Mexico	M
University of North Florida	M
University of Oregon	M
University of Pittsburgh	O
University of Redlands	M
University of St. Thomas (MN)	M,O
The University of Scranton	M
University of South Carolina	M
The University of Texas at Arlington	M,D
University of the Sacred Heart	M
University of Wisconsin–Madison	M
Utah State University	M
Valdosta State University	M
Virginia Commonwealth University	M
Webster University	M
Western New England College	M
Widener University	M
Wilkes University	M
Wilmington College	M
York College of Pennsylvania	M

■ HUMAN SERVICES

Abilene Christian University	M
Andrews University	M
Antioch New England Graduate School	M
Bellevue University	M
Brandeis University	M
California State University, Sacramento	M
Chestnut Hill College	M,D
The College of New Rochelle	O
Concordia University (IL)	M,O
DePaul University	M
Drury University	M
Florida State University	M,D,O
Framingham State College	M
Georgia State University	M
Hood College	M
Indiana University Northwest	M,O
Kansas State University	M,D
Lehigh University	M,D,O
Lesley University	M,O
Lincoln University (PA)	M
Lindenwood University	M
Louisiana State University in Shreveport	M
Minnesota State University, Mankato	M
Minnesota State University Moorhead	M
Montclair State University	M
Murray State University	M
National-Louis University	M,O
Pontifical Catholic University of Puerto Rico	M
Rider University	M
Roberts Wesleyan College	M
Sage Graduate School	M
St. Edward's University	M,O
St. Mary's University of San Antonio	M,D,O
Springfield College	M
State University of New York at Oswego	M
Syracuse University	M
Universidad del Turabo	M
University of Baltimore	M
University of Bridgeport	M
University of Colorado at Colorado Springs	M
University of Illinois at Springfield	M
University of Maryland, Baltimore County	M,D
University of Massachusetts Boston	M
University of Oklahoma	M
Walden University	D
Wayne State University	O
West Virginia University	M
Youngstown State University	M

■ HYDRAULICS

Auburn University	M,D
Colorado State University	M,D
Texas A&M University	M,D
University of Missouri–Rolla	M,D
University of Washington	M,D

■ HYDROLOGY

Auburn University	M,D
California State University, Bakersfield	M
Clemson University	M
Colorado State University	M,D
Cornell University	M,D
Idaho State University	M
Illinois State University	M
New Mexico Institute of Mining and Technology	M,D
Rensselaer Polytechnic Institute	M
Syracuse University	M,D
Texas A&M University	M,D
The University of Arizona	M,D
University of California, Davis	M,D
University of Hawaii at Manoa	M,D
University of Idaho	M
University of Illinois at Chicago	M,D
University of Missouri–Rolla	M,D
University of Nevada, Reno	M,D
University of New Hampshire	M,D
University of Southern Mississippi	M,D
University of South Florida	M,D,O
University of Washington	M,D
West Virginia University	M,D
Wright State University	M

■ ILLUSTRATION

California State University, Long Beach	M
Kent State University	M
Syracuse University	M
University of Utah	M
Western Connecticut State University	M

■ IMMUNOLOGY

Boston University	D
Brown University	M,D
California Institute of Technology	D
Case Western Reserve University	M,D
Colorado State University	M,D
Cornell University	M,D
Creighton University	M,D
Dartmouth College	D
Duke University	D
East Carolina University	D
Emory University	D
Florida State University	M,D
Georgetown University	D
The George Washington University	D
Harvard University	D
Indiana University–Purdue University Indianapolis	M,D
Iowa State University of Science and Technology	M,D
Johns Hopkins University	M,D
Kansas State University	M,D
Long Island University, C.W. Post Campus	M
Loyola University Chicago	M,D
Massachusetts Institute of Technology	D
Mayo Graduate School	D
MCP Hahnemann University	M,D
New York University	D
North Carolina State University	M,D
Northwestern University	D
The Ohio State University	M,D
Purdue University	M,D
Rutgers, The State University of New Jersey, New Brunswick	M,D
Saint Louis University	D
Stanford University	D
State University of New York at Albany	M,D
Stony Brook University, State University of New York	D
Temple University	M,D
Tufts University	D
Tulane University	M,D
University at Buffalo, The State University of New York	D
The University of Arizona	M,D
University of California, Berkeley	M,D
University of California, Davis	M,D
University of California, Los Angeles	M,D
University of California, San Diego	D
University of California, San Francisco	D
University of Chicago	D
University of Florida	M,D
University of Illinois at Chicago	D
The University of Iowa	M,D
University of Kansas	D
University of Kentucky	D
University of Louisville	M,D
University of Maryland	M,D
University of Miami	D
University of Michigan	D
University of Minnesota, Duluth	M,D
University of Missouri–Columbia	M,D
The University of North Carolina at Chapel Hill	M,D
University of North Dakota	M,D
University of Pennsylvania	D
University of Pittsburgh	M,D
University of Rochester	M,D
University of South Alabama	D
University of South Dakota	M,D
University of Southern California	M,D
University of Southern Maine	M
University of South Florida	D
The University of Texas at Austin	D
University of Utah	D
University of Virginia	D
University of Washington	D
Vanderbilt University	M,D
Virginia Commonwealth University	M,D,O
Wake Forest University	D
Washington University in St. Louis	D
Wayne State University	M,D
West Virginia University	M,D
Wright State University	M
Yale University	D
Yeshiva University	D

■ INDUSTRIAL/MANAGEMENT ENGINEERING

Arizona State University	M,D
Auburn University	M,D

Bradley University M
California Polytechnic State University, San Luis Obispo M
California State University, Fresno M
California State University, Northridge M
Central Missouri State University M,O
Central Washington University M
Clemson University M,D
Cleveland State University M,D
Colorado State University M,D
Columbia University M,D,O
Cornell University M,D
East Carolina University M
Eastern Michigan University M
Florida Agricultural and Mechanical University M
Florida International University M
Florida State University M,D
Georgia Institute of Technology M,D
Illinois State University M
Indiana State University M
Iowa State University of Science and Technology M,D
Kansas State University M,D
Lamar University M,D
Lehigh University M,D
Louisiana State University and Agricultural and Mechanical College M,D
Louisiana Tech University M,D
Loyola Marymount University M
Mississippi State University M,D
Montana State University–Bozeman M,D
New Jersey Institute of Technology M,D
New Mexico State University M,D
North Carolina Agricultural and Technical State University M,D
North Carolina State University M,D
North Dakota State University M
Northeastern University M,D
Northern Illinois University M
Northwestern University M,D
The Ohio State University M,D
Ohio University M
Oklahoma State University M,D
Oregon State University M,D
The Pennsylvania State University University Park Campus M,D
Polytechnic University, Brooklyn Campus M
Polytechnic University, Westchester Graduate Center M
Purdue University M,D
Rensselaer Polytechnic Institute M
Rochester Institute of Technology M
Rutgers, The State University of New Jersey, New Brunswick M,D
St. Mary's University of San Antonio M
South Dakota State University M
Southwest Texas State University M
Stanford University M,D
State University of New York at Binghamton M,D
State University of New York College at Buffalo M
Tennessee Technological University M,D
Texas A&M University M,D
Texas A&M University–Commerce M
Texas A&M University–Kingsville M
Texas Tech University M,D
University at Buffalo, The State University of New York M,D
The University of Alabama M
The University of Alabama in Huntsville M,D
The University of Arizona M,D
University of Arkansas M,D
University of California, Berkeley M,D
University of Central Florida M,D,O
University of Cincinnati M,D
University of Dayton M
University of Florida M,D,O
University of Houston M,D
University of Illinois at Chicago M,D
University of Illinois at Urbana–Champaign M,D
The University of Iowa M,D
University of Louisville M,D
University of Massachusetts Amherst M,D
University of Massachusetts Lowell M,D
The University of Memphis M
University of Miami M,D
University of Michigan M,D,O
University of Michigan–Dearborn M
University of Minnesota, Twin Cities Campus M,D
University of Missouri–Columbia M,D
University of Nebraska–Lincoln M,D
University of New Haven M,O
University of Oklahoma M,D
University of Pittsburgh M,D
University of Puerto Rico, Mayagüez Campus M
University of Rhode Island M
University of Southern California M,D,O
University of Southern Colorado M
University of South Florida M,D
The University of Tennessee M,D
The University of Texas at Arlington M,D
The University of Texas at Austin M,D
The University of Texas at El Paso M
University of Toledo M,D
University of Washington M,D
University of Wisconsin–Madison M,D
Virginia Polytechnic Institute and State University M,D
Wayne State University M,D
Western Carolina University M
Western Michigan University M
Western New England College M
West Virginia University M,D
Wichita State University M,D
Youngstown State University M

■ INDUSTRIAL AND LABOR RELATIONS

Case Western Reserve University M,D
Cleveland State University M
Cornell University M,D
Georgia State University M,D
Indiana University of Pennsylvania M
Inter American University of Puerto Rico, Metropolitan Campus M
Inter American University of Puerto Rico, San Germán Campus M
Iowa State University of Science and Technology M
Loyola University Chicago M
Michigan State University M,D
Middle Tennessee State University M,D
New York Institute of Technology M,O
The Ohio State University M,D
The Pennsylvania State University University Park Campus M
Rutgers, The State University of New Jersey, New Brunswick M,D
Saint Francis University M
State University of New York Empire State College M
Stony Brook University, State University of New York M,O
The University of Akron M
University of California, Berkeley D
University of Cincinnati M
University of Illinois at Urbana–Champaign M,D
University of Louisville M
University of Massachusetts Amherst M
University of Minnesota, Twin Cities Campus M,D
University of New Haven M
University of North Texas M,D
University of Oregon M
University of Rhode Island M
University of Wisconsin–Madison M,D
University of Wisconsin–Milwaukee M
Virginia Commonwealth University M
Wayne State University M
West Virginia University M

■ INDUSTRIAL AND MANUFACTURING MANAGEMENT

Bentley College M,O
Bernard M. Baruch College of the City University of New York M,D
Boston University M,D,O
California Polytechnic State University, San Luis Obispo M
Carnegie Mellon University M,D
Case Western Reserve University M,D
Central Connecticut State University M
Central Michigan University M
Central Missouri State University M
Clarkson University M
Clemson University M,D
Columbia University D
DePaul University M
Eastern Michigan University M
Fairleigh Dickinson University, Florham-Madison Campus M
Fairleigh Dickinson University, Teaneck–Hackensack Campus M
Florida Institute of Technology M
The George Washington University M
Georgia State University M,D
Illinois Institute of Technology M
Inter American University of Puerto Rico, Metropolitan Campus M
Lawrence Technological University M
Lynchburg College M
Massachusetts Institute of Technology M
Michigan State University M,D
Michigan Technological University M
New Jersey Institute of Technology M,D
New York University M
Northeastern State University M
Northern Illinois University M
Northwestern University M
The Pennsylvania State University University Park Campus M,D
Polytechnic University, Brooklyn Campus M
Polytechnic University, Westchester Graduate Center M
Purdue University M,D
Regis University M,O
Rensselaer Polytechnic Institute M,D
Rochester Institute of Technology M
San Diego State University M
San Jose State University M
Southeastern Oklahoma State University M
Stevens Institute of Technology M,O
Stony Brook University, State University of New York M,O
Syracuse University D
Texas Tech University M,D
The University of Alabama M,D
University of Arkansas M
University of Cincinnati M,D
University of Colorado at Boulder M,D

University of Colorado at Colorado Springs M
University of Massachusetts Lowell M
University of Minnesota, Twin Cities Campus M,D
University of North Dakota M
University of North Texas M,D
University of Rhode Island M,D
University of St. Thomas (MN) M,O
University of Southern Indiana M
The University of Tennessee M,D
The University of Tennessee at Chattanooga M
University of Toledo M,D
University of Wisconsin–Madison M
University of Wisconsin–Platteville M
Washington University in St. Louis M,D
Wright State University M

■ INDUSTRIAL AND ORGANIZATIONAL PSYCHOLOGY

Alliant International University M,D
Angelo State University M
Appalachian State University M
Bernard M. Baruch College of the City University of New York M,D,O
Bowling Green State University M,D
Brooklyn College of the City University of New York M,D
California State University, San Bernardino M
Central Michigan University M,D
Central Washington University M
Claremont Graduate University M,D
Clemson University D
Cleveland State University M
Colorado State University D
DePaul University M,D
Emporia State University M
Fairleigh Dickinson University, Florham-Madison Campus M
Florida Institute of Technology M,D
George Mason University M,D
The George Washington University D
Goddard College M
Hofstra University M
Illinois Institute of Technology M,D
Illinois State University M,D,O
Indiana University–Purdue University Indianapolis M,D
John F. Kennedy University M,O
Kean University M,O
Lamar University M
Louisiana State University and Agricultural and Mechanical College M,D
Louisiana Tech University M,D,O
Marshall University M
Middle Tennessee State University M,O
Minnesota State University, Mankato M
Montclair State University M
National-Louis University M,O
New York University M,D,O
Ohio University D
Old Dominion University D
The Pennsylvania State University University Park Campus M,D
Pontifical Catholic University of Puerto Rico M
Radford University M,O
Rensselaer Polytechnic Institute M
Rice University M,D
Roosevelt University M,D
Rutgers, The State University of New Jersey, New Brunswick M,D
St. Mary's University of San Antonio M
San Diego State University M,D
San Jose State University M
Southern Illinois University Edwardsville M
Springfield College M,O
State University of New York at Albany M,D
Teachers College, Columbia University M,D
Temple University M,D
Texas A&M University M,D
The University of Akron M,D
University of Baltimore M,D
University of Central Florida M,D
University of Connecticut M,D
University of Detroit Mercy M
University of Houston D
University of Illinois at Urbana–Champaign M,D
University of Maryland, College Park M,D
University of Michigan D
University of Minnesota, Twin Cities Campus D
University of Missouri–St. Louis M,D,O
University of Nebraska at Omaha M,D,O
University of New Haven M,O
The University of North Carolina at Charlotte M
University of North Texas M,D
University of South Florida D
The University of Tennessee D
The University of Tennessee at Chattanooga M
University of Tulsa M,D
University of Wisconsin–Oshkosh M
Valdosta State University M,O
Virginia Polytechnic Institute and State University M,D
Wayne State University M,D
West Chester University of Pennsylvania M
Western Michigan University M,D,O
William Carey College M
Wright State University M,D
Xavier University M,D

■ INDUSTRIAL DESIGN

Auburn University M
Illinois Institute of Technology M,D
North Carolina State University M
The Ohio State University M
Pratt Institute M
Rochester Institute of Technology M
San Francisco State University M
San Jose State University M
University of Cincinnati M
University of Illinois at Chicago M
University of Illinois at Urbana–Champaign M
University of Notre Dame M

■ INDUSTRIAL HYGIENE

Central Missouri State University M,O
Purdue University M,D
San Diego State University M,D
Texas A&M University M
The University of Alabama at Birmingham D
University of Cincinnati M,D
University of Michigan M,D
University of Minnesota, Twin Cities Campus M,D
University of New Haven M
The University of North Carolina at Chapel Hill M,D
University of South Carolina M,D
University of Washington M,D
Wayne State University M,O

■ INFORMATION SCIENCE

Alcorn State University M
American InterContinental University (DC) M
American University M,O
Arkansas Tech University M
Ball State University M
Barry University M
Bradley University M
Brooklyn College of the City University of New York M,D
California State University, Fullerton M
Carnegie Mellon University M,D
Case Western Reserve University M,D
Claremont Graduate University M,D
Clark Atlanta University M
Clarkson University M
The College of Saint Rose M
DePaul University M
DeSales University M
Drexel University M,D,O
East Carolina University M
East Tennessee State University M
Edinboro University of Pennsylvania O
Florida Gulf Coast University M
Florida Institute of Technology M,D
George Mason University M
Georgia Southwestern State University M
Grand Valley State University M
Harvard University M,O
Hood College M
Indiana University Bloomington M,D,O
Kansas State University M,D
Kennesaw State University M
Kutztown University of Pennsylvania M
Lamar University M
Lehigh University M,D
Long Island University, C.W. Post Campus M
Marist College M
Marshall University M
Montclair State University M,O
New Jersey Institute of Technology M,D
New York University M,D
Northeastern University M
Northwestern University M
Nova Southeastern University M,D
The Ohio State University M,D
Pace University, New York City Campus M,D,O
Pace University, White Plains M,D,O
The Pennsylvania State University Great Valley Campus M
The Pennsylvania State University University Park Campus D
Polytechnic University, Brooklyn Campus M
Polytechnic University, Westchester Graduate Center M
Princeton University M,D
Regis University M,O
Rensselaer Polytechnic Institute M
Rivier College M
Robert Morris College M,D
Rochester Institute of Technology M
Sacred Heart University M,O
St. Mary's University of San Antonio M
Saint Xavier University M
San Jose State University M
Shippensburg University of Pennsylvania M
Southern Methodist University M,D
State University of New York at Albany M,D,O
State University of New York Institute of Technology at Utica/Rome M
Stevens Institute of Technology M,O

Syracuse University	M,D
Tarleton State University	M
Temple University	M,D
Towson University	O
Trevecca Nazarene University	M
The University of Alabama at Birmingham	M,D
University of California, Irvine	M,D
University of Colorado at Colorado Springs	M
University of Delaware	M,D
University of Florida	M,D,O
University of Great Falls	M
University of Hawaii at Manoa	D
University of Houston	M,D
University of Houston–Clear Lake	M
University of Mary Hardin-Baylor	M
University of Maryland, Baltimore County	M,D
University of Michigan–Dearborn	M
University of Minnesota, Twin Cities Campus	M,D
University of New Haven	M
The University of North Carolina at Charlotte	M,D
University of North Florida	M
University of North Texas	M,D
University of Oregon	M,D
University of Pennsylvania	M,D
University of Pittsburgh	M,D,O
University of South Alabama	M
The University of Tennessee	M,D
University of Washington	M,D
Virginia Polytechnic Institute and State University	M

■ INFORMATION STUDIES

The Catholic University of America	M
Central Connecticut State University	M
Central Missouri State University	M,O
Clark Atlanta University	M,O
College of St. Catherine	M
Dominican University	M,O
Drexel University	M,D,O
Emporia State University	M,D
Florida State University	M,D,O
Indiana University–Purdue University Indianapolis	M
Long Island University, C.W. Post Campus	M,D,O
Louisiana State University and Agricultural and Mechanical College	M,O
Mansfield University of Pennsylvania	M
Metropolitan State University	M
Montana State University–Billings	M
North Carolina Central University	M
Pratt Institute	M,O
Queens College of the City University of New York	M,O
Rutgers, The State University of New Jersey, New Brunswick	M,D
St. John's University (NY)	M,O
San Jose State University	M
Simmons College	M,D,O
Southern Connecticut State University	M,O
Syracuse University	M,D
Texas Woman's University	M,D
University at Buffalo, The State University of New York	M,O
The University of Alabama	M,O
The University of Arizona	M,D
University of California, Berkeley	M,D
University of California, Los Angeles	M,D,O
University of Denver	M
University of Hawaii at Manoa	M,D,O
University of Illinois at Urbana–Champaign	M,D,O
The University of Iowa	M
University of Maryland, College Park	M,D
University of Michigan	M,D
University of Missouri–Columbia	M
The University of North Carolina at Chapel Hill	M,D,O
The University of North Carolina at Greensboro	M
University of North Texas	M,D
University of Oklahoma	M,O
University of Pittsburgh	M,D,O
University of Puerto Rico, Río Piedras	M,O
University of Rhode Island	M
University of South Carolina	M,O
University of South Florida	M
The University of Tennessee	M
The University of Texas at Austin	M,D
University of Wisconsin–Madison	M,D,O
University of Wisconsin–Milwaukee	M,O
Wayne State University	M,O

■ INORGANIC CHEMISTRY

Boston College	M,D
Brandeis University	M,D
Brigham Young University	M,D
California State University, Fullerton	M
California State University, Los Angeles	M
Case Western Reserve University	M,D
Clark Atlanta University	M,D
Clarkson University	M,D
Cleveland State University	M,D
Columbia University	M,D
Cornell University	D
Florida State University	M,D
Georgetown University	M,D
The George Washington University	M,D
Harvard University	M,D
Howard University	M,D
Illinois Institute of Technology	M,D
Indiana University Bloomington	M,D
Kansas State University	M,D
Kent State University	M,D
Marquette University	M,D
Massachusetts Institute of Technology	D
Miami University	M,D
Michigan State University	M,D
Northeastern University	M,D
Oregon State University	M,D
Purdue University	M,D
Rensselaer Polytechnic Institute	M,D
Rice University	M,D
Rutgers, The State University of New Jersey, Newark	M,D
Rutgers, The State University of New Jersey, New Brunswick	M,D
San Jose State University	M
Seton Hall University	M,D
South Dakota State University	M,D
Southern University and Agricultural and Mechanical College	M
State University of New York at Binghamton	M,D
Tufts University	M,D
The University of Akron	M,D
University of Cincinnati	M,D
University of Georgia	M,D
University of Louisville	M,D
University of Maryland, College Park	M,D
University of Miami	M,D
University of Michigan	D
University of Missouri–Columbia	M,D
University of Missouri–Kansas City	M,D
University of Missouri–St. Louis	M,D
The University of Montana–Missoula	M,D
University of Nebraska–Lincoln	M,D
University of Notre Dame	M,D
University of Southern Mississippi	M,D
University of South Florida	M,D
The University of Tennessee	M,D
The University of Texas at Austin	M,D
University of Toledo	M,D
Wake Forest University	M,D
Washington State University	M,D
West Virginia University	M,D
Yale University	D

■ INSURANCE

California State University, Northridge	M
Georgia State University	M,D
The Pennsylvania State University University Park Campus	M,D
Temple University	M,D
University of North Texas	M,D
University of Pennsylvania	M,D
University of St. Thomas (MN)	M,O
University of Wisconsin–Madison	M,D
Virginia Commonwealth University	M

■ INTERDISCIPLINARY STUDIES

Alliant International University	M
American University	M
Angelo State University	M
Antioch New England Graduate School	M
Arizona State University West	M
Baylor University	M,D
Boise State University	M
Boston University	M,D
Bowling Green State University	M,D
California State University, Bakersfield	M
California State University, Chico	M
California State University, Fullerton	M
California State University, Hayward	M,O
California State University, Long Beach	M
California State University, Los Angeles	M
California State University, Northridge	M
California State University, Sacramento	M
California State University, San Bernardino	M
California State University, Stanislaus	M
Central Washington University	M
Claremont Graduate University	M
Clarkson University	M
DePaul University	M
Eastern Washington University	M
Emory University	D
Fitchburg State College	O
Fresno Pacific University	M
George Mason University	M
Goddard College	M
Hofstra University	M
Idaho State University	M
Iowa State University of Science and Technology	M
John F. Kennedy University	M,O
Lesley University	M,O
Long Island University, C.W. Post Campus	M
Loyola College in Maryland	M
Marquette University	D
Marylhurst University	M
Minnesota State University, Mankato	M
New Mexico State University	M,D
New York University	M
Norwich University	M,O
The Ohio State University	M
Ohio University	M,D
Oregon State University	M

Rochester Institute of Technology M
San Diego State University M
San Jose State University M
Sonoma State University M
Southern Methodist University M
Southwest Texas State University M
Stanford University M,D
State University of New York College at Buffalo M
Stephen F. Austin State University M
Teachers College, Columbia University M,D
Texas A&M International University M
Texas A&M University–Corpus Christi M
Texas A&M University–Texarkana M
Texas Tech University M
The Union Institute D
University of Alaska Anchorage M
University of Alaska Fairbanks M,D
The University of Arizona M,D,O
University of Cincinnati D
University of Houston–Victoria M
University of Idaho M
University of Illinois at Springfield M
University of Louisville M
University of Minnesota, Twin Cities Campus M,D
University of Missouri–Kansas City D
The University of Montana–Missoula M,D
University of Northern Colorado M,D,O
University of North Texas M,D
University of Oklahoma M,D
University of Oregon M
University of South Dakota M
The University of Texas at Arlington M
The University of Texas at Brownsville M
The University of Texas at Dallas M
The University of Texas at El Paso M
The University of Texas–Pan American M
University of the Incarnate Word M
University of Wisconsin–Milwaukee D
Virginia Commonwealth University M
Virginia State University M
Wayne State University M,D
West Texas A&M University M
Wright State University M

■ INTERIOR DESIGN

Colorado State University M
Columbia College Chicago M
Cornell University M
Drexel University M
Florida State University M
The George Washington University M
Indiana University Bloomington M
Iowa State University of Science and Technology M
Louisiana Tech University M
Marymount University M
Michigan State University M,D
Minnesota State University, Mankato M
New School University M
The Ohio State University M
Pratt Institute M
Rochester Institute of Technology M
San Diego State University M
San Jose State University M
Suffolk University M
The University of Alabama M
University of Central Oklahoma M
University of Cincinnati M
University of Florida M
University of Georgia M,D
University of Houston M
University of Kentucky M
University of Massachusetts Amherst M
The University of Memphis M
University of Minnesota, Twin Cities Campus M,D
The University of North Carolina at Greensboro M
University of North Texas M,D
University of Oregon M
Virginia Commonwealth University M
Virginia Polytechnic Institute and State University M,D
Washington State University M

■ INTERNATIONAL AFFAIRS

Alliant International University M
American University M,D,O
Angelo State University M
Antioch University McGregor M
Baylor University M
Boston University M,O
Brandeis University M,D
Brigham Young University M
California State University, Fresno M
California State University, Sacramento M
California State University, Stanislaus M
The Catholic University of America M
Central Connecticut State University M
Central Michigan University M,O
City College of the City University of New York M
Claremont Graduate University M,D
Clark Atlanta University M,D
Columbia University M
Cornell University D
Creighton University M
DePaul University M
Dominican University of California M
East Carolina University M
Fairleigh Dickinson University, Teaneck–Hackensack Campus M
Florida International University M,D
Florida State University M
George Mason University M
Georgetown University M,D
The George Washington University M
Georgia Institute of Technology M
Harvard University M,D
Johns Hopkins University M,D,O
Kansas State University M
Kent State University M,D
Lesley University M,O
Long Island University, Brooklyn Campus M,O
Long Island University, C.W. Post Campus M
Loyola University Chicago M,D
Marquette University M
Michigan State University M,D
Monterey Institute of International Studies M
Morgan State University M
New School University M
New York University M,D,O
North Carolina State University M
Northeastern University M,D
Northwestern University O
Ohio University M
Oklahoma City University M
Oklahoma State University M
Old Dominion University M,D
Princeton University M,D
Rutgers, The State University of New Jersey, Camden M
Rutgers, The State University of New Jersey, Newark M
Rutgers, The State University of New Jersey, New Brunswick D
St. John Fisher College M
St. Mary's University of San Antonio M
Salve Regina University M
San Francisco State University M
School for International Training M,O
Seton Hall University M
Southwest Missouri State University M
Southwest Texas State University M
Stanford University M
Syracuse University M
Texas A&M University M
Troy State University M
Tufts University M,D
University of California, Berkeley M
University of California, San Diego M,D
University of California, Santa Cruz D
University of Central Oklahoma M
University of Chicago M
University of Colorado at Boulder M,D
University of Connecticut M
University of Delaware M,D
University of Denver M,D
University of Detroit Mercy M
University of Florida M,D
University of Kentucky M
University of Miami M,D
University of Missouri–St. Louis O
University of New Orleans M,D
University of Notre Dame D
University of Oklahoma M
University of Oregon M
University of Pennsylvania M
University of Pittsburgh M,D
University of Rhode Island M,O
University of San Diego M
University of South Carolina M,D
University of Southern California M,D
University of the Pacific P,M,D
University of Virginia M,D
University of Washington M
University of Wyoming M
Virginia Polytechnic Institute and State University M
Webster University M
West Virginia University M,D
Yale University M

■ INTERNATIONAL AND COMPARATIVE EDUCATION

American University M
Boston University M
Claremont Graduate University M,D
Concordia University (CA) M
Florida International University M
Florida State University M,D,O
The George Washington University M
Harvard University M,D,O
Indiana University Bloomington M,D,O
Iowa State University of Science and Technology M,D
Lesley University M,O
Louisiana State University and Agricultural and Mechanical College M,D
Loyola University Chicago M,D
Lynn University M,D
New York University M,D
School for International Training M,O
Stanford University M,D
Teachers College, Columbia University M,D
Tufts University M,D
University of Bridgeport M,O
University of Massachusetts Amherst M,D,O
University of Minnesota, Twin Cities Campus M,D,O
University of Pittsburgh M,D
University of San Francisco M,D
University of Southern California M,D
Wright State University M

■ INTERNATIONAL BUSINESS

Alliant International University	M,D
American University	M
Azusa Pacific University	M
Baldwin-Wallace College	M
Baylor University	M
Bentley College	M,O
Bernard M. Baruch College of the City University of New York	M
Boston University	M
Brandeis University	M,D
California Lutheran University	M
California State University, Fullerton	M
California State University, Hayward	M
California State University, Los Angeles	M
Central Connecticut State University	M
Central Michigan University	M
Claremont Graduate University	M
Clark Atlanta University	M,D
Clark University	M
Columbia University	M
Concordia University Wisconsin	M
Dallas Baptist University	M
DePaul University	M
Dominican University of California	M
Drury University	M
Eastern Michigan University	M
Fairfield University	M,O
Fairleigh Dickinson University, Florham-Madison Campus	M
Fairleigh Dickinson University, Teaneck–Hackensack Campus	M
Florida International University	M
Florida Metropolitan University–Tampa Campus	M
The George Washington University	M,D
Georgia State University	M,D
Hawaii Pacific University	M
Hofstra University	M
Hope International University	M
Illinois Institute of Technology	M
Indiana University Bloomington	M
Iona College	M,O
Johns Hopkins University	M,D,O
Johnson & Wales University	M
Long Island University, C.W. Post Campus	M,O
Loyola College in Maryland	M
Lynn University	M
Madonna University	M
Marymount University	M,O
Maryville University of Saint Louis	M,O
Mercy College	M
Metropolitan State University	M
Montclair State University	M
Monterey Institute of International Studies	M
National University	M
New School University	M
New York Institute of Technology	M,O
New York University	M,D,O
Nova Southeastern University	M,D
Oklahoma City University	M
Oral Roberts University	M
Our Lady of the Lake University of San Antonio	M
Pace University, New York City Campus	M
Pace University, White Plains Campus	M
Pepperdine University	M
Philadelphia University	M
Point Park College	M
Portland State University	M
Quinnipiac University	M
Regis University	M,O
Rochester Institute of Technology	M
Roosevelt University	M
Rutgers, The State University of New Jersey, Newark	M,D
St. Edward's University	M,O
St. John's University (NY)	M
Saint Joseph's University	M
Saint Louis University	M
Saint Peter's College	M
St. Thomas University	M,O
San Diego State University	M
School for International Training	M,O
Seattle University	M,O
Seton Hall University	M,O
Southeastern University	M
State University of New York at New Paltz	M
Suffolk University	M
Sul Ross State University	M
Temple University	M,D
Texas A&M International University	M
Texas Tech University	M,D
Tufts University	M,D
The University of Akron	M
University of Chicago	M
University of Cincinnati	M
University of Colorado at Denver	M
University of Connecticut	M,D
University of Denver	M
The University of Findlay	M
University of Florida	M
University of Hawaii at Manoa	D
University of Kentucky	M
University of La Verne	M
University of Maryland University College	M
The University of Memphis	M
University of Minnesota, Twin Cities Campus	M
University of New Haven	M
University of New Mexico	M
The University of North Carolina at Greensboro	M,O
University of Oklahoma	M
University of Pennsylvania	M
University of Pittsburgh	M
University of Rhode Island	M,D
University of St. Thomas (MN)	M,O
University of San Francisco	M
The University of Scranton	M
University of South Carolina	M
University of Southern California	M
The University of Texas at Dallas	M,D
University of the Incarnate Word	M,D
University of Toledo	M
University of Tulsa	M
University of Washington	O
University of Wisconsin–Madison	M
Wagner College	M
Washington State University	M,D,O
Webster University	M
Western International University	M
Western New England College	M
Whitworth College	M
Wilkes University	M
Wright State University	M

■ INTERNATIONAL DEVELOPMENT

American University	M,D,O
Andrews University	M
Brandeis University	M
Brigham Young University	M
Clark Atlanta University	M,D
Clark University	M
Cornell University	M
Duke University	M
Fordham University	M,O
The George Washington University	M
Harvard University	M
Hope International University	M
Johns Hopkins University	M,D,O
New School University	M
Ohio University	M
Rutgers, The State University of New Jersey, Camden	M
Tufts University	M,D
Tulane University	M,D
University of Florida	M,D,O
University of Pittsburgh	M
University of Rhode Island	M,O

■ INTERNATIONAL HEALTH

Boston University	M,O
Emory University	M
The George Washington University	M
Harvard University	M,D
Johns Hopkins University	M,D
Loma Linda University	M
Tufts University	M,D
Tulane University	M,D
The University of Alabama at Birmingham	D
University of Michigan	M,D
Yale University	M

■ INTERNET AND INTERACTIVE MULTIMEDIA

Abilene Christian University	M
Alfred University	M
Chapman University	M
City University	M,O
Duquesne University	M
Florida State University	M,D
Georgetown University	M
Georgia Institute of Technology	M
Georgia State University	M,D
Indiana University Bloomington	M
Indiana University–Purdue University Indianapolis	M
Long Island University, C.W. Post Campus	M
New Mexico Highlands University	M
New York University	M
Pratt Institute	M
Quinnipiac University	M
Regis University	M,O
Robert Morris College	M
Rochester Institute of Technology	O
Sacred Heart University	M,O
San Diego State University	M
Strayer University	M
Syracuse University	M
Towson University	O
University of Miami	M
University of Southern California	M,D
Virginia Commonwealth University	M
Western Illinois University	M,O

■ ITALIAN

Boston College	M,D
Brown University	M,D
The Catholic University of America	M
Columbia University	M,D
Florida State University	M,D
Harvard University	M,D
Hunter College of the City University of New York	M
Indiana University Bloomington	M,D
Johns Hopkins University	M,D
Long Island University, C.W. Post Campus	M
New York University	M,D
Northwestern University	D,O

The Ohio State University M,D
Queens College of the City University of New York M
Rutgers, The State University of New Jersey, New Brunswick M,D
San Francisco State University M
Stanford University M,D
State University of New York at Albany M
State University of New York at Binghamton M
Stony Brook University, State University of New York M,D
University of California, Berkeley M,D
University of California, Los Angeles M,D
University of Chicago M,D
University of Connecticut M,D
University of Illinois at Urbana–Champaign M,D
University of Minnesota, Twin Cities Campus M,D
The University of North Carolina at Chapel Hill M,D
University of Notre Dame M
University of Oregon M
University of Pennsylvania M,D
University of Pittsburgh M
The University of Tennessee D
University of Virginia M
University of Washington M,D
University of Wisconsin–Madison M,D
University of Wisconsin–Milwaukee M
Wayne State University M
Yale University D

■ JEWISH STUDIES

Brandeis University M,D
Brooklyn College of the City University of New York M
Brown University M,D
Columbia University M,D
Cornell University M,D
Emory University M
Gratz College M
Harvard University M,D
New York University M,D
Seton Hall University M
Touro College M
University of California, San Diego M,D
University of Chicago M,D
University of Denver M
The University of Montana–Missoula M
University of Wisconsin–Madison M,D
University of Wisconsin–Milwaukee M
Washington University in St. Louis M
Yeshiva University M,D

■ JOURNALISM

American University M
Arizona State University M
Arkansas State University M
Arkansas Tech University M
Austin Peay State University M
Ball State University M
Baylor University M
Boston University M
California State University, Fullerton M
California State University, Northridge M
Columbia College Chicago M
Columbia University M
Emerson College M
Florida Agricultural and Mechanical University M
Georgia College and State University M
Indiana University Bloomington M,D
Iona College M,O
Iowa State University of Science and Technology M
Kent State University M
Marquette University M
Marshall University M
Michigan State University M,D
Morehead State University M
New York University M,D,O
Norfolk State University M
Northeastern University M
Northwestern University M
The Ohio State University M
Ohio University M,D
Point Park College M
Polytechnic University, Brooklyn Campus M
Quinnipiac University M
Regent University M
Roosevelt University M
South Dakota State University M
Stanford University M,D
Syracuse University M
Temple University M
Texas A&M University M
Texas Christian University M
Texas Southern University M
The University of Alabama M
University of Alaska Fairbanks M
The University of Arizona M
University of Arkansas M
University of Arkansas at Little Rock M
University of California, Berkeley M
University of Colorado at Boulder M,D
University of Florida M,D
University of Georgia M,D
University of Illinois at Springfield M
University of Illinois at Urbana–Champaign M
The University of Iowa M
University of Kansas M
University of Maryland, College Park M,D
The University of Memphis M
University of Miami M,D
University of Mississippi M
University of Missouri–Columbia M,D
The University of Montana–Missoula M
University of Nebraska–Lincoln M
University of Nevada, Reno M
University of North Texas M
University of Oklahoma M
University of Oregon M,D
University of South Carolina M,D
University of Southern California M,O
The University of Tennessee M,D
The University of Texas at Austin M,D
University of the Sacred Heart M
University of Wisconsin–Madison M,D
University of Wisconsin–Milwaukee M
West Virginia University M

■ KINESIOLOGY AND MOVEMENT STUDIES

Angelo State University M
Armstrong Atlantic State University M
Barry University M
Boston University M,D,O
Bowling Green State University M
California Polytechnic State University, San Luis Obispo M
California State Polytechnic University, Pomona M
California State University, Fresno M
California State University, Long Beach M
California State University, Northridge M
Florida State University M,D
Georgia Southern University M
Indiana University Bloomington M,D,O
Inter American University of Puerto Rico, San Germán Campus M
James Madison University M
Kansas State University M
Lamar University M
Louisiana State University and Agricultural and Mechanical College M,D
Michigan State University M,D
Midwestern State University M
New York University M,D
Oregon State University M
The Pennsylvania State University University Park Campus M,D
Sonoma State University M
Southeastern Louisiana University M
Southern Arkansas University–Magnolia M
Southern Illinois University Edwardsville M,O
Springfield College M
Teachers College, Columbia University M,D
Temple University M,D
Texas A&M University M,D
Texas A&M University–Kingsville M
Texas Christian University M
Texas Woman's University M,D
University of Arkansas M,D
University of Central Arkansas M
University of Colorado at Boulder M,D
University of Delaware M,D
University of Florida D
University of Hawaii at Manoa M
University of Illinois at Chicago M
University of Illinois at Urbana–Champaign M,D
University of Kentucky M,D
University of Maine M,O
University of Maryland, College Park M,D
University of Michigan M,D,O
University of Minnesota, Twin Cities Campus M,D
University of Nevada, Las Vegas M
University of New Hampshire M
The University of North Carolina at Chapel Hill M,D
University of North Dakota M
University of Northern Colorado M,D
University of North Texas M
University of Oregon M,D
University of Pittsburgh M,D
University of Southern California M,D
The University of Texas at Austin M,D
The University of Texas at El Paso M
The University of Texas at Tyler M
The University of Texas–Pan American M
University of Wisconsin–Madison M,D
University of Wisconsin–Milwaukee M
Virginia Polytechnic Institute and State University M,D
Washington State University M
Washington University in St. Louis D
West Chester University of Pennsylvania M,O
Western Washington University M

■ LANDSCAPE ARCHITECTURE

Ball State University M
California State Polytechnic University, Pomona M
Colorado State University M,D
Cornell University M
Florida International University M
Harvard University M,D
Iowa State University of Science and Technology M

Kansas State University	M
Louisiana State University and Agricultural and Mechanical College	M
Mississippi State University	M
Morgan State University	M
North Carolina State University	M
The Ohio State University	M
Oklahoma State University	M
The Pennsylvania State University University Park Campus	M
State University of New York College of Environmental Science and Forestry	M
Texas A&M University	M,D
Texas Tech University	M
The University of Arizona	M
University of California, Berkeley	M
University of Colorado at Denver	M
University of Florida	M
University of Georgia	M
University of Illinois at Urbana–Champaign	M
University of Massachusetts Amherst	M
University of Michigan	M,D
University of Minnesota, Twin Cities Campus	M
University of New Mexico	M
University of Oklahoma	M
University of Oregon	M
University of Pennsylvania	M,O
University of Southern California	M
The University of Texas at Arlington	M
University of Virginia	M
University of Washington	M
University of Wisconsin–Madison	M
Utah State University	M
Virginia Polytechnic Institute and State University	M
Washington State University	M,D

■ LATIN AMERICAN STUDIES

American University	M,O
Arizona State University	M,D
Brown University	M,D
California State University, Los Angeles	M
Columbia University	O
Duke University	D,O
Florida International University	M
Georgetown University	M
The George Washington University	M
Indiana University Bloomington	M
Johns Hopkins University	M,D,O
La Salle University	M
New York University	M
The Ohio State University	M,D,O
Ohio University	M
Princeton University	D
San Diego State University	M
Southern Methodist University	M
Stanford University	M
State University of New York at Albany	M,O
Tulane University	M,D
The University of Alabama	M,O
The University of Arizona	M
University of California, Berkeley	M,D
University of California, Los Angeles	M
University of California, San Diego	M
University of California, Santa Barbara	M,D
University of Central Florida	M,O
University of Chicago	M
University of Connecticut	M
University of Florida	M,O
University of Illinois at Urbana–Champaign	M
University of Kansas	M
University of New Mexico	M,D
The University of North Carolina at Chapel Hill	M,D,O
University of Pittsburgh	O
The University of Texas at Austin	M,D
University of Wisconsin–Madison	M
Vanderbilt University	M
West Virginia University	M,D

■ LAW

American University	P,M
Arizona State University	P
Barry University	P
Baylor University	P
Boston College	P
Boston University	P,M
Brigham Young University	P,M
Campbell University	P
Capital University	P,M
Case Western Reserve University	P,M
The Catholic University of America	P
Chapman University	P
City University of New York School of Law at Queens College	P
Cleveland State University	P,M
The College of William and Mary	P,M
Columbia University	P,M,D
Cornell University	P,M,D
Creighton University	P
DePaul University	P,M
Drake University	P
Duke University	P,M,D
Duquesne University	P
Emory University	P,M
Florida State University	P
Fordham University	P,M
George Mason University	P
Georgetown University	P,M,D
The George Washington University	P,M,D
Georgia State University	P
Gonzaga University	P
Hamline University	P,M
Harvard University	P,M,D
Hofstra University	P,M
Howard University	P,M
Illinois Institute of Technology	P,M
Inter American University of Puerto Rico, Metropolitan Campus	P
John F. Kennedy University	P
Louisiana State University and Agricultural and Mechanical College	P,M
Loyola Marymount University	P,M
Loyola University Chicago	P,M,D
Loyola University New Orleans	P
Marquette University	P
Mercer University	P
Mississippi College	P
New College of California	P
New York University	P,M,D
North Carolina Central University	P
Northeastern University	P
Northern Illinois University	P
Northern Kentucky University	P
Northwestern University	P,M,O
Nova Southeastern University	P
The Ohio State University	P
Oklahoma City University	P
Pace University, White Plains Campus	P,M,D
Pepperdine University	P
Pontifical Catholic University of Puerto Rico	P
Quinnipiac University	P
Regent University	P,M
Rutgers, The State University of New Jersey, Camden	P
Rutgers, The State University of New Jersey, Newark	P
St. John's University (NY)	P,M
Saint Louis University	P,M
St. Mary's University of San Antonio	P
St. Thomas University	P,M
Samford University	P,D
Santa Clara University	P,M,O
Seattle University	P
Seton Hall University	P,M
Southern Illinois University Carbondale	P
Southern Methodist University	P,M,D
Southern University and Agricultural and Mechanical College	P
Stanford University	P,M,D
Stetson University	P
Suffolk University	P
Syracuse University	P
Temple University	P,M
Texas Southern University	P
Texas Tech University	P
Texas Wesleyan University	P
Touro College	P,M
Tulane University	P,M,D
University at Buffalo, The State University of New York	P,M
The University of Akron	P,M
The University of Alabama	P,M
The University of Arizona	P,M
University of Arkansas	P,M
University of Arkansas at Little Rock	P
University of Baltimore	P,M
University of California, Berkeley	P,M,D
University of California, Davis	P,M
University of California, Los Angeles	P,M
University of Chicago	P,M,D
University of Cincinnati	P
University of Colorado at Boulder	P
University of Connecticut	P
University of Dayton	P
University of Denver	P,M
University of Detroit Mercy	P
University of Florida	P,M,D
University of Georgia	P,M
University of Hawaii at Manoa	P
University of Houston	P,M
University of Idaho	P
University of Illinois at Urbana–Champaign	P,M,D
The University of Iowa	P,M
University of Kansas	P
University of Kentucky	P
University of La Verne	P
University of Louisville	P
University of Maryland	P
University of Maryland, College Park	
The University of Memphis	P
University of Miami	P,M
University of Michigan	P,M,D
University of Minnesota, Twin Cities Campus	P,M
University of Mississippi	P
University of Missouri–Columbia	P,M
University of Missouri–Kansas City	P,M
The University of Montana–Missoula	P
University of Nebraska–Lincoln	P,M
University of Nevada, Las Vegas	P
University of New Mexico	P
The University of North Carolina at Chapel Hill	P
University of North Dakota	P
University of Notre Dame	P,M,D
University of Oklahoma	P
University of Oregon	P
University of Pennsylvania	P,M,D
University of Pittsburgh	P,M

University of Puerto Rico, Río Piedras P
University of Richmond P
University of San Diego P,M,O
University of San Francisco P
University of South Carolina P
University of South Dakota P
University of Southern California P
University of Southern Maine P
The University of Tennessee P
The University of Texas at Austin P,M
University of the District of Columbia P
University of the Pacific P,M,D
University of Toledo P
University of Tulsa P,M
University of Utah P,M
University of Virginia P,M,D
University of Washington P,M,D
University of Wisconsin–Madison P,M,D
University of Wyoming P
Valparaiso University P,M
Vanderbilt University P,M
Villanova University P
Wake Forest University P,M
Washburn University of Topeka P
Washington University in St. Louis P,M,D
Wayne State University P,M
Western New England College P
West Virginia University P
Widener University P,M,D
Yale University P,M,D
Yeshiva University P,M

■ LEGAL AND JUSTICE STUDIES

American University M
Arizona State University M,D
Boston University M
Capital University M
Case Western Reserve University P,M
The Catholic University of America D,O
DePaul University M
Governors State University M
Hofstra University P,M
Illinois Institute of Technology M
Marymount University M,O
Montclair State University M,O
New York University D
Northeastern University M,D
Pace University, White Plains Campus P,M,D
Prairie View A&M University M,D
Rutgers, The State University of New Jersey, New Brunswick D
Southwest Texas State University M
University of Baltimore M
University of California, Berkeley D
University of Denver M
University of Illinois at Springfield M
University of Nebraska–Lincoln M
University of Nevada, Reno M
University of Pennsylvania M
University of Pittsburgh M,O
University of San Diego P,M,O
University of the Pacific P,M,D
University of Washington P,M,D
University of Wisconsin–Madison M
Webster University M,O
West Virginia University M

■ LEISURE STUDIES

Aurora University M
Boston University M
Bowling Green State University M
California State University, Long Beach M
California State University, Northridge M
Central Michigan University M
East Carolina University M
Gallaudet University M
Howard University M
Indiana University Bloomington M,D,O
Murray State University M
New York University M,D,O
Oklahoma State University M,D
The Pennsylvania State University University Park Campus M,D
San Francisco State University M
San Jose State University M
Southern Connecticut State University M
Southwest Texas State University M
State University of New York College at Brockport M
Temple University M
Universidad Metropolitana M
University of Connecticut M,D
University of Georgia M,D
University of Hawaii at Manoa M
University of Illinois at Urbana–Champaign M,D
The University of Iowa M,D
The University of Memphis M
University of Minnesota, Twin Cities Campus M,D
University of Mississippi M,D
University of Nevada, Las Vegas M
The University of North Carolina at Chapel Hill M
University of Northern Iowa M
University of North Texas M,O
University of South Alabama M
University of Toledo M
University of Utah M,D
University of West Florida M
Washington State University M

■ LIBERAL STUDIES

Abilene Christian University M
Alliant International University M
Antioch University McGregor M
Arkansas Tech University M
Auburn University Montgomery M
Baker University M
Benedictine University M
Boston University M
Bradley University M
Brooklyn College of the City University of New York M
Christian Brothers University M
Clark University M
College of Notre Dame of Maryland M
College of Our Lady of the Elms M
College of Staten Island of the City University of New York M
Columbia University M
Converse College M
Creighton University M
Dallas Baptist University M
Dartmouth College M
DePaul University M
Duke University M
Duquesne University M
Florida Atlantic University M
Fordham University M
Fort Hays State University M
George Mason University M
Georgetown University M
Hamline University M
Harvard University M,O
Henderson State University M
Houston Baptist University M
Indiana University–Purdue University Fort Wayne M
Indiana University South Bend M
Jacksonville State University M
Johns Hopkins University M,O
Kean University M
Kent State University M
Lock Haven University of Pennsylvania M
Louisiana State University and Agricultural and Mechanical College M
Louisiana State University in Shreveport M
Manhattanville College M
Minnesota State University Moorhead M
Mississippi College M
Monmouth University M
New School University M
North Carolina State University M
North Central College M
Northern Arizona University M
Northwestern University M
Oklahoma City University M
Plattsburgh State University of New York M
Queens College of the City University of New York M
Regis University M,O
Rollins College M
Roosevelt University M
Rutgers, The State University of New Jersey, Camden M
Rutgers, The State University of New Jersey, Newark M
St. Edward's University M
Saint Mary's College of California M
San Diego State University M
Southwest Texas State University M
Spring Hill College M
State University of New York at Albany M
State University of New York College at Brockport M
State University of New York Empire State College M
Stony Brook University, State University of New York M,O
Temple University M
Texas Christian University M
Thomas Edison State College M
Towson University M
Tulane University M
University of Arkansas at Little Rock M
University of Central Florida M
University of Delaware M
University of Denver M
University of Detroit Mercy M
University of Great Falls M
University of Maine M
University of Miami M
University of Michigan–Dearborn M
University of Missouri–Kansas City M
University of New Hampshire M
The University of North Carolina at Charlotte M
The University of North Carolina at Greensboro M
The University of North Carolina at Wilmington M
University of Oklahoma M
University of Richmond M
University of St. Thomas (TX) M
University of Southern Indiana M
University of South Florida M
University of Toledo M
Ursuline College M
Valparaiso University M
Vanderbilt University M
Villanova University M
Wake Forest University M
Washburn University of Topeka M
West Virginia University M

Wichita State University M
Widener University M
Winthrop University M

■ LIBRARY SCIENCE

Appalachian State University M,O
The Catholic University of America M
Central Missouri State University M,O
Chicago State University M
Clarion University of Pennsylvania M,O
Clark Atlanta University M,O
College of St. Catherine M
Dominican University M,O
Drexel University M,D,O
East Carolina University M,O
Emporia State University M,D
Florida State University M,D,O
Gratz College O
Indiana University Bloomington M,D,O
Indiana University–Purdue University Indianapolis M
Inter American University of Puerto Rico, San Germán Campus M
Kent State University M
Kutztown University of Pennsylvania M,O
Long Island University, C.W. Post Campus M,D,O
Louisiana State University and Agricultural and Mechanical College M,O
Mansfield University of Pennsylvania M
North Carolina Central University M
Old Dominion University M
Pratt Institute M,O
Queens College of the City University of New York M,O
Rutgers, The State University of New Jersey, New Brunswick M
St. John's University (NY) M,O
Sam Houston State University M
San Jose State University M
Simmons College M,D,O
Southern Arkansas University–Magnolia M
Southern Connecticut State University M,O
Spalding University M
State University of New York at Albany M,D,O
Syracuse University M,O
Tennessee Technological University M
Texas Woman's University M,D
Trevecca Nazarene University M
University at Buffalo, The State University of New York M,O
The University of Alabama M,O
The University of Arizona M,D
University of California, Los Angeles M,D,O
University of Central Arkansas M
University of Denver M
University of Hawaii at Manoa M,D,O
University of Illinois at Urbana–Champaign M,D,O
The University of Iowa M
University of Kentucky M
University of Maryland, College Park M,D
University of Michigan M,D
University of Missouri–Columbia M
The University of North Carolina at Chapel Hill M,D,O
The University of North Carolina at Greensboro M
University of North Texas M,D
University of Oklahoma M,O
University of Pittsburgh M,D,O
University of Puerto Rico, Río Piedras M,O
University of Rhode Island M
University of South Carolina M,O
University of Southern Mississippi M,O
University of South Florida M
The University of Tennessee M
The University of Texas at Austin M,D
University of Washington M,D
University of Wisconsin–Madison M,D,O
University of Wisconsin–Milwaukee M,O
Wayne State University M,O
Wright State University M

■ LIMNOLOGY

Baylor University M,D
Cornell University D
University of Alaska Fairbanks M,D
University of Florida M,D
University of Wisconsin–Madison M,D
William Paterson University of New Jersey M

■ LINGUISTICS

Arizona State University M,D
Ball State University D
Biola University M,D,O
Boston College M
Boston University M,D
Brigham Young University M,O
Brown University M,D
California State University, Fresno M
California State University, Fullerton M
California State University, Long Beach M
California State University, Northridge M
California State University, San Bernardino M
Carnegie Mellon University M,D
Cornell University M,D
Eastern Michigan University M
Florida International University M
Gallaudet University M
George Mason University M
Georgetown University M,D,O
Georgia State University M
Harvard University M,D
Hofstra University M
Indiana State University M
Indiana University Bloomington M,D,O
Indiana University of Pennsylvania M,D
Louisiana State University and Agricultural and Mechanical College M,D
Massachusetts Institute of Technology D
Michigan State University M,D
Montclair State University M
New York University M,D
Northeastern Illinois University M
Northern Arizona University M,D
Northwestern University M,D
Oakland University M
The Ohio State University M,D
Ohio University M
Old Dominion University M
Purdue University M,D
Queens College of the City University of New York M
Rice University M,D
Rutgers, The State University of New Jersey, New Brunswick D
San Diego State University M,O
San Francisco State University M
San Jose State University M,O
Southern Illinois University Carbondale M
Stanford University M,D
Stony Brook University, State University of New York M,D
Syracuse University M
Teachers College, Columbia University M,D
Temple University M
Texas Tech University M,D
University at Buffalo, The State University of New York M,D
The University of Alabama M,D
The University of Arizona M,D
University of California, Berkeley M,D
University of California, Davis M
University of California, Irvine M,D
University of California, Los Angeles M,D
University of California, San Diego D
University of California, Santa Barbara D
University of California, Santa Cruz M,D
University of Chicago M,D
University of Colorado at Boulder M,D
University of Connecticut M,D
University of Delaware M,D
University of Florida M,D,O
University of Georgia M,D
University of Hawaii at Manoa M,D
University of Houston M,D
University of Illinois at Chicago M
University of Illinois at Urbana–Champaign M,D
The University of Iowa M,D
University of Kansas M,D
University of Louisville M
University of Maryland, Baltimore County M
University of Maryland, College Park M,D
University of Massachusetts Amherst M,D
University of Massachusetts Boston M
University of Michigan M,D
University of Minnesota, Twin Cities Campus M,D
University of Missouri–St. Louis M
The University of Montana–Missoula M
University of New Hampshire M,D
University of New Mexico M,D
The University of North Carolina at Chapel Hill M,D
University of North Dakota M
University of Oregon M,D
University of Pennsylvania M,D
University of Pittsburgh M,D
University of Puerto Rico, Río Piedras M
University of South Carolina M,D,O
University of Southern California M,D
University of South Florida M
The University of Tennessee D
The University of Texas at Arlington M,D
The University of Texas at Austin M,D
The University of Texas at El Paso M
University of Utah M
University of Virginia M
University of Washington M,D
University of Wisconsin–Madison M,D
Wayne State University M
West Virginia University M
Yale University D

■ LOGISTICS

Arizona State University M,D
California State University, Hayward M
Case Western Reserve University M,D
Colorado Technical University M,D
Florida Institute of Technology M
George Mason University M
The George Washington University M
Georgia College and State University M
Long Island University, C.W. Post Campus M,O
Massachusetts Institute of Technology M,D
Michigan State University M,D
The Pennsylvania State University University Park Campus M,D

Texas A&M International University M
Universidad del Turabo M
University of Arkansas M
University of Minnesota, Twin Cities Campus M,D
University of New Haven M,O
The University of Tennessee M,D
The University of Texas at Arlington M
University of Washington O
University of Wisconsin–Madison M
Wright State University M

■ MANAGEMENT INFORMATION SYSTEMS

Alliant International University M,D
American University M
Arizona State University M,D
Auburn University M,D
Baldwin-Wallace College M
Baylor University M
Bellevue University M
Benedictine University M
Bentley College M,O
Bernard M. Baruch College of the City University of New York M
Boise State University M
Boston University M,D
Bowie State University M,O
Brigham Young University M
California Lutheran University M
California State University, Dominguez Hills M
California State University, Fullerton M
California State University, Hayward M
California State University, Los Angeles M
California State University, Northridge M
California State University, Sacramento M
Carnegie Mellon University M,D
Case Western Reserve University M,D
Central Michigan University M,O
Central Missouri State University M
Charleston Southern University M
City University M,O
Claremont Graduate University M,D
Clarkson University M
Clark University M
Cleveland State University M
Colorado State University M
Colorado Technical University M,D
Columbus State University M
Concordia University Wisconsin M
Creighton University M
Dallas Baptist University M
DePaul University M
Dominican University M
Duquesne University M
Eastern Michigan University M
Fairfield University M,O
Fairleigh Dickinson University, Florham-Madison Campus M
Fairleigh Dickinson University, Teaneck–Hackensack Campus M
Ferris State University M
Florida Agricultural and Mechanical University M
Florida Institute of Technology M
Florida International University D
Fordham University M
Fort Hays State University M
Friends University M
The George Washington University M
Georgia Southwestern State University M
Georgia State University M,D
Governors State University M
Harvard University D
Hawaii Pacific University M
Hofstra University M
Holy Family College M
Houston Baptist University M
Illinois Institute of Technology M
Indiana University Bloomington M,D
Indiana University South Bend M
Jackson State University M
Johns Hopkins University M,O
Kean University M
Kennesaw State University M
Kent State University D
Lawrence Technological University M
Lesley University M
Long Island University, C.W. Post Campus M,O
Louisiana State University and Agricultural and Mechanical College M,D
Loyola University Chicago M
Marymount University M,O
Maryville University of Saint Louis M,O
Marywood University M
Metropolitan State University M
Miami University M
Michigan State University M,D
Middle Tennessee State University M
Mississippi State University M
Montclair State University M
New Jersey Institute of Technology M
New York Institute of Technology M,O
New York University M,D,O
North Carolina State University M
North Central College M
Northeastern University M
Northern Arizona University M
Northern Illinois University M
Northwestern University M
Northwest Missouri State University M
Nova Southeastern University M,D
The Ohio State University M,D
Oklahoma City University M
Oklahoma State University M,D
Pace University, New York City Campus M
Pace University, White Plains Campus M
The Pennsylvania State University Harrisburg Campus of the Capital College M
The Pennsylvania State University University Park Campus M
Philadelphia University M
Purdue University M,D
Quinnipiac University M
Regis University M,O
Rensselaer Polytechnic Institute M,D
Rivier College M
Robert Morris College M,D
Roosevelt University M
Rutgers, The State University of New Jersey, Newark M,D
Sacred Heart University M,O
St. Edward's University M,O
St. John's University (NY) M,O
Saint Joseph's University M
Saint Louis University M,D
St. Mary's University of San Antonio M
Saint Peter's College M
San Diego State University M
San Jose State University M
Seattle Pacific University M
Seton Hall University M,O
Shenandoah University M,O
Southeastern University M
Southern Illinois University Edwardsville M
Southwest Missouri State University M
State University of New York at Albany M
Stevens Institute of Technology M,D,O
Stony Brook University, State University of New York M,O
Strayer University M
Syracuse University M,D
Temple University M
Texas A&M International University M
Texas A&M University M,D
Texas Tech University M,D,O
Towson University O
Troy State University Dothan M
Troy State University Montgomery M
University at Buffalo, The State University of New York M,D
The University of Akron M
The University of Arizona M
University of Arkansas M
University of Baltimore M
University of Cincinnati M,D
University of Colorado at Colorado Springs M
University of Colorado at Denver M
University of Denver M
University of Detroit Mercy M
University of Florida M,D
University of Illinois at Chicago M,D
University of Illinois at Springfield M
The University of Iowa M
University of Kansas M,D
University of La Verne M
University of Mary Hardin-Baylor M
University of Maryland University College M
The University of Memphis M,D
University of Miami M,O
University of Minnesota, Twin Cities Campus M,D
University of Mississippi M,D
University of Missouri–St. Louis M,O
University of Nebraska at Omaha M
University of New Haven M
University of New Mexico M
The University of North Carolina at Chapel Hill D
The University of North Carolina at Greensboro M
University of North Texas M,D
University of Oklahoma M
University of Oregon M
University of Pennsylvania M,D
University of Pittsburgh M
University of Rhode Island M,D
University of St. Thomas (MN) M,O
University of San Francisco M
University of Southern California M
University of Southern Mississippi M
University of South Florida M
The University of Texas at Arlington M,D
The University of Texas at Austin D
The University of Texas at San Antonio M
The University of Texas–Pan American M,D
University of the Sacred Heart M
University of Toledo M,D
University of Tulsa M
University of Virginia M
University of Wisconsin–Madison M
University of Wisconsin–Oshkosh M
University of Wisconsin–Whitewater M
Utah State University M,D
Virginia Commonwealth University M,D
Webster University M
Western International University M
Western New England College M
Worcester Polytechnic Institute M,O

Wright State University M
York College of Pennsylvania M

■ MANAGEMENT OF TECHNOLOGY

Alliant International University M,D
Bentley College M,O
Boston University M
Brigham Young University M
California Polytechnic State University, San Luis Obispo M
Carlow College M
Carnegie Mellon University M,D
Central Missouri State University D
Colorado State University M,D
Dallas Baptist University M
Embry-Riddle Aeronautical University, Extended Campus M
Fairfield University M
Fairleigh Dickinson University, Florham-Madison Campus M
Fairleigh Dickinson University, Teaneck–Hackensack Campus M
George Mason University M,D
The George Washington University M,D
Georgia Institute of Technology M
Illinois Institute of Technology M
Iona College M,O
La Salle University M
Marquette University M,D
Marshall University M
Mercer University M
Murray State University M
National University M
New Jersey Institute of Technology M
New York University M,D,O
North Carolina Agricultural and Technical State University M
North Carolina State University D
Northern Kentucky University M
Pacific Lutheran University M
Polytechnic University, Brooklyn Campus M
Portland State University M,D
Rensselaer Polytechnic Institute M,D
Rhode Island College M
Saginaw Valley State University M
St. Ambrose University M,D
Southwest Texas State University M
Stevens Institute of Technology M,D,O
Stony Brook University, State University of New York M,O
Texas A&M University–Commerce M
University of Bridgeport M
University of Colorado at Boulder M,D
University of Denver M
University of Maryland University College M
University of Miami M,D
University of Minnesota, Twin Cities Campus M
University of New Haven M
University of New Mexico M
University of Pennsylvania M
The University of Texas at Arlington M
The University of Texas at San Antonio M
University of Tulsa M
University of Wisconsin–Stout M
Vanderbilt University M,D

■ MANAGEMENT STRATEGY AND POLICY

Alliant International University M,D
Azusa Pacific University M
Bernard M. Baruch College of the City University of New York M,D
Brenau University M
Case Western Reserve University M,D
Claremont Graduate University M
DePaul University M
Dominican University of California M
Drexel University M,D,O
The George Washington University M,D
Illinois Institute of Technology M
Lamar University M
Manhattanville College M
Marymount University M,O
Michigan State University M,D
Northwestern University D
Purdue University M,D
Regent University M,D,O
Simmons College M
Stevens Institute of Technology M
Syracuse University D
Temple University M,D
Towson University O
The University of Arizona M
University of Florida M,D
University of Minnesota, Twin Cities Campus M,D
University of New Haven M
The University of North Carolina at Chapel Hill D
University of North Texas M,D

■ MANUFACTURING ENGINEERING

Boston University M,D
Bowling Green State University M
Bradley University M
Brigham Young University M
California Polytechnic State University, San Luis Obispo M
Colorado State University M,D
Cornell University M,D
Drexel University M,D
Eastern Kentucky University M
East Tennessee State University M
Florida Atlantic University M
Illinois Institute of Technology M,D
Kansas State University M,D
Lawrence Technological University M
Lehigh University M
Louisiana Tech University M,D
Marquette University M,D
Massachusetts Institute of Technology M
Michigan State University M,D
Minnesota State University, Mankato M
North Carolina State University M
North Dakota State University M
Northeastern University M,D
Northwestern University M
Ohio University M,D
Oklahoma State University M
Old Dominion University M,D
Oregon State University M
The Pennsylvania State University University Park Campus M
Polytechnic University, Brooklyn Campus M
Polytechnic University, Westchester Graduate Center M
Portland State University M
Purdue University M,D
Rensselaer Polytechnic Institute M
Rochester Institute of Technology M
Southern Illinois University Carbondale M
Southern Methodist University M,D
Stanford University M,D
Syracuse University M
Tufts University O
University of California, Los Angeles M
University of Central Florida M,D,O
University of Colorado at Colorado Springs M
University of Detroit Mercy M,D
University of Florida M,D,O
University of Houston M
The University of Iowa M,D
University of Kentucky M
University of Maryland, College Park M,D
University of Massachusetts Amherst M
The University of Memphis M
University of Michigan M,D
University of Michigan–Dearborn M,D
University of Minnesota, Twin Cities Campus M
University of Missouri–Columbia M,D
University of Missouri–Rolla M
University of Nebraska–Lincoln M,D
University of New Mexico M,D
University of Pittsburgh M
University of Rhode Island M
University of St. Thomas (MN) M,O
University of Southern California M
University of Southern Maine M
The University of Tennessee M,D
The University of Texas at Austin M,D
The University of Texas at El Paso M
University of Wisconsin–Madison M
Villanova University M,O
Wayne State University M
Western Michigan University M
Western New England College M
Wichita State University M,D
Worcester Polytechnic Institute M,D,O

■ MARINE AFFAIRS

Duke University M,D
East Carolina University D
Florida Institute of Technology M,D
Louisiana State University and Agricultural and Mechanical College M,D
Nova Southeastern University M,D
Oregon State University M
Stevens Institute of Technology M
University of Delaware M,D
University of Maine M
University of Miami M
University of Rhode Island M,D
University of San Diego M
University of Washington M
University of West Florida M

■ MARINE BIOLOGY

California State University, Stanislaus M
Florida Institute of Technology M
Florida State University M,D
Massachusetts Institute of Technology M,D,O
Murray State University M
Nova Southeastern University M,D
Rutgers, The State University of New Jersey, New Brunswick M,D
San Francisco State University M
Southwest Texas State University M
University of Alaska Fairbanks M,D
University of California, San Diego M,D
University of California, Santa Barbara M,D
University of Colorado at Boulder M,D
University of Guam M
University of Hawaii at Manoa M,D
University of Maine M,D
University of Massachusetts Dartmouth M
University of Miami M,D
The University of North Carolina at Wilmington M
University of Oregon M,D
University of Southern California M,D

University of Southern Mississippi	M,D
University of South Florida	M,D
Western Illinois University	M,O

■ MARINE SCIENCES

California State University, Fresno	M
California State University, Hayward	M
California State University, Sacramento	M
The College of William and Mary	M,D
Duke University	M,D
Florida Institute of Technology	M,D
Murray State University	M
North Carolina State University	M,D
Nova Southeastern University	M,D
Oregon State University	M
San Jose State University	M
Stony Brook University, State University of New York	M
University of Alaska Fairbanks	M,D
University of California, San Diego	M,D
University of California, Santa Barbara	M,D
University of California, Santa Cruz	M,D
University of Connecticut	M,D
University of Delaware	M,D
University of Florida	M,D
University of Georgia	M,D
University of Maine	M,D
University of Maryland	M,D
University of Maryland, Baltimore County	M,D
University of Maryland, College Park	M,D
University of Maryland Eastern Shore	M,D
University of Massachusetts Boston	D
University of Miami	M,D
The University of North Carolina at Chapel Hill	M,D
University of Puerto Rico, Mayagüez Campus	M,D
University of San Diego	M
University of South Alabama	M,D
University of South Carolina	M,D
University of Southern California	M,D
University of Southern Mississippi	M,D
University of South Florida	M,D
The University of Texas at Austin	M,D
University of Wisconsin–Madison	M,D

■ MARKETING

Alabama Agricultural and Mechanical University	M
Alliant International University	M,D
American University	M
Andrews University	M
Arizona State University	M,D
Bayamón Central University	M
Bentley College	M,O
Bernard M. Baruch College of the City University of New York	M,D
Boston University	M,D,O
California Lutheran University	M
California State University, Fullerton	M
California State University, Hayward	M
California State University, Los Angeles	M
California State University, Northridge	M
Carnegie Mellon University	D
Case Western Reserve University	M,D
Central Michigan University	M
City University	M,O
Claremont Graduate University	M
Clark Atlanta University	M
Clark University	M
Columbia University	M,D
Concordia University Wisconsin	M
Cornell University	D
Dallas Baptist University	M
Delta State University	M
DePaul University	M
Drexel University	M,D,O
Eastern College	M
Eastern Michigan University	M
Fairfield University	M,O
Fairleigh Dickinson University, Florham-Madison Campus	M
Fairleigh Dickinson University, Teaneck–Hackensack Campus	M
Florida Agricultural and Mechanical University	M
Fordham University	M
The George Washington University	M,D
Georgia State University	M,D
Hawaii Pacific University	M
Hofstra University	M
Illinois Institute of Technology	M
Indiana University Bloomington	M,D
Inter American University of Puerto Rico, Metropolitan Campus	M
Inter American University of Puerto Rico, San Germán Campus	M
Iona College	M,O
Johns Hopkins University	M,O
Kennesaw State University	M
Kent State University	D
Lindenwood University	M
Long Island University, C.W. Post Campus	M,O
Louisiana State University and Agricultural and Mechanical College	M,D
Louisiana Tech University	M,D
Loyola College in Maryland	M
Loyola University Chicago	M
Maryville University of Saint Louis	M,O
Mercy College	M
Metropolitan State University	M
Miami University	M
Michigan State University	M,D
Montclair State University	M
National University	M
New Mexico State University	D
New York Institute of Technology	M,O
New York University	M,D,O
Northeastern Illinois University	M
Northwestern University	M,D
Oklahoma City University	M
Oklahoma State University	M,D
Oral Roberts University	M
Pace University, New York City Campus	M
Pace University, White Plains Campus	M
The Pennsylvania State University University Park Campus	M,D
Philadelphia University	M
Pontifical Catholic University of Puerto Rico	M,D
Purdue University	M,D
Quinnipiac University	M
Regis University	M,O
Rensselaer Polytechnic Institute	M,D
Robert Morris College	M
Rutgers, The State University of New Jersey, Newark	M,D
Sage Graduate School	M
St. Bonaventure University	M,O
St. Cloud State University	M
St. Edward's University	M,O
St. John's University (NY)	M,O
Saint Joseph's University	M
Saint Louis University	M,D
Saint Peter's College	M
St. Thomas Aquinas College	M
Saint Xavier University	M,O
San Diego State University	M
Seton Hall University	M,O
Southeastern University	M
State University of New York at Albany	M
State University of New York at New Paltz	M
Stephen F. Austin State University	M
Syracuse University	D
Temple University	M,D
Texas A&M University	M,D
Texas Tech University	M,D
Universidad del Turabo	M
Universidad Metropolitana	M
The University of Akron	M
The University of Alabama	M,D
The University of Arizona	M
University of Baltimore	M
University of California, Berkeley	D
University of Central Florida	D
University of Cincinnati	M,D
University of Colorado at Boulder	M,D
University of Colorado at Colorado Springs	M
University of Colorado at Denver	M
University of Connecticut	M,D
University of Denver	M
The University of Findlay	M
University of Florida	M,D
University of Houston	D
University of Illinois at Chicago	D
The University of Iowa	D
University of La Verne	M
The University of Memphis	M,D
University of Minnesota, Twin Cities Campus	M,D
University of Missouri–St. Louis	M,O
University of Nebraska–Lincoln	M,D
University of New Haven	M
University of New Mexico	M
The University of North Carolina at Chapel Hill	D
The University of North Carolina at Greensboro	M,D
University of North Texas	M,D
University of Oregon	M,D
University of Pennsylvania	M,D
University of Rhode Island	M,D
University of St. Thomas (MN)	M,O
University of San Francisco	M
The University of Scranton	M
The University of Tennessee	M,D
The University of Tennessee at Chattanooga	M
The University of Texas at Arlington	M,D
The University of Texas at Austin	D
University of the Sacred Heart	M
University of Toledo	M
University of Utah	D
University of Wisconsin–Madison	M
Vanderbilt University	D
Virginia Commonwealth University	M
Virginia Polytechnic Institute and State University	M,D
Wagner College	M
Webster University	M
Western International University	M
Western New England College	M
Wilkes University	M
Worcester Polytechnic Institute	M,O
Wright State University	M
Yale University	D
York College of Pennsylvania	M
Youngstown State University	M

■ MARKETING RESEARCH

Hofstra University	M

Pace University, New York City Campus M
Pace University, White Plains Campus M
Southern Illinois University Edwardsville M
University of Georgia M
The University of Texas at Arlington M
University of Wisconsin–Madison M

■ MARRIAGE AND FAMILY THERAPY

Abilene Christian University M
Alliant International University M,D
Antioch New England Graduate School M
Appalachian State University M,O
Azusa Pacific University M,D
Barry University M,O
Brigham Young University M,D
California Baptist University M
California Lutheran University M
California State University, Bakersfield M,O
California State University, Dominguez Hills M
California State University, Fresno M
California State University, Northridge M,O
Central Connecticut State University M
Chapman University M
The College of New Jersey O
Converse College O
East Carolina University M
Eastern Nazarene College M
Edgewood College M
Fairfield University M
Fitchburg State College M,O
Florida State University M,D
Friends University M
Geneva College M
George Fox University M
Harding University M
Hardin-Simmons University M
Hofstra University M,O
Hope International University M
Idaho State University M,O
Indiana State University M,D,O
Iona College M,O
Iowa State University of Science and Technology M,D
Kean University M,O
Kutztown University of Pennsylvania M
La Salle University D
Loma Linda University M,D
Long Island University, C.W. Post Campus M,O
Loyola Marymount University M
MCP Hahnemann University M,D
Michigan State University M,D
Montclair State University M
Northwestern University M
Notre Dame de Namur University M
Nova Southeastern University M,D,O
Pacific Lutheran University M
Palm Beach Atlantic College M
Prairie View A&M University M
Purdue University M,D
Purdue University Calumet M
Saint Joseph College M
Saint Louis University M,D
St. Mary's University of San Antonio M,D,O
St. Thomas University M
San Francisco State University M
Santa Clara University M
Seattle Pacific University M
Seton Hall University M,D,O
Sonoma State University M
Southern Connecticut State University M
Southern Nazarene University M
Springfield College M,O
State University of New York College at Oneonta M,O
Stetson University M
Syracuse University M,D
Texas Tech University M,D
Texas Woman's University M,D
Trevecca Nazarene University M
The University of Akron M
The University of Alabama at Birmingham M
University of Florida M,D,O
University of Great Falls M
University of Houston–Clear Lake M
University of La Verne M
University of Louisiana at Monroe M,D
University of Maryland, College Park M
University of Miami M
University of Mobile M
University of Nevada, Las Vegas M
University of New Hampshire M
The University of North Carolina at Greensboro M,D,O
University of Oregon M
University of Pittsburgh O
University of Rochester M
University of San Diego M
University of San Francisco M,D
University of Southern California M,D,O
University of Southern Mississippi M,D
University of Wisconsin–Stout M
Utah State University M
Valdosta State University M
Virginia Polytechnic Institute and State University M,D
Wayne State University M,D,O
Western Illinois University M,O

■ MASS COMMUNICATION

American University M
Auburn University M
Boston University M
Bowling Green State University M,D
Brigham Young University M
California State University, Chico M
California State University, Fresno M
California State University, Northridge M
Central Michigan University M
The College of Saint Rose M
Emerson College M
Florida International University M
Florida State University M,D
Fordham University M
The George Washington University M
Grambling State University M
Howard University M,D
Hunter College of the City University of New York M
Indiana University Bloomington M,D
Iowa State University of Science and Technology M
Jackson State University M
Kansas State University M
Kent State University M
Lindenwood University M
Louisiana State University and Agricultural and Mechanical College M
Loyola University New Orleans M
Marquette University M
Marshall University M
Miami University M
Middle Tennessee State University M
Murray State University M
New School University M
Norfolk State University M
North Dakota State University M
Oklahoma State University M,D
The Pennsylvania State University University Park Campus M,D
Point Park College M
St. Cloud State University M
San Diego State University M
San Jose State University M
Seton Hall University M
Southern Illinois University Edwardsville M
Southern University and Agricultural and Mechanical College M
Southwest Texas State University M
Stephen F. Austin State University M
Syracuse University D
Temple University D
Texas Christian University M
Texas Tech University M
University of Colorado at Boulder M,D
University of Connecticut M
University of Denver M
University of Florida M,D
University of Georgia M,D
University of Houston M
University of Illinois at Chicago M
The University of Iowa M,D
University of Louisiana at Lafayette M
University of Maryland, College Park D
University of Michigan D
University of Minnesota, Twin Cities Campus M,D
University of Nebraska–Lincoln M
University of Nevada, Las Vegas M
The University of North Carolina at Chapel Hill M,D
University of Oklahoma M
University of Puerto Rico, Río Piedras M
University of South Dakota M
University of Southern California M,D
University of South Florida M
University of the Sacred Heart M
University of Wisconsin–Madison M,D
University of Wisconsin–Milwaukee M
University of Wisconsin–Stevens Point M
University of Wisconsin–Superior M
University of Wisconsin–Whitewater M
Virginia Commonwealth University M

■ MATERIALS ENGINEERING

Arizona State University M,D
Auburn University M,D
California State University, Northridge M
Carnegie Mellon University M,D
Case Western Reserve University M,D
Clemson University M,D
Colorado State University M,D
Columbia University M,D
Cornell University M,D
Dartmouth College M,D
Drexel University M,D
Georgia Institute of Technology M,D
Howard University M,D
Illinois Institute of Technology M,D
Iowa State University of Science and Technology M,D
Johns Hopkins University M,D
Lehigh University M,D
Marquette University M,D
Massachusetts Institute of Technology M,D,O
Michigan State University M,D
Michigan Technological University M,D
New Jersey Institute of Technology M,D
New Mexico Institute of Mining and Technology M,D
North Carolina State University M,D
Northwestern University M,D,O
The Ohio State University M,D

Old Dominion University	M
The Pennsylvania State University University Park Campus	M,D
Purdue University	M,D
Rensselaer Polytechnic Institute	M,D
Rochester Institute of Technology	M
San Jose State University	M
Stanford University	M,D,O
Stevens Institute of Technology	M,D,O
Stony Brook University, State University of New York	M,D
Texas A&M University	M,D
Tuskegee University	D
The University of Alabama	M,D
The University of Alabama at Birmingham	M,D
The University of Alabama in Huntsville	M
The University of Arizona	M,D
University of California, Berkeley	M,D
University of California, Irvine	M,D
University of California, Los Angeles	M,D
University of California, Santa Barbara	M,D
University of Central Florida	M,D
University of Cincinnati	M,D
University of Dayton	M,D
University of Delaware	M,D
University of Florida	M,D,O
University of Houston	M,D
University of Illinois at Chicago	M,D
University of Illinois at Urbana–Champaign	M,D
University of Maryland, College Park	M,D
University of Michigan	M,D
University of Minnesota, Twin Cities Campus	M,D
University of Nebraska–Lincoln	M,D
University of Pennsylvania	M,D
University of Pittsburgh	M,D
University of Southern California	M
The University of Tennessee	M,D
The University of Texas at Arlington	M,D
The University of Texas at Austin	M,D
The University of Texas at El Paso	D
University of Utah	M,D
University of Washington	M,D
Virginia Polytechnic Institute and State University	M,D
Washington State University	M,D
Washington University in St. Louis	M,D
Wayne State University	M,D,O
Western Michigan University	M
Worcester Polytechnic Institute	M,D,O
Wright State University	M

■ MATERIALS SCIENCES

Alabama Agricultural and Mechanical University	M,D
Alfred University	M,D
Arizona State University	M,D
Brown University	M,D
California Institute of Technology	M,D
California Polytechnic State University, San Luis Obispo	M
Carnegie Mellon University	M,D
Case Western Reserve University	M,D
Clemson University	M,D
Columbia University	M,D,O
Cornell University	M,D
Dartmouth College	M,D
Duke University	M,D
The George Washington University	M,D
Howard University	M,D
Iowa State University of Science and Technology	M,D
Jackson State University	M
Johns Hopkins University	M,D
Lehigh University	M,D
Marquette University	M,D
Massachusetts Institute of Technology	M,D,O
Michigan State University	M,D
New Jersey Institute of Technology	M,D
Norfolk State University	M
North Carolina State University	M,D
Northwestern University	M,D,O
The Ohio State University	M,D
Ohio University	D
Old Dominion University	M
Oregon State University	M
The Pennsylvania State University University Park Campus	M,D
Polytechnic University, Brooklyn Campus	M
Polytechnic University, Westchester Graduate Center	M
Princeton University	
Rensselaer Polytechnic Institute	M,D
Rice University	M,D
Rochester Institute of Technology	M
Rutgers, The State University of New Jersey, New Brunswick	M,D
Southwest Missouri State University	M
Stanford University	M,D,O
Stevens Institute of Technology	M,D,O
Stony Brook University, State University of New York	M,D
Syracuse University	M,D
University at Buffalo, The State University of New York	M
The University of Alabama	D
The University of Alabama at Birmingham	D
The University of Alabama in Huntsville	M,D
The University of Arizona	M,D
University of California, Berkeley	M,D
University of California, Davis	M,D,O
University of California, Irvine	M,D
University of California, Los Angeles	M,D
University of California, San Diego	M,D
University of California, Santa Barbara	M,D
University of Central Florida	M,D
University of Cincinnati	M,D
University of Connecticut	M,D
University of Delaware	M,D
University of Denver	M,D
University of Florida	M,D,O
University of Illinois at Urbana–Champaign	M,D
University of Kentucky	M,D
University of Maryland, College Park	M,D
University of Michigan	M,D
University of Minnesota, Twin Cities Campus	M,D
University of New Hampshire	M
The University of North Carolina at Chapel Hill	M,D
University of North Texas	M,D
University of Pennsylvania	M,D
University of Pittsburgh	M,D
University of Rochester	M,D
University of Southern California	M,D,O
The University of Tennessee	M,D
The University of Texas at Arlington	M,D
The University of Texas at Austin	M,D
The University of Texas at El Paso	D
University of Utah	M,D
University of Vermont	M,D
University of Virginia	M,D
University of Washington	M,D
University of Wisconsin–Madison	M,D
Vanderbilt University	M,D
Virginia Polytechnic Institute and State University	M,D
Washington State University	M,D
Washington University in St. Louis	M,D
Wayne State University	M,D,O
Western Michigan University	M
Worcester Polytechnic Institute	M,D,O
Wright State University	M

■ MATERNAL/CHILD NURSING

Baylor University	M
Boston College	M,D
Case Western Reserve University	M
The Catholic University of America	M,D
Columbia University	M,O
Duke University	M,O
Emory University	M
Florida Atlantic University	M,O
Georgia State University	M,D
Gwynedd-Mercy College	M
Hardin-Simmons University	M
Hunter College of the City University of New York	M,O
Indiana University–Purdue University Indianapolis	M
Johns Hopkins University	M,O
Kent State University	M
Lehman College of the City University of New York	M
Loma Linda University	M
Loyola University Chicago	M
Marquette University	M,O
Molloy College	M,O
New York University	M,O
Northeastern University	M,O
Pontifical Catholic University of Puerto Rico	M
Rutgers, The State University of New Jersey, Newark	M,D
Saint Joseph College	M,O
Seton Hall University	M
Stony Brook University, State University of New York	M,O
Texas Woman's University	M,D
University at Buffalo, The State University of New York	M,D,O
University of Central Florida	M
University of Cincinnati	M,D
University of Colorado at Colorado Springs	M
University of Delaware	M,O
University of Illinois at Chicago	M
University of Maryland	M,D
University of Michigan	M
University of Minnesota, Twin Cities Campus	M
University of Missouri–Kansas City	M,D
University of New Mexico	M,O
University of Pennsylvania	M,O
University of Pittsburgh	M
University of San Diego	M,D,O
University of South Alabama	M
University of Southern Mississippi	M,D
The University of Texas at El Paso	M
Vanderbilt University	M,D
Villanova University	M,O
Virginia Commonwealth University	M,D,O
Wayne State University	M
Wichita State University	M
Wright State University	M

■ MATERNAL AND CHILD HEALTH

Boston University	M,O
Columbia University	M
The George Washington University	M
Harvard University	M,D
Tulane University	M,D
The University of Alabama at Birmingham	M

University of California, Berkeley M
University of Minnesota, Twin Cities Campus M
The University of North Carolina at Chapel Hill M,D
Wheelock College M

■ MATHEMATICAL AND COMPUTATIONAL FINANCE

Boston University M,D
Carnegie Mellon University M,D
Florida State University M,D
New York University M,D
Purdue University M,D
Rice University M,D
Stanford University M,D
University of Chicago M

■ MATHEMATICAL PHYSICS

New Mexico Institute of Mining and Technology M,D
Princeton University D
University of Colorado at Boulder M,D
Virginia Polytechnic Institute and State University M,D

■ MATHEMATICS

Adelphi University M,D
Alabama State University M,O
American University M
Andrews University M
Appalachian State University M
Arizona State University M,D
Arkansas State University M
Auburn University M,D
Ball State University M
Baylor University M
Boston College M
Boston University M,D
Bowling Green State University M,D,O
Brandeis University D
Brigham Young University M,D
Brooklyn College of the City University of New York M,D
Brown University M,D
California Institute of Technology D
California Polytechnic State University, San Luis Obispo M
California State Polytechnic University, Pomona M
California State University, Fresno M
California State University, Fullerton M
California State University, Hayward M
California State University, Long Beach M
California State University, Los Angeles M
California State University, Northridge M
California State University, Sacramento M
California State University, San Bernardino M
California State University, San Marcos M
Carnegie Mellon University M,D
Case Western Reserve University M,D
Central Connecticut State University M
Central Michigan University M,D
Central Missouri State University M
Central Washington University M
Chicago State University M
City College of the City University of New York M
Clarkson University M,D
Clemson University M,D
Cleveland State University M
Colorado State University M,D
Columbia University M,D
Cornell University D
Creighton University M
Dartmouth College D
Drexel University M,D
Duke University D
Duquesne University M
East Carolina University M
Eastern Illinois University M
Eastern Kentucky University M
Eastern Michigan University M
Eastern New Mexico University M
Eastern Washington University M
East Tennessee State University M
Edinboro University of Pennsylvania O
Emory University M,D
Emporia State University M
Fairfield University M
Fayetteville State University M
Florida Atlantic University M,D
Florida International University M
Florida State University M,D
George Mason University M
The George Washington University M,D
Georgia Institute of Technology M,D
Georgian Court College M
Georgia Southern University M
Georgia State University M
Harvard University M,D
Howard University M,D
Hunter College of the City University of New York M
Idaho State University M,D
Illinois State University M
Indiana State University M
Indiana University Bloomington M,D
Indiana University of Pennsylvania M
Indiana University–Purdue University Fort Wayne M
Indiana University–Purdue University Indianapolis M,D
Iowa State University of Science and Technology M,D
Jackson State University M
Jacksonville State University M
John Carroll University M
Johns Hopkins University M,D
Kansas State University M,D
Kean University M
Kent State University M,D
Kutztown University of Pennsylvania M
Lamar University M
Lehigh University M,D
Lehman College of the City University of New York M
Long Island University, C.W. Post Campus M
Louisiana State University and Agricultural and Mechanical College M,D
Louisiana Tech University M
Loyola University Chicago M
Maharishi University of Management M
Marquette University M,D
Marshall University M
Massachusetts Institute of Technology D
McNeese State University M
Miami University M
Michigan State University M,D
Michigan Technological University M,D
Middle Tennessee State University M
Minnesota State University, Mankato M
Mississippi College M
Mississippi State University M,D
Montana State University–Bozeman M,D
Montclair State University M
Morgan State University M
Murray State University M
New Jersey Institute of Technology M,D
New Mexico Institute of Mining and Technology M
New Mexico State University M,D
New York University M,D
Nicholls State University M
North Carolina Central University M
North Carolina State University M,D
North Dakota State University M,D
Northeastern Illinois University M
Northeastern University M,D
Northern Arizona University M
Northern Illinois University M,D
Northwestern University D
Oakland University M,D,O
The Ohio State University M,D
Ohio University M,D
Oklahoma State University M,D
Old Dominion University M,D
Oregon State University M,D
The Pennsylvania State University University Park Campus M,D
Pittsburg State University M
Polytechnic University, Brooklyn Campus M,D
Portland State University M,D
Prairie View A&M University M
Princeton University D
Purdue University M,D
Purdue University Calumet M
Queens College of the City University of New York M
Rensselaer Polytechnic Institute M,D
Rhode Island College M,O
Rice University M,D
Roosevelt University M
Rowan University M
Rutgers, The State University of New Jersey, Camden M
Rutgers, The State University of New Jersey, Newark D
Rutgers, The State University of New Jersey, New Brunswick M,D
St. Cloud State University M
St. John's University (NY) M
Saint Louis University M,D
Salem State College M
Sam Houston State University M
San Diego State University M,D
San Francisco State University M
San Jose State University M
Shippensburg University of Pennsylvania M
South Dakota State University M
Southeast Missouri State University M
Southern Connecticut State University M
Southern Illinois University Carbondale M,D
Southern Illinois University Edwardsville M
Southern Methodist University M,D
Southern Oregon University M
Southern University and Agricultural and Mechanical College M
Southwest Missouri State University M
Southwest Texas State University M
Stanford University M,D
State University of New York at Albany M,D
State University of New York at Binghamton M,D
State University of New York at New Paltz M
State University of New York College at Brockport M

State University of New York College at Potsdam M
Stephen F. Austin State University M
Stevens Institute of Technology M,D
Stony Brook University, State University of New York M,D
Syracuse University M,D
Tarleton State University M
Temple University M,D
Tennessee State University M
Tennessee Technological University M
Texas A&M International University M
Texas A&M University M,D
Texas A&M University–Commerce M
Texas A&M University–Corpus Christi M
Texas A&M University–Kingsville M
Texas Christian University M
Texas Southern University M
Texas Tech University M,D
Texas Woman's University M
Truman State University M
Tufts University M,D
Tulane University M,D
University at Buffalo, The State University of New York M,D
The University of Akron M
The University of Alabama M,D
The University of Alabama at Birmingham M,D
The University of Alabama in Huntsville M,D
University of Alaska Fairbanks M,D
The University of Arizona M,D
University of Arkansas M,D
University of California, Berkeley M,D,O
University of California, Davis M,D
University of California, Irvine M,D
University of California, Los Angeles M,D
University of California, Riverside M,D
University of California, San Diego M,D
University of California, Santa Barbara M,D
University of California, Santa Cruz M,D
University of Central Arkansas M
University of Central Florida M,D
University of Central Oklahoma M
University of Chicago M,D
University of Cincinnati M,D
University of Colorado at Boulder M,D
University of Connecticut M,D
University of Delaware M,D
University of Denver M,D
University of Detroit Mercy M
University of Florida M,D
University of Georgia M,D
University of Hawaii at Manoa M,D
University of Houston M,D
University of Houston–Clear Lake M
University of Idaho M,D
University of Illinois at Chicago M,D
University of Illinois at Urbana–Champaign M,D
The University of Iowa M,D
University of Kansas M,D
University of Kentucky M,D
University of Louisiana at Lafayette M,D
University of Louisville M
University of Maine M
University of Maryland, College Park M,D
University of Massachusetts Amherst M,D
University of Massachusetts Lowell M,D
The University of Memphis M,D
University of Miami M,D
University of Michigan M,D
University of Minnesota, Twin Cities Campus M,D
University of Mississippi M,D
University of Missouri–Columbia M,D
University of Missouri–Kansas City M,D
University of Missouri–Rolla M,D
University of Missouri–St. Louis M,D,O
The University of Montana–Missoula M,D
University of Nebraska at Omaha M
University of Nebraska–Lincoln M,D
University of Nevada, Las Vegas M
University of Nevada, Reno M
University of New Hampshire M,D
University of New Mexico M,D
University of New Orleans M
The University of North Carolina at Chapel Hill M,D
The University of North Carolina at Charlotte M,D
The University of North Carolina at Greensboro M
The University of North Carolina at Wilmington M
University of North Dakota M
University of Northern Colorado M,D
University of Northern Iowa M
University of North Florida M
University of North Texas M,D
University of Notre Dame M,D
University of Oklahoma M,D
University of Oregon M,D
University of Pennsylvania M,D
University of Pittsburgh M,D
University of Puerto Rico, Mayagüez Campus M
University of Puerto Rico, Río Piedras M
University of Rhode Island M,D
University of Rochester M,D
University of South Alabama M
University of South Carolina M,D
University of South Dakota M
University of Southern California M,D
University of Southern Mississippi M
University of South Florida M,D
The University of Tennessee M,D
The University of Texas at Arlington M,D
The University of Texas at Austin M,D
The University of Texas at Dallas M,D
The University of Texas at El Paso M
The University of Texas at San Antonio M
The University of Texas at Tyler M
The University of Texas–Pan American M
University of the District of Columbia M
University of the Incarnate Word M,D
University of Toledo M,D
University of Tulsa M
University of Utah M,D
University of Vermont M,D
University of Virginia M,D
University of Washington M,D
University of West Florida M
University of Wisconsin–Madison M,D
University of Wisconsin–Milwaukee M,D
University of Wyoming M,D
Utah State University M,D
Vanderbilt University M,D
Villanova University M
Virginia Commonwealth University M,O
Virginia Polytechnic Institute and State University M,D
Virginia State University M
Wake Forest University M
Washington State University M,D
Washington University in St. Louis M,D
Wayne State University M,D
West Chester University of Pennsylvania M
Western Carolina University M
Western Connecticut State University M
Western Illinois University M
Western Kentucky University M
Western Michigan University M,D
Western Washington University M
West Texas A&M University M
West Virginia University M,D
Wichita State University M,D
Wilkes University M
Winthrop University M
Worcester Polytechnic Institute M,D,O
Wright State University M
Yale University M,D
Youngstown State University M

■ MATHEMATICS EDUCATION

Alabama State University M,O
Albany State University M
Alfred University M
American University D
Arcadia University M,O
Arkansas State University M
Arkansas Tech University M
Armstrong Atlantic State University M
Auburn University M,D,O
Ball State University M
Bemidji State University M
Boise State University M
Boston College M
Boston University M,D,O
Bowling Green State University M,D,O
Bridgewater State College M
Brooklyn College of the City University of New York M,D
California State University, Bakersfield M
California State University, Dominguez Hills M
California State University, Fullerton M
California University of Pennsylvania M
Campbell University M
Central Missouri State University M
The Citadel, The Military College of South Carolina M
Clarion University of Pennsylvania M
Clemson University M
The College of William and Mary M
Columbus State University M,O
Cornell University M,D
Delta State University M
DePaul University M
DeSales University M
East Carolina University M
Eastern Illinois University M
Eastern Kentucky University M
Eastern Washington University M
Edinboro University of Pennsylvania M
Fayetteville State University M
Fitchburg State College M
Florida Gulf Coast University M
Florida Institute of Technology M,D,O
Florida International University M
Florida State University M,D,O
Fort Hays State University M
Framingham State College M
Fresno Pacific University M
Georgia College and State University M,O
Georgia Southern University M,O
Georgia State University M,D,O
Harvard University M,D,O
Henderson State University M
Hofstra University M
Hood College M
Hunter College of the City University of New York M
Illinois State University D
Indiana University Bloomington M,D
Indiana University of Pennsylvania M
Indiana University–Purdue University Indianapolis M

Iona College	M
Iowa State University of Science and Technology	M,D
Jackson State University	M
Jacksonville University	M
Johns Hopkins University	M,D,O
Kean University	M,O
Kutztown University of Pennsylvania	M,O
Lehman College of the City University of New York	M
LeMoyne-Owen College	M
Long Island University, Brooklyn Campus	M
Long Island University, C.W. Post Campus	M
Louisiana Tech University	M,D,O
Loyola Marymount University	M
Manhattanville College	M
Marquette University	M,D
McNeese State University	M
Mercer University	M,O
Miami University	M
Michigan State University	M,D
Middle Tennessee State University	M
Millersville University of Pennsylvania	M
Minnesota State University, Mankato	M
Minot State University	M
Mississippi College	M
Montclair State University	M,D
Morgan State University	D
National-Louis University	M,O
New Jersey City University	M
New York University	M,D
North Carolina Agricultural and Technical State University	M
North Carolina State University	M,D
Northeastern Illinois University	M
Northeastern University	M
Northern Arizona University	M
Northern Michigan University	M
North Georgia College & State University	M,O
Northwestern State University of Louisiana	M,O
Northwest Missouri State University	M
Nova Southeastern University	M,O
Ohio University	M,D
Oregon State University	M,D
Plattsburgh State University of New York	M
Plymouth State College	M
Portland State University	M,D
Providence College	M
Purdue University	M,D,O
Queens College of the City University of New York	M,O
Quinnipiac University	M
Rider University	O
Rollins College	M
Rowan University	M
Rutgers, The State University of New Jersey, New Brunswick	M,D
Sage Graduate School	M
St. John Fisher College	M
Saint Joseph's University	M
Salem State College	M,O
Salisbury State University	M
San Diego State University	M,D
San Francisco State University	M
Slippery Rock University of Pennsylvania	M
South Carolina State University	M
Southern University and Agricultural and Mechanical College	D
Southwestern Oklahoma State University	M
Southwest Texas State University	M
Stanford University	M,D
State University of New York at Albany	M,D
State University of New York at Binghamton	M
State University of New York College at Brockport	M
State University of New York College at Buffalo	M
State University of New York College at Cortland	M
State University of New York College at Fredonia	M
State University of West Georgia	M,O
Stephen F. Austin State University	M
Syracuse University	M,D,O
Teachers College, Columbia University	M,D
Temple University	M,D
Texas A&M University	M,D
Texas Woman's University	M
Towson University	M
University at Buffalo, The State University of New York	M,D,O
University of Alaska Fairbanks	M,D
University of Arkansas	M
University of California, Berkeley	M,D
University of California, San Diego	D
University of Central Florida	M
University of Central Oklahoma	M
University of Cincinnati	M,D
University of Connecticut	M,D
University of Detroit Mercy	M
University of Florida	M,D,O
University of Georgia	M,D,O
University of Houston	M,D
University of Idaho	M,D
University of Illinois at Chicago	M
University of Illinois at Urbana–Champaign	M,D
University of Massachusetts Lowell	D
University of Miami	M
University of Michigan	M,D
University of Minnesota, Twin Cities Campus	M
University of Missouri–Columbia	M,D
University of Missouri–Rolla	M,D
The University of Montana–Missoula	M,D
University of Nevada, Las Vegas	M,D,O
University of Nevada, Reno	M
University of New Hampshire	M,D
The University of North Carolina at Chapel Hill	M
The University of North Carolina at Charlotte	M,D
The University of North Carolina at Greensboro	M
The University of North Carolina at Pembroke	M
University of Northern Colorado	M,D
University of Northern Iowa	M
University of North Florida	M
University of Oklahoma	M,D
University of Pittsburgh	M,D
University of Puerto Rico, Río Piedras	M,D
University of Rio Grande	M
University of South Carolina	M,D
University of South Florida	M,D,O
The University of Tennessee	M,D,O
The University of Texas at Austin	M,D
The University of Texas at Dallas	M
The University of Texas at San Antonio	M
The University of Texas at Tyler	M
University of Toledo	M,D
University of Tulsa	M
University of Vermont	M,D
University of Washington	M,D
The University of West Alabama	M
University of West Florida	M
University of Wisconsin–Eau Claire	M
University of Wisconsin–Madison	M
University of Wisconsin–Oshkosh	M
University of Wisconsin–River Falls	M
University of Wyoming	M,D
Vanderbilt University	M,D
Virginia State University	M
Washington State University	M,D
Washington University in St. Louis	M,D
Wayne State College	M
Webster University	M
Western Carolina University	M
Western Connecticut State University	M
Western Illinois University	M,O
Western Michigan University	M,D
Western Oregon University	M
West Virginia University	M,D
Wheeling Jesuit University	M
Widener University	M,D
Wilkes University	M
Wright State University	M
Xavier University	M

■ MECHANICAL ENGINEERING

Alfred University	M
Arizona State University	M,D
Auburn University	M,D
Boise State University	M
Boston University	M,D
Bradley University	M
Brigham Young University	M,D
Brown University	M,D
California Institute of Technology	M,D,O
California State University, Chico	M
California State University, Fresno	M
California State University, Fullerton	M
California State University, Long Beach	M
California State University, Los Angeles	M
California State University, Northridge	M
California State University, Sacramento	M
Carnegie Mellon University	M,D
Case Western Reserve University	M,D
The Catholic University of America	M
City College of the City University of New York	M,D
Clarkson University	M,D
Clemson University	M,D
Cleveland State University	M,D
Colorado State University	M,D
Columbia University	M,D
Cornell University	M,D
Dartmouth College	M,D
Drexel University	M,D
Duke University	M,D
Florida Agricultural and Mechanical University	M,D
Florida Atlantic University	M,D
Florida Institute of Technology	M,D
Florida International University	M,D
Florida State University	M,D
Gannon University	M
The George Washington University	M,D,O
Georgia Institute of Technology	M,D
Howard University	M,D
Illinois Institute of Technology	M,D
Indiana University–Purdue University Indianapolis	M
Iowa State University of Science and Technology	M,D
Johns Hopkins University	M,D
Kansas State University	M,D
Lamar University	M,D
Lehigh University	M,D

Louisiana State University and Agricultural and Mechanical College M,D
Louisiana Tech University M,D
Loyola Marymount University M
Manhattan College M
Marquette University M,D
Massachusetts Institute of Technology M,D,O
McNeese State University M
Mercer University M
Michigan State University M,D
Michigan Technological University M,D
Minnesota State University, Mankato M
Mississippi State University M,D
Montana State University–Bozeman M,D
New Jersey Institute of Technology M,D,O
New Mexico State University M,D
North Carolina Agricultural and Technical State University M,D
North Carolina State University M,D
North Dakota State University M
Northeastern University M,D
Northern Illinois University M
Northwestern University M,D
Oakland University M
The Ohio State University M,D
Ohio University M,D
Oklahoma State University M,D
Old Dominion University M,D
Oregon State University M,D
The Pennsylvania State University University Park Campus M,D
Polytechnic University, Brooklyn Campus M,D
Portland State University M,D
Princeton University M,D
Purdue University M,D
Rensselaer Polytechnic Institute M,D
Rice University M,D
Rochester Institute of Technology M
Rutgers, The State University of New Jersey, New Brunswick M,D
Saint Louis University M
San Diego State University M,D
San Jose State University M
Santa Clara University M,D,O
South Dakota State University M
Southern Illinois University Carbondale M
Southern Illinois University Edwardsville M
Southern Methodist University M,D
Stanford University M,D,O
State University of New York at Binghamton M,D
Stevens Institute of Technology M,D,O
Stony Brook University, State University of New York M,D,O
Syracuse University M,D
Temple University M
Tennessee Technological University M,D
Texas A&M University M,D
Texas A&M University–Kingsville M
Texas Tech University M,D
Tufts University M,D
Tulane University M,D
Tuskegee University M
University at Buffalo, The State University of New York M,D
The University of Akron M,D
The University of Alabama M,D
The University of Alabama at Birmingham M,D
The University of Alabama in Huntsville M,D
University of Alaska Fairbanks M
The University of Arizona M,D
University of Arkansas M,D
University of Bridgeport M
University of California, Berkeley M,D
University of California, Davis M,D,O
University of California, Irvine M,D
University of California, Los Angeles M,D
University of California, San Diego M,D
University of California, Santa Barbara M,D
University of Central Florida M,D,O
University of Cincinnati M,D
University of Colorado at Boulder M,D
University of Colorado at Colorado Springs M
University of Colorado at Denver M
University of Connecticut M,D
University of Dayton M,D
University of Delaware M,D
University of Denver M,D
University of Detroit Mercy M,D
University of Florida M,D,O
University of Hawaii at Manoa M,D
University of Houston M,D
University of Idaho M,D
University of Illinois at Chicago M,D
University of Illinois at Urbana–Champaign M,D
The University of Iowa M,D
University of Kansas M,D
University of Kentucky M,D
University of Louisiana at Lafayette M
University of Louisville M
University of Maine M
University of Maryland, Baltimore County M,D
University of Maryland, College Park M,D
University of Massachusetts Amherst M,D
University of Massachusetts Dartmouth M
University of Massachusetts Lowell M,D
The University of Memphis M,D
University of Miami M,D
University of Michigan M,D
University of Michigan–Dearborn M
University of Minnesota, Twin Cities Campus M,D
University of Missouri–Columbia M,D
University of Missouri–Rolla M,D
University of Nebraska–Lincoln M,D
University of Nevada, Las Vegas M,D
University of Nevada, Reno M,D
University of New Hampshire M,D
University of New Haven M
University of New Mexico M,D
University of New Orleans M
The University of North Carolina at Charlotte M,D
University of North Dakota M
University of Notre Dame M,D
University of Oklahoma M,D
University of Pennsylvania M,D
University of Pittsburgh M,D
University of Puerto Rico, Mayagüez Campus M
University of Rhode Island M,D
University of Rochester M,D
University of South Alabama M
University of South Carolina M,D
University of Southern California M,D,O
University of South Florida M,D
The University of Tennessee M,D
The University of Texas at Arlington M,D
The University of Texas at Austin M,D
The University of Texas at El Paso M
The University of Texas at San Antonio M
University of Toledo M,D
University of Tulsa M,D
University of Utah M,D
University of Vermont M,D
University of Virginia M,D
University of Washington M,D
University of Wisconsin–Madison M,D
University of Wyoming M,D
Utah State University M,D
Vanderbilt University M,D
Villanova University M,O
Virginia Polytechnic Institute and State University M,D
Washington State University M,D
Washington University in St. Louis M,D
Wayne State University M,D
Western Michigan University M,D
Western New England College M
West Virginia University M,D
Wichita State University M,D
Widener University M
Worcester Polytechnic Institute M,D,O
Wright State University M
Yale University M,D
Youngstown State University M

■ MECHANICS

Brown University M,D
California Institute of Technology M,D
California State University, Fullerton M
California State University, Northridge M
Case Western Reserve University M,D
The Catholic University of America M,D
Clemson University M,D
Colorado State University M,D
Columbia University M,D,O
Cornell University M,D
Drexel University M,D
Georgia Institute of Technology M,D
Howard University M,D
Idaho State University M,D
Iowa State University of Science and Technology M,D
Johns Hopkins University M,D
Lehigh University M,D
Louisiana State University and Agricultural and Mechanical College M,D
Michigan State University M,D
Michigan Technological University M
Mississippi State University M
New Mexico Institute of Mining and Technology M
North Dakota State University M
Northwestern University M,D
The Ohio State University M,D
Old Dominion University M,D
The Pennsylvania State University University Park Campus M,D
Rensselaer Polytechnic Institute M,D
Rutgers, The State University of New Jersey, New Brunswick M,D
San Diego State University M,D
San Jose State University M
Southern Illinois University Carbondale M,D
The University of Alabama M,D
The University of Arizona M,D
University of California, Berkeley M,D
University of California, San Diego M,D
University of Cincinnati M,D
University of Connecticut D
University of Dayton M
University of Florida M,D,O
University of Illinois at Urbana–Champaign M,D
University of Kentucky M,D
University of Maryland, College Park M,D
University of Massachusetts Lowell M,D
University of Michigan M,D

University of Minnesota, Twin Cities Campus	M,D
University of Missouri–Rolla	M,D
University of Nebraska–Lincoln	M,D
University of Pennsylvania	M,D
University of Rhode Island	M,D
University of Southern California	M
The University of Tennessee	M,D
The University of Texas at Austin	M,D
University of Virginia	M
University of Wisconsin–Madison	M,D
Virginia Polytechnic Institute and State University	M,D
Yale University	M,D

■ MEDIA STUDIES

American University	M
Arkansas State University	M
Austin Peay State University	M
Boston University	M
California State University, Fullerton	M
Carnegie Mellon University	M
Central Michigan University	M
City College of the City University of New York	M
Columbia College Chicago	M
Emerson College	M
Governors State University	M
Hunter College of the City University of New York	M
Indiana State University	M
Kutztown University of Pennsylvania	M
Marquette University	M
Massachusetts Institute of Technology	M,D
Michigan State University	M,D
Monmouth University	M,O
New College of California	M
New School University	M
New York University	M,D
Norfolk State University	M
Northwestern University	M,D
Ohio University	M,D
The Pennsylvania State University University Park Campus	M
Queens College of the City University of New York	M
Regent University	M
Saginaw Valley State University	M
San Diego State University	M
San Francisco State University	M
Suffolk University	M
Syracuse University	M
Temple University	M,D
Texas Christian University	M
Texas Southern University	M
University at Buffalo, The State University of New York	M
The University of Alabama	M
The University of Arizona	M
University of Chicago	M,D
University of Colorado at Boulder	D
University of Denver	M
University of Florida	M,D
University of Oklahoma	M
University of South Carolina	M
University of Southern California	M
The University of Tennessee	M,D
The University of Texas at Austin	M,D
Wayne State University	M,D
Webster University	M
William Paterson University of New Jersey	M

■ MEDICAL/SURGICAL NURSING

Angelo State University	M
Boston College	M,D
Case Western Reserve University	M
The Catholic University of America	M,D
College of Mount Saint Vincent	M,O
College of Staten Island of the City University of New York	M
Columbia University	M,O
Duke University	M,O
Emory University	M
Florida Atlantic University	M,O
Gannon University	M,O
George Mason University	M,D
Georgia State University	M,D
Gwynedd-Mercy College	M
Hunter College of the City University of New York	M
Indiana University–Purdue University Indianapolis	M
Johns Hopkins University	M,O
Kent State University	M
La Roche College	M
La Salle University	M,O
Lehman College of the City University of New York	M
Loyola University Chicago	M
Madonna University	M
Marquette University	M,O
Marymount University	M,O
Molloy College	M,O
Mount Saint Mary College	M
New York University	M,O
Oakland University	M
Pontifical Catholic University of Puerto Rico	M
Rutgers, The State University of New Jersey, Newark	M,D
Sage Graduate School	M
Saint Xavier University	M,O
Seton Hall University	M
Southern Illinois University Edwardsville	M
Stony Brook University, State University of New York	M,O
Texas Woman's University	M,D
University at Buffalo, The State University of New York	M,D,O
University of Central Florida	M
University of Cincinnati	M,D
University of Colorado at Colorado Springs	M
University of Hawaii at Manoa	M,D,O
University of Illinois at Chicago	M
University of Maryland	M,D
University of Miami	M,D
University of Michigan	M
University of Minnesota, Twin Cities Campus	M
University of Missouri–Kansas City	M,D
University of New Mexico	M,O
The University of North Carolina at Charlotte	M
University of Pennsylvania	M
University of San Diego	M,D,O
University of San Francisco	M
The University of Scranton	M
University of South Alabama	M
University of South Carolina	M
University of Southern Maine	M,O
University of Southern Mississippi	M,D
The University of Tennessee at Chattanooga	M
The University of Texas at El Paso	M
The University of Texas–Pan American	M
Vanderbilt University	M,D
Villanova University	M,O
Virginia Commonwealth University	M,D,O
Wayne State University	M
Western Connecticut State University	M
Wichita State University	M
Wright State University	M

■ MEDICAL ILLUSTRATION

Johns Hopkins University	M
Rochester Institute of Technology	M
University of Illinois at Chicago	M
University of Michigan	M

■ MEDICAL INFORMATICS

Columbia University	M,D
Emory University	M
Harvard University	P,M,D
Massachusetts Institute of Technology	M
Stanford University	M,D
University of California, Davis	M
University of California, San Francisco	M,D
University of Utah	M,D
University of Washington	M

■ MEDICAL MICROBIOLOGY

Creighton University	M,D
The Ohio State University	M,D
Rutgers, The State University of New Jersey, New Brunswick	M,D
University of Georgia	M,D
University of Hawaii at Manoa	M,D
University of Minnesota, Duluth	M,D
University of South Florida	D
University of Washington	M,D
University of Wisconsin–Madison	D

■ MEDICAL PHYSICS

Columbia University	M,D
East Carolina University	M,D
Harvard University	M,D
Massachusetts Institute of Technology	D
MCP Hahnemann University	M,D
Oakland University	M,D
Purdue University	M,D
University of California, Los Angeles	M,D
University of Central Arkansas	M
University of Chicago	D
University of Colorado at Boulder	M,D
University of Florida	M,D,O
University of Kentucky	M
University of Minnesota, Twin Cities Campus	M,D
University of Missouri–Columbia	M,D
University of Wisconsin–Madison	M,D
Vanderbilt University	M
Wayne State University	M,D
Wright State University	M

■ MEDICINAL AND PHARMACEUTICAL CHEMISTRY

Duquesne University	M,D
Florida Agricultural and Mechanical University	M,D
Idaho State University	M,D
Long Island University, Brooklyn Campus	M
Long Island University, C.W. Post Campus	M
The Ohio State University	M,D
Purdue University	M,D
Rutgers, The State University of New Jersey, New Brunswick	M,D
St. John's University (NY)	M,D
Temple University	M,D
University at Buffalo, The State University of New York	M,D
University of California, San Francisco	D
University of Connecticut	M,D

University of Florida	M,D
University of Georgia	M,D
University of Kansas	M,D
University of Minnesota, Twin Cities Campus	M,D
University of Mississippi	M,D
University of Rhode Island	M,D
University of the Pacific	M,D
University of Toledo	M,D
University of Utah	M,D
University of Washington	D
West Virginia University	M,D

■ MEDIEVAL AND RENAISSANCE STUDIES

Arizona State University	O
The Catholic University of America	M,D,O
Columbia University	M
Cornell University	D
Duke University	O
Fordham University	M,D
Harvard University	M,D
Indiana University Bloomington	M,D
Marquette University	M,D
Rutgers, The State University of New Jersey, New Brunswick	D
Southern Methodist University	M
University of Connecticut	M,D
University of Minnesota, Twin Cities Campus	M,D
University of Notre Dame	M,D
Western Michigan University	M
Yale University	M,D

■ METALLURGICAL ENGINEERING AND METALLURGY

Georgia Institute of Technology	M,D
Illinois Institute of Technology	M,D
Massachusetts Institute of Technology	M,D,O
Michigan State University	M,D
Michigan Technological University	M,D
The Ohio State University	M,D
The Pennsylvania State University University Park Campus	M,D
Purdue University	M,D
Rensselaer Polytechnic Institute	M,D
Rutgers, The State University of New Jersey, New Brunswick	M,D
The University of Alabama	M,D
The University of Alabama at Birmingham	M,D
University of California, Berkeley	M,D
University of California, Los Angeles	M,D
University of Cincinnati	M,D
University of Connecticut	M,D
University of Florida	M,D,O
University of Idaho	M,D
University of Missouri–Rolla	M,D
University of Nevada, Reno	M,D,O
University of Pittsburgh	M,D
The University of Texas at El Paso	M
University of Utah	M,D
University of Wisconsin–Madison	M,D

■ METEOROLOGY

Florida Institute of Technology	M,D
Florida State University	M,D
Iowa State University of Science and Technology	M,D
Massachusetts Institute of Technology	M,D
North Carolina State University	M,D
The Pennsylvania State University University Park Campus	M,D
San Jose State University	M
Texas A&M University	M,D
University of Hawaii at Manoa	M,D
University of Maryland, College Park	M,D
University of Miami	M,D
University of Oklahoma	M,D
University of Utah	M,D
Yale University	D

■ MICROBIOLOGY

Arizona State University	M,D
Auburn University	M,D
Boston University	M,D
Brandeis University	M,D
Brigham Young University	M,D
Brown University	M,D
California State University, Fullerton	M
California State University, Long Beach	M
California State University, Los Angeles	M
Case Western Reserve University	D
The Catholic University of America	M,D
Clemson University	M,D
Colorado State University	M,D
Columbia University	M,D
Cornell University	D
Dartmouth College	
Duke University	D
East Carolina University	D
East Tennessee State University	M,D
Emory University	D
Emporia State University	M
Florida State University	M,D
Georgetown University	D
Georgia State University	M,D
Harvard University	D
Howard University	D
Idaho State University	M,D
Illinois Institute of Technology	M,D
Illinois State University	M,D
Indiana State University	M,D
Indiana University Bloomington	M,D
Indiana University–Purdue University Indianapolis	M,D
Iowa State University of Science and Technology	M,D
Johns Hopkins University	M,D
Kansas State University	M,D
Loma Linda University	M,D
Long Island University, C.W. Post Campus	M
Louisiana State University and Agricultural and Mechanical College	M,D
Loyola University Chicago	M,D
Marquette University	M,D
Massachusetts Institute of Technology	D
MCP Hahnemann University	M,D
Miami University	M,D
Michigan State University	M,D
Montana State University–Bozeman	M,D
New York University	M,D
North Carolina State University	M,D
North Dakota State University	M,D
Northwestern University	D
The Ohio State University	M,D
Ohio University	M,D
Oklahoma State University	M,D
Oregon State University	M,D
The Pennsylvania State University University Park Campus	M,D
Purdue University	M,D
Quinnipiac University	M
Rensselaer Polytechnic Institute	M,D
Rutgers, The State University of New Jersey, New Brunswick	M,D
Saint Louis University	D
San Diego State University	M
San Francisco State University	M
Seton Hall University	M
South Dakota State University	M
Southern Illinois University Carbondale	M,D
Stanford University	D
Stony Brook University, State University of New York	D
Temple University	M,D
Texas A&M University	M,D
Texas Tech University	M,D
Tufts University	D
Tulane University	M,D
University at Buffalo, The State University of New York	M,D
The University of Alabama at Birmingham	D
The University of Arizona	M,D
University of California, Berkeley	D
University of California, Davis	M,D
University of California, Irvine	D
University of California, Los Angeles	M,D
University of California, Riverside	M,D
University of California, San Francisco	D
University of Central Florida	M
University of Cincinnati	D
University of Colorado at Boulder	M,D
University of Connecticut	M,D
University of Delaware	M,D
University of Florida	M,D
University of Georgia	M,D
University of Hawaii at Manoa	M,D
University of Idaho	M,D
University of Illinois at Chicago	D
University of Illinois at Urbana–Champaign	M,D
The University of Iowa	M,D
University of Kansas	M,D
University of Kentucky	D
University of Louisville	M,D
University of Maine	M,D
University of Maryland	M,D
University of Maryland, College Park	M,D
University of Massachusetts Amherst	M,D
The University of Memphis	M,D
University of Miami	D
University of Michigan	D
University of Minnesota, Twin Cities Campus	M,D
University of Missouri–Columbia	M,D
The University of Montana–Missoula	M,D
University of New Hampshire	M,D
University of New Mexico	M,D
The University of North Carolina at Chapel Hill	M,D
University of North Dakota	M,D
University of Oklahoma	M,D
University of Pennsylvania	D
University of Pittsburgh	M,D
University of Rhode Island	M,D
University of Rochester	M,D
University of South Alabama	D
University of South Dakota	M,D
University of Southern California	M,D
University of Southern Mississippi	M,D
University of South Florida	M
The University of Tennessee	M,D
The University of Texas at Austin	M,D
University of Utah	
University of Vermont	M,D
University of Virginia	D
University of Washington	D
University of Wisconsin–La Crosse	M
University of Wisconsin–Madison	D
University of Wisconsin–Oshkosh	M
Utah State University	M,D
Vanderbilt University	M,D

Virginia Commonwealth University	M,D,O
Virginia Polytechnic Institute and State University	M,D
Wagner College	M
Wake Forest University	D
Washington State University	M,D
Washington University in St. Louis	D
Wayne State University	M,D
West Virginia University	M,D
Wright State University	M
Yale University	D
Yeshiva University	D

■ MIDDLE SCHOOL EDUCATION

Alaska Pacific University	M
Albany State University	M
Armstrong Atlantic State University	M
Augusta State University	M,O
Averett University	M
Ball State University	M
Bellarmine University	M
Brenau University	M,O
Campbell University	M
Central Michigan University	M
College of Mount Saint Vincent	M,O
Columbus State University	M,O
Cumberland College	M
Drury University	M
East Carolina University	M
Eastern Illinois University	M
Eastern Michigan University	M
Eastern Nazarene College	M,O
Edinboro University of Pennsylvania	M
Emory University	M,D,O
Fayetteville State University	M
Fitchburg State College	M
Fort Valley State University	M
Gardner-Webb University	M
George Mason University	M
Georgia College and State University	M,O
Georgia Southern University	M,O
Georgia Southwestern State University	M,O
Georgia State University	M,D,O
James Madison University	M
Kennesaw State University	M
Kent State University	M
Lesley University	M,D,O
Lynchburg College	M
Mary Baldwin College	M
Maryville University of Saint Louis	M
Mercer University	M,O
Middle Tennessee State University	M,O
Morehead State University	M
Morgan State University	M
Murray State University	M,O
Newman University	M
North Carolina Agricultural and Technical State University	M
North Carolina State University	M
Northern Kentucky University	M
North Georgia College & State University	M,O
Northwest Missouri State University	M
Ohio University	M,D
Old Dominion University	M,O
Pacific University	M
Quinnipiac University	M
Saginaw Valley State University	M
St. Cloud State University	M
St. John Fisher College	M
Salem State College	M
Shenandoah University	M,D,O
Siena Heights University	M
Southeast Missouri State University	M
Spalding University	M
State University of West Georgia	M,O
Tufts University	M,O
University of Arkansas	M,D,O
University of Arkansas at Little Rock	M,O
University of Dayton	M
University of Florida	M,D,O
University of Georgia	M,D,O
University of Louisville	M
University of Nebraska at Kearney	M
University of Nevada, Las Vegas	M,D,O
The University of North Carolina at Charlotte	M
The University of North Carolina at Pembroke	M
University of Northern Iowa	M
University of St. Francis (IL)	M
University of South Florida	M
University of West Florida	M
University of Wisconsin–Milwaukee	M
University of Wisconsin–Platteville	M
Valdosta State University	M,O
Virginia Commonwealth University	M,O
Western Carolina University	M
Western Kentucky University	M,O
Western Michigan University	M
Westfield State College	M
Widener University	M,D
Winthrop University	M
Worcester State College	M,O
Youngstown State University	M

■ MILITARY AND DEFENSE STUDIES

California State University, San Bernardino	M
Georgetown University	M
The George Washington University	M
Hawaii Pacific University	M
Johns Hopkins University	M,D,O
Norwich University	M,O
Southwest Missouri State University	M
University of Pittsburgh	M

■ MINERAL/MINING ENGINEERING

Columbia University	D,O
Michigan Technological University	M,D
New Mexico Institute of Mining and Technology	M
The Pennsylvania State University University Park Campus	M,D
Southern Illinois University Carbondale	M
University of Alaska Fairbanks	M,O
The University of Arizona	M,D
University of California, Berkeley	M,D
University of Idaho	M,D
University of Kentucky	M,D
University of Missouri–Rolla	M,D
University of Nevada, Reno	M,O
University of North Dakota	M
The University of Texas at Austin	M
University of Utah	M,D
Virginia Polytechnic Institute and State University	M,D
West Virginia University	M,D

■ MINERAL ECONOMICS

Michigan Technological University	M
The Pennsylvania State University University Park Campus	M,D
The University of Texas at Austin	M

■ MINERALOGY

Cornell University	M,D
Indiana University Bloomington	M,D
University of Illinois at Chicago	M,D
University of Michigan	M,D
Yale University	D

■ MISSIONS AND MISSIOLOGY

Abilene Christian University	M
Biola University	M,D,O
Concordia University (CA)	M
Gardner-Webb University	P
Grand Rapids Baptist Seminary	P,M,D
Oral Roberts University	P,M,D
Regent University	P,M,D
Simpson College and Graduate School	M

■ MOLECULAR BIOLOGY

Arizona State University	M,D
Boston University	M,D
Brandeis University	M,D
Brigham Young University	M,D
Brown University	M,D
California Institute of Technology	D
Carnegie Mellon University	M,D
Case Western Reserve University	M,D
Central Connecticut State University	M,O
Colorado State University	M,D
Columbia University	M,D
Cornell University	D
Dartmouth College	
Duke University	D,O
East Carolina University	M
Emory University	D
Florida Institute of Technology	M
Florida State University	M,D
Fordham University	M,D
George Mason University	M
Georgetown University	D
The George Washington University	M,D
Harvard University	D
Howard University	M,D
Indiana University Bloomington	M,D
Indiana University–Purdue University Indianapolis	M,D
Iowa State University of Science and Technology	M,D
Johns Hopkins University	M,D
Kansas State University	M,D
Kent State University	M,D
Lehigh University	D
Loyola University Chicago	M,D
Maharishi University of Management	M,D
Marquette University	M,D
Mayo Graduate School	D
MCP Hahnemann University	M,D
Michigan State University	M,D
Mississippi State University	M,D
Montana State University–Bozeman	M,D
Montclair State University	M,O
New Mexico State University	M,D
New York University	D
North Dakota State University	M,D
Northwestern University	D
The Ohio State University	M,D
Ohio University	M,D
Oklahoma State University	M,D
Oregon State University	D
The Pennsylvania State University University Park Campus	M,D
Princeton University	D
Purdue University	M,D
Quinnipiac University	M
Rensselaer Polytechnic Institute	M,D
Rutgers, The State University of New Jersey, New Brunswick	M,D
Saint Joseph College	M
Saint Louis University	D
Salem International University	M
San Diego State University	M,D
San Francisco State University	M

Southern Illinois University Carbondale M,D
Southwest Missouri State University M
State University of New York at Albany M,D
Stony Brook University, State University of New York M,D
Temple University D
Texas A&M University D
Texas Woman's University M,D
Tufts University D
Tulane University M,D
University at Buffalo, The State University of New York D
The University of Alabama at Birmingham
The University of Arizona M,D
University of Arkansas M,D
University of California, Berkeley D
University of California, Davis M,D
University of California, Irvine D
University of California, Los Angeles M,D
University of California, Riverside M,D
University of California, San Diego D
University of California, San Francisco D
University of California, Santa Barbara M,D
University of California, Santa Cruz D
University of Central Florida M
University of Chicago D
University of Cincinnati M,D
University of Colorado at Boulder M,D
University of Delaware M,D
University of Florida D
University of Georgia M,D
University of Hawaii at Manoa M,D
University of Idaho M,D
University of Illinois at Chicago M,D
University of Illinois at Urbana–Champaign
The University of Iowa D
University of Kansas M,D
University of Louisville M,D
University of Maine M,D
University of Maryland D
University of Maryland, Baltimore County M,D
University of Maryland, College Park D
University of Massachusetts Amherst D
The University of Memphis M,D
University of Miami D
University of Michigan M,D
University of Minnesota, Duluth M,D
University of Minnesota, Twin Cities Campus M,D
University of Missouri–Kansas City M,D
University of Missouri–St. Louis M,D,O
University of Nevada, Reno M,D
University of New Hampshire M,D
University of New Haven M
University of New Mexico M,D
The University of North Carolina at Chapel Hill M,D
University of North Texas M,D
University of Notre Dame M,D
University of Oregon M,D
University of Pennsylvania D
University of Pittsburgh D
University of Rochester M,D
University of South Alabama D
University of South Carolina M,D
University of South Dakota M,D
University of Southern California M,D
University of Southern Maine M
University of Southern Mississippi M,D
University of South Florida D
The University of Texas at Austin D
The University of Texas at Dallas M,D
University of Utah D
University of Vermont M,D
University of Virginia D
University of Washington D
University of Wisconsin–Madison M,D
University of Wisconsin–Parkside M
University of Wyoming M,D
Utah State University M,D
Vanderbilt University D
Virginia Commonwealth University M,D,O
Virginia Polytechnic Institute and State University M,D
Wake Forest University D
Washington State University M,D
Washington University in St. Louis D
Wayne State University M,D
West Virginia University M,D
William Paterson University of New Jersey M
Wright State University M
Yale University D
Yeshiva University D

■ MOLECULAR MEDICINE

Boston University D
Cornell University M,D
Johns Hopkins University D
The Pennsylvania State University University Park Campus M,D
University of Cincinnati D
University of Rochester
University of Virginia D
University of Washington M,D
Wake Forest University D
Yale University D

■ MULTILINGUAL AND MULTICULTURAL EDUCATION

Adelphi University M
Azusa Pacific University M
Boston University M,O
Brooklyn College of the City University of New York M
Brown University M,D
California Baptist University M
California State University, Bakersfield M
California State University, Chico M
California State University, Dominguez Hills M
California State University, Fullerton M
California State University, Los Angeles M,D
California State University, Sacramento M
California State University, San Bernardino M
California State University, Stanislaus M
Chicago State University M
City College of the City University of New York M
College of Mount Saint Vincent M,O
The College of New Rochelle M,O
College of Santa Fe M
Columbia College Chicago M
Eastern College M
Eastern Michigan University M
Eastern Nazarene College M,O
Emmanuel College M
Fairfield University M,O
Fairleigh Dickinson University, Teaneck–Hackensack Campus M
Florida State University M,D,O
Fordham University M,D,O
Fresno Pacific University M
George Mason University M
Georgetown University M,D,O
Heritage College M
Hofstra University M
Houston Baptist University M
Hunter College of the City University of New York M
Immaculata College M
Iona College M
Kean University M,O
Lehman College of the City University of New York M
Lesley University M,O
Long Island University, Brooklyn Campus M
Long Island University, C.W. Post Campus M
Loyola Marymount University M
Mercy College M,O
Minnesota State University, Mankato M,O
National University M
New Jersey City University M
New York University M,D,O
Northeastern Illinois University M
Northern Arizona University M
The Pennsylvania State University University Park Campus M,D
Prescott College M
Queens College of the City University of New York M,O
Rhode Island College M
St. John's University (NY) M
Salem State College M
Sam Houston State University M,O
San Diego State University M
School for International Training M
Seton Hall University M,O
Southern Connecticut State University M
Southern Methodist University M
Southwest Texas State University M
State University of New York College at Brockport M
State University of New York College at Buffalo M
Sul Ross State University M
Teachers College, Columbia University M
Texas A&M International University M
Texas A&M University M,D
Texas A&M University–Kingsville M,D
Texas Southern University M,D
Texas Tech University M,D,O
Universidad del Turabo M
University of Alaska Fairbanks M,O
The University of Arizona M,D,O
University of California, Berkeley M,D,O
University of Colorado at Boulder M,D
University of Connecticut M,D
University of Delaware M,D
The University of Findlay M
University of Florida M,D,O
University of Houston M,D
University of Houston–Clear Lake M
University of La Verne O
University of Maryland, Baltimore County M,D
University of Massachusetts Amherst M,D,O
University of Massachusetts Boston M
University of Minnesota, Twin Cities Campus M
University of New Mexico D
University of Pennsylvania M,D
University of San Francisco M,D
The University of Tennessee M,D,O
The University of Texas at Brownsville M
The University of Texas at San Antonio M,D
The University of Texas–Pan American M
University of Washington M,D
Utah State University M
Washington State University M,D

Western Oregon University	M
Xavier University	M

■ MUSEUM EDUCATION

The College of New Rochelle	O
The George Washington University	M
The University of Montana–Missoula	M

■ MUSEUM STUDIES

Baylor University	M
Boston University	M,D,O
California State University, Chico	M
California State University, Fullerton	M,O
Case Western Reserve University	M,D
City College of the City University of New York	M
Colorado State University	M
Duquesne University	M
Florida State University	M,D,O
The George Washington University	M,O
Hampton University	M
Harvard University	M,O
John F. Kennedy University	M,O
New York University	M,D,O
Rutgers, The State University of New Jersey, New Brunswick	M,D
San Francisco State University	M
Seton Hall University	M
State University of New York College at Oneonta	M
Syracuse University	M
Texas Tech University	M
Tufts University	O
University of California, Riverside	M,D
University of Central Oklahoma	M
University of Colorado at Boulder	M
University of Delaware	O
University of Denver	M
University of Florida	M
University of Kansas	M
University of Missouri–St. Louis	M,O
University of Nebraska–Lincoln	M
University of New Hampshire	M,D
The University of North Carolina at Greensboro	M,O
University of South Carolina	M,O
University of Washington	M
University of Wisconsin–Milwaukee	M,O
Wayne State University	M,O

■ MUSIC

Alabama Agricultural and Mechanical University	M
Alabama State University	M
Andrews University	M
Appalachian State University	M
Arizona State University	M,D
Arkansas State University	M,O
Auburn University	M
Austin Peay State University	M
Azusa Pacific University	M
Baylor University	M
Belmont University	M
Bethel College (MN)	M
Boise State University	M
Boston University	M,D,O
Bowling Green State University	M
Brandeis University	M,D,O
Brigham Young University	M
Brooklyn College of the City University of New York	M,D
Brown University	M,D
Butler University	M
California State University, Chico	M
California State University, Fresno	M
California State University, Fullerton	M
California State University, Hayward	M
California State University, Long Beach	M
California State University, Los Angeles	M
California State University, Northridge	M
California State University, Sacramento	M
Campbellsville University	M
Carnegie Mellon University	M
Case Western Reserve University	M,D
The Catholic University of America	M,D
Central Michigan University	M
Central Missouri State University	M
Central Washington University	M
City College of the City University of New York	M
Claremont Graduate University	M,D
Cleveland State University	M
The College of Saint Rose	M
Colorado State University	M
Columbia University	M,D
Concordia University (IL)	M,O
Concordia University Wisconsin	M
Converse College	M
Cornell University	D
Dartmouth College	M
DePaul University	M,O
Duke University	M,D
Duquesne University	M,O
East Carolina University	M
Eastern Illinois University	M
Eastern Kentucky University	M
Eastern Michigan University	M
Eastern Washington University	M
Emory University	M
Emporia State University	M
Florida Atlantic University	M
Florida International University	M
Florida State University	M,D
Gardner-Webb University	P
George Mason University	M
Georgia Southern University	M
Georgia State University	M
Golden Gate Baptist Theological Seminary	P,M,D,O
Gratz College	M,O
Hardin-Simmons University	M
Harvard University	M,D
Holy Names College	M,O
Hope International University	M
Howard University	M
Hunter College of the City University of New York	M
Illinois State University	M
Indiana State University	M
Indiana University Bloomington	M,D
Indiana University of Pennsylvania	M
Indiana University–Purdue University Indianapolis	M
Indiana University South Bend	M
Ithaca College	M
Jacksonville State University	M
James Madison University	M
Johns Hopkins University	M,D,O
Kansas State University	M
Kent State University	M,D
Lamar University	M
Lehman College of the City University of New York	M
Long Island University, C.W. Post Campus	M
Louisiana State University and Agricultural and Mechanical College	M,D
Loyola University New Orleans	M
Lynn University	O
Mansfield University of Pennsylvania	M
Marshall University	M
Marywood University	M
Meredith College	M
Miami University	M
Michigan State University	M,D
Middle Tennessee State University	M
Minnesota State University, Mankato	M
Minnesota State University Moorhead	M
Mississippi College	M
Montclair State University	M
Morehead State University	M
Morgan State University	M
Murray State University	M
New Mexico State University	M
New York University	M,D,O
Norfolk State University	M
Northeastern Illinois University	M
Northern Arizona University	M
Northern Illinois University	M,O
Northwestern State University of Louisiana	M
Northwestern University	M,D,O
Notre Dame de Namur University	M
Oakland University	M
The Ohio State University	M,D
Ohio University	M
Oklahoma City University	M
Oklahoma State University	M
The Pennsylvania State University University Park Campus	M
Pittsburg State University	M
Portland State University	M
Princeton University	D
Purchase College, State University of New York	M
Queens College of the City University of New York	M
Radford University	M
Rhode Island College	M
Rice University	M,D
Rider University	M
Roosevelt University	M,O
Rowan University	M
Rutgers, The State University of New Jersey, Newark	M
Rutgers, The State University of New Jersey, New Brunswick	M,D,O
St. Cloud State University	M
Samford University	M
Sam Houston State University	M
San Diego State University	M
San Francisco State University	M
San Jose State University	M
Santa Clara University	M
Shenandoah University	M,D,O
Southeastern Louisiana University	M
Southern Illinois University Carbondale	M
Southern Illinois University Edwardsville	M
Southern Methodist University	M
Southern Oregon University	M
Southwestern Oklahoma State University	M
Southwest Missouri State University	M
Southwest Texas State University	M
Stanford University	M,D
State University of New York at Binghamton	M
State University of New York at New Paltz	M
State University of New York College at Fredonia	M
State University of New York College at Potsdam	M
State University of West Georgia	M
Stephen F. Austin State University	M

Stony Brook University, State University of New York M,D
Syracuse University M
Temple University M,D
Texas A&M University–Commerce M
Texas Christian University M
Texas Southern University M
Texas Tech University M,D
Texas Woman's University M
Towson University M
Truman State University M
Tufts University M
Tulane University M
University at Buffalo, The State University of New York M,D
The University of Akron M
The University of Alabama M,D,O
University of Alaska Fairbanks M
The University of Arizona M,D
University of Arkansas M
University of California, Berkeley M,D
University of California, Davis M,D
University of California, Irvine M
University of California, Los Angeles M,D
University of California, Riverside M
University of California, San Diego M,D
University of California, Santa Barbara M,D
University of California, Santa Cruz M
University of Central Arkansas M
University of Central Oklahoma M
University of Chicago M,D
University of Cincinnati M,D,O
University of Colorado at Boulder M,D
University of Connecticut M,D
University of Delaware M
University of Denver M
University of Florida M,D
University of Georgia M,D
University of Hartford M,D,O
University of Hawaii at Manoa M,D
University of Houston M,D
University of Idaho M
University of Illinois at Urbana–Champaign M,D
The University of Iowa M,D
University of Kansas M,D
University of Kentucky M,D
University of Louisiana at Lafayette M
University of Louisiana at Monroe M
University of Louisville M,D
University of Maine M
University of Maryland, College Park M,D
University of Massachusetts Amherst M,D
University of Massachusetts Lowell M
The University of Memphis M,D
University of Miami M,D
University of Michigan M,D
University of Minnesota, Duluth M
University of Minnesota, Twin Cities Campus M,D
University of Mississippi M,D
University of Missouri–Columbia M
University of Missouri–Kansas City M,D
The University of Montana–Missoula M
University of Montevallo M
University of Nebraska at Omaha M
University of Nebraska–Lincoln M,D
University of Nevada, Las Vegas M
University of Nevada, Reno M
University of New Hampshire M
University of New Mexico M
University of New Orleans M
The University of North Carolina at Chapel Hill M,D
The University of North Carolina at Greensboro M,D
University of North Dakota M
University of Northern Colorado M,D
University of Northern Iowa M
University of North Texas M,D
University of Notre Dame M
University of Oklahoma M,D
University of Oregon M,D
University of Pennsylvania M,D
University of Pittsburgh M,D
University of Portland M
University of Redlands M
University of Rhode Island M
University of Rochester M,D
University of South Carolina M,D,O
University of South Dakota M
University of Southern California M,D
University of Southern Mississippi M,D
University of South Florida M,D
The University of Tennessee M
The University of Tennessee at Chattanooga M
The University of Texas at Arlington M
The University of Texas at Austin M,D
The University of Texas at El Paso M
The University of Texas at San Antonio M
The University of Texas at Tyler M
University of the Pacific M
University of Toledo M
University of Utah M,D
University of Virginia M
University of Washington M,D
University of Wisconsin–Madison M,D
University of Wisconsin–Milwaukee M
University of Wyoming M
Valparaiso University M
Virginia Commonwealth University M
Washington State University M
Washington University in St. Louis M,D
Wayne State University M,O
Webster University M
West Chester University of Pennsylvania M
Western Carolina University M
Western Illinois University M
Western Michigan University M
Western Washington University M
West Texas A&M University M
West Virginia University M,D
Wichita State University M
William Paterson University of New Jersey M
Winthrop University M
Yale University M,D,O
Youngstown State University M

■ MUSIC EDUCATION

Alabama Agricultural and Mechanical University M
Alabama State University M
Albany State University M
Appalachian State University M
Arcadia University M,O
Arkansas State University M,O
Auburn University M,D,O
Austin Peay State University M
Azusa Pacific University M
Ball State University M,D
Baylor University M
Belmont University M
Boise State University M
Boston University M,D
Bowling Green State University M
Brigham Young University M
Brooklyn College of the City University of New York M,D
Butler University M
California State University, Fresno M
California State University, Fullerton M
California State University, Los Angeles M
California State University, Northridge M
Campbellsville University M
Carnegie Mellon University M
Case Western Reserve University M,D
The Catholic University of America M,D
Central Connecticut State University M
Central Michigan University M
Claremont Graduate University M,D
Cleveland State University M
The College of Saint Rose M
Colorado State University M
Columbus State University M
Converse College M
Delta State University M
DePaul University M
Duquesne University M,O
East Carolina University M
Eastern Kentucky University M
Eastern Nazarene College M,O
Eastern Washington University M
East Tennessee State University M
Emporia State University M
Florida International University M
Florida State University M,D
George Mason University M
Georgia Southern University M,O
Georgia State University M,D,O
Hardin-Simmons University M
Hofstra University M
Holy Names College M,O
Howard University M
Hunter College of the City University of New York M
Indiana State University M
Indiana University Bloomington M,D,O
Indiana University of Pennsylvania M
Ithaca College M
Jackson State University M
Jacksonville State University M
Jacksonville University M
James Madison University M
Kansas State University M
Kent State University M,D
Lamar University M
Long Island University, C.W. Post Campus M
Louisiana State University and Agricultural and Mechanical College M,D
Manhattanville College M
Marywood University M
McNeese State University M
Miami University M
Michigan State University M,D
Minnesota State University Moorhead M
Minot State University M
Mississippi College M
Montclair State University M
Morehead State University M
Murray State University M
Nazareth College of Rochester M
New Jersey City University M
New York University M,D,O
Norfolk State University M
Northern Arizona University M
Northwestern University M,D
Northwest Missouri State University M
Notre Dame de Namur University M,O
Oregon State University M
The Pennsylvania State University University Park Campus M,D
Pittsburg State University M
Portland State University M

Queens College of the City University of New York	M,O
Radford University	M
Rhode Island College	M
Rider University	M
Rollins College	M
Roosevelt University	M,O
Rowan University	M
St. Cloud State University	M
Salisbury State University	M
Samford University	M,D,O
Sam Houston State University	M
Shenandoah University	M,D,O
Silver Lake College	M
Southeast Missouri State University	M
Southern Illinois University Carbondale	M
Southern Illinois University Edwardsville	M
Southern Methodist University	M
Southwest Texas State University	M
State University of New York at New Paltz	M
State University of New York College at Fredonia	M
State University of New York College at Potsdam	M
State University of West Georgia	M
Syracuse University	M
Teachers College, Columbia University	M,D
Temple University	M,D
Tennessee State University	M
Texas A&M University–Commerce	M
Texas A&M University–Kingsville	M
Texas Christian University	M
Texas Tech University	M,D,O
Texas Woman's University	M
Towson University	M,O
University at Buffalo, The State University of New York	M,D,O
The University of Akron	M
The University of Alabama	M,D,O
University of Alaska Fairbanks	M
The University of Arizona	M,D
University of Central Arkansas	M
University of Central Florida	M
University of Central Oklahoma	M
University of Cincinnati	M,D
University of Colorado at Boulder	M,D
University of Connecticut	M,D
University of Delaware	M
University of Denver	M
University of Florida	M,D
University of Georgia	M,D,O
University of Hartford	M,D,O
University of Houston	M,D
The University of Iowa	M,D
University of Kansas	M,D
University of Louisiana at Lafayette	M
University of Louisville	M
University of Maryland, College Park	M,D
University of Massachusetts Lowell	M
The University of Memphis	M,D
University of Miami	M,D,O
University of Michigan	D
University of Minnesota, Duluth	M
University of Missouri–Kansas City	M,D
University of Missouri–St. Louis	M
The University of Montana–Missoula	M
University of Nebraska at Kearney	M
University of Nevada, Las Vegas	M
University of New Hampshire	M
The University of North Carolina at Chapel Hill	M
The University of North Carolina at Greensboro	M,D
University of North Dakota	M
University of Northern Colorado	M,D
University of Northern Iowa	M
University of North Florida	M
University of North Texas	M,D
University of Oklahoma	M,D
University of Oregon	M,D
University of Rochester	M,D
University of St. Thomas (MN)	M
University of South Alabama	M
University of South Carolina	M,D
University of Southern California	M,D
University of Southern Mississippi	M,D
University of South Florida	M,D
The University of Tennessee	M
The University of Texas at El Paso	M
The University of Texas at Tyler	M
University of Toledo	M
University of Washington	M,D
University of Wisconsin–Madison	M,D
University of Wisconsin–Stevens Point	M
University of Wyoming	M
Valdosta State University	M
Virginia Commonwealth University	M
Wayne State College	M
Wayne State University	M,O
Webster University	M
West Chester University of Pennsylvania	M
Western Connecticut State University	M
Western Kentucky University	M
West Virginia University	M,D
Wichita State University	M
Winthrop University	M
Wright State University	M
Xavier University	M
Youngstown State University	M

■ NATURAL RESOURCES

Ball State University	M
Colorado State University	D
Cornell University	M,D
Duke University	M,D
Humboldt State University	M
Montana State University–Bozeman	M,D
North Carolina State University	M,D
The Ohio State University	M,D
Purdue University	M,D
Texas A&M University	M,D
The University of Arizona	M,D
University of Connecticut	M
University of Florida	M,D
University of Georgia	M,D
University of Illinois at Urbana–Champaign	M,D
University of Maine	M,D
University of Michigan	M,D,O
The University of Montana–Missoula	M
University of Nebraska–Lincoln	M
University of New Hampshire	M,D
University of Rhode Island	M,D
University of Wisconsin–Stevens Point	M
University of Wyoming	M,D
Utah State University	M
Virginia Polytechnic Institute and State University	M,D
Washington State University	M,D
West Virginia University	D

■ NATUROPATHIC MEDICINE

University of Bridgeport	D

■ NEAR AND MIDDLE EASTERN LANGUAGES

Brigham Young University	M
The Catholic University of America	M,D
Columbia University	M,D
Georgetown University	M,D
Harvard University	M,D
Indiana University Bloomington	M,D
The Ohio State University	M
University of California, Los Angeles	M,D
University of Chicago	M,D
University of Michigan	M,D
The University of Texas at Austin	M,D
University of Wisconsin–Madison	M,D
Yale University	M,D

■ NEAR AND MIDDLE EASTERN STUDIES

Brandeis University	M,D
Brigham Young University	M
Columbia University	M,D,O
Cornell University	M,D
Georgetown University	M,O
Gratz College	O
Harvard University	M,D
Johns Hopkins University	M,D,O
New York University	M,D
Princeton University	M,D
The University of Arizona	M,D
University of California, Berkeley	M,D,O
University of California, Los Angeles	M,D
University of Chicago	M,D
University of Michigan	M,D
University of Pennsylvania	M,D
The University of Texas at Austin	M,D
University of Utah	M,D
University of Virginia	M
University of Washington	M,D
Washington University in St. Louis	M
Wayne State University	M

■ NEUROSCIENCE

Arizona State University	M,D
Baylor University	M,D
Boston University	M,D
Brandeis University	M,D
Brown University	D
California Institute of Technology	M,D
Carnegie Mellon University	
Case Western Reserve University	D
College of Staten Island of the City University of New York	D
Colorado State University	M,D
Columbia University	M,D
Cornell University	D
Dartmouth College	D
Duke University	D
Emory University	D
Florida State University	D
Georgetown University	D
The George Washington University	D
Georgia State University	M,D
Harvard University	D
Indiana University Bloomington	D
Indiana University–Purdue University Indianapolis	M,D
Iowa State University of Science and Technology	M,D
Johns Hopkins University	D
Kent State University	M,D
Lehigh University	D
Loyola University Chicago	M,D
Maharishi University of Management	M,D
Marquette University	M,D
Massachusetts Institute of Technology	D
Mayo Graduate School	D
MCP Hahnemann University	D
Michigan State University	D
New York University	M,D
Northwestern University	M,D

The Ohio State University	D
The Pennsylvania State University University Park Campus	M,D
Princeton University	D
Purdue University	M,D
Rutgers, The State University of New Jersey, Newark	D
Rutgers, The State University of New Jersey, New Brunswick	D
Saint Louis University	M,D
Stanford University	D
State University of New York at Albany	M,D
Stony Brook University, State University of New York	D
Syracuse University	M,D
Teachers College, Columbia University	M
Tufts University	D
Tulane University	M,D
University at Buffalo, The State University of New York	M,D
The University of Alabama at Birmingham	M,D
The University of Arizona	D
University of California, Berkeley	D
University of California, Davis	D
University of California, Irvine	M,D
University of California, Los Angeles	D
University of California, Riverside	D
University of California, San Diego	D
University of California, San Francisco	D
University of Chicago	D
University of Cincinnati	D
University of Colorado at Boulder	M,D
University of Connecticut	M,D
University of Delaware	D
University of Florida	M,D
University of Hartford	M
University of Hawaii at Manoa	M,D
University of Illinois at Chicago	M,D
University of Illinois at Urbana–Champaign	D
The University of Iowa	M,D
University of Kentucky	D
University of Louisville	M,D
University of Maryland	M,D
University of Maryland, Baltimore County	M,D
University of Maryland, College Park	D
University of Massachusetts Amherst	M,D
University of Miami	M,D
University of Michigan	D
University of Minnesota, Twin Cities Campus	M,D
University of New Mexico	M,D
The University of North Carolina at Chapel Hill	D
University of Oregon	M,D
University of Pennsylvania	D
University of Pittsburgh	M,D
University of Rochester	M,D
University of South Alabama	D
University of South Dakota	M,D
University of Southern California	M,D
The University of Texas at Austin	M,D
The University of Texas at Dallas	M
The University of Texas at San Antonio	D
University of Utah	M,D
University of Vermont	D
University of Virginia	D
University of Washington	D
University of Wisconsin–Madison	M,D
Vanderbilt University	D
Virginia Commonwealth University	M,D,O
Wake Forest University	D
Washington State University	M,D
Washington University in St. Louis	D
Wayne State University	D
Yale University	D
Yeshiva University	D

■ NONPROFIT MANAGEMENT

Boston University	M
Carlow College	M
Case Western Reserve University	M,O
College of Notre Dame of Maryland	M
The College of Saint Rose	O
DePaul University	M,O
Eastern College	M
Hamline University	M
Hope International University	M
Indiana University Northwest	M,O
Indiana University–Purdue University Indianapolis	M
Lesley University	M
Metropolitan State University	M
New School University	M
New York University	M,D,O
North Central College	M
Oral Roberts University	M
Pace University, White Plains Campus	M
Regis University	M,O
St. Cloud State University	M
St. Edward's University	M,O
San Francisco State University	M
Seattle University	M
Seton Hall University	M
Suffolk University	M,O
Trinity College (DC)	M
Tufts University	O
University of Central Florida	M,O
The University of Memphis	M
University of Missouri–St. Louis	M,O
The University of North Carolina at Greensboro	M,O
University of Pittsburgh	M
University of St. Thomas (MN)	M,O
University of San Francisco	M
Worcester State College	M

■ NORTHERN STUDIES

University of Alaska Fairbanks	M,D

■ NUCLEAR ENGINEERING

Cornell University	M,D
Georgia Institute of Technology	M,D
Idaho State University	M,D
Kansas State University	M,D
Louisiana State University and Agricultural and Mechanical College	M
Massachusetts Institute of Technology	M,D,O
North Carolina State University	M,D
The Ohio State University	M,D
Oregon State University	M,D
The Pennsylvania State University University Park Campus	M,D
Purdue University	M,D
Rensselaer Polytechnic Institute	M,D
Texas A&M University	M,D
The University of Arizona	M,D
University of California, Berkeley	M,D
University of Cincinnati	M,D
University of Florida	M,D,O
University of Idaho	M,D
University of Illinois at Urbana–Champaign	M,D
University of Maryland, College Park	M,D
University of Michigan	M,D,O
University of Missouri–Columbia	M,D
University of Missouri–Rolla	M,D
University of New Mexico	M,D
The University of Tennessee	M,D
University of Utah	M,D
University of Virginia	M,D
University of Wisconsin–Madison	M,D

■ NURSE ANESTHESIA

Barry University	M
California State University, Long Beach	M
Case Western Reserve University	M
Columbia University	M,O
DePaul University	M
Duke University	M,O
Emory University	M
Gannon University	M,O
Gonzaga University	M
La Roche College	M
MCP Hahnemann University	M
Mount Marty College	M
Newman University	M
Northeastern University	M
Oakland University	M
Saint Joseph's University	M
Saint Mary's University of Minnesota	M
Southern Illinois University Edwardsville	M
Southwest Missouri State University	M
Texas Wesleyan University	M
University at Buffalo, The State University of New York	M,D,O
The University of Alabama at Birmingham	M
University of Cincinnati	M,D
University of Detroit Mercy	M
University of Kansas	M
University of Michigan–Flint	M
University of New England	M
The University of North Carolina at Greensboro	M,O
University of Pittsburgh	M
The University of Scranton	M
University of South Carolina	M
The University of Tennessee at Chattanooga	M
University of Wisconsin–La Crosse	M
Villanova University	M,O
Virginia Commonwealth University	M
Wayne State University	M,O
Webster University	M
Xavier University of Louisiana	M

■ NURSE MIDWIFERY

Boston University	M,O
Case Western Reserve University	M
Columbia University	M
Emory University	M
Georgia Southwestern State University	M
Illinois State University	M,O
Loyola University Chicago	M
Marquette University	M,O
New York University	M,O
Philadelphia University	M
Stony Brook University, State University of New York	M,O
University of Cincinnati	M,D
University of Illinois at Chicago	M
University of Miami	M,D
University of Michigan	M
University of Minnesota, Twin Cities Campus	M
University of New Mexico	M,O
University of Pennsylvania	M
The University of Texas at El Paso	M
Vanderbilt University	M,D

■ NURSING—GENERAL

Abilene Christian University	M
Adelphi University	M,O
Albany State University	M
Alcorn State University	M
Andrews University	M
Arizona State University	M
Arkansas State University	M
Armstrong Atlantic State University	M
Azusa Pacific University	M
Ball State University	M
Barry University	D
Baylor University	M
Bellarmine University	M
Belmont University	M
Bethel College (MN)	M
Bloomsburg University of Pennsylvania	M
Boston College	M,D
Bowie State University	M
Bradley University	M
Brenau University	M
Brigham Young University	M
California State University, Bakersfield	M
California State University, Chico	M
California State University, Dominguez Hills	M
California State University, Fresno	M
California State University, Fullerton	M
California State University, Long Beach	M
California State University, Los Angeles	M
California State University, Sacramento	M
Capital University	M
Cardinal Stritch University	M
Carlow College	M,O
Case Western Reserve University	M,D
The Catholic University of America	M,D
Central Missouri State University	M
Clarion University of Pennsylvania	M
Clemson University	M
College Misericordia	M
College of Mount Saint Vincent	M,O
The College of New Jersey	M
The College of New Rochelle	M,O
College of St. Catherine	M
The College of St. Scholastica	M
Columbia University	M,D,O
Concordia University Wisconsin	M
Coppin State College	M
Creighton University	M
Delta State University	M
DePaul University	M
DeSales University	M
Dominican University of California	M
Duke University	M,O
Duquesne University	M,D
East Carolina University	M
Eastern Kentucky University	M
Eastern Washington University	M
East Tennessee State University	M,O
Edgewood College	M
Edinboro University of Pennsylvania	M
Emory University	M,D
Fairfield University	M,O
Fairleigh Dickinson University, Teaneck–Hackensack Campus	M
Florida Atlantic University	M,O
Florida Gulf Coast University	M
Florida International University	M
Florida State University	M
Fort Hays State University	M
Franciscan University of Steubenville	M
Gannon University	M,O
George Mason University	M,D
Georgetown University	M
Georgia College and State University	M
Georgia Southern University	M,O
Georgia Southwestern State University	M
Georgia State University	M,D
Gonzaga University	M
Governors State University	M
Grambling State University	M
Grand Valley State University	M
Gwynedd-Mercy College	M
Hampton University	M
Harding University	M
Hardin-Simmons University	M
Hawaii Pacific University	M
Holy Family College	M
Holy Names College	M
Houston Baptist University	M
Howard University	M,O
Hunter College of the City University of New York	M,O
Husson College	M
Idaho State University	M,O
Illinois State University	M,O
Indiana State University	M
Indiana University of Pennsylvania	M
Indiana University–Purdue University Fort Wayne	M
Indiana University–Purdue University Indianapolis	M,D
Indiana University South Bend	M
Indiana Wesleyan University	M,O
Jacksonville State University	M
Johns Hopkins University	M,D,O
Kean University	M
Kennesaw State University	M
Kent State University	M
Lamar University	M
La Roche College	M
La Salle University	M,O
Lehman College of the City University of New York	M
Lewis University	M,O
Loma Linda University	M,O
Long Island University, Brooklyn Campus	M,O
Long Island University, C.W. Post Campus	M,O
Loyola University Chicago	M,D
Loyola University New Orleans	M
Madonna University	M
Marquette University	M,O
Marshall University	M
Maryville University of Saint Louis	M
Marywood University	M
McNeese State University	M
MCP Hahnemann University	M
Mercy College	M
Metropolitan State University	M
Michigan State University	M,D
Midwestern State University	M
Millersville University of Pennsylvania	M
Minnesota State University, Mankato	M
Mississippi University for Women	M,O
Molloy College	M,O
Monmouth University	M,O
Montana State University–Bozeman	M
Mount Marty College	M
Mount Saint Mary College	M
Murray State University	M
National University	M
Nazareth College of Rochester	M
New Jersey City University	M
Newman University	M
New Mexico State University	M
New York University	M,D,O
Niagara University	M
Northeastern University	M,O
Northern Arizona University	M
Northern Illinois University	M
Northern Kentucky University	M
Northern Michigan University	M
North Georgia College & State University	M
North Park University	M
Northwestern State University of Louisiana	M
Oakland University	M,O
The Ohio State University	M,D
Old Dominion University	M,O
Pace University, New York City Campus	M,O
Pace University, Pleasantville/Briarcliff Campus	M,O
Pacific Lutheran University	M
The Pennsylvania State University University Park Campus	M,D
Pittsburg State University	M
Pontifical Catholic University of Puerto Rico	M
Prairie View A&M University	M
Purdue University Calumet	M
Queens College	M
Quinnipiac University	M
Radford University	M
Regis College (MA)	M,O
Regis University	M
Rivier College	M
Rutgers, The State University of New Jersey, Newark	M,D
Sacred Heart University	M
Sage Graduate School	M,O
Saginaw Valley State University	M
St. John Fisher College	M,O
Saint Joseph College	M,O
Saint Joseph's College (ME)	M
Saint Louis University	D
Saint Peter's College	M
Saint Xavier University	M,O
Salem State College	M
Salisbury State University	M
Samford University	M
San Diego State University	M
San Francisco State University	M
San Jose State University	M
Seattle Pacific University	M,O
Seattle University	M,O
Seton Hall University	M
Shenandoah University	M
Simmons College	M,O
Slippery Rock University of Pennsylvania	M
South Dakota State University	M
Southeastern Louisiana University	M
Southeast Missouri State University	M
Southern Connecticut State University	M
Southern Illinois University Edwardsville	M
Southern University and Agricultural and Mechanical College	M
Southwest Missouri State University	M
Spalding University	M
State University of New York at Binghamton	M,D,O
State University of New York at New Paltz	M
State University of New York Institute of Technology at Utica/Rome	M,O
Stony Brook University, State University of New York	M,O
Syracuse University	M
Temple University	M
Tennessee State University	M
Texas A&M University–Corpus Christi	M
Texas Woman's University	M,D
Towson University	M,O
Troy State University	M

University at Buffalo, The State University of New York M,D,O
The University of Akron M,D
The University of Alabama at Birmingham M,D
The University of Alabama in Huntsville M
University of Alaska Anchorage M
The University of Arizona M,D
University of California, Los Angeles M,D
University of California, San Francisco M,D
University of Central Arkansas M
University of Central Florida M
University of Cincinnati M,D
University of Colorado at Colorado Springs M
University of Connecticut M,D
University of Delaware M,O
University of Evansville M
University of Florida M,D
University of Hartford M
University of Hawaii at Manoa M,D,O
University of Illinois at Chicago M,D
The University of Iowa M,D
University of Kansas M,D
University of Kentucky M,D
University of Louisiana at Lafayette M
University of Louisville M
University of Maine M,O
University of Mary M
University of Maryland M,D
University of Massachusetts Amherst M,D
University of Massachusetts Boston M,D
University of Massachusetts Dartmouth M,O
University of Massachusetts Lowell M,D
University of Miami M,D
University of Michigan M,D,O
University of Michigan–Flint M
University of Minnesota, Twin Cities Campus M,D
University of Missouri–Columbia M,D
University of Missouri–Kansas City M,D
University of Missouri–St. Louis M,D
University of Mobile M
University of Nevada, Las Vegas M
University of Nevada, Reno M
University of New Hampshire M
University of New Mexico M,O
The University of North Carolina at Chapel Hill M,D
The University of North Carolina at Greensboro M,O
The University of North Carolina at Wilmington M
University of North Dakota M
University of Northern Colorado M
University of North Florida M
University of Pennsylvania M,D,O
University of Pittsburgh M,D
University of Portland M,O
University of Rhode Island M,D
University of Rochester M,D,O
University of Saint Francis (IN) M
University of San Diego M,D,O
University of San Francisco M
The University of Scranton M
University of South Alabama M
University of South Carolina M,D,O
University of Southern California M,O
University of Southern Indiana M
University of Southern Maine M,O
University of Southern Mississippi M,D
University of South Florida M,D
The University of Tampa M
The University of Tennessee M,D
The University of Tennessee at Chattanooga M
The University of Texas at Arlington M
The University of Texas at Austin M,D
The University of Texas at El Paso M
The University of Texas at Tyler M
The University of Texas–Pan American M
University of the Incarnate Word M
University of Utah M,D
University of Vermont M
University of Virginia M,D
University of Washington M,D
University of Wisconsin–Eau Claire M
University of Wisconsin–Madison M,D
University of Wisconsin–Milwaukee M,D
University of Wisconsin–Oshkosh M
University of Wyoming M
Ursuline College M
Valdosta State University M
Valparaiso University M
Vanderbilt University M,D
Villanova University M,O
Virginia Commonwealth University M,D,O
Viterbo University M
Wagner College M
Washington State University M
Wayne State University M,D,O
Webster University M
West Chester University of Pennsylvania M
Western Carolina University M
Western Connecticut State University M
Western Kentucky University M
Westminster College (UT) M
West Texas A&M University M
West Virginia University M,D,O
Wheeling Jesuit University M
Wichita State University M
Widener University M,D,O
Wilkes University M
William Paterson University of New Jersey M
Wilmington College M
Winona State University M
Wright State University M
Xavier University M
Yale University M,D,O
Youngstown State University M

■ NURSING AND HEALTHCARE ADMINISTRATION

Barry University M
Baylor University M
Bellarmine University M
Bowie State University M
Capital University M
Carlow College M,O
The Catholic University of America M,D
College of Mount Saint Vincent M,O
The College of New Rochelle M,O
DeSales University M
Duke University M,O
Duquesne University M
Florida Atlantic University M,O
Gannon University M,O
George Mason University M,D
Indiana University–Purdue University Fort Wayne M
Indiana University–Purdue University Indianapolis M
Johns Hopkins University M
Kent State University M
Lamar University M
La Roche College M
La Salle University M,O
Lewis University M,O
Loma Linda University M,O
Long Island University, Brooklyn Campus M
Loyola University Chicago M
Madonna University M
Marymount University M,O
Minnesota State University, Mankato M
Molloy College M,O
Mount Saint Mary College M
Northeastern University M
Pacific Lutheran University M
Queens College M
Rivier College M
Sacred Heart University M
Saginaw Valley State University M
Saint Xavier University M,O
San Francisco State University M
San Jose State University M
Seton Hall University M
Southern Connecticut State University M
Spalding University M
State University of New York Institute of Technology at Utica/Rome M
Texas A&M University–Corpus Christi M
University at Buffalo, The State University of New York M,D,O
University of Cincinnati M,D
University of Connecticut M,D
University of Delaware M,O
University of Hawaii at Manoa M,D,O
University of Illinois at Chicago M
University of Maryland M,D
University of Massachusetts Lowell D
University of Michigan M
University of Minnesota, Twin Cities Campus M
University of Missouri–Kansas City M,D
University of New Mexico M,O
The University of North Carolina at Greensboro M,O
University of Pennsylvania M,D
University of Pittsburgh M
University of Portland M,O
University of Rhode Island M,D
University of San Diego M,D,O
University of San Francisco M
University of South Carolina M
University of Southern Maine M,O
University of Southern Mississippi M,D
The University of Tampa M
The University of Tennessee at Chattanooga M
The University of Texas at Arlington M
The University of Texas at El Paso M
Valdosta State University M
Vanderbilt University M,D
Villanova University M,O
Virginia Commonwealth University M,D,O
Wichita State University M
Wright State University M
Xavier University M

■ NURSING EDUCATION

Barry University M
Bellarmine University M
Bowie State University M
The Catholic University of America M,D
The College of New Rochelle M,O
Concordia University Wisconsin M
Duquesne University M
Eastern Michigan University M
Eastern Washington University M
Florida State University M
Indiana Wesleyan University M,O
Kent State University M
La Salle University M,O
Lewis University M,O
Midwestern State University M
Minnesota State University, Mankato M
Molloy College M,O

Mount Saint Mary College	M
New York University	M,O
Saginaw Valley State University	M
San Francisco State University	M
San Jose State University	M
Seton Hall University	M
Southern Connecticut State University	M
Teachers College, Columbia University	M,D
University of Central Florida	M
University of Connecticut	M,D
University of Mary	M
University of Maryland	M,D
University of Minnesota, Twin Cities Campus	M
University of Missouri–Kansas City	M,D
University of Northern Colorado	M
University of Pittsburgh	M
University of Rhode Island	M,D
The University of Tennessee at Chattanooga	M
The University of Texas at Arlington	M
Villanova University	M,O
Wayne State University	O
West Chester University of Pennsylvania	M
Wichita State University	M

■ NUTRITION

Andrews University	M
Auburn University	M,D
Boston University	M,D,O
Bowling Green State University	M
Brigham Young University	M
Brooklyn College of the City University of New York	M
California State Polytechnic University, Pomona	M
California State University, Chico	M
California State University, Fresno	M
California State University, Long Beach	M
California State University, Los Angeles	M
Case Western Reserve University	M,D
Central Michigan University	M
Central Washington University	M
Chapman University	M
Colorado State University	M,D
Columbia University	M,D
Cornell University	M,D
Drexel University	M,D
East Carolina University	M
Eastern Illinois University	M
Eastern Kentucky University	M
East Tennessee State University	M
Emory University	D
Florida International University	M,D
Florida State University	M,D
Framingham State College	M
Georgia State University	M
Harvard University	D
Howard University	M,D
Hunter College of the City University of New York	M
Immaculata College	M
Indiana State University	M
Indiana University of Pennsylvania	M
Indiana University–Purdue University Indianapolis	M
Iowa State University of Science and Technology	M,D
Johns Hopkins University	M,D
Kansas State University	M,D
Kent State University	M
Lehman College of the City University of New York	M
Loma Linda University	M,D
Long Island University, C.W. Post Campus	M,O
Louisiana Tech University	M
Marywood University	M
Michigan State University	M,D
Middle Tennessee State University	M
Mississippi State University	M,D
Montclair State University	M
Mount Mary College	M
New York Institute of Technology	M
New York University	M,D
North Carolina Agricultural and Technical State University	M
North Carolina State University	M,D
North Dakota State University	M,D
Northern Illinois University	M
The Ohio State University	M,D
Ohio University	M
Oklahoma State University	M,D
Oregon State University	M,D
The Pennsylvania State University University Park Campus	M,D
Purdue University	M,D
Rutgers, The State University of New Jersey, New Brunswick	M,D
Sage Graduate School	M
Saint Louis University	M
San Diego State University	M
San Jose State University	M
Simmons College	M,O
South Carolina State University	M
Southern Illinois University Carbondale	M
Syracuse University	M,D
Texas A&M University	M,D
Texas Southern University	M
Texas Tech University	M,D
Texas Woman's University	M,D
Tufts University	M,D
Tulane University	M
Tuskegee University	M
University at Buffalo, The State University of New York	M
The University of Akron	M
The University of Alabama	M
The University of Alabama at Birmingham	M,D,O
The University of Arizona	M,D
University of Bridgeport	M
University of California, Berkeley	M,D
University of California, Davis	M,D
University of Central Oklahoma	M
University of Chicago	D
University of Cincinnati	M
University of Connecticut	M,D
University of Delaware	M
University of Florida	M,D
University of Georgia	M,D
University of Hawaii at Manoa	M
University of Illinois at Chicago	M,D
University of Illinois at Urbana–Champaign	M,D
University of Kansas	M
University of Kentucky	M,D
University of Maine	M,D
University of Maryland, College Park	M,D
University of Massachusetts Amherst	M
The University of Memphis	M
University of Michigan	M
University of Minnesota, Twin Cities Campus	M,D
University of Missouri–Columbia	M,D
University of Nebraska–Lincoln	M,D
University of Nevada, Reno	M
University of New Hampshire	M,D
University of New Haven	M
University of New Mexico	M
The University of North Carolina at Chapel Hill	M,D
The University of North Carolina at Greensboro	M,D
University of North Florida	M,O
University of Rhode Island	M,D
University of Southern California	M
University of Southern Mississippi	M,D
The University of Tennessee	M
The University of Tennessee at Martin	M
The University of Texas at Austin	M,D
University of the Incarnate Word	M
University of Utah	M
University of Vermont	M
University of Washington	M,D
University of Wisconsin–Madison	M,D
University of Wisconsin–Stevens Point	M
University of Wisconsin–Stout	M
University of Wyoming	M
Utah State University	M,D
Virginia Polytechnic Institute and State University	M,D
Washington State University	M,D
Wayne State University	M,D
West Virginia University	M,D
Winthrop University	M

■ OCCUPATIONAL HEALTH NURSING

Capital University	M
University of Cincinnati	M,D
University of Massachusetts Lowell	M
University of Michigan	M
University of Minnesota, Twin Cities Campus	M,D
The University of North Carolina at Chapel Hill	M,D
University of Pennsylvania	M
Vanderbilt University	M,D

■ OCCUPATIONAL THERAPY

Barry University	M
Belmont University	M
Boston University	M,D,O
College Misericordia	M
College of St. Catherine	M
The College of St. Scholastica	M
Colorado State University	M
Columbia University	M
Concordia University Wisconsin	M
Creighton University	D
Duquesne University	M
East Carolina University	M
Eastern Kentucky University	M
Eastern Michigan University	M
Florida International University	M
Gannon University	M
Governors State University	M
Grand Valley State University	M
Idaho State University	M
Ithaca College	M
Kean University	M
Maryville University of Saint Louis	M
Mercy College	M
Milligan College	M
Mount Mary College	M
New York Institute of Technology	M
New York University	M,D
Nova Southeastern University	M,D
Pacific University	M
Philadelphia University	M
Rockhurst University	M
Sacred Heart University	M
St. Ambrose University	M
Saint Francis University	M
Saint Louis University	M

San Jose State University M
Seton Hall University M
Shenandoah University M
Springfield College M,O
Temple University M
Texas Woman's University M,D
Touro College M
Towson University M
Tufts University M,O
University at Buffalo, The State University of New York M
The University of Alabama at Birmingham M
University of Central Arkansas M
University of Florida M
University of Illinois at Chicago M
University of Indianapolis M
University of Kansas M
University of Mary M
University of New England M
University of New Hampshire M
University of New Mexico M
The University of North Carolina at Chapel Hill M,D
University of South Dakota M
University of Southern California M,D
University of Southern Indiana M
University of Southern Maine M
University of Utah M
University of Washington M
University of Wisconsin–Milwaukee M
Virginia Commonwealth University M
Washington University in St. Louis M
Wayne State University M
Western Michigan University M
West Virginia University M
Worcester State College M

■ OCEAN ENGINEERING

Florida Atlantic University M,D
Florida Institute of Technology M,D
Massachusetts Institute of Technology M,D,O
Oregon State University M
Stevens Institute of Technology M,D
Texas A&M University M,D
University of California, Berkeley M,D
University of California, San Diego M,D
University of Connecticut M,D
University of Delaware M,D
University of Florida M,D,O
University of Hawaii at Manoa M,D
University of Miami M,D
University of Michigan M,D,O
University of New Hampshire M,D
University of Rhode Island M,D
University of Southern California M
Virginia Polytechnic Institute and State University M

■ OCEANOGRAPHY

Columbia University M,D
Cornell University D
Florida Institute of Technology M,D
Florida State University M,D
Johns Hopkins University M,D
Louisiana State University and Agricultural and Mechanical College M,D
Massachusetts Institute of Technology M,D,O
North Carolina State University M,D
Nova Southeastern University M,D
Old Dominion University M,D
Oregon State University M,D
Princeton University D
Rutgers, The State University of New Jersey, New Brunswick M,D
Stony Brook University, State University of New York M,D,O
Texas A&M University M,D
University of Alaska Fairbanks M,D
University of California, San Diego M,D
University of Connecticut M,D
University of Delaware M,D
University of Georgia M,D
University of Hawaii at Manoa M,D
University of Maine M,D
University of Miami M,D
University of Michigan M,D
University of New Hampshire M,D
University of Puerto Rico, Mayagüez Campus M,D
University of Rhode Island M,D
University of Southern California M,D
University of South Florida M,D
University of Washington M,D
University of Wisconsin–Madison M,D
Yale University D

■ ONCOLOGY

Brown University M,D
Duke University D
Emory University M
Georgetown University
The George Washington University D
Harvard University D
Kansas State University M,D
Mayo Graduate School D
MCP Hahnemann University M,D
New York University D
Northwestern University D
Stanford University D
University at Buffalo, The State University of New York D
The University of Arizona D
University of California, San Diego D
University of Chicago D
The University of North Carolina at Chapel Hill
University of Pennsylvania D
University of South Florida D
University of Utah M,D
University of Wisconsin–Madison D
Vanderbilt University M,D
Wake Forest University D
Wayne State University M,D
West Virginia University M,D

■ ONCOLOGY NURSING

Case Western Reserve University M
Columbia University M,O
Duke University M,O
Emory University M
Loyola University Chicago M
University of Delaware M,O
University of Minnesota, Twin Cities Campus M
University of Pennsylvania M

■ OPERATIONS RESEARCH

Bernard M. Baruch College of the City University of New York M
California State University, Fullerton M
California State University, Hayward M
Carnegie Mellon University D
Case Western Reserve University M,D
Claremont Graduate University M,D
Clemson University M,D
The College of William and Mary M
Columbia University M,D,O
Cornell University M,D
Florida Institute of Technology M,D
George Mason University M
Georgia Institute of Technology M
Georgia State University M,D
Idaho State University M,D
Indiana University–Purdue University Fort Wayne M
Iowa State University of Science and Technology M,D
Kansas State University M,D
Louisiana Tech University M,D
Massachusetts Institute of Technology M,D
Miami University M
Michigan State University M,D
New Mexico Institute of Mining and Technology M
New York University M,D,O
North Carolina State University M,D
North Dakota State University M,D
Northeastern University M,D
Northwestern University M,D
Old Dominion University M,D
Oregon State University M,D
Princeton University M,D
Purdue University M,D
Rensselaer Polytechnic Institute M,D
Rutgers, The State University of New Jersey, New Brunswick D
St. Mary's University of San Antonio M
Southern Methodist University M,D
The University of Alabama in Huntsville M
University of Arkansas M
University of California, Berkeley M,D
University of California, Los Angeles M,D
University of Central Florida M,D,O
University of Delaware M,D
University of Florida M,D,O
University of Illinois at Chicago D
The University of Iowa M,D
University of Massachusetts Amherst M,D
University of Miami M,D
University of Michigan M,D,O
University of New Haven M
The University of North Carolina at Chapel Hill M,D
University of Southern California M
The University of Texas at Austin M,D
Virginia Commonwealth University M
Virginia Polytechnic Institute and State University M,D
Wayne State University M,D
Western Michigan University M

■ OPTICAL SCIENCES

Alabama Agricultural and Mechanical University M,D
Cleveland State University M
Indiana University Bloomington M,D
The Ohio State University M,D
Oklahoma State University M,D
Rochester Institute of Technology M,D
Tufts University O
The University of Alabama in Huntsville D
The University of Arizona M,D
University of Arkansas M,D
University of Central Florida M,D,O
University of Colorado at Boulder M,D
University of Dayton M,D
University of Maryland, Baltimore County M,D
University of Massachusetts Lowell M,D
University of New Mexico M,D
University of Rochester M,D

■ OPTOMETRY

Ferris State University P

Indiana University Bloomington	P
Inter American University of Puerto Rico, Metropolitan Campus	P
Northeastern State University	P
Nova Southeastern University	P
The Ohio State University	P
Pacific University	P
The University of Alabama at Birmingham	P
University of California, Berkeley	P
University of Houston	P
University of Missouri–St. Louis	P

■ ORAL AND DENTAL SCIENCES

Boston University	M,D,O
Case Western Reserve University	M,O
Columbia University	M
The George Washington University	M
Harvard University	M,D,O
Indiana University–Purdue University Indianapolis	M,D
Loma Linda University	M,O
Marquette University	M
New York University	M,D,O
The Ohio State University	M,D
Saint Louis University	M
Stony Brook University, State University of New York	P,D,O
Temple University	M,O
Tufts University	M,O
University at Buffalo, The State University of New York	M,D,O
The University of Alabama at Birmingham	M
University of California, Los Angeles	M,D
University of California, San Francisco	M,D
University of Connecticut	M
University of Detroit Mercy	M,O
University of Florida	M,D,O
University of Illinois at Chicago	M
The University of Iowa	M,D,O
University of Kentucky	M
University of Louisville	M
University of Maryland	M,D
University of Michigan	M,D,O
University of Minnesota, Twin Cities Campus	M,D
University of Missouri–Kansas City	M,D,O
The University of North Carolina at Chapel Hill	M,D
University of Pittsburgh	M,O
University of Rochester	M
University of Southern California	M,D
University of the Pacific	M
University of Washington	M,D
West Virginia University	M

■ ORGANIC CHEMISTRY

Boston College	M,D
Brandeis University	M,D
Brigham Young University	M,D
California State University, Fullerton	M
California State University, Los Angeles	M
Case Western Reserve University	M,D
Clark Atlanta University	M,D
Clarkson University	M,D
Cleveland State University	M,D
Columbia University	M,D
Cornell University	D
Florida State University	M,D
Georgetown University	M,D
The George Washington University	M,D
Harvard University	M,D
Howard University	M,D
Illinois Institute of Technology	M,D
Kansas State University	M,D
Kent State University	M,D
Marquette University	M,D
Massachusetts Institute of Technology	D
Miami University	M,D
Michigan State University	M,D
Northeastern University	M,D
Old Dominion University	M
Oregon State University	M,D
Purdue University	M,D
Rensselaer Polytechnic Institute	M,D
Rice University	M,D
Rutgers, The State University of New Jersey, Newark	M,D
Rutgers, The State University of New Jersey, New Brunswick	M,D
San Jose State University	M
Seton Hall University	M,D
South Dakota State University	M,D
Southern University and Agricultural and Mechanical College	M
State University of New York at Binghamton	M,D
Stevens Institute of Technology	M,D,O
Tufts University	M,D
The University of Akron	M,D
University of Cincinnati	M,D
University of Georgia	M,D
University of Louisville	M,D
University of Maryland, College Park	M,D
University of Miami	M,D
University of Michigan	D
University of Missouri–Columbia	M,D
University of Missouri–Kansas City	M,D
University of Missouri–St. Louis	M,D
The University of Montana–Missoula	M,D
University of Nebraska–Lincoln	M,D
University of Notre Dame	M,D
University of Southern Mississippi	M,D
University of South Florida	M,D
The University of Tennessee	M,D
The University of Texas at Austin	M,D
University of Toledo	M,D
Wake Forest University	M,D
Washington State University	M,D
Washington University in St. Louis	D
West Virginia University	M,D
Yale University	D

■ ORGANIZATIONAL BEHAVIOR

Antioch University McGregor	M
Benedictine University	M
Bernard M. Baruch College of the City University of New York	M,D
Boston College	D
Boston University	M,D,O
Brigham Young University	M
California Lutheran University	M
Carnegie Mellon University	D
Case Western Reserve University	M,D
Cornell University	M,D
Drexel University	M,D,O
Fairleigh Dickinson University, Florham-Madison Campus	M
George Mason University	M
The George Washington University	M,D
Harvard University	D
Indiana University Bloomington	D
Michigan State University	M,D
Northwestern University	D
Polytechnic University, Brooklyn Campus	M
Polytechnic University, Westchester Graduate Center	M
Purdue University	M,D
Silver Lake College	M
Syracuse University	D
University of California, Berkeley	D
The University of North Carolina at Chapel Hill	D
University of Pennsylvania	M

■ ORGANIZATIONAL MANAGEMENT

American International College	M
American University	M
Antioch University Los Angeles	M
Antioch University Seattle	M
Argosy University-Sarasota	D
Benedictine University	D
Bernard M. Baruch College of the City University of New York	M,D
Bethel College (MN)	M
Biola University	M
Boston College	D
Bowling Green State University	M
Carnegie Mellon University	D
Chapman University	M
Charleston Southern University	M
College Misericordia	M
College of Mount St. Joseph	M
College of St. Catherine	M
Colorado Technical University	M,D
Dallas Baptist University	M
Dominican University	M
Eastern Connecticut State University	M
Eastern Michigan University	M
Geneva College	M
George Fox University	M
George Mason University	M
The George Washington University	M
Gonzaga University	M
Hawaii Pacific University	M
Immaculata College	M
John F. Kennedy University	M,O
Loyola University Chicago	M
Manhattanville College	M
Marian College of Fond du Lac	M
Marymount University	M,O
Mercy College	M
Metropolitan State University	M
Newman University	M
New School University	M
Northwestern University	D
Pfeiffer University	M
Regent University	M,D,O
Regis College (MA)	M
Regis University	M,O
Rutgers, The State University of New Jersey, Newark	M
Saginaw Valley State University	M
St. Ambrose University	M
St. Edward's University	M
Spring Arbor University	M
State University of New York at Albany	D
Trevecca Nazarene University	M
University of Colorado at Boulder	M,D
University of Colorado at Colorado Springs	M
University of La Verne	M,D,O
University of North Texas	M,D
University of Pennsylvania	M
University of San Francisco	M
The University of Scranton	M
The University of Tennessee at Chattanooga	M
University of the Incarnate Word	M,D
Vanderbilt University	M,D

■ OSTEOPATHIC MEDICINE

Michigan State University	P
New York Institute of Technology	P
Nova Southeastern University	P

Ohio University P
University of New England P

■ PAPER AND PULP ENGINEERING

Georgia Institute of Technology O
Miami University M
North Carolina State University M,D
Oregon State University M,D
University of Washington M,D
Western Michigan University M

■ PARASITOLOGY

New York University M,D
Purdue University M,D
Texas A&M University M,D
Tulane University M,D,O
University of Georgia M,D
University of Notre Dame M,D
University of Pennsylvania D
University of Washington M,D
West Virginia University M,D
Yale University D

■ PASTORAL MINISTRY AND COUNSELING

Abilene Christian University M,D
Argosy University-Sarasota M,D,O
Ashland University P,M,D
Azusa Pacific University P,M,D
Barry University M,D
Bayamón Central University P,M
Boston College M,D,O
Chaminade University of Honolulu M
College of Mount St. Joseph M
Colorado Christian University M
Fordham University M,O
Freed-Hardeman University M
Gannon University M,O
Gardner-Webb University P
George Fox University P,M,D
Golden Gate Baptist Theological Seminary P,M,D,O
Gonzaga University P,M
Grand Rapids Baptist Seminary P,M,D
Harding University M
Hardin-Simmons University M
Holy Names College M,O
Hope International University M
Houston Baptist University M
Iona College M,O
La Salle University M
Loyola College in Maryland M,D,O
Loyola Marymount University M
Loyola University Chicago M
Malone College M
Marygrove College M
Olivet Nazarene University M
Oral Roberts University P,M,D
Providence College M
St. Ambrose University M
St. John's University (NY) P,M,O
Saint Joseph College M,O
Saint Joseph's College (ME) M
Saint Mary's University of Minnesota M,O
St. Mary's University of San Antonio M
St. Thomas University M,O
Santa Clara University M
Seattle University M
Seton Hall University P,M,O
Southern Wesleyan University M
Spalding University M
Texas Christian University P,M,D,O
University of Dayton M,D
University of Portland M
University of St. Thomas (MN) M,D
University of San Diego M
University of San Francisco M
Wake Forest University M
Xavier University of Louisiana M

■ PATHOBIOLOGY

Auburn University M
Brown University M,D
Columbia University M,D
Johns Hopkins University D
Kansas State University M,D
MCP Hahnemann University D
The Ohio State University M,D
The Pennsylvania State University University Park Campus M,D
Purdue University M,D
Texas A&M University M,D
The University of Arizona M,D
University of Cincinnati D
University of Connecticut M,D
University of Illinois at Urbana–Champaign M,D
University of Missouri–Columbia M,D
University of Rochester
University of Southern California M,D
University of Washington M,D
University of Wyoming M
Wake Forest University M,D

■ PATHOLOGY

Boston University D
Brown University M,D
Case Western Reserve University M,D
Colorado State University M,D
Columbia University M,D
Duke University M,D
East Carolina University D
Georgetown University M,D
Harvard University D
Indiana University–Purdue University Indianapolis M,D
Iowa State University of Science and Technology M,D
Johns Hopkins University D
Michigan State University M,D
New York University M,D
North Carolina State University M,D
The Ohio State University M,D
Oregon State University M
Purdue University M,D
Quinnipiac University M
Saint Louis University M,D
State University of New York at Albany M,D
Stony Brook University, State University of New York D
Temple University D
Texas A&M University M,D
University at Buffalo, The State University of New York M,D
The University of Alabama at Birmingham D
University of California, Davis M,D
University of California, Los Angeles M,D
University of California, San Diego D
University of California, San Francisco D
University of Chicago D
University of Cincinnati D
University of Florida M,D
University of Georgia M,D
University of Illinois at Chicago M,D
The University of Iowa M
University of Kansas M,D
University of Maryland M,D
University of Michigan D
University of New Mexico M,D
The University of North Carolina at Chapel Hill D
University of Pittsburgh M,D
University of Rochester M,D
University of Southern California M,D
University of South Florida D
University of Utah D
University of Vermont M
University of Washington M,D
University of Wisconsin–Madison D
Vanderbilt University D
Virginia Commonwealth University M,D
Washington State University M,D
Wayne State University D
Yale University D
Yeshiva University D

■ PEDIATRIC NURSING

Baylor University M
Case Western Reserve University M
The Catholic University of America M,D
Columbia University M,O
Duke University M,O
Emory University M
Georgia State University M,D
Gwynedd-Mercy College M
Hunter College of the City University of New York M,O
Indiana University–Purdue University Indianapolis M
Johns Hopkins University M,O
Kent State University M
Lehman College of the City University of New York M
Loma Linda University M
Loyola University Chicago M
Marquette University M,O
Molloy College M,O
New York University M,O
Northeastern University M,O
Seton Hall University M
Stony Brook University, State University of New York M,O
Texas Woman's University M,D
University at Buffalo, The State University of New York M,D,O
University of Central Florida M
University of Delaware M,O
University of Illinois at Chicago M
University of Maryland M,D
University of Michigan M
University of Minnesota, Twin Cities Campus M
University of Missouri–Kansas City M,D
University of Pennsylvania M
University of Pittsburgh M
University of San Diego M,D,O
Vanderbilt University M,D
Villanova University M,O
Virginia Commonwealth University M,D,O
Wayne State University M
Wright State University M

■ PETROLEUM ENGINEERING

Louisiana State University and Agricultural and Mechanical College M,D
New Mexico Institute of Mining and Technology M,D
The Pennsylvania State University University Park Campus M,D
Stanford University M,D,O
Texas A&M University M,D
Texas A&M University–Kingsville M
Texas Tech University M
University of Alaska Fairbanks M

University of California, Berkeley M,D
University of Houston M,D
University of Kansas M,D
University of Louisiana at Lafayette M
University of Missouri–Rolla M,D
University of Oklahoma M,D
University of Pittsburgh M,D
University of Southern California M,D,O
The University of Texas at Austin M,D
University of Tulsa M,D
University of Utah M,D
University of Wyoming M,D
West Virginia University M,D

■ PHARMACEUTICAL ADMINISTRATION

Duquesne University M
Fairleigh Dickinson University, Florham-Madison Campus M
Fairleigh Dickinson University, Teaneck–Hackensack Campus M
Florida Agricultural and Mechanical University M,D
Idaho State University P,M,D
Long Island University, Brooklyn Campus M
The Ohio State University M,D
St. John's University (NY) M
Seton Hall University M,O
University of Florida M,D
University of Georgia M,D
University of Houston P,M,D
University of Illinois at Chicago M,D
University of Maryland D
University of Michigan M,D
University of Minnesota, Twin Cities Campus M,D
University of Mississippi M,D
University of New Mexico M,D
University of Rhode Island M
University of Toledo M
University of Wisconsin–Madison M,D
West Virginia University M,D

■ PHARMACEUTICAL SCIENCES

Auburn University M,D
Butler University P,M
Campbell University P,M
Creighton University M,D
Duquesne University M,D
Florida Agricultural and Mechanical University M,D
Idaho State University M,D
Long Island University, Brooklyn Campus M,D
Mercer University P,D
North Dakota State University M,D
Northeastern University M,D
The Ohio State University M,D
Oregon State University P,M,D
Purdue University M,D
Rutgers, The State University of New Jersey, New Brunswick M,D
St. John's University (NY) M,D
South Dakota State University M
Temple University M,D
University at Buffalo, The State University of New York M,D
The University of Arizona M,D
University of California, San Francisco D
University of Cincinnati M,D
University of Connecticut M,D
University of Georgia M,D
University of Houston P,M,D
University of Illinois at Chicago M,D
The University of Iowa M,D
University of Kansas M
University of Kentucky M,D
University of Louisiana at Monroe P,M,D
University of Maryland D
University of Michigan M,D
University of Minnesota, Twin Cities Campus M,D
University of Mississippi M,D
University of Missouri–Kansas City M
The University of Montana–Missoula M,D
University of New Mexico M,D
The University of North Carolina at Chapel Hill M,D
University of Pittsburgh M,D
University of Rhode Island M,D
University of South Carolina M,D
University of Southern California M,D
The University of Texas at Austin M,D
University of the Pacific M,D
University of Toledo M
University of Washington M,D
University of Wisconsin–Madison M,D
Virginia Commonwealth University P,M,D
Wayne State University M,D
West Virginia University M,D

■ PHARMACOLOGY

Auburn University M
Boston University M,D
Brown University M,D
Case Western Reserve University D
Columbia University M,D
Cornell University M,D
Creighton University M,D
Dartmouth College D
Duke University D
Duquesne University M,D
East Carolina University D
East Tennessee State University M,D
Emory University D
Florida Agricultural and Mechanical University M,D
Georgetown University D
The George Washington University D
Harvard University D
Howard University M,D
Idaho State University M,D
Indiana University Bloomington M,D
Indiana University–Purdue University Indianapolis M,D
Johns Hopkins University D
Kent State University M,D
Loma Linda University M,D
Long Island University, Brooklyn Campus M
Loyola University Chicago M,D
Mayo Graduate School D
MCP Hahnemann University M,D
Michigan State University M,D
New York University M,D
North Carolina State University M,D
Northeastern University M,D
Northwestern University D
Nova Southeastern University M
The Ohio State University M,D
Purdue University M,D
Rutgers, The State University of New Jersey, New Brunswick D
St. John's University (NY) M,D
Saint Louis University M,D
Southern Illinois University Carbondale M,D
Stanford University D
Stony Brook University, State University of New York D
Temple University M,D
Tufts University D
Tulane University M,D
University at Buffalo, The State University of New York M,D
The University of Alabama at Birmingham D
The University of Arizona M,D
University of California, Davis M,D
University of California, Irvine M,D
University of California, Los Angeles M,D
University of California, San Diego D
University of California, San Francisco D
University of Chicago D
University of Cincinnati D
University of Connecticut M,D
University of Florida M,D
University of Georgia M,D
University of Hawaii at Manoa M,D
University of Houston P,M,D
University of Illinois at Chicago D
The University of Iowa M,D
University of Kansas M,D
University of Kentucky D
University of Louisville M,D
University of Maryland M,D
University of Miami D
University of Michigan D
University of Minnesota, Duluth M,D
University of Minnesota, Twin Cities Campus M,D
University of Mississippi M,D
University of Missouri–Columbia M,D
The University of Montana–Missoula M,D
University of Nevada, Reno M,D
The University of North Carolina at Chapel Hill D
University of North Dakota M,D
University of Pennsylvania D
University of Pittsburgh D
University of Rhode Island M,D
University of Rochester M,D
University of South Alabama D
University of South Dakota M,D
University of Southern California M,D
University of South Florida D
University of the Pacific M,D
University of Toledo M
University of Utah M,D
University of Vermont M,D
University of Virginia D
University of Washington M,D
University of Wisconsin–Madison M,D
Vanderbilt University D
Virginia Commonwealth University M,D,O
Wake Forest University D
Washington State University M,D
Wayne State University M,D
West Virginia University M,D
Wright State University M
Yale University D
Yeshiva University D

■ PHARMACY

Auburn University P
Butler University P,M
Campbell University P,M
Creighton University P
Drake University P
Duquesne University P
Ferris State University P
Florida Agricultural and Mechanical University P
Howard University P
Idaho State University P,M,D
Long Island University, Brooklyn Campus P
Mercer University P,D
Northeastern University P

Nova Southeastern University P
The Ohio State University P
Oregon State University P,M,D
Palm Beach Atlantic College P
Purdue University P
Rutgers, The State University of New Jersey, New Brunswick P
St. John's University (NY) P
Samford University P
Shenandoah University P
South Dakota State University P
Southwestern Oklahoma State University P
Temple University P
Texas Southern University P
University at Buffalo, The State University of New York P
The University of Arizona P,M,D
University of California, San Francisco P
University of Cincinnati P
University of Florida P
University of Georgia P
University of Houston P,M,D
University of Illinois at Chicago P
The University of Iowa P
University of Kentucky P
University of Maryland P,D
University of Michigan P
University of Minnesota, Twin Cities Campus P
University of Mississippi P
University of Missouri–Kansas City P
University of New Mexico P
University of Pittsburgh P
University of Rhode Island P
University of South Carolina P
University of Southern California P
The University of Texas at Austin P
University of the Pacific P
University of Toledo P
University of Utah P,M
University of Washington P
University of Wisconsin–Madison P
Virginia Commonwealth University P
Washington State University P
Wayne State University P,M
West Virginia University P,M,D
Wilkes University P
Xavier University of Louisiana P

■ PHILANTHROPIC STUDIES

Indiana University–Purdue University Indianapolis M
Saint Mary's University of Minnesota M
Suffolk University M

■ PHILOSOPHY

American University M
Arizona State University M
Baylor University M
Boston College M,D
Boston University M,D
Bowling Green State University M,D
Brown University M,D
California State University, Long Beach M
California State University, Los Angeles M
Carnegie Mellon University M,D
The Catholic University of America M,D,O
Claremont Graduate University M,D
Cleveland State University M
Colorado State University M
Columbia University M,D
Cornell University D
DePaul University M,D
Duke University D
Duquesne University M,D
Emory University D
Florida State University M,D
Fordham University M,D
Franciscan University of Steubenville M
Georgetown University M,D
The George Washington University M
Georgia State University M
Gonzaga University M
Harvard University M,D
Howard University M
Indiana University Bloomington M,D
Johns Hopkins University M,D
Kent State University M
Louisiana State University and Agricultural and Mechanical College M
Loyola University Chicago M,D
Marquette University M,D
Massachusetts Institute of Technology D
Miami University M
Michigan State University M,D
Montclair State University M,D
New School University M,D
New York University M,D
Northern Illinois University M
Northwestern University D
The Ohio State University M,D
Ohio University M
Oklahoma City University M
Oklahoma State University M,D
The Pennsylvania State University University Park Campus M,D
Princeton University D
Purdue University M,D
Rensselaer Polytechnic Institute M
Rice University M,D
Rutgers, The State University of New Jersey, New Brunswick D
Saint Louis University M,D
San Diego State University M
San Francisco State University M,O
San Jose State University M,O
Southern Illinois University Carbondale M,D
Stanford University M,D
State University of New York at Albany M,D
State University of New York at Binghamton M,D
Stony Brook University, State University of New York M,D,O
Syracuse University M,D
Temple University M,D
Texas A&M University M
Texas Tech University M
Tufts University M
Tulane University M,D
University at Buffalo, The State University of New York M,D
The University of Arizona M,D
University of Arkansas M,D
University of California, Berkeley D
University of California, Davis M,D
University of California, Irvine M,D
University of California, Los Angeles M,D
University of California, Riverside M,D
University of California, San Diego D
University of California, Santa Barbara D
University of Chicago M,D
University of Cincinnati M,D
University of Colorado at Boulder M,D
University of Connecticut M,D
University of Denver M
University of Florida M,D
University of Georgia M,D
University of Hawaii at Manoa M,D
University of Houston M
University of Illinois at Chicago M,D
University of Illinois at Urbana–Champaign M,D
The University of Iowa M,D
University of Kansas M,D
University of Kentucky M,D
University of Louisville M
University of Maryland, Baltimore County M,O
University of Maryland, College Park M,D
University of Massachusetts Amherst M,D
The University of Memphis M,D
University of Miami M,D
University of Michigan M,D
University of Minnesota, Twin Cities Campus M,D
University of Mississippi M
University of Missouri–Columbia M,D
University of Missouri–St. Louis M
The University of Montana–Missoula M
University of Nebraska–Lincoln M,D
University of Nevada, Reno M
University of New Mexico M,D
The University of North Carolina at Chapel Hill M,D
University of North Texas M
University of Notre Dame D
University of Oklahoma M,D
University of Oregon M,D
University of Pennsylvania M,D
University of Pittsburgh M,D
University of Puerto Rico, Río Piedras M
University of Rhode Island M
University of Rochester M,D
University of St. Thomas (TX) M,D
University of South Carolina M,D
University of Southern California M,D
University of Southern Mississippi M
University of South Florida M,D
The University of Tennessee M,D
The University of Texas at Arlington M
The University of Texas at Austin M,D
University of Toledo M
University of Utah M,D
University of Virginia M,D
University of Washington M,D
University of Wisconsin–Madison M,D
University of Wisconsin–Milwaukee M
University of Wyoming M
Vanderbilt University M,D
Villanova University M,D
Virginia Polytechnic Institute and State University M
Washington University in St. Louis M,D
Wayne State University M,D
West Chester University of Pennsylvania M
Western Kentucky University M
Western Michigan University M
Yale University D

■ PHOTOGRAPHY

Barry University M
Bradley University M
Brooklyn College of the City University of New York M,D
California State University, Fullerton M,O
California State University, Los Angeles M
Claremont Graduate University M
Columbia College Chicago M
Columbia University M
Cornell University M
The George Washington University M
Howard University M

Illinois Institute of Technology	M,D
Illinois State University	M
Indiana State University	M
Indiana University Bloomington	M
James Madison University	M
Lamar University	M
Louisiana State University and Agricultural and Mechanical College	M
Louisiana Tech University	M
Ohio University	M
The Pennsylvania State University University Park Campus	M
Pratt Institute	M
Rochester Institute of Technology	M
San Jose State University	M
Southern Methodist University	M
State University of New York at New Paltz	M
Syracuse University	M
Temple University	M
Texas Woman's University	M
The University of Alabama	M
University of Colorado at Boulder	M
University of Houston	M
University of Illinois at Chicago	M
The University of Memphis	M
University of Miami	M
The University of Montana–Missoula	M
University of New Orleans	M
University of North Texas	M,D
University of Notre Dame	M
University of Oklahoma	M
The University of Tennessee	M
University of Utah	M
Virginia Commonwealth University	M
Washington State University	M
Washington University in St. Louis	M
Yale University	M

■ PHYSICAL CHEMISTRY

Boston College	M,D
Brandeis University	M,D
Brigham Young University	M,D
California State University, Fullerton	M
California State University, Los Angeles	M
Case Western Reserve University	M,D
Clark Atlanta University	M,D
Clarkson University	M,D
Cleveland State University	M,D
Columbia University	M,D
Cornell University	D
Florida State University	M,D
Georgetown University	M,D
The George Washington University	M,D
Harvard University	M,D
Howard University	M,D
Illinois Institute of Technology	M,D
Indiana University Bloomington	M,D
Kansas State University	M,D
Kent State University	M,D
Marquette University	M,D
Massachusetts Institute of Technology	D
Miami University	M,D
Michigan State University	M,D
Northeastern University	M,D
The Ohio State University	M,D
Old Dominion University	M
Oregon State University	M,D
Princeton University	M,D
Purdue University	M,D
Rensselaer Polytechnic Institute	M,D
Rice University	M,D
Rutgers, The State University of New Jersey, Newark	M,D
Rutgers, The State University of New Jersey, New Brunswick	M,D
San Jose State University	M
Seton Hall University	M,D
South Dakota State University	M,D
Southern University and Agricultural and Mechanical College	M
State University of New York at Binghamton	M,D
Stevens Institute of Technology	M,D,O
Tufts University	M,D
The University of Akron	M,D
University of Cincinnati	M,D
University of Colorado at Boulder	M,D
University of Georgia	M,D
University of Louisville	M,D
University of Maryland, College Park	M,D
University of Miami	M,D
University of Michigan	D
University of Missouri–Columbia	M,D
University of Missouri–Kansas City	M,D
University of Missouri–St. Louis	M,D
The University of Montana–Missoula	M,D
University of Nebraska–Lincoln	M,D
University of Nevada, Reno	D
University of Notre Dame	M,D
University of Puerto Rico, Río Piedras	M,D
University of Southern California	D
University of Southern Mississippi	M,D
University of South Florida	M,D
The University of Tennessee	M,D
The University of Texas at Austin	M,D
University of Toledo	M,D
University of Utah	M,D
Wake Forest University	M,D
Washington State University	M,D
West Virginia University	M,D
Yale University	D

■ PHYSICAL EDUCATION

Adams State College	M
Adelphi University	M,O
Alabama Agricultural and Mechanical University	M
Alabama State University	M
Albany State University	M
Alcorn State University	M,O
Appalachian State University	M
Arizona State University	M
Arkansas State University	M,O
Arkansas Tech University	M
Ashland University	M
Auburn University	M,D,O
Auburn University Montgomery	M,O
Azusa Pacific University	M
Ball State University	M,D
Barry University	M
Baylor University	M
Bemidji State University	M
Boston University	M,D,O
Bridgewater State College	M
Brigham Young University	M,D
Brooklyn College of the City University of New York	M
California Polytechnic State University, San Luis Obispo	M
California State University, Chico	M
California State University, Dominguez Hills	M
California State University, Fullerton	M
California State University, Hayward	M
California State University, Long Beach	M
California State University, Los Angeles	M
California State University, Sacramento	M
California State University, Stanislaus	M
Campbell University	M
Canisius College	M
Central Connecticut State University	M
Central Michigan University	M
Central Missouri State University	M
Central Washington University	M
Chicago State University	M
The Citadel, The Military College of South Carolina	M
Cleveland State University	M
The College of New Jersey	M
Columbus State University	M
Delta State University	M
DePaul University	M
Drury University	M
Eastern Illinois University	M
Eastern Kentucky University	M
Eastern Michigan University	M
Eastern Nazarene College	M,O
Eastern New Mexico University	M
Eastern Washington University	M
East Stroudsburg University of Pennsylvania	M
East Tennessee State University	M
Edinboro University of Pennsylvania	O
Emporia State University	M
Florida Agricultural and Mechanical University	M
Florida International University	M
Florida State University	M,D,O
Fort Hays State University	M
Frostburg State University	M
Gardner-Webb University	M
Georgia College and State University	M,O
Georgia Southern University	M,O
Georgia Southwestern State University	M,O
Georgia State University	M
Hardin-Simmons University	M
Henderson State University	M
Hofstra University	M
Humboldt State University	M
Idaho State University	M
Illinois State University	M
Indiana State University	M
Indiana University Bloomington	M,D,O
Indiana University of Pennsylvania	M
Inter American University of Puerto Rico, Metropolitan Campus	M
Inter American University of Puerto Rico, San Germán Campus	M
Iowa State University of Science and Technology	M,D
Jackson State University	M
Jacksonville State University	M,O
Kent State University	M,D
Long Island University, Brooklyn Campus	M
Longwood College	M
Loras College	M
Louisiana Tech University	M,D,O
Marshall University	M
McNeese State University	M
Michigan State University	M,D
Middle Tennessee State University	M,D
Minnesota State University, Mankato	M,O
Mississippi State University	M
Montclair State University	M
Morehead State University	M
Murray State University	M
New Mexico Highlands University	M
North Carolina Agricultural and Technical State University	M
North Carolina Central University	M
North Dakota State University	M
Northern Arizona University	M
Northern Illinois University	M
Northern State University	M

North Georgia College & State University M,O
Northwest Missouri State University M
The Ohio State University M,D
Ohio University M
Oklahoma State University M,D
Old Dominion University M
Oregon State University M
Pittsburg State University M
Plymouth State College M
Prairie View A&M University M
Purdue University M,D
Queens College of the City University of New York M
Rowan University M
St. Cloud State University M
Saint Mary's College of California M
San Diego State University M
San Francisco State University M
San Jose State University M
Seattle Pacific University M
Slippery Rock University of Pennsylvania M
South Dakota State University M
Southern Connecticut State University M
Southern Illinois University Carbondale M
Southwestern Oklahoma State University M
Southwest Texas State University M
Springfield College M,D,O
State University of New York College at Brockport M
State University of New York College at Cortland M
State University of West Georgia M,O
Stephen F. Austin State University M
Stony Brook University, State University of New York M,O
Sul Ross State University M
Tarleton State University M,O
Teachers College, Columbia University M,D
Temple University M,D
Tennessee State University M
Tennessee Technological University M
Texas A&M University M,D
Texas A&M University–Commerce M
Texas Christian University M
Texas Southern University M
Texas Tech University M,D,O
Universidad Metropolitana M
The University of Akron M
The University of Alabama at Birmingham M
University of Arkansas M
University of Central Florida M
University of Colorado at Boulder M,D
University of Dayton M
University of Florida D
University of Georgia M,D,O
University of Houston M,D
University of Idaho M,D
The University of Iowa M,D
University of Kansas M,D
University of Louisiana at Monroe M
University of Louisville M
University of Maine M,O
University of Massachusetts Amherst M,D,O
University of Minnesota, Twin Cities Campus M,D
The University of Montana–Missoula M
University of Nebraska at Kearney M
University of Nebraska at Omaha M
University of Nebraska–Lincoln M
University of Nevada, Reno M
University of New Mexico M,D
University of New Orleans M,O
The University of North Carolina at Chapel Hill M
The University of North Carolina at Pembroke M
University of Northern Colorado M,D
University of Northern Iowa M
University of Rhode Island M
University of South Alabama M,O
University of South Carolina M,D
University of South Dakota M
University of Southern Mississippi M,D
University of South Florida M
The University of Tennessee at Chattanooga M
The University of Texas at El Paso M
The University of Texas of the Permian Basin M
University of the Incarnate Word M
University of Toledo D
University of Virginia M,D
The University of West Alabama M
University of West Florida M
University of Wisconsin–La Crosse M
University of Wyoming M
Utah State University M
Valdosta State University M
Virginia Commonwealth University M
Virginia Polytechnic Institute and State University M,D,O
Wayne State College M
Wayne State University M
West Chester University of Pennsylvania M,O
Western Carolina University M
Western Illinois University M
Western Kentucky University M
Western Michigan University M
Western Washington University M
Westfield State College M,O
West Virginia University M,D
Whitworth College M
Wichita State University M
Winthrop University M
Wright State University M

■ PHYSICAL THERAPY

Alabama State University M
American International College M
Andrews University M
Angelo State University M
Arcadia University D
Arkansas State University M
Armstrong Atlantic State University M
Azusa Pacific University M
Baylor University M
Belmont University M,D
Boston University M,D
Bradley University M
California State University, Fresno M
California State University, Long Beach M
California State University, Northridge M
Central Michigan University M
Chapman University D
Clarkson University M
College Misericordia M
College of Mount St. Joseph M
College of St. Catherine M
The College of St. Scholastica M
College of Staten Island of the City University of New York M
Columbia University M
Concordia University Wisconsin M
Creighton University D
Duke University M
Duquesne University M
East Carolina University M
Eastern Washington University M
East Tennessee State University M
Elon University M
Emory University M
Florida Gulf Coast University M
Florida International University M
Gannon University M
The George Washington University M
Georgia State University M
Governors State University M
Grand Valley State University M
Hampton University D
Hardin-Simmons University M
Hunter College of the City University of New York M
Husson College M
Idaho State University M
Indiana University–Purdue University Indianapolis M
Ithaca College M
Loma Linda University M,D
Long Island University, Brooklyn Campus M
Marquette University M
Marymount University M
Maryville University of Saint Louis M
MCP Hahnemann University M,D,O
Mercy College M
Mount St. Mary's College M
New York Institute of Technology M
New York University M,D
Northern Arizona University M
Northern Illinois University M
North Georgia College & State University M
Northwestern University D
Nova Southeastern University M,D
Oakland University M,O
Ohio University M
Old Dominion University M
Pacific University M
Quinnipiac University M
Regis University D
Rockhurst University M
Rutgers, The State University of New Jersey, Camden M
Sacred Heart University M
Sage Graduate School M
St. Ambrose University M
Saint Francis University M
Saint Louis University M
San Francisco State University M
Shenandoah University M
Simmons College M,D
Slippery Rock University of Pennsylvania D
Southwest Baptist University M
Southwest Missouri State University M
Southwest Texas State University M
Springfield College M
Temple University M,D
Texas Woman's University M,D
Touro College M
University at Buffalo, The State University of New York M,D
The University of Alabama at Birmingham M
University of California, San Francisco M
University of Central Arkansas M,D
University of Central Florida M
University of Cincinnati M
University of Delaware M
The University of Findlay M
University of Florida M
University of Hartford M
University of Illinois at Chicago M
University of Indianapolis M

The University of Iowa	M,D
University of Kansas	M
University of Kentucky	M
University of Mary	M
University of Maryland Eastern Shore	M
University of Massachusetts Lowell	M
University of Miami	M,D
University of Michigan–Flint	M
University of Minnesota, Twin Cities Campus	M,D
University of Missouri–Columbia	M
The University of Montana–Missoula	M
University of Nevada, Las Vegas	M
University of New England	M
University of New Mexico	M
The University of North Carolina at Chapel Hill	M,D
University of North Dakota	M
University of North Florida	M,O
University of Pittsburgh	M
University of Rhode Island	M
University of South Dakota	M
University of Southern California	M,D
The University of Tennessee at Chattanooga	M
The University of Texas at El Paso	M
University of the Pacific	M
University of Utah	M
University of Vermont	M
University of Washington	M
University of Wisconsin–La Crosse	M
Virginia Commonwealth University	M,D,O
Walsh University	M
Washington University in St. Louis	D,O
Wayne State University	M
Western Carolina University	M
West Virginia University	M
Wheeling Jesuit University	M
Wichita State University	M
Widener University	M
Youngstown State University	M

■ PHYSICIAN ASSISTANT STUDIES

Arcadia University	M
Barry University	M
Central Michigan University	M
DeSales University	M
Duke University	M
Duquesne University	M
Emory University	M
Gannon University	M
The George Washington University	M
Grand Valley State University	M
King's College	M
Lock Haven University of Pennsylvania	M
Loma Linda University	M
Marquette University	M
MCP Hahnemann University	M
Northeastern University	M
Pacific University	M
Philadelphia University	M
Quinnipiac University	M
Saint Francis University	M
Saint Louis University	M
Seton Hall University	M
Southwest Missouri State University	M
Towson University	M
Trevecca Nazarene University	M
University of Detroit Mercy	M
University of Florida	M
The University of Iowa	M
University of New England	M
University of South Alabama	M
Wayne State University	M
Western Michigan University	M
Yale University	M

■ PHYSICS

Adelphi University	M
Alabama Agricultural and Mechanical University	M,D
American University	M
Arizona State University	M,D
Auburn University	M,D
Ball State University	M
Baylor University	M,D
Boston College	M,D
Boston University	M,D
Bowling Green State University	M
Brandeis University	M,D
Brigham Young University	M,D
Brooklyn College of the City University of New York	M,D
Brown University	M,D
California Institute of Technology	D
California State University, Fresno	M
California State University, Fullerton	M
California State University, Long Beach	M
California State University, Los Angeles	M
California State University, Northridge	M
Carnegie Mellon University	M,D
Case Western Reserve University	M,D
The Catholic University of America	M,D
Central Connecticut State University	M
Central Michigan University	M
City College of the City University of New York	M,D
Clark Atlanta University	M
Clarkson University	M,D
Clark University	M,D
Clemson University	M,D
Cleveland State University	M
The College of William and Mary	M,D
Colorado State University	M,D
Columbia University	M,D
Cornell University	M,D
Creighton University	M
Dartmouth College	M,D
Delaware State University	M
DePaul University	M
Drexel University	M,D
Duke University	D
East Carolina University	M,D
Eastern Michigan University	M
Emory University	D
Emporia State University	M
Florida Agricultural and Mechanical University	M
Florida Atlantic University	M,D
Florida Institute of Technology	M,D
Florida International University	M,D
Florida State University	M,D
George Mason University	M
The George Washington University	D
Georgia Institute of Technology	M,D
Georgia State University	M,D
Hampton University	M,D
Harvard University	M,D
Howard University	M,D
Hunter College of the City University of New York	M,D
Idaho State University	M
Illinois Institute of Technology	M,D
Indiana State University	M
Indiana University Bloomington	M,D
Indiana University of Pennsylvania	M
Indiana University–Purdue University Indianapolis	M,D
Iowa State University of Science and Technology	M,D
John Carroll University	M
Johns Hopkins University	D
Kansas State University	M,D
Kent State University	M,D
Lehigh University	M,D
Louisiana State University and Agricultural and Mechanical College	M,D
Louisiana Tech University	M,D
Marshall University	M
Massachusetts Institute of Technology	M,D
Miami University	M
Michigan State University	M,D
Michigan Technological University	M,D
Minnesota State University, Mankato	M
Mississippi State University	M,D
Montana State University–Bozeman	M,D
Morgan State University	M
New Mexico Institute of Mining and Technology	M,D
New Mexico State University	M,D
New York University	M,D
North Carolina State University	M,D
North Dakota State University	M,D
Northeastern University	M,D
Northern Illinois University	M,D
Northwestern University	M,D
Oakland University	M,D
The Ohio State University	M,D
Ohio University	M,D
Oklahoma State University	M,D
Old Dominion University	M,D
Oregon State University	M,D
The Pennsylvania State University University Park Campus	M,D
Pittsburg State University	M
Polytechnic University, Brooklyn Campus	M,D
Portland State University	M,D
Princeton University	D
Purdue University	M,D
Queens College of the City University of New York	M
Rensselaer Polytechnic Institute	M,D
Rice University	M,D
Rutgers, The State University of New Jersey, New Brunswick	M,D
Sam Houston State University	M
San Diego State University	M
San Francisco State University	M
San Jose State University	M
South Dakota State University	M
Southern Illinois University Carbondale	M
Southern Illinois University Edwardsville	M
Southern Methodist University	M,D
Southern University and Agricultural and Mechanical College	M
Southwest Texas State University	M
Stanford University	D
State University of New York at Albany	M,D
State University of New York at Binghamton	M
State University of New York at New Paltz	M
Stephen F. Austin State University	M
Stevens Institute of Technology	M,D,O
Stony Brook University, State University of New York	M,D
Syracuse University	M,D
Temple University	M,D
Texas A&M University	M,D
Texas A&M University–Commerce	M
Texas Christian University	M,D
Texas Tech University	M,D
Tufts University	M,D
Tulane University	M,D

University at Buffalo, The State University of New York	M,D
The University of Akron	M
The University of Alabama	M,D
The University of Alabama at Birmingham	M,D
The University of Alabama in Huntsville	M,D
University of Alaska Fairbanks	M,D
The University of Arizona	M,D
University of Arkansas	M,D
University of California, Berkeley	D
University of California, Davis	M,D
University of California, Irvine	M,D
University of California, Los Angeles	M,D
University of California, Riverside	M,D
University of California, San Diego	M,D
University of California, Santa Barbara	D
University of California, Santa Cruz	M,D
University of Central Florida	M,D
University of Chicago	M,D
University of Cincinnati	M,D
University of Colorado at Boulder	M,D
University of Colorado at Colorado Springs	M
University of Connecticut	M,D
University of Delaware	M,D
University of Denver	M,D
University of Florida	M,D
University of Georgia	M,D
University of Hawaii at Manoa	M,D
University of Houston	M,D
University of Idaho	M,D
University of Illinois at Chicago	M,D
University of Illinois at Urbana–Champaign	M,D
The University of Iowa	M,D
University of Kansas	M,D
University of Kentucky	M,D
University of Louisiana at Lafayette	M
University of Louisville	M
University of Maine	M,D
University of Maryland, Baltimore County	M,D
University of Maryland, College Park	M,D
University of Massachusetts Amherst	M,D
University of Massachusetts Dartmouth	M
University of Massachusetts Lowell	M,D
The University of Memphis	M
University of Miami	M,D
University of Michigan	M,D
University of Minnesota, Duluth	M
University of Minnesota, Twin Cities Campus	M,D
University of Mississippi	M,D
University of Missouri–Columbia	M,D
University of Missouri–Kansas City	M,D
University of Missouri–Rolla	M,D
University of Missouri–St. Louis	M,D
University of Nebraska–Lincoln	M,D
University of Nevada, Las Vegas	M,D
University of Nevada, Reno	M,D
University of New Hampshire	M,D
University of New Mexico	M,D
University of New Orleans	M
The University of North Carolina at Chapel Hill	M,D
University of North Dakota	M,D
University of North Texas	M,D
University of Notre Dame	D
University of Oklahoma	M,D
University of Oregon	M,D
University of Pennsylvania	D
University of Pittsburgh	M,D
University of Puerto Rico, Mayagüez Campus	M
University of Puerto Rico, Río Piedras	M,D
University of Rhode Island	M,D
University of Rochester	M,D
University of South Carolina	M,D
University of Southern California	M,D
University of Southern Mississippi	M
University of South Florida	M,D
The University of Tennessee	M,D
The University of Texas at Arlington	M,D
The University of Texas at Austin	M,D
The University of Texas at Dallas	M,D
The University of Texas at El Paso	M
The University of Texas at Tyler	M
University of Toledo	M,D
University of Utah	M,D
University of Vermont	M
University of Virginia	M,D
University of Washington	M,D
University of Wisconsin–Madison	M,D
University of Wisconsin–Milwaukee	M,D
University of Wisconsin–Oshkosh	M
Utah State University	M,D
Vanderbilt University	M,D
Virginia Commonwealth University	M
Virginia Polytechnic Institute and State University	M,D
Virginia State University	M
Wake Forest University	M,D
Washington State University	M,D
Washington University in St. Louis	M,D
Wayne State University	M,D
Western Carolina University	M
Western Illinois University	M
Western Michigan University	M,D
West Virginia University	M,D
Wichita State University	M
Wilkes University	M
Worcester Polytechnic Institute	M,D
Wright State University	M
Yale University	D

■ PHYSIOLOGY

Arizona State University	M,D
Auburn University	M
Ball State University	M
Boston University	M,D
Brown University	M,D
Case Western Reserve University	M,D
Clemson University	M,D
Colorado State University	M,D
Columbia University	M,D
Cornell University	M,D
Dartmouth College	D
Duke University	D
East Carolina University	D
East Tennessee State University	M,D
Florida State University	M,D
Georgetown University	M,D
Georgia State University	M,D
Harvard University	M,D
Howard University	D
Illinois State University	M,D
Indiana State University	M,D
Indiana University Bloomington	M,D
Indiana University–Purdue University Indianapolis	M,D
Iowa State University of Science and Technology	M,D
Johns Hopkins University	M,D
Kansas State University	M,D
Kent State University	M,D
Loma Linda University	M,D
Loyola University Chicago	M,D
Maharishi University of Management	M,D
Marquette University	M,D
Michigan State University	M,D
Mississippi State University	M,D
New York University	M,D
North Carolina State University	M,D
Northwestern University	M
The Ohio State University	M,D
The Pennsylvania State University University Park Campus	M,D
Purdue University	M,D
Rutgers, The State University of New Jersey, New Brunswick	D
Saint Louis University	M,D
Salisbury State University	M
San Francisco State University	M
Southern Illinois University Carbondale	M,D
Southern Illinois University Edwardsville	M,O
Stanford University	D
Stony Brook University, State University of New York	D
Teachers College, Columbia University	M,D
Temple University	M,D
Texas A&M University	M,D
Tufts University	D
Tulane University	M,D
University at Buffalo, The State University of New York	M,D
The University of Alabama at Birmingham	D
The University of Arizona	D
University of California, Berkeley	M,D
University of California, Davis	M,D
University of California, Irvine	D
University of California, Los Angeles	M,D
University of California, San Diego	D
University of California, San Francisco	D
University of Chicago	D
University of Cincinnati	M,D
University of Colorado at Boulder	M,D
University of Connecticut	M,D
University of Delaware	M,D
University of Florida	D
University of Georgia	M,D
University of Hawaii at Manoa	M,D
University of Illinois at Chicago	M,D
University of Illinois at Urbana–Champaign	M,D
The University of Iowa	M,D
University of Kansas	M,D
University of Kentucky	D
University of Louisville	M,D
University of Maryland	D
University of Miami	D
University of Michigan	D
University of Minnesota, Duluth	M,D
University of Minnesota, Twin Cities Campus	M,D
University of Missouri–Columbia	M,D
University of Missouri–St. Louis	M,D,O
University of Nevada, Reno	M,D
University of New Mexico	M,D
The University of North Carolina at Chapel Hill	D
University of North Dakota	M,D
University of Notre Dame	M,D
University of Pennsylvania	D
University of Pittsburgh	M,D
University of Rochester	M,D
University of South Alabama	D
University of South Dakota	M,D
University of Southern California	M,D
University of South Florida	M,D
The University of Tennessee	M,D
University of the Pacific	M,D
University of Utah	D
University of Vermont	M,D
University of Virginia	D
University of Washington	D
University of Wisconsin–Madison	M,D

University of Wyoming M,D
Vanderbilt University D
Virginia Commonwealth University M,D,O
Wake Forest University D
Wayne State University M,D
West Virginia University M,D
William Paterson University of New Jersey M
Wright State University M
Yale University D
Yeshiva University D

■ PLANETARY AND SPACE SCIENCES

California Institute of Technology M,D
Columbia University M,D
Cornell University D
Florida Institute of Technology M,D
Harvard University M,D
Johns Hopkins University M,D
Massachusetts Institute of Technology M,D
Rensselaer Polytechnic Institute M,D
Stony Brook University, State University of New York M,D
The University of Arizona M,D
University of California, Los Angeles M,D
University of Chicago M,D
University of Hawaii at Manoa M,D
University of Michigan M,D
University of New Mexico M,D
University of North Dakota M
University of Pittsburgh M,D
Washington University in St. Louis M,D
Western Connecticut State University M

■ PLANT MOLECULAR BIOLOGY

Cornell University D
University of California, Los Angeles M,D
University of California, Riverside M,D
University of California, San Diego D
University of Connecticut M,D
University of Delaware M,D
University of Florida M,D

■ PLANT PATHOLOGY

Auburn University M,D
Colorado State University M,D
Cornell University M,D
Iowa State University of Science and Technology M,D
Kansas State University M,D
Louisiana State University and Agricultural and Mechanical College M,D
Michigan State University M,D
Mississippi State University M,D
Montana State University–Bozeman M,D
New Mexico State University M
North Carolina State University M,D
North Dakota State University M,D
The Ohio State University M,D
Oklahoma State University M,D
Oregon State University M,D
The Pennsylvania State University University Park Campus M,D
Purdue University M,D
Rutgers, The State University of New Jersey, New Brunswick M,D
South Dakota State University M
Texas A&M University M,D
The University of Arizona M,D
University of Arkansas M
University of California, Davis M,D
University of California, Riverside M,D
University of Florida M,D
University of Georgia M,D
University of Hawaii at Manoa M,D
University of Idaho M,D
University of Kentucky M,D
University of Maine M
University of Minnesota, Twin Cities Campus M,D
University of Missouri–Columbia M,D
University of Rhode Island M,D
The University of Tennessee M
University of Wisconsin–Madison M,D
Virginia Polytechnic Institute and State University M,D
Washington State University M,D
West Virginia University M,D

■ PLANT PHYSIOLOGY

Colorado State University M,D
Cornell University D
Iowa State University of Science and Technology M,D
Oregon State University M,D
The Pennsylvania State University University Park Campus M,D
Purdue University D
Rutgers, The State University of New Jersey, New Brunswick M,D
University of Colorado at Boulder M,D
University of Hawaii at Manoa M,D
University of Kentucky D
The University of Tennessee M,D
Virginia Polytechnic Institute and State University M,D
Washington State University M,D

■ PLASMA PHYSICS

Columbia University M,D
Princeton University D
University of Colorado at Boulder M,D
West Virginia University M,D

■ PODIATRIC MEDICINE

Barry University P
Temple University P

■ POLITICAL SCIENCE

American University M,D
Appalachian State University M
Arizona State University M,D
Arkansas State University M,O
Auburn University M,D
Auburn University Montgomery M
Ball State University M
Baylor University M,D
Boston College M,D
Boston University M,D
Bowling Green State University
Brandeis University M,D
Brooklyn College of the City University of New York M,D
Brown University M,D
California Institute of Technology D
California State University, Chico M
California State University, Fullerton M
California State University, Long Beach M
California State University, Los Angeles M
California State University, Northridge M
California State University, Sacramento M
Case Western Reserve University M,D
The Catholic University of America M,D
Central Michigan University M
Claremont Graduate University M,D
Clark Atlanta University M,D
The College of Saint Rose M
Colorado State University M,D
Columbia University M,D
Converse College M
Cornell University D
Duke University M,D
Eastern Illinois University M
Eastern Kentucky University M
East Stroudsburg University of Pennsylvania M
Emory University D
Fairleigh Dickinson University, Teaneck–Hackensack Campus M
Fayetteville State University M
Florida Atlantic University M
Florida International University M,D
Florida State University M,D
Fordham University M,D
Georgetown University M,D
The George Washington University M,D
Georgia Southern University M
Georgia State University M,D
Governors State University M
Harvard University M,D
Howard University M,D
Idaho State University M,D
Illinois State University M
Indiana State University M
Indiana University Bloomington M,D
Indiana University of Pennsylvania M
Iowa State University of Science and Technology M
Jackson State University M
Jacksonville State University M
Johns Hopkins University M,D
Kansas State University M
Kent State University M,D
Lamar University M
Lehigh University M
Long Island University, Brooklyn Campus M
Long Island University, C.W. Post Campus M
Louisiana State University and Agricultural and Mechanical College M,D
Loyola University Chicago M,D
Marquette University M
Marshall University M
Massachusetts Institute of Technology M,D
Miami University M,D
Michigan State University M,D
Midwestern State University M
Minnesota State University, Mankato M
Mississippi College M
Mississippi State University M,D
New Mexico Highlands University M
New Mexico State University M
New School University M,D
New York University M,D
North Dakota State University M
Northeastern Illinois University M
Northeastern University M,D
Northern Arizona University M,D
Northern Illinois University M,D
Northwestern University M,D
The Ohio State University M,D,O
Ohio University M
Oklahoma State University M
The Pennsylvania State University University Park Campus M,D
Portland State University M,D
Princeton University D
Purdue University M,D
Purdue University Calumet M
Rice University M,D
Roosevelt University M

Rutgers, The State University of New Jersey, Newark M
Rutgers, The State University of New Jersey, New Brunswick M,D
St. John's University (NY) M
St. Mary's University of San Antonio M
Sam Houston State University M
San Diego State University M
San Francisco State University M
Sonoma State University M
Southern Connecticut State University M
Southern Illinois University Carbondale M,D
Southern University and Agricultural and Mechanical College M
Southwest Texas State University M
Stanford University M,D
State University of New York at Albany M,D
State University of New York at Binghamton M,D
Stony Brook University, State University of New York M,D
Suffolk University M
Sul Ross State University M
Syracuse University M,D
Tarleton State University M
Teachers College, Columbia University M,D
Temple University M,D
Texas A&M International University M
Texas A&M University M,D
Texas A&M University–Kingsville M
Texas Tech University M,D
Texas Woman's University M
Troy State University Dothan M
Tulane University M,D
University at Buffalo, The State University of New York M,D
The University of Akron M
The University of Alabama M,D
The University of Arizona M,D
University of Arkansas M
University of California, Berkeley D
University of California, Davis M,D
University of California, Irvine M,D
University of California, Los Angeles M,D
University of California, Riverside M,D
University of California, San Diego M,D
University of California, Santa Barbara M,D
University of Central Florida M
University of Central Oklahoma M
University of Chicago D
University of Cincinnati M,D
University of Colorado at Boulder M,D
University of Colorado at Denver M
University of Connecticut M,D
University of Delaware M,D
University of Detroit Mercy M
University of Florida M,D,O
University of Georgia M,D
University of Hawaii at Manoa M,D
University of Houston M,D
University of Idaho M,D
University of Illinois at Chicago M,D
University of Illinois at Springfield M
University of Illinois at Urbana–Champaign M,D
The University of Iowa M,D
University of Kansas M,D
University of Kentucky M,D
University of Louisville M
University of Maryland, College Park M,D
University of Massachusetts Amherst M,D
University of Massachusetts Boston O
The University of Memphis M
University of Miami M
University of Michigan M,D
University of Minnesota, Twin Cities Campus M,D
University of Mississippi M,D
University of Missouri–Columbia M,D
University of Missouri–Kansas City M,D
University of Missouri–St. Louis M,D
The University of Montana–Missoula M
University of Nebraska at Omaha M
University of Nebraska–Lincoln M,D
University of Nevada, Las Vegas M
University of Nevada, Reno M,D
University of New Hampshire M
University of New Mexico M,D
University of New Orleans M,D
The University of North Carolina at Chapel Hill M,D
The University of North Carolina at Greensboro M
University of Northern Iowa M
University of North Texas M,D
University of Notre Dame D
University of Oklahoma M,D
University of Oregon M,D
University of Pennsylvania M,D
University of Pittsburgh M,D
University of Rhode Island M,O
University of Rochester M,D
University of South Carolina M,D
University of South Dakota M
University of Southern California M,D
University of Southern Mississippi M
University of South Florida M
The University of Tennessee M,D
The University of Texas at Arlington M
The University of Texas at Austin M,D
The University of Texas at Brownsville M
The University of Texas at El Paso M
The University of Texas at San Antonio M
University of Toledo M
University of Utah M,D
University of Vermont M
University of Virginia M,D
University of Washington M,D
University of West Florida M
University of Wisconsin–Madison M,D
University of Wisconsin–Milwaukee M,D
University of Wyoming M
Utah State University M
Vanderbilt University M,D
Villanova University M
Virginia Polytechnic Institute and State University M
Washington State University M,D
Washington University in St. Louis M,D
Wayne State University M,D
Western Illinois University M
Western Michigan University M,D
Western Washington University M
West Texas A&M University M
West Virginia University M,D
Wichita State University M
Yale University D

■ POLYMER SCIENCE AND ENGINEERING

Carnegie Mellon University M,D
Case Western Reserve University M,D
Clemson University M,D
Cornell University M,D
Eastern Michigan University M
Georgia Institute of Technology M
Illinois Institute of Technology
Lehigh University M,D
North Dakota State University M,D
The Pennsylvania State University University Park Campus M,D
Polytechnic University, Brooklyn Campus M
Princeton University M,D
Rensselaer Polytechnic Institute M,D
Rutgers, The State University of New Jersey, New Brunswick M,D
San Jose State University M
The University of Akron M,D
University of Cincinnati M,D
University of Connecticut M,D
University of Detroit Mercy M
University of Florida M,D,O
University of Massachusetts Amherst M,D
University of Massachusetts Lowell M,D
University of Missouri–Kansas City M,D
University of Southern Mississippi M,D
The University of Tennessee M,D
University of Wisconsin–Madison M,D
Wayne State University M,D,O

■ PORTUGUESE

Brigham Young University M
Harvard University M,D
Indiana University Bloomington M,D
New York University M,D
The Ohio State University M,D
Tulane University M,D
University of California, Los Angeles M
University of California, Santa Barbara M,D
University of Minnesota, Twin Cities Campus M,D
University of New Mexico M,D
The University of North Carolina at Chapel Hill M,D
The University of Tennessee D
The University of Texas at Austin M,D
University of Washington M
University of Wisconsin–Madison M,D
Vanderbilt University M,D
Yale University M,D

■ PROJECT MANAGEMENT

Carnegie Mellon University M,D
City University M,O
Denver Technical College M
The George Washington University M,D
Lesley University M,O
Mississippi State University M,D
Montana State University–Bozeman M,D
Northwestern University M
Regis University M,O
Stevens Institute of Technology M,O
Texas A&M University M,D
Thomas Edison State College M
University of Wisconsin–Platteville M
Western Carolina University M
Wright State University M

■ PSYCHIATRIC NURSING

Boston College M,D
Case Western Reserve University M
The Catholic University of America M,D
Columbia University M,O
Fairfield University M,O
Georgia State University M,D
Hunter College of the City University of New York M
Husson College M
Indiana University–Purdue University Indianapolis M
Kent State University M
Molloy College M,O
New York University M,O
Northeastern University M,O
Pontifical Catholic University of Puerto Rico M

Rutgers, The State University of New Jersey, Newark	M,D
Sage Graduate School	M
Saint Joseph College	M,O
Saint Xavier University	M,O
Southern Illinois University Edwardsville	M
Stony Brook University, State University of New York	M,O
Texas Woman's University	M,D
University at Buffalo, The State University of New York	M,D,O
University of Cincinnati	M,D
University of Delaware	M,O
University of Illinois at Chicago	M
University of Maryland	M,D
University of Massachusetts Lowell	M
University of Miami	M,D
University of Michigan	M
University of Minnesota, Twin Cities Campus	M
University of Pennsylvania	M
University of Pittsburgh	M
University of South Alabama	M
University of South Carolina	M,O
University of Southern Maine	M,O
University of Southern Mississippi	M,D
The University of Texas at El Paso	M
Vanderbilt University	M,D
Virginia Commonwealth University	M,D,O
Wayne State University	M
Wichita State University	M

■ PSYCHOLOGY—GENERAL

Abilene Christian University	M
Adelphi University	M,D,O
Alabama Agricultural and Mechanical University	M,O
Alliant International University	M,D
American International College	M,D,O
American University	M,D
Andrews University	M,D,O
Angelo State University	M
Anna Maria College	M,O
Antioch New England Graduate School	M
Antioch University Los Angeles	M
Antioch University McGregor	M
Antioch University Seattle	M
Appalachian State University	M,O
Arcadia University	M
Argosy University-Sarasota	M,D,O
Arizona State University	D
Assumption College	M,O
Auburn University	M,D
Auburn University Montgomery	M
Augusta State University	M
Austin Peay State University	M
Avila College	M
Azusa Pacific University	M,D
Ball State University	M
Barry University	M,O
Bayamón Central University	M
Baylor University	M,D
Bethel College (MN)	M
Biola University	M,D
Boston College	D
Boston University	M,D
Bowling Green State University	M,D
Brandeis University	M,D
Bridgewater State College	M
Brigham Young University	M,D
Brooklyn College of the City University of New York	M,D
Brown University	M,D
California Lutheran University	M
California Polytechnic State University, San Luis Obispo	M
California State Polytechnic University, Pomona	M
California State University, Bakersfield	M,O
California State University, Chico	M
California State University, Dominguez Hills	M
California State University, Fresno	M
California State University, Fullerton	M
California State University, Long Beach	M
California State University, Los Angeles	M
California State University, Northridge	M
California State University, Sacramento	M
California State University, San Bernardino	M
California State University, San Marcos	M
California State University, Stanislaus	M
Cameron University	M
Cardinal Stritch University	M
Carnegie Mellon University	D
Case Western Reserve University	D
Castleton State College	M
The Catholic University of America	M,D
Central Connecticut State University	M
Central Michigan University	M,D,O
Central Missouri State University	M,O
Central Washington University	M
Chapman University	M
Chestnut Hill College	M,D
The Citadel, The Military College of South Carolina	M
City College of the City University of New York	M,D
Claremont Graduate University	M,D
Clark University	D
Clemson University	M,D
Cleveland State University	M,O
College of St. Joseph	M
College of Staten Island of the City University of New York	D
The College of William and Mary	M,D
Colorado State University	D
Columbia University	M,D
Concordia University (IL)	M,O
Coppin State College	M
Cornell University	D
Dartmouth College	D
DePaul University	M,D
Drexel University	M,D
Duke University	D
Duquesne University	M,D
East Carolina University	M
East Central University	M
Eastern Illinois University	M,O
Eastern Kentucky University	M,O
Eastern Michigan University	M
Eastern New Mexico University	M
Eastern Washington University	M
East Tennessee State University	M
Edinboro University of Pennsylvania	M
Emory University	D
Emporia State University	M
Fairfield University	M,O
Fairleigh Dickinson University, Florham-Madison Campus	M
Fairleigh Dickinson University, Teaneck–Hackensack Campus	M,D
Fayetteville State University	M
Florida Agricultural and Mechanical University	M
Florida Atlantic University	M,D
Florida Institute of Technology	M,D
Florida International University	M,D
Florida State University	M,D
Fordham University	D
Fort Hays State University	M,O
Framingham State College	M
Francis Marion University	M
Frostburg State University	M
Gallaudet University	M,D,O
Gardner-Webb University	M
Geneva College	M
George Fox University	M,D
George Mason University	M,D
Georgetown University	D
The George Washington University	D
Georgia College and State University	M
Georgia Institute of Technology	M,D
Georgia Southern University	M
Georgia Southwestern State University	M
Georgia State University	D
Governors State University	M
Hardin-Simmons University	M
Harvard University	M,D
Hofstra University	M,D,O
Hood College	M
Hope International University	M
Houston Baptist University	M
Howard University	M,D
Humboldt State University	M
Hunter College of the City University of New York	M
Idaho State University	M,D
Illinois Institute of Technology	M,D
Illinois School of Professional Psychology, Chicago Northwest Campus	M,D
Illinois State University	M,D,O
Immaculata College	M,D,O
Indiana State University	M,D
Indiana University Bloomington	D
Indiana University of Pennsylvania	M,D
Indiana University–Purdue University Indianapolis	M,D
Indiana University South Bend	M
Inter American University of Puerto Rico, Metropolitan Campus	M
Inter American University of Puerto Rico, San Germán Campus	M
Iona College	M
Iowa State University of Science and Technology	M,D
Jackson State University	D
Jacksonville State University	M
James Madison University	M,D,O
John F. Kennedy University	M,D,O
Johns Hopkins University	D
Kansas State University	M,D
Kean University	M,O
Kent State University	M,D
Lamar University	M
La Salle University	D
Lehigh University	D
Lesley University	M,O
Lewis University	M
Long Island University, Brooklyn Campus	M,D
Long Island University, C.W. Post Campus	M,D
Loras College	M
Louisiana State University and Agricultural and Mechanical College	M,D
Louisiana Tech University	M,D,O
Loyola College in Maryland	M,D,O
Loyola Marymount University	M
Loyola University Chicago	M,D
Madonna University	M
Maharishi University of Management	M,D
Marist College	M,O
Marquette University	M,D

Marshall University	M
Marymount University	M,O
Marywood University	M,D
Massachusetts Institute of Technology	D
McNeese State University	M
Miami University	D
Michigan State University	M,D
Middle Tennessee State University	M,O
Midwestern State University	M
Millersville University of Pennsylvania	M
Minnesota State University, Mankato	M
Minnesota State University Moorhead	M,O
Mississippi College	M
Mississippi State University	M,D
Monmouth University	M,O
Montana State University–Billings	M
Montana State University–Bozeman	M
Montclair State University	M,O
Morehead State University	M
Murray State University	M
National-Louis University	M,O
National University	M,O
New College of California	M
New Jersey City University	M,O
New Mexico Highlands University	M
New Mexico State University	M,D
New School University	M,D
New York University	M,D,O
Norfolk State University	M,D
North Carolina Central University	M
North Carolina State University	M,D
North Dakota State University	M,D
Northeastern State University	M
Northeastern University	M,D,O
Northern Arizona University	M
Northern Illinois University	M,D
Northwestern Oklahoma State University	M
Northwestern State University of Louisiana	M
Northwestern University	D
Northwest Missouri State University	M
Notre Dame de Namur University	M
Nova Southeastern University	M,D,O
The Ohio State University	D
Ohio University	D
Oklahoma State University	M,D
Our Lady of the Lake University of San Antonio	M,D
Pace University, New York City Campus	M,D
Pace University, White Plains Campus	M
Pacific University	M,D
The Pennsylvania State University Harrisburg Campus of the Capital College	M
The Pennsylvania State University University Park Campus	M,D
Pittsburg State University	M
Plattsburgh State University of New York	M,O
Portland State University	M,D
Princeton University	D
Purdue University	D
Queens College of the City University of New York	M
Radford University	M,O
Regis University	M,O
Rensselaer Polytechnic Institute	M
Rhode Island College	M
Rice University	M,D
Roosevelt University	M,D
Rowan University	M
Rutgers, The State University of New Jersey, Newark	D
Rutgers, The State University of New Jersey, New Brunswick	M,D
Sage Graduate School	M
St. Bonaventure University	M
St. Cloud State University	M
St. John's University (NY)	M,D
Saint Joseph College	M,O
Saint Joseph's University	M
Saint Louis University	M,D
Saint Mary College	M
St. Mary's University of San Antonio	M
Saint Xavier University	M,O
Salem State College	M
Salisbury State University	M
Sam Houston State University	M,D
San Diego State University	M,D
San Francisco State University	M
San Jose State University	M
Seattle University	M
Seton Hall University	M,D,O
Shippensburg University of Pennsylvania	M
Southeastern Louisiana University	M
Southern Connecticut State University	M
Southern Illinois University Carbondale	M,D
Southern Illinois University Edwardsville	M
Southern Methodist University	M,D
Southern Nazarene University	M
Southern Oregon University	M
Southern University and Agricultural and Mechanical College	M
Southwest Missouri State University	M
Southwest Texas State University	M
Spalding University	M,D
Stanford University	D
State University of New York at Albany	M,D
State University of New York at Binghamton	M,D
State University of New York at New Paltz	M
State University of New York College at Brockport	M
State University of West Georgia	M
Stephen F. Austin State University	M
Stony Brook University, State University of New York	M,D
Suffolk University	D
Sul Ross State University	M
Syracuse University	M,D
Temple University	D
Tennessee State University	M,D
Texas A&M International University	M
Texas A&M University	M,D
Texas A&M University–Commerce	M,D
Texas A&M University–Corpus Christi	M
Texas A&M University–Kingsville	M
Texas Christian University	M,D
Texas Tech University	M,D
Texas Woman's University	M,D
Towson University	M,O
Tufts University	M,D
Tulane University	M,D
The Union Institute	D
University at Buffalo, The State University of New York	M,D
The University of Akron	M,D
The University of Alabama	D
The University of Alabama at Birmingham	M,D
The University of Alabama in Huntsville	M
University of Alaska Anchorage	M
University of Alaska Fairbanks	M
The University of Arizona	M,D
University of Arkansas	M,D
University of Arkansas at Little Rock	M
University of Baltimore	M,D
University of California, Berkeley	D
University of California, Davis	D
University of California, Irvine	M,D
University of California, Los Angeles	M,D
University of California, Riverside	D
University of California, San Diego	D
University of California, Santa Barbara	M,D
University of California, Santa Cruz	D
University of Central Arkansas	M,D
University of Central Florida	M,D
University of Central Oklahoma	M
University of Chicago	D
University of Cincinnati	M,D
University of Colorado at Boulder	M,D
University of Colorado at Colorado Springs	M
University of Colorado at Denver	M
University of Connecticut	M,D
University of Dayton	M
University of Delaware	D
University of Denver	D
University of Detroit Mercy	M,D,O
University of Florida	M,D
University of Georgia	M,D
University of Hartford	M
University of Hawaii at Manoa	M,D
University of Houston	D
University of Houston–Clear Lake	M
University of Houston–Victoria	M
University of Idaho	M
University of Illinois at Chicago	D
University of Illinois at Springfield	M
University of Illinois at Urbana–Champaign	M,D
The University of Iowa	M,D
University of Kansas	M,D
University of Kentucky	M,D
University of La Verne	M,D
University of Louisiana at Lafayette	M
University of Louisiana at Monroe	M,O
University of Louisville	M,D
University of Maine	M,D
University of Mary Hardin-Baylor	M
University of Maryland, Baltimore County	M,D
University of Maryland, College Park	M,D
University of Massachusetts Amherst	M,D
University of Massachusetts Dartmouth	M
University of Massachusetts Lowell	M
The University of Memphis	M,D
University of Miami	M,D
University of Michigan	D,O
University of Minnesota, Twin Cities Campus	M,D
University of Mississippi	M,D
University of Missouri–Columbia	M,D
University of Missouri–Kansas City	M,D
University of Missouri–St. Louis	M,D,O
The University of Montana–Missoula	M,D,O
University of Nebraska at Omaha	M,D,O
University of Nebraska–Lincoln	M,D
University of Nevada, Las Vegas	M,D
University of Nevada, Reno	M,D
University of New Hampshire	D
University of New Mexico	M,D
University of New Orleans	M,D
The University of North Carolina at Chapel Hill	D
The University of North Carolina at Charlotte	M
The University of North Carolina at Greensboro	M,D
The University of North Carolina at Wilmington	M
University of North Dakota	M,D
University of Northern Colorado	M

University of Northern Iowa M
University of North Florida M
University of North Texas M,D
University of Notre Dame D
University of Oklahoma M,D
University of Oregon M,D
University of Pennsylvania D
University of Pittsburgh M,D
University of Puerto Rico, Río Piedras M,D
University of Rhode Island M,D
University of Richmond M
University of Rochester M,D
University of Saint Francis (IN) M
University of St. Thomas (MN) M,D
University of South Alabama M
University of South Carolina M,D
University of South Dakota M,D
University of Southern California M,D
University of Southern Mississippi M,D,O
University of South Florida D
The University of Tennessee M,D
The University of Tennessee at Chattanooga M
The University of Texas at Arlington M,D
The University of Texas at Austin D
The University of Texas at Brownsville M
The University of Texas at El Paso M,D
The University of Texas at San Antonio M
The University of Texas at Tyler M,O
The University of Texas of the Permian Basin M
The University of Texas–Pan American M
University of the Pacific M
University of Toledo M,D
University of Tulsa M,D
University of Utah M,D
University of Vermont D
University of Virginia M,D
University of Washington D
University of West Florida M
University of Wisconsin–Eau Claire M,O
University of Wisconsin–La Crosse M,O
University of Wisconsin–Madison D
University of Wisconsin–Milwaukee M,D
University of Wisconsin–Oshkosh M
University of Wisconsin–Stout M
University of Wisconsin–Whitewater M
University of Wyoming M,D
Utah State University M,D
Valdosta State University M,O
Valparaiso University M
Vanderbilt University M,D
Villanova University M
Virginia Commonwealth University D
Virginia Polytechnic Institute and State University M,D
Virginia State University M
Wake Forest University M
Walden University M,D
Washburn University of Topeka M
Washington State University M,D
Washington University in St. Louis M,D
Wayne State University M,D
West Chester University of Pennsylvania M
Western Carolina University M
Western Illinois University M,O
Western Kentucky University M,O
Western Michigan University M,D,O
Western Washington University M
Westfield State College M
West Texas A&M University M
West Virginia University M,D
Wichita State University M,D
Widener University
Wilmington College M
Winthrop University M,O
Wright State University M,D
Xavier University M,D
Yale University M,D
Yeshiva University M,D

■ PUBLIC HEALTH—GENERAL

Arcadia University M
Armstrong Atlantic State University M
Benedictine University M
Boise State University M
Boston University M,D,O
Bowling Green State University M
Brooklyn College of the City University of New York M
California State University, Fresno M
California State University, Northridge M
Case Western Reserve University M
Cleveland State University M,D
Columbia University M,D
East Stroudsburg University of Pennsylvania M
East Tennessee State University M,O
Emerson College M
Emory University M,D
Florida Agricultural and Mechanical University M,D
Florida International University M
The George Washington University M,D
Georgia Southern University M
Harvard University M,D,O
Hunter College of the City University of New York M
Idaho State University M,O
Indiana University Bloomington M,D,O
Johns Hopkins University M,D,O
Kent State University M
Loma Linda University M,D
MCP Hahnemann University M
Morgan State University D
New Mexico State University M
New York University M,D,O
Northern Arizona University M
Northern Illinois University M
Northwestern University M
Nova Southeastern University M
The Ohio State University M,D
Old Dominion University M,O
Oregon State University M
Portland State University M
Rutgers, The State University of New Jersey, New Brunswick M,D
Saint Louis University M,D
Saint Xavier University M,O
San Diego State University M,D
San Francisco State University M
San Jose State University M,O
Southern Connecticut State University M
State University of New York at Albany M,D
Temple University M
Tufts University M
Tulane University M,D,O
University at Buffalo, The State University of New York M,D
The University of Akron M,D
The University of Alabama at Birmingham M,D
The University of Arizona M
University of California, Berkeley M,D
University of California, Los Angeles M,D
University of California, San Diego D
University of Connecticut M
University of Denver M
University of Florida M
University of Hawaii at Manoa M
University of Illinois at Chicago M,D
University of Illinois at Springfield M
The University of Iowa M,D
University of Kansas M
University of Kentucky M,D
University of Maryland, College Park M,D
University of Massachusetts Amherst M,D
University of Miami M
University of Michigan M,D
University of Minnesota, Twin Cities Campus M,D
University of New Mexico M
The University of North Carolina at Chapel Hill M,D
University of Northern Colorado M
University of Pittsburgh M,D,O
University of Rochester M
University of South Carolina M
University of Southern California M
University of Southern Mississippi M
University of South Florida M,D
The University of Tennessee M
University of Toledo M
University of Utah M
University of Washington M,D
University of Wisconsin–Eau Claire M
University of Wisconsin–La Crosse M
Vanderbilt University M
Virginia Commonwealth University M
West Chester University of Pennsylvania M
Western Kentucky University M
West Virginia University M
Wichita State University M
Yale University M,D

■ PUBLIC HISTORY

Appalachian State University M
Arizona State University M,D
California State University, Sacramento M
Eastern Illinois University M
Florida State University M,D
Indiana University–Purdue University Indianapolis M
New York University M,D,O
North Carolina State University M
Northeastern University M,D
Rutgers, The State University of New Jersey, Camden M
Simmons College
Sonoma State University M
State University of New York at Albany M,D,O
University of Arkansas at Little Rock M
University of Houston M,D
University of Illinois at Springfield M
University of Kansas M
University of Massachusetts Amherst M,D
University of Massachusetts Boston M
University of New Orleans M
University of South Carolina M,O
The University of Texas at Austin M
Wayne State University M,D,O

■ PUBLIC POLICY AND ADMINISTRATION

Albany State University M
Alfred University M
American International College M
American University M,D
Angelo State University M
Anna Maria College M
Appalachian State University M
Arizona State University M,D
Arkansas State University M,O
Auburn University M,D
Auburn University Montgomery M,D

Augusta State University	M
Ball State University	M
Baylor University	M
Bernard M. Baruch College of the City University of New York	M
Boise State University	M
Boston University	M
Bowie State University	M
Bowling Green State University	M
Brandeis University	D
Bridgewater State College	M
Brigham Young University	M
Brooklyn College of the City University of New York	M
California Lutheran University	M
California State University, Bakersfield	M
California State University, Chico	M
California State University, Dominguez Hills	M
California State University, Fresno	M
California State University, Fullerton	M
California State University, Hayward	M
California State University, Long Beach	M,O
California State University, Los Angeles	M
California State University, Northridge	M
California State University, Sacramento	M
California State University, San Bernardino	M
California State University, Stanislaus	M
Carnegie Mellon University	M,D
Central Michigan University	M,O
Central Missouri State University	M,O
Chaminade University of Honolulu	M
City University	M,O
Claremont Graduate University	M,D
Clark Atlanta University	M
Clark University	M,O
Clemson University	M,D,O
Cleveland State University	M,D
The College of William and Mary	M
Columbia University	M
Columbus State University	M
Concordia University Wisconsin	M
Cornell University	M
Cumberland University	M
DePaul University	M
Drake University	M
Duke University	M
Duquesne University	M,O
East Carolina University	M
Eastern Kentucky University	M
Eastern Michigan University	M
Eastern Washington University	M
Fairleigh Dickinson University, Teaneck–Hackensack Campus	M
Florida Atlantic University	M,D
Florida Gulf Coast University	M
Florida Institute of Technology	M
Florida International University	M,D
Florida State University	M,D,O
Framingham State College	M
Gannon University	M,O
George Mason University	M,D
Georgetown University	M
The George Washington University	M,D
Georgia College and State University	M
Georgia Institute of Technology	M,D
Georgia Southern University	M
Georgia State University	M,D
Governors State University	M
Grambling State University	M
Grand Valley State University	M
Hamline University	M
Harvard University	M,D
Howard University	M
Idaho State University	M
Illinois Institute of Technology	M
Indiana State University	M
Indiana University Bloomington	M,D
Indiana University Northwest	M,O
Indiana University of Pennsylvania	M
Indiana University–Purdue University Fort Wayne	M,O
Indiana University–Purdue University Indianapolis	M,O
Indiana University South Bend	M
Iowa State University of Science and Technology	M
Jackson State University	M,D
Jacksonville State University	M
James Madison University	M
Johns Hopkins University	M
Kansas State University	M
Kean University	M
Kennesaw State University	M
Kent State University	M
Kentucky State University	M
Kutztown University of Pennsylvania	M
Lamar University	M
Long Island University, Brooklyn Campus	M
Long Island University, C.W. Post Campus	M,O
Louisiana State University and Agricultural and Mechanical College	M
Marist College	M,O
Marywood University	M
Metropolitan State University	M
Michigan State University	M,D
Midwestern State University	M
Minnesota State University, Mankato	M
Minnesota State University Moorhead	M
Mississippi State University	M,D
Montana State University–Bozeman	M
Monterey Institute of International Studies	M
Murray State University	M
National University	M
New Mexico Highlands University	M
New School University	D
New York University	M,D,O
North Carolina Central University	M
North Carolina State University	M,D
Northeastern University	M,D
Northern Arizona University	M,D
Northern Illinois University	M
Northern Kentucky University	M
Northern Michigan University	M
North Georgia College & State University	M
Northwestern University	D
Notre Dame de Namur University	M
Nova Southeastern University	M,D
Oakland University	M
The Ohio State University	M,D
Ohio University	M
Oklahoma City University	M
Oklahoma State University	M
Old Dominion University	M
Pace University, White Plains Campus	M
Park University	M
The Pennsylvania State University Harrisburg Campus of the Capital College	M,D
Pepperdine University	M
Piedmont College	M
Pontifical Catholic University of Puerto Rico	M
Portland State University	M,D
Princeton University	M,D
Regent University	M
Roosevelt University	M
Rutgers, The State University of New Jersey, Camden	M
Rutgers, The State University of New Jersey, Newark	M,D
Rutgers, The State University of New Jersey, New Brunswick	M
Sage Graduate School	M
St. Edward's University	M,O
Saint Louis University	M,D
Saint Mary's University of Minnesota	M
St. Mary's University of San Antonio	M
St. Thomas University	M,O
San Diego State University	M
San Francisco State University	M
San Jose State University	M
Savannah State University	M
Seattle University	M
Seton Hall University	M
Shenandoah University	M,O
Shippensburg University of Pennsylvania	M
Sonoma State University	M
Southeastern University	M
Southeast Missouri State University	M
Southern Illinois University Carbondale	M
Southern University and Agricultural and Mechanical College	M,D
Southwest Missouri State University	M
Southwest Texas State University	M
State University of New York at Albany	M,D,O
State University of New York at Binghamton	M,D
State University of New York College at Brockport	M
State University of New York Empire State College	M
State University of West Georgia	M
Stephen F. Austin State University	M
Stony Brook University, State University of New York	M,O
Suffolk University	M,O
Sul Ross State University	M
Syracuse University	M,D
Tennessee State University	M,D
Texas A&M International University	M
Texas A&M University	M
Texas A&M University–Corpus Christi	M
Texas Southern University	M
Texas Tech University	M,D
Troy State University	M
Tufts University	M
Tulane University	M
The University of Akron	M
The University of Alabama	M,D
The University of Alabama at Birmingham	M
The University of Alabama in Huntsville	M
University of Alaska Anchorage	M
University of Alaska Southeast	M
The University of Arizona	M,D
University of Arkansas	M,D
University of Arkansas at Little Rock	M
University of Baltimore	M,D
University of California, Berkeley	M,D
University of California, Los Angeles	M
University of Central Florida	M,D,O
University of Chicago	M,D
University of Cincinnati	M,D
University of Colorado at Boulder	M,D
University of Colorado at Colorado Springs	M
University of Colorado at Denver	M,D
University of Connecticut	M

University of Dayton M
University of Delaware M,D
University of Detroit Mercy M
The University of Findlay M
University of Florida M,D,O
University of Georgia M,D
University of Guam M
University of Hawaii at Manoa M,O
University of Houston–Clear Lake M
University of Idaho M
University of Illinois at Chicago M,D
University of Illinois at Springfield M,D
University of Kansas M
University of Kentucky M,D
University of La Verne M,D
University of Louisville M
University of Maine M
University of Maryland, Baltimore County M,D
University of Maryland, College Park M,D
University of Massachusetts Amherst M
University of Massachusetts Boston M
The University of Memphis M
University of Michigan M,D
University of Michigan–Dearborn M
University of Michigan–Flint M
University of Minnesota, Twin Cities Campus M
University of Missouri–Columbia M
University of Missouri–Kansas City M,D
University of Missouri–St. Louis M,D,O
The University of Montana–Missoula M
University of Nebraska at Omaha M,D
University of Nevada, Las Vegas M
University of Nevada, Reno M
University of New Hampshire M
University of New Haven M
University of New Mexico M
University of New Orleans M
The University of North Carolina at Chapel Hill M,D
The University of North Carolina at Charlotte M
The University of North Carolina at Greensboro M,O
The University of North Carolina at Pembroke M
University of North Dakota M
University of Northern Iowa M
University of North Florida M
University of North Texas M
University of Oklahoma M
University of Oregon M
University of Pennsylvania M,D
University of Pittsburgh M,D
University of Puerto Rico, Río Piedras M
University of Rhode Island M
University of San Francisco M
University of South Alabama M
University of South Carolina M
University of South Dakota M
University of Southern California M,D,O
University of Southern Maine M,D
University of South Florida M
The University of Tennessee M
The University of Tennessee at Chattanooga M
The University of Texas at Arlington M,D
The University of Texas at Austin M,D
The University of Texas at Dallas M
The University of Texas at San Antonio M
The University of Texas at Tyler M
The University of Texas–Pan American M
University of the District of Columbia M
University of the Pacific P,M,D
University of the Virgin Islands M
University of Toledo M
University of Utah M,O
University of Vermont M
University of Washington M
University of West Florida M
University of Wisconsin–Madison M
University of Wisconsin–Milwaukee M
University of Wisconsin–Oshkosh M
University of Wisconsin–Whitewater M
University of Wyoming M
Valdosta State University M
Villanova University M
Virginia Commonwealth University M,D,O
Virginia Polytechnic Institute and State University M,D,O
Washington State University M
Washington University in St. Louis M
Wayne State University M
Webster University M
West Chester University of Pennsylvania M
Western Carolina University M
Western International University M
Western Kentucky University M
Western Michigan University M,D
West Virginia University M,D
Wichita State University M
Widener University M
Wilmington College M
Wright State University M

■ PUBLISHING

Drexel University M
Emerson College M
New York University M
Northwestern University M
Pace University, New York City Campus M
Rochester Institute of Technology M
University of Baltimore M

■ QUALITY MANAGEMENT

California State University, Dominguez Hills M
Case Western Reserve University M,D
Dowling College M,O
Eastern Michigan University M
Hawaii Pacific University M
Loyola University New Orleans M
Madonna University M
Marian College of Fond du Lac M
North Carolina State University M
The Pennsylvania State University University Park Campus M
Rutgers, The State University of New Jersey, New Brunswick M,D
San Jose State University M
The University of Akron M
University of Central Florida M,O
University of Dubuque M

■ QUANTITATIVE ANALYSIS

California State University, Hayward M
Clark Atlanta University M
Drexel University M,D,O
Fairleigh Dickinson University, Teaneck–Hackensack Campus M
Hofstra University M
Louisiana Tech University M,D
Loyola College in Maryland M
New York University M,D,O
Purdue University M,D
St. John's University (NY) M,O
Saint Louis University M,D
Texas Tech University M,D
Troy State University Dothan M
University of Cincinnati M,D
University of Missouri–St. Louis M,O
The University of North Carolina at Chapel Hill D
University of Oregon M,D
University of Rhode Island M,D
The University of Texas at Arlington M,D
Virginia Commonwealth University M

■ RADIATION BIOLOGY

Auburn University M
Colorado State University M,D
Florida State University M,D
Georgetown University M
University of California, Irvine M,D
The University of Iowa M,D

■ RANGE SCIENCE

Brigham Young University M,D
Colorado State University M,D
Kansas State University M,D
Montana State University–Bozeman M
New Mexico State University M,D
North Dakota State University M,D
Oregon State University M,D
Sul Ross State University M
Texas A&M University M,D
Texas A&M University–Kingsville M
Texas Tech University M,D
The University of Arizona M,D
University of California, Berkeley M,D
University of Idaho M,D
University of Wyoming M,D
Utah State University M,D

■ READING EDUCATION

Abilene Christian University M
Adelphi University M,O
Alabama State University M,O
Albany State University M
Alfred University M
American International College M,D,O
Andrews University M
Angelo State University M
Anna Maria College M
Appalachian State University M
Arcadia University M,O
Arkansas State University M,O
Ashland University M
Auburn University M,D,O
Auburn University Montgomery M,O
Austin Peay State University M,O
Averett University M
Baldwin-Wallace College M
Ball State University M,D
Barry University M,O
Bloomsburg University of Pennsylvania M
Boise State University M
Boston College M,O
Boston University M,D,O
Bowie State University M
Bowling Green State University M,O
Bridgewater State College M,O
Brigham Young University M,D
Brooklyn College of the City University of New York M
Butler University M,O
California Baptist University M
California Lutheran University M
California Polytechnic State University, San Luis Obispo M
California State University, Bakersfield M
California State University, Chico M
California State University, Fresno M
California State University, Fullerton M

California State University, Los Angeles M
California State University, Sacramento M
California State University, San Bernardino M
California State University, Stanislaus M
California University of Pennsylvania M
Canisius College M
Cardinal Stritch University M
Carthage College M,O
Castleton State College M,O
Central Connecticut State University M,O
Central Michigan University M
Central Missouri State University M,O
Central Washington University M
Chapman University M
Chicago State University M
The Citadel, The Military College of South Carolina M
City College of the City University of New York M,O
City University M,O
Claremont Graduate University M,D
Clarion University of Pennsylvania M
Clemson University M
Cleveland State University M
College of Mount St. Joseph M
The College of New Jersey M
The College of New Rochelle M
College of Our Lady of the Elms M,O
College of St. Joseph M
The College of Saint Rose M
The College of William and Mary M
Concordia University (CA) M
Concordia University (IL) M,O
Concordia University (NE) M
Concordia University Wisconsin M
Cumberland College M
Dallas Baptist University M
DePaul University M
Dowling College M
Duquesne University M
East Carolina University M
Eastern Connecticut State University M
Eastern Kentucky University M
Eastern Michigan University M
Eastern Nazarene College M,O
Eastern Washington University M
East Stroudsburg University of Pennsylvania M
East Tennessee State University M
Edinboro University of Pennsylvania M,O
Emporia State University M
Ferris State University M
Florida Atlantic University M
Florida Gulf Coast University M
Florida International University M
Florida State University M,D,O
Fordham University M,D,O
Framingham State College M
Fresno Pacific University M
Frostburg State University M
Gannon University M,O
George Mason University M
Georgian Court College M
Georgia Southern University M,O
Georgia Southwestern State University M,O
Georgia State University M,O
Governors State University M
Grand Canyon University M
Grand Valley State University M
Gwynedd-Mercy College M
Hardin-Simmons University M
Harvard University M,D,O
Henderson State University M
Hofstra University M,D,O
Holy Family College M
Hood College M
Houston Baptist University M
Howard University M,O
Hunter College of the City University of New York M,O
Idaho State University M,O
Illinois State University M
Indiana State University M,D,O
Indiana University Bloomington M,D,O
Indiana University of Pennsylvania M
Indiana University–Purdue University Indianapolis M
Jacksonville University M
James Madison University M
Johns Hopkins University M,D,O
Johnson State College M
Kean University M,O
Kent State University M
King's College M
Kutztown University of Pennsylvania M
Lake Erie College M
Lamar University M,O
Lehman College of the City University of New York M
Lesley University M,D,O
Liberty University M,D
Long Island University, Brooklyn Campus M
Long Island University, C.W. Post Campus M,O
Longwood College M
Louisiana Tech University M,D,O
Loyola College in Maryland M,O
Loyola Marymount University M
Loyola University New Orleans M
Lynchburg College M
Madonna University M
Malone College M
Manhattanville College M
Marshall University M,O
Marygrove College M
Marywood University M
McNeese State University M
Mercer University M,O
Mercy College M,O
Miami University M
Michigan State University M
Middle Tennessee State University M
Midwestern State University M
Millersville University of Pennsylvania M
Minnesota State University, Mankato M
Minnesota State University Moorhead M
Monmouth University M,O
Montana State University–Billings M
Montclair State University M
Morehead State University M
Murray State University M
National-Louis University M,D,O
Nazareth College of Rochester M
New Jersey City University M
New Mexico State University M,D,O
New York University M,D,O
Niagara University M
North Carolina Agricultural and Technical State University M
Northeastern Illinois University M
Northeastern State University M
Northern Arizona University M
Northern Illinois University M,D
Northern State University M
Northwestern Oklahoma State University M
Northwestern State University of Louisiana M,O
Northwest Missouri State University M
Nova Southeastern University M,O
Oakland University M,D,O
Ohio University M,D
Old Dominion University M
Pacific Lutheran University M
The Pennsylvania State University University Park Campus M,D
Pittsburg State University M
Plattsburgh State University of New York M
Plymouth State College M
Portland State University M
Providence College M
Purdue University M,D,O
Queens College of the City University of New York M
Radford University M
Rhode Island College M,O
Rider University M
Rivier College M
Rockford College M
Roosevelt University M,D
Rowan University M
Rutgers, The State University of New Jersey, New Brunswick M,D
Sage Graduate School M
Saginaw Valley State University M
St. Bonaventure University M
St. Cloud State University M
St. John Fisher College M
St. John's University (NY) M,O
Saint Joseph's University M
Saint Martin's College M
Saint Mary's College of California M
St. Mary's University of San Antonio M
Saint Michael's College M,O
Saint Peter's College M
St. Thomas Aquinas College M,O
Saint Xavier University M,O
Salem State College M
Salisbury State University M
Sam Houston State University M,O
San Diego State University M
San Francisco State University M,O
Seattle Pacific University M
Shippensburg University of Pennsylvania M
Siena Heights University M
Slippery Rock University of Pennsylvania M
Sonoma State University M
Southern Connecticut State University M,O
Southern Oregon University M
Southwest Missouri State University M
Southwest Texas State University M
Spalding University M
State University of New York at Albany M,D,O
State University of New York at Binghamton M
State University of New York at New Paltz M
State University of New York at Oswego M
State University of New York College at Brockport M
State University of New York College at Buffalo M
State University of New York College at Cortland M
State University of New York College at Fredonia M
State University of New York College at Geneseo M
State University of New York College at Oneonta M
State University of New York College at Potsdam M
State University of West Georgia M

Sul Ross State University	M
Syracuse University	M,D,O
Tarleton State University	M,O
Teachers College, Columbia University	M
Temple University	M,D
Tennessee Technological University	M,O
Texas A&M International University	M
Texas A&M University	M,D
Texas A&M University–Commerce	M,D
Texas A&M University–Kingsville	M
Texas Southern University	M,D
Texas Tech University	M,D,O
Texas Woman's University	M,D
Towson University	M
University at Buffalo, The State University of New York	M,D,O
The University of Arizona	M,D,O
University of Arkansas at Little Rock	M,O
University of Bridgeport	M,O
University of California, Berkeley	M,D,O
University of Central Arkansas	M
University of Central Florida	M
University of Central Oklahoma	M
University of Cincinnati	M,D
University of Connecticut	M,D
University of Dayton	M
University of Florida	M,D,O
University of Georgia	M,D,O
University of Guam	M
University of Houston	M,D
University of Houston–Clear Lake	M
University of Illinois at Chicago	M,D
University of La Verne	M
University of Louisiana at Monroe	M
University of Louisville	M
University of Maine	M,D,O
University of Mary Hardin-Baylor	M
University of Maryland, College Park	M,D,O
University of Massachusetts Amherst	M,D,O
University of Massachusetts Lowell	M,D,O
The University of Memphis	M,D
University of Miami	M,D,O
University of Michigan	M,D
University of Missouri–Kansas City	M,D,O
University of Missouri–St. Louis	M,D
University of Nebraska at Kearney	M
University of Nebraska at Omaha	M
University of New Hampshire	M,D
University of North Alabama	M
The University of North Carolina at Chapel Hill	D
The University of North Carolina at Charlotte	M
The University of North Carolina at Pembroke	M
The University of North Carolina at Wilmington	M
University of North Dakota	M
University of Northern Colorado	M
University of Northern Iowa	M
University of North Texas	M,D
University of Oklahoma	M,D
University of Pennsylvania	M,D
University of Pittsburgh	M,D
University of Rhode Island	M
University of Rio Grande	M
University of Saint Francis (IN)	M
University of St. Thomas (MN)	M,D,O
The University of Scranton	M
University of Sioux Falls	M
University of South Alabama	M
University of South Carolina	M,D,O
University of Southern California	M,D
University of Southern Maine	M,O
University of Southern Mississippi	M,D,O
University of South Florida	M,D,O
The University of Tennessee	M,D,O
The University of Tennessee at Chattanooga	M,O
The University of Texas at Brownsville	M
The University of Texas at Tyler	M,O
The University of Texas of the Permian Basin	M
The University of Texas–Pan American	M
University of the Incarnate Word	M
University of Vermont	M
University of Washington	M,D
University of West Florida	M
University of Wisconsin–Eau Claire	M
University of Wisconsin–La Crosse	M
University of Wisconsin–Milwaukee	M
University of Wisconsin–Oshkosh	M
University of Wisconsin–River Falls	M
University of Wisconsin–Stevens Point	M
University of Wisconsin–Superior	M
University of Wisconsin–Whitewater	M
Valdosta State University	M,O
Vanderbilt University	M,D
Virginia Commonwealth University	M
Walla Walla College	M
Washburn University of Topeka	M
Washington State University	M,D
Wayne State University	M,D,O
West Chester University of Pennsylvania	M
Western Carolina University	M
Western Connecticut State University	M
Western Illinois University	M,O
Western Kentucky University	M
Western Michigan University	M
Western New Mexico University	M
Westfield State College	M
West Texas A&M University	M
West Virginia University	M
Wheelock College	M
Whitworth College	M
Widener University	M,D
William Paterson University of New Jersey	M
Wilmington College	M,D
Winthrop University	M
Worcester State College	M,O
Xavier University	M
Youngstown State University	M

■ REAL ESTATE

American University	M
California State University, Northridge	M
California State University, Sacramento	M
Columbia University	M
Cornell University	M
The George Washington University	M
Georgia State University	M,D
Johns Hopkins University	M,O
Massachusetts Institute of Technology	M
New York University	M
The Pennsylvania State University University Park Campus	M,D
Texas A&M University	M
University of California, Berkeley	D
University of Cincinnati	M
University of Colorado at Boulder	M,D
University of Denver	M
University of Florida	M,D
The University of Memphis	M,D
University of North Texas	M,D
University of Pennsylvania	M,D
University of St. Thomas (MN)	M,O
University of Southern California	M
The University of Texas at Arlington	M,D
University of Wisconsin–Madison	M
Virginia Commonwealth University	M,O
Webster University	M

■ RECREATION AND PARK MANAGEMENT

Adams State College	M
Arizona State University	M
Aurora University	M
Baylor University	M
Bowling Green State University	M
Brigham Young University	M
California State University, Chico	M
California State University, Long Beach	M
California State University, Northridge	M
California State University, Sacramento	M
Central Michigan University	M
Central Washington University	M
Clemson University	M,D
Cleveland State University	M
Colorado State University	M,D
Delta State University	M
East Carolina University	M
Eastern Kentucky University	M
Florida Agricultural and Mechanical University	M
Florida International University	M
Florida State University	M
Fort Hays State University	M
Frostburg State University	M
Georgia Southern University	M
Hardin-Simmons University	M
Howard University	M
Indiana University Bloomington	M,D,O
Lehman College of the City University of New York	M
Michigan State University	M,D
Middle Tennessee State University	M,D
Morehead State University	M
Murray State University	M
New York University	M,D,O
North Carolina Central University	M
North Carolina State University	M
Ohio University	M
Old Dominion University	M
Purdue University	M,D
San Francisco State University	M
San Jose State University	M
South Dakota State University	M
Southern Connecticut State University	M
Southern Illinois University Carbondale	M
Southern University and Agricultural and Mechanical College	M
Southwestern Oklahoma State University	M
Southwest Texas State University	M
Springfield College	M
State University of New York College at Brockport	M
State University of New York College at Cortland	M
Temple University	M
Tennessee State University	M
Texas A&M University	M,D
Universidad Metropolitana	M
University of Arkansas	M,D
University of Florida	M,D
University of Georgia	M,D
University of Idaho	M
University of Minnesota, Twin Cities Campus	M,D
University of Missouri–Columbia	M
The University of Montana–Missoula	M
University of Nebraska at Omaha	M
University of Nebraska–Lincoln	M
University of New Mexico	M,D,O
The University of North Carolina at Chapel Hill	M

The University of North Carolina at Greensboro	M
University of North Texas	M,O
University of Rhode Island	M
University of South Alabama	M
University of Southern Mississippi	M,D
The University of Tennessee	M
University of Toledo	M
University of Utah	M,D
University of Wisconsin–La Crosse	M
Utah State University	M,D
Virginia Commonwealth University	M
Virginia Polytechnic Institute and State University	M,D
Washington State University	M
Wayne State University	M
Western Illinois University	M
Western Kentucky University	M
West Virginia University	M
Wright State University	M

■ REHABILITATION COUNSELING

Arkansas State University	M,O
Assumption College	M,O
Barry University	M,O
Boston University	M,D,O
Bowling Green State University	M
California State University, Fresno	M
California State University, Los Angeles	M
California State University, San Bernardino	M
Central Connecticut State University	M
Coppin State College	M
East Central University	M
Edinboro University of Pennsylvania	M,O
Emporia State University	M
Florida State University	M,D,O
Fort Valley State University	M
The George Washington University	M,D
Georgia State University	M,O
Hofstra University	M,O
Hunter College of the City University of New York	M
Illinois Institute of Technology	M,D
Indiana University–Purdue University Indianapolis	M,D
Jackson State University	M,O
Kent State University	M,O
La Salle University	D
Maryville University of Saint Louis	M
Michigan State University	M,D,O
Minnesota State University, Mankato	M
Montana State University–Billings	M
New York University	M,D
Northeastern University	M
Ohio University	M,D
St. Cloud State University	M
St. John's University (NY)	M,O
San Diego State University	M
San Francisco State University	M
South Carolina State University	M
Southern Illinois University Carbondale	M,D
Southern University and Agricultural and Mechanical College	M
Springfield College	M,O
State University of New York at Albany	M
Syracuse University	M,D
University at Buffalo, The State University of New York	M,D,O
The University of Alabama	M,D,O
The University of Alabama at Birmingham	M
The University of Arizona	M,D,O
University of Arkansas	M,D
University of Cincinnati	M,D,O
University of Florida	M
University of Illinois at Urbana–Champaign	M
The University of Iowa	M,D
University of Kentucky	M
University of Louisiana at Lafayette	M
University of Maryland, College Park	M,D,O
The University of Memphis	M,D
University of Nevada, Las Vegas	M
The University of North Carolina at Chapel Hill	M,D
University of Northern Colorado	M,D
University of North Texas	M
University of Puerto Rico, Río Piedras	M
The University of Scranton	M
University of South Carolina	M
University of South Florida	M
The University of Tennessee	M
The University of Texas–Pan American	M
University of Wisconsin–Madison	M,D
University of Wisconsin–Milwaukee	M
University of Wisconsin–Stout	M
Utah State University	M
Virginia Commonwealth University	M,O
Wayne State University	M,D,O
Western Michigan University	M
Western Oregon University	M
Western Washington University	M
West Virginia University	M
Wilmington College	M
Wright State University	M

■ REHABILITATION SCIENCES

Boston University	M,D
East Carolina University	M
East Stroudsburg University of Pennsylvania	M
Northeastern Illinois University	M
St. Ambrose University	M
University at Buffalo, The State University of New York	D
University of Delaware	M
University of Florida	D
University of Illinois at Urbana–Champaign	M
University of Minnesota, Twin Cities Campus	M,D
University of North Texas	M
University of Pittsburgh	M,D,O
University of Washington	M
University of Wisconsin–La Crosse	M
University of Wisconsin–Madison	M
Wayne State University	M

■ RELIABILITY ENGINEERING

The University of Arizona	M
University of Maryland, College Park	M,D

■ RELIGION

Arizona State University	M
Azusa Pacific University	P,M,D
Bayamón Central University	P,M
Baylor University	M,D
Biola University	P,M,D
Boston University	M,D
Brown University	M,D
Cardinal Stritch University	M
The Catholic University of America	M,D,O
Chestnut Hill College	M
Claremont Graduate University	M,D
College of Our Lady of the Elms	M
Colorado Christian University	M
Columbia University	M,D
Concordia University (IL)	M,O
Duke University	M,D
Edgewood College	M
Emory University	D
Florida International University	M
Florida State University	M,D
Fordham University	M,O
George Fox University	P,M,D
The George Washington University	M
Gonzaga University	P,M
Grand Rapids Baptist Seminary	P,M,D
Hardin-Simmons University	M
Harvard University	M,D
Holy Names College	M,O
Indiana State University	M
Indiana University Bloomington	M,D
John Carroll University	M
La Salle University	M
La Sierra University	M
Liberty University	M
Lipscomb University	P,M
Loras College	M
Loyola University New Orleans	M
Miami University	M
Mount St. Mary's College	M
New York University	M,O
Northwest Nazarene University	M
Oklahoma City University	M
Olivet Nazarene University	M
Pepperdine University	P,M
Point Loma Nazarene University	M
Princeton University	D
Providence College	M
Rice University	M,D
Sacred Heart University	M
Santa Clara University	M
Seton Hall University	M
Southern Methodist University	M,D
Southern Nazarene University	M
Southwest Missouri State University	M
Spalding University	M
Stanford University	M,D
Syracuse University	M,D
Temple University	M,D
Trevecca Nazarene University	M
University of California, Berkeley	D
University of California, Santa Barbara	M,D
University of Chicago	P,M,D
University of Colorado at Boulder	M
University of Denver	M,D
University of Detroit Mercy	M
University of Florida	M
University of Georgia	M
University of Hawaii at Manoa	M
The University of Iowa	M,D
University of Kansas	M
University of Missouri–Columbia	M
The University of North Carolina at Chapel Hill	M,D
University of North Texas	M
University of Notre Dame	M
University of Pennsylvania	D
University of Pittsburgh	M,D
University of St. Thomas (MN)	M
University of South Carolina	M
University of Southern California	M,D
University of South Florida	M
The University of Tennessee	M,D
University of the Incarnate Word	M
University of Virginia	M,D
University of Washington	M
Vanderbilt University	M,D
Wake Forest University	M
Washington University in St. Louis	M
Wayland Baptist University	M
Western Kentucky University	M
Western Michigan University	M,D
Yale University	D

■ RELIGIOUS EDUCATION

Andrews University	M,D,O
Ashland University	P,M,D
Azusa Pacific University	P,M,D
Biola University	P,M,D
Boston College	M,D,O
Campbell University	P,M
The Catholic University of America	M,D
Concordia University (NE)	M
Fordham University	M,O
Gardner-Webb University	P
George Fox University	P,M,D
Golden Gate Baptist Theological Seminary	P,M,D,O
Grand Rapids Baptist Seminary	P,M,D
Gratz College	M,O
La Sierra University	M
Loyola University Chicago	M
North Park Theological Seminary	M
Notre Dame de Namur University	M,O
Nova Southeastern University	M,O
Oklahoma City University	M
Oral Roberts University	P,M,D
Pfeiffer University	M
Pontifical Catholic University of Puerto Rico	M,D
Teachers College, Columbia University	M,D
University of Portland	M
University of St. Thomas (MN)	M,D
University of San Francisco	M,D
Xavier University	M
Yeshiva University	M,D,O

■ REPRODUCTIVE BIOLOGY

Cornell University	M,D
Johns Hopkins University	M,D
Northwestern University	D
University of Hawaii at Manoa	M,D
University of Wyoming	M,D
West Virginia University	M,D

■ ROMANCE LANGUAGES

Appalachian State University	M
The Catholic University of America	M,D
Clark Atlanta University	M
Columbia University	M,D
Cornell University	D
New York University	M,D
Southern Connecticut State University	M
Stony Brook University, State University of New York	M,D
Texas Tech University	M,D
The University of Alabama	M,D
University of California, Berkeley	D
University of California, Los Angeles	M,D
University of Georgia	M,D
University of Miami	D
University of Michigan	D
University of Missouri–Columbia	M,D
University of Missouri–Kansas City	M
University of New Orleans	M
The University of North Carolina at Chapel Hill	M,D
University of Notre Dame	M
University of Oregon	M,D
University of Pennsylvania	M,D
The University of Texas at Austin	M,D
University of Washington	M,D
Washington University in St. Louis	M,D

■ RURAL PLANNING AND STUDIES

California State University, Chico	M
Cornell University	M
Iowa State University of Science and Technology	M,D
State University of West Georgia	M
University of Alaska Fairbanks	M,D
University of Wyoming	M

■ RURAL SOCIOLOGY

Auburn University	M,D
Cornell University	M,D
Iowa State University of Science and Technology	M,D
North Carolina State University	M,D
The Ohio State University	M,D
The Pennsylvania State University University Park Campus	M,D
South Dakota State University	M,D
University of Missouri–Columbia	M,D
The University of Montana–Missoula	M
The University of Tennessee	M
University of Wisconsin–Madison	M,D

■ RUSSIAN

American University	M,O
Boston College	M
Brigham Young University	M
Brown University	M,D
Columbia University	M,D
Harvard University	M,D
Michigan State University	M,D
Monterey Institute of International Studies	M
New York University	M
The Pennsylvania State University University Park Campus	M
San Francisco State University	M
Stanford University	M,D
State University of New York at Albany	M,O
Stony Brook University, State University of New York	M,D
The University of Arizona	M
University of California, Berkeley	M,D
University of Illinois at Urbana–Champaign	M,D
The University of Iowa	M
University of Maryland, Baltimore County	M
University of Maryland, College Park	M
University of Michigan	M,D
The University of North Carolina at Chapel Hill	M,D
University of Oregon	M
The University of Tennessee	D
University of Washington	M,D

■ SAFETY ENGINEERING

Central Missouri State University	M,O
Embry-Riddle Aeronautical University	M
Murray State University	M
New Jersey Institute of Technology	M
Texas A&M University	M
University of Minnesota, Duluth	M
University of Wisconsin–Stout	M
West Virginia University	M

■ SCANDINAVIAN LANGUAGES

Brigham Young University	M
Harvard University	M,D
University of California, Berkeley	M,D
University of California, Los Angeles	M,D
University of Minnesota, Twin Cities Campus	M,D
University of Washington	M,D
University of Wisconsin–Madison	M,D

■ SCHOOL NURSING

Capital University	M
Kutztown University of Pennsylvania	O
La Salle University	M,O
Monmouth University	M,O
Seton Hall University	M
University of Minnesota, Twin Cities Campus	M
Wright State University	M

■ SCHOOL PSYCHOLOGY

Abilene Christian University	M
Alabama Agricultural and Mechanical University	M,O
Alfred University	M,D,O
American International College	M,O
Andrews University	M,O
Appalachian State University	M,O
Arcadia University	M
Argosy University-Sarasota	M,D,O
Auburn University	M,D,O
Austin Peay State University	M
Ball State University	M,D,O
Barry University	M,O
Bowling Green State University	M
Brigham Young University	M,D
Brooklyn College of the City University of New York	M,O
Butler University	M,O
California State University, Los Angeles	M
California State University, Sacramento	M
California University of Pennsylvania	M
Central Connecticut State University	M
Central Michigan University	D,O
Central Washington University	M
The Citadel, The Military College of South Carolina	O
City University	M,O
Cleveland State University	M,O
The College of New Rochelle	M
College of St. Joseph	M
The College of Saint Rose	M,O
The College of William and Mary	M,O
Duquesne University	M,O
East Carolina University	
Eastern Illinois University	O
Eastern Kentucky University	M,O
Eastern Washington University	M
Edinboro University of Pennsylvania	O
Emporia State University	M,O
Fairfield University	M,O
Fairleigh Dickinson University, Teaneck–Hackensack Campus	M,D
Florida Agricultural and Mechanical University	M
Florida International University	O
Florida State University	M,O
Fordham University	M,D,O
Fort Hays State University	O
Francis Marion University	M
Fresno Pacific University	M
Gallaudet University	M,O
Gardner-Webb University	M
George Mason University	M
Georgia Southern University	M,O
Georgia State University	M,D,O
Hofstra University	M,D,O
Howard University	M,D,O
Idaho State University	M,O
Illinois State University	D,O
Immaculata College	M,D,O
Indiana State University	M,D,O
Indiana University Bloomington	M,D,O
Indiana University of Pennsylvania	D
Iona College	M
James Madison University	M,O
Kean University	M,O
Kent State University	M,D,O

La Sierra University M,O
Lehigh University D,O
Lesley University M,O
Long Island University, Brooklyn Campus M
Louisiana State University and Agricultural and Mechanical College M,D
Louisiana State University in Shreveport O
Loyola Marymount University M
Loyola University Chicago M,D
Marist College M,O
Marshall University O
Miami University M,O
Michigan State University M,D,O
Middle Tennessee State University M,O
Millersville University of Pennsylvania M
Minnesota State University Moorhead M,O
National-Louis University M,D,O
National University M
New Jersey City University O
New York University M,D,O
Nicholls State University M,O
Northeastern University M,D,O
Northern Arizona University M,D
Nova Southeastern University M
Pace University, New York City Campus M,D
The Pennsylvania State University University Park Campus M,D
Pittsburg State University O
Plattsburgh State University of New York M,O
Pontifical Catholic University of Puerto Rico M,D
Queens College of the City University of New York M,O
Radford University O
Rhode Island College O
Rochester Institute of Technology M,O
Rowan University M,O
Rutgers, The State University of New Jersey, New Brunswick M,D
St. John's University (NY) M,D
Sam Houston State University M
San Diego State University M
Seattle Pacific University O
Seattle University O
Seton Hall University O
Southern Connecticut State University M,O
Southern Illinois University Edwardsville O
Southwest Texas State University M
State University of New York at Albany M,D,O
State University of New York at Oswego M,O
Stephen F. Austin State University M
Syracuse University D
Tarleton State University M
Teachers College, Columbia University M,D
Temple University M,D
Tennessee State University M,D
Texas A&M University D
Texas Woman's University M,D
Towson University M,O
Trinity University M
Tufts University M,O
University at Buffalo, The State University of New York M,D,O
The University of Akron M,D
The University of Alabama M,D,O
The University of Alabama at Birmingham M
University of California, Berkeley D
University of California, Santa Barbara M,D
University of Central Arkansas M,D
University of Central Florida O
University of Cincinnati M,D
University of Colorado at Denver O
University of Connecticut M,D
University of Dayton M
University of Delaware M,D
University of Denver M,D,O
University of Detroit Mercy M,O
University of Florida M,D,O
University of Georgia M,D,O
University of Hartford M
University of Houston–Clear Lake M
University of Idaho O
University of Kansas D,O
University of Louisiana at Monroe O
University of Maryland, College Park M,D,O
University of Massachusetts Amherst D
University of Massachusetts Boston M,O
The University of Memphis M,D
University of Minnesota, Twin Cities Campus M,D,O
The University of Montana–Missoula M,O
University of Nebraska at Kearney M,O
University of Nebraska at Omaha M,D,O
University of Nevada, Las Vegas M,D,O
The University of North Carolina at Chapel Hill M,D
The University of North Carolina at Greensboro M,D,O
University of Northern Colorado D,O
University of Northern Iowa M,O
University of North Texas M,D
University of Oregon M,D
University of Pennsylvania D
University of Rhode Island M,D
University of South Carolina D
University of Southern Maine M
University of South Florida D,O
The University of Tennessee M,D,O
The University of Tennessee at Chattanooga M
The University of Texas at Austin M,D
The University of Texas at Tyler M,O
The University of Texas–Pan American M,D
University of the Pacific M,D
University of Toledo M,O
University of Washington M,D
University of Wisconsin–Eau Claire M,O
University of Wisconsin–La Crosse M,O
University of Wisconsin–River Falls M
University of Wisconsin–Stout M,O
University of Wisconsin–Whitewater M
Utah State University M,D
Valdosta State University M,O
Valparaiso University M
Wayne State University M,D,O
Western Carolina University M
Western Illinois University M,O
Western Kentucky University M,O
Western Michigan University M,D,O
Wichita State University M,D,O
Wilmington College M
Yeshiva University D

■ SCIENCE EDUCATION

Alabama State University M,O
Albany State University M
Alfred University M
Andrews University M
Antioch New England Graduate School M
Arcadia University M,O
Arizona State University M,D
Arkansas State University M,D,O
Armstrong Atlantic State University M
Auburn University M,D,O
Averett University M
Ball State University M,D
Bemidji State University M
Bloomsburg University of Pennsylvania M
Boise State University M,D
Boston College M
Boston University M,D,O
Bowling Green State University M,D,O
Bridgewater State College M
Brigham Young University M,D
Brooklyn College of the City University of New York M
Brown University M
California State University, Fullerton M
California University of Pennsylvania M
Carthage College M,O
Central Connecticut State University M
Central Michigan University M
Charleston Southern University M
The Citadel, The Military College of South Carolina M
City College of the City University of New York M
Clarion University of Pennsylvania M
Clark Atlanta University M,D
Clemson University M
College of Our Lady of the Elms M,O
The College of William and Mary M
Columbus State University M,O
Cornell University M,D
Delaware State University M
DePaul University M
DeSales University M
East Carolina University M
Eastern Connecticut State University M
Eastern Kentucky University M
Eastern Michigan University M
Eastern Washington University M
East Stroudsburg University of Pennsylvania M
Edinboro University of Pennsylvania M
Fayetteville State University M
Fitchburg State College M
Florida Gulf Coast University M
Florida Institute of Technology M,D,O
Florida International University M
Florida State University M,D,O
Fresno Pacific University M
Gannon University M,O
Georgia College and State University M,O
Georgia Southern University M,O
Georgia State University M,D,O
Grambling State University M
Harvard University M,D,O
Henderson State University M
Hofstra University M
Hood College M
Hunter College of the City University of New York M
Illinois Institute of Technology M,D
Indiana State University M
Indiana University Bloomington M,D,O
Indiana University–Purdue University Indianapolis M
Inter American University of Puerto Rico, Metropolitan Campus M
Inter American University of Puerto Rico, San Germán Campus M
Iona College M
Jackson State University M,D
Johns Hopkins University M,D,O
Kean University M,O
Kutztown University of Pennsylvania M,O
Lawrence Technological University M
Lebanon Valley College M
Lehman College of the City University of New York M

LeMoyne-Owen College	M
Long Island University, C.W. Post Campus	M
Louisiana Tech University	M,D,O
Loyola Marymount University	M
Manhattanville College	M
McNeese State University	M
Mercer University	M,O
Michigan State University	M,D
Middle Tennessee State University	M
Minot State University	M
Mississippi College	M
Montana State University–Bozeman	M,D,O
Montana State University–Northern	M
Montclair State University	M,O
Morgan State University	D
National-Louis University	M,O
New Mexico Institute of Mining and Technology	M
New York University	M
Niagara University	M,O
North Carolina Agricultural and Technical State University	M
North Carolina State University	M,D
Northeastern University	M
Northern Arizona University	M,D
Northern Michigan University	M
North Georgia College & State University	M,O
Northwestern State University of Louisiana	M,O
Northwest Missouri State University	M
Notre Dame de Namur University	M,O
Nova Southeastern University	M,O
Oregon State University	M,D
The Pennsylvania State University University Park Campus	M,D
Plattsburgh State University of New York	M
Portland State University	M,D
Purdue University	M,D,O
Purdue University Calumet	M
Queens College of the City University of New York	M,O
Quinnipiac University	M
Rhode Island College	M
Rider University	O
Rowan University	M
Rutgers, The State University of New Jersey, New Brunswick	M,D
Sage Graduate School	M
Saginaw Valley State University	M
St. John Fisher College	M
Saint Joseph's University	M
Salem State College	M,O
Salisbury State University	M
San Diego State University	M,D
Slippery Rock University of Pennsylvania	M
South Carolina State University	M
Southeast Missouri State University	M
Southern Connecticut State University	M,O
Southern University and Agricultural and Mechanical College	D
Southwestern Oklahoma State University	M
Southwest Missouri State University	M
Southwest Texas State University	M
Stanford University	M,D
State University of New York at Albany	M,D
State University of New York at Binghamton	M
State University of New York College at Brockport	M
State University of New York College at Buffalo	M
State University of New York College at Cortland	M
State University of West Georgia	M,O
Stevens Institute of Technology	O
Stony Brook University, State University of New York	M,O
Syracuse University	M,D,O
Teachers College, Columbia University	M,D
Temple University	M,D
Texas A&M University	M,D
Texas Woman's University	M,D
Tuskegee University	M
University at Buffalo, The State University of New York	M,D,O
University of Alaska Fairbanks	M,D
University of California, Berkeley	M,D
University of California, Los Angeles	M,D
University of California, San Diego	D
University of Central Florida	M
University of Connecticut	M,D
University of Florida	M,D,O
University of Georgia	M,D,O
University of Houston	M,D
University of Idaho	M,D
The University of Iowa	M,D
University of Maine	M,O
University of Massachusetts Amherst	D
University of Massachusetts Lowell	D
University of Miami	M
University of Michigan	M,D
University of Minnesota, Twin Cities Campus	M
University of Missouri–Rolla	M,D
The University of Montana–Missoula	M,D
University of Nebraska at Kearney	M
University of New Orleans	M
The University of North Carolina at Chapel Hill	M
The University of North Carolina at Pembroke	M
University of Northern Colorado	M,D
University of Northern Iowa	M,O
University of North Florida	M
University of Oklahoma	M,D
University of Pittsburgh	M,D
University of Puerto Rico, Río Piedras	M,D
University of South Alabama	M
University of South Carolina	M,D
University of Southern Mississippi	M,D
University of South Florida	M,D,O
The University of Tennessee	M,D,O
The University of Texas at Austin	M,D
The University of Texas at Dallas	M
The University of Texas at Tyler	M
University of Toledo	M,D
University of Tulsa	M
University of Utah	M,D
University of Vermont	M,D
University of Virginia	M,D
University of Washington	M,D
The University of West Alabama	M
University of West Florida	M
University of Wisconsin–Eau Claire	M
University of Wisconsin–Madison	M
University of Wisconsin–Oshkosh	M
University of Wisconsin–River Falls	M
University of Wyoming	M
Vanderbilt University	M,D
Wayne State College	M
Wayne State University	M,D,O
Webster University	M
West Chester University of Pennsylvania	M
Western Carolina University	M
Western Illinois University	M,O
Western Kentucky University	M
Western Michigan University	M,D
Western Oregon University	M
Western Washington University	M
Wheeling Jesuit University	M
Widener University	M,D
Wilkes University	M
Wright State University	M

■ SECONDARY EDUCATION

Abilene Christian University	M
Adams State College	M
Adelphi University	M
Alabama Agricultural and Mechanical University	M,O
Alabama State University	M,O
Alcorn State University	M,O
Alfred University	M
American International College	M,D,O
American University	M,O
Andrews University	M
Appalachian State University	M
Arcadia University	M,O
Arizona State University West	M
Armstrong Atlantic State University	M
Auburn University	M,D,O
Auburn University Montgomery	M,O
Augusta State University	M,O
Austin Peay State University	M,O
Ball State University	M
Belmont University	M
Boston College	M
Bowie State University	M
Bridgewater State College	M
Brooklyn College of the City University of New York	M
Brown University	M
Butler University	M,O
California State University, Bakersfield	M
California State University, Long Beach	M
California State University, Los Angeles	M
California State University, Northridge	M
California State University, San Bernardino	M
California State University, Stanislaus	M
Campbell University	M
Canisius College	M
Carson-Newman College	M
Centenary College of Louisiana	M
Central Michigan University	M
Central Missouri State University	M,O
Chadron State College	M,O
Charleston Southern University	M
Chicago State University	M
The Citadel, The Military College of South Carolina	M
Clemson University	M
Cleveland State University	M
The College of New Jersey	M
College of Our Lady of the Elms	M,O
The College of Saint Rose	M
College of Staten Island of the City University of New York	M
The College of William and Mary	M
Columbus State University	M,O
Concordia University (OR)	M
Converse College	M
Cumberland College	M,O
DePaul University	M
Dowling College	M
Drake University	M
Drury University	M
Duquesne University	M
Eastern Kentucky University	M
Eastern Michigan University	M
Eastern Nazarene College	M,O
Eastern Oregon University	M

East Stroudsburg University of Pennsylvania	M
East Tennessee State University	M
Edinboro University of Pennsylvania	M
Emmanuel College	M
Emory University	M,D,O
Emporia State University	M
Fayetteville State University	M
Fitchburg State College	M
Florida Agricultural and Mechanical University	M
Florida Gulf Coast University	M
Fordham University	M,D,O
Fort Hays State University	M
Francis Marion University	M
Friends University	M
Frostburg State University	M
Gallaudet University	M,D,O
Gannon University	M
George Mason University	M
The George Washington University	M
Georgia College and State University	M,O
Georgia Southwestern State University	M,O
Grand Canyon University	M
Grand Valley State University	M
Harding University	M
Harvard University	M,D,O
Henderson State University	M
Hofstra University	M
Holy Family College	M
Hood College	M
Houston Baptist University	M
Howard University	M,O
Hunter College of the City University of New York	M
Immaculata College	M,D,O
Indiana State University	M,D,O
Indiana University Bloomington	M,D,O
Indiana University Northwest	M
Indiana University–Purdue University Fort Wayne	M
Indiana University–Purdue University Indianapolis	M
Indiana University South Bend	M
Indiana University Southeast	M
Iona College	M
Jackson State University	M,D,O
Jacksonville State University	M,O
Jacksonville University	O
James Madison University	M
John Carroll University	M
Johns Hopkins University	M
Kansas State University	M
Kent State University	M
Kutztown University of Pennsylvania	M,O
Lamar University	M,O
Lehigh University	M,D,O
Liberty University	M,D
Lincoln University (MO)	M
Long Island University, C.W. Post Campus	M
Longwood College	M
Louisiana State University and Agricultural and Mechanical College	M,D,O
Louisiana Tech University	M,D,O
Loyola Marymount University	M
Loyola University New Orleans	M
Lynchburg College	M
Maharishi University of Management	M
Manhattanville College	M
Mansfield University of Pennsylvania	M
Marshall University	M
Marymount University	M
Maryville University of Saint Louis	M
McNeese State University	M
Mercy College	M,O
Miami University	M
Michigan State University	M,D
Middle Tennessee State University	M,O
Minnesota State University, Mankato	M,O
Mississippi College	M
Mississippi State University	M,D,O
Montana State University–Billings	M
Morehead State University	M
Mount Saint Mary College	M
Mount St. Mary's College	M
Murray State University	M,O
National-Louis University	M
Nazareth College of Rochester	M
New School University	M
Niagara University	M
Norfolk State University	M
Northern Arizona University	M
Northern Illinois University	M,D
Northern Kentucky University	M
Northern Michigan University	M
Northern State University	M
North Georgia College & State University	M,O
Northwestern Oklahoma State University	M
Northwestern State University of Louisiana	M,O
Northwestern University	M,D
Northwest Missouri State University	M,O
Notre Dame de Namur University	M,O
Old Dominion University	M,O
Olivet Nazarene University	M
Pacific Lutheran University	M
Pacific University	M
Piedmont College	M
Pittsburg State University	M
Plattsburgh State University of New York	M
Plymouth State College	M
Portland State University	M
Purdue University Calumet	M
Queens College of the City University of New York	M,O
Quinnipiac University	M
Rhode Island College	M
Rivier College	M
Rochester Institute of Technology	M
Rockford College	M
Rollins College	M
Roosevelt University	M,D
Rowan University	M
Sacred Heart University	M,O
Saginaw Valley State University	M
St. Bonaventure University	M
St. Cloud State University	M
St. John's University (NY)	M
Saint Joseph's University	M
St. Thomas Aquinas College	M
Saint Xavier University	M,O
Salem International University	M
Salem State College	M
Salisbury State University	M
Sam Houston State University	M,D,O
San Diego State University	M
San Francisco State University	M,O
San Jose State University	M
Seattle Pacific University	M
Seton Hall University	M
Shenandoah University	M,D,O
Siena Heights University	M
Simmons College	M
Slippery Rock University of Pennsylvania	M
South Carolina State University	M
Southeastern Oklahoma State University	M
Southeast Missouri State University	M
Southern Arkansas University–Magnolia	M
Southern Illinois University Edwardsville	M
Southern Oregon University	M
Southern University and Agricultural and Mechanical College	M
Southwestern Oklahoma State University	M
Southwest Missouri State University	M
Southwest Texas State University	M
Springfield College	M
Spring Hill College	M
State University of New York at Binghamton	M
State University of New York at New Paltz	M
State University of New York at Oswego	M
State University of New York College at Brockport	M
State University of New York College at Cortland	M
State University of New York College at Fredonia	M
State University of New York College at Geneseo	M
State University of New York College at Oneonta	M
State University of New York College at Potsdam	M
State University of West Georgia	M,O
Stephen F. Austin State University	M,D
Suffolk University	M
Sul Ross State University	M
Tarleton State University	M,O
Temple University	M,D
Tennessee Technological University	M,O
Texas A&M International University	M
Texas A&M University–Commerce	M,D
Texas A&M University–Corpus Christi	M
Texas A&M University–Kingsville	M
Texas A&M University–Texarkana	M
Texas Christian University	M
Texas Southern University	M,D
Texas Tech University	M,D,O
Towson University	M
Trinity College (DC)	M
Troy State University	M,O
Tufts University	M,O
University at Buffalo, The State University of New York	M,D,O
The University of Akron	M,D
The University of Alabama	M,D,O
The University of Alabama at Birmingham	M
University of Alaska Southeast	M
The University of Arizona	M,D,O
University of Arkansas	M,O
University of Arkansas at Little Rock	M
University of Bridgeport	M,O
University of Central Arkansas	M
University of Central Florida	M
University of Central Oklahoma	M
University of Cincinnati	M
University of Connecticut	M,D
University of Dayton	M
University of Delaware	M,D
University of Florida	M,D,O
University of Georgia	M,D,O
University of Great Falls	M
University of Guam	M
University of Hartford	M
University of Hawaii at Manoa	M
University of Houston	M,D
University of Idaho	M,D,O
University of Illinois at Chicago	M,D

University of Indianapolis	M
The University of Iowa	M,D
University of Louisiana at Monroe	M,O
University of Louisville	M,O
University of Maine	M,O
University of Mary	M
University of Maryland, Baltimore County	M,D
University of Maryland, College Park	M,D,O
University of Massachusetts Amherst	M,D,O
University of Massachusetts Boston	M,D,O
The University of Memphis	M,D
University of Mississippi	M,D,O
University of Missouri–Kansas City	M,D,O
University of Missouri–St. Louis	M,D
University of Montevallo	M,O
University of Nebraska at Omaha	M
University of Nevada, Las Vegas	M,D,O
University of Nevada, Reno	M,D,O
University of New Hampshire	M
University of New Mexico	M
University of North Alabama	M
The University of North Carolina at Chapel Hill	M
The University of North Carolina at Charlotte	M
The University of North Carolina at Wilmington	M
University of North Dakota	D
University of North Florida	M
University of North Texas	M
University of Oklahoma	M,D
University of Pennsylvania	M
University of Pittsburgh	M,D
University of Portland	M
University of Puerto Rico, Río Piedras	M,D
University of Rhode Island	M
The University of Scranton	M
University of South Alabama	M,O
University of South Carolina	M,D,O
University of South Dakota	M
University of Southern Indiana	M
University of Southern Mississippi	M,D,O
University of South Florida	D
The University of Tennessee	M,D,O
The University of Tennessee at Chattanooga	M,O
The University of Texas at Tyler	M
The University of Texas of the Permian Basin	M
The University of Texas–Pan American	M
University of the Incarnate Word	M
University of Toledo	M,D,O
University of Utah	M
The University of West Alabama	M
University of West Florida	M
University of Wisconsin–Eau Claire	M
University of Wisconsin–La Crosse	M
University of Wisconsin–Milwaukee	M
University of Wisconsin–Platteville	M
University of Wyoming	M
Utah State University	M
Valdosta State University	M,O
Vanderbilt University	M,D
Villanova University	M
Virginia Commonwealth University	M,O
Wagner College	M
Wake Forest University	M
Washington State University	M,D
Washington University in St. Louis	M
Wayne State University	M,D,O
West Chester University of Pennsylvania	M
Western Carolina University	M
Western Illinois University	M
Western Kentucky University	M,O
Western New Mexico University	M
Western Oregon University	M
Western Washington University	M
Westfield State College	M
West Texas A&M University	M
West Virginia University	M,D
Wilkes University	M
William Carey College	M
Winthrop University	M
Worcester State College	M,O
Wright State University	M
Xavier University	M
Youngstown State University	M

■ SLAVIC LANGUAGES

Boston College	M
Brown University	M,D
Columbia University	M,D
Duke University	M,D
Florida State University	M
Harvard University	M,D
Indiana University Bloomington	M,D
New York University	M
Northwestern University	D
The Ohio State University	M,D,O
Princeton University	D
Stanford University	M,D
Stony Brook University, State University of New York	M
University of California, Berkeley	M,D
University of California, Los Angeles	M,D
University of Chicago	M,D
University of Illinois at Chicago	M,D
University of Illinois at Urbana–Champaign	M,D
University of Kansas	M,D
University of Michigan	M,D
The University of North Carolina at Chapel Hill	M,D
University of Pittsburgh	M,D
University of Southern California	M,D
The University of Texas at Austin	M,D
University of Virginia	M,D
University of Washington	M,D
University of Wisconsin–Madison	M,D
University of Wisconsin–Milwaukee	M
Yale University	M,D

■ SOCIAL PSYCHOLOGY

American University	M
Andrews University	M
Arcadia University	M
Arizona State University	D
Auburn University	M,D,O
Ball State University	M
Bowling Green State University	M,D
Brandeis University	M,D
Brooklyn College of the City University of New York	M,D
California State University, Fullerton	M
Carnegie Mellon University	D
Central Connecticut State University	M
Claremont Graduate University	M,D
Clark University	D
The College of New Rochelle	M
College of St. Joseph	M
Columbia University	M,D
Cornell University	M,D
DePaul University	M,D
Fairleigh Dickinson University, Florham-Madison Campus	M
Florida Agricultural and Mechanical University	M
Francis Marion University	M
The George Washington University	D
Harvard University	M,D
Henderson State University	M
Hofstra University	M,D
Howard University	M,D
Hunter College of the City University of New York	M
Indiana University Bloomington	D
Iowa State University of Science and Technology	M,D
Lamar University	M
Lesley University	M,O
Loyola University Chicago	M,D
Marist College	M,O
Miami University	D
Montclair State University	M
New College of California	M
New York University	M,D,O
Norfolk State University	M
North Georgia College & State University	M
Northwestern University	D
The Ohio State University	D
Pace University, New York City Campus	M,D
The Pennsylvania State University Harrisburg Campus of the Capital College	M
The Pennsylvania State University University Park Campus	M,D
Rutgers, The State University of New Jersey, Newark	D
Rutgers, The State University of New Jersey, New Brunswick	D
Sage Graduate School	M
St. Edward's University	M,O
Saint Joseph College	M,O
Saint Martin's College	M
Southeast Missouri State University	M
Southern Illinois University Edwardsville	M
State University of New York at Albany	M,D
State University of New York College at Oneonta	M,O
Stony Brook University, State University of New York	D
Syracuse University	D
Teachers College, Columbia University	M,D
Temple University	D
University at Buffalo, The State University of New York	M,D
The University of Alabama	M,D,O
University of Alaska Fairbanks	M
University of California, Santa Cruz	D
University of Central Arkansas	M
University of Cincinnati	M,D
University of Connecticut	M,D
University of Dayton	M
University of Delaware	D
University of Houston	D
University of Illinois at Urbana–Champaign	M,D
University of La Verne	D
University of Maine	M,D
University of Maryland, College Park	M,D
University of Massachusetts Lowell	M
University of Michigan	D
University of Minnesota, Duluth	M
University of Minnesota, Twin Cities Campus	D
University of Missouri–Kansas City	D
University of Nevada, Reno	D
University of New Haven	M,O
The University of North Carolina at Chapel Hill	D
The University of North Carolina at Charlotte	M
The University of North Carolina at Greensboro	M,D

University of Oklahoma	M
University of Oregon	M,D
University of Pennsylvania	D
University of Rochester	M,D
The University of Scranton	M
University of South Carolina	D
University of Wisconsin–Madison	D
University of Wisconsin–Superior	M
Washington University in St. Louis	M,D
Wayne State University	M,D
Western Illinois University	M,O
Wichita State University	M,D
Wilmington College	M

■ SOCIAL SCIENCES

Appalachian State University	M
Arkansas Tech University	M
Ball State University	M
California Institute of Technology	M,D
California State University, Chico	M
California State University, Fullerton	M
California State University, San Bernardino	M
California University of Pennsylvania	M
Campbellsville University	M
Carnegie Mellon University	D
Central Connecticut State University	M
Columbia University	M
Eastern Michigan University	M
Edinboro University of Pennsylvania	M
Florida Agricultural and Mechanical University	M
Florida State University	M
Henderson State University	M
Humboldt State University	M
Johns Hopkins University	M,D
Long Island University, Brooklyn Campus	M,O
Long Island University, C.W. Post Campus	M
Massachusetts Institute of Technology	D
Michigan State University	M,D
Mississippi College	M
Montclair State University	M
New School University	M,D
Northwestern University	O
Ohio University	M
Old Dominion University	M
Pittsburg State University	M
Queens College of the City University of New York	M
Regis University	M,O
San Francisco State University	M
San Jose State University	M
Southern Oregon University	M
State University of New York at Binghamton	M
State University of New York College at Fredonia	M
Stony Brook University, State University of New York	M,O
Syracuse University	M,D
Texas A&M International University	M
Texas A&M University–Commerce	M
Towson University	M
University at Buffalo, The State University of New York	M
University of California, Irvine	M,D
University of California, Santa Cruz	D
University of Chicago	M,D
University of Colorado at Denver	M
University of Illinois at Springfield	M
University of Michigan	D
The University of Texas at Tyler	M

■ SOCIAL SCIENCES EDUCATION

Alabama State University	M,O
Albany State University	M
Alfred University	M
Andrews University	M
Arcadia University	M,O
Arkansas State University	M,O
Arkansas Tech University	M
Armstrong Atlantic State University	M
Auburn University	M,D,O
Boston College	M
Boston University	M,D,O
Bridgewater State College	M
Brooklyn College of the City University of New York	M
Brown University	M
California State University, San Bernardino	M
California State University, Stanislaus	M
Campbell University	M
Carthage College	M,O
Central Missouri State University	M
Chadron State College	M,O
Chaminade University of Honolulu	M
Charleston Southern University	M
The Citadel, The Military College of South Carolina	M
Claremont Graduate University	M,D
Clemson University	M
The College of William and Mary	M
Columbus State University	M,O
Delta State University	M
East Carolina University	M
Eastern Kentucky University	M
Eastern Washington University	M
East Stroudsburg University of Pennsylvania	M
Edinboro University of Pennsylvania	M
Emporia State University	M
Fayetteville State University	M
Fitchburg State College	M
Florida Gulf Coast University	M
Florida International University	M
Florida State University	M,D,O
Framingham State College	M
Georgia College and State University	M,O
Georgia Southern University	M,O
Georgia State University	M,D,O
Grambling State University	M
Henderson State University	M
Hofstra University	M
Hunter College of the City University of New York	M
Indiana University Bloomington	M,D,O
Iona College	M
Kutztown University of Pennsylvania	M,O
Lehman College of the City University of New York	M
Longwood College	M
Louisiana Tech University	M,D,O
Loyola Marymount University	M
Manhattanville College	M
McNeese State University	M
Mercer University	M,O
Miami University	M
Michigan State University	M,D
Minnesota State University, Mankato	M
Montclair State University	M
New Jersey Institute of Technology	M
New York University	M,D
North Carolina Agricultural and Technical State University	M
Northeastern University	M
North Georgia College & State University	M,O
Northwestern State University of Louisiana	M
Northwest Missouri State University	M
Notre Dame de Namur University	M,O
Nova Southeastern University	M,O
Ohio University	M,D
The Pennsylvania State University University Park Campus	M,D
Plattsburgh State University of New York	M
Portland State University	M
Princeton University	D
Purdue University	M,D,O
Queens College of the City University of New York	M,O
Quinnipiac University	M
Rider University	O
Rockford College	M
Rutgers, The State University of New Jersey, New Brunswick	M,D,O
Sage Graduate School	M
Salem State College	M,O
Salisbury State University	M
South Carolina State University	M
Southeast Missouri State University	M
Southwestern Oklahoma State University	M
Southwest Texas State University	M,D
Stanford University	M,D
State University of New York at Binghamton	M
State University of New York College at Brockport	M
State University of New York College at Buffalo	M
State University of New York College at Cortland	M
State University of West Georgia	M,O
Stony Brook University, State University of New York	M,O
Syracuse University	M,O
Teachers College, Columbia University	M,D
Texas A&M University–Commerce	M
University at Buffalo, The State University of New York	M,D,O
University of Central Florida	M
University of Connecticut	M,D
University of Denver	M,D
University of Florida	M,D,O
University of Georgia	M,D,O
University of Houston	M,D
University of Idaho	M,D
University of Indianapolis	M
University of Maine	M,O
University of Michigan	M,D
University of Minnesota, Twin Cities Campus	M
The University of North Carolina at Chapel Hill	M
The University of North Carolina at Pembroke	M
University of Oklahoma	M,D
University of Pittsburgh	M,D
University of Puerto Rico, Río Piedras	M,D
University of South Carolina	M,D,O
University of Southern Mississippi	M,D,O
University of South Florida	M
The University of Tennessee	M,D,O
The University of Texas at Tyler	M
University of Vermont	M
University of Washington	M,D
The University of West Alabama	M
University of Wisconsin–Eau Claire	M
University of Wisconsin–Madison	M,D
University of Wisconsin–River Falls	M
Virginia Commonwealth University	M,O
Wayne State College	M
Wayne State University	M,D,O
Webster University	M
Western Carolina University	M
Western Illinois University	M,O

Western Kentucky University	M
Western Oregon University	M
Widener University	M,D
Wilkes University	M
Worcester State College	M

■ SOCIAL WORK

Adelphi University	M,D
Alabama Agricultural and Mechanical University	M
Andrews University	M
Arizona State University	M,D
Arizona State University West	M
Augsburg College	M
Aurora University	M
Barry University	M,D
Baylor University	M
Boise State University	M
Boston College	M,D
Boston University	M,D,O
Brigham Young University	M
California State University, Bakersfield	M
California State University, Fresno	M
California State University, Long Beach	M
California State University, Los Angeles	M
California State University, Sacramento	M
California State University, San Bernardino	M
California State University, Stanislaus	M
California University of Pennsylvania	M
Case Western Reserve University	M,D,O
The Catholic University of America	M,D
Chicago State University	M
Clark Atlanta University	M,D
Cleveland State University	M
College of St. Catherine	M
Colorado State University	M
Columbia University	M,D
Delaware State University	M
Delta State University	M
East Carolina University	M
Eastern Michigan University	M
Eastern Washington University	M
Edinboro University of Pennsylvania	M
Florida Atlantic University	M
Florida Gulf Coast University	M
Florida International University	M,D
Florida State University	M,D
Fordham University	M,D
Gallaudet University	M
Georgia State University	M
Governors State University	M
Grambling State University	M
Grand Valley State University	M
Gratz College	M,O
Howard University	M,D
Hunter College of the City University of New York	M,D
Illinois State University	M
Indiana University Northwest	M
Indiana University–Purdue University Indianapolis	M,D
Indiana University South Bend	M
Inter American University of Puerto Rico, Metrópolitan Campus	M
Jackson State University	M,D
Kean University	M
Loma Linda University	M,D
Louisiana State University and Agricultural and Mechanical College	M,D
Loyola University Chicago	M,D
Marywood University	M
Michigan State University	M,D
Monmouth University	M
Nazareth College of Rochester	M
Newman University	M
New Mexico Highlands University	M
New Mexico State University	M
New York University	M,D
Norfolk State University	M,D
North Carolina Agricultural and Technical State University	M
The Ohio State University	M,D
Ohio University	M
Our Lady of the Lake University of San Antonio	M
Pontifical Catholic University of Puerto Rico	M
Portland State University	M,D
Radford University	M
Rhode Island College	M
Roberts Wesleyan College	M
Rutgers, The State University of New Jersey, New Brunswick	M,D
St. Ambrose University	M
Saint Louis University	M
Salem State College	M
San Diego State University	M
San Francisco State University	M
San Jose State University	M
Savannah State University	M
Simmons College	M,D
Southern Connecticut State University	M
Southern Illinois University Carbondale	M
Southern Illinois University Edwardsville	M
Southern University at New Orleans	M
Southwest Missouri State University	M
Southwest Texas State University	M
Spalding University	M
Springfield College	M
State University of New York at Albany	M,D
State University of New York College at Brockport	M
Stephen F. Austin State University	M
Stony Brook University, State University of New York	M,D
Syracuse University	M
Temple University	M
Texas A&M University–Commerce	M
Tulane University	M,D
University at Buffalo, The State University of New York	M,D
The University of Akron	M
The University of Alabama	M,D
University of Alaska Anchorage	M
University of Arkansas at Little Rock	M
University of California, Berkeley	M,D
University of California, Los Angeles	M,D
University of Central Florida	M,O
University of Chicago	M,D
University of Cincinnati	M
University of Connecticut	M
University of Denver	M,D
University of Georgia	M,D
University of Hawaii at Manoa	M,D
University of Houston	M,D
University of Illinois at Chicago	M,D
University of Illinois at Urbana–Champaign	M,D
The University of Iowa	M,D
University of Kentucky	M,D
University of Louisville	M,D
University of Maine	M
University of Maryland	M,D
University of Michigan	M,D
University of Minnesota, Duluth	M
University of Minnesota, Twin Cities Campus	M,D
University of Missouri–Columbia	M
University of Missouri–Kansas City	M
University of Missouri–St. Louis	M,O
University of Nebraska at Omaha	M
University of Nevada, Las Vegas	M
University of Nevada, Reno	M
University of New England	M
University of New Hampshire	M
The University of North Carolina at Chapel Hill	M,D
The University of North Carolina at Charlotte	M
The University of North Carolina at Greensboro	M
University of North Dakota	M
University of Northern Iowa	M
University of Oklahoma	M
University of Pennsylvania	M,D
University of Pittsburgh	M,D,O
University of Puerto Rico, Río Piedras	M
University of St. Thomas (MN)	M
University of South Carolina	M,D
University of Southern California	M,D
University of Southern Indiana	M
University of Southern Mississippi	M
University of South Florida	M
The University of Tennessee	M,D
The University of Texas at Arlington	M,D
The University of Texas at Austin	M,D
The University of Texas–Pan American	M
University of Utah	M,D
University of Vermont	M
University of Washington	M,D
University of Wisconsin–Madison	M,D
University of Wisconsin–Milwaukee	M
University of Wyoming	M
Valdosta State University	M
Virginia Commonwealth University	M,D
Walla Walla College	M
Washington University in St. Louis	M,D
Wayne State University	M,O
West Chester University of Pennsylvania	M
Western Michigan University	M
West Virginia University	M
Wheelock College	M
Wichita State University	M
Widener University	M
Yeshiva University	M,D

■ SOCIOLOGY

American University	M,D
Arizona State University	M,D
Arkansas State University	M,O
Auburn University	M
Ball State University	M
Baylor University	M,D
Bethel College (MN)	M
Boston College	M,D
Boston University	M,D
Bowling Green State University	M,D
Brandeis University	M,D
Brigham Young University	M,D
Brooklyn College of the City University of New York	M,D
Brown University	M,D
California State University, Bakersfield	M
California State University, Dominguez Hills	M,O
California State University, Fullerton	M
California State University, Hayward	M
California State University, Los Angeles	M
California State University, Northridge	M
California State University, Sacramento	M
California State University, San Marcos	M
Case Western Reserve University	D

The Catholic University of America	M,D
Central Michigan University	M
Central Missouri State University	M
City College of the City University of New York	M
Clark Atlanta University	M
Clemson University	M
Cleveland State University	M
Colorado State University	M,D
Columbia University	M,D
Converse College	M
Cornell University	M,D
DePaul University	M
Duke University	M,D
East Carolina University	M
Eastern Michigan University	M
East Tennessee State University	M
Emory University	D
Fayetteville State University	M
Florida Atlantic University	M
Florida International University	M,D
Florida State University	M,D
Fordham University	M,D
George Mason University	M
The George Washington University	M
Georgia Southern University	M
Georgia Southwestern State University	M
Georgia State University	M,D
Harvard University	M,D
Howard University	M,D
Humboldt State University	M
Hunter College of the City University of New York	M
Idaho State University	M
Illinois State University	M
Indiana State University	M
Indiana University Bloomington	M,D
Indiana University of Pennsylvania	M
Indiana University–Purdue University Fort Wayne	M
Iowa State University of Science and Technology	M,D
Jackson State University	M
Johns Hopkins University	D
Kansas State University	M,D
Kent State University	M,D
Lehigh University	M
Lincoln University (MO)	M
Louisiana State University and Agricultural and Mechanical College	M,D
Loyola University Chicago	M,D
Marshall University	M
Michigan State University	M,D
Middle Tennessee State University	M
Minnesota State University, Mankato	M
Mississippi College	M
Mississippi State University	M,D
Montclair State University	M
Morehead State University	M
Morgan State University	M
New Mexico Highlands University	M
New Mexico State University	M
New School University	M,D
New York University	M,D
Norfolk State University	M
North Carolina Central University	M
North Carolina State University	M,D
North Dakota State University	M
Northeastern University	M,D
Northern Arizona University	M
Northern Illinois University	M
Northwestern University	D
The Ohio State University	M,D
Ohio University	M
Oklahoma State University	M,D
Old Dominion University	M
Our Lady of the Lake University of San Antonio	M
The Pennsylvania State University University Park Campus	M,D
Portland State University	M,D
Prairie View A&M University	M
Princeton University	D
Purdue University	M,D
Queens College of the City University of New York	M
Roosevelt University	M
Rutgers, The State University of New Jersey, New Brunswick	M,D
St. John's University (NY)	M
Sam Houston State University	M
San Diego State University	M
Southern Connecticut State University	M
Southern Illinois University Carbondale	M,D
Southern Illinois University Edwardsville	M
Southern University and Agricultural and Mechanical College	M
Southwest Texas State University	M
Stanford University	D
State University of New York at Albany	M,D,O
State University of New York at Binghamton	M,D
State University of New York at New Paltz	M
State University of New York Institute of Technology at Utica/Rome	M
State University of West Georgia	M
Stony Brook University, State University of New York	M,D
Syracuse University	M,D
Teachers College, Columbia University	M,D
Temple University	M,D
Texas A&M International University	M
Texas A&M University	M,D
Texas A&M University–Commerce	M
Texas A&M University–Kingsville	M
Texas Southern University	M
Texas Tech University	M
Texas Woman's University	M,D
Tulane University	M,D
University at Buffalo, The State University of New York	M,D
The University of Akron	M,D
The University of Alabama at Birmingham	M,D
The University of Arizona	M,D
University of Arkansas	M
University of California, Berkeley	D
University of California, Davis	M,D
University of California, Irvine	M,D
University of California, Los Angeles	M,D
University of California, Riverside	D
University of California, San Diego	D
University of California, San Francisco	D
University of California, Santa Barbara	M,D
University of California, Santa Cruz	D
University of Central Florida	M,O
University of Chicago	D
University of Cincinnati	M,D
University of Colorado at Boulder	M,D
University of Colorado at Colorado Springs	M
University of Colorado at Denver	M
University of Connecticut	M,D
University of Delaware	M,D
University of Denver	M,D
University of Florida	M,D
University of Georgia	M,D
University of Hawaii at Manoa	M,D
University of Houston	M
University of Houston–Clear Lake	M
University of Illinois at Chicago	M,D
University of Illinois at Urbana–Champaign	M,D
University of Indianapolis	M
The University of Iowa	M,D
University of Kansas	M,D
University of Kentucky	M,D
University of Louisville	M
University of Maryland, Baltimore County	M,O
University of Maryland, College Park	M,D
University of Massachusetts Amherst	M,D
University of Massachusetts Boston	M
University of Massachusetts Lowell	M
The University of Memphis	M
University of Miami	M,D
University of Michigan	M,D
University of Minnesota, Duluth	M
University of Minnesota, Twin Cities Campus	M,D
University of Mississippi	M
University of Missouri–Columbia	M,D
University of Missouri–Kansas City	M,D
University of Missouri–St. Louis	M
The University of Montana–Missoula	M
University of Nebraska at Omaha	M
University of Nebraska–Lincoln	M,D
University of Nevada, Las Vegas	M,D
University of Nevada, Reno	M
University of New Hampshire	M,D
University of New Mexico	M,D
University of New Orleans	M
The University of North Carolina at Chapel Hill	M,D
The University of North Carolina at Charlotte	M
The University of North Carolina at Greensboro	M
University of North Dakota	M
University of Northern Colorado	M
University of Northern Iowa	M
University of North Texas	M,D
University of Notre Dame	D
University of Oklahoma	M,D
University of Oregon	M,D
University of Pennsylvania	M,D
University of Pittsburgh	M,D
University of Puerto Rico, Río Piedras	M
University of South Alabama	M
University of South Carolina	M,D
University of South Dakota	M
University of Southern California	M,D
University of South Florida	M
The University of Tennessee	M,D
The University of Texas at Arlington	M
The University of Texas at Austin	M,D
The University of Texas at Dallas	M
The University of Texas at El Paso	M
The University of Texas at San Antonio	M
The University of Texas–Pan American	M
University of Toledo	M
University of Virginia	M,D
University of Washington	M,D
University of Wisconsin–Madison	M,D
University of Wisconsin–Milwaukee	M
University of Wyoming	M
Utah State University	M,D
Valdosta State University	M
Vanderbilt University	M,D
Virginia Commonwealth University	M,O
Virginia Polytechnic Institute and State University	M,D
Washington State University	M,D
Wayne State University	M,D

West Chester University of Pennsylvania M,O
Western Illinois University M
Western Kentucky University M
Western Michigan University M,D
Western Washington University M
West Virginia University M
Wichita State University M
William Paterson University of New Jersey M
Yale University D

■ SOFTWARE ENGINEERING

Andrews University M
Auburn University M,D
Azusa Pacific University M,O
California State University, Sacramento M
Carnegie Mellon University M,D
Central Michigan University M,O
DePaul University M
Drexel University M
East Tennessee State University M
Embry-Riddle Aeronautical University M
Fairfield University M
Florida Institute of Technology M,D
Florida State University M,D
Gannon University M
George Mason University M
Grand Valley State University M
Illinois Institute of Technology M,D
Jacksonville State University M
Kansas State University M
Mercer University M
Monmouth University M,O
National University M
Oakland University M
The Pennsylvania State University Great Valley Campus M
Rochester Institute of Technology M
San Jose State University M
Santa Clara University M,D,O
Seattle University M
Southern Methodist University M,D
Southwest Texas State University M
Stevens Institute of Technology O
Stony Brook University, State University of New York M,D,O
Texas Christian University M
Texas Tech University M,D
Towson University O
University of Colorado at Colorado Springs M
University of Connecticut M,D
University of Houston–Clear Lake M
University of Maryland, College Park M
University of Maryland University College M
University of Michigan–Dearborn M
University of Minnesota, Twin Cities Campus M
University of Missouri–Kansas City M,D
University of Nebraska–Lincoln M
University of New Haven M
University of St. Thomas (MN) M,O
The University of Scranton M
University of Southern California M
The University of Texas at Arlington M,D
Wayne State University M,D
West Virginia University M
Widener University M

■ SPANISH

American University M,O
Arizona State University M,D
Auburn University M
Baylor University M
Boston College M,D
Boston University M,D
Bowling Green State University M
Brigham Young University M
Brooklyn College of the City University of New York M
California State University, Bakersfield M
California State University, Fresno M
California State University, Fullerton M
California State University, Long Beach M
California State University, Los Angeles M
California State University, Northridge M
California State University, Sacramento M
California State University, San Marcos M
The Catholic University of America M,D
Central Connecticut State University M
Central Michigan University M
City College of the City University of New York M
Cleveland State University M
Colorado State University M
Columbia University M,D
Duke University D
Eastern Michigan University M
Emory University D,O
Florida Atlantic University M
Florida International University M,D
Florida State University M,D
Georgetown University M,D
Georgia State University M
Harvard University M,D
Howard University M
Hunter College of the City University of New York M
Illinois State University M
Indiana State University M
Indiana University Bloomington M,D
Inter American University of Puerto Rico, Metropolitan Campus M
Iona College M
Johns Hopkins University M,D
Kansas State University M
Kent State University M
Lehman College of the City University of New York M
Long Island University, C.W. Post Campus M
Louisiana State University and Agricultural and Mechanical College M
Loyola University Chicago M
Marquette University M
Miami University M
Michigan State University M,D
Millersville University of Pennsylvania M
Minnesota State University, Mankato M
Montclair State University M
Monterey Institute of International Studies M
New Mexico Highlands University M
New Mexico State University M
New York University M,D
Northern Illinois University M
Nova Southeastern University M,O
The Ohio State University M,D
Ohio University M
The Pennsylvania State University University Park Campus M,D
Portland State University M
Princeton University D
Purdue University M,D
Queens College of the City University of New York M
Rice University M
Roosevelt University M
Rutgers, The State University of New Jersey, New Brunswick M,D
St. John's University (NY) M
Saint Louis University M
San Diego State University M
San Francisco State University M
San Jose State University M
Seton Hall University M
Simmons College M
Southern Connecticut State University M
Southwest Missouri State University M
Southwest Texas State University M
Stanford University M,D
State University of New York at Albany M,D
State University of New York at Binghamton M,O
Stony Brook University, State University of New York M,D
Syracuse University M
Temple University M,D
Texas A&M International University M
Texas A&M University M
Texas A&M University–Commerce M,D
Texas A&M University–Kingsville M
Texas Tech University M,D
Tulane University M,D
University at Buffalo, The State University of New York M,D
The University of Akron M
The University of Alabama M,D
The University of Arizona M,D
University of Arkansas M
University of California, Berkeley M,D
University of California, Davis M,D
University of California, Irvine M,D
University of California, Los Angeles M
University of California, Riverside M,D
University of California, San Diego M,D
University of California, Santa Barbara M,D
University of Central Florida M
University of Chicago M,D
University of Cincinnati M,D
University of Colorado at Boulder M,D
University of Connecticut M,D
University of Delaware M
University of Denver M
University of Florida M,D
University of Georgia M
University of Hawaii at Manoa M
University of Houston M,D
University of Idaho M
The University of Iowa M,D
University of Kansas M,D
University of Kentucky M,D
University of Louisville M
University of Maryland, Baltimore County M
University of Maryland, College Park M,D
University of Massachusetts Amherst M,D
The University of Memphis M
University of Miami D
University of Michigan D
University of Minnesota, Twin Cities Campus M,D
University of Mississippi M
University of Missouri–Columbia M,D
The University of Montana–Missoula M
University of Nebraska–Lincoln M,D
University of Nevada, Las Vegas M
University of Nevada, Reno M
University of New Hampshire M
University of New Mexico M,D
The University of North Carolina at Chapel Hill M,D
The University of North Carolina at Greensboro M

University of Northern Colorado M
University of Northern Iowa M
University of North Texas M
University of Notre Dame M
University of Oklahoma M,D
University of Oregon M
University of Pennsylvania M,D
University of Pittsburgh M,D
University of Rhode Island M
University of Rochester M
University of South Carolina M
University of South Florida M
The University of Tennessee M,D
The University of Texas at Arlington M
The University of Texas at Austin M,D
The University of Texas at Brownsville M
The University of Texas at El Paso M
The University of Texas at San Antonio M
The University of Texas–Pan American M
University of Toledo M
University of Utah M,D
University of Virginia M,D
University of Washington M
University of Wisconsin–Madison M,D
University of Wisconsin–Milwaukee M
University of Wyoming M
Vanderbilt University M,D
Villanova University M
Washington State University M
Washington University in St. Louis M,D
Wayne State University M
West Chester University of Pennsylvania M
Western Michigan University M
West Virginia University M
Wichita State University M
Winthrop University M
Yale University M,D

■ SPECIAL EDUCATION

Adams State College M
Adelphi University M,O
Alabama Agricultural and Mechanical University M,O
Alabama State University M
Albany State University M
Alcorn State University M,O
American International College M,D,O
American University M
Appalachian State University M
Arcadia University M,O
Arizona State University M
Arizona State University West M
Arkansas State University M
Armstrong Atlantic State University M
Ashland University M
Assumption College M
Auburn University M,D,O
Auburn University Montgomery M,O
Augusta State University M,O
Austin Peay State University M,O
Averett University M
Azusa Pacific University M
Baldwin-Wallace College M
Ball State University M,D,O
Barry University M,D,O
Bayamón Central University M
Bellarmine University M
Bemidji State University M
Benedictine University M
Bloomsburg University of Pennsylvania M
Boise State University M
Boston College M,O
Boston University M,D,O
Bowie State University M
Bowling Green State University M
Bradley University M
Brenau University M,O
Bridgewater State College M
Brigham Young University M,D
Brooklyn College of the City University of New York M
Butler University M,O
California Baptist University M
California Lutheran University M
California Polytechnic State University, San Luis Obispo M
California State University, Bakersfield M
California State University, Chico M
California State University, Dominguez Hills M
California State University, Fresno M
California State University, Fullerton M
California State University, Hayward M
California State University, Long Beach M
California State University, Los Angeles M,D
California State University, Northridge M
California State University, Sacramento M
California State University, San Bernardino M
California State University, Stanislaus M
California University of Pennsylvania M
Canisius College M
Cardinal Stritch University M
Castleton State College M,O
Central Connecticut State University M
Central Michigan University M
Central Missouri State University M,O
Central Washington University M
Chapman University M
Cheyney University of Pennsylvania M
Chicago State University M
City College of the City University of New York M
Clarion University of Pennsylvania M
Clemson University M
Cleveland State University M
College of Mount St. Joseph M
The College of New Jersey M
The College of New Rochelle M
College of Our Lady of the Elms M,O
College of St. Joseph M
The College of Saint Rose M
College of Santa Fe M
College of Staten Island of the City University of New York M
The College of William and Mary M
Columbus State University M,O
Converse College M
Coppin State College M
Cumberland College M
Delaware State University M
Delta State University M
DePaul University M
Dominican University M
Dowling College M
Drake University M
Duquesne University M
East Carolina University M
Eastern Illinois University M
Eastern Kentucky University M
Eastern Michigan University M,O
Eastern Nazarene College M,O
Eastern New Mexico University M
Eastern Washington University M
East Stroudsburg University of Pennsylvania M
East Tennessee State University M
Edgewood College M,O
Edinboro University of Pennsylvania M
Elon University M
Emporia State University M
Fairfield University M,O
Fairleigh Dickinson University, Teaneck–Hackensack Campus M
Fayetteville State University M
Fitchburg State College M
Florida Atlantic University M,D
Florida Gulf Coast University M
Florida International University M,D
Florida State University M,D,O
Fontbonne College M
Fordham University M,D,O
Fort Hays State University M
Framingham State College M
Francis Marion University M
Fresno Pacific University M
Frostburg State University M
Gallaudet University M,D,O
Geneva College M
George Mason University M
The George Washington University M,D,O
Georgia College and State University M
Georgian Court College M
Georgia Southern University M,O
Georgia State University M,D,O
Gonzaga University M
Governors State University M
Grand Valley State University M
Hampton University M
Henderson State University M
Heritage College M
Hofstra University M,O
Hood College M
Houston Baptist University M
Howard University M,O
Hunter College of the City University of New York M
Idaho State University M,O
Illinois State University M,D
Immaculata College M,D,O
Indiana State University M,D,O
Indiana University Bloomington M,D,O
Indiana University of Pennsylvania M
Indiana University–Purdue University Indianapolis M
Indiana University South Bend M
Inter American University of Puerto Rico, Metropolitan Campus M
Inter American University of Puerto Rico, San Germán Campus M
Iowa State University of Science and Technology M,D
Jackson State University M,O
Jacksonville State University M,O
Jacksonville University M,O
James Madison University M
Johns Hopkins University M,D,O
Johnson State College M
Kansas State University M,D
Kean University M
Keene State College M,O
Kennesaw State University M
Kent State University M,D,O
Kutztown University of Pennsylvania M,O
Lamar University M,D,O
La Sierra University M,D,O
Lehigh University M,D,O
Lehman College of the City University of New York M
Lesley University M,D,O
Liberty University M,D
Long Island University, Brooklyn Campus M
Long Island University, C.W. Post Campus M,O
Longwood College M
Loras College M

Louisiana Tech University	M,D,O
Loyola College in Maryland	M,O
Loyola Marymount University	M
Loyola University Chicago	M
Lynchburg College	M
Lynn University	M,D
Madonna University	M
Malone College	M
Manhattan College	M,O
Manhattanville College	M
Marshall University	M
Marygrove College	M
Marymount University	M
Marywood University	M
McNeese State University	M
Mercy College	M,O
Miami University	M
Michigan State University	M,D,O
Middle Tennessee State University	M
Midwestern State University	M
Millersville University of Pennsylvania	M
Minnesota State University, Mankato	M
Minnesota State University Moorhead	M
Minot State University	M
Mississippi State University	M,D,O
Monmouth University	M,O
Montana State University–Billings	M
Montclair State University	M
Morehead State University	M
Mount Saint Mary College	M
Mount St. Mary's College	M
Murray State University	M
National-Louis University	M,O
National University	M
Nazareth College of Rochester	M
New Jersey City University	M
New Mexico Highlands University	M
New Mexico State University	M
New York University	M,O
North Carolina Central University	M
North Carolina State University	M
Northeastern Illinois University	M
Northeastern State University	M
Northeastern University	M
Northern Arizona University	M
Northern Illinois University	M
Northern Michigan University	M
Northern State University	M
North Georgia College & State University	M,O
Northwestern State University of Louisiana	M,O
Northwestern University	M,D
Northwest Missouri State University	M
Northwest Nazarene University	M
Notre Dame de Namur University	M,O
Oakland University	M,O
Ohio University	M,D
Old Dominion University	M
Our Lady of the Lake University of San Antonio	M
Pacific Lutheran University	M
The Pennsylvania State University Great Valley Campus	M
The Pennsylvania State University University Park Campus	M,D
Pittsburg State University	M
Plattsburgh State University of New York	M
Portland State University	M
Prairie View A&M University	M
Pratt Institute	M
Providence College	M
Purdue University	M,D,O
Queens College of the City University of New York	M
Radford University	M
Rhode Island College	M,O
Rivier College	M
Rochester Institute of Technology	M,O
Rockford College	M
Rowan University	M
Rutgers, The State University of New Jersey, New Brunswick	M
Sage Graduate School	M
Saginaw Valley State University	M
St. Ambrose University	M
St. Bonaventure University	M
St. Cloud State University	M,O
St. John Fisher College	M
St. John's University (NY)	M,O
Saint Joseph College	M
Saint Joseph's University	M
Saint Louis University	M,D
Saint Martin's College	M
Saint Mary's College of California	M
Saint Mary's University of Minnesota	M
Saint Michael's College	M,O
St. Thomas Aquinas College	M,O
Saint Xavier University	M,O
Salem State College	M
Sam Houston State University	M,O
San Diego State University	M
San Francisco State University	M,D,O
San Jose State University	M
Santa Clara University	M
Shippensburg University of Pennsylvania	M
Simmons College	M,O
Slippery Rock University of Pennsylvania	M
Sonoma State University	M
South Carolina State University	M
Southeastern Louisiana University	M
Southeast Missouri State University	M
Southern Connecticut State University	M,O
Southern Illinois University Carbondale	M
Southern Illinois University Edwardsville	M
Southern Oregon University	M
Southern University and Agricultural and Mechanical College	M,D
Southwestern Oklahoma State University	M
Southwest Missouri State University	M
Southwest Texas State University	M
State University of New York at Albany	M
State University of New York at Binghamton	M
State University of New York at New Paltz	M
State University of New York at Oswego	M
State University of New York College at Buffalo	M
State University of New York College at Geneseo	M
State University of New York College at Potsdam	M
State University of West Georgia	M,O
Stephen F. Austin State University	M
Stetson University	M
Syracuse University	M,D
Tarleton State University	M,O
Teachers College, Columbia University	M,D
Temple University	M,D
Tennessee State University	M,D
Tennessee Technological University	M,O
Texas A&M University	M,D
Texas A&M University–Commerce	M,D
Texas A&M University–Corpus Christi	M
Texas A&M University–Kingsville	M
Texas A&M University–Texarkana	M
Texas Christian University	M
Texas Southern University	M,D
Texas Tech University	M,D,O
Texas Woman's University	M,D
Trinity College (DC)	M
Troy State University	M,O
Universidad del Turabo	M
Universidad Metropolitana	M
University at Buffalo, The State University of New York	M,D,O
The University of Akron	M
The University of Alabama	M,D,O
The University of Alabama at Birmingham	M
University of Alaska Anchorage	M
The University of Arizona	M,D,O
University of Arkansas	M
University of Arkansas at Little Rock	M
University of California, Berkeley	D
University of California, Los Angeles	D
University of Central Arkansas	M
University of Central Florida	M
University of Central Oklahoma	M
University of Cincinnati	M,D
University of Colorado at Colorado Springs	M
University of Colorado at Denver	M
University of Connecticut	M,D
University of Dayton	M
University of Delaware	M,D
University of Detroit Mercy	M
The University of Findlay	M
University of Florida	M,D,O
University of Georgia	M,D,O
University of Guam	M
University of Hartford	M
University of Hawaii at Manoa	M,D
University of Houston	M,D
University of Idaho	M,O
University of Illinois at Chicago	M,D
University of Illinois at Urbana–Champaign	M,D,O
The University of Iowa	M,D
University of Kansas	M,D
University of Kentucky	M,D,O
University of La Verne	M
University of Louisiana at Monroe	M
University of Louisville	M,D,O
University of Maine	M,O
University of Mary	M
University of Maryland, College Park	M,D,O
University of Maryland Eastern Shore	M
University of Massachusetts Amherst	M,D,O
University of Massachusetts Boston	M
The University of Memphis	M,D
University of Miami	M,D,O
University of Michigan–Dearborn	M
University of Minnesota, Twin Cities Campus	M,D,O
University of Missouri–Columbia	M,D,O
University of Missouri–Kansas City	M,D,O
University of Missouri–St. Louis	M
University of Nebraska at Kearney	M
University of Nebraska at Omaha	M
University of Nebraska–Lincoln	M
University of Nevada, Las Vegas	M,D,O
University of Nevada, Reno	M,D,O
University of New Hampshire	M
University of New Mexico	M,D,O
University of New Orleans	M,D,O
University of North Alabama	M
The University of North Carolina at Chapel Hill	M
The University of North Carolina at Charlotte	M

The University of North Carolina at Greensboro	M
The University of North Carolina at Wilmington	M
University of North Dakota	M,D
University of Northern Colorado	M,D
University of Northern Iowa	M
University of North Florida	M
University of North Texas	M,D
University of Oklahoma	M,D
University of Oregon	M,D
University of Pittsburgh	M,D
University of Portland	M
University of Puerto Rico, Río Piedras	M
University of Rio Grande	M
University of Saint Francis (IN)	M
University of St. Thomas (MN)	M
University of South Alabama	M,O
University of South Carolina	M,D
University of South Dakota	M
University of Southern California	M,D
University of Southern Maine	M
University of Southern Mississippi	M,D,O
University of South Florida	M,D,O
The University of Tennessee	M,D,O
The University of Tennessee at Chattanooga	M,O
The University of Texas at Austin	M,D
The University of Texas at Brownsville	M
The University of Texas at Tyler	M,O
The University of Texas of the Permian Basin	M
The University of Texas–Pan American	M,D
University of the District of Columbia	M
University of the Incarnate Word	M
University of Toledo	M,D,O
University of Utah	M,D
University of Vermont	M
University of Virginia	M,D,O
University of Washington	M,D
The University of West Alabama	M
University of West Florida	M
University of Wisconsin–Eau Claire	M
University of Wisconsin–La Crosse	M
University of Wisconsin–Madison	M,D
University of Wisconsin–Milwaukee	M
University of Wisconsin–Oshkosh	M
University of Wisconsin–Superior	M
University of Wisconsin–Whitewater	M
Utah State University	M,D,O
Valdosta State University	M,O
Valparaiso University	M
Vanderbilt University	M,D
Virginia Commonwealth University	M
Virginia Polytechnic Institute and State University	D,O
Wagner College	M
Walla Walla College	M
Washburn University of Topeka	M
Washington University in St. Louis	M,D
Wayne State College	M
Wayne State University	M,D,O
Webster University	M
West Chester University of Pennsylvania	M
Western Carolina University	M
Western Connecticut State University	M
Western Illinois University	M
Western Kentucky University	M
Western Michigan University	M,D
Western New Mexico University	M
Western Oregon University	M
Western Washington University	M
Westfield State College	M
West Virginia University	M,D
Wheelock College	M
Whitworth College	M
Wichita State University	M
Widener University	M,D
William Carey College	M
William Paterson University of New Jersey	M
Wilmington College	M,D
Winona State University	M
Winthrop University	M
Wright State University	M
Xavier University	M
Youngstown State University	M

■ SPEECH AND INTERPERSONAL COMMUNICATION

Abilene Christian University	M
Arizona State University	M,D
Arkansas State University	M,O
Austin Peay State University	M
Ball State University	M
Bowling Green State University	M,D
Brooklyn College of the City University of New York	M,D
California State University, Chico	M
California State University, Fresno	M
California State University, Fullerton	M
California State University, Hayward	M
California State University, Los Angeles	M
California State University, Northridge	M
Carnegie Mellon University	M,D
The Catholic University of America	M,D
Central Michigan University	M
Central Missouri State University	M
Colorado State University	M
Eastern Illinois University	M
Eastern Michigan University	M
Emerson College	M
Florida State University	M,D
Georgia College and State University	M
Idaho State University	M
Indiana University Bloomington	M,D
Iowa State University of Science and Technology	M,D
Kansas State University	M
Louisiana State University and Agricultural and Mechanical College	M,D
Louisiana Tech University	M
Marquette University	M
Miami University	M
Minnesota State University, Mankato	M
Montclair State University	M
Morehead State University	M
New York University	M,O
Norfolk State University	M
North Dakota State University	M
Northeastern Illinois University	M
Northwestern University	M,D
Ohio University	M,D
The Pennsylvania State University University Park Campus	M,D
Portland State University	M
Rensselaer Polytechnic Institute	M,D
St. Mary's University of San Antonio	M
San Francisco State University	M
San Jose State University	M
Southern Illinois University Carbondale	M,D
Southern Illinois University Edwardsville	M
Southwest Texas State University	M
Syracuse University	M
Temple University	M
Texas A&M University	M,D
Texas A&M University–Commerce	M
Texas Christian University	M
Texas Southern University	M
The University of Alabama	M
University of Arkansas at Little Rock	M
University of California, Berkeley	D
University of Connecticut	M
University of Denver	M,D
University of Georgia	M,D
University of Hawaii at Manoa	M
University of Houston	M
University of Illinois at Urbana–Champaign	M,D
The University of Iowa	M,D
University of Maryland, College Park	M,D
University of Minnesota, Twin Cities Campus	M,D
University of Nevada, Reno	M
The University of North Carolina at Greensboro	M
University of South Dakota	M
University of Southern California	M,D
The University of Tennessee	M,D
The University of Texas–Pan American	M
University of Washington	M,D
University of Wisconsin–Stevens Point	M
University of Wisconsin–Superior	M
Wake Forest University	M
Wayne State University	M,D
Western Kentucky University	M

■ SPORT PSYCHOLOGY

Cleveland State University	M
Florida State University	M,D,O
John F. Kennedy University	M
Purdue University	M,D
Southern Connecticut State University	M
Springfield College	M,D,O
University of Florida	D
West Virginia University	M,D

■ SPORTS ADMINISTRATION

Appalachian State University	M
Barry University	M
Belmont University	M
Boise State University	M
Bowling Green State University	M
Brooklyn College of the City University of New York	M
Canisius College	M
Central Michigan University	M
Cleveland State University	M
Eastern Kentucky University	M
East Stroudsburg University of Pennsylvania	M
Florida Atlantic University	M
Florida State University	M,D,O
The George Washington University	M
Georgia Southern University	M
Georgia State University	M
Gonzaga University	M
Grambling State University	M
Hardin-Simmons University	M
Idaho State University	M
Indiana State University	M
Indiana University Bloomington	M,D,O
Indiana University of Pennsylvania	M
Lynn University	M
Millersville University of Pennsylvania	M
Mississippi State University	M
Montana State University–Billings	M
Montclair State University	M
Morehead State University	M
North Carolina State University	M
North Dakota State University	M
Northwestern State University of Louisiana	M
Ohio University	M
Old Dominion University	M

Robert Morris College	M
St. Cloud State University	M
St. Edward's University	M,O
St. Thomas University	M
Seton Hall University	M,O
Southeast Missouri State University	M
Southwest Texas State University	M
Springfield College	M,D,O
Temple University	M
University of Denver	M
University of Miami	M
University of New Haven	M
University of New Orleans	M,O
The University of North Carolina at Chapel Hill	M
University of Oklahoma	M
University of Rhode Island	M,D
University of St. Thomas (MN)	M,O
University of San Francisco	M
University of Southern Mississippi	M,D
The University of Tennessee	M
University of the Incarnate Word	M,D
University of Wisconsin–La Crosse	M
Wayne State College	M
Wayne State University	M
West Chester University of Pennsylvania	M,O
Western Illinois University	M
Western Michigan University	M
West Virginia University	M,D
Whitworth College	M
Wichita State University	M
Xavier University	M

■ STATISTICS

American University	M,D,O
Arizona State University	M,D
Auburn University	M,D
Ball State University	M
Baylor University	M,D
Bernard M. Baruch College of the City University of New York	M
Bowling Green State University	M,D,O
Brigham Young University	M
California State University, Fullerton	M
California State University, Hayward	M
California State University, Sacramento	M
Carnegie Mellon University	M,D
Case Western Reserve University	M,D
Central Connecticut State University	M
Claremont Graduate University	M,D
Clemson University	M,D
Colorado State University	M,D
Columbia University	M,D
Cornell University	M,D
Creighton University	M
DePaul University	M
Duke University	D
Florida International University	M
Florida State University	M,D
George Mason University	M
The George Washington University	M,D
Georgia Institute of Technology	M,D
Harvard University	M,D
Indiana University Bloomington	M,D
Indiana University–Purdue University Indianapolis	M,D
Iowa State University of Science and Technology	M,D
Kansas State University	M,D
Kean University	M
Lehigh University	M
Louisiana State University and Agricultural and Mechanical College	M
Louisiana Tech University	M
Marquette University	M,D
McNeese State University	M
Miami University	M
Michigan State University	M,D
Minnesota State University, Mankato	M
Mississippi State University	M,D
Montana State University–Bozeman	M,D
Montclair State University	M,O
New Mexico State University	M
New York University	M,D,O
North Carolina State University	M,D
North Dakota State University	M,D
Northern Arizona University	M
Northern Illinois University	M
Northwestern University	M,D
Oakland University	M,D,O
The Ohio State University	M,D
Oklahoma State University	M,D
Oregon State University	M,D
The Pennsylvania State University University Park Campus	M,D
Princeton University	M,D
Purdue University	M,D
Rensselaer Polytechnic Institute	M
Rice University	M,D
Rochester Institute of Technology	M,O
Rutgers, The State University of New Jersey, New Brunswick	M,D
St. John's University (NY)	M
Sam Houston State University	M
San Diego State University	M
Southern Illinois University Carbondale	M,D
Southern Illinois University Edwardsville	M
Southern Methodist University	M,D
Stanford University	M,D
State University of New York at Albany	M,D,O
State University of New York at Binghamton	M,D
Stephen F. Austin State University	M
Stevens Institute of Technology	M,O
Stony Brook University, State University of New York	M,D
Syracuse University	M
Temple University	M,D
Texas A&M University	M,D
Texas Tech University	M,D
Tulane University	M,D
The University of Akron	M
The University of Alabama	M,D
The University of Arizona	M,D
University of Arkansas	M
University of Arkansas at Little Rock	M
University of California, Berkeley	M,D
University of California, Davis	M,D
University of California, Los Angeles	M,D
University of California, Riverside	M,D
University of California, San Diego	M,D
University of California, Santa Barbara	M,D
University of Central Florida	M
University of Central Oklahoma	M
University of Chicago	M,D
University of Cincinnati	M,D
University of Connecticut	M,D
University of Florida	M,D
University of Georgia	M,D
University of Houston–Clear Lake	M
University of Idaho	M
University of Illinois at Chicago	M,D
University of Illinois at Urbana–Champaign	M,D
The University of Iowa	M,D
University of Kansas	M,D
University of Kentucky	M,D
University of Maryland, Baltimore County	M,D
University of Maryland, College Park	M,D
University of Massachusetts Amherst	M,D
The University of Memphis	M,D
University of Miami	M,D
University of Michigan	M,D
University of Minnesota, Twin Cities Campus	M,D
University of Missouri–Columbia	M,D
University of Missouri–Kansas City	M,D
University of Nebraska–Lincoln	M,D
University of Nevada, Las Vegas	M
University of Nevada, Reno	M
University of New Hampshire	M,D
University of New Mexico	M,D
The University of North Carolina at Chapel Hill	M,D
The University of North Carolina at Charlotte	M,D
University of North Florida	M
University of Pennsylvania	M,D
University of Pittsburgh	M,D
University of Puerto Rico, Mayagüez Campus	M
University of Rhode Island	M,D
University of Rochester	M,D
University of South Carolina	M,D,O
University of Southern California	M
The University of Tennessee	M,D
The University of Texas at Austin	M
The University of Texas at Dallas	M,D
The University of Texas at El Paso	M
The University of Texas at San Antonio	M
University of Toledo	M,D
University of Utah	M
University of Vermont	M
University of Virginia	M,D
University of Washington	M,D
University of West Florida	M
University of Wisconsin–Madison	M,D
University of Wyoming	M,D
Utah State University	M
Villanova University	M
Virginia Commonwealth University	M,O
Virginia Polytechnic Institute and State University	M,D
Washington University in St. Louis	M,D
Wayne State University	M,D
Western Michigan University	M,D
West Virginia University	M,D
Wichita State University	M,D
Worcester Polytechnic Institute	M,D,O
Wright State University	M
Yale University	M,D

■ STRUCTURAL BIOLOGY

Brandeis University	D
Cornell University	M,D
Iowa State University of Science and Technology	M,D
Northwestern University	D
Stanford University	D
State University of New York at Albany	M,D
Stony Brook University, State University of New York	D
Syracuse University	D
Tulane University	M,D
University of Illinois at Urbana–Champaign	D
University of Pennsylvania	D
University of Washington	D

■ STRUCTURAL ENGINEERING

Auburn University	M,D
California State University, Northridge	M

The Catholic University of America M,D
Colorado State University M,D
Cornell University M,D
Howard University M
Iowa State University of Science and Technology M,D
Louisiana State University and Agricultural and Mechanical College M,D
Marquette University M,D
Michigan Technological University D
Northwestern University M,D
Ohio University M
The Pennsylvania State University University Park Campus M,D
Princeton University M,D
Rensselaer Polytechnic Institute M,D
Texas A&M University M,D
Tufts University M,D
University at Buffalo, The State University of New York M,D
University of California, Berkeley M,D
University of California, Los Angeles M,D
University of California, San Diego M,D
University of Central Florida M,D,O
University of Colorado at Boulder M,D
University of Dayton M
University of Delaware M,D
University of Maine M,D
The University of Memphis M,D
University of Missouri–Columbia M,D
University of Missouri–Rolla M,D
University of North Dakota M
University of Oklahoma M,D
University of Rhode Island M,D
University of Southern California M
University of Virginia M,D
University of Washington M,D
Washington University in St. Louis M,D

■ SURVEYING SCIENCE AND ENGINEERING

The Ohio State University M,D

■ SUSTAINABLE DEVELOPMENT

Brandeis University M
Carnegie Mellon University M
New College of California M
Prescott College M
School for International Training M,O
Slippery Rock University of Pennsylvania M
University of Georgia M,D
University of Maryland, College Park M
University of Washington P,M,D
University of Wisconsin–Madison M
Western Illinois University M,O

■ SYSTEMS ENGINEERING

Auburn University M,D
Boston University M,D
California Institute of Technology M,D
California State University, Fullerton M
Case Western Reserve University M,D
Embry-Riddle Aeronautical University M
Florida Atlantic University M
George Mason University M
The George Washington University M,D,O
Georgia Institute of Technology M,D
Iowa State University of Science and Technology M
Lehigh University M
Louisiana State University in Shreveport M
Massachusetts Institute of Technology M,O
North Carolina Agricultural and Technical State University M,D
Northeastern University M
Oakland University M,D
The Ohio State University M,D
Ohio University M
Oklahoma State University M
The Pennsylvania State University Great Valley Campus M
Polytechnic University, Brooklyn Campus M
Polytechnic University, Westchester Graduate Center M
Purdue University M,D
Rensselaer Polytechnic Institute M,D
Rochester Institute of Technology M
Rutgers, The State University of New Jersey, New Brunswick M,D
San Jose State University M
Southern Methodist University M,D
Stanford University M
Texas Tech University M,D
The University of Arizona M,D
University of Central Florida M,D,O
University of Connecticut M,D
University of Florida M,D,O
University of Houston M,D
University of Idaho M,D
University of Illinois at Urbana–Champaign M
University of Maryland, College Park M
University of Massachusetts Lowell M,D
The University of Memphis M
University of Michigan M,D
University of Michigan–Dearborn M
University of Minnesota, Twin Cities Campus M
University of Missouri–Rolla M
University of Pennsylvania M,D
University of Pittsburgh M
University of Rhode Island M,D
University of St. Thomas (MN) M,O
University of Southern California M,D,O
University of Southern Colorado M
University of Virginia M,D
University of West Florida M
Virginia Polytechnic Institute and State University M
Washington University in St. Louis D

■ SYSTEMS SCIENCE

Fairleigh Dickinson University, Teaneck–Hackensack Campus M
Florida Institute of Technology M
Louisiana State University and Agricultural and Mechanical College M
Louisiana State University in Shreveport M
Miami University M
Portland State University D
Southern Methodist University M,D
State University of New York at Binghamton M,D
Syracuse University M,D
University of Michigan–Dearborn M
Washington University in St. Louis M,D

■ TAXATION

American University M
Arizona State University M
Bentley College M,O
Bernard M. Baruch College of the City University of New York M
Boston University P,M
California State University, Fullerton M
California State University, Hayward M
California State University, Los Angeles M
Capital University M
Case Western Reserve University P,M
DePaul University M
Drexel University M
Duquesne University M
Fairfield University M,O
Fairleigh Dickinson University, Florham-Madison Campus M
Fairleigh Dickinson University, Teaneck–Hackensack Campus M
Florida Atlantic University M
Florida Gulf Coast University M
Florida International University M
Fontbonne College M
Fordham University M
Georgetown University P,M,D
Georgia State University M
Grand Valley State University M
Hofstra University M
Illinois Institute of Technology P,M
King's College M
Long Island University, Brooklyn Campus M
Long Island University, C.W. Post Campus M
Loyola Marymount University P,M
Mississippi State University M
Northeastern University M,O
Northern Illinois University M
Old Dominion University M
Pace University, New York City Campus M
Pace University, White Plains Campus M
Philadelphia University M
Regent University P,M
Robert Morris College M
St. John Fisher College M
St. John's University (NY) M,O
St. Thomas University P,M
Saint Xavier University M,O
San Francisco State University M
San Jose State University M
Seton Hall University M,O
Southeastern University M
Southern Methodist University P,M,D
State University of New York at Albany M
Suffolk University M,O
Temple University P,M
The University of Akron M
The University of Alabama M
University of Baltimore P,M
University of Central Florida M
University of Colorado at Boulder M,D
University of Denver M
University of Florida M
University of Hartford M
University of Houston M,D
The University of Memphis M
University of Miami M
University of Minnesota, Twin Cities Campus M
University of Mississippi M,D
University of Missouri–Kansas City M
University of Missouri–St. Louis M,O
University of New Haven M
University of New Mexico M
University of New Orleans M
University of San Diego P,M,O
University of South Carolina M
University of Southern California M
The University of Texas at Arlington M,D
The University of Texas at San Antonio M

University of the Sacred Heart M
University of Tulsa M
University of Washington P,M,D
Villanova University M
Virginia Commonwealth University M,D
Wayne State University M
Widener University M

■ TECHNICAL WRITING

Boise State University M
Bowling Green State University M
Carnegie Mellon University M
Colorado State University M
Drexel University M
Florida Institute of Technology M
Georgia State University M,D
Illinois Institute of Technology M
James Madison University M
Metropolitan State University M
Miami University M
Michigan Technological University M,D
New Jersey Institute of Technology M
North Carolina State University M
Northeastern University M,O
Oregon State University M
Polytechnic University, Brooklyn Campus M
Regis University M,O
Rensselaer Polytechnic Institute M
San Jose State University M
Southwest Texas State University M
Texas Tech University M,D
University of Arkansas at Little Rock M
University of Central Florida M,O
University of Colorado at Denver M
University of Minnesota, Twin Cities Campus M,D
The University of North Carolina at Greensboro M,D,O
University of Washington M

■ TECHNOLOGY AND PUBLIC POLICY

California State University, Los Angeles M
Carnegie Mellon University M,D
Colorado State University M,D
Eastern Michigan University M
George Mason University M
The George Washington University M
Massachusetts Institute of Technology M,D
Northwestern University M,O
Rensselaer Polytechnic Institute M,D
St. Cloud State University M
University of Minnesota, Twin Cities Campus M
University of Pennsylvania M,D
The University of Texas at Austin M
Washington University in St. Louis M,D
Western Illinois University M

■ TELECOMMUNICATIONS

Azusa Pacific University M,O
Boston University M
Columbia University M,D,O
DePaul University M
Drexel University M
George Mason University M
The George Washington University M
Illinois Institute of Technology M,D
Iona College M,O
Michigan State University M,D
New Jersey Institute of Technology M,D,O
North Carolina State University M
Northwestern University M,O
Pace University, New York City Campus M,D,O
Pace University, White Plains Campus M,D,O
The Pennsylvania State University University Park Campus M
Polytechnic University, Brooklyn Campus M
Polytechnic University, Westchester Graduate Center M
Regis University M,O
Rochester Institute of Technology M
Roosevelt University M
Saint Mary's University of Minnesota M
Southern Methodist University M,D
State University of New York Institute of Technology at Utica/Rome M
Syracuse University M
Texas Tech University M,D
University of Arkansas M
University of California, San Diego M,D
University of Colorado at Boulder M
University of Denver M
University of Louisiana at Lafayette M
University of Maryland, College Park M
University of Missouri–Kansas City M,D
University of Pennsylvania M
University of Pittsburgh M,O
The University of Texas at Dallas M,D
Western Illinois University M,O
Widener University M

■ TELECOMMUNICATIONS MANAGEMENT

Alaska Pacific University M
Canisius College M
Illinois Institute of Technology M
Murray State University M
National University M
Northwestern University M,O
Oklahoma State University M
Polytechnic University, Brooklyn Campus M
Regis University M,O
San Diego State University M
Stevens Institute of Technology M,D,O
Syracuse University M
University of Colorado at Boulder M
University of Denver M
University of Maryland University College M
University of Miami M,O
University of Missouri–St. Louis M,D,O
University of Pennsylvania M
University of San Francisco M
Webster University M

■ TEXTILE DESIGN

California State University, Los Angeles M
Central Washington University M
Colorado State University M
Cornell University M,D
Drexel University M
Illinois State University M
Indiana University Bloomington M
James Madison University M
Kent State University M
New School University M
Philadelphia University M
Rochester Institute of Technology M
San Jose State University M
Southern Illinois University Edwardsville M
Sul Ross State University M
Syracuse University M
Temple University M
Texas Woman's University M
University of California, Davis M
University of Cincinnati M
University of Minnesota, Twin Cities Campus M,D
The University of North Carolina at Greensboro M,D
University of North Texas M,D
Western Michigan University M

■ TEXTILE SCIENCES AND ENGINEERING

Auburn University M,D
Clemson University M,D
Cornell University M,D
Georgia Institute of Technology M,D
North Carolina State University M,D
Philadelphia University M
University of Massachusetts Dartmouth M

■ THEATER

Antioch University McGregor M
Arizona State University M,D
Arkansas State University M,O
Austin Peay State University M
Baylor University M
Boston University M,O
Bowling Green State University M,D
Brandeis University M
Brigham Young University M
Brooklyn College of the City University of New York M
Brown University M
California State University, Fullerton M
California State University, Long Beach M
California State University, Los Angeles M
California State University, Northridge M
California State University, Sacramento M
Carnegie Mellon University M
Case Western Reserve University M,D
The Catholic University of America M
Central Michigan University M
Central Missouri State University M
Central Washington University M
Claremont Graduate University M,D
Columbia University M,D
Cornell University D
DePaul University M,O
Eastern Michigan University M
Emerson College M
Florida Atlantic University M
Florida State University M,D
The George Washington University M
Humboldt State University M
Hunter College of the City University of New York M
Idaho State University M
Illinois State University M
Indiana State University M
Indiana University Bloomington M,D
Kent State University M
Lamar University M
Lesley University M,O
Lindenwood University M
Long Island University, C.W. Post Campus M
Louisiana State University and Agricultural and Mechanical College M,D
Miami University M
Michigan State University M,D
Minnesota State University, Mankato M
Montana State University–Billings M
Montclair State University M

Morehead State University	M
New School University	M
New York University	M,D,O
North Dakota State University	M
Northern Illinois University	M
Northwestern University	M,D
The Ohio State University	M,D
Ohio University	M
Oklahoma City University	M
Oklahoma State University	M
The Pennsylvania State University University Park Campus	M
Pittsburg State University	M
Portland State University	M
Purchase College, State University of New York	M
Purdue University	M
Regent University	M
Rhode Island College	M
Roosevelt University	M
Rowan University	M
Rutgers, The State University of New Jersey, New Brunswick	M
San Diego State University	M
San Francisco State University	M
San Jose State University	M
South Dakota State University	M
Southern Illinois University Carbondale	M,D
Southern Methodist University	M
Southwest Missouri State University	M
Southwest Texas State University	M
Stanford University	D
State University of New York at Albany	M
State University of New York at Binghamton	M
Stephen F. Austin State University	M
Stony Brook University, State University of New York	M
Syracuse University	M
Temple University	M
Texas A&M University–Commerce	M
Texas Tech University	M,D
Texas Woman's University	M
Towson University	M,O
Tufts University	M,D
Tulane University	M
The University of Akron	M
The University of Alabama	M
The University of Arizona	M
University of Arkansas	M
University of California, Berkeley	D,O
University of California, Davis	M,D
University of California, Irvine	M,D
University of California, Los Angeles	M,D
University of California, San Diego	M,D
University of California, Santa Barbara	M,D
University of California, Santa Cruz	O
University of Cincinnati	M
University of Colorado at Boulder	M,D
University of Colorado at Denver	M
University of Connecticut	M
University of Delaware	M
University of Florida	M
University of Georgia	M,D
University of Hawaii at Manoa	M,D
University of Houston	M
University of Idaho	M
University of Illinois at Chicago	M
University of Illinois at Urbana–Champaign	M,D
The University of Iowa	M
University of Kansas	M,D
University of Kentucky	M
University of Louisville	M
University of Maine	M
University of Maryland, College Park	M,D
University of Massachusetts Amherst	M
The University of Memphis	M
University of Michigan	M,D
University of Minnesota, Twin Cities Campus	M,D
University of Mississippi	M
University of Missouri–Columbia	M,D
University of Missouri–Kansas City	M
The University of Montana–Missoula	M
University of Nebraska at Omaha	M
University of Nebraska–Lincoln	M,D
University of Nevada, Las Vegas	M
University of New Mexico	M
University of New Orleans	M
The University of North Carolina at Chapel Hill	M
The University of North Carolina at Greensboro	M
University of North Dakota	M
University of Northern Iowa	M
University of North Texas	M
University of Oklahoma	M
University of Oregon	M,D
University of Pittsburgh	M,D
University of Portland	M
University of San Diego	M
University of South Carolina	M
University of South Dakota	M
University of Southern California	M
University of Southern Mississippi	M
University of South Florida	M
The University of Tennessee	M
The University of Texas at Austin	M,D
The University of Texas at El Paso	M
The University of Texas–Pan American	M
University of Utah	M,D
University of Virginia	M
University of Washington	M,D
University of Wisconsin–Madison	M,D
University of Wisconsin–Milwaukee	M
University of Wisconsin–Superior	M
Utah State University	M
Villanova University	M
Virginia Commonwealth University	M
Virginia Polytechnic Institute and State University	M
Washington State University	M
Washington University in St. Louis	M
Wayne State University	M,D
Western Illinois University	M
Western Washington University	M
West Virginia University	M
Yale University	M,D,O

■ THEOLOGY

Abilene Christian University	P,M
Anderson University	P,M,D
Andrews University	P,M,D
Ashland University	P,M,D
Azusa Pacific University	P,M,D
Barry University	M,D
Bayamón Central University	P,M
Baylor University	P,D
Biola University	P,M,D
Boston College	M,D
Boston University	P,M,D
Campbellsville University	M
Campbell University	P,M
The Catholic University of America	P,M,D,O
Claremont Graduate University	M,D
College of Mount St. Joseph	M
College of St. Catherine	M
Concordia University (CA)	M
Creighton University	M
Duke University	P,M
Duquesne University	M,D
Emory University	P,M,D
Fordham University	M,D
Franciscan University of Steubenville	M
Freed-Hardeman University	M
Friends University	M
George Fox University	P,M,D
Georgian Court College	M
Golden Gate Baptist Theological Seminary	P,M,D,O
Gonzaga University	P,M
Grand Rapids Baptist Seminary	P,M,D
Hardin-Simmons University	P
Harvard University	P,M,D
Houston Baptist University	M
Howard University	P,M,D
Indiana Wesleyan University	M
La Salle University	M
Liberty University	P,M,D
Lipscomb University	P,M
Loyola Marymount University	M
Loyola University Chicago	P,M,D
Loyola University New Orleans	M
Marquette University	M,D
Marylhurst University	M
Mercer University	P
Mount Saint Mary's College and Seminary	P,M
North Park Theological Seminary	P,M,D,O
Oakland City University	P,D
Olivet Nazarene University	M
Oral Roberts University	P,M,D
Palm Beach Atlantic College	M
Pontifical Catholic University of Puerto Rico	M
Providence College	M
Regent University	P,M,D
St. Bonaventure University	M,O
St. John's University (NY)	P,M,O
Saint Louis University	M,D
St. Mary's University of San Antonio	M
Saint Michael's College	M,O
Samford University	P,M,D
Seattle University	P,M,O
Seton Hall University	P,M,O
Simpson College and Graduate School	M
Southern Methodist University	P,M,D
Southern Nazarene University	M
Spring Hill College	M
Texas Christian University	P,M,D,O
University of Chicago	P,M,D
University of Dayton	M,D
University of Dubuque	P,M,D
University of Mary Hardin-Baylor	M
University of Mobile	M
University of Notre Dame	P,M,D
University of St. Thomas (MN)	P,M,D
University of St. Thomas (TX)	P,M
University of San Diego	M
University of San Francisco	M
The University of Scranton	M
Ursuline College	M
Valparaiso University	M
Vanderbilt University	P,M
Villanova University	M
Wheeling Jesuit University	M
Xavier University	M
Xavier University of Louisiana	M
Yale University	P,M

■ THEORETICAL CHEMISTRY

Cornell University	D
Georgetown University	M,D
Howard University	M,D
Illinois Institute of Technology	M,D
The University of Tennessee	M,D
West Virginia University	M,D

■ THEORETICAL PHYSICS

Cornell University M,D
Harvard University M,D
Rutgers, The State University of New Jersey, New Brunswick M,D
West Virginia University M,D

■ THEORY AND CRITICISM OF FILM, TELEVISION, AND VIDEO

American University M
Boston University M
Chapman University M
Claremont Graduate University M,D
College of Staten Island of the City University of New York M
Columbia University M
Emory University M
New York University M,D
Ohio University M
San Francisco State University M
University of Chicago M,D
The University of Iowa M,D
University of Kansas M,D
University of Miami M,D
University of Southern California M,D

■ THERAPIES—DANCE, DRAMA, AND MUSIC

Antioch New England Graduate School M
Colorado State University M
Columbia College Chicago M
East Carolina University M
Florida State University M,D
Immaculata College M
Lesley University M,O
MCP Hahnemann University M
Michigan State University M,D
Montclair State University M
New York University M,D
Ohio University M
Pratt Institute M
Shenandoah University M,D,O
Southern Methodist University M
Temple University M,D
Texas Woman's University M
University of Kansas M,D
University of Miami M,D,O

■ TOXICOLOGY

American University M,O
Brown University M,D
Case Western Reserve University M,D
Columbia University M,D
Cornell University M,D
Dartmouth College D
Duke University O
Duquesne University M,D
Florida Agricultural and Mechanical University M,D
The George Washington University M
Indiana University–Purdue University Indianapolis M,D
Iowa State University of Science and Technology M,D
Johns Hopkins University D
Long Island University, Brooklyn Campus M
Louisiana State University and Agricultural and Mechanical College M
Massachusetts Institute of Technology M,D
Michigan State University M,D
North Carolina State University M,D
Northeastern University M,D
Northwestern University D
The Ohio State University M,D
Oregon State University M,D
Purdue University M,D
Rutgers, The State University of New Jersey, New Brunswick M,D
St. John's University (NY) M,D
San Diego State University M,D
State University of New York at Albany M,D
Texas A&M University M,D
Texas Southern University M,D
Texas Tech University M,D
University at Buffalo, The State University of New York M,D
The University of Alabama at Birmingham D
The University of Arizona M,D
University of California, Davis M,D
University of California, Irvine M,D
University of California, Los Angeles D
University of California, Riverside M,D
University of Cincinnati M,D
University of Connecticut M,D
University of Florida M,D,O
University of Georgia M,D
University of Kansas M,D
University of Kentucky M,D
University of Louisville M,D
University of Maryland M,D
University of Maryland, College Park M,D
University of Maryland Eastern Shore M,D
University of Michigan M,D
University of Minnesota, Duluth M,D
University of Minnesota, Twin Cities Campus M,D
University of Mississippi M,D
University of Nebraska–Lincoln M,D
University of New Mexico M,D
The University of North Carolina at Chapel Hill M,D
University of Rhode Island M,D
University of Rochester M,D
University of Southern California M,D
University of Utah M,D
University of Washington M,D
University of Wisconsin–Madison M,D
Utah State University M,D
Vanderbilt University
Virginia Commonwealth University M,D,O
Washington State University M,D
Wayne State University M,D,O
West Virginia University M,D
Wright State University M

■ TRANSCULTURAL NURSING

Augsburg College M
Capital University M
New Jersey City University M
Wayne State University O

■ TRANSLATION AND INTERPRETATION

American University M,O
Gallaudet University M
Georgia State University O
Monterey Institute of International Studies M
Rutgers, The State University of New Jersey, New Brunswick M,D
State University of New York at Albany M,O
State University of New York at Binghamton M,O
University of Arkansas M
The University of Iowa M
University of Puerto Rico, Río Piedras M,O

■ TRANSPERSONAL AND HUMANISTIC PSYCHOLOGY

Duquesne University M,D
John F. Kennedy University M
Seattle University M

■ TRANSPORTATION AND HIGHWAY ENGINEERING

Auburn University M,D
Cornell University M,D
Howard University M
Iowa State University of Science and Technology M,D
Louisiana State University and Agricultural and Mechanical College M,D
Marquette University M,D
Massachusetts Institute of Technology M,D
New Jersey Institute of Technology M,D
Northwestern University M,D
The Pennsylvania State University University Park Campus M,D
Polytechnic University, Brooklyn Campus M
Princeton University M,D
Rensselaer Polytechnic Institute M,D
Texas A&M University M,D
Texas Southern University M
University of Arkansas M
University of California, Berkeley M,D
University of California, Davis M,D
University of California, Irvine M,D
University of Central Florida M,D,O
University of Dayton M
University of Delaware M,D
The University of Memphis M,D
University of Missouri–Columbia M,D
University of Oklahoma M,D
University of Pennsylvania M,D
University of Rhode Island M,D
University of Southern California M
University of Virginia M,D
University of Washington M,D
Villanova University M
Washington University in St. Louis D

■ TRANSPORTATION MANAGEMENT

Arizona State University O
Central Missouri State University M,O
Florida Institute of Technology M
George Mason University M
Iowa State University of Science and Technology M
Massachusetts Institute of Technology M,D
Middle Tennessee State University M
Morgan State University M
New Jersey Institute of Technology M,D
Polytechnic University, Brooklyn Campus M
Polytechnic University, Westchester Graduate Center M
San Jose State University M
University of Arkansas M
University of California, Davis M,D
The University of Tennessee M,D
University of Virginia M,D
University of Washington O

■ TRAVEL AND TOURISM

Central Michigan University M,O

Clemson University M,D
The George Washington University M
Michigan State University M,D
New York University M
North Carolina State University M
Purdue University M,D
Rochester Institute of Technology M
Temple University M
University of Denver M
University of Hawaii at Manoa M
University of Massachusetts Amherst M
University of New Haven M
University of South Carolina M
The University of Tennessee M
University of Wisconsin–Stout M
Virginia Polytechnic Institute and State University M,D
Western Illinois University M

■ URBAN DESIGN

City College of the City University of New York M
Columbia University M
Cornell University M,D
Harvard University M
New York Institute of Technology M
Pratt Institute M
Rice University M,D
University at Buffalo, The State University of New York M
University of California, Berkeley M,D
University of California, Los Angeles M,D
University of Colorado at Denver M
University of Miami M
University of Michigan M
University of Washington M,D,O
Washington University in St. Louis M

■ URBAN EDUCATION

Cleveland State University D
College of Mount Saint Vincent M,O
Columbia College Chicago M
Concordia University (IL) M,O
DePaul University M
Florida International University M
Georgia State University M
Harvard University M,D,O
Morgan State University D
New Jersey City University M
Norfolk State University M
Northeastern Illinois University M
Old Dominion University D
Saint Peter's College M
Temple University M,D
Texas Southern University M,D
University of Massachusetts Boston M,D,O
University of Wisconsin–Milwaukee M,D
Virginia Commonwealth University D

■ URBAN STUDIES

Boston University M
Brooklyn College of the City University of New York M
Cleveland State University M,D
East Tennessee State University M
Georgia State University M
Hunter College of the City University of New York M
Long Island University, Brooklyn Campus M
Massachusetts Institute of Technology M,D
Michigan State University M,D
Minnesota State University, Mankato M
New Jersey City University M
New School University M
Norfolk State University M
Old Dominion University M,D
Portland State University M,D
Queens College of the City University of New York M
Rutgers, The State University of New Jersey, Newark M,D
Saint Louis University M
Savannah State University M
Southern Connecticut State University M
State University of New York at Albany M,D,O
Temple University M
Tufts University M
The University of Akron M,D
University of Central Oklahoma M
University of Delaware M,D
University of Louisville D
University of New Orleans M,D
University of Wisconsin–Milwaukee M,D
Wright State University M

■ VETERINARY MEDICINE

Auburn University P
Colorado State University P
Cornell University P
Iowa State University of Science and Technology P
Kansas State University P
Louisiana State University and Agricultural and Mechanical College P
Michigan State University P
Mississippi State University P
North Carolina State University P
The Ohio State University P
Oklahoma State University P
Oregon State University P
Purdue University P
Texas A&M University P
Tufts University P
Tuskegee University P
University of California, Davis P
University of Florida P
University of Georgia P
University of Illinois at Urbana–Champaign P
University of Maryland, College Park P
University of Minnesota, Twin Cities Campus P
University of Missouri–Columbia P
University of Pennsylvania P
The University of Tennessee P
University of Wisconsin–Madison P
Virginia Polytechnic Institute and State University P
Washington State University P

■ VETERINARY SCIENCES

Auburn University M,D
Colorado State University M,D
Cornell University M,D
Iowa State University of Science and Technology M,D
Kansas State University M
Louisiana State University and Agricultural and Mechanical College M,D
MCP Hahnemann University M
Michigan State University M,D
Mississippi State University M,D
Montana State University–Bozeman M,D
North Carolina State University M,D
North Dakota State University M,D
The Ohio State University M,D
Oklahoma State University M,D
Oregon State University M,D
The Pennsylvania State University University Park Campus M,D
Purdue University M,D
Texas A&M University M,D
Tufts University M,D
Tuskegee University M
The University of Arizona M,D
University of California, Davis M,O
University of Florida M,D,O
University of Georgia M,D
University of Idaho M,D
University of Illinois at Urbana–Champaign M,D
University of Kentucky M,D
University of Maryland, College Park D
University of Massachusetts Amherst M,D
University of Minnesota, Twin Cities Campus M,D
University of Missouri–Columbia M,D
University of Nebraska–Lincoln M,D
University of Washington M
University of Wisconsin–Madison M,D
Utah State University M,D
Virginia Polytechnic Institute and State University M,D
Washington State University M,D
West Virginia University M

■ VIROLOGY

Cornell University M,D
Harvard University D
Johns Hopkins University M,D
Kansas State University M,D
Loyola University Chicago M,D
Purdue University M,D
Rutgers, The State University of New Jersey, New Brunswick M,D
University of California, San Diego D
University of Chicago D
The University of Iowa M,D
University of Pennsylvania D
University of Pittsburgh M,D
University of Virginia D
West Virginia University M,D

■ VISION SCIENCES

Emory University M
Indiana University Bloomington M,D
Pacific University M
The University of Alabama at Birmingham M,D
The University of Alabama in Huntsville M,D
University of California, Berkeley M,D
University of Chicago D
University of Houston M,D
University of Louisville D
University of Missouri–St. Louis M,D

■ VOCATIONAL AND TECHNICAL EDUCATION

Alabama Agricultural and Mechanical University M
Alcorn State University M,O
Appalachian State University M
Ball State University M
Bemidji State University M
Bowling Green State University M
Brigham Young University M
California Baptist University M
California State University, Long Beach M
California State University, Sacramento M
California State University, San Bernardino M

California University of Pennsylvania M
Central Connecticut State University M
Central Michigan University M
Central Missouri State University M,O
Chicago State University M
Clemson University M,D
Colorado State University M,D
Drake University M
East Carolina University M
Eastern Kentucky University M
Eastern Michigan University M
Eastern Washington University M
Ferris State University M
Fitchburg State College M
Florida Agricultural and Mechanical University M
Florida International University M
Florida State University D,O
Georgia Southern University M,O
Georgia State University M,D,O
Idaho State University M
Indiana State University M,D,O
Inter American University of Puerto Rico, Metropolitan Campus M
Iowa State University of Science and Technology M,D
Jackson State University M
James Madison University M
Kent State University M,O
Louisiana State University and Agricultural and Mechanical College M,D
Marshall University M
Middle Tennessee State University M
Millersville University of Pennsylvania M
Mississippi State University M,D,O
Montana State University–Northern M
Montclair State University M
Morehead State University M
Murray State University M
North Carolina Agricultural and Technical State University M
North Carolina State University M,D,O
Northern Arizona University M
Nova Southeastern University D
The Ohio State University D
Oklahoma State University M,D,O
Old Dominion University M,O
Oregon State University M
The Pennsylvania State University University Park Campus M,D
Pittsburg State University M,O
Purdue University M,D,O
Rhode Island College M
Rutgers, The State University of New Jersey, New Brunswick M,D,O
Sam Houston State University M
South Carolina State University M
Southern Illinois University Carbondale M,D
Southwestern Oklahoma State University M
Southwest Missouri State University M
Southwest Texas State University M
State University of New York at Oswego M
State University of New York College at Buffalo M
Sul Ross State University M
Temple University M,D
Texas A&M University M,D
Texas A&M University–Commerce M,D
Texas A&M University–Corpus Christi M
The University of Akron M
University of Alaska Anchorage M
University of Arkansas M,D,O
University of Central Florida M
University of Connecticut M,D
University of Georgia M,D,O
University of Idaho M,D,O
University of Illinois at Urbana–Champaign M,D,O
University of Kentucky M,D,O
University of Louisville M,D
University of Maryland Eastern Shore M
University of Minnesota, Twin Cities Campus M,D
University of Missouri–Columbia M,D,O
University of Nevada, Las Vegas M,D,O
University of New Hampshire M
University of Northern Iowa M,D
University of North Texas M,D,O
University of South Carolina M,D
University of Southern Maine M
University of Southern Mississippi M
University of South Florida M,D,O
The University of Texas at Tyler M
University of Toledo M,D,O
University of West Florida M
University of Wisconsin–Madison M,D
University of Wisconsin–Platteville M
University of Wisconsin–Stout M,O
Utah State University M
Valdosta State University M,D,O
Virginia Polytechnic Institute and State University M,D,O
Virginia State University M,O
Wayne State College M
Western Michigan University M
Western Washington University M
Westfield State College M
West Virginia University M,D
Wright State University M

■ WATER RESOURCES

Albany State University M
Colorado State University M,D
Duke University M,D
Iowa State University of Science and Technology M,D
Johns Hopkins University M,D
Montclair State University M,O
Rutgers, The State University of New Jersey, New Brunswick M,D
South Dakota State University D
The University of Arizona M,D
University of Florida M,D
University of Illinois at Chicago M,D
University of Kansas M,D
University of Minnesota, Twin Cities Campus M,D
University of Missouri–Rolla M,D
University of Nevada, Las Vegas M
University of New Hampshire M,D
University of New Mexico M
University of Oklahoma M,D
University of Vermont M
University of Wisconsin–Madison M
University of Wyoming M,D
Utah State University M,D

■ WATER RESOURCES ENGINEERING

California Polytechnic State University, San Luis Obispo M
Cornell University M,D
Louisiana State University and Agricultural and Mechanical College M,D
Marquette University M,D
New Mexico Institute of Mining and Technology M
Ohio University M
Oregon State University M,D
The Pennsylvania State University University Park Campus M,D
Princeton University D
Texas A&M University M,D
Tufts University M,D
University of California, Berkeley M,D
University of California, Los Angeles M,D
University of Central Florida M,D,O
University of Colorado at Boulder M,D
University of Delaware M,D
University of Kansas M,D
University of Maryland, College Park M,D
The University of Memphis M,D
University of Missouri–Columbia M,D
University of Southern California M
The University of Texas at Austin M
University of Virginia M,D
Utah State University M,D
Villanova University M
Virginia Polytechnic Institute and State University M,D

■ WESTERN EUROPEAN STUDIES

Boston College M,D
Brown University M,D
The Catholic University of America M
Claremont Graduate University M,D
Columbia University M,O
East Carolina University M
Georgetown University M
The George Washington University M
Indiana University Bloomington M,D,O
Johns Hopkins University M,D,O
New York University M
University of California, Santa Barbara M
University of Connecticut M
University of Nevada, Reno D
Washington University in St. Louis M

■ WOMEN'S HEALTH NURSING

Case Western Reserve University M
Columbia University M,O
Emory University M
Georgia Southern University M,O
Georgia State University M,D
Indiana University–Purdue University Indianapolis M
Loyola University Chicago M
Pacific Lutheran University M
Seton Hall University M
Stony Brook University, State University of New York M,O
Texas Woman's University M,D
University at Buffalo, The State University of New York M,D,O
University of Cincinnati M,D
University of Delaware M,O
University of Missouri–Kansas City M,D
University of Pennsylvania M
University of South Carolina O
The University of Texas at El Paso M
Vanderbilt University M,D
Virginia Commonwealth University M,D,O

■ WOMEN'S STUDIES

Brandeis University M
Claremont Graduate University M,D
Clark Atlanta University M,D
Clark University D
DePaul University O
Duke University O
Eastern Michigan University M
Emory University D,O
Florida Atlantic University M
The George Washington University M,D

Georgia State University	M
Minnesota State University, Mankato	M
New College of California	M
Northwestern University	
The Ohio State University	M
Roosevelt University	M
Rutgers, The State University of New Jersey, New Brunswick	M,D
San Diego State University	M
San Francisco State University	M
Southern Connecticut State University	M
State University of New York at Albany	M
Stony Brook University, State University of New York	M,O
Syracuse University	O
Texas Woman's University	M
Towson University	M
The University of Alabama	M
The University of Arizona	M
University of California, Los Angeles	M,D
University of Central Florida	M,O
University of Cincinnati	M,O
The University of Iowa	D
University of Maryland, College Park	M,D
University of Massachusetts Boston	O
University of Michigan	D,O
University of Missouri–St. Louis	O
The University of North Carolina at Greensboro	M,D,O
University of Northern Iowa	M
University of Pittsburgh	O
University of South Carolina	O
University of South Florida	M
University of Washington	M,D

■ WRITING

Abilene Christian University	M
American University	M
Antioch University Los Angeles	M,O
Antioch University McGregor	M
Arizona State University	M
Ball State University	M,D
Boise State University	M
Boston University	M,D
Bowling Green State University	M
Brooklyn College of the City University of New York	M
Brown University	M
California State University, Chico	M
California State University, Fresno	M
California State University, Long Beach	M
California State University, Sacramento	M
California State University, San Marcos	M
Carnegie Mellon University	M
Central Michigan University	M
Chapman University	M
City College of the City University of New York	M
Claremont Graduate University	M,D
Clemson University	M
Colorado State University	M
Columbia College Chicago	M
Columbia University	M
Cornell University	M,D
DePaul University	M
Eastern Michigan University	M
Eastern Washington University	M
Emerson College	M
Florida International University	M
Florida State University	M,D
George Mason University	M
Georgia State University	M,D
Goddard College	M
Hofstra University	M
Hunter College of the City University of New York	M
Illinois State University	M
Indiana University Bloomington	M,D
Indiana University of Pennsylvania	M,D
Johns Hopkins University	M
Kennesaw State University	M
Long Island University, Brooklyn Campus	M
Longwood College	M
Louisiana State University and Agricultural and Mechanical College	M,D
Loyola Marymount University	M
Maharishi University of Management	M
Manhattanville College	M
McNeese State University	M
Miami University	M,D
Michigan State University	M,D
Minnesota State University, Mankato	M
Minnesota State University Moorhead	M
National-Louis University	M
New College of California	M
New Mexico Highlands University	M
New Mexico State University	M,D
New School University	M
New York University	M
Northeastern Illinois University	M
Northeastern University	M,D,O
Northern Arizona University	M
Northern Michigan University	M
Northwestern University	M
Norwich University	M,O
Oklahoma City University	M
Old Dominion University	M
The Pennsylvania State University University Park Campus	M,D
Purdue University	M,D
Queens College of the City University of New York	M
Rensselaer Polytechnic Institute	M,D
Rivier College	M
Roosevelt University	M
Rowan University	M
Rutgers, The State University of New Jersey, New Brunswick	M
Saint Mary's College of California	M
Saint Xavier University	M,O
Salisbury State University	M
San Diego State University	M
San Francisco State University	M
Sonoma State University	M
Southern Illinois University Carbondale	M
Southwest Texas State University	M
Syracuse University	M,D
Temple University	M
Towson University	M
The University of Alabama	M,D
University of Alaska Anchorage	M
University of Alaska Fairbanks	M
The University of Arizona	M
University of Arkansas	M
University of Arkansas at Little Rock	M
University of Baltimore	M
University of California, Davis	M,D
University of California, Irvine	M,D
University of Central Florida	M,O
University of Central Oklahoma	M
University of Colorado at Boulder	M,D
University of Houston	M,D
University of Idaho	M
University of Illinois at Chicago	M,D
The University of Iowa	M,D
University of Louisiana at Lafayette	M,D
University of Maryland, College Park	M,D
University of Massachusetts Amherst	M,D
University of Massachusetts Dartmouth	M
The University of Memphis	M,D
University of Michigan	M
University of Missouri–St. Louis	M
The University of Montana–Missoula	M
University of Nevada, Las Vegas	M,D
University of New Hampshire	M,D
University of New Orleans	M
The University of North Carolina at Greensboro	M
The University of North Carolina at Wilmington	M
University of Notre Dame	M,D
University of Oregon	M
University of Pennsylvania	M,D
University of St. Thomas (MN)	M,O
University of San Francisco	M
University of South Carolina	M,D
University of Southern California	M
The University of Texas at Austin	M
The University of Texas at El Paso	M
University of Utah	M,D
University of Virginia	M
Utah State University	M
Virginia Commonwealth University	M
Warren Wilson College	M
Washington University in St. Louis	M
Wayne State University	M,D
Western Illinois University	M
Western Kentucky University	M
Western Michigan University	M,D
Westminster College (UT)	M
West Virginia University	M,D
Wichita State University	M
Wright State University	M

■ ZOOLOGY

Auburn University	M,D
Brigham Young University	M,D
Clemson University	M,D
Colorado State University	M,D
Cornell University	D
Eastern Illinois University	M
Emporia State University	M
Illinois State University	M,D
Indiana University Bloomington	M,D
Iowa State University of Science and Technology	M,D
Kent State University	M,D
Louisiana State University and Agricultural and Mechanical College	M,D
Miami University	M,D
Michigan State University	M,D
Montana State University–Bozeman	M,D
North Carolina State University	M,D
North Dakota State University	M,D
Ohio University	M,D
Oklahoma State University	M,D
Oregon State University	M,D
Southern Illinois University Carbondale	M,D
Texas A&M University	M,D
Texas Tech University	M,D
University of Alaska Fairbanks	M,D
University of California, Davis	M
University of Chicago	D
University of Colorado at Boulder	M,D
University of Connecticut	M,D
University of Florida	M,D
University of Hawaii at Manoa	M,D
University of Idaho	M,D
University of Maine	M,D
University of Maryland, College Park	M,D
University of New Hampshire	M,D
University of North Dakota	M,D
University of Oklahoma	M,D

University of Rhode Island	M,D
University of South Florida	M
University of Washington	D
University of Wisconsin–Madison	M,D
University of Wisconsin–Oshkosh	M
University of Wyoming	M,D
Virginia Polytechnic Institute and State University	M,D
Washington State University	M,D
Western Illinois University	M,O

Profiles of Institutions Offering Graduate and Professional Work

Alabama

■ ALABAMA AGRICULTURAL AND MECHANICAL UNIVERSITY

Normal, AL 35762

http://www.aamu.edu/

State-supported, coed, university. *Computer facilities:* 1,000 computers available on campus for general student use. A campuswide network can be accessed from student residence rooms and from off campus. Internet access is available. *Library facilities:* J. F. Drake Learning Resources Center. *General application contact:* Director of Institutional Research and Interim Dean, School of Graduate Studies, 256-858-8170.

School of Graduate Studies

School of Agricultural and Environmental Sciences
Programs in:
agribusiness • MS
agricultural and environmental sciences • MS, MURP, PhD
animal sciences • MS
environmental science • MS
family and consumer sciences • MS
food science • MS, PhD
plant and soil science • PhD
urban and regional planning • MURP

School of Arts and Sciences
Programs in:
arts and sciences • MS, MSW, PhD
biology • MS
computer science • MS
physics • MS, PhD
social work • MSW

School of Business
Programs in:
business • MBA, MS
economics and finance • MS
management and marketing • MBA

School of Education
Programs in:
communicative disorders • M Ed, MS
early childhood education • M Ed, MS, Ed S
education • M Ed, Ed S
elementary and early childhood education • M Ed, MS, Ed S
elementary education • M Ed, MS, Ed S
health and physical education • M Ed, MS
higher administration • MS
music • MS
music education • M Ed, MS
physical education • M Ed, MS
psychology and counseling • MS, Ed S
secondary education • M Ed, MS, Ed S
special education • M Ed, MS

School of Engineering and Technology
Programs in:
engineering and technology • M Ed, MS
industry and education • MS
trade and industrial education • M Ed

■ ALABAMA STATE UNIVERSITY

Montgomery, AL 36101-0271

http://www.alasu.edu/

State-supported, coed, comprehensive institution. *Enrollment:* 187 full-time matriculated graduate/professional students (120 women), 734 part-time matriculated graduate/professional students (555 women). *Graduate faculty:* 44 full-time (20 women), 12 part-time/adjunct (3 women). *Computer facilities:* 380 computers available on campus for general student use. A campuswide network can be accessed from off campus. Internet access and online class registration, e-mail are available. *Library facilities:* Levi Watkins Learning Center. *Graduate expenses:* Tuition, state resident: part-time $120 per hour. Tuition, nonresident: part-time $240 per hour. Required fees: $120 per hour. *General application contact:* Dr. Annette Marie Allen, Dean of Graduate Studies, 334-229-4275.

School of Graduate Studies
Dr. Annette Marie Allen, Dean

College of Arts and Sciences
Dr. Thelma Ivery, Acting Dean
Programs in:
arts and sciences • MA, MS, Ed S
biology • MS
biology education • Ed S
history • MA
mathematics • MS, Ed S
physical therapy • MS

College of Business Administration
Dr. Percy Vaughn, Dean
Programs in:
accountancy • MS
business administration • MS

College of Education
Dr. Daniel Vertrees, Dean
Programs in:
biology education • M Ed
early childhood education • M Ed, Ed S
education • M Ed, MS, Ed S
educational administration • M Ed, Ed S
elementary education • M Ed, Ed S
English education • M Ed
general counseling • MS
guidance and counseling • M Ed, MS, Ed S
health, physical education, recreation, and safety • M Ed
history education • M Ed
library educational media • M Ed, Ed S
mathematics education • M Ed
physical education • M Ed
reading education • M Ed
school counseling • M Ed, Ed S
secondary education • M Ed, Ed S
special education • M Ed

School of Music
Dr. Horace B. Lamar, Dean
Program in:
music education • MME

■ AUBURN UNIVERSITY

Auburn, Auburn University, AL 36849-0002

http://www.auburn.edu/

State-supported, coed, university. CGS member. *Enrollment:* 2,097 full-time matriculated graduate/professional students (1,136 women), 1,437 part-time matriculated graduate/professional students (617 women). *Graduate faculty:* 993 full-time (208 women). *Computer facilities:* 600 computers available on campus for general student use. A campuswide network can be accessed from student residence rooms and from off campus. Online class registration is available. *Library facilities:* R. B. Draughon Library plus 2 others. *Graduate expenses:* Tuition, state resident: full-time $3,050; part-time $126 per credit hour. Tuition, nonresident: full-time $9,150; part-time $378 per credit hour. Required fees: $265 per term. *General application contact:* Dr. Stephen L. McFarland, Interim Dean of the Graduate School, 334-844-4700.

Find an in-depth description at www.petersons.com/graduate.

College of Veterinary Medicine
Dr. Timothy R. Boosinger, Dean
Program in:5984
veterinary medicine • DVM, MS, PhD

Graduate Programs in Veterinary Medicine
Programs in:
anatomy and histology • MS
anatomy, physiology and pharmacology • MS
biomedical sciences • PhD
clinical sciences • MS
large animal surgery and medicine • MS
pathobiology • MS
physiology and pharmacology • MS
radiology • MS
small animal surgery and medicine • MS
veterinary medicine • MS, PhD

Graduate School
Dr. John F. Pritchett, Dean
Programs in:
integrated textile and apparel sciences • MS, PhD
sociology • MA, MS
textile science • MS

College of Agriculture
Dr. Luther Waters, Dean
Programs in:
agricultural economics and rural sociology • M Ag, MS, PhD
agriculture • M Ag, M Aq, MS, PhD
agronomy and soils • M Ag, MS, PhD
animal and dairy sciences • M Ag, MS, PhD
biosystems engineering • MS, PhD
entomology • M Ag, MS, PhD
fisheries and allied aquacultures • M Aq, MS, PhD
horticulture • M Ag, MS, PhD
plant pathology • M Ag, MS, PhD
poultry science • M Ag, MS, PhD

College of Architecture, Design, and Construction
Dan D. Bennett, Dean
Programs in:
architecture, design, and construction • MBS, MCP, MID, MLA
building science • MBS
community planning • MCP
construction management • MBS
industrial design • MID

College of Business
Dr. John S. Jahera, Interim Dean
Programs in:
accountancy • M Acc
business • M Acc, MBA, MMIS, MS, PhD
business administration • MBA
economics • MS, PhD
human relations management • PhD
management • MS
management information systems • MMIS, PhD

College of Education
Dr. Richard C. Kunkel, Dean
Programs in:
adult education • M Ed, MS, Ed D
business education • M Ed, MS, PhD
community agency counseling • M Ed, MS, Ed D, PhD, Ed S
counseling psychology • PhD
counselor education • Ed D, PhD
curriculum and instruction • M Ed, MS, Ed D, Ed S
curriculum supervision • M Ed, MS, Ed D, Ed S
early childhood education • M Ed, MS, PhD, Ed S
education • M Ed, MS, Ed D, PhD, Ed S
educational psychology • PhD
elementary education • M Ed, MS, PhD, Ed S
foreign languages • M Ed, MS
health and human performance • M Ed, MS, Ed D, PhD, Ed S
higher education administration • M Ed, MS, Ed D, Ed S
media instructional design • MS
media specialist • M Ed
music education • M Ed, MS, PhD, Ed S
postsecondary education • PhD
reading education • PhD, Ed S
rehabilitation and special education • M Ed, MS, PhD, Ed S
school administration • M Ed, MS, Ed D, Ed S
school counseling • M Ed, MS, Ed D, PhD, Ed S
school psychometry • M Ed, MS, Ed D, PhD, Ed S
secondary education • M Ed, MS, PhD, Ed S

College of Engineering
Dr. Larry Benefield, Dean
Programs in:
aerospace engineering • MAE, MS, PhD
chemical engineering • M Ch E, MS, PhD
computer science and software engineering • MS, MSWE, PhD
construction engineering and management • MCE, MS, PhD
electrical and computer engineering • MEE, MS, PhD
engineering • M Ch E, M Mtl E, MAE, MCE, MEE, MIE, MME, MS, MSWE, PhD
environmental engineering • MCE, MS, PhD
geotechnical/materials engineering • MCE, MS, PhD
hydraulics/hydrology • MCE, MS, PhD
industrial and systems engineering • MIE, MS, PhD
materials engineering • M Mtl E, MS, PhD
mechanical engineering • MME, MS, PhD
structural engineering • MCE, MS, PhD
transportation engineering • MCE, MS, PhD

College of Human Sciences
Dr. June Henton, Dean
Programs in:
apparel and textiles • MS
human development and family studies • MS, PhD
human sciences • MS, PhD
nutrition and food science • MS, PhD

College of Liberal Arts
Dr. Rebekah Pindzola, Acting Dean
Programs in:
audiology • MCD, MS
communication • MA, MSC
English • MA, PhD
French • MA, MFS
history • MA, PhD
liberal arts • MA, MCD, MFS, MHS, MM, MPA, MS, MSC, PhD
mass communications • MA, MSC
music • MM
psychology • MS, PhD
public administration • MPA, PhD
Spanish • MA, MHS
speech pathology • MCD, MS

College of Sciences and Mathematics
Dr. Stewart W. Schneller, Dean
Programs in:
botany • MS, PhD
chemistry • MS, PhD
discrete and statistical sciences • M Prob S, MAM, MS, PhD
geology and geography • MS
mathematics • MAM, MS, PhD
microbiology • MS, PhD
physics • MS, PhD
sciences and mathematics • M Prob S, MAM, MS, PhD
zoology • MS, PhD

School of Forestry and Wildlife Sciences
Richard W. Brinker, Dean
Program in:
forestry and wildlife sciences • MF, MS, PhD

School of Pharmacy
Dr. R. Lee Evans, Dean
Program in:
pharmacy • Pharm D, MS, PhD

■ AUBURN UNIVERSITY MONTGOMERY

Montgomery, AL 36124-4023

http://www.aum.edu/

State-supported, coed, comprehensive institution. *Enrollment:* 264 full-time matriculated graduate/professional students (173 women), 538 part-time matriculated graduate/professional students (347 women). *Graduate faculty:* 116 full-time (43 women), 9 part-time/adjunct (4 women). *Computer facilities:* 300 computers available on campus for general student use. A campuswide network can be accessed from student residence rooms and from off campus. Internet access and online class registration are available. *Library facilities:* Auburn University Montgomery Library. *Graduate expenses:* Full-time $2,880; part-time $120 per credit hour. Tuition, state resident: full-time $2,880; part-time $120 per credit hour. Tuition, nonresident: full-time $8,640; part-time $360 per credit hour. $8,640 full-time. *General application contact:* Michele M. Moore, Associate Director of Enrollment Services, 334-244-3614.

School of Business
Dr. Keith W. Lantz, Dean
Program in:
business • MBA

School of Education
Dr. Janet S. Warren, Dean
Programs in:
counseling • M Ed, Ed S
early childhood education • M Ed, Ed S
education • M Ed, Ed S
education administration • M Ed, Ed S
elementary education • M Ed, Ed S
physical education • M Ed
reading education • M Ed, Ed S
secondary education • M Ed, Ed S
special education • M Ed, Ed S

School of Liberal Arts
Dr. Larry C. Mullins, Dean
Program in:
liberal arts • MLA

School of Sciences
Dr. Robert H. Elliott, Dean
Programs in:
justice and public safety • MSJPS
political science • MPS
psychology • MSPG
public administration • MPA, PhD
sciences • MPA, MPS, MSJPS, MSPG, PhD

■ JACKSONVILLE STATE UNIVERSITY

Jacksonville, AL 36265-1602

http://www.jsu.edu/

State-supported, coed, comprehensive institution. *Enrollment:* 277 full-time matriculated graduate/professional students (188 women), 912 part-time matriculated graduate/professional students (619 women). *Graduate faculty:* 157 full-time (48 women). *Computer facilities:* 330 computers available on campus for general student use. A campuswide network can be accessed from off campus. Internet access is available. *Library facilities:* Houston Cole Library. *Graduate expenses:* Tuition: full-time $1,320. *General application contact:* Dr. William D. Carr, Dean of the College of Graduate Studies and Continuing Education, 256-782-5329.

College of Graduate Studies and Continuing Education
Dr. William D. Carr, Dean
Programs in:
general studies • MA
public administration • MPA

College of Arts and Sciences
Programs in:
arts and sciences • MA, MS
biology • MS
computer systems and software design • MS
criminal justice • MS
English • MA
history • MA
mathematics • MS
music • MA
political science • MA
psychology • MS

College of Commerce and Business Administration
Program in:
commerce and business administration • MBA

College of Education
Programs in:
early childhood education • MS Ed, Ed S
education • MA, MS, MS Ed, Ed S
elementary education • MS Ed, Ed S
guidance and counseling • MS, Ed S
health and physical education • MS Ed, Ed S
instructional media • MS Ed
music education • MA
school administration • MS Ed, Ed S
secondary education • MS Ed, Ed S
special education • MS Ed, Ed S

College of Nursing
Prof. Beth Hembree, Director of Graduate Studies
Program in:
nursing • MSN

■ SAMFORD UNIVERSITY

Birmingham, AL 35229-0002

http://www.samford.edu/

Independent-religious, coed, university. *Enrollment:* 1,249 full-time matriculated graduate/professional students (634 women), 245 part-time matriculated graduate/professional students (150 women). *Graduate faculty:* 113 full-time (36 women), 33 part-time/adjunct (9 women). *Computer facilities:* 350 computers available on campus for general student use. A campuswide network can be accessed from student residence rooms. *Library facilities:* Samford University Library plus 3 others. *Graduate expenses:* Tuition: part-time $383 per credit hour. *General application contact:* Dr. Phil Kimrey, Dean of Admissions and Financial Aid, 205-726-2871.

Beeson School of Divinity
Dr. Timothy George, Dean
Program in:
theology • M Div, MTS, D Min

Cumberland School of Law
Michael D. Floyd, Acting Dean
Program in:
law • JD, SJD

Howard College of Arts and Sciences
Dr. J. Roderick Davis, Dean
Program in:
arts and sciences • MSEM

Ida V. Moffett School of Nursing
Dr. Marian K. Baur, Dean
Program in:
nursing • MSN

McWhorter School of Pharmacy
Dr. Joe Dean, Dean
Program in:
pharmacy • Pharm D

School of Business
Dr. Carl Bellas, Dean
Program in:
business • M Acc, MBA

School of Education
Dr. Ruth Ash, Dean
Programs in:
early childhood education • MS Ed, Ed D, Ed S
educational administration • MS Ed, Ed D, Ed S

elementary education • MS Ed, Ed D, Ed S
music education • MS Ed

School of Music
Dr. Milburn Price, Dean
Program in:
music • MM, MME

■ SPRING HILL COLLEGE
Mobile, AL 36608-1791
http://www.shc.edu/

Independent-religious, coed, comprehensive institution. *Enrollment:* 21 full-time matriculated graduate/professional students (16 women), 236 part-time matriculated graduate/professional students (164 women). *Graduate faculty:* 16 full-time (4 women), 10 part-time/adjunct (4 women). *Computer facilities:* 141 computers available on campus for general student use. A campuswide network can be accessed from student residence rooms and from off campus. Internet access is available. *Library facilities:* Thomas Byrne Memorial Library. *Graduate expenses:* Tuition: part-time $195 per credit hour. Part-time tuition and fees vary according to program. *General application contact:* Dr. Gary Norsworthy, Dean of Life Long Learning and Graduate Programs, 334-380-3066.

Graduate Programs
Dr. Gary Norsworthy, Dean of Life Long Learning and Graduate Programs
Programs in:
business administration • MBA
early childhood education • MAT, MS Ed
elementary education • MAT, MS Ed
liberal arts • MLA
secondary education • MAT, MS Ed
theology • MA, MPS, MTS

■ TROY STATE UNIVERSITY
Troy, AL 36082
http://www.troyst.edu/

State-supported, coed, comprehensive institution. *Enrollment:* 2,115 full-time matriculated graduate/professional students (1,341 women), 2,813 part-time matriculated graduate/professional students (1,617 women). *Graduate faculty:* 267 full-time (116 women), 466 part-time/adjunct (197 women). *Computer facilities:* 487 computers available on campus for general student use. A campuswide network can be accessed from student residence rooms and from off campus. Internet access is available. *Library facilities:* Wallace Library. *Graduate expenses:* Tuition, state resident: full-time $3,120; part-time $130 per term. Tuition, nonresident: full-time $6,240; part-time $260 per term. Required fees: $276; $8 per hour. Tuition and fees vary according to course load. *General application contact:* Brenda Campbell, Director of Graduate Admissions, 334-670-3178.

Graduate School
Dr. Dianne Barron, Dean, Graduate Study and Research

College of Arts and Sciences
Dr. Robert Pullen, Dean
Programs in:
administration of criminal justice • MS
arts and sciences • MS
corrections • MS
environmental analysis and management • MS
international relations • MS
police administration • MS
public administration • MS

College of Health and Human Services
Dr. Brenda Riley, Acting Dean
Programs in:
health and human services • MS
nursing • MS

School of Education
Dr. Anita Hardin, Dean
Programs in:
counseling and human development • MS
counselor education • MS
early childhood education • MS, Ed S
education • MS, Ed S
educational leadership/administration • MS
elementary education • MS, Ed S
emotional conflict • MS
foundations of education • MS
guidance services • MS
learning disabilities • MS
mental retardation • MS
mild learning handicapped • MS, Ed S
N–12 education • MS, Ed S
secondary education • MS, Ed S

University College
Dr. Rodney Cox, Dean
Programs in:
business administration • MBA
management • MS
personnel management • MS

■ TROY STATE UNIVERSITY DOTHAN
Dothan, AL 36304-0368
http://www.tsud.edu/

State-supported, coed, comprehensive institution. *Enrollment:* 97 full-time matriculated graduate/professional students (70 women), 297 part-time matriculated graduate/professional students (210 women). *Graduate faculty:* 52 full-time (17 women), 12 part-time/adjunct (3 women). *Computer facilities:* 150 computers available on campus for general student use. A campuswide network can be accessed. Internet access is available. *Library facilities:* Troy State University Dotham Library. *Graduate expenses:* Tuition: part-time $135 per hour. *General application contact:* Reta Cordell, Director of Admissions and Records, 334-983-6556 Ext. 228.

Graduate School
Dr. Barbara Alford, Executive Vice President

College of Arts and Sciences
Dr. Alan Belsches, Dean
Programs in:
arts and sciences • MS
history and political sciences • MS

School of Business
Dr. Adair Gilbert, Dean
Programs in:
accounting • MBA, MS
business • MBA, MS
business education • MS
business law • MS
computer information systems • MS
finance • MS
general business • MBA
human resource management • MBA, MS
quantitative methods • MS

School of Education
Dr. Cynthia Lumpkin, Dean
Programs in:
counseling and psychology • MS, Ed S
curriculum and instruction • MS, Ed S
education • MS, MS Ed, Ed S
leadership, foundations, and technology • MS, Ed S

■ TROY STATE UNIVERSITY MONTGOMERY
Montgomery, AL 36103-4419
http://www.tsum.edu/

State-supported, coed, comprehensive institution. *Enrollment:* 131 full-time

Troy State University Montgomery (continued)

matriculated graduate/professional students (81 women), 316 part-time matriculated graduate/professional students (223 women). *Graduate faculty:* 22 full-time (6 women), 18 part-time/adjunct (7 women). *Computer facilities:* 190 computers available on campus for general student use. A campuswide network can be accessed from off campus. Internet access and online class registration are available. *Library facilities:* Troy State University Montgomery Library. *Graduate expenses:* Tuition, state resident: full-time $2,160; part-time $120 per credit hour. Tuition, nonresident: full-time $4,320; part-time $240 per credit hour. Required fees: $60; $30 per semester. Full-time tuition and fees vary according to program. *General application contact:* Dr. Kimberly A. Combs, Interim Dean of Graduate Division, 334-241-9581.

Graduate Programs

Dr. Kimberly A. Combs, Interim Dean of Graduate Division

Division of Business
Dr. Jimmy Simpson, Acting Dean
Programs in:
- business administration • MBA
- computer and information science • MS
- human resources management • MS
- management • MS

Division of Counseling, Education, and Psychology
Dr. Donald Thompson, Dean
Programs in:
- adult education • MS
- counseling • MS, Ed S
- counseling and human development • MS, Ed S
- elementary education • MS
- general education administration • Ed S
- teaching • MA

■ TUSKEGEE UNIVERSITY

Tuskegee, AL 36088
http://www.tusk.edu/

Independent, coed, comprehensive institution. *Enrollment:* 315 full-time matriculated graduate/professional students (195 women), 44 part-time matriculated graduate/professional students (21 women). *Graduate faculty:* 112 full-time (17 women), 11 part-time/adjunct (5 women). *Computer facilities:* 1,000 computers available on campus for general student use. A campuswide network can be accessed from student residence rooms and from off campus. Internet access and online class registration are available. *Library facilities:* Hollis B. Frissell Library plus 3 others. *Graduate expenses:* Tuition: full-time $9,928. Required fees: $156. *General application contact:* William E. Mathis, Director of Admissions, 334-727-8580.

Graduate Programs

Dr. William L. Lester, Provost
Program in:
- general science education • M Ed, MS

College of Agricultural, Environmental and Natural Sciences
Dr. Walter A. Hill, Dean
Programs in:
- agricultural and resource economics • MS
- agricultural, environmental and natural sciences • MS
- animal and poultry sciences • MS
- biology • MS
- chemistry • MS
- environmental sciences • MS
- food and nutritional sciences • MS
- plant and soil sciences • MS

College of Engineering, Architecture and Physical Sciences
Dr. Legand L. Burge, Acting Dean
Programs in:
- electrical engineering • MSEE
- engineering, architecture and physical sciences • MSEE, MSME, PhD
- material science engineering • PhD
- mechanical engineering • MSME

College of Veterinary Medicine and Allied Health
Dr. Alfonza Atkinson, Dean
Programs in:
- veterinary medicine • DVM, MS
- veterinary medicine and allied health • DVM, MS

■ THE UNIVERSITY OF ALABAMA

Tuscaloosa, AL 35487
http://www.ua.edu/

State-supported, coed, university. CGS member. *Enrollment:* 2,007 full-time matriculated graduate/professional students (1,014 women), 1,378 part-time matriculated graduate/professional students (919 women). *Graduate faculty:* 450 full-time, 274 part-time/adjunct. *Computer facilities:* 1,450 computers available on campus for general student use. A campuswide network can be accessed from student residence rooms and from off campus. Internet access is available. *Library facilities:* Amelia Gayle Gorgas Library plus 8 others. *Graduate expenses:* Tuition, state resident: full-time $3,014. Tuition, nonresident: full-time $8,162. *General application contact:* Libby Williams, Admissions Supervisor, 205-348-5921.

Graduate School

Dr. Ronald Rogers, Dean

College of Arts and Sciences
Dr. Robert D. Olin, Dean
Programs in:
- acting • MFA
- administration • DMA
- American studies • MA
- anthropology • MA
- applied linguistics • PhD
- applied mathematics • PhD
- art history • MA
- arts and sciences • MA, MATESOL, MFA, MM, MPA, MS, MSCJ, DMA, Ed D, PhD, Certificate, Ed S
- audiology • MS
- biological sciences • MS, PhD
- chemistry • MS, PhD
- clinical psychology • PhD
- cognitive psychology • PhD
- composition • DMA
- costume design • MFA
- creative writing • MFA
- criminal justice • MSCJ
- directing • MFA
- French • MA, PhD
- French and Spanish • PhD
- geography • MS
- geological sciences • MS, PhD
- German • MA
- history • MA, PhD
- Latin American studies • MA, Certificate
- literature • MA, PhD
- mathematics • MA
- music education • Ed D, Ed S
- musicology • MM
- performance • MM, DMA
- physics • MS, PhD
- playwriting/dramaturgy • MFA
- political science • MA, MPA, PhD
- public administration • MPA
- pure mathematics • PhD
- rhetoric and composition • MA, PhD
- Romance languages • MA, PhD
- scene design/technical production • MFA
- Spanish • MA, PhD
- speech-language pathology • MS
- stage management • MFA
- studio art • MA, MFA
- teaching English to speakers of other languages • MATESOL
- theatre • MFA
- theatre management/administration • MFA
- theory and criticism • MA
- women's studies • MA

College of Communication and Information Sciences
Dr. Matthew D. Bunker, Acting Associate Dean for Graduate Studies and Research
Programs in:
advertising and public relations • MA
book arts • MFA
communication and information sciences • MA, MFA, MLIS, PhD, Ed S
communication studies • MA
journalism • MA
library and information studies • MLIS, Ed S
telecommunication and film • MA

College of Education
Dr. John Dolly, Dean
Programs in:
community counseling • MA
counselor education • MA, Ed D, PhD, Ed S
early childhood education • MA, Ed S
education • MA, Ed D, PhD, Ed S
educational leadership • MA, Ed S
educational leadership, policy, and technology studies • MA, Ed D
educational psychology • MA, Ed D, PhD, Ed S
educational research • PhD
elementary education • MA, Ed D, PhD, Ed S
higher education administration • MA, Ed D, PhD, Ed S
human performance • MA, PhD, Ed S
instructional leadership • Ed D, PhD
music education • MA, Ed D, Ed S
rehabilitative counseling • MA
school counseling • MA
school psychology • MA, Ed D, PhD, Ed S
secondary education • MA, Ed D, PhD, Ed S
special education • MA, Ed D, PhD, Ed S

College of Engineering
Timothy J. Greene, Dean
Programs in:
aerospace engineering and mechanics • MSAE, MSESM, PhD
chemical engineering • MS Ch E, PhD
civil engineering • MSCE, PhD
computer science • MSCS, PhD
electrical engineering • MSEE, PhD
engineering • MS Ch E, MS Met E, MSAE, MSCE, MSCS, MSE, MSEE, MSESM, MSIE, MSME, PhD
environmental engineering • MSE
industrial engineering • MSE, MSIE
materials science • PhD
mechanical engineering • MSME, PhD
metallurgical and materials engineering • MS Met E, PhD

College of Human Environmental Sciences
Dr. Judy L. Bonner, Dean
Programs in:
clothing, textiles, and interior design • MSHES
consumer sciences • MSHES
health education and promotion • PhD
health studies • MA
human development and family studies • MSHES
human environmental sciences • MA, MSHES, PhD
human nutrition and hospitality management • MSHES

The Manderson Graduate School of Business
J. Barry Mason, Dean
Programs in:
accounting • M Acc, PhD
applied statistics • MS, PhD
banking and finance • MA, MSC, PhD
business • Exec MBA, M Acc, MA, MBA, MS, MSC, MTA, PhD
business administration • Exec MBA, MBA
economics • MA, MSC, PhD
management science • MA, MBA, MSC, PhD
manufacturing management • MA, MBA, PhD
marketing • MA, PhD
marketing and management • MSC
production management • MA, MBA, PhD
tax accounting • MTA

School of Social Work
Dr. James P. Adams, Dean
Program in:
social work • MSW, PhD

School of Law
Kenneth C. Randall, Dean
Program in:
law • JD, LL M, LL M in Tax

■ THE UNIVERSITY OF ALABAMA AT BIRMINGHAM
Birmingham, AL 35294
http://www.uab.edu/

State-supported, coed, university. CGS member. *Enrollment:* 3,116 full-time matriculated graduate/professional students (1,614 women), 886 part-time matriculated graduate/professional students (582 women). *Computer facilities:* 400 computers available on campus for general student use. A campuswide network can be accessed from off campus. Internet access and online class registration are available. *Library facilities:* Mervyn Sterne Library plus 1 other. *Graduate expenses:* Tuition, state resident: full-time $3,027; part-time $107 per credit hour. Tuition, nonresident: full-time $5,595; part-time $214 per credit hour. Required fees: $5 per credit hour. One-time fee: $23 part-time. *General application contact:* Julie Bryant, Director of Graduate Admissions, 205-934-8227.

Find an in-depth description at www.petersons.com/graduate.

Graduate School
Dr. Joan F. Lorden, Dean
Programs in:
basic medical sciences • MSBMS
biochemistry • PhD
biochemistry and molecular genetics • PhD
biophysical sciences • PhD
cell biology • PhD
medical genetics • PhD
microbiology • PhD
neurobiology • PhD
neuroscience • PhD
pathology • PhD
pharmacology • PhD
physiology and biophysics • PhD
toxicology • PhD

Graduate School of Management
Dr. Robert E. Holmes, Dean
Program in:
management • M Acct, MBA, PhD

School of Arts and Humanities
Bert Brouwer, Dean
Programs in:
art history • MA
arts and humanities • MA
English • MA

School of Education
Dr. Michael J. Froning, Dean
Programs in:
agency counseling • MA
allied health sciences • MA Ed
arts education • MA Ed
counseling • MA, MA Ed
curriculum and instruction • Ed S
early childhood education • MA Ed, PhD
education • MA, MA Ed, Ed D, PhD, Ed S
educational leadership • MA Ed, Ed D, PhD, Ed S
elementary education • MA Ed
health education • MA Ed
health education/health promotion • MA Ed, PhD
high school education • MA Ed
marriage and family counseling • MA

The University of Alabama at Birmingham (continued)
- physical education • MA Ed
- rehabilitation counseling • MA
- school counseling • MA
- school psychology • MA Ed
- special education • MA Ed

School of Engineering
Dr. Linda C. Lucas, Interim Dean
Programs in:
- biomedical engineering • MSBME, PhD
- civil and environmental engineering • MSCE, PhD
- electrical and computer engineering • MSEE, PhD
- engineering • MS Mt E, MSBME, MSCE, MSEE, MSME, PhD
- materials engineering • MS Mt E, PhD
- materials science • PhD
- mechanical engineering • MSME, PhD

School of Health Related Professions
Dr. C. Michael Brooks, Interim Dean
Programs in:
- administration-health services • PhD
- clinical laboratory science • MSCLS
- clinical nutrition • MS
- clinical nutrition and dietetics • MS, Certificate
- dietetic internship • Certificate
- health administration • MSHA
- health informatics • MS
- health related professions • MNA, MS, MSCLS, MSHA, PhD, Certificate
- nurse anesthesia • MNA
- nutrition sciences • PhD
- occupational therapy • MS
- physical therapy • MS

School of Natural Sciences and Mathematics
Dr. James B. McClintock, Dean
Programs in:
- applied mathematics • PhD
- biology • MS, PhD
- chemistry • MS, PhD
- computer and information sciences • MS, PhD
- mathematics • MS
- natural sciences and mathematics • MS, PhD
- physics • MS, PhD

School of Nursing
Dr. Rachel Z. Booth, Dean
Program in:
- nursing • MSN, PhD

School of Public Health
Dr. Eli I. Capilouto, Dean
Programs in:
- biomathematics • MS, PhD
- biostatistics • MS, PhD
- environmental health • PhD
- environmental toxicology • PhD
- epidemiology • PhD
- health care organization and policy • MPH, MSPH
- health education promotion • PhD
- health education/promotion • PhD
- industrial hygiene • PhD
- maternal and child health • MSPH
- public health • MPH, MS, MSPH, PhD

School of Social and Behavioral Sciences
Dr. Tennant S. McWilliams, Dean
Programs in:
- anthropology • MA
- behavioral neuroscience • PhD
- clinical psychology • PhD
- criminal justice • MSCJ
- developmental psychology • PhD
- forensic science • MSFS
- history • MA
- medical psychology • PhD
- medical sociology • PhD
- psychology • MA, PhD
- public administration • MPA
- social and behavioral sciences • MA, MPA, MSCJ, MSFS, PhD
- sociology • MA

School of Dentistry
Dr. Mary Lynne Capilouto, Dean
Program in:
- dentistry • DMD, MS, MSBMS, PhD

School of Medicine
Dr. William B. Deal, Vice President/Dean, School of Medicine
Program in:
- medicine • MD, MSBMS, PhD

School of Optometry
Dr. Jimmy D. Bartlett, Interim Dean
Programs in:
- optometry • OD, MS, PhD
- vision science • MS, PhD

■ THE UNIVERSITY OF ALABAMA IN HUNTSVILLE
Huntsville, AL 35899
http://www.uah.edu/

State-supported, coed, university. CGS member. *Enrollment:* 470 full-time matriculated graduate/professional students (214 women), 686 part-time matriculated graduate/professional students (268 women). *Graduate faculty:* 211 full-time (50 women), 15 part-time/adjunct (4 women). *Computer facilities:* 520 computers available on campus for general student use. A campuswide network can be accessed from student residence rooms and from off campus. Internet access and online class registration are available. *Library facilities:* University of Alabama in Huntsville Library. *Graduate expenses:* Tuition, state resident: full-time $4,088; part-time $153 per hour. Tuition, nonresident: full-time $8,394; part-time $314 per hour. *General application contact:* Dr. Gordon Emslie, Dean of Graduate Studies, 256-890-6002.

School of Graduate Studies
Dr. Gordon Emslie, Dean
Programs in:
- materials science • MS, PhD
- optical science and engineering • PhD

College of Administrative Science
Programs in:
- accountancy • M Acc
- management • MSM

College of Engineering
Dr. Jorge Aunon, Dean
Programs in:
- chemical and materials engineering • MSE
- civil and environmental engineering • MSE
- computer engineering • PhD
- electrical and computer engineering • MSE
- electrical engineering • PhD
- engineering • MSE, MSOR, PhD
- industrial engineering • MSE, PhD
- mechanical engineering • MSE, PhD
- operations research • MSOR
- optical science and engineering • PhD

College of Liberal Arts
Dr. Sue Kirkpatrick, Dean
Programs in:
- English • MA
- history • MA
- liberal arts • MA
- psychology • MA
- public affairs • MA

College of Nursing
Dr. Fay Raines, Dean
Program in:
- nursing • MSN

College of Science
Dr. Jack Fix, Dean
Programs in:
- applied mathematics • PhD
- atmospheric and environmental science • MS, PhD
- biological sciences • MS
- chemistry • MS
- computer science • MS, PhD
- mathematics • MA, MS
- physics • MS, PhD
- science • MA, MS, PhD

■ UNIVERSITY OF MOBILE
Mobile, AL 36663-0220
http://www.umobile.edu/

Independent-religious, coed, comprehensive institution. *Enrollment:* 44 full-time matriculated graduate/professional students (33 women), 150 part-time matriculated graduate/professional students (102 women). *Graduate faculty:* 28 full-time (15 women), 36 part-time/adjunct (17 women). *Computer facilities:* 100 computers available on campus for general student use. A campuswide network can be accessed from off campus. Internet access is available. *Library facilities:* J. L. Bedsole Library plus 2 others. *Graduate expenses:* Tuition: full-time $3,276; part-time $182 per semester hour. *General application contact:* Dr. Kaye F. Brown, Dean, Graduate Programs, 334-442-2289.

Graduate Programs
Dr. Kaye F. Brown, Dean
Programs in:
- biblical/theological studies • MA
- business administration • MBA
- marriage and family counseling • MA
- nursing • MSN
- teacher education • MA

■ UNIVERSITY OF MONTEVALLO
Montevallo, AL 35115
http://www.montevallo.edu/

State-supported, coed, comprehensive institution. *Computer facilities:* 250 computers available on campus for general student use. A campuswide network can be accessed from student residence rooms and from off campus. *Library facilities:* Carmichael Library. *General application contact:* Coordinator for Graduate Studies, 205-665-6350.

College of Arts and Sciences
Programs in:
- arts and sciences • MA, MS
- English • MA
- speech pathology and audiology • MS

College of Education
Programs in:
- early childhood education • M Ed
- education • M Ed, Ed S
- educational administration • M Ed, Ed S
- elementary education • M Ed
- guidance and counseling • M Ed
- secondary education • M Ed, Ed S
- teacher leader • Ed S

College of Fine Arts
Programs in:
- fine arts • MM
- music • MM

■ UNIVERSITY OF NORTH ALABAMA
Florence, AL 35632-0001
http://www.una.edu/

State-supported, coed, comprehensive institution. *Enrollment:* 103 full-time matriculated graduate/professional students (63 women), 478 part-time matriculated graduate/professional students (325 women). *Graduate faculty:* 49 part-time/adjunct (12 women). *Computer facilities:* 500 computers available on campus for general student use. A campuswide network can be accessed from student residence rooms and from off campus. Internet access is available. *Library facilities:* Collier Library. *Graduate expenses:* Tuition, state resident: full-time $2,016; part-time $112 per credit hour. Tuition, nonresident: full-time $4,032; part-time $224 per credit hour. Required fees: $150; $7 per credit hour. *General application contact:* Kim Mauldin, Director of Admissions, 256-765-4221.

College of Arts and Sciences
Dr. Elliot Pood, Dean
Programs in:
- arts and sciences • MA, MSCJ
- criminal justice • MSCJ
- English • MA

College of Business
Dr. Kerry Gatlin, Dean
Program in:
- business • MBA

College of Education
Dr. Fred L. Hattabaugh, Dean
Programs in:
- counseling • MA, MA Ed
- early childhood education • MA Ed
- education • MA, MA Ed, Ed S
- education leadership • Ed S
- elementary education • MA Ed, Ed S
- learning disabilities • MA Ed
- mentally retarded • MA Ed
- mild learning handicapped • MA Ed
- non-school-based counseling • MA
- non-school-based teaching • MA
- principalship • MA Ed
- principalship, superintendency, and supervision of instruction • MA Ed
- reading specialization • MA Ed
- secondary education • MA Ed
- special education • MA Ed
- superintendency • MA Ed
- supervision of instruction • MA Ed

■ UNIVERSITY OF SOUTH ALABAMA
Mobile, AL 36688-0002
http://www.southalabama.edu/

State-supported, coed, university. CGS member. *Enrollment:* 1,543 full-time matriculated graduate/professional students (986 women), 898 part-time matriculated graduate/professional students (630 women). *Graduate faculty:* 455 full-time (108 women), 27 part-time/adjunct (9 women). *Computer facilities:* 325 computers available on campus for general student use. A campuswide network can be accessed from student residence rooms and from off campus. Internet access is available. *Library facilities:* University Library plus 1 other. *Graduate expenses:* Tuition, state resident: full-time $2,760. Tuition, nonresident: full-time $5,520. Required fees: $241. *General application contact:* Dr. James L. Wolfe, Associate Vice President for Research and Dean of the Graduate School, 334-460-6310.

Find an in-depth description at www.petersons.com/graduate.

College of Medicine
Dr. Robert A. Kreisberg, Interim Dean
Programs in:
- biochemistry and molecular biology • PhD
- cellular biology and neuroscience • PhD
- medicine • MD, PhD
- microbiology and immunology • PhD
- pharmacology • PhD
- physiology • PhD

Graduate School
Dr. James L. Wolfe, Associate Vice President for Research and Dean

College of Allied Health Professions
Dr. Daniel Sellers, Interim Dean
Programs in:
- allied health professions • MHS, MPT, MS, PhD
- communication sciences and disorders • PhD
- physical therapy • MPT
- physician assistant studies • MHS
- speech and hearing sciences • MS

University of South Alabama (continued)

College of Arts and Sciences
Dr. John Friedl, Dean
Programs in:
- arts and sciences • MA, MPA, MS, PhD, Certificate
- biological sciences • MS
- communication arts • MA
- English • MA
- gerontology • Certificate
- history • MA
- marine sciences • MS, PhD
- mathematics • MS
- psychology • MS
- public administration • MPA
- sociology • MA

College of Education
George E. Uhlig, Dean
Programs in:
- art/music education • M Ed
- business education • M Ed
- counseling • M Ed, MS, Ed S
- early childhood education • M Ed, Ed S
- education • M Ed, MS, PhD, Ed S
- education of the emotionally disturbed • M Ed
- education of the gifted • M Ed
- educational administration • M Ed, Ed S
- educational media • M Ed, MS
- elementary education • M Ed, Ed S
- exercise technology • MS
- health education • M Ed
- instructional design • MS
- instructional design and development • PhD
- learning disability • M Ed
- leisure services • MS
- mentally retarded • M Ed
- multihandicapped education • M Ed
- natural science education • M Ed
- physical education • M Ed, Ed S
- reading • M Ed
- science education • M Ed
- secondary education • M Ed, Ed S
- special education • M Ed, Ed S
- therapeutic recreation • MS

College of Engineering
Dr. David T. Hayhurst, Dean
Programs in:
- chemical engineering • MS Ch E
- computer and electrical engineering • MSEE
- engineering • MS Ch E, MSEE, MSME
- mechanical engineering • MSME

College of Nursing
Dr. Debra C. Davis, Dean
Programs in:
- adult health nursing • MSN
- community mental health nursing • MSN
- maternal child nursing • MSN

Division of Computer and Information Sciences
Dr. David Feinstein, Dean
Programs in:
- computer science • MS
- information science • MS

Mitchell College of Business
Dr. Carl Moore, Dean
Programs in:
- accounting • M Acct
- business • M Acct, MBA
- general management • MBA

■ THE UNIVERSITY OF WEST ALABAMA
Livingston, AL 35470
http://www.uwa.edu/

State-supported, coed, comprehensive institution. *Enrollment:* 15 full-time matriculated graduate/professional students (10 women), 314 part-time matriculated graduate/professional students (248 women). *Graduate faculty:* 50 full-time (14 women), 3 part-time/adjunct (0 women). *Computer facilities:* 250 computers available on campus for general student use. A campuswide network can be accessed from student residence rooms and from off campus. Internet access is available. *Library facilities:* Julia Tutwiler Library. *Graduate expenses:* Tuition, state resident: part-time $110 per semester hour. *General application contact:* Dr. Joe B. Wilkins, Dean of Graduate Studies, 205-652-3647 Ext. 421.

School of Graduate Studies
Dr. Joe B. Wilkins, Dean

College of Education
Dr. Ann Jones, Dean
Programs in:
- continuing education • MSCE
- early childhood education • M Ed
- education • M Ed, MAT, MSCE
- elementary education • M Ed
- guidance and counseling • M Ed, MSCE
- library media • M Ed
- physical education • M Ed, MAT
- school administration • M Ed
- secondary education • M Ed, MAT
- special education • M Ed

College of Liberal Arts
Dr. Roy Underwood, Chairperson
Programs in:
- history • MAT
- language arts • MAT
- liberal arts • MAT
- social science • MAT

College of Natural Sciences and Mathematics
Richard D. Holland, Dean
Programs in:
- biological sciences • MAT
- mathematics • MAT
- natural sciences and mathematics • MAT

Alaska

■ ALASKA PACIFIC UNIVERSITY
Anchorage, AK 99508-4672
http://www.alaskapacific.edu/

Independent, coed, comprehensive institution. *Enrollment:* 88 full-time matriculated graduate/professional students (58 women), 82 part-time matriculated graduate/professional students (41 women). *Graduate faculty:* 15 full-time (5 women), 7 part-time/adjunct (3 women). *Computer facilities:* 35 computers available on campus for general student use. A campuswide network can be accessed. Internet access is available. *Library facilities:* Consortium Library. *Graduate expenses:* Tuition: full-time $9,840; part-time $410 per credit hour. Required fees: $160; $40 per semester. *General application contact:* Dale Montague, Director of Admissions, 907-564-8248.

Graduate Programs
Dr. Charles B. Fahl, Academic Dean
Programs in:
- business administration • MBA
- counseling psychology • MSCP
- environmental science • MSES
- teaching (K-8) • MAT
- telecommunication management • MBATM

■ UNIVERSITY OF ALASKA ANCHORAGE
Anchorage, AK 99508-8060
http://www.uaa.alaska.edu/

State-supported, coed, comprehensive institution. CGS member. *Computer facilities:* 500 computers available on campus for general student use. A campuswide network can be accessed from student residence rooms and from off campus. Internet access is available. *Library facilities:* Consortium Library. *General application contact:* Director for Enrollment Services, 907-786-1558.

College of Arts and Sciences
Programs in:
- arts and sciences • MA, MFA, MS
- biological sciences • MS
- clinical psychology • MS
- creative writing and literary arts • MFA
- English • MA
- interdisciplinary studies • MA, MS

College of Business and Public Policy
Programs in:
- business administration • MBA
- business and public policy • MBA, MPA
- public administration • MPA

College of Health, Education, and Social Welfare
Programs in:
- health, education, and social welfare • M Ed, MAT, MS, MSW, Certificate
- substance abuse disorders • Certificate

School of Education
Programs in:
- adult education • M Ed
- counseling and guidance • M Ed
- education • M Ed, MAT
- educational leadership • M Ed
- master teacher • M Ed
- special education • M Ed
- teaching • MAT

School of Nursing
Program in:
- nursing and health science • MS

School of Social Work
Program in:
- social work • MSW

Community and Technical College
Program in:
- vocational education • MS

School of Engineering
Programs in:
- arctic engineering • MS
- civil engineering • MCE, MS
- engineering • MCE, MS
- engineering management • MS
- environmental quality engineering • MS
- environmental quality science • MS
- science management • MS

■ UNIVERSITY OF ALASKA FAIRBANKS
Fairbanks, AK 99775
http://www.uaf.edu/

State-supported, coed, university. CGS member. *Enrollment:* 507 full-time matriculated graduate/professional students (244 women), 266 part-time matriculated graduate/professional students (151 women). *Graduate faculty:* 316 full-time (119 women), 111 part-time/adjunct (50 women). *Computer facilities:* 500 computers available on campus for general student use. A campuswide network can be accessed from student residence rooms and from off campus. Internet access is available. *Library facilities:* Rasmuson Library plus 8 others. *Graduate expenses:* Tuition, state resident: full-time $4,128. $8,064 full-time. Required fees: $960. *General application contact:* Nancy Dix, Interim Director of Admissions, 907-474-7500.

Graduate School
Dr. Joe Kan, Dean
Programs in:
- Alaska native and rural development • MS, PhD
- interdisciplinary studies • MA, MS, PhD

College of Liberal Arts
Dr. John Leipzig, Interim Dean
Programs in:
- Alaskan ethnomusicology • MA
- anthropology • MA, PhD
- art • MA, MFA
- community psychology • MA
- creative writing • MFA
- English • MA
- journalism • MA
- liberal arts • MA, MAT, MFA, PhD
- music • MAT
- music education • MA
- music history • MA
- music theory • MA
- Northern studies • MA, PhD
- performance • MA

College of Rural Alaska
Dr. Ralph Gabrielli, Executive Dean
Program in:
- Alaska native and rural development • MS, PhD

College of Science, Engineering and Mathematics
Dr. David Woodall, Dean
Programs in:
- arctic engineering • MS
- atmospheric science • MS, PhD
- biochemistry • MS, PhD
- biological sciences • MAT, MS, PhD
- biology • MAT, MS, PhD
- botany • MS, PhD
- chemistry • MA, MAT, MS
- civil engineering • MCE, MS
- computer science • MS
- electrical engineering • MEE, MS
- engineering management • MS
- environmental quality engineering • MS
- environmental quality science • MS
- geology • MS, PhD
- geophysics • MS, PhD
- geoscience • MAT
- mathematics • MAT, MS, PhD
- mechanical engineering • MS
- physics • MS, PhD
- science management • MS
- science, engineering and mathematics • MA, MAT, MCE, MEE, MS, PhD
- space physics • MS, PhD
- wildlife biology and management • MS, PhD
- zoology • MS, PhD

School of Agriculture and Land Resources Management
Dr. Carol Lewis, Interim Dean
Program in:
- natural resources management • MS

School of Education
Dr. Roger Norris-Tull, Director
Programs in:
- cross-cultural education • M Ed, Ed S
- curriculum and instruction • M Ed
- educational administration • M Ed
- guidance and counseling • M Ed
- language and literature • M Ed

School of Fisheries and Ocean Sciences
Dr. Vera Alexander, Dean
Programs in:
- fisheries • MS, PhD
- fisheries and ocean sciences • MS, PhD
- marine biology • MS
- oceanography • MS, PhD

School of Management
Dr. James Collins, Dean
Programs in:
- business administration • MBA
- management • MBA, MS
- resource economics • MS

School of Mineral Engineering
Robert Carlson, Interim Dean
Programs in:
- geological engineering • MS, EM
- mineral engineering • MS, EM
- mineral preparation engineering • MS
- mining engineering • MS, EM
- petroleum engineering • MS

■ UNIVERSITY OF ALASKA SOUTHEAST
Juneau, AK 99801
http://www.jun.alaska.edu/

State-supported, coed, comprehensive institution. *Enrollment:* 55 full-time matriculated graduate/professional

University of Alaska Southeast (continued)
students (35 women), 82 part-time matriculated graduate/professional students (64 women). *Graduate faculty:* 12 full-time (6 women), 12 part-time/adjunct (7 women). *Computer facilities:* 75 computers available on campus for general student use. A campuswide network can be accessed from student residence rooms and from off campus. Internet access is available. *Library facilities:* Egan Memorial Library. *Graduate expenses:* Tuition, state resident: full-time $3,440; part-time $172 per credit. Tuition, nonresident: full-time $6,720; part-time $336 per credit. Required fees: $38 per term. Tuition and fees vary according to course load. *General application contact:* Greg Wagner, Recruiter, 907-465-6239.

Graduate Programs
Dr. Roberta Stell, Vice Chancellor for Academic Affairs
Programs in:
early childhood education • M Ed
educational technology • M Ed
elementary education • M Ed, MAT
public administration • MPA
secondary education • M Ed, MAT

Arizona

■ ARIZONA STATE UNIVERSITY

Tempe, AZ 85287
http://www.asu.edu/

State-supported, coed, university. CGS member. *Enrollment:* 5,626 full-time matriculated graduate/professional students (2,598 women), 2,352 part-time matriculated graduate/professional students (1,289 women). *Graduate faculty:* 1,831 full-time (664 women), 134 part-time/adjunct (61 women). *Computer facilities:* A campuswide network can be accessed from student residence rooms and from off campus. Internet access is available. *Library facilities:* Hayden Library plus 4 others. *Graduate expenses:* Tuition, state resident: part-time $119 per credit hour. Tuition, nonresident: part-time $405 per credit hour. Required fees: $18 per semester. *General application contact:* Graduate Admissions, 480-965-6113.

College of Law
Patricia D. White, Dean
Program in:
law • JD

Graduate College
Dr. Bianca L. Bernstein, Dean
Programs in:
creative writing • MFA
curriculum and instruction • PhD
exercise science • PhD
gerontology • Certificate
justice studies • PhD
public administration • DPA
science and engineering of materials • PhD
speech and hearing science • PhD
statistics • MS
transportation systems • Certificate

College of Architecture and Environmental Design
Dr. John Meunier, Dean
Programs in:
architecture • M Arch
architecture and environmental design • M Arch, MEP, MS, MSD, PhD
building design • MS
design • PhD
history, theory, and criticism • PhD
planning • PhD

College of Business
Dr. Larry E. Penley, Dean
Programs in:
accountancy • M Accy, PhD
business • M Accy, M Tax, MBA, MHSA, MS, PhD
business administration • MBA
economics • MS, PhD
finance • PhD
health administration and policy • MHSA
health services research • PhD
information management • MS, PhD
management • PhD
marketing • PhD
supply chain management • PhD
taxation • M Tax

College of Education
Dr. David Berliner, Dean
Programs in:
counseling • M Ed, MC
counseling psychology • PhD
curriculum and instruction • M Ed, MA, Ed D
education • M Ed, MA, MC, Ed D, PhD
educational administration and supervision • M Ed, Ed D
educational leadership and policy studies • M Ed, MA, Ed D, PhD
educational psychology • M Ed, MA, PhD
higher and post-secondary education • M Ed, Ed D
learning and instructional technology • M Ed, MA, PhD
psychology in education • M Ed, MA, MC, PhD
social and philosophical foundations of education • MA
special education • M Ed, MA

College of Engineering and Applied Sciences
Dr. Peter E. Crouch, Dean
Programs in:
aerospace engineering • MS, MSE, PhD
bioengineering • MS, PhD
chemical engineering • MS, MSE, PhD
civil engineering • MS, MSE, PhD
computer science • MCS, MS, PhD
construction • MS
electrical engineering • MS, MSE, PhD
engineering and applied sciences • M Eng, MCS, MS, MSE, PhD
engineering science • MS, MSE, PhD
industrial engineering • MS, MSE, PhD
materials science and engineering • MS, MSE, PhD
mechanical engineering • MS, MSE, PhD

College of Fine Arts
Dr. J. Robert Wills, Dean
Programs in:
art • MA, MFA
dance • MFA
fine arts • MA, MFA, MM, DMA, PhD
music • MA, MM, DMA
theater • MA, MFA, PhD

College of Liberal Arts and Sciences
Dr. Gary S. Krahenbuhl, Dean
Programs in:
anthropology • MA, PhD
applied mathematics • MA, PhD
Asian history • MA, PhD
behavior • MS, PhD
behavioral neuroscience • PhD
biology • MNS
biology education • MS, PhD
British history • MA, PhD
cell and developmental biology • MS, PhD
chemistry and biochemistry • MNS, MS, PhD
clinical psychology • PhD
cognitive/behavioral systems • PhD
communication disorders • MS
computational, statistical, and mathematical biology • MS, PhD
conservation • MS, PhD
demography and population studies • MA, PhD

developmental psychology • PhD
ecology • MS, PhD
English • MA, PhD
environmental psychology • PhD
European history • MA, PhD
evolution • MS, PhD
exercise science and physical education • MPE, MS
family resources and human development • MS
family science • PhD
French • MA
genetics • MS, PhD
geography • MA, PhD
geological engineering • MS, PhD
German • MA
history and philosophy of biology • MS, PhD
humanities • MA
Latin American studies • MA, PhD
liberal arts and sciences • MA, MNS, MPE, MS, MTESL, PhD, Certificate
mathematics • MA, MNS, PhD
medieval studies • Certificate
microbiology • MNS, MS, PhD
molecular and cellular biology • MS, PhD
natural science • MNS
neuroscience • MS, PhD
philosophy • MA
physics and astronomy • MNS, MS, PhD
physiology • MS, PhD
plant biology • MNS, MS, PhD
political science • MA, PhD
public history • MA
quantitative research methods • PhD
religious studies • MA
Renaissance studies • Certificate
social psychology • PhD
sociology • MA, PhD
Spanish • MA, PhD
statistics • MA, PhD
teaching English as a second language • MTESL
U.S. history • PhD
U.S. western history • MA

College of Nursing
Dr. Barbara H. Durand, Dean
Program in:
nursing • MS

College of Public Programs
Dr. Anne L. Schneider, Dean
Programs in:
communication • PhD
journalism and telecommunication • MMC
justice studies • MS
public affairs • MPA, DPA
public programs • MA, MMC, MPA, MS, MSW, DPA, PhD
recreation • MS
social work • MSW, PhD
speech and interpersonal communication • MA

■ ARIZONA STATE UNIVERSITY WEST

Phoenix, AZ 85069-7100
http://www.west.asu.edu/

State-supported, coed, upper-level institution. *Enrollment:* 145 full-time matriculated graduate/professional students (70 women), 471 part-time matriculated graduate/professional students (256 women). *Graduate faculty:* 56 full-time (26 women), 44 part-time/adjunct (14 women). *Computer facilities:* 391 computers available on campus for general student use. A campuswide network can be accessed from off campus. Internet access is available. *Library facilities:* ASU West Library. *Graduate expenses:* Part-time $119 per credit. Tuition, state resident: full-time $2,272. Tuition, nonresident: full-time $9,728; part-time $405 per credit. Tuition and fees vary according to program. *General application contact:* Marge A. Runyan, Coordinator, Graduate College, 602-543-4567.

Find an in-depth description at www.petersons.com/graduate.

College of Arts and Sciences
Dr. Andrew Kirby, Director
Program in:
interdisciplinary studies • MA

College of Education
Dr. Michael Awender, Dean
Programs in:
educational administration and supervision • M Ed
elementary education • M Ed
secondary education • M Ed
special education • M Ed

College of Human Services
Dr. Mark Searle, Dean
Programs in:
communication studies • MA
criminal justice • MA
human services • MA, MSW
social work • MSW

School of Management
Dr. David Van Fleet, Director
Program in:
management • MBA

■ GRAND CANYON UNIVERSITY

Phoenix, AZ 85061-1097
http://www.grand-canyon.edu/

Independent-religious, coed, comprehensive institution. *Computer facilities:* 119 computers available on campus for general student use. Internet access is available. *Library facilities:* Fleming Library. *General application contact:* Director of Admissions, 602-589-2855 Ext. 2811.

College of Business
Program in:
business • MBA

College of Education
Programs in:
elementary education • M Ed, MA
reading education • MA
secondary education • M Ed
teaching • MAT
teaching English as a second language • MA

■ NORTHERN ARIZONA UNIVERSITY

Flagstaff, AZ 86011
http://www.nau.edu/

State-supported, coed, university. CGS member. *Enrollment:* 1,285 full-time matriculated graduate/professional students (845 women), 3,208 part-time matriculated graduate/professional students (2,232 women). *Graduate faculty:* 1,367 full-time (896 women), 3,154 part-time/adjunct (2,244 women). *Computer facilities:* 620 computers available on campus for general student use. A campuswide network can be accessed from student residence rooms and from off campus. Internet access and online class registration are available. *Library facilities:* Cline Library. *Graduate expenses:* Tuition, state resident: full-time $2,346; part-time $129 per credit hour. Tuition, nonresident: full-time $11,124. *General application contact:* Dr. Patricia Baron, Director of Graduate Admissions, 520-523-4348.

Find an in-depth description at www.petersons.com/graduate.

Graduate College
Dr. Tom McPoil, Interim Vice Provost for Research and Graduate Studies

Center for Excellence in Education
Dr. Melvin E. Hall, Executive Director
Programs in:
bilingual/multicultural education • M Ed
community college • M Ed
counseling • M Ed, MA
counseling psychology • Ed D
curriculum and instruction • Ed D

Northern Arizona University (continued)
- early childhood education • M Ed
- educational leadership • Ed D
- educational technology • M Ed
- elementary education • M Ed
- excellence in education • M Ed, MA, MVE, Ed D
- learning and instruction • Ed D
- reading and learning disabilities • M Ed
- school leadership • M Ed
- school psychology • Ed D
- secondary education • M Ed
- special education • M Ed
- vocational education • MVE

College of Arts and Sciences
Suzanne Shipley, Dean
Programs in:
- applied linguistics • PhD
- applied physics • MS
- arts and sciences • MA, MAT, MLS, MS, PhD
- biology • MS, PhD
- biology education • MAT
- chemistry • MS
- creative writing • MA
- earth science • MAT, MS
- English • MA
- general English • MA
- geology • MS
- history • MA, PhD
- liberal studies • MLS
- literature • MA
- mathematics • MAT, MS
- physical science • MAT
- quaternary studies • MS
- rhetoric • MA
- statistics • MS
- teaching English as a second language • MA
- teaching English as a second language/applied linguistics • MA, PhD

College of Business Administration
Dr. Patricia Meyers, Dean
Programs in:
- general management • MBA
- management • MSM
- management information systems • MBA

College of Ecosystem Science and Management
Dr. Donald G. Arganbright, Interim Dean
Programs in:
- ecosystem science and management • MA, MSF, PhD
- forestry • MSF, PhD
- rural geography • MA

College of Engineering
Dr. Mason Somerville, Dean
Program in:
- engineering • M Eng

College of Health Professions
Dr. James Blagg, Dean
Programs in:
- health education and health promotion • MPH
- health professions • MA, MPH, MPT, MS, MSN
- nursing • MSN
- physical education • MA
- physical therapy • MPT
- speech pathology • MS

College of Social and Behavioral Sciences
M. Susanna Maxwell, Dean
Programs in:
- anthropology • MA
- applied health psychology • MA
- applied sociology • MA
- archaeology • MA
- criminal justice • MS
- general • MA
- political science • MA, PhD
- public administration • MPA
- public policy • PhD
- social and behavioral sciences • MA, MPA, MS, PhD

School of Performing Arts
Dr. John Barton, Interim Dean
Programs in:
- choral conducting • MM
- instrumental conducting • MM
- instrumental performance • MM
- music education • MM
- music history • MM
- theory and composition • MM
- vocal performance • MM

■ PRESCOTT COLLEGE
Prescott, AZ 86301-2990
http://www.prescott.edu/

Independent, coed, comprehensive institution. *Enrollment:* 128 full-time matriculated graduate/professional students (83 women), 19 part-time matriculated graduate/professional students (10 women). *Graduate faculty:* 9 full-time (5 women), 78 part-time/adjunct (49 women). *Computer facilities:* 30 computers available on campus for general student use. A campuswide network can be accessed. *Library facilities:* Prescott College Library. *Graduate expenses:* Tuition: full-time $9,900; part-time $275 per credit. *General application contact:* Abbey Carpenter, Admissions Counselor, 800-628-6364.

Find an in-depth description at www.petersons.com/graduate.

Graduate Programs
Dr. Steve Walters, Dean
Programs in:
- adventure education/wilderness leadership • MA
- agroecology • MA
- bilingual education • MA
- counseling and psychology • MA
- ecopsychology • MA
- education • MA
- environmental education • MA
- environmental studies • MA
- humanities • MA
- multicultural education • MA
- Southwestern regional history • MA
- sustainability • MA

■ THE UNIVERSITY OF ARIZONA
Tucson, AZ 85721
http://www.arizona.edu/

State-supported, coed, university. CGS member. *Enrollment:* 4,681 full-time matriculated graduate/professional students (2,291 women), 1,269 part-time matriculated graduate/professional students (686 women). *Graduate faculty:* 1,392 full-time (362 women), 103 part-time/adjunct (32 women). *Computer facilities:* 1,750 computers available on campus for general student use. A campuswide network can be accessed from student residence rooms and from off campus. Internet access is available. *Library facilities:* University of Arizona Main Library plus 5 others. *Graduate expenses:* Tuition, state resident: part-time $126 per unit. Tuition, nonresident: part-time $412 per unit. Tuition and fees vary according to program. *General application contact:* Graduate Admissions Office, 520-621-3132.

College of Medicine
Programs in:
- biochemistry • MS, PhD
- cell biology and anatomy • PhD
- medicine • MD, MPH, MS, PhD
- microbiology and immunology • MS, PhD
- public health • MPH

Graduate College
Gary Pivo, Dean
Programs in:
- American Indian studies • MA
- applied mathematics • MS, PMS, PhD
- arid land resource sciences • PhD
- cancer biology • PhD
- comparative cultural and literary studies • MA, PhD

epidemiology • MS, PhD
genetics • MS, PhD
gerontological studies • MS, Certificate
insect science • PhD
mathematical sciences • PMS
neuroscience • PhD
nutritional sciences • PhD
pharmacology and toxicology • PhD
physiological sciences • PhD
planning • MS
public health • MPH
second language acquisition and teaching • PhD

College of Agriculture and Life Sciences
Dr. Eugene G. Sander, Dean
Programs in:
agricultural and biosystems engineering • MS, PhD
agricultural and resource economics • MS
agricultural education • M Ag Ed, MS
agriculture and life sciences • M Ag Ed, MHE Ed, ML Arch, MS, PhD
animal sciences • MS, PhD
dietetics • MS
entomology • MS, PhD
family and consumer sciences • MS
family studies and human development • PhD
forest-watershed management • MS, PhD
nutritional sciences • MS
pathobiology • MS, PhD
plant pathology • MS, PhD
plant sciences • MS, PhD
range management • MS, PhD
renewable natural resources • ML Arch, MS, PhD
retailing and consumer sciences • MS, PhD
soil, water and environmental science • MS, PhD
wildlife and fisheries science • MS, PhD

College of Architecture, Planning and Landscape Architecture
Dr. Richard Eribes, Dean
Programs in:
architecture, planning and landscape architecture • M Arch, ML Arch
landscape architecture • ML Arch

College of Business and Public Administration
Dr. Mark A. Zupan, Acting Dean
Programs in:
accounting • M Ac
business administration • MBA
business and public administration • M Ac, MA, MBA, MPA, MS, PhD
economics • MA, PhD
finance • MS
management • PhD
management and policy • MS
management information systems • MS
marketing • MS
public administration • MPA
public administration and policy • PhD

College of Education
Dr. John Taylor, Dean
Programs in:
bilingual education • M Ed
bilingual/multicultural education • MA
education • M Ed, MA, MS, MT, Ed D, PhD, Ed S
educational administration • M Ed, MA, Ed D, PhD, Ed S
educational psychology • MA, PhD
elementary education • M Ed, MT, Ed D
higher education • M Ed, MA, Ed D, PhD
language, reading and culture • MA, Ed D, PhD, Ed S
reading • M Ed, MA, Ed D, PhD, Ed S
secondary education • M Ed, MT, Ed D, Ed S
special education and rehabilitation • M Ed, MA, MS, Ed D, PhD, Ed S
teaching and teacher education • MA, Ed D, PhD, Ed S

College of Engineering and Mines
Dr. Ernest Smerdon, Dean
Programs in:
aerospace engineering • MS, PhD
chemical engineering • MS, PhD
civil engineering • MS, PhD
electrical and computer engineering • MS, PhD
engineering and mines • MS, PhD
engineering mechanics • MS, PhD
environmental engineering • MS, PhD
geological and geophysical engineering • MS, PhD
hydrology • MS, PhD
industrial engineering • MS
materials science and engineering • MS, PhD
mechanical engineering • MS, PhD
mining engineering • MS, PhD
nuclear engineering • MS, PhD
reliability and quality engineering • MS
systems and industrial engineering • PhD
systems engineering • MS
water resource administration • MS, PhD

College of Fine Arts
Dr. Maurice Sevigny, Dean
Programs in:
studio art • MFA
art education • MA
art history • MA
composition • MM, A Mus D
conducting • MM, A Mus D
fine arts • MA, MFA, MM, A Mus D, PhD
media arts • MA
music education • MM, PhD
music theory • MM, PhD
musicology • MM
performance • MM, A Mus D
theatre arts • MA, MFA

College of Humanities
Dr. Charles M. Tatum, Dean
Programs in:
classics • MA
creative writing • MFA
East Asian studies • MA, PhD
English • M Ed, MA, PhD
English as a second language • MA
French • M Ed, MA, PhD
German • M Ed, MA
humanities • M Ed, MA, MFA, PhD
rhetoric, composition and teaching of English • PhD
Russian • M Ed, MA
Spanish • M Ed, MA, PhD

College of Nursing
Dr. Suzanne Van Ort, Dean
Program in:
nursing • MS, PhD

College of Pharmacy
Dr. J. Lyle Bootman, Dean
Programs in:
pharmaceutical sciences • MS, PhD
pharmacology and toxicology • MS, PhD
pharmacy • Pharm D, MS, PhD

College of Science
Dr. Eugene H. Levy, Dean
Programs in:
astronomy • MS, PhD
atmospheric sciences • MS, PhD
botany • MS, PhD
chemistry • MA, MS, PhD
computer science • MS, PhD
ecology and evolutionary biology • MS, PhD
geosciences • MS, PhD
mathematics • M Ed, MA, MS, PhD
molecular and cellular biology • MS, PhD
physics • M Ed, MS, PhD
planetary sciences • MS, PhD
science • M Ed, MA, MS, PhD
speech and hearing sciences • MS, PhD
statistics • MS, PhD

College of Social and Behavioral Sciences
Dr. Holly Smith, Dean
Programs in:
anthropology • MA, PhD

The University of Arizona (continued)
communication • MA, PhD
geography • MA, PhD
history • M Ed, MA, PhD
journalism • MA
Latin American studies • MA
library science • MA, PhD
linguistics • MA, PhD
Near Eastern studies • MA, PhD
philosophy • MA, PhD
political science • MA, PhD
psychology • MA, PhD
social and behavioral sciences • M Ed, MA, PhD
sociology • MA, PhD
women's studies • MA

James E. Rogers College of Law
Toni M. Massaro, Dean
Programs in:
international indigenous peoples' rights and policy • LL M
international trade law • LL M
law • JD

Optical Sciences Center
Dr. James Wyant, Director
Program in:
optical sciences • MS, PhD

■ WESTERN INTERNATIONAL UNIVERSITY

Phoenix, AZ 85021-2718
http://www.wintu.edu/

Proprietary, coed, comprehensive institution. *Enrollment:* 526 full-time matriculated graduate/professional students (262 women). *Graduate faculty:* 82 part-time/adjunct (26 women). *Computer facilities:* 30 computers available on campus for general student use. A campuswide network can be accessed. Internet access is available. *Library facilities:* Learning Resource Center. *Graduate expenses:* Tuition: full-time $9,360; part-time $260 per credit. *General application contact:* Karen Janitell, Director of Enrollment, 602-943-2311 Ext. 126.

Graduate Programs in Business
Kay Look, Director of Academic Affairs and Curriculum
Programs in:
business • MBA, MPA, MS
finance • MBA
information technology • MBA, MS
international business • MBA
management • MBA
marketing • MBA
public administration • MPA

Arkansas

■ ARKANSAS STATE UNIVERSITY

Jonesboro, State University, AR 72467
http://www.astate.edu/

State-supported, coed, comprehensive institution. CGS member. *Enrollment:* 244 full-time matriculated graduate/professional students (157 women), 896 part-time matriculated graduate/professional students (592 women). *Graduate faculty:* 269 full-time (78 women), 9 part-time/adjunct (6 women). *Computer facilities:* 556 computers available on campus for general student use. A campuswide network can be accessed from student residence rooms and from off campus. Internet access and online class registration are available. *Library facilities:* Dean B. Ellis Library. *Graduate expenses:* Tuition, state resident: full-time $3,192; part-time $133 per hour. Tuition, nonresident: full-time $8,040; part-time $335 per hour. Required fees: $526; $19 per hour. $25 per semester. Tuition and fees vary according to course load. *General application contact:* Dr. Thomas G. Wheeler, Dean of the Graduate School, 870-972-3029.

Graduate School
Dr. Thomas G. Wheeler, Dean of the Graduate School

College of Agriculture
Dr. Calvin Shumway, Interim Dean
Programs in:
agricultural education • MSA, SCCT
agriculture • MSA
vocational-technical administration • MS, SCCT

College of Arts and Sciences
Dr. Linda Pritchard, Dean
Programs in:
arts and sciences • MA, MPA, MS, MSE, PhD, SCCT
biology • MS
biology education • MSE, SCCT
chemistry • MS
chemistry education • MSE, SCCT
computer science • MS
English • MA
English education • MSE, SCCT
environmental sciences • PhD
history • MA, SCCT
mathematics • MS, MSE
political science • MA, SCCT
public administration • MPA
social science • MSE
sociology • MA, SCCT

College of Business
Dr. Jan Duggar, Dean
Programs in:
business • EMBA, MBA, MSE, SCCT
business administration • EMBA, MBA, SCCT
business education • MSE, SCCT

College of Communications
Dr. Russell Shain, Dean
Programs in:
communications • MA, MSMC
journalism • MSMC
radio-television • MSMC
speech communication • MA
theater • MA

College of Education
Dr. John Beineke, Dean
Programs in:
counselor education • MSE, Ed S
early childhood education • MSE
early childhood services • MS
education • MRC, MS, MSE, Ed D, Ed S, SCCT
educational administration • MSE, Ed S
educational leadership • Ed D
elementary education • MSE
emotionally disturbed • MSE
gifted, talented, and creative • MSE
instructional specialist (4-12) • MSE
instructional specialist (P-4) • MSE
physical education • MS, MSE, SCCT
reading • MSE, SCCT
rehabilitation counseling • MRC

College of Fine Arts
Dr. Daniel Reeves, Dean
Programs in:
art • MA
fine arts • MA, MM, MME, SCCT
music education • MME, SCCT
performance • MM
speech communication • MA, SCCT
theater arts • MA, SCCT

College of Nursing and Health Professions
Dr. Susan Hanrahan, Dean
Programs in:
aging studies • Certificate
communication disorders • MCD
nursing • MSN
physical therapy • MPT

■ ARKANSAS TECH UNIVERSITY

Russellville, AR 72801-2222
http://www.atu.edu/

State-supported, coed, comprehensive institution. *Enrollment:* 99 full-time matriculated graduate/professional

students, 212 part-time matriculated graduate/professional students. *Graduate faculty:* 109 full-time (37 women), 31 part-time/adjunct (17 women). *Computer facilities:* 258 computers available on campus for general student use. A campuswide network can be accessed from student residence rooms and from off campus. Internet access and online class registration are available. *Library facilities:* Ross Pendergraft Library and Technology Center. *Graduate expenses:* Tuition, state resident: part-time $116 per credit hour. Tuition, nonresident: part-time $232 per credit hour. Required fees: $60 per semester. *General application contact:* Dr. Eldon G. Clary, Dean of Graduate Studies, 501-968-0398.

Graduate Studies
Dr. Eldon G. Clary, Dean
Programs in:
fisheries and wildlife biology • MS
information technology • MS

School of Education
Dr. Dennis W. Fleniken, Dean
Programs in:
education • M Ed, MSE
educational leadership • M Ed
elementary education • M Ed
English • M Ed
gifted education • MSE
instructional improvement • M Ed
instructional technology • M Ed
mathematics • M Ed
physical education • M Ed
social studies • M Ed

School of Liberal Arts
Dr. Georgena Duncan, Dean
Programs in:
communications • MLA
English • MA
fine arts • MLA
history • MA
multi-media journalism • MA
social sciences • MLA

School of Physical and Life Science
Dr. Richad Cohoon, Dean
Program in:
fisheries and wildlife biology • MS

School of System Science
Dr. Jack Hamm, Dean
Program in:
information technology • MS

■ HARDING UNIVERSITY

Searcy, AR 72149-0001

http://www.harding.edu/

Independent-religious, coed, comprehensive institution. *Enrollment:* 71 full-time matriculated graduate/professional students (38 women), 362 part-time matriculated graduate/professional students (279 women). *Graduate faculty:* 3 full-time (0 women), 90 part-time/adjunct (23 women). *Computer facilities:* 150 computers available on campus for general student use. A campuswide network can be accessed from student residence rooms and from off campus. Internet access and online class registration are available. *Library facilities:* Brackett Library plus 1 other. *Graduate expenses:* Tuition: full-time $4,905; part-time $273 per credit hour. Required fees: $250; $125 per semester. Tuition and fees vary according to course load, degree level, reciprocity agreements, student level and student's religious affiliation. *General application contact:* Dr. Jim Nichols, Director of Graduate Studies, 501-279-4315.

College of Bible and Religion
Dr. Tom Alexander, Dean
Programs in:
Bible and religion • MA, MS
marriage and family therapy • MS
ministry • MA

School of Business
Dr. Randy McLeod, Dean
Program in:
business • MBA

School of Education
Dr. Jim Nichols, Director of Graduate Studies
Programs in:
education • M Ed, MSE
elementary education • M Ed
elementary school administration • M Ed
secondary education • M Ed, MSE

School of Nursing
Dr. Cathleen M. Schultz, Dean
Program in:
nursing • MSN

■ HENDERSON STATE UNIVERSITY

Arkadelphia, AR 71999-0001

http://www.hsu.edu/

State-supported, coed, comprehensive institution. *Enrollment:* 51 full-time matriculated graduate/professional students (30 women), 316 part-time matriculated graduate/professional students (218 women). *Graduate faculty:* 110 full-time (23 women), 9 part-time/adjunct (6 women). *Computer facilities:* 125 computers available on campus for general student use. A campuswide network can be accessed from student residence rooms and from off campus. *Library facilities:* Huie Library. *Graduate expenses:* Tuition, state resident: full-time $3,024; part-time $126 per credit. Tuition, nonresident: full-time $6,048; part-time $252 per credit. Required fees: $100 per semester. *General application contact:* Dr. Johnnie Jones Roebuck, Graduate Dean, 870-230-5126.

Graduate Studies
Dr. Johnnie Jones Roebuck, Dean
Programs in:
English • MLA
liberal arts • MLA
social studies • MLA

School of Business Administration
Dr. Gary Linn, Dean
Program in:
business administration • MBA

School of Education
Dr. Charles Green, Dean
Programs in:
art education • MSE
biology education • MSE
community counseling • MS
early childhood/special education • MSE
education • MS, MSE
education of the mildly handicapped • MSE
elementary school administration • MSE
elementary school counseling • MSE
English education • MSE
general elementary education • MSE
mathematics education • MSE
physical education • MSE
reading • MSE
secondary school administration • MSE
secondary school counseling • MSE
social sciences education • MSE

■ SOUTHERN ARKANSAS UNIVERSITY–MAGNOLIA

Magnolia, AR 71753

http://www.saumag.edu/

State-supported, coed, comprehensive institution. *Enrollment:* 15 full-time matriculated graduate/professional students (11 women), 117 part-time matriculated graduate/professional students (98 women). *Graduate faculty:* 39 full-time (18 women), 1 part-time/adjunct (0 women). *Computer facilities:* 150 computers available on campus for general student use. A campuswide network can be accessed from off campus. Internet access is available. *Library facilities:* Magale Library. *Graduate expenses:* Tuition, state resident: part-time $119 per credit hour. Tuition, nonresident:

Southern Arkansas University–Magnolia (continued)
part-time $173 per credit hour. Required fees: $120. *General application contact:* Dr. John R. Jones, Dean, Graduate Studies, 870-235-4055.

Graduate Programs
Dr. John R. Jones, Dean, Graduate Studies
Programs in:
agency counseling • M Ed
education • M Ed
library media and information specialist • M Ed

■ UNIVERSITY OF ARKANSAS

Fayetteville, AR 72701-1201
http://www.uark.edu/

State-supported, coed, university. CGS member. *Enrollment:* 1,432 full-time matriculated graduate/professional students (695 women), 1,412 part-time matriculated graduate/professional students (669 women). *Graduate faculty:* 844 full-time (207 women), 139 part-time/adjunct (41 women). *Computer facilities:* 1,415 computers available on campus for general student use. A campuswide network can be accessed from student residence rooms and from off campus. Internet access is available. *Library facilities:* David W. Mullins Library plus 5 others. *Graduate expenses:* Tuition, state resident: full-time $3,384; part-time $188 per credit. Tuition, nonresident: full-time $8,010; part-time $445 per credit. Tuition and fees vary according to class time, course level, course load, degree level, program and student level. *General application contact:* Information Contact, 501-575-4401.

Graduate School
Dr. Patricia R. Koski, Associate Dean
Programs in:
cell and molecular biology • MS, PhD
microelectronics and photonics • MS, PhD
public policy • PhD

College of Business Administration
Dr. Doyle Williams, Dean
Programs in:
accounting • M Acc
business administration • M Acc, MA, MBA, MIS, MTLM, PhD
economics • MA, PhD
information systems • MIS
transportation and logistics management • MTLM

College of Education and Health Professions
M. Reed Greenwood, Associate Dean
Programs in:
adult education • M Ed, Ed D, Ed S
childhood education • MAT
communication disorders • MS
counseling education • MS, PhD, Ed S
curriculum and instruction • PhD
education • M Ed, Ed D, Ed S
education and health professions • M Ed, MAT, MS, Ed D, PhD, Ed S
educational administration • M Ed, Ed D, Ed S
educational technology • M Ed
elementary education • M Ed, Ed S
health science • MS, PhD
higher education • M Ed, Ed D, Ed S
kinesiology • MS, PhD
middle-level education • MAT
physical education • M Ed, MAT
recreation • M Ed, Ed D
rehabilitation • MS, PhD
secondary education • M Ed, MAT, Ed S
special education • M Ed, MAT
vocational education • M Ed, MAT, Ed D, Ed S

College of Engineering
Dr. Otto Loewer, Dean
Programs in:
biological and agricultural engineering • MSBAE, MSE, PhD
chemical engineering • MS Ch E, MSE, PhD
civil engineering • MSCE, MSE, PhD
computer systems engineering • MSCSE, MSE, PhD
electrical engineering • MSEE, PhD
engineering • MS, MS Ch E, MS En E, MS Tc E, MSBAE, MSCE, MSCSE, MSE, MSEE, MSIE, MSME, MSOR, MSTE, PhD
environmental engineering • MS En E, MSE
industrial engineering • MSE, MSIE, PhD
mechanical engineering • MSE, MSME, PhD
operations management • MS
operations research • MSE, MSOR
telecommunications engineering • MS Tc E
transportation engineering • MSE, MSTE

Dale Bumpers College of Agricultural, Food and Life Sciences
Dr. Greg Weideman, Interim Dean
Programs in:
agricultural and extension education • MS
agricultural economics • MS
agricultural education • MAT
agricultural, food and life sciences • MAT, MS, PhD
agronomy • MS, PhD
animal science • MS, PhD
entomology • MS, PhD
food science • MS, PhD
general agriculture • MS
horticulture • MS
human environmental sciences • MS
plant pathology • MS
plant science • PhD
poultry science • MS, PhD

J. William Fulbright College of Arts and Sciences
Dr. Randall Woods, Interim Dean
Programs in:
anthropology • MA
applied physics • MS
art • MFA
arts and sciences • MA, MFA, MM, MPA, MS, PhD
biology • MA, MS, PhD
chemistry • MS, PhD
communication • MA
comparative literature • MA, PhD
computer science • MS, PhD
creative writing • MFA
drama • MA, MFA
English • MA, PhD
environmental dynamics • PhD
French • MA
geography • MA
geology • MS
German • MA
history • MA, PhD
journalism • MA
mathematics • MS, PhD
music • MM
philosophy • MA, PhD
physics • MA, MS, PhD
political science • MA
psychology • MA, PhD
public administration • MPA
secondary mathematics • MA
sociology • MA
Spanish • MA
statistics • MS
translation • MFA

School of Law
Robert Moberly, Dean
Programs in:
agricultural law • LL M
law • JD

■ UNIVERSITY OF ARKANSAS AT LITTLE ROCK

Little Rock, AR 72204-1099
http://www.ualr.edu/

State-supported, coed, university. CGS member. *Computer facilities:* 500 computers available on campus for general student use. A campuswide network can be accessed from off campus. Internet access is available. *Library facilities:* Ottenheimer Library plus 1 other. *General application contact:* Dean of the Graduate School, 501-569-8661.

Graduate School

College of Arts, Humanities, and Social Science
Programs in:
applied psychology • MAP
art education • MA
art history • MA
arts, humanities, and social science • MA, MALS, MAP
expository writing • MA
liberal studies • MALS
public history • MA
studio art • MA
technical writing • MA

College of Business Administration
Program in:
business administration • MBA

College of Education
Programs in:
adult education • M Ed
counselor education • M Ed
early childhood education • M Ed, Ed S
early childhood special education • M Ed
education • M Ed, MA, Ed D, Ed S
education of hearing impaired children • M Ed
educational administration • M Ed, Ed D, Ed S
educational administration and supervision • M Ed, Ed D, Ed S
higher education administration • Ed D
instructional resources • M Ed
middle childhood education • M Ed, Ed S
reading • M Ed, Ed S
rehabilitation for the blind • MA
school counseling • M Ed
secondary education • M Ed
special education • M Ed
teaching of the mildly disabled student • M Ed
teaching persons with severe disabilities • M Ed
teaching the gifted and talented • M Ed
teaching the visually impaired child • M Ed

College of Information Science and Systems Engineering
Programs in:
computer science • MS
information science and systems engineering • MA, MS, PhD
instrumental sciences • MS, PhD

College of Professional Studies
Programs in:
applied gerontology • CG
clinical social work • MSW
criminal justice • MA
gerontology • MA
health services administration • MHSA
interpersonal communications • MA
journalism • MA
organizational communications • MA
professional studies • MA, MHSA, MPA, MSW, CG
public administration • MPA
social program administration • MSW
social work • MA, MSW, CG

College of Science and Mathematics
Programs in:
applied mathematics • MS
chemistry • MA, MS
science and mathematics • MA, MS

William H. Bowen School of Law

Charles W. Goldner, Dean
Program in:
law • JD

■ UNIVERSITY OF CENTRAL ARKANSAS

Conway, AR 72035-0001

http://www.uca.edu/

State-supported, coed, comprehensive institution. CGS member. *Enrollment:* 389 full-time matriculated graduate/professional students (275 women), 499 part-time matriculated graduate/professional students (396 women). *Graduate faculty:* 216 full-time (71 women), 11 part-time/adjunct (7 women). *Computer facilities:* 500 computers available on campus for general student use. A campuswide network can be accessed from student residence rooms and from off campus. Internet access is available. *Library facilities:* Torreyson Library. *Graduate expenses:* Tuition, state resident: full-time $1,336; part-time $148 per hour. Tuition, nonresident: full-time $2,754; part-time $306 per hour. Required fees: $19 per term. $24 per term. Tuition and fees vary according to campus/location and program. *General application contact:* Dr. Elaine M. McNiece, Associate Provost and Dean of the Graduate School, 501-450-3124.

Graduate School

Dr. Elaine M. McNiece, Associate Provost

College of Education
Dr. Jane McHaney, Dean
Programs in:
business education • MSE
community service counseling • MS
counseling psychology • MS
early childhood education • MSE
early childhood special education • MSE
education • MS, MSE, PhD
education media and library science • MS
elementary education • MSE
elementary education for the gifted • MSE
elementary school counseling • MS
mildly handicapped • MSE
moderately/profoundly handicapped • MSE
reading education • MSE
school counseling • MS
school psychology • MS, PhD
secondary school counseling • MS
seriously emotionally disturbed • MSE
special education • MSE
student personnel services in higher education • MS

College of Fine Arts and Communication
Dr. Robert G. Everding, Dean
Programs in:
choral conducting • MM
fine arts and communication • MM
instrumental conducting • MM
music education • MM
music theory • MM
performance • MM

College of Health and Applied Sciences
Dr. Neil Hattlestad, Dean
Programs in:
family and consumer sciences • MS
health and applied sciences • MS, MSN, DPT, PhD
health education • MS
health systems • MS
kinesiology • MS
nursing • MSN
occupational therapy • MS
physical therapy • MS, DPT, PhD
speech-language pathology • MS

College of Liberal Arts
Maurice Lee, Dean
Programs in:
English • MA
foreign languages • MSE
history • MA
liberal arts • MA, MSE

College of Natural Sciences and Math
Dr. Ron Toll, Dean
Programs in:
biological science • MS
mathematics • MA
natural sciences and math • MA, MS

University of Central Arkansas (continued)

Graduate School of Management, Leadership, and Administration
Dr. Ira Saltz, Associate Dean
Programs in:
business administration • IMBA, MBA
educational leadership • Ed S
elementary school leadership • MSE
management, leadership and administration • IMBA, MBA, MSE, Ed S
secondary school leadership • MSE

California

■ ALLIANT INTERNATIONAL UNIVERSITY

San Diego, CA 92131-1799
http://www.usiu.edu/

Independent, coed, university. *Enrollment:* 487 full-time matriculated graduate/professional students (282 women), 336 part-time matriculated graduate/professional students (184 women). *Graduate faculty:* 53 full-time (20 women), 69 part-time/adjunct (29 women). *Computer facilities:* 80 computers available on campus for general student use. A campuswide network can be accessed from student residence rooms. Internet access and online class registration are available. *Library facilities:* Walter Library. *Graduate expenses:* Tuition: part-time $385 per summer. Required fees: $117 per quarter. Tuition and fees vary according to degree level and program. *General application contact:* Susan Topham, Director of Admissions, 858-635-4772.

Find an in-depth description at www.petersons.com/graduate.

College of Arts and Sciences
Dr. Ramona Kunard, Dean
Programs in:
arts and sciences • MA, MS, Ed D, Psy D
clinical psychology • Psy D
counseling psychology • MA
educational administration • MA, Ed D
industrial organizational psychology • MS
industrial/organizational psychology • MA, Psy D
international relations • MA
marriage and family therapy • MA, Psy D
teaching • MA
teaching English to speakers of other languages • MA, Ed D
technology and learning • MA, Ed D

College of Business Administration
Dr. Mink H. Stavenga, Dean
Programs in:
business administration • MBA
information and technology management • DBA
international business • MIBA, DBA
strategic business • DBA

■ ANTIOCH UNIVERSITY LOS ANGELES

Marina del Rey, CA 90292-7090
http://www.antiochla.edu/

Independent, coed, upper-level institution. *Enrollment:* 270 full-time matriculated graduate/professional students (194 women), 153 part-time matriculated graduate/professional students (117 women). *Graduate faculty:* 14 full-time (10 women), 76 part-time/adjunct (40 women). *Computer facilities:* 12 computers available on campus for general student use. A campuswide network can be accessed from off campus. Internet access is available. *Graduate expenses:* Tuition: full-time $3,700; part-time $355 per unit. One-time fee: $350. Tuition and fees vary according to program. *General application contact:* Director of Admissions, 310-578-1080 Ext. 100.

Graduate Programs
Dr. Mark Schulman, President and Dean of Academic Affairs
Programs in:
clinical psychology • MA
creative writing • MFA
education • MA
human resource development • MA
leadership • MA
organizational development • MA
pedagogy of creative writing • Certificate
psychology • MA

■ AZUSA PACIFIC UNIVERSITY

Azusa, CA 91702-7000
http://www.apu.edu/

Independent-religious, coed, comprehensive institution. CGS member. *Enrollment:* 1,170 full-time matriculated graduate/professional students (692 women), 1,874 part-time matriculated graduate/professional students (1,116 women). *Graduate faculty:* 206 full-time (81 women), 356 part-time/adjunct (156 women). *Computer facilities:* 300 computers available on campus for general student use. A campuswide network can be accessed from off campus. Internet access is available. *Library facilities:* Marshburn Memorial Library plus 2 others. *Graduate expenses:* Tuition: part-time $380 per unit. Full-time tuition and fees vary according to degree level and program. *General application contact:* 626-812-3016.

Find an in-depth description at www.petersons.com/graduate.

Graduate Studies

College of Liberal Arts and Sciences
Dr. David Weeks, Dean
Programs in:
applied computer science and technology • MS
client/server technology • Certificate
computer information systems • Certificate
computer science • Certificate
end-user training and support • Certificate
liberal arts and sciences • MA, MPT, MS, MSE, Certificate
physical therapy • MPT
software engineering • MSE
teaching English to speakers of other languages • MA, Certificate
technical programming • Certificate
telecommunications • Certificate

Graduate School of Theology
Dr. Lane Scott, Interim Dean
Programs in:
Christian education • MA
Christian nonprofit leadership • MA
pastoral studies • MAPS
religion • MA
theology • M Div, D Min

School of Business and Management
Dr. Ilene Bezjiah, Dean
Programs in:
business administration • MBA
human and organizational development • MA
human resource development • MHRD
international business • MBA
organizational management • MAOM
strategic management • MBA

School of Education and Behavioral Studies
Dr. Alice Watkins, Dean
Programs in:

clinical psychology • MA, Psy D
college student affairs • M Ed
curriculum and instruction in a multicultural setting • MA
education and behavioral studies • M Ed, MA, MFT, Ed D, Psy D
educational leadership and administration • Ed D
educational technology • M Ed
family therapy • MFT
language development • MA
physical education • M Ed
pupil personnel services • MA
school administration • MA
social science leadership studies • MA
special education • MA
teaching • MA

School of Music
Dr. Duane Funderburk, Dean
Programs in:
conducting • M Mus
education • M Mus

School of Nursing
Dr. Rose Liegler, Dean
Program in:
nursing • MSN

■ BIOLA UNIVERSITY

La Mirada, CA 90639-0001
http://www.biola.edu/

Independent-religious, coed, university. *Enrollment:* 487 full-time matriculated graduate/professional students (161 women), 750 part-time matriculated graduate/professional students (292 women). *Graduate faculty:* 70 full-time (18 women), 71 part-time/adjunct (27 women). *Computer facilities:* 115 computers available on campus for general student use. A campuswide network can be accessed from student residence rooms and from off campus. Internet access and online class registration are available. *Library facilities:* Rose Memorial Library. *Graduate expenses:* Tuition: full-time $15,862; part-time $327 per unit. One-time fee: $50 part-time. Tuition and fees vary according to degree level and program. *General application contact:* Roy M. Allinson, Director of Graduate Admissions, 562-903-4752.

Rosemead School of Psychology
Dr. Patricia Pike, Administrative Dean
Program in:
psychology • MA, PhD, Psy D

School of Arts and Sciences
Dr. Pete Menjares, Chair of Education Department
Program in:
arts and sciences • MA Ed

School of Business
Larry D. Strand, Dean
Program in:
business • MBA

School of Intercultural Studies
Dr. Douglas Pennoyer, Dean
Programs in:
applied linguistics • MA
intercultural studies • MAICS, PhD
missiology • D Miss
missions • MA
teaching English to speakers of other languages • MA, Certificate

School of Professional Studies
Dr. Ed Norman, Dean
Programs in:
Christian apologetics • MA
organizational leadership • MA

Talbot School of Theology
Dr. Dennis Dirks, Dean
Programs in:
Bible exposition • MA
biblical and theological studies • MA
Christian education • MACE
Christian ministry and leadership • MA
divinity • M Div
education • PhD
ministry • MA Min
New Testament • MA
Old Testament • MA
philosophy of religion and ethics • MA
theology • Th M, D Min

■ CALIFORNIA BAPTIST UNIVERSITY

Riverside, CA 92504-3206
http://www.calbaptist.edu/

Independent-religious, coed, comprehensive institution. *Enrollment:* 151 full-time matriculated graduate/professional students (109 women), 383 part-time matriculated graduate/professional students (269 women). *Graduate faculty:* 19 full-time (9 women), 8 part-time/adjunct (3 women). *Computer facilities:* 132 computers available on campus for general student use. A campuswide network can be accessed from student residence rooms and from off campus. Internet access, intranet are available. *Library facilities:* Annie Gabriel Library. *Graduate expenses:* Tuition: full-time $8,736; part-time $364 per unit. Required fees: $160 per semester. Tuition and fees vary according to course load and program. *General application contact:* Gail Ronveaux, Director of Graduate Services, 909-343-4249.

Graduate Program in Business Administration
Dr. Bob Jabs, Chair
Program in:
business administration • MBA

Graduate Program in Education
Dr. Mary Crist, Chair
Programs in:
cross-cultural language academic development • MA Ed
educational leadership • MS Ed
educational technology • MS Ed
English education • MA Ed
reading • MS Ed
special education • MS Ed
sport leadership • MS Ed
teaching and curriculum • MS Ed

Graduate Program in Marriage, Family, and Child Counseling
Dr. Gary Collins, Director
Program in:
counseling psychology • MS

■ CALIFORNIA INSTITUTE OF TECHNOLOGY

Pasadena, CA 91125-0001
http://www.caltech.edu/

Independent, coed, university. CGS member. *Enrollment:* 1,100 full-time matriculated graduate/professional students (251 women). *Graduate faculty:* 339 full-time (47 women), 56 part-time/adjunct (17 women). *Computer facilities:* 600 computers available on campus for general student use. A campuswide network can be accessed from student residence rooms and from off campus. Internet access is available. *Library facilities:* Millikan Library plus 10 others. *Graduate expenses:* Tuition: full-time $19,743. *General application contact:* Natalie Gilmore, Graduate Office, 626-395-3812.

Division of Biology
Dr. Elliot M. Meyerowitz, Chairman
Programs in:
biochemistry and molecular biophysics • PhD
cell biology and biophysics • PhD
developmental biology • PhD
genetics • PhD
immunology • PhD
molecular biology • PhD
neurobiology • PhD

Division of Chemistry and Chemical Engineering
Programs in:
biochemistry • PhD
chemical engineering • MS, PhD
chemistry • PhD

California Institute of Technology (continued)

Division of Engineering and Applied Science
Dr. Richard M. Murray, Chair
Programs in:
aeronautics • MS, PhD, Engr
applied and computational mathematics • MS, PhD
applied mechanics • MS, PhD
applied physics • MS, PhD
civil engineering • MS, PhD
computation and neural systems • MS, PhD
computer science • MS, PhD
control and dynamical systems • MS, PhD
electrical engineering • MS, PhD
engineering science • PhD
environmental science and engineering • MS, PhD
materials science • MS, PhD
mechanical engineering • MS, PhD

Division of Geological and Planetary Sciences
Dr. Edward M. Stolper, Chair
Programs in:
cosmochemistry • PhD
geobiology • PhD
geochemistry • MS, PhD
geology • MS, PhD
geophysics • MS, PhD
planetary science • MS, PhD

Division of Physics, Mathematics and Astronomy
Programs in:
astronomy • PhD
mathematics • PhD
physics • PhD

Division of the Humanities and Social Sciences
John O. Ledyard, Chairman
Programs in:
economics • PhD
humanities and social sciences • MS, PhD
political science • PhD
social science • MS

■ CALIFORNIA LUTHERAN UNIVERSITY

Thousand Oaks, CA 91360-2787

http://www.clunet.edu/

Independent-religious, coed, comprehensive institution. *Enrollment:* 470 full-time matriculated graduate/professional students (351 women), 480 part-time matriculated graduate/professional students (332 women). *Graduate faculty:* 38 full-time (17 women), 106 part-time/adjunct (49 women). *Computer facilities:* 135 computers available on campus for general student use. A campuswide network can be accessed from student residence rooms and from off campus. Internet access is available. *Library facilities:* Pearson Library. *Graduate expenses:* Tuition: part-time $360 per credit. One-time fee: $50. Tuition and fees vary according to program. *General application contact:* 805-493-3127.

Graduate Studies
Dr. Pamela M. Jolicoeur, Provost and Dean of the Faculty
Programs in:
clinical psychology • MS
marital and family therapy • MS
public policy and administration • MPPA

School of Business
Dr. Ronald Hagler, Director
Programs in:
finance • MBA
healthcare management • MBA
international business • MBA
management information systems • MBA
marketing • MBA
organizational behavior • MBA
small business/entrepreneurship • MBA

School of Education
Dr. Carol Bartell, Dean
Programs in:
counseling and guidance • MS
curriculum and instruction • MA
education • M Ed
educational administration • MA
reading education • MA
special education • MS
teacher preparation • Certificate

■ CALIFORNIA POLYTECHNIC STATE UNIVERSITY, SAN LUIS OBISPO

San Luis Obispo, CA 93407

http://www.calpoly.edu/

State-supported, coed, comprehensive institution. *Enrollment:* 595 full-time matriculated graduate/professional students (325 women), 415 part-time matriculated graduate/professional students (243 women). *Graduate faculty:* 344 full-time, 291 part-time/adjunct. *Computer facilities:* 1,880 computers available on campus for general student use. A campuswide network can be accessed from student residence rooms and from off campus. *Library facilities:* Kennedy Library. *Graduate expenses:* Tuition, state resident: full-time $2,293; part-time $266 per unit. Tuition, nonresident: full-time $3,699; part-time $293 per unit. *General application contact:* Jim Maraviglia, Admissions Office, 805-756-2311.

Find an in-depth description at www.petersons.com/graduate.

College of Agriculture
Dr. Mark Shelton, Graduate Coordinator
Program in:
agriculture • MS

College of Architecture and Environmental Design
Martin Harms, Dean
Programs in:
architecture • MS Arch
architecture and environmental design • MCRP, MS Arch
city and regional planning • MCRP

College of Engineering
Dr. Peter Y. Lee, Dean
Programs in:
aeronautical engineering • MSAE
biochemical engineering • MS
civil and environmental engineering • MS
computer science • MSCS
electrical engineering • MS
engineering • MS, MSAE, MSCS
industrial engineering • MS
integrated technology management • MS
materials engineering • MS
water engineering • MS

College of Liberal Arts
Harold Hellenbrand, Dean
Programs in:
English • MA
liberal arts • MA, MS
psychology • MS

College of Science and Mathematics
Philip S. Bailey, Dean
Programs in:
biological sciences • MS
kinesiology • MS
mathematics • MS
science and mathematics • MS

Orfalea College of Business
Dr. William Pendergast, Dean
Programs in:
agribusiness management • MBA
engineering management • MA, MBA
industrial and technical studies • MA
industrial technology • MA

Center for Teacher Education
Dr. Bonnie Konopak, Director
Programs in:
counseling • MA
curriculum and instruction • MA
education • MA
educational administration • MA
reading • MA
special education • MA

■ CALIFORNIA STATE POLYTECHNIC UNIVERSITY, POMONA

Pomona, CA 91768-2557
http://www.csupomona.edu/

State-supported, coed, comprehensive institution. CGS member. *Enrollment:* 528 full-time matriculated graduate/professional students (273 women), 526 part-time matriculated graduate/professional students (254 women). *Graduate faculty:* 670 full-time (211 women), 513 part-time/adjunct (218 women). *Computer facilities:* 1,864 computers available on campus for general student use. A campuswide network can be accessed from student residence rooms and from off campus. Internet access is available. *Library facilities:* University Library. *Graduate expenses:* Tuition, nonresident: part-time $164 per unit. Required fees: $306 per quarter. *General application contact:* Dena Bennett, Assistant Director of Admissions, 909-869-2991.

Academic Affairs
Dr. Jane Ollenburger, Vice President for Academic Affairs

College of Agriculture
Dr. Wayne R. Bidlack, Dean
Programs in:
agricultural science • MS
animal science • MS
foods and nutrition • MS

College of Business Administration
Dr. Eric J. McLaughlin, Director
Program in:
business administration • MBA, MSBA

College of Engineering
Dr. Ed Hohmann, Interim Dean
Programs in:
electrical engineering • MSEE
engineering • MSE

College of Environmental Design
Linda Sanders, Dean
Programs in:
architecture • M Arch
environmental design • M Arch, M Land Arch, MURP
landscape architecture • M Land Arch
urban and regional planning • MURP

College of Letters, Arts, and Social Sciences
Dr. Barbara J. Way, Interim Dean
Programs in:
economics • MS
English • MA
kinesiology • MS
letters, arts, and social sciences • MA, MS
psychology • MS

College of Science
Dr. Simon J. Bernau, Dean
Programs in:
applied mathematics • MS
biological sciences • MS
chemistry • MS
computer science • MS
pure mathematics • MS
science • MS

School of Education and Integrative Studies
Dr. Richard A. Navarro, Dean
Program in:
education and integrative studies • MA

■ CALIFORNIA STATE UNIVERSITY, BAKERSFIELD

Bakersfield, CA 93311-1099
http://www.csubak.edu/

State-supported, coed, comprehensive institution. CGS member. *Enrollment:* 236 full-time matriculated graduate/professional students (151 women), 258 part-time matriculated graduate/professional students (170 women). *Graduate faculty:* 165 full-time (96 women), 103 part-time/adjunct (63 women). *Computer facilities:* 600 computers available on campus for general student use. A campuswide network can be accessed from student residence rooms and from off campus. Internet access is available. *Library facilities:* Walter W. Stiern Library. *Graduate expenses:* Tuition, nonresident: full-time $5,904. Required fees: $1,887. One-time fee: $55 full-time. Tuition and fees vary according to program. *General application contact:* Dr. George Hibbard, Dean of Students, 661-664-2161.

Division of Graduate Studies and Research
Dr. Janice Chavez, Interim Dean
Programs in:
administration • MS
counseling psychology • MS
interdisciplinary studies • MA

School of Business and Public Administration
Dr. Henry Lowenstein, Dean
Programs in:
business administration • MBA
business and public administration • MBA, MPA, MSA
health care management • MSA
public administration • MPA

School of Education
Dr. Sheryl Santos, Dean
Programs in:
bilingual/bicultural education • MA
counseling • MS
counseling and personnel services • MA
curriculum and instruction • MA
education administration • MA
elementary curriculum and instruction • MA
reading education • MA
secondary curriculum and instruction • MA
special education • MA

School of Humanities and Social Sciences
Dr. Marla Iyasere, Dean
Programs in:
anthropology • MA
English • MA
family and child counseling • MFCC
history • MA
humanities and social sciences • MA, MS, MSW, MFCC
psychology • MS
social work • MSW
sociology • MA
Spanish • MA

School of Natural Sciences, Mathematics, and Engineering
Dr. Thomas Meyer, Interim Dean
Programs in:
geology • MS
hydrology • MS
natural sciences, mathematics, and engineering • MA, MS
nursing • MS
secondary school mathematics teaching • MA

■ CALIFORNIA STATE UNIVERSITY, CHICO

Chico, CA 95929-0722
http://www.csuchico.edu/

State-supported, coed, comprehensive institution. CGS member. *Enrollment:* 628

California State University, Chico (continued)
full-time matriculated graduate/professional students (317 women), 321 part-time matriculated graduate/professional students (202 women). *Graduate faculty:* 589 full-time (180 women), 227 part-time/adjunct (116 women). *Computer facilities:* 1,000 computers available on campus for general student use. A campuswide network can be accessed from student residence rooms and from off campus. Internet access, student account information are available. *Library facilities:* Meriam Library. *Graduate expenses:* Tuition, state resident: full-time $1,054. Tuition, nonresident: full-time $2,530. *General application contact:* Dr. Robert M. Jackson, Dean, Graduate and International Programs, 530-898-6880.

Find an in-depth description at www.petersons.com/graduate.

Graduate School
Dr. Robert M. Jackson, Dean, Graduate and International Programs
Programs in:
- applied mechanical engineering • MS
- interdisciplinary studies • MA, MS
- simulation science • MS

College of Behavioral and Social Sciences
Dr. Jeanne L. Thomas, Dean
Programs in:
- behavioral and social sciences • MA, MPA, MRTP, MS
- counseling • MS
- geography • MA
- health administration • MPA
- museum studies • MA
- political science • MA
- psychology • MA
- public administration • MPA
- rural and town planning • MRTP
- social science • MA

College of Business
Marc Siegall, Dean
Programs in:
- accountancy • MSA
- business • MBA, MSA
- business administration • MBA

College of Communication and Education
Dr. Stephen King, Dean
Programs in:
- communication and education • M Ed, MA
- education • MA
- human communication • MA
- information and communication studies • MA
- physical education • MA
- public communication • MA
- recreation administration • MA
- speech pathology and audiology • MA
- teaching international languages • M Ed

College of Engineering, Computer Science, and Technology
Dr. Kenneth Derucher, Dean
Programs in:
- computer science • MS
- electrical engineering • MS
- engineering, computer science, and technology • MS

College of Humanities and Fine Arts
Dr. Donald J. Heinz, Dean
Programs in:
- art • MA
- creative writing • MA
- English • MA
- history • MA
- humanities and fine arts • MA
- music • MA

College of Natural Sciences
Dr. Roger Lederer, Dean
Programs in:
- biological sciences • MS
- botany • MS
- earth sciences • MS
- environmental science • MS
- geosciences • MS
- natural sciences • MS
- nursing • MS
- nutrition education • MS
- nutritional science • MS

School of Agriculture
Thomas E. Dickinson, Dean
Program in:
- agriculture • MS

■ CALIFORNIA STATE UNIVERSITY, DOMINGUEZ HILLS

Carson, CA 90747-0001
http://www.csudh.edu/

State-supported, coed, comprehensive institution. CGS member. *Enrollment:* 1,197 full-time matriculated graduate/professional students (853 women), 2,620 part-time matriculated graduate/professional students (1,910 women). *Graduate faculty:* 292 full-time, 243 part-time/adjunct. *Computer facilities:* 200 computers available on campus for general student use. *Library facilities:* Leo F. Cain Educational Resource Center. *Graduate expenses:* Tuition, state resident: full-time $1,818. *General application contact:* Linda Wise, Associate Director, 310-243-3613.

Find an in-depth description at www.petersons.com/graduate.

College of Arts and Sciences
Dr. Selase Williams, Dean
Programs in:
- applied behavioral science • MA
- arts and sciences • MA, MS, Certificate
- biology • MA
- clinical psychology • MA
- English • MA
- general psychology • MA
- gerontology • MA
- human cytogenic technology • Certificate
- humanities • MA
- marriage, family, and child counseling • MS
- negotiation and conflict resolution • MA, Certificate
- quality assurance • MS
- rhetoric and composition • Certificate
- social research • Certificate
- sociology • MA
- teaching English as a second language • Certificate

School of Business and Public Administration
Dr. Donald Bates, Dean
Programs in:
- business and public administration • MBA, MPA
- computer information systems • MBA
- public administration • MPA

School of Education
Dr. Billie Blair, Dean
Programs in:
- computer-based education • MA, Certificate
- counseling • MA
- education • MA, Certificate
- educational administration • MA
- individualized education • MA
- learning handicapped • MA
- multicultural education • MA
- physical education • MA
- severely handicapped • MA
- special education • MA
- teaching mathematics • MA
- teaching/curriculum • MA

School of Health
Abel Whittemore, Dean
Programs in:
- clinical sciences • MS, Certificate
- health • MS, MSN, Certificate
- nursing • MSN

■ CALIFORNIA STATE UNIVERSITY, FRESNO

Fresno, CA 93740-8027

http://www.csufresno.edu/

State-supported, coed, comprehensive institution. CGS member. *Enrollment:* 941 full-time matriculated graduate/professional students (619 women), 919 part-time matriculated graduate/professional students (542 women). *Graduate faculty:* 429 full-time (142 women), 33 part-time/adjunct (12 women). *Computer facilities:* 853 computers available on campus for general student use. A campuswide network can be accessed from off campus. Internet access, common applications are available. *Library facilities:* Henry Madden Library. *Graduate expenses:* Tuition, state resident: part-time $246 per unit. Required fees: $1,840; $605 per semester. Tuition and fees vary according to course load. *General application contact:* Shirlee C. Fulton, Administrative Analyst/Specialist, 559-278-2448.

Division of Graduate Studies
Dr. Vivian A. Vidoli, Dean
Program in:
- animal science • MA

College of Agricultural Sciences and Technology
Dr. Daniel P. Bartell, Dean
Programs in:
- agricultural sciences and technology • MA, MS
- agriculture • MS
- child, family and consumer sciences • MS
- industrial technology • MS
- plant science • MS

College of Arts and Humanities
Dr. Luis F. Costa, Dean
Programs in:
- art and design • MA
- arts and humanities • MA, MFA
- communication • MA
- composition theory • MA
- creative writing • MFA
- linguistics • MA
- literature • MA
- mass communication • MA
- music • MA
- music education • MA
- nonfiction prose • MA
- performance • MA
- Spanish • MA

College of Engineering and Computer Science
Dr. Karl Longley, Dean
Programs in:
- civil engineering • MS
- computer science • MS
- electrical engineering • MS
- engineering and computer science • MS
- mechanical engineering • MS

College of Health and Human Services
Benjamin Cuellar, Dean
Programs in:
- communicative disorders • MA
- environmental/occupational health • MPH
- exercise science • MA
- health administration • MPH
- health and human services • MA, MPH, MPT, MS, MSW
- health promotion • MPH
- nursing • MS
- physical therapy • MPT
- social work education • MSW

College of Science and Mathematics
Dr. Kin-Ping Wong, Dean
Programs in:
- biology • MA
- chemistry • MS
- geology • MS
- marine sciences • MS
- mathematics • MA
- physics • MS
- psychology • MA, MS
- science and mathematics • MA, MS

College of Social Sciences
Dr. Ellen Gruenbaum, Dean
Programs in:
- criminology • MS
- history • MA
- international relations • MA
- public administration • MPA
- social sciences • MA, MPA, MS

School of Education and Human Development
Dr. Paul Shaker, Dean
Programs in:
- counseling and student services • MA
- education • MA
- education and human development • MA, MS, Ed D
- educational leadership • Ed D
- marriage and family therapy • MS
- rehabilitation counseling • MS
- special education • MA

Sid Craig School of Business
Dr. Fred Evans, Dean
Programs in:
- business • MBA
- business administration • MBA

■ CALIFORNIA STATE UNIVERSITY, FULLERTON

Fullerton, CA 92834-9480

http://www.fullerton.edu/

State-supported, coed, comprehensive institution. CGS member. *Enrollment:* 457 full-time matriculated graduate/professional students (270 women), 2,797 part-time matriculated graduate/professional students (1,748 women). *Graduate faculty:* 608 full-time (218 women), 946 part-time/adjunct. *Computer facilities:* 1,000 computers available on campus for general student use. A campuswide network can be accessed from student residence rooms and from off campus. Internet access is available. *Library facilities:* California State University, Fullerton Library. *Graduate expenses:* Tuition, nonresident: full-time $5,904; part-time $246 per unit. Required fees: $1,887; $629 per semester. *General application contact:* Gladys M. Fleckles, Director, Graduate Studies, 714-278-2618.

Graduate Studies
Dr. Keith Boyum, Acting Associate Vice President, Academic Programs
Program in:
- interdisciplinary studies • MA

College of Business and Economics
Dr. Anil Puri, Dean
Programs in:
- accounting • MBA, MS
- business administration • MBA
- business and economics • MA, MBA, MS
- business economics • MBA
- economics • MA
- finance • MBA
- international business • MBA
- management • MBA
- management information systems • MS
- management science • MBA, MS
- marketing • MBA
- operations research • MS
- statistics • MS
- taxation • MS

College of Communications
Dr. Rick Pullen, Dean
Programs in:
- advertising • MA
- communications • MA
- communicative disorders • MA
- journalism education • MA
- news editorial • MA
- photo communication • MA
- public relations • MA
- radio, television and film • MA
- speech communication • MA
- technical communication • MA
- theory and process • MA

California State University, Fullerton (continued)

College of Engineering and Computer Science
Dr. Richard Rocke, Acting Dean
Programs in:
- applications administrative information systems • MS
- applications mathematical methods • MS
- civil engineering and engineering mechanics • MS
- computer science • MS
- electrical engineering • MS
- engineering and computer science • MS
- engineering science • MS
- information processing systems • MS
- mechanical engineering • MS
- systems engineering • MS

College of Human Development and Community Service
Dr. Judith Ramirez, Acting Dean
Programs in:
- bilingual/bicultural education • MS
- counseling • MS
- educational leadership • MS
- elementary curriculum and instruction • MS
- human development and community service • MS
- nursing • MS
- physical education • MS
- reading • MS
- special education • MS

College of Humanities and Social Sciences
Dr. Thomas Klammer, Dean
Programs in:
- American studies • MA
- analysis of specific language structures • MA
- anthropological linguistics • MA
- anthropology • MA
- applied linguistics • MA
- clinical/community psychology • MS
- communication and semantics • MA
- comparative literature • MA
- disorders of communication • MA
- English • MA
- environmental education and communication • MS
- environmental policy and planning • MS
- environmental sciences • MS
- experimental phonetics • MA
- French • MA
- geography • MA
- German • MA
- history • MA
- humanities and social sciences • MA, MPA, MS
- political science • MA
- psychology • MA
- public administration • MPA
- social sciences • MA
- sociology • MA
- Spanish • MA
- teaching English to speakers of other languages • MS
- technological studies • MS

College of Natural Science and Mathematics
Dr. Kolf Jayaweera, Dean
Programs in:
- analytical chemistry • MS
- applied mathematics • MA
- biochemistry • MS
- biological science • MA
- botany • MA
- geochemistry • MS
- geological sciences • MS
- inorganic chemistry • MS
- mathematics • MA
- mathematics for secondary school teachers • MA
- microbiology • MA
- natural science and mathematics • MA, MS
- organic chemistry • MS
- physical chemistry • MS
- physics • MA
- teaching science • MA

College of the Arts
Jerry Samuelson, Dean
Programs in:
- acting • MFA
- acting and directing • MA
- art • MA, MFA
- art history • MA
- arts • MA, MFA, MM, Certificate
- dance • MA
- design • MA
- directing • MFA
- dramatic literature/criticism • MA
- museum studies • Certificate
- music education • MA
- music history and literature • MA
- oral interpretation • MA
- performance • MM
- playwriting • MA
- technical theater • MA
- technical theater and design • MFA
- television • MA
- theatre for children • MA
- theatre history • MA
- theory-composition • MM

■ CALIFORNIA STATE UNIVERSITY, HAYWARD

Hayward, CA 94542-3000
http://www.csuhayward.edu/

State-supported, coed, comprehensive institution. CGS member. *Enrollment:* 1,268 full-time matriculated graduate/professional students (904 women), 1,854 part-time matriculated graduate/professional students (1,114 women). *Graduate faculty:* 368 full-time (117 women). *Computer facilities:* 700 computers available on campus for general student use. A campuswide network can be accessed from student residence rooms and from off campus. Internet access and online class registration are available. *Library facilities:* California State University, Hayward Library plus 1 other. *Graduate expenses:* Tuition, state resident: full-time $2,408; part-time $392 per course. Tuition, nonresident: full-time $7,656; part-time $656 per course. *General application contact:* Jennifer Rice, Graduate Program Coordinator, 510-885-3286.

Graduate Programs
Dr. Carl Bellone, Dean
Program in:
- interdisciplinary studies • MA, MS, Certificate

School of Arts, Letters, and Social Sciences
Dr. Michael Good, Dean
Programs in:
- anthropology • MA
- arts, letters, and social sciences • MA, MPA, MS
- English • MA
- geography • MA
- history • MA
- music • MA
- public administration • MPA
- sociology • MA
- speech communication • MA
- speech pathology • MS

School of Business and Economics
Dr. Jay Tontz, Dean
Programs in:
- accounting • MBA
- business and economics • MA, MBA, MS
- computer information systems • MBA
- e-business • MBA
- economics • MA, MBA
- finance • MBA
- human resources management • MBA
- international business • MBA
- management sciences • MBA
- marketing management • MBA
- new ventures/small business management • MBA
- operations research • MBA
- quantitative business methods • MS
- supply chain management • MBA
- taxation • MBA, MS

School of Education
Dr. Arthurlene Towner, Dean
Programs in:
- counseling • MS
- education • MS

educational leadership • MS
physical education • MS
special education • MS
teacher education • MS

School of Science
Dr. Michael Leung, Dean
Programs in:
biochemistry • MS
biological sciences • MS
chemistry • MS
computer science • MS
geology • MS
marine sciences • MS
mathematics • MS
science • MS
statistics • MS

■ CALIFORNIA STATE UNIVERSITY, LONG BEACH

Long Beach, CA 90840

http://www.csulb.edu/

State-supported, coed, comprehensive institution. CGS member. *Enrollment:* 1,483 full-time matriculated graduate/professional students (968 women), 2,327 part-time matriculated graduate/professional students (1,319 women). *Graduate faculty:* 773 full-time (265 women), 894 part-time/adjunct (466 women). *Computer facilities:* 2,000 computers available on campus for general student use. A campuswide network can be accessed from off campus. Internet access is available. *Library facilities:* University Library. *Graduate expenses:* Tuition, state resident: full-time $1,506; part-time $438 per semester. Required fees: $316; $158 per semester. *General application contact:* Dr. Henry C. Fung, Associate Vice President for Academic Affairs for Graduate Studies, Research, and Community Service Outreach, 562-985-4128.

Graduate Studies
Dr. Henry C. Fung, Dean
Program in:
interdisciplinary studies • MA, MS

College of Business Administration
Dr. Luis Ma. R. Calingo, Dean
Program in:
business administration • MBA

College of Education
Dr. Jean Houck, Dean
Programs in:
counseling • MS, Certificate
education • MA, MS, Certificate
educational administration • MA
educational psychology • MA
elementary education • MA
secondary education • MA
social and multicultural foundations of education • MA
special education • MS

College of Engineering
Dr. Michael Mahoney, Interim Dean
Programs in:
aerospace engineering • MSAE
civil engineering • MSCE, MSE, CE
computer engineering • MS
computer science • MS
electrical engineering • MSE, MSEE
engineering • MS, MSAE, MSCE, MSE, MSEE, MSME, PhD, CE
mechanical engineering • MSE, MSME

College of Health and Human Services
Dr. Donald Lauda, Dean
Programs in:
audiology • MA
community health education • MPH
criminal justice • MS
gerontology • MS
health and human services • MA, MPA, MPH, MPT, MS, MSW, Certificate
health care administration • MS, Certificate
health science • MS
home economics • MA
kinesiology and physical education • MA
nurse anesthesiology • MS
nursing • MS
nutritional sciences • MS
occupational studies • MA
physical therapy • MPT
public policy and administration • MPA, Certificate
recreation and leisure studies • MS
social work • MSW
speech pathology • MA

College of Liberal Arts
Dr. Dorothy Abrahamse, Dean
Programs in:
anthropology • MA
Asian American studies • Certificate
Asian studies • MA
communication studies • MA
creative writing • MFA
economics • MA
English • MA
French • MA
geography • MA
German • MA
history • MA
liberal arts • MA, MFA, MS, Certificate
linguistics • MA
philosophy • MA
political science • MA
psychology • MA, MS
Spanish • MA

College of Natural Sciences
Dr. Glenn Nagel, Dean
Programs in:
applied mathematics • MA
biochemistry • MS
biological sciences • MS
chemistry • MS
geological sciences • MS
mathematics • MA
medical technology • MPH
metals physics • MS
microbiology • MPH, MS
natural sciences • MA, MPH, MS, Certificate
nurse epidemiology • MPH
physics • MS

College of the Arts
Kristi Jones, Interim Dean
Programs in:
art education • MA
art history • MA
arts • MA, MFA, MM
crafts • MA, MFA
dance • MFA
illustration • MA, MFA
music • MA, MM
pictorial arts • MA, MFA
theatre arts • MA, MFA

■ CALIFORNIA STATE UNIVERSITY, LOS ANGELES

Los Angeles, CA 90032-8530

http://www.calstatela.edu/

State-supported, coed, comprehensive institution. CGS member. *Enrollment:* 1,168 full-time matriculated graduate/professional students (787 women), 2,529 part-time matriculated graduate/professional students (1,584 women). *Graduate faculty:* 477 full-time, 656 part-time/adjunct. *Computer facilities:* 1,500 computers available on campus for general student use. A campuswide network can be accessed from off campus. Internet access is available. *Library facilities:* John K. Kennedy Memorial Library. *Graduate expenses:* Tuition, state resident: full-time $1,860; part-time $576 per quarter. Tuition, nonresident: full-time $7,704; part-time $164 per unit. *General application contact:* Dr. Theodore Crovello, Dean of Graduate Studies, 323-343-3820.

Graduate Studies
Dr. Theodore Crovello, Dean
Program in:
interdisciplinary studies • MA, MS

California State University, Los Angeles (continued)

Charter College of Education
Dr. Allen Mori, Dean
Programs in:
adult and continuing education • MA
applied behavior analysis • MS
community college counseling • MS
computer education • MA
counseling • MS
early childhood education for the handicapped • MA
education • MA, MS, PhD
education of handicapped adolescents and young adults • MA
education of the communication handicapped • MA
education of the learning handicapped • MA
education of the physically handicapped • MA
education of the severely handicapped • MA
education of the visually handicapped • MA
educational administration • MA
educational foundations and interdivisional studies • MA
elementary teaching • MA
gifted education • MA
instructional technology • MA
multicultural and multilingual special education • MA
orientation and mobility specialist for the blind • MA
psychological foundations • MA
reading • MA
rehabilitation counseling • MS
resource specialist • MA
school counseling and school psychology • MS
secondary teaching • MA
social foundations • MA
special education • PhD
special interests • MA
teaching English to speakers of other languages • MA

College of Arts and Letters
Carl Selkin, Dean
Programs in:
art • MA
arts and letters • MA, MFA, MM
English • MA
fine arts • MFA
French • MA
music composition • MM
music education • MA
musicology • MA
performance • MM
philosophy • MA
Spanish • MA
speech communication • MA
theater arts • MA

College of Business and Economics
Dr. Timothy Haight, Dean
Programs in:
accountancy • MS
accounting • MBA
analytical quantitative economics • MA
business and economics • MA, MBA, MS
business economics • MA, MBA, MS
business information systems • MBA
economics • MA
finance and banking • MBA, MS
finance and law • MBA, MS
health care management • MS
information systems • MBA, MS
international business • MBA, MS
management • MBA, MS
management information systems • MS
marketing • MBA, MS
office management • MBA

College of Engineering and Technology
Dr. Raymond Landis, Dean
Programs in:
civil engineering • MS
electrical engineering • MS
engineering and technology • MA, MS
industrial and technical studies • MA
mechanical engineering • MS

College of Health and Human Services
Dr. James Kelly, Acting Dean
Programs in:
child development • MA
communicative disorders • MA
criminal justice • MS
criminalistics • MS
health and human services • MA, MS, MSW
health science • MA
hearing • MA
home economics • MA
nursing • MS
nutritional science • MS
physical education • MA
social work • MSW
speech • MA

College of Natural and Social Sciences
Dr. David Soltz, Dean
Programs in:
analytical chemistry • MS
anthropology • MA
biochemistry • MS
biology • MS
chemistry • MS
geography • MA
geology • MS
history • MA
inorganic chemistry • MS
Latin American studies • MA
mathematics • MS
Mexican-American studies • MA
natural and social sciences • MA, MS
organic chemistry • MS
physical chemistry • MS
physics • MS
political science • MA
psychology • MA, MS
public administration • MS
sociology • MA

■ CALIFORNIA STATE UNIVERSITY, NORTHRIDGE

Northridge, CA 91330
http://www.csun.edu/

State-supported, coed, comprehensive institution. CGS member. *Enrollment:* 1,226 full-time matriculated graduate/professional students (856 women), 1,759 part-time matriculated graduate/professional students (1,076 women). *Graduate faculty:* 812 full-time, 838 part-time/adjunct. *Computer facilities:* A campuswide network can be accessed from off campus. Internet access and online class registration are available. *Library facilities:* Oviatt Library. *Graduate expenses:* Tuition, state resident: part-time $438 per semester. Tuition, nonresident: part-time $246 per unit. Required fees: $631 per semester. *General application contact:* Dr. Mack Johnson, Associate Vice President, 818-677-2138.

Graduate Studies
Dr. Mack Johnson, Associate Vice President
Program in:
interdisciplinary studies • MA, MS

College of Arts, Media, and Communications
William P. Toutant, Interim Dean
Programs in:
art • MA, MFA
art history • MA
arts • MA, MFA
arts, media, and communications • MA, MFA, MM
composition • MM
mass communication • MA
music education • MA
music theory • MA
musicology • MA
news communication • MA
performance • MM
speech communication • MA
theater • MA

College of Business Administration and Economics
Dr. William Hosek, Dean
Programs in:
administrative/office management • MBA
business administration • MBA

business administration and economics • MBA, MS
business education • MBA, MS
finance, real estate and insurance • MBA
management • MBA
management of information systems • MBA
management science • MBA
marketing • MBA
production and management systems analysis • MS

College of Education
Dr. Philip J. Rusche, Head
Programs in:
administration and supervision • MA
counseling • MS
counseling and guidance • MS, MFCC
early childhood special education • MA
education • MA, MS, MFCC
education of the deaf and hard of hearing • MA
education of the gifted • MA
education of the learning handicapped • MA
education of the severely handicapped • MA
educational psychology and counseling • MA
educational therapy • MA
elementary education • MA
foundations • MA
genetic counseling • MS
marriage, family and child counseling • MFCC
secondary education • MA

College of Engineering and Computer Science
Dr. Laurence Caretto, Interim Dean
Programs in:
aerospace engineering • MS
applied engineering • MS
applied mechanics • MSE
biomedical engineering • MS
civil engineering • MS
communications/radar engineering • MS
computer science • MS
control engineering • MS
digital/computer engineering • MS
electronics engineering • MS
engineering and computer science • MS
engineering management • MS
industrial engineering • MS
machine design • MS
materials engineering • MS
mechanical engineering • MS
mechanics • MS
microwave/antenna engineering • MS
structural engineering • MS
thermofluids • MS

College of Health and Human Development
Dr. Ann Stutts, Dean
Programs in:
communicative disorders and sciences • MA
environmental health • MS
family environmental sciences • MS
health administration • MS
health and human development • MA, MPH, MS
health education • MPH, MS
health science • MS
kinesiology • MA
leisure studies and recreation • MS
physical therapy • MS
public health • MPH

College of Humanities
Dr. Jorge Garcia, Dean
Programs in:
Chicano studies • MA
English • MA
humanities • MA
linguistics • MA
Spanish • MA

College of Science and Mathematics
Dr. Edward J. Carroll, Interim Dean
Programs in:
biology • MS
chemistry • MS
genetic counseling • MS
geological sciences • MS
mathematics • MS
physics • MS
science and mathematics • MS

College of Social and Behavioral Sciences
Dr. William Flores, Dean
Programs in:
anthropology • MA
geography • MA
history • MA
political science • MA
psychology • MA
public administration • MPA
social and behavioral sciences • MA, MPA
sociology • MA

■ CALIFORNIA STATE UNIVERSITY, SACRAMENTO
Sacramento, CA 95819-6048
http://www.csus.edu/

State-supported, coed, comprehensive institution. CGS member. *Enrollment:* 2,116 full-time matriculated graduate/professional students (1,506 women), 2,188 part-time matriculated graduate/professional students (1,379 women). *Graduate faculty:* 399 full-time, 222 part-time/adjunct. *Computer facilities:* 700 computers available on campus for general student use. A campuswide network can be accessed from student residence rooms and from off campus. Internet access and online class registration are available. *Library facilities:* California State University, Sacramento Library. *Graduate expenses:* Tuition, state resident: full-time $979. Tuition, nonresident: full-time $2,455. *General application contact:* Bonnie Pesely, Coordinator of Graduate Admissions, 916-278-6470.

Graduate Studies
Dr. Ric Brown, Associate Vice President of Research, Graduate and Extended Programs
Program in:
special majors • MA, MS

College of Arts and Letters
Dr. William J. Sullivan, Dean
Programs in:
arts and letters • MA, MM
communication studies • MA
creative writing • MA
foreign languages • MA
French • MA
German • MA
music • MM
public history • MA
Spanish • MA
studio art • MA
teaching English to speakers of other languages • MA
theater arts • MA
theatre and dance • MA

College of Business Administration
Dr. Fel Ramey, Dean
Programs in:
accountancy • MS
business administration • MBA
human resources • MBA
management information science • MS
urban land development • MBA

College of Education
Dr. Catherine Emihovich, Dean
Programs in:
bilingual/cross-cultural education • MA
career counseling • MS
curriculum and instruction • MA
early childhood education • MA
education • MA, MS
educational administration • MA
generic counseling • MS
guidance • MA
reading education • MA
school counseling • MS
school psychology • MS
special education • MA
vocational rehabilitation • MS

California State University, Sacramento (continued)

College of Engineering and Computer Science
Dr. Braja Das, Dean
Programs in:
- civil engineering • MS
- computer systems • MS
- electrical engineering • MS
- engineering and computer science • MS
- mechanical engineering • MS
- software engineering • MS

College of Health and Human Services
Dr. Marilyn Hopkins, Dean
Programs in:
- audiology • MS
- criminal justice • MS
- family and children's services • MSW
- health and human services • MS, MSW
- health care • MSW
- mental health • MSW
- nursing • MS
- physical education • MS
- recreation administration • MS
- social justice and corrections • MSW
- speech pathology • MS

College of Natural Sciences and Mathematics
Marion O'Leary, Dean
Programs in:
- biological sciences • MA, MS
- chemistry • MS
- immunohematology • MS
- marine science • MS
- mathematics and statistics • MA
- natural sciences and mathematics • MA, MS

College of Social Sciences and Interdisciplinary Studies
Joseph F. Sheley, Dean
Programs in:
- anthropology • MA
- counseling psychology • MA
- government • MA
- international affairs • MA
- public policy and administration • MPPA
- social sciences • MA, MPPA
- sociology • MA

■ CALIFORNIA STATE UNIVERSITY, SAN BERNARDINO

San Bernardino, CA 92407-2397
http://www.csusb.edu/

State-supported, coed, comprehensive institution. CGS member. *Enrollment:* 1,396 full-time matriculated graduate/professional students (912 women), 860 part-time matriculated graduate/professional students (549 women). *Computer facilities:* 1,300 computers available on campus for general student use. A campuswide network can be accessed from student residence rooms and from off campus. Internet access is available. *Library facilities:* Pfau Library. *Graduate expenses:* Tuition, nonresident: part-time $164 per unit. Required fees: $292 per quarter. *General application contact:* Lydia Ortega, Director of Admissions, 909-880-5200.

Graduate Studies
Program in:
- interdisciplinary studies • MA

College of Business and Public Administration
Programs in:
- business administration • MBA
- business and public administration • MBA, MPA
- public administration • MPA

School of Education
Programs in:
- bilingual/cross-cultural education • MA
- counseling/guidance • MS
- counselor education • MA, MS
- elementary education • MA
- English as a second language • MA
- environmental education • MA
- history and English for secondary teachers • MA
- instructional technology • MA
- reading • MA
- rehabilitation counseling • MA
- school administration • MA
- secondary education • MA
- special education • MA
- special education and rehabilitation counseling • MA
- vocational education • MA

School of Humanities
Programs in:
- English as a second language/linguistics • MA
- English composition • MA
- humanities • MA

School of Natural Sciences
Programs in:
- biology • MS
- computer science • MS
- health services administration • MS
- mathematics • MA
- natural sciences • MA, MS

School of Social and Behavioral Sciences
Programs in:
- clinical/counseling psychology • MS
- criminal justice • MA
- general/experimental psychology • MA
- human development • MA
- industrial organizational psychology • MS
- life span developmental psychology • MA
- national security studies • MA
- psychology • MS
- social and behavioral sciences • MA, MS, MSW, MUP
- social sciences • MA
- social work • MSW

■ CALIFORNIA STATE UNIVERSITY, SAN MARCOS

San Marcos, CA 92096-0001
http://ww2.csusm.edu/

State-supported, coed, comprehensive institution. *Enrollment:* 164 full-time matriculated graduate/professional students (82 women), 289 part-time matriculated graduate/professional students (207 women). *Graduate faculty:* 92 full-time (40 women), 18 part-time/adjunct (8 women). *Computer facilities:* 487 computers available on campus for general student use. A campuswide network can be accessed from student residence rooms and from off campus. Internet access and online class registration are available. *Library facilities:* Library and Information Services. *Graduate expenses:* Tuition, nonresident: part-time $246 per unit. Required fees: $1,898; $606 per semester. *General application contact:* Admissions, 760-750-4848.

College of Arts and Sciences
Miriam Schustack, Acting Dean
Programs in:
- arts and sciences • MA, MS
- biological sciences • MS
- computer science • MS
- literature and writing studies • MA
- mathematics • MS
- psychology • MA
- sociological practice • MA
- Spanish • MA

College of Business Administration
Mohamed Moustafa, Dean, City of Business Administration
Programs in:
- business management • MBA
- government management • MBA

College of Education
Dr. Steve Lilly, Dean
Program in:
- education • MA

■ CALIFORNIA STATE UNIVERSITY, STANISLAUS

Turlock, CA 95382
http://www.csustan.edu/

State-supported, coed, comprehensive institution. CGS member. *Enrollment:* 571 matriculated graduate/professional students (367 women). *Graduate faculty:* 6. *Computer facilities:* 150 computers available on campus for general student use. A campuswide network can be accessed from student residence rooms and from off campus. Internet access is available. *Library facilities:* Vasche Library. *Graduate expenses:* Tuition, nonresident: full-time $890; part-time $105 per unit. *General application contact:* Mary Coker, Director, Graduate Studies, 209-667-3129.

Graduate Programs

Dr. Diana Mayer Demetrulias, Dean of Graduate Studies
Program in:
- interdisciplinary studies • MA, MS

College of Arts, Letters, and Sciences
Dr. Mary P. Cullinan, Dean
Programs in:
- arts, letters, and sciences • MA, MPA, MS, MSW
- behavior analysis psychology • MS
- counseling psychology • MS
- criminal justice • MA
- English • MA
- general psychology • MA
- history • MA
- international relations • MA
- marine science • MS
- public administration • MPA
- secondary school history teaching • MA
- social work • MSW
- teaching English to speakers of other languages • MA

College of Business Administration
Amin Elmallah, Dean
Program in:
- business administration • MBA

College of Education
Dr. Irma Guzman Wagner, Dean
Programs in:
- curriculum and instruction • MA Ed
- education • MA Ed
- educational administration • MA Ed
- educational technology • MA Ed
- elementary education • MA Ed
- multilingual education • MA Ed
- physical education • MA Ed
- reading education • MA Ed
- school counseling • MA Ed
- secondary education • MA Ed
- special education • MA Ed

■ CHAPMAN UNIVERSITY

Orange, CA 92866
http://www.chapman.edu/

Independent-religious, coed, comprehensive institution. *Enrollment:* 2,900 matriculated graduate/professional students. *Graduate faculty:* 313. *Computer facilities:* 278 computers available on campus for general student use. A campuswide network can be accessed from off campus. Internet access is available. *Library facilities:* Thurmond Clarke Memorial Library plus 1 other. *Graduate expenses:* Tuition: part-time $500 per credit. Part-time tuition and fees vary according to program. *General application contact:* Saundra R. Hoover, Director of Graduate Admissions, 714-997-6786.

Find an in-depth description at www.petersons.com/graduate.

Graduate Studies

Dr. Barbara E. G. Mulch, Vice Provost and Dean
Programs in:
- criminal justice • MA
- food science and nutrition • MS
- human resources • MS
- organizational leadership • MA

Division of Psychology
Dr. John Flowers, Chair
Programs in:
- counseling psychology • MA
- marriage and family therapy • MA
- pre-clinical • MA

The George L. Argyros School of Business and Economics
Dr. Richard McDowell, Dean
Program in:
- business and economics • Exec MBA, MBA

School of Communication Arts
Dr. Myron Yeager, Dean
Programs in:
- communication arts • MA, MFA
- creative writing • MFA
- literature • MA
- teaching literature and composition • MA

School of Education
Dr. Jim Brown, Dean
Programs in:
- career counseling • MA
- curriculum and instruction • MA
- education • MA
- educational administration • MA
- educational psychology • MA
- learning handicapped • MA
- reading education • MA
- school counseling • MA
- severely handicapped • MA
- special education • MA

School of Film and Television
Robert Bassett, Dean
Programs in:
- film and television • MA, MFA
- film studies • MA
- new media • MFA
- producing • MFA
- production • MFA
- screenwriting • MFA

School of Law
Parham Williams, Dean
Program in:
- law • JD

School of Physical Therapy
Dr. Donald L. Gabard, Chair
Program in:
- physical therapy • DPT

■ CLAREMONT GRADUATE UNIVERSITY

Claremont, CA 91711-6160
http://www.cgu.edu/

Independent, coed, graduate-only institution. CGS member. *Graduate faculty:* 82 full-time (24 women), 88 part-time/adjunct (46 women). *Computer facilities:* 91 computers available on campus for general student use. A campuswide network can be accessed from off campus. Internet access is available. *Library facilities:* Honnold Library plus 3 others. *Graduate expenses:* Tuition: full-time $21,580; part-time $913 per unit. Required fees: $150. *General application contact:* Rosa Delia Rosas, Admissions Coordinator, 909-621-8069.

Graduate Programs

Dr. Ann Weaver Hart, Vice President for Academic Affairs/Provost
Programs in:
- applied women's studies • MA
- arts • MA, MFA, DCM, DMA, PhD
- church music • MA, DCM
- composition • MA, DMA
- drawing • MA, MFA
- engineering mathematics • PhD
- filmmaking • MA, MFA
- financial engineering • MS
- history • MA
- interdisciplinary studies • MA
- music education • MA
- musicology • MA, PhD
- operations research and statistics • MA, MS
- painting • MA, MFA
- performance • MA, DMA
- performance/installation • MA, MFA
- photography • MA, MFA
- physical applied mathematics • MA, MS

Claremont Graduate University (continued)

- printmaking • MA, MFA
- pure mathematics • MA, MS, PhD
- scientific computing • MA, MS
- sculpture • MA, MFA
- systematics and evolution of higher plants • MA, PhD
- systems and control theory • MA, MS

Center for the Arts
Programs in:

- arts • MA, MFA, DCM, DMA, PhD
- church music • MA, DCM
- composition • MA, DMA
- drawing • MA, MFA
- filmmaking • MA, MFA
- history • MA
- music education • MA
- musicology • MA, PhD
- painting • MA, MFA
- performance • MA, DMA
- performance/installation • MA, MFA
- photography • MA, MFA
- printmaking • MA, MFA
- sculpture • MA, MFA

Center for the Humanities
Constance Jordan, Dean
Programs in:

- American studies • MA, PhD
- cultural studies • MA, PhD
- English • M Phil, MA, PhD
- European studies • MA, PhD
- history • MA, PhD
- humanities • M Phil, MA, PhD
- literature and creative writing • MA
- literature and film • MA
- literature and theatre • MA
- philosophy and education • MA, PhD
- philosophy and social theory • MA, PhD
- philosophy of religion • MA, PhD
- Western philosophy • MA, PhD

Independent Programs
Programs in:

- applied women's studies • MA
- engineering mathematics • PhD
- financial engineering • MS
- operations research and statistics • MA, MS
- physical applied mathematics • MA, MS
- pure mathematics • MA, MS, PhD
- scientific computing • MA, MS
- systematics and evolution of higher plants • MA, PhD
- systems and control theory • MA, MS

Peter F. Drucker Graduate School of Management
Cornelis Dekluyver, Dean
Programs in:

- advanced management • MSAM
- business administration • MBA
- executive management • EMBA, MA, MSAM, PhD, Certificate
- finance • MBA
- financial engineering • MS
- international business • MBA
- management • MBA
- marketing • MBA
- strategic management • MBA

School of Behavioral and Organizational Sciences
Dale Berger, Dean
Programs in:

- cognitive psychology • MA, PhD
- developmental psychology • MA, PhD
- human resources design • MS
- organizational behavior • MA, PhD
- program design, management, and evaluation • MA
- social environmental psychology • PhD
- social psychology • MA

School of Educational Studies
David Drew, Dean
Programs in:

- comparative and intercultural studies • MA, PhD
- cross-cultural studies • MA, PhD
- curriculum and teaching • MA, PhD
- evaluation and quantitative analysis • MA, PhD
- growth and development • MA, PhD
- higher education • MA, PhD
- organization and administration • MA, PhD
- reading and language development • MA, PhD
- teaching/learning process • MA, PhD

School of Information Science
Lorne Olfman, Dean
Programs in:

- information systems • MIS
- management of information systems • MSMIS, PhD

School of Politics and Economics
Dean McHenry, Interim Dean
Programs in:

- business and financial economics • MA, PhD
- economics • PhD
- international economic policy and management • MA, PhD
- international political economy • MAIPE
- international studies • MAIS
- political economy and public policy • MA, PhD
- political science • PhD
- politics • MAP
- politics and economics • MA, MAIPE, MAIS, MAP, MAPEB, MAPP, PhD
- politics, economics, and business • MAPEB
- public policy • MAPP

School of Religion
Karen Jo Torjensen, Dean
Programs in:

- Hebrew Bible • MA, PhD
- history of Christianity • MA, PhD
- New Testament • MA, PhD
- philosophy of religion and theology • MA, PhD
- theology, ethics and culture • MA, PhD
- women's studies in religion • MA, PhD

■ CONCORDIA UNIVERSITY

Irvine, CA 92612-3299
http://www.cui.edu/

Independent-religious, coed, comprehensive institution. *Enrollment:* 78 full-time matriculated graduate/professional students (29 women), 64 part-time matriculated graduate/professional students (39 women). *Graduate faculty:* 13 full-time (3 women), 12 part-time/adjunct (3 women). *Computer facilities:* 42 computers available on campus for general student use. A campuswide network can be accessed from student residence rooms. *Library facilities:* Concordia University Library. *Graduate expenses:* Tuition: part-time $340 per unit. *General application contact:* Dr. Barbara Morton, Dean, School of Education, 949-854-8002 Ext. 1326.

MBA Entrepreneurial
Dr. Richard Harms, Director
Program in:

- business administration • MBA

School of Education
Dr. Barbara Morton, Dean
Programs in:

- Christian leadership • MA
- curriculum and instruction • MA
- education • M Ed
- educational administration • MA

School of Theology
Rev. Dr. James V. Bachman, Dean
Programs in:

- Christian leadership • MA
- family life • MA
- mission planating • MA
- Reformation theology • MA
- research and theology • MA
- theology and culture • MA

■ DOMINICAN UNIVERSITY OF CALIFORNIA

San Rafael, CA 94901-2298
http://www.dominican.edu/

Independent-religious, coed, comprehensive institution. *Enrollment:* 127 full-time matriculated graduate/professional students (103 women), 210 part-time matriculated graduate/professional students (156 women). *Graduate faculty:* 25 full-time (13 women), 47 part-time/adjunct (28 women). *Computer facilities:* 52 computers available on campus for general student use. A campuswide network can be accessed from student residence rooms and from off campus. Internet access is available. *Library facilities:* Archbishop Alemany Library plus 1 other. *Graduate expenses:* Tuition: full-time $14,040; part-time $585 per unit. *General application contact:* Kris Thornton, Director of Admissions, 415-257-1338.

■ FRESNO PACIFIC UNIVERSITY

Fresno, CA 93702-4709
http://www.fresno.edu/

Independent-religious, coed, comprehensive institution. *Enrollment:* 74 full-time matriculated graduate/professional students (62 women), 921 part-time matriculated graduate/professional students (647 women). *Graduate faculty:* 27 full-time (11 women), 76 part-time/adjunct (34 women). *Computer facilities:* 68 computers available on campus for general student use. A campuswide network can be accessed from student residence rooms and from off campus. *Library facilities:* Hiebert Library. *Graduate expenses:* Tuition: full-time $6,960; part-time $290 per unit. Tuition and fees vary according to course level and program. *General application contact:* Edith D. Thiessen, Director of Graduate Admissions, 559-453-2256.

Graduate School

Dr. Rod Janzen, Interim Dean
Programs in:
- administration • MA Ed
- administrative leadership • MA
- administrative services • MA Ed
- bilingual/cross-cultural education • MA Ed
- conflict management and peacemaking • MA
- curriculum and teaching • MA Ed
- educational technology • MA Ed
- foundations, curriculum and teaching • MA Ed
- individualized study • MA
- integrated mathematics/science education • MA Ed
- language development • MA Ed
- language, literacy, and culture • MA Ed
- learning handicapped • MA Ed
- mathematics education • MA Ed
- mathematics/science/computer education • MA Ed
- middle school mathematics • MA Ed
- multilingual contexts • MA Ed
- physical and health impairments • MA Ed
- pupil personnel • MA Ed
- reading • MA Ed
- reading/English as a second language • MA Ed
- reading/language arts • MA Ed
- school counseling • MA Ed
- school library media • MA Ed
- school psychology • MA Ed
- secondary school mathematics • MA Ed
- severely handicapped • MA Ed
- special education • MA Ed
- teaching English to speakers of other languages • MA

■ GOLDEN GATE BAPTIST THEOLOGICAL SEMINARY

Mill Valley, CA 94941-3197
http://www.ggbts.edu/

Independent-religious, coed, graduate-only institution. *Graduate faculty:* 25 full-time (2 women), 18 part-time/adjunct (8 women). *Computer facilities:* 15 computers available on campus for general student use. A campuswide network can be accessed from off campus. Internet access and online class registration are available. *Graduate expenses:* Tuition: full-time $1,380; part-time $115 per credit hour. Tuition and fees vary according to student's religious affiliation. *General application contact:* Karen White, Admissions Counselor, 415-380-1600.

Graduate and Professional Programs

Dr. Rodrick Durst, Dean of Academic Affairs
Programs in:
- Christian education • MACE, Dip CS
- church music • MACM, MMCM
- divinity • M Div
- early childhood education • Certificate
- intercultural ministries • MAIM
- ministry • D Min
- theological studies • MATS
- theology • Th M, Dip CS
- worship leadership • MA

■ HOLY NAMES COLLEGE

Oakland, CA 94619-1699
http://www.hnc.edu/

Independent-religious, coed, primarily women, comprehensive institution. *Enrollment:* 125 full-time matriculated graduate/professional students (111 women), 219 part-time matriculated graduate/professional students (177 women). *Graduate faculty:* 23 full-time (16 women), 33 part-time/adjunct (22 women). *Computer facilities:* 69 computers available on campus for general student use. A campuswide network can be accessed from student residence rooms and from off campus. Internet access is available. *Library facilities:* Cushing Library. *Graduate expenses:* Tuition: part-time $445 per unit. Required fees: $120; $120 per year. *General application contact:* 510-436-1317.

Graduate Division

Dr. David Fike, Vice President for Academic Affairs
Programs in:
- community health nursing/case manager • MS
- counseling psychology with emphasis in pastoral counseling • MA
- education • M Ed
- English • MA
- family nurse practitioner • MS
- Kodály music education • Certificate
- management • MBA
- music education with a Kodály emphasis • MM
- pastoral counseling • MA, Certificate
- performance • MM
- piano pedagogy • MM
- piano pedagogy with Suzuki emphasis • Certificate
- teaching English as a second language • Certificate

Sophia Center: Spirituality for the New Millennium

Dr. James Conlon, Program Director
Programs in:
- creation spirituality • Certificate
- culture and creation spirituality • MA

■ HOPE INTERNATIONAL UNIVERSITY

Fullerton, CA 92831-3138

http://www.hiu.edu/

Independent-religious, coed, comprehensive institution. *Enrollment:* 95 full-time matriculated graduate/professional students (54 women), 118 part-time matriculated graduate/professional students (45 women). *Graduate faculty:* 8 full-time (2 women), 29 part-time/adjunct (14 women). *Computer facilities:* 32 computers available on campus for general student use. A campuswide network can be accessed from off campus. Internet access is available. *Library facilities:* Hurst Memorial Library. *Graduate expenses:* Tuition: full-time $6,030; part-time $335 per unit. Required fees: $80. *General application contact:* Dr. Stanley Mutunga, Dean, School of Graduate Studies, 800-762-1294 Ext. 2626.

School of Graduate Studies

Dr. Stanley Mutunga, Dean

Programs in:

- church music • MA, MCM
- congregational leadership • MA
- counseling • MA
- education • ME
- intercultural studies/urban ministries • MA
- international development • MBA, MSM
- marriage and family therapy • MFT
- marriage, family, and child counseling • MA
- nonprofit management • MBA
- psychology • MA

■ HUMBOLDT STATE UNIVERSITY

Arcata, CA 95521-8299

http://www.humboldt.edu/

State-supported, coed, comprehensive institution. CGS member. *Enrollment:* 335 full-time matriculated graduate/professional students (188 women), 133 part-time matriculated graduate/professional students (76 women). *Graduate faculty:* 313 full-time (96 women), 229 part-time/adjunct (112 women). *Computer facilities:* 600 computers available on campus for general student use. A campuswide network can be accessed from student residence rooms and from off campus. Internet access and online class registration are available. *General application contact:* Admissions and Records Office, 707-826-4402.

Graduate Studies

Ron A. Fritzsche, Interim Dean

College of Arts, Humanities, and Social Sciences

Dr. Karen Carlton, Dean

Programs in:

- arts, humanities, and social sciences • MA, MFA
- English • MA
- social science • MA
- sociology • MA
- theatre arts • MA, MFA

College of Natural Resources and Sciences

Dr. Jim Howard, Interim Dean

Programs in:

- biological sciences • MA
- environmental systems • MS
- natural resources • MS
- natural resources and sciences • MA, MS
- psychology • MA

College of Professional Studies

Dr. John Costello, Dean

Programs in:

- business and economics • MBA
- physical education • MA
- professional studies • MA, MBA

■ JOHN F. KENNEDY UNIVERSITY

Orinda, CA 94563-2603

http://www.jfku.edu/

Independent, coed, comprehensive institution. *Enrollment:* 633 full-time matriculated graduate/professional students (425 women), 725 part-time matriculated graduate/professional students (569 women). *Graduate faculty:* 29 full-time (13 women), 805 part-time/adjunct (483 women). *Computer facilities:* 50 computers available on campus for general student use. *Library facilities:* Robert M. Fisher Library. *Graduate expenses:* Tuition: full-time $8,667; part-time $321 per unit. Required fees: $27; $9 per quarter. *General application contact:* Ellena Bloedorn, Director of Admissions, 925-258-2213.

Find an in-depth description at www.petersons.com/graduate.

Graduate School for Holistic Studies

K. Sue Duncan, Dean

Programs in:

- arts and consciousness • MA
- consciousness studies • MA
- holistic health education • MA
- holistic studies • MA, MFA, Certificate
- studio arts • MFA
- transformative arts • MA
- transpersonal counseling psychology • MA

Graduate School of Professional Psychology

Dr. H. Keith McConnell, Dean

Programs in:

- conflict resolution • Certificate
- counseling psychology • MA
- organizational psychology • MA, Certificate
- professional psychology • MA, Psy D, Certificate
- psychology • Psy D
- sport psychology • MA

School of Law

Michael Guarino, Dean

Program in:

- law • JD

School of Liberal Arts

Jeremiah Hallisey, Dean

Programs in:

- liberal arts • MA, MAT, Certificate
- museum studies • MA, Certificate
- teaching • MAT

School of Management

Josephina Baltodano, Dean

Programs in:

- business administration • MBA
- career development • MA, Certificate
- management • MA
- organizational leadership • Certificate

■ LA SIERRA UNIVERSITY

Riverside, CA 92515-8247

http://www.lasierra.edu/

Independent-religious, coed, comprehensive institution. *Enrollment:* 98 full-time matriculated graduate/professional students (60 women), 79 part-time matriculated graduate/professional students (46 women). *Graduate faculty:* 29. *Computer facilities:* 125 computers available on campus for general student use. A campuswide network can be accessed from student residence rooms and from off campus. Internet access and online class registration are available. *Library facilities:* University Library plus 1 other. *Graduate expenses:* Tuition: part-time $350 per unit. *General application contact:* Dr. Tom Smith, Director of Admissions, 909-785-2176.

College of Arts and Sciences
Dr. James Beach, Dean
Programs in:
arts and sciences • MA
English • MA

School of Business and Management
Dr. John Thomas, Chair
Programs in:
business administration and management • MBA
executive business administration • EMBA
leadership, values, and ethics for business and management • Certificate

School of Education
Dr. Norman Powell, Chair
Programs in:
administration and leadership • MA, Ed D, Ed S
counseling • MA
curriculum and instruction • MA, Ed D, Ed S
education • MA, Ed D, Ed S
educational psychology • Ed S
school psychology • Ed S
special education • MA

School of Religion
Dr. John Jones, Dean
Programs in:
religion • MA
religious education • MA
religious studies • MA

■ LOMA LINDA UNIVERSITY

Loma Linda, CA 92350
http://www.llu.edu/

Independent-religious, coed, university. CGS member. *Enrollment:* 1,997 full-time matriculated graduate/professional students (1,002 women), 361 part-time matriculated graduate/professional students (252 women). *Graduate faculty:* 994 full-time (320 women), 275 part-time/adjunct (95 women). *Computer facilities:* A campuswide network can be accessed from student residence rooms and from off campus. Internet access and online class registration, on-line courses are available. *Library facilities:* Del E. Webb Memorial Library. *Graduate expenses:* Tuition: part-time $240 per credit hour. Tuition and fees vary according to program. *General application contact:* Dr. W. Barton Rippon, Dean of the Graduate School, 909-824-4528.

Graduate School
Dr. W. Barton Rippon, Dean
Programs in:
adult and aging family nursing • MS
biology • MS, PhD
biomedical and clinical ethics • MA
clinical nutrition • MS
clinical psychology • PhD, Psy D
endodontics • MS, Certificate
family studies • MA, Certificate
geology • MS
growing family nursing • MS
implant dentistry • MS, Certificate
marriage and family therapy • MS, DMFT, PhD
nursing administration • MS, Certificate
nursing management • Certificate
nutrition care management • MS
nutritional science • MS
oral and maxillofacial surgery • MS, Certificate
orthodontics • MS, Certificate
periodontics • MS
social policy and research • PhD
social work • MSW

Graduate Programs in Medicine
Dr. Daniel Giang, Associate Dean
Programs in:
anatomy • MS, PhD
biochemistry • MS, PhD
medicine • MS, PhD
microbiology • MS, PhD
pharmacology • MS, PhD
physiology • MS, PhD

School of Allied Health Professions
Dr. Joyce Hopp, Dean
Programs in:
allied health professions • MHIS, MPT, MRED, MS, DPT
health information systems • MHIS
physical therapy • MPT, DPT
physician assistant • MRED
speech-language pathology and audiology • MS

School of Dentistry
Dr. Charles Goodacre, Dean
Program in:
dentistry • DDS

School of Medicine
Dr. Brian Bull, Dean
Program in:
medicine • MD

School of Public Health
Dr. Richard Hart, Dean
Programs in:
biostatistics • MPH, MSPH
environmental and occupational health • MPH, MSPH
epidemiology • MPH, Dr PH
health administration • MHA, MPH
health promotion and education • MPH, Dr PH
international health • MPH
public health • MHA, MPH, MSPH, Dr PH
public health nutrition • MPH, Dr PH

■ LOYOLA MARYMOUNT UNIVERSITY

Los Angeles, CA 90045-2659

Independent-religious, coed, comprehensive institution. CGS member. *Enrollment:* 770 full-time matriculated graduate/professional students (401 women), 334 part-time matriculated graduate/professional students (184 women). *Graduate faculty:* 296 full-time (96 women), 332 part-time/adjunct (162 women). *Computer facilities:* 200 computers available on campus for general student use. A campuswide network can be accessed from student residence rooms and from off campus. Internet access is available. *Library facilities:* Charles von der Ahe Library plus 1 other. *Graduate expenses:* Tuition: part-time $575 per credit hour. Required fees: $254. *General application contact:* Chake Kouyoumjian, Director, Graduate Admissions Office, 310-338-2721.

Find an in-depth description at www.petersons.com/graduate.

Graduate Division
Dr. Joseph G. Jabbra, Academic Vice President and Chair of Graduate Council

College of Business Administration
Dr. John T. Wholihan, Dean
Program in:
business administration • MBA

College of Communication and Fine Arts
Thomas P. Kelly, Dean
Programs in:
communication and fine arts • MA
film production • MA

College of Liberal Arts
Dr. Kenyon Chan, Dean
Programs in:
counseling psychology • MA
creative writing • MA
liberal arts • MA
literature • MA
marital and family therapy • MA
pastoral studies • MA
theology • MA

Loyola Marymount University (continued)

College of Science and Engineering
Dr. Gerald S. Jakubowski, Dean
Programs in:
civil engineering • MS, MSE
computer science • MS
electrical engineering • MSE
engineering and production management • MS
environmental science • MS
mechanical engineering • MSE
science and engineering • MS, MSE

School of Education
Dr. Albert P. Koppes, Director
Programs in:
administration • M Ed
bilingual and bicultural education • MA
biology education • MAT
catholic school administration • MA
child/adolescent literacy • MA
communications • MAT
counseling • MA
education • M Ed, MA, MAT
elementary education • MA
English education • MAT
general education • M Ed
history education • MAT
learning and teaching • MAT
literacy and language • M Ed
mathematics education • MAT
multicultural education • MA
reading/language arts • M Ed
school psychology • MA
secondary education • MA
social studies education • MAT
special education • MA

Loyola Law School
David W. Burcham, Dean
Programs in:
law • JD
taxation • LL M

■ MONTEREY INSTITUTE OF INTERNATIONAL STUDIES

Monterey, CA 93940-2691
http://www.miis.edu/

Independent, coed, graduate-only institution. *Enrollment:* 548 full-time matriculated graduate/professional students (365 women), 63 part-time matriculated graduate/professional students (40 women). *Graduate faculty:* 73 full-time (35 women), 40 part-time/adjunct (12 women). *Graduate expenses:* Tuition: full-time $19,998. Required fees: $50. *General application contact:* Admissions Office, 831-647-4123.

Fisher Graduate School of International Business
Dr. Lisbeth Claus, Acting Dean
Program in:
international business • MBA

Graduate School of International Policy Studies
Dr. Philip Morgan, Dean
Programs in:
commercial diplomacy • MA
international environmental policy • MA
international management • MPA
international policy studies • MA, MPA
international policy studies and English for non-native speakers • MA
international policy studies and French • MA
international policy studies and German • MA
international policy studies and Japanese • MA
international policy studies and Mandarin • MA
international policy studies and Russian • MA
international policy studies and Spanish • MA

Graduate School of Language and Educational Linguistics
Dr. Ruth Larimer, Dean
Programs in:
language and educational linguistics • MATESOL, MATFL
peace corps master's internationalist in TESOL • MATESOL
teaching English to speakers of other languages • MATESOL
teaching foreign language • MATFL

Graduate School of Translation and Interpretation
Dr. Diane De Terra, Dean
Programs in:
conference interpretation • MA
translation • MA
translation and interpretation • MA

■ MOUNT ST. MARY'S COLLEGE

Los Angeles, CA 90049-1599
http://www.msmc.la.edu/

Independent-religious, coed, primarily women, comprehensive institution. *Computer facilities:* 85 computers available on campus for general student use. A campuswide network can be accessed from student residence rooms and from off campus. *Library facilities:* Charles Williard Coe Memorial Library. *General application contact:* Dean of the Graduate Division, 213-477-2500.

Find an in-depth description at www.petersons.com/graduate.

Graduate Division
Programs in:
administrative studies • MS
counseling psychology • MS
elementary education • MS
physical therapy • MPT
religious studies • MA
secondary education • MS
special education • MS

■ NATIONAL UNIVERSITY

La Jolla, CA 92037-1011
http://www.nu.edu/

Independent, coed, comprehensive institution. CGS member. *Enrollment:* 7,739 full-time matriculated graduate/professional students (4,873 women), 3,992 part-time matriculated graduate/professional students (2,367 women). *Graduate faculty:* 113 full-time (41 women), 2,078 part-time/adjunct (933 women). *Computer facilities:* 2,152 computers available on campus for general student use. A campuswide network can be accessed from off campus. Internet access and online class registration are available. *Library facilities:* Central Library. *Graduate expenses:* Tuition: full-time $8,640; part-time $960 per course. One-time fee: $60. Tuition and fees vary according to campus/location. *General application contact:* Nancy Rohland, Director of Enrollment Management, 858-642-8180.

Find an in-depth description at www.petersons.com/graduate.

Academic Affairs
Dr. Susan Harris, Vice President

School of Arts and Sciences
Dr. Mary Elizabeth Shutler, Dean
Programs in:
art therapy • Certificate
arts and sciences • MA, MFA, MS, Certificate
counseling psychology • MA
human behavior • MA
instructional technology • MS
nursing • MS

School of Business and Technology
Dr. Shahram Azordegan, Dean
Programs in:
accounting • MBA
biotechnology • MBA

business and technology • GMBA, MA, MBA, MCJ, MFS, MHCA, MPA, MS
criminal justice • MCJ, MPA
electronic commerce • MBA, MS
environmental management • MBA
financial management • MBA
forensic science • MFS
general business administration • MBA
global business administration • GMBA
health care administration • MBA, MHCA
human resource management • MA
human resources administration • MBA
international business • MBA
management • MA
marketing • MBA
public administration • MBA, MPA
software engineering • MS
space commerce • MBA
technology management • MBA, MS
telecommunications systems management • MS

School of Education
Dr. Ellen Curtis-Pierce, Dean
Programs in:
cross-cultural teaching • M Ed
education • MS
educational administration • MS
educational counseling • MS
educational technology • MS
school psychology • MS
special education • MS
teaching • MA

■ NEW COLLEGE OF CALIFORNIA

San Francisco, CA 94102-5206
http://www.newcollege.edu/

Independent, coed, comprehensive institution. *Computer facilities:* 10 computers available on campus for general student use. *Library facilities:* New College Library. *General application contact:* 415-437-3460.

Find an in-depth description at www.petersons.com/graduate.

School of Humanities
Program in:
humanities • MA, MFA

Division of Humanities
Programs in:
culture, ecology, and sustainable community • MA
humanities and leadership • MA
media studies • MA
poetics • MA, MFA
poetics and writing • MFA
psychology • MA
women's spirituality • MA
writing and consciousness • MA

School of Law
Program in:
law • JD

School of Psychology
Dr. Ali Chavoshian, Dean
Programs in:
feminist clinical psychology • MA
social-clinical psychology • MA

■ NOTRE DAME DE NAMUR UNIVERSITY

Belmont, CA 94002-1997
http://www.cnd.edu/

Independent-religious, coed, comprehensive institution. CGS member. *Enrollment:* 224 full-time matriculated graduate/professional students (176 women), 462 part-time matriculated graduate/professional students (339 women). *Graduate faculty:* 19 full-time (15 women), 102 part-time/adjunct (70 women). *Computer facilities:* 50 computers available on campus for general student use. A campuswide network can be accessed from off campus. Internet access is available. *Library facilities:* College of Notre Dame Library. *Graduate expenses:* Tuition: part-time $497 per unit. Required fees: $30 per term. *General application contact:* Barbara Sterner, Assistant to the Graduate Dean for Admissions, 650-508-3527.

Graduate School
Dr. Elaine L. Cohen, Dean
Programs in:
art therapy • MAAT, MAMFT
business administration • MBA
chemical dependency • MACP
counseling psychology • MACP
curriculum and instruction • M Ed
educational technology • M Ed
educational technology administration • MS
electronic business management • MS
elementary education • M Ed, Certificate
English • MA
gerontology • MA
humanities • MA
management • MSM
marital and family therapy • MACP
music • MM
pedagogy • MM
performance • MM
public administration • MPA
secondary education • M Ed, MAT, Certificate
special education • MA, Certificate
teaching art • MAT
teaching biology • MAT
teaching English • MAT
teaching French • MAT
teaching music • MAT
teaching religious studies • MAT
teaching social sciences • MAT

■ PEPPERDINE UNIVERSITY

Malibu, CA 90263-0002
http://www.pepperdine.edu/

Independent-religious, coed, university. CGS member. *Enrollment:* 874 full-time matriculated graduate/professional students (403 women), 147 part-time matriculated graduate/professional students (68 women). *Graduate faculty:* 74 full-time (18 women), 30 part-time/adjunct (12 women). *Computer facilities:* 292 computers available on campus for general student use. A campuswide network can be accessed from student residence rooms. *Library facilities:* Payson Library plus 2 others. *Graduate expenses:* Tuition: full-time $15,700; part-time $785 per unit. Tuition and fees vary according to degree level and program. *General application contact:* Paul Long, Dean of Enrollment Management, 310-506-4392.

Malibu Graduate Business Programs
Dr. James A. Goodrich, Associate Dean
Programs in:
business administration • MBA
international business • MIB

School of Law
Dr. Richardson Lynn, Dean
Programs in:
dispute resolution • MDR
law • JD, MDR

School of Public Policy
Dr. James Wilburn, Dean
Program in:
public policy • MPP

Seaver College
Dr. David Baird, Dean
Programs in:
American studies • MA
communication • MA
history • MA
ministry • MS
religion • M Div, MA

■ POINT LOMA NAZARENE UNIVERSITY

San Diego, CA 92106-2899

http://www.ptloma.edu/

Independent-religious, coed, comprehensive institution. *Enrollment:* 280 full-time matriculated graduate/professional students (188 women), 149 part-time matriculated graduate/professional students (99 women). *Graduate faculty:* 10 full-time (6 women), 40 part-time/adjunct (16 women). *Computer facilities:* 125 computers available on campus for general student use. A campuswide network can be accessed from student residence rooms and from off campus. *Library facilities:* Ryan Library. *Graduate expenses:* Tuition: full-time $11,100; part-time $450 per unit. Required fees: $25 per unit. One-time fee: $25. Tuition and fees vary according to degree level and program. *General application contact:* Dr. Darrel Falk, Associate Provost for Research and Dean of Graduate and Continuing Education, 619-849-2629.

Graduate Programs

Dr. Darrel Falk, Associate Provost for Research and Dean of Graduate and Continuing Education

Programs in:

- business • MBA
- education • MA, Ed S
- religion • M Min, MA

■ SAINT MARY'S COLLEGE OF CALIFORNIA

Moraga, CA 94556

http://www.stmarys-ca.edu/

Independent-religious, coed, comprehensive institution. *Enrollment:* 465 full-time matriculated graduate/professional students (290 women), 639 part-time matriculated graduate/professional students (511 women). *Graduate faculty:* 42 full-time (26 women), 356 part-time/adjunct (250 women). *Computer facilities:* 250 computers available on campus for general student use. A campuswide network can be accessed from student residence rooms and from off campus. Internet access is available. *Library facilities:* St. Albert Hall plus 1 other. *Graduate expenses:* Tuition: full-time $14,472; part-time $555 per credit. *General application contact:* Michael Beseda, Vice President, Enrollment Services, 925-631-4277.

Graduate Business Programs

Dr. Ted Tsukahara, Interim Dean

Programs in:

- business administration • MBA
- economics and business administration • MBA
- executive business administration • MBA

School of Education

Dr. Nancy L. Sorenson, Dean

Programs in:

- early childhood education and Montessori teacher training • M Ed, MA
- education • M Ed, MA
- educational leadership • MA
- graduate counseling • MA
- reading leadership • MA
- special education • M Ed, MA

School of Extended Education

Dr. Dean Elias, Dean

Programs in:

- extended education • MA, MS
- health services administration • MS
- liberal studies • MA

School of Liberal Arts

Francis Sweeney, Dean

Programs in:

- creative writing • MFA
- health, physical education, and recreation • MA
- liberal arts • MA, MFA

■ SAN DIEGO STATE UNIVERSITY

San Diego, CA 92182

http://www.sdsu.edu/

State-supported, coed, university. CGS member. *Computer facilities:* 400 computers available on campus for general student use. A campuswide network can be accessed from student residence rooms and from off campus. Internet access and online class registration are available. *Library facilities:* Malcolm A. Love Library. *General application contact:* Associate Dean, Graduate Division, 619-594-4162.

Graduate and Research Affairs

Program in:

- interdisciplinary studies • MA, MS

College of Arts and Letters

Programs in:

- anthropology • MA
- arts and letters • MA, MFA, PhD, CAL
- Asian studies • MA
- creative writing • MFA
- economics • MA
- English • MA
- French • MA
- geography • MA, PhD
- history • MA
- Latin American studies • MA
- liberal arts • MA
- linguistics and Oriental languages • MA, CAL
- philosophy • MA
- political science • MA
- sociology • MA
- Spanish • MA
- women's studies • MA

College of Education

Programs in:

- counseling and school psychology • MS
- education • MA, MS, PhD
- educational administration and supervision • MA
- educational technology • MA
- elementary curriculum and instruction • MA
- policy studies in language and cross cultural education • MA
- reading education • MA
- rehabilitation counseling • MS
- secondary curriculum and instruction • MA
- special education • MA

College of Engineering

Programs in:

- aerospace engineering • MS
- civil engineering • MS
- electrical engineering • MS
- engineering • MS, PhD
- engineering mechanics • MS
- engineering sciences and applied mechanics • PhD
- flight dynamics • MS
- fluid dynamics • MS
- mechanical engineering • MS

College of Health and Human Services

Programs in:

- communicative disorders • MA
- environmental health • MPH, MS
- epidemiology • MPH, PhD
- health and human services • MA, MPH, MS, MSW, PhD
- health promotion • MPH
- health services administration • MPH
- industrial hygiene • MS
- language and communicative disorders • PhD
- nursing • MS
- social work • MSW
- toxicology • MS

College of Professional Studies and Fine Arts

Programs in:

- advertising and public relations • MA
- art history • MA

city planning • MCP
communication • MA
criminal justice administration • MPA
criminal justice and criminology • MS
critical-cultural studies • MA
drama • MA, MFA
exercise physiology • MA
interaction studies • MA
intercultural and international studies • MA
music and dance • MA, MM
new media studies • MA
news and information studies • MA
nutritional science • MS
physical education • MS
professional studies and fine arts • MA, MCP, MFA, MM, MPA, MS
public administration • MPA
studio arts • MA, MFA
telecommunications and media management • MA
television, film, and new media production • MA

College of Sciences
Programs in:
applied mathematics • MS
astronomy • MS
biology • MA, MS
cell and molecular biology • PhD
chemistry • MA, MS, PhD
clinical psychology • MS, PhD
computer science • MS
ecology • PhD
geological sciences • MS
industrial and organizational psychology • MS
mathematics • MA
mathematics and science education • PhD
microbiology • MS
molecular biology • MA, MS
physics • MA, MS
program evaluation • MS
psychology • MA
radiological physics • MS
sciences • MA, MS, PhD
statistics • MS

Graduate School of Business
Programs in:
accountancy • MBA, MS
business • MBA, MS
business administration • MBA
finance • MBA, MS
human resources management • MS
information and decision systems • MBA, MS
international business • MBA, MS
management science • MS
marketing • MBA, MS
product operations management • MS

■ SAN FRANCISCO STATE UNIVERSITY
San Francisco, CA 94132-1722
http://www.sfsu.edu/

State-supported, coed, comprehensive institution. CGS member. *Computer facilities:* 1,474 computers available on campus for general student use. A campuswide network can be accessed from student residence rooms and from off campus. *Library facilities:* J. Paul Leonard Library plus 2 others. *General application contact:* Associate Dean, Graduate Studies, 415-338-2234.

Graduate Division

College of Behavioral and Social Sciences
Programs in:
anthropology • MA
behavioral and social sciences • MA, MPA, MS
economics • MA
geography • MA
history • MA
international relations • MA
nonprofit administration • MPA
policy analysis • MPA
political science • MA
psychology • MA, MS
public management • MPA
social science • MA
urban administration • MPA

College of Business
Programs in:
business • MBA, MS
business administration • MBA
taxation • MS

College of Creative Arts
Programs in:
art • MFA
art history • MA
broadcast and electronic communication arts • MA
cinema • MFA
cinema studies • MA
creative arts • MA, MFA, MM
industrial arts • MA
music • MA, MM
theatre arts • MA, MFA

College of Education
Programs in:
adult education • MA, AC
communicative disorders • MS
early childhood education • MA
education • MA, MS, Ed D, PhD, AC
educational administration • MA, AC
educational technology • MA
elementary education • MA
language and literacy education • MA
mathematics education • MA
secondary education • MA, AC
special education • MA, Ed D, PhD, AC
special interest • MA
training systems development • AC

College of Ethnic Studies
Program in:
ethnic studies • MA

College of Health and Human Services
Programs in:
case management • MS
counseling • MS
ethnogerontology • MA
health and human services • MA, MPH, MS, MSW
health education • MPH
healthy aging • MA
home economics • MA
life-long learning • MA
long-term care administration • MA
marriage and family counseling • MS
marriage, family, and child counseling • MS
nursing administration • MS
nursing education • MS
physical education • MA
physical therapy • MS
recreation and leisure studies • MS
rehabilitation counseling • MS
social work education • MSW

College of Humanities
Programs in:
Chinese • MA
classics • MA
composition • MA, Certificate
creative writing • MA, MFA
English as a foreign/second language • MA
French • MA
German • MA
humanities • MA, MFA, Certificate
Italian • MA
Japanese • MA
linguistics • MA
literature • MA
museum studies • MA
philosophy • MA
Russian • MA
Spanish • MA
speech and communication studies • MA
teaching composition • Certificate
teaching critical thinking • Certificate
teaching post-secondary reading • Certificate
women's studies • MA
world and comparative literature • MA

College of Science and Engineering
Programs in:
applied geosciences • MS
biomedical laboratory science • MS

San Francisco State University (continued)

- cell and molecular biology • MA
- chemistry • MS
- computer science • MS
- conservation biology • MA
- ecology and systematic biology • MA
- engineering • MS
- marine biology • MA
- mathematics • MA
- microbiology • MA
- physics and astrophysics • MS
- physiology and behavioral biology • MA
- science and engineering • MA, MS

■ SAN JOSE STATE UNIVERSITY

San Jose, CA 95192-0001

http://www.sjsu.edu/

State-supported, coed, comprehensive institution. CGS member. *Enrollment:* 2,242 full-time matriculated graduate/professional students (1,593 women), 3,278 part-time matriculated graduate/professional students (1,954 women). *Graduate faculty:* 933 full-time (216 women), 488 part-time/adjunct (152 women). *Computer facilities:* 993 computers available on campus for general student use. A campuswide network can be accessed from student residence rooms and from off campus. Internet access and online class registration are available. *Library facilities:* Robert D. Clark Library plus 1 other. *Graduate expenses:* Tuition, state resident: full-time $1,506. Tuition, nonresident: full-time $1,998. *General application contact:* Dr. Nabil A. Ibrahim, Graduate Studies Officer, 408-924-2480.

Graduate Studies

Dr. Nabil A. Ibrahim, Associate Vice President

Programs in:

- human factors/ergonomics • MS
- interdisciplinary studies • MA, MS
- library and information science • MLIS

College of Applied Arts and Sciences

Dr. Michael Ego, Dean

Programs in:

- administration of justice • MS
- applied arts and sciences • MA, MPH, MS, Certificate
- community health nursing • MS
- gerontology • MS
- gerontology nurse practitioner • MS
- health administration • Certificate
- health science • MA
- mass communication • MS
- nutritional science • MS
- occupational therapy • MS
- physical education • MA
- public health • MPH
- recreation and leisure studies • MS

College of Business

Dr. David Conroth, Dean

Programs in:

- accountancy • MS
- business • MBA, MS
- business administration, information management, and manufacturing management • MBA
- taxation • MS
- transportation management • MS

College of Education

Dr. Susan Myers, Acting Dean

Programs in:

- administration/higher education • MA, Certificate
- audiology • MA
- child development • MA
- counseling • MA
- education • MA, Certificate
- education for the hearing impaired • MA
- education for the severely handicapped • MA
- elementary education • MA
- instructional technology • MA, Certificate
- learning handicapped • MA
- secondary education • MA
- special education • MA
- speech pathology • MA

College of Engineering

Dr. Don Kirk, Dean

Programs in:

- aerospace engineering • MS
- chemical engineering • MS
- civil engineering and applied mechanics • MS
- computer engineering • MS
- computer software • MS
- computerized robots and computer applications • MS
- electrical engineering • MS
- engineering • MS
- general engineering • MS
- information and systems engineering • MS
- materials engineering • MS
- mechanical engineering • MS
- microprocessors and microcomputers • MS
- quality assurance • MS

College of Humanities and Arts

Dr. Carmen Sigler, Acting Dean

Programs in:

- art education • MA
- art history • MA
- drama • MA
- environmental design • MA
- French • MA
- graphic arts • MA
- humanities and arts • MA, MFA, Certificate
- industrial design • MA
- interior design • MA
- linguistics • MA, Certificate
- literature • MA
- music • MA
- music performance • MA
- philosophy • MA, Certificate
- pictorial arts • MFA
- plastic arts • MFA
- Spanish • MA
- teaching English as a second language • MA
- technical writing • MA
- textiles • MA

College of Science

Dr. Gerry Selter, Dean

Programs in:

- analytical chemistry • MS
- biochemistry • MS
- biological sciences • MA, MS
- chemistry • MA
- computer science • MS
- geology • MS
- inorganic chemistry • MS
- marine science • MS
- mathematics • MA, MS
- meteorology • MS
- organic chemistry • MS
- physical chemistry • MS
- physics • MS
- polymer chemistry • MS
- radiochemistry • MS
- science • MA, MS

College of Social Sciences

Dr. Lela Noble, Dean

Programs in:

- clinical psychology • MS
- counseling • MS
- criminology • MA
- economics • MA
- environmental studies • MS
- geography • MA
- history • MA
- industrial psychology • MS
- public administration • MPA
- research psychology • MA
- social sciences • MA, MPA, MS
- speech communication • MA

College of Social Work

Dr. Sylvia Andrew, Dean

Programs in:

- Mexican-American studies • MA
- social work • MA, MSW, MUP
- urban and regional planning • MUP

■ SANTA BARBARA COLLEGE OF ORIENTAL MEDICINE

Santa Barbara, CA 93101

Private, coed, graduate-only institution. *General application contact:* Registrar, 805-898-1180.

Program in Acupuncture and Oriental Medicine

Program in:
acupuncture and Oriental medicine • M Ac OM

■ SANTA CLARA UNIVERSITY

Santa Clara, CA 95053
http://www.scu.edu/

Independent-religious, coed, university. CGS member. *Enrollment:* 1,274 full-time matriculated graduate/professional students (693 women), 1,457 part-time matriculated graduate/professional students (543 women). *Graduate faculty:* 180 full-time (54 women), 111 part-time/adjunct (34 women). *Computer facilities:* 535 computers available on campus for general student use. A campuswide network can be accessed from student residence rooms and from off campus. *Library facilities:* Orradre Library plus 1 other. *Graduate expenses:* Tuition: part-time $571 per term. *General application contact:* Richard J. Toomey, Dean, Enrollment Management, 408-554-4505.

College of Arts and Sciences

Dr. Peter A. Facione, Dean
Programs in:
arts and sciences • MA
catechetics • MA
liturgical music • MA
pastoral liturgy • MA
spirituality • MA

Division of Counseling Psychology and Education

Dr. Peter A. Facione, Administrator
Programs in:
counseling psychology • MA
counseling psychology and education • MA, Certificate
education • MA
educational administration • MA
health psychology • MA
marriage, family, and child counseling • MA
multiple subject teaching • Certificate
pastoral counseling • MA
single subject teaching • Certificate
special education • MA

Leavey School of Business

Dr. Barry Posner, Dean
Programs in:
agribusiness • MBA
business administration • EMBA, MBA

School of Engineering

Dr. Terry E. Shoup, Dean
Programs in:
applied mathematics • MSAM
ASIC design and test • Certificate
civil engineering • MSCE
computer science and engineering • MSCSE, PhD
data storage technologies • Certificate
electrical engineering • MSEE, PhD, Engineer
engineering • MS, MSAM, MSCE, MSCSE, MSE, MSE Mgt, MSEE, MSME, PhD, Certificate, Engineer
engineering management • MSE Mgt
high performance computing • Certificate
mechanical engineering • MSME, PhD, Engineer
software engineering • MS, Certificate

School of Law

Mack Player, Dean
Program in:
law • JD, LL M, Certificate

■ SIMPSON COLLEGE AND GRADUATE SCHOOL

Redding, CA 96003-8606
http://www.simpsonca.edu/

Independent-religious, coed, comprehensive institution. *Graduate faculty:* 17 full-time (3 women), 9 part-time/adjunct (3 women). *Computer facilities:* 26 computers available on campus for general student use. A campuswide network can be accessed from student residence rooms and from off campus. Internet access is available. *Library facilities:* Start-Kilgour Memorial Library. *General application contact:* Murry Evans, Vice President for Enrollment Management and Marketing, 530-224-5606.

Graduate School

Dr. Judith Fortune, Vice President for Academic Affairs
Programs in:
Christian ministry • MA
curriculum and instruction • MA
missiology • MA

■ SONOMA STATE UNIVERSITY

Rohnert Park, CA 94928-3609
http://www.sonoma.edu/

State-supported, coed, comprehensive institution. *Enrollment:* 181 full-time matriculated graduate/professional students (134 women), 311 part-time matriculated graduate/professional students (233 women). *Graduate faculty:* 270 full-time (115 women), 267 part-time/adjunct (149 women). *Computer facilities:* 300 computers available on campus for general student use. A campuswide network can be accessed from student residence rooms and from off campus. Internet access is available. *Library facilities:* Jean and Charles Schultz Information Center. *Graduate expenses:* Tuition, nonresident: part-time $246 per unit. Required fees: $2,080. *General application contact:* Elaine Sundberg, Director, Graduate Studies, 707-664-2215.

Institute of Interdisciplinary Studies

Dr. Gardner Rust, Coordinator
Program in:
interdisciplinary studies • MA, MS

School of Arts and Humanities

Dr. William Babula, Dean
Programs in:
American literature • MA
arts and humanities • MA
creative writing • MA
English literature • MA
world literature • MA

School of Business and Economics

Dr. Ahmad Hosseini, Interima Dean
Programs in:
business administration • MBA
business and economics • MBA

School of Education

Dr. Phyllis Fernlund, Dean
Programs in:
curriculum and instruction • MA
early childhood and elementary education • MA
education • MA
educational leadership • MA
reading • MA
special education • MA

School of Natural Sciences

Dr. Saeid Rahimi, Interim Dean
Programs in:
environmental biology • MA
family nurse practitioner • MS

Sonoma State University (continued)
general biology • MA
kinesiology • MA
natural sciences • MA, MS

School of Social Sciences
Dr. Robert Karlsrud, Dean
Programs in:
counseling • MA
cultural resources management • MA
history • MA
marriage, family, and child counseling • MA
political science • MA
public administration • MPA
pupil personnel services • MA
social sciences • MA, MPA

■ STANFORD UNIVERSITY

Stanford, CA 94305-9991
http://www.stanford.edu/

Independent, coed, university. CGS member. *Enrollment:* 6,318 full-time matriculated graduate/professional students (2,293 women), 1,382 part-time matriculated graduate/professional students (472 women). *Graduate faculty:* 1,670 full-time (342 women). *Computer facilities:* 1,000 computers available on campus for general student use. A campuswide network can be accessed from student residence rooms and from off campus. Internet access and online class registration are available. *Library facilities:* Green Library plus 18 others. *Graduate expenses:* Tuition: full-time $24,441. Required fees: $72. Full-time tuition and fees vary according to program. Part-time tuition and fees vary according to course load. *General application contact:* Mary Lue Eiche, Graduate Admissions Support Section, 650-723-4291.

Graduate School of Business
Robert L. Joss, Dean
Program in:
business • MBA, PhD

Law School
Kathleen M. Sullivan, Dean
Program in:
law • JD, JSM, MLS, JSD

School of Earth Sciences
Franklin M. Orr, Dean
Programs in:
earth sciences • MS, PhD, Eng
earth systems • MS
geological and environmental sciences • MS, PhD, Eng
geophysics • MS, PhD
petroleum engineering • MS, PhD, Eng

School of Education
Deborah J. Stipek, Dean
Programs in:
administration and policy analysis • Ed D, PhD
anthropology of education • PhD
art education • AM, PhD
child and adolescent development • PhD
counseling psychology • PhD
dance education • AM
economics of education • PhD
education • AM, Ed D, PhD
educational linguistics • PhD
educational psychology • PhD
English education • AM, PhD
evaluation • AM
general curriculum studies • AM, PhD
higher education • PhD
history of education • PhD
interdisciplinary studies • PhD
international comparative education • AM, PhD
international education administration and policy analysis • AM
languages education • AM
learning, design and technology • AM, PhD
mathematics education • AM
mathematics educations • PhD
philosophy of education • PhD
policy analysis • AM
prospective principal's program • AM
science education • AM, PhD
social studies education • AM, PhD
sociology of education • PhD
symbolic systemis in education • PhD
teacher education • AM, PhD

School of Engineering
James D. Plummer, Dean
Programs in:
aeronautics and astronautics • MS, PhD, Eng
biomechanical engineering • MS
chemical engineering • MS, PhD, Eng
civil and environmental engineering • MS, PhD, Eng
computer science • MS, PhD
electrical engineering • MS, PhD, Eng
engineering • MS, PhD, Eng
management science and engineering • MS, PhD
management science and engineering and electrical engineering • MS
manufacturing systems engineering • MS
materials science and engineering • MS, PhD, Eng
mechanical engineering • MS, PhD, Eng
product design • MS
scientific computing and computational mathematics • MS, PhD

School of Humanities and Sciences
Malcolm R. Beasley, Dean
Programs in:
anthropological sciences • AM, MS, PhD
applied physics • MS, PhD
art • MFA, PhD
biological sciences • MS, PhD
biophysics • PhD
chemistry • PhD
Chinese • AM, PhD
classics • AM, PhD
communication theory and research • PhD
comparative literature • PhD
computer-based music theory and acoustics • AM, PhD
cultural and social anthropology • AM, PhD
documentary film and video • AM
drama • PhD
economics • PhD
English • AM, PhD
financial mathematics • MS
French • AM, PhD
German studies • AM, PhD
history • AM, PhD
humanities • AM
humanities and sciences • AM, MFA, MS, DMA, PhD
international policy studies • AM
Italian • AM, PhD
Japanese • AM, PhD
journalism • AM
linguistics • AM, PhD
mathematiacs • PhD
mathematics • MS
modern thought and literature • PhD
music composition • AM, DMA
music history • AM
music, science, and technology • AM
musicology • PhD
philosophy • AM, PhD
physics • PhD
political science • AM, PhD
psychology • PhD
religious studies • AM, PhD
Russian • AM
Slavic languages and literatures • PhD
sociology • PhD
Spanish • AM, PhD
statistics • MS, PhD

Center for East Asian Studies
Jean Oi, Director
Program in:
East Asian studies • AM

Center for Latin American Studies
Terry L. Karl, Director
Program in:
Latin American studies • AM

Center for Russian and East European Studies
Nancy Kollman, Director
Program in:
- Russian and East European studies • AM

School of Medicine
Philip A. Pizzo, Dean
Program in:
- medicine • MD, MS, PhD

Graduate Programs in Medicine
Programs in:
- biochemistry • PhD
- biomedical informatics • MS, PhD
- cancer biology • PhD
- developmental biology • PhD
- epidemiology • MS, PhD
- genetics • PhD
- health services research • MS
- immunology • PhD
- medicine • MS, PhD
- microbiology and immunology • PhD
- molecular and cellular physiology • PhD
- molecular pharmacology • PhD
- neurosciences • PhD
- structural biology • PhD

■ UNIVERSITY OF CALIFORNIA, BERKELEY
Berkeley, CA 94720-1500
http://www.berkeley.edu/

State-supported, coed, university. CGS member. *Computer facilities:* 600 computers available on campus for general student use. A campuswide network can be accessed from student residence rooms and from off campus. Internet access and online class registration are available. *Library facilities:* Doe Library plus 30 others. *General application contact:* 510-642-7405.

Graduate Division
Programs in:
- ancient history and Mediterranean archaeology • MA, PhD
- applied science and technology • PhD
- Asian studies • PhD
- bioengineering • PhD
- biophysics • MA, PhD
- Buddhist studies • PhD
- business administration/Asian studies • MA, PhD
- business administration/international and area studies • MA
- comparative biochemistry • PhD
- demography • MA, PhD
- dramatic art • PhD, C Phil
- East Asian studies • MA
- endocrinology • MA, PhD
- energy and resources • MA, MS, PhD
- ethnic studies • PhD
- folklore • MA
- French • PhD
- international and area studies • MA
- Italian • PhD
- journalism-Asian studies • MA, PhD
- journalism/international and area studies • MA
- Latin American studies • MA, PhD
- law-Asian studies • MA, PhD
- law/international and area studies • MA
- logic and the methodology of science • PhD
- microbiology • PhD
- neuroscience • PhD
- Northeast Asian studies • MA
- nutrition • MS, PhD
- ocean engineering • M Eng, MS, D Eng, PhD
- public policy/international and area studies • MA
- range management • MS
- Romance philology • PhD
- South Asian studies • MA
- Southeast Asian studies • MA
- Spanish • PhD
- vision science • MS, PhD
- wood science and technology • MS, PhD

College of Chemistry
Programs in:
- chemical engineering • MS, PhD
- chemistry • MS, PhD

College of Engineering
Programs in:
- ceramic sciences and engineering • M Eng, MS, D Eng, PhD
- computer science • MS, PhD
- construction engineering and management • M Eng, MS, D Eng, PhD
- electrical engineering • M Eng, MS, D Eng, PhD
- engineering • M Eng, MS, D Eng, PhD
- engineering geoscience • M Eng, MS, D Eng, PhD
- environmental quality and environmental water resources engineering • M Eng, MS, D Eng, PhD
- geotechnical engineering • M Eng, MS, D Eng, PhD
- industrial engineering and operations research • M Eng, MS, D Eng, PhD
- materials engineering • M Eng, MS, D Eng, PhD
- mechanical engineering • M Eng, MS, D Eng, PhD
- mineral engineering • M Eng, MS, D Eng, PhD
- nuclear engineering • M Eng, MS, PhD
- petroleum engineering • M Eng, MS, D Eng, PhD
- physical metallurgy • M Eng, MS, D Eng, PhD
- structural engineering, mechanics and materials • M Eng, MS, D Eng, PhD
- transportation engineering • M Eng, MS, D Eng, PhD

College of Environmental Design
Programs in:
- architecture • M Arch
- building science and urban design • MS, PhD
- city and regional planning • MCP, PhD
- design • MA
- design theories and methods • MS, PhD
- environmental design • M Arch, MA, MCP, MLA, MS, MUD, PhD
- environmental design in developing countries • MS, PhD
- environmental planning • MLA, PhD
- history of architecture and urban design • MS, PhD
- landscape architecture • MLA
- landscape design and site planning • MLA
- social basis of architecture and urban design • MS, PhD
- structures and construction • MS, PhD
- the building process • MS, PhD
- urban and community design • MLA
- urban design • MUD

College of Letters and Science
Programs in:
- African American studies • PhD
- anthropology • PhD
- applied mathematics • PhD
- art practice • MFA
- astrophysics • PhD
- Chinese language • PhD
- classical archaeology • MA, PhD
- classics • MA, PhD
- comparative literature • MA, PhD
- Czech • MA, PhD
- economics • PhD
- endocrinology • PhD
- English • PhD
- French • PhD
- geography • PhD
- geology • MA, MS, PhD
- geophysics • MA, MS, PhD
- German • MA, PhD
- Greek • MA
- Hindi-Urdu • MA, PhD
- Hispanic languages and literatures • MA, PhD
- history • PhD, C Phil

University of California, Berkeley (continued)

history of art • PhD
integrative biology • PhD
Italian studies • MA, PhD
Japanese language • PhD
Latin • MA
letters and science • MA, MFA, MS, PhD, C Phil
linguistics • MA, PhD
Malay-Indonesian • MA, PhD
mathematics • MA, PhD, C Phil
medical anthropology • PhD
molecular and cell biology • PhD
music • MA, PhD
Near Eastern religions • PhD
Near Eastern studies • MA, PhD, C Phil
philosophy • PhD
physics • PhD
Polish • MA, PhD
political science • PhD
psychology • PhD
rhetoric • PhD
Russian • MA, PhD
Sanskrit • MA, PhD
Scandinavian languages and literatures • MA, PhD
Serbo-Croatian • MA, PhD
sociology • PhD
South Asian civilization • MA
statistics • MA, PhD
Tamil • MA, PhD

College of Natural Resources
Programs in:
agricultural and environmental chemistry • MS, PhD
agricultural and resource economics and policy • PhD
environmental science, policy, and management • MS, PhD
forestry • MF
natural resources • MA, MF, MS, PhD
plant biology • PhD
range management • MS

Graduate School of Journalism
Program in:
journalism • MJ

Graduate School of Public Policy
Program in:
public policy • MPP, PhD

Haas School of Business
Laura D'Andrea Tyson, Dean
Programs in:
accounting • PhD
business • MBA, MFE, PhD, MBA/MFE
business administration • MBA
business administration and financial engineering • MBA/MFE
business and public policy • PhD
finance • PhD
financial engineering • MFE
marketing • PhD
organizational behavior and industrial relations • PhD
real estate • PhD

School of Education
Programs in:
advanced reading and language leadership • MA
developmental teacher education • MA
education • MA, Ed D, PhD, Certificate
education in mathematics, science, and technology • MA, PhD
education with a multiple subject credential • MA
education/single subject teaching: mathematics • MA
education/single subject teaching: science • MA
educational leadership • Ed D
English • Certificate
human development and education • MA, PhD
language, literacy, and culture • MA, Ed D, PhD
policy • MA
policy research • PhD
program evaluation and assessment • Ed D
quantitative methods in education • PhD
school psychology • PhD
science and mathematics • PhD
science and mathematics education • MA
social and cultural analysis and social theory • MA, PhD
special education • PhD

School of Information Management and Systems
Program in:
information management and systems • MIMS, PhD

School of Public Health
Programs in:
biostatistics • MPH
environmental health sciences • MPH, MS, PhD
epidemiology • MPH, MS, PhD
epidemiology/biostatistics • MPH
health and medical sciences • MS
health and social behavior • MPH
health policy and management • MPH
health services and policy analysis • PhD
infectious diseases • MPH, PhD
infectious diseases and immunity • PhD
interdisciplinary • MPH
maternal and child health • MPH
public health • MA, MPH, MS, Dr PH, PhD
public health nutrition • MPH

School of Social Welfare
Program in:
social welfare • MSW, PhD

School of Law
Programs in:
jurisprudence and social policy • PhD
law • JD, LL M, JSD
law/business administration • JD, LL M, JSD, PhD

School of Optometry
Dr. Anthony J. Adams, Dean
Program in:
optometry • OD

■ UNIVERSITY OF CALIFORNIA, DAVIS

Davis, CA 95616
http://www.ucdavis.edu/

State-supported, coed, university. CGS member. *Enrollment:* 4,615 full-time matriculated graduate/professional students (2,331 women), 12 part-time matriculated graduate/professional students (5 women). *Graduate faculty:* 1,371 full-time, 231 part-time/adjunct. *Computer facilities:* 600 computers available on campus for general student use. A campuswide network can be accessed from student residence rooms and from off campus. Internet access, software packages are available. *Library facilities:* Peter J. Shields Library plus 5 others. *Graduate expenses:* Tuition, nonresident: full-time $10,244. Required fees: $4,591.

Find an in-depth description at www.petersons.com/graduate.

Graduate School of Management
Robert H. Smiley, Dean
Program in:
management • MBA

Graduate Studies
Christina González, Dean
Programs in:
acting • MFA
agricultural and environmental chemistry • MS, PhD
agricultural and resource economics • MS, PhD

animal behavior • MS, PhD
animal science • MAM, MS
anthropology • MA, PhD
applied linguistics • MA
applied mathematics • MS, PhD
art • MFA
art history • MA
atmospheric sciences • MS, PhD
avian sciences • MS
biochemistry and molecular biology • MS, PhD
biophysics • MS, PhD
cell and developmental biology • PhD
chemistry • MS, PhD
child development • MS
community development • MS
comparative literature • PhD
comparative pathology • MS, PhD
composition • MA, PhD
conducting • MA, PhD
creative writing • MA
cultural studies • MA, PhD
dramatic art • PhD
ecology • MS, PhD
economics • MA, PhD
education • Ed D
English • MA, PhD
entomology • MS, PhD
epidemiology • MS, PhD
exercise science • MS
food science • MS, PhD
French • PhD
genetics • MS, PhD
geography • MA, PhD
geology • MS, PhD
German • MA, PhD
history • MA, PhD
horticulture, agronomy, and vegetable crops • MS
human development • PhD
hydrologic sciences • MS, PhD
immunology • MS, PhD
instructional studies • PhD
international agricultural development • MS
linguistics • MA
mathematics • MA, MAT, PhD
medical informatics • MS
microbiology • MS, PhD
musicology • MA, PhD
Native American studies • MA, PhD
neuroscience • PhD
nutrition • MS, PhD
pharmacology/toxicology • MS, PhD
philosophy • MA, PhD
physics • MS, PhD
physiology • MS, PhD
plant biology • MS, PhD
plant pathology • MS, PhD
plant protection and pest management • MS
political science • MA, PhD
population biology • PhD
psychological studies • PhD
psychology • PhD
sociocultural studies • PhD
sociology • MA, PhD
soil science • MS, PhD
Spanish • MA, PhD
statistics • MS, PhD
textile arts and costume design • MFA
textiles • MS

College of Engineering
Dr. Zuhair A. Munir, Interim Dean
Programs in:
aeronautical engineering • M Engr, MS, D Engr, PhD, Certificate
applied science • MS, PhD
biological and agricultural engineering • M Engr, MS, D Engr, PhD
biomedical engineering • MS, PhD
chemical engineering • MS, PhD
civil and environmental engineering • M Engr, MS, D Engr, PhD, Certificate
computer science • MS, PhD
electrical and computer engineering • MS, PhD
engineering • M Engr, MS, D Engr, PhD, Certificate
materials science • MS, PhD, Certificate
mechanical engineering • M Engr, MS, D Engr, PhD, Certificate
transportation and technology policy • MS, PhD

School of Law
Program in:
law • JD, LL M

School of Medicine
Program in:
medicine • MD

School of Veterinary Medicine
Program in:
veterinary medicine • DVM, MPVM, Certificate

■ UNIVERSITY OF CALIFORNIA, IRVINE

Irvine, CA 92697
http://www.uci.edu/

State-supported, coed, university. CGS member. *Enrollment:* 3,105 full-time matriculated graduate/professional students (1,192 women), 124 part-time matriculated graduate/professional students (27 women). *Graduate faculty:* 1,624. *Computer facilities:* 500 computers available on campus for general student use. A campuswide network can be accessed from student residence rooms and from off campus. Internet access and online class registration are available. *Library facilities:* Main Library plus 1 other. *Graduate expenses:* Tuition, nonresident: full-time $10,244; part-time $10,244. Required fees: $5,484; $3,941 per year. $1,314 per term. Tuition and fees vary according to course load, program and student level. *General application contact:* 949-824-4611.

College of Medicine
Dr. Thomas Cesario, Dean
Program in:
medicine • MD, MS, PhD

Graduate Programs in Medicine
Dr. Thomas Cesario, Dean, College of Medicine
Programs in:
biological sciences • MS, PhD
environmental toxicology • MS, PhD
genetic counseling • MS
medicine • MS, PhD
pharmacology and toxicology • MS, PhD
radiological sciences • MS, PhD

Office of Research and Graduate Studies
William H. Parker, Vice Chancellor for Research and Dean of Graduate Studies
Programs in:
educational administration • Ed D
information and computer science • MS, PhD

Graduate School of Management
David H. Blake, Dean
Program in:
management • MBA, PhD

School of Biological Sciences
Dr. Susan V. Bryant, Dean
Program in:
biological sciences • MS, PhD

School of Engineering
Dr. Nicolaos G. Alexopoulos, Dean
Programs in:
biomedical engineering • MS, PhD
chemical and biochemical engineering • MS, PhD
civil engineering • MS, PhD
computer networks and distributed computing • MS, PhD
computer systems and software • MS, PhD
electrical engineering • MS, PhD
engineering • MS, PhD
environmental engineering • MS, PhD
mechanical and aerospace engineering • MS, PhD

School of Humanities
Karen Lawrence, Dean
Programs in:
art history • PhD
Chinese • MA, PhD
classics • MA, PhD

University of California, Irvine (continued)
comparative literature • MA, PhD
East Asian cultures • MA, PhD
English • MA, PhD
French • MA, PhD
German • MA, PhD
history • MA, PhD
humanities • MA, MAT, MFA, PhD
Japanese • MA, PhD
philosophy • MA, PhD
Spanish • MA, MAT, PhD
visual studies • PhD
writing • MFA

School of Physical Sciences
Ronald Stern, Dean
Programs in:
chemistry • MS, PhD
earth system science • MS, PhD
mathematics • MS, PhD
physical sciences • MS, PhD
physics • MS, PhD

School of Social Ecology
C. Ronald Huff, Dean
Programs in:
criminology, law and society • PhD
environmental analysis and design • PhD
environmental health science and policy • MS, PhD
health psychology • PhD
human development • PhD
social ecology • MA, PhD
urban and regional planning • MURP, PhD

School of Social Sciences
William Schonfeld, Dean
Programs in:
anthropology • MA, PhD
demographic and social analysis • MA
economics • MA, PhD
logic and philosophy of science • PhD
political sciences • PhD
psychology • PhD
social networks • MA, PhD
social science • MA, PhD
social sciences • MA, PhD
sociology and social relations • MA, PhD
transportation science • MA, PhD

School of the Arts
Jill Beck, Dean
Programs in:
accounting • MFA
acting • MFA
arts • MFA, PhD
choral conducting • MFA
composition and technology • MFA
dance • MFA
design and stage management • MFA
directing • MFA
drama and theatre • PhD
guitar/lute performance • MFA
instrument performance • MFA
jazz composition • MFA
jazz instrumental performance • MFA
piano performance • MFA
studio art • MFA
vocal performance • MFA

■ UNIVERSITY OF CALIFORNIA, LOS ANGELES

Los Angeles, CA 90095
http://www.ucla.edu/

State-supported, coed, university. CGS member. *Enrollment:* 8,392 full-time matriculated graduate/professional students (3,986 women). *Computer facilities:* A campuswide network can be accessed from student residence rooms and from off campus. *Library facilities:* University Research Library plus 13 others. *Graduate expenses:* Tuition, nonresident: full-time $10,434. Required fees: $4,406. *General application contact:* Graduate Admissions, 310-825-1711.

Graduate Division
Dr. Claudia Mitchell-Kernan, Dean
Program in:
East Asian studies • MA

College of Letters and Science
Dr. Brian P. Copenhaver, Provost
Programs in:
African studies • MA
Afro-American studies • MA
American Indian studies • MA
anthropology • MA, PhD
applied linguistics • PhD
applied linguistics and teaching English as a second language • MA
archaeology • MA, PhD
art history • MA, PhD
Asian-American studies • MA
astronomy • MAT, MS, PhD
atmospheric sciences • MS, PhD
biochemistry and molecular biology • MS, PhD
biology • MA, PhD
chemistry • MS, PhD
classics • MA, PhD
comparative literature • MA, PhD
East Asian languages and cultures • MA, PhD
economics • MA, PhD
English • MA, PhD
French and Francophone studies • MA, PhD
geochemistry • MS, PhD
geography • MA, PhD
geology • MS, PhD
geophysics and space physics • MS, PhD
German • MA
Germanic languages • MA, PhD
Greek • MA
Hispanic languages and literature • PhD
history • MA, PhD
Indo-European studies • PhD
Islamic studies • MA, PhD
Italian • MA, PhD
Latin • MA
Latin American studies • MA
letters and science • MA, MAT, MS, PhD, Certificate
linguistics • MA, PhD
mathematics • MA, MAT, PhD
microbiology and molecular genetics • PhD
molecular and cellular life sciences • PhD
molecular biology • PhD
musicology • MA, PhD
Near Eastern languages and cultures • MA, PhD
philosophy • MA, PhD
physics • MAT, MS, PhD
physics education • MAT
physiological science • MS, PhD
plant molecular biology • PhD
political science • MA, PhD
Portuguese • MA
psychology • MA, PhD
Romance linguistics and literature • MA, PhD
Scandinavian • MA, PhD
Slavic languages and literatures • MA, PhD
sociology • MA, PhD
Spanish • MA
statistics • MS, PhD
women's studies • MS, PhD

Graduate School of Education and Information Studies
Dr. Herold Levine, Interim Dean
Programs in:
archive and preservation management • MLIS
education • M Ed, MA, Ed D, PhD
education and information studies • M Ed, MA, MLIS, Ed D, PhD, Certificate
educational leadership • Ed D
information access • MLIS
information organization • MLIS
information policy and management • MLIS
information systems • MLIS
library and information science • PhD, Certificate
special education • PhD

John E. Anderson Graduate School of Management
Dr. John Mamer, Dean
Program in:
management • MBA, MS, PhD

School of Engineering and Applied Science
Dr. Stephen E. Jacobsen, Associate Dean, Academic and Student Affairs
Programs in:
aerospace engineering • MS, PhD
biomedical engineering • MS, PhD
ceramics engineering • MS, PhD
chemical engineering • MS, PhD
computer science • MS, PhD
electrical engineering • MS, PhD
engineering and applied science • MS, PhD
environmental engineering • MS, PhD
geotechnical engineering • MS, PhD
manufacturing engineering • MS
mechanical engineering • MS, PhD
metallurgy • MS, PhD
operations research • MS, PhD
structures • MS, PhD
water resource systems engineering • MS, PhD

School of Nursing
Marie J. Cowan, Acting Dean
Program in:
nursing • MSN, PhD

School of Public Health
Dr. Linda Rosenstock, Dean
Programs in:
biostatistics • MS, PhD
environmental health sciences • MS, PhD
environmental science and engineering • D Env
epidemiology • MS, PhD
health services • MS, PhD
molecular toxicology • PhD
public health • MS, PhD
public health for health professionals • MPH

School of Public Policy and Social Research
Barbara Nelson, Dean
Programs in:
public policy • MPP
public policy and social research • MA, MPP, MSW, PhD
social welfare • MSW, PhD
urban planning • MA, PhD

School of the Arts and Architecture
Dr. Daniel Neuman, Dean
Programs in:
architecture and urban design • M Arch, MA, PhD
art • MA, MFA
arts and architecture • M Arch, MA, MFA, MM, DMA, PhD
composition • MA, PhD
culture and performance • MA, PhD
dance • MA, MFA
design/media arts • MFA
ethnomusicology • MA, PhD
performance • MM, DMA

School of Theater, Film and Television
Robert Rosen, Dean
Programs in:
film and television • MA, MFA, PhD
film, television, and digital media • MA, MFA, PhD
theater • MFA, PhD

School of Dentistry
Dr. Wyatt R. Hume, Dean
Programs in:
dentistry • DDS, MS, PhD, Certificate
oral biology • MS, PhD

School of Law
Dr. Jonathan Varat, Dean
Program in:
law • JD, LL M

School of Medicine
Dr. Gerald S. Levey, Dean/Provost
Program in:
medicine • MD, MA, MS, PhD

Graduate Programs in Medicine
David I. Meyer, Associate Dean
Programs in:
anatomy and cell biology • PhD
biological chemistry • MS, PhD
biomathematics • MS, PhD
biomedical physics • MS, PhD
experimental pathology • MS, PhD
human genetics • MS, PhD
medicine • MA, MS, PhD
microbiology and immunology • MS, PhD
molecular and medical pharmacology • MS, PhD
molecular, cell and developmental biology • MA, PhD
neuroscience • PhD
physiology • MS, PhD

■ UNIVERSITY OF CALIFORNIA, RIVERSIDE
Riverside, CA 92521-0102
http://www.ucr.edu/

State-supported, coed, university. CGS member. *Enrollment:* 1,394 full-time matriculated graduate/professional students (662 women), 45 part-time matriculated graduate/professional students (13 women). *Graduate faculty:* 470 full-time (110 women). *Computer facilities:* 600 computers available on campus for general student use. A campuswide network can be accessed from student residence rooms and from off campus. Internet access and online class registration are available. *Library facilities:* Tomás Rivera Library plus 6 others. *Graduate expenses:* Tuition, state resident: full-time $5,098; part-time $3,649 per year. Tuition, nonresident: full-time $15,282; part-time $8,613 per year. Full-time tuition and fees vary according to degree level. Part-time tuition and fees vary according to course load. *General application contact:* Graduate Admissions, 909-787-3313.

Find an in-depth description at www.petersons.com/graduate.

Graduate Division
Dr. Neal Schiller, Dean

A. Gary Anderson Graduate School of Management
Donald Dye, Dean
Program in:
management • MBA

College of Engineering
Dr. Satish K. Tripathi, Dean
Programs in:
chemical and environmental engineering • MS, PhD
computer science • MS, PhD
electrical engineering • MS, PhD
engineering • MS, PhD

College of Humanities, Arts and Social Sciences
Dr. Patricia O'Brien, Dean
Programs in:
anthropology • MA, MS, PhD
archival management • MA
art history • MA
comparative literature • MA, PhD
dance history and theory • PhD
economics • MA, PhD
English • MA, PhD
historic preservation • MA
history • MA, PhD
humanities, arts and social sciences • MA, MS, PhD
museum curatorship • MA
music • MA
philosophy • MA, PhD
political science • MA, PhD
psychology • PhD
sociology • PhD
Spanish • MA, PhD

College of Natural and Agricultural Sciences
Dr. Michael Clegg, Dean
Programs in:
applied mathematics • MS
applied statistics • PhD
biochemistry and molecular biology • MS, PhD
biology • MS, PhD
biomedical sciences • PhD
botany • MS
cell, molecular, and developmental biology • MS, PhD
chemistry • MS, PhD
entomology • MS, PhD
environmental sciences • MS, PhD

University of California, Riverside (continued)

- environmental toxicology • MS, PhD
- genomics and bioinformatics • PhD
- geological sciences • MS, PhD
- mathematics • MA, MS, PhD
- microbiology • MS, PhD
- molecular genetics, evolutionary and population genetics • PhD
- natural and agricultural sciences • MA, MS, PhD
- neuroscience • PhD
- physics • MS, PhD
- plant biology • PhD
- plant biology • plant genetics • PhD
- plant pathology • MS, PhD
- plant science • MS
- soil and water sciences • MS, PhD
- statistics • MS

School of Education
Dr. Robert Calfee, Dean
Program in:

- education • MA, PhD

■ UNIVERSITY OF CALIFORNIA, SAN DIEGO

La Jolla, CA 92093
http://www.ucsd.edu/

State-supported, coed, university. CGS member. *Enrollment:* 3,119 matriculated graduate/professional students (1,206 women). *Graduate faculty:* 1,800. *Computer facilities:* 1,020 computers available on campus for general student use. A campuswide network can be accessed from student residence rooms and from off campus. Internet access and online class registration, e-mail are available. *Library facilities:* Geisel Library plus 7 others. *Graduate expenses:* Tuition, nonresident: full-time $10,434. Required fees: $4,883. *General application contact:* Graduate Admissions Office, 858-534-1193.

Graduate Studies and Research

Richard Attiyeh, Dean
Programs in:

- acting • MFA
- aerospace engineering • MS, PhD
- anthropology • PhD
- applied mathematics • MA
- applied mechanics • MS, PhD
- applied ocean science • MS, PhD
- applied physics • MS, PhD
- bilingual education • MA
- bioengineering • M Eng, MS, PhD
- bioinformatics • PhD
- biological oceanography • MS, PhD
- biophysics • MS, PhD
- chemical engineering • MS, PhD
- chemistry • MS, PhD
- clinical psychology • PhD
- cognitive science • PhD
- cognitive science/anthropology • PhD
- cognitive science/communication • PhD
- cognitive science/computer science and engineering • PhD
- cognitive science/linguistics • PhD
- cognitive science/neuroscience • PhD
- cognitive science/philosophy • PhD
- cognitive science/psychology • PhD
- cognitive science/sociology • PhD
- communication • MA, PhD
- communication theory and systems • MS, PhD
- comparative literature • MA, PhD
- computer engineering • MS, PhD
- computer science • MS, PhD
- curriculum design • MA
- design • MFA
- directing • MFA
- drama and theatre • PhD
- economics • PhD
- economics and international affairs • PhD
- electrical engineering • M Eng
- electronic circuits and systems • MS, PhD
- engineering physics • MS, PhD
- ethnic studies • PhD
- French literature • MA, PhD
- geochemistry and marine chemistry • MS, PhD
- German literature • MA, PhD
- history • MA, PhD
- intelligent systems, robotics and control • MS, PhD
- Judaic studies • MA
- language and communicative disorders • PhD
- Latin American studies • MA
- linguistics • PhD
- literature • PhD
- literatures in English • MA, PhD
- marine biology • MS, PhD
- materials science • MS, PhD
- mathematics • MA, PhD
- mathematics and science education • PhD
- mechanical engineering • MS, PhD
- music • MA, DMA, PhD
- philosophy • PhD
- photonics • MS, PhD
- physical oceanography and geological sciences • MS, PhD
- physics • MS, PhD
- physics/materials physics • MS
- playwriting • MFA
- political science • PhD
- political science and international affairs • PhD
- psychology • PhD
- public health and epidemiology • PhD
- science studies • PhD
- signal and image processing • MS, PhD
- sociology • PhD
- Spanish literature • MA, PhD
- stage management • MFA
- statistics • MS
- structural engineering • MS, PhD
- theatre • PhD
- visual arts • MFA

Division of Biology
Dr. Eduardo Macagno, Dean
Programs in:

- biochemistry • PhD
- biology • MS
- cell and developmental biology • PhD
- computational neurobiology • PhD
- ecology, behavior, and evolution • PhD
- genetics and molecular biology • PhD
- immunology, virology, and cancer biology • PhD
- molecular and cellular biology • PhD
- neurobiology • PhD
- plant molecular biology • PhD
- signal transduction • PhD

Graduate School of International Relations and Pacific Studies
Dr. Andrew MacIntyre, Interim Dean
Programs in:

- economics and international affairs • PhD
- Pacific international affairs • MPIA
- political science and international affairs • PhD

School of Medicine

Programs in:

- cell and molecular biology • PhD
- • medical scientist training
- medicine • MD, PhD
- molecular pathology • PhD
- neuroscience • PhD
- neurosciences • PhD
- pharmacology • PhD
- physiology • PhD
- regulatory biology • PhD

■ UNIVERSITY OF CALIFORNIA, SAN FRANCISCO

San Francisco, CA 94143
http://www.ucsf.edu/

State-supported, coed, graduate-only institution. CGS member. *General application contact:* Dean of Graduate Studies, 415-476-2310.

Graduate Division
Programs in:
- anatomy • PhD
- biochemistry and molecular biology • PhD
- bioengineering • PhD
- biophysics • PhD
- cell biology • PhD
- developmental biology • PhD
- endocrinology • PhD
- experimental pathology • PhD
- genetics • PhD
- history of health sciences • MA, PhD
- medical anthropology • PhD
- microbiology and immunology • PhD
- neuroscience • PhD
- oral biology • MS, PhD
- physical therapy • MPT
- physiology • PhD

School of Nursing
Programs in:
- nursing • MS, PhD
- sociology • PhD

School of Dentistry
Program in:
- dentistry • DDS

School of Medicine
Dr. Haile T. Debas, Dean
Program in:
- medicine • MD

School of Pharmacy
Mary Anne Koda Kimble, Dean
Programs in:
- biological and medical informatics • MS, PhD
- chemistry and chemical biology • PhD
- pharmaceutical sciences and pharmacogenomics • PhD
- pharmacy • Pharm D, MS, PhD

■ UNIVERSITY OF CALIFORNIA, SANTA BARBARA

Santa Barbara, CA 93106
http://www.ucsb.edu/

State-supported, coed, university. CGS member. *Computer facilities:* 3,000 computers available on campus for general student use. A campuswide network can be accessed from off campus. *Library facilities:* Davidson Library. *General application contact:* Director of Graduate Outreach Admissions and Retention, 805-893-3803.

Graduate Division

College of Engineering
Programs in:
- chemical engineering • MS, PhD
- computer science • MS, PhD
- electrical and computer engineering • MS, PhD
- engineering • MS, PhD
- materials • MS, PhD
- mechanical and environmental engineering • MS, PhD

College of Letters and Sciences
Programs in:
- anthropology • MA, PhD
- applied mathematics • MA
- art history • MA, PhD
- art studio • MFA
- biochemistry and molecular biology • PhD
- chemistry and biochemistry • MA, MS, PhD
- classics • MA, PhD
- communication • PhD
- comparative literature • MA, PhD
- dramatic art • MA, PhD
- East Asian languages and cultural studies • MA
- ecology, evolution, and marine biology • MA, PhD
- economics • MA, PhD
- English • PhD
- French • MA, PhD
- geography • MA, PhD
- geological sciences • MA, PhD
- geophysics • MS
- Germanic languages and literature • MA, PhD
- Hispanic languages and literature • PhD
- history • MA, PhD
- history of science • PhD
- humanities and fine arts • MA, MFA, MM, DMA, PhD
- Latin American and Iberian studies • MA
- letters and science • MA, MFA, MM, MS, DMA, PhD
- linguistics • PhD
- marine science • MS, PhD
- mathematics • MA, PhD
- mathematics, life, and physical sciences • MA, MS, PhD
- molecular, cellular, and developmental biology • MA, PhD
- music • MA, MM, DMA, PhD
- performance • MM, DMA
- philosophy • PhD
- physics • PhD
- political science • MA, PhD
- Portuguese • MA
- psychology • MA, PhD
- religious studies • MA, PhD
- social science • MA, PhD
- sociology • MA, PhD
- Spanish • MA
- statistics and applied probability • MA, PhD

Donald Bren School of Environmental Science and Management
Program in:
- environmental science and management • MESM, PhD

Graduate School of Education
Programs in:
- clinical/school/counseling psychology • M Ed, PhD
- education • M Ed, MA, PhD
- school psychology • M Ed

■ UNIVERSITY OF CALIFORNIA, SANTA CRUZ

Santa Cruz, CA 95064
http://www.ucsc.edu/

State-supported, coed, university. CGS member. *Computer facilities:* 200 computers available on campus for general student use. A campuswide network can be accessed from student residence rooms and from off campus. Internet access is available. *Library facilities:* McHenry Library plus 9 others. *General application contact:* Graduate Admissions, 831-459-2301.

Graduate Division

Division of Arts
Programs in:
- arts • MA, Certificate
- music • MA
- theatre arts • Certificate

Division of Humanities
Programs in:
- history • PhD
- history of consciousness • PhD
- humanities • MA, PhD
- linguistics • MA, PhD
- literature • MA, PhD

Division of Natural Sciences
Programs in:
- applied mathematics • MA, PhD
- astronomy and astrophysics • PhD
- chemistry • MS, PhD
- computer engineering • MS, PhD
- computer science • MS, PhD
- earth sciences • MS, PhD
- marine sciences • MS
- mathematics • MA, PhD
- molecular, cellular, and developmental biology • PhD
- natural sciences • MA, MS, PhD, Certificate
- ocean sciences • PhD
- physics • MS, PhD
- science communication • Certificate

Division of Social Sciences
Programs in:
- anthropology • MA, PhD

University of California, Santa Cruz (continued)

applied economics • MS
developmental psychology • PhD
education • MA, Certificate
environmental studies • PhD
experimental psychology • PhD
international economics • PhD
social psychology • PhD
social sciences • MA, MS, PhD, Certificate
sociology • PhD

■ UNIVERSITY OF LA VERNE

La Verne, CA 91750-4443
http://www.ulv.edu/

Independent, coed, university. *Enrollment:* 961 full-time matriculated graduate/professional students (633 women), 1,408 part-time matriculated graduate/professional students (845 women). *Graduate faculty:* 54 full-time (25 women), 247 part-time/adjunct (109 women). *Computer facilities:* 150 computers available on campus for general student use. A campuswide network can be accessed from student residence rooms and from off campus. Internet access, on-line grade information are available. *Library facilities:* Wilson Library plus 1 other. *Graduate expenses:* Tuition: full-time $6,480; part-time $360 per semester hour. Required fees: $60. Tuition and fees vary according to course load, degree level and program. *General application contact:* Jo Nell Baker, Director, Graduate Admissions and Academic Services, 909-593-3511 Ext. 4504.

College of Arts and Sciences

Dr. John Gingrich, Dean
Programs in:

arts and sciences • MS, Psy D
clinical-community psychology • Psy D
counseling • MS
counseling in higher education • MS
general counseling • MS
gerontology • MS
marriage, family and child counseling • MS
psychology • Psy D

School of Business and Global Studies

Verne Orr, Interim Dean
Programs in:

accounting • MBA
business and global studies • MBA, MBA-EP, MS
business organizational management • MS
executive management • MBA-EP
finance • MBA, MBA-EP
health services management • MBA
information technology • MBA, MBA-EP
international business • MBA, MBA-EP
leadership • MBA-EP
managed care • MBA
management • MBA, MBA-EP
marketing • MBA, MBA-EP

School of Continuing Education

Dr. James C. Manolis, Dean
Programs in:

advanced teaching • M Ed
business • MBA-EP
continuing education • M Ed, MBA-EP, MHA, MS, Credential
cross cultural language and academic development • Credential
educational management • M Ed
multiple subject • Credential
reading • M Ed
school counseling • MS
single subject • Credential

School of Education and Organizational Leadership

Dr. Leonard Pellicer, Dean
Programs in:

advanced teaching skills • M Ed
child development • MS
child development/child life • MS
child life • MS
education • M Ed
education (special emphasis) • M Ed
education and organizational leadership • M Ed, MS, Ed D, Credential
educational leadership • Ed D
educational management • M Ed, Credential
leadership and management • MS
preliminary administrative services • Credential
professional administrative services • Credential
pupil personnel services • Credential
reading • M Ed, Credential
reading and language arts specialist • Credential
school counseling • MS, Credential
teacher education • Credential

School of Public Affairs and Health Administration

Dr. Jack W. Meek, Dean
Programs in:

business administration • MS
counseling • MS
gerontology • MS
gerontology administration • MS
health administration • MHA
health services management • MS
healthcare information management • MHA
managed care • MHA
public administration • MPA, MS, DPA
public affairs and health administration • MHA, MPA, MS, DPA

■ UNIVERSITY OF REDLANDS

Redlands, CA 92373-0999
http://www.redlands.edu/

Independent, coed, comprehensive institution. *Computer facilities:* 277 computers available on campus for general student use. A campuswide network can be accessed from student residence rooms and from off campus. Internet access is available. *Library facilities:* Armacost Library.

Alfred North Whitehead College for Lifelong Learning

Programs in:

administrative services • MA
business administration • MBA
curriculum and instruction • MA
management and business • MAHRM, MBA
management and human resources • MAHRM
pupil personnel services • MA

Graduate Studies

Program in:

communicative disorders • MS

School of Music

Program in:

music • MM

■ UNIVERSITY OF SAN DIEGO

San Diego, CA 92110-2492
http://www.sandiego.edu/

Independent-religious, coed, university. CGS member. *Enrollment:* 1,175 full-time matriculated graduate/professional students (630 women), 863 part-time matriculated graduate/professional students (473 women). *Graduate faculty:* 159 full-time (64 women), 135 part-time/adjunct (65 women). *Computer facilities:* 260 computers available on campus for general student use. A campuswide network can be accessed from student residence rooms and from off campus. Internet access and online class registration are available. *Library facilities:* Helen K. and James S. Copley Library plus 1 other. *Graduate expenses:* Tuition: full-time $12,150; part-time $675 per credit. Tuition and fees vary according to course load and degree level. *General application contact:* Mary Jane Tiernan, Director of Graduate Admissions, 619-260-4524.

Find an in-depth description at www.petersons.com/graduate.

College of Arts and Sciences
Dr. Patrick Drinan, Dean
Programs in:
- arts and sciences • MA, MFA, MS
- dramatic arts • MFA
- history • MA
- international relations • MA
- marine science • MS
- pastoral care and counseling • MA
- practical theology • MA

Hahn School of Nursing and Health Sciences
Dr. Janet Rodgers, Dean
Programs in:
- adult nurse practitioner • MSN, Post Master's Certificate
- case management for vulnerable populations • MSN
- family nurse practitioner • MSN, Post Master's Certificate
- health care systems • MSN
- nursing science • PhD
- pediatric nurse practitioner • MSN, Post Master's Certificate

School of Business Administration
Dr. Curtis Cook, Dean
Programs in:
- business administration • IMBA, MBA
- electronic commerce • MSEC
- executive leadership • MSEL
- global leadership • MSGL

School of Education
Dr. Paula A. Cordeiro, Dean
Programs in:
- counseling • MA
- education • M Ed, MA, MAT, Ed D
- educational leadership • M Ed
- leadership studies • MA, Ed D
- learning and teaching • M Ed, MAT, Ed D
- marital and family therapy • MA

School of Law
Daniel B. Rodriguez, Dean
Programs in:
- business and corporate law • LL M
- comparative law • LL M
- general studies • LL M
- international law • LL M
- law • JD
- taxation • LL M, Diploma

■ UNIVERSITY OF SAN FRANCISCO
San Francisco, CA 94117-1080
http://www.usfca.edu/

Independent-religious, coed, university. *Enrollment:* 2,069 full-time matriculated graduate/professional students (1,227 women), 747 part-time matriculated graduate/professional students (443 women). *Graduate faculty:* 459. *Computer facilities:* 250 computers available on campus for general student use. A campuswide network can be accessed from student residence rooms and from off campus. Internet access and online class registration are available. *Library facilities:* Gleeson Library plus 2 others. *Graduate expenses:* Tuition: full-time $13,248; part-time $746 per unit. Tuition and fees vary according to degree level, campus/location and program. *General application contact:* 415-422-6563.

Find an in-depth description at www.petersons.com/graduate.

College of Arts and Sciences
Dr. Stanley Nel, Dean
Programs in:
- arts and sciences • MA, MFA, MS
- Asia Pacific studies • MA
- biology • MS
- chemistry • MS
- computer science • MS
- economics • MA
- environmental management • MS
- sports and fitness management • MA
- theology • MA
- writing • MA, MFA

College of Professional Studies
Dr. Larry Brewster, Dean
Programs in:
- health services administration • MPA
- human resources and organization development • MHROD
- information systems • MS
- nonprofit administration • MNA
- professional studies • MHROD, MNA, MPA, MS
- public administration • MPA

Graduate School of Management
Dr. Gary Williams, Dean
Programs in:
- executive business administration • EMBA
- finance and banking • MBA
- international business • MBA
- management • MBA
- marketing • MBA
- professional business administration • MBA
- telecommunications management and policy • MBA

School of Education
Dr. Paul Warren, Dean
Programs in:
- Catholic school teaching • MA
- counseling • MA
- counseling psychology • Psy D
- education • MA, Ed D, Psy D
- educational technology • MA
- international and multicultural education • MA, Ed D
- learning and instruction • MA, Ed D
- multicultural literature for children and young adults • MA
- organization and leadership • MA, Ed D
- private school administration • Ed D
- teaching English as a second language • MA

School of Law
Jeffrey Brand, Dean
Program in:
- law • JD

School of Nursing
Dr. John Lantz, Dean
Programs in:
- advanced practice nursing-nurse practitioner and clinical nurse specialist • MSN
- nursing administration • MSN

■ UNIVERSITY OF SOUTHERN CALIFORNIA
Los Angeles, CA 90089
http://www.usc.edu/

Independent, coed, university. CGS member. *Enrollment:* 9,390 full-time matriculated graduate/professional students (4,499 women), 3,778 part-time matriculated graduate/professional students (1,570 women). *Graduate faculty:* 1,614 full-time (435 women), 818 part-time/adjunct (539 women). *Computer facilities:* 2,300 computers available on campus for general student use. A campuswide network can be accessed from student residence rooms and from off campus. Internet access, on-line degree progress, grades, financial aid summary are available. *Library facilities:* Doheny Memorial Library plus 22 others. *Graduate expenses:* Tuition: full-time $23,664; part-time $797 per semester hour. Required fees: $460. Part-time tuition and fees vary according to course

University of Southern California (continued)

load, program and student level. *General application contact:* Dr. Jonathan Kotler, Dean of Graduate Studies, 213-740-9033.

Find an in-depth description at www.petersons.com/graduate.

Graduate School

Dr. Jonathan Kotler, Director, Graduate and Professional Programs

Annenberg School for Communication
Programs in:
broadcast journalism • MA
communication • MA, PhD
communication management • MA
international journalism • MA, Certificate
print journalism • MA
public relations • MA

College of Letters, Arts and Sciences
Joseph Aoun, Dean
Programs in:
anthropology • PhD
applied demography • MS
applied mathematics • MA, MS, PhD
art history • MA, PhD, Certificate
chemical physics • PhD
chemistry • MA, MS, PhD
classics • MA, PhD
clinical psychology • PhD
comparative literature • MA, PhD
computational linguistics • MS
earth sciences • MS, PhD
East Asian languages and cultures • MA, PhD
East Asian studies • MA
economic development programming • MA
economics • MA, PhD
English • MA, PhD
environmental studies • MA, MS
French • MA, PhD
geography • MA, MS, PhD
history • MA, PhD
international relations • MA, PhD
kinesiology • MA, MS, PhD
letters, arts and sciences • MA, MPW, MS, PhD, Certificate
linguistics • MA, PhD
marine biology and biological oceanography • MS, PhD
marriage and family therapy • PhD
mathematics • MA, PhD
molecular biology • MS, PhD
neurobiology • PhD
neuroscience • PhD
philosophy • MA, PhD
physics • MA, MS, PhD
political economy • MA
political economy and public policy • PhD
political science • MA, PhD
professional writing • MPW
psychology • MA, PhD
Slavic languages and literatures • MA, PhD
social anthropology • PhD
social ethics • MA, PhD
sociology • MA, MS, PhD
statistics • MS
visual anthropology • MA

Leonard Davis School of Gerontology
Dr. Elizabeth Zelinski, Dean
Program in:
gerontology • MS, PhD, Certificate

Marshall School of Business
Dr. Randolph Westerfield, Dean
Programs in:
accounting • M Acc
business • M Acc, MBA, MBT, MS, PhD
business administration • MBA, MS, PhD
business taxation • MBT
finance and business economics • MBA
information and operations management • MS
international business • MBA

School of Architecture
Dr. Robert Timme, Dean
Programs in:
architecture • M Arch
building science • MBS
landscape architecture • ML Arch

School of Cinema-Television
Dr. Elizabeth Daley, Dean
Programs in:
cinema-television • MA, MFA, PhD
critical studies • MA, PhD
film and video production • MFA
film, video, and computer animation • MFA
interactive media • MFA
producing • MFA
screen and television writing • MFA

School of Education
Dr. Guilbert Hentschke, Dean
Programs in:
administration and policy • PhD
college student personnel services • MS
communication handicapped • MS
counseling psychology • MS, PhD
curriculum and instruction • Ed D, PhD
curriculum and teaching • MS
education • MS, Ed D, PhD, MFCC
educational leadership • MS
educational psychology • PhD
instructional technology • MS
international and intercultural education • MS
language, literacy, and learning • PhD
learning handicapped • MS
marriage, family and child counseling • MFCC
pupil personnel services (K–12) • MS
teaching English as a second language • MS

School of Engineering
Dr. Leonard Silverman, Dean
Programs in:
aerospace and mechanical engineering • MS, PhD, Engr
applied mechanics • MS
biomedical engineering • MS, PhD
biomedical imaging and telemedicine • MS
chemical engineering • MS, PhD, Engr
civil engineering • MS, PhD, Engr
computer aided engineering • ME, Certificate
computer engineering • MS, PhD
computer networks • MS
computer science • MS, PhD
construction engineering • MS
construction management • MCM
earthquake engineering • MS
electrical engineering • MS, PhD, Engr
engineering • MCM, ME, MS, PhD, Certificate, Engr
engineering management • MS
environmental engineering • MS, PhD
industrial and systems engineering • MS, PhD, Engr
manufacturing engineering • MS
materials engineering • MS
materials science • MS, PhD, Engr
multimedia and creative technologies • MS
ocean engineering • MS
operations research • MS
petroleum engineering • MS, PhD, Engr
robotics and automation • MS
software engineering • MS
soil mechanics and foundations • MS
structural engineering • MS
structural mechanics • MS
systems architecture and engineering • MS
transportation engineering • MS
VLSI design • MS
water resources • MS

School of Fine Arts
Ruth Weisberg, Dean
Programs in:
fine arts • MFA, MPAS
public art studies • MPAS

School of Health Affairs
Joseph P. Van Der Meulen, Vice President
Programs in:
biokinesiology • MS, PhD

health affairs • MA, MS, DPT, PhD, Certificate
nursing • MS, Certificate
occupational science • PhD
occupational therapy • MA
physical therapy • MS, DPT

School of Policy, Planning and Development
Dr. Daniel A. Mazmanian, Dean
Programs in:
health administration • MHA
planning • M Pl
planning and development studies • MPDS, DPDS
policy, planning and development • M Pl, MHA, MPA, MPDS, MPP, MRED, DPA, DPDS, PhD, Certificate
public administration • MPA, DPA, PhD, Certificate
public policy • MPP
real estate development • MRED
urban and regional planning • PhD

School of Social Work
Dr. Marilyn S. Flynn, Dean
Program in:
social work • MSW, PhD

School of Theatre
Dr. Robert Scales, Dean
Programs in:
design • MFA
playwriting • MFA

Thorton School of Music
Dr. Larry Livingston, Dean
Programs in:
choral and church music • MM, DMA
conducting • MM
early music performance • MA
historical musicology • PhD
history and literature • MA
jazz • MM
music • MA, MM, MM Ed, DMA, PhD
music education • MM, MM Ed, DMA
performance • MM, DMA
theory and composition • MA, MM, DMA, PhD

Keck School of Medicine
Dr. Stephen J. Ryan, Dean
Program in:
medicine • MD, MPH, MS, PhD

Graduate Programs in Medicine
Dr. John T. Nicoloff, Interim Associate Dean for Scientific Affairs
Programs in:
anatomy and cell biology • MS, PhD
applied biostatistics/epidemiology • MS
biochemistry and molecular biology • MS, PhD
biometry/epidemiology • MPH
biostatistics • MS, PhD
cell and neurobiology • MS, PhD
epidemiology • PhD
experimental and molecular pathology • MS
health behavior research • MPH, PhD
health promotion • MPH
medicine • MPH, MS, PhD
molecular biology and epidemiological methods • MS
molecular microbiology and immunology • MS, PhD
pathobiology • PhD
physiology and biophysics • MS, PhD
preventive nutrition • MPH
public health • MPH

Law School
Dr. Matthew L. Spitzer, Dean
Program in:
law • JD

School of Dentistry
Dr. Harold Slavkin, Dean
Programs in:
craniofacial biology • MS, PhD
dentistry • DDS, MS, PhD, Certificate

School of Pharmacy
Dr. Timothy M. Chan, Dean
Programs in:
molecular pharmacology and toxicology • MS, PhD
pharmaceutical economics and policy • MS, PhD
pharmaceutical sciences • MS, PhD
pharmacy • Pharm D, MS, PhD
regulatory sciences • MS

■ UNIVERSITY OF THE PACIFIC

Stockton, CA 95211-0197
http://www.uop.edu/

Independent, coed, university. CGS member. *Enrollment:* 1,927 full-time matriculated graduate/professional students (1,043 women), 557 part-time matriculated graduate/professional students (291 women). *Graduate faculty:* 378 full-time, 230 part-time/adjunct. *Computer facilities:* 274 computers available on campus for general student use. A campuswide network can be accessed from student residence rooms and from off campus. Internet access and online class registration are available. *Library facilities:* Holt Memorial Library plus 1 other. *General application contact:* Dr. Denis J. Meerdink, Research and Graduate Studies, 209-946-2261.

Graduate School
Dr. Denis J. Meerdink, Dean
Programs in:
biochemistry • MS, PhD
biological sciences • MS
chemistry • MS, PhD
communication • MA
physical therapy • MS
psychology • MA
speech-language pathology • MA
sport sciences • MA

Conservatory of Music
Dr. Steven Anderson, Dean
Program in:
music • MA, MM

Eberhardt School of Business
Dr. Mark Plovnick, Dean
Program in:
business • MBA

School of Education
Dr. Jack Nagle, Dean
Programs in:
counseling • MA
counseling psychology • Ed D
curriculum and instruction • MA
education • M Ed
educational administration and foundations • MA, Ed D
educational psychology • MA, Ed D
educational research • MA
school psychology • Ed D

McGeorge School of Law
John G. Sprankling, Dean
Programs in:
government and public policy • LL M
international waters resources law • LL M, JSD
law • JD
transnational business practice • LL M

School of Dentistry
Dr. Arthur A. Dugoni, Dean
Programs in:
dentistry • DDS, MSD
international dental studies • DDS
orthodontics • MSD

School of Pharmacy
Dr. Philip Oppenheimer, Dean
Programs in:
biopharmaceutics/pharmacokinetics • MS, PhD
clinical pharmacy • MS, PhD
industrial pharmacy • MS, PhD
medicinal chemistry • MS, PhD
nuclear pharmacy • MS, PhD
Pharmaceutical Sciences • MS, PhD
pharmaceutics and medicinal chemistry • MS, PhD
pharmacology • MS, PhD
pharmacy • Pharm D, MS, PhD

University of the Pacific (continued)
pharmacy practice • MS, PhD
physiology • MS, PhD
physiology/pharmacology • MS, PhD

■ WOODBURY UNIVERSITY

Burbank, CA 91504-1099
http://www.woodbury.edu/

Independent, coed, comprehensive institution. *Computer facilities:* 116 computers available on campus for general student use. A campuswide network can be accessed from off campus. Internet access is available. *Library facilities:* Los Angeles Times Library. *General application contact:* Graduate Admissions Assistant, 818-767-0888 Ext. 264.

Business Administration Program

Program in:
business administration • MBA

Colorado

■ ADAMS STATE COLLEGE

Alamosa, CO 81102
http://www.adams.edu/

State-supported, coed, comprehensive institution. *Computer facilities:* 261 computers available on campus for general student use. A campuswide network can be accessed from student residence rooms and from off campus. Internet access and online class registration are available. *Library facilities:* Nielsen Library. *General application contact:* Dean of Graduate Studies, 719-587-7936.

Graduate Studies

School of Arts and Letters
Programs in:
art • MA
arts and letters • MA

School of Education and Graduate Studies
Programs in:
counseling • MA
education and graduate studies • MA
elementary education • MA
health, physical education, and recreation • MA
secondary education • MA
special education • MA

■ COLORADO CHRISTIAN UNIVERSITY

Lakewood, CO 80226-7499
http://www.ccu.edu/

Independent-religious, coed, comprehensive institution. *Computer facilities:* 13 computers available on campus for general student use. A campuswide network can be accessed from student residence rooms and from off campus. Internet access is available. *Library facilities:* Clifton Fowler Library plus 1 other. *General application contact:* Director of Graduate Studies, 303-963-3404.

Program in Counseling

Program in:
biblical counseling • MA

Program in Curriculum and Instruction

Program in:
curriculum and instruction • MA

■ COLORADO STATE UNIVERSITY

Fort Collins, CO 80523-0015
http://www.colostate.edu/

State-supported, coed, university. CGS member. *Enrollment:* 2,286 full-time matriculated graduate/professional students (1,293 women), 1,751 part-time matriculated graduate/professional students (881 women). *Graduate faculty:* 993 full-time (247 women). *Computer facilities:* A campuswide network can be accessed from student residence rooms and from off campus. Internet access is available. *Library facilities:* William E. Morgan Library plus 3 others. *Graduate expenses:* Tuition, state resident: full-time $1,386; part-time $154 per credit. Tuition, nonresident: full-time $5,439; part-time $604 per credit. Required fees: $33 per semester. *General application contact:* Graduate School, 970-491-6817.

College of Veterinary Medicine and Biomedical Sciences

Dr. James L. Voss, Dean
Programs in:
anatomy and neurobiology • MS, PhD
cell and molecular biology • MS, PhD
cellular and molecular biology • MS, PhD
clinical sciences • MS, PhD
environmental health • MS, PhD
health physics • MS, PhD
immunology • MS, PhD
mammalian radiobiology • MS, PhD
microbiology • MS, PhD
nuclear-waste management • MS
pathology • MS, PhD
physiology • MS, PhD
radiobiology • MS
radioecology • MS, PhD
radiological health sciences • MS, PhD
radiology • MS, PhD
veterinary medicine • DVM
veterinary medicine and biomedical sciences • DVM, MS, PhD
veterinary radiology • MS

Graduate School

James L. Fry, Dean
Programs in:
cell and molecular biology • MS, PhD
ecology • MS, PhD

College of Agricultural Sciences
Dr. James C. Heird, Associate Dean
Programs in:
agricultural and resource economics • M Agr, MS, PhD
agricultural sciences • M Agr, MS, PhD
animal breeding and genetics • MS, PhD
animal nutrition • MS, PhD
animal reproduction • MS, PhD
animal sciences • M Agr
crop science • MS, PhD
entomology • MS, PhD
floriculture • M Agr, MS, PhD
horticultural food crops • M Agr, MS, PhD
livestock handling • MS, PhD
meats • MS, PhD
nursery and landscape management • M Agr, MS, PhD
plant genetics • MS, PhD
plant pathology • MS, PhD
plant physiology • MS, PhD
production management • MS, PhD
soil science • MS, PhD
turf management • M Agr, MS, PhD
weed science • MS, PhD

College of Applied Human Sciences
Nancy Hartley, Dean
Programs in:
apparel and merchandising • MS
applied human sciences • M Ed, MS, MSW, PhD
automotive pollution control • MS
construction management • MS
education and human resource studies • M Ed, PhD
food science • MS, PhD
health and exercise science • MS
historic preservation • MS

human development and family studies • MS
industrial technology management • MS
interior design • MS
nutrition • MS, PhD
occupational therapy • MS
social work • MSW
student affairs • MS
technology education and training • MS
technology of industry • PhD

College of Business
Dr. Daniel Costello, Dean
Programs in:
accounting • MS
business • MBA, MS
business administration • MBA
computer information systems • MS
management • MBA, MS

College of Engineering
Dr. Neal Gallagher, Dean
Programs in:
atmospheric science • MS, PhD
bioengineering • MS, PhD
bioresource and agricultural engineering • MS, PhD
chemical engineering • MS, PhD
electrical and computer engineering • M Elec E, MS, PhD
energy and environmental engineering • MS, PhD
energy conversion • MS, PhD
engineering • M Elec E, MS, PhD
engineering management • MS
environmental engineering • MS, PhD
heat and mass transfer • MS, PhD
hydraulics and wind engineering • MS, PhD
industrial and manufacturing systems engineering • MS, PhD
mechanical engineering • MS, PhD
mechanics and materials • MS, PhD
structural and geotechnical engineering • MS, PhD
water resources planning and management • MS, PhD
water resources, hydrologic and environmental sciences • MS, PhD

College of Liberal Arts
Robert Hoffert, Dean
Programs in:
American history • MA
anthropology • MA
applied music • MM
archival science • MA
Asian history • MA
communication development • MA
conducting • MM
creative writing • MFA
drawing • MFA
economics • MA, PhD
English • MA
English as a second language • MA
European history • MA
fibers • MFA
French • MA
French/TESL • MA
German • MA
German/TESL • MA
graphic design • MFA
historic preservation • MA
Latin American history • MA
liberal arts • MA, MFA, MM, MS, PhD
literature • MA
metalsmithing • MFA
music education • MM
music history and literature • MM
music theory • MM
music therapy • MM
painting • MFA
philosophy • MA
political science • MA, PhD
printmaking • MFA
sculpture • MFA
sociology • MA, PhD
Spanish • MA
Spanish/TESL • MA
speech communication • MA
teaching • MA
technical communication • MS

College of Natural Resources
A. A. Dyer, Dean
Programs in:
commercial recreation and tourism • MS
earth resources • PhD
fishery and wildlife biology • MS, PhD
fluvial geomorphology • MS
forestry • MF, MS, PhD
geology • MS, PhD
human dimensions in natural resources • PhD
hydrogeology • MS
natural resources • MF, MS, PhD
petrology/geochemistry and economic geology • MS
rangeland ecosystem science • MS, PhD
recreation resource management • MS, PhD
resource interpretation • MS
stratigraphy/sedimentology • MS
structure/tectonics • MS
watershed science • MS, PhD

College of Natural Sciences
John C. Raich, Dean
Programs in:
biochemistry and molecular biology • MS, PhD
botany • MS, PhD
chemistry • MS, PhD
computer science • MS, PhD
counseling psychology • PhD
general/experimental psychology • PhD
industrial-organizational psychology • PhD
mathematics • MS, PhD
natural sciences • MS, PhD
physics • MS, PhD
statistics • MS, PhD
zoology • MS, PhD

■ COLORADO TECHNICAL UNIVERSITY

Colorado Springs, CO 80907-3896

http://www.coloradotech.edu

Proprietary, coed, comprehensive institution. *Computer facilities:* 130 computers available on campus for general student use. A campuswide network can be accessed from off campus. Internet access is available. *Library facilities:* Colorado Technical University Library. *General application contact:* Graduate Admissions, 719-590-6720.

Graduate Studies
Programs in:
business administration • MBA
business management • MSM
computer engineering • MSCE
computer science • MSCS, DCS
electrical engineering • MSEE
health science management • MSM
human resources management • MSM
logistics management • MSM
management • DM
management information systems • MSM
organizational leadership • MSM

■ REGIS UNIVERSITY

Denver, CO 80221-1099

http://www.regis.edu/

Independent-religious, coed, comprehensive institution. *Enrollment:* 3,500 matriculated graduate/professional students. *Graduate faculty:* 575. *Computer facilities:* 300 computers available on campus for general student use. A campuswide network can be accessed from student residence rooms and from off campus. *Library facilities:* Dayton Memorial Library. *Graduate expenses:* Tuition: part-time $310 per credit. *General application contact:* 303-458-4080.

Find an in-depth description at www.petersons.com/graduate.

Regis College
Dr. Steve Doty, Dean
Program in:
education • MA

Regis University (continued)

School for Healthcare Professions
Dr. Patricia Ladewig, Academic Dean
Programs in:
healthcare professions • MSN, MSPT, DPT
nursing • MSN
physical therapy • DPT

School for Professional Studies
Dr. Jim Dorris, Acting Associate Dean
Programs in:
accounting • MBA
adult learning, training and development • MLS, Certificate
business administration • MBA, Certificate
database technologies • MSCIT, Certificate
e-commerce engineering • MSCIT, Certificate
electronic commerce • MBA
executive international management • Certificate
executive leadership • Certificate
finance • MBA
international business • MBA, Certificate
language and communication • MLS
leadership • Certificate
licensed professional counselor • MLS
management of technology • MSCIT
market strategy • MBA
networking technologies • MSCIT
networking technology • Certificate
nonprofit management • MNM
object-oriented technologies • MSCIT
object-oriented technology • Certificate
operations management • MBA
organizational leadership • MSM
physicians practice • MBA, Certificate
program management • Certificate
project leadership and management • Certificate
psychology • MLS
resource development • Certificate
social science • MLS
strategic business • Certificate
strategic human resource • Certificate
technical communication • Certificate

■ UNIVERSITY OF COLORADO AT BOULDER

Boulder, CO 80309
http://www.colorado.edu/

State-supported, coed, university. CGS member. *Enrollment:* 3,419 full-time matriculated graduate/professional students (1,565 women), 933 part-time matriculated graduate/professional students (449 women). *Graduate faculty:* 1,037 full-time (305 women). *Computer facilities:* 1,700 computers available on campus for general student use. A campuswide network can be accessed from student residence rooms and from off campus. Internet access and online class registration, standard and academic software, student government voting are available. *Library facilities:* Norlin Library plus 5 others.

Graduate School
Carol Lynch, Dean
Programs in:
museum • MS
museum and field studies • MBS

College of Arts and Sciences
Peter D. Spear, Dean
Programs in:
animal behavior • MA, PhD
anthropology • MA, PhD
applied mathematics • MS, PhD
aquatic biology • MA, PhD
art history • MA
arts and sciences • MA, MFA, MS, PhD
astrophysical and geophysical fluid dynamics • MS, PhD
astrophysics • MS, PhD
audiology • MA, PhD
behavioral genetics • MA, PhD
biochemistry • PhD
cellular structure and function • MA, PhD
chemical physics • PhD
chemistry • MS, PhD
Chinese • MA
classics • MA, PhD
communication • MA, PhD
comparative literature • MA, PhD
dance • MFA
developmental biology • MA, PhD
drawing • MFA
ecology • MA, PhD
economics • MA, PhD
English literature • MA, PhD
French • MA, PhD
geography • MA, PhD
geology • MS, PhD
geophysics • PhD
German • MA
history • MA, PhD
international affairs • MA
Japanese • MA
kinesiology • PhD
linguistics • MA, PhD
liquid crystal science and technology • PhD
mathematical physics • PhD
mathematics • MA, MS, PhD
medical physics • PhD
microbiology • MA, PhD
molecular biology • MA, PhD
neurobiology • MA, PhD
optical sciences and engineering • PhD
painting • MFA
philosophy • MA, PhD
photography • MFA
physical education • MS
physics • MS, PhD
plant and animal physiology • MA, PhD
plant and animal systematics • MA, PhD
plasma physics • MS, PhD
political science • MA, PhD
population biology • MA, PhD
population genetics • MA, PhD
printmaking • MFA
psychology • MA, PhD
public policy analysis • MA
religious studies • MA
sculpture • MFA
sociology • MA, PhD
Spanish • MA, PhD
speech-language pathology • MA, PhD
theatre • MA, PhD

College of Engineering and Applied Science
Ross Corotis, Dean
Programs in:
aerospace engineering sciences • ME, MS, PhD
building systems • MS, PhD
chemical engineering • ME, MS, PhD
computer science • ME, MS, PhD
construction engineering and management • MS, PhD
electrical engineering • ME, MS, PhD
engineering and applied science • ME, MS, PhD
engineering management • ME
environmental engineering • MS, PhD
geoenvironmental engineering • MS, PhD
geotechnical engineering • MS, PhD
mechanical engineering • ME, MS, PhD
structural engineering • MS, PhD
telecommunications • ME, MS
water resource engineering • MS, PhD

College of Music
Daniel P. Sher, Dean
Programs in:
church music • M Mus
composition • M Mus, D Mus A
conducting • M Mus, D Mus A
music education • M Mus Ed, PhD
music literature • M Mus
musicology • PhD
pedagogy • M Mus, D Mus A
performance • M Mus, D Mus A

School of Education
Lorrie Shepard, Interim Dean
Programs in:
education • MA, PhD
educational and psychological studies • MA, PhD
instruction and curriculum • MA, PhD
research and evaluation methodologies • PhD
social multicultural and bilingual foundations • MA, PhD

School of Journalism and Mass Communication
Robert Trager, Director, Graduate Program
Programs in:
communication • PhD
integrated marketing communications • MA
mass communication research • MA
media studies • PhD
newsgathering • MA

Graduate School of Business Administration
Larry Singell, Dean
Programs in:
accounting • MS
business administration • MBA, PhD
business self designed • MBA
entrepreneurship • MBA
finance • MBA, PhD
marketing • MBA, PhD
operations management • MBA
organization management • MBA, PhD
real estate • MBA
taxation • MS
technology and innovation management • MBA

School of Law
Harold H. Bruff, Dean
Program in:
law • JD

■ UNIVERSITY OF COLORADO AT COLORADO SPRINGS

Colorado Springs, CO 80933-7150
http://www.uccs.edu/

State-supported, coed, comprehensive institution. *Enrollment:* 869 full-time matriculated graduate/professional students (467 women), 651 part-time matriculated graduate/professional students (358 women). *Graduate faculty:* 167 full-time (57 women), 38 part-time/adjunct (13 women). *Computer facilities:* 350 computers available on campus for general student use. A campuswide network can be accessed from student residence rooms and from off campus. *Library facilities:* University of Colorado at Colorado Springs Kraemer Family Library. *Graduate expenses:* Tuition, state resident: full-time $2,385; part-time $150 per credit. Tuition, nonresident: full-time $8,156; part-time $505 per credit. Required fees: $13 per credit. $141 per semester. One-time fee: $28. Tuition and fees vary according to course load and program. *General application contact:* Laverne Gonzales, Administrative Assistant, 719-262-3417.

Beth-El College of Nursing
Barbara Joyce-Nagata, Chair
Programs in:
adult health nurse practitioner and clinical specialist • MSN
family practitioner • MSN
neonatal nurse practitioner and clinical specialist • MSN

Graduate School
Dr. David Schmidt, Dean

College of Education
Dr. David Nelson, Dean
Programs in:
counseling and human services • MA
curriculum and instruction • MA
educational administration • MA
educational leadership • MA
special education • MA

College of Engineering and Applied Science
Dr. Ronald Sega, Dean
Programs in:
applied mathematics • MS
computer science • MS, PhD
electrical engineering • MS, PhD
engineering and applied science • ME, MS, PhD
engineering management • ME
information operations • ME
manufacturing • ME
mechanical engineering • MS
software engineering • ME
space operations • ME

College of Letters, Arts and Sciences
Dr. Elizabeth Grobsmith, Dean
Programs in:
basic science • MBS
communications • MA
history • MA
letters, arts and sciences • MA, MBS, MS
physics • MBS, MS
psychology • MA
sociology • MA

Graduate School of Business Administration
Dr. Joseph Rallo, Dean
Programs in:
accounting • MBA
finance • MBA
information systems • MBA
marketing • MBA
organizational management • MBA
production management • MBA

Graduate School of Public Affairs
Dr. Kathleen Beatty, Dean
Programs in:
criminal justice • MCJ
public administration • MPA

■ UNIVERSITY OF COLORADO AT DENVER

Denver, CO 80217-3364
http://www.cudenver.edu/

State-supported, coed, university. CGS member. *Enrollment:* 1,340 full-time matriculated graduate/professional students (702 women), 2,667 part-time matriculated graduate/professional students (1,503 women). *Graduate faculty:* 343 full-time (124 women). *Computer facilities:* 577 computers available on campus for general student use. A campuswide network can be accessed from off campus. Internet access and online class registration are available. *Library facilities:* Auraria Library. *Graduate expenses:* Tuition, state resident: full-time $3,158; part-time $190 per credit. Tuition, nonresident: full-time $12,742; part-time $764 per credit. Required fees: $425; $425 per term. One-time fee: $25. *General application contact:* Annette Beck, Program Specialist, 303-556-2663.

College of Architecture and Planning
Patricia O'Leary, Dean
Programs in:
architecture • M Arch
architecture and planning • M Arch, MLA, MUD, MURP, PhD
design and planning • PhD
landscape architecture • MLA
urban and regional planning • MURP
urban design • MUD

Graduate School
Mark Gelernter, Interim Vice Chancellor for Academic and Student Affairs

University of Colorado at Denver (continued)

College of Engineering and Applied Science
Peter Jenkins, Dean
Programs in:
civil engineering • MS, PhD
computer science • MS
electrical engineering • MS
engineering • ME
engineering and applied science • ME, MS, PhD
mechanical engineering • MS

College of Liberal Arts and Sciences
Jim Smith, Dean
Programs in:
anthropology • MA
applied mathematics • MS, PhD
basic science • MBS
biology • MA
chemistry • MS
communication • MA
economics • MA
environmental science • MS
health and behavioral science • PhD
history • MA
humanities • MH
liberal arts and sciences • MA, MBS, MH, MS, MSS, PhD
literature • MA
political science • MA
psychology • MA
social sciences • MSS
sociology • MA
teaching English as a second language • MA
teaching of writing • MA
technical communication • MS

School of Education
G. Thomas Bellamy, Dean
Programs in:
administration, supervision, and curriculum development • MA
counseling psychology and counselor education • MA
curriculum and instruction • MA
early childhood education • MA
education • MA, PhD, Ed S
educational administration, curriculum and supervision • Ed S
educational psychology • MA
information and learning technologies • MA
leadership and innovation • PhD
school psychology • Ed S
special education • MA

Graduate School of Business Administration
Jean Claude Bosch, Dean
Programs in:
accounting • MS
business administration • Exec MBA, Exec MS, MBA, MS, MSIB
finance • MS
health administration • Exec MBA, MS
information systems management • MS
international business • MSIB
management • MS
marketing • MS

Graduate School of Public Affairs
Kathleen Beatty, Dean
Programs in:
criminal justice • MCJ
public administration • Exec MPA, MPA, PhD
public affairs • Exec MPA, MCJ, MPA, PhD

■ UNIVERSITY OF DENVER
Denver, CO 80208
http://www.du.edu/

Independent, coed, university. CGS member. *Enrollment:* 3,490 matriculated graduate/professional students. *Graduate faculty:* 978. *Computer facilities:* 750 computers available on campus for general student use. A campuswide network can be accessed from student residence rooms and from off campus. *Library facilities:* Penrose Library. *Graduate expenses:* Tuition: full-time $20,052; part-time $557 per credit hour. Required fees: $159; $4 per credit hour. Part-time tuition and fees vary according to course load and program. *General application contact:* 360-871-2706.

Find an in-depth description at www.petersons.com/graduate.

College of Education
Dr. Lester F. Goodchild, Dean
Programs in:
counseling psychology • MA, PhD
curriculum and instruction • MA, PhD
educational psychology • MA, PhD, Ed S
higher education and adult studies • MA, PhD
school administration • PhD

College of Law
Mary E. Ricketson, Dean
Programs in:
American and comparative law • LL M
law • JD, LL M, MRLS, MSLA, MT
legal administration • MSLA
natural resources law • LL M, MRLS
taxation • LL M, MT

Daniels College of Business
James R. Griesemer, Dean
Programs in:
business • M Acc, MBA, MIM, MRECM, MS, MSF, MSIT, MSM, MSMC, MSMGEN, MSRTM
business administration • MBA
education management • MSM
finance • MBA, MS, MSF
health care management • MSM
information technology and electronic commerce • MBA, MIM, MSIT
international business/management • MIM
management and communications • MSMC
management and general engineering • MSMGEN
management and telecommunications • MSMC
marketing • MBA, MIM
public health management • MSM
resort and tourism management • MS, MSRTM
sports management • MSM

School of Accountancy
Dr. Ronald Kucic, Director
Programs in:
accountancy • M Acc
accounting • MBA

School of Real Estate and Construction Management
Dr. Mark Levine, Director
Program in:
real estate • MBA

Graduate School of International Studies
Dr. Tom Farer, Dean
Program in:
international studies • MA, MIM, PhD

Graduate School of Professional Psychology
Dr. Peter Buirski, Dean
Program in:
clinical psychology • Psy D

Graduate School of Social Work
Dr. Catherine Alter, Dean
Program in:
social work • MSW, PhD

Graduate Studies
Dr. Barry Hughes, Vice Provost
Program in:
international and intercultural communication • MA

Faculty of Arts and Humanities/Social Sciences
Dr. Gregg Kvistad, Dean
Programs in:

anthropology • MA
applied research and evaluation • MS
art history • MA
art history/museum studies • MA
arts and humanities/social sciences • MA, MFA, MS, PhD
composition • MA
conducting • MA
economics • MA
education • MA
English • MA, PhD
French • MA
German • MA
history • MA
intern studies • MA
Judaic studies • MA
music education • MA
music history and literature • MA
Orff-Schulwerk • MA
performance • MA
philosophy • MA
piano pedagogy • MA
psychology • PhD
religious studies • MA, PhD
sociology • MA, PhD
Spanish • MA
studio art • MFA
Suzuki pedagogy • MA
theory • MA

Faculty of Natural Sciences, Mathematics and Engineering
Dr. Robert Coombe, Dean
Programs in:
applied mathematics • MA, MS
biological sciences • MS, PhD
chemistry • MA, MS, PhD
computer science • MS
computer science and engineering • MS
electrical engineering • MS
geography • MA, PhD
management and general engineering • MSMGEN
materials science • PhD
mathematics and computer science • PhD
mechanical engineering • MS
natural sciences, mathematics and engineering • MA, MS, MSMGEN, PhD
physics and astronomy • MS, PhD

School of Communication
Dr. Michael Wirth, Chairperson
Programs in:
advertising management • MS
communication • MA, MS, PhD
digital media studies • MA
human communication studies • MA, PhD
mass communications • MA
public relations • MS
video production • MA

University College
James R. Griesemer, Dean
Programs in:
applied communication • MSS
computer information systems • MCIS
environmental policy and management • MEPM
healthcare systems • MHS
liberal studies • MLS
library and information services • MLIS
public health • MPH
technology management • MoTM
telecommunications • MTEL

■ UNIVERSITY OF NORTHERN COLORADO

Greeley, CO 80639
http://www.unco.edu/

State-supported, coed, university. CGS member. *Enrollment:* 1,079 full-time matriculated graduate/professional students (775 women), 318 part-time matriculated graduate/professional students (233 women). *Graduate faculty:* 242 full-time (103 women). *Computer facilities:* 1,100 computers available on campus for general student use. A campuswide network can be accessed from student residence rooms and from off campus. Internet access and online class registration are available. *Library facilities:* James A. Michener Library plus 2 others. *Graduate expenses:* Tuition, state resident: full-time $2,451; part-time $136 per credit hour. Tuition, nonresident: full-time $9,961; part-time $593 per credit hour. Required fees: $657; $37 per credit hour. *General application contact:* Dorothy Eckas, Graduate Student Adviser, 970-351-1806.

Find an in-depth description at www.petersons.com/graduate.

Graduate School
Dr. Allen Huang, Associate Vice President for Research and Dean of the Graduate School
Programs in:
interdisciplinary education • MA
interdisciplinary studies • MA, MS, DA, Ed D, Ed S

College of Arts and Sciences
Dr. Sandra Flake, Dean
Programs in:
arts and sciences • MA, PhD
biological education • PhD
biological sciences • MA
chemical education • MA, PhD
chemical research • MA
communication • MA
earth sciences • MA
educational mathematics • MA, PhD
English • MA
history • MA
mathematics • MA, PhD
psychology • MA
sociology • MA
Spanish • MA

College of Education
Dr. Eugene Sheehan, Interim Dean
Programs in:
agency counseling • MA
applied statistics and research methods • MS, PhD
college student personnel administration • PhD
counseling psychology • Psy D
counselor education • Ed D
counselor education and counseling psychology • MA, Ed D, Psy D
early childhood education • MA
education • MA, MS, Ed D, PhD, Psy D, Ed S
education of gifted • MA
educational leadership • MA, Ed D, Ed S
educational media • MA
educational psychology • MA, PhD
educational technology • MA, PhD
elementary education • MA, Ed D
elementary school counseling • MA
reading education • MA
school psychology • PhD, Ed S
secondary and postsecondary school counseling • MA
special education • MA, Ed D

College of Health and Human Sciences
Dr. Vincent Scalia, Dean
Programs in:
communication disorders • MA
community health • MPH
family nurse practitioner • MS
gerontology • MA
health and human sciences • MA, MPH, MS, Ed D, PhD
kinesiology and physical education • MA, Ed D
nursing education • MS
rehabilitation counseling • MA, PhD

College of Performing and Visual Arts
Dr. Kathleen Rountree, Dean
Programs in:
music • MM, MME, DA
performing and visual arts • MA, MM, MME, DA
visual arts • MA

■ UNIVERSITY OF SOUTHERN COLORADO

Pueblo, CO 81001-4901
http://www.uscolo.edu/

State-supported, coed, comprehensive institution. *Enrollment:* 76 full-time matriculated graduate/professional

University of Southern Colorado (continued)
students (35 women), 53 part-time matriculated graduate/professional students (18 women). *Graduate faculty:* 44 full-time (13 women), 4 part-time/adjunct (1 woman). *Computer facilities:* 521 computers available on campus for general student use. A campuswide network can be accessed from student residence rooms and from off campus. Internet access is available. *Library facilities:* University of Southern Colorado Library. *Graduate expenses:* Part-time $93 per credit. Tuition, state resident: full-time $1,674; part-time $93 per credit. Tuition, nonresident: full-time $7,907; part-time $439 per credit. Required fees: $424; $23 per credit. Tuition and fees vary according to program. *General application contact:* Pamela L. Anastassiou, Director, Admissions and Records, 719-549-2461.

College of Education, Engineering and Professional Studies
Dr. Hector R. Carrasco, Dean
Programs in:
- education, engineering and professional studies • MS
- industrial and systems engineering • MS

College of Science and Mathematics
Dr. Ernest E. Allen, Dean
Program in:
- science and mathematics • MS

Hasan School of Business
Dr. Rex D. Fuller, Dean
Program in:
- business • MBA

Program in Applied Natural Science
Program in:
- applied natural science • MS

Connecticut

■ CENTRAL CONNECTICUT STATE UNIVERSITY

New Britain, CT 06050-4010
http://www.ccsu.edu/

State-supported, coed, comprehensive institution. CGS member. *Enrollment:* 529 full-time matriculated graduate/professional students (339 women), 1,576 part-time matriculated graduate/professional students (1,079 women). *Computer facilities:* 230 computers available on campus for general student use. A campuswide network can be accessed from student residence rooms and from off campus. Internet access is available. *Library facilities:* Burritt Library plus 1 other. *Graduate expenses:* Tuition, state resident: full-time $2,668; part-time $195 per credit. Tuition, nonresident: full-time $7,436. Required fees: $1,794. One-time fee: $50 part-time. Part-time tuition and fees vary according to course level and course load. *General application contact:* Kevin Oliva, Graduate Admissions, 860-832-2350.

Find an in-depth description at www.petersons.com/graduate.

School of Graduate Studies
Kevin Oliva, Graduate Admissions
Programs in:
- international studies • MS
- social science • MS

School of Arts and Sciences
Dr. June B. Higgins, Dean
Programs in:
- art education • MS
- arts and sciences • MA, MS, Certificate
- biological sciences • MA, MS
- cell and molecular biology • Certificate
- community psychology • MA
- computer science • MS
- criminal justice • MS
- earth science • MS
- English • MA, MS
- French • MA
- general science • MS
- geography • MS
- graphic information design • MA
- history • MA, MS
- mathematics • MA, MS
- music education • MS
- natural science chemistry • MS
- natural sciences • MS
- organizational communication • MS
- physics • MS
- pre health • Certificate
- psychology • MA
- science and science education • MS
- Spanish • MA, MS
- teaching English to speakers of other languages • MS

School of Business
Dr. Dan Miller, Dean
Programs in:
- business • MBA, MS
- business education • MS
- international business administration • MBA

School of Education and Professional Studies
Dr. Ellen Whitford, Dean
Programs in:
- early childhood education • MS
- education and professional studies • MS, Certificate, Sixth Year Certificate
- education leadership • MS
- educational foundations policy • MS
- educational leadership • Sixth Year Certificate
- educational technology • MS
- educational technology and media • MS
- elementary education • MS, Certificate
- marriage and family therapy • MS
- physical education • MS
- reading • MS, Sixth Year Certificate
- rehabilitation/mental counseling • MS
- school counseling • MS
- special education • MS
- student development in higher education • MS

School of Technology
Dr. Zdzislaw Kremens, Dean
Programs in:
- industrial • technical management • MS
- technology • MS
- technology education • MS

■ EASTERN CONNECTICUT STATE UNIVERSITY

Willimantic, CT 06226-2295
http://www.easternct.edu/

State-supported, coed, comprehensive institution. *Computer facilities:* 518 computers available on campus for general student use. A campuswide network can be accessed from student residence rooms and from off campus. Internet access is available. *Library facilities:* J. Eugene Smith Library. *General application contact:* Dean, 860-465-5293.

School of Education and Professional Studies
Programs in:
- accounting • MS
- early childhood education • MS
- education and professional studies • MS
- elementary education • MS
- organizational management • MS
- reading and language arts • MS
- science education • MS

■ FAIRFIELD UNIVERSITY

Fairfield, CT 06430-5195
http://www.fairfield.edu/

Independent-religious, coed, comprehensive institution. *Enrollment:* 169 full-time matriculated graduate/professional students (114 women), 846 part-time matriculated graduate/professional students (480 women). *Graduate faculty:* 99 full-time (40 women), 52 part-time/adjunct (21 women). *Computer facilities:* 150 computers available on campus for general student use. A campuswide network can be accessed from student residence rooms and from off campus. Internet access and online class registration are available. *Library facilities:* Dimenna-Nyselius Library. *Graduate expenses:* Tuition: full-time $18,000; part-time $370 per credit hour. Required fees: $25 per term. Tuition and fees vary according to program.

Charles F. Dolan School of Business

Dr. Winston Tellis, Acting Dean
Programs in:
accounting • MBA, CAS
finance • MBA, CAS
financial management • MSFM
healthcare management • MBA
human resource management • CAS
information technology • MBA, CAS
international business • MBA, CAS
marketing • MBA, CAS
taxation • MBA, CAS

College of Arts and Sciences

Dr. Beverly Kahn, Acting Dean
Programs in:
American studies • MA
arts and sciences • MA, MS
mathematics and quantitative methods • MS

Graduate School of Education and Allied Professions

Dr. Margaret Deignan, Dean
Programs in:
applied psychology • MA
community counseling • MA
computers in education • MA, CAS
counselor education • CAS
early childhood education • MA, CAS
education and allied professions • MA, CAS
educational media • MA, CAS
elementary education • MA
marriage and family therapy • MA
school counseling • MA
school psychology • MA, CAS
special education • MA, CAS
teaching and foundation • MA, CAS
TESOL, foreign language and bilingual/multicultural education • MA, CAS

School of Engineering

Dr. Evangelos Hadjimichael, Dean
Programs in:
management of technology • MS
software engineering • MS

School of Nursing

Dr. Kathleen Wheeler, Director
Programs in:
family nurse practitioner • MSN, CAS
psychiatric nurse practitioner • MSN, CAS

■ QUINNIPIAC UNIVERSITY

Hamden, CT 06518-1940
http://www.quinnipiac.edu/

Independent, coed, comprehensive institution. *Enrollment:* 949 full-time matriculated graduate/professional students (545 women), 685 part-time matriculated graduate/professional students (384 women). *Graduate faculty:* 76 full-time (28 women), 34 part-time/adjunct (15 women). *Computer facilities:* 200 computers available on campus for general student use. A campuswide network can be accessed from student residence rooms and from off campus. Internet access is available. *Library facilities:* Arnold Bernhard Library plus 1 other. *Graduate expenses:* Tuition: part-time $430 per credit hour. Required fees: $20 per term. Tuition and fees vary according to program. *General application contact:* 800-462-1944.

Find an in-depth description at www.petersons.com/graduate.

College of Liberal Arts

Dr. David Stineback, Dean
Programs in:
biology • MAT
chemistry • MAT
elementary school teaching • MAT
English • MAT
French • MAT
history/social studies • MAT
liberal arts • MAT
mathematics • MAT
physics • MAT
Spanish • MAT

Lender School of Business

Dr. Phillip Frese, Dean
Programs in:
accounting • MBA
business • MBA, MHA
computer information systems • MBA
economics • MBA
finance • MBA
health administration • MHA
health management • MBA
international business • MBA
long-term care administration • MHA
management • MBA
marketing • MBA

School of Communications

Dr. Raymond Foery, Interim Dean
Programs in:
communications • MS
e-media • MS
journalism • MS

School of Health Sciences

Dr. Joseph Woods, Dean
Programs in:
advanced clinical practice • MSPT
biomedical sciences • MHS
forensic nursing • MSN
health sciences • MHS, MS, MSN, MSPT
laboratory management • MHS
microbiology • MHS
molecular and cell biology • MS
neurorehabilitation • MSPT
nurse practitioner • MSN
orthopedic physical therapy • MSPT
pathologists' assistant • MHS
physician assistant • MHS

School of Law

David S. King, Interim Dean
Program in:
law • JD

■ SACRED HEART UNIVERSITY

Fairfield, CT 06432-1000
http://www.sacredheart.edu/

Independent-religious, coed, comprehensive institution. *Enrollment:* 457 full-time matriculated graduate/professional students (330 women), 1,198 part-time matriculated graduate/professional students (747 women). *Graduate faculty:* 64 full-time (26 women), 104 part-time/adjunct (56 women). *Computer facilities:* 110 computers available on campus for general student use. A campuswide network can be accessed from student residence rooms and from off campus. Internet access and online class registration, Intranet are available. *Library facilities:* Ryan-Matura Library. *Graduate expenses:* Tuition: part-time $425 per credit.

Sacred Heart University (continued)
Required fees: $90 per term. *General application contact:* Linda B. Kirby, Dean of Graduate Admissions, 203-365-7619.

Find an in-depth description at www.petersons.com/graduate.

Graduate Studies

College of Arts and Sciences
Dr. Claire Paolini, Dean
Programs in:
- arts and sciences • MA, MS, CPS
- chemistry • MS
- computer science • MS, CPS
- e-commerce • CPS
- information technology • MS, CPS
- multimedia • CPS
- religious studies • MA

College of Business
Dr. Mary Trefry, Interim Director
Programs in:
- business administration • MBA
- health care administration • MBA
- health systems management • MA

College of Education and Health Professions
Dr. Patricia Walker, Dean
Programs in:
- administration • CAS
- education • CAS
- education and health professions • MAT, MOT, MSN, MSPT, CAS
- elementary education • MAT
- family nurse practitioner • MSN
- occupational therapy • MOT
- patient care services • MSN
- physical therapy • MSPT
- secondary education • MAT

■ SAINT JOSEPH COLLEGE
West Hartford, CT 06117-2700
http://www.sjc.edu/

Independent-religious, women only, comprehensive institution. *Enrollment:* 61 full-time matriculated graduate/professional students (52 women), 391 part-time matriculated graduate/professional students (359 women). *Graduate faculty:* 36 full-time (22 women), 28 part-time/adjunct (20 women). *Computer facilities:* 150 computers available on campus for general student use. A campuswide network can be accessed from student residence rooms and from off campus. Internet access is available. *Library facilities:* Pope Pius XII Library plus 1 other. *Graduate expenses:* Tuition: full-time $8,100. Required fees: $300. *General application contact:* Monica Gat, Graduate Recruiter, 860-231-5261.

Graduate Division
Dr. Clark Hendley, Associate Dean
Programs in:
- biology • MS
- biology/chemistry • MS
- chemistry • MS
- community counseling • MA
- early childhood education • MA
- education • MA
- family health nurse practitioner • MS
- family health nursing • MS
- human development/gerontology • MA
- marriage and family therapy • MA
- nursing • Post Master's Certificate
- psychiatric/mental health nursing • MS
- special education • MA
- spirituality • Certificate

■ SOUTHERN CONNECTICUT STATE UNIVERSITY
New Haven, CT 06515-1355
http://www.southernct.edu/

State-supported, coed, comprehensive institution. CGS member. *Computer facilities:* 300 computers available on campus for general student use. A campuswide network can be accessed from student residence rooms and from off campus. Internet access is available. *Library facilities:* Hilton C. Buley Library. *General application contact:* Assistant to the Dean, 203-392-5337.

Find an in-depth description at www.petersons.com/graduate.

School of Graduate Studies

School of Arts and Sciences
Programs in:
- art education • MS
- arts and sciences • MA, MS, Diploma
- biology • MS
- biology for nurse anesthetists • MS
- chemistry • MS
- English • MA, MS
- environmental education • MS
- French • MA
- history • MA, MS
- mathematics • MS
- multicultural-bilingual education/teaching English to speakers of other languages • MS
- political science • MS
- psychology • MA
- Romance languages • MA
- science education • MS, Diploma
- sociology • MS
- Spanish • MA
- women's studies • MA

School of Business
Programs in:
- business • MBA
- business administration • MBA

School of Communication, Information and Library Science
Programs in:
- communication, information and library science • MLS, MS, Diploma
- instructional technology • MS
- library science • MLS
- library/information studies • Diploma

School of Education
Programs in:
- classroom teacher specialist • Diploma
- community counseling • MS
- counseling • Diploma
- education • MS, MS Ed, Diploma
- educational leadership • Diploma
- elementary education • MS
- foundational studies • Diploma
- human performance • MS
- physical education • MS
- reading • MS, Diploma
- research, measurement and quantitative analysis • MS
- school counseling • MS
- school health education • MS
- school psychology • MS, Diploma
- special education • MS Ed, Diploma
- sport psychology • MS

School of Health and Human Services
Programs in:
- audiology • MS
- health and human services • MFT, MPH, MS, MSN, MSW
- marriage and family therapy • MFT
- nursing administration • MSN
- nursing education • MSN
- public health • MPH
- recreation and leisure studies • MS
- social work • MSW
- speech pathology • MS
- urban studies • MS

■ UNIVERSITY OF BRIDGEPORT
Bridgeport, CT 06601
http://www.bridgeport.edu/

Independent, coed, comprehensive institution. CGS member. *Enrollment:* 872 full-time matriculated graduate/professional students (418 women), 965 part-time matriculated graduate/professional students (556 women). *Graduate faculty:* 92 full-time (18 women), 232 part-time/adjunct (93 women). *Computer facilities:* 350 computers available on campus for general student use. A campuswide network can be accessed from student residence rooms and from off campus.

Library facilities: Wahlstrom Library. *Graduate expenses:* Tuition: full-time $14,150; part-time $365 per credit hour. Required fees: $800; $50 per term. Tuition and fees vary according to course load, degree level and program. *General application contact:* Barbara L. Maryak, Dean of Admissions, 203-576-4552.

Find an in-depth description at www.petersons.com/graduate.

College of Chiropractic
Dr. Francis A. Zolli, Dean
Programs in:
acupuncture • MS
chiropractic • DC

College of Naturopathic Medicine
Dr. Peter Allen Martin, Dean
Program in:
naturopathic medicine • ND

Division of Allied Health Technology
Dr. Blonnie Y. Thompson, Director
Program in:
allied health technology • MS

Human Nutrition Institute
Dr. Blonnie Y. Thompson, Director, Division of Allied Health Technology
Program in:
human nutrition • MS

School of Business
Dr. Glenn A. Bassett, Director
Programs in:
business • MBA, MS
business administration • MBA

School of Education and Human Resources
Dr. James J. Ritchie, Dean
Program in:
education and human resources • MS, Ed D, Diploma

Division of Counseling and Human Resources
Dr. Joseph E. Nechasek, Director
Programs in:
community agency counseling • MS
human resource development and counseling • MS

Division of Education
Dr. Allen P. Cook, Associate Dean
Programs in:
computer specialist • MS, Diploma
early childhood education • MS, Diploma
education • MS
educational management • Ed D, Diploma
elementary education • MS, Diploma
international education • MS, Diploma
reading specialist • MS, Diploma
secondary education • MS, Diploma

School of Engineering and Design
Dr. Tarek M. Sobh, Director
Programs in:
computer engineering • MS
computer science • MS
electrical engineering • MS
engineering and design • MS
mechanical engineering • MS
technology management • MS

■ UNIVERSITY OF CONNECTICUT
Storrs, CT 06269
http://www.uconn.edu/

State-supported, coed, university. CGS member. *Computer facilities:* 1,800 computers available on campus for general student use. A campuswide network can be accessed from student residence rooms and from off campus. Internet access and online class registration, e-mail are available. *Library facilities:* Homer Babbidge Library plus 3 others. *General application contact:* Director of Graduate Admissions, 860-486-3617.

Find an in-depth description at www.petersons.com/graduate.

Graduate School
Programs in:
biomedical science • PhD
dental science • M Dent Sc
public health • MPH

College of Agriculture and Natural Resources
Programs in:
agricultural and resource economics • MS, PhD
agriculture and natural resources • MS, PhD
animal science • MS, PhD
natural resources: land, water, and air • MS
nutritional sciences • MS, PhD
pathobiology • MS, PhD
plant and soil sciences • MS, PhD

College of Liberal Arts and Sciences
Programs in:
African studies • MA
anthropology • MA, PhD
behavioral neuroscience • PhD
biochemistry • MS, PhD
biophysics • MS, PhD
biopsychology • MA, PhD
biotechnology • MS
botany • MS, PhD
cell and developmental biology • MS, PhD
chemistry • MS, PhD
clinical psychology • PhD
cognition/instruction psychology • PhD
communication • MA
communication processes and marketing communication • PhD
comparative literature and cultural studies • MA, PhD
developmental psychobiology • MS, PhD
developmental psychology • PhD
ecological psychology • PhD
ecology • MS, PhD
ecology and evolutionary biology • MS, PhD
economics • MA, PhD
English • MA, PhD
entomology • MS, PhD
French • MA, PhD
general experimental psychology • PhD
genetics • MS, PhD
geography • MS, PhD
geology • MS, PhD
geophysics • MS, PhD
German • MA, PhD
history • MA, PhD
industrial and organizational psychology • PhD
international studies • MA
interpersonal communication • MA
Italian • MA, PhD
language psychology • PhD
Latin American studies • MA
liberal arts and sciences • MA, MPA, MS, PhD
linguistics • MA, PhD
mass communication • MA
mathematics • MS, PhD
medieval studies • MA, PhD
microbiology • MS, PhD
molecular and cell biology • MS, PhD
neurobiology • MS, PhD
neuroscience • MA
nonverbal communication • MA
oceanography • MS, PhD
organizational communication • MA
philosophy • MA, PhD
physics • MS, PhD
physiology • MS, PhD
physiology and neurobiology • MS, PhD
plant molecular and cell biology • MS, PhD
political science • MA, PhD
public affairs • MPA
Slavic and East European studies • MA
social psychology • PhD

University of Connecticut (continued)

sociology • MA, PhD
Spanish • MA, PhD
speech, language, and hearing • MA, PhD
statistics • MS, PhD
systematics • MS, PhD
Western European studies • MA
zoology • MS, PhD

School of Allied Health Professions
Program in:
allied health professions • MS

School of Business Administration
Programs in:
accounting • MBA, PhD
finance • PhD
general business administration • MBA
health care management • MBA
human resources management • MBA
international studies and business administration • MBA, PhD
management • MBA, PhD
marketing • MBA, PhD

School of Education
Programs in:
adult and vocational education • MA, PhD
bilingual and bicultural education • MA, PhD
cognition and instruction • PhD
counseling psychology • MA, PhD
curriculum and instruction • MA, PhD
education • MA, PhD
educational administration • MA, PhD
educational psychology • MA, PhD
educational studies • MA, PhD
elementary education • MA, PhD
English education • MA, PhD
evaluation and measurement • MA, PhD
foreign languages education • MA, PhD
gifted and talented • MA, PhD
history and social science education • MA, PhD
instructional media and technology • MA, PhD
leisure science • MA, PhD
mathematics education • MA, PhD
professional higher education administration • MA, PhD
reading education • MA, PhD
school psychology • MA, PhD
science education • MA, PhD
secondary education • MA, PhD
special education • MA, PhD
sport science • MA, PhD

School of Engineering
Programs in:
aerospace engineering • MS, PhD
applied mechanics • PhD
artificial intelligence • MS, PhD
biological engineering • MS
biomedical engineering • MS, PhD
chemical engineering • MS, PhD
chemistry • MS, PhD
civil engineering • MS, PhD
computer architecture • MS, PhD
computer science • MS, PhD
control and communication systems • MS, PhD
electromagnetics and physical electronics • MS, PhD
engineering • MS, PhD
environmental engineering • MS, PhD
fluid dynamics • PhD
material science • MS, PhD
mechanical engineering • MS, PhD
metallurgy • MS, PhD
ocean engineering • MS, PhD
operating systems • MS, PhD
polymer science • MS, PhD
robotics • MS, PhD
software engineering • MS, PhD

School of Family Studies
Programs in:
family studies • MA, MS, PhD
human development and family relations • MA, PhD

School of Fine Arts
Programs in:
art and art history • MFA
composition • M Mus
conducting • M Mus, DMA
dramatic arts • MA, MFA
fine arts • M Mus, MA, MFA, DMA, PhD
historical musicology • MA
music education • M Mus, PhD
music theory and history • PhD
performance • M Mus, DMA
psychomusicology • PhD
theory • MA

School of Nursing
Programs in:
nurse education • MS
nursing • PhD
nursing management • MS

School of Pharmacy
Programs in:
medicinal chemistry • MS, PhD
pharmaceutics • MS, PhD
pharmacology and toxicology • MS, PhD
pharmacy • MS, PhD

School of Social Work
Program in:
social work • MSW

School of Law
Ellen Keane Rutt, Associate Dean, Admissions and Career Services
Program in:
law • JD

■ UNIVERSITY OF HARTFORD

West Hartford, CT 06117-1599
http://www.hartford.edu/

Independent, coed, comprehensive institution. CGS member. *Enrollment:* 528 full-time matriculated graduate/professional students (340 women), 747 part-time matriculated graduate/professional students (471 women). *Graduate faculty:* 115 full-time (34 women), 89 part-time/adjunct (35 women). *Computer facilities:* 380 computers available on campus for general student use. A campuswide network can be accessed from student residence rooms and from off campus. *Library facilities:* Mortenson Library. *Graduate expenses:* Tuition: full-time $6,840; part-time $380 per hour. Required fees: $55 per term. *General application contact:* Kellie Westenfeld, Coordinator of Graduate Application, 860-768-4371.

Barney School of Business and Public Administration
Corine T. Norgaard, Dean
Programs in:
accounting • MSPA
business administration • EMBA, MBA
business and public administration • EMBA, MBA, MSPA, MST
taxation • MST

College of Arts and Sciences
Dr. Edward Gray, Dean
Programs in:
arts and sciences • MA, MS, Psy D
biology • MS
clinical practices • MA
communication • MA
general experimental psychology • MA
neuroscience • MS
school psychology • MS

Graduate Institute of Professional Psychology
Dr. David L. Singer, Director
Program in:
clinical psychology • Psy D

College of Education, Nursing, and Health Professions
Dr. David A. Caruso, Dean
Programs in:
administration and supervision • M Ed, CAGS, Sixth Year Certificate
counseling • M Ed, MS, Sixth Year Certificate
early childhood education • M Ed
education, nursing, and health professions • M Ed, MS, MSN,

MSPT, Ed D, CAGS, Sixth Year Certificate
educational computing and technology • M Ed
educational leadership • Ed D
elementary education • M Ed
nursing • MSN
physical therapy • MS
secondary education • M Ed
special education • M Ed

College of Engineering
Alan Hadad, Dean
Program in:
engineering • M Eng

Hartford Art School
Tom Bradley, Associate Dean
Program in:
art • MFA

Hartt School of Music
Dr. Malcolm Morrison, Dean
Programs in:
choral conducting • MM Ed
composition • MM, DMA, Artist Diploma, Diploma
conducting • MM, DMA, Artist Diploma, Diploma
early childhood education • MM Ed
instrumental conducting • MM Ed
Kodály • MM Ed
music • CAGS
music education • DMA, PhD
music history • MM
music theory • MM
opera • MM, Artist Diploma, Diploma
pedagogy • MM Ed
performance • MM, MM Ed, DMA, Artist Diploma, Diploma
research • MM Ed
technology • MM Ed

■ UNIVERSITY OF NEW HAVEN

West Haven, CT 06516-1916
http://www.newhaven.edu/

Independent, coed, university. CGS member. *Computer facilities:* 800 computers available on campus for general student use. A campuswide network can be accessed from student residence rooms and from off campus. Internet access, e-mail are available. *Library facilities:* Marvin K. Peterson Library. *General application contact:* Director of Admissions and Operations, 203-932-7133.

Find an in-depth description at www.petersons.com/graduate.

Graduate School

College of Arts and Sciences
Programs in:
arts and sciences • MA, MS, Certificate
cellular and molecular biology • MS
community psychology • MA, Certificate
education • MS
environmental sciences • MS
executive tourism and hospitality • MS
hotel, restaurant, tourism and dietetics administration • MS
human nutrition • MS
industrial and organizational psychology • MA, Certificate

School of Business
Programs in:
accounting • MBA
business • EMBA, MBA, MPA, MS
business administration • EMBA, MBA
business policy and strategy • MBA
corporate taxation • MS
finance • MBA
finance and financial services • MS
financial accounting • MS
health care administration • MS
health care management • MBA, MPA
human resources management • MBA
industrial relations • MS
international business • MBA
managerial accounting • MS
marketing • MBA
personnel and labor relations • MPA
public relations • MBA
public taxation • MS
sports management • MBA
taxation • MS
technology management • MBA

School of Engineering and Applied Science
Programs in:
applications software • MS
civil engineering design • Certificate
electrical engineering • MSEE
engineering and applied science • MS, MSEE, MSIE, MSME, Certificate
environmental engineering • MS
industrial engineering • MSIE
logistics • Certificate
management information systems • MS
mechanical engineering • MSME
operations research • MS
systems software • MS

School of Public Safety and Professional Studies
Programs in:
advanced investigation • MS
aviation science • MS
correctional counseling • MS
criminal justice management • MS
criminalistics • MS
fire science • MS
forensic science • MS
industrial hygiene • MS
occupational safety and health management • MS
public safety and professional studies • MS
security management • MS

■ WESTERN CONNECTICUT STATE UNIVERSITY

Danbury, CT 06810-6885
http://www.wcsu.edu/

State-supported, coed, comprehensive institution. *Enrollment:* 22 full-time matriculated graduate/professional students (16 women), 611 part-time matriculated graduate/professional students (432 women). *Graduate faculty:* 46 full-time (18 women), 6 part-time/adjunct (1 woman). *Computer facilities:* 400 computers available on campus for general student use. A campuswide network can be accessed from student residence rooms and from off campus. Internet access is available. *Library facilities:* Ruth Haas Library plus 1 other. *Graduate expenses:* Tuition, state resident: full-time $2,668; part-time $195 per credit. Tuition, nonresident: full-time $7,436. Required fees: $1,763; $30 per term. Part-time tuition and fees vary according to course load. *General application contact:* Chris Shankle, Associate Director of Graduate Admissions, 203-837-8244.

Division of Graduate Studies
William Hawkins, Enrollment Management Officer

Ancell School of Business and Public Administration
Dr. Allen Morton, Dean
Programs in:
accounting • MBA
business administration • MBA
business and public administration • MBA, MHA, MS
health administration • MHA
justice administration • MS

School of Arts and Sciences
Dr. Carol Hawkes, Dean
Programs in:
arts and sciences • MA, MFA
biological and environmental sciences • MA
earth and planetary sciences • MA

Western Connecticut State University (continued)
- English • MA
- history • MA
- illustration • MFA
- mathematics and computer science • MA
- painting • MFA
- theoretical mathematics • MA

School of Professional Studies
Dr. Lawrence Huntley, Interim Dean
Programs in:
- adult nurse practitioner • MSN
- clinical nurse specialist • MSN
- community counseling • MS
- counselor education • MS
- curriculum • MS
- English education • MS
- instructional technology • MS
- mathematics education • MS
- music education • MS
- professional studies • MS, MSN
- reading • MS
- school counseling • MS
- special education • MS

■ YALE UNIVERSITY
New Haven, CT 06520
http://www.yale.edu/

Independent, coed, university. CGS member. *Computer facilities:* 350 computers available on campus for general student use. A campuswide network can be accessed from student residence rooms and from off campus. *Library facilities:* Sterling Memorial Library plus 20 others. *General application contact:* Admissions Information, 203-432-2772.

Divinity School
Program in:
- divinity • M Div, MAR, STM

Graduate School of Arts and Sciences
Dr. Susan Hockfield, Dean
Programs in:
- African studies • MA
- African-American studies • MA, PhD
- American studies • MA, PhD
- anthropology • MA, PhD
- applied mathematics • M Phil, MS, PhD
- applied mechanics and mechanical engineering • M Phil, MS, PhD
- applied physics • MS, PhD
- archaeological studies • MA
- arts and sciences • M Phil, MA, MS, PhD
- astronomy • MS, PhD
- biophysical chemistry • PhD
- cell biology • PhD
- cellular and molecular physiology • PhD
- chemical engineering • MS, PhD
- classics • PhD
- comparative literature • PhD
- computer science • PhD
- developmental biology • PhD
- East Asian languages and literatures • PhD
- East Asian studies • MA
- ecology and evolutionary biology • PhD
- economics • PhD
- electrical engineering • MS, PhD
- English language and literature • MA, PhD
- environmental sciences • PhD
- experimental pathology • PhD
- forestry • PhD
- French • MA, PhD
- genetics • PhD
- geochemistry • PhD
- geophysics • PhD
- Germanic language and literature • MA, PhD
- history • MA, PhD
- history of art • PhD
- history of medicine and the life sciences • MS, PhD
- immunobiology • PhD
- inorganic chemistry • PhD
- international and development economics • MA
- international relations • MA
- Italian language and literature • PhD
- linguistics • PhD
- mathematics • MS, PhD
- mechanical engineering • M Phil, MS, PhD
- medieval studies • MA, PhD
- meteorology • PhD
- mineralogy and crystallography • PhD
- molecular biology • PhD
- molecular biophysics and biochemistry • MS, PhD
- music • MA, PhD
- Near Eastern languages and civilizations • MA, PhD
- neurobiology • PhD
- neuroscience • PhD
- oceanography • PhD
- organic chemistry • PhD
- paleoecology • PhD
- paleontology and stratigraphy • PhD
- petrology • PhD
- pharmacology • PhD
- philosophy • PhD
- physical chemistry • PhD
- physics • PhD
- plant sciences • PhD
- political science • PhD
- psychology • MS, PhD
- religious studies • PhD
- Renaissance studies • PhD
- Russian and East European studies • MA
- Slavic languages and literatures • MA, PhD
- sociology • PhD
- Spanish and Portuguese • MA, PhD
- statistics • MS, PhD
- structural geology • PhD

School of Architecture
Robert A. M. Stern, Dean
Program in:
- architecture • M Arch, M Env Des

School of Art
Richard Benson, Dean
Programs in:
- graphic design • MFA
- painting/printmaking • MFA
- photography • MFA
- sculpture • MFA

School of Drama
Dr. Stan Wojewodski, Dean/Artistic Director
Program in:
- drama • MFA, DFA, Certificate

School of Forestry and Environmental Studies
Program in:
- forestry and environmental studies • MES, MF, MFS, DFES, PhD

School of Medicine
Programs in:
- biostatistics • MPH, MS, PhD
- chronic disease epidemiology • MPH, PhD
- environmental health • MPH, PhD
- epidemiology of microbial diseases • MPH, PhD
- global health • MPH
- health policy and administration • MPH, PhD
- medicine • MD, MMS, MPH, MS, PhD
- parasitology • PhD
- physician associate • MMS

Combined Program in Biological and Biomedical Sciences (BBS)
Dr. Lynn Cooley, Director
Programs in:
- biological and biomedical sciences • PhD
- biological sciences • PhD
- cell biology and molecular physiology • PhD
- genetics, development, and molecular biology • PhD
- immunology • PhD
- microbiology • PhD
- molecular biophysics and biochemistry • PhD
- neuroscience • PhD
- pharmacological sciences and molecular medicine • PhD

School of Music
Robert Blocker, Dean
Program in:
music • MM, MMA, DMA, AD, Certificate

School of Nursing
Program in:
nursing • MSN, DN Sc, Post Master's Certificate

Yale Law School
Anthony T. Kronman, Dean
Program in:
law • JD, LL M, MSL, JSD

Yale School of Management
Jeffrey E. Garten, Dean
Programs in:
accounting • PhD
business administration • MBA
financial economics • PhD
management • MBA, PhD
marketing • PhD

Delaware

■ DELAWARE STATE UNIVERSITY

Dover, DE 19901-2277
http://www.dsc.edu/

State-supported, coed, comprehensive institution. *Computer facilities:* 641 computers available on campus for general student use. A campuswide network can be accessed from student residence rooms and from off campus. Internet access and online class registration, online grade access, e-mail are available. *Library facilities:* William C. Jason Library. *General application contact:* Dean of Graduate Studies and Research, 302-739-5143.

Graduate Programs
Programs in:
applied chemistry • MS
biology • MS
biology education • MS
business administration • MBA
chemistry • MS
curriculum and instruction • MA
education • MA
physics • MS
physics teaching • MS
science education • MA
social work • MSW
special education • MA

■ UNIVERSITY OF DELAWARE

Newark, DE 19716
http://www.udel.edu/

State-related, coed, university. CGS member. *Enrollment:* 2,146 full-time matriculated graduate/professional students (1,032 women), 806 part-time matriculated graduate/professional students (461 women). *Graduate faculty:* 998 full-time (340 women), 20 part-time/adjunct (15 women). *Computer facilities:* 900 computers available on campus for general student use. A campuswide network can be accessed from student residence rooms and from off campus. *Library facilities:* Hugh Morris Library plus 3 others. *Graduate expenses:* Tuition, state resident: part-time $243 per semester hour. Tuition, nonresident: part-time $708 per semester hour. Required fees: $191 per semester. *General application contact:* Mary Martin, Assistant Provost for Graduate Studies, 302-831-8916.

Find an in-depth description at www.petersons.com/graduate.

College of Agriculture and Natural Resources
Dr. Robin Morgan, Acting Dean
Programs in:
agricultural and resource economics • MS
agriculture and natural resources • MS, PhD
animal sciences • MS, PhD
entomology and applied ecology • MS, PhD
food sciences • MS
horticulture • MS
operations research • MS, PhD
plant and soil sciences • MS, PhD

College of Arts and Science
Dr. Mark W. Huddleston, Acting Dean
Programs in:
acting • MFA
American civilization • PhD
applied mathematics • MA, MS, PhD
art • MA, MFA
art history • MA, PhD
arts and science • MA, MALS, MFA, MM, MPT, MS, PhD, Certificate
biochemistry • MA, MS, PhD
biopsychology • PhD
biotechnology • MS, PhD
cell and extracellular matrix biology • MS, PhD
cell and systems physiology • MS, PhD
chemistry • MA, MS, PhD
climatology • PhD
clinical psychology • PhD
cognitive psychology • PhD
communication • MA
computer and information sciences • MS, PhD
criminology • MA, PhD
early American culture • MA
ecology and evolution • MS, PhD
English education • MA
English literature • MA
foreign language pedagogy • MA
French • MA
geography • MA, MS
geology • MS, PhD
German • MA
history • MA, PhD
international relations • MA
liberal studies • MALS
linguistics • MA, PhD
literature • PhD
mathematics • MA, MS, PhD
microbiology • MS, PhD
molecular biology and genetics • MS, PhD
museum studies • Certificate
music education • MM
neuroscience and biology • PhD
neuroscience and psychology • PhD
performance • MM
physical therapy • MPT
physics and astronomy • MS, PhD
plant biology • MS, PhD
political science • MA, PhD
practicing art conservation • MS
social psychology • PhD
sociology • MA, PhD
Spanish • MA
stage management • MFA
technical production • MFA

College of Business and Economics
Michael J. Ginzberg, Dean
Programs in:
accounting • MS
business administration • MBA
business and economics • MA, MBA, MS, PhD
economics • MA, MS, PhD
economics for educators • MA

College of Engineering
Dr. Eric W. Kaler, Dean
Programs in:
chemical engineering • M Ch E, PhD
electrical and computer engineering • MEE, PhD
engineering • M Ch E, MAS, MCE, MEE, MEM, MMSE, MSME, PhD
environmental engineering • MAS, MCE, PhD
geotechnical engineering • MAS, MCE, PhD

University of Delaware (continued)
- materials science and engineering • MMSE, PhD
- mechanical engineering • MEM, MSME, PhD
- ocean engineering • MAS, MCE, PhD
- railroad engineering • MAS, MCE, PhD
- structural engineering • MAS, MCE, PhD
- transportation engineering • MAS, MCE, PhD
- water resource engineering • MAS, MCE, PhD

College of Health and Nursing Sciences
Dr. Betty J. Paulanka, Dean
Programs in:
- applied nutrition • MS
- biomechanics • MS
- biomechanics and movement science • MS, PhD
- cardiac rehabilitation • MS
- cardiopulmonary clinical nurse specialist • MSN, PMC
- cardiopulmonary clinical nurse specialist/adult nurse practitioner • MSN, PMC
- exercise physiology • MS
- family nurse practitioner • MSN, PMC
- general human nutrition • MS
- gerontology clinical nurse specialist • MSN, PMC
- gerontology clinical nurse specialist geriatric nurse practitioner • PMC
- gerontology clinical nurse specialist/ geriatric nurse practitioner • MSN
- health and nursing sciences • MS, MSN, PhD, PMC
- health promotion • MS
- health services administation • PMC
- health services administration • MSN
- nursing administration • PMC
- nursing of children clinical nurse specialist • MSN, PMC
- nursing of children clinical nurse specialist/pediatric nurse practitioner • MSN, PMC
- nutrient metabolism and utilization • MS
- oncology/immune deficiency clinical nurse specialist • MSN, PMC
- oncology/immune deficiency clinical nurse specialist/adult nurse practitioner • MSN, PMC
- perinatal/women's health clinical nurse specialist • MSN, PMC
- perinatal/women's health clinical nurse specialist/women's health nurse practitioner • MSN, PMC
- psychiatric nursing clinical nurse specialist • PMC

College of Human Services, Education and Public Policy
Dr. Daniel Rich, Dean
Programs in:
- college counseling • M Ed
- family studies • PhD
- human services, education and public policy • M Ed, MA, MI, MPA, MS, Ed D, PhD
- individual and family studies • MS
- student affairs practice in higher education • M Ed

Center for Energy and Environmental Policy
Dr. Richard T. Sylves, Director
Programs in:
- environmental and energy policy • MS, PhD
- urban affairs and public policy • MA, PhD

School of Education
Dr. Christopher M. Clark, Director
Programs in:
- cognition and instruction • MA
- cognition, development, and instruction • PhD
- curriculum and instruction • M Ed, PhD
- educational leadership • M Ed, Ed D
- educational policy • MA, PhD
- English as a second language/ bilingualism • MA
- exceptional children • M Ed
- exceptionality • PhD
- instruction • MI
- measurements, statistics, and evaluation • MA, PhD
- school counseling • M Ed
- school psychology • MA
- secondary education • M Ed

School of Urban Affairs and Public Policy
Dr. Jeffrey A. Raffel, Director
Programs in:
- community development and nonprofit leadership • MA
- energy and environmental policy • MA
- governance, planning and management • PhD
- historic preservation • MA
- public administration • MPA
- social and urban policy • PhD
- technology, environment and society • PhD
- urban affairs and public policy • MA, MPA, PhD

College of Marine Studies
Dr. Carolyn A. Thoroughgood, Dean
Programs in:
- marine policy • MS
- marine studies • MS
- oceanography • MS

Delaware Biotechnology Institute
Dr. David S. Weir, Director
Program in:
- biotechnology • PhD

■ WILMINGTON COLLEGE
New Castle, DE 19720-6491
http://www.wilmcoll.edu/

Independent, coed, comprehensive institution. *Enrollment:* 247 full-time matriculated graduate/professional students (161 women), 1,124 part-time matriculated graduate/professional students (771 women). *Graduate faculty:* 48 full-time, 150 part-time/adjunct. *Computer facilities:* 100 computers available on campus for general student use. Internet access is available. *Library facilities:* Robert C. and Dorothy M. Peoples Library plus 1 other. *Graduate expenses:* Tuition: part-time $256 per credit hour. *General application contact:* Michael Lee, Director of Admissions and Financial Aid, 302-328-9407 Ext. 102.

Division of Behavioral Science
Dr. John Liptak, Chair
Programs in:
- community counseling • MS
- criminal justice studies • MS
- rehabilitation counseling • MS
- student affairs and college counseling • MS

Division of Business
Andrew LaFond, Chair
Programs in:
- business administration • MBA
- human resource management • MS
- management • MS
- public administration • MS

Division of Education
Dr. Barbara Raetsch, Chair
Programs in:
- elementary and secondary school counseling • M Ed
- elementary special education • M Ed
- elementary studies • M Ed
- innovation and leadership • Ed D
- reading • M Ed
- school leadership • M Ed

Division of Nursing
Dr. Betty Caffo, Chair
Programs in:
- family nurse practitioner • MSN
- gerontology • MSN
- nursing • MSN

District of Columbia

■ AMERICAN UNIVERSITY

Washington, DC 20016-8001
http://www.american.edu/

Independent-religious, coed, university. CGS member. *Enrollment:* 2,450 full-time matriculated graduate/professional students (1,491 women), 2,227 part-time matriculated graduate/professional students (1,312 women). *Graduate faculty:* 414 full-time (147 women), 215 part-time/adjunct (78 women). *Computer facilities:* 600 computers available on campus for general student use. A campuswide network can be accessed from student residence rooms and from off campus. Internet access, online course support are available. *Library facilities:* Bender Library plus 1 other. *Graduate expenses:* Tuition: full-time $13,644; part-time $758 per credit. Required fees: $180. *General application contact:* Elizabeth P. Bickell, Office of Graduate Affairs and Admissions, 202-885-6000.

Find an in-depth description at www.petersons.com/graduate.

College of Arts and Sciences

Dr. Kay Mussell, Dean
Programs in:
- anthropology • MA, PhD
- applied anthropology • MA
- applied economics • Certificate
- applied mathematics • MA
- applied sociology • MA
- applied statistics • Certificate
- art history • MA
- arts and sciences • MA, MAT, MFA, MS, PhD, Certificate
- arts management • MA, Certificate
- biology • MA, MS
- chemistry • MS, PhD
- clinical psychology • PhD
- computer science • MS
- creative writing • MFA
- dance • MA
- development banking • MA
- economics • MA, PhD
- environmental science • MS
- environmental studies • MA
- experimental psychology • PhD
- experimental/biological psychology • MA
- financial economics for public policy • MA
- French studies • MA, Certificate
- general psychology • MA
- health fitness management • MS
- history • MA, PhD
- information systems • MS, Certificate
- international training and education • MA
- literature • MA
- mathematics • MA
- mathematics education • PhD
- painting, sculpture and printmaking • MFA
- personality/social psychology • MA
- philosophy • MA
- philosophy and social policy • MA
- physics • MS
- psychology • MA
- Russian studies • MA, Certificate
- social research • Certificate
- sociology • MA, PhD
- sociology/justice • PhD
- Spanish: Latin American studies • MA, Certificate
- statistical computing • MS
- statistics • MA, MS, PhD, Certificate
- statistics for policy analysis • MS
- teaching English to speakers of other languages • MA, Certificate
- toxicology • MS, Certificate
- translation • Certificate

School of Education

Dr. Charles Tesconi, Dean
Programs in:
- education • MA, MAT, PhD, Certificate
- educational leadership • MA
- educational technology • MA
- elementary education • MAT
- English for speakers of other languages • MAT
- learning disabilities • MA
- secondary teaching • MAT, Certificate
- specialized studies • MA

Kogod School of Business

Dr. Myron Roomkin, Dean
Programs in:
- accounting • MBA, MS
- business • MBA, MS
- business administration • MBA
- business management information systems • MS
- entrepreneurship and management • MBA
- finance • MBA, MS
- human resource management • MBA
- international business • MBA
- management of global information technology • MBA
- marketing information and technology • MBA
- marketing management • MBA
- real estate • MBA
- taxation • MS

School of Communication

Prof. Glenn Harnden, Acting Dean
Programs in:
- broadcast journalism • MA
- communication • MA, MFA
- film and electronic media • MFA
- film and video production • MA
- interactive journalism • MA
- journalism and public affairs • MA
- print journalism • MA
- producing for film and video • MA
- public communication • MA

School of International Service

Dr. Louis W. Goodman, Dean
Programs in:
- comparative and regional studies • MA
- development management • MS
- environmental policy • MA
- international communication • MA
- international development • MA
- international development management • Certificate
- international economic policy • MA
- international economic relations • Certificate
- international peace and conflict resolution • MA
- international politics • MA
- international relations • PhD
- U.S. foreign policy • MA

School of Public Affairs

Dr. Walter Broadmax, Dean
Programs in:
- justice • MS
- organization development • MSOD
- organizational development • Certificate
- personnel and human resource management • MS
- political science • MA, PhD
- public administration • MPA, PhD
- public affairs • MA, MPA, MPP, MS, MSOD, PhD, Certificate
- public financial management • Certificate
- public management • Certificate
- public policy • MPP
- sociology/justice • PhD

Washington College of Law

Claudio Grossman, Dean
Programs in:
- international legal studies • LL M
- law • JD
- law and government • LL M

■ THE CATHOLIC UNIVERSITY OF AMERICA

Washington, DC 20064
http://www.cua.edu/

Independent-religious, coed, university. CGS member. *Computer facilities:* 450 computers available on campus for

The Catholic University of America (continued)
general student use. A campuswide network can be accessed from student residence rooms and from off campus. Internet access and online class registration are available. *Library facilities:* Mullen Library plus 7 others. *General application contact:* Director of Graduate Admissions, 202-319-5227.

Find an in-depth description at www.petersons.com/graduate.

The Benjamin T. Rome School of Music

Programs in:
- accompanying and chamber music • MM
- chamber music • DMA
- composition • MM, DMA
- instrumental conducting • MM, DMA
- liturgical music • M Lit M, DMA
- music • M Lit M, MA, MM, DMA, PhD
- music education • MM, DMA
- musicology • MA, PhD
- orchestral instruments • MM, DMA
- organ • MM, DMA
- performance • MM, DMA
- piano pedagogy • MM, DMA
- vocal accompanying • DMA
- vocal pedagogy • MM
- vocal performance • MM
- voice pedagogy and performance • DMA

Columbus School of Law

Program in:
- law • JD

National Catholic School of Social Service

Program in:
- social service • MSW, PhD

School of Architecture and Planning

Program in:
- architecture and planning • M Arch, M Arch Studies

School of Arts and Sciences

Programs in:
- accounting • MA
- acting, directing, and playwriting • MFA
- administration, curriculum, and policy studies • MA
- American government • MA, PhD
- anthropology • MA, PhD
- applied experimental psychology • PhD
- arts and sciences • MA, MFA, MS, MTS, PhD, Certificate
- Byzantine studies • MA, Certificate
- Catholic school leadership • MA
- cell and microbial biology • MS, PhD
- cell biology • MS, PhD
- chemistry • MS, PhD
- classics • MA
- clinical laboratory science • MS, PhD
- clinical psychology • PhD
- comparative literature • MA, PhD
- congressional studies • MA
- counselor education • MA
- early Christian studies • MA, PhD, Certificate
- economics • MA
- educational administration • PhD
- educational psychology • PhD
- English as a second language • MA
- English language and literature • MA, PhD
- financial management • MA
- French • MA, PhD
- general psychology • MA
- German • MA
- Greek and Latin • PhD
- history • MA, PhD
- human development • PhD
- human factors • MA
- human resource management • MA
- international affairs • MA
- international political economics • MA
- Irish studies • MA
- Italian • MA
- Latin • MA
- learning and instruction • MA
- medieval studies • MA, PhD, Certificate
- microbiology • MS, PhD
- physics • MS, PhD
- policy studies • PhD
- political theory • MA, PhD
- psychology/law • MA, PhD
- rhetoric • MA, PhD
- Romance languages and literatures • MA, PhD
- Semitic and Egyptian languages and literature • MA, PhD
- sociology • MA, PhD
- Spanish • MA, PhD
- teacher education • MA
- theatre history and criticism • MA
- world politics • MA, PhD

School of Engineering

Programs in:
- biomedical engineering • MBE, MS Engr, PhD
- civil engineering • MCE, D Engr
- construction management • MCE, MS Engr
- design • D Engr, PhD
- design and robotics • MME, D Engr, PhD
- electrical engineering and computer science • MEE, MS Engr, D Engr, PhD
- engineering • MBE, MCE, MEE, MME, MS Engr, D Engr, PhD
- engineering management • MS Engr
- environmental engineering • MCE, MS Engr
- fluid and solid mechanics • PhD
- fluid mechanics and thermal science • MME, D Engr, PhD
- geotechnical engineering • MCE
- mechanical design • MME
- ocean and structural acoustics • MME, MS Engr, PhD
- structures and structural mechanics • MCE, PhD

School of Library and Information Science

Program in:
- library and information science • MSLS

School of Nursing

Programs in:
- advanced practice nursing • MSN
- clinical nursing • DN Sc

School of Philosophy

Program in:
- philosophy • MA, PhD, Ph L

School of Religious Studies

Programs in:
- biblical studies • MA, PhD
- canon law • JCD, JCL
- church history • MA, PhD
- history of religion • MA
- liturgical studies • MA, PhD, STD, STL
- religion • MA, MRE, PhD
- religious education • MA, MRE, PhD
- religious studies • M Div, STB, MA, MRE, D Min, JCD, PhD, STD, JCL, STL
- theology • M Div, STB, MA, D Min, PhD, STD, STL

■ GALLAUDET UNIVERSITY

Washington, DC 20002-3625
http://www.gallaudet.edu/

Independent, coed, university. CGS member. *Computer facilities:* 240 computers available on campus for general student use. A campuswide network can be accessed from student residence rooms and from off campus. Online class registration is available. *Library facilities:* Merrill Learning Center. *General application contact:* Coordinator of Prospective Graduate Student Services, 202-651-5647.

The Graduate School

College of Arts and Sciences
Programs in:
- arts and sciences • MA, MSW, PhD, Psy S
- clinical psychology • PhD
- developmental psychology • MA
- school psychology • MA, Psy S
- social work • MSW

School of Communication
Programs in:
- audiology • Au D
- communication • MA, MS, Au D
- interpretation • MA
- linguistics • MA
- speech and language pathology • MS

School of Education and Human Services
Programs in:
- administration • MS
- administration and supervision • PhD, Ed S
- community counseling • MA
- early childhood education • MA, Ed S
- education and human services • MA, MS, PhD, Certificate, Ed S
- education of deaf and hard of hearing students and multihandicapped deaf and hard of hearing students • MA, Ed S
- elementary education • MA, Ed S
- individualized program of study • PhD
- instructional supervision • Ed S
- integrating technology in the classroom • Certificate
- leadership training • MS
- leisure services administration • MS
- mental health counseling • MA
- parent/infant specialty • MA, Ed S
- school counseling • MA
- secondary education • MA, Ed S
- special education administration • PhD

■ GEORGETOWN UNIVERSITY
Washington, DC 20057
http://www.georgetown.edu/

Independent-religious, coed, university. CGS member. *Computer facilities:* 360 computers available on campus for general student use. A campuswide network can be accessed from student residence rooms and from off campus. Internet access and online class registration, online grade reports are available. *Library facilities:* Lauinger Library plus 6 others. *General application contact:* Dean of the Graduate School, 202-687-5974.

Graduate School of Arts and Sciences
Programs in:
- American government • MA, PhD
- analytical chemistry • MS, PhD
- Arab studies • MA, Certificate
- Arabic language, literature, and linguistics • MS, PhD
- bilingual education • Certificate
- biochemistry • MS, PhD
- biochemistry and molecular biology • PhD
- biology • MS, PhD
- biomedical sciences • MS, PhD
- biostatistics and epidemiology • MS
- British and American literature • MA
- cell biology • PhD
- chemical physics • MS, PhD
- communication, culture, and technology • MA
- comparative government • PhD
- demography • MA
- economics • PhD
- German • MS, PhD
- health physics • MS
- history • MA, PhD
- inorganic chemistry • MS, PhD
- international relations • PhD
- linguistics • MS, PhD
- microbiology and immunology • PhD
- national security studies • MA
- neuroscience • PhD
- organic chemistry • MS, PhD
- pathology • MS, PhD
- pharmacology • PhD
- philosophy • MA, PhD
- physical chemistry • MS, PhD
- physiology and biophysics • MS, PhD
- political theory • PhD
- psychology • PhD
- radiobiology • MS
- Russian and East European studies • MA
- Spanish • MS, PhD
- teaching English as a second language • MAT, Certificate
- teaching English as a second language and bilingual education • MAT
- theoretical chemistry • MS, PhD

BMW Center for German and European Studies
Program in:
- German and European studies • MA

Center for Latin American Studies
Program in:
- Latin American studies • MA

Edmund A. Walsh School of Foreign Service
Program in:
- foreign service • MS

The Georgetown Public Policy Institute
Program in:
- public policy • MPP

McDonough School of Business
Program in:
- business administration • MBA

School for Summer and Continuing Education
Program in:
- summer and continuing education • MALS

School of Nursing and Health Studies
Program in:
- nursing • MS

Law Center
Programs in:
- advocacy • LL M
- common law studies • LL M
- general • LL M
- international and comparative law • LL M
- labor and employment law • LL M
- law • JD, SJD
- securities regulation • LL M
- taxation • LL M

School of Medicine
Program in:
- medicine • MD

■ THE GEORGE WASHINGTON UNIVERSITY
Washington, DC 20052
http://www.gwu.edu/

Independent, coed, university. CGS member. *Enrollment:* 5,318 full-time matriculated graduate/professional students (2,817 women), 5,226 part-time matriculated graduate/professional students (2,644 women). *Graduate faculty:* 1,396 full-time (469 women), 2,643 part-time/adjunct (891 women). *Computer facilities:* 550 computers available on campus for general student use. A campuswide network can be accessed from student residence rooms and from off campus. *Library facilities:* Gelman Library plus 2 others. *Graduate expenses:* Tuition: full-time $13,680; part-time $760 per credit hour. *General application contact:* Kristin Williams, Director, Graduate Enrollment Support Services, 202-994-0467.

Find an in-depth description at www.petersons.com/graduate.

Columbian School of Arts and Sciences
Dr. Lester Lefton, Dean
Programs in:
- American • MA
- American literature • MA, PhD

The George Washington University (continued)
- American studies • MA, PhD
- analytical chemistry • MS, PhD
- anthropology • MA
- applied mathematics • MA, MS
- applied social psychology • PhD
- applied statistics • MS
- art history • MA
- art history-museum training • MA
- art therapy • MA
- arts and sciences • MA, MFA, MFS, MPP, MS, MSFS, PhD, Psy D, Certificate
- baroque • MA
- biochemistry and molecular biology • MS, PhD
- biology • MS, PhD
- biostatistics • MS, PhD
- ceramics • MFA
- chemical toxicology • MS
- classical acting • MFA
- classical art and archaeology • MA
- clinical psychology • PhD, Psy D
- cognitive neuropsychology • PhD
- computational mathematics • MS
- computational physics • MS
- computational science • MS
- computational statistics and stochastic modeling • MS
- contemporary • MA
- crime and commerce • MA
- criminal justice • MA
- design • MFA
- economics • MA, PhD
- eighteenth-century art • MA
- English literature • MA, PhD
- environmental and resource policy • MA
- epidemiology • MS, PhD
- folklife • MA
- forensic molecular biology • MFS
- forensic sciences • MFS, MSFS
- geochemistry • MS
- geography and regional science • MA
- geology • MS, PhD
- Hinduism and Islam • MA
- historic preservation • MA
- history • MA, PhD
- history and public policy • MA
- history of religion • MA
- hominid paleobiology • MS, PhD
- human resource management • MA
- human sciences • PhD
- industrial and engineering statistics • MS
- industrial-organizational psychology • PhD
- inorganic chemistry • MS, PhD
- interior design • MFA
- legislative affairs • MA
- material culture • MA
- materials science • MS, PhD
- mathematical statistics • MS
- mathematics • MA, PhD
- medieval • MA
- museum studies • MA, Certificate
- nineteenth-century art • MA
- organic chemistry • MS, PhD
- organizational management • MA
- painting • MFA
- philosophy and social policy • MA
- photography • MFA
- physical chemistry • MS, PhD
- physics • PhD
- political science • MA, PhD
- printmaking • MFA
- public policy • MA, MPP, PhD
- public policy-women's studies • MA
- Renaissance • MA
- sculpture • MFA
- security management • MA
- sociology • MA
- speech pathology • MA
- statistical computing • MS
- statistics • MS, PhD
- telecommunication studies • MA
- theatre/design • MFA
- visual communication • MFA
- women's studies • MA

Graduate School of Political Management
Dr. Christopher Arterton, Dean
Program in:
- political management • MA

Institute for Biomedical Sciences
Programs in:
- biochemistry • PhD
- genetics • MS, PhD
- immunology • PhD
- molecular and cellular oncology • PhD
- neuroscience • PhD
- pharmacology • PhD

School of Media and Public Affairs
Jean Folkerts, Director
Program in:
- media and public affairs • MA

Elliott School of International Affairs
Dr. Harry Harding, Dean
Programs in:
- Asian studies • MA
- European studies • MA
- international affairs • MA
- international development studies • MA
- international policy and practice • MA
- international trade and investment policy • MA
- Latin American studies • MA
- Russian and East European studies • MA
- science, technology, and public policy • MA
- security policy studies • MA

Graduate School of Education and Human Development
Dr. Mary Hatwood Futrell, Dean
Programs in:
- counseling • PhD, Ed S
- counseling: school, community and rehabilitation • MA Ed, PhD
- curriculum and instruction • MA Ed, Ed D, Ed S
- education administration and policy studies • Ed D
- education and human development • M Ed, MA Ed, MAT, Ed D, PhD, Certificate, Ed S
- education policy studies • MA Ed
- educational human development • MA Ed
- educational leadership and administration • MA Ed
- educational technology leadership • MA Ed
- elementary education • M Ed
- executive leadership • Ed D
- higher education administration • MA Ed, Ed D, Ed S
- human resource development • MA Ed, Ed D, Ed S
- infant special education • MA Ed
- international education • MA Ed
- museum education • MAT
- secondary education • M Ed
- special education • Ed D, Ed S
- special education of seriously emotionally disturbed students • MA Ed
- special education/early childhood • MA Ed
- transitional special education • MA Ed, Certificate

Law School
Michael K. Young, Dean
Program in:
- law • JD, LL M, SJD

School of Business and Public Management, Full Time MBA Program
Dr. Susan Philips, Dean
Programs in:
- accountancy • M Accy, PhD
- budget and public finance • MPA
- business and public management • M Accy, MBA, MPA, MS, MSF, MSIST, MTA, PhD
- business economics and public policy • MBA
- destination management • MTA
- event management • MTA
- executive, legislative, and regulatory management • MPA
- finance • MSF, PhD
- finance and investments • MBA
- human resources management • MBA
- information systems management • MBA

international business • MBA, PhD
logistics, operations, and materials management • MBA
management and organizations • PhD
management decision making • MBA, PhD
management information systems technology • MSIST
management of science, technology, and innovation • MBA
managing public organizations • MPA
managing state and local governments • MPA
marketing • MBA, PhD
organizational behavior and development • MBA
policy analysis and evaluation • MPA
project management • MS
public administration • MBA, MPA, PhD
real estate development • MBA
sport management • MTA
strategic management and public policy • PhD
tourism administration • MTA
tourism and hospitality management • MBA
travel marketing • MTA

School of Engineering and Applied Science
Dr. Timothy Tong, Dean
Programs in:
civil and environmental engineering • MS, D Sc, App Sc, Engr
computer science • MS, D Sc, App Sc, Engr
electrical and computer engineering • MS, D Sc, App Sc, Engr
engineering and applied science • MEM, MS, D Sc, App Sc, Engr
engineering management and systems engineering • MEM, MS, D Sc, App Sc, Engr
mechanical and aerospace engineering • MS, D Sc, App Sc, Engr

School of Medicine and Health Sciences
Dr. John F. Williams, Vice President for Academic Affairs
Programs in:
medicine • MD
medicine and health sciences • MD, MSHS
oral biology • MSHS
physical therapy • MSHS
physician assistant • MSHS

School of Public Health and Health Services
Dr. Richard Riegelman, Dean
Programs in:
administrative medicine • MPH
community-oriented primary care • MPH
environmental-occupational health • MPH
epidemiology-biostatistics • MPH
exercise science • MS
health promotion • MPH
health promotion-disease prevention • MPH
health services management and policy • MHSA, Specialist
international health • MPH
management • MPH
maternal and child health • MPH
policy • MPH
policy and programs • MPH
public health • Dr PH
public health and health services • MHSA, MPH, MS, MSHS, Dr PH, Specialist

■ HOWARD UNIVERSITY
Washington, DC 20059-0002
http://www.howard.edu/

Independent, coed, university. CGS member. *Computer facilities:* A campuswide network can be accessed from off campus. Internet access and online class registration are available. *Library facilities:* Founders Library plus 8 others. *General application contact:* Associate Dean for Student Relations, 202-806-6800.

College of Dentistry
Dr. Charles F. Sanders, Dean
Program in:
dentistry • DDS, Certificate

College of Engineering, Architecture, and Computer Sciences
Program in:
engineering, architecture, and computer sciences • M Arch, M Eng, MCS, MS, MS Arch, PhD

School of Architecture and Design
Programs in:
architecture • M Arch, MS Arch
architecture and design • M Arch, MS Arch

School of Engineering and Computer Science
Programs in:
aerospace engineering/dynamics and controls • M Eng, PhD
applied mechanics • M Eng, PhD
CAD/CAM and robotics • M Eng, PhD
chemical engineering • MS
electrical engineering • M Eng, PhD
engineering and computer science • M Eng, MCS, MS, PhD
environmental and water resources • M Eng
fluid and thermal sciences • M Eng, PhD
geotechnical engineering • M Eng
materials science and engineering • MS, PhD
structural engineering • M Eng
systems and computer science • MCS
transportation systems engineering • M Eng

College of Fine Arts
Programs in:
applied music • MM
art history • MA
ceramics • MFA
design • MFA
experimental studio • MFA
fine arts • MFA
jazz studies • MM
music • MM Ed
music education • MM Ed
painting • MFA
performance • MM
photography • MFA
printmaking • MFA
sculpture • MFA

College of Medicine
Programs in:
biochemistry and molecular biology • PhD
biotechnology • MS
medicine • MD, MS, PhD

College of Pharmacy, Nursing and Allied Health Sciences
Program in:
pharmacy, nursing and allied health sciences • Pharm D, MSN, Certificate

Division of Nursing
Programs in:
nurse practitioner • Certificate
primary family health nursing • MSN

Division of Pharmacy
Program in:
pharmacy • Pharm D

Graduate School of Arts and Sciences
Programs in:
African studies • MA, PhD
analytical chemistry • MS, PhD
anatomy • MS, PhD
applied mathematics • MS, PhD
arts and sciences • M Eng, MA, MAPA, MCS, MS, PhD
atmospheric sciences • MS, PhD
biochemistry • MS, PhD
biology • MS, PhD
biophysics • PhD
clinical psychology • PhD

Howard University (continued)

developmental psychology • PhD
economics • MA, PhD
English • MA, PhD
exercise physiology • MS
experimental psychology • PhD
French • MA
genetics and human genetics • MS, PhD
history • MA, PhD
inorganic chemistry • MS, PhD
mathematics • MS, PhD
microbiology • PhD
neuropsychology • PhD
nutrition • MS, PhD
organic chemistry • MS, PhD
personality psychology • PhD
pharmacology • MS, PhD
philosophy • MA
physical chemistry • MS, PhD
physics • MS, PhD
physiology • PhD
political science • MA, PhD
polymer chemistry • MS, PhD
psychology • MS
public administration • MAPA
public affairs • MA
recreation and leisure studies • MS
school and community health education • MS
social psychology • PhD
sociology • MA, PhD
Spanish • MA
theoretical chemistry • MS, PhD

School of Business
Dr. Barron H. Harvey, Dean
Programs in:
business • MBA
general management • MBA
health services administration • MBA

School of Communications
Programs in:
audiology • MS
communication sciences and disorders • PhD
communications • MA, MFA, MS, PhD
film • MFA
intercultural communication • MA, PhD
mass communication • MA, PhD
organizational communication • MA, PhD
speech pathology • MS

School of Divinity
Program in:
theology • M Div, MARS, D Min

School of Education
Programs in:
counseling psychology • M Ed, MA, Ed D, PhD, CAGS
early childhood education • M Ed, MA, MAT, CAGS
education • M Ed, MA, MAT, MS, Ed D, PhD, CAGS
educational administration • M Ed, MA, CAGS
educational psychology • M Ed, MA, Ed D, PhD, CAGS
educational supervision • M Ed, MA, CAGS
elementary education • M Ed
guidance and counseling • M Ed, MA, Ed D, PhD, CAGS
human development • MS
reading • M Ed, MA, MAT, CAGS
school psychology • M Ed, MA, Ed D, PhD, CAGS
secondary curriculum and instruction • M Ed, MA, MAT, CAGS
special education • M Ed, MA, CAGS

School of Law
Ruby Sherrod, Dean
Program in:
law • JD, LL M

School of Social Work
Program in:
social work • MSW, PhD

■ SOUTHEASTERN UNIVERSITY

Washington, DC 20024-2788
http://www.seu.edu/

Independent, coed, comprehensive institution. *Computer facilities:* 137 computers available on campus for general student use. A campuswide network can be accessed from off campus. *Library facilities:* The Learning Resources Center plus 1 other. *General application contact:* Director of Admissions, 202-265-5343.

Find an in-depth description at www.petersons.com/graduate.

College of Graduate Studies
Programs in:
accounting • MBA
business • MBA, MPA, MS
computer science • MS
financial management • MBA
government program management • MPA
health services administration • MPA
international management • MBA
management • MBA
management information systems • MBA
marketing • MBA
taxation • MS

■ STRAYER UNIVERSITY

Washington, DC 20005-2603
http://www.strayer.edu/

Proprietary, coed, comprehensive institution. CGS member. *Enrollment:* 1,018 full-time matriculated graduate/professional students (511 women), 799 part-time matriculated graduate/professional students (418 women). *Graduate faculty:* 61 full-time (7 women), 51 part-time/adjunct (17 women). *Computer facilities:* 1,000 computers available on campus for general student use. A campuswide network can be accessed. Internet access and online class registration are available. *Library facilities:* Wilkes Library plus 13 others. *Graduate expenses:* Tuition: full-time $7,560; part-time $280 per credit hour. *General application contact:* Betty G. Shuford, Administrative Dean, Region I, 202-408-2400.

Graduate School
Dr. Joel O. Nwagbaraocha, Director of Graduate Studies
Programs in:
business administration • MS
communications technology • MS
information systems • MS
professional accounting • MS

■ TRINITY COLLEGE

Washington, DC 20017-1094
http://www.trinitydc.edu/

Independent-religious, women only, comprehensive institution. *Enrollment:* 83 full-time matriculated graduate/professional students (66 women), 332 part-time matriculated graduate/professional students (281 women). *Graduate faculty:* 11 full-time (9 women), 32 part-time/adjunct (23 women). *Computer facilities:* 80 computers available on campus for general student use. A campuswide network can be accessed from student residence rooms and from off campus. Internet access and online class registration are available. *Library facilities:* Sister Helen Sheehan Library plus 1 other. *Graduate expenses:* Tuition: full-time $11,242; part-time $845 per credit. Tuition and fees vary according to program. *General application contact:* Carri Commer, Director of Graduate Admissions, 202-884-9400.

Find an in-depth description at www.petersons.com/graduate.

School of Education
Dr. Gloria Grantham, Dean
Programs in:
administration • MA
arts and sciences • MA
communications • MA
community counseling • MA
curriculum and instruction • M Ed
early childhood education • MAT
education • M Ed, MA, MAT, MSA
educational administration • MSA
elementary education • MAT
guidance and counseling • MA
health • MA
human resources development • MSA
human resources management • MSA
non-profit management • MSA
secondary education • MAT
special education • MAT
student development in higher education • MA

College of Arts and Sciences
Loretta M. Shpunt, Ph.D., Interim Chief Academic Administrator
Programs in:
arts and sciences • MA
communications • MA

School of Professional Studies
Dr. Sara Murray Thompson, Dean
Programs in:
administration • MA
health • MA
human resources development • MSA
human resources management • MSA
non-profit management • MSA

■ UNIVERSITY OF THE DISTRICT OF COLUMBIA
Washington, DC 20008-1175
http://www.udc.edu/

District-supported, coed, comprehensive institution. CGS member. *Enrollment:* 205 full-time matriculated graduate/professional students (133 women), 103 part-time matriculated graduate/professional students (78 women). *Graduate faculty:* 30. *Computer facilities:* 50 computers available on campus for general student use. A campuswide network can be accessed. *Library facilities:* Learning Resources Division Library plus 1 other. *Graduate expenses:* Tuition, district resident: part-time $198 per credit hour. Tuition, nonresident: part-time $329 per credit hour. One-time fee: $135 part-time. *General application contact:* LaVerne Hill Flannigan, Processor, Graduate Applications, 202-274-5008.

College of Arts and Sciences
Dr. Rachael Petty, Dean
Program in:
arts and sciences • MA, MS, MST

Division of Arts and Education
Dr. Rachael Petty, Dean
Programs in:
arts and education • MA, MS
early childhood education • MA
English • MA
special education • MA
speech and language pathology • MS

Division of Science and Mathematics
Dr. Freddie Dixon, Head
Programs in:
mathematics • MST
science and mathematics • MA, MST

Division of Urban Affairs, Social, and Behavioral Sciences
Dr. Sheilla Hammon-Martin, Head
Programs in:
counseling • MA
urban affairs, social, and behavioral sciences • MA

David A. Clarke School of Law
Katherine S. Broderick, Dean
Program in:
law • JD

School of Business and Public Administration
Dr. Herbert Quigley, Dean
Programs in:
business administration • MBA
business and public administration • MBA, MPA
public administration • MPA

Florida

■ ARGOSY UNIVERSITY-SARASOTA
Sarasota, FL 34235-8246
http://www.sarasota.edu/

Independent, coed, university. *Graduate faculty:* 24 full-time (11 women), 17 part-time/adjunct (5 women). *Graduate expenses:* Tuition: full-time $2,166; part-time $361 per credit. Tuition and fees vary according to program. *General application contact:* Elmina Taylor, Admissions Representative, 800-331-5995 Ext. 221.

Find an in-depth description at www.petersons.com/graduate.

College of Behavioral Sciences
Dr. Douglas G. Riedmiller, Dean
Programs in:
behavioral sciences • MA, Ed D, Ed S
counseling psychology • Ed D
guidance counseling • MA
mental health counseling • MA
organizational leadership • Ed D
pastoral community counseling • Ed D
school counseling • Ed S

College of Business Administration
Dr. Pete R. Simmons, Dean
Program in:
business • MBA, DBA

College of Education
Dr. Nancy Hoover, Dean
Programs in:
curriculum and instruction • Ed D, Ed S
education • Ed D, Ed S
educational leadership • Ed D, Ed S

■ BARRY UNIVERSITY
Miami Shores, FL 33161-6695
http://www.barry.edu/

Independent-religious, coed, university. *Enrollment:* 1,249 full-time matriculated graduate/professional students (798 women), 1,624 part-time matriculated graduate/professional students (1,178 women). *Graduate faculty:* 128 full-time (67 women), 86 part-time/adjunct. *Computer facilities:* 250 computers available on campus for general student use. A campuswide network can be accessed from student residence rooms and from off campus. Internet access is available. *Library facilities:* Monsignor William Barry Memorial Library plus 1 other. *Graduate expenses:* Tuition: full-time $8,910; part-time $495 per credit hour. Full-time tuition and fees vary according to course load, degree level and program. *General application contact:* Marcia Nance, Dean, Enrollment Services, 305-899-3112.

Find an in-depth description at www.petersons.com/graduate.

Andreas School of Business
Dr. Jack Scarborough, Dean
Programs in:
business • MBA
e-commerce • MS

Barry University (continued)

School of Adult and Continuing Education
Sr. Loretta Mulry,, OP, Dean
Programs in:
adult and continuing education • MS
information technology • MS

School of Arts and Sciences
Dr. Laura Armesto, Dean
Programs in:
arts and sciences • EMS, MA, MFA, MS, D Min, Certificate, SSP
broadcasting • Certificate
clinical psychology • MS
communication • EMS, MA
organizational communication • MS
pastoral ministry for Hispanics • MA
pastoral theology • MA
photography • MA, MFA
school psychology • MS, SSP
theology • MA, D Min

School of Education
Sr. Evelyn Piche, OP, Dean
Programs in:
counseling • PhD
education • MAT, MS, PhD, Ed S
educational computing and technology • PhD
educational leadership • MS, Ed S
elementary education • MS
exceptional student education • PhD
guidance and counseling • MS, Ed S
higher education administration • PhD
human resource development • PhD
leadership • PhD
marriage and family counseling • MS, Ed S
mental health counseling • MS, Ed S
Montessori education • MS, Ed S
pre-kindergarten and primary education • MS
reading • MS, Ed S
rehabilitation counseling • MS, Ed S
teaching • MAT

School of Graduate Medical Sciences
Dr. Chet Evans, Academic Dean
Programs in:
medical sciences • DPM, MCMS
physician assistant • MCMS
podiatric medicine • DPM

School of Human Performance and Leisure Sciences
Dr. G. Jean Cerra, Vice Provost, Academic Services
Programs in:
athletic training • MS
biomechanics • MS
exercise science • MS
human performance and leisure sciences • MS
sport management • MS

School of Law
Stanley Talcott, Dean
Program in:
law • JD

School of Natural and Health Sciences
Sr. John Karen Frei, Dean
Programs in:
anesthesiology • MS
biology • MS
biomedical sciences • MS
health services administration • MS
natural and health sciences • MS
occupational therapy • MS

School of Nursing
Dr. Judith Ann Balcerski, Dean
Programs in:
advanced nursing completion • MSN
nurse practitioner • MSN
nursing • MSN, PhD
nursing administration • MSN
nursing education • MSN

School of Social Work
Dr. Stephen Holloway, Dean
Program in:
social work • MSW, PhD

■ EMBRY-RIDDLE AERONAUTICAL UNIVERSITY

Daytona Beach, FL 32114-3900
http://www.embryriddle.edu/

Independent, coed, primarily men, comprehensive institution. *Enrollment:* 131 full-time matriculated graduate/professional students (33 women), 143 part-time matriculated graduate/professional students (31 women). *Graduate faculty:* 35 full-time (4 women), 5 part-time/adjunct (0 women). *Computer facilities:* A campuswide network can be accessed from student residence rooms and from off campus. *Library facilities:* Jack R. Hunt Memorial Library. *Graduate expenses:* Tuition: full-time $13,140; part-time $730 per credit. Required fees: $125 per semester. *General application contact:* Christine Castetter, Data Analyst, 386-226-6225.

Daytona Beach Campus Graduate Program
Dr. John Watret, Dean of Student Academics
Programs in:
aeronautical science • MAS
aeronautics • MAS, MBAA, MSAE, MSE, MSHFS, MSSS
aerospace engineering • MSAE
business administration in aviation • MBAA
human factors engineering • MSHFS
safety science • MSSS
software engineering • MSE
systems engineering • MSHFS

■ EMBRY-RIDDLE AERONAUTICAL UNIVERSITY, EXTENDED CAMPUS

Daytona Beach, FL 32114-3900
http://www.embryriddle.edu/

Independent, coed, primarily men, comprehensive institution. *Enrollment:* 50 full-time matriculated graduate/professional students (12 women), 2,279 part-time matriculated graduate/professional students (368 women). *Graduate faculty:* 119 full-time (13 women), 2,717 part-time/adjunct (445 women). *Library facilities:* Jack R. Hunt Memorial Library. *Graduate expenses:* Tuition: full-time $5,880; part-time $245 per credit. *General application contact:* Pam Thomas, Director of Admissions and Records, 386-226-6910.

Graduate Resident Centers
Dr. Leon E. Flancher, Chancellor
Programs in:
aeronautical science • MAS
aviation administration and management • MBAA
technical management • MSTM

■ FLORIDA AGRICULTURAL AND MECHANICAL UNIVERSITY

Tallahassee, FL 32307-3200
http://www.famu.edu/

State-supported, coed, university. CGS member. *Computer facilities:* A campuswide network can be accessed from student residence rooms and from off campus. Internet access is available. *Library facilities:* Coleman Memorial Library plus 5 others. *General application contact:* Dean of Graduate Studies, Research, and Continuing Education, 850-599-3315.

Division of Graduate Studies, Research, and Continuing Education

College of Allied Health Sciences

College of Arts and Sciences
Programs in:
applied social science • MASS
arts and sciences • MASS, MS
biology • MS
chemistry • MS
community psychology • MS
physics • MS
school psychology • MS
social and behavioral sciences • MASS

College of Education
Programs in:
administration and supervision • M Ed, MS Ed, PhD
adult education • M Ed, MS Ed
business education • MBE
early childhood and elementary education • M Ed, MS Ed
education • M Ed, MBE, MS Ed, PhD
guidance and counseling • M Ed, MS Ed
health, physical education, and recreation • M Ed, MS Ed
industrial education • M Ed, MS Ed
secondary education • M Ed, MS Ed

College of Engineering Science, Technology, and Agriculture
Programs in:
agricultural and extension education • M Ed, MS Ed
engineering science, technology, and agriculture • M Ed, MS Ed

College of Pharmacy and Pharmaceutical Sciences
Programs in:
environmental toxicology • PhD
medicinal chemistry • MS, PhD
pharmaceutics • MS, PhD
pharmacology/toxicology • MS, PhD
pharmacy administration • MS
pharmacy and pharmaceutical sciences • Pharm D, MPH, MS, PhD
public health • MPH

FAMU-FSU College of Engineering
Programs in:
chemical engineering • MS, PhD
civil engineering • MS, PhD
electrical engineering • MS, PhD
engineering • MS, PhD
environmental engineering • MS, PhD
industrial engineering • MS
mechanical engineering • MS, PhD

School of Architecture
Program in:
architecture • M Arch, MS Arch

School of Business and Industry
Programs in:
accounting • MBA
finance • MBA
management information systems • MBA
marketing • MBA

School of Journalism Media and Graphic Arts
Program in:
journalism • MS

■ FLORIDA ATLANTIC UNIVERSITY
Boca Raton, FL 33431-0991
http://www.fau.edu/

State-supported, coed, university. CGS member. *Enrollment:* 1,038 full-time matriculated graduate/professional students (564 women), 1,581 part-time matriculated graduate/professional students (994 women). *Graduate faculty:* 850 full-time (339 women), 11 part-time/adjunct (2 women). *Computer facilities:* 400 computers available on campus for general student use. A campuswide network can be accessed from student residence rooms and from off campus. Internet access and online class registration are available. *Library facilities:* S. E. Wimberly Library. *Graduate expenses:* Tuition, nonresident: full-time $12,843. *General application contact:* Steve Todish, Graduate Studies—Admissions, 561-297-3624.

Find an in-depth description at www.petersons.com/graduate.

Charles E. Schmidt College of Science
Dr. John Wiesenfeld, Dean
Programs in:
biological sciences • MBS, MS, MST
chemistry and biochemistry • MS, MST, PhD
environmental sciences • MS
geography • MA, MAT
geology • MS
mathematical science • MS, MST, PhD
physics • MS, MST, PhD
psychology • MA, PhD
science • MA, MAT, MBS, MS, MST, PhD

Center for Complex Systems and Brain Sciences
Dr. J. A. Scott Kelso, Director
Program in:
complex systems and brain sciences • PhD

College of Architecture, Urban and Public Affairs
Dr. Rosalyn Carter, Dean
Programs in:
architecture, urban and public affairs • MJPM, MNM, MPA, MSW, MURP, PhD
criminology and criminal justice • MJPM
social work • MSW
urban and regional planning • MURP

School of Public Administration
Dr. Hugh T. Miller, Director
Program in:
public administration • MNM, MPA, PhD

College of Business
Dr. Bruce Mallen, Dean
Programs in:
business • Exec MBA, M Ac, M Tax, MA, MBA, MS, MSIB, MST, PhD
business administration • Exec MBA, MBA, MSIB, PhD
economics • MS, MST
sport management • MBA

School of Accounting
Dr. Carl Borgia, Director, School of Accounting
Programs in:
accounting • M Ac, M Tax
taxation • M Tax

College of Education
Dr. Jerry Lafferty, Dean
Programs in:
adult/community education • M Ed, Ed D, Ed S
counselor education • M Ed, Ed S
curriculum and instruction • M Ed, Ed D, Ed S
early childhood education • M Ed
education • M Ed, MA, MAT, MS, MST, Ed D, Ed S
educational leadership • M Ed, Ed D, Ed S
elementary education • M Ed
execptional student education • M Ed
exercise science and health promotion • M Ed, MS
foundations of education • M Ed
foundations-educational research • M Ed
foundations-educational technology • M Ed
higher education management • Ed D
reading teacher education • M Ed
special education • Ed D
speech-language pathology • MS

Florida Atlantic University (continued)

College of Engineering
Dr. John Jurewicz, Dean
Programs in:
civil engineering • MS
computer engineering • MS, PhD
computer science • MS, PhD
electrical engineering • MS, PhD
engineering • MS, PhD
manufacturing systems engineering • MS
mechanical engineering • MS, PhD
ocean engineering • MS, PhD

College of Liberal Arts
John Childrey, Associate Dean
Programs in:
computer arts • MFA
graphic design • MFA
liberal studies • MLBLST
music • MA
teaching English • MA

College of Nursing
Dr. Anne Boykin, Dean
Programs in:
adult practitioner • MS, Post Master's Certificate
family practitioner • MS, Post Master's Certificate
gerontology • MS, Post Master's Certificate
nursing • MS, Post Master's Certificate
nursing administration • MS

Dorothy F. Schmidt College of Arts and Letters
Dr. James Lamare, Dean
Programs in:
American literature • MA
anthropology • MA, MAT
art education • MAT
arts and letters • MA, MAT, MFA, PhD
ceramics • MFA
communication • MA
comparative literature • MA
comparative studies • PhD
English literature • MA
fantasy and science fiction • MA
French • MA
German • MA
history • MA
multicultural literature • MA
music • MA
political science • MA, MAT
sociology • MA, MAT
Spanish • MA
teaching French • MAT
teaching German • MAT
teaching Spanish • MAT
theatre • MFA

Women's Studies Center
Dr. Leslie Terry, Acting Director
Program in:
women's studies • MA

■ FLORIDA GULF COAST UNIVERSITY

Fort Myers, FL 33965-6565

http://www.fgcu.edu/

State-supported, coed, comprehensive institution. *Enrollment:* 136 full-time matriculated graduate/professional students (67 women), 333 part-time matriculated graduate/professional students (242 women). *Graduate faculty:* 74 full-time (32 women), 13 part-time/adjunct (8 women). *Computer facilities:* 323 computers available on campus for general student use. A campuswide network can be accessed from student residence rooms and from off campus. Internet access and online class registration, online admissions and advising are available. *Library facilities:* Library Services. *Graduate expenses:* Full-time $3,556; part-time $148 per credit. Tuition, state resident: full-time $3,556; part-time $148 per credit. Tuition, nonresident: full-time $1,264; part-time $527 per credit. Required fees: $700. *General application contact:* Marc Laviolette, Graduate Admissions Coordinator, 941-590-7878.

College of Business
Richard Pegnetter, Dean
Programs in:
accounting and taxation • MS
business • MBA, MS
business administration • MBA
computer and information systems • MS

College of Education
Lawrence Byrnes, Dean
Programs in:
behavior disorders • MA
biology • MAT
counselor education • M Ed, MA
education • M Ed, MA, MAT
educational leadership • M Ed
educational technology • M Ed, MA
elementary education • M Ed, MA
English • MAT
mathematics • MAT
mental retardation • MA
reading education • M Ed
social sciences • MAT
specific learning disabilities • MA
varying exceptionalities • MA

College of Health Professions
Cecilia Rokusek, Dean
Programs in:
health professions • MS, MSN
health science • MS
nursing • MSN
physical therapy • MS

College of Public and Social Services
John McGaha, Director
Programs in:
criminal justice • MPA
environmental policy • MPA
general public administration • MPA
management • MPA
public and social services • MPA, MSW
social work • MSW

■ FLORIDA INSTITUTE OF TECHNOLOGY

Melbourne, FL 32901-6975

http://www.fit.edu/

Independent, coed, university. CGS member. *Enrollment:* 399 full-time matriculated graduate/professional students (166 women), 1,763 part-time matriculated graduate/professional students (639 women). *Graduate faculty:* 116 full-time (25 women), 176 part-time/adjunct (52 women). *Computer facilities:* 600 computers available on campus for general student use. A campuswide network can be accessed from student residence rooms and from off campus. Internet access and online class registration are available. *Library facilities:* Evans Library. *Graduate expenses:* Tuition: part-time $610 per credit. Tuition and fees vary according to campus/location and program. *General application contact:* Dr. Carolyn P. Farrior, Director of Graduate Admissions, 321-674-7118.

Find an in-depth description at www.petersons.com/graduate.

Graduate School
Dr. Robert L. Sullivan, Vice President for Research and Graduate Programs

College of Engineering
Dr. J. Ronald Bailey, Dean
Programs in:
aerospace engineering • MS, PhD
biological oceanography • MS
chemical engineering • MS, PhD
chemical oceanography • MS
civil engineering • MS, PhD
coastal zone management • MS
computer engineering • MS
computer information systems • MS
computer science • MS, PhD
electrical engineering • MS, PhD
engineering • MS, PhD
engineering management • MS
environmental resource management • MS
environmental science • MS, PhD
geological oceanography • MS

mechanical engineering • MS, PhD
meteorology • MS
ocean engineering • MS, PhD
oceanography • MS, PhD
physical oceanography • MS
software engineering • MS

College of Science and Liberal Arts
Dr. Gordon L. Nelson, Dean
Programs in:
applied mathematics • MS, PhD
biology • PhD
biotechnology • MS
cell and molecular biology • MS
chemistry • MS, PhD
computer science education • MS
ecology • MS
environmental education • MS
general science education • MS, Ed S
marine biology • MS
mathematics education • MS, Ed D, PhD, Ed S
operations research • MS, PhD
physics • MS, PhD
science and liberal arts • MS, Ed D, PhD, Ed S
science education • Ed D, PhD
space science • MS, PhD
technical and professional communication • MS

School of Aeronautics
Dr. Nathaniel Villaire, Chairman of Graduate Studies
Programs in:
airport development and management • MSA
applied airport safety • MSA
aviation human factors • MS

School of Business
Dr. A. Thomas Hollingsworth, Dean
Programs in:
accounting • MBA
business administration • MBA

School of Extended Graduate Studies
Programs in:
acquisition and contract management • MS, MSM, PMBA
aerospace engineering • MS
business administration • PMBA
computer information systems • MS
computer science • MS
electrical engineering • MS
engineering management • MS
health management • MS
health sciences management • MSM
human resource management • MSM, PMBA
human resources management • MS
information systems • MSM, PMBA
logistics management • MS, MSM
management • MS
material acquisition management • MS
mechanical engineering • MS
operations research • MS
public administration • MPA
space systems • MS
space systems management • MS
transportation management • MSM

School of Psychology
Dr. Carol L. Philpot, Dean
Programs in:
applied behavior analysis • MS
clinical psychology • Psy D
industrial/organizational psychology • MS, PhD

■ FLORIDA INTERNATIONAL UNIVERSITY
Miami, FL 33199
http://www.fiu.edu/

State-supported, coed, university. CGS member. *Enrollment:* 1,772 full-time matriculated graduate/professional students (1,015 women), 2,362 part-time matriculated graduate/professional students (1,412 women). *Graduate faculty:* 766 full-time (276 women). *Computer facilities:* 600 computers available on campus for general student use. A campuswide network can be accessed from student residence rooms and from off campus. Internet access and online class registration are available. *Library facilities:* University Park Library plus 2 others. *Graduate expenses:* Tuition, state resident: part-time $151 per credit. Tuition, nonresident: part-time $530 per credit. Required fees: $54 per term. *General application contact:* Carmen Brown, Director of Admissions, 305-348-2363.

Find an in-depth description at www.petersons.com/graduate.

College of Arts and Sciences
Dr. Arthur W. Herriott, Dean
Programs in:
African-new world studies • MA
arts and sciences • MA, MFA, MM, MS, PhD
biological management • MS
biological sciences • MS, PhD
chemistry • MS, PhD
comparative sociology • MA
creative writing • MFA
developmental psychology • PhD
earth sciences • MS, PhD
economics • MA, PhD
energy • MS
English • MA
forensic science • MS
general psychology • MS
history • MA, PhD
international relations • PhD
international studies • MA
Latin American and Caribbean studies • MA
linguistics • MA
mathematical sciences • MS
physics • MS, PhD
political science • MS, PhD
pollution • MS
psychology • MS
religious studies • MA
sociology • PhD
Spanish • MA, PhD
statistics • MS
visual arts • MFA

School of Computer Science
Dr. Jainendra Navlakha, Director
Program in:
computer science • MS, PhD

School of Music
Fredrick Kaufman, Director
Programs in:
music • MM
music education • MS

College of Business Administration
Dr. Joyce J. Elam, Dean
Programs in:
business administration • M Acc, MBA, MIB, MS, MSF, MST, PhD
decision sciences and information systems • PhD
finance • MSF
international business • MIB

School of Accounting
Dr. Mortimer Dittenhofer, Director
Programs in:
accounting • M Acc
taxation • MST

College of Education
Dr. Linda P. Blanton, Dean
Programs in:
adult education • MS, Ed D
art education • MS
community college teaching • Ed D
counselor education • MS
curriculum and instruction • Ed D, Ed S
early childhood education • MS
education • MA, MS, Ed D, Ed S
educational administration and supervision • Ed D
educational leadership • Ed D, Ed S
elementary education • MS
emotional disturbances • MS
English education • MS
English for non-English speakers • MS
exceptional student education • Ed D
health education • MS
health occupations education • MS
higher education administration • Ed S
home economics education • MS

Florida International University (continued)

human resource development • MS
international development education • MS
mathematics education • MS
modern language education • MS
non-school based home economics education • MS
parks and recreation administration • MS
physical education • MS
reading education • MS
school psychology • Ed S
science education • MS
social studies education • MS
specific learning disabilities • MS
technical education • MS
urban education • MS
vocational home economics education • MS
vocational industrial education • MS

College of Engineering
Dr. Richard K. Irey, Acting Dean
Programs in:
biomedical engineering • MS
civil engineering • MS, PhD
computer engineering • MS
construction management • MS
electrical engineering • MS, PhD
engineering • MS, PhD
environmental and urban systems • MS
environmental engineering • MS
industrial engineering • MS
mechanical engineering • MS, PhD

College of Health and Urban Affairs
Dr. Ronald M. Berkman, Dean
Program in:
health and urban affairs • MHSA, MPA, MPH, MS, MSN, MSW, PhD

School of Health
Dr. Carol Pyles, Director
Programs in:
dietetics and nutrition • MS, PhD
health • MPH, MS, MSN, PhD
occupational therapy • MS
physical therapy • MS
public health • MPH
speech-language pathology • MS

School of Nursing
Dr. Divina Grossman, Director
Program in:
nursing • MSN

School of Policy and Management
Dr. Gloria Deckard, Director
Programs in:
criminal justice • MS
health services administration • MHSA
policy and management • MHSA, MPA, MS, PhD
public administration • MPA, PhD

School of Social Work
Dr. Ray Thomlison, Director
Program in:
social work • MSW, PhD

School of Architecture
William McMinn, Dean
Programs in:
architecture • MS
landscape architecture • MS

School of Hospitality Management
Dr. Joseph West, Dean
Program in:
hotel and food service management • MS

School of Journalism and Mass Communication
Dr. J. Arthur Heise, Dean
Program in:
mass communication • MS

■ FLORIDA METROPOLITAN UNIVERSITY–BRANDON CAMPUS

Tampa, FL 33619
http://www.fmu.edu/

Proprietary, coed, comprehensive institution. *Computer facilities:* 81 computers available on campus for general student use. A campuswide network can be accessed. Internet access is available. *Library facilities:* Tampa College Library. *General application contact:* 813-621-0041.

Program in Business Administration
Program in:
business administration • MBA

Program in Criminal Justice
Program in:
criminal justice • MS

■ FLORIDA METROPOLITAN UNIVERSITY–NORTH ORLANDO CAMPUS

Orlando, FL 32810-5674
http://www.fmu.edu/

Proprietary, coed, comprehensive institution. *Enrollment:* 6 full-time matriculated graduate/professional students (4 women), 35 part-time matriculated graduate/professional students (18 women). *Graduate faculty:* 1 full-time (0 women), 6 part-time/adjunct (0 women). *Computer facilities:* 25 computers available on campus for general student use. A campuswide network can be accessed. Internet access is available. *Library facilities:* Orlando College Library. *Graduate expenses:* Tuition: full-time $7,500. *General application contact:* Charlene Donnelly, Director of Admissions, 407-628-5870 Ext. 108.

Division of Business Administration
Program in:
business administration • MBA

■ FLORIDA METROPOLITAN UNIVERSITY–PINELLAS CAMPUS

Clearwater, FL 33759
http://www.fmu.edu/

Proprietary, coed, comprehensive institution. *Computer facilities:* 42 computers available on campus for general student use. A campuswide network can be accessed. Internet access is available. *Library facilities:* Laurel Raffel Memorial Library. *General application contact:* 727-725-2688.

Program in Business Administration
Program in:
business administration • MBA

Program in Criminal Justice
Program in:
criminal justice • MS

■ FLORIDA METROPOLITAN UNIVERSITY–TAMPA CAMPUS

Tampa, FL 33614-5899
http://www.cci.edu/

Proprietary, coed, comprehensive institution. *Computer facilities:* 113 computers available on campus for general student use. Internet access is available. *Library facilities:* Tampa College Library. *General application contact:* Director of Admissions, 813-879-6000 Ext. 36.

Department of Business Administration
Programs in:
human resources • MBA
international business • MBA

■ FLORIDA STATE UNIVERSITY

Tallahassee, FL 32306
http://www.fsu.edu/

State-supported, coed, university. CGS member. *Enrollment:* 4,167 full-time matriculated graduate/professional students (2,171 women), 2,169 part-time matriculated graduate/professional students (1,347 women). *Graduate faculty:* 999 full-time (307 women), 10 part-time/adjunct (4 women). *Computer facilities:* 1,249 computers available on campus for general student use. A campuswide network can be accessed from student residence rooms and from off campus. Internet access and online class registration, Web pages are available. *Library facilities:* Robert Manning Strozier Library plus 6 others. *Graduate expenses:* Tuition, state resident: part-time $153 per credit hour. Tuition, nonresident: part-time $532 per credit hour. Required fees: $133 per credit hour. *General application contact:* Melanie Booker, Assistant Director for Graduate Admissions, 850-644-3420.

Find an in-depth description at www.petersons.com/graduate.

College of Law

Donald J. Weidner, Dean
Program in:
law • JD

Graduate Studies

Dr. Alan R. Mabe, Associate Vice President and Dean

College of Arts and Sciences
Dr. Donald J. Foss, Dean
Programs in:
American and Florida studies • MA
analytical chemistry • MS, PhD
anthropology • MA, MS, PhD
applied behavior analysis • MS
applied mathematics • MA, MS, PhD
applied statistics • MS
arts and sciences • MA, MS, PhD
biochemistry • MS, PhD
cell biology • MS, PhD
chemical physics • MS, PhD
classical archaeology • MA
classical civilization • MA, PhD
classics • MA
clinical psychology • PhD
cognitive and behavioral science • PhD
computer and network system administration • MA, MS
computer science • MA, MS, PhD
developmental biology • MS, PhD
ecology • MS, PhD
English • MA, PhD
evolutionary biology • MS, PhD
financial mathematics • PhD
French • MA, PhD
genetics • MS, PhD
geological sciences • MS, PhD
geophysical fluid dynamics • PhD
German • MA
Greek • MA
Greek and Latin • MA
historical administration • MA
history • MA, PhD
humanities • PhD
immunology • MS, PhD
inorganic chemistry • MS, PhD
Italian • MA
Latin • MA
literature • MA, PhD
marine biology • MS, PhD
mathematical sciences • MA, MS
mathematical statistics • MS, PhD
meteorology • MS, PhD
microbiology • MS, PhD
molecular biology • MS, PhD
molecular biophysics • PhD
neuroscience • PhD
oceanography • MS, PhD
organic chemistry • MS, PhD
philosophy • MA, PhD
physical chemistry • MS, PhD
physics • MS, PhD
physiology • MS, PhD
plant sciences • MS, PhD
pure mathematics • MA, MS, PhD
radiation biology • MS, PhD
religion • MA, PhD
Slavic languages and literatures • MA
Slavic languages/Russian • MA
software engineering • MA, MS
Spanish • MA, PhD
writing • MA, PhD

College of Business
Dr. Pamela L. Perrewé, Associate Dean for Graduate Studies
Programs in:
accounting • M Acc
business administration • MBA, PhD
management • MS

College of Communication
Dr. John K. Mayo, Dean
Programs in:
communication • Adv M, MA, MS, PhD
communication sciences and disorders • Adv M, MS, PhD
interactive and new communication technology • MA, MS
management communication • MA, MS
mass communication • MA, MS, PhD
policy and political communications • MS
policy political communication • MA
rhetorical and communication theory • MA, MS
speech communication • PhD

College of Education
Dr. Robert C. Clark, Dean
Programs in:
adapted physical education • MS
adult education • MS, Ed D, PhD, Ed S
comprehensive vocational education • PhD, Ed S
counseling and human systems • MS, Ed S
counseling psychology • PhD
early childhood education • MS, Ed D, PhD, Ed S
education • MS, Ed D, PhD, Ed S
educational administration/leadership • MS, Ed D, PhD, Ed S
educational psychology • MS, PhD, Ed S
elementary education • MS, Ed D, PhD, Ed S
emotional disturbance/learning disabilities • MS
English education • MS, PhD, Ed S
foundations of education • MS, PhD, Ed S
health education • MS
higher education • MS, Ed D, PhD, Ed S
history and philosophy of education • MS, PhD, Ed S
institutional research • MS, Ed D, PhD, Ed S
instructional systems • MS, PhD, Ed S
international and intercultural education • MS, PhD, Ed S
learning and cognition • MS, PhD, Ed S
mathematics education • MS, PhD, Ed S
measurement and statistics • MS, PhD, Ed S
mental retardation • MS
multilingual-multicultural education • MS, PhD, Ed S
open and distance learning • MS
policy planning and analysis • MS, Ed D, PhD, Ed S
program evaluation • MS, PhD, Ed S
reading education/language arts • MS, Ed D, PhD, Ed S
recreation and leisure services administration • MS
rehabilitation services • MS, Ed D, PhD, Ed S
school psychology • MS, Ed S
science education • MS, PhD, Ed S
social science and education • PhD, Ed S
social science education • MS, Ed D, PhD, Ed S
special education • PhD, Ed S
sports administration • MS, Ed D, PhD, Ed S

Florida State University (continued)
sports psychology • MS, PhD, Ed S
teacher education • MS, Ed D, PhD, Ed S
visual disabilities • MS

College of Human Sciences
Dr. Penny A. Ralston, Dean
Programs in:
child development • MS, PhD
exercise science • MS, PhD
family and consumer sciences education • MS, PhD
family relations • MS, PhD
human sciences • MS, PhD
marriage and the family • PhD
nutrition and food science • PhD
nutrition and food sciences • MS
textiles and consumer sciences • MS, PhD

College of Social Sciences
Dr. Marie E. Cowart, Dean
Programs in:
Asian studies • MA
economics • MS, PhD
geography • MA, MS, PhD
health policy research • MA, MS, PhD
international affairs • MA, MS
political science • MA, MS, PhD
public administration and policy • MPA, PhD, Certificate
Russian and East European studies • MA
social science • MA, MS
social sciences • MA, MPA, MS, MSP, PhD, Certificate
sociology • MA, MS, PhD
study of population • MS, Certificate
urban and regional planning • MSP, PhD

FAMU/FSU College of Engineering
Programs in:
chemical engineering • MS, PhD
civil engineering • MS, PhD
electrical engineering • MS, PhD
engineering • MS, PhD
environmental engineering • MS, PhD
industrial engineering • MS, PhD
mechanical engineering • MS, PhD

School of Criminology and Criminal Justice
Daniel Maier-Katkin, Dean
Program in:
criminology and criminal justice • MA, MSC, PhD

School of Information Studies
Dr. Jane B. Robbins, Dean
Programs in:
information studies • PhD
library and information studies • MS, PhD, Specialist

School of Motion Picture, Television, and Recording Arts
Dr. Raymond Fielding, Dean
Program in:
motion picture, television, and recording arts • MFA

School of Music
Jon R. Piersol, Dean
Programs in:
accompanying • MM
arts administration • MA
choral conducting • MM
composition • MM, DM
ethnomusicology • MM
instrumental accompanying • MM
instrumental conducting • MM
jazz studies • MM
music education • MM Ed, Ed D, PhD
music theory • MM, PhD
music therapy • MM
musicology • MM, PhD
opera • MM
performance • MM, DM
piano pedagogy • MM
vocal accompanying • MM

School of Nursing
Dr. Evelyn Singer, Dean
Program in:
family nursing • MSN

School of Social Work
Dr. Frederick W. Seidl, Interim Dean
Programs in:
clinical social work • MSW
marriage and the family • PhD
social policy and administration • MSW
social work • PhD

School of Theatre
Dr. John J. Deal, Interim Dean
Programs in:
acting • MFA
directing • MFA
lighting, costume, and scenic design • MFA
technical production • MFA
theater management • MFA
theatre • MA, MS, PhD

School of Visual Arts and Dance
Dr. Jerry L. Draper, Dean
Programs in:
art education • MA, MS, Ed D, PhD, Ed S
art history • MA, PhD
dance • MFA
interior design • MA, MFA, MS
museum studies • Certificate
studio art • MFA
visual arts and dance • MA, MFA, MS, Ed D, PhD, Certificate, Ed S

■ JACKSONVILLE UNIVERSITY

Jacksonville, FL 32211-3394
http://www.ju.edu/

Independent, coed, comprehensive institution. *Computer facilities:* 300 computers available on campus for general student use. A campuswide network can be accessed from student residence rooms and from off campus. *Library facilities:* Carl S. Swisher Library. *General application contact:* Director of Admissions, 904-745-7000.

College of Arts and Sciences
Program in:
arts and sciences • MAT, Certificate

School of Education
Programs in:
art • MAT
computer education • MAT
early childhood education • Certificate
educational leadership • MAT
elementary education • MAT
English • MAT
exceptional child education • Certificate
foreign language • MAT
French • MAT
gifted education • Certificate
integrated learning with educational technology • MAT
mathematics • MAT
music • MAT
reading • MAT
secondary education • Certificate
Spanish • MAT

Davis College of Business
Programs in:
business • Exec MBA, MBA
business administration • Exec MBA, MBA

■ LYNN UNIVERSITY

Boca Raton, FL 33431-5598
http://www.lynn.edu/

Independent, coed, comprehensive institution. *Computer facilities:* 150 computers available on campus for general student use. A campuswide network can be accessed from student residence rooms and from off campus. *Library facilities:* Eugene M. and Christine E. Lynn Library. *General application contact:* Graduate Admission Coordinator, 800-544-8035 Ext. 7849.

Find an in-depth description at www.petersons.com/graduate.

School of Graduate Studies
Programs in:
aging studies • Certificate
biomechanical trauma • MS
criminal justice administration • MS
health care administration • MS, Certificate
music performance • Diploma

College of Education
Programs in:
educational leadership with a global perspective • PhD
ESOL and varying exceptionalities • M Ed
varying exceptionalities • M Ed

School of Business
Programs in:
hospitality administration • MBA
international business • MBA
sports and athletics administration • MBA

■ NOVA SOUTHEASTERN UNIVERSITY
Fort Lauderdale, FL 33314-7721
http://www.nova.edu/

Independent, coed, university. CGS member. *Enrollment:* 6,154 full-time matriculated graduate/professional students (3,751 women), 8,323 part-time matriculated graduate/professional students (5,506 women). *Graduate faculty:* 429 full-time (145 women), 941 part-time/adjunct (417 women). *Computer facilities:* 800 computers available on campus for general student use. A campuswide network can be accessed from student residence rooms and from off campus. Internet access and online class registration are available. *Library facilities:* Einstein Library plus 4 others. *Graduate expenses:* Tuition: full-time $7,240; part-time $406 per credit. Required fees: $200. Tuition and fees vary according to course load and program. *General application contact:* 800-541-6682.

Center for Psychological Studies
Dr. Ronald F. Levant, Dean
Programs in:
clinical psychology • PhD, Psy D, SPS
mental health counseling • MS
psychological studies • MS, PhD, Psy D, SPS
psychopharmacology • MS
school guidance and counseling • MS

Fischler Graduate School of Education and Human Services
Dr. H. Wells Singleton, Provost/Dean
Programs in:
adult education • Ed D
audiology • Au D
child and youth care administration • MS
child and youth studies • Ed D
computer science education • MS, Ed S
computing and information technology • Ed D
early childhood education administration • MS
education and human services • MA, MS, Au D, Ed D, SLPD, Ed S
education technology • MS, Ed S
educational leaders • Ed D
educational leadership (administration K–12) • MS, Ed S
educational media • MS, Ed S
educational technology • MS
elementary education • MS, Ed S
English • MS, Ed S
family support studies • MS
gifted education • MS
health care education • Ed D
higher education • Ed D
instructional technology and distance education • MS, Ed D
mathematics • MS, Ed S
pre-kindergarten/primary • Ed S
prekindergarten/primary • MS
reading • MS, Ed S
science • MS, Ed S
social studies • MS, Ed S
Spanish language • MS
speech-language pathology • MS, SLPD
substance abuse counseling and education • MS
teaching and learning • MA
teaching English to speakers of other languages • MS, Ed S
varying exceptionalities • MS, Ed S
vocational, occupational and technical education • Ed D

Health Professions Division
Dr. Morton Terry, Chancellor
Program in:
health professions • DMD, DO, OD, Pharm D, MBS, MOT, MPH, MPT, Dr OT, Dr Sc PT, PhD

College of Allied Health
Dr. Raul Cuadrado, Director
Programs in:
allied health • MOT, MPH, MPT, Dr OT, Dr Sc PT, PhD
occupational therapy • MOT, Dr OT, PhD
physical therapy • MPT, Dr Sc PT
public health • MPH

College of Dental Medicine
Dr. Seymour Oliet, Dean
Program in:
dental medicine • DMD

College of Medical Sciences
Dr. Harold E. Laubach, Dean
Program in:
biomedical sciences • MBS

College of Optometry
Dr. David S. Loshin, Dean
Program in:
optometry • OD

College of Osteopathic Medicine
Dr. Anthony J. Silavgni, Dean
Program in:
osteopathic medicine • DO

College of Pharmacy
Dr. William Hardigan, Dean
Program in:
pharmacy • Pharm D

Oceanographic Center
Dr. Richard Dodge, Dean
Programs in:
coastal-zone management • MS
marine biology • MS, PhD
marine environmental science • MS
oceanography • PhD

School of Computer and Information Sciences
Dr. Edward Lieblein, Dean
Programs in:
computer information systems • MS, PhD
computer science • MS, PhD
computing technology in education • MS, Ed D, PhD
information science • PhD
information systems • PhD
management information systems • MS

School of Social and Systemic Studies
Dr. Honggang Yang, Dean
Programs in:
dispute resolution • MS, PhD, Certificate
family therapy • MS, PhD, Certificate
social and systemic studies • MS, PhD, Certificate

Shepard Broad Law Center
Joseph D. Harbaugh, Dean
Program in:
law • JD

Nova Southeastern University (continued)

Wayne Huizenga Graduate School of Business and Entrepreneurship
Dr. Randolph A. Pohlman, Dean
Programs in:
accounting • M Acc
business administration • MBA, DBA
business and entrepreneurship • M Acc, MBA, MIBA, MPA, MS, MSHRM, MT, DBA, DIBA, DPA
health services administration • MS
human resources management • MSHRM
international business administration • MIBA, DIBA
public administration • MPA, DPA

■ PALM BEACH ATLANTIC COLLEGE

West Palm Beach, FL 33416-4708
http://www.pbac.edu/

Independent-religious, coed, comprehensive institution. *Enrollment:* 139 full-time matriculated graduate/professional students (104 women), 199 part-time matriculated graduate/professional students (87 women). *Graduate faculty:* 25 full-time (7 women), 18 part-time/adjunct (13 women). *Computer facilities:* A campuswide network can be accessed from student residence rooms and from off campus. *Library facilities:* E. C. Blomeyer Library. *Graduate expenses:* Tuition: part-time $285 per course. *General application contact:* Carolanne M. Brown, Director of Graduate Admissions, 800-281-3466.

MacArthur School of Continuing Education
Dr. Dawn Hodges, Dean
Program in:
human resource development • MS

Rinker School of Business
Dr. Bob Myers, Acting Dean
Program in:
business • MBA

School of Education and Behavioral Studies
Dr. Dona Thornton, Dean
Programs in:
counseling psychology • MSCP
elementary education • M Ed

School of Ministry
Dr. Kenneth L. Mahanes, Vice President of Religious Life and Dean
Program in:
ministry • MA

School of Pharmacy
Dr. Scott Swigart, Dean
Program in:
pharmacy • Pharm D

■ ROLLINS COLLEGE

Winter Park, FL 32789-4499
http://www.rollins.edu/

Independent, coed, comprehensive institution. *Enrollment:* 274 full-time matriculated graduate/professional students (134 women), 448 part-time matriculated graduate/professional students (279 women). *Graduate faculty:* 34 full-time (9 women), 23 part-time/adjunct (9 women). *Computer facilities:* 200 computers available on campus for general student use. A campuswide network can be accessed from student residence rooms and from off campus. Internet access is available. *Library facilities:* Olin Library. *Graduate expenses:* Tuition: part-time $361 per credit hour. *General application contact:* Information Contact, 407-646-2000.

Crummer Graduate School of Business
Dr. Craig M. McAllester, Dean
Program in:
business • MBA

Hamilton Holt School
Dr. Patricia A. Lancaster, Dean
Programs in:
corporate communications and technology • MA
elementary education • M Ed, MAT
human resources • MA
liberal studies • MLS
mental health counseling • MA
school counseling • MA
secondary education • MAT

■ SAINT LEO UNIVERSITY

Saint Leo, FL 33574-6665
http://www.saintleo.edu/

Independent-religious, coed, comprehensive institution. *Enrollment:* 198 full-time matriculated graduate/professional students (116 women), 53 part-time matriculated graduate/professional students (32 women). *Graduate faculty:* 2 full-time (1 woman), 9 part-time/adjunct (5 women). *Computer facilities:* 570 computers available on campus for general student use. A campuswide network can be accessed from student residence rooms and from off campus. Internet access is available. *Library facilities:* Cannon Memorial Library. *Graduate expenses:* Tuition: full-time $4,860; part-time $270 per semester hour. Tuition and fees vary according to class time and program. *General application contact:* Martin Smith, Director of Graduate Admission, 352-588-8283.

Graduate Business Studies
Dr. Susan D. Steiner, Director
Program in:
business • MBA

Graduate Studies in Education
Dr. Charles Hale, Director
Program in:
education • M Ed

■ ST. THOMAS UNIVERSITY

Miami, FL 33054-6459
http://www.stu.edu/

Independent-religious, coed, comprehensive institution. *Computer facilities:* 60 computers available on campus for general student use. A campuswide network can be accessed. *Library facilities:* St. Thomas University Library plus 1 other. *General application contact:* Associate Director of Graduate Admissions, 305-628-6614.

Find an in-depth description at www.petersons.com/graduate.

School of Graduate Studies
Programs in:
accounting • MBA
business administration • M Acc, MBA, Certificate
elementary education • MS
general management • MSM, Certificate
guidance and counseling • MS, Certificate
health management • MBA, MSM, Certificate
human resource management • MSM, Certificate
international business • MBA, MSM, Certificate
justice administration • MSM, Certificate
management • MBA
marriage and family therapy • MS
mental health counseling • MS
public management • MSM, Certificate
sports administration • MBA

Institute of Pastoral Ministries
Program in:
pastoral ministries • MA, Certificate

School of Law
Dr. John Makdisi, Dean
Programs in:
international human rights • LL M
international taxation • LL M
law • JD

■ STETSON UNIVERSITY
DeLand, FL 32720-3781
http://www.stetson.edu/

Independent, coed, comprehensive institution. *Enrollment:* 743 full-time matriculated graduate/professional students (407 women), 247 part-time matriculated graduate/professional students (146 women). *Graduate faculty:* 64 full-time (22 women), 42 part-time/adjunct (15 women). *Computer facilities:* 262 computers available on campus for general student use. A campuswide network can be accessed from student residence rooms and from off campus. Internet access is available. *Library facilities:* DuPont-Ball Library plus 2 others. *Graduate expenses:* Tuition: part-time $410 per credit hour. Tuition and fees vary according to program. *General application contact:* Pat LeClaire, Office of Graduate Studies, 386-822-7075.

College of Arts and Sciences
Dr. Grady Ballenger, Dean
Programs in:
arts and sciences • M Ed, MA, MAT, MS, Ed S
career teaching • Ed S
education • MA
educational leadership • M Ed, Ed S
elementary education • M Ed
exceptional student education • M Ed
marriage and family therapy • MS
mental health counseling • MS
school guidance and family consultation • MS
varying exceptionalities • M Ed

Division of Humanities
Program in:
English • MA, MAT

College of Law
Dr. W. Gary Vause, Dean
Program in:
law • JD

School of Business Administration
Dr. Paul Dasher, Dean
Programs in:
accounting • M Acc
business administration • M Acc, MBA

■ UNIVERSITY OF CENTRAL FLORIDA
Orlando, FL 32816
http://www.ucf.edu/

State-supported, coed, university. CGS member. *Enrollment:* 1,899 full-time matriculated graduate/professional students (1,093 women), 3,699 part-time matriculated graduate/professional students (2,175 women). *Graduate faculty:* 794 full-time (292 women), 700 part-time/adjunct (360 women). *Computer facilities:* 1,191 computers available on campus for general student use. A campuswide network can be accessed from student residence rooms and from off campus. Internet access and online class registration are available. *Library facilities:* University Library. *Graduate expenses:* Tuition, state resident: full-time $3,659; part-time $152 per credit. Tuition, nonresident: full-time $12,749; part-time $531 per credit. Required fees: $106; $53 per term. *General application contact:* Dr. Patricia Bishop, Vice Provost and Dean of Graduate Studies, 407-823-2766.

Find an in-depth description at www.petersons.com/graduate.

College of Arts and Sciences
K. L. Seidel, Dean
Programs in:
applied sociology • MA
arts and sciences • MA, MALS, MS, PhD, Certificate
biological sciences • MS
clinical psychology • MA, MS, PhD
conservation biology • Certificate
creative writing • MA
domestic violence • Certificate
foreign languages • MA, Certificate
gender studies • Certificate
history • MA
human factors psychology • PhD
industrial chemistry • MS
industrial/organizational psychology • MS, PhD
liberal studies • MALS
literature • MA
mathematical science • MS
mathematics • PhD
Mayan studies • Certificate
physics • MS, PhD
political science • MA
professional writing • Certificate
Spanish • MA
statistical computing • MS
teaching English as a second language • MA, Certificate
technical writing • MA

School of Communication
Dr. M. D. Meeske, Chair
Program in:
communication • MA

College of Business Administration
Dr. Thomas Keon, Acting Dean
Programs in:
business administration • MBA
economics • MAAE
finance • PhD
management • PhD
marketing • PhD
taxation • MST

School of Accounting
Dr. Andrew J. Judd, Director
Program in:
accounting • MS

College of Education
Dr. Sandra Robinson, Dean
Programs in:
art education • M Ed, MA
business education • M Ed, MA
counselor education • M Ed, MA
curriculum and instruction • Ed D, PhD, Ed S
education • M Ed, MA, Ed D, PhD, Certificate, Ed S
educational leadership • M Ed, MA, Ed D, Ed S
elementary and secondary education • M Ed
elementary education • M Ed, MA
English language education • M Ed, MA
exceptional student education • M Ed, MA
foreign language education • M Ed, MA
initial teacher professional preparation • Certificate
instructional technology • M Ed, MA, PhD
mathematics education • M Ed, MA
music education • M Ed, MA
physical education • M Ed, MA
pre-kindergarten handicapped endorsement • Certificate
reading • M Ed
school psychology • Ed S
science education • M Ed, MA
social science education • M Ed, MA
teaching excellence • Certificate
vocational education • M Ed, MA

College of Engineering and Computer Sciences
Dr. Martin Wanielista, Dean
Programs in:
aerospace engineering • MSAE
air pollution control • Certificate
applied operations research • Certificate
CAD/CAM technology • Certificate
civil engineering • MS, MSCE, PhD, Certificate
computational methods in mechanics • Certificate
computer science • MS, PhD

University of Central Florida (continued)
computer-integrated manufacturing • MS
design for usability • Certificate
drinking water treatment • Certificate
engineering • MS, MS Cp E, MS Env E, MSAE, MSCE, MSEE, MSIE, MSME, MSMSE, PhD, Certificate
engineering management • MS
environmental engineering • MS, MS Env E, PhD, Certificate
geotechnical engineering • Certificate
hazardous waste management • Certificate
HVAC engineering • Certificate
industrial engineering • MSIE
industrial engineering and management systems • PhD
industrial ergonomics and safety • Certificate
launch/spacecraft vehicle processing • Certificate
materials characterization • Certificate
materials failure analysis • Certificate
materials science and engineering • MSMSE, PhD
mechanical engineering • MSME, PhD, Certificate
operations research • MS
product assurance engineering • MS
project engineering • Certificate
quality assurance • Certificate
simulation systems • MS
structural engineering • Certificate
surface water modeling • Certificate
systems simulations for engineers • Certificate
thermofluids • MSME, PhD
training simulation • Certificate
transportation engineering • Certificate
wastewater treatment • Certificate

School of Electrical Engineering and Computer Science
Dr. Erol Gelenbe, Chair
Programs in:
antennas and propagation • Certificate
communications systems • Certificate
computer engineering • MS Cp E, PhD, Certificate
digital signal processing • Certificate
electrical engineering • MSEE, PhD, Certificate
electronic circuits • Certificate

College of Health and Public Affairs
Dr. Belinda R. McCarthy, Dean
Programs in:
communicative disorders • MA
crime analysis • Certificate
criminal justice • MS
health and public affairs • MA, MPA, MS, MSN, MSW, PhD, Certificate
health care information systems • Certificate
health services administration • MS
managed care • Certificate
medical group management • Certificate
microbiology • MS
molecular biology • MS
non-profit management • Certificate
physical therapy • MS
public administration • MPA, Certificate
public affairs • PhD
risk quality management • Certificate

School of Nursing
E. Stullenbarger, Chair
Programs in:
adult practitioner • MSN
family practitioner • MSN
nursing • MSN
nursing and health profession education • MSN

School of Social Work
Dr. Mary Van Hook, Director
Programs in:
gerontology • Certificate
non-profit management • Certificate
social work • MSW

School of Optics
Dr. Eric W. Van Stryland, Interim Director
Programs in:
applied optics • Certificate
lasers • Certificate
optical communication • Certificate
optics • MS, PhD

■ UNIVERSITY OF FLORIDA
Gainesville, FL 32611
http://www.ufl.edu/

State-supported, coed, university. CGS member. *Enrollment:* 8,813 full-time matriculated graduate/professional students (4,040 women), 1,902 part-time matriculated graduate/professional students (950 women). *Graduate faculty:* 2,792. *Computer facilities:* 447 computers available on campus for general student use. A campuswide network can be accessed from student residence rooms and from off campus. *Library facilities:* George A. Smathers Library plus 15 others. *Graduate expenses:* Tuition, state resident: full-time $3,640; part-time $152 per credit hour. Tuition, nonresident: full-time $12,730; part-time $530 per credit hour. Tuition and fees vary according to course level, course load and program. *General application contact:* Gary O. Hartge, Coordinator, Office of Data Management, 352-392-1562.

Find an in-depth description at www.petersons.com/graduate.

College of Dentistry
Dr. Frank A. Catalanotto, Dean
Programs in:
dentistry • DMD
endodontics • MS, Certificate
foreign trained dentistry • Certificate
orthodontics • MS, Certificate
periodontics • MS, Certificate
prosthodontics • MS, Certificate

College of Medicine
Dr. Kenneth I. Berns, Vice President and Dean
Programs in:
medicine • MD, MPAS, MPH, MS, PhD
physician assistant studies • MPAS

Interdisciplinary Program in Biomedical Sciences
Dr. Colin Sumners, Associate Dean for Graduate Education
Programs in:
anatomy and cell biology • PhD
biochemistry and molecular biology • PhD
biomedical sciences • MS, PhD
clinical chemistry • MS
clinical investigation • MS
genetics • PhD
immunology and microbiology • PhD
immunology and molecular pathology • PhD
molecular cell biology • PhD
molecular genetics and microbiology • MS, PhD
neuroscience • MS, PhD
oral biology • PhD
pharmacology and therapeutics • PhD
physiology • PhD
physiology and pharmacology • PhD

College of Pharmacy
Dr. William H. Riffee, Dean
Programs in:
medicinal chemistry • MSP, PhD
pharmaceutics • MSP, PhD
pharmacodynamics • MSP, PhD
pharmacology • PhD
pharmacy • MSP, PhD
pharmacy health care administration • MS, MSP, PhD

College of Veterinary Medicine
Programs in:
forensic toxicology • Certificate
veterinary medical science • MS, PhD
veterinary medicine • DVM, MS, PhD, Certificate

Fredric G. Levin College of Law
Prof. Jon Mills, Interim Dean and Professor of Law
Programs in:
comparative law • LL M CL
law • JD, LL M, LL M CL, LL M T, SJD
taxation • LL M T

Graduate School
Dr. Winfred M. Phillips, Vice President of Research and Dean of Graduate School

College of Agriculture and Life Sciences
Dr. Jimmy G. Cheek, Dean
Programs in:
agribusiness • MAB
agricultural education and communication • M Ag, MS, PhD
agriculture and life sciences • M Ag, MAB, MFAS, MFRC, MS, DPM, PhD
agronomy • MS, PhD
animal sciences • M Ag, MS, PhD
cell biology • MS, PhD
entomology and nematology • MS, PhD
environmental horticulture • MS, PhD
fisheries and aquatic science • MFAS, MS, PhD
food and resource economics • M Ag, MS, PhD
food science and human nutrition • MS, PhD
forest resources and conservation • MFRC, MS, PhD
fruit crops • MS, PhD
microbiology • MS, PhD
microbiology and cell science • M Ag
plant molecular and cellular biology • MS, PhD
plant pathology • MS, PhD
soil and water science • M Ag, MS, PhD
vegetable crops and crop science • MS, PhD
wildlife ecology • MS, PhD

College of Design, Construction and Planning
Dr. Jay Stein, Interim Dean
Programs in:
building construction • MBC, MICM, MSBC
design, construction and planning • M Arch, MAURP, MBC, MICM, MID, MLA, MS, MSAS, MSBC, PhD
interior design • MID
landscape architecture • MLA, MS
urban and regional planning • MAURP

College of Education
Dr. Gerardo Gonzalez, Interim Dean
Programs in:
bilingual education • M Ed, MAE, Ed D, PhD, Ed S
computer education • M Ed, MAE, Ed D, PhD, Ed S
curriculum and instructional leadership • Ed D, PhD, Ed S
early childhood education • M Ed, MAE, Ed D, PhD, Ed S
economics education • M Ed, MAE, Ed D, PhD, Ed S
education • M Ed, MAE, Ed D, PhD, Ed S
educational administration • M Ed, MAE, Ed D, PhD, Ed S
educational leadership • PhD
educational psychology • M Ed, Ed D, PhD, Ed S
educational psychololgy • MAE
elementary education • M Ed, MAE, Ed D, PhD, Ed S
English education • M Ed, MAE, Ed D, PhD, Ed S
foreign language education • M Ed, MAE, Ed D, PhD, Ed S
higher education • Ed D, PhD, Ed S
marriage and family counseling • M Ed, Ed D, PhD, Ed S
mathematics education • M Ed, MAE, Ed D, PhD, Ed S
media and instructional design • M Ed, MAE, Ed D, PhD, Ed S
mental health counseling • M Ed, Ed D, PhD, Ed S
middle school education • M Ed, MAE, Ed D, PhD, Ed S
reading and language arts • M Ed, MAE, Ed D, PhD, Ed S
school counseling and guidance • M Ed, Ed D, Ed S
school psychology • MAE, Ed D, PhD
school psycyology • Ed S
science education • M Ed, MAE, Ed D, PhD, Ed S
secondary education • M Ed, MAE, Ed D, PhD, Ed S
social studies education • M Ed, MAE, Ed D, PhD, Ed S
special education • M Ed, MAE, Ed D, PhD, Ed S
statistics, measurement and evaluation methodology • Ed S
statistics, measurement, and evaluation methodology • M Ed, MAE, Ed D, PhD
student counseling and guidance • PhD
student personnel services in higher education • M Ed, Ed D, PhD, Ed S

College of Engineering
Dr. M. J. Ohanian, Interim Vice President of Research and Dean of Graduate School
Programs in:
aerospace engineering • ME, MS, PhD, Certificate, Engr
agricultural and biological engineering • ME, MS, PhD, Engr
agricultural operations management • MS, PhD
biomedical engineering • ME, MS, PhD, Certificate, Engr
ceramic science and engineering • ME, MS, PhD, Engr
chemical engineering • ME, MS, PhD, Engr
civil engineering • MCE, ME, MS, PhD, Engr
coastal and oceanographic engineering • ME, MS, PhD, Engr
computer and information science and engineering • ME
computer organization • MS, PhD, Engr
electrical and computer engineering • ME, MS, PhD, Engr
engineering • MCE, ME, MS, PhD, Certificate, Engr
engineering management • ME, MS
engineering physics • ME, MS, PhD, Engr
engineering science and engineering mechanics • ME, MS, PhD, Engr
environmental engineering sciences • ME, MS, PhD, Engr
facilities layout decision support systems energy • PhD
health physics • MS, PhD
health systems • ME, MS
industrial engineering • PhD, Engr
information systems • MS, PhD, Engr
manufacturing systems engineering • ME, MS, PhD, Certificate
materials science and engineering • ME, MS, PhD, Certificate, Engr
mechanical engineering • ME, MS, PhD, Certificate, Engr
medical physics • MS, PhD
metallurgical and materials engineering • ME, MS, PhD, Engr
metallurgical engineering • ME, MS, PhD, Engr
nuclear engineering sciences • ME, PhD, Engr
nuclear sciences engineering • MS
operations research • ME, MS, PhD, Engr
polymer science and engineering • ME, MS, PhD, Engr
production planning and control engineering management • PhD
quality and reliability assurance • ME, MS
software systems • MS, PhD, Engr
systems engineering • PhD, Engr

College of Fine Arts
Dr. Donald McGlothlin, Dean
Programs in:
art • MFA

University of Florida (continued)

art education • MA
art history • MA
fine arts • MA, MFA, MM, PhD
museology • MA
music • MA, MM, PhD
music education • MM, PhD
theatre and dance • MFA

College of Health and Human Performance
Dr. Patrick J. Bird, Dean
Programs in:
athletics training/sport medicine • PhD
biomechanics • PhD
exercise and sport science • MESS, MSESS, PhD
exercise physiology • PhD
health and human performance • MESS, MHSE, MPH, MSESS, MSHSE, MSRS, PhD
health behavior • PhD
health science education • MHSE, MSHSE, PhD
motor learning control • PhD
natural resource recreation • PhD
public health • MPH
recreation • MSRS
recreation, parks and tourism • PhD
sport and exercise psychology • PhD
therapeutic recreation • PhD
tourism • PhD

College of Health Professions
Dr. Robert Frank, Dean
Programs in:
audiology • Au D
clinical and health psychology • PhD
health administration • EMHA, MHA
health professions • EMHA, MHA, MHS, MPH, MPT, Au D, PhD
health services research • PhD
occupational therapy • MHS
physical therapy • MPT
rehabilitation counseling • MHS
rehabilitation sciences • PhD

College of Journalism and Communications
Dr. Terry Hynes, Dean
Programs in:
advertising • MAMC, PhD
documentary • MAMC
international communication • MAMC
journalism • MAMC, PhD
mass communication • MAMC
political communication • MAMC
public relations • MAMC, PhD
sports communication • MAMC
telecommunication • MAMC, PhD

College of Liberal Arts and Sciences
Dr. Neil Sullivan, Dean
Programs in:
African studies • Certificate
anthropology • MA, MAT, PhD
applied mathematics • MS, PhD
astronomy • MS, PhD
botany • M Ag, MS, PhD
botany education • MST
chemistry • MS, MST, PhD
classical studies • MA, PhD
communication sciences and disorders • MA, PhD
creative writing • MFA
English • MA, PhD
French • MA, MAT, PhD
geography • MA, MAT, MS, MST, PhD
geology • MS, PhD
geology education • MST
German • MA, PhD
history • MA, PhD
international development policy • MA
international relations • MA, MAT, PhD
Latin American studies • MA, MAT, Certificate
liberal arts and sciences • M Ag, M Stat, MA, MAT, MFA, MS, MS Stat, MST, Au D, PhD, Certificate
linguistics • MA, PhD
mathematics • MA, MS, PhD
mathematics teaching • MAT, MST
philosophy • MA, MAT, PhD
physics • MS, PhD
physics education • MST
political campaigning • MA, Certificate
political science • MA, MAT, PhD
psychology • MA, MAT, MS, MST, PhD
public affairs • MA, Certificate
religion • MA
sociology • MA, PhD
Spanish • MA, PhD
statistics • M Stat, MS Stat, PhD
teaching English as a second language • Certificate
zoology • MS, MST, PhD

College of Natural Resources and Environment
Dr. Stephen R. Humphrey, Dean
Programs in:
interdisciplinary ecology • MS, PhD
natural resources and environment • MS, PhD

College of Nursing
Dr. Kathleen A. Long, Dean
Program in:
nursing • MS Nsg, PhD

Graduate Engineering and Research Center (GERC)
Dr. Pasquale M. Sforza, Director
Programs in:
aerospace engineering • ME, MS, PhD, Engr
electrical and computer engineering • ME, MS, PhD, Engr
engineering mechanics • ME, MS, PhD, Engr
industrial and systems engineering • ME, MS, PhD, Engr

Warrington College of Business Administration
Dr. John Kraft, Dean
Programs in:
accounting • M Acc, PhD
business administration • M Acc, MA, MAIB, MBA, MS, MSM, PhD
decision and information sciences • MA, MS, PhD
economics • MA, MS, PhD
finance • PhD
finance, real estate and urban analysis • MA
human resources management • PhD
international business • MAIB
management • MA, MS, PhD
marketing • MA, MS, PhD
strategy • PhD

■ UNIVERSITY OF MIAMI
Coral Gables, FL 33124
http://www.miami.edu/

Independent, coed, university. CGS member. *Enrollment:* 4,276 full-time matriculated graduate/professional students (2,038 women), 732 part-time matriculated graduate/professional students (453 women). *Graduate faculty:* 1,118 full-time (266 women), 5 part-time/adjunct (1 woman). *Computer facilities:* 2,000 computers available on campus for general student use. A campuswide network can be accessed from student residence rooms and from off campus. Internet access and online class registration, online student account and grade information are available. *Library facilities:* Otto G. Richter Library plus 6 others. *Graduate expenses:* Tuition: part-time $960 per credit hour. *General application contact:* Office of Graduate Studies, 305-284-4154.

Find an in-depth description at www.petersons.com/graduate.

Graduate School
Dr. Steven G. Ullmann, Dean

College of Arts and Sciences
Dr. Daniel L. Pals, Interim Dean
Programs in:
applied developmental psychology • PhD
art history • MA
arts and sciences • MA, MALS, MFA, MS, DA, PhD

behavioral neuroscience • PhD
biology • MS, PhD
ceramics/glass • MFA
chemistry • MS
clinical psychology • PhD
computer science • MS
English • MA, MFA, PhD
French • PhD
genetics and evolution • MS, PhD
graphic design/multimedia • MFA
health psychology • PhD
history • MA, PhD
inorganic chemistry • PhD
liberal studies • MALS
mathematics • MA, DA, PhD
organic chemistry • PhD
painting • MFA
philosophy • MA, MALS, PhD
photography/digital imaging • MFA
physical chemistry • PhD
physics • MS, DA, PhD
printmaking • MFA
psychology • MS
Romance languages • PhD
sculpture • MFA
sociology • MA, PhD
Spanish • PhD
tropical biology, ecology, and behavior • MS, PhD

College of Engineering
Dr. M. Lewis Temares, Dean
Programs in:
architectural engineering • MSAE
biomedical engineering • MSBE, PhD
civil engineering • MSCE, DA, PhD
electrical and computer engineering • MSECE, PhD
engineering • MS, MSAE, MSBE, MSCE, MSECE, MSEVH, MSIE, MSME, MSOES, DA, PhD
environmental health and safety • MS, MSEVH, MSOES
ergonomics • PhD
industrial engineering • MSIE, PhD
management of technology • MS
mechanical engineering • MS, MSME, DA, PhD
occupational ergonomics and safety • MSOES

Rosenstiel School of Marine and Atmospheric Science
Dr. Otis Brown, Dean
Programs in:
applied marine physics • MS, PhD
atmospheric science • MS, PhD
marine affairs • MA, MS
marine and atmospheric chemistry • MS, PhD
marine and atmospheric science • MA, MS, PhD
marine biology and fisheries • MS, PhD
marine geology and geophysics • MS, PhD
ocean engineering • MS
physical oceanography • MS, PhD

School of Architecture
Teofilo Victoria, Director, Graduate Studies
Programs in:
architecture • M Arch
computing in design • M Arch
suburb and town design • M Arch

School of Business Administration
Dr. Harold W. Berkman, Vice Dean
Programs in:
accounting • MBA
business administration • Exec MBA, MA, MBA, MP Acc, MPA, MS, MS Tax, PhD, Certificate
computer information systems • MS
economic development • MA, PhD
financial economics • PhD
human resource economics • MA, PhD
international economics • MA, PhD
management science • MS, PhD
political science • MPA
professional accounting • MP Acc
taxation • MS Tax
telecommunications management • Certificate

School of Communication
Edward J. Pfister, Dean
Programs in:
communication • PhD
communication studies • MA
motion pictures • MA, MFA
public relations • MA
television broadcast and print journalism • MA

School of Education
Dr. Samuel Yarger, Dean
Programs in:
counseling • MS Ed
counseling psychology • PhD
early childhood special education • MS Ed, Ed S
education • MS Ed, PhD, Ed S
educational research and evaluation • MS Ed, PhD
educational research/exercise physiology • PhD
elementary education • MS Ed, PhD, Ed S
emotional handicaps/learning disabilities • MS Ed, Ed S
exercise physiology • MS Ed, PhD
higher education/enrollment management • MS Ed
marriage and family therapy • MS Ed
mathematics/science resource • MS Ed
mental health counseling • MS Ed
pre-K through primary education • MS Ed, Ed S
reading • PhD
reading and learning disabilities • MS Ed, Ed S
research and evaluation • MS Ed
research in education and behavioral sciences • PhD
special education • PhD
sports administration • MS Ed
sports medicine • MS Ed
teaching and learning • PhD
teaching English to speakers of other languages • MS Ed, PhD, Ed S

School of International Studies
Dr. Andres S. Gomez, Interim Dean
Program in:
international studies • MA, PhD

School of Music
Dr. James William Hipp, Dean
Programs in:
accompanying and chamber music • MM, DMA
choral conducting • MM, DMA
composition • MM, DMA
electronic music • MM
instrumental conducting • MM, DMA
instrumental performance • MM, DMA
jazz composition • DMA
jazz pedagogy • MM
jazz performance • MM, DMA
keyboard performance and pedagogy • MM, DMA
media writing and production • MM
multiple woodwinds • MM, DMA
music • MM, MS, DMA, PhD, Spec M
music business and entertainment industries • MM
music education • MM, PhD, Spec M
music engineering • MS
music therapy • MM
musicology • MM
piano performance • MM, DMA
studio jazz writing • MM
vocal performance • MM, DMA

School of Nursing
Dr. Diane Horner, Dean
Programs in:
nursing • PhD
primary health care • MSN

School of Law
Michael Goodnight, Assistant Dean of Admissions
Programs in:
comparative law • LL M
estate planning • LL M
international law • LL M
law • JD
ocean and coastal law • LL M
real property and development • LL M

School of Medicine
Dr. John G. Clarkson, Vice President for Medical Affairs and Dean

University of Miami (continued)
Program in:
medicine • MD, MPH, MS, MSPT, DPT, PhD

Graduate Programs in Medicine
Dr. Richard J. Bookman, Associate Dean for Graduate Studies
Programs in:
biochemistry and molecular biology • PhD
biomedical studies • PhD
epidemiology • PhD
medicine • MPH, MS, MSPT, DPT, PhD
microbiology and immunology • PhD
molecular and cellular pharmacology • PhD
molecular cell and developmental biology • PhD
neuroscience • PhD
physical therapy • MS, MSPT, DPT, PhD
physiology and biophysics • PhD
public health • MPH

■ UNIVERSITY OF NORTH FLORIDA

Jacksonville, FL 32224-2645

http://www.unf.edu/

State-supported, coed, comprehensive institution. *Enrollment:* 441 full-time matriculated graduate/professional students (292 women), 1,154 part-time matriculated graduate/professional students (770 women). *Graduate faculty:* 279 full-time (107 women). *Computer facilities:* 700 computers available on campus for general student use. A campuswide network can be accessed from student residence rooms and from off campus. Internet access and online class registration, applications software are available. *Library facilities:* Thomas G. Carpenter Library. *Graduate expenses:* Full-time $2,991; part-time $125 per credit. Tuition, state resident: full-time $2,991; part-time $125 per credit. Tuition, nonresident: full-time $11,648; part-time $485 per credit. $11,648 full-time. Required fees: $33 per credit. *General application contact:* Jim Owen, Assistant Director of Graduate Studies, 904-620-1360.

College of Arts and Sciences
Dr. Henry Camp, Interim Dean
Programs in:
arts and sciences • MA, MAC, MPA, MS, MSCJ
counseling psychology • MAC
criminal justice • MSCJ
English • MA
general psychology • MA
history • MA
mathematical sciences • MS
public administration • MPA
statistics • MS

College of Business Administration
Dr. Earle C. Traynham, Dean
Programs in:
accounting • M Acct
business administration • MBA
human resource management • MHRM
management, marketing, and logistics • MBA, MHRM

College of Computer Sciences and Engineering
Dr. Neal Coulter, Dean
Program in:
computer and information sciences • MS

College of Education
Dr. Kathrine Kasten, Dean
Programs in:
administration • M Ed
counselor education • M Ed
education • M Ed, Ed D
educational leadership • M Ed, Ed D
elementary education • M Ed
mathematics education • M Ed
music education • M Ed
science education • M Ed
secondary education • M Ed
special education • M Ed

College of Health
Dr. Pamela Chally, Dean
Programs in:
addictions counseling • MSH
advanced practice nursing • MSN
aging studies • Certificate
community health • MPH
employee health services • MSH
health • MHA, MPH, MPT, MSH, MSN, Certificate
health administration • MHA
health care administration • MSH
human ecology and nutrition • MSH
human performance • MSH
physical therapy • MPT

■ UNIVERSITY OF SOUTH FLORIDA

Tampa, FL 33620-9951

http://www.usf.edu/

State-supported, coed, university. CGS member. *Computer facilities:* 500 computers available on campus for general student use. A campuswide network can be accessed from student residence rooms and from off campus. Internet access and online class registration are available. *Library facilities:* Tampa Campus Library plus 2 others. *General application contact:* Dean, Graduate School, 813-974-2846.

Find an in-depth description at www.petersons.com/graduate.

College of Medicine
Program in:
medicine • MD, PhD

Graduate Programs in Medical Sciences
Programs in:
anatomy • PhD
biochemistry and molecular biology • PhD
medical microbiology and immunology • PhD
medical sciences • PhD
pathology • PhD
physiology and biophysics • PhD

Graduate School
Program in:
marine science • MS, PhD

College of Arts and Sciences
Programs in:
aging studies • PhD
American studies • MA
analytical chemistry • MS, PhD
applied anthropology • MA, PhD
applied linguistics • MA
applied mathematics • PhD
applied physics • MS
arts and sciences • MA, MLA, MPA, MS, MSW, PhD, Adv C
audiology • MS
aural rehabilitation • MS
biochemistry • MS, PhD
biology • PhD
botany • MS
cellular and molecular biology • PhD
clinical psychology • PhD
communication • MA, PhD
criminology • MA, PhD
ecology • PhD
engineering science/physics • MS, PhD
English • MA, PhD
experimental psychology • PhD
French • MA
geography • MA
geology • MS, PhD
gerontology • MA
history • MA
hydrogeology • MS, Adv C
industrial/organizational psychology • PhD
inorganic chemistry • MS, PhD
languages and linguistics • MA
liberal arts • MLA
library and information sciences • MA
linguistics • MA

marine biology • MS, PhD
mass communications • MA
mathematics • MA, PhD
microbiology • MS
organic chemistry • MS, PhD
philosophy • MA, PhD
physical chemistry • MS, PhD
physics • MA, MS
physiology • PhD
political science • MA
public administration • MPA
rehabilitation and mental health counseling • MA
religious studies • MA
school library media • MA
social work • MSW
sociology • MA
Spanish • MA
speech pathology • MS
teaching English as a second language • MA
women's studies • MA
zoology • MS

College of Business Administration
Programs in:
accounting • M Acc
business • PhD
business administration • Exec MBA, M Acc, MA, MBA, MS, PhD
business administration for physicians • Exec MBA
economics • MA
management • MS
management information systems • MS

College of Education
Programs in:
adult education • MA, Ed D, PhD, Ed S
business and office education • MA
college student affairs • M Ed
counselor education • MA, Ed S
distributive and marketing education • MA
early childhood education • M Ed, PhD, Ed S
education • M Ed, MA, Ed D, PhD, Ed S
education of the emotionally disturbed • MA
education of the mentally handicapped • MA
educational leadership • M Ed, Ed D, Ed S
educational measurement and research • M Ed, PhD, Ed S
elementary education • MA, Ed D, PhD, Ed S
English education • M Ed, MA, PhD
foreign language education • M Ed, MA
gifted education • MA
higher education • PhD, Ed S
industrial technical education • MA
instructional computing • M Ed, PhD
interdisciplinary education • PhD, Ed S
junior college teaching • MA
learning disabilities • MA
mathematics education • M Ed, MA, PhD, Ed S
middle school education • M Ed
music education • MA, PhD
physical education • MA
reading education • MA, PhD, Ed S
school psychology • PhD, Ed S
science education • M Ed, MA, PhD, Ed S
secondary education • PhD
social science education • M Ed, MA
special education • Ed D, PhD, Ed S
theater education • MA
varying exceptionalities • MA
vocational education • Ed D, PhD, Ed S

College of Engineering
Programs in:
chemical engineering • M Ch E, ME, MS Ch E, MSE, PhD
civil engineering • MCE, MSCE, PhD
computer engineering • M Cp E, MS Cp E
computer science • MCS, MSCS
computer science and engineering • PhD
electrical engineering • ME, MEE, MSE, MSEE, PhD
engineering • ME, MSE
engineering management • ME, MSE, MSEM, MSIE
engineering science • PhD
environmental engineering • MEVE, MSEV
industrial engineering • ME, MSE, MSEM, MSIE, PhD
mechanical engineering • MME, MSE, MSME, PhD

College of Fine Arts
Programs in:
art • MFA
art education • MA
art history • MA
choral conducting • MM
composition • MM
fine arts • MA, MFA, MM, PhD
instrumental conducting (wind instruments) • MM
jazz studies • MM
music education • MA, PhD
performance • MM
theory • MM

College of Nursing
Program in:
nursing • MS, PhD

College of Public Health
Programs in:
community and family health • MPH, MSPH, PhD
environmental and occupational health • MPH, MSPH, PhD
epidemiology and biostatistics • MPH, MSPH, PhD
health policy and management • MHA, MPH, MSPH, PhD
public health • MHA, MPH, MSPH, PhD
public health practice • MPH

School of Architecture and Community Design
Program in:
architecture and community design • M Arch

H. Lee Moffitt Cancer Center and Research Institute
Dr. Julie Dieu, Professor and Director
Program in:
oncology • PhD

■ THE UNIVERSITY OF TAMPA

Tampa, FL 33606-1490
http://www.utampa.edu/

Independent, coed, comprehensive institution. *Enrollment:* 111 full-time matriculated graduate/professional students (55 women), 451 part-time matriculated graduate/professional students (232 women). *Graduate faculty:* 142 full-time (49 women), 159 part-time/adjunct (87 women). *Computer facilities:* 250 computers available on campus for general student use. A campuswide network can be accessed from student residence rooms and from off campus. Internet access is available. *Library facilities:* Merl Kelce Library. *Graduate expenses:* Tuition: part-time $325 per credit hour. *General application contact:* Barbara P. Strickler, Vice President for Enrollment, 800-733-4773.

John H. Sykes College of Business
Dr. Joseph E. McCann, Dean
Program in:
business • MBA

Nursing Program
Dr. Nancy Ross, Director
Programs in:
family nurse practitioner • MSN
nursing administration • MSN

■ UNIVERSITY OF WEST FLORIDA

Pensacola, FL 32514-5750
http://uwf.edu/

State-supported, coed, comprehensive institution. CGS member. *Enrollment:* 390

University of West Florida (continued)
full-time matriculated graduate/professional students (260 women), 991 part-time matriculated graduate/professional students (630 women). *Graduate faculty:* 165 full-time (50 women), 47 part-time/adjunct (23 women). *Computer facilities:* A campuswide network can be accessed from student residence rooms and from off campus. Internet access and online class registration are available. *Library facilities:* Pace Library. *Graduate expenses:* Tuition, state resident: part-time $156 per credit hour. Tuition, nonresident: part-time $535 per credit hour. *General application contact:* Susie Neeley, Director of Admissions, 850-474-2230.

College of Arts and Sciences: Arts
Dr. Martha D. Saunders, Dean
Programs in:
- applied politics • MA
- arts and sciences: arts • MA, MAT
- communication arts • MA
- English • MA
- history • MA
- humanities • MA
- political science • MA
- psychology • MA

College of Arts and Sciences: Sciences
Dr. Katheryn K. Fouché, Associate Dean
Programs in:
- arts and sciences: sciences • MA, MAT, MS, MST
- biology • MS
- biology education • MST
- coastal zone studies • MS
- computer science • MS
- general biology • MS, MST
- mathematics • MA
- mathematics education • MAT
- statistics • MA
- systems and control engineering • MS

College of Business
Dr. F. Edward Ranelli, Dean
Programs in:
- accounting • MA
- business • MA, MBA
- business administration • MBA

College of Professional Studies
Dr. Wesley Little, Dean
Programs in:
- alternative education • M Ed
- clinical teaching • MA
- curriculum and instruction • M Ed
- curriculum and instruction/alternative education • M Ed
- education • M Ed, MA, MPA, MS, Ed D, Ed S
- elementary education • M Ed
- habilitative science • MA
- middle and secondary level education • M Ed
- primary education • M Ed
- reading • M Ed
- special education-clinical teaching • MA
- vocational education • M Ed

Division of Administrative Studies
Dr. Kato B. Keeton, Chairperson
Program in:
- public administration • MPA

Division of Diversity Studies and Applied Research
Dr. Janet Pilcher, Chairperson
Programs in:
- curriculum and instruction • Ed D, Ed S
- educational leadership • M Ed, Ed S

Division of Health, Leisure, and Exercise Science
Dr. C. B. Williamson, Chairperson
Programs in:
- health and community education • MS
- health, leisure, and sports • MS
- physical education • MS

Georgia

ALBANY STATE UNIVERSITY

Albany, GA 31705-2717
http://asuweb.asurams.edu/asu/

State-supported, coed, comprehensive institution. CGS member. *Enrollment:* 91 full-time matriculated graduate/professional students (66 women), 305 part-time matriculated graduate/professional students (217 women). *Graduate faculty:* 58 full-time (11 women), 32 part-time/adjunct (27 women). *Computer facilities:* 1,000 computers available on campus for general student use. A campuswide network can be accessed from student residence rooms and from off campus. Internet access, email are available. *Library facilities:* James Pendergrast Memorial Library. *Graduate expenses:* Tuition, state resident: full-time $2,252. Tuition, nonresident: full-time $9,008. *General application contact:* Diane P. Frink, Graduate Admissions Counselor, 229-430-5718.

College of Arts and Sciences
Dr. Ellis Sykes, Dean
Programs in:
- arts and sciences • MPA, MS
- community and economic development • MPA
- criminal justice • MPA
- fiscal management • MPA
- general management • MPA
- health administration and policy • MPA
- human resources management • MPA
- public policy • MPA
- water resource management and policy • MPA

College of Education
Dr. Wilburn Campbell, Dean
Programs in:
- biology • M Ed
- business education • M Ed
- chemistry • M Ed
- early childhood education • M Ed
- education • M Ed, Certificate, Ed S
- educational administration and supervision • M Ed, Certificate, Ed S
- English education • M Ed
- health and physical education • M Ed
- mathematics education • M Ed
- middle grades education • M Ed
- music education • M Ed
- reading education • M Ed
- school counseling • M Ed
- social science education • M Ed
- special education • M Ed

College of Health Professions
Dr. Lucille B. Wilson, Dean
Program in:
- nursing • MS

School of Business
Dr. Rosa Okpara, Chairperson
Program in:
- water policy • MBA

ARMSTRONG ATLANTIC STATE UNIVERSITY

Savannah, GA 31419-1997
http://www.armstrong.edu/

State-supported, coed, comprehensive institution. CGS member. *Enrollment:* 139 full-time matriculated graduate/professional students (104 women), 317 part-time matriculated graduate/professional students (257 women). *Graduate faculty:* 158. *Computer facilities:* 160 computers available on campus for general student use. A campuswide network can be accessed from student residence rooms and from off campus. Internet access and online class registration are available. *Library facilities:* Lane Library. *Graduate expenses:* Full-time $2,252; part-time $94 per hour. Tuition, state resident: full-time $2,252; part-time $94 per hour. Tuition, nonresident: full-time $6,758; part-time $282 per hour. Required fees: $366; $183 per semester. $183 per semester. *General application contact:* Dr. Emma T. Simon, Dean of Graduate Studies, 912-927-5377.

Find an in-depth description at www.petersons.com/graduate.

School of Graduate Studies
Dr. Emma T. Simon, Dean of Graduate Studies
Programs in:
athletic training • MS
criminal justice • MS
education • M Ed
elementary education • M Ed
health services administration • MHSA
history • MA
middle grades education • M Ed
nursing • MSN
physical therapy • MSPT
public health • MPH
secondary education • M Ed
special education • M Ed
sports health sciences • MS

■ AUGUSTA STATE UNIVERSITY

Augusta, GA 30904-2200
http://www.aug.edu/

State-supported, coed, comprehensive institution. *Enrollment:* 73 full-time matriculated graduate/professional students, 240 part-time matriculated graduate/professional students. *Graduate faculty:* 59 full-time (33 women), 1 part-time/adjunct (0 women). *Computer facilities:* 160 computers available on campus for general student use. A campuswide network can be accessed from off campus. Internet access and online class registration are available. *Library facilities:* Reese Library plus 1 other. *Graduate expenses:* Tuition, state resident: part-time $94 per hour. Tuition, nonresident: part-time $376 per hour. Required fees: $122 per semester. *General application contact:* Katherine Sweeney, Director of Admissions and Registrar, 706-737-1405.

Graduate Studies
Dr. Bill E. Bompart, Vice President for Academic Affairs

College of Arts and Sciences
Dr. Elizabeth B. House, Dean
Programs in:
arts and sciences • MPA, MS
psychology • MS
public administration • MPA

College of Business Administration
Jackson K. Widener, Dean
Program in:
business administration • MBA

College of Education
Dr. Robert Freeman, Dean
Programs in:
counseling/guidance • M Ed, Ed S
early childhood education • M Ed, Ed S
education • M Ed, Ed S
educational leadership • M Ed, Ed S
middle grades education • M Ed, Ed S
secondary education • M Ed, Ed S
special education • M Ed, Ed S

■ BRENAU UNIVERSITY

Gainesville, GA 30501-3697
http://www.brenau.edu/

Independent, women only, comprehensive institution. *Enrollment:* 230 full-time matriculated graduate/professional students (185 women), 567 part-time matriculated graduate/professional students (417 women). *Graduate faculty:* 42 full-time (26 women), 37 part-time/adjunct (15 women). *Computer facilities:* 120 computers available on campus for general student use. A campuswide network can be accessed from student residence rooms and from off campus. Internet access is available. *Library facilities:* Trustee Library. *Graduate expenses:* Tuition: full-time $4,842; part-time $269 per credit hour. Tuition and fees vary according to program. *General application contact:* Kathy Cobb, Director of Graduate Admissions, 770-534-6162.

Graduate Programs
Dr. Helen Ray, Dean

School of Business and Mass Communication
Dr. Diane Garsombke, Dean
Programs in:
accounting • MBA
healthcare management • MBA
leadership development • MBA
management • MBA

School of Education and Human Development
Dr. William B. Ware, Dean
Programs in:
early childhood education • M Ed, Ed S
learning disabilities • M Ed
middle grades education • M Ed, Ed S

School of Health and Science
Dr. Rudi Kiefer, Head
Programs in:
family nurse practitioner • MSN
occupational therapy • MS

■ CLARK ATLANTA UNIVERSITY

Atlanta, GA 30314
http://www.cau.edu/

Independent-religious, coed, university. CGS member. *Computer facilities:* 300 computers available on campus for general student use. A campuswide network can be accessed from off campus. *Library facilities:* Robert W. Woodruff Library. *General application contact:* Graduate Program Assistant, 404-880-8709.

Find an in-depth description at www.petersons.com/graduate.

School of Arts and Sciences
Programs in:
African-American studies • MA
Africana women's studies • MA, DA
applied mathematics • MS
arts and sciences • MA, MPA, MS, DA, PhD
biology • MS, PhD
computer and information science • MS
computer science • MS
criminal justice • MA
economics • MA
English • MA
history • MA
humanities • DA
inorganic chemistry • MS, PhD
organic chemistry • MS, PhD
physical chemistry • MS, PhD
physics • MS
political science • MA, PhD
public administration • MPA
Romance languages • MA
science education • DA
sociology • MA

School of Business Administration
Programs in:
business administration • MBA
decision science • MBA
finance • MBA
marketing • MBA

Clark Atlanta University (continued)

School of Education

Programs in:
- counseling • MA, PhD
- curriculum • MA, Ed S
- education • MA, Ed D, PhD, Ed S
- education psychology • MA
- educational leadership • MA, Ed D, Ed S
- exceptional student education • MA, Ed S

School of International Affairs and Development

Programs in:
- international affairs and development • PhD
- international business and development • MA
- international development administration • MA
- international development education and planning • MA
- international relations • MA
- regional studies • MA

School of Library and Information Studies

Dr. Arthur C. Gunn, Dean

Program in:
- library and information studies • MSLS, SLS

School of Social Work

Program in:
- social work • MSW, PhD

■ COLUMBUS STATE UNIVERSITY

Columbus, GA 31907-5645

http://www.colstate.edu/

State-supported, coed, comprehensive institution. *Enrollment:* 188 full-time matriculated graduate/professional students (111 women), 545 part-time matriculated graduate/professional students (284 women). *Graduate faculty:* 102 full-time (37 women), 7 part-time/adjunct (1 woman). *Computer facilities:* 300 computers available on campus for general student use. A campuswide network can be accessed from student residence rooms and from off campus. Internet access and online class registration are available. *Library facilities:* Simon Schwob Memorial Library. *Graduate expenses:* Tuition, state resident: full-time $846; part-time $376 per credit hour. Tuition, nonresident: full-time $3,384; part-time $1,504 per credit hour. Required fees: $197 per semester. Tuition and fees vary according to course load and campus/location. *General application contact:* Katie Thornton, Graduate Admissions Specialist, 706-568-2279.

Graduate Studies

Dr. Thomas Z. Jones, Vice President for Academic Affairs

College of Arts and Letters

Dr. William L. Chappell, Acting Dean

Programs in:
- art education • M Ed
- arts and letters • M Ed, MM, MPA
- music education • MM
- public administration • MPA

College of Business

Dr. Robert S. Johnson, Dean

Program in:
- business • MBA

College of Education

Dr. Thomas E. Harrison, Dean

Programs in:
- community counseling • MS
- early childhood education • M Ed, Ed S
- education • M Ed, MS, Ed S
- educational leadership • M Ed, Ed S
- middle grades education • M Ed, Ed S
- physical education • M Ed
- school counseling • M Ed, Ed S
- secondary education • M Ed, Ed S
- special education • M Ed, Ed S

College of Science

Dr. Arthur G. Cleveland, Dean

Programs in:
- applied computer science • MS
- environmental science • MS
- information technology management • MS
- science • MS

■ EMORY UNIVERSITY

Atlanta, GA 30322-1100

http://www.emory.edu/

Independent-religious, coed, university. CGS member. *Enrollment:* 4,283 full-time matriculated graduate/professional students (2,392 women), 783 part-time matriculated graduate/professional students (502 women). *Graduate faculty:* 1,931 full-time, 400 part-time/adjunct. *Computer facilities:* 600 computers available on campus for general student use. A campuswide network can be accessed from student residence rooms and from off campus. Internet access and online class registration are available. *Library facilities:* Robert W. Woodruff Library plus 7 others. *Graduate expenses:* Tuition: full-time $23,770; part-time $990 per hour. Required fees: $251; $180 per term. Part-time tuition and fees vary according to course load.

Find an in-depth description at www.petersons.com/graduate.

Candler School of Theology

Russell E. Richey, Dean

Program in:
- theology • M Div, MTS, Th M, Th D

Graduate School of Arts and Sciences

Dr. Robert A. Paul, Dean

Programs in:
- anthropology • PhD
- art history • PhD
- arts and sciences • M Ed, MA, MAT, MM, MS, MSM, PhD, Certificate, DAST
- biostatistics • PhD
- chemistry • PhD
- clinical psychology • PhD
- cognition and development • PhD
- comparative literature • Certificate
- economics • PhD
- English • PhD
- film studies • MA
- French • PhD
- history • PhD
- Jewish studies • MA
- mathematics • PhD
- mathematics/computer science • MS
- music • MM, MSM
- nursing • PhD
- philosophy • PhD
- physics • PhD
- political science • PhD
- psychobiology • PhD
- sociology • PhD
- Spanish • PhD
- women's studies • Certificate

Division of Biological and Biomedical Sciences

Dr. Bryan D. Noe, Director

Programs in:
- biochemistry, cell and developmental biology • PhD
- biological and biomedical sciences • PhD
- genetics and molecular biology • PhD
- immunology and molecular pathogenesis • PhD
- microbiology and molecular genetics • PhD
- molecular and systems pharmacology • PhD
- neuroscience • PhD
- nutrition and health sciences • PhD
- population biology, ecology, and evolution • PhD

Division of Educational Studies
Dr. Eleanor C. Main, Director
Programs in:
educational studies • MA, PhD, DAST
middle grades teaching • M Ed, MAT
secondary teaching • M Ed, MAT

Division of Epidemiology
Dr. John Boring, Director
Program in:
quantitative epidemiology • PhD

Division of Religion
Dr. Steven M. Tipton, Director
Program in:
religion • PhD

Graduate Institute of Liberal Arts
Dr. Dana White, Acting Chair
Program in:
liberal arts • PhD

Nell Hodgson Woodruff School of Nursing
Dr. Marla E. Salmon, Dean
Programs in:
adult health • MSN
family nurse midwifery • MSN
international health • MSN
leadership in healthcare • MSN
nursing systems • MSN
public health nursing • MSN
women's health nurse practitioner • MSN

Roberto C. Goizueta Business School
Thomas S. Robertson, Dean
Program in:
business • EMBA, MBA

The Rollins School of Public Health
Dr. James W. Curran, Dean
Programs in:
behavioral sciences and health education • MPH
biostatistics • MPH, MSPH, PhD
environmental/occupational health • MPH, MSPH
epidemiology • MPH, MS, MSPH, PhD
health policy and management • MPH
international health • MPH
public health • MPH, MS, MSPH, PhD
public health informatics • MSPH

School of Law
Howard O. Hunter, Dean
Program in:
law • JD, LL M

School of Medicine
Dr. Thomas J. Lawley, Dean
Programs in:
anesthesiology/patient monitoring systems • MM Sc
medicine • MD, MM Sc, MPT, Certificate
ophthalmic technology • MM Sc
physical therapy • MM Sc, MPT
physician assistant • MM Sc
radiation oncology physics • MM Sc

■ FORT VALLEY STATE UNIVERSITY
Fort Valley, GA 31030-3298
http://www.fvsu.edu/

State-supported, coed, comprehensive institution. *Computer facilities:* 633 computers available on campus for general student use. A campuswide network can be accessed from off campus. On-line grade reports available. *Library facilities:* Henry A. Hunt Memorial Library plus 2 others. *General application contact:* Dean of Admissions and Enrollment Management, 912-825-6307.

Graduate Division
Programs in:
early childhood education • MS
guidance and counseling • MS, Ed S
mental health counseling • MS
middle grades education • MS
vocational rehabilitation counseling • MS

■ GEORGIA COLLEGE AND STATE UNIVERSITY
Milledgeville, GA 31061
http://www.gcsu.edu/

State-supported, coed, comprehensive institution. *Enrollment:* 687 full-time matriculated graduate/professional students (474 women), 409 part-time matriculated graduate/professional students (295 women). *Graduate faculty:* 109 full-time, 50 part-time/adjunct. *Computer facilities:* 375 computers available on campus for general student use. A campuswide network can be accessed from student residence rooms and from off campus. Internet access and online class registration are available. *Library facilities:* Ina Dillard Russell Library. *Graduate expenses:* Tuition, state resident: full-time $7,988. *General application contact:* Dr. Ken Jones, Dean of the Graduate School, 478-445-1228.

Graduate School
Dr. Ken Jones, Dean of the Graduate School

College of Arts and Sciences
Dr. Bernie L. Patterson, Dean
Programs in:
arts and sciences • MA, MPA, MS, MSA, MSLS
biology • MS
English, speech and journalism • MA
history • MA
logistics • MSA, MSLS
logistics management • MSA
logistics systems • MSLS
psychology • MS
public administration • MPA
public administration and public affairs • MPA, MS
public affairs • MS

The J. Whitney Bunting School of Business
Dr. Jo Ann Jones, Dean
Program in:
business • MBA, MIS

School of Education
Dr. Les Crawford, Dean
Programs in:
administration and supervision • M Ed, Ed S
behavior disorders • M Ed
early childhood education • M Ed, Ed S
education • M Ed, MAT, Ed S
English education • M Ed
instructional technology • M Ed
interrelated teaching • M Ed
learning disabilities • M Ed
mathematics education • M Ed
mental retardation • M Ed
middle grades education • M Ed, Ed S
natural science education • M Ed, Ed S
secondary education • MAT
social science education • M Ed, Ed S
special education • M Ed

School of Health Sciences
Dr. Pamela Levi, Dean
Programs in:
health and physical education • M Ed, Ed S
health sciences • M Ed, MSN, Ed S
nursing • MSN

■ GEORGIA INSTITUTE OF TECHNOLOGY
Atlanta, GA 30332-0001
http://www.gatech.edu/

State-supported, coed, university. CGS member. *Computer facilities:* 1,450 computers available on campus for general student use. A campuswide network can be accessed from student residence rooms and from off campus. Internet access and online class registration are available. *Library facilities:* Library

Georgia Institute of Technology (continued)
and Information Center. *General application contact:* Manager, Graduate Academic and Enrollment Services, 404-894-4612.

Graduate Studies and Research
Programs in:
algorithms, combinatorics, and optimization • PhD
statistics • MS Stat

College of Architecture
Programs in:
architecture • M Arch, MCP, MS, PhD
city planning • MCP

College of Computing
Programs in:
algorithms, combinatorics, and optimization • PhD
computer science • MS, MSCS, PhD
human computer interaction • MSHCI

College of Engineering
Programs in:
aerospace engineering • MS, MSAE, PhD
algorithms, combinatorics, and optimization • PhD
biomedical engineering • MS Bio E
ceramic engineering • MSMSE, PhD
chemical engineering • MS Ch E, PhD
civil engineering • MS, MS Bio E, MSCE, PhD
construction management • MS, MSCE, PhD
electrical and computer engineering • MS, MSEE, PhD
engineering • MS, MS Bio E, MS Ch E, MS Env E, MS Poly, MS Stat, MS Text, MSAE, MSCE, MSEE, MSESM, MSHP, MSHS, MSIE, MSME, MSMSE, MSNE, MSOR, MST Ch, MSTE, PhD, Certificate
engineering science and mechanics • MS, MSESM, PhD
environmental engineering • MS, MS Env E, PhD
health physics • MSHP
health systems • MSHS
industrial and systems engineering • MS, MS Stat, MSIE, PhD
industrial engineering • MS, MSIE
materials engineering • MS
mechanical engineering • MS, MS Bio E, MSME, PhD
metallurgy • MSMSE, PhD
nuclear engineering • MSNE, PhD
nuclear engineering and health physics • MSHP, MSNE, PhD
operations research • MSOR
polymers • MS Poly
pulp and paper engineering • Certificate
statistics • MS Stat
textile chemistry • MS, MST Ch
textile engineering • MS, MSTE, PhD
textiles • MS, MS Text

College of Sciences
Programs in:
algorithms, combinatorics, and optimization • PhD
applied mathematics • MS
applied physics • MSA Phy
atmospheric chemistry • MS, PhD
atmospheric dynamics and physics • MS, PhD
biology • MS, MS Biol, PhD
chemistry and biochemistry • MS, MS Chem, PhD
earth and atmospheric sciences • MSEAS
geochemistry • MS, PhD
human computer interaction • MSHCI
mathematics • MS Math, PhD
physics • MS, MS Phys, PhD
psychology • MS, MS Psy, PhD
sciences • MS, MS Biol, MS Chem, MS Math, MS Phys, MS Psy, MS Stat, MSA Phy, MSEAS, MSHCI, PhD
solid-earth geophysics • MS, PhD
statistics • MS Stat

Dupree College of Management
Programs in:
management • MS, MS Mgt, MSMOT, PhD
management of technology • MSMOT

Ivan Allen College of Policy and International Affairs
Programs in:
economics • MS
history of technology • MSHT, PhD
human computer interaction • MSHCI
information design and technology • MSIDT
international affairs • MS Int A
policy and international affairs • MS, MS Int A, MS Pub P, MSHCI, MSHT, MSIDT, PhD
public policy • MS Pub P, PhD

■ GEORGIA SOUTHERN UNIVERSITY
Statesboro, GA 30460
http://www.gasou.edu/

State-supported, coed, comprehensive institution. CGS member. *Enrollment:* 298 full-time matriculated graduate/professional students (196 women), 906 part-time matriculated graduate/professional students (596 women). *Graduate faculty:* 328 full-time (113 women), 28 part-time/adjunct (18 women). *Computer facilities:* 1,100 computers available on campus for general student use. A campuswide network can be accessed from student residence rooms and from off campus. Internet access is available. *Library facilities:* Henderson Library. *Graduate expenses:* Tuition, state resident: full-time $1,692; part-time $94 per semester hour. Tuition, nonresident: full-time $6,768; part-time $376 per semester hour. Required fees: $312 per term. Tuition and fees vary according to course load. *General application contact:* Dr. John R. Diebolt, Associate Graduate Dean, 912-681-5384.

Jack N. Averitt College of Graduate Studies
Dr. G. Lane Van Tassell, Associate Vice President for Academic Affairs and Dean of Graduate Studies and Research

Allen E. Paulson College of Science and Technology
Dr. Jimmy Solomon, Dean
Programs in:
biology • MS
mathematics • MS
science and technology • M Tech, MS
technology • M Tech

College of Business Administration
Dr. Carl W. Gooding, Dean
Programs in:
accounting • M Acc
business administration • M Acc, MBA

College of Education
Dr. Arnold Cooper, Dean
Programs in:
art education • M Ed, Ed S
business education • M Ed
counselor education • M Ed, Ed S
curriculum studies • Ed D
early childhood education • M Ed, Ed S
education • M Ed, Ed D, Ed S
educational administration • Ed D
educational leadership • M Ed, Ed D, Ed S
English education • M Ed, Ed S
French education • M Ed
German education • M Ed
health and physical education • M Ed, Ed S
higher education • M Ed
instructional technology • M Ed, Ed S
mathematics • M Ed, Ed S

middle grades education • M Ed, Ed S
music education • M Ed, Ed S
reading education • M Ed, Ed S
school psychology • M Ed, Ed S
science education • M Ed, Ed S
social science education • M Ed, Ed S
Spanish education • M Ed
special education • M Ed, Ed S
technology education • M Ed, Ed S

College of Health and Professional Studies
Dr. Frederick Whitt, Dean
Programs in:
health and professional studies • MHSA, MPH, MS, MSN, Certificate
health services administration • MHSA
kinesiology • MS
public health • MPH
recreation administration • MS
rural community health nurse specialist • MSN, Certificate
rural family nurse practitioner • MSN, Certificate
sport management • MS
women's health nurse practitioner • Certificate

College of Liberal Arts and Social Sciences
Dr. Jeffrey Buller, Interim Dean
Programs in:
English • MA
fine arts • MFA
history • MA
liberal arts and social sciences • MA, MFA, MM, MPA, MS
music • MM
political science • MA
psychology • MS
public administration • MPA
sociology • MA

■ GEORGIA SOUTHWESTERN STATE UNIVERSITY

Americus, GA 31709-4693
http://www.gsw.edu/

State-supported, coed, comprehensive institution. *Enrollment:* 118 full-time matriculated graduate/professional students (79 women), 523 part-time matriculated graduate/professional students (460 women). *Graduate faculty:* 71 full-time (26 women). *Computer facilities:* 336 computers available on campus for general student use. A campuswide network can be accessed from off campus. Internet access and online class registration are available. *Library facilities:* James Earl Carter Library. *Graduate expenses:* Tuition, state resident: full-time $1,126; part-time $94 per credit. Tuition, nonresident: full-time $4,505; part-time $376 per credit. Required fees: $536. *General application contact:* Dr. Cathy L. Rozmus, Vice President for Academic Affairs, 913-931-2275.

Graduate Studies
Dr. Cathy L. Rozmus, Vice President for Academic Affairs

School of Arts and Sciences
Dr. Harold J. Nichols, Dean
Programs in:
arts and sciences • MSA
social administration • MSA

School of Business
Dr. John G. Kooti, Dean
Programs in:
business administration • MSA
computer information systems • MSA
social administration • MSA

School of Computer and Information Science
Dr. Boris V. Peltsverger, Interim Dean
Programs in:
computer information systems • MS
computer science • MS

School of Education
Dr. Kirt Myers, Dean
Programs in:
business education • M Ed
early childhood education • M Ed, Ed S
health and physical education • M Ed
middle grades education • M Ed, Ed S
reading • M Ed
secondary education • M Ed

School of Nursing
Dr. Judith Malachowski, Acting Dean
Program in:
midwifery • MSN

■ GEORGIA STATE UNIVERSITY

Atlanta, GA 30303-3083
http://www.gsu.edu/

State-supported, coed, university. CGS member. *Enrollment:* 3,488 full-time matriculated graduate/professional students (2,644 women), 3,691 part-time matriculated graduate/professional students (2,194 women). *Graduate faculty:* 952 full-time (409 women), 61 part-time/adjunct (44 women). *Computer facilities:* 500 computers available on campus for general student use. A campuswide network can be accessed from student residence rooms and from off campus. *Library facilities:* Pullen Library plus 1 other. *Graduate expenses:* Tuition, state resident: full-time $3,006; part-time $125 per credit hour. Tuition, nonresident: full-time $10,024; part-time $417 per credit hour. Required fees: $616; $616 per year. Tuition and fees vary according to course load, degree level and program. *General application contact:* Gretchen Young, Interim Director of Admissions, 404-651-2469.

Andrew Young School of Policy Studies
Dr. Roy Bahl, Dean
Programs in:
economics • MA, PhD
human resource development • MS, PhD
policy studies • MA, MPA, MS, PhD
public administration • MPA
public policy • PhD
urban policy studies • MS

College of Arts and Sciences
Dr. Ahmed T. Abdelal, Dean
Programs in:
anthropology • MA
applied and environmental microbiology • MS, PhD
applied linguistics • MA
arts and sciences • M Mu, MA, MA Ed, MAT, MFA, MHP, MS, PhD, Certificate
astronomy • PhD
cell biology and physiology • MS, PhD
chemistry • MS, PhD
communication • MA, PhD
composition • MA, PhD
computer science • MS, PhD
creative writing • MA, MFA, PhD
English • MA, PhD
fiction • MFA
French • MA, Certificate
geography • MA
geology • MS
German • MA, Certificate
heritage preservation • MHP
history • MA, PhD
literature • MA, PhD
mathematics • MA, MAT, MS
molecular genetics and biochemistry • MS, PhD
neurobiology • MS, PhD
philosophy • MA
physics • MS, PhD
poetry • MFA
political science • MA, PhD
psychology • PhD
rhetoric • MA, PhD
sociology • MA, PhD
Spanish • MA, Certificate
technical and professional writing • MA, PhD
translation and interpretation • Certificate

Georgia State University (continued)
School of Art and Design
Prof. John McWilliams, Director
Programs in:
- art education • MA Ed
- art history • MA
- studio art • MFA

School of Music
Dr. John Haberlen, Director
Program in:
- music • M Mu

Women's Studies Institute
Dr. Linda A. Bell, Director
Program in:
- women's studies • MA

College of Education
Dr. Ron P. Colarusso, Interim Dean
Programs in:
- art education • Ed S
- communication disorders • M Ed
- counseling • PhD
- counseling psychology • PhD
- early childhood education • M Ed, PhD, Ed S
- education • M Ed, MLM, MS, PhD, Ed S
- education of behavior/learning disabled • M Ed
- education of the hearing impaired • M Ed
- educational leadership • M Ed, PhD, Ed S
- educational psychology • MS, PhD
- educational research • MS, PhD
- English education • M Ed, Ed S
- exceptionalities • PhD
- exercise science • MS
- foreign language education • Ed S
- health and physical education • M Ed
- higher education • PhD
- instructional technology • MS, PhD, Ed S
- language and literacy education • M Ed, PhD
- library media technology • MLM, PhD, Ed S
- library science/media • MLM, MS, PhD, Ed S
- mathematics education • M Ed, PhD, Ed S
- middle childhood education • M Ed, PhD, Ed S
- multiple/severe disabilities • M Ed
- music education • Ed S
- professional counseling • MS, PhD, Ed S
- reading instruction • M Ed, Ed S
- rehabilitation counseling • MS, Ed S
- research, measurements and statistics • PhD
- school counseling • M Ed, Ed S
- school psychology • M Ed, PhD, Ed S
- science education • M Ed, PhD, Ed S
- secondary education • M Ed, PhD, Ed S
- social foundations of education • MS, PhD
- social science education • Ed S
- social studies education • M Ed, PhD
- special education • Ed S
- sport science • PhD
- sports administration • MS
- sports medicine • MS
- teaching English as a second language • M Ed
- urban teacher leadership • MS
- vocational education • M Ed

College of Health and Human Sciences
Dr. Susan Kelley, Dean
Programs in:
- advanced nutrition • MS
- advanced physical therapy • MS
- advanced respiratory care • MS
- community partnerships • MSW
- criminal justice • MS
- health and human sciences • MPT, MS, MSW, PhD
- physical therapy • MPT

School of Nursing
Dr. Patsy L. Ruchala, Associate Director of Graduate Programs
Programs in:
- adult health • MS
- child health • MS
- family nurse practitioner • MS
- health promotion, protection and restoration • PhD
- perinatal/women's health • MS
- psychiatric/mental health • MS

College of Law
Dr. Janice C. Griffith, Dean
Program in:
- law • JD

J. Mack Robinson College of Business
Dr. Sidney E. Harris, Dean
Programs in:
- actuarial science • MAS, MBA
- business • MAS, MBA, MHA, MIB, MPA, MS, MSHA, MSRE, MTX, PhD
- computer information systems • MBA, MS, PhD
- decision sciences • MBA, MS
- entrepreneurship • MBA
- finance • MBA, MS, PhD
- general business administration • MBA
- management • MBA, MS, PhD
- marketing • MBA, MS, PhD
- operations management • PhD
- personal financial planning • MBA, MS
- real estate • MBA, MSRE, PhD
- risk management and insurance • MBA, MS, PhD

Institute of Health Administration
Dr. Andrew T. Sumner, Director
Program in:
- health administration • MBA, MHA, MSHA, PhD

Institute of International Business
Dr. Karen D. Loch, Director
Program in:
- international business • MBA, MIB, PhD

School of Accountancy
Dr. Jane Mutchler, Director
Programs in:
- accountancy • MBA, MPA, MTX, PhD
- taxation • MTX

W. T. Beebe Institute of Personnel and Employee Relations
Dr. Richard H. Deane, Director
Program in:
- personnel and employee relations • MBA, MS, PhD

■ KENNESAW STATE UNIVERSITY
Kennesaw, GA 30144-5591
http://www.kennesaw.edu/

State-supported, coed, comprehensive institution. CGS member. *Enrollment:* 413 full-time matriculated graduate/professional students (230 women), 783 part-time matriculated graduate/professional students (451 women). *Graduate faculty:* 116 full-time (59 women), 17 part-time/adjunct (9 women). *Computer facilities:* 542 computers available on campus for general student use. A campuswide network can be accessed from off campus. Internet access and online class registration are available. *Library facilities:* Horace W. Sturgis Library. *Graduate expenses:* Tuition: full-time $2,252; part-time $94 per credit hour. Required fees: $131 per term. One-time fee: $232 full-time. *General application contact:* Dawn Mann, Assistant Director of Graduate Admissions, 770-420-4377.

College of Health and Social Service
Dr. Julia Perkins, Dean
Programs in:
- health and social service • MSN
- primary care nurse practitioner • MSN

College of Humanities and Social Sciences
Dr. Linda M. Noble, Dean
Programs in:
conflict management • MSCM
humanities and social sciences • MAPW, MPA, MSCM
professional writing • MAPW
public administration • MPA

College of Science and Mathematics
Dr. Laurence I. Peterson, Dean
Programs in:
information systems • MSIS
science and mathematics • MSIS

Leland and Clarice C. Bagwell College of Education
Dr. Ann Smith, Interim Dean
Programs in:
early childhood • M Ed
education • M Ed
middle grades • M Ed
special education • M Ed

Michael J. Coles College of Business
Dr. Timothy Mescon, Dean
Programs in:
accounting • M Acc, MBA
business • M Acc, MBA, MBA-EP, MBA-PE
business administration • MBA, MBA-EP, MBA-PE
business information systems management • MBA
entrepreneurship • MBA
finance • MBA
human resources management and development • MBA
marketing • MBA

■ MERCER UNIVERSITY

Macon, GA 31207-0003
http://www.mercer.edu/

Independent-religious, coed, comprehensive institution. *Enrollment:* 889 full-time matriculated graduate/professional students (549 women), 730 part-time matriculated graduate/professional students (421 women). *Graduate faculty:* 98 full-time (30 women), 31 part-time/adjunct (15 women). *Computer facilities:* 140 computers available on campus for general student use. A campuswide network can be accessed from student residence rooms and from off campus. Internet access is available. *Library facilities:* Jack Tarver Library plus 3 others. *Graduate expenses:* Tuition: part-time $313 per hour. Tuition and fees vary according to campus/location and program. *General application contact:* 478-301-2700.

Graduate Studies, Cecil B. Day Campus

James and Carolyn McAfee School of Theology
Dr. R. Alan Culpepper, Dean
Program in:
theology • M Div

School of Education
Dr. Richard T. Sietsema, Dean
Programs in:
early childhood education • M Ed, Ed S
middle grades education • M Ed, Ed S

Southern School of Pharmacy
Dr. Hewitt W. Matthews, Dean
Program in:
pharmacy • Pharm D, PhD

Stetson School of Business and Economics
Dr. W. Carl Joiner, Dean
Programs in:
business administration • MBA, XMBA
health care management • MS
technology management • MS

Graduate Studies, Macon Campus

School of Education
Dr. Richard T. Sietsema, Dean
Programs in:
early childhood education • M Ed, Ed S
English education • M Ed
mathematics education • M Ed
middle grades education • M Ed, Ed S
reading specialist • M Ed
science education • M Ed
social sciences education • M Ed

School of Engineering
Dr. M. Dayne Aldridge, Dean
Programs in:
biomedical engineering • MSE
electrical engineering • MSE
engineering management • MSE
mechanical engineering • MSE
software engineering • MSE
software systems • MS
technical management • MS

Stetson School of Business and Economics
Dr. W. Carl Joiner, Dean
Program in:
business and economics • MBA

School of Medicine
Dr. W. Douglas Skelton, Vice President for Health Affairs/Dean
Program in:
medicine • MD, MFS, MPH

Walter F. George School of Law
R. Lawrence Dessem, Dean
Program in:
law • JD

■ NORTH GEORGIA COLLEGE & STATE UNIVERSITY

Dahlonega, GA 30597-1001
http://www.ngcsu.edu/

State-supported, coed, comprehensive institution. *Enrollment:* 106 full-time matriculated graduate/professional students (70 women), 275 part-time matriculated graduate/professional students (212 women). *Graduate faculty:* 69 full-time (21 women), 14 part-time/adjunct (9 women). *Computer facilities:* 500 computers available on campus for general student use. A campuswide network can be accessed from student residence rooms and from off campus. *Library facilities:* Stewart Library. *Graduate expenses:* Tuition, state resident: full-time $2,320; part-time $97 per credit hour. Tuition, nonresident: full-time $6,966; part-time $387 per credit hour. Tuition and fees vary according to course load, campus/location and program. *General application contact:* Dr. Steve Ross, Coordinator of Graduate Admissions, 706-864-1916.

Graduate School
Programs in:
community counseling • MS
early childhood education • M Ed
educational administration • Ed S
family practitioner • MSN
middle grades education • M Ed
physical therapy • MS
public administration • MPA
secondary education • M Ed
special education • M Ed

■ PIEDMONT COLLEGE

Demorest, GA 30535-0010
http://www.piedmont.edu/

Independent-religious, coed, comprehensive institution. *Enrollment:* 188 full-time matriculated graduate/professional students (148 women), 514 part-time matriculated graduate/professional students (444 women). *Graduate faculty:* 82 full-time (37 women), 85 part-time/adjunct (37 women). *Computer facilities:* 100 computers available on campus for general student use. A campuswide network can be accessed from student residence

Piedmont College (continued)
rooms and from off campus. Internet access, e-mail are available. *Library facilities:* Arrendale Library. *Graduate expenses:* Tuition: full-time $4,140; part-time $230 per credit hour. *General application contact:* Carol E. Kokesh, Director of Graduate Studies, 706-778-8500 Ext. 1181.

Department of Social Sciences
Dr. Kenneth E. Melichar, Chair
Program in:
public administration • MPA

Division of Education
Dr. Jane McFerrin, Dean, School of Education
Programs in:
early childhood education • MA, MAT
secondary education • MA, MAT

School of Business
Dr. William Piper, Head
Program in:
business • MBA

■ SAVANNAH STATE UNIVERSITY

Savannah, GA 31404
http://www.savstate.edu/

State-supported, coed, comprehensive institution. *Computer facilities:* 440 computers available on campus for general student use. A campuswide network can be accessed. Internet access is available. *Library facilities:* Asa H. Gordon Library. *General application contact:* Director of Admissions, 912-356-2181.

Program in Public Administration
Program in:
public administration • MPA

Program in Social Work
Program in:
social work • MSW

Program in Urban Studies
Program in:
urban studies • MS

■ STATE UNIVERSITY OF WEST GEORGIA

Carrollton, GA 30118
http://www.westga.edu/

State-supported, coed, comprehensive institution. CGS member. *Enrollment:* 325 full-time matriculated graduate/professional students (220 women), 1,525 part-time matriculated graduate/professional students (1,191 women). *Graduate faculty:* 230 full-time (92 women), 17 part-time/adjunct (5 women). *Computer facilities:* A campuswide network can be accessed from student residence rooms and from off campus. Internet access and online class registration are available. *Library facilities:* Irvine Sullivan Ingram Library. *Graduate expenses:* Tuition, state resident: full-time $1,072; part-time $146 per credit hour. Tuition, nonresident: full-time $3,610; part-time $428 per credit hour. Required fees: $259; $14 per credit hour. $100 per semester. *General application contact:* Dr. Jack O. Jenkins, Dean, Graduate School, 770-836-6419.

Graduate School
Dr. Jack O. Jenkins, Dean

College of Arts and Sciences
Dr. Richard G. Miller, Dean
Programs in:
art education • M Ed
arts and sciences • M Ed, MA, MM, MPA, MS
biology • MS
English language and literature • MA
gerontology • MA
history • MA
music education • MM
music performance • MM
psychology • MA
public administration • MPA
rural and small town planning • MS
sociology • MA

College of Education
Dr. Price M. Michael, Interim Dean
Programs in:
administration and supervision • M Ed, Ed S
counseling and guidance • M Ed, Ed S
early childhood education • M Ed, Ed S
education • M Ed, Ed D, Ed S
French • M Ed
media • M Ed, Ed S
middle grades education • M Ed, Ed S
physical education • M Ed, Ed S
reading education • M Ed
school improvement • Ed D
secondary education—English • M Ed, Ed S
secondary education—foreign language • M Ed
secondary education—mathematics • M Ed, Ed S
secondary education—science • M Ed, Ed S
secondary education—social studies • M Ed, Ed S
Spanish • M Ed
special education-curriculum specialist • Ed S
special education-emotionally handicapped • M Ed, Ed S
special education-learning disabled • M Ed
special education-mentally handicapped • M Ed
speech-language pathology • M Ed

Richards College of Business
Dr. Jack E. Johnson, Dean
Programs in:
accounting • MP Acc
business • M Ed, MBA, MP Acc, Ed S
business administration • MBA
business education • M Ed, Ed S

■ UNIVERSITY OF GEORGIA

Athens, GA 30602
http://www.uga.edu/

State-supported, coed, university. CGS member. *Enrollment:* 3,714 full-time matriculated graduate/professional students (2,009 women), 1,859 part-time matriculated graduate/professional students (1,264 women). *Graduate faculty:* 1,495 full-time (396 women). *Computer facilities:* 2,500 computers available on campus for general student use. A campuswide network can be accessed from student residence rooms and from off campus. Internet access and online class registration, e-mail, Web pages are available. *Library facilities:* Ilah Dunlap Little Memorial Library plus 2 others. *Graduate expenses:* Tuition, state resident: full-time $1,971; part-time $132 per hour. Tuition, nonresident: full-time $6,705; part-time $528 per hour. Required fees: $393 per semester. *General application contact:* Dr. Jan Sandor, Director of Graduate Admissions, 706-542-1739.

Find an in-depth description at www.petersons.com/graduate.

College of Pharmacy
Dr. Svein Oie, Dean
Programs in:
experimental therapeutics • PhD
experimental therapeutics • MS
medicinal chemistry • MS, PhD
pharmaceutics • MS, PhD
pharmacology • MS, PhD

pharmacy • Pharm D, MS, PhD
pharmacy care administration • MS, PhD
toxicology • MS, PhD

College of Veterinary Medicine
Dr. Keith W. Prasse, Dean
Programs in:
avian medicine • MAM
medical microbiology • MS, PhD
medical microbiology and parasitology • MS, PhD
parasitology • MS, PhD
pathology • MS, PhD
pharmacology • MS, PhD
physiology • MS, PhD
physiology and pharmacology • MS, PhD
toxicology • MS, PhD
veterinary anatomy • MS
veterinary anatomy and radiology • MS
veterinary medicine • DVM, MAM, MS, PhD

Graduate School
Dr. Gordhan L. Patel, Dean

College of Agricultural and Environmental Sciences
Dr. Gale A. Buchanan, Dean
Programs in:
agricultural and environmental sciences • MA Ext, MAE, MCCS, MFT, MPPPM, MS, PhD
agricultural economics • MAE, MS, PhD
agricultural engineering • MS
agricultural extension • MA Ext
agronomy • MS, PhD
animal and dairy science • PhD
animal nutrition • PhD
animal science • MS
biological and agricultural engineering • PhD
biological engineering • MS
crop and soil sciences • MCCS
dairy science • MS
entomology • MS, PhD
environmental economics • MS
environmental health • MS
food science • MS, PhD
food technology • MFT
horticulture • MS, PhD
plant pathology • MS, PhD
plant protection and pest management • MPPPM
poultry science • MS, PhD
toxicology • MS, PhD

College of Arts and Sciences
Dr. Wyatt W. Anderson, Dean
Programs in:
analytical chemistry • MS, PhD
anthropology • MA, PhD
applied mathematical science • MAMS
art • MFA, PhD
art history • MA
artificial intelligence • MS
arts and sciences • MA, MAMS, MAT, MFA, MM, MPA, MS, DMA, DPA, PhD
biochemistry and molecular biology • MS, PhD
botany • MS, PhD
cellular biology • MS, PhD
classics • MA
comparative literature • MA, PhD
computer science • MS, PhD
conservation ecology and sustainable development • MS
drama • MFA, PhD
ecology • MS, PhD
English • MA, MAT, PhD
French • MA, MAT
genetics • MS, PhD
geography • MA, MS, PhD
geology • MS, PhD
German • MA
Greek • MA
history • MA, PhD
inorganic chemistry • MS, PhD
Latin • MA
linguistics • MA, PhD
marine sciences • MS, PhD
mathematics • MA, PhD
microbiology • MS, PhD
music • MA, MM, DMA, PhD
organic chemistry • MS, PhD
philosophy • MA, PhD
physical chemistry • MS, PhD
physics • MS, PhD
political science • MA, PhD
psychology • MS, PhD
public administration • MPA, DPA
religion • MA
Romance languages • MA, MAT, PhD
sociology • MA, PhD
Spanish • MA, MAT
speech communication • MA, PhD
statistics • MS, PhD

College of Education
Dr. Louis A. Castenell, Dean
Programs in:
adult education • M Ed, MA, Ed D, PhD, Ed S
agricultural education • M Ed
art education • MA Ed, Ed D, Ed S
business education • M Ed
college student affairs administration • M Ed
communication sciences and disorders • M Ed, MA, PhD, Ed S
computer-based education • M Ed
counseling and student personnel services • PhD
counseling psychology • PhD
early childhood education • M Ed, PhD, Ed S
education • MA
education of the gifted • Ed D
educational leadership • M Ed, MA, Ed D, Ed S
educational psychology • M Ed, MA, PhD
elementary and middle school education • M Ed, PhD, Ed S
elementary education • PhD
English education • M Ed, Ed S
exercise science • M Ed, Ed D, PhD
family and consumer sciences education • M Ed
guidance and counseling • M Ed
health and human performance • M Ed, MA, Ed D, PhD, Ed S
health promotion and behavior • PhD
health promotion and behavior and safety education • M Ed
higher education • Ed D, PhD
human resource and organization development • M Ed
human resources and organization development • M Ed
instructional technology • M Ed, PhD, Ed S
language education • PhD
marketing education • M Ed
mathematics education • M Ed, Ed D, PhD, Ed S
middle school education • M Ed, PhD, Ed S
music education • MM Ed, Ed D, Ed S
occupational studies • M Ed, Ed D, PhD, Ed S
physical education and sport studies • M Ed, MA, Ed D, PhD, Ed S
reading education • M Ed, MA, Ed D, PhD, Ed S
recreation and leisure studies • M Ed, MA, Ed D
safety education • Ed S
school psychology and school psychometry • Ed S
science education • M Ed, Ed D, PhD, Ed S
social foundations of education • PhD
social science education • M Ed, Ed D, PhD
special education • M Ed, MA, Ed D, PhD, Ed S
teaching additional languages • M Ed, Ed S
technological studies • M Ed

College of Family and Consumer Sciences
Dr. Sharon Y. Nickols, Dean
Programs in:
child and family development • MFCS, MS, PhD
family and consumer sciences • MFCS, MS, PhD
foods and nutrition • MFCS, MS, PhD
housing and consumer economics • MS, PhD
textiles, merchandising, and interiors • MS, PhD

University of Georgia (continued)

School of Environmental Design
John F. Crowley, Dean
Programs in:
environmental design • MHP, MLA
historic preservation • MHP
landscape architecture • MLA

School of Forest Resources
Dr. Arnett C. Mace, Dean
Program in:
forest resources • MFR, MS, PhD

School of Journalism and Mass Communication
John Soloski, Dean
Programs in:
journalism and mass communication • MA
mass communication • MMC, PhD

School of Social Work
Dr. Bonnie L. Yegidis, Dean
Programs in:
nonprofit organizations • MA
social work • MSW, PhD

Terry College of Business
Dr. P. George Benson, Dean
Programs in:
accounting • M Acc
business • M Acc, MA, MBA, MIT, MMR, PhD
business administration • MA, MBA, PhD
economics • MA, PhD
marketing research • MMR

School of Law
David E. Shipley, Dean
Program in:
law • JD, LL M

■ VALDOSTA STATE UNIVERSITY

Valdosta, GA 31698
http://www.valdosta.edu/

State-supported, coed, university. CGS member. *Enrollment:* 428 full-time matriculated graduate/professional students (392 women), 881 part-time matriculated graduate/professional students (633 women). *Graduate faculty:* 217 full-time (74 women). *Computer facilities:* 2,400 computers available on campus for general student use. A campuswide network can be accessed from student residence rooms and from off campus. Internet access and online class registration are available. *Library facilities:* Odom Library. *Graduate expenses:* Tuition, state resident: full-time $1,692; part-time $94 per credit hour. Tuition, nonresident: full-time $5,076; part-time $282 per credit hour. Required fees: $279 per semester. One-time fee: $50. *General application contact:* Dr. Ernestine H. Clark, Dean, 229-333-5694.

Graduate School
Dr. Ernestine H. Clark, Dean

College of Arts and Sciences
Dr. Mary Kay Corbitt, Acting Dean
Programs in:
arts and sciences • MA, MPA, MS
city management • MPA
criminal justice • MS
English • MA
history • MA
marriage and family therapy • MS
public human resources • MPA
public sector • MPA
sociology • MS

College of Business Administration
Dr. Kenneth L. Stanley, Dean
Program in:
business administration • MBA

College of Education
Dr. Thomas Reed, Acting Dean
Programs in:
adult and vocational education • Ed D
business education • M Ed, Ed S
clinical/counseling psychology • MS
communication disorders • M Ed
early childhood education • M Ed, Ed S
education • M Ed, MAE, MME, MS, Ed D, Ed S
educational leadership • M Ed, Ed D, Ed S
industrial/organizational psychology • MS
kinesiology and physical education • M Ed
middle grades education • M Ed, Ed S
reading • M Ed, Ed S
school counseling • M Ed, Ed S
school psychology • M Ed, Ed S
secondary education • M Ed, Ed S
special education • M Ed, Ed S
vocational education • M Ed

College of Fine Arts
Dr. Lanny D. Milbrandt, Head
Programs in:
art education • MAE
fine arts • MAE, MME
music education • MME

College of Nursing
Dr. Maryann Reichenbach, Dean
Programs in:
administration • MSN
community health nursing • MSN

Division of Social Work
Dr. Peggy Cleveland, Director
Program in:
social work • MSW

Guam

■ UNIVERSITY OF GUAM

Mangilao, GU 96923
http://uog.edu

Territory-supported, coed, comprehensive institution. *Computer facilities:* 150 computers available on campus for general student use. *General application contact:* Dean, Graduate School and Research, 671-735-2173.

Graduate School and Research

College of Arts and Sciences
Programs in:
arts and sciences • MA, MS
ceramics • MA
environmental science • MS
graphics • MA
Micronesian studies • MA
painting • MA
tropical marine biology • MS

College of Business and Public Administration
Programs in:
business administration • MBA
business and public administration • MBA, MPA
public administration • MPA

College of Education
Programs in:
administration and supervision • M Ed
counseling • MA
education • M Ed, MA
instructional leadership • MA
language and literacy • M Ed
secondary education • M Ed
special education • M Ed
teaching English to speakers of other languages • M Ed

Hawaii

■ CHAMINADE UNIVERSITY OF HONOLULU

Honolulu, HI 96816-1578
http://www.chaminade.edu/

Independent-religious, coed, comprehensive institution. *Enrollment:* 367 full-time matriculated graduate/professional students (243 women), 257 part-time matriculated graduate/professional students (158 women). *Graduate faculty:* 25 full-time (13 women), 31 part-time/adjunct (16 women). *Computer facilities:* 50 computers available on campus for general student use. A campuswide network can be accessed from off campus. *Library facilities:* Sullivan Library. *Graduate expenses:* Tuition: part-time $372 per credit hour. *General application contact:* Dr. Michael Fassiotto, Director, 808-739-4674.

Graduate Programs
Dr. Michael Fassiotto, Director
Programs in:
business administration • MBA
counseling psychology • MSCP
criminal justice administration • MSCJA
pastoral leadership • MPL
public administration • MPA
social science via peace education • M Ed

■ HAWAII PACIFIC UNIVERSITY

Honolulu, HI 96813-2785

http://www.hpu.edu/

Independent, coed, comprehensive institution. *Enrollment:* 672 full-time matriculated graduate/professional students (305 women), 568 part-time matriculated graduate/professional students (263 women). *Graduate faculty:* 47 full-time (19 women), 38 part-time/adjunct (18 women). *Computer facilities:* 418 computers available on campus for general student use. A campuswide network can be accessed from student residence rooms and from off campus. Internet access is available. *Library facilities:* Meader Library plus 2 others. *Graduate expenses:* Tuition: full-time $7,020; part-time $4,680 per year. *General application contact:* Leina Danao, Admissions Coordinator, 808-544-1120.

Find an in-depth description at www.petersons.com/graduate.

Division of Arts and Sciences
Dr. Leslie Correa, Associate Vice President and Dean
Program in:
diplomacy and military studies • MA

Division of Business Administration
Dr. Rodney Romig, Dean
Programs in:
accounting • MBA
finance • MBA
human resource management • MBA
information systems • MBA
international business • MBA
management • MBA
marketing • MBA
not-for-profit management • MBA
quality management • MBA
travel industry management • MBA

Division of Communication
Dr. Helen Varner, Dean
Program in:
communication • MA

Division of International Studies
Dr. Jeanne Rellahan, Dean
Program in:
teaching English as a second language • MA

Division of Nursing
Dr. Carol Winters-Moorhead, Dean
Programs in:
community clinical nurse specialist • MSN
family nurse practitioner • MSN

Division of Professional Studies
Dr. Larry Zimmerman, Acting Dean
Programs in:
human resource management • MA
information systems management • MSIS
information systems technology • MSIS
management • MA
organizational change • MA

■ UNIVERSITY OF HAWAII AT MANOA

Honolulu, HI 96822

http://www.uhm.hawaii.edu/

State-supported, coed, university. CGS member. *Enrollment:* 2,470 full-time matriculated graduate/professional students (1,373 women), 1,658 part-time matriculated graduate/professional students (964 women). *Graduate faculty:* 1,320 full-time (356 women), 192 part-time/adjunct (28 women). *Computer facilities:* 1,000 computers available on campus for general student use. A campuswide network can be accessed from student residence rooms and from off campus. Internet access, telephone registration are available. *Library facilities:* Hamilton Library plus 6 others. *General application contact:* Raymond Jarman, Assistant Dean, 808-956-8950.

Graduate Division
Dr. Alan H. Teramura, Senior Vice President for Research and Dean of the Graduate Division
Programs in:
cell, molecular, and neuro sciences • MS, PhD
ecology, evolution and conservation biology • MS, PhD
marine biology • MS, PhD
travel industry management • MS

College of Arts and Sciences
Programs in:
advanced library and information science • Certificate
American studies • MA, PhD
anthropology • MA, PhD
art • MA
art history • MA
arts and humanities • M Mus, MA, MFA, PhD
arts and sciences • M Mus, MA, MFA, MLI Sc, MPA, MS, MURP, PhD, Certificate
Asian and Asian-Western theatre • PhD
botany • MS, PhD
chemistry • MS, PhD
classics • MA
clinical psychology • PhD
communication • MA
communication and information science • PhD
community planning and social policy • MURP
computer science • PhD
dance • MA, MFA
dance and theatre • PhD
East Asian languages and literature • MA, PhD
economics • MA, PhD
English • MA, PhD
English as a second language • MA
environmental planning and management • MURP
French • MA
geography • MA, PhD
German • MA
history • MA, PhD
information and computer sciences • MS
land use and infrastructure planning • MURP
language, linguistics and literature • MA, PhD
library and information science • MLI Sc, PhD, Certificate
linguistics • MA, PhD
mathematics • MA, PhD
microbiology • MS, PhD
music • M Mus, MA, PhD
natural sciences • MA, MLI Sc, MS, PhD, Certificate
philosophy • MA, PhD
physics and astronomy • MS, PhD
political science • MA, PhD
psychology • MA, PhD
public administration • MPA, Certificate
religion • MA
second language acquisition • PhD

University of Hawaii at Manoa (continued)

social sciences • MA, MPA, MURP, PhD, Certificate
sociology • MA, PhD
Spanish • MA
speech • MA
theatre • MA, MFA
urban and regional planning in Asia and Pacific • MURP
visual arts • MFA
zoology • MS, PhD

College of Business Administration
David McClain, Dean
Programs in:
accountancy • M Acc
business administration • EMBA, MBA
China focused business administration • EMBA
executive business administration • EMBA
international management • PhD
Japan focused business administration • EMBA

College of Education
Dr. Randy A. Hitz, Dean
Programs in:
counselor education • M Ed
curriculum and instruction • PhD
education • M Ed, M Ed T, MS, PhD
education in teaching • M Ed T
educational administration • PhD
educational foundations • PhD
educational policy studies • PhD
educational psychology • M Ed, PhD
educational technology • M Ed
elementary education • M Ed
exceptionalities • PhD
kinesiology and leisure science • MS
secondary education • M Ed
special education • M Ed

College of Engineering
Dr. Wai-Fah Chen, Dean
Programs in:
civil engineering • MS, PhD
electrical engineering • MS, PhD
engineering • MS, PhD
mechanical engineering • MS, PhD

College of Health Sciences and Social Welfare
Programs in:
clinical nurse specialist • MS
health sciences and social welfare • MS, MSW, PhD, Certificate
nurse practitioner • MS
nursing • PhD, Certificate
nursing administration • MS
social welfare • PhD
social work • MSW

College of Tropical Agriculture and Human Resources
Dr. H. Michael Harrington, Interim Dean
Programs in:
agricultural and resource economics • MS, PhD
agronomy and soil sciences • MS, PhD
animal sciences • MS
biosystems engineering • MS
botanical sciences • MS, PhD
entomology • MS, PhD
food science • MS
horticulture • MS, PhD
nutritional science • MS
plant pathology • MS, PhD
tropical agriculture and human resources • MS, PhD

School of Architecture
W. H. Raymond Yeh, Dean
Program in:
architecture • D Arch

School of Hawaiian, Asian and Pacific Studies
Willa Tanabe, Dean
Programs in:
Asian studies • MA
Pacific Island studies • MA

School of Ocean and Earth Science and Technology
C. Barry Raleigh, Dean
Programs in:
high-pressure geophysics and geochemistry • MS, PhD
hydrogeology and engineering geology • MS, PhD
marine geology and geophysics • MS, PhD
meteorology • MS, PhD
ocean and earth science and technology • MS, PhD
ocean and resources engineering • MS, PhD
oceanography • MS, PhD
planetary geosciences and remote sensing • MS, PhD
seismology and solid-earth geophysics • MS, PhD
volcanology, petrology, and geochemistry • MS, PhD

School of Travel Industry Management
Dr. Pauline J. Sheldon, Interim Dean
Program in:
travel industry management • MS

John A. Burns School of Medicine
Dr. Edwin L. Cadmen, Dean
Programs in:
medicine • MD, MPH, MS, PhD
public health sciences and epidemiology • MPH, MS

Graduate Programs in Biomedical Sciences
Programs in:
biochemistry • MS, PhD
biomedical sciences • MS, PhD
biophysics • MS, PhD
genetics and molecular biology • MS, PhD
pharmacology • MS, PhD
physiology • MS, PhD
reproductive biology • PhD
speech pathology and audiology • MS
tropical medicine • MS, PhD

William S. Richardson School of Law
Lawrence C. Foster, Dean
Program in:
law • JD

Idaho

■ BOISE STATE UNIVERSITY
Boise, ID 83725-0399
http://www.boisestate.edu/

State-supported, coed, comprehensive institution. *Enrollment:* 306 full-time matriculated graduate/professional students (196 women), 942 part-time matriculated graduate/professional students (591 women). *Graduate faculty:* 394 full-time (108 women), 172 part-time/adjunct (60 women). *Computer facilities:* 900 computers available on campus for general student use. A campuswide network can be accessed from student residence rooms and from off campus. Internet access and online class registration are available. *Library facilities:* Albertsons Library. *Graduate expenses:* Tuition, nonresident: full-time $3,000. Required fees: $157 per credit. *General application contact:* Dr. John R. Pelton, Dean, Graduate College, 208-426-3647.

Graduate College
College of Arts and Sciences
Programs in:
applied geophysics • MS
art • MA
arts and sciences • MA, MFA, MM, MS, PhD
biology • MA, MS
computer science • MS
creative writing • MFA
earth science • MS

- English • MA
- fine arts, creative writing • MFA
- fine arts, visual arts • MFA
- geology • MS
- geophysics • PhD
- interdisciplinary studies • MA, MS
- music • MM
- music education • MM
- pedagogy • MM
- performance • MM
- raptor biology • MS
- technical communication • MA
- visual arts • MFA

College of Business and Economics
Programs in:
- accountancy • MS
- business administration • MBA
- business and economics • MBA, MS
- management information systems • MS

College of Education
Programs in:
- athletic administration • MPE
- curriculum and instruction • MA
- early childhood education • MA
- education • MA, MPE, MS, Ed D
- educational technology • MS
- exercise and sport studies • MS
- mathematics education • MS
- physical education • MPE
- reading • MA
- school counseling • MA
- special education • MA

College of Engineering
Programs in:
- civil engineering • MS
- computer engineering • MS
- electrical engineering • MS
- engineering • MS
- instructional and performance technology • MS
- mechanical engineering • MS

College of Health Science
Programs in:
- health science • MHS
- health studies • MHS

College of Social Science and Public Affairs
Programs in:
- communication • MA
- criminal justice administration • MA
- environmental and natural resources policy and administration • MPA
- general public administration • MPA
- history • MA
- social science and public affairs • MA, MPA, MSW
- social work • MSW
- state and local government policy and administration • MPA

■ IDAHO STATE UNIVERSITY
Pocatello, ID 83209

State-supported, coed, university. CGS member. *Computer facilities:* 300 computers available on campus for general student use. A campuswide network can be accessed from student residence rooms and from off campus. *Library facilities:* Eli M. Oboler Library. *General application contact:* Dean, 208-282-2150.

Office of Graduate Studies
Programs in:
- biology • MNS
- chemistry • MNS
- general interdisciplinary • M Ed, MA
- geology • MNS
- mathematics • MNS
- physics • MNS
- waste management and environmental science • MS

College of Arts and Sciences
Programs in:
- anthropology • MA, MS
- art • MFA
- arts and sciences • MA, MFA, MNS, MPA, MS, DA, PhD
- biology • MS, DA, PhD
- chemistry • MNS, MS
- clinical psychology • PhD
- English • MA, DA
- geology • MS
- geophysics/hydrology • MS
- mathematics • MS, DA
- microbiology • MS
- natural science • MNS
- physics • MS
- political science • MA, DA
- psychology • MS
- public administration • MPA
- sociology • MA
- speech communication • MA
- theatre • MA

College of Business
Programs in:
- business administration • MBA
- computer information systems • MS

College of Education
Programs in:
- athletic administration • MPE
- child and family studies • M Ed
- curriculum and instruction • M Ed
- education • M Ed, MPE, Ed D, Ed S
- educational administration • M Ed, Ed S
- educational leadership • Ed D
- human exceptionality • M Ed
- industrial training management • M Ed
- instructional technology • M Ed
- literacy • M Ed
- school psychology • Ed S
- special education •
- vocational program ...ement • M Ed

College of Engineering
Programs in:
- engineering and applied s... • PhD
- engineering structures and m...nics • MS
- environmental engineering • M...
- measurement and control engineering • MS
- nuclear science and engineering • MS
- waste management and environmental science • MS

College of Health Professions
Programs in:
- audiology • MS
- counseling • M Coun, Ed S
- counselor education and counseling • PhD
- deaf education • MS
- family medicine • Certificate
- health education • MHE
- health professions • M Coun, MHE, MOT, MPH, MPT, MS, PhD, Certificate, Ed S
- marriage and family counseling • M Coun
- mental health counseling • M Coun
- nursing • MS, Certificate
- occupational therapy • MOT
- physical therapy • MPT
- public health • MPH
- school counseling • M Coun
- speech language pathology • MS
- student affairs and college counseling • M Coun

College of Pharmacy
Programs in:
- biopharmaceutical analysis • PhD
- biopharmaceutics • PhD
- pharmaceutical chemistry • MS
- pharmaceutical science • PhD
- pharmaceutics • MS
- pharmacognosy • MS
- pharmacokinetics • PhD
- pharmacology • MS, PhD
- pharmacy • Pharm D
- pharmacy administration • MS, PhD

■ NORTHWEST NAZARENE UNIVERSITY
Nampa, ID 83686-5897
http://www.nnu.edu/

Independent-religious, coed, comprehensive institution. *Computer facilities:* 400 computers available on campus for general student use. A campuswide network can be accessed from student residence rooms and from off campus. Internet access, various software packages are available. *Library*

...sity

Northwest Nazaren... (continued)
...ibrary. *General facilities:* John E... ector, Graduate and application con... 08-467-8345.

Continuing St... dies

Graduat...

Program... ministration • MBA
busin... and instruction • M Ed
curri... nal leadership • M Ed
edu... onal child • M Ed
ex... on • M Min
...ool counseling • M Ed

UNIVERSITY OF IDAHO

Moscow, ID 83844-2282
http://www.uidaho.edu/

State-supported, coed, university. CGS member. *Enrollment:* 1,635 full-time matriculated graduate/professional students (469 women), 1,240 part-time matriculated graduate/professional students (573 women). *Graduate faculty:* 599. *Computer facilities:* 750 computers available on campus for general student use. A campuswide network can be accessed from student residence rooms and from off campus. Internet access and online class registration are available. *Library facilities:* University of Idaho Library plus 1 other. *Graduate expenses:* Tuition, state resident: full-time $2,720. Tuition, nonresident: full-time $8,720. Required fees: $540. *General application contact:* Dr. Roger P. Wallins, Associate Dean of the College of Graduate Studies, 208-885-6243.

Find an in-depth description at www.petersons.com/graduate.

College of Graduate Studies

Dr. Charles R. Hatch, Dean

College of Agriculture
Dr. Larry Branen, Dean
Programs in:
- agricultural and extension education • MS
- agricultural economics • MS
- agriculture • M Engr, MS, PhD
- animal physiology • PhD
- biochemistry • MS, PhD
- biological and agricultural engineering • M Engr, MS, PhD
- entomology • MS, PhD
- food science • MS
- home economics • MS
- microbiology • MS, PhD
- microbiology, molecular biology and biochemistry • MS, PhD
- plant protection • MS, PhD
- plant science • MS, PhD
- soil science • MS, PhD
- veterinary science • MS

College of Art and Architecture
Programs in:
- architecture • M Arch, MA
- art • MFA
- art and architecture • M Arch, MA, MAT, MFA
- art education • MAT

College of Business and Economics
Dr. Byron Dangerfield, Dean
Programs in:
- accounting • M Acct
- business and economics • M Acct, MS
- economics • MS

College of Education
Dr. Dale Gentry, Dean
Programs in:
- adult education • M Ed, MS, Ed D, PhD
- business education • M Ed
- counseling and human services • M Ed, MS, Ed D, PhD, CHSS
- education • MAT, Ed D, PhD, Ed S
- educational administration • M Ed
- elementary education • M Ed
- industrial technology education • M Ed, MS, Ed D, PhD
- physical education • M Ed, MS, PhD
- professional-technical education • M Ed, Ed D, PhD, Ed Sp PTE
- recreation • MS
- school psychology • SPS
- secondary education • M Ed, MS
- special education • M Ed, MS, Sp Ed S
- teacher education • M Ed, MAT, MS, Ed D, PhD, EAS, Ed S, Sp Ed S
- vocational education • MS

College of Engineering
Dr. David E. Thompson, Dean
Programs in:
- chemical engineering • M Engr, MS, PhD
- civil engineering • M Engr, MS, PhD
- computer engineering • M Engr, MS
- computer science • MS, PhD
- electrical engineering • M Engr, MS, PhD
- engineering • M Engr, MS, PhD
- environmental engineering • M Engr, MS
- mechanical engineering • M Engr, MS, PhD
- nuclear engineering • M Engr, MS, PhD
- systems engineering • M Engr

College of Letters and Science
Dr. Kurt O. Olsson, Dean
Programs in:
- anthropology • MA
- biological sciences • M Nat Sci
- botany • MS, PhD
- chemistry • MS, PhD
- chemistry education • MAT
- creative writing • MFA
- English • MA, MAT
- English education • MAT
- environmental science • MS
- French • MAT
- history • MA, PhD
- history education • MAT
- interdisciplinary studies • MA, MS
- letters and science • M Mus, M Nat Sci, MA, MAT, MFA, MPA, MS, PhD
- mathematics • MAT, MS, PhD
- mathematics education • MAT
- music • M Mus, MA
- physics • MS, PhD
- physics education • MAT
- political science • MA, PhD
- psychology • MS
- public administration • MPA
- Spanish • MAT
- statistics • MS
- teaching English as a second language • MA
- theatre arts • MFA
- waste management • MS
- zoology • MS, PhD

College of Mines and Earth Resources
Dr. Earl H. Bennett, Dean
Programs in:
- geography • MS, PhD
- geography education • MAT
- geological engineering • MS
- geology • MS, PhD
- geophysics • MS
- hydrology • MS
- metallurgical engineering • MS, PhD
- metallurgy • MS
- metallurgy engineering • MS
- mines and earth resources • MAT, MS, PhD
- mining engineering • MS, PhD
- mining engineering: metallurgy • PhD

College of Natural Resources
Dean
Programs in:
- fishery management • MS
- fishery resources • MS, PhD
- forest products • MS, PhD
- forest resources • MS, PhD
- forestry, wildlife, and range sciences • PhD
- natural resources • MS, PhD
- rangeland ecology and management • MS, PhD
- resource recreation and tourism • MS, PhD
- wildlife resources • MS, PhD

College of Law

John A. Miller, Dean
Program in:
- law • JD

Illinois

■ ILLINOIS SCHOOL OF PROFESSIONAL PSYCHOLOGY, CHICAGO NORTHWEST CAMPUS

Rolling Meadows, IL 60008
http://www.aspp.edu/

Proprietary, coed, graduate-only institution. *Computer facilities:* 5 computers available on campus for general student use. A campuswide network can be accessed. Internet access is available. *Library facilities:* Learning Resource Center. *General application contact:* Coordinator of Student Enrollment, 847-290-7400.

Graduate Programs

Programs in:
- clinical psychology • MA, Psy D
- professional counseling • MA

■ AURORA UNIVERSITY

Aurora, IL 60506-4892
http://www.aurora.edu/

Independent, coed, comprehensive institution. *Enrollment:* 352 full-time matriculated graduate/professional students (273 women), 723 part-time matriculated graduate/professional students (516 women). *Graduate faculty:* 34 full-time (18 women), 38 part-time/adjunct (19 women). *Computer facilities:* 90 computers available on campus for general student use. A campuswide network can be accessed from student residence rooms and from off campus. Internet access is available. *Library facilities:* Charles B. Phillips Library plus 1 other. *Graduate expenses:* Tuition: part-time $442 per semester hour. Tuition and fees vary according to course load, degree level, campus/location and program. *General application contact:* Jane Zimmerman, Graduate Recruitment Coordinator, 800-742-5281.

College of Education

Dr. Gary Jewel, Dean
Programs in:
- curriculum and instruction • Ed D
- education • MAT
- education and administration • Ed D
- educational leadership • MEL

George Williams College

Dr. Rita Yerkes, Dean

School of Professional Studies

Programs in:
- administration of leisure services • MS
- outdoor pursuits recreation administration • MS
- outdoor therapeutic recreation administration • MS
- therapeutic recreation administration • MS

School of Social Work

Dr. Sandra Alcorn, Dean
Program in:
- social work • MSW

John and Judy Dunham College of Business

Dr. Ronald Benson, Dean
Program in:
- business • MBA

■ BENEDICTINE UNIVERSITY

Lisle, IL 60532-0900
http://www.ben.edu/

Independent-religious, coed, comprehensive institution. *Computer facilities:* 125 computers available on campus for general student use. A campuswide network can be accessed from student residence rooms and from off campus. *Library facilities:* Lownik Library. *General application contact:* Director, Center for Adult Programs and Services, 630-829-6200.

Find an in-depth description at www.petersons.com/graduate.

Graduate Programs

Programs in:
- business • EMBA
- business administration • MBA
- counseling psychology • MS
- curriculum and instruction and collaborative teaching • M Ed
- elementary education • MA Ed
- exercise physiology • MS
- fitness management • MS
- liberal studies • MA
- management and organizational behavior • MS
- management information systems • MS
- organizational development • PhD
- public health • MPH
- special education • MA Ed

■ BRADLEY UNIVERSITY

Peoria, IL 61625-0002
http://www.bradley.edu/

Independent, coed, comprehensive institution. CGS member. *Enrollment:* 183 full-time matriculated graduate/professional students, 652 part-time matriculated graduate/professional students. *Graduate faculty:* 251. *Computer facilities:* 2,000 computers available on campus for general student use. A campuswide network can be accessed from student residence rooms and from off campus. Internet access is available. *Library facilities:* Cullom-Davis Library. *General application contact:* Barbara Friedhoff, Director of Graduate Admissions, 309-677-2371.

Find an in-depth description at www.petersons.com/graduate.

Graduate School

Dean of the Graduate School

College of Communications and Fine Arts

Dr. Jeffrey Huberman, Dean
Programs in:
- ceramics • MA, MFA
- communications and fine arts • MA, MFA
- painting • MA, MFA
- photography • MA, MFA
- printmaking • MA, MFA
- sculpture • MA, MFA

College of Education and Health Sciences

Dr. Joan Sattler, Dean
Programs in:
- curriculum and instruction • MA
- education and health sciences • MA, MPT, MSN
- education and learning disabilities • MA
- human development counseling • MA
- leadership in educational administration • MA
- leadership in human services administration • MA
- nursing • MSN
- physical therapy • MPT

College of Engineering and Technology

Dr. Richard Johnson, Dean
Programs in:
- civil engineering and construction • MSCE
- electrical engineering • MSEE
- engineering and technology • MSCE, MSEE, MSIE, MSME, MSMFE
- industrial and manufacturing engineering and technology • MSIE, MSMFE
- mechanical engineering • MSME

College of Liberal Arts and Sciences

Dr. Claire Etaugh, Dean
Programs in:

Bradley University (continued)
- biology • MS
- chemistry • MS
- computer information systems • MS
- computer science • MS
- English • MA
- liberal arts and sciences • MA, MLS, MS
- liberal studies • MLS

Foster College of Business Administration
Dr. Rob Baer, Dean
Programs in:
- accounting • MS
- business administration • MBA, MS

■ CHICAGO STATE UNIVERSITY
Chicago, IL 60628
http://www.csu.edu/

State-supported, coed, comprehensive institution. *Enrollment:* 312 full-time matriculated graduate/professional students (210 women), 1,542 part-time matriculated graduate/professional students (1,072 women). *Graduate faculty:* 133 full-time (67 women), 87 part-time/adjunct (49 women). *Computer facilities:* 40 computers available on campus for general student use. *Library facilities:* Paul and Emily Douglas Library. *Graduate expenses:* Tuition, state resident: part-time $110 per credit hour. Tuition, nonresident: part-time $329 per credit hour. Required fees: $164 per credit hour. *General application contact:* Daphne G. Townsend, Admissions and Records Officer II, 773-995-2404.

Graduate Studies
Dr. Ellen F. Rosen, Dean of Graduate Studies

College of Arts and Sciences
Dr. Rachel Lindsey, Dean
Programs in:
- arts and sciences • MA, MS, MSW
- biological sciences • MS
- counseling • MA
- criminal justice • MS
- English • MA
- geography • MA
- history, philosophy, and political science • MA
- mathematics and computer science • MS
- social work and sociology • MSW

College of Education
Dr. Sandra Westbrooks, Acting Dean
Programs in:
- bilingual/bicultural education • MS Ed
- early childhood education • MAT, MS Ed
- education • MA, MAT, MS, MS Ed
- educational leadership • MA
- elementary education • MAT, MS Ed
- general administration • MA
- higher education administration • MA
- library science and communications media • MS
- physical education • MS Ed
- reading • MS Ed
- secondary education • MAT, MS Ed
- special education • MS Ed
- teaching in non-school settings • MS Ed
- teaching of reading • MS Ed
- technology and education • MS Ed

■ COLUMBIA COLLEGE CHICAGO
Chicago, IL 60605-1996
http://www.colum.edu/

Independent, coed, comprehensive institution. CGS member. *Computer facilities:* 730 computers available on campus for general student use. A campuswide network can be accessed. Internet access is available. *Library facilities:* Columbia College Library. *General application contact:* Associate Dean of the Graduate School, 312-663-1600 Ext. 5260.

Find an in-depth description at www.petersons.com/graduate.

Graduate School
Programs in:
- architectural studies • MFA
- arts, entertainment, and media management • MA
- creative writing • MFA
- dance/movement therapy • MA
- elementary • MAT
- English • MAT
- film and video • MFA
- interdisciplinary arts • MA, MAT
- interdisciplinary book and paper arts • MFA
- interior design • MFA
- media management • MA
- multicultural education • MA
- music business • MA
- performing arts management • MA
- photography • MA, MFA
- public affairs journalism • MA
- teaching of writing • MA
- urban teaching • MA
- visual arts management • MA

■ CONCORDIA UNIVERSITY
River Forest, IL 60305-1499
http://www.curf.edu/

Independent-religious, coed, comprehensive institution. CGS member. *Enrollment:* 278 full-time matriculated graduate/professional students, 342 part-time matriculated graduate/professional students. *Graduate faculty:* 68 full-time (24 women), 49 part-time/adjunct (18 women). *Computer facilities:* 70 computers available on campus for general student use. A campuswide network can be accessed from student residence rooms and from off campus. Internet access is available. *Library facilities:* Klinck Memorial Library. *Graduate expenses:* Tuition: part-time $460 per credit. *General application contact:* Dr. Donald E. Gnewuch, Dean of Graduate Studies, 708-209-3454.

Graduate Studies
Dr. Donald E. Gnewuch, Dean
Programs in:
- church music • MCM, CAS
- curriculum and instruction • MA, CAS
- early childhood education • MA, Ed D, CAS
- educational leadership • Ed D
- gerontology • MA, CAS
- human services • MA, CAS
- professional counseling • MA, CAS
- psychology • MA, CAS
- reading education • MA, CAS
- religion • MA, CAS
- school administration • MA, CAS
- school counseling • MA, CAS
- supervision of instruction • MA, CAS
- teaching • MAT, CAS
- urban teaching • MA

■ DEPAUL UNIVERSITY
Chicago, IL 60604-2287
http://www.depaul.edu/

Independent-religious, coed, university. CGS member. *Enrollment:* 4,397 full-time matriculated graduate/professional students (2,135 women), 3,715 part-time matriculated graduate/professional students (1,781 women). *Graduate faculty:* 598 full-time (213 women), 952 part-time/adjunct (406 women). *Computer facilities:* 850 computers available on campus for general student use. A campuswide network can be accessed from student residence rooms and from off campus. Internet access and online class registration are available. *Library facilities:* John T. Richardson Library plus

2 others. *Graduate expenses:* Tuition: part-time $345 per hour. *General application contact:* 312-362-6709.

Find an in-depth description at www.petersons.com/graduate.

Charles H. Kellstadt Graduate School of Business
Karen M. Stark, Assistant Dean and Director
Programs in:
business • M Acc, MA, MBA, MS, MSA, MSF, MSHR, MSMA, MSMIS, MST
business economics • MBA
economics • MA
entrepreneurship • MBA
finance • MBA, MSF
human resource management • MBA, MSHR
international business • MBA
international marketing and finance • MBA
leadership and change management • MBA
management planning and strategy • MBA
marketing • MBA
marketing analysis • MS
operations management • MBA

School of Accountancy
Dr. Ray Whittington, Director
Programs in:
accountancy • M Acc, MBA, MSA, MSMIS, MST
accounting • M Acc, MBA, MSA
management information systems • MSMIS
systems • MBA
taxation • MST

College of Law
Wayne Lewis, Acting Dean
Program in:
law • JD, LL M

College of Liberal Arts and Sciences
Michael Mezey, Dean
Programs in:
advanced practice nursing • MS
applied physics • MS
applied statistics • MS
association management • MS
biochemistry • MS
biological sciences • MA, MS
chemistry • MS
child clinical psychology • MA, PhD
clinical psychology • MA, PhD
community clinical psychology • MA, PhD
community psychology • PhD
corporate communication • MA
English • MA
experimental psychology • MA, PhD
financial administration management • Certificate
fundraising and philanthropy • MS
general psychology • MS
health administration • Certificate
health law and policy • MS
healthcare administration • MS
higher education administration • MS
history • MA
industrial/organizational psychology • MA, PhD
interdisciplinary studies • MA, MS
international studies • MA
liberal arts and sciences • MA, MBA, MPS, MS, PhD, Certificate
liberal studies • MA
mathematics education • MA
metropolitan planning • MS, Certificate
multicultural communication • MA
non-profit administration • MS
nonprofit organization management • MS
nurse anesthesia • MS
philosophy • MA, PhD
polymer chemistry and coating • MS
public administration • MS
public policy • MS
public service management • MS
public services • Certificate
sociology • MA
teaching of physics • MS
technology • MS
women's studies • Certificate
writing • MA

School for New Learning
Dr. Russ Rogers, Program Director
Programs in:
applied technology • MA
integrated professional studies • MA

School of Computer Science, Telecommunications, and Information Systems
Dr. Helmut Epp, Dean
Programs in:
computer science • MS, PhD
computer science, telecommunications, and information systems • MA, MBA, MS, MSMIS, PhD
e-commerce technology • MS
human-computer interaction • MS
information systems • MS
software engineering • MS
telecommunications systems • MS

School of Education
Dr. Sandra Jackson, Dean
Programs in:
administration and supervision • M Ed, MA
agencies, family concerns, and higher education • M Ed, MA
Catholic school leadership • M Ed, MA
curriculum studies/development • M Ed, MA, Ed D
education • M Ed, MA, Ed D
educational leadership • Ed D
elementary education • M Ed, MA
elementary schools • M Ed, MA
human development and learning • MA
human services management • M Ed, MA
physical education • M Ed, MA
reading and learning disabilities • M Ed, MA
secondary education • M Ed, MA
secondary schools • M Ed, MA

School of Music
Dr. Donald E. Casey, Dean
Programs in:
applied music (performance) • MM, Certificate
composition • MM
music • MM, Certificate
music composition • MM
music education • MM
performance • MM

The Theatre School
John Culbert, Chair
Programs in:
acting • MFA, Certificate
costume design • MFA
directing • MFA
lighting design • MFA
scenic design • MFA
theatre • MFA, Certificate

■ DOMINICAN UNIVERSITY
River Forest, IL 60305-1099
http://www.dom.edu/

Independent-religious, coed, comprehensive institution. *Enrollment:* 168 full-time matriculated graduate/professional students (119 women), 1,021 part-time matriculated graduate/professional students (806 women). *Graduate faculty:* 32 full-time (18 women), 94 part-time/adjunct (50 women). *Computer facilities:* 199 computers available on campus for general student use. A campuswide network can be accessed from student residence rooms and from off campus. Internet access, email are available. *Library facilities:* Rebecca Crown Library. *Graduate expenses:* Tuition: part-time $355 per credit hour. Tuition and fees vary according to program.

Dominican University (continued)

Graduate School of Business
Dr. Molly Burke, Dean
Programs in:
- accounting • MSA
- business administration • MBA
- computer information systems • MSCIS
- management information systems • MSMIS
- organization management • MSOM

Graduate School of Education
Sr. Colleen McNicholas, Dean
Programs in:
- curriculum and instruction • MA Ed
- early childhood education • MS
- education • MAT
- educational administration • MA
- special education • MS

Graduate School of Library and Information Science
Prudence Dalrymple, Dean
Programs in:
- library and information science • MLIS, MSMIS, CSS
- management information systems • MSMIS

■ EASTERN ILLINOIS UNIVERSITY

Charleston, IL 61920-3099
http://www.eiu.edu/

State-supported, coed, comprehensive institution. CGS member. *Computer facilities:* 1,202 computers available on campus for general student use. A campuswide network can be accessed from student residence rooms and from off campus. Internet access and online class registration are available. *Library facilities:* Booth Library. *General application contact:* Acting Dean, Graduate School, 217-581-2220.

Find an in-depth description at www.petersons.com/graduate.

Graduate School

College of Arts and Humanities
Programs in:
- art • MA
- arts and humanities • MA
- English • MA
- historical administration • MA
- history • MA
- music • MA
- speech-communication • MA

College of Education and Professional Studies
Programs in:
- education and professional studies • MS, MS Ed, Ed S
- educational administration and supervision • MS Ed, Ed S
- educational psychology and guidance • MS Ed
- elementary education • MS Ed
- junior high education • MS Ed
- physical education • MS
- special education • MS Ed

College of Sciences
Programs in:
- biological sciences • MS
- botany • MS
- chemistry • MS
- clinical psychology • MA
- communication disorders and sciences • MS
- economics • MA
- environmental biology • MS
- mathematics • MA
- mathematics education • MA
- political science • MA
- school psychology • SSP
- sciences • MA, MS, SSP
- zoology • MS

Lumpkin College of Business and Applied Sciences
Programs in:
- business administration • MBA
- business and applied sciences • MA, MBA, MS, MS Ed
- dietetics • MS
- gerontology • MA
- home economics • MS
- technology • MS

■ GOVERNORS STATE UNIVERSITY

University Park, IL 60466-0975
http://www.govst.edu/

State-supported, coed, upper-level institution. *Enrollment:* 207 full-time matriculated graduate/professional students (133 women), 2,865 part-time matriculated graduate/professional students (2,136 women). *Graduate faculty:* 150 full-time (54 women), 160 part-time/adjunct (74 women). *Computer facilities:* 142 computers available on campus for general student use. A campuswide network can be accessed from off campus. *Library facilities:* University Library. *Graduate expenses:* Tuition, state resident: full-time $2,424; part-time $101 per credit hour. Tuition, nonresident: full-time $7,272; part-time $303 per credit hour. Required fees: $120 per semester. *General application contact:* William T. Craig, Admissions Officer, 708-534-4492.

College of Arts and Sciences
Dr. Roger Oden, Dean
Program in:
- arts and sciences • MA, MS

Division of Liberal Arts
Dr. Joyce Kennedy, Chairperson
Programs in:
- art • MA
- communication studies • MA
- English • MA
- instructional and training technology • MA
- liberal arts • MA
- media communication • MA
- political and justice studies • MA

Division of Science
Dr. Edwin Cehelnik, Chairperson
Programs in:
- analytical chemistry • MS
- computer science • MS
- environmental biology • MS
- science • MS

College of Business and Public Administration
Dr. William Nowlin, Dean
Programs in:
- accounting • MS
- business administration • MBA
- business and public administration • MBA, MPA, MS
- management information systems • MS
- public administration • MPA

College of Education
Dr. Diane Alexander, Dean
Program in:
- education • MA

Division of Education
Dr. Larry Freeman, Chairperson
Programs in:
- early childhood education • MA
- education • MA
- educational administration and supervision • MA
- multi-categorical special education • MA
- reading • MA

Division of Psychology and Counseling
Dr. Addison Woodward, Chairperson
Programs in:
- counseling • MA
- psychology • MA
- psychology and counseling • MA

College of Health Professions
Dr. Amerfil Wang, Interim Dean
Programs in:
- health professions • MHA, MHS, MOT, MPT, MSN, MSW
- social work • MSW

Division of Health Administration and Human Services
Dr. Cheryl Mejta, Chairperson
Programs in:
- addictions studies • MHS
- health administration • MHA
- health administration and human services • MHA, MHS

Division of Nursing and Health Science
Dr. Sandra Mayfield, Chairperson
Programs in:
- communication disorders • MHS
- nursing • MSN
- nursing and health science • MHS, MOT, MPT, MSN
- occupational therapy • MOT
- physical therapy • MPT

■ ILLINOIS INSTITUTE OF TECHNOLOGY

Chicago, IL 60616-3793
http://www.iit.edu/

Independent, coed, university. CGS member. *Computer facilities:* 450 computers available on campus for general student use. A campuswide network can be accessed from student residence rooms and from off campus. Internet access and online class registration are available. *Library facilities:* Paul V. Galvin Library plus 5 others. *General application contact:* Dean of Graduate College, 312-567-3024.

Find an in-depth description at www.petersons.com/graduate.

Center for Law and Financial Markets

Programs in:
- financial markets and regulation • MS
- financial markets and regulations • MS
- financial markets and trading • MS
- financial services law • LL M

Chicago-Kent College of Law

Henry H. Perritt, Dean
Programs in:
- financial services • LL M
- international law • LL M
- law • JD
- taxation • LL M

Graduate College

Armour College of Engineering and Sciences
Programs in:
- analytical chemistry • MAC, MS, PhD
- biochemistry • MS
- biology • MS, PhD
- biomedical engineering • PhD
- biotechnology • MS
- cell biology • MS
- chemical engineering • M Ch E, MS, PhD
- chemistry • M Chem, MAC, MS, PhD
- civil and architectural engineering • M Geoenv E, M Trans E, MCEM, MGE, MPW, MS, MSE, PhD
- computer science • MS, PhD
- computer systems engineering • MS
- electrical and computer engineering • MECE
- electrical engineering • MS, PhD
- engineering and sciences • M Ch E, M Chem, M Env E, M Geoenv E, M Trans E, MAC, MCEM, MECE, MGE, MHP, MMAE, MME, MMME, MPA, MPW, MS, MSE, MST, MTSE, PhD
- environmental engineering • M Env E, MS, PhD
- food safety and technology • M Eng, MS
- health physics • MHP
- inorganic chemistry • MS, PhD
- manufacturing engineering • MME, MS
- mechanical and aerospace engineering • MMAE, MS, PhD
- metallurgical and materials engineering • MMME, MS, PhD
- microbiology • MS
- organic chemistry • MS, PhD
- physical chemistry • MS, PhD
- physics • MHP, MS, PhD
- polymer chemistry • MS, PhD
- social sciences • MPA, MPW
- teaching • MST
- technical communication and information design • MS
- telecommunications and software engineering • MTSE
- theoretical chemistry • MS, PhD

College of Architecture
Program in:
- architecture • M Arch, D Arch

Institute of Design
Programs in:
- communication design • M Des, MS, PhD
- photography • M Des
- product design • M Des, MS, PhD

Institute of Psychology
Programs in:
- clinical psychology • PhD
- industrial/organizational psychology • PhD
- personnel/human resource development • MS
- psychology • MS
- rehabilitation counseling • MS
- rehabilitation psychology • PhD

Stuart Graduate School of Business
Programs in:
- business • MBA, MS, PhD
- environmental management • MS
- finance • MBA
- information management • MBA
- international business • MBA
- management science • MBA
- marketing • MBA
- marketing communication • MS
- operations and technology management • MS
- operations management • MBA
- organization and management • MBA
- strategic management • MBA
- telecommunications management • MBA

■ ILLINOIS STATE UNIVERSITY

Normal, IL 61790-2200
http://www.ilstu.edu/

State-supported, coed, university. CGS member. *Enrollment:* 983 full-time matriculated graduate/professional students (596 women), 1,330 part-time matriculated graduate/professional students (849 women). *Graduate faculty:* 517 full-time (175 women), 18 part-time/adjunct (5 women). *Computer facilities:* 2,100 computers available on campus for general student use. A campuswide network can be accessed from student residence rooms and from off campus. Internet access is available. *Library facilities:* Milner Library. *Graduate expenses:* Tuition, state resident: full-time $2,599; part-time $107 per credit hour. Tuition, nonresident: full-time $7,898; part-time $325 per credit hour. Required fees: $1,117; $47 per credit hour. *General application contact:* Dr. Gary McGinnis, Associate Vice President of Research, Graduate Studies, and International Education.

Find an in-depth description at www.petersons.com/graduate.

Graduate School

Dr. Gary McGinnis, Associate Vice President of Research, Graduate Studies and International Education

College of Applied Science and Technology
Dr. J. Robert Rossman, Dean
Programs in:
- agribusiness • MS
- applied computer science • MS
- applied science and technology • MA, MS

Illinois State University (continued)
- criminal justice sciences • MA, MS
- environmental health and safety • MS
- family and consumer sciences • MA, MS
- health education • MS
- industrial technology • MS
- physical education • MS

College of Arts and Sciences
Dr. Paul Schollaert, Dean
Programs in:
- arts and sciences • MA, MS, MSW, PhD, SSP
- biological sciences • MS
- biology • PhD
- biotechnology • MS
- botany • PhD
- chemistry • MS
- communication • MA, MS
- ecology • PhD
- economics • MA, MS
- English • MA, MS, PhD
- English studies • PhD
- French • MA
- French and German • MA
- French and Spanish • MA
- genetics • PhD
- geohydrology • MS
- German • MA
- German and Spanish • MA
- history • MA, MS
- mathematics • MA, MS
- mathematics education • PhD
- microbiology • PhD
- physiology • PhD
- political science • MA, MS
- psychology • MA, MS
- school psychology • PhD, SSP
- social work • MSW
- sociology • MA, MS
- Spanish • MA
- speech pathology and audiology • MA, MS
- writing • MA, MS
- zoology • PhD

College of Business
Dr. Dixie Mills, Dean
Programs in:
- accounting • MPA, MS
- business • MBA, MPA, MS
- business administration • MBA

College of Education
Dr. Sally Pancrazio, Dean
Programs in:
- curriculum and instruction • MS, MS Ed, Ed D
- education • MS, MS Ed, Ed D, PhD
- educational administration and foundations • MS, MS Ed, Ed D, PhD
- educational policies • Ed D
- guidance and counseling • MS, MS Ed
- postsecondary education • Ed D
- reading education • MS Ed
- special education • MS, MS Ed, Ed D
- supervision • Ed D

College of Fine Arts
Dr. Roosevelt Newson, Dean
Programs in:
- art history • MA, MS
- ceramics • MFA, MS
- drawing • MFA, MS
- fibers • MFA, MS
- fine arts • MA, MFA, MM, MM Ed, MS
- glass • MFA, MS
- graphic design • MFA, MS
- metals • MFA, MS
- music • MM, MM Ed
- painting • MFA, MS
- photography • MFA, MS
- printmaking • MFA, MS
- sculpture • MFA, MS
- theater • MA, MFA, MS

Mennonite College of Nursing
Nancy Ridenour, Dean
Programs in:
- family nurse practitioner • PMC
- nursing • MSN

■ LEWIS UNIVERSITY
Romeoville, IL 60446
http://www.lewisu.edu/

Independent-religious, coed, comprehensive institution. *Computer facilities:* 287 computers available on campus for general student use. A campuswide network can be accessed from student residence rooms and from off campus. Internet access and online class registration are available. *Library facilities:* Lewis University Library. *General application contact:* Director, Graduate Admissions, 815-836-5520.

College of Arts and Sciences
Programs in:
- arts and sciences • M Ed, MA, MAE, MS, CAS
- counseling psychology • MA
- criminal/social justice • MS
- school counseling and guidance • MA

School of Education
Programs in:
- education • M Ed, MAE
- education administration • CAS

College of Business
Program in:
- business • MBA

College of Nursing
Programs in:
- case management • MSN
- community health • MSN
- nursing administration • MSN, Certificate
- nursing education • MSN

■ LOYOLA UNIVERSITY CHICAGO
Chicago, IL 60611-2196
http://www.luc.edu/

Independent-religious, coed, university. CGS member. *Enrollment:* 2,959 full-time matriculated graduate/professional students (1,766 women), 2,505 part-time matriculated graduate/professional students (1,685 women). *Graduate faculty:* 1,382. *Computer facilities:* 318 computers available on campus for general student use. A campuswide network can be accessed from student residence rooms and from off campus. Internet access is available. *Library facilities:* Cudahy Library plus 3 others. *Graduate expenses:* Tuition: part-time $360 per semester hour. Part-time tuition and fees vary according to course level. *General application contact:* Marianne Gramza, Assistant Dean and Director of Graduate Admissions, 773-508-3396.

Find an in-depth description at www.petersons.com/graduate.

Graduate School
Dr. William Yost, Acting Dean
Programs in:
- American politics and policy • MA, PhD
- applied social psychology • MA, PhD
- applied sociology • MA
- biochemistry • MS, PhD
- biology • MS
- cell and molecular physiology • MS, PhD
- cell biology, neurobiology and anatomy • MS, PhD
- chemistry • MS, PhD
- classical studies • PhD
- clinical psychology • PhD
- computer science • MS
- criminal justice • MA
- developmental psychology • PhD
- English • MA, PhD
- Greek • MA
- history • MA, PhD
- immunology • MS, PhD
- international studies • MA, PhD
- Latin • MA
- mathematical sciences • MS
- microbiology • MS, PhD
- molecular biology • PhD

neurochemistry • PhD
neuroscience • MS, PhD
organizational development • MSOD
perception • PhD
pharmacology and experimental therapeutics • MS, PhD
philosophy • MA, PhD
political theory and philosophy • MA, PhD
sociology • MA, PhD
Spanish • MA
theology • MA, PhD
training and development • MSTD
virology • MS, PhD

Institute of Human Resources and Industrial Relations
Dr. Homer H. Johnson, Director
Program in:
human resources and industrial relations • MSHR, MSIR

Institute of Pastoral Studies
Dr. Camilla Burns, Director
Programs in:
divinity • M Div
pastoral counseling • MA
pastoral studies • MPS
religious education • M Rel Ed

Marcella Niehoff School of Nursing
Programs in:
acute care clinical nurse specialist • MSN
acute care nurse practitioner • MSN
adult nurse practitioner • MSN
cardiovascular health and disease clinical nurse specialist • MSN
emergency nurse practitioner • MSN
health systems management • MSN
nurse midwifery • MSN
nursing • PhD
oncology clinical nurse specialist • MSN
pediatric clinical nurse specialist • MSN
pediatric nurse practitioner • MSN
women's health • MSN
women's health nurse practitioner • MSN

Graduate School of Business
Dr. John Nicholas, Associate Dean
Programs in:
accountancy • MS
business administration • MBA
information systems and operations management • MS
information systems management • MS
integrated marketing communication • MS

School of Education
Dr. Margaret L. Fong, Dean
Programs in:
administration/supervision • M Ed, MA, Ed D, PhD
college student personnel • M Ed
community counseling • M Ed, MA
comparative-international education • M Ed, MA, Ed D, PhD
counseling psychology • PhD
cultural and educational policy studies • M Ed, MA, Ed D, PhD
curriculum and instruction • M Ed, MA, Ed D
education • M Ed, MA, MS, Ed D, PhD
educational psychology • M Ed, MA, PhD
higher education • Ed D, PhD
history of education • M Ed, MA, Ed D, PhD
instructional leadership • M Ed
philosophy of education • M Ed, MA, Ed D, PhD
research methods • M Ed, MA, PhD
school counseling • M Ed
school psychology • M Ed, PhD
sociology of education • M Ed, MA, Ed D, PhD
special education • M Ed

School of Law
Nina S. Appel, Dean
Programs in:
business law • LL M, MJ
child and family law • LL M, MJ
health law • LL M, MJ, D Law, SJD
law • JD

School of Social Work
Dr. Joseph A. Walsh, Dean
Program in:
social work • MSW, PhD

Stritch School of Medicine
Dr. Stephen Slogoff, Dean
Program in:
medicine • MD

■ NATIONAL-LOUIS UNIVERSITY
Evanston, IL 60201-1796
http://www.nl.edu/

Independent, coed, university. *Computer facilities:* A campuswide network can be accessed from off campus. Internet access is available. *Library facilities:* NLU Library plus 5 others. *General application contact:* Vice President for University Services, 800-443-5522 Ext. 5127.

College of Arts and Sciences
Program in:
arts and sciences • M Ad Ed, MA, MS, Ed D, Certificate

Division of Health and Human Services
Programs in:
addictions counseling • MS, Certificate
addictions treatment • Certificate
career counseling and development studies • Certificate
community wellness and prevention • MS, Certificate
counseling • MS, Certificate
eating disorders counseling • Certificate
employee assistance programs • MS, Certificate
gerontology administration • Certificate
gerontology counseling • MS, Certificate
human services administration • MS, Certificate
long-term care administration • Certificate

Division of Language and Academic Development
Programs in:
adult education • M Ad Ed, Ed D, Certificate
adult education and developmental studies • M Ad Ed, Certificate
developmental studies • M Ad Ed

Division of Liberal Arts and Sciences
Programs in:
cultural psychology • MA
health psychology • MA
human development • MA
liberal arts and sciences • MA, MS, Certificate
organizational psychology • MA
psychology • Certificate
written communication • MS

College of Management and Business
Programs in:
business administration • MBA
human resource management and development • MS
management and business • MBA, MS
managerial leadership • MS

National College of Education, McGaw Graduate School
Programs in:
administration and supervision • M Ed, CAS, Ed S
curriculum and instruction • M Ed, MS Ed, CAS, Ed S
curriculum and social inquiry • Ed D
early childhood administration • M Ed, CAS
early childhood curriculum and instruction specialist • M Ed, MS Ed, CAS

National-Louis University (continued)
early childhood education • M Ed, MAT, CAS
early childhood leadership and advocacy • M Ed
education • M Ed, MAT, MS Ed, Ed D, CAS, Ed S
educational leadership • Ed D
educational leadership/superintendent endorsement • Ed D
educational psychology • CAS
educational psychology/human learning and development • M Ed, MS Ed
educational psychology/school psychology • M Ed, Ed D
elementary education • MAT
general special education • M Ed, MS Ed, CAS
human learning and development • Ed D
language and literacy • M Ed, MS Ed, CAS
learning disabilities • M Ed, MS Ed, CAS
learning disabilities/behavior disorders • M Ed, MAT, MS Ed, CAS
mathematics education • M Ed, MS Ed, CAS
reading and language • Ed D
reading recovery • CAS
reading specialist • M Ed, MS Ed, CAS
science education • M Ed, MS Ed, CAS
secondary education • MAT
technology in education • M Ed, MS Ed, CAS

■ NORTH CENTRAL COLLEGE

Naperville, IL 60566-7063

http://www.noctrl.edu/

Independent-religious, coed, comprehensive institution. *Enrollment:* 58 full-time matriculated graduate/professional students (27 women), 357 part-time matriculated graduate/professional students (180 women). *Graduate faculty:* 40 full-time, 22 part-time/adjunct. *Computer facilities:* 200 computers available on campus for general student use. A campuswide network can be accessed from student residence rooms and from off campus. Internet access, software packages are available. *Library facilities:* Oesterle Library. *Graduate expenses:* Tuition: full-time $16,995; part-time $455 per credit hour. Required fees: $180. *General application contact:* Frank Johnson, Director of Graduate Programs, 630-637-5840.

Graduate Programs
Barbara E. Illg, Associate Dean
Programs in:
business administration • MBA
computer science • MS
education • MA Ed
leadership studies • MLD
liberal studies • MALS
management information systems • MS

■ NORTHEASTERN ILLINOIS UNIVERSITY

Chicago, IL 60625-4699

http://www.neiu.edu/

State-supported, coed, comprehensive institution. CGS member. *Enrollment:* 238 full-time matriculated graduate/professional students (150 women), 1,354 part-time matriculated graduate/professional students (964 women). *Graduate faculty:* 257 full-time (103 women), 164 part-time/adjunct (77 women). *Computer facilities:* 300 computers available on campus for general student use. A campuswide network can be accessed from off campus. Internet access and online class registration, productivity software are available. *Library facilities:* Ronald Williams Library. *Graduate expenses:* Tuition, state resident: part-time $117 per credit hour. Tuition, nonresident: part-time $323 per credit hour. *General application contact:* Dr. Mohan K. Sood, Dean of the Graduate College, 773-442-6010.

Graduate College
Dr. Mohan K. Sood, Dean of the Graduate College

College of Arts and Sciences
Dr. Hode Mahmoudi, Acting Dean
Programs in:
arts and sciences • MA, MS
biology • MS
chemistry • MS
composition/writing • MA
computer science • MS
earth science • MS
English • MA
exercise science and cardiac rehabilitation • MS
geography and environmental studies • MA
gerontology • MA
history • MA
linguistics • MA
literature • MA
mathematics • MA, MS
mathematics for elementary school teachers • MA
music • MA
political science • MA
speech • MA

College of Business and Management
Dr. Allen N. Shub, Acting Dean
Programs in:
accounting • MBA, MSA
accounting, business law, and finance • MSA
finance • MBA
management • MBA
marketing • MBA

College of Education
Dr. Michael Carl, Dean
Programs in:
bilingual/bicultural education • MAT, MSI
early childhood special education • MA
educating children with behavior disorders • MA
educating individuals with mental retardation • MA
education • M Ed, MA, MAT, MSI
educational administration and supervision • MA
educational leadership • MA
gifted education • MA
guidance and counseling • MA
human resource development • MA
inner city studies • MA
instruction • MSI
language arts • MAT, MSI
reading • MA
special education • MA
teaching • MAT
teaching children with learning disabilities • MA

■ NORTHERN ILLINOIS UNIVERSITY

De Kalb, IL 60115-2854

http://www.niu.edu/

State-supported, coed, university. CGS member. *Enrollment:* 1,789 full-time matriculated graduate/professional students (971 women), 2,964 part-time matriculated graduate/professional students (1,801 women). *Graduate faculty:* 715 full-time (245 women), 50 part-time/adjunct (13 women). *Computer facilities:* 1,200 computers available on campus for general student use. A campuswide network can be accessed from student residence rooms and from off campus. *Library facilities:* Founders Memorial Library plus 8 others. *Graduate expenses:* Tuition, state resident: full-time $3,120; part-time $130 per credit hour. Tuition, nonresident: full-time $6,240; part-time $260 per credit hour. Required fees: $110; $46 per credit hour. *General application contact:* Graduate School Office, 815-753-0395.

Find an in-depth description at www.petersons.com/graduate.

College of Law
LeRoy Pernell, Dean
Program in:
law • JD

Graduate School
Dr. Jerrold Zar, Dean and Associate Provost for Graduate Studies and Research

College of Business
Dr. David K. Graf, Dean
Programs in:
accountancy • MAS, MST
business • MAS, MBA, MS, MST
business administration • MBA
management information systems • MS

College of Education
Dr. Alfonzo Thurman, Dean
Programs in:
adult continuing education • MS Ed, Ed D
counseling • MS Ed, Ed D
curriculum and instruction • MS Ed, Ed D
curriculum and supervision • MS Ed
early childhood education • MS Ed
education • MS Ed, Ed D, Ed S
educational administration • MS Ed, Ed D, Ed S
educational psychology • MS Ed, Ed D
elementary education • MS Ed, Ed D
foundations of education • MS Ed
instructional technology • MS Ed, Ed D
outdoor teacher education • MS Ed
physical education • MS Ed
reading • MS Ed, Ed D
school business management • MS Ed
secondary education • MS Ed, Ed D
special education • MS Ed

College of Engineering and Engineering Technology
Dr. Romualdas Kasuba, Dean
Programs in:
electrical engineering • MS
engineering and engineering technology • MS
industrial engineering • MS
industrial management • MS
mechanical engineering • MS

College of Health and Human Sciences
Dr. James Lankford, Dean
Programs in:
applied family and child studies • MS
communicative disorders • MA
health and human sciences • MA, MPH, MPT, MS
nursing • MS
nutrition and dietetics • MS
physical therapy • MPT
public health • MPH

College of Liberal Arts and Sciences
Dr. Frederick Kitterle, Dean
Programs in:
anthropology • MA
biological sciences • MS, PhD
chemistry • MS, PhD
communication studies • MA
computer science • MS
economics • MA, PhD
English • MA, PhD
French • MA
geography • MS
geology • MS, PhD
history • MA, PhD
liberal arts and sciences • MA, MPA, MS, PhD
mathematical sciences • PhD
mathematics • MS
philosophy • MA
physics • MS, PhD
political science • MA, PhD
psychology • MA, PhD
public administration • MPA
sociology • MA
Spanish • MA
statistics • MS

College of Visual and Performing Arts
Dr. Harold Kafer, Dean
Programs in:
art • MA, MFA, MS
music • MM, Performer's Certificate
theatre and dance • MFA
visual and performing arts • MA, MFA, MM, MS, Performer's Certificate

■ NORTH PARK THEOLOGICAL SEMINARY

Chicago, IL 60625-4895

http://www.northpark.edu/sem/

Independent-religious, coed, graduate-only institution. *Computer facilities:* A campuswide network can be accessed from off campus. Internet access is available. *Library facilities:* North Park Consolidated Library. *General application contact:* Associate Director, 800-964-0101.

Graduate and Professional Programs
Programs in:
Christian studies • Certificate
preaching • D Min
religious education • MACE
theological studies • MATS
theology • M Div

■ NORTH PARK UNIVERSITY

Chicago, IL 60625-4895

http://www.northpark.edu/

Independent-religious, coed, comprehensive institution. *Computer facilities:* 105 computers available on campus for general student use. A campuswide network can be accessed from student residence rooms and from off campus. *Library facilities:* Consolidated Library plus 4 others. *General application contact:* Vice President for Admissions and Financial Aid, 773-244-5500.

Center for Management Education
Program in:
management education • MBA, MM

School of Community Development
Program in:
community development • MA

School of Education
Program in:
education • MA

School of Nursing
Program in:
nursing • MS

■ NORTHWESTERN UNIVERSITY

Evanston, IL 60208

http://www.northwestern.edu/

Independent, coed, university. CGS member. *Enrollment:* 5,781 full-time matriculated graduate/professional students (2,668 women), 1,689 part-time matriculated graduate/professional students (558 women). *Graduate faculty:* 1,807 full-time (453 women), 151 part-time/adjunct (33 women). *Computer facilities:* 661 computers available on campus for general student use. A campuswide network can be accessed from student residence rooms and from off campus. Internet access and online class registration are available. *Library facilities:* University Library plus 6 others. *Graduate expenses:* Tuition: full-time $23,301; part-time $2,764 per unit. Required fees: $812. One-time fee: $812 part-time.

Northwestern University (continued)
General application contact: Dorothea Reid, Coordinator of Graduate Admissions, 847-491-8532.

The Graduate School
Richard I. Morimoto, Dean
Programs in:
- clinical psychology • PhD
- genetic counseling • MS
- marital and family therapy • MS
- public health • MPH
- telecommunications science, management, and policy • MA, MS, Certificate

Division of Interdepartmental Programs
Programs in:
- African studies • Certificate
- international and comparative studies • Certificate
- law and social science • Certificate
- liberal studies • MA
- literature • MA
- sociology and organization behavior • PhD

Institute for Neuroscience
Enrico Mugnaini, Director
Program in:
- neuroscience • PhD

Judd A. and Marjorie Weinberg College of Arts and Sciences
Eric J. Sundquist, Dean
Programs in:
- anthropology • PhD
- art history • PhD
- arts and sciences • MA, MFA, MS, PhD, Certificate
- astrophysics • PhD
- biochemistry • PhD
- biochemistry, molecular biology, and cell biology • PhD
- biotechnology • PhD
- brain, behavior and cognition • PhD
- cell and molecular biology • PhD
- chemistry • PhD
- clinical psychology • PhD
- cognitive psychology • PhD
- comparative literary studies • PhD
- developmental biology and genetics • PhD
- economics • MA, PhD
- eighteenth-century studies • Certificate
- English • MA, PhD
- French • PhD
- French and comparative literature • PhD
- geological sciences • MS, PhD
- German literature and critical thought • PhD
- history • PhD
- hormone action and signal transduction • PhD
- Italian studies • Certificate
- linguistics • MA, PhD
- mathematics • PhD
- molecular biophysics • PhD
- neurobiology and physiology • MS
- neuroscience • PhD
- personality • PhD
- philosophy • PhD
- physics • MS, PhD
- political science • MA, PhD
- Slavic languages and literature • PhD
- social psychology • PhD
- sociology • PhD
- statistics • MS, PhD
- structural biology • PhD
- structural biology, biochemistry, and biophysics • PhD
- visual arts • MFA

Kellogg Graduate School of Management
Donald P. Jacobs, Dean
Programs in:
- accounting • PhD
- biotechnology • MS
- business administration • MBA
- finance • PhD
- management • MBA, MMM, MS, PhD
- management and organizations • PhD
- managerial economics and strategy • PhD
- manufacturing management • MMM
- marketing • PhD

School of Education and Social Policy
Mark D. Hoffman, Assistant Dean
Programs in:
- advanced teaching • MS
- corporate training and development • MS
- education • MS
- education and social policy • MS
- education and social policy-counseling psychology • MA
- education and social policy-learning sciences • MA, PhD
- elementary teaching • MS
- higher education administration • MS
- human development and social policy • PhD
- school administration • MS
- secondary teaching • MS

School of Speech
Barbara O'Keefe, Dean
Programs in:
- audiology and hearing sciences • MA, PhD
- communication studies • MA, PhD
- communication systems • MSC
- directing • MFA
- learning disabilities • MA, PhD
- managerial communication • MSC
- performance studies • MA, PhD
- radio/television/film • MA, MFA, PhD
- speech • MA, MFA, MSC, PhD
- speech and language pathology • MA, PhD
- speech and language pathology and learning disabilities • MA
- stage design • MFA
- theatre • MA
- theatre and drama • PhD

Law School
David E. VanZandt, Dean
Program in:
- law • JD, LL M

Medical School
Programs in:
- cancer biology • PhD
- cell biology • PhD
- clinical investigation • MSCI
- developmental biology • PhD
- evolutionary biology • PhD
- immunology and microbial pathogenesis • PhD
- medicine • MD, MS, MSCI, DPT, PhD
- molecular biology and genetics • PhD
- neurobiology • PhD
- pharmacology and toxicology • PhD
- physical therapy • DPT, PhD
- structural biology and biochemistry • PhD

Medill School of Journalism
Programs in:
- advertising/sales promotion • MSIMC
- broadcast journalism • MSJ
- direct, database and e-commerce marketing • MSIMC
- general studies • MSIMC
- integrated marketing communications • MSIMC
- magazine publishing • MSJ
- new media • MSJ
- public relations • MSIMC
- reporting and writing • MSJ

Robert R. McCormick School of Engineering and Applied Science
John Birge, Dean
Programs in:
- applied mathematics • MS, PhD
- biomedical engineering • MS, PhD
- biosolid mechanics • MS, PhD
- chemical engineering • MS, PhD
- computer science • MS, PhD
- electrical and computer engineering • MS, PhD
- electronic materials • Certificate
- engineering and applied science • MEM, MIT, MME, MMM, MPM, MS, PhD, Certificate

engineering management • MEM
environmental health engineering • MS, PhD
fluid mechanics • MS, PhD
geotechnical engineering • MS, PhD
health physics/radiological health • MS, PhD
industrial engineering and management science • MS, PhD
information technology • MIT
manufacturing engineering • MME
materials science and engineering • MS, PhD
mechanical engineering • MS, PhD
operations research • MS, PhD
project management • MPM
solid mechanics • MS, PhD
structural engineering • MS, PhD
structural mechanics • MS, PhD
transportation systems engineering • MS, PhD

School of Music
Bernard J. Dobroski, Dean
Programs in:
collaborative arts • DM
conducting • MM, DM
jazz pedagogy • MM
keyboard • MM, DM, CP
music • MM, DM, PhD, CP
music composition • MM, DM
music education • MM, PhD
music technology • MM, PhD
music theory • MM, PhD
musicology • MM, PhD
opera production • MM
performance • MM
piano performance and pedagogy • MM
string performance and pedagogy • MM
strings • MM, DM
strings, winds and percussion • CP
voice • MM, DM, CP
winds and percussion • MM, DM

■ OLIVET NAZARENE UNIVERSITY

Bourbonnais, IL 60914-2271
http://www.olivet.edu/

Independent-religious, coed, comprehensive institution. *Computer facilities:* 100 computers available on campus for general student use. Internet access and online class registration are available. *Library facilities:* Benner Library. *General application contact:* Dean of the Graduate School, 815-939-5291.

Graduate School
Programs in:
business administration • MBA
practical ministries • MPM

Division of Education
Programs in:
curriculum and instruction • MAE
elementary education • MAT
secondary education • MAT

Division of Religion and Philosophy
Programs in:
biblical literature • MA
religion • MA
theology • MA

Institute for Church Management
Programs in:
church management • MCM
pastoral counseling • MPC

■ QUINCY UNIVERSITY

Quincy, IL 62301-2699
http://www.quincy.edu/

Independent-religious, coed, comprehensive institution. *Enrollment:* 87 full-time matriculated graduate/professional students (26 women), 60 part-time matriculated graduate/professional students (37 women). *Graduate faculty:* 8 full-time (3 women), 5 part-time/adjunct (3 women). *Computer facilities:* 200 computers available on campus for general student use. A campuswide network can be accessed from student residence rooms and from off campus. Internet access and online class registration are available. *Library facilities:* Brenner Library. *Graduate expenses:* Tuition: part-time $420 per credit hour. *General application contact:* Kevin Brown, Director of Admissions, 217-228-5210.

Division of Business
Dr. Richard Magliari, Director, MBA Program
Program in:
business • MBA

Division of Education
Dr. Alice Mills, Chair
Program in:
education • MS Ed

■ ROCKFORD COLLEGE

Rockford, IL 61108-2393
http://www.rockford.edu/

Independent, coed, comprehensive institution. *Computer facilities:* 65 computers available on campus for general student use. A campuswide network can be accessed from student residence rooms. Internet access is available. *Library facilities:* Howard Colman Library. *General application contact:* Dean, Continuing and Graduate Education, 815-226-4013.

Graduate Studies
Programs in:
art education • MAT
business administration • MBA
elementary education • MAT
English • MAT
history • MAT
learning disabilities • MAT
political science • MAT
reading • MAT
secondary education • MAT
social sciences • MAT

■ ROOSEVELT UNIVERSITY

Chicago, IL 60605-1394
http://www.roosevelt.edu/

Independent, coed, comprehensive institution. *Computer facilities:* 380 computers available on campus for general student use. A campuswide network can be accessed from off campus. Internet access and online class registration are available. *Library facilities:* Murray-Green Library plus 4 others. *General application contact:* Coordinator of Graduate Admissions, 312-341-3612.

Find an in-depth description at www.petersons.com/graduate.

Graduate Division

College of Arts and Sciences
Programs in:
applied economics • MA
arts and sciences • MA, MFA, MPA, MS, MSC, MSIMC, MSJ, MST, Psy D
chemistry • MS
clinical professional psychology • MA
clinical psychology • MA, Psy D
communication • MSIMC, MSJ
computer science • MSC
computer science and telecommunications • MSC, MST
creative writing • MFA
economics • MA
English • MA
general psychology • MA
history • MA
industrial/organizational psychology • MA
integrated marketing communications • MSIMC
journalism • MSJ
liberal studies • MA, MFA
mathematical sciences • MS
policy studies • MA, MPA
political science • MA
public administration • MPA
science and mathematics • MS
sociology • MA
sociology-gerontology • MA
Spanish • MA
telecommunications • MST
women's studies • MA

Roosevelt University (continued)

College of Education
Programs in:
early childhood education • MA
educational administration and supervision • MA, Ed D
elementary education • MA
guidance and counseling • MA
reading education • MA
secondary education • MA

College of the Performing Arts
Programs in:
directing and dramaturgy • MFA
music • MM
music education • MM Ed
musical theatre • MFA
performing arts • MA, MFA, MM, MM Ed, Diploma
piano pedagogy • Diploma
theatre • MA, MFA
theatre-directing • MA
theatre-performance • MFA

Evelyn T. Stone University College
Programs in:
general studies • MGS
hospitality management • MS
training and development • MA

Walter E. Heller College of Business Administration
Programs in:
accounting • MSA
business administration • MBA, MSA, MSIB, MSIS
information systems • MSIS
international business • MSIB

■ SAINT XAVIER UNIVERSITY

Chicago, IL 60655-3105

http://www.sxu.edu/

Independent-religious, coed, comprehensive institution. *Enrollment:* 454 full-time matriculated graduate/professional students (369 women), 1,364 part-time matriculated graduate/professional students (1,103 women). *Graduate faculty:* 98. *Computer facilities:* 261 computers available on campus for general student use. A campuswide network can be accessed from student residence rooms and from off campus. Internet access is available. *Library facilities:* Byrne Memorial Library. *Graduate expenses:* Tuition: full-time $8,550; part-time $475 per credit. Required fees: $40 per term. Tuition and fees vary according to course load and program. *General application contact:* Beth Gierach, Vice President of Enrollment Services, 773-298-3050.

Graduate Studies
Vice President of Academic Affairs

Graham School of Management
Dr. John Eber, Dean
Programs in:
employee health benefits • Certificate
finance • MBA, MS
financial planning • MBA, Certificate
financial trading and practice • MBA, Certificate
generalist/administration • MBA
health administration • MBA, MS
managed care • Certificate
management • MBA, MS
marketing • MBA
public health • MPH
taxation • MBA

School of Arts and Sciences
Dr. Lawrence Frank, Dean
Programs in:
adult counseling • Certificate
applied computer science in Internet information systems • MS
arts and sciences • MA, MS, CAS, Certificate
child/adolescent counseling • Certificate
core counseling • Certificate
counseling psychology • MA
English • CAS
literary studies • MA
speech-language pathology • MS
teaching of writing • MA
writing pedagogy • CAS

School of Education
Dr. Beverly Gulley, Dean
Programs in:
curriculum and instruction • MA
early childhood education • MA
education • CAS
educational administration • MA
elementary education • MA
field-based education • MA
general educational studies • MA
individualized program • MA
learning disabilities • MA
reading • MA
secondary education • MA

School of Nursing
Beth Gierach, Managing Director of Admission
Programs in:
adult health clinical nurse specialist • MS
family nurse practitioner • MS, PMC
leadership in community health nursing • MS
psychiatric-mental health clinical nurse specialist • MS
psychiatric-mental health clinical specialist • PMC

■ SOUTHERN ILLINOIS UNIVERSITY CARBONDALE

Carbondale, IL 62901-6806

http://www.siu.edu/siuc/

State-supported, coed, university. CGS member. *Enrollment:* 2,357 full-time matriculated graduate/professional students (942 women), 2,198 part-time matriculated graduate/professional students (1,202 women). *Graduate faculty:* 1,074 full-time (262 women), 112 part-time/adjunct. *Computer facilities:* 1,426 computers available on campus for general student use. A campuswide network can be accessed from student residence rooms and from off campus. Internet access and online class registration are available. *Library facilities:* Morris Library plus 1 other. *Graduate expenses:* Tuition, state resident: full-time $3,964. Tuition, nonresident: full-time $6,837. Required fees: $1,090. *General application contact:* Associate Dean of the Graduate School, 618-536-7791.

Find an in-depth description at www.petersons.com/graduate.

Graduate School
Acting Dean

College of Agriculture
David Shoup, Dean
Programs in:
agribusiness economics • MS
agriculture • MS
animal science • MS
food and nutrition • MS
forestry • MS
horticultural science • MS
plant and soil science • MS

College of Business and Administration
Dan Worrell, Dean
Programs in:
accountancy • M Acc, PhD
business administration • MBA, PhD

College of Education
Dr. Keith Hillkirk, Dean
Programs in:
behavioral analysis and therapy • MS
communication disorders and sciences • MS
counselor education • MS Ed, PhD
curriculum and instruction • MS Ed, PhD
education • MS, MS Ed, MSW, PhD, Rh D
educational administration • MS Ed, PhD
educational psychology • MS Ed, PhD

health education • MS Ed, PhD
higher education • MS Ed
human learning and development • MS Ed
measurement and statistics • PhD
physical education • MS Ed
recreation • MS Ed
rehabilitation • Rh D
rehabilitation administration and services • MS
rehabilitation counseling • MS
social work • MSW
special education • MS Ed
workforce education and development • MS Ed, PhD

College of Engineering
Dr. George Swisher, Dean
Programs in:
civil engineering and mechanics • MS
electrical engineering • MS
electrical systems • PhD
engineering • MS, PhD
fossil energy • PhD
manufacturing systems • MS
mechanical engineering and energy processes • MS
mechanics • PhD
mining engineering • MS

College of Liberal Arts
Dr. Shirley Scott Clay, Dean
Programs in:
administration of justice • MA
anthropology • MA, PhD
applied linguistics • MA
ceramics • MFA
clinical psychology • MA, MS, PhD
composition • MA, PhD
composition and theory • MM
counseling psychology • MA, MS, PhD
creative writing • MFA
drawing • MFA
economics • MA, MS, PhD
experimental psychology • MA, MS, PhD
fiber/weaving • MFA
foreign languages and literatures • MA
geography • MS, PhD
glass • MFA
history • MA, PhD
history and literature • MM
jewelry • MFA
liberal arts • MA, MFA, MM, MPA, MS, PhD
literature • MA, PhD
metals/blacksmithing • MFA
music education • MM
opera/music theater • MM
painting • MFA
performance • MM
philosophy • MA, PhD
piano pedagogy • MM
political science • MA, PhD
printmaking • MFA
public administration • MPA
rhetoric • MA, PhD
sculpture • MFA
sociology • MA, PhD
speech communication • MA, MS, PhD
speech/theater • PhD
teaching English as a second language • MA
theater • MFA

College of Mass Communication and Media Arts
Dr. Gerald C. Stone, Director of Graduate Studies
Program in:
mass communication and media arts • MA, MFA, PhD

College of Science
Jack Parker, Dean
Programs in:
biological sciences • MS
chemistry and biochemistry • MS, PhD
computer science • MS
geology • MS, PhD
mathematics • MA, MS, PhD
molecular biology, microbiology, and biochemistry • MS, PhD
physics • MS
plant biology • MS, PhD
science • MA, MS, PhD
statistics • MS
zoology • MS, PhD

School of Law
Thomas F. Guernsey, Dean
Program in:
law • JD

School of Medicine
Dr. Carl J. Getto, Dean and Provost
Programs in:
medicine • MD, MS, PhD
pharmacology • MS, PhD
physiology • MS, PhD

■ SOUTHERN ILLINOIS UNIVERSITY EDWARDSVILLE

Edwardsville, IL 62026-0001
http://www.siue.edu/

State-supported, coed, comprehensive institution. CGS member. *Enrollment:* 877 full-time matriculated graduate/professional students (383 women), 1,418 part-time matriculated graduate/professional students (897 women). *Graduate faculty:* 512 full-time (192 women), 200 part-time/adjunct (127 women). *Computer facilities:* 550 computers available on campus for general student use. A campuswide network can be accessed from student residence rooms and from off campus. Internet access is available. *Library facilities:* Lovejoy Library. *Graduate expenses:* Part-time $113 per credit hour. Tuition, state resident: full-time $1,017; part-time $226 per credit hour. Tuition, nonresident: full-time $2,034. Required fees: $287. One-time fee: $126 part-time. *General application contact:* Dr. Stephen L. Hansen, Dean of Graduate Studies and Research, 618-650-3010.

Find an in-depth description at www.petersons.com/graduate.

Graduate Studies and Research
Dr. Stephen L. Hansen, Dean of Graduate Studies and Research

College of Arts and Sciences
Dixie Engelman, Interim Dean
Programs in:
American and English literature • MA
art therapy counseling • MA
arts and sciences • MA, MFA, MM, MPA, MS, MSW
biological sciences • MA, MS
ceramics • MFA
chemistry • MS
drawing • MFA
environmental sciences • MS
fiber/fabrics • MFA
geography • MA, MS
history • MA
mass communication • MS
mathematics and statistics • MS
music education • MM
music performance • MM
painting • MFA
physics • MS
printmaking • MFA
public administration • MPA
sculpture • MFA
social work • MSW
sociology • MA
speech communication • MA
teaching English as a second language • MA
teaching of writing • MA

School of Business
Dr. M. Robert Carver, Dean
Programs in:
accountancy • MSA
business • MA, MBA, MMR, MS, MSA
business administration • MBA
e-business • MBA
economics and finance • MA, MS
management information systems • MBA
marketing research • MBA, MMR

School of Education
Dr. Mary Polite, Dean
Programs in:

Southern Illinois University Edwardsville (continued)

clinical adult • MS
community school • MS
education • MA, MS, MS Ed, Certificate, Ed S
educational administration and supervision • MS Ed, Ed S
elementary education • MS Ed
exercise physiology • Certificate
general academic • MA
industrial organizational • MS
instructional technology • MS Ed
kinesiology and health education • MS Ed
pedigogy/administration • Certificate
school psychology • Ed S
secondary education • MS Ed
special education and communication disorders • MS Ed
speech pathology • MS
sports and exercise behavior • Certificate

School of Engineering
Dr. Paul Seaburg, Dean
Programs in:
civil engineering • MS
computer information systems • MS
electrical engineering • MS
engineering • MS
mechanical engineering • MS

School of Nursing
Dr. Felissa Lashley, Dean
Programs in:
community health nursing • MS
medical-surgical nursing • MS
nurse anesthesia • MS
nurse practitioner nursing • MS
psychiatric nursing • MS

School of Dental Medicine
Dr. Patrick Ferrillo, Dean
Program in:
dental medicine • DMD

■ UNIVERSITY OF CHICAGO

Chicago, IL 60637-1513
http://www.uchicago.edu/

Independent, coed, university. CGS member. *Enrollment:* 6,559 full-time matriculated graduate/professional students (2,842 women), 1,900 part-time matriculated graduate/professional students (477 women). *Graduate faculty:* 2,111 full-time (582 women), 728 part-time/adjunct (219 women). *Computer facilities:* 1,000 computers available on campus for general student use. A campuswide network can be accessed from student residence rooms and from off campus. *Library facilities:* Joseph Regenstein Library plus 8 others. *Graduate expenses:* Tuition: full-time $26,046. Required fees: $1,239. *General application contact:* Kathy Skipper, Manager, Office of Graduate Affairs, 773-702-7813.

Divinity School
Dr. Richard A. Rosengarten, Dean
Program in:
theology • M Div, AM, AMRS, PhD

Division of Social Sciences
Dr. Richard Saller, Dean
Programs in:
anthropology • PhD
economics • PhD
history • PhD
human development • PhD
international relations • AM
Latin American and Caribbean studies • AM
Middle Eastern studies • AM
political science • PhD
psychology • PhD
social sciences • AM, PhD
social thought • PhD
sociology • PhD

Division of the Biological Sciences
Dr. Bryce Weir, Acting Dean
Programs in:
biochemistry and molecular biology • PhD
biological sciences • MS, PhD
cancer biology • PhD
cell physiology • PhD
cellular and molecular physiology • PhD
cellular differentiation • PhD
developmental biology • PhD
developmental endocrinology • PhD
developmental genetics • PhD
developmental neurobiology • PhD
ecology and evolution • PhD
evolutionary biology • PhD
functional and evolutionary biology • PhD
gene expression • PhD
genetics • PhD
health studies • MS
human genetics • PhD
human nutrition and nutritional biology • PhD
immunology • PhD
medical physics • PhD
molecular genetics and cell biology • PhD
neurobiology • PhD
neurobiology, pharmacology and physiology • PhD
ophthalmology and visual science • PhD
organismal biology and anatomy • PhD
pathology • PhD
pharmacological and physiological sciences • PhD
virology • PhD

Division of the Humanities
Thomas B. Thuerer, Dean of Students
Programs in:
ancient Mediterranean world • AM, PhD
ancient philosophy • AM, PhD
anthropology and linguistics • PhD
art history • AM, PhD
cinema and media studies • AM, PhD
classical archaeology • AM, PhD
classical languages and literatures • AM, PhD
comparative literature • AM, PhD
conceptual and historical studies of science • AM, PhD
East Asian languages and civilizations • AM, PhD
English language and literature • AM, PhD
French • AM, PhD
general studies in the humanities • AM
Germanic languages and literatures • AM, PhD
history of culture • AM, PhD
humanities • AM, MFA, PhD
Italian • AM, PhD
Jewish history and culture • AM, PhD
Jewish studies • AM
linguistics • AM, PhD
music • AM, PhD
Near Eastern languages and civilizations • AM, PhD
New Testament and early Christian culture • AM, PhD
philosophy • AM, PhD
Slavic languages and literatures • AM, PhD
South Asian languages and civilizations • AM, PhD
Spanish • AM, PhD
visual arts • MFA

Division of the Physical Sciences
David Oxtoby, Dean
Programs in:
applied mathematics • SM, PhD
astronomy and astrophysics • SM, PhD
atmospheric sciences • SM, PhD
chemistry • SM, PhD
computer science • SM, PhD
earth sciences • SM, PhD
financial mathematics • MS
mathematics • SM, PhD
paleobiology • PhD
physical sciences • MS, SM, PhD
physics • SM, PhD
planetary and space sciences • SM, PhD
statistics • SM, PhD

Graduate Program in Health Administration and Policy
Program in:
health administration and policy • AM, MBA, MPP, Certificate

Graduate School of Business
Robert S. Hamada, Dean
Programs in:
accounting • MBA
business administration • EMBA, MBA, PhD
international business administration • IEMBA, IMBA

The Irving B. Harris Graduate School of Public Policy Studies
Programs in:
environmental science and policy • MS
public policy studies • AM, MPP, PhD

The Law School
Saul Levmore, Dean
Program in:
law • JD, LL M, MCL, DCL, JSD

Pritzker School of Medicine
Program in:
medicine • MD

School of Social Service Administration
Peggy Berndt, Dean
Programs in:
social service administration • PhD
social work • AM

■ UNIVERSITY OF ILLINOIS AT CHICAGO

Chicago, IL 60607-7128

http://www.uic.edu/

State-supported, coed, university. CGS member. *Enrollment:* 2,974 full-time matriculated graduate/professional students (1,561 women), 2,336 part-time matriculated graduate/professional students (1,463 women). *Graduate faculty:* 1,319 full-time (326 women), 94 part-time/adjunct (15 women). *Computer facilities:* 600 computers available on campus for general student use. A campuswide network can be accessed from student residence rooms and from off campus. *Library facilities:* University Library plus 8 others. *Graduate expenses:* Tuition, state resident: full-time $3,864; part-time $644 per hour. Tuition, nonresident: full-time $10,908; part-time $1,818 per hour. Required fees: $1,568; $784 per term. Tuition and fees vary according to program. *General application contact:* Graduate College Receptionist, 312-413-2550.

College of Dentistry
Dale W. Eisenmann, Acting Dean
Programs in:
dentistry • DDS, MS
oral sciences • MS

College of Medicine
Gerald S. Moss, Dean
Programs in:
anatomy and cell biology • MS, PhD
biochemistry and molecular biology • MS, PhD
genetics • PhD
health professions education • MHPE
medicine • MD, MHPE, MS, PhD
microbiology and immunology • PhD
molecular genetics • PhD
pathology • MS, PhD
pharmacology • PhD
physiology and biophysics • MS, PhD
surgery • MS

College of Pharmacy
Rosalie Sagraves, Dean
Programs in:
forensic science • MS
medicinal chemistry • MS, PhD
pharmaceutics • MS, PhD
pharmacodynamics • MS, PhD
pharmacognosy • MS, PhD
pharmacy • Pharm D, MS, PhD
pharmacy administration • MS, PhD

Graduate College
Dr. Clark Hulse, Acting Dean
Program in:
neuroscience • PhD

College of Architecture and Art
Dr. Judith Kirshner, Dean
Programs in:
architecture • M Arch
architecture and art • M Arch, MA, MFA, PhD
art history • MA, PhD
art therapy • MA
electronic visualization • MFA
film animation • MFA
graphic design • MFA
industrial design • MFA
photography • MFA
studio arts • MFA
theatre • MA

College of Associated Health Professions
Dean
Programs in:
associated health professions • MAMS, MS, PhD
biomedical visualization • MAMS
disability and human development • MS
disability studies • PhD
human nutrition and dietetics • MS, PhD
kinesiology • MS
medical laboratory sciences • MS
occupational therapy • MS
physical therapy • MS

College of Business Administration
Wim Wiewiel, Acting Dean
Programs in:
accounting • MS
business administration • MBA
business economics • PhD
economics • MA, PhD
finance • PhD
human resource management • PhD
human resources management • PhD
management information systems • MS, PhD
marketing • PhD
public policy analysis • PhD

College of Education
Connie Bridge, Dean
Programs in:
curriculum and instruction • PhD
education • M Ed, PhD
educational policy and administration • PhD
instructional leadership • M Ed
leadership and administration • M Ed
special education • M Ed, PhD

College of Engineering
Lawrence A. Kennedy, Dean
Programs in:
bioengineering • MS, PhD
chemical engineering • MS, PhD
civil and materials engineering • MS, PhD
computer science and engineering • MS, PhD
electrical engineering • MS, PhD
engineering • MS, PhD
industrial engineering • MS
industrial engineering and operations research • PhD
mechanical engineering • MS, PhD

College of Liberal Arts and Sciences
Stanley Fish, Dean
Programs in:
anthropology • MA, PhD
applied linguistics • teaching English as a second language • MA
applied mathematics • MS, DA, PhD
cell and developmental biology • PhD
chemistry • MS, PhD
communication • MA
computer science • MS, DA, PhD
criminal justice • MA
crystallography • MS, PhD
ecology and evolution • MS, DA, PhD
English • MA, PhD

University of Illinois at Chicago (continued)

environmental and urban geography • MA
environmental geology • MS, PhD
environmental studies • MA
French • MA
genetics and development • PhD
geochemistry • MS, PhD
geology • MS, PhD
geomorphology • MS, PhD
geophysics • MS, PhD
geotechnical engineering and geosciences • PhD
German • MA, PhD
Hispanic studies • MA, PhD
history • MA, MAT, PhD
hydrogeology • MS, PhD
language, literacy, and rhetoric • PhD
liberal arts and sciences • MA, MAT, MPA, MS, MST, DA, PhD
linguistics • MA
low-temperature and organic geochemistry • MS, PhD
mass communication • MA
mineralogy • MS, PhD
molecular biology • MS, PhD
neurobiology • MS, PhD
paleoclimatology • MS, PhD
paleontology • MS, PhD
petrology • MS, PhD
philosophy • MA, PhD
physics • MS, PhD
plant biology • MS, DA, PhD
political science • MA
probability and statistics • MS, DA, PhD
psychology • PhD
public policy analysis • PhD
pure mathematics • MS, DA, PhD
quaternary geology • MS, PhD
sedimentology • MS, PhD
Slavic languages and literatures • PhD
Slavic studies • MA
sociology • MA, PhD
teaching of mathematics • MST
urban geography • MA
water resources • MS, PhD

College of Nursing
Dr. Joyce Johnson, Dean
Programs in:
maternity nursing/nurse midwifery • MS
medical-surgical nursing • MS
mental health nursing • MS
nursing • MS, PhD
nursing administration • MS
nursing research • PhD
pediatric nursing • MS
perinatal nursing • MS
public health nursing • MS

College of Urban Planning and Public Affairs
Wim Wiewiel, Acting Dean
Programs in:
public administration • MPA, PhD
public policy analysis • PhD
urban planning and policy • MUPP
urban planning and public affairs • MPA, MUPP, PhD

Jane Addams College of Social Work
C. F. Hairston, Dean
Program in:
social work • MSW, PhD

School of Public Health
Dr. Susan Scrimshaw, Dean
Programs in:
biostatistics • MS, PhD
community health sciences • MPH, MS, Dr PH, PhD
environmental and occupational health sciences • MPH, MS, Dr PH, PhD
epidemiology and biostatistics • MPH, MS, Dr PH, PhD
health resources management • MPH, MS, Dr PH, PhD

■ UNIVERSITY OF ILLINOIS AT SPRINGFIELD

Springfield, IL 62794-9243
http://www.uis.edu/

State-supported, coed, upper-level institution. CGS member. *Enrollment:* 317 full-time matriculated graduate/professional students (185 women), 1,507 part-time matriculated graduate/professional students (855 women). *Graduate faculty:* 164 full-time (62 women), 79 part-time/adjunct (33 women). *Computer facilities:* 160 computers available on campus for general student use. A campuswide network can be accessed from student residence rooms and from off campus. Internet access is available. *Library facilities:* Brookens Library. *Graduate expenses:* Tuition, state resident: part-time $108 per semester hour. Tuition, nonresident: part-time $323 per semester hour. Required fees: $3.5 per semester hour. $47 per semester. *General application contact:* 217-206-6626.

Find an in-depth description at www.petersons.com/graduate.

Graduate Programs
Dr. Wayne Penn, Provost/Vice Chancellor for Academic Affairs

College of Business and Management
Dr. Paul McDevitt, Dean
Programs in:
accountancy • MA
business administration • MBA
business and management • MA, MBA
economics • MA
management information systems • MA

College of Education and Human Services
Dr. Larry Stonecipher, Dean
Programs in:
alcoholism and substance abuse • MA
child and family studies • MA
education and human services • MA, MPH
educational leadership • MA
gerontology • MA
human development counseling • MA
social services administration • MA

College of Liberal Arts and Sciences
William Bloemer, Dean
Programs in:
arts and sciences • MA
biology • MA
clinical psychology • MA
communication • MA
computer science • MA
English • MA
general psychology • MA
individual option • MA
public history • MA

College of Public Affairs and Administration
Glen Cope, Dean
Programs in:
community arts management • MA
environmental studies • MA
legal studies • MA
political studies • MA
public administration • MPA, DPA
public affairs and administration • MA, MPA, MPH, DPA
public affairs reporting • MA
public health • MPH

■ UNIVERSITY OF ILLINOIS AT URBANA–CHAMPAIGN

Champaign, IL 61820
http://www.uiuc.edu/

State-supported, coed, university. CGS member. *Enrollment:* 8,109 full-time matriculated graduate/professional students (3,593 women). *Graduate faculty:* 1,727 full-time, 131 part-time/adjunct. *Computer facilities:* 3,000 computers available on campus for general student use. A campuswide network can be accessed from student residence rooms and from off campus. Internet access and online class registration are available. *Library facilities:* University Library plus 40 others. *Graduate expenses:* Tuition, state resident: full-time $5,636. Tuition, nonresident: full-time $13,146. *General application contact:* Richard Wheeler, Dean, 217-333-0035.

College of Law
Thomas M. Mengler, Dean
Program in:
law • JD, LL M, MCL, JSD

College of Veterinary Medicine
Victor E. Valli, Dean
Programs in:
veterinary biosciences • MS, PhD
veterinary clinical medicine • MS, PhD
veterinary medicine • DVM, MS, PhD
veterinary pathobiology • MS, PhD

Graduate College
Richard Wheeler, Dean
Programs in:
atmospheric science • MS, PhD
biophysics and computational biology • PhD

College of Agricultural, Consumer and Environmental Sciences
David L. Chicoine, Dean
Programs in:
agricultural and consumer economics • MS, PhD
agricultural, consumer and environmental sciences • AM, MS, PhD
animal sciences • MS, PhD
crop sciences • MS, PhD
extension education • MS
food science and human nutrition • MS, PhD
human and community development • AM, MS, PhD
natural resources and environmental science • MS, PhD
nutritional sciences • MS, PhD

College of Applied Life Studies
Tanya Gallagher, Director of Graduate Studies
Programs in:
applied life studies • AM, MS, MSPH, MST, PhD
community health • MSPH, PhD
kinesiology • MS, MST, PhD
leisure studies • MS, PhD
rehabilitation • MS
rehabilitation education services • MS
speech and hearing science • AM, MS, PhD

College of Commerce and Business Administration
William Bryan, Interim Dean
Programs in:
accountancy • MAS, MS, MSA, PhD
business administration • MBA, MSBA, PhD
commerce and business administration • MAS, MBA, MS, MSA, MSBA, PhD
economics • MS, PhD
finance • MS, PhD

College of Communications
Kim B. Rotzoll, Dean
Programs in:
advertising • MS
communications • PhD
journalism • MS

College of Education
Susan A. Fowler, Dean
Programs in:
curriculum and instruction • AM, Ed M, MS, Ed D, PhD, AC
education • AM, Ed M, MS, Ed D, PhD, AC
education, organization and leadership • AM, Ed M, MS, Ed D, PhD, AC
educational policy studies • AM, Ed M, MS, Ed D, PhD, AC
educational psychology • AM, Ed M, MS, Ed D, PhD, AC
human resource education • AM, Ed M, MS, Ed D, PhD, AC
special education • AM, Ed M, MS, Ed D, PhD, AC

College of Engineering
Dr. William R. Schowalter, Dean
Programs in:
aeronautical and astronautical engineering • MS, PhD
agricultural engineering • MS, PhD
civil engineering • MS, PhD
computer engineering • MS, PhD
computer science • MCS, MS, MST, PhD
electrical engineering • MS, PhD
engineering • MCS, MS, MST, PhD
environmental engineering • MS, PhD
environmental engineering and environmental science • MS, PhD
environmental science • MS, PhD
health physics • MS, PhD
industrial engineering • MS, PhD
materials science and engineering • MS, PhD
mechanical engineering • MS, PhD
nuclear engineering • MS, PhD
physics • MS, PhD
systems engineering and engineering design • MS
theoretical and applied mechanics • MS, PhD

College of Fine and Applied Arts
Kathleen F. Conlin, Dean
Programs in:
architecture • M Arch
art and design • AM, MFA, Ed D, PhD
art education • AM, Ed D
art history • AM, PhD
dance • AM
fine and applied arts • AM, M Arch, M Mus, MFA, MLA, MS, MUP, DMA, Ed D, PhD
graphic design • MFA
industrial design • MFA
landscape architecture • MLA
music • M Mus, MS, DMA, Ed D, PhD
regional planning • PhD
theatre • AM, MFA, PhD
urban and regional planning • MUP

College of Liberal Arts and Sciences
Jesse Delia, Dean
Programs in:
African studies • AM
anthropology • AM, PhD
applied mathematics • MS
applied measurement • MS
astronomy • MS, PhD
biochemistry • MS, PhD
biological psychology • AM, PhD
cell and structural biology • PhD
chemical engineering • MS, PhD
chemical sciences • MS, PhD
chemistry • MS, PhD
classics • AM, PhD
clinical psychology • AM, PhD
cognitive psychology • AM, PhD
comparative literature • AM, MAT, PhD
demography • AM, PhD
developmental psychology • AM, PhD
earth sciences • MS, PhD
East Asian languages and cultures • AM, PhD
ecology, ethnology, and evolution • PhD
engineering psychology • MS
English • AM, PhD
English as an international language • AM
entomology • MS, PhD
French • AM, MAT, PhD
geochemistry • MS, PhD
geography • AM, MS, PhD
geology • MS, PhD
geophysics • MS, PhD
Germanic languages and literatures • AM, MAT, PhD
history • AM, PhD
insect pest management • MS
Italian • AM, PhD
Latin American and Caribbean studies • AM
liberal arts and sciences • AM, MAT, MS, PhD

University of Illinois at Urbana–Champaign (continued)
- life sciences • MS, PhD
- linguistics • AM, PhD
- mathematics • MS, PhD
- microbiology • MS, PhD
- molecular and integrative physiology • MS, PhD
- neuroscience • PhD
- perception and performance psychology • AM, PhD
- personality-social-organizational • AM, PhD
- personnel psychology • MS
- philosophy • AM, PhD
- plant biology • MS, PhD
- political science • AM, PhD
- quantitative psychology • AM, PhD
- Russian • AM, MAT, PhD
- Russian and East European studies • AM
- Slavic languages and literatures • AM, MAT, PhD
- sociology • AM, PhD
- Spanish • MAT
- speech communication • AM, MAT, PhD
- statistics • MS, PhD
- teaching of mathematics • MS

Graduate School of Library and Information Science
Dr. Leigh S. Estabrook, Dean
Program in:
- library and information science • MS, PhD, CAS

Institute of Labor and Industrial Relations
Dr. Peter Feuille, Director
Programs in:
- human resources • MHRIR, PhD
- labor and industrial relations • MHRIR, PhD

School of Social Work
Jill Doner Kagle, Dean
Program in:
- social work • MSW, PhD

■ UNIVERSITY OF ST. FRANCIS

Joliet, IL 60435-6169

http://www.stfrancis.edu/

Independent-religious, coed, comprehensive institution. *Enrollment:* 54 full-time matriculated graduate/professional students (36 women), 1,176 part-time matriculated graduate/professional students (946 women). *Graduate faculty:* 6 full-time (2 women), 62 part-time/adjunct (24 women). *Computer facilities:* 147 computers available on campus for general student use. A campuswide network can be accessed from student residence rooms. Internet access and online class registration are available. *Library facilities:* University of St. Francis Library. *Graduate expenses:* Tuition: part-time $325 per credit hour. Tuition and fees vary according to program. *General application contact:* Dr. R. Joy Thompson, Dean, College of Graduate Studies, 800-735-4723.

College of Graduate Studies
Dr. Lyle Hicks, Dean
Programs in:
- business administration • MBA, MSM
- continuing education training management • MS
- curriculum in instruction in middle schools • MS
- education • M Ed
- health services administration • MS
- long-term care administration • Certificate

■ WESTERN ILLINOIS UNIVERSITY

Macomb, IL 61455-1390

http://www.wiu.edu/

State-supported, coed, comprehensive institution. CGS member. *Enrollment:* 684 full-time matriculated graduate/professional students (369 women), 1,046 part-time matriculated graduate/professional students (749 women). *Graduate faculty:* 392 full-time (118 women), 16 part-time/adjunct (3 women). *Computer facilities:* 700 computers available on campus for general student use. A campuswide network can be accessed from off campus. Course registration available. *Library facilities:* Western Illinois University Library plus 4 others. *Graduate expenses:* Tuition, state resident: full-time $2,376; part-time $99 per semester hour. Tuition, nonresident: full-time $4,752; part-time $198 per semester hour. Required fees: $29 per semester hour. *General application contact:* Barbara Baily, Director of Graduate Studies, 309-298-1806.

School of Graduate Studies
Barbara Baily, Director of Graduate Studies

College of Arts and Sciences
Dr. Phyllis Rippey, Dean
Programs in:
- arts and sciences • MA, MS, Certificate, SSP
- biological sciences • MS
- chemistry • MS
- clinical/community mental health • MS
- community development • Certificate
- general psychology • MS
- geography • MA
- gerontology • MA
- history • MA
- literature and language • MA
- mathematics • MS
- physics • MS
- political science • MA
- psychology • MS, SSP
- school psychology • SSP
- sociology • MA
- writing • MA
- zoo and aquarium studies • Certificate

College of Business and Technology
Dr. David Beveridge, Dean
Programs in:
- accountancy • M Acct
- business administration • MBA
- business and technology • M Acct, MA, MBA, MS
- computer science • MS
- economics • MA
- engineering technology • MS

College of Education and Human Services
Dr. David Taylor, Dean
Programs in:
- college student personnel • MS
- counseling • MS Ed
- counselor education • MS Ed, Certificate
- distance learning • Certificate
- early childhood education • Certificate
- education administration and supervision • MS Ed, Ed S
- education and human services • MA, MAT, MS, MS Ed, Certificate, Ed S
- educational and interdisciplinary studies • MS Ed
- elementary education • MS Ed, Certificate
- graphics application • Certificate
- health education • MS
- instructional technology and telecommunications • MS
- language literacy • Certificate
- law enforcement and justice administration • MA
- marriage and family counseling • Certificate
- mathematics • Certificate
- multimedia • Certificate
- physical education • MS
- Police Executive Certification • Certificate
- reading • MS Ed, Certificate
- recreation, park, and tourism administration • MS
- science • Certificate

secondary education • MAT
social studies • Certificate
special education • MS Ed
sport management • MS
technology integration in education • Certificate
training development • Certificate

College of Fine Arts and Communication
Dr. James M. Butterworth, Dean
Programs in:
communication • MA
communication sciences and disorders • MS
fine arts and communication • MA, MFA, MS
music • MA
theatre • MFA

Indiana

■ ANDERSON UNIVERSITY

Anderson, IN 46012-3495
http://www.anderson.edu/

Independent-religious, coed, comprehensive institution. *Computer facilities:* 200 computers available on campus for general student use. A campuswide network can be accessed from student residence rooms and from off campus. Microcomputer software available. *Library facilities:* Robert A. Nicholson Library. *General application contact:* Director of Advancement and Recruitment, 765-641-3005.

School of Education

School of Theology
Program in:
theology • M Div, MA, MRE, D Min

■ BALL STATE UNIVERSITY

Muncie, IN 47306-1099
http://www.bsu.edu/

State-supported, coed, university. CGS member. *Enrollment:* 911 full-time matriculated graduate/professional students (509 women), 1,101 part-time matriculated graduate/professional students (644 women). *Graduate faculty:* 624. *Computer facilities:* 1,500 computers available on campus for general student use. A campuswide network can be accessed from student residence rooms and from off campus. *Library facilities:* Bracken Library plus 3 others. *Graduate expenses:* Tuition, state resident: full-time $3,864; part-time $2,436 per year. Tuition, nonresident: full-time $10,324; part-time $6,126 per year. Required fees: $6 per credit hour. *General application contact:* Dr. Deborah W. Balogh, Dean, 765-285-1300.

Graduate School
Dr. Deborah W. Balogh, Dean

College of Applied Science and Technology
Dr. Donald Smith, Dean
Programs in:
applied gerontology • MA
applied science and technology • MA, MAE, MS, PhD
family and consumer sciences • MA, MAE, MS
human bioenergetics • PhD
industry and technology • MA, MAE
nursing • MS
physical education • MA, MAE, PhD
wellness management • MS

College of Architecture and Planning
Jeffrey Hall, Acting Dean
Programs in:
architecture • M Arch
architecture and planning • M Arch, MLA, MS, MURP
historic preservation • M Arch, MS
landscape architecture • MLA
urban planning • MURP

College of Business
Dr. Neil A. Palomba, Dean
Programs in:
accounting • MS
business • MA, MAE, MBA, MS
business administration • MBA
business education and office administration • MAE

College of Communication, Information, and Media
Dr. Scott Olson, Dean
Programs in:
communication, information, and media • MA, MS
information and communication sciences • MS
journalism • MA
public relations • MA
speech, public address, forensics, and rhetoric • MA

College of Fine Arts
Dr. Robert Kvam, Interim Dean (per 2A)
Programs in:
art • MA
art education • MA, MAE
fine arts • MA, MAE, MM, DA
music education • MA, MM, DA

College of Sciences and Humanities
Dr. Ronald L. Johnstone, Dean
Programs in:
actuarial science • MA
anthropology • MA
applied linguistics • PhD
biology • MA, MAE, MS
biology education • Ed D
chemistry • MA, MS
clinical psychology • MA
computer science • MA, MS
earth sciences • MA
English • MA, PhD
geology • MA, MS
health education • MA, MAE
history • MA
linguistics • MA, PhD
linguistics and teaching English to speakers of other languages • MA
mathematical statistics • MA
mathematics • MA, MAE, MS
mathematics education • MAE
natural resources • MA, MS
physics • MA, MS
physiology • MA, MS
political science • MA
psychological science • MA
public administration • MPA
sciences and humanities • MA, MAE, MPA, MS, Au D, Ed D, PhD
social sciences • MA
sociology • MA
speech pathology and audiology • MA, Au D
teaching English to speakers of other languages • MA

Teachers College
Dr. Roy Weaver, Dean
Programs in:
adult and community education • MA
adult education • MA, Ed D
adult, community, and higher education • Ed D
counseling psychology • MA, PhD
curriculum • MAE, Ed S
curriculum and instruction • MAE, Ed S
early childhood education • MAE, Ed D
education • MA, MAE, Ed D, PhD, Ed S
educational administration • MAE, Ed D
educational psychology • MA, PhD, Ed S
educational studies • MA, MAE, Ed D, Ed S
elementary education • MAE, Ed D, PhD
executive development • MA
junior high/middle school education • MAE
reading education • MAE, Ed D
school psychology • MA, PhD, Ed S
school superintendency • Ed S
secondary education • MA
social psychology • MA
special education • MA, MAE, Ed D, Ed S
student affairs administration in higher education • MA

■ BUTLER UNIVERSITY

Indianapolis, IN 46208-3485
http://www.butler.edu/

Independent, coed, comprehensive institution. *Enrollment:* 379 full-time matriculated graduate/professional students (261 women), 629 part-time matriculated graduate/professional students (305 women). *Graduate faculty:* 68 full-time (17 women), 43 part-time/adjunct (22 women). *Computer facilities:* 250 computers available on campus for general student use. A campuswide network can be accessed from student residence rooms and from off campus. Internet access, e-mail are available. *Library facilities:* Irwin Library System plus 1 other. *Graduate expenses:* Tuition: part-time $240 per hour. Part-time tuition and fees vary according to program and student level. *General application contact:* Lindsay Lamar, Assistant Director Student Services, 317-940-8100.

College of Business Administration

Dr. Richard Fetter, Interim Dean
Program in:
- business administration • MBA

College of Education

Dr. Robert Rider, Dean
Programs in:
- administration • MS, Ed S
- counseling psychology • Ed S
- elementary education • MS
- reading • MS
- school counseling • MS, Ed S
- school psychology • MS, Ed S
- secondary education • MS
- special education • MS

College of Liberal Arts and Sciences

Dr. Steven Kaplan, Dean
Programs in:
- English • MA
- history • MA
- liberal arts and sciences • MA, MS

College of Pharmacy

Dr. Patricia Chase, Dean
Program in:
- pharmaceutical science • Pharm D, MS

Jordan College of Fine Arts

Dr. Michael Sells
Programs in:
- composition • MM
- conducting • MM
- fine arts • MM
- music • MM
- music education • MM
- music history • MM
- organ • MM
- performance • MM

■ INDIANA STATE UNIVERSITY

Terre Haute, IN 47809-1401
http://web.indstate.edu/

State-supported, coed, university. CGS member. *Computer facilities:* A campuswide network can be accessed from student residence rooms and from off campus. Internet access is available. *Library facilities:* Cunningham Memorial Library plus 2 others. *General application contact:* Dean, School of Graduate Studies, 800-444-GRAD.

Find an in-depth description at www.petersons.com/graduate.

School of Graduate Studies

College of Arts and Sciences
Programs in:
- art history • MA
- arts and sciences • MA, MFA, MM, MME, MPA, MS, PhD, Psy D, CAS
- ceramics • MA, MFA, MS
- chemistry • MS
- child and family relations • MS
- clinical laboratory sciences • MS
- clinical psychology • Psy D
- clothing and textiles • MS
- communication studies • MA, MS
- composition • MA
- criminology • MA, MS
- dietetics • MS
- drawing • MA, MFA, MS
- earth sciences • MS
- ecology • MA, MS, PhD
- economic geography • PhD
- economics • MA, MS
- English • MA, MS
- French • MA, MS
- general psychology • MA, MS
- geography • MA
- graphic design • MA, MFA, MS
- history • MA, MS
- home management • MS
- interdisciplinary humanities • MA
- language • CAS
- linguistics/teaching English as a second language • MA, MS
- literature • CAS
- mathematics • MA, MS
- metalry • MA, MFA, MS
- microbiology • MA, MS, PhD
- music • MM
- music education • MA, MME, MS
- music history and literature • MA
- music performance • MS
- music theory • MA
- nutrition and foods • MS
- painting • MA, MFA, MS
- photography • MA, MFA, MS
- physical geography • PhD
- physics • MA, MS
- physiology • MA, MS, PhD
- political science • MA, MS
- printmaking • MA, MFA, MS
- public administration • MPA
- radio, television and film • MA, MS
- religion • MA
- rhetoric • CAS
- science education • MA, MS
- sculpture • MA, MFA, MS
- sociology • MA, MS
- Spanish • MA, MS
- theatre • MA, MS

School of Business
Program in:
- business • MA, MBA, MS, PhD, Ed S

School of Education
Programs in:
- counseling psychology • PhD
- counselor education • PhD
- curriculum and instruction • M Ed, PhD
- director of special education • M Ed
- early childhood education • M Ed, PhD, Ed S
- education • M Ed, MA, MS, PhD, Ed S
- educational administration • PhD, Ed S
- educational media • MA, MS, Ed S
- educational psychology • MA, MS
- elementary education • M Ed, PhD, Ed S
- elementary school administration • M Ed
- gifted/talented education • MA, MS, Ed S
- guidance • PhD, Ed S
- higher education • MA, MS
- industrial arts education • PhD
- marriage and family counseling • MA, MS
- reading education • M Ed, PhD, Ed S
- school counseling • M Ed
- school psychology • M Ed, PhD, Ed S
- secondary education • M Ed, MS, PhD, Ed S
- secondary school administration • M Ed
- special education • MA, MS, PhD
- speech pathology and audiology • MA, MS

School of Health and Human Performance
Programs in:
- athletic training • MA, MS

health and human performance • MA, MS
health program and facility administration • MA, MS
occupational safety management • MA, MS
physical education • MA, MS
recreation and sport management • MA, MS
school health and safety • MA, MS

School of Nursing
Program in:
nursing • MS

School of Technology
Programs in:
curriculum and instruction • PhD
electronics and computer technology • MA, MS
human resource development • MS
industrial technology • MA, MS
technology • MA, MS, PhD
technology education • MA, MS
vocational technical education • MA, MS

■ INDIANA UNIVERSITY BLOOMINGTON

Bloomington, IN 47405
http://www.iub.edu/

State-supported, coed, university. CGS member. *Computer facilities:* 1,500 computers available on campus for general student use. A campuswide network can be accessed from student residence rooms and from off campus. Internet access, various software packages are available. *Library facilities:* Indiana University Library plus 32 others. *General application contact:* 812-855-2666.

Graduate School

College of Arts and Sciences
Programs in:
acting • MFA
Afro-American studies • MA
American studies • PhD
analytical chemistry • PhD
anthropology • MA, PhD
apparel studies • MS
applied linguistics (teaching English as a second language) • MA, Certificate
applied mathematics–numerical analysis • MA, PhD
art education • MAT
arts administration • MA
arts and sciences • MA, MAT, MFA, MS, PhD, Certificate
astronomy • MA, PhD
astrophysics • PhD
biochemistry and molecular biology • MS, PhD
biogeochemistry • MS, PhD
biological chemistry • PhD
biology and behavior • PhD
biology teaching • MAT
Central Eurasian studies • MA, PhD
ceramics • MFA
chemistry • MAT, MS
Chinese language and literature • MA, PhD
classical studies • MA, MAT, PhD
clinical science • PhD
cognitive psychology • PhD
communication and culture • MA, MAT, PhD
comparative literature • MA, MAT, PhD
computer science • MS, PhD
computer science/cognitive science • PhD
computer science/logic • PhD
costume design • MFA
creative writing • MFA
cross-cultural studies of crime and justice • MA, PhD
developmental psychology • PhD
directing • MFA
East Asian studies • MA
East European studies • Certificate
ecology • MA, PhD
economics • MA, MAT, PhD
English • MA, PhD
English education • MAT
environmental geosciences • MS, PhD
evolution, ecology, and behavior • MA, PhD
evolutionary biology • MA, PhD
fine arts • MA, MAT, MFA, PhD
folklore • MA, PhD
French • MA, MAT, PhD
French linguistics • MA, PhD
French literature • MA, PhD
genetics • PhD
geobiology, stratigraphy, and sedimentology • MS, PhD
geochemistry • MS, PhD
geochemistry, mineralogy, and petrology • MS, PhD
geography • MA, MAT, PhD
geophysics • MS, PhD
geophysics, tectonics, and structural geology • MS, PhD
German literature and linguistics • PhD
German studies • MA, PhD
graphic design • MFA
Hispanic linguistics • MA, PhD
Hispanic literature • MA, PhD
history • MA, MAT, PhD
history and philosophy of science • MA, PhD
history of art • MA, PhD
inorganic chemistry • PhD
interior design • MS
Italian • MA, PhD
Japanese language and literature • MA, PhD
jewelry/metalsmithing • MFA
justice systems and processes • MA, PhD
Latin American and Caribbean studies • MA
law and society • MA, PhD
lighting design • MFA
linguistics • PhD
literature • MA, PhD
Luso-Brazilian literature • MA, PhD
mass communication • PhD
mathematics education • MAT
medieval German studies • PhD
microbiology • MA, PhD
molecular, cellular, and developmental biology • PhD
nature of crime • MA, PhD
Near Eastern languages and cultures • MA, PhD
neural sciences • PhD
painting • MFA
philosophy • MA, PhD
photography • MFA
physical chemistry • PhD
physics • MAT, MS, PhD
plant sciences, molecular and organismal biology • MA, PhD
playwriting • MFA
political science • MA, PhD
printmaking • MFA
probability-statistics • MA, PhD
religious studies • MA, PhD
Russian and East European studies • MA
Russian area studies • Certificate
scenic design • MFA
sculpture • MFA
Slavic languages and literatures • MA, MAT, PhD
social psychology • PhD
sociology • MA, PhD
speech and hearing sciences • MA, MAT, PhD
teaching French • MAT
teaching German • MAT
teaching Spanish • MAT
technology • MFA
telecommunications • MA, MS
textiles • MFA
theatre and drama • MAT
theatre history • MA, PhD
theory • MA, PhD
West European studies • MA, PhD, Certificate
zoology • MA, PhD

School of Journalism
Programs in:
journalism • MA
mass communication • PhD

Kelley School of Business

Programs in:
accounting • DBA, PhD
business • EMBA, MBA, MPA, MS, MSIS, DBA, PhD

Indiana University Bloomington (continued)

business economics and public policy • DBA, PhD
decision systems • DBA, PhD
entrepreneurship • MBA
finance • MBA, DBA, PhD
human resources management • MBA
international business • MBA
management • MBA, DBA, PhD
management information systems • MBA, DBA, PhD
marketing • MBA, DBA, PhD
operations management • MBA, DBA, PhD
organizational behavior • DBA, PhD
production/operations leaders program • MBA
professional accountancy • MPA
systems and accounting • MS, MSIS

Medical Sciences Program
Programs in:
anatomy and cell biology • MA, PhD
pharmacology • MS, PhD
physiology • MA, PhD

School of Education
Programs in:
art education • MS Ed
counseling/counselor education • MS Ed, Ed D, PhD
curriculum and instruction • Ed D, PhD
education • MM Ed, MS Ed, D Mus Ed, Ed D, PhD, Ed S
educational leadership and policy • PhD
educational psychology • MS Ed, Ed D, PhD
elementary education • MS Ed, Ed S
higher education • Ed D, PhD
higher education and student affairs administration • MS Ed
history and philosophy of education • MS Ed
history, philosophy, and policy studies in education • PhD
instructional systems technology • MS Ed, PhD, Ed S
international and comparative education • MS Ed
language education • MS Ed, Ed D, PhD, Ed S
music education • MM Ed, D Mus Ed
school administration • MS Ed, Ed D, Ed S
school psychology • Ed S
science and environmental education • Ed D
secondary education • MS Ed, Ed S
social studies education • MS Ed
special education • MS Ed, Ed D, PhD, Ed S

School of Health, Physical Education and Recreation
Programs in:
adapted physical education • MS
administration • MS
applied health science • MS
applied sport science • MS
athletic administration/sport management • MS
athletic training • MS
biomechanics • MS
clinical exercise physiology • MS
exercise physiology • MS
health and safety • HSD, HS Dir
health behavior • PhD
health, physical education and recreation • MPH, MS, HSD, PED, PhD, Re D, HS Dir, PE Dir, Re Dir
human performance • PhD
leisure behavior • PhD
motor control • MS
motor development • MS
motor learning • MS
outdoor recreation and resource management • MS
park and recreation management • MS
physical education • PED, PE Dir
public health • MPH
recreation • Re D, Re Dir
social science of sport • MS
sport management • MS
sports management • MS
therapeutic recreation • MS

School of Informatics
Programs in:
bioinformatics • MS
chemical informatics • MS
human computer interaction • MS
media arts and science • MS
new media • MS

School of Library and Information Science
Program in:
library and information science • MIS, MLS, PhD, Spec

School of Music
Programs in:
ballet • MS
instrumentation science • MS
music • MA, MAT, MM, MS, DM, PhD
musicology • MA, PhD

School of Optometry
Programs in:
optometry • OD, MS, PhD
visual sciences and physiological optics • MS, PhD

School of Public and Environmental Affairs
Programs in:
environmental science • MSES, PhD
public affairs • EMPA, MPA, PhD
public and environmental affairs • EMPA, MPA, MSES, PhD
public policy • PhD

■ INDIANA UNIVERSITY NORTHWEST

Gary, IN 46408-1197

http://www.indiana.edu/

State-supported, coed, comprehensive institution. *Computer facilities:* 250 computers available on campus for general student use. A campuswide network can be accessed from off campus. Internet access and online class registration are available. *Library facilities:* IUN Library. *General application contact:* Interim Executive Vice Chancellor for Academic Affairs, 219-980-6967.

Division of Business and Economics
Programs in:
accountancy • M Acc
accounting • Certificate
business administration • MBA

Division of Education
Programs in:
elementary education • MS Ed
secondary education • MS Ed

Division of Public and Environmental Affairs
Programs in:
criminal justice • MPA
health services administration • MPA
human services administration • MPA
management of public affairs • MPA
non-profit management • NPMC
public management • PMC

Program in Social Work
Program in:
social work • MSW

■ INDIANA UNIVERSITY–PURDUE UNIVERSITY FORT WAYNE

Fort Wayne, IN 46805-1499

http://www.ipfw.edu/

State-supported, coed, comprehensive institution. *Enrollment:* 55 full-time matriculated graduate/professional students (33 women), 565 part-time matriculated graduate/professional students (326 women). *Graduate faculty:*

82 full-time (24 women), 12 part-time/adjunct (6 women). *Computer facilities:* 285 computers available on campus for general student use. A campuswide network can be accessed from off campus. Internet access and online class registration, students academic records are available. *Library facilities:* Helmke Library. *Graduate expenses:* Full-time $2,648; part-time $147 per credit hour. Tuition, state resident: full-time $2,648; part-time $147 per credit hour. Tuition, nonresident: full-time $5,882; part-time $327 per credit hour. $5,882 full-time. Required fees: $142; $7.9 per credit hour. Tuition and fees vary according to course load. *General application contact:* Kim Pegan, Secretary for Graduate Studies, 219-481-6144.

Division of Public and Environmental Affairs
Dr. William Ludwin, Assistant Dean
Programs in:
- management of public affairs • MPA
- public management • Certificate

School of Arts and Sciences
Dr. Van Coufoudakis, Dean
Programs in:
- applied mathematics • MS
- arts and sciences • MA, MAT, MLS, MS
- biology • MS
- chemistry • MS
- English • MA, MAT
- liberal studies • MLS
- mathematics • MS
- operations research • MS
- professional communication • MA, MS
- sociological practice • MA

School of Business and Management Sciences
Dr. John L. Wellington, Dean
Program in:
- business • MBA

School of Education
Dr. Roberta B. Wiener, Dean
Programs in:
- counselor education • MS Ed
- education • MS Ed
- educational administration • MS Ed
- elementary education • MS Ed
- secondary education • MS Ed

School of Engineering, Technology, and Computer Science
Dr. G. Allen Pugh, Dean
Programs in:
- applied computer science • MS
- engineering, technology, and computer science • MS

School of Health Sciences
Dr. James E. Jones, Dean
Programs in:
- health sciences • MS
- nursing administration • MS

■ INDIANA UNIVERSITY–PURDUE UNIVERSITY INDIANAPOLIS

Indianapolis, IN 46202-2896
http://www.indiana.edu/

State-supported, coed, university. *Computer facilities:* 500 computers available on campus for general student use. A campuswide network can be accessed from off campus. Internet access is available. *Library facilities:* University Library plus 5 others. *General application contact:* Director, Graduate Studies and Associate Dean, 317-274-4023.

Center on Philanthropy
Programs in:
- nonprofit management • MPA
- philanthropic studies • MA

Herron School of Art
Program in:
- art education • MAE

School of Business
Program in:
- business • MBA, MPA

School of Dentistry
Programs in:
- dental materials • MS, MSD
- dental sciences • PhD
- dentistry • DDS, MS, MSD, PhD
- diagnostic sciences • MS, MSD
- endodontics • MSD
- operative dentistry • MSD
- oral and maxillofacial surgery • MSD
- oral biology • PhD
- orthodontics • MS, MSD
- pediatric dentistry • MSD
- periodontics • MSD
- preventive dentistry • MS, MSD
- prosthodontics • MSD

School of Education
Programs in:
- counseling and counselor education • MS
- education • MS
- educational leadership and school administration • MS
- elementary education • MS
- higher education and student affairs • MS
- instructional systems technology • MS
- language education • MS
- secondary education • MS
- special education • MS

School of Engineering and Technology
Programs in:
- biomedical engineering • MS Bm E, PhD
- electrical engineering • MSEE
- engineering • MS, MSE
- engineering and technology • MS, MS Bm E, MSE, MSEE, MSME, PhD
- mechanical engineering • MSME

School of Liberal Arts
Programs in:
- economics • MA
- English • MA
- history • MA
- liberal arts • MA
- public history • MA
- teaching English • MA

School of Library and Information Science
Program in:
- library and information science • MIS, MLS

School of Medicine
Programs in:
- anatomy and cell biology • MS, PhD
- biochemistry and molecular biology • MS, PhD
- health sciences education • MS
- medical and molecular genetics • MS, PhD
- medical biophysics • MS, PhD
- medical neurobiology • MS, PhD
- medicine • MD, MS, PhD
- microbiology and immunology • MS, PhD
- nutrition and dietetics • MS
- pathology and laboratory medicine • MS, PhD
- pharmacology • MS, PhD
- physical therapy • MS
- physiology and biophysics • MS, PhD
- therapeutic outcomes research • MS
- toxicology • MS, PhD

School of Music
Program in:
- music technology • MS

School of New Media
Program in:
- media arts and science • MS

School of Nursing
Programs in:
- acute care nurse practitioner • MSN
- adult clinical nurse specialist • MSN
- adult nurse practitioner • MSN
- community health nursing • MSN
- family nurse practitioner • MSN
- nursing • MSN, PhD
- nursing administration • MSN

Indiana University–Purdue University Indianapolis (continued)

nursing science • PhD
pediatric • MSN
pediatric nursing practitioner • MSN
psychiatric and mental health nursing • MSN
women's health nurse practitioner • MSN

School of Public and Environmental Affairs
Programs in:
environmental planning • M Pl
health administration • MHA
health planning • M Pl
planning and information science • M Pl
planning and public policy • M Pl
public affairs • MPA, Certificate
public and environmental affairs • M Pl, MHA, MPA, Certificate
urban development planning • M Pl

School of Science
Programs in:
applied mathematics • MS, PhD
applied statistics • MS
biology • MS, PhD
chemistry • MS, PhD
clinical rehabilitation psychology • MS, PhD
computer science • MS
geology • MS
industrial/organizational psychology • MS
mathematics • MS, PhD
physics • MS, PhD
psychobiology of addictions • PhD
science • MS, PhD

School of Social Work
Program in:
social work • MSW, PhD

■ INDIANA UNIVERSITY SOUTH BEND

South Bend, IN 46634-7111
http://www.indiana.edu/

State-supported, coed, comprehensive institution. *Enrollment:* 108 full-time matriculated graduate/professional students (62 women), 729 part-time matriculated graduate/professional students (490 women). *Graduate faculty:* 113 full-time (42 women), 27 part-time/adjunct (14 women). *Computer facilities:* 200 computers available on campus for general student use. Internet access is available. *Library facilities:* Franklin D. Schurz Library plus 1 other. *Graduate expenses:* Tuition, state resident: full-time $3,005; part-time $137 per credit hour. Tuition, nonresident: full-time $6,657; part-time $333 per credit hour. $6,464 full-time. Required fees: $3 per credit hour. $50 per semester. Tuition and fees vary according to course level and program. *General application contact:* Dr. Linda M. Fritshner, Acting Associate Vice Chancellor for Academic Affairs, 219-237-4338.

College of Liberal Arts and Sciences
Dr. Miriam Shillingsburg, Dean
Programs in:
applied psychology • MA
liberal arts and sciences • MA, MLS
liberal studies • MLS

Division of Nursing and Health Professions
Dr. Lawrence Garber, Interim Dean
Program in:
family nurse practitioner • MSN

Program in Social Work
Dr. Paul R. Newcomb, Director
Program in:
social work • MSW

School of Business and Economics
Dr. Bill N. Schwartz, Dean
Programs in:
accounting • MSA
business administration • MBA
business and economics • MBA, MIT, MSA
management information technologies • MIT

School of Education
Dr. Gwynn Mettetal, Interim Dean
Programs in:
counseling and human services • MS Ed
education • MS Ed
elementary education • MS Ed
secondary education • MS Ed
special education • MS Ed

School of Public and Environmental Affairs
Dr. William P. Hojnacki, Assistant Dean
Programs in:
public affairs • MPA
public and environmental affairs • MPA

School of the Arts
Dr. Thomas Miller, Dean
Program in:
music • MM

■ INDIANA UNIVERSITY SOUTHEAST

New Albany, IN 47150-6405
http://www.indiana.edu/

State-supported, coed, comprehensive institution. *Enrollment:* 5 full-time matriculated graduate/professional students (3 women), 414 part-time matriculated graduate/professional students (321 women). *Graduate faculty:* 21 full-time (14 women), 14 part-time/adjunct (7 women). *Computer facilities:* 200 computers available on campus for general student use. A campuswide network can be accessed from off campus. Internet access is available. *Library facilities:* Main library plus 1 other. *Graduate expenses:* Tuition, state resident: part-time $135 per credit hour. Tuition, nonresident: part-time $310 per credit hour. Required fees: $9 per credit hour. *General application contact:* Dr. Carolyn A. Babione, Graduate Coordinator, 812-941-2594.

Division of Education
Dr. Steven Gilbert, Dean
Programs in:
counselor education • MS Ed
elementary education • MS Ed
secondary education • MS Ed

■ INDIANA WESLEYAN UNIVERSITY

Marion, IN 46953-4974
http://www.indwes.edu/

Independent-religious, coed, comprehensive institution. *Enrollment:* 2,008 full-time matriculated graduate/professional students, 104 part-time matriculated graduate/professional students. *Graduate faculty:* 23 full-time, 547 part-time/adjunct. *Computer facilities:* 163 computers available on campus for general student use. A campuswide network can be accessed from student residence rooms. Internet access is available. *Library facilities:* Goodman Library. *Graduate expenses:* Tuition: part-time $265 per credit hour. One-time fee: $200 part-time.

College of Adult and Professional Studies
Dr. Mark Smith, Dean
Programs in:
business administration • MBA
curriculum and instruction • M Ed
management • MS
teacher education • M Ed

Graduate Programs
Dr. David Wright, Vice President
Programs in:
counseling • MA
ministry • MA
nursing education • MS, Post Master's Certificate

Division of Nursing Education
Dr. Susan Stranahan, Director of Graduate Nursing
Programs in:
community health development • MS
community health nursing • MS
nursing • Post Master's Certificate
nursing education • MS
primary care nursing • MS

■ OAKLAND CITY UNIVERSITY

Oakland City, IN 47660-1099

http://www.oak.edu/

Independent-religious, coed, comprehensive institution. *Enrollment:* 190 full-time matriculated graduate/professional students (11 women), 107 part-time matriculated graduate/professional students (8 women). *Graduate faculty:* 7 full-time (1 woman), 6 part-time/adjunct (1 woman). *Computer facilities:* 70 computers available on campus for general student use. Internet access is available. *Library facilities:* Founders Memorial Library. *Graduate expenses:* Tuition: full-time $5,205. Required fees: $320. *General application contact:* Counselor for Graduate Admissions, 812-749-1241.

Chapman School of Religious Studies
Dr. Ray Barber, Dean
Program in:
religious studies • M Div, D Min

School of Adult Degrees
Dr. Ora Johnson, Executive Vice President
Program in:
management • MS Mgt

School of Education
Dr. Bernard M. Marley, Dean
Program in:
teaching • MA

■ PURDUE UNIVERSITY

West Lafayette, IN 47907

http://www.purdue.edu/

State-supported, coed, university. CGS member. *Enrollment:* 5,011 full-time matriculated graduate/professional students (2,017 women), 1,488 part-time matriculated graduate/professional students (600 women). *Graduate faculty:* 1,741 full-time (400 women), 92 part-time/adjunct (29 women). *Computer facilities:* 2,100 computers available on campus for general student use. A campuswide network can be accessed from student residence rooms and from off campus. Internet access is available. *Library facilities:* Hicks Undergraduate Library plus 14 others. *Graduate expenses:* Tuition, state resident: full-time $3,772; part-time $135 per credit hour. Tuition, nonresident: full-time $12,804; part-time $422 per credit hour. Tuition and fees vary according to campus/location and program. *General application contact:* Graduate School Admissions, 765-494-2600.

Graduate School
Dr. Gary E. Isom, Vice President for Research and Dean
Programs in:
biochemistry and molecular biology • PhD
neuroscience • PhD
plant biology • PhD

Krannert Graduate School of Management
Dr. R. A. Cosier, Dean
Programs in:
accounting • MS, PhD
applied optimization • PhD
applied statistics • PhD
economics • MS, PhD
finance • MSM, PhD
general management • MSM
human resource management • MS
industrial administration • MSIA
management • EMS
management information systems • MSM, PhD
management science • MSM
marketing • MSM, PhD
operations management • MSM, PhD
organizational behavior and human resource management • PhD
quantitative methods • MSM, PhD
strategic management • MSM, PhD

School of Agriculture
Dr. Victor L. Lechtenberg, Dean
Programs in:
agribusiness • EMBA
agricultural economics • MS, PhD
agriculture • EMBA, M Agr, MS, MSF, PhD
agronomy • MS, PhD
animal sciences • MS, PhD
aquaculture, fisheries, aquatic science • MSF
aquaculture, fisheries, aquatic sciences • MS, PhD
biochemistry • MS, PhD
botany and plant pathology • MS, PhD
entomology • MS, PhD
food science • MS, PhD
forest biology • MS, MSF, PhD
horticulture • M Agr, MS, PhD
natural resources and environmental policy • MS, MSF
natural resources environmental policy • PhD
outdoor recreation and tourism • MS, MSF, PhD
quantitative resource analysis • MS, MSF, PhD
wildlife science • MS, MSF, PhD
wood science and technology • MS, MSF, PhD

School of Consumer and Family Sciences
Dr. Dennis A. Savaiano, Dean
Programs in:
consumer and family sciences • MS, PhD
consumer behavior • MS, PhD
developmental studies • MS, PhD
family and consumer economics • MS, PhD
family studies • MS, PhD
food sciences • MS, PhD
hospitality and tourism management • MS, PhD
marriage and family therapy • MS, PhD
nutrition • MS, PhD
retail management • MS, PhD
textile science • MS, PhD

School of Education
Dr. Marilyn J. Haring, Dean
Programs in:
administration • MS Ed, PhD, Ed S
agricultural and extension education • PhD, Ed S
agriculture and extension education • MS, MS Ed
art education • PhD
consumer and family sciences and extension education • MS Ed, PhD, Ed S
counseling and development • MS Ed, PhD
curriculum studies • MS Ed, PhD, Ed S
education • MS, MS Ed, PhD, Ed S
education of the gifted • MS Ed
educational psychology • MS Ed, PhD
educational technology • MS Ed, PhD, Ed S
elementary education • MS Ed
foreign language education • MS Ed, PhD, Ed S

Purdue University (continued)
- foundations of education • MS Ed, PhD
- higher education administration • MS Ed, PhD
- industrial technology • PhD, Ed S
- language arts • MS Ed, PhD, Ed S
- literacy • MS Ed, PhD, Ed S
- mathematics/science education • MS, MS Ed, PhD, Ed S
- social studies • MS Ed, PhD
- social studies education • Ed S
- special education • MS Ed, PhD
- vocational/industrial education • MS Ed, PhD, Ed S
- vocational/technical education • MS Ed, PhD, Ed S

School of Health Sciences
Dr. G. A. Sandison, Head
Programs in:
- environmental health • MS, PhD
- health physics • MS, PhD
- health sciences • MS, PhD
- industrial hygiene • MS, PhD
- medical physics • MS, PhD
- toxicology • MS, PhD

School of Liberal Arts
Dr. Margaret M. Rowe, Dean
Programs in:
- American studies • MA, PhD
- anthropology • MS, PhD
- art and design • MA
- audiology • MS, PhD
- communication • MA, MS, PhD
- comparative literature • MA, PhD
- creative writing • MFA
- exercise, human physiology of movement and sport • PhD
- French • MA, MAT, PhD
- French education • MAT
- German • MA, MAT, PhD
- German education • MAT
- health and fitness • MS
- health promotion • MS
- health promotion and disease prevention • PhD
- history • MA, PhD
- liberal arts • MA, MAT, MFA, MS, PhD
- linguistics • MS, PhD
- literature • MA, PhD
- movement and sport science • MS
- pedagogy and administration • MS
- pedagogy of physical activity and health • PhD
- philosophy • MA, PhD
- political science • MA, PhD
- psychological sciences • PhD
- psychology of sport and exercise, and motor behavior • PhD
- sociology • MS, PhD
- Spanish • MA, MAT, PhD
- Spanish education • MAT
- speech and hearing science • MS, PhD
- speech-language pathology • MS, PhD
- theatre • MA, MFA

School of Science
Dr. Harry A. Morrison, Dean
Programs in:
- analytical chemistry • MS, PhD
- applied statistics • MS
- biochemistry • MS, PhD
- biophysics • PhD
- cell and developmental biology • PhD
- chemical education • MS, PhD
- computer sciences • MS, PhD
- earth and atmospheric sciences • MS, PhD
- ecology • MS, PhD
- ecology, evolutionary and population biology • MS, PhD
- evolutionary biology • MS, PhD
- genetics • MS, PhD
- inorganic chemistry • MS, PhD
- mathematics • MS, PhD
- microbiology • MS, PhD
- molecular biology • PhD
- neurobiology • MS, PhD
- organic chemistry • MS, PhD
- physical chemistry • MS, PhD
- physics • MS, PhD
- plant physiology • PhD
- population biology • MS, PhD
- science • MS, PhD
- statistics • PhD
- statistics and computer science • MS
- statistics/computational finance • MS
- theoretical statistics • MS

School of Technology
Dr. Don K. Gentry, Dean
Program in:
- technology • MS

Schools of Engineering
Dr. Richard J. Schwartz, Dean
Programs in:
- aeronautics and astronautics • MS, MSAAE, MSE, PhD
- agricultural and biological engineering • MS, MSABE, MSE, PhD
- biomedical engineering • MS Bm E, PhD
- chemical engineering • MS, PhD
- civil engineering • MS, MSCE, MSE, PhD
- computer engineering • MS, PhD
- continuing engineering education • MS, MSE
- electrical engineering • MS, PhD
- engineering • MS, MS Bm E, MS Met E, MSAAE, MSABE, MSCE, MSE, MSIE, MSME, MSNE, PhD
- human factors in industrial engineering • MS, MSIE, PhD
- manufacturing engineering • MS, MSIE, PhD
- materials engineering • MS, MSE, PhD
- mechanical engineering • MS, MSE, MSME, PhD
- metallurgical engineering • MS Met E
- nuclear engineering • MS, MSNE, PhD
- operations research • MS, MSIE, PhD
- systems engineering • MS, MSIE, PhD

School of Pharmacy and Pharmacal Sciences
Dr. Charles O. Rutledge, Dean
Programs in:
- analytical medicinal chemistry • PhD
- clinical pharmacy • MS, PhD
- computational and biophysical medicinal chemistry • PhD
- industrial and physical pharmacy • PhD
- medicinal and bioorganic chemistry • PhD
- medicinal biochemistry and molecular biology • PhD
- medicinal chemistry and molecular pharmacology • MS, PhD
- molecular pharmacology and toxicology • PhD
- natural products and pharmacognosy • PhD
- nuclear pharmacy • MS
- pharmacy administration • MS, PhD
- pharmacy and pharmacal sciences • Pharm D, MS, PhD
- pharmacy practice • MS, PhD
- radiopharmaceutical chemistry and nuclear pharmacy • PhD

School of Veterinary Medicine
Dr. Alan H. Rebar, Dean
Programs in:
- anatomy • MS, PhD
- bacteriology • MS, PhD
- basic medical sciences • MS, PhD
- epidemiology • MS, PhD
- immunology • MS, PhD
- infectious diseases • MS, PhD
- microbiology • MS, PhD
- parasitology • MS, PhD
- pathology • MS, PhD
- pharmacology • MS, PhD
- physiology • MS, PhD
- toxicology • MS, PhD
- veterinary clinical sciences • MS, PhD
- veterinary medicine • DVM, MS, PhD
- veterinary pathobiology • MS, PhD
- virology • MS, PhD

■ PURDUE UNIVERSITY CALUMET

Hammond, IN 46323-2094
http://www.calumet.purdue.edu/

State-supported, coed, comprehensive institution. *Computer facilities:* 250 computers available on campus for general student use. A campuswide network can be accessed. Internet access is available. *Library facilities:* Purdue Calumet Library. *General application contact:* Associate Vice Chancellor for Academic Affairs, 219-989-2257.

Graduate School

School of Education
Programs in:
counseling and personnel services • MS Ed
educational administration • MS Ed
elementary education • MS Ed
instructional development • MS Ed
media sciences • MS Ed
secondary education • MS Ed

School of Engineering, Mathematics, and Science
Programs in:
biology • MS
biology teaching • MS
engineering • MSE
engineering, mathematics, and science • MS, MSE
mathematics • MS

School of Liberal Arts and Sciences
Programs in:
communication • MA
English • MA
history and political science • MA
liberal arts and sciences • MA, MS
marriage and family therapy • MS

School of Management
Programs in:
accountancy • M Acc
business administration • MBA

School of Nursing
Program in:
nursing • MS

■ UNIVERSITY OF EVANSVILLE
Evansville, IN 47722-0002
http://www.evansville.edu/

Independent-religious, coed. *Computer facilities:* 360 computers available on campus for general student use. A campuswide network can be accessed from student residence rooms and from off campus. *Library facilities:* Bower Suhrheinrich Library plus 1 other. *General application contact:* Associate Vice President for Admission and Financial Aid, 812-479-2683.

Graduate Programs

College of Education and Health Sciences
Programs in:
education • MA, MS Coun
nursing • MS

■ UNIVERSITY OF INDIANAPOLIS
Indianapolis, IN 46227-3697
http://www.uindy.edu/

Independent-religious, coed, comprehensive institution. *Computer facilities:* 218 computers available on campus for general student use. A campuswide network can be accessed from student residence rooms and from off campus. Internet access is available. *Library facilities:* Krannert Memorial Library. *General application contact:* Vice President and Provost, 317-788-3213.

Graduate School
Programs in:
accounting • M Acc
business administration • MBA
occupational therapy • MS

College of Arts and Sciences
Programs in:
applied sociology • MA
art • MA
arts and sciences • MA, MS
biology • MS
English language and literature • MA
history • MA

Krannert School of Physical Therapy
Program in:
physical therapy • MHS, MS

School of Education
Programs in:
education • MA
elementary education • MA
secondary education • MA

■ UNIVERSITY OF NOTRE DAME
Notre Dame, IN 46556
http://www.nd.edu/

Independent-religious, coed, university. CGS member. *Enrollment:* 1,404 full-time matriculated graduate/professional students (536 women), 53 part-time matriculated graduate/professional students (20 women). *Graduate faculty:* 576 full-time (117 women), 48 part-time/adjunct (9 women). *Computer facilities:* 880 computers available on campus for general student use. A campuswide network can be accessed from student residence rooms and from off campus. Internet access is available. *Library facilities:* University Libraries of Notre Dame plus 8 others. *Graduate expenses:* Tuition: full-time $23,080; part-time $1,282 per credit hour. Required fees: $155. *General application contact:* Dr. Terrence J. Akai, Director of Graduate Admissions, 219-631-7706.

Find an in-depth description at www.petersons.com/graduate.

Graduate School
Dr. James L. Merz, Vice President

College of Arts and Letters
Dr. Mark W. Roche, Dean
Programs in:
art history • MA
arts and letters • M Div, M Ed, MA, MFA, MM, MMS, MTS, PhD
ceramics • MFA
cognitive psychology • PhD
counseling psychology • PhD
creative writing • MFA
design • MFA
developmental psychology • PhD
early Christian studies • MA
economics • MA, PhD
educational initiatives • M Ed
English • MA, PhD
French • MA
German • MA
government and international studies • PhD
graphic design • MFA
history • MA, PhD
history and philosophy of science • MA, PhD
humanities • M Div, MA, MFA, MM, MMS, MTS, PhD
industrial design • MFA
international peace studies • MA
Italian studies • MA
medieval studies • MMS, PhD
music • MA, MM
painting • MFA
philosophy • PhD
photography • MFA
printmaking • MFA
quantitative psychology • PhD
Romance literatures • MA
sculpture • MFA
social science • M Ed, MA, PhD
sociology • PhD
Spanish • MA
studio art • MFA
theology • M Div, MA, MTS, PhD

College of Engineering
Dr. Frank P. Incropera, Dean
Programs in:
aerospace and mechanical engineering • PhD
aerospace engineering • MS
bioengineering • MS

University of Notre Dame (continued)
chemical engineering • MS, PhD
civil engineering • MS
civil engineering and geological sciences • PhD
computer science and engineering • MS, PhD
electrical engineering • MS, PhD
engineering • MEME, MS, PhD
environmental engineering • MS
geological sciences • MS
mechanical engineering • MEME, MS

College of Science
Dr. Francis J. Castellino, Dean
Programs in:
aquatic ecology, evolution and environmental biology • MS, PhD
biochemistry • MS, PhD
cellular and molecular biology • MS, PhD
genetics • MS, PhD
inorganic chemistry • MS, PhD
mathematics • MSAM, PhD
organic chemistry • MS, PhD
physical chemistry • MS, PhD
physics • PhD
physiology • MS, PhD
science • MS, MSAM, PhD
vector biology and parasitology • MS, PhD

School of Architecture
Norman Crowe, Director of Graduate Studies
Program in:
architecture • M Arch

Law School
Patricia A. O'Hara, Dean
Programs in:
comparative law • LL M
human rights • JSD
international law • LL M
law • JD

Mendoza College of Business
Dr. Carolyn Y. Woo, Dean
Programs in:
accountancy • MS
business • EMBA, MBA, MS
business administration • MBA
executive business administration • EMBA

■ UNIVERSITY OF SAINT FRANCIS

Fort Wayne, IN 46808-3994
http://www.sf.edu/

Independent-religious, coed, comprehensive institution. *Enrollment:* 33 full-time matriculated graduate/professional students (23 women), 153 part-time matriculated graduate/professional students (105 women). *Graduate faculty:* 20 full-time (13 women), 5 part-time/adjunct (4 women). *Computer facilities:* 135 computers available on campus for general student use. Internet access is available. *Library facilities:* University Library plus 1 other. *Graduate expenses:* Tuition: full-time $7,020; part-time $390 per credit hour. Required fees: $420; $9 per credit hour. $75 per term. One-time fee: $20 full-time. *General application contact:* David McMahan, Director of Admissions, 219-434-3264.

Graduate School
Dr. Marcia Sauter, Chair
Programs in:
business administration • MBA, MS
fine art • MA
general psychology • MS
mental health counseling • MS
nursing • MSN
reading • MS Ed
school counseling • MS Ed
special education • MS Ed

■ UNIVERSITY OF SOUTHERN INDIANA

Evansville, IN 47712-3590
http://www.usi.edu/

State-supported, coed, comprehensive institution. CGS member. *Enrollment:* 84 full-time matriculated graduate/professional students (64 women), 306 part-time matriculated graduate/professional students (196 women). *Graduate faculty:* 69 full-time (21 women), 8 part-time/adjunct (6 women). *Computer facilities:* 750 computers available on campus for general student use. A campuswide network can be accessed from student residence rooms and from off campus. Internet access and online class registration are available. *Library facilities:* David L. Rice Library plus 1 other. *Graduate expenses:* Tuition, state resident: full-time $1,289; part-time $143 per credit hour. Tuition, nonresident: full-time $2,588; part-time $287 per credit hour. Required fees: $60; $23 per semester. *General application contact:* Dr. Peggy F. Harrel, Director, Graduate Studies, 812-465-7015.

Graduate Studies
Dr. Peggy F. Harrel, Director

School of Business
Dr. Philip C. Fisher, Dean
Programs in:
accounting and business law • MSA
business • MBA, MSA
business administration • MBA

School of Education and Human Services
Dr. Thomas Pickering, Dean
Programs in:
education and human services • MS, MSW
elementary education • MS
secondary education • MS
social work • MSW

School of Liberal Arts
Dr. Iain L. Crawford, Dean
Programs in:
liberal arts • MA
liberal studies • MA

School of Nursing and Health Professions
Dr. Nadine Coudret, Dean
Programs in:
health administration • MHA
nursing and health professions • MHA, MSN, MSOT
occupational therapy • MSOT

School of Science and Engineering Technology
Dr. Jerome Cain, Dean
Programs in:
industrial management • MS
science and engineering • MS

■ VALPARAISO UNIVERSITY

Valparaiso, IN 46383-6493
http://www.valpo.edu/

Independent-religious, coed, comprehensive institution. *Enrollment:* 444 full-time matriculated graduate/professional students (226 women), 157 part-time matriculated graduate/professional students (91 women). *Computer facilities:* 580 computers available on campus for general student use. A campuswide network can be accessed from student residence rooms and from off campus. Internet access is available. *Library facilities:* Moellering Library plus 1 other. *Graduate expenses:* Tuition: full-time $17,100; part-time $270 per credit hour. Required fees: $536. Tuition and fees vary according to program. *General application contact:* Dr. David L. Rowland, Dean, Graduate Studies and Continuing Education, 219-464-5313.

Graduate Division
Dr. David L. Rowland, Dean, Graduate Studies and Continuing Education
Programs in:
applied behavioral science • MA

clinical mental health counseling • MA
counseling • MA
emotionally handicapped • M Ed, MS Sp Ed
English • MALS
history • MALS
human behavior and society • MALS
learning disabilities • MS Sp Ed
learning disability • M Ed
mild disabilities • M Ed, MS Sp Ed
mild mentally handicapped • M Ed, MS Sp Ed
music • MALS, MM
psychological foundations • MA
psychology • MALS
school psychology • MA
special education • M Ed, MS Sp Ed
teaching and learning • M Ed
theology • MALS

College of Nursing
Dr. Janet Brown, Dean
Program in:
nursing • MSN

School of Law
Jay Conison, Dean
Program in:
law • JD, LL M

Iowa

■ DRAKE UNIVERSITY
Des Moines, IA 50311-4516
http://www.drake.edu/

Independent, coed, university. *Enrollment:* 1,582 matriculated graduate/professional students. *Graduate faculty:* 252 full-time (91 women), 41 part-time/adjunct. *Computer facilities:* 1,081 computers available on campus for general student use. A campuswide network can be accessed from student residence rooms and from off campus. Internet access is available. *Library facilities:* Cowles Library plus 1 other. *Graduate expenses:* Tuition: part-time $340 per credit hour. *General application contact:* A. J. Martin, Graduate Coordinator, 515-271-3181.

Find an in-depth description at www.petersons.com/graduate.

College of Arts and Sciences
Dr. Susan E. Wright, Dean
Program in:
arts and sciences • MA

College of Business and Public Administration
Antone F. Alber, Dean
Program in:
business and public administration • M Acc, MBA, MPA

College of Pharmacy and Health Sciences
Dr. Stephen G. Hoag, Dean
Programs in:
pharmacy • Pharm D
pharmacy and health sciences • Pharm D

Law School
C. Peter Goplerud, Dean
Program in:
law • JD

School of Education
Dr. James L. Romig, Dean
Programs in:
adult education • MS, MSE, Ed D, Ed S
adult education, training and development • MS
counseling • MSE
early childhood education • MSE
education • MAT, MS, MSE, MST, Ed D, Ed S
education leadership • MSE, Ed D, Ed S
elementary education • MSE, MST
guidance counseling • MSE
secondary education • MAT
special education • MSE
teacher education • MSE, Ed S
vocational rehabilitation • MS

■ IOWA STATE UNIVERSITY OF SCIENCE AND TECHNOLOGY
Ames, IA 50011
http://www.iastate.edu/

State-supported, coed, university. CGS member. *Enrollment:* 2,362 full-time matriculated graduate/professional students (897 women), 2,002 part-time matriculated graduate/professional students (868 women). *Graduate faculty:* 1,424 full-time, 107 part-time/adjunct. *Computer facilities:* 2,600 computers available on campus for general student use. A campuswide network can be accessed from student residence rooms and from off campus. E-mail, network services available. *Library facilities:* University Library plus 1 other. *Graduate expenses:* Tuition, state resident: full-time $1,726; part-time $192 per credit. Tuition, nonresident: full-time $5,082; part-time $565 per credit. Required fees: $6 per credit. *General application contact:* Dr. James R. Bloedel, Dean of the Graduate College, 515-294-6344.

Find an in-depth description at www.petersons.com/graduate.

College of Veterinary Medicine
Dr. Norman Cheville, Dean
Programs in:
biomedical sciences • MS, PhD
veterinary anatomy • MS, PhD
veterinary clinical sciences • MS
veterinary medicine • DVM, MS, PhD
veterinary microbiology • MS, PhD
veterinary microbiology and preventive medicine • MS, PhD
veterinary pathology • MS, PhD
veterinary physiology • MS, PhD
veterinary preventive medicine • MS

Graduate College
Dr. James R. Bloedel, Dean of the Graduate College
Programs in:
bioinformatics and computational biology • MS, PhD
ecology and evolutionary biology • MS, PhD
family and consumer sciences • MFCS
genetics • MS, PhD
immunobiology • MS, PhD
industrial relations • MS
interdisciplinary graduate studies • MA, MS
interdisciplinary studies • M Ag, M Eng, MA, MBA, MFCS, MS, PhD
molecular, cellular, and developmental biology • MS, PhD
neuroscience • MS, PhD
plant physiology • MS, PhD
systems engineering • M Eng
toxicology • MS, PhD
transportation • MS
water resources • MS, PhD

College of Agriculture
Dr. Richard F. Ross, Interim Dean
Programs in:
agricultural education and studies • MS, PhD
agricultural meteorology • MS, PhD
agriculture • M Ag, MS, PhD
agronomy • MS
animal breeding and genetics • MS, PhD
animal ecology • MS, PhD
animal nutrition • MS, PhD
animal physiology • MS
animal psychology • PhD
animal science • MS, PhD
biochemistry • MS, PhD
biophysics • MS, PhD

Iowa State University of Science and Technology (continued)

crop production and physiology • MS, PhD
entomology • MS, PhD
fisheries biology • MS, PhD
forestry • MS, PhD
genetics • MS, PhD
horticulture • MS, PhD
meat science • MS, PhD
microbiology • MS, PhD
molecular, cellular, and developmental biology • MS, PhD
plant breeding • MS, PhD
plant pathology • MS, PhD
soil science • MS, PhD
toxicology • MS, PhD
wildlife biology • MS, PhD

College of Business
Dr. Benjamin J. Allen, Dean
Programs in:
accounting • M Acc
business • M Acc, MBA, MS
business administration • MBA, MS

College of Design
Mark Engelbrecht, Dean
Programs in:
architectural studies • MSAS
architecture • M Arch
art and design • MA
community and regional planning • MCRP
design • M Arch, MA, MCRP, MFA, MLA, MS, MSAS
graphic design • MFA
integrated visual arts • MFA
interior design • MA, MFA
landscape architecture • MLA
transportation • MS

College of Education
Dr. Walter H. Gmelch, Dean
Programs in:
counselor education • M Ed, MS
curriculum and instructional technology • M Ed, MS, PhD
education • M Ed
educational administration • M Ed, MS
educational leadership • PhD
elementary education • M Ed, MS
exercise and sport science • MS
health and human performance • PhD
higher education • M Ed, MS
historical, philosophical and comparative studies in education • M Ed, MS
industrial education and technology • MS, PhD
organizational learning and human resource development • M Ed, MS
research and evaluation • MS
special education • M Ed, MS
vocational-technical education • M Ed

College of Engineering
Dr. James L. Melsa, Dean
Programs in:
aerospace engineering • M Eng, MS, PhD
agricultural and biosystems engineering • M Eng, MS, PhD
chemical engineering • M Eng, MS, PhD
civil engineering • MS, PhD
computer engineering • MS, PhD
electrical engineering • MS, PhD
engineering • M Eng, MS, PhD
engineering mechanics • M Eng, MS, PhD
industrial engineering • MS, PhD
materials science and engineering • MS, PhD
mechanical engineering • MS, PhD
operations research • MS

College of Family and Consumer Sciences
Dr. Carol B. Meeks, Dean
Programs in:
family and consumer sciences • M Ed, MFCS, MS, PhD
family and consumer sciences education and studies • M Ed, MS, PhD
food science and technology • MS, PhD
hotel, restaurant and institution management • MFCS, MS, PhD
human development and family studies • MFCS, MS, PhD
marriage and family therapy • PhD
nutrition • MS, PhD
textiles and clothing • MFCS, MS, PhD

College of Liberal Arts and Sciences
Dr. Peter Rabideau, Dean
Programs in:
agricultural economics • MS, PhD
agricultural history and rural studies • PhD
anthropology • MA
applied mathematics • MS, PhD
botany • MS, PhD
chemistry • MS, PhD
cognitive psychology • PhD
computer science • MS, PhD
counseling psychology • PhD
earth science • MS, PhD
economics • MS, PhD
English • MA
general psychology • MS
geology • MS, PhD
history • MA
history of technology and science • MA, PhD
journalism and mass communication • MS
liberal arts and sciences • MA, MPA, MS, MSM, PhD
mathematics • MS, PhD
meteorology • MS, PhD
physics and astronomy • MS, PhD
political science • MA
public administration • MPA
rhetoric and professional communication • PhD
rural sociology • MS, PhD
school mathematics • MSM
social psychology • PhD
sociology • MS, PhD
statistics • MS, PhD
water resources • MS, PhD
zoology and genetics • MS, PhD

■ LORAS COLLEGE

Dubuque, IA 52004-0178
http://www.loras.edu/

Independent-religious, coed, comprehensive institution. *Enrollment:* 13 full-time matriculated graduate/professional students (9 women), 86 part-time matriculated graduate/professional students (59 women). *Graduate faculty:* 31 full-time, 5 part-time/adjunct. *Computer facilities:* 100 computers available on campus for general student use. A campuswide network can be accessed from student residence rooms and from off campus. Internet access is available. *Library facilities:* Wahlert Memorial Library plus 1 other. *Graduate expenses:* Tuition: part-time $375 per credit. *General application contact:* 319-588-7236.

Graduate Division
Linda Crossett, Director
Programs in:
educational administration: elementary and secondary • MA
effective teaching • MA
English • MA
pastoral studies • MM
physical education • MA
psychology • MA
religious education • MM
special education • MA
theology • MA

■ MAHARISHI UNIVERSITY OF MANAGEMENT

Fairfield, IA 52557
http://www.mum.edu/

Independent, coed, university. *Computer facilities:* 120 computers available on campus for general student use. A campuswide network can be accessed from student residence rooms and from off campus. Internet access is available. *Library facilities:* Maharishi University of Management Library plus 1 other. *General application contact:* Dean of Graduate Studies, 515-472-1111.

Graduate Studies
Programs in:
art • MA
business administration • MBA, PhD
ceramics/sculpture • MFA
computer science • MS
drawing/painting • MFA
elementary education • MA
English • MA
foundations of education • MA
mathematics • MS
neuroscience of human consciousness • MS, PhD
physiology, molecular, and cell biology • MS, PhD
professional writing • MA
psychology • MS, PhD
science of creative intelligence • MA, PhD
secondary education • MA

■ MARYCREST INTERNATIONAL UNIVERSITY

Davenport, IA 52804-4096

http://www.mcrest.edu/

Independent, coed, comprehensive institution. *Enrollment:* 22 full-time matriculated graduate/professional students (7 women), 319 part-time matriculated graduate/professional students (276 women). *Graduate faculty:* 6 full-time (3 women), 43 part-time/adjunct (23 women). *Computer facilities:* 110 computers available on campus for general student use. A campuswide network can be accessed from student residence rooms and from off campus. Internet access and online class registration are available. *Library facilities:* Cone Library plus 1 other. *Graduate expenses:* Tuition: full-time $8,100; part-time $450 per semester hour. Required fees: $500; $12 per semester hour. *General application contact:* Meg Farber, Admissions Director, 319-327-9609.

College of Chiropractic
Dr. Doug Davison, Executive Dean
Program in:
chiropractic • DC

Graduate Studies
Gary Monnard, Academic Dean and Vice President for Academic Affairs
Programs in:
computer science • MS
education • MA
reading specialist • MA
teaching • MAT

■ ST. AMBROSE UNIVERSITY

Davenport, IA 52803-2898

http://www.sau.edu/

Independent-religious, coed, comprehensive institution. *Enrollment:* 286 full-time matriculated graduate/professional students (204 women), 609 part-time matriculated graduate/professional students (328 women). *Graduate faculty:* 56 full-time (19 women), 35 part-time/adjunct (7 women). *Computer facilities:* 190 computers available on campus for general student use. A campuswide network can be accessed from student residence rooms and from off campus. Internet access and online class registration, on-line course syllabi, class listings are available. *Library facilities:* O'Keefe Library plus 1 other. *Graduate expenses:* Tuition: full-time $13,890; part-time $432 per credit. One-time fee: $200. Full-time tuition and fees vary according to degree level, program and student's religious affiliation. Part-time tuition and fees vary according to degree level, campus/location and student's religious affiliation. *General application contact:* Suzanne Humphrey, Assistant Dean for Graduate Studies, 563-333-6308.

College of Arts and Sciences
Dr. Paul Koch, Dean
Programs in:
arts and sciences • MOL, MPS, MSW
leadership studies • MOL
pastoral studies • MPS
social work • MSW

College of Business
Dr. Richard M. Dienesch, Dean
Programs in:
accounting • M Ac
business • M Ac, MBA, MBAH, DBA
business administration • DBA
health care administration • MBAH
management generalist • MBA
technical management • MBA

College of Human Services
Dr. Daniel Bozik, Dean
Programs in:
criminal justice • MCJ
human services • M Ed, MCJ, MOS, MOT, MPT, MS
information technology management • MS
juvenile justice • MCJ
occupational therapy • MOT
orthotic science • MOS
physical therapy • MPT
special education • M Ed

■ UNIVERSITY OF DUBUQUE

Dubuque, IA 52001-5099

http://www.dbq.edu/

Independent-religious, coed, comprehensive institution. *Enrollment:* 192 full-time matriculated graduate/professional students (66 women), 120 part-time matriculated graduate/professional students (61 women). *Graduate faculty:* 21 full-time (6 women), 12 part-time/adjunct (4 women). *Computer facilities:* 100 computers available on campus for general student use. A campuswide network can be accessed from off campus. Internet access, intranet are available. *Library facilities:* Charles C. Myer's Library. *Graduate expenses:* Tuition: part-time $355 per hour. Required fees: $90 per semester. *General application contact:* Dr. Rodney Foth, Associate Dean for Academic Affairs, 563-589-3205.

Program in Business Administration
Dr. Roderic Hewlett, Director
Programs in:
aviation management • MBA
business administration • MBA
finance • MBA
quality management • MBA

Program in Communication
Dr. Kelly Foth, Chair
Program in:
communication • MA

Theological Seminary
Program in:
theology • M Div, MAR, D Min

■ THE UNIVERSITY OF IOWA

Iowa City, IA 52242-1316

http://www.uiowa.edu/

State-supported, coed, university. CGS member. *Enrollment:* 5,622 full-time matriculated graduate/professional students (2,713 women), 2,386 part-time matriculated graduate/professional students (1,206 women). *Graduate faculty:* 1,618 full-time (430 women), 96 part-time/adjunct (22 women). *Computer facilities:* 1,200 computers available on campus for general student use. A campuswide network can be accessed from student residence rooms and from

The University of Iowa (continued)
off campus. Internet access and online class registration, online degree process, grades, financial aid summary are available. *Library facilities:* Main Library plus 12 others. *Graduate expenses:* Tuition, state resident: full-time $3,750; part-time $192 per semester hour. Tuition, nonresident: full-time $11,420. Required fees: $126 per semester. Tuition and fees vary according to course load and program. *General application contact:* Betty Wood, Assistant Director of Admissions, 319-335-1525.

College of Dentistry
Dr. David C. Johnsen, Dean
Programs in:
- dental public health • MS
- dentistry • DDS, MS, PhD, Certificate
- endodontics • MS, Certificate
- operative dentistry • MS, Certificate
- oral and maxillofacial surgery • MS, Certificate
- oral pathology, radiology and medicine • MS, Certificate
- oral science • MS, PhD
- orthodontics • MS, Certificate
- pediatric dentistry • MS, Certificate
- periodontics • MS, Certificate
- preventive and community dentistry • MS
- prosthodontics • MS, Certificate
- stomatology • MS, Certificate

College of Law
Program in:
- law • JD, LL M

College of Medicine
Dr. Robert P. Kelch, Dean, College of Medicine, and Vice President for Statewide Health Services
Programs in:
- biosciences • PhD
- medicine • MD, MA, MHA, MPAS, MPH, MPT, MS, PhD
- translational biomedical research • MS, PhD

Graduate Programs in Medicine
Programs in:
- anatomy and cell biology • PhD
- biochemistry • MS, PhD
- free radical and radiation biology • MS, PhD
- general microbiology and microbial physiology • MS, PhD
- immunology • MS, PhD
- medicine • MA, MHA, MPAS, MPH, MPT, MS, PhD
- microbial genetics • MS, PhD
- pathogenic bacteriology • MS, PhD
- pathology • MS
- pharmacology • MS, PhD
- physical therapy • MA, MPT
- physician assistant • MPAS
- physiology and biophysics • PhD
- physiology and biophysiology • MS
- rehabilitation science • PhD
- virology • MS, PhD

College of Pharmacy
Program in:
- pharmacy • Pharm D, MS, PhD

Graduate College
John C. Keller, Interim Dean
Programs in:
- applied mathematical and computational sciences • PhD
- genetics • PhD
- immunology • PhD
- molecular biology • PhD
- neuroscience • PhD
- second language acquisition • PhD
- urban and regional planning • MA, MS

College of Education
Sondra Bowman Damico, Dean
Programs in:
- art education • MA, MAT, PhD
- counselor education • MA, PhD
- early childhood and elementary education • MA, PhD
- early childhood education • MA
- education • MA, MAT, PhD, Ed S
- educational administration • MA, PhD, Ed S
- elementary education • PhD
- foreign language education • MAT
- higher education • MA, PhD, Ed S
- instructional design and technology • MA, PhD, Ed S
- music education • MA, PhD
- psychological and quantitative foundations • MA, PhD, Ed S
- rehabilitation counseling • MA, PhD
- secondary education • MA, MAT, PhD
- social foundations • MA, PhD
- special education • MA, PhD

College of Engineering
Dr. P. Barry Butler, Dean
Programs in:
- biomedical engineering • MS, PhD
- chemical and biochemical engineering • MS, PhD
- civil and environmental engineering • MS, PhD
- electrical and computer engineering • MS, PhD
- engineering • MS, PhD
- engineering design and manufacturing • MS, PhD
- ergonomics • MS, PhD
- information and engineering management • MS, PhD
- mechanical engineering • MS, PhD
- operations research • MS, PhD
- quality engineering • MS, PhD

College of Liberal Arts
Linda Maxson, Dean
Programs in:
- African American world studies • MA
- American studies • MA, PhD
- anthropology • MA, PhD
- art • MA, MFA
- art history • MA, PhD
- Asian civilizations • MA
- astronomy • MS
- bibliography • PhD
- biological sciences • MS, PhD
- chemistry • MS, PhD
- classics • MA, PhD
- communication and mass communication • MA
- communication research • MA, PhD
- comparative literature • MA, PhD
- comparative literature translation • MFA
- computer science • MCS, MS, PhD
- dance • MFA
- development support communication • MA
- English • MFA, PhD
- exercise science • MS, PhD
- expository writing • MA
- film and video production • MA, MFA
- film studies • MA, PhD
- French • MA, PhD
- geography • MA, PhD
- geoscience • MS, PhD
- German • MA, PhD
- history • MA, PhD
- leisure studies • MA
- liberal arts • MA, MAMS, MCS, MFA, MS, MSW, DMA, PhD
- linguistics • MA, PhD
- literary criticism • PhD
- literary history • PhD
- literary studies • MA
- mass communication • PhD
- mathematics • MS, PhD
- music • MA, MFA, DMA, PhD
- neural and behavioral sciences • PhD
- nonfiction writing • MFA
- pedagogy • PhD
- philosophy • MA, PhD
- physical education • PhD
- physical education and sports studies • MA, PhD
- physics • MS, PhD
- political science • MA, PhD
- professional journalism • MA
- psychology • MA, PhD
- religion • MA, PhD
- rhetorical studies • MA, PhD
- rhetorical theory and stylistics • PhD
- Russian • MA
- science education • MS, PhD
- social work • MSW, PhD
- sociology • MA, PhD
- Spanish • MA, PhD
- speech and hearing science • PhD

speech pathology and audiology • MA
statistics and actuarial science • MS, PhD
theatre arts • MFA
women's studies • PhD
writer's workshop • MFA
writing • PhD

College of Nursing
Melanie Dreher, Dean
Program in:
nursing • MSN, PhD

College of Public Health
Dr. James A. Merchant, Dean
Programs in:
biostatistics • MS, PhD
epidemiology • MS, PhD
health management and policy • MHA, PhD
occupational and environmental health • MS, PhD
preventive medicine and environmental health • MPH, MS, PhD
public health • MHA, MPH, MS, PhD

Henry B. Tippie College of Business
Prof. Gary C. Fethke, Dean
Programs in:
accountancy • M Ac
business • M Ac, MA, MBA, PhD
business administration • PhD
economics • PhD
finance • PhD
management • MBA
management information systems • MA
management sciences • PhD
marketing • PhD

School of Library and Information Science
Joseph Kearney, Director
Program in:
library and information science • MA

■ UNIVERSITY OF NORTHERN IOWA

Cedar Falls, IA 50614
http://www.uni.edu/

State-supported, coed, comprehensive institution. CGS member. *Enrollment:* 525 full-time matriculated graduate/professional students (333 women), 684 part-time matriculated graduate/professional students (462 women). *Graduate faculty:* 536. *Computer facilities:* 884 computers available on campus for general student use. A campuswide network can be accessed from student residence rooms and from off campus. Internet access and online class registration, course registration, student account and grade information are available. *Library facilities:* Rod Library plus 1 other. *Graduate expenses:* Tuition, state resident: full-time $3,452; part-time $192 per credit hour. Tuition, nonresident: full-time $8,508. Required fees: $224; $112 per semester. *General application contact:* Dr. John W. Somervill, Graduate Dean, 319-273-2748.

Graduate College
Dr. John W. Somervill, Dean
Programs in:
public policy • MPP
women's studies • MA

College of Education
Dr. Thomas J. Switzer, Dean
Programs in:
communication and training technology • MA Ed
counseling • MA, MA Ed, Ed D
curriculum and instruction • MA Ed, Ed D
early childhood education • MA Ed
education • MA, MA Ed, Ed D, Ed S
education of the gifted • MA Ed
educational administration • Ed D
educational leadership • MA Ed, Ed D
educational media • MA Ed
educational psychology • MA Ed
educational technology • MA
elementary education • MA Ed
elementary principal • MA Ed
health education • MA
health, physical education, and leisure services • MA
middle school/junior high education • MA
physical education • MA
postsecondary education • MA Ed
reading • MA Ed
school counseling • MA Ed
school library media studies • MA
school psychology • Ed S
secondary principal • MA Ed
special education • MA Ed
youth agency administration • MA

College of Humanities and Fine Arts
Dr. James F. Lubker, Dean
Programs in:
art • MA
art education • MA
audiology • MA
communication studies • MA
composition • MM
conducting • MM
English • MA
French • MA
German • MA
humanities and fine arts • MA, MM
jazz pedagogy • MM
music • MA
music education • MM
music history • MM
performance • MM
Spanish • MA
speech pathology • MA
teaching English to speakers of other languages • MA
theatre • MA
two languages • MA

College of Natural Sciences
Dr. Joel Haack, Interim Dean
Programs in:
biology • MA, MS
chemistry • MA
computer science • MS
environmental science/technology • MS
industrial technology • MA, DIT
mathematics • MA
mathematics for elementary and middle school • MA
natural sciences • MA, MS, DIT, SP
science education • MA

College of Social and Behavioral Sciences
Dr. Julia Wallace, Acting Dean
Programs in:
geography • MA
history • MA
political science • MA
psychology • MA
social and behavioral sciences • MA, MSW
social work • MSW
sociology • MA

School of Business Administration
Dr. Willis Greer, Dean
Program in:
business administration • MBA

Kansas

■ BAKER UNIVERSITY

Baldwin City, KS 66006-0065
http://www.bakeru.edu/

Independent-religious, coed, comprehensive institution. *Enrollment:* 712 full-time matriculated graduate/professional students (337 women), 205 part-time matriculated graduate/professional students (141 women). *Graduate faculty:* 15 full-time (5 women), 175 part-time/adjunct (57 women). *Computer facilities:* 151 computers available on campus for general student use. A campuswide network can be accessed from student residence rooms and from off campus. Internet access is available. *Library facilities:* Collins Library. *Graduate expenses:* Tuition: full-time $9,045; part-time $195 per credit. Required fees: $105; $105 per year. Tuition and fees vary according to course load and program.

Baker University (continued)
General application contact: Dr. Donald B. Clardy, Dean, School of Professional and Graduate Studies, 913-491-4432.

School of Professional and Graduate Studies
Dr. Donald B. Clardy, Dean
Programs in:
- business • MBA, MSM
- education • MA Ed, MASL
- liberal arts • MLA

■ BENEDICTINE COLLEGE
Atchison, KS 66002-1499
http://www.benedictine.edu/

Independent-religious, coed, comprehensive institution. *Enrollment:* 25 full-time matriculated graduate/professional students (2 women), 35 part-time matriculated graduate/professional students (18 women). *Graduate faculty:* 4 full-time (0 women), 9 part-time/adjunct (3 women). *Computer facilities:* 80 computers available on campus for general student use. A campuswide network can be accessed from student residence rooms and from off campus. Internet access is available. *Library facilities:* Benedictine College Library. *Graduate expenses:* Tuition: full-time $16,000. *General application contact:* Kelly Vowels, Dean of Enrollment Management, 913-367-5340 Ext. 2476.

Executive Master of Business Administration Program
Carol Shomin, Chair
Program in:
- executive business administration • EMBA

Program in Educational Administration
Dr. Dianna Henderson, Director
Program in:
- educational administration • MA

■ EMPORIA STATE UNIVERSITY
Emporia, KS 66801-5087
http://www.emporia.edu/

State-supported, coed, comprehensive institution. CGS member. *Enrollment:* 305 full-time matriculated graduate/professional students (184 women), 559 part-time matriculated graduate/professional students (408 women). *Graduate faculty:* 204 full-time (62 women), 79 part-time/adjunct (48 women). *Computer facilities:* 283 computers available on campus for general student use. A campuswide network can be accessed from student residence rooms and from off campus. Internet access and online class registration, various software packages are available. *Library facilities:* William Allen White Library. *Graduate expenses:* Part-time $115 per credit hour. Tuition, state resident: full-time $2,556; part-time $282 per credit hour. Tuition, nonresident: full-time $6,572. *General application contact:* Heather Mc Murphey, Admissions Coordinator, 800-950-GRAD.

Find an in-depth description at www.petersons.com/graduate.

School of Graduate Studies
Dr. Timothy M. Downs, Dean, School of Graduate Studies

College of Liberal Arts and Sciences
Dr. Lendley C. Black, Dean
Programs in:
- American history • MAT
- anthropology • MAT
- botany • MS
- chemistry • MS
- earth science • MS
- economics • MAT
- English • MA
- environmental biology • MS
- general biology • MS
- geography • MAT
- history • MA
- liberal arts and sciences • MA, MAT, MM, MS
- mathematics • MS
- microbial and cellular biology • MS
- music education • MM
- performance • MM
- physical science • MS
- physics • MS
- political science • MAT
- social sciences • MAT
- social studies education • MAT
- sociology • MAT
- world history • MAT
- zoology • MS

School of Business
Dr. Sajjad Hashmi, Dean
Programs in:
- business • MBA, MS
- business administration • MBA
- business education • MS

School of Library and Information Management
Dr. Robert J. Grover, Dean
Programs in:
- library and information science • PhD
- library science • MLS

The Teachers College
Dr. Teresa Mehring, Dean
Programs in:
- art therapy • MS
- behavior disorders • MS
- clinical psychology • MS
- counselor education • MS
- curriculum and instruction • MS
- early childhood education • MS
- education • MS, Ed S
- educational administration • MS
- elementary education • MS
- general psychology • MS
- gifted, talented, and creative • MS
- health, physical education and recreation • MS
- industrial/organizational psychology • MS
- instructional design and technology • MS
- interrelated special education • MS
- learning disabilities • MS
- mental health counseling • MS
- mental retardation • MS
- psychology • MS
- rehabilitation counseling • MS
- school counseling • MS
- school psychology • MS, Ed S
- secondary education • MS
- special education • MS
- student personnel • MS

■ FORT HAYS STATE UNIVERSITY
Hays, KS 67601-4099
http://www.fhsu.edu/

State-supported, coed, comprehensive institution. CGS member. *Enrollment:* 154 full-time matriculated graduate/professional students (90 women), 495 part-time matriculated graduate/professional students (356 women). *Graduate faculty:* 126 full-time (32 women). *Computer facilities:* 550 computers available on campus for general student use. A campuswide network can be accessed from student residence rooms and from off campus. Internet access is available. *Library facilities:* Forsyth Library. *Graduate expenses:* Tuition, state resident: part-time $101 per credit hour. Tuition, nonresident: part-time $268 per credit hour. *General application contact:* Dr. Tom Jackson, Dean of the Graduate School, 785-628-4236.

Graduate School
Dr. Tom Jackson, Dean

College of Arts and Sciences
Dr. Paul Faber, Interim Dean
Programs in:

arts and sciences • MA, MAT, MFA, MLS, MS, Ed S
communication • MS
English • MA
geology • MS
history • MA
liberal studies • MLS
mathematics • MAT
psychology • MS
school psychology • Ed S
studio art • MFA

College of Business and Leadership
Dr. Richard Peters, Dean
Programs in:
accounting • MBA
business • MBA
computer information systems • MBA
economics • MBA
finance • MBA

College of Education
Dr. Tom Buttery, Dean
Programs in:
counseling • MS
education • MS, Ed S
education administration • MS, Ed S
elementary education • MS
instructional technology • MS
secondary education • MS
special education • MS

College of Health and Life Sciences
Dr. Tony Fernandez, Dean
Programs in:
biology • MS
health and life sciences • MS, MSN
health, physical education, and recreation • MS
nursing • MSN
speech-language pathology • MS

■ FRIENDS UNIVERSITY

Wichita, KS 67213
http://www.friends.edu/

Independent, coed, comprehensive institution. *Enrollment:* 623 matriculated graduate/professional students. *Graduate faculty:* 61. *Computer facilities:* 190 computers available on campus for general student use. A campuswide network can be accessed from student residence rooms and from off campus. *Library facilities:* Edmund Stanley Library plus 3 others. *Graduate expenses:* Tuition: part-time $412 per credit hour. Tuition and fees vary according to campus/location and program. *General application contact:* Tony Myers.

Graduate Programs
Dr. G. Robert Dove, Vice President of Academic Affairs

College of Arts and Sciences
Programs in:
arts and sciences • MACM, MAT, MSES, MSFT, MSL
Christian ministries • MACM
elementary education • MAT
environmental studies • MSES
family therapy • MSFT
school leadership • MSL
secondary education • MAT

College of Business
Dr. Al Saber, Dean
Programs in:
business • EMBA, MMIS, MSM
executive business administration • EMBA
management • MSM
management information systems • MMIS

College of Continuing Education
Dean
Program in:
human resource development/occupational development • MHRDOD

■ KANSAS STATE UNIVERSITY

Manhattan, KS 66506
http://www.ksu.edu/

State-supported, coed, university. CGS member. *Enrollment:* 3,681 matriculated graduate/professional students (2,076 women). *Graduate faculty:* 1,100. *Computer facilities:* 556 computers available on campus for general student use. A campuswide network can be accessed from student residence rooms and from off campus. Internet access and online class registration are available. *Library facilities:* Hale Library plus 3 others. *Graduate expenses:* Tuition, state resident: part-time $110 per credit hour. Tuition, nonresident: part-time $350 per credit hour. Required fees: $257 per semester. Tuition and fees vary according to course level, course load and degree level. *General application contact:* Dr. James Guikema, Associate Dean, 785-532-7927.

Find an in-depth description at www.petersons.com/graduate.

College of Veterinary Medicine
Ralph Richardson, Dean
Programs in:
anatomy • MS
anatomy and physiology • MS, PhD
clinical sciences • MS
diagnostic medicine/pathobiology • MS, PhD
physiology • MS, PhD
veterinary medicine • DVM, MS, PhD
veterinary medicine and surgery • MS

Graduate School
Ron Trewyn, Dean
Programs in:
food science • MS, PhD
genetics • MS, PhD

College of Agriculture
Marc Johnson, Dean
Programs in:
agricultural economics • MAB, MS, PhD
agriculture • MAB, MS, PhD
animal nutrition • MS, PhD
animal reproduction • MS, PhD
animal sciences and industry • MS, PhD
crop science • MS, PhD
entomology • MS, PhD
genetics • MS, PhD
grain science and industry • MS, PhD
horticulture • MS, PhD
meat science • MS, PhD
plant pathology • MS, PhD
range management • MS, PhD
soil science • MS, PhD
weed science • MS, PhD

College of Architecture, Planning and Design
Dennis Law, Dean
Programs in:
architecture • M Arch
architecture, planning and design • M Arch, MA, MLA, MRCP
environmental planning and management • MA
landscape architecture • MLA
regional and community planning • MRCP

College of Arts and Sciences
Peter Nicholls, Dean
Programs in:
analytical chemistry • MS
art • MFA
arts and sciences • MA, MFA, MM, MPA, MS, PhD
biochemistry • MS, PhD
cell biology • MS, PhD
chemistry • PhD
developmental biology and physiology • MS, PhD
economics • MA, PhD
English • MA
French • MA
geography • MA, PhD
geology • MS
German • MA
history • MA, PhD
inorganic chemistry • MS
international relations • MA

Kansas State University (continued)
kinesiology • MS
mass communications • MS
mathematics • MS, PhD
microbiology and immunology • MS, PhD
molecular biology and genetics • MS, PhD
music education • MM
music history and literature • MM
organic chemistry • MS
performance • MM
performance with pedagogy emphasis • MM
physical chemistry • MS
physics • MS, PhD
political science • MA
psychology • MS, PhD
public administration • MPA
sociology • MA, PhD
Spanish • MA
speech • MA
statistics • MS, PhD
systematics and ecology • MS, PhD
theory and composition • MM
virology and oncology • MS, PhD

College of Business Administration
Yar M. Ebadi, Interim Dean
Programs in:
accounting • M Acc
business administration • M Acc, MBA

College of Education
Michael Holen, Dean
Programs in:
counselor education • Ed D, PhD
curriculum and instruction • Ed D, PhD
education • MS, Ed D, PhD
educational administration and leadership • MS, Ed D
educational psychology • Ed D
elementary education • MS
foundations and adult education • MS, Ed D, PhD
school counseling • MS
secondary education • MS
special education • MS, Ed D
student affairs in higher education • PhD
student personnel services • MS

College of Engineering
Terry S. King, Dean
Programs in:
architectural engineering • MS
bioengineering • MS, PhD
biological and agricultural engineering • MS, PhD
chemical engineering • MS, PhD
civil engineering • MS, PhD
communications • MS, PhD
computer engineering • MS, PhD
computer science • MS, PhD
control systems • MS, PhD
electric energy systems • MS, PhD
engineering • PhD
engineering management • MEM
industrial and manufacturing systems engineering • PhD
industrial engineering • MS
instrumentation • MS, PhD
mechanical engineering • MS
nuclear engineering • MS
operations research • MS
signal processing • MS, PhD
software engineering • MSE

College of Human Ecology
Dr. Carol Kellett, Dean
Programs in:
apparel and textiles • MS
dietetics • MS
family studies and human services • MS
food science • MS, PhD
food service and hospitality management • MS, PhD
human ecology • PhD
nutrition • MS, PhD

■ MIDAMERICA NAZARENE UNIVERSITY
Olathe, KS 66062-1899
http://www.mnu.edu/

Independent-religious, coed, comprehensive institution. *Enrollment:* 185 full-time matriculated graduate/professional students (116 women). *Graduate faculty:* 23 full-time, 14 part-time/adjunct. *Computer facilities:* 85 computers available on campus for general student use. A campuswide network can be accessed from student residence rooms and from off campus. Internet access is available. *Library facilities:* Mabee Library. *Graduate expenses:* Tuition: full-time $13,400. Required fees: $652. Full-time tuition and fees vary according to program. *General application contact:* Gina Harvey, Secretary, Graduate Studies in Management, 913-782-3276.

Find an in-depth description at www.petersons.com/graduate.

Graduate Studies in Counseling
Roy Rotz, Director
Program in:
counseling • MAC

Graduate Studies in Education
Dr. Jim Burns, Director
Programs in:
curriculum and instruction • M Ed
educational technology • M Ed

Graduate Studies in Management
Dr. Mary E. Jones, Director
Program in:
management • MBA

■ NEWMAN UNIVERSITY
Wichita, KS 67213-2097
http://www.newmanu.edu/

Independent-religious, coed, comprehensive institution. *Computer facilities:* 90 computers available on campus for general student use. *Library facilities:* Ryan Library. *General application contact:* Coordinator of Graduate Admissions, 316-942-4291 Ext. 355.

Division of Nursing
Programs in:
nurse anesthesia • MS
nursing • MS

Graduate School of Social Work
Program in:
social work • MSW

Masters in Business Administration
Program in:
organizational leadership • MS

Program in Education
Programs in:
adult education • MS Ed
building leadership • MS Ed
elementary/middle-level education • MS Ed
English as a second language • MS Ed

■ PITTSBURG STATE UNIVERSITY
Pittsburg, KS 66762
http://www.pittstate.edu/

State-supported, coed, comprehensive institution. CGS member. *Enrollment:* 331 full-time matriculated graduate/professional students (160 women), 865 part-time matriculated graduate/professional students (544 women). *Graduate faculty:* 288 full-time (106 women), 76 part-time/adjunct (32 women). *Computer facilities:* 213 computers available on campus for general student use. A campuswide network can be accessed from student residence rooms and from off campus. Internet access and online class registration are available. *Library facilities:* Leonard H. Axe Library plus 2 others. *Graduate expenses:* Tuition, state resident: full-time $1,302; part-time $111 per credit hour.

Tuition, nonresident: full-time $3,310; part-time $278 per credit hour. *General application contact:* Marvene Darraugh, Administrative Officer, 316-235-4220.

Graduate School

Dr. Oliver Hensley, Dean of Graduate Studies and Research

College of Arts and Sciences
Dr. Orville Brill, Dean
Programs in:
- applied communication • MA
- applied physics • MS
- art education • MA
- arts and sciences • MA, MM, MS, MSN
- biology • MS
- chemistry • MS
- communication education • MA
- English • MA
- history • MA
- instrumental music education • MM
- mathematics • MS
- music history/music literature • MM
- nursing • MSN
- performance • MM
- physics • MS
- professional physics • MS
- social science • MS
- studio art • MA
- theatre • MA
- theory and composition • MM
- vocal music education • MM

College of Education
Dr. Steve Scott, Dean
Programs in:
- behavioral disorders • MS
- classroom reading teacher • MS
- community college and higher education • Ed S
- counseling • MS
- counselor education • MS
- early childhood education • MS
- education • MS, Ed S
- educational leadership • MS, Ed S
- educational technology • MS
- elementary education • MS
- general school administration • Ed S
- learning disabilities • MS
- mentally retarded • MS
- physical education • MS
- psychology • MS
- reading • MS
- reading specialist • MS
- school psychology • Ed S
- secondary education • MS
- special education teaching • MS

College of Technology
Dr. Tom Baldwin, Dean
Programs in:
- engineering technology • MET
- human resource development and technical teacher education • MS
- industrial education • Ed S
- technology • MS
- technology education • MS

Kelce College of Business
Dr. Ronald Clement, Dean
Programs in:
- accounting • MBA
- business • MBA
- general administration • MBA

■ SAINT MARY COLLEGE
Leavenworth, KS 66048-5082
http://www.smcks.edu/

Independent-religious, coed, comprehensive institution. *Computer facilities:* 95 computers available on campus for general student use. A campuswide network can be accessed from student residence rooms. Internet access is available. *Library facilities:* De Paul Library. *General application contact:* Graduate Dean, 913-758-6158.

Graduate Programs

Programs in:
- business administration • MBA
- curriculum and instruction • MA
- education • MA
- management • MS
- psychology • MA
- teaching • MA

■ UNIVERSITY OF KANSAS
Lawrence, KS 66045
http://www.ku.edu

State-supported, coed, university. CGS member. *Enrollment:* 4,185 full-time matriculated graduate/professional students (2,240 women), 2,687 part-time matriculated graduate/professional students (1,502 women). *Graduate faculty:* 1,192 full-time (352 women), 124 part-time/adjunct (52 women). *Computer facilities:* 938 computers available on campus for general student use. A campuswide network can be accessed from student residence rooms and from off campus. Internet access is available. *Library facilities:* Watson Library plus 11 others. *Graduate expenses:* Part-time $110 per credit hour. Tuition, state resident: full-time $2,644; part-time $110 per credit hour. Tuition, nonresident: full-time $8,406; part-time $350 per credit hour. Required fees: $458; $33 per credit hour. Tuition and fees vary according to course load, campus/location and program. *General application contact:* 785-864-4141.

Graduate School

Dana Carlin, Dean

College of Liberal Arts and Sciences
Kathleen McCluskey-Fawcett, Interim Dean
Programs in:
- American studies • MA, PhD
- anthropology • MA, PhD
- applied mathematics and statistics • MA, PhD
- biochemistry and biophysics • MA, MS, PhD
- biological sciences • MA, MS, PhD
- chemistry • MS, PhD
- child language • MA, PhD
- classics • MA
- clinical child psychology • MA, PhD
- communication studies • MA, PhD
- computational physics and astronomy • MS
- developmental and child psychology • PhD
- early childhood education • MA, PhD
- East Asian languages and cultures • MA
- economics • MA, PhD
- English • MA, PhD
- French • MA, PhD
- geography • MA, PhD
- geology • MS, PhD
- German • MA, PhD
- gerontology • MA, PhD
- historical administration and museum studies • MHAMS
- history • MA, PhD
- history of art • MA, PhD
- human development • MA, MHD
- indigenous nations studies • MA
- Latin American studies • MA
- liberal arts and sciences • MA, MHAMS, MHD, MPA, MS, PhD
- linguistics • MA, PhD
- mathematics • MA, PhD
- microbiology • MA, MS, PhD
- molecular, cellular, and developmental biology • MA, MS, PhD
- philosophy • MA, PhD
- physics • MS, PhD
- political science • MA, PhD
- psychology • MA, PhD
- public administration • MPA
- religious studies • MA
- Russian and East European studies • MA
- Slavic languages and literatures • MA, PhD
- sociology • MA, PhD
- Spanish • MA, PhD
- speech-language-hearing: sciences and disorders • MA, PhD
- theatre and film • MA, PhD

School of Architecture and Urban Design
John Gaunt, Dean
Programs in:
- architecture • M Arch

University of Kansas (continued)
architecture and urban design • M Arch, MUP
urban planning • MUP

School of Business
William L. Fuerst, Dean
Programs in:
accounting and information systems • MAIS, PhD
business • MAIS, MBA, MS, PhD
business administration • MBA, MS

School of Education
Angela Lumpkin, Dean
Programs in:
counseling psychology • MS, PhD
curriculum and instruction • MA, MS Ed, Ed D, PhD
education • MA, MS, MS Ed, Ed D, PhD, Ed S
educational administration • MS Ed
educational policy and leadership • MS Ed, Ed D, PhD
educational psychology and research • MS Ed, PhD
foundations of education • MS Ed
health education • MS Ed
higher education • MS Ed
physical education • MS Ed, Ed D, PhD
school psychology • PhD, Ed S
special education • MS Ed, Ed D, PhD

School of Engineering
Carl E. Locke, Dean
Programs in:
aerospace engineering • ME, MS, DE, PhD
architectural engineering • MS
chemical engineering • MS
chemical/petroleum engineering • PhD
civil engineering • MS, DE, PhD
computer engineering • MS
computer science • MS, PhD
construction management • MS
electrical engineering • MS, DE, PhD
engineering • ME, MS, DE, PhD
engineering management • MS
environmental engineering • MS, PhD
environmental science • MS, PhD
mechanical engineering • MS, DE, PhD
petroleum engineering • MS
water resources engineering • MS
water resources science • MS

School of Fine Arts
Toni-Marie Montgomery, Dean
Programs in:
art • MFA
church music • MM, DMA
composition • MM, DMA
conducting • MM, DMA
design • MFA
fine arts • MA, MFA, MM, MME, DMA, PhD
music education • PhD
music education and music therapy • MME, PhD
music theory • MM, PhD
musicology • MM, PhD
opera • MM
performance • MM, DMA
visual arts education • MA

School of Journalism and Mass Communications
James Gentry, Dean
Program in:
journalism • MS

School of Pharmacy
Jack Fincham, Dean
Programs in:
medicinal chemistry • MS, PhD
pharmaceutical chemistry • MS, PhD
pharmacology • MS, PhD
pharmacy • MS, PhD
pharmacy practice • MS
toxicology • MS, PhD

Graduate Studies Medical Center
Dr. Allen Rawitch, Vice Chancellor for Academic Affairs and Dean of Graduate Studies
Programs in:
anatomy and cell biology • MA, PhD
anthropology • MA, PhD
biochemistry and molecular biology • MS, PhD
biomedical and basic sciences • MA, MPH, MS, PhD
health policy management • MHSA
microbiology, molecular genetics and immunology • PhD
molecular and integrative physiology • MS, PhD
pathology and laboratory medicine • MA, PhD
pharmacology • MS, PhD
preventive medicine • MPH
toxicology • MS, PhD

School of Allied Health
Dr. Karen L. Miller, Dean
Programs in:
allied health • MA, MS, PhD
audiology • MA, PhD
dietetics and nutrition • MS
education of the deaf • MS
nurse anesthesia education • MS
occupational therapy education • MS
physical therapy education • MS
speech and hearing science • PhD
speech-language pathology • MA, PhD

School of Nursing
Dr. Karen L. Miller, Dean
Program in:
nursing • MS, PhD

School of Law
Stephen R. McAllister, Dean
Program in:
law • JD

School of Medicine
Dr. Deborah Powell, Executive Dean
Program in:
medicine • MD

School of Social Welfare
Ann Weick, Dean
Program in:
social welfare • MSW, PhD

■ WASHBURN UNIVERSITY OF TOPEKA

Topeka, KS 66621
http://www.washburn.edu/

City-supported, coed, comprehensive institution. *Enrollment:* 615 full-time matriculated graduate/professional students (336 women), 414 part-time matriculated graduate/professional students (238 women). *Graduate faculty:* 76 full-time (27 women), 44 part-time/adjunct (10 women). *Computer facilities:* 200 computers available on campus for general student use. A campuswide network can be accessed from off campus. Internet access and online class registration are available. *Library facilities:* Mabee Library plus 2 others. *Graduate expenses:* Tuition, state resident: part-time $145 per credit hour. Tuition, nonresident: part-time $274 per credit hour. Required fees: $14 per semester. *General application contact:* Nancy Tate, Interim Dean, 785-231-1010 Ext. 1561.

College of Arts and Sciences
Nancy Tate, Interim Dean
Programs in:
arts and sciences • M Ed, MA, MLS
clinical psychology • MA
curriculum and instruction • M Ed
educational administration • M Ed
liberal studies • MLS
reading • M Ed
special education • M Ed

School of Business
Dr. Juli Ann Mazachek, Dean
Program in:
business • MBA

School of Law
Dennis R. Honabach, Dean
Program in:
law • JD

■ WICHITA STATE UNIVERSITY

Wichita, KS 67260
http://www.wichita.edu/

State-supported, coed, university. CGS member. *Enrollment:* 1,009 full-time matriculated graduate/professional students (464 women), 1,873 part-time matriculated graduate/professional students (1,086 women). *Graduate faculty:* 440 full-time (156 women), 39 part-time/adjunct (22 women). *Computer facilities:* 1,500 computers available on campus for general student use. A campuswide network can be accessed from student residence rooms and from off campus. Internet access is available. *Library facilities:* Ablah Library plus 2 others. *Graduate expenses:* Part-time $629 per term. Tuition, state resident: full-time $1,888. Tuition, nonresident: full-time $6,129; part-time $2,043 per term. Required fees: $345; $115 per term. $17 per term. Tuition and fees vary according to course load. *General application contact:* Dr. Susan K. Kovar, Dean of the Graduate School, 316-978-3095.

Find an in-depth description at www.petersons.com/graduate.

Graduate School

Dr. Susan K. Kovar, Dean of the Graduate School

College of Education
Dr. Jon Engelhardt, Dean
Programs in:
- communications sciences • MA, PhD
- counseling • M Ed
- curriculum and instruction • M Ed
- education • M Ed, MA, Ed D, PhD, Ed S
- education administration • M Ed, Ed D
- educational psychology • M Ed
- physical education • M Ed
- school psychology • Ed S
- special education • M Ed
- sports administration • M Ed

College of Engineering
Dr. Dennis Siginer, Dean
Programs in:
- aerospace engineering • MS, PhD
- electrical engineering • MS, PhD
- engineering • MEM, MS, PhD
- industrial and manufacturing engineering • MEM, MS, PhD
- mechanical engineering • MS, PhD

College of Fine Arts
Dr. Walter Myers, Dean
Programs in:
- art education • MA
- fine arts • MA, MFA, MM, MME
- music • MM
- music education • MME
- studio arts • MFA

College of Health Professions
Dr. Peter A. Cohen, Dean
Programs in:
- clinical specialization • MSN
- health professions • MPH, MPT, MSN
- health sciences • MPH, MPT
- nursing administration • MSN
- physical therapy • MPT
- public health • MPH
- teaching of nursing • MSN

Fairmount College of Liberal Arts and Sciences
Dr. David C. Glenn-Lewin, Dean
Programs in:
- anthropology • MA
- applied mathematics • PhD
- biological sciences • MS
- chemistry • MS, PhD
- communication • MA
- community/clinical psychology • PhD
- computer science • MS
- creative writing • MA, MFA
- criminal justice • MA
- English • MA, MFA
- environmental science • MS
- geology • MS
- gerontology • MA
- history • MA
- human factors • PhD
- liberal arts and sciences • MA, MFA, MPA, MS, MSW, PhD
- liberal studies • MA
- mathematics • MS
- physics • MS
- political science • MA
- public administration • MPA
- social work • MSW
- sociology • MA
- Spanish • MA
- statistics • MS

W. Frank Barton School of Business
Dr. John Beehler, Dean
Programs in:
- accountancy • MPA
- business • EMBA, MBA, MS
- business economics • MA
- economic analysis • MA
- economics • MA
- professional accountancy • MPA

Kentucky

■ BELLARMINE UNIVERSITY

Louisville, KY 40205-0671
http://www.bellarmine.edu/

Independent-religious, coed, comprehensive institution. *Computer facilities:* 160 computers available on campus for general student use. A campuswide network can be accessed from student residence rooms. Internet access is available. *Library facilities:* W.L. Lyons Brown Library. *General application contact:* Registrar, 502-452-8133.

Allan and Donna Lansing School of Nursing and Health Sciences
Programs in:
- advanced community health nursing • MSN
- nursing administration • MSN
- nursing and health sciences • MSN
- nursing education • MSN

College of Education
Programs in:
- early elementary education • MA, MAT
- elementary education • MA
- learning and behavior disorders • MA
- middle school education • MA, MAT

W. Fielding Rubel School of Business
Program in:
- business • EMBA, MBA

■ CAMPBELLSVILLE UNIVERSITY

Campbellsville, KY 42718-2799
http://www.campbellsvil.edu/

Independent-religious, coed, comprehensive institution. *Enrollment:* 17 full-time matriculated graduate/professional students (5 women), 84 part-time matriculated graduate/professional students (43 women). *Graduate faculty:* 25 full-time (5 women), 9 part-time/adjunct (0 women). *Computer facilities:* 120 computers available on campus for general student use. Internet access is available. *Library facilities:* Montgomery Library plus 2 others. *Graduate expenses:* Tuition: full-time $5,850; part-time $325 per credit. Required fees: $70; $35 per unit. *General application contact:* Trent Argo, Director of Admissions, 270-789-5220.

Campbellsville University (continued)
College of Arts and Sciences
Mary Wilgus

School of Business Administration
Dr. Barry Griffin, MBA Director
Program in:
business administration • MBA

School of Education
Dr. James E. Pirkle, Dean
Program in:
education • MA Ed

School of Music
Dr. J. Robert Gaddis, Dean
Programs in:
church music • MM
music • MA
music education • MM

School of Theology
Dr. Walter C. Jackson, Dean
Programs in:
Christian studies • MA
theology • M Th

■ CUMBERLAND COLLEGE
Williamsburg, KY 40769-1372
http://cc.cumber.edu/

Independent-religious, coed, comprehensive institution. *Computer facilities:* 300 computers available on campus for general student use. A campuswide network can be accessed from student residence rooms and from off campus. Internet access and online class registration are available. *Library facilities:* Norma Perkins Hagan Memorial Library. *General application contact:* Director, Graduate Programs in Education, 606-549-2200 Ext. 4432.

Graduate Programs in Education
Programs in:
early childhood education • MA Ed
early elementary K-4 • MA Ed
elementary education • MA Ed
elementary/secondary principalship • Certificate
elementary/secondary teaching • Certificate
middle school 5-8 • MA Ed
middle school education • MA Ed
reading specialist • MA Ed
secondary general education • MA Ed
special education • MA Ed

■ EASTERN KENTUCKY UNIVERSITY
Richmond, KY 40475-3102
http://www.eku.edu/

State-supported, coed, comprehensive institution. CGS member. *Computer facilities:* 500 computers available on campus for general student use. Internet access is available. *Library facilities:* John Grant Crabbe Library plus 2 others. *General application contact:* Acting Dean, 859-622-1744.

The Graduate School

College of Allied Health and Nursing
Programs in:
allied health and nursing • MS, MSN
occupational therapy • MS
rural community health care • MSN
rural health family nurse practitioner • MSN

College of Applied Arts and Technology
Programs in:
applied arts and technology • MS
community nutrition • MS
industrial education • MS
industrial training • MS
manufacturing technology • MS
technology education • MS
vocational administration • MS

College of Arts and Humanities
Programs in:
arts and humanities • MA, MM
choral conducting • MM
English • MA
performance • MM
theory/composition • MM

College of Business and Technology
Program in:
business • MBA

College of Education
Programs in:
administration and supervision • Ed S
agricultural education • MA Ed
allied health sciences education • MA Ed
art education • MA Ed
biological sciences education • MA Ed
business education • MA Ed
chemistry education • MA Ed
communication disorders • MA Ed
community counseling • MA
earth science education • MA Ed
education • MA, MA Ed, Ed S
elementary counseling • MA Ed
elementary education general • MA Ed
English education • MA Ed
general science education • MA Ed
geography education • MA Ed
history education • MA Ed
home economics education • MA Ed
industrial education • MA Ed
mathematical sciences education • MA Ed
music education • MA Ed
physical education • MA Ed
physics education • MA Ed
political science education • MA Ed
psychology education • MA Ed
reading • MA Ed
school health education • MA Ed
secondary and higher education • MA Ed
secondary counseling • MA Ed
sociology education • MA Ed
special education • MA Ed
student personnel counseling • MA, Ed S

College of Health, Physical Education, Recreation and Athletics
Programs in:
health, physical education, recreation and athletics • MS
physical education • MS
recreation and park administration • MS
sports administration • MS

College of Law Enforcement
Programs in:
corrections and juvenile services • MS
criminal justice • MS
criminal justice education • MS
law enforcement • MS
loss prevention administration • MS
police studies • MS

College of Natural and Mathematical Sciences
Programs in:
biological sciences • MS
chemistry • MS
ecology • MS
geology • MS, PhD
mathematical sciences • MS
natural and mathematical sciences • MS, PhD

College of Social and Behavioral Sciences
Programs in:
clinical psychology • MS
community development • MPA
community health administration • MPA
general public administration • MPA
history • MA
political science • MA
school psychology • Psy S
social and behavioral sciences • MA, MPA, MS, Psy S

■ KENTUCKY STATE UNIVERSITY

Frankfort, KY 40601

http://www.kysu.edu/

State-related, coed, comprehensive institution. *Enrollment:* 46 full-time matriculated graduate/professional students (24 women), 60 part-time matriculated graduate/professional students (30 women). *Graduate faculty:* 6 full-time (0 women). *Computer facilities:* 230 computers available on campus for general student use. A campuswide network can be accessed from off campus. Internet access, e-mail are available. *Library facilities:* Blazer Library. *Graduate expenses:* Tuition, state resident: full-time $2,308; part-time $135 per credit hour. Tuition, nonresident: full-time $6,926; part-time $392 per credit hour. Required fees: $30 per semester. *General application contact:* Cornelia F. Calhoun, Assistant to the Dean, 502-597-6117 Ext. 6105.

College of Arts and Sciences
Dr. Paul Bibbins, Dean
Program in:
- aquaculture • MS

School of Public Administration
Dr. Gashaw Lake, Dean
Program in:
- public administration • MPA

■ MOREHEAD STATE UNIVERSITY

Morehead, KY 40351

http://www.moreheadstate.edu/

State-supported, coed, comprehensive institution. CGS member. *Enrollment:* 189 full-time matriculated graduate/professional students (103 women), 692 part-time matriculated graduate/professional students (483 women). *Graduate faculty:* 139 full-time (46 women). *Computer facilities:* 1,000 computers available on campus for general student use. A campuswide network can be accessed from student residence rooms and from off campus. Internet access and online class registration are available. *Library facilities:* Camden Carroll Library. *Graduate expenses:* Tuition, state resident: full-time $1,355; part-time $156 per hour. Tuition, nonresident: full-time $3,645; part-time $405 per hour. *General application contact:* Betty R. Cowsert, Graduate Admissions/Records Manager, 606-783-2039.

Graduate Programs
Dr. Marc Glasser, Dean of Graduate and Undergraduate Programs

Caudill College of Humanities
Dr. Lemuel Berry, Dean
Programs in:
- advertising/publications • MA
- art education • MA
- electronic media • MA
- English • MA
- humanities • MA, MM
- journalism • MA
- music education • MM
- music performance • MM
- speech • MA
- studio art • MA
- theatre • MA

College of Business
Dr. Robert L. Albert, Dean
Program in:
- business • MBA

College of Education and Behavioral Sciences
Dr. Michael Seelig, Interim Dean
Programs in:
- adult and higher education • MA, Ed S
- clinical psychology • MA
- counseling psychology • MA
- criminology • MA
- curriculum and instruction • Ed S
- education and behavioral sciences • MA, MA Ed, MS, Ed S
- elementary education • MA Ed
- exercise physiology • MA
- experimental/general psychology • MA
- general sociology • MA
- guidance and counseling • MA Ed, Ed S
- health, physical education and recreation • MA
- instructional leadership • Ed S
- middle school education • MA Ed
- reading • MA Ed
- recreation and sports administration • MA
- school administration • MA
- secondary education • MA Ed
- social gerontology • MA
- special education • MA Ed

College of Science and Technology
Dr. Gerald DeMoss, Dean
Programs in:
- biology • MS
- science and technology • MS
- vocational education/technology • MS

■ MURRAY STATE UNIVERSITY

Murray, KY 42071-0009

http://www.murraystate.edu/

State-supported, coed, comprehensive institution. CGS member. *Enrollment:* 439 full-time matriculated graduate/professional students (256 women), 1,225 part-time matriculated graduate/professional students (886 women). *Graduate faculty:* 319 full-time (77 women). *Computer facilities:* 1,500 computers available on campus for general student use. A campuswide network can be accessed from student residence rooms and from off campus. Internet access is available. *Library facilities:* Harry Lee Waterfield Library plus 1 other. *Graduate expenses:* Tuition, state resident: full-time $2,674; part-time $156 per hour. Tuition, nonresident: full-time $7,446; part-time $418 per hour. *General application contact:* Dr. Sandra Flynn, University Coordinator of Graduate Studies, 270-762-3895.

Find an in-depth description at www.petersons.com/graduate.

College of Business and Public Affairs
Dr. Dannie Harrison, Dean
Programs in:
- business administration • MBA
- business and public affairs • MA, MBA, MPA, MS
- economics • MS
- mass communications • MA, MS
- organizational communication • MA, MS
- public affairs • MPA
- telecommunications systems management • MS

College of Education
Dr. Jack Rose, Dean
Programs in:
- adolescent, career and special education • MA, MA Ed, MS, Ed S
- community and agency counseling • Ed S
- early childhood education • MS
- education • MA, MA Ed, MS, Ed D, PhD, Ed S
- elementary education • MA Ed, Ed S
- guidance and counseling • MA Ed, Ed S
- health, physical education, and recreation • MA
- human services • MS
- industrial and technical education • MS
- learning disabilities • MA Ed

Murray State University (continued)
- middle school education • MA Ed, Ed S
- physical education • MA
- reading and writing • MA Ed
- school administration • MA Ed, Ed S
- secondary education • MA Ed, Ed S
- special education • MA Ed

College of Health Sciences and Human Services
Dr. Elizabeth Blodgett, Dean
Programs in:
- health sciences and human services • MA, MS, MSN
- nursing • MSN
- occupational safety and health • MS
- recreation and leisure services • MA
- speech language pathology • MS

College of Humanities and Fine Arts
Dr. Sandra Jordan, Dean
Programs in:
- clinical psychology • MA, MS
- English • MA
- history • MA
- humanities and fine arts • MA, MME, MS
- music education • MME
- psychology • MA, MS
- teaching English to speakers of other languages • MA

College of Science, Engineering and Technology
Dr. John Mateja, Dean
Programs in:
- biological sciences • MAT, MS, PhD
- chemistry • MAT, MS
- geosciences • MA, MS
- management of technology • MS
- mathematics • MA, MAT, MS
- science, engineering and technology • MA, MAT, MS, PhD
- water science • MS

School of Agriculture
Dr. James Rudolph, Head
Program in:
- agriculture • MS

■ NORTHERN KENTUCKY UNIVERSITY

Highland Heights, KY 41099
http://www.nku.edu/

State-supported, coed, comprehensive institution. *Enrollment:* 266 full-time matriculated graduate/professional students (131 women), 774 part-time matriculated graduate/professional students (479 women). *Graduate faculty:* 91 full-time (47 women). *Computer facilities:* 600 computers available on campus for general student use. A campuswide network can be accessed from student residence rooms and from off campus. Internet access and online class registration are available. *Library facilities:* Steely Library plus 2 others. *Graduate expenses:* Tuition, state resident: full-time $2,760; part-time $138 per semester hour. Tuition, nonresident: full-time $7,440; part-time $398 per semester hour. *General application contact:* Peg Griffin, Graduate Coordinator, 859-572-6364.

Salmon P. Chase College of Law
Prof. Gerald A. St. Amand, Dean
Program in:
- law • JD

School of Graduate Programs
Dr. Paul Reichardt, Associate Provost
Programs in:
- accountancy • M Acct
- business administration • MBA
- elementary education • MA Ed
- middle school education • MA Ed
- nursing • MSN
- public administration • MPA
- secondary education • MA Ed
- technology • MST

■ SPALDING UNIVERSITY

Louisville, KY 40203-2188
http://www.spalding.edu/

Independent-religious, coed, comprehensive institution. CGS member. *Computer facilities:* 80 computers available on campus for general student use. A campuswide network can be accessed. Internet access is available. *Library facilities:* Spalding Library. *General application contact:* 502-585-7105.

Find an in-depth description at www.petersons.com/graduate.

Graduate Studies

College of Arts and Sciences
Programs in:
- arts and sciences • MA
- ministry studies • MA
- religious studies • MA

School of Education
Programs in:
- 5–8 • MA, MAT
- 9–12 • MA, MAT
- education • MA, MAT, Ed D
- guidance • MA
- K–4 • MA, MAT
- leadership education • Ed D
- reading specialist • MA
- school media librarianship • MA

School of Nursing and Health Sciences
Programs in:
- administration • MSN
- family nurse practitioner • MSN

School of Professional Psychology and Social Work
Programs in:
- clinical psychology • MA, Psy D
- psychology and social work • MA, MSW, Psy D
- social work • MSW

■ UNIVERSITY OF KENTUCKY

Lexington, KY 40506-0032
http://www.uky.edu/

State-supported, coed, university. CGS member. *Enrollment:* 3,780 full-time matriculated graduate/professional students (1,883 women), 2,752 part-time matriculated graduate/professional students (1,615 women). *Graduate faculty:* 1,373 full-time (305 women), 140 part-time/adjunct (11 women). *Computer facilities:* 1,400 computers available on campus for general student use. A campuswide network can be accessed from student residence rooms and from off campus. Internet access and online class registration, various software packages are available. *Library facilities:* William T. Young Library plus 15 others. *Graduate expenses:* Tuition, state resident: full-time $3,766; part-time $197 per hour. Tuition, nonresident: full-time $10,626; part-time $578 per hour. Required fees: $336; $6 per credit hour. *General application contact:* Dr. Constance L. Wood, Associate Dean, 606-257-4613.

Find an in-depth description at www.petersons.com/graduate.

College of Dentistry
Dr. Leon A. Assael, Dean
Program in:
- dentistry • DMD, MS

College of Law
Alla W. Vestal, Dean
Program in:
- law • JD

College of Medicine
Kimberly Scott, Head
Program in:
- medicine • MD, MPH, MS, Dr PH, PhD

College of Pharmacy
Dr. Kenneth B. Roberts, Dean
Programs in:
pharmaceutical sciences • MS, PhD
pharmacy • Pharm D, MS, PhD

Graduate School
Programs in:
anatomy and neurobiology • PhD
biomedical engineering • MSBE, PhD
dentistry • MS
gerontology • PhD
health administration • MHA
integrated biomedical sciences • MPH, Dr PH, PhD
microbiology and immunology • PhD
molecular and biomedical pharmacology • PhD
molecular and cellular biochemistry • PhD
nutritional sciences • PhD
physiology • PhD
public administration • MPA, PhD
public health • MPH, Dr PH
toxicology • MS, PhD

College of Architecture
Programs in:
architecture • MHP
historic preservation • MHP

College of Communications and Information Studies
Programs in:
communication • MA, PhD
communications and information studies • MA, MSLS, PhD
library science • MA, MSLS

College of Human Environmental Sciences
Programs in:
family studies • MSFAM
human environment: interior design, merchandising, and textiles • MAIDM, MAIND, MATEX, MSIDM
human environmental sciences • MAIDM, MAIND, MATEX, MS, MSFAM, MSIDM
nutrition and food science • MS

College of Nursing
Program in:
nursing • MSN, PhD

College of Social Work
Program in:
social work • MSW, PhD

Graduate School Programs from the College of Agriculture
Programs in:
agricultural economics • MS, PhD
agriculture • MS, MS Ag, MSFOR, PhD
animal sciences • MS, PhD
crop science • MS, MS Ag, PhD
entomology • MS, PhD
forestry • MSFOR
plant and soil science • MS
plant pathology • MS, PhD
plant physiology • PhD
soil science • PhD
veterinary science • MS, PhD

Graduate School Programs from the College of Allied Health
Programs in:
allied health • MSCD, MSCNU, MSHP, MSPT, MSRMP
clinical nutrition • MSCNU
communication disorders • MSCD
health physics • MSHP
physical therapy • MSPT
radiological medical physics • MSRMP

Graduate School Programs from the College of Arts and Sciences
Programs in:
anthropology • MA, PhD
arts and sciences • MA, MS, MS Ag, PhD
biological sciences • MS, PhD
chemistry • MS, PhD
classical languages and literatures • MA
English • MA, PhD
French • MA
geography • MA, PhD
geology • MS, PhD
German • MA
history • MA, PhD
mathematics • MA, MS, PhD
philosophy • MA, PhD
physics and astronomy • MS, PhD
political science • MA, PhD
psychology • MA, PhD
sociology • MA, MS Ag, PhD
Spanish • MA, PhD
statistics • MS, PhD

Graduate School Programs from the College of Business and Economics
Programs in:
accounting • MSACC
business administration • MBA, PhD
business and economics • MBA, MS, MSACC, PhD
economics • MS, PhD

Graduate School Programs from the College of Education
Programs in:
administration and supervision • Ed D, Ed S
clinical and college teaching • MS Ed
curriculum and instruction • Ed D
education • MA Ed, MRC, MS, MS Ed, MSVE, Ed D, PhD, Ed S
educational and counseling psychology • MA Ed, MS Ed, Ed D, PhD, Ed S
educational policy studies and evaluation • MS Ed, Ed D, PhD
instruction and administration • Ed D
kinesiology and health promotion • MS, Ed D
rehabilitation counseling • MRC
special education • MA Ed, MS Ed, Ed D, Ed S
vocational education • MA Ed, MS Ed, MSVE, Ed D, Ed S

Graduate School Programs from the College of Engineering
Programs in:
agricultural engineering • MSAE, PhD
chemical engineering • MS Ch E, PhD
civil engineering • MCE, MSCE, PhD
computer science • MS, PhD
electrical engineering • MSEE, PhD
engineering • M Eng, MCE, MME, MS, MS Ch E, MS Min, MSAE, MSCE, MSEE, MSEM, MSMAE, MSME, MSMSE, PhD
engineering mechanics • MSEM, PhD
manufacturing systems engineering • MSMSE
materials science • MSMAE, PhD
mechanical engineering • MSME, PhD
mining engineering • MME, MS Min, PhD

Graduate School Programs from the College of Fine Arts
Programs in:
art education • MA
art history • MA
art studio • MFA
fine arts • MA, MFA, MM, DMA, PhD
music • MA, MM, DMA, PhD
theatre • MA

Patterson School of Diplomacy and International Commerce
Program in:
diplomacy and international commerce • MA

■ UNIVERSITY OF LOUISVILLE

Louisville, KY 40292-0001
http://www.louisville.edu/

State-supported, coed, university. CGS member. *Computer facilities:* 250 computers available on campus for general student use. A campuswide network can be accessed from student residence rooms and from off campus. Internet

University of Louisville (continued)
access is available. *Library facilities:* William F. Ekstrom Library plus 5 others. *General application contact:* Director of Admissions, 502-852-6495.

Find an in-depth description at www.petersons.com/graduate.

Graduate School
Program in:
interdisciplinary studies • MA, MS

College of Arts and Sciences
Programs in:
analytical chemistry • MS, PhD
art history • MA, PhD
arts and sciences • MA, MFA, MS, PhD
biology • MS
chemical physics • PhD
clinical psychology • PhD
English • MA
English literature • MA
English rhetoric and composition • PhD
environmental biology • PhD
experimental psychology • PhD
fine arts • MA
foreign language education • MA
French • MA
German • MA
history • MA
humanities • MA
inorganic chemistry • MS, PhD
justice administration • MS
linguistics • MA
mathematics • MA
organic chemistry • MS, PhD
performance • MFA
philosophy • MA
physical chemistry • MS, PhD
physics • MS
political science • MA
production • MFA
psychology • MA
sociology • MA
Spanish • MA
theatre arts • MA

College of Business and Public Administration
Programs in:
business • MBA
business and public administration • MA, MBA, MPA, PhD
labor and public management • MPA
public administration • MPA
public policy • MPA
systems science • MA
urban and public affairs • PhD
urban and regional development • MPA

Raymond A. Kent School of Social Work
Program in:
social work • MSSW, PhD

School of Allied Health Sciences
Programs in:
allied health sciences • MA
expressive therapies • MA

School of Education
Programs in:
administration • Ed S
art education • M Ed
business education • MAT
college student personnel services • M Ed
community counseling • M Ed
counseling and student personnel • Ed D
early childhood education • M Ed
early elementary education • MAT
education • M Ed, MA, MAT, MS, Ed D, Ed S
educational administration • M Ed, Ed D
educational supervision • Ed D, Ed S
elementary education • M Ed, MA, MAT, Ed S
elementary school guidance • M Ed
exercise physiology • MS
guidance and personnel • Ed S
higher education • MA, Ed S
human resources development • M Ed
middle school education • M Ed
music education • MAT
physical education • M Ed, MAT
reading education • M Ed
secondary education • M Ed, MA, MAT, Ed S
secondary school guidance • M Ed
special education • M Ed, Ed D, Ed S
supervision of human resources development • Ed D

School of Music
Programs in:
music education • MAT, MME
music history • MA, MM, PhD
music literature • PhD
music performance • MM
music theory and composition • MM
musicology • PhD

School of Nursing
Program in:
nursing • MSN

Speed Scientific School
Programs in:
chemical engineering • M Eng, MS, PhD
civil and environmental engineering • M Eng, MS, PhD
computer science and engineering • PhD
electrical engineering • M Eng, MS
engineering • M Eng, MS, PhD
engineering mathematics and computer science • M Eng, MS
industrial engineering • M Eng, MS, PhD
mechanical engineering • M Eng, MS

Louis D. Brandeis School of Law
Laura Rothstein, Dean
Program in:
humanities • JD

School of Dentistry
Programs in:
dentistry • DMD, MS
oral biology • MS

School of Medicine
Programs in:
communicative disorders • MS
medicine • MD, MS, PhD
ophthalmology and visual sciences • PhD

Integrated Programs in Biomedical Sciences
Programs in:
anatomical sciences and neurobiology • MS, PhD
biochemistry and molecular biology • MS, PhD
biomedical sciences • MS, PhD
microbiology and immunology • MS, PhD
pharmacology and toxicology • MS, PhD
physiology and biophysics • MS, PhD

■ WESTERN KENTUCKY UNIVERSITY
Bowling Green, KY 42101-3576
http://www.wku.edu/

State-supported, coed, comprehensive institution. CGS member. *Enrollment:* 443 full-time matriculated graduate/professional students (287 women), 1,156 part-time matriculated graduate/professional students (835 women). *Graduate faculty:* 312 full-time (110 women), 37 part-time/adjunct (16 women). *Computer facilities:* 100 computers available on campus for general student use. A campuswide network can be accessed from student residence rooms and from off campus. Internet access and online class registration, on-line grade reports are available. *Library facilities:* Helm-Cravens Library plus 3 others. *Graduate expenses:* Full-time $2,350; part-time $148 per credit. Tuition, nonresident: full-time $6,660; part-time $388 per credit. Full-time tuition and fees vary according to program. *General application contact:* Dr. Elmer Gray, Dean, Graduate Studies, 270-745-2446.

Find an in-depth description at www.petersons.com/graduate.

Graduate Studies
Dr. Elmer Gray, Dean
Program in:
administration • MA

College of Education and Behavioral Sciences
Dr. Karen Adams, Dean
Programs in:
business education • MA Ed
communication disorders • MS
early childhood education • MA Ed
education • Ed S
education and behavioral sciences • MA, MA Ed, MS, Ed S
educational leadership • MA Ed, Ed S
elementary education • MA Ed, Ed S
exceptional child education • MA Ed
guidance and counseling • MA Ed, Ed S
library media education • MS
middle grades education • MA Ed
physical education • MA Ed, MS
psychology • MA
reading • MA Ed
recreation • MS
school administration • Ed S
school business administration • MA Ed
school psychology • Ed S
secondary education • MA Ed, Ed S

Gordon Ford College of Business
Dr. Robert Jefferson, Dean
Program in:
business administration • MBA

Ogden College of Science, and Engineering
Dr. Martin Houston, Dean
Programs in:
agriculture • MA Ed, MS
biology • MA Ed, MS
chemistry • MA Ed, MS
computer science • MS
environmental health • MS
geography and geology • MS
gerontology • MS
healthcare administration • MHA
mathematics • MA Ed, MS
nursing • MSN
public health • MPH, MSFS
public health education • MPH, MSFS
science, technology, and health • MA Ed, MHA, MPH, MS, MSFS, MSN

Potter College of Arts, Humanities and Social Sciences
Dr. David Lee, Dean
Programs in:
art education • MA Ed
arts and humanities • MA, MA Ed, MS
communication • MA
communication education • MA Ed
English • MA Ed
folk studies • MA
French • MA Ed
German • MA Ed
government • MA Ed
historic preservation • MA
history • MA, MA Ed
humanities • MA
literature • MA
music • MA Ed
sociology • MA, MA Ed
Spanish • MA Ed
teaching English as a second language • MA
writing • MA

Louisiana

■ CENTENARY COLLEGE OF LOUISIANA

Shreveport, LA 71134-1188
http://www.centenary.edu/

Independent-religious, coed, comprehensive institution. *Enrollment:* 7 full-time matriculated graduate/professional students (2 women), 170 part-time matriculated graduate/professional students (109 women). *Graduate faculty:* 9 full-time (4 women), 4 part-time/adjunct (2 women). *Computer facilities:* A campuswide network can be accessed from student residence rooms and from off campus. Internet access is available. *Library facilities:* Magale Library plus 1 other. *Graduate expenses:* Tuition: part-time $400 per course. Part-time tuition and fees vary according to program. *General application contact:* Dr. Earl W. Fleck, Provost and Dean, 318-869-5104.

Graduate Programs
Dr. Earl W. Fleck, Provost and Dean
Programs in:
administration • M Ed
elementary education • M Ed, MAT
secondary education • M Ed, MAT
supervision of instruction • M Ed

Frost School of Business
Dean
Program in:
business • MBA

■ GRAMBLING STATE UNIVERSITY

Grambling, LA 71245
http://www.gram.edu/

State-supported, coed, comprehensive institution. CGS member. *Enrollment:* 235 full-time matriculated graduate/professional students (156 women), 192 part-time matriculated graduate/professional students (143 women). *Graduate faculty:* 48 full-time (17 women), 10 part-time/adjunct (8 women). *Computer facilities:* 250 computers available on campus for general student use. A campuswide network can be accessed from student residence rooms and from off campus. Internet access is available. *Library facilities:* A. C. Lewis Memorial Library. *General application contact:* Jacklen Greer, Administrative Assistant, Division of Graduate Studies, 318-274-2158.

Division of Graduate Studies

College of Education
Dr. Andolyn B. Harrison, Dean
Programs in:
curriculum and instruction • Ed D
developmental education • MS, Ed D
early childhood education • MS
educational leadership • Ed D
elementary education • MS
sports administration • MS

College of Liberal Arts
Dr. Allen Williams, Dean
Programs in:
criminal justice • MS
humanities • MA
mass communication • MA
public administration • MPA
social sciences • MAT

College of Science and Technology
Dr. Connie Walton, Dean
Program in:
natural sciences • MAT

School of Nursing
Dr. Betty E. Smith, Dean
Program in:
family nurse practitioner • MSN

School of Social Work
Dr. Birdex Copeland, Dean
Program in:
social work • MSW

■ LOUISIANA STATE UNIVERSITY AND AGRICULTURAL AND MECHANICAL COLLEGE

Baton Rouge, LA 70803
http://www.lsu.edu/

State-supported, coed, university. CGS member. *Enrollment:* 2,897 full-time matriculated graduate/professional students (1,450 women), 1,347 part-time matriculated graduate/professional students (759 women). *Graduate faculty:*

Louisiana State University and Agricultural and Mechanical College (continued)

1,102 full-time (215 women), 27 part-time/adjunct (7 women). *Computer facilities:* 7,000 computers available on campus for general student use. A campuswide network can be accessed from student residence rooms and from off campus. Internet access and online class registration, e-mail are available. *Library facilities:* Troy H. Middleton Library plus 7 others. *Graduate expenses:* Tuition, state resident: full-time $1,281. Tuition, nonresident: full-time $3,931. Tuition and fees vary according to course load and program. *General application contact:* Office of Graduate Admissions, 225-578-2311.

Graduate School
George M. Strain, Interim Dean
Program in:
- linguistics • MA, PhD

Center for Coastal, Energy and Environmental Resources
Dr. Russell L. Chapman, Interim Executive Director
Programs in:
- coastal, energy and environmental resources • MS, PhD
- environmental planning and management • MS
- environmental toxicology • MS
- nuclear science and engineering • MS
- oceanography and coastal sciences • MS, PhD

College of Agriculture
Dr. Kenneth Koonce, Dean
Programs in:
- agricultural economics and agribusiness • MS, PhD
- agriculture • M App St, MS, MSBAE, PhD
- agronomy • MS, PhD
- animal science • MS, PhD
- applied statistics • M App St
- biological and agricultural engineering • MSBAE
- comprehensive vocational education • MS, PhD
- dairy science • MS, PhD
- engineering science • MS, PhD
- entomology • MS, PhD
- extension and international education • MS, PhD
- fisheries • MS
- food science • MS, PhD
- forestry • MS, PhD
- horticulture • MS, PhD
- human ecology • MS, PhD
- industrial education • MS
- plant health • MS, PhD
- poultry science • MS
- vocational agriculture education • MS, PhD
- vocational business education • MS
- vocational home economics education • MS
- wildlife • MS
- wildlife and fisheries science • PhD

College of Arts and Sciences
Dr. Mary Jane Collins, Dean
Programs in:
- anthropology • MA
- arts and sciences • MA, MALA, MFA, MS, PhD
- biological psychology • MA, PhD
- clinical psychology • MA, PhD
- cognitive psychology • MA, PhD
- communication sciences and disorders • MA, PhD
- comparative literature • MA, PhD
- creative writing • MFA
- developmental psychology • MA, PhD
- English • MA, PhD
- French literature and linguistics • MA, PhD
- geography • MA, MS, PhD
- history • MA, PhD
- industrial/organizational psychology • MA, PhD
- liberal arts • MALA
- mathematics • MS, PhD
- philosophy • MA
- political science • MA, PhD
- school psychology • MA, PhD
- sociology • MA, PhD
- Spanish • MA
- speech communication • MA, PhD

College of Basic Sciences
Dr. Harold Silverman, Chairman
Programs in:
- astronomy • PhD
- astrophysics • PhD
- basic sciences • MNS, MS, MSSS, PhD
- biochemistry • MS, PhD
- chemistry • MS, PhD
- computer science • MSSS, PhD
- geology and geophysics • MS, PhD
- microbiology • MS, PhD
- natural sciences • MNS
- physics • MS, PhD
- plant biology • MS, PhD
- systems science • MSSS
- zoology • MS, PhD

College of Design
Christos A. Saccopoulas, Dean
Programs in:
- architecture • MS
- art history • MA
- ceramics • MFA
- design • MA, MFA, MLA, MS
- graphic design • MFA
- landscape architecture • MLA
- painting and drawing • MFA
- photography • MFA
- printmaking • MFA
- sculpture • MFA
- studio art • MFA

College of Education
Dr. Barbara Fuhrmann, Dean
Programs in:
- counseling • M Ed, MA, Ed S
- curriculum and instruction • MA, PhD, Ed S
- education • M Ed, MA, MS, PhD, Ed S
- educational administration • M Ed, MA, PhD, Ed S
- educational technology • MA
- elementary education • M Ed
- higher education • PhD
- kinesiology • MS, PhD
- research methodology • PhD
- secondary education • M Ed

College of Engineering
Dr. Pius J. Egbelu, Dean
Programs in:
- chemical engineering • MS Ch E, PhD
- electrical and computer engineering • MSEE, PhD
- engineering • MS Ch E, MS Pet E, MSCE, MSEE, MSES, MSIE, MSME, PhD
- engineering science • MSES, PhD
- environmental engineering • MSCE, PhD
- geotechnical engineering • MSCE, PhD
- industrial engineering • MSIE
- mechanical engineering • MSME, PhD
- petroleum engineering • MS Pet E, PhD
- structural engineering and mechanics • MSCE, PhD
- transportation engineering • MSCE, PhD
- water resources • MSCE, PhD

College of Music and Dramatic Arts
Dr. Ronald Ross, Dean
Programs in:
- acting • MFA
- directing • MFA
- music • MM, DMA, PhD
- music and dramatic arts • MFA, MM, DMA, PhD
- music education • PhD
- theatre • PhD
- theatre design/technology • MFA

E.J. Ourso College of Business Administration
Dr. Thomas D. Clark, Dean
Programs in:
- accounting • MS, PhD
- business administration • PhD
- economics • MS, PhD
- finance • MS

information systems and decision sciences • MS
marketing • MS
public administration • MPA

Manship School of Mass Communication
Dr. John Maxwell Hamilton, Dean
Program in:
mass communication • MMC

School of Library and Information Science
Dr. Beth M. Paskoff, Dean
Program in:
library and information science • MLIS, CLIS

Paul M. Hebert Law Center
John J. Costonis, Chancellor
Program in:
law • JD, LL M, MCL

School of Social Work
Dr. Kenneth A. Millar, Dean
Program in:
social work • MSW, PhD

School of Veterinary Medicine
Dr. Michael G. Groves, Dean
Programs in:
comparative veterinary biomedical sciences • MS, PhD
epidemiology and community health • MS, PhD
veterinary anatomy and cell biology • MS, PhD
veterinary clinical sciences • MS
veterinary medicine • DVM, MS, PhD
veterinary microbiology and parasitology • MS, PhD
veterinary pathology • MS, PhD

■ LOUISIANA STATE UNIVERSITY IN SHREVEPORT

Shreveport, LA 71115-2399
http://www.lsus.edu/

State-supported, coed, comprehensive institution. *Enrollment:* 127 full-time matriculated graduate/professional students (95 women), 559 part-time matriculated graduate/professional students (364 women). *Graduate faculty:* 84 full-time (30 women), 29 part-time/adjunct (13 women). *Computer facilities:* A campuswide network can be accessed from off campus. Internet access is available. *Library facilities:* Noel Memorial Library. *Graduate expenses:* Tuition, state resident: part-time $95 per semester hour. Tuition, nonresident: part-time $300 per semester hour. Required fees: $55 per semester hour. *General application contact:* Julie A. Wilkins, Registrar and Director of Admissions, 318-797-5061.

College of Business Administration
Program in:
business administration • MBA

College of Education
Programs in:
education • M Ed, SSP
school psychology • SSP

College of Liberal Arts
Programs in:
human services administration • MS
liberal arts • MA, MS

College of Sciences
Program in:
systems technology • MST

■ LOUISIANA TECH UNIVERSITY

Ruston, LA 71272
http://www.latech.edu/

State-supported, coed, university. *Computer facilities:* 1,800 computers available on campus for general student use. A campuswide network can be accessed from student residence rooms and from off campus. *Library facilities:* Prescott Memorial Library. *General application contact:* Dean of the Graduate School, 318-257-2924.

Graduate School

College of Administration and Business
Programs in:
administration and business • MBA, MPA, DBA
business administration • MBA
business economics • MBA, DBA
finance • MBA, DBA
management • MBA, DBA
marketing • MBA, DBA
professional accountancy • MBA, MPA, DBA
quantitative analysis • MBA, DBA

College of Applied and Natural Sciences
Programs in:
applied and natural sciences • MS
biological sciences • MS
dietetics • MS
human ecology • MS

College of Education
Programs in:
counseling • MA, Ed S
counseling psychology • PhD
curriculum and instruction • MS, Ed D
education • M Ed, MA, MS, Ed D, PhD, Ed S
educational leadership • Ed D
health and physical education • MS
industrial/organizational psychology • MA
reading • Ed S
secondary education • M Ed
special education • MA

College of Engineering and Science
Programs in:
applied computational analysis and modeling • PhD
biomedical engineering • MS, PhD
chemical engineering • MS, D Eng
chemistry • MS
civil engineering • MS, D Eng
computer science • MS
electrical engineering • MS, D Eng
engineering • D Eng
engineering and science • MS, D Eng, PhD
industrial engineering • MS, D Eng
manufacturing systems engineering • MS
mathematics and statistics • MS
mechanical engineering • MS, D Eng
operations research • MS
physics • MS

College of Liberal Arts
Programs in:
art and graphic design • MFA
English • MA
history • MA
interior design • MFA
liberal arts • MA, MFA
photography • MFA
speech • MA
speech pathology and audiology • MA
studio art • MFA

■ LOYOLA UNIVERSITY NEW ORLEANS

New Orleans, LA 70118-6195
http://www.loyno.edu/

Independent-religious, coed, comprehensive institution. *Enrollment:* 658 full-time matriculated graduate/professional students (291 women), 946 part-time matriculated graduate/professional students (563 women). *Graduate faculty:* 255 full-time (96 women), 131 part-time/adjunct (54 women). *Computer facilities:* 300 computers available on campus for general student use. A campuswide network can be accessed from student residence rooms and from off campus. Internet access and online class registration are available. *Library facilities:* University

Loyola University New Orleans (continued)
Library plus 1 other. *Graduate expenses:* Tuition: part-time $464 per credit hour. Required fees: $142 per semester. Tuition and fees vary according to course load, degree level and program. *General application contact:* Deborah C. Stieffel, Dean of Admissions and Enrollment Management, 504-865-3240.

College of Arts and Sciences
Dr. Frank E. Scully, Dean
Programs in:
arts and sciences • MA, MCJ, MS
counseling • MS
criminal justice • MCJ
elementary education • MS
mass communication • MA
reading education • MS
religious studies • MA
secondary education • MS

College of Music
Dr. Edward J. Kvet, Dean
Program in:
music • MM, MME, MMT

Institute for Ministry
Dr. Barbara J. Fleischer, Director
Program in:
ministry • MPS, MRE

Joseph A. Butt, S.J., College of Business Administration
Dr. J. Patrick O'Brien, Dean
Programs in:
business administration • MBA, MQM
quality management • MQM

Program in Nursing
Dr. Billie Ann Wilson, Director
Program in:
family nurse practitioner • MSN

School of Law
James M. Klebba, Interim Dean
Program in:
law • JD

■ MCNEESE STATE UNIVERSITY
Lake Charles, LA 70609

State-supported, coed, comprehensive institution. *Computer facilities:* 354 computers available on campus for general student use. A campuswide network can be accessed from off campus. Internet access and online class registration are available. *Library facilities:* Frazer Memorial Library plus 2 others. *General application contact:* Admissions Counselor, 318-475-5147.

Graduate School

College of Business
Programs in:
business • MBA
business administration • MBA

College of Education
Programs in:
administration and supervision • M Ed, Ed S
counseling and guidance • M Ed
early childhood education • M Ed
education • M Ed, MA, Ed S
educational technology • M Ed
elementary education • M Ed
health and physical education • M Ed
psychology • MA
reading education • M Ed
secondary education • M Ed
special education • M Ed

College of Engineering and Technology
Programs in:
chemical engineering • M Eng
civil engineering • M Eng
electrical engineering • M Eng
mechanical engineering • M Eng

College of Liberal Arts
Programs in:
creative writing • MFA
English • MA
liberal arts • MA, MFA, MM Ed
music education • MM Ed

College of Nursing
Program in:
nursing • MSN

College of Science
Programs in:
biology • MS
chemistry • MS
computer science • MS
environmental sciences • MS
mathematics • MS
science • MS
statistics • MS

■ NICHOLLS STATE UNIVERSITY
Thibodaux, LA 70310
http://www.nicholls.edu/

State-supported, coed, comprehensive institution. *Enrollment:* 93 full-time matriculated graduate/professional students (67 women), 687 part-time matriculated graduate/professional students (527 women). *Graduate faculty:* 105 full-time (35 women). *Computer facilities:* 204 computers available on campus for general student use. A campuswide network can be accessed from student residence rooms and from off campus. Internet access is available. *Library facilities:* Allen J. Ellender Memorial Library. *Graduate expenses:* Tuition, state resident: full-time $2,368; part-time $105 per hour. Tuition, nonresident: full-time $7,816. $7,936 full-time. Full-time tuition and fees vary according to course level, course load and reciprocity agreements. *General application contact:* Dr. J. B. Stroud, Director, 504-449-7014.

Graduate Studies
Dr. J. B. Stroud, Director

College of Arts and Sciences
Dr. Thomas Mortillaro, Dean
Programs in:
applied mathematics • MS
arts and sciences • MS

College of Business Administration
Dr. Ridley Gros, Dean
Program in:
business administration • MBA

College of Education
Dr. O. Cleveland Hill, Dean
Programs in:
administration and supervision • M Ed
counselor education • M Ed
curriculum and instruction • M Ed
education • M Ed, MA, SSP
psychological counseling • MA
school psychology • SSP

■ NORTHWESTERN STATE UNIVERSITY OF LOUISIANA
Natchitoches, LA 71497
http://www.nsula.edu/

State-supported, coed, comprehensive institution. CGS member. *Enrollment:* 253 full-time matriculated graduate/professional students (159 women), 765 part-time matriculated graduate/professional students (616 women). *Graduate faculty:* 55 full-time (32 women), 12 part-time/adjunct (8 women). *Computer facilities:* 687 computers available on campus for general student use. A campuswide network can be accessed from student residence rooms and from off campus. Internet access and online class registration are available. *Library facilities:* Eugene P. Watson Memorial Library. *Graduate expenses:* Tuition: part-time $359 per hour. *General application contact:* Dr. Anthony J. Scheffler, Dean, Graduate Studies, Research, and Information Systems, 318-357-5851.

Graduate Studies and Research
Dr. Anthony J. Scheffler, Dean, Graduate Studies, Research, and Information Systems

Programs in:
- art • MA
- clinical psychology • MS
- English • MA
- English education • M Ed
- health promotion • M Ed
- history • MA
- music • MM
- social sciences education • M Ed
- sport administration • M Ed

College of Education
Dr. John Tollett, Chair
Programs in:
- business and distributive education • M Ed
- counseling and guidance • M Ed, Ed S
- early childhood education • M Ed
- educational administration/supervision • M Ed, Ed S
- educational technology • M Ed, Ed S
- elementary teaching • M Ed, Ed S
- home economics education • M Ed
- human services • M Ed, MA, Ed S
- mathematics education • M Ed
- reading • M Ed, Ed S
- science education • M Ed
- secondary teaching • M Ed, Ed S
- special education • M Ed, Ed S
- student personnel services • MA

College of Nursing
Dr. Norann Planchock, Director
Program in:
- nursing • MSN

■ SOUTHEASTERN LOUISIANA UNIVERSITY

Hammond, LA 70402
http://www.selu.edu/

State-supported, coed, comprehensive institution. *Enrollment:* 332 full-time matriculated graduate/professional students (203 women), 668 part-time matriculated graduate/professional students (552 women). *Graduate faculty:* 194. *Computer facilities:* 702 computers available on campus for general student use. A campuswide network can be accessed from off campus. Internet access and online class registration are available. *Library facilities:* Sims Memorial Library. *Graduate expenses:* Tuition, state resident: full-time $2,374. Tuition, nonresident: full-time $6,370. $6,490 full-time. *General application contact:* Josie Mercante, Associate Director of Admissions, 985-549-2066.

College of Arts and Sciences
Dr. John S. Miller, Dean
Programs in:
- arts and sciences • M Mus, MA, MS
- biological sciences • MS
- English • MA
- history • MA
- music theory • M Mus
- performance • M Mus
- psychology • MA

College of Business and Technology
Dr. Michael Budden, Dean
Program in:
- business and technology • MBA

College of Education and Human Development
Dr. Martha Head, Interim Dean
Programs in:
- administration and supervision • M Ed
- counselor education • M Ed
- curriculum and instruction • M Ed
- education and human development • M Ed, MA, MS
- special education • M Ed

College of Nursing and Health Studies
Dr. Donnie Booth, Dean
Programs in:
- communication sciences and disorders • MS
- kinesiology and health studies • MA
- nursing • MSN
- nursing and health studies • MA, MS, MSN

■ SOUTHERN UNIVERSITY AND AGRICULTURAL AND MECHANICAL COLLEGE

Baton Rouge, LA 70813
http://www.subr.edu/

State-supported, coed, comprehensive institution. CGS member. *Computer facilities:* 835 computers available on campus for general student use. A campuswide network can be accessed from student residence rooms and from off campus. Internet access and online class registration are available. *Library facilities:* John B. Cade Library plus 2 others. *General application contact:* Director of Graduate Admissions and Recruitment, 225-771-5390.

Find an in-depth description at www.petersons.com/graduate.

Graduate School
Program in:
- science/mathematics education • PhD

College of Agricultural, Family and Consumer Sciences
Program in:
- urban forestry • MS

College of Arts and Humanities
Programs in:
- arts and humanities • MA
- mass communications • MA
- social sciences • MA

College of Business
Programs in:
- accountancy • MPA
- business • MPA

College of Education
Programs in:
- administration and supervision • M Ed
- counselor education • MA
- education • M Ed, MA, MS
- elementary education • M Ed
- media • M Ed
- mental health counseling • MA
- secondary education • M Ed
- therapeutic recreation • MS

College of Sciences
Programs in:
- analytical chemistry • MS
- biochemistry • MS
- biology • MS
- environmental sciences • MS
- information systems • MS
- inorganic chemistry • MS
- mathematics • MS
- micro/minicomputer architecture • MS
- operating systems • MS
- organic chemistry • MS
- physical chemistry • MS
- physics • MS
- rehabilitation counseling • MS
- sciences • MA, MS
- social sciences • MA

School of Public Policy and Urban Affairs
Programs in:
- public administration • MPA
- public policy • PhD
- public policy and urban affairs • MA, MPA, PhD
- social sciences • MA

Special Education Institute
Program in:
- special education • M Ed, PhD

School of Nursing
Program in:
- nursing • MSN

Southern University Law Center
Program in:
- law • JD

■ SOUTHERN UNIVERSITY AT NEW ORLEANS

New Orleans, LA 70126-1009
http://www.gnofn.org/~zaire/suno4.htm

State-supported, coed, comprehensive institution. *Computer facilities:* 100 computers available on campus for general student use. *Library facilities:* Leonard Washington Library. *General application contact:* Director of Student Affairs, 504-286-5376.

School of Social Work

Program in:
social work • MSW

■ TULANE UNIVERSITY

New Orleans, LA 70118-5669
http://www.tulane.edu/

Independent, coed, university. CGS member. *Enrollment:* 4,105 full-time matriculated graduate/professional students (2,073 women), 673 part-time matriculated graduate/professional students (273 women). *Graduate faculty:* 958 full-time, 322 part-time/adjunct. *Computer facilities:* A campuswide network can be accessed from student residence rooms and from off campus. *Library facilities:* Howard Tilton Memorial Library plus 8 others. *Graduate expenses:* Tuition: full-time $24,675. Required fees: $2,210. *General application contact:* Kay D. Orrill, Assistant Dean, 504-865-5100.

Find an in-depth description at www.petersons.com/graduate.

A. B. Freeman School of Business

Dr. James W. McFarland, Dean
Program in:
business • EMBA, M Acct, MBA, PhD

Graduate School

Kay D. Orrill, Assistant Dean
Programs in:
anthropology • MA, MS, PhD
applied development • MA, PhD
applied mathematics • MS
art • MFA
art history • MA
biology • MS, PhD
chemistry • MS, PhD
civic and cultural management • MA
classical studies • MA
economics • MA, PhD
English • MA, PhD
French and Italian • MA, PhD
geology • MS, PhD
history • MA, PhD
liberal arts • MLA
mathematics • MS, PhD
music • MA, MFA
paleontology • PhD
philosophy • MA, PhD
physics • MS, PhD
political science • MA, PhD
psychology • MS, PhD
sociology • MA, MAD, PhD
Spanish and Portuguese • MA, PhD
statistics • MS
theatre and dance • MFA

Roger Thayer Stone Center for Latin American Studies

Dr. Thomas Reese, Executive Director
Program in:
Latin American studies • MA, PhD

School of Architecture

Program in:
architecture • M Arch, MPS

School of Engineering

Dr. Nicholas Altiero, Acting Dean
Programs in:
biomedical engineering • MS, MSE, PhD, Sc D
chemical engineering • MS, MSE, PhD, Sc D
civil and environmental engineering • MS, MSE, PhD, Sc D
computer science • MS, MSCS, PhD, Sc D
electrical engineering • MS, MSE, PhD, Sc D
engineering • MS, MSCS, MSE, PhD, Sc D
mechanical engineering • MS, MSE, PhD, Sc D

School of Law

Lawrence Ponoroff, Dean
Programs in:
admiralty • LL M
energy and environment • LL M
international and comparative law • LL M
law • LL M

School of Medicine

Dr. Ian L. Taylor, Dean
Program in:
medicine • MD, MPHTM, MS, MSPH, PhD, Sc D, Diploma

Graduate Programs in Medicine

Programs in:
biochemistry • MS, PhD
clinical tropical medicine and travelers health • Diploma
human genetics • MS, PhD
medicine • MPHTM, MS, MSPH, PhD, Sc D, Diploma
microbiology and immunology • MS, PhD
molecular and cellular biology • PhD
neuroscience • MS, PhD
parasitology • MS, MSPH, PhD, Sc D
pharmacology • MS, PhD
physiology • MS, PhD
public health and tropical medicine • MPHTM
structural and cellular biology • MS, PhD

School of Public Health and Tropical Medicine

Dr. Ann C. Anderson, Acting Dean
Programs in:
biostatistics • MS, MSPH, PhD, Sc D
environmental health sciences • MPH, MSPH, Sc D
epidemiology • MPH, MS, Dr PH, PhD
health communication/education • MPH
health systems management • MHA, MMM, MPH, Dr PH
international health and development • MADH, MPH, Dr PH
maternal and child health • MPH, Dr PH
nutrition • MPH
population studies • MPH
public health and tropical medicine • MADH, MHA, MMM, MPH, MPHTM, MS, MSPH, Dr PH, PhD, Sc D, Diploma

School of Social Work

Dr. Suzanne England, Dean
Program in:
social work • MSW, PhD

■ UNIVERSITY OF LOUISIANA AT LAFAYETTE

Lafayette, LA 70504
http://www.louisiana.edu/

State-supported, coed, university. CGS member. *Enrollment:* 756 full-time matriculated graduate/professional students (355 women), 460 part-time matriculated graduate/professional students (283 women). *Graduate faculty:* 339 full-time (96 women). *Computer facilities:* 548 computers available on campus for general student use. A campuswide network can be accessed from off campus. Internet access and online class registration are available. *Library facilities:* Edith Garland Dupre Library. *Graduate expenses:* Tuition, state resident: full-time $2,275; part-time $79 per credit hour. Tuition, nonresident: full-time $9,227; part-time $368 per credit hour. $9,363 full-time. *General application contact:* Dr. Lewis Pyenson, Dean, 337-482-6965.

Graduate School
Dr. Lewis Pyenson, Dean

College of Applied Life Sciences
Dr. Linda Vincent, Dean
Programs in:
- applied life sciences • MS
- human resources • MS

College of Business Administration
Dr. Michael Fronmueller, Acting Dean
Programs in:
- business administration • MBA
- health care administration • MBA
- health care certification • MBA

College of Education
Dr. Lucindia B. Chance, Dean
Programs in:
- administration and supervision • M Ed
- curriculum and instruction • M Ed
- education • M Ed
- education of the gifted • M Ed
- guidance and counseling • M Ed

College of Engineering
Dr. Anthony B. Ponter, Dean
Programs in:
- chemical engineering • MSE
- civil engineering • MSE
- computer engineering • MS, PhD
- computer science • MS, PhD
- engineering • MS, MSE, MSET, MSTC, PhD
- engineering management • MSET
- mechanical engineering • MSE
- petroleum engineering • MSE
- telecommunications • MSTC

College of Liberal Arts
Dr. A. David Barry, Dean
Programs in:
- British and American literature • MA
- communicative disorders • MS
- creative writing • PhD
- francophone studies • PhD
- French • MA
- history and geography • MA
- liberal arts • MA, MS, PhD
- literature • PhD
- mass communications • MS
- psychology • MS
- rehabilitation counseling • MS
- rhetoric • PhD

College of Nursing
Dr. Gail Poirrier, Acting Dean
Program in:
- nursing • MSN

College of Sciences
Dr. Duane D. Blumberg, Dean
Programs in:
- applied physics • MS
- biology • MS
- cognitive science • PhD
- computer science • MS
- environmental and evolutionary biology • PhD
- geology • MS
- mathematics • MS, PhD
- physics • MS
- sciences • MS, PhD

College of the Arts
H. Gordon Brooks, Dean
Programs in:
- arts • MM
- conducting • MM
- pedagogy • MM
- vocal and instrumental performance • MM

■ UNIVERSITY OF LOUISIANA AT MONROE
Monroe, LA 71209-0001
http://www.nlu.edu/

State-supported, coed, comprehensive institution. *Computer facilities:* 1,400 computers available on campus for general student use. A campuswide network can be accessed from off campus. *Library facilities:* Sandel Library. *General application contact:* Dean, Graduate Studies and Research, 318-342-1036.

Graduate Studies and Research

College of Allied Health and Rehabilitation Professions
Programs in:
- allied health and rehabilitation professions • MA
- communicative disorders • MA

College of Business Administration
Program in:
- business administration • MBA

College of Education
Programs in:
- administration and supervision • M Ed, Ed S
- counseling • M Ed, Ed S
- curriculum and instruction • Ed D, Ed S
- education • M Ed, MA, MS, Ed D, PhD, Ed S, SSP
- educational leadership • Ed D
- elementary education • M Ed, Ed S
- English education • M Ed
- health and human performance • M Ed, MS
- marriage and family therapy • MA, PhD
- psychology • MS
- reading • M Ed
- school psychology • SSP
- secondary education • M Ed, Ed S
- special education • M Ed
- substance abuse counseling • MA

College of Liberal Arts
Programs in:
- communication • MA
- criminal justice • MA
- English • MA
- gerontological studies • CGS
- gerontology • MA
- history • MA
- liberal arts • MA, MM, CGS
- music • MM

College of Pharmacy and Health Sciences
Programs in:
- pharmaceutical sciences • MS
- pharmacy • PhD
- pharmacy and health sciences • Pharm D, MS, PhD

College of Pure and Applied Sciences
Programs in:
- biology • MS
- chemistry • MS
- geosciences • MS
- pure and applied sciences • MS

■ UNIVERSITY OF NEW ORLEANS
New Orleans, LA 70148
http://www.uno.edu/

State-supported, coed, university. CGS member. *Enrollment:* 1,299 full-time matriculated graduate/professional students (680 women), 2,659 part-time matriculated graduate/professional students (1,718 women). *Graduate faculty:* 440. *Computer facilities:* 1,084 computers available on campus for general student use. A campuswide network can be accessed from student residence rooms and from off campus. Internet access is available. *Library facilities:* Earl K. Long Library. *Graduate expenses:* Tuition: full-time $1,306; part-time $134 per hour. *General application contact:* Dr. Robert Cashner, Dean, Graduate School, 504-280-6836.

Graduate School
Dr. Robert Cashner, Dean

College of Business Administration
Dr. Tim Ryan, Dean
Programs in:
- accounting • MS
- business administration • MBA, MHCM, MS, PhD

University of New Orleans (continued)
financial economics • PhD
health care management • MHCM
taxation • MS

College of Education
Dr. James Meza, Chairperson
Programs in:
adapted physical education • MA
counselor education • M Ed, PhD, Certificate
curriculum and instruction • M Ed, PhD, Certificate
education • M Ed, MA, PhD, Certificate
educational leadership and foundations • M Ed, PhD, Certificate
exercise physiology • MA
gerontology • Certificate
health and physical education • Certificate
physical education • M Ed
science, pedagogy and coaching sport management • MA
special education • M Ed, PhD, Certificate

College of Engineering
Dr. John N. Crisp, Dean
Programs in:
civil engineering • MS
electrical engineering • MS
engineering • MS, PhD, Certificate
engineering and applied sciences • PhD
engineering management • MS, Certificate
mechanical engineering • MS
naval architecture and marine engineering • MS

College of Liberal Arts
Fredrick P. Barton, Associate Dean
Programs in:
applied sociology • MA
archives and records administration • MA
arts administration • MA
communications • MA, MFA
creative writing • MFA
drama • MFA
English • MA
geography • MA
graphic design • MFA
graphics • MFA
history • MA
international relations • MA
liberal arts • MA, MFA, MM, PhD
music • MM
painting • MFA
photography • MFA
political science • MA, PhD
Romance languages • MA
sculpture • MFA
sociology • MA

College of Sciences
Dr. Joe King, Dean
Programs in:
applied physics • MS
applied psychology • PhD
biological sciences • MS
chemistry • MS, PhD
computer science • MS
conservation biology • PhD
geology • MS
geophysics • MS
mathematics • MS
physics • MS
psychology • MS
science teaching • MA
sciences • MA, MS, PhD

College of Urban and Public Affairs
Dr. Robert K. Whelan, Graduate Coordinator
Programs in:
public administration and policy • MPA
urban and public affairs • MPA, MS, MURP, PhD
urban and regional planning • MURP
urban studies • MS, PhD

■ XAVIER UNIVERSITY OF LOUISIANA

New Orleans, LA 70125-1098
http://www.xula.edu/

Independent-religious, coed, comprehensive institution. CGS member. *Enrollment:* 654 full-time matriculated graduate/professional students (441 women), 64 part-time matriculated graduate/professional students (52 women). *Graduate faculty:* 5 full-time (2 women), 72 part-time/adjunct (32 women). *Computer facilities:* 250 computers available on campus for general student use. A campuswide network can be accessed from student residence rooms and from off campus. *Library facilities:* Xavier Library plus 1 other. *Graduate expenses:* Tuition: part-time $200 per semester hour. *General application contact:* Marlene C. Robinson, Director of Graduate Admissions, 504-483-7487.

College of Pharmacy
Dr. Wayne T. Harris, Dean
Program in:
pharmacy • Pharm D

Graduate School
Dr. Alvin J. Richard, Dean
Programs in:
administration and supervision • MA
curriculum and instruction • MA
guidance and counseling • MA
nurse anesthesiology • MS

Institute for Black Catholic Studies
Sr. Eva Regina Martin, Director
Program in:
pastoral theology • Th M

Maine

■ HUSSON COLLEGE

Bangor, ME 04401-2999
http://www.husson.edu/

Independent, coed, comprehensive institution. *Computer facilities:* 135 computers available on campus for general student use. A campuswide network can be accessed from student residence rooms and from off campus. Internet access is available. *Library facilities:* Husson College Library. *General application contact:* Dean of Graduate Studies, 207-941-7062.

Graduate Studies Division
Programs in:
business • MSB
family nurse practitioner • MSN
nursing • MSN
physical therapy • MSPT
psychiatric nursing • MSN

■ SAINT JOSEPH'S COLLEGE

Standish, ME 04084-5263
http://www.sjcme.edu/

Independent-religious, coed, comprehensive institution. *Computer facilities:* 71 computers available on campus for general student use. A campuswide network can be accessed from student residence rooms and from off campus. Internet access is available. *Library facilities:* Wellehan Library. *General application contact:* Admissions Department, 800-752-4723.

Department of Nursing
Program in:
nursing • MS

Program in Health Services Administration
Program in:
health services administration • MHSA

Program in Pastoral Studies
Program in:
pastoral studies • MA

Program in Teacher Education
Program in:
teacher education • MS

■ UNIVERSITY OF MAINE

Orono, ME 04469
http://www.umaine.edu/

State-supported, coed, university. CGS member. *Computer facilities:* 520 computers available on campus for general student use. A campuswide network can be accessed from student residence rooms and from off campus. Internet access and online class registration, on-line grade information, e-mail are available. *Library facilities:* Fogler Library. *General application contact:* Director of the Graduate School, 207-581-3218.

Find an in-depth description at www.petersons.com/graduate.

Graduate School
Program in:
liberal studies • MA

College of Business, Public Policy and Health
Programs in:
business • MBA
business, public policy and health • MBA, MPA, MS, MSW, CAS
nursing • MS, CAS
public administration • MPA
social work • MSW

College of Education and Human Development
Programs in:
counselor education • M Ed, MS, CAS
educational leadership • M Ed, Ed D, CAS
elementary education • M Ed, MAT, MS, CAS
higher education • M Ed, MS, Ed D, CAS
human development • MS
human development and family studies • MS
kinesiology and physical education • M Ed, MS, CAS
literacy education • M Ed, MS, Ed D, CAS
science education • M Ed, MS, CAS
secondary education • M Ed, MAT, MS, CAS
social studies education • M Ed, MS, CAS
special education • M Ed, CAS

College of Engineering
Programs in:
chemical engineering • MS, PhD
civil engineering • MS, PhD
computer engineering • MS
electrical engineering • MS, PhD
engineering • MS, PhD
mechanical engineering • MS
spatial information science and engineering • MS, PhD

College of Liberal Arts and Sciences
Programs in:
chemistry • MS, PhD
clinical psychology • PhD
communication • MA
communication sciences and disorders • MA
computer science • MS, PhD
developmental psychology • MA
economics • MA
engineering physics • M Eng
English • MA
experimental psychology • MA, PhD
French • MA, MAT
history • MA, PhD
liberal arts and sciences • M Eng, MA, MAT, MM, MS, PhD
mathematics • MA
music • MM
physics • MS, PhD
social psychology • MA
theatre • MA

College of Natural Sciences, Forestry, and Agriculture
Programs in:
animal sciences • MPS, MS
bio-resource engineering • MS
biochemistry • MPS, MS
biochemistry and molecular biology • PhD
biological sciences • PhD
botany and plant pathology • MS
ecology and environmental science • MS, PhD
ecology and environmental sciences • MS, PhD
entomology • MS
food and nutritional sciences • PhD
food science and human nutrition • MS
forest resources • PhD
forestry • MF, MS
geological sciences • MS, PhD
horticulture • MS
marine biology • MS, PhD
marine policy • MS
microbiology • MPS, MS, PhD
natural sciences, forestry, and agriculture • MF, MPS, MS, MWC, PhD
oceanography • MS, PhD
plant science • PhD
plant, soil, and environmental sciences • MS
resource economics and policy • MS
resource utilization • MS
wildlife conservation • MWC
wildlife ecology • MS, PhD
zoology • MS, PhD

Institute for Quaternary Studies
Program in:
quaternary studies • MS

■ UNIVERSITY OF NEW ENGLAND

Biddeford, ME 04005-9526
http://www.une.edu/

Independent, coed, comprehensive institution. *Enrollment:* 978 full-time matriculated graduate/professional students (584 women), 417 part-time matriculated graduate/professional students (346 women). *Graduate faculty:* 53 full-time (29 women), 84 part-time/adjunct (40 women). *Computer facilities:* 76 computers available on campus for general student use. A campuswide network can be accessed from off campus. Internet access is available. *Library facilities:* Ketchum Library plus 1 other. *Graduate expenses:* Tuition: full-time $12,640. Required fees: $230. *General application contact:* Patricia T. Cribby, Dean of Admissions and Enrollment Management, 207-283-0171 Ext. 2297.

College of Arts and Sciences
Jacque Carter, Director
Programs in:
arts and sciences • MS Ed, MSOT
education • MS Ed
occupational therapy • MSOT

College of Health Professions
Dr. Vernon Moore, Dean
Programs in:
health professions • MPA, MS, MSPT, MSW
nurse anesthesia • MS
physical therapy • MSPT
physician assistant • MPA
social work • MSW

College of Osteopathic Medicine
Dr. Stephen Shannon, Dean
Program in:
osteopathic medicine • DO

■ UNIVERSITY OF SOUTHERN MAINE

Portland, ME 04104-9300
http://www.usm.maine.edu/

State-supported, coed, comprehensive institution. *Enrollment:* 938 full-time matriculated graduate/professional students (605 women), 1,156 part-time

University of Southern Maine (continued)
matriculated graduate/professional students (806 women). *Graduate faculty:* 140. *Computer facilities:* 440 computers available on campus for general student use. A campuswide network can be accessed from student residence rooms and from off campus. Internet access and online class registration are available. *Library facilities:* University of Southern Maine Library plus 4 others. *Graduate expenses:* Part-time $193 per credit hour. Tuition, nonresident: part-time $538 per credit hour. *General application contact:* Mary Sloan, Assistant Director of Graduate Studies, 207-780-4336.

College of Arts and Science
Dr. F. C. McGrath, Dean
Programs in:
- American and New England studies • MA
- arts and science • MA

College of Education and Human Development
Programs in:
- adult education • MS, CAS
- counselor education • MS, CAS
- education and human development • MS, MS Ed, CAS, Certificate
- educational leadership • MS Ed, CAS, Certificate
- English as a second language • MS Ed, CAS
- extended teacher education • MS Ed, Certificate
- industrial/technology education • MS Ed
- literacy education • MS Ed, CAS
- school psychology • MS
- special education • MS

College of Nursing and Health Professions
Dr. Jane Marie Kirschling, Dean
Programs in:
- adult health nursing • PMC
- clinical nurse specialist adult health care management • MS
- clinical nurse specialist psychiatric-mental health nursing • MS
- family nursing • PMC
- nurse practitioner adult health nursing • MS
- nurse practitioner family nursing • MS
- nurse practitioner psychiatric/mental health nursing • MS
- psychiatric-mental health nursing • PMC

Edmund S. Muskie School of Public Service
Karl R. Braithwaite, Dean
Programs in:
- community planning and development • MCPD, Certificate
- health policy and management • MS, Certificate
- public policy and management • MPPM, PhD
- public service • MCPD, MPPM, MS, PhD, Certificate

Program in Occupational Therapy
Roxie M. Black, Director
Program in:
- occupational therapy • MOT

School of Applied Science, Engineering, and Technology
Dr. John R. Wright, Dean
Programs in:
- applied immunology and molecular biology • MS
- applied science, engineering, and technology • MS
- computer science • MS
- manufacturing systems • MS

School of Business
Dr. John W. Bay, Dean
Programs in:
- accounting • MSA
- business administration • MBA

University of Maine School of Law
Colleen A. Khoury, Dean
Program in:
- law • JD

Maryland

■ BOWIE STATE UNIVERSITY
Bowie, MD 20715-9465
http://www.bowiestate.edu/

State-supported, coed, comprehensive institution. CGS member. *Computer facilities:* A campuswide network can be accessed from student residence rooms and from off campus. Internet access and online class registration are available. *Library facilities:* Thurgood Marshall Library. *General application contact:* Graduate Dean, 301-464-6586.

Graduate Programs
Programs in:
- administration of nursing services • MS
- business administration • M Adm Mgt
- computer science • MS
- counseling psychology • MA
- elementary education • M Ed
- family nurse practitioner • MS
- guidance and counseling • M Ed
- human resource development • MA
- information systems analyst • Certificate
- management information systems • MS
- nursing education • MS
- organizational communication • MA, Certificate
- public administration • M Adm Mgt
- reading education • M Ed
- school administration and supervision • M Ed
- secondary education • M Ed
- special education • M Ed
- teaching • MAT

■ COLLEGE OF NOTRE DAME OF MARYLAND
Baltimore, MD 21210-2476
http://www.ndm.edu/

Independent-religious, women only, comprehensive institution. *Enrollment:* 896 part-time matriculated graduate/professional students (725 women). *Graduate faculty:* 28 full-time (16 women), 48 part-time/adjunct (32 women). *Computer facilities:* 80 computers available on campus for general student use. A campuswide network can be accessed from student residence rooms and from off campus. Internet access, online classroom assignments and information are available. *Library facilities:* Loyola/Notre Dame Library. *Graduate expenses:* Tuition: part-time $280 per credit. *General application contact:* Kathy Nikolaidis, Admissions Secretary, 410-532-5317.

Graduate Studies
Sr. Margaret E. Mahoney, PhD, Director
Programs in:
- communicating in contemporary culture • MA
- leadership in teaching • MA
- liberal studies • MA
- management • MA
- nonprofit management • MA
- studies in aging • MA
- teaching • MA
- teaching English to speakers of other languages • MA

■ COPPIN STATE COLLEGE

Baltimore, MD 21216-3698
http://www.coppin.edu/

State-supported, coed, comprehensive institution. CGS member. *Enrollment:* 29 full-time matriculated graduate/professional students (17 women), 769 part-time matriculated graduate/professional students (595 women). *Graduate faculty:* 25 full-time (15 women), 31 part-time/adjunct (22 women). *Computer facilities:* 130 computers available on campus for general student use. A campuswide network can be accessed from off campus. Internet access is available. *Library facilities:* Parlett L. Moore Library. *Graduate expenses:* Tuition, state resident: full-time $3,576; part-time $149 per credit hour. Tuition, nonresident: full-time $6,360; part-time $265 per credit hour. Required fees: $589. *General application contact:* Vell Lyles, Associate Vice President for Enrollment Management, 410-383-5821.

Division of Graduate Studies
Dr. Jerusa Wilson, Dean

Division of Arts and Sciences
Dr. Clyde Mathura, Dean
Programs in:
- arts and sciences • M Ed, MS
- criminal justice • MS
- rehabilitation • M Ed

Division of Education
Dr. Julius Chapman, Chair
Programs in:
- adult and general education • M Ed, MS
- curriculum and instruction • M Ed, MAT
- special education • M Ed

Helene Fuld School of Nursing
Dr. Marcella Copes, Dean
Program in:
- nurse practitioner • MS

■ FROSTBURG STATE UNIVERSITY

Frostburg, MD 21532-1099
http://www.frostburg.edu/

State-supported, coed, comprehensive institution. *Enrollment:* 188 full-time matriculated graduate/professional students (98 women), 675 part-time matriculated graduate/professional students (364 women). *Graduate faculty:* 89 full-time (37 women), 14 part-time/adjunct (7 women). *Computer facilities:* 577 computers available on campus for general student use. A campuswide network can be accessed from student residence rooms and from off campus. Internet access and online class registration are available. *Library facilities:* Lewis J. Ort Library. *Graduate expenses:* Tuition, state resident: full-time $3,240; part-time $180 per credit hour. Tuition, nonresident: full-time $3,744; part-time $208 per credit hour. Required fees: $612; $33 per credit hour. $9 per term. *General application contact:* Patricia C. Spiker, Director of Graduate Services, 301-687-7053.

Graduate School
Patricia C. Spiker, Director of Graduate Services

College of Business
Dr. Steve Wilkinson, Dean
Programs in:
- business • MBA
- business administration • MBA

College of Education
Dr. Susan Arisman, Dean
Programs in:
- curriculum and instruction • M Ed
- education • M Ed, MA, MS
- educational administration • M Ed
- educational technology • M Ed
- elementary • M Ed
- elementary education • M Ed
- elementary teaching • MA
- human performance • MS
- interdisciplinary education • M Ed
- parks and recreational management • MS
- reading • M Ed
- school counseling • M Ed
- secondary • M Ed
- secondary education • M Ed
- special education • M Ed

College of Liberal Arts and Sciences
Dr. Fred Yaffe, Dean
Programs in:
- applied computer science • MS
- applied ecology and conservation biology • MS
- counseling psychology • MS
- fisheries and wildlife management • MS
- liberal arts and sciences • MA, MS
- modern humanities • MA

■ HOOD COLLEGE

Frederick, MD 21701-8575
http://www.hood.edu/

Independent, women only, comprehensive institution. CGS member. *Enrollment:* 52 full-time matriculated graduate/professional students (35 women), 803 part-time matriculated graduate/professional students (553 women). *Graduate faculty:* 94. *Computer facilities:* 222 computers available on campus for general student use. A campuswide network can be accessed from student residence rooms and from off campus. Internet access is available. *Library facilities:* Beneficial-Hodson Library and Information Technology Center. *Graduate expenses:* Tuition: part-time $310 per credit. Required fees: $20 per term. *General application contact:* Dr. Ann Boyd, Dean of the Graduate School, 301-696-3600.

Graduate School
Dr. Ann Boyd, Dean
Programs in:
- administration and management • MBA
- biomedical science • MS
- computer and information sciences • MS
- curriculum and instruction • MS
- educational leadership • MS
- environmental biology • MS
- psychology • MA
- thanatology • MA

■ JOHNS HOPKINS UNIVERSITY

Baltimore, MD 21218-2699
http://www.jhu.edu/

Independent, coed, university. CGS member. *Enrollment:* 11,799 matriculated graduate/professional students. *Graduate faculty:* 2,425 full-time (833 women), 3,438 part-time/adjunct (1,013 women). *Computer facilities:* 185 computers available on campus for general student use. A campuswide network can be accessed from student residence rooms and from off campus. Internet access is available. *Library facilities:* Milton S. Eisenhower Library plus 6 others. *Graduate expenses:* Tuition: full-time $24,930; part-time $1,675 per course. Tuition and fees vary according to program. *General application contact:* Nicole Kendzejewki, Graduate Admissions Coordinator, 410-516-8174.

Find an in-depth description at www.petersons.com/graduate.

G. W. C. Whiting School of Engineering
Dr. Ilene J. Busch-Vishniac, Dean
Programs in:
- biomedical engineering • MSE, PhD
- chemical engineering • MS, MSE, PhD
- civil engineering • MCE, MSE, PhD
- computer science • MSE, PhD
- discrete mathematics • MA, MSE, PhD

Johns Hopkins University (continued)

electrical and computer engineering • MSE, PhD
engineering • M Mat SE, MA, MCE, MS, MSE, PhD
geography and environmental engineering • MA, MS, MSE, PhD
materials science and engineering • M Mat SE, MSE, PhD
mechanical engineering • MS, MSE, PhD
operations research/optimization/decision science • MA, MSE, PhD
statistics/probability/stochastic processes • MA, MSE, PhD

Paul H. Nitze School of Advanced International Studies
Steven Syabo, Dean
Programs in:
emerging markets • Certificate
interdisciplinary studies • MA, PhD
international public policy • MIPP

Peabody Conservatory of Music
Dr. Robert Sirota, Director
Program in:
music • MM, DMA, AD, GPD

Program in Molecular Biophysics
Dr. David E. Draper, Director
Program in:
molecular biophysics • PhD

School of Hygiene and Public Health
Dr. Alfred Sommer, Dean
Programs in:
biochemistry • MPH, PhD
biophysics • PhD
biostatistics • MPH
cancer epidemiology • MHS, Sc M, Dr PH, PhD, Sc D
clinical epidemiology • MHS, Sc M, Dr PH, PhD, Sc D
clinical investigation • MHS, Sc M, PhD
clinical trials • MHS, Sc M, Dr PH, PhD, Sc D
community health and health systems • MHS, PhD, Sc D
disease control • MHS, PhD, Sc D
environmental health engineering • MHS, Sc M, Dr PH, PhD, Sc D
environmental health sciences • MPH
epidemiology • MHS, MPH, Sc M, Dr PH, PhD, Sc D
finance and administration • MHS
genetic counseling • Sc M
genetics • MHS, Sc M, Dr PH, PhD, Sc D
health and public policy • MHS, PhD, Sc D
health economics • PhD, Sc D
health education • MHS
health policy • MHS
health policy and management • MPH
health policy/prevention policy • PhD, Sc D
health services research • MHS, PhD, Sc D
human nutrition • MHS, PhD, Sc D
hygiene and public health • MHS, MPH, Sc M, Dr PH, PhD, Sc D, Certificate
infectious disease epidemiology • MHS, Sc M, Dr PH, PhD, Sc D
international health • MPH, Dr PH
long-term care • PhD, Sc D
mental hygiene • MPH
molecular microbiology and immunology • MPH
occupational and environmental health • Dr PH, PhD
occupational/environmental epidemiology • MHS, Sc M, Dr PH, PhD, Sc D
physiology • Sc M, PhD
population and family health sciences • MPH
public health • MPH, Certificate
radiation health sciences • MHS, Sc M, Dr PH, PhD, Sc D
reproductive biology • MHS, Sc M, PhD
social and behavioral sciences • MHS, Sc M, PhD, Sc D
social sciences and public health • MHS, PhD, Sc D
toxicological sciences • PhD
vaccine development • Sc M, PhD, Sc D

School of Medicine
Dr. Edward D. Miller, Dean of Medical Faculty and Chief Executive Officer
Programs in:
art as applied to medicine • MA
medicine • MD, MA, MS, MSE, PhD

Graduate Programs in Medicine
Dr. Peter Maloney, Associate Dean for Graduate Student Affairs
Programs in:
biochemistry, cellular and molecular biology • PhD
biological chemistry • PhD
biophysics and biophysical chemistry • MS, PhD
cell biology and anatomy • PhD
cellular and molecular medicine • PhD
cellular and molecular physiology • PhD
human genetics and molecular biology • PhD
immunology • PhD
medicine • MA, MS, PhD
molecular biology and genetics • PhD
neuroscience • PhD
pathobiology • PhD
pharmacology and molecular sciences • PhD
physiology • PhD

School of Nursing
Dr. Sue K. Donaldson, Dean
Programs in:
advanced practice nursing-nurse practitioner • MSN
clinical specialist • MSN
clinical specialist and health systems management • MSN
community health nursing • MSN
health systems management • MSN
nurse practitioner • Certificate
nursing • MSN, DN Sc, PhD, Certificate
nursing science • DN Sc

School of Professional Studies in Business and Education
Dr. Ralph Fessler, Dean
Program in:
continuing studies • MAT, MBA, MS, Ed D, CAGS, Certificate, Post Master's Certificate

Division of Business and Management
Dr. Pete Peterson, Interim Associate Dean
Programs in:
advanced technology • Post Master's Certificate
business administration • MBA
change management • Certificate
electronic commerce • Post Master's Certificate
electronics business • Post Master's Certificate
finance • MS
information and telecommunication systems • Certificate
information and telecommunication systems for business • MS
information systems • Post Master's Certificate
investments • Certificate
leadership development • Certificate
marketing • MS
organization development and human resources • MS
police executive leadership • MS
real estate • MS
senior and housing care • Certificate
skilled facilitator • Certificate
telecommunication systems • Post Master's Certificate
the business of medicine • Certificate
the business of nursing • Certificate

Division of Education
Rochelle Ingram, Chair
Programs in:
- addictions counseling • Post Master's Certificate
- administration and supervision • MS
- assistive technology • Certificate
- autism • Certificate
- career counseling • Post Master's Certificate
- clinical community counseling • Post Master's Certificate
- counseling • MS, Ed D, CAGS
- counseling at-risk students • Post Master's Certificate
- discipline and positive behavior management • Certificate
- early childhood education • MAT
- earth and space science education/ mathematics education • MS
- earth/space science • Certificate
- education • MAT, MS, Ed D, CAGS, Certificate, Post Master's Certificate
- elementary education • MAT
- general education • MS, Ed D
- gifted education • MS, Certificate
- inclusion • Certificate
- instructional technology for web-based professional development and training • Certificate
- leadership in technology integration • Certificate
- learning disabilities • CAGS
- organizational counseling • Post Master's Certificate
- reading • MS, Certificate
- school administration and supervision • Certificate
- secondary education • MAT
- severe disabilities • Certificate
- severely and profoundly handicapped • CAGS
- special education • MS, Ed D
- teacher leadership • MS
- teaching in higher education • Certificate
- technology for educators • MS
- technology for internet-based and multimedia instruction • Certificate
- technology-based curriculum design and development • Certificate
- transition planning • Certificate

Zanvyl Krieger School of Arts and Sciences
Dr. Richard E. McCarty, Dean
Programs in:
- anthropology • PhD
- arts and sciences • MA, MLA, PhD, CAGS
- astronomy • PhD
- biochemistry • PhD
- biophysics • MA, PhD
- cell biology • PhD
- chemistry • MA, PhD
- classics • MA, PhD
- cognitive science • PhD
- developmental biology • PhD
- economics • PhD
- English and American literature • PhD
- experimental psychology • PhD
- French • PhD
- genetic biology • PhD
- geochemistry • MA, PhD
- geology • MA, PhD
- geophysics • MA, PhD
- German • PhD
- groundwater • MA, PhD
- history • PhD
- history of art • MA, PhD
- history of science • PhD
- Italian • MA, PhD
- liberal arts • MLA, CAGS
- mathematics • PhD
- molecular biology • PhD
- Near Eastern studies • MA, PhD
- oceanography • MA, PhD
- philosophy • MA, PhD
- physics • PhD
- planetary atmosphere • MA, PhD
- political science • MA, PhD
- psychology • PhD
- sociology • PhD
- Spanish • MA, PhD
- writing • MA

Humanities Center
Michael Fried, Chair
Program in:
- comparative literature and intellectual history • PhD

Institute for Policy Studies
Dr. Sandra J. Newman, Director
Program in:
- policy studies • MA

■ LOYOLA COLLEGE IN MARYLAND
Baltimore, MD 21210-2699
http://www.loyola.edu/

Independent-religious, coed, comprehensive institution. *Enrollment:* 625 full-time matriculated graduate/professional students (355 women), 1,972 part-time matriculated graduate/professional students (1,197 women). *Graduate faculty:* 65 full-time (31 women), 97 part-time/adjunct (33 women). *Computer facilities:* 292 computers available on campus for general student use. A campuswide network can be accessed from student residence rooms and from off campus. Internet access is available. *Library facilities:* Loyola/Notre Dame Library. *Graduate expenses:* Tuition: part-time $244 per credit. Tuition and fees vary according to program and student level. *General application contact:* Scott Greatorex, Director, Graduate Admissions, 410-617-5020 Ext. 2407.

Graduate Programs
Rev. Harold Ridley, SJ, President

College of Arts and Sciences
Dr. James Buckley, Dean
Programs in:
- arts and sciences • M Ed, MA, MES, MS, PhD, Psy D, CAS
- clinical psychology • MA, MS, Psy D, CAS
- counseling psychology • MA, MS, CAS
- curriculum and instruction • M Ed, MA, CAS
- education technology • M Ed
- educational management and supervision • M Ed, MA, CAS
- employee assistance and substance abuse • CAS
- engineering science • MES, MS
- foundations of education • M Ed, MA, CAS
- general psychology • MA, CAS
- guidance and counseling • M Ed, MA, CAS
- modern studies • MA
- Montessori education • M Ed
- pastoral counseling • MS, PhD, CAS
- reading • M Ed, MA, CAS
- special education • M Ed, MA, CAS
- speech pathology and audiology • MS, CAS
- spiritual and pastoral care • MA

The Joseph A. Sellinger S.J. School of Business and Management
John Moran, Associate Dean
Programs in:
- business and management • MBA, MIB, MSF, XMBA
- decision sciences • MBA
- economics • MBA
- executive business administration • MBA, XMBA
- finance • MBA
- international business • MIB
- marketing/management • MBA

■ MORGAN STATE UNIVERSITY
Baltimore, MD 21251
http://www.morgan.edu/

State-supported, coed, university. CGS member. *Enrollment:* 282 full-time matriculated graduate/professional students, 302 part-time matriculated graduate/professional students. *Graduate faculty:* 172 full-time, 10 part-time/adjunct. *Computer facilities:* 65 computers available on campus for general student use. A campuswide network can be accessed from student residence rooms

Morgan State University (continued)
and from off campus. Internet access and online class registration, engineering lab supercomputer are available. *Library facilities:* Morris Soper Library. *Graduate expenses:* Tuition, state resident: part-time $193 per credit. Tuition, nonresident: part-time $364 per credit. Required fees: $40 per credit. *General application contact:* Dr. James E. Waller, Admissions and Programs Officer, 443-885-3185.

School of Graduate Studies
Dr. Maurice C. Taylor, Dean, Graduate Studies and Research
Program in:
public health • Dr PH

College of Liberal Arts
Dr. Burney J. Hollis, Dean
Programs in:
African-American studies • MA
economics • MA
English • MA
history • MA, PhD
international studies • MA
liberal arts • MA, MS, PhD
mathematics • MA
music • MA
sociology • MA, MS

Earl G. Graves School of Business and Management
Dr. Otis A. Thomas, Dean
Programs in:
business administration • PhD
business and management • MBA, PhD

Institute of Architecture and Planning
Melvin L. Mitchell, Director
Programs in:
architecture • M Arch, MS Arch
city and regional planning • MCRP
landscape architecture • MASLA, MLA

School of Computer, Mathematical, and Natural Sciences
Dr. T. Joan Robinson, Dean
Programs in:
bio-environmental science • PhD
computer, mathematical, and natural sciences • MS, PhD
science • MS, PhD

School of Education and Urban Studies
Dr. Patricia L. Morris-Welch, Dean
Programs in:
education and urban studies • MAT, MS, Ed D, PhD
educational administration and supervision • MS
elementary and middle school education • MS
higher education administration • PhD
mathematics education • Ed D
teaching • MAT
urban educational leadership • Ed D

School of Engineering
Dr. Eugene DeLoatch, Dean
Programs in:
engineering • MS, D Eng
transportation • MS

■ MOUNT SAINT MARY'S COLLEGE AND SEMINARY
Emmitsburg, MD 21727-7799
http://www.msmary.edu/

Independent-religious, coed, comprehensive institution. *Enrollment:* 192 full-time matriculated graduate/professional students (21 women), 167 part-time matriculated graduate/professional students (100 women). *Graduate faculty:* 27 full-time (7 women), 25 part-time/adjunct (10 women). *Computer facilities:* 118 computers available on campus for general student use. A campuswide network can be accessed from student residence rooms and from off campus. Internet access and online class registration are available. *Library facilities:* Phillips Library. *Graduate expenses:* Tuition: part-time $270 per credit. Required fees: $200; $5 per credit. Tuition and fees vary according to program. *General application contact:* Dr. Stan Werne, Dean of Academic Services, 301-447-5355.

Graduate Seminary
Rev. Kevin Rhoades, Vice President/Rector
Program in:
theology • M Div, MA

Program in Business
Lori White Drega, Director
Program in:
business • MBA

Program in Education
Liz Monohan, Director
Program in:
education • M Ed

■ SALISBURY STATE UNIVERSITY
Salisbury, MD 21801-6837
http://www.ssu.edu/

State-supported, coed, comprehensive institution. *Enrollment:* 110 full-time matriculated graduate/professional students (62 women), 428 part-time matriculated graduate/professional students (311 women). *Graduate faculty:* 108 full-time (34 women). *Computer facilities:* 200 computers available on campus for general student use. A campuswide network can be accessed from student residence rooms and from off campus. Internet access is available. *Library facilities:* Blackwell Library plus 1 other. *Graduate expenses:* Tuition: part-time $168 per credit hour. Required fees: $4 per credit hour. *General application contact:* Jane H. Dané, Dean of Admissions, 410-543-6161.

Graduate Division
Programs in:
applied health physiology • MS
business administration • MBA
composition • MA
early childhood education • M Ed
educational administration • M Ed
elementary education • M Ed
English • M Ed
geography • M Ed
history • M Ed
literature • MA
mathematics • M Ed
media and technology • M Ed
music • M Ed
nursing • MS
psychology • M Ed
public school administration • MS Ed
reading education • M Ed
science • M Ed
secondary education • M Ed
teaching • MAT
teaching English to speakers of other languages • MA

■ TOWSON UNIVERSITY
Towson, MD 21252-0001
http://www.towson.edu/

State-supported, coed, comprehensive institution. CGS member. *Enrollment:* 665 full-time matriculated graduate/professional students (496 women), 2,159 part-time matriculated graduate/professional students (1,643 women). *Graduate faculty:* 136 full-time (54 women), 19 part-time/adjunct (12 women). *Computer facilities:* 1,013 computers available on campus for general student use. A campuswide network can be accessed from student residence rooms and from off campus. Internet access is available. *Library facilities:* Cook Library. *Graduate expenses:* Tuition, state resident: part-time $203 per credit. Tuition, nonresident: part-time $410 per credit. Required fees: $44 per credit. Tuition and fees vary according to program. *General application contact:* 410-704-2501.

Find an in-depth description at www.petersons.com/graduate.

Graduate School
Dr. Jin Gong, Dean of Graduate Education and Research
Programs in:
- administration and supervision • Certificate
- allied health professions • MS
- applied and industrial mathematics • MS
- applied gerontology • MS
- art education • M Ed
- audiology • Au D
- biology • MS
- clinical psychology • MA
- clinician-administrator transition • Certificate
- communications management • MS
- computer science • MS
- counseling psychology • MA
- Dalcroze • Certificate
- early childhood education • M Ed
- elementary education • M Ed
- environmental science • MS, Certificate
- experimental psychology • MA
- geography and environmental planning • MA
- human resource development • MS
- humanities • MA
- information security and assurance • Certificate
- information systems management • Certificate
- instructional technology • MS, Ed D
- interdisciplinary theatre • Certificate
- Internet application development • Certificate
- internet application development • Certificate
- Kodály • Certificate
- liberal and professional studies • MA
- litigation consulting • Certificate
- management and leadership development • Certificate
- mathematics education • MS
- music education • MS
- music performance • MM
- networking technologies • Certificate
- occupational science • Sc D
- occupational therapy • MS
- Orff • Certificate
- physician assistant studies • MS
- professional writing • MS
- psychology • MA
- reading education • M Ed
- school psychology • MA, CAS
- secondary education • M Ed
- social science • MS
- software engineering • Certificate
- speech-language pathology and audiology • MS
- strategic public relations and integrated communications • Certificate
- studio arts • MFA
- teaching • MAT
- theatre • MFA
- women's studies • MS

■ UNIVERSITY OF BALTIMORE

Baltimore, MD 21201-5779
http://www.ubalt.edu/

State-supported, coed, upper-level institution. *Enrollment:* 1,322 full-time matriculated graduate/professional students (710 women), 1,040 part-time matriculated graduate/professional students (611 women). *Graduate faculty:* 214 full-time (63 women), 161 part-time/adjunct (48 women). *Computer facilities:* 135 computers available on campus for general student use. A campuswide network can be accessed from off campus. Internet access is available. *Library facilities:* Langsdale Library plus 1 other. *Graduate expenses:* Tuition, state resident: full-time $5,076; part-time $282 per credit. Tuition, nonresident: full-time $7,560; part-time $420 per credit. Required fees: $628; $22 per credit. $60 per semester. Tuition and fees vary according to course load and degree level. *General application contact:* Jeffrey Zavrotny, Assistant Director of Admissions, 410-837-4777.

Graduate School
Ronald Legon, Provost

College of Liberal Arts
Dr. Carl Stenberg, Dean
Programs in:
- applied assessment and consulting • Psy D
- applied psychology • MS
- communications design • DCD
- counseling • MS
- criminal justice • MS
- government and public administration • MPA, DPA
- human services administration • MS
- industrial and organizational psychology • MS
- legal and ethical studies • MA
- liberal arts • MA, MPA, MS, DCD, DPA, Psy D
- negotiations and conflict management • MS
- publications design • MA

School of Business
Dr. John Hatfield, Dean
Programs in:
- accounting • MS
- business • MBA, MS
- business administration • MBA
- business/management information systems • MS
- business/marketing and venturing • MS
- finance • MS
- taxation • MS

School of Law
Eric Schneider, Dean
Programs in:
- law • JD
- taxation • LL M

■ UNIVERSITY OF MARYLAND

Baltimore, MD 21201-1627
http://www.umaryland.edu/

State-supported, coed, graduate-only institution. CGS member. *Graduate faculty:* 1,296 full-time, 338 part-time/adjunct. *Computer facilities:* A campuswide network can be accessed. Internet access is available. *Library facilities:* Health Sciences and Human Services Library. *Graduate expenses:* Tuition, state resident: full-time $6,576. Tuition, nonresident: full-time $11,736. Required fees: $388. Full-time tuition and fees vary according to course load, degree level and program. *General application contact:* Keith T. Brooks, Director, Graduate Admissions and Records, 410-706-7131.

Find an in-depth description at www.petersons.com/graduate.

Graduate School
Dr. Joann A. Boughman, Vice President for Academic Affairs and Dean
Programs in:
- dental hygiene • MS
- marine-estuarine-environmental sciences • MS, PhD
- medical and research technology • MS
- oral and craniofacial biological sciences • MS, PhD
- oral biology • MS
- oral pathology • MS, PhD
- pharmaceutical sciences • PhD
- pharmacy administration • PhD
- pharmacy practice and science • PhD
- social work • MSW, PhD

Graduate Programs in Medicine
Dr. Donald E. Wilson, Dean and Vice President for Medical Affairs

University of Maryland (continued)
Programs in:
anatomy and neurobiology • MS, PhD
applied professional ethics-medicine • MA
biochemistry • PhD
epidemiology and preventive medicine • MS, PhD
human genetics • MS, PhD
medical pathology • PhD
medicine • MA, MS, PhD
membrane biology • PhD
microbiology and immunology • MS, PhD
molecular and cell biology • PhD
neuroscience • PhD
neuroscience and cognitive sciences • MS, PhD
pathology • MS
pharmacology • PhD
pharmacology and experimental therapeutics • MS
physiology • PhD
reproductive endocrinology • PhD
toxicology • PhD

School of Nursing
Dr. Barbara Heller, Dean
Programs in:
community health nursing • MS
direct nursing • PhD
gerontological nursing • MS
indirect nursing • PhD
maternal-child nursing • MS
medical-surgical nursing • MS
nursing • PhD
nursing administration • MS
nursing education • MS
nursing health policy • MS
primary care nursing • MS
psychiatric nursing • MS

Professional Program in Dentistry
Dr. Richard R. Ranney, Dean
Program in:
dentistry • DDS, PhD

Professional Program in Medicine
Dr. Donald E. Wilson, Dean and Vice President for Medical Affairs
Program in:
medicine • MD

Professional Program in Pharmacy
Dr. Robert S. Beardsley, Associate Dean for Student Affairs
Program in:
pharmacy • Pharm D

School of Law
Karen H. Rothenberg, Dean
Program in:
law • JD

■ UNIVERSITY OF MARYLAND, BALTIMORE COUNTY

Baltimore, MD 21250-5398
http://www.umbc.edu/

State-supported, coed, university. CGS member. *Enrollment:* 765 full-time matriculated graduate/professional students, 893 part-time matriculated graduate/professional students. *Graduate faculty:* 423. *Computer facilities:* 500 computers available on campus for general student use. A campuswide network can be accessed from student residence rooms and from off campus. Internet access and online class registration, student account and grade information are available. *Library facilities:* Albin O. Kuhn Library and Gallery plus 1 other. *Graduate expenses:* Part-time $268 per credit. Tuition, nonresident: part-time $470 per credit. *General application contact:* Associate Dean, 410-455-3579.

Find an in-depth description at www.petersons.com/graduate.

Graduate School
Dr. Scott A. Bass, Dean and Vice Provost for Research
Programs in:
administration, planning, and policy • MS
applied and professional ethics • MA, Certificate
applied behavioral analysis • MA
applied developmental psychology • PhD
applied mathematics • MS, PhD
applied molecular biology • MS
applied physics • MS, PhD
applied sociology • MA, Certificate
atmospheric physics • MS, PhD
biochemistry • PhD
biological sciences • MS, PhD
biomedical and biobehavioral aspects of aging • PhD
chemistry • PhD
early childhood education • MA
economic policy analysis • MA
education • MA, MS
elementary education • MA
English as a second language/bilingual education • MA
epidemiology of aging • PhD
French • MA
German • MA
historical studies • MA
imaging and digital arts • MFA
information systems • MS, PhD
instructional systems development • MA
language, literacy, and culture • PhD
law and social policy of aging • PhD
literacy, language and culture • PhD
marine-estuarine-environmental sciences • MS, PhD
medical sociology • MA
modern languages and linguistics • MA
molecular and cell biology • PhD
neuroscience • PhD
neurosciences and cognitive sciences • MS, PhD
policy sciences • MPS, PhD
post-baccalaureate teacher education • MA
preventive medicine and epidemiology • MS
psychology/human services • MA, PhD
Russian • MA
secondary education • MA
social and behavioral aspects of aging • PhD
Spanish • MA
statistics • MS, PhD
training systems • MA

College of Engineering
Dr. Shlomo Carmi, Dean
Programs in:
chemical and biochemical engineering • MS, PhD
computer science • MS, PhD
electrical engineering • MS, PhD
engineering • MS, PhD
engineering management • MS
mechanical engineering • MS, PhD

■ UNIVERSITY OF MARYLAND, COLLEGE PARK

College Park, MD 20742
http://www.maryland.edu/

State-supported, coed, university. CGS member. *Enrollment:* 4,919 full-time matriculated graduate/professional students (2,236 women), 2,907 part-time matriculated graduate/professional students (1,483 women). *Graduate faculty:* 2,690 full-time (852 women), 914 part-time/adjunct (376 women). *Computer facilities:* 899 computers available on campus for general student use. A campuswide network can be accessed from student residence rooms and from off campus. Internet access and online class registration, student account information, financial aid summary are available. *Library facilities:* McKeldin Library plus 6 others. *Graduate expenses:* Tuition, state resident: part-time $278 per credit. Tuition, nonresident: part-time $430 per credit. Required fees: $687; $414 per year. Tuition and fees vary according to course load, campus/location and program. *General application contact:* Trudy Lindsey, Director, Graduate Admissions and Records, 301-405-4198.

Graduate Studies and Research
Dr. William W. Destler, Dean
Programs in:
- business and management/public management
- geography, library, and information services
- history, library, and information services

neurosciences and cognitive sciences • PhD

A. James Clark School of Engineering
Dr. Nariman Farvardin, Dean
Programs in:
aerospace engineering • M Eng
chemical engineering • M Eng
civil and environmental engineering • M Eng, MS, PhD
civil engineering • M Eng
electrical and computer engineering • M Eng, MS, PhD
electrical engineering • M Eng, MS, PhD
electronic packaging and reliability • MS, PhD
engineering • M Eng, ME, MS, PhD
fire protection engineering • M Eng
manufacturing and design • MS, PhD
materials science and engineering • M Eng, MS, PhD
mechanical engineering • M Eng
mechanics and materials • MS, PhD
nuclear engineering • ME, MS, PhD
reliability engineering • M Eng, MS, PhD
systems engineering • M Eng
telecommunications • MS
thermal and fluid sciences • MS, PhD

College of Agriculture and Natural Resources
Dr. Thomas Fretz, Dean
Programs in:
agriculture and natural resources • DVM, MS, PhD
agriculture economics • MS, PhD
agronomy • MS, PhD
animal sciences • MS, PhD
biological resources engineering • MS, PhD
food science • MS, PhD
horticulture • MS, PhD
nutrition • MS, PhD
poultry science • MS, PhD
resource economics • MS, PhD
veterinary medical sciences • PhD
veterinary medicine • DVM, PhD

College of Arts and Humanities
Dr. James Harris, Dean
Programs in:
American studies • MA, PhD
art • MFA
art history • MA, PhD
arts and humanities • M Ed, MA, MFA, MM, DMA, Ed D, PhD
classics • MA
communications • MA, PhD
comparative literature • MA, PhD
creative writing • MA, PhD
dance • MFA
English language and literature • MA, PhD
French language and literature • MA, PhD
Germanic language and literature • MA, PhD
history • MA, PhD
linguistics • MA, PhD
music • M Ed, MA, MM, DMA, Ed D, PhD
philosophy • MA, PhD
Russian language and literature • MA
Spanish • MA, PhD
theatre • MA, MFA, PhD
women's studies • MA, PhD

College of Behavioral and Social Sciences
Dr. Irwin L. Goldstein, Dean
Programs in:
American politics • MA, PhD
applied anthropology • MAA
audiology • MA, PhD
behavioral and social sciences • MA, MAA, MS, PhD
clinical psychology • PhD
comparative politics • MA, PhD
criminology and criminal justice • MA, PhD
developmental psychology • PhD
economics • MA, PhD
experimental psychology • PhD
geography • MA, PhD
industrial psychology • MA, MS, PhD
international relations • MA, PhD
language pathology • MA, PhD
political economy • MA, PhD
political theory • MA, PhD
social psychology • PhD
sociology • MA, PhD
speech • MA, PhD
survey methodology • MS, PhD

College of Computer, Mathematical and Physical Sciences
Dr. Stephen Halperin, Dean
Programs in:
applied mathematics • MS, PhD
astronomy • MS, PhD
chemical physics • MS, PhD
computer science • MS, PhD
computer, mathematical and physical sciences • MA, MS, MSWE, PhD
geology • MS, PhD
mathematical statistics • MA, PhD
mathematics • MA, PhD
meteorology • MS, PhD
physics • MS, PhD
software engineering • MS, MSWE

College of Education
Dr. Edna Szymanski, Dean
Programs in:
college student personnel • M Ed, MA
college student personnel administration • PhD
community counseling • CAGS
community/career counseling • M Ed, MA
counseling and personnel services • M Ed, MA, PhD
counseling psychology • PhD
counselor education • PhD
curriculum and educational communications • M Ed, MA, Ed D, PhD
early childhood/elementary education • M Ed, MA, Ed D, PhD, CAGS
education • M Ed, MA, Ed D, PhD, CAGS
human development • M Ed, MA, Ed D, PhD, CAGS
measurement • MA, PhD
program evaluation • MA, PhD
reading • M Ed, MA, PhD, CAGS
rehabilitation counseling • M Ed, MA
school counseling • M Ed, MA
school psychology • M Ed, MA, PhD
secondary education • M Ed, MA, Ed D, PhD, CAGS
social foundations of education • M Ed, MA, Ed D, PhD, CAGS
special education • M Ed, MA, Ed D, PhD, CAGS
statistics • MA, PhD
teaching English to speakers of other languages • M Ed

College of Health and Human Performance
Dr. Jerry Wrenn, Interim Dean
Programs in:
community health • MPH
family studies • MS
health and human performance • MA, MPH, MS, Ed D, PhD
health education • MA, Ed D, PhD
kinesiology • MA, PhD
marriage and family therapy • MS

College of Information Studies
Dr. Ann E. Prentice, Dean
Program in:
information studies • MLS, PhD

University of Maryland, College Park (continued)

College of Life Sciences
Dr. Norman M. Allewell, Dean
Programs in:
- analytical chemistry • MS, PhD
- biochemistry • MS, PhD
- biology • MS, PhD
- cell biology and molecular genetics • MS, PhD
- chemistry • MS, PhD
- entomology • MS, PhD
- inorganic chemistry • MS, PhD
- life sciences • MLS, MS, PhD
- marine-estuarine-environmental sciences • MS, PhD
- microbiology • MS, PhD
- molecular and cell biology • PhD
- organic chemistry • MS, PhD
- physical chemistry • MS, PhD
- plant biology • MS, PhD
- sustainable development and conservation biology • MS
- toxicology • MS, PhD
- zoology • MS, PhD

Phillip Merrill College of Journalism
Thomas Kunkel, Dean
Programs in:
- advertising • MA, PhD
- broadcast journalism • MA, PhD
- international communication • MA, PhD
- journalism • MA
- journalism education • MA, PhD
- mass communication • PhD
- mass communication research • MA, PhD
- political communication • MA, PhD
- public affairs reporting • MA, PhD
- public communication • MA, PhD
- public relations • MA, PhD
- science communication • MA, PhD

Robert H. Smith School of Business
Dr. Howard Frank, Dean
Programs in:
- business • MBA, MS, PhD
- business administration • MBA
- business and management • MS, PhD

School of Architecture
Steven Hurtt, Dean
Programs in:
- architecture • M Arch, MA, MCP
- community planning • MCP

School of Public Affairs
Dr. Susan C. Schwab, Dean
Programs in:
- policy studies • PhD
- public affairs • MPM, MPP, PhD
- public management • MPM
- public policy • MPP

■ UNIVERSITY OF MARYLAND EASTERN SHORE

Princess Anne, MD 21853-1299
http://www.umes.edu/

State-supported, coed, university. CGS member. *Enrollment:* 241 matriculated graduate/professional students (160 women). *Graduate faculty:* 107. *Computer facilities:* 120 computers available on campus for general student use. A campuswide network can be accessed. *Library facilities:* Frederick Douglass Library. *Graduate expenses:* Tuition, state resident: part-time $151 per credit hour. Tuition, nonresident: part-time $272 per credit hour. Required fees: $25 per semester. *General application contact:* Terrance L. Hicks, Admissions and Advisement Coordinator, 410-651-8626.

Find an in-depth description at www.petersons.com/graduate.

Graduate Programs
Dr. C. Dennis Ignasias, Dean of Graduate Studies
Programs in:
- agriculture education and extension • MS
- applied computer science • MS
- career and technology education • M Ed
- food and agricultural sciences • MS
- guidance and counseling • M Ed
- marine estuarine • MS, PhD
- marine-estuarine-environmental sciences • MS, PhD
- physical therapy • MPT
- special education • M Ed
- teaching • MAT
- toxicology • MS, PhD

■ UNIVERSITY OF MARYLAND UNIVERSITY COLLEGE

Adelphi, MD 20783
http://www.umuc.edu/

State-supported, coed, comprehensive institution. CGS member. *Enrollment:* 336 full-time matriculated graduate/professional students (160 women), 4,666 part-time matriculated graduate/professional students (2,294 women). *Graduate faculty:* 143 part-time/adjunct (22 women). *Computer facilities:* 375 computers available on campus for general student use. A campuswide network can be accessed from off campus. *Library facilities:* Information and Library Services plus 1 other. *Graduate expenses:* Tuition, state resident: full-time $5,238; part-time $291 per credit. Tuition, nonresident: full-time $8,550; part-time $475 per credit. *General application contact:* Coordinator, Graduate Admissions, 301-985-7155.

Graduate School of Management and Technology
Dr. Christina A. Hannah, Acting Associate Vice President and Dean of Graduate Studies
Programs in:
- computer systems management • MS
- distance education • MDE
- environmental management • MS
- international management • Exec MIM, MIM
- management • MS
- management and technology • Exec MIM, Exec MS, M Sw E, MDE, MIM, MS
- software engineering • M Sw E
- technology management • Exec MS, MS
- telecommunications management • MS

Massachusetts

■ AMERICAN INTERNATIONAL COLLEGE

Springfield, MA 01109-3189
http://www.aic.edu/

Independent, coed, comprehensive institution. *Computer facilities:* 100 computers available on campus for general student use. A campuswide network can be accessed. Internet access is available. *Library facilities:* James J. Shea Jr. Library. *General application contact:* Dean, 413-747-6525.

School of Continuing Education and Graduate Studies
Programs in:
- organization development • MSOD
- physical therapy • MPT
- public administration • MPA

School of Business Administration
Program in:
- business administration • MBA

School of Psychology and Education
Programs in:
- administration • M Ed, CAGS
- child development • MA, Ed D
- clinical psychology • MS
- criminal justice studies • MS

educational psychology • MA, Ed D
elementary education • M Ed, CAGS
human resource development • MA, CAGS
psychology and education • M Ed, MA, MS, Ed D, CAGS
reading • M Ed, CAGS
school psychology • MA, CAGS
secondary education • M Ed, CAGS
special education • M Ed, CAGS

■ ANNA MARIA COLLEGE

Paxton, MA 01612
http://www.annamaria.edu/

Independent-religious, coed, comprehensive institution. *Enrollment:* 6 full-time matriculated graduate/professional students (4 women), 321 part-time matriculated graduate/professional students (162 women). *Graduate faculty:* 35 full-time (21 women), 61 part-time/adjunct (21 women). *Computer facilities:* 57 computers available on campus for general student use. A campuswide network can be accessed from student residence rooms and from off campus. Internet access, on-line class schedules, student account information are available. *Library facilities:* Mondor-Eagen Library. *Graduate expenses:* Tuition: part-time $300 per credit. *General application contact:* Ann Kwek, Assistant Director of Admissions for Graduate Programs and the Department of Professional Studies, 508-849-3361.

Graduate Division

Dr. Cynthia Patterson, Dean
Programs in:
biological studies • MA
business administration • MBA, AC
counseling psychology • MA, CAGS
criminal justice • MA
early childhood development • M Ed
elementary education • M Ed
emergency response planning • MS
fire science • MA
occupational and environmental health and safety • MS
psychology • MA, CAGS
reading • M Ed

■ ASSUMPTION COLLEGE

Worcester, MA 01609-1296
http://www.assumption.edu/

Independent-religious, coed, comprehensive institution. *Enrollment:* 60 full-time matriculated graduate/professional students (48 women), 213 part-time matriculated graduate/professional students (149 women). *Graduate faculty:* 38 full-time (12 women), 37 part-time/adjunct (10 women). *Computer facilities:* 190 computers available on campus for general student use. A campuswide network can be accessed from student residence rooms and from off campus. Internet access is available. *Library facilities:* Emmanuel d'Alzon Library. *Graduate expenses:* Tuition: full-time $3,015; part-time $1,005 per course. Required fees: $150; $150 per year. *General application contact:* Adrian O. Dumas, Director of Graduate Enrollment Management and Services, 508-767-7365.

Find an in-depth description at www.petersons.com/graduate.

Graduate School

Dr. MaryLou Anderson, Dean of the College
Programs in:
business studies • MBA, CPS
counseling psychology • MA, CAGS
special education • MA

Institute for Social and Rehabilitation Services

Dr. William Talley, Director
Program in:
rehabilitation counseling • MA, CAGS

■ BENTLEY COLLEGE

Waltham, MA 02452-4705
http://www.bentley.edu/

Independent, coed, comprehensive institution. CGS member. *Enrollment:* 356 full-time matriculated graduate/professional students (153 women), 1,056 part-time matriculated graduate/professional students (479 women). *Graduate faculty:* 227 full-time (72 women), 184 part-time/adjunct. *Computer facilities:* 3,349 computers available on campus for general student use. A campuswide network can be accessed from student residence rooms and from off campus. Internet access and online class registration are available. *Library facilities:* Soloman R. Baker Library. *Graduate expenses:* Tuition: full-time $17,920; part-time $747 per credit hour. Required fees: $65; $65 per year. *General application contact:* Simone L. Booth, Director of Graduate Admissions, 781-891-2108.

The Elkin B. McCallum Graduate School of Business

Dr. Patricia M. Flynn, Dean
Programs in:
accountancy • MBA
accounting • MSA, Certificate
accounting information systems • MSAIS, Certificate
advanced accountancy • MBA
business • IAMBA, MBA, MSA, MSAIS, MSCIS, MSF, MSGFA, MSHFID, MSIAM, MSPFP, MST, Advanced Certificate, Certificate
business administration • Advanced Certificate
business communication • MBA
business data analysis • MBA, Certificate
business economics • MBA
business ethics • MBA, Certificate
e-business • MBA, Certificate
entrepreneurial studies • MBA
finance • MBA
global financial analysis • MSGFA
human factors in information design • MSHFID
information age business administration • IAMBA
information age marketing • MSIAM, Certificate
international business • MBA
management • MBA
management information systems • MBA, MSCIS
management of technology • MBA
marketing • MBA
operations management • MBA
personal financial planning • MSPFP, Advanced Certificate, Certificate
taxation • MBA

■ BOSTON COLLEGE

Chestnut Hill, MA 02467-3800
http://www.bc.edu/

Independent-religious, coed, university. CGS member. *Enrollment:* 2,293 full-time matriculated graduate/professional students (1,417 women), 2,370 part-time matriculated graduate/professional students (1,274 women). *Graduate faculty:* 641. *Computer facilities:* 200 computers available on campus for general student use. A campuswide network can be accessed from student residence rooms and from off campus. *Library facilities:* Thomas P. O'Neill Library plus 6 others. *Graduate expenses:* Tuition: part-time $736 per credit. *General application contact:* Stephanie Autenrieth, Assistant Dean for Student Services, 617-552-3265.

Find an in-depth description at www.petersons.com/graduate.

Boston College (continued)

Graduate School of Arts and Sciences
Dr. Michael A. Smyer, Dean
Programs in:
analytical chemistry • MS, PhD
arts and sciences • MA, MS, PhD, CAES, CAGS
biochemistry • MS, PhD
biology • MS, PhD
chemistry • MS
classics • MA
economics • MA, PhD
English • MA, PhD, CAGS
European national studies • MA
French • MA, PhD
geology and geophysics • MS
Greek • MA
history • MA, PhD
inorganic chemistry • MS, PhD
Italian • MA
Latin • MA
linguistics • MA
mathematics • MA
medieval language • PhD
medieval studies • MA
organic chemistry • MS, PhD
philosophy • MA, PhD
physical chemistry • MS, PhD
physics • MS, PhD
political science • MA, PhD
psychology • PhD
Russian and Slavic languages and literature • MA
Slavic studies • MA
sociology • MA, PhD
Spanish • MA, PhD
theology • MA, PhD

Institute of Religious Education and Pastoral Ministry
Dr. Mary Anne Hinsdale, Chairperson
Programs in:
church leadership • MA
nursing and pastoral ministry • MA, PhD, CAES
pastoral ministry • MA
religious education • MA, PhD, CAES
social justice/social ministry • MA
youth ministry • MA

Graduate School of Social Work
Program in:
social work • MSW, PhD

Law School
John Garvey, Dean
Program in:
law • JD

Lynch Graduate School of Education
Dr. Mary Brabeck, Dean
Programs in:
biology • MST
Catholic school leadership • M Ed, CAES
chemistry • MST
counseling psychology • MA, PhD
curriculum and instruction • M Ed, PhD, CAES
developmental and educational psychology • MA, PhD
early childhood education/teacher option • M Ed
early childhood/specialist option • MA
education • M Ed, MA, MAT, MST, Ed D, PhD, CAES
educational administration • M Ed, Ed D, PhD, CAES
educational research, measurement, and evaluation • M Ed, PhD, CAES
elementary teaching • M Ed
English • MAT
geology • MST
higher education administration • MA, PhD
history • MAT
Latin and classics • MAT
mathematics • MST
moderate special needs • M Ed, CAES
multiple disabilities and deaf/blindness • M Ed, CAES
physics • MST
professional school administrator • PhD
reading specialist • M Ed, CAES
religious education • M Ed, CAES
Romance languages • MAT
secondary education • M Ed, MAT, MST
secondary teaching • M Ed
severe special needs • M Ed
visual impairment studies • M Ed, CAES

School of Nursing
Dr. Barbara Munro, Dean
Programs in:
adult health nursing • MS
community health nursing • MS
family health • MS
gerontology • MS
maternal/child health nursing • MS
nursing • PhD
nursing and pastoral ministry • MS, PhD
psychiatric-mental health nursing • MS

The Wallace E. Carroll School of Management
Dr. Robert A. Taggart, Associate Dean for Graduate Programs
Programs in:
business administration • MBA
finance • MSF, PhD
management • MBA, MSF, PhD
organization studies • PhD

■ BOSTON UNIVERSITY
Boston, MA 02215
http://www.bu.edu/

Independent, coed, university. CGS member. *Enrollment:* 7,341 full-time matriculated graduate/professional students (3,850 women), 2,790 part-time matriculated graduate/professional students (1,430 women). *Graduate faculty:* 3,222. *Computer facilities:* 750 computers available on campus for general student use. A campuswide network can be accessed from student residence rooms and from off campus. Internet access, research and educational networks are available. *Library facilities:* Mugar Memorial Library plus 18 others. *Graduate expenses:* Tuition: full-time $24,700. Required fees: $234.

Find an in-depth description at www.petersons.com/graduate.

College of Communication
Brent Baker, Dean
Programs in:
broadcast journalism • MS
business and economics journalism • MS
communication • MFA, MS
film production • MFA
film studies • MFA
mass communication • MS
print journalism • MS
public relations • MS
science journalism • MS
screenwriting • MFA
television • MS
television management • MS

College of Engineering
Dr. David Campbell, Dean
Programs in:
aerospace engineering • MS, PhD
biomedical engineering • MS, PhD
computer engineering • PhD
computer systems engineering • MS
electrical engineering • MS, PhD
engineering • MS, PhD
general engineering • MS
manufacturing engineering • MS, PhD
mechanical engineering • MS, PhD
systems engineering • PhD

Graduate School of Arts and Sciences
J. Scott Whittaker, Associate Dean
Programs in:
French language and literature • MA
African American studies • MA
African studies • Certificate
American and New England studies • PhD

anthropology • MA, PhD
applied linguistics • MA, PhD
archaeology • MA, PhD
art history • MA, PhD
arts and sciences • MA, MAEP, MAPE, PhD, Certificate
astronomy • MA, PhD
biology • MA, PhD
biostatistics • MA, PhD
cellular biophysics • PhD
chemistry • MA, PhD
classical studies • MA, PhD
cognitive and neural systems • MA, PhD
composition • MA
computer science • MA, PhD
creative writing • MA
earth sciences • MA, PhD
economic policy • MAEP
economics • MA, PhD
editorial • MA, PhD
energy and environmental analysis • MA
English • MA, PhD
environmental remote sensing and geographic information systems • MA
French language and literature • PhD
geography • MA, PhD
Hispanic language and literature • MA, PhD
history • MA, PhD
international relations • MA
international relations and enivronmental policy • MA
international relations and environmental policy management • MA
international relations and international communication • MA
mathematical finance • MA
mathematics • MA, PhD
molecular biology, cell biology, and biochemistry • MA, PhD
museum studies • Certificate
music education • MA
music history/theory • PhD
musicology • MA, PhD
neuroscience • MA, PhD
philosophy • MA, PhD
physics • MA, PhD
political economy • MAPE
political science • MA, PhD
preservation studies • MA
psychology • MA, PhD
religious and theological studies • MA, PhD
sociology • MA, PhD
sociology and social work • PhD

Editorial Institute
Christopher Ricks, Co-Director
Program in:
editorial • MA, PhD

Henry M. Goldman School of Dental Medicine
Dr. Spencer Frankl, Dean
Programs in:
advanced general dentistry • CAGS
dental medicine • DMD, MS, MSD, D Sc, D Sc D, PhD, CAGS
dental public health • MS, MSD, D Sc D, CAGS
dentistry • DMD, MS, MSD, D Sc, D Sc D, PhD, CAGS
endodontics • MSD, D Sc D, CAGS
implantology • CAGS
nutritional science • MS, D Sc
operative dentistry • MSD, D Sc D, CAGS
oral and maxillofacial surgery • MSD, D Sc D, CAGS
oral biology • MSD, D Sc, D Sc D, PhD
orthodontics • MSD, D Sc D, CAGS
pediatric dentistry • MSD, D Sc D, CAGS
periodontology • MSD, D Sc D, CAGS
prosthodontics • MSD, D Sc D, CAGS

Metropolitan College
John F. Ebersole, Dean
Programs in:
actuarial science • MS
arts administration • MS
city planning • MCP
computer information systems • MS
computer science • MS
criminal justice • MCJ
electronic commerce • MSAS
financial economics • MSAS
innovation and technology • MSAS
liberal arts • MLA
multinational commerce • MSAS
telecommunications • MS
urban affairs • MUA

Sargent College of Health and Rehabilitation Sciences
Dr. Alan M. Jette, Dean
Programs in:
applied anatomy and physiology • MS, D Sc
audiology • D Sc
health and rehabilitation sciences • MS, MSOT, MSPT, D Sc, DPT, CAGS
movement and rehabilitation sciences • MS, D Sc
nutrition • MS
occupational therapy • MS, MSOT, CAGS
physical therapy • MSPT, DPT
rehabilitation counseling • MS, D Sc, CAGS
speech-language pathology • MS, D Sc, CAGS
therapeutic studies • D Sc

School for the Arts
Walt Meissner, Acting Dean
Programs in:
art education • MFA
arts • MFA, MM, DMA, Artist Diploma, Certificate
collaborative piano • MM, DMA
composition • MM, DMA
conducting • MM, Artist Diploma
costume design • MFA
costume production • MFA
directing • MFA
graphic design • MFA
historical performance • MM, DMA, Artist Diploma
lighting design • MFA
music education • MM, DMA
music history and literature • MM
music theory • MM
opera performance • Certificate
painting • MFA
performance • MM, DMA, Artist Diploma
scene design • MFA
sculpture • MFA
studio teaching • MFA
technical production • MFA, Certificate
theatre crafts • Certificate
theatre education • MFA

School of Education
Dr. Edwin J. Delattre, Dean
Programs in:
administration, training, and policy studies • Ed D
bilingual education • Ed M, CAGS
counseling • Ed M, CAGS
counseling psychology • Ed D
curriculum and teaching • Ed M, MAT, Ed D, CAGS
developmental studies • Ed M, Ed D, CAGS
early childhood education • Ed M, Ed D, CAGS
education • Ed M, MAT, Ed D, CAGS
education of the deaf • Ed M, CAGS
educational administration • Ed M
educational media and technology • Ed M, Ed D, CAGS
elementary education • Ed M
English and language arts education • Ed M, Ed D, CAGS
health education • Ed M, CAGS
human movement • Ed M, Ed D, CAGS
human resource education • Ed M, CAGS
international educational development • Ed M
Latin and classical studies • MAT
leisure education • Ed M
mathematics education • Ed M, MAT, Ed D, CAGS

Boston University (continued)
- modern foreign language education • Ed M, MAT
- policy, planning and administration • Ed D
- policy, planning, and administration • Ed M, CAGS
- reading education • Ed M, Ed D, CAGS
- science education • Ed M, MAT, Ed D, CAGS
- social studies education • Ed M, MAT, Ed D, CAGS
- special education • Ed M, Ed D, CAGS
- special education and social work • Ed M, Ed D, CAGS
- teaching of English to speakers of other languages • Ed M, CAGS

School of Law
Ronald A. Cass, Dean
Programs in:
- American law • LL M
- banking law • LL M
- law • JD
- taxation • LL M

School of Management
Janelle Heineke, Associate Dean
Programs in:
- accounting • DBA
- advanced accounting • Certificate
- business administration • Exec MBA
- finance • DBA
- general management • MBA
- health-care management • MBA
- information systems • MSIS, DBA
- investment management • MSIM
- management policy • DBA
- marketing • DBA
- nonprofit management • MBA
- operations management • DBA
- organizational behavior • DBA
- public and nonprofit management • MBA
- public management • MBA

School of Medicine
Dr. Aram V. Chobanian, Dean
Program in:
- medicine • MD, MA, PhD

Division of Graduate Medical Sciences
Dr. Carl Franzblau, Associate Dean
Programs in:
- anatomy and neurobiology • MA, PhD
- behavioral neurosciences • PhD
- biochemistry • MA, PhD
- cell and molecular biology • PhD
- experimental pathology • PhD
- immunology • PhD
- medical sciences • MA, PhD
- mental health counseling and behavioral medicine • MA
- microbiology • MA, PhD
- molecular medicine • PhD
- pharmacology and experimental therapeutics • MA, PhD
- physiology • MA, PhD
- physiology and biophysics • MA, PhD

School of Public Health
Dr. Robert F. Meenan, Dean
Programs in:
- biostatistics • MA, MPH, PhD
- environmental health • MPH, D Sc
- epidemiology • M Sc, MPH, D Sc
- health behavior, health promotion, and disease prevention • MPH
- health law • MPH
- health services • MPH
- international health • MPH, Certificate
- maternal and child health • MPH
- nurse midwifery education • Certificate
- public health • M Sc, MA, MPH, D Sc, PhD, Certificate

School of Social Work
Wilma Peebles-Wilkins, Dean
Programs in:
- clinical practice with groups • MSW
- clinical practice with individuals and families • MSW
- macro social work practice • MSW
- social work and sociology • PhD

School of Theology
Dr. Robert Neville, Dean
Program in:
- theology • M Div, D Min/MSW, MSM, MTS, STM, D Min, Th D

University Professors Program
Claudio Véliz, Director
Program in:
- interdisciplinary studies • MA, PhD

■ BRANDEIS UNIVERSITY
Waltham, MA 02454-9110
http://www.brandeis.edu/

Independent, coed, university. CGS member. *Enrollment:* 942 full-time matriculated graduate/professional students (492 women), 473 part-time matriculated graduate/professional students (198 women). *Graduate faculty:* 360 full-time (117 women), 181 part-time/adjunct (91 women). *Computer facilities:* 104 computers available on campus for general student use. A campuswide network can be accessed from student residence rooms and from off campus. Internet access and online class registration, educational software are available. *Library facilities:* Goldfarb Library plus 2 others. *Graduate expenses:* Tuition: full-time $25,392; part-time $3,174 per course. *General application contact:* Margaret Haley, Assistant Dean, Graduate Admissions, 781-736-3410.

Find an in-depth description at www.petersons.com/graduate.

Graduate School of Arts and Sciences
Dr. Milton Kornfeld, Associate Dean of Arts and Sciences for Graduate Education
Programs in:
- American history • MA, PhD
- anthropology • MA, PhD
- anthropology and women's studies • MA
- arts and sciences • MA, MAMM, MFA, MS, PhD, AD, Certificate
- biochemistry • MS, PhD
- biophysics and structural biology • PhD
- cell biology • PhD
- classical studies • MA
- cognitive neuroscience • PhD
- comparative history • MA, PhD
- composition and theory • MA, MFA, PhD
- developmental biology • PhD
- English and American literature • PhD
- English and women's studies • MA
- general psychology • MA
- genetic counseling • MS
- genetics • PhD
- inorganic chemistry • MS, PhD
- Jewish communal service • MA, MAMM
- mathematics • PhD
- microbiology • PhD
- molecular and cell biology • MS, PhD
- molecular biology • PhD
- music and women's studies • MA, MFA
- musicology • MA, MFA, PhD
- Near Eastern and Judaic studies • MA, PhD
- Near Eastern and Judaic studies and sociology • PhD
- near Eastern and Judaic studies and sociology • MA, PhD
- Near Eastern and Judaic studies and women's studies • MA
- Near Eastern and Judiac studies and sociology • MA
- neurobiology • PhD
- neuroscience • MS, PhD
- organic chemistry • MS, PhD
- physical chemistry • MS, PhD
- physics • MS, PhD
- politics • MA, PhD
- postbaccalaureate premedical • Certificate
- social policy and sociology • PhD

social/developmental psychology • PhD
sociology • MA, PhD
sociology and women's studies • MA
studio art • Certificate
theater arts • MFA

Michtom School of Computer Science
Dr. James Pustejovsky, Director of Graduate Studies
Program in:
computer science • MA, PhD

Graduate School of International Economics and Finance
Dr. Peter Petri, Dean
Programs in:
finance • MSF
international business • MBAi
international economics and finance • MA, PhD

The Heller School for Social Policy and Management
Dr. Jack Shonkoff, Dean
Programs in:
child, youth, and family services • MBA, MM
elder and disabled services • MBA, MM
health care administratiaon • MM
health care administration • MBA
human services • MBA, MM
social policy • PhD
social policy and management • MA, MAMM, MBA, MM, PhD
sustainable international development • MA

■ BRIDGEWATER STATE COLLEGE

Bridgewater, MA 02325-0001
http://www.bridgew.edu/

State-supported, coed, comprehensive institution. CGS member. *Enrollment:* 1,800 matriculated graduate/professional students. *Graduate faculty:* 140 full-time. *Computer facilities:* 534 computers available on campus for general student use. A campuswide network can be accessed from student residence rooms and from off campus. Internet access and online class registration, student account information, application software are available. *Library facilities:* Clement Maxwell Library. *Graduate expenses:* Tuition: part-time $70 per credit. Required fees: $66 per credit. *General application contact:* James Plotner, Assistant Dean, Graduate Admissions, 508-531-1300.

Graduate School
Dr. Edward Minnock, Dean
Programs in:
accounting and finance • MSM
management • MSM

School of Arts and Sciences
Dr. Howard London, Dean
Programs in:
art • MAT
arts and sciences • MA, MAT, MPA, MS
biological sciences • MAT
chemical sciences • MAT
computer science • MS
earth sciences • MAT
English • MA, MAT
history • MAT
mathematics • MAT
physical sciences • MAT
physics • MAT
political science • MPA
psychology • MA

School of Education and Allied Science
Dr. Ronald Cromwell, Dean
Programs in:
counseling • M Ed, CAGS
early childhood education • M Ed
education • M Ed, MAT, MS, CAGS
educational leadership • M Ed, CAGS
elementary education • M Ed
health promotion • M Ed, MAT
instructional technology • M Ed
library media • M Ed
physical education • MAT, MS
reading • M Ed, CAGS
secondary education • MAT
special education • M Ed

School of Management
Dr. Dorothy Oppenheim, Acting Dean
Programs in:
accounting and finance • MSM
management • MSM

■ CLARK UNIVERSITY

Worcester, MA 01610-1477
http://www.clarku.edu/

Independent, coed, university. CGS member. *Enrollment:* 433 full-time matriculated graduate/professional students (231 women), 223 part-time matriculated graduate/professional students (114 women). *Graduate faculty:* 169 full-time (57 women). *Computer facilities:* 70 computers available on campus for general student use. A campuswide network can be accessed from student residence rooms and from off campus. Internet access, on-line course support are available. *Library facilities:* Robert Hutchings Goddard Library plus 4 others. *Graduate expenses:* Tuition: full-time $23,300; part-time $728 per credit. *General application contact:* Audrey Rawson, Graduate School Coordinator, 508-793-7676.

Find an in-depth description at www.petersons.com/graduate.

Graduate School
David P. Angel, Dean of Graduate Studies and Research
Programs in:
biology • MA, PhD
chemistry • MA, PhD
clinical psychology • PhD
developmental psychology • PhD
economics • PhD
education • MA Ed
English • MA
environmental science and policy • MA
geographic information sciences, environment and development • MA
geography • PhD
history • MA, CAGS
holocaust history • PhD
international development and social change • MA
physics • MA, PhD
social-personality psychology • PhD
women's studies • PhD

College of Professional and Continuing Education
Dr. Thomas Massey, Director
Programs in:
liberal studies • MALA
professional and continuing education • MALA, MPA, MSPC, CAGS, Certificate
professional communications • MSPC
public administration • MPA, Certificate

Graduate School of Management
Dr. Edward Ottensmeyer, Dean
Programs in:
accounting • MBA
finance • MBA
global business • MBA
health care management • MBA
health services • MBA
management • MBA
management of information technology • MBA
marketing • MBA

■ COLLEGE OF OUR LADY OF THE ELMS

Chicopee, MA 01013-2839
http://www.elms.edu/

Independent-religious, coed, primarily women, comprehensive institution. *Enrollment:* 22 full-time matriculated graduate/professional students (all women), 103

College of Our Lady of the Elms (continued)

part-time matriculated graduate/professional students (93 women). *Graduate faculty:* 21 full-time (13 women), 11 part-time/adjunct (6 women). *Computer facilities:* 76 computers available on campus for general student use. A campuswide network can be accessed from student residence rooms and from off campus. Internet access is available. *Library facilities:* Alumnae Library. *Graduate expenses:* Tuition: full-time $6,300; part-time $350 per credit. Required fees: $20 per term. *General application contact:* Michael Crowley, Director of Admission Office, 413-594-2761 Ext. 238.

Department of Education
Sr. Carla Oleska, Dean of Enrollment Services
Programs in:
early childhood education • MAT
education • CAGS
elementary education • MAT
English as a second language • MAT
general education administration • M Ed
reading • MAT
secondary education • MAT
special education • MAT

Program in Liberal Arts
Sr. Carla Oleska, Dean of Enrollment Services
Program in:
liberal arts • MALA

Religious Studies Department
Sr. Carla Oleska, Dean of Enrollment Services
Program in:
religious studies • MAAT

■ EASTERN NAZARENE COLLEGE

Quincy, MA 02170-2999
http://www.enc.edu/

Independent-religious, coed, comprehensive institution. *Computer facilities:* 98 computers available on campus for general student use. A campuswide network can be accessed from student residence rooms and from off campus. Internet access is available. *Library facilities:* Nease Library. *General application contact:* Graduate Enrollment Counselor, 617-745-3870.

Graduate Studies
Program in:
family counseling • MA

Division of Education
Programs in:
bilingual education • M Ed, Certificate
early childhood education • M Ed, Certificate
elementary education • M Ed, Certificate
English as a second language • M Ed, Certificate
instructional enrichment and development • M Ed, Certificate
middle school education • M Ed, Certificate
moderate special needs education • M Ed, Certificate
music education • M Ed, Certificate
physical education • M Ed, Certificate
principal • Certificate
program development and supervision • M Ed, Certificate
secondary education • M Ed, Certificate
special education administrator • Certificate
supervisor • Certificate
teacher of reading • M Ed, Certificate

■ EMERSON COLLEGE

Boston, MA 02116-4624
http://www.emerson.edu/

Independent, coed, comprehensive institution. CGS member. *Enrollment:* 703 full-time matriculated graduate/professional students (532 women), 203 part-time matriculated graduate/professional students (136 women). *Graduate faculty:* 109 full-time, 199 part-time/adjunct. *Computer facilities:* 265 computers available on campus for general student use. A campuswide network can be accessed from student residence rooms and from off campus. Internet access and online class registration are available. *Library facilities:* Emerson Library plus 1 other. *Graduate expenses:* Tuition: full-time $9,760; part-time $610 per credit. *General application contact:* Lynn Terrell, Director of Graduate Admission, 617-824-8610.

Find an in-depth description at www.petersons.com/graduate.

Graduate Studies
Donna Schroth, Dean

School of Communication
Dr. Stuart J. Sigman, Dean
Programs in:
broadcast journalism • MA
communication • MA, MS
communication sciences and disorders • MS
global marketing communication and advertising • MA
health communication • MA
integrated journalism • MA
integrated marketing communication • MA
management and organizational communication • MA
political communication • MA
print/multimedia journalism • MA
print/multimedia journalism, broadcast journalism, integrated journalism • MA
speech communication • MA
speech-language pathology • MS

School of the Arts
Grafton J. Nunes, Dean
Programs in:
arts • MA, MFA
audio production • MA
audio, television/video, and new media production • MA
creative writing • MFA
new media production • MA
publishing and writing • MA
television/video production • MA
theatre education • MA

■ EMMANUEL COLLEGE

Boston, MA 02115
http://www.emmanuel.edu/

Independent-religious, coed, comprehensive institution. *Enrollment:* 20 full-time matriculated graduate/professional students, 210 part-time matriculated graduate/professional students. *Graduate faculty:* 4 full-time (all women), 135 part-time/adjunct (64 women). *Computer facilities:* 115 computers available on campus for general student use. A campuswide network can be accessed from student residence rooms. Internet access, software applications are available. *Library facilities:* Cardinal Cushing Library. *Graduate expenses:* Tuition: part-time $430 per credit. *General application contact:* Valerie Healey, Center for Adult Studies, 617-735-9902.

Graduate Programs
Programs in:
elementary education • MAT
human resource management • MA
management • MSM
multi-cultural education • MAT
school administration • M Ed
secondary education • MAT

■ FITCHBURG STATE COLLEGE

Fitchburg, MA 01420-2697
http://www.fsc.edu/

State-supported, coed, comprehensive institution. CGS member. *Enrollment:* 150 full-time matriculated graduate/professional students (126 women), 591 part-time matriculated graduate/professional students (456 women). *Graduate faculty:* 150 part-time/adjunct (48 women). *Computer facilities:* 500 computers available on campus for general student use. A campuswide network can be accessed from student residence rooms and from off campus. Internet access is available. *Library facilities:* Hammond Library. *Graduate expenses:* Tuition, state resident: part-time $150 per credit. Required fees: $7 per credit. $65 per term. *General application contact:* James DuPont, Director of Admissions, 978-665-3144.

Find an in-depth description at www.petersons.com/graduate.

Division of Graduate and Continuing Education
Dr. Dorothy Boisvert, Interim Dean
Programs in:
- adolescent and family therapy • Certificate
- arts in education • M Ed
- business administration • MBA
- child protective services • Certificate
- communications/media • MS
- computer science • MS
- criminal justice • MS
- early childhood education • M Ed
- educational leadership and management • M Ed, CAGS
- elementary education • M Ed
- elementary school guidance counseling • MS
- forensic case work • Certificate
- forensic nursing • MS
- general studies education • M Ed
- guided study • M Ed
- interdisciplinary studies • CAGS
- mental health counseling • MS
- middle school education • M Ed
- occupational education • M Ed
- school guidance counselor • Certificate
- science education • M Ed
- secondary education • M Ed
- secondary school guidance counseling • MS
- teacher leadership • CAGS
- teaching biology • MA, MAT
- teaching earth science • MAT
- teaching English • MA, MAT
- teaching history • MA, MAT
- teaching mathematics • MAT
- teaching students with intensive special needs • M Ed
- teaching students with special needs • M Ed
- technology education • M Ed

■ FRAMINGHAM STATE COLLEGE

Framingham, MA 01701-9101
http://www.framingham.edu/

State-supported, coed, comprehensive institution. *Enrollment:* 52 full-time matriculated graduate/professional students, 815 part-time matriculated graduate/professional students. *Graduate faculty:* 24 full-time, 39 part-time/adjunct. *Computer facilities:* 575 computers available on campus for general student use. A campuswide network can be accessed from student residence rooms and from off campus. Internet access and online class registration, TELNET are available. *Library facilities:* Whittemore Library. *Graduate expenses:* Tuition, state resident: part-time $550 per course. *General application contact:* Dr. Arnold Good, Associate Dean, 508-626-4562.

Graduate Programs
Dr. Arnold Good, Associate Dean
Programs in:
- business administration • MA
- counseling • MA
- curriculum and instructional technology • M Ed
- educational leadership • MA
- English • M Ed
- food science and nutrition science • MS
- health care administration • MA
- history • M Ed
- human resources administration • MA
- human services administration • MA
- literacy and language • M Ed
- mathematics • M Ed
- nutrition education • M Ed
- public administration • MA
- special education • M Ed
- teaching English as a second language • M Ed

■ HARVARD UNIVERSITY

Cambridge, MA 02138
http://www.harvard.edu/

Independent, coed, university. CGS member. *Enrollment:* 10,793 full-time matriculated graduate/professional students (4,986 women), 1,028 part-time matriculated graduate/professional students (580 women). *Graduate faculty:* 2,347. *Computer facilities:* A campuswide network can be accessed from student residence rooms and from off campus. Internet access is available. *Library facilities:* Widener Library plus 90 others. *Graduate expenses:* Tuition: full-time $22,694. Required fees: $745.

Find an in-depth description at www.petersons.com/graduate.

Business School
Programs in:
- business • MBA, DBA, PhD
- business administration • DBA
- business economics • PhD
- information and technology management • PhD
- organizational behavior • PhD

Divinity School
Fr. J. Bryan Hehir, Chair of the Executive Committee
Program in:
- theology • M Div, MTS, Th M, PhD, Th D

Extension School
Michael Shinagel, Dean
Programs in:
- applied sciences • CAS
- English for graduate and professional studies • DGP
- information technology • ALM
- liberal arts • ALM
- museum studies • CMS
- premedical studies • Diploma
- public health • CPH
- publication and communication • CPC
- special studies in administration and management • CSS
- technology of education • Certificate

Graduate School of Arts and Sciences
Programs in:
- African history • PhD
- Akkadian and Sumerian • AM, PhD
- American history • PhD
- ancient art • PhD
- ancient Near Eastern art • PhD
- ancient, medieval, early modern, and modern Europe • PhD
- anthropology and Middle Eastern studies • PhD
- Arabic • AM, PhD
- archaeology • PhD
- architecture • PhD
- Armenian • AM, PhD
- arts and sciences • MD, AM, ME, MFS, SM, PhD, Sc D
- astronomy • AM, PhD
- astrophysics • AM, PhD
- baroque art • PhD
- biblical history • AM, PhD

Harvard University (continued)
biochemical chemistry • AM, PhD
biological anthropology • PhD
biological chemistry and molecular pharmacology • PhD
biological sciences in public health • PhD
biology • PhD
biophysics • PhD
business economics • AM, PhD
Byzantine art • PhD
Byzantine Greek • PhD
cell biology • PhD
chemical physics • PhD
chemistry • AM
Chinese • AM, PhD
Chinese studies • AM
classical archaeology • AM, PhD
classical art • PhD
classical philology • AM, PhD
classical philosophy • PhD
comparative literature • PhD
composition • AM, PhD
critical theory • AM, PhD
descriptive linguistics • AM, PhD
diplomatic history • PhD
earth and planetary sciences • AM, PhD
East Asian history • PhD
economic and social history • PhD
economics • AM, PhD
economics and Middle Eastern studies • PhD
eighteenth-century literature • AM, PhD
experimental pathology • PhD
experimental physics • AM, PhD
fine arts and Middle Eastern studies • PhD
forest science • MFS
French • AM, PhD
genetics • PhD
German • AM, PhD
health policy • PhD
Hebrew • AM, PhD
historical linguistics • AM, PhD
history and East Asian languages • PhD
history and Middle Eastern studies • PhD
history of American civilization • PhD
history of science • AM, PhD
immunology • PhD
Indian art • PhD
Indian philosophy • AM, PhD
Indo-Muslim culture • AM, PhD
Inner Asian and Altaic studies • PhD
inorganic chemistry • AM, PhD
intellectual history • PhD
Iranian • AM, PhD
Irish • AM, PhD
Islamic art • PhD
Italian • AM, PhD
Japanese • AM, PhD
Japanese and Chinese art • PhD
Japanese studies • AM
Jewish history and literature • AM, PhD
Korean • AM, PhD
Korean studies • AM
landscape architecture • PhD
Latin American history • PhD
legal anthropology • AM
literature: nineteenth-century to the present • AM, PhD
mathematics • AM, PhD
medical anthropology • AM
medical engineering/medical physics • PhD, Sc D
medieval art • PhD
medieval Latin • PhD
medieval literature and language • AM, PhD
microbiology and molecular genetics • PhD
modern art • PhD
modern British and American literature • AM, PhD
molecular and cellular biology • PhD
Mongolian • AM, PhD
Mongolian studies • AM
musicology • AM
musicology and ethnomusicology • PhD
Near Eastern history • PhD
neurobiology • PhD
oceanic history • PhD
oral literature • PhD
organic chemistry • AM, PhD
organizational behavior • PhD
Pali • AM, PhD
pathology • PhD
Persian • AM, PhD
philosophy • PhD
physical chemistry • AM, PhD
physics • AM
Polish • AM, PhD
political economy and government • PhD
political science • AM, PhD
Portuguese • AM, PhD
psychology • AM, PhD
public policy • PhD
regional studies–Middle East • AM
regional studies-Russia, Eastern Europe, and Central Asia • AM
Renaissance and modern architecture • PhD
Renaissance art • PhD
Renaissance literature • AM, PhD
Russian • AM, PhD
Sanskrit • AM, PhD
Scandinavian • AM, PhD
Semitic philology • AM, PhD
Serbo-Croatian • AM, PhD
Slavic philology • AM, PhD
social anthropology • AM, PhD
social change and development • AM
social psychology • AM, PhD
sociology • AM, PhD
Spanish • AM, PhD
statistics • AM, PhD
study of religion • AM, PhD
Syro-Palestinian archaeology • AM, PhD
theoretical linguistics • AM, PhD
theoretical physics • AM, PhD
theory • AM, PhD
Tibetan • AM, PhD
Turkish • AM, PhD
Ukrainian • AM, PhD
urban planning • PhD
Urdu • AM, PhD
Vietnamese • AM, PhD
Vietnamese studies • AM
virology • PhD
Welsh • AM, PhD

Division of Engineering and Applied Sciences
Programs in:
applied mathematics • ME, SM, PhD
applied physics • ME, SM, PhD
computer science • ME, SM, PhD
computing technology • PhD
engineering science • ME
engineering sciences • SM, PhD
medical engineering/medical physics • PhD, Sc D

Graduate School of Design
Programs in:
architecture • M Arch
design • M Arch, M Des S, MAUD, MLA, MLAUD, MUP, Dr DES, PhD
design studies • M Des S
landscape architecture • MLA
urban planning • MUP
urban planning and design • MAUD, MLAUD

Graduate School of Education
Jerome T. Murphy, Dean
Programs in:
acquisition of language and culture • Ed M
administration, planning and social policy • Ed M, CAS
arts in education • Ed M
children and adolescents at risk • Ed M
cognitive development • Ed M
community and lifelong learning • Ed D
education • Ed M, Ed D, CAS
education in the community • Ed D
elementary and secondary education • Ed D
experienced teachers program • Ed M, CAS
higher education • Ed M, Ed D
human development and psychology • Ed M, Ed D, CAS
individualized program • Ed M
international education • Ed M, Ed D
language and literacy • Ed M, Ed D, CAS

learning and teaching • Ed M, Ed D
methodology in developmental research • Ed M
mid-career mathematics and science (teaching certification) • Ed M, CAS
philosophy of education and curriculum theory • Ed D
research • Ed D
risk and prevention • Ed M, CAS
schools and schooling • Ed D
teaching and curriculum (teaching certification) • Ed M
technology in education • Ed M
urban superintendency • Ed D

John F. Kennedy School of Government
Dr. Joseph Nye, Dean
Programs in:
government • MPA, MPAID, MPP, MPPUP, PhD
political economy and government • PhD
public administration • MPA
public administration and international development • MPAID
public policy • MPP, PhD
public policy and urban planning • MPPUP

Law School
Program in:
law • JD, LL M, SJD

Medical School
Dr. Joseph B. Martin, Dean
Program in:
medicine • MD, SM, PhD, Sc D

Division of Health Sciences and Technology
Programs in:
applied physics • PhD
engineering sciences • PhD
medical engineering/medical physics • PhD, Sc D
medical informatics • SM
medical sciences • MD
physics • PhD
speech and hearing sciences • PhD, Sc D

Division of Medical Sciences
Program in:
medical sciences • PhD

School of Dental Medicine
Dr. R. Bruce Donoff, Dean
Programs in:
advanced general dentistry • Certificate
dental medicine • DMD, M Med Sc, D Med Sc, Certificate
general practice residency • Certificate
oral biology • M Med Sc, D Med Sc
oral surgery • Certificate
pediatric dentistry • Certificate

School of Public Health
Programs in:
biostatistics • SM, SD
cancer cell biology • PhD
clinical effectiveness • MPH
environmental epidemiology • SM, DPH, SD
environmental health • SM
environmental science and engineering • SM, SD
epidemiology • SM, DPH, SD
epidemiology/international nutrition • DPH, SD
family and community health • MPH
health and social behavior • SM, DPH, SD
health care management • MPH
health policy and management • SM, DPH, SD
immunology and infectious diseases • DPH, SD
international health • MPH
law and public health • MPH
maternal and child health • SM, DPH, SD
occupational and environmental health • MPH
occupational health • MOH, SM, DPH, SD
physiology • SD
population and international health • SM, DPH, SD
public health • MOH, MPH, SM, DPH, PhD, SD
quantitative methods • MPH

Division of Biological Sciences
Program in:
biological sciences • PhD

■ LESLEY UNIVERSITY
Cambridge, MA 02138-2790
http://www.lesley.edu/

Independent, coed, primarily women, comprehensive institution. CGS member. *Enrollment:* 374 full-time matriculated graduate/professional students (321 women), 4,646 part-time matriculated graduate/professional students (4,021 women). *Graduate faculty:* 101 full-time (77 women), 804 part-time/adjunct (470 women). *Computer facilities:* 150 computers available on campus for general student use. A campuswide network can be accessed from student residence rooms and from off campus. Internet access is available. *Library facilities:* Eleanor DeWolfe Ludcke Library. *Graduate expenses:* Tuition: full-time $15,200; part-time $475 per credit. One-time fee: $15. Tuition and fees vary according to program. *General application contact:* Hugh Norwood, Dean of Admissions and Enrollment Planning, 800-999-1959.

Find an in-depth description at www.petersons.com/graduate.

Graduate School of Arts and Social Sciences
Dr. Martha B. McKenna, Dean
Programs in:
clinical mental health counseling • MA
counseling psychology • MA, CAGS
creative arts in learning • M Ed, CAGS
development project administration • MA
ecological literacy • MS
environmental education • MS
expressive therapies • MA, CAGS
independent studies • M Ed
independent study • MA
individually designed • MA
intercultural conflict resolution • MA
intercultural health and human services • MA
intercultural relations • MA, CAGS
intercultural training and consulting • MA
interdisciplinary studies • MA
international education exchange • MA
international student advising • MA
managing culturally diverse human resources • MA
multicultural education • MA

School of Education
Dr. William L. Dandridge, Dean
Programs in:
computers in education • M Ed, CAGS
curriculum and instruction • M Ed, CAGS
early childhood education • M Ed
educational administration • M Ed, CAGS
educational studies • PhD
elementary education • M Ed
individually designed • M Ed
intensive special needs • M Ed
middle school education • M Ed
reading • M Ed, CAGS
special needs • M Ed, CAGS

School of Management
Programs in:
fundraising management • MSM
health services management • MSM
human resources management • MSM
management • MSM
management of information technology • MSM
training and development • MS

■ MASSACHUSETTS INSTITUTE OF TECHNOLOGY

Cambridge, MA 02139-4307
http://web.mit.edu/

Independent, coed, university. CGS member. *Enrollment:* 5,691 full-time matriculated graduate/professional students (1,553 women), 73 part-time matriculated graduate/professional students (17 women). *Graduate faculty:* 933 full-time (149 women), 14 part-time/adjunct (1 woman). *Computer facilities:* 950 computers available on campus for general student use. A campuswide network can be accessed from student residence rooms and from off campus. *Library facilities:* Main library plus 10 others. *Graduate expenses:* Tuition: full-time $26,050. *General application contact:* Marilee Jones, Dean of Admissions, 617-253-2917.

Operations Research Center
Dr. James B. Orlin, Co-Director
Program in:
- operations research • SM, PhD

Program in Oceanography/Applied Ocean Science and Engineering
Prof. Paola Rizzoli, Director
Programs in:
- applied ocean sciences • PhD
- biological oceanography • PhD, Sc D
- chemical oceanography • PhD, Sc D
- civil and environmental and oceanographic engineering • PhD
- electrical and oceanographic engineering • PhD
- geochemistry • PhD
- geophysics • PhD
- marine biology • PhD
- marine geochemistry • PhD, Sc D
- marine geology • PhD, Sc D
- marine geophysics • PhD
- mechanical and oceanographic engineering • PhD
- ocean engineering • PhD
- oceanographic engineering • M Eng, MS, PhD, Sc D, Eng
- paleoceanography • PhD
- physical oceanography • PhD, Sc D

School of Architecture and Planning
William Mitchell, Dean
Programs in:
- architecture • M Arch, SM Arch S, SM Vis S, SMBT, PhD
- architecture and planning • M Arch, MCP, MS, MSRED, SM Arch S, SM Vis S, SMBT, PhD
- city planning • MCP
- media arts and sciences • MS, PhD
- urban and regional planning • PhD
- urban and regional studies • PhD
- urban studies and planning • MS

Center for Real Estate
William C. Wheaton, Director
Program in:
- real estate • MSRED

School of Engineering
Thomas L. Magnanti, Dean
Programs in:
- aeronautics and astronautics • M Eng, SM, PhD, Sc D, EAA
- bioengineering • PhD
- chemical engineering • SM, PhD, Sc D
- civil and environmental engineering • M Eng, SM, PhD, Sc D, CE, EE
- computer science • EE
- electrical engineering • EE
- electrical engineering and computer science • M Eng, SM, PhD, Sc D
- engineering • M Eng, MBA, MST, SM, PhD, Sc D, CAS, CE, EAA, EE, EE, Mat E, Mech E, Met E, NE, Naval E, Ocean E
- materials engineering • Mat E
- materials science and engineering • SM, PhD, Sc D
- mechanical engineering • SM, PhD, Sc D, Mech E
- metallurgical engineering • Met E
- naval architecture and marine engineering • SM
- naval engineering • Naval E
- nuclear engineering • SM, PhD, Sc D, NE
- nuclear systems engineering • M Eng
- ocean engineering • M Eng, SM, PhD, Sc D, Ocean E
- ocean systems management • SM
- radiological health and industrial radiation engineering • M Eng
- radiological sciences • PhD, Sc D
- toxicology • SM, PhD, Sc D

Center for Transportation Studies
Yossi Sheffi, Director
Programs in:
- logistics • M Eng
- transportation • MST, PhD

Engineering Systems Division
Prof. Daniel Roos, Director
Programs in:
- engineering • SM
- engineering and management • SM
- engineering systems • MBA, SM, PhD, CAS
- management • MBA, SM
- system design and management • CAS
- technology and policy • SM, PhD

School of Humanities, Arts and Social Sciences
Philip S. Khoury, Dean
Programs in:
- comparative media studies • SM
- economics • MA, PhD
- history and social study of science and technology • PhD
- humanities, arts and social science • MA, SM, PhD
- linguistics • PhD
- philosophy • PhD
- political science • SM, PhD

School of Science
Robert J. Silbey, Dean
Programs in:
- atmospheres, oceans, and climate • SM, PhD, Sc D
- biochemistry • PhD
- biological chemistry • PhD, Sc D
- biological oceanography • PhD
- biophysics • PhD
- cellular and developmental biology • PhD
- cellular/molecular neuroscience • PhD
- cognitive neuroscience • PhD
- cognitive science • PhD
- computational neuroscience • PhD
- computationals cognitive science • PhD
- genetics • PhD
- geology and geochemistry • SM, PhD, Sc D
- geophysics • SM, PhD, Sc D
- immunology • PhD
- inorganic chemistry • PhD, Sc D
- mathematics • PhD, Sc D
- microbiology • PhD
- neurobiology • PhD
- organic chemistry • PhD, Sc D
- physical chemistry • PhD, Sc D
- physics • SM, PhD, Sc D
- planetary science • SM, PhD, Sc D
- science • SM, PhD, Sc D
- systems neuroscience • PhD

Sloan School of Management
Richard L. Schmalensee, Dean
Program in:
- management • MBA, MS, SM, PhD

Whitaker College of Health Sciences and Technology
Programs in:
- health sciences and technology • MD, SM, PhD, Sc D
- medical engineering • PhD
- medical engineering and medical physics • Sc D
- medical informatics • SM
- medical physics • PhD
- medical sciences • MD
- speech and hearing sciences • PhD, Sc D

■ NORTHEASTERN UNIVERSITY

Boston, MA 02115-5096
http://www.neu.edu/

Independent, coed, university. CGS member. *Enrollment:* 2,673 full-time matriculated graduate/professional students (1,481 women), 1,636 part-time matriculated graduate/professional students (734 women). *Graduate faculty:* 769 full-time (273 women). *Computer facilities:* A campuswide network can be accessed from student residence rooms and from off campus. Internet access is available. *Library facilities:* Snell Library plus 6 others. *Graduate expenses:* Tuition: part-time $480 per quarter hour.

Find an in-depth description at www.petersons.com/graduate.

Bouvé College of Health Sciences Graduate School

Dr. Ena Vazquez-Nuttall, Director
Programs in:
applied behavior analysis • MS
applied educational psychology • MS
audiology • MS
biomedical sciences • MS
cardiopulmonary science (perfusion technology) • MS
clinical exercise physiology • MS
college student development and counseling • MS
counseling psychology • MS, PhD, CAGS
medical laboratory science • PhD
medicinal chemistry • PhD
pharmaceutics • PhD
pharmacology • PhD
pharmacy • Pharm D
pharmacy and health sciences • Pharm D, MS, MS Ed, PhD, CAGS, CAS
physician assistant • MS
rehabilitation counseling • MS
school counseling • MS
school psychology • MS, PhD, CAGS
special needs and intensive special needs • MS Ed
speech-language pathology • MS
toxicology • MS, PhD

School of Nursing

Dr. Margery Chisholm, Interim Dean
Programs in:
community health nursing • MS, CAS
critical care-acute care nurse practitioner • MS, CAS
critical care-neonatal nurse practitioner • MS, CAS
nurse anesthesia • MS
nursing • MS, CAS
nursing administration • MS
primary care nursing • MS, CAS
psychiatric-mental health nursing • MS, CAS

College of Arts and Sciences

Dr. Edward L. Jarroll, Interim Associate Dean and Director of the Graduate School
Programs in:
American government and politics • MA
analytical chemistry • PhD
arts and sciences • M Ed, MA, MAT, MAW, MPA, MS, MTPW, PhD, Certificate
biology • MS, PhD
chemistry • MS, PhD
comparative government and politics • MA
development administration • MPA
economics • MA
English • MA, PhD
experimental psychology • MA, PhD
health administration and policy • MPA
history • MA, PhD
inorganic chemistry • PhD
international relations • MA
law, policy, and society • MS, PhD
management information systems • MPA
mathematics • MS, PhD
organic chemistry • PhD
physical chemistry • PhD
physics • MS, PhD
political theory • MA
public administration • MPA
public and international affairs • PhD
public history • MA
sociology and anthropology • MA, PhD
state and local government • MPA
technical and professional writing • MTPW, Certificate
technical writing training • Certificate
writing • MA, MAW

School of Education

Dr. James W. Fraser, Dean/Director
Programs in:
biology • MAT
chemistry • MAT
curriculum and instruction • M Ed
economics • MAT
English • MAT
history • MAT
mathematics • MAT
physics • MAT
political science • MAT
sociology • MAT

School of Journalism

Prof. Laurel Leff, Graduate Coordinator
Program in:
journalism • MA

College of Computer Science

Dr. Larry A. Finkelstein, Dean
Program in:
computer science • MS, PhD

College of Criminal Justice

Jack McDevitt, Director
Program in:
criminal justice • MS

College of Engineering

Dr. Yaman Yener, Associate Dean for Research and Graduate Education
Programs in:
chemical engineering • MS, PhD
civil and environmental engineering • MS, PhD
computer systems engineering • MS
electrical and computer engineering • MS, PhD
engineering • MS, PhD
engineering management • MS
industrial engineering • MS, PhD
information systems • MS
mechanical engineering • MS, PhD
operations research • MS

Graduate School of Business Administration

Therese M. Hofmann, Associate Dean and Director
Programs in:
business administration • EMBA, MBA, MSF, MST, CAGS
finance • MSF

Graduate School of Professional Accounting

Elizabeth Lawrence, Director
Programs in:
professional accounting • MST, CAGS
taxation • MST, CAGS

School of Law

Roger I. Abrams, Dean
Program in:
law • JD

■ REGIS COLLEGE

Weston, MA 02493
http://www.regiscollege.edu/

Independent-religious, women only, comprehensive institution. *Enrollment:* 77 full-time matriculated graduate/professional students (73 women), 177 part-time matriculated graduate/professional students (172 women). *Graduate faculty:* 13 full-time (10 women), 26 part-time/adjunct (18 women). *Computer facilities:* 133 computers available on campus for general

Regis College (continued)
student use. A campuswide network can be accessed from student residence rooms. Internet access is available. *Library facilities:* Regis College Library. *Graduate expenses:* Tuition: full-time $17,500; part-time $425 per credit. Required fees: $140; $70 per semester. *General application contact:* Donna Gibbons, Director of Admissions, 781-768-7059.

Department of Education
Dr. Leona McCaughey-Oreszak, Chair
Program in:
education • MAT

Department of Management and Leadership
Dr. Phillip F. Jutras, Chair
Program in:
leadership and organizational change • MS

Division of Nursing
Dr. Amy Anderson, Chair
Program in:
nursing • MS, Certificate

■ SALEM STATE COLLEGE
Salem, MA 01970-5353
http://www.salemstate.edu/

State-supported, coed, comprehensive institution. CGS member. *Computer facilities:* 150 computers available on campus for general student use. *Library facilities:* Salem State College Library. *General application contact:* Dean of the Graduate School, 978-542-6323.

Graduate School
Programs in:
bilingual education • M Ed
business administration • MBA
chemistry • MAT
counseling and psychological services • MS
early childhood education • M Ed
education • CAGS
elementary education • M Ed
English • MA, MAT
English as a second language • MAT
geo-information science • MS
geography • MA, MAT
guidance and counseling • M Ed
history • MAT
library media studies • M Ed
mathematics • MAT
middle school education • M Ed
nursing • MSN
reading • M Ed
school administration • M Ed
secondary education • M Ed
social work • MSW
special education • M Ed
teaching English as a second language K–9 • M Ed
technology in education • M Ed

■ SIMMONS COLLEGE
Boston, MA 02115
http://www.simmons.edu/

Independent, coed, primarily women, comprehensive institution. *Enrollment:* 650 full-time matriculated graduate/professional students (585 women), 1,462 part-time matriculated graduate/professional students (1,245 women). *Graduate faculty:* 119 full-time, 159 part-time/adjunct. *Computer facilities:* 250 computers available on campus for general student use. A campuswide network can be accessed from student residence rooms and from off campus. Internet access is available. *Library facilities:* Beatley Library plus 5 others. *Graduate expenses:* Tuition: part-time $637 per semester hour. Required fees: $20. *General application contact:* Director, Graduate Studies Admission, 617-521-2910.

Competitive Intelligence Center
Dr. Jerry P. Miller, Director
Program in:
competitive intelligence • Master in Competitive Intelligence

Graduate School
Dr. Lynne Goodstein, Dean

College of Arts and Sciences and Professional Studies
Programs in:
arts and sciences and professional studies • M Phil, MA, MAT, MS, MS Ed, CAGS, Ed S
assistive technology • MS Ed, Ed S
behavioral education • MS Ed, Ed S
children's literature • MA
communications management • MS
education • MAT, MS Ed, CAGS, Ed S
educational leadership • MS Ed, CAGS
elementary school education • MAT
English • M Phil, MA
gender/cultural studies • MA
general purposes • CAGS
inclusion specialist • MS Ed
intensive special needs • MS Ed
language-based learning disabilities • MS Ed, Ed S
secondary education • MAT
Spanish • MA
special education • MS Ed, Ed S
special needs • MS Ed
teacher preparation • MAT
teaching English as a second language • MAT

Graduate School for Health Studies
Dean
Programs in:
health care administration • MS, CAGS
health studies • MS, DPT, CAGS, Certificate
nutrition and health promotion • MS, Certificate
physical therapy • MS, DPT
primary health care • MS, CAGS

Graduate School of Library and Information Science
Dr. James Matarazzo, Dean
Programs in:
library and information science • MS, DA, Certificate
school library media specialist • Certificate

Graduate School of Management
Dr. Patricia O'Brien, Dean
Program in:
management • MBA

School of Social Work
Dr. Joseph M. Regan, Dean
Program in:
clinical social work • MSW, PhD

■ SPRINGFIELD COLLEGE
Springfield, MA 01109-3797
http://www.spfldcol.edu/

Independent, coed, comprehensive institution. *Enrollment:* 1,048 full-time matriculated graduate/professional students (700 women), 290 part-time matriculated graduate/professional students (201 women). *Graduate faculty:* 156 full-time (78 women), 98 part-time/adjunct (46 women). *Computer facilities:* 95 computers available on campus for general student use. A campuswide network can be accessed from student residence rooms and from off campus. Internet access is available. *Library facilities:* Babson Library. *Graduate expenses:* Tuition: full-time $9,324; part-time $518 per semester hour. Required fees: $25. One-time fee: $25. Tuition and fees vary according to course load, campus/location and program. *General application contact:* Donald James Shaw, Director of Graduate Admissions, 413-748-3225.

Find an in-depth description at www.petersons.com/graduate.

School of Graduate Studies
Dr. Betty L. Mann, Dean
Programs in:
- adapted physical education • M Ed, MPE, MS, CAS
- advanced level coaching • M Ed, MPE, MS, CAS
- alcohol rehabilitation/substance abuse counseling • M Ed, MS, CAS
- applied exercise science • M Ed, MPE, MS
- art therapy • M Ed, MS, CAS
- athletic administration • M Ed, MPE, MS, CAS
- athletic counseling • M Ed, MS, CAS
- biomechanics • M Ed, MPE, MS
- clinical masters in physical education • M Ed, MPE, MS
- counseling and secondary education • M Ed, MS
- deaf counseling • M Ed, MS, CAS
- developmental disabilities • M Ed, MS, CAS
- education • M Ed, MS
- exercise physiology • M Ed, MPE, MS
- general counseling • M Ed, MS, CAS
- general counseling and casework • M Ed, MS, CAS
- general physical education • DPE
- health care management • M Ed, MS
- health promotion/wellness management • M Ed, MS, CAS
- human services • MS
- industrial/organizational psychology • MS, CAS
- interdisciplinary studies • M Ed, MPE, MS
- marriage and family therapy • M Ed, MS, CAS
- mental health counseling • M Ed, MS, CAS
- occupational therapy • M Ed, MS, CAS
- outdoor recreational management • M Ed, MS
- physical therapy • MS
- psychiatric rehabilitation/mental health counseling • M Ed, MS, CAS
- recreational management • M Ed, MS
- school guidance and counseling • M Ed, MS, CAS
- social work • MSW
- special services • M Ed, MS, CAS
- sport management • M Ed, MPE, MS, CAS
- sport psychology • M Ed, MPE, MS, DPE, CAS
- sport studies • M Ed, MPE, MS, CAS
- sports injury prevention and management • M Ed, MPE, MS
- student personnel in higher education • M Ed, MS, CAS
- teaching and administration • M Ed, MPE, MS, CAS
- therapeutic recreational management • M Ed, MS
- vocational evaluation and work adjustment • M Ed, MS, CAS

■ SUFFOLK UNIVERSITY
Boston, MA 02108-2770
http://www.suffolk.edu/

Independent, coed, comprehensive institution. *Enrollment:* 1,351 full-time matriculated graduate/professional students (732 women), 2,076 part-time matriculated graduate/professional students (1,011 women). *Graduate faculty:* 299 full-time (126 women), 438 part-time/adjunct (199 women). *Computer facilities:* 300 computers available on campus for general student use. A campuswide network can be accessed from student residence rooms and from off campus. Internet access is available. *Library facilities:* Mildred Sawyer Library plus 3 others. *Graduate expenses:* Tuition: full-time $12,240. Tuition and fees vary according to program. *General application contact:* Judith Reynolds, Director of Graduate Admissions, 617-573-8302.

College of Arts and Sciences
Dr. Michael Ronayne, Dean
Programs in:
- arts and sciences • M Ed, MA, MID, MS, MSIE, PhD, CAGS
- adult and organizational learning • MS, CAGS
- clinical-developmental psychology • PhD
- communication • MA
- computer science • MS
- counseling and human relations • M Ed, MS, CAGS
- criminal justice • MS
- educational administration • M Ed
- foundations of education • M Ed, CAGS
- higher education administration • M Ed, CAGS
- human resources • MS, CAGS
- international economics • MSIE
- leadership • CAGS
- mental health counseling • MS
- political science • MS
- school counseling • M Ed
- secondary school teaching • MS

New England School of Art and Design
William M. Davis, Chair
Program in:
- interior design • MA

Frank Sawyer School of Management
John F. Brennan, Dean
Programs in:
- accounting • MSA, GDPA
- banking and financial services • MS
- business administration • MBA, APC
- disability studies • MPA
- entrepreneurial studies • MBA
- executive business administration • EMBA
- finance • MSF
- health administration • MHA, MPA
- management • EMBA, M Ph M, MBA, MBAH, MHA, MPA, MS, MSA, MSF, MST, APC, CASPA, GDPA
- nonprofit management • MPA
- public administration • CASPA
- public finance and human resources • MPA
- state and local government • MPA
- taxation • MST

Law School
Gail N. Ellis, Dean of Admissions
Programs in:
- civil litigation • JD
- financial services • JD
- health care/biotechnology law • JD
- high technology/intellectual property law • JD

■ TUFTS UNIVERSITY
Medford, MA 02155
http://www.tufts.edu/

Independent, coed, university. CGS member. *Enrollment:* 3,605 full-time matriculated graduate/professional students (2,010 women), 687 part-time matriculated graduate/professional students (361 women). *Graduate faculty:* 641 full-time (229 women), 417 part-time/adjunct (185 women). *Computer facilities:* 254 computers available on campus for general student use. A campuswide network can be accessed from student residence rooms and from off campus. Internet access and online class registration are available. *Library facilities:* Tisch Library plus 1 other. *Graduate expenses:* Tuition: full-time $26,853. *General application contact:* Darla Pires, Admissions Coordinator, 617-627-2750.

Find an in-depth description at www.petersons.com/graduate.

Tufts University (continued)

Division of Graduate and Continuing Studies and Research

Programs in:
- bioengineering • Certificate
- biotechnology • Certificate
- biotechnology engineering • Certificate
- community environmental studies • Certificate
- computer science • Certificate
- computer science minor • Certificate
- electro-optics technology • Certificate
- environmental management • Certificate
- human-computer interaction • Certificate
- management of community organizations • Certificate
- manufacturing engineering • Certificate
- microwave and wireless engineering • Certificate
- museum studies • Certificate
- occupational therapy • Certificate
- premedical studies • Certificate
- program evaluation • Certificate

Graduate School of Arts and Sciences

Programs in:
- analytical chemistry • MS, PhD
- applied developmental psychology • PhD
- art history • MA
- arts and sciences • MA, MAT, ME, MFA, MS, MSEM, MSEM, PhD, CAGS
- biology • MS, PhD
- bioorganic chemistry • MS, PhD
- chemical engineering • ME, MS, PhD
- child development • MA, CAGS
- civil engineering • MS, PhD
- classical archaeology • MA
- classics • MA
- community development • MA
- computer science • MS, PhD
- dance • MA, PhD
- drama • MA
- dramatic literature and criticism • PhD
- early childhood education • MAT
- economics • MA
- education • CAGS
- electrical engineering • MS, PhD
- elementary education • MAT
- engineering • ME, MS, MSEM, MSEM, PhD
- engineering management • MSEM
- English • MA, PhD
- environmental chemistry • MS, PhD
- environmental engineering • MS, PhD
- environmental policy • MA
- ethnomusicology • MA
- French • MA
- German • MA
- health and human welfare • MA
- history • MA, PhD
- housing policy • MA
- human factors • MS
- inorganic chemistry • MS, PhD
- international environment/development policy • MA
- mathematics • MA, MS, PhD
- mechanical engineering • ME, MS, PhD
- middle and secondary education • MA, MAT
- music history and literature • MA
- music theory and composition • MA
- occupational therapy • MA, MS
- organic chemistry • MS, PhD
- philosophy • MA
- physical chemistry • MS, PhD
- physics • MS, PhD
- psychology • MS, PhD
- public policy and citizen participation • MA
- school psychology • MA, CAGS
- secondary education • MA
- studio art • MFA
- theater history • PhD

Fletcher School of Law and Diplomacy

Stephen W. Bosworth, Dean

Program in:
- law and diplomacy • MA, MAHA, MALD, PhD

Sackler School of Graduate Biomedical Sciences

Dr. Louis Lasagna, Dean

Programs in:
- biochemistry • PhD
- biomedical sciences • MS, PhD
- cell, molecular and developmental biology • PhD
- cellular and molecular physiology • PhD
- clinical care research • MS, PhD
- genetics • PhD
- immunology • PhD
- molecular microbiology • PhD
- neuroscience • PhD
- pharmacology and experimental therapeutics • PhD

Division of Clinical Care Research

Dr. Harry P. Selker, Program Director

Program in:
- clinical care research • MS, PhD

School of Dental Medicine

Programs in:
- dental medicine • DMD, MS, Certificate
- dentistry • Certificate

School of Medicine

Dr. John Harrington, Dean

Programs in:
- health communication • MS
- medicine • MD, MPH, MS
- public health • MPH

School of Nutrition Science and Policy

Program in:
- nutrition • MS, PhD

School of Veterinary Medicine

Programs in:
- animals and public policy • MS
- comparative biomedical sciences • PhD
- veterinary medicine • DVM, MS, PhD

■ UNIVERSITY OF MASSACHUSETTS AMHERST

Amherst, MA 01003

http://www.umass.edu/

State-supported, coed, university. CGS member. *Enrollment:* 2,013 full-time matriculated graduate/professional students (1,077 women), 2,319 part-time matriculated graduate/professional students (1,166 women). *Graduate faculty:* 1,161 full-time (322 women), 130 part-time/adjunct (59 women). *Computer facilities:* A campuswide network can be accessed from student residence rooms and from off campus. On-line course and grade information available. *Library facilities:* W. E. B. Du Bois Library plus 3 others. *Graduate expenses:* Tuition, state resident: full-time $2,640; part-time $110 per credit. Tuition, nonresident: full-time $9,937; part-time $414 per credit. One-time fee: $110. *General application contact:* Jean Ames, Supervisor of Admissions, 413-545-0721.

Find an in-depth description at www.petersons.com/graduate.

Graduate School

Dr. Charlena M. Seymour, Dean

Programs in:
- interdisciplinary studies • MS, PhD
- neuroscience and behavior • MS, PhD
- organismic and evolutionary biology • MS, PhD
- plant biology • MS, PhD

College of Engineering

Dr. Joseph I. Goldstein, Dean

Programs in:
- chemical engineering • MS, PhD
- civil engineering • MS, PhD
- electrical and computer engineering • MS, PhD
- engineering • MS, PhD
- engineering management • MS
- environmental engineering • MS

industrial engineering and operations research • MS, PhD
manufacturing engineering • MS
mechanical engineering • MS, PhD

College of Food and Natural Resources
Dr. Cleve Willis, Director
Programs in:
entomology • MS, PhD
food and natural resources • MLA, MRP, MS, PhD
food science • MS, PhD
forestry and wood technology • MS, PhD
hotel, restaurant, and travel administration • MS
landscape architecture • MLA
landscape architecture and regional planning • MLA, MRP, PhD
mammalian and avian biology • MS, PhD
microbiology • MS, PhD
plant science • PhD
regional planning • MRP, PhD
resource economics • MS, PhD
soil science • MS, PhD
sport studies • MS, PhD
wildlife and fisheries conservation • MS, PhD

College of Humanities and Fine Arts
Dr. Lee Edwards, Dean
Programs in:
Afro-American studies • MA, PhD
ancient history • MA
art • MA, MFA, MS
art education • MA
art history • MA
British Empire history • MA
Chinese • MA
comparative literature • MA, PhD
creative writing • MFA
English and American literature • MA, PhD
European • medieval and modern history • MA, PhD
French and Francophone studies • MA, MAT
Germanic languages and literatures • MA, PhD
Hispanic literatures and linguistics • MA, PhD
humanities and fine arts • MA, MAT, MFA, MM, MS, PhD
interior design • MS
Islamic history • MA
Italian studies • MAT
Japanese • MA
Latin American history • MA, PhD
Latin and classical humanities • MAT
linguistics • MA, PhD
modern global history • MA
music • MM, PhD
philosophy • MA, PhD
public history • MA
science and technology history • MA
studio art • MFA
theater • MFA
U.S. history • MA, PhD

College of Natural Sciences and Mathematics
Dr. Robert Hallock, Dean
Programs in:
applied mathematics • MS
astronomy • MS, PhD
biochemistry • MS, PhD
biological chemistry • PhD
biology • MA, MS, PhD
cell and developmental biology • PhD
chemistry • MS, PhD
computer science • MS, PhD
geography • MS
geology • MS, PhD
geosciences • PhD
mathematics and statistics • MS, PhD
natural sciences and mathematics • MA, MS, PhD
physics • MS, PhD
polymer science and engineering • MS, PhD

College of Social and Behavioral Sciences
Dr. Glen Gordon, Dean
Programs in:
anthropology • MA, PhD
clinical psychology • MS, PhD
communication • MA, PhD
economics • MA, PhD
labor studies • MS
political science • MA, PhD
public policy and administration • MPA
social and behavioral sciences • MA, MPA, MS, PhD
sociology • MA, PhD

Isenberg School of Management
Programs in:
business administration • PMBA
management • MBA, MS, PMBA, PhD

School of Education
Dr. Bailey Jackson, Dean
Programs in:
cultural diversity and curriculum reform • M Ed, Ed D, CAGS
early childhood education and development • M Ed, Ed D, CAGS
education • M Ed, Ed D, PhD, CAGS
educational administration • M Ed, Ed D, CAGS
elementary teacher education • M Ed, Ed D, CAGS
higher education • M Ed, Ed D, CAGS
international education • M Ed, Ed D, CAGS
mathematics, science, and instructional technology • M Ed, Ed D, CAGS
physical education teacher education • M Ed, Ed D, CAGS
reading and writing • M Ed, Ed D, CAGS
research and evaluation methods • M Ed, Ed D, CAGS
school psychology • PhD
school psychology and school counseling • M Ed, Ed D, CAGS
science education • Ed D
secondary teacher education • M Ed, Ed D, CAGS
social justice education • M Ed, Ed D, CAGS
special education • M Ed, Ed D, CAGS

School of Nursing
Dr. Eileen T. Breslin, Dean
Program in:
nursing • MS, PhD

School of Public Health and Health Sciences
Dr. Stephen Gelhbach, Dean
Programs in:
communication disorders • MA, PhD
exercise science • MS, PhD
nutrition • MS
public health • MPH, MS, PhD
public health and health sciences • MA, MPH, MS, PhD

■ UNIVERSITY OF MASSACHUSETTS BOSTON

Boston, MA 02125-3393
http://www.umb.edu/

State-supported, coed, university. CGS member. *Enrollment:* 770 full-time matriculated graduate/professional students (532 women), 1,739 part-time matriculated graduate/professional students (1,167 women). *Graduate faculty:* 448 full-time (172 women). *Computer facilities:* 260 computers available on campus for general student use. A campuswide network can be accessed from off campus. Internet access and online class registration are available. *Library facilities:* Joseph P. Healey Library. *Graduate expenses:* Tuition, state resident: full-time $5,180; part-time $108 per credit. Tuition, nonresident: full-time $9,758; part-time $407 per credit. Required fees: $1,040; $166 per semester. *General application contact:* Lisa Lavely, Director of Graduate Admissions and Records, 617-287-6400.

Find an in-depth description at www.petersons.com/graduate.

University of Massachusetts Boston (continued)

Office of Graduate Studies and Research
Dr. Ismael Ramírez-Soto, Dean of Graduate Studies
Programs in:
public affairs • MS
public policy • PhD

College of Arts and Sciences
Dr. Ismael Ramírez-Soto, Dean of Graduate Studies
Programs in:
American studies • MA
applied physics • MS
applied sociology • MA
archival methods • MA
arts • MA, PhD
arts and sciences • MA, MS, PhD
bilingual education • MA
biology • MS
biotechnology and biomedical science • MS
chemistry • MS
clinical psychology • PhD
computer science • MS, PhD
English • MA
English as a second language • MA
environmental biology • PhD
environmental sciences • MS
environmental, coastal and ocean sciences • PhD
foreign language pedagogy • MA
historical archaeology • MA
history • MA
sciences • MS, PhD

College of Management
Dr. Philip Quaglieri, Dean
Programs in:
business administration • MBA
management • MBA

College of Nursing
Dr. Brenda Cherry, Dean
Programs in:
nursing • MS, PhD

College of Public and Community Service
Dr. Ismael Ramírez-Soto, Dean of Graduate Studies
Programs in:
dispute resolution • MA, Certificate
gerontology • PhD
human services • MS
public and community service • MA, MS, PhD, Certificate

Division of Continuing Education
Dr. Theresa Mortimer, Associate Provost
Programs in:
continuing education • Certificate
women in politics and government • Certificate

Graduate College of Education
Dr. Clara Jennings, Dean
Programs in:
counseling • M Ed, CAGS
critical and creative thinking • MA, Certificate
education • M Ed, Ed D
educational administration • M Ed, CAGS
elementary and secondary education/ certification • M Ed
higher education administration • Ed D
instructional design • M Ed
school psychology • M Ed, CAGS
special education • M Ed
teacher certification • M Ed
urban school leadership • Ed D

■ UNIVERSITY OF MASSACHUSETTS DARTMOUTH

North Dartmouth, MA 02747-2300

http://www.umassd.edu/

State-supported, coed, comprehensive institution. *Enrollment:* 227 full-time matriculated graduate/professional students (92 women), 321 part-time matriculated graduate/professional students (198 women). *Graduate faculty:* 250 full-time (73 women), 78 part-time/adjunct (37 women). *Computer facilities:* 368 computers available on campus for general student use. A campuswide network can be accessed from student residence rooms and from off campus. Internet access and online class registration are available. *Library facilities:* University of Massachusetts Dartmouth Library. *Graduate expenses:* Tuition, state resident: full-time $2,071; part-time $86 per credit. Tuition, nonresident: full-time $7,995; part-time $333 per credit. Required fees: $2,888; $120 per credit. Full-time tuition and fees vary according to course load, program and reciprocity agreements. *General application contact:* Carol A. Novo, Graduate Admissions Office, 508-999-8026.

Find an in-depth description at www.petersons.com/graduate.

Graduate School
Dr. Richard J. Panofsky, Associate Vice Chancellor for Academic Affairs/ Graduate Studies

Charlton College of Business
Dr. Ronald D. McNeil, Dean
Programs in:
business • MBA
business administration • MBA

College of Arts and Sciences
Ann Carey, Interim Dean
Programs in:
arts and sciences • MA, MAT, MS
biology • MS
chemistry • MS
clinical psychology • MA
general psychology • MA
marine biology • MS
professional writing • MA
teaching • MAT

College of Engineering
Dr. Farhad Azadivar, Dean
Programs in:
computer engineering • MS, Certificate
computer science • MS
electrical engineering • MS, PhD, Certificate
engineering • MS, PhD, Certificate
mechanical engineering • MS
physics • MS
textile chemistry • MS
textile technology • MS

College of Nursing
Dr. Elisabeth Pennington, Dean
Program in:
nursing • MS, PMC

College of Visual and Performing Arts
Dr. John C. Laughton, Dean
Programs in:
art education • MAE
artisanry • MFA
fine arts • MFA
visual and performing arts • MAE, MFA
visual design • MFA

■ UNIVERSITY OF MASSACHUSETTS LOWELL

Lowell, MA 01854-2881

http://www.uml.edu/

State-supported, coed, university. CGS member. *Enrollment:* 613 full-time matriculated graduate/professional students (253 women), 1,890 part-time matriculated graduate/professional students (895 women). *Graduate faculty:* 405 full-time (119 women), 115 part-time/adjunct (45 women). *Computer facilities:* 4,000 computers available on campus for general student use. A campuswide network can be accessed from student residence rooms and from off campus. *Library facilities:* O'Leary Library plus 2 others. *Graduate expenses:* Tuition: part-time $225 per credit. *General application contact:* 978-934-2380.

Find an in-depth description at www.petersons.com/graduate.

Graduate School
Dr. Jerome L. Hojnacki, Dean

College of Arts and Sciences
Dr. Robert Tamarin, Co-Dean
Programs in:
- applied mathematics • MS
- applied mechanics • PhD
- applied physics • MS, PhD
- arts and sciences • MA, MM, MMS, MS, MS Eng, PhD, Sc D
- biochemistry • PhD
- biological sciences • MS
- biotechnology • MS
- chemistry • MS, PhD
- community and social psychology • MA
- computational mathematics • PhD
- computer science • MS, PhD, Sc D
- criminal justice • MA
- energy engineering • PhD
- environmental studies • PhD
- mathematics • MS
- music education • MM
- music theory • MM
- performance • MM
- physics • MS, PhD
- polymer sciences • MS, PhD
- radiological sciences and protection • MS, PhD
- regional economic and social development • MS
- sound recording technology • MMS

College of Education
Dr. Donald Pierson, Dean
Programs in:
- curriculum and instruction • M Ed, Ed D, CAGS
- education • M Ed, Ed D, CAGS
- educational administration • M Ed, Ed D, CAGS
- language arts and literacy • Ed D
- leadership in schooling • Ed D
- math and science education • Ed D
- reading and language • M Ed, Ed D, CAGS

College of Health Professions
Dr. Janice Stecchi, Dean
Programs in:
- administration of nursing services • PhD
- adult psychiatric nursing • MS
- advanced practice • MS
- clinical laboratory studies • MS
- family and community health nursing • MS
- gerontological nursing • MS
- health professions • MS, PhD
- health promotion • PhD
- health services administration • MS
- occupational health nursing • MS
- physical therapy • MS

College of Management
Dr. Kathryn Verreault, Dean
Programs in:
- business administration • MBA
- management • MBA, MMS
- manufacturing management • MMS

James B. Francis College of Engineering
Dr. Krishna Vedula, Dean
Programs in:
- chemical engineering • MS Eng
- chemistry • PhD
- civil engineering • MS Eng
- computer engineering • MS Eng, D Eng
- electrical engineering • MS Eng, D Eng
- energy engineering • MS Eng
- engineering • MS, MS Eng, D Eng, PhD, Sc D
- environmental studies • MS Eng
- mechanical engineering • MS Eng, D Eng
- plastics engineering • MS Eng, D Eng
- systems engineering • MS Eng, D Eng
- work environment • MS, Sc D

■ WESTERN NEW ENGLAND COLLEGE
Springfield, MA 01119-2654
http://www.wnec.edu/

Independent, coed, comprehensive institution. *Graduate faculty:* 61 full-time (16 women), 80 part-time/adjunct (23 women). *Computer facilities:* 250 computers available on campus for general student use. A campuswide network can be accessed from student residence rooms and from off campus. Internet access is available. *Library facilities:* D'Amour Library plus 1 other. *Graduate expenses:* Tuition: part-time $409 per credit. Required fees: $9 per credit. $20 per semester. *General application contact:* Dr. Janet Castleman, Director of Continuing Education, 413-782-1750.

School of Business
Dr. Stanley Kowalski, Dean
Programs in:
- accounting • MBA, MSA
- business administration • general • MBA
- business administration • weekend and accelerated • MBA
- criminal justice administration • MSCJA
- finance • MBA
- health care management • MBA
- human resources • MBA
- information systems • MSIS
- international business • MBA
- management information systems • MBA
- marketing • MBA
- procurement and contracting • MBA
- systems management • MSSM

School of Engineering
Dr. Eric W. Haffner, Dean
Programs in:
- electrical engineering • MSEE
- engineering • MSEE, MSEM, MSME
- industrial and manufacturing engineering • MSEM
- mechanical engineering • MSME

School of Law
Donald J. Dunn, Dean
Program in:
- law • JD

■ WESTFIELD STATE COLLEGE
Westfield, MA 01086
http://www.wsc.ma.edu/

State-supported, coed, comprehensive institution. *Enrollment:* 24 full-time matriculated graduate/professional students (16 women), 270 part-time matriculated graduate/professional students (190 women). *Graduate faculty:* 21 full-time (9 women), 29 part-time/adjunct (10 women). *Computer facilities:* 230 computers available on campus for general student use. A campuswide network can be accessed from student residence rooms and from off campus. Internet access is available. *Library facilities:* Ely Library. *Graduate expenses:* Tuition, state resident: full-time $2,610; part-time $145 per credit. Tuition, nonresident: full-time $2,790; part-time $155 per credit. Required fees: $100 per term. Tuition and fees vary according to course level, course load and degree level. *General application contact:* Russ Leary, Admissions Clerk, 413-572-8022.

Division of Graduate Studies and Continuing Education
Dr. Catherine Lilly, Dean
Programs in:
- counseling/clinical psychology • MA
- criminal justice • MS
- early childhood education • M Ed
- elementary education • M Ed
- English • MA
- history • M Ed
- intensive special needs education • M Ed
- middle school education • M Ed
- occupational education • M Ed

Westfield State College (continued)
- physical education • M Ed
- reading • M Ed
- school administration • M Ed, CAGS
- secondary education • M Ed
- special education • M Ed
- special needs education • M Ed
- technology for educators • M Ed

■ WHEELOCK COLLEGE

Boston, MA 02215

http://www.wheelock.edu/

Independent, coed, primarily women, comprehensive institution. *Enrollment:* 176 full-time matriculated graduate/professional students (166 women), 263 part-time matriculated graduate/professional students (255 women). *Graduate faculty:* 36 full-time (30 women), 32 part-time/adjunct (27 women). *Computer facilities:* 120 computers available on campus for general student use. A campuswide network can be accessed from student residence rooms and from off campus. Internet access is available. *Library facilities:* Wheelock College Library. *Graduate expenses:* Tuition: part-time $575 per credit. Tuition and fees vary according to course load and campus/location. *General application contact:* Deborah A. Sheehan, Director of Graduate Admissions and Student Financial Planning, 617-879-2178.

Graduate School

Dean

Programs in:
- child development and early childhood education • MS
- child life and family centered care • MS
- development and intervention • MS
- early childhood education • MS
- education • MS, MSW, CAGS
- elementary education • MS
- family studies • CAGS
- family support and parent education • MS
- family, culture, and society • MS
- language, literacy, and reading • MS
- leadership and policy in early care and education • MS, CAGS
- school leadership • MS
- social work and education • MSW
- teacher as a leader • MS
- teaching students with special needs • MS

■ WORCESTER POLYTECHNIC INSTITUTE

Worcester, MA 01609-2280

http://www.wpi.edu/

Independent, coed, university. CGS member. *Enrollment:* 441 full-time matriculated graduate/professional students (103 women), 334 part-time matriculated graduate/professional students (82 women). *Graduate faculty:* 189 full-time (30 women), 50 part-time/adjunct (7 women). *Computer facilities:* 1,000 computers available on campus for general student use. A campuswide network can be accessed from student residence rooms and from off campus. Internet access and online class registration are available. *Library facilities:* Gordon Library. *Graduate expenses:* Tuition: full-time $14,060; part-time $703 per credit. *General application contact:* Database Coordinator, 508-831-5248.

Find an in-depth description at www.petersons.com/graduate.

Graduate Studies

Jeanne M. Gosselin, Director

Programs in:
- applied mathematics • MS
- applied statistics • MS
- biochemistry • MS, PhD
- biology • MS
- biomedical engineering • M Eng, MS, PhD, Certificate
- biomedical sciences • PhD
- biotechnology • MS, PhD
- chemical engineering • MS, PhD
- chemistry • MS, PhD
- civil and environmental engineering • M Eng, MS, PhD, Advanced Certificate, Certificate
- clinical engineering • MS
- computer science • MS, PhD, Advanced Certificate, Certificate
- electrical and computer engineering • MS, PhD, Advanced Certificate, Certificate
- engineering • M Eng, MBA, MME, MS, PhD, Advanced Certificate, Certificate
- fire protection engineering • MS, PhD, Advanced Certificate, Certificate
- management • MBA, Certificate
- manufacturing engineering • MS, PhD, Certificate
- marketing and technological innovation • MS
- materials science and engineering • MS, PhD
- mathematical science • PhD, Certificate
- mathematics • MME
- mechanical engineering • M Eng, MS, PhD, Advanced Certificate
- operations and information technology • MS
- physics • MS, PhD
- power systems engineering • MS, PhD

■ WORCESTER STATE COLLEGE

Worcester, MA 01602-2597

http://www.worcester.edu/

State-supported, coed, comprehensive institution. *Computer facilities:* 250 computers available on campus for general student use. A campuswide network can be accessed from student residence rooms. Internet access is available. *Library facilities:* Learning Resources Center. *General application contact:* Graduate Admissions Counselor, 508-929-8120.

Find an in-depth description at www.petersons.com/graduate.

Graduate Studies

Programs in:
- biotechnology • MS
- early childhood education • M Ed
- elementary education • M Ed
- English • M Ed
- health education • M Ed
- history • M Ed
- leadership and administration • M Ed
- middle school education • M Ed, Certificate
- non-profit management • MS
- occupational therapy • MOT
- reading • M Ed, Certificate
- secondary education • M Ed, Certificate
- speech-language pathology • MS

Michigan

■ ANDREWS UNIVERSITY

Berrien Springs, MI 49104

http://www.andrews.edu/

Independent-religious, coed, university. CGS member. *Enrollment:* 491 full-time matriculated graduate/professional students (154 women), 365 part-time matriculated graduate/professional students (147 women). *Graduate faculty:* 162 full-time (49 women), 20 part-time/adjunct (13 women). *Computer facilities:* 130 computers available on campus for general student use. A campuswide network can be accessed from student residence rooms and from off campus. Internet access is available. *Library facilities:* James White Library plus 2 others. *Graduate expenses:* Tuition: part-time $490 per credit. Required fees: $121 per semester. *General application contact:* Eileen Lesher, Supervisor of Graduate Admission, 800-253-2874.

School of Graduate Studies
Dr. Linda S. Thorman, Dean
Program in:
international development • MSA

College of Arts and Sciences
Dr. William Richardson, Dean
Programs in:
allied health • MSMT
arts and sciences • M Mus, MA, MAT, MPT, MS, MSA, MSMT, MSPT, MSW
biology • MAT, MS
communication • MA
community services management • MSA
English • MA, MAT
history • MA, MAT
mathematics and physical science • MS
modern languages • MAT
music • M Mus, MA
nursing • MS
nutrition • MS
physical therapy • MPT, MSPT
social work • MSW

College of Technology
Dr. M. Wesley Schultz, Head
Programs in:
software engineering • MS
technology • MS

School of Business
Dr. Ann Gibson, Dean
Programs in:
business • MBA, MSA
management and marketing • MBA, MSA

School of Education
Dr. Karen R. Graham, Dean
Programs in:
community counseling • MA
counseling psychology • PhD
curriculum and instruction • MA, Ed D, PhD, Ed S
education • MA, MAT, Ed D, PhD, Ed S
educational administration and leadership • MA, Ed D, PhD, Ed S
educational and developmental psychology • MA
educational psychology • Ed D, PhD
elementary education • MAT
leadership • Ed D, PhD
reading • MA
religious education • MA, Ed D, PhD, Ed S
school counseling • MA
school psychology • Ed D, Ed S
secondary education • MAT
teacher education • MAT

Seventh-day Adventist Theological Seminary
Dr. John K. McVay, Dean
Program in:
theology • M Div, M Th, MA, D Min, PhD, Th D

■ AQUINAS COLLEGE
Grand Rapids, MI 49506-1799
http://www.aquinas.edu/

Independent-religious, coed, comprehensive institution. *Enrollment:* 141 full-time matriculated graduate/professional students (100 women), 443 part-time matriculated graduate/professional students (302 women). *Graduate faculty:* 37 full-time (20 women), 55 part-time/adjunct (35 women). *Computer facilities:* 85 computers available on campus for general student use. A campuswide network can be accessed. *Library facilities:* Woodhouse Library. *Graduate expenses:* Tuition: full-time $6,300; part-time $350 per credit. *General application contact:* Mary Kwiatkowski, Executive Assistant, School of Management.

Graduate School of Management
Dr. Lawrence Pfaff, Dean
Program in:
management • M Mgt

School of Education
Dr. V. James Garofalo, Dean
Program in:
education • MAT

■ CENTRAL MICHIGAN UNIVERSITY
Mount Pleasant, MI 48859
http://www.cmich.edu/

State-supported, coed, university. CGS member. *Enrollment:* 1,013 full-time matriculated graduate/professional students (622 women), 1,161 part-time matriculated graduate/professional students (709 women). *Graduate faculty:* 707 full-time (243 women). *Computer facilities:* 1,500 computers available on campus for general student use. A campuswide network can be accessed from student residence rooms and from off campus. Internet access and online class registration are available. *Library facilities:* Park Library plus 1 other. *Graduate expenses:* Tuition, state resident: part-time $163 per semester. Tuition, nonresident: part-time $323 per semester. Required fees: $208 per semester. Tuition and fees vary according to degree level and program. *General application contact:* Dr. James Hageman, Dean, College of Graduate Studies, 989-774-6467.

Find an in-depth description at www.petersons.com/graduate.

College of Extended Learning
Dr. Gary Peer, Interim Dean
Programs in:
audiology • Au D
education • MA
educational administration • MA
extended learning • MA, MSA, Au D, Certificate
general administration • MSA
health services administration • MSA, Certificate
hospitality and tourism • MSA, Certificate
human resources administration • MSA, Certificate
humanities • MA
information resource management • MSA, Certificate
international administration • MSA, Certificate
public administration • MSA, Certificate
software engineering administration • MSA, Certificate

College of Graduate Studies
Dr. James Hageman, Dean, College of Graduate Studies

College of Business Administration
Dr. John Schleede, Dean
Programs in:
accounting • MBA
business administration • MA, MBA, MBE, MS
business education • MBE
economics • MA
finance and law • MBA
information systems • MS
management • MBA
marketing and hospitality services administration • MBA

College of Communication and Fine Arts
Dr. Sue Ann Martin, Dean
Programs in:
art • MA, MFA
broadcast and cinematic arts • MA
communication and fine arts • MA, MFA, MM, MSA
interpersonal and public communication • MA

Central Michigan University (continued)
- music education and supervision • MM
- music performance • MM
- oral interpretation • MA
- theatre • MA

College of Education and Human Services
Dr. Steven Russell, Dean
Programs in:
- classroom teaching • MA
- community leadership • MA
- counseling • MA
- early childhood education • MA
- education and human services • MA, MS, MSA, Ed D, Ed S
- educational administration • MA, Ed S
- educational leadership • Ed D
- educational technology • MA
- elementary education • MA
- human development and family studies • MA
- library media • MA
- library, media, and technology • MA
- media and technology • MA
- middle level education • MA
- nutrition and dietetics • MS
- professional counseling • MA
- reading improvement • MA
- reading in the elementary school • MA
- recreation and park administration • MA
- school guidance personnel • MA
- school principalship • MA
- secondary education • MA
- special education • MA
- teaching senior high • MA
- therapeutic recreation • MA

College of Health Professions
Dr. Stephen Kopp, Dean
Programs in:
- athletic administration • MA
- audiology • Au D
- coaching • MA
- exercise science • MA
- health professions • MA, MS, MSA, Au D, Certificate
- health promotion and program management • MA
- physical therapy • MS
- physician assistant • MS
- speech and language pathology • MA
- sport administration • MA
- teaching • MA

College of Humanities and Social and Behavioral Sciences
Dr. Gary Shapiro, Dean
Programs in:
- applied experimental psychology • PhD
- clinical psychology • Psy D
- composition and communication • MA
- creative writing • MA
- English language and literature • MA
- general, applied, and experimental psychology • MS, PhD
- general/experimental psychology • MS
- history • MA, PhD
- humanities and social and behavioral sciences • MA, MPA, MS, PhD, Psy D, Certificate, S Psy S
- industrial/organizational psychology • MA, PhD
- political science • MA
- public administration • MPA
- public management • MPA
- school psychology • PhD, S Psy S
- social and criminal justice • MA
- sociology • MA
- Spanish • MA
- state and local government • MPA
- teaching English to speakers of other languages • MA

College of Science and Technology
Dr. Robert E. Kohrman, Dean
Programs in:
- biology • MS
- chemistry • MS
- computer science • MS
- conservation biology • MS
- industrial education • MA
- industrial management and technology • MA
- mathematics • MA, MAT, PhD
- physics • MS
- science and technology • MA, MAT, MS, PhD
- teaching chemistry • MA

Interdisciplinary Programs
Programs in:
- general administration • MSA
- health service administration • MSA
- hospitality and tourism administration • MSA
- human resource administration • MSA
- humanities • MA
- information resource administration • MSA
- interdisciplinary studies • MA, MSA
- international administration • MSA
- leadership • MSA
- organizational communications • MSA
- public administration • MSA
- recreation and park administration • MSA
- software engineering • MSA
- sports administration • MSA

■ EASTERN MICHIGAN UNIVERSITY
Ypsilanti, MI 48197
http://www.emich.edu/

State-supported, coed, comprehensive institution. CGS member. *Enrollment:* 1,291 full-time matriculated graduate/professional students (828 women), 4,081 part-time matriculated graduate/professional students (2,667 women). *Graduate faculty:* 687 full-time (279 women). *Computer facilities:* 525 computers available on campus for general student use. A campuswide network can be accessed from student residence rooms and from off campus. Internet access is available. *Library facilities:* Bruce T. Halle Library. *Graduate expenses:* Tuition, state resident: part-time $160 per credit. Tuition, nonresident: part-time $360 per credit. Required fees: $20 per credit. $40 per term. Tuition and fees vary according to course level and degree level. *General application contact:* Mary Ann Shichtman, Associate Director of Admissions, 734-487-3400.

Graduate School
Dr. Robert Holkeboer, Dean

College of Arts and Sciences
Dr. Barry Fish, Dean
Programs in:
- applied economics • MA
- art • MA
- art education • MA
- arts administration • MA
- arts and sciences • MA, MFA, MLS, MPA, MS
- biology • MS
- chemistry • MS
- children's literature • MA
- clinical/behavioral services • MS
- communication • MA
- computer science • MS
- criminology and criminal justice • MA
- development, trade and planning • MA
- drama/theatre for the young • MA, MFA
- economics • MA
- English • MA
- English linguistics • MA
- fine arts • MFA
- foreign languages • MA
- French • MA
- general psychology • MS
- general science • MS
- geography • MA, MS
- German • MA
- historic preservation • MS
- history • MA
- interpretation/performance studies • MA
- language and international trade • MA
- literature • MA
- mathematics • MA
- music • MA
- physics • MS
- physics education • MS

psychology • MS
public administration • MPA
social science • MA, MLS
social science and American culture • MLS
sociology • MA
Spanish • MA
Spanish (bilingual-bicultural education) • MA
studio art • MA
teaching English to speakers of other languages • MA
theatre arts • MA
women's studies • MLS
written communication • MA

College of Business
Dr. Earl Potter, Dean
Programs in:
accounting • MSA
accounting and taxation • MBA
accounting, financial, and operational control • MBA
business • MBA, MSA, MSHROD, MSIS
business administration • MBA
computer information systems • MBA
computer-based information systems • MSIS
finance • MBA
human resources management and organizational development • MSHROD
international business • MBA
management of human resources • MBA
management organizational development • MBA
marketing • MBA
production and operations management • MBA
strategic quality management • MBA

College of Education
Dr. Jerry Robbins, Dean
Programs in:
advanced counseling • MA
community counseling • MA
curriculum and instruction • MA
early childhood education • MA
education • MA, MS, Ed D, Sp Ed
educational leadership • MA, Ed D, Sp Ed
educational psychology • MA
elementary education • MA
guidance and counseling • MA, Sp Ed
K–12 curriculum • MA
middle school education • MA
physical education • MS
reading • MA
school counseling • MA, Sp Ed
secondary curriculum • MA
secondary school teaching • MA
social foundations of education • MA
special education • MA, Sp Ed
speech and language pathology • MA

College of Health and Human Services
Dr. Elizabeth King, Dean
Programs in:
health and human services • MOT, MS, MSN, MSW
human, environmental, and consumer resources • MS
nursing education • MSN
occupational therapy • MOT, MS
social work • MSW

College of Technology
Dr. John Dugger, Dean
Programs in:
business education • MBE
industrial technology • MS
liberal studies in technology • MLS
polymer technology • MS
technology • MA, MBE, MLS, MS
technology education • MA

■ FERRIS STATE UNIVERSITY

Big Rapids, MI 49307
http://www.ferris.edu/

State-supported, coed, comprehensive institution. *Enrollment:* 615 matriculated graduate/professional students. *Graduate faculty:* 70 full-time (20 women), 78 part-time/adjunct (31 women). *Computer facilities:* 276 computers available on campus for general student use. A campuswide network can be accessed from student residence rooms and from off campus. Internet access and online class registration are available. *Library facilities:* Ferris Library for Information, Technology and Education. *Graduate expenses:* Tuition, state resident: full-time $6,000; part-time $250 per credit hour. Tuition, nonresident: full-time $11,880; part-time $495 per credit hour. *General application contact:* Craig Westman, Associate Dean Enrollment Services/Director Admissions and Records, 231-581-2100.

College of Business
Jim Maas, Acting Dean
Programs in:
business • MSISM
information systems management • MSISM

College of Education
Dr. Nancy Cooley, Dean
Programs in:
administration • M Ed, MSCTE
curriculum and instruction • M Ed
education • M Ed, MS, MSCTE
education technology • MSCTE
elementary education • M Ed
instructor • MSCTE
post-secondary administration • MSCTE
reading • M Ed
subject matter option • M Ed
training and development • MSCTE

School of Criminal Justice
Dr. Frank Crowe, Acting Director
Program in:
criminal justice • MS

College of Pharmacy
Dr. Ian Mathison, Dean
Program in:
pharmacy • Pharm D

Michigan College of Optometry
Dr. Kevin L. Alexander, Dean
Program in:
optometry • OD

■ GRAND RAPIDS BAPTIST SEMINARY

Grand Rapids, MI 49525-5897
http://www.cornerstone.edu/grbs.nsf/

Independent-religious, coed, graduate-only institution. *Graduate faculty:* 9 full-time (0 women), 6 part-time/adjunct (1 woman). *Computer facilities:* A campuswide network can be accessed from student residence rooms and from off campus. Internet access and online class registration are available. *Library facilities:* Miller Library. *Graduate expenses:* Tuition: part-time $277 per credit hour. *General application contact:* Peter G. Osborn, Director of Admissions, 616-222-1422 Ext. 1251.

Graduate Programs
Dr. Robert W. Nienhuis, Executive Vice President
Programs in:
biblical counseling • MA
chaplaincy • M Div
Christian education • M Div, MA, MRE
education/management • D Min
intercultural studies • MA
missions • M Div, MRE
New Testament • MA, MTS, Th M
Old Testament • MA, MTS, Th M
pastoral studies • M Div, MRE
religious education • MRE
systematic theology • MA
theology • MTS, Th M

■ GRAND VALLEY STATE UNIVERSITY

Allendale, MI 49401-9403

http://www.gvsu.edu/

State-supported, coed, comprehensive institution. *Enrollment:* 577 full-time matriculated graduate/professional students (407 women), 1,513 part-time matriculated graduate/professional students (1,011 women). *Graduate faculty:* 146 full-time (67 women), 224 part-time/adjunct (109 women). *Computer facilities:* 2,600 computers available on campus for general student use. A campuswide network can be accessed from student residence rooms and from off campus. Internet access and online class registration, transcript, degree audit are available. *Library facilities:* James H. Zumberge Library plus 2 others. *Graduate expenses:* Tuition, state resident: full-time $4,800; part-time $200 per credit. Tuition, nonresident: full-time $10,320; part-time $430 per credit. Tuition and fees vary according to course level and course load. *General application contact:* Tory Parsons, Associate Director for Graduate Recruitment, 616-895-2025.

Find an in-depth description at www.petersons.com/graduate.

Division of Arts and Humanities
Dr. Gary Stark, Dean
Program in:
arts and humanities • MS

School of Communications
Dr. Alex Nesterenko, Director
Program in:
communications • MS

Russell B. Kirkhof School of Nursing
Dr. Phyllis Gendler, Acting Dean
Program in:
nursing • MSN

School of Education
Dr. Robert Hagerty, Dean
Programs in:
early childhood education • M Ed
education • M Ed
education of the gifted and talented • M Ed
educational leadership • M Ed
educational technology • M Ed
elementary education • M Ed
learning disabilities • M Ed
pre-primary impaired • M Ed
reading/language arts • M Ed
secondary, adult and higher education • M Ed
special education administration • M Ed

School of Social Work
Dr. Rodney Mulder, Dean
Program in:
social work • MSW

Science and Mathematics Division
Dr. P. Douglas Kindschi, Dean
Programs in:
biomedical and health sciences • MHS
engineering • MSE
information systems • MS
science and mathematics • MHS, MPAS, MS, MSE
software engineering • MS

School of Health Professions
Dr. Jane Toot, Director
Programs in:
health professions • MPAS, MS
occupational therapy • MS
physical therapy • MS
physician assistant studies • MPAS

Seymour and Esther Padnos School of Engineering
Dr. Paul Plotkowski, Director
Program in:
engineering • MSE

Seidman School of Business
Dr. David E. Mielke, Dean
Programs in:
business • MBA, MST
business administration • MBA
taxation • MST

Social Science Division
Dr. Jonathan R. White, Dean
Program in:
social science • MPA, MS

School of Criminal Justice
Dr. James Houston, Director
Program in:
criminal justice • MS

School of Public and Nonprofit Administration
Dr. Danny L. Balfour, Director
Program in:
public and nonprofit administration • MPA

■ LAWRENCE TECHNOLOGICAL UNIVERSITY

Southfield, MI 48075-1058

http://www.ltu.edu/

Independent, coed, comprehensive institution. *Enrollment:* 78 full-time matriculated graduate/professional students (27 women), 1,035 part-time matriculated graduate/professional students (375 women). *Graduate faculty:* 68 full-time (14 women), 56 part-time/adjunct (17 women). *Computer facilities:* 400 computers available on campus for general student use. A campuswide network can be accessed from student residence rooms and from off campus. *Library facilities:* Lawrence Technological University Library plus 1 other. *Graduate expenses:* Tuition: part-time $440 per credit hour. Required fees: $100 per semester. *General application contact:* Lisa Kujawa, Director of Admissions, 248-204-3160.

College of Architecture and Design
Dr. Neville Clouten, Dean
Program in:
architecture and design • M Arch

College of Arts and Sciences
Dr. James Rodgers, Dean
Programs in:
computer science • MS
science education • MSE

College of Engineering
Dr. Laird Johnston, Dean
Programs in:
automotive engineering • MAE
civil engineering • MCE
manufacturing systems • MEMS

College of Management
Dr. Lou DeGennaro, Dean
Programs in:
business administration • MBA
industrial operations • MS
information systems • MS

■ MADONNA UNIVERSITY

Livonia, MI 48150-1173

http://www.munet.edu/

Independent-religious, coed, comprehensive institution. *Enrollment:* 155 full-time matriculated graduate/professional students (55 women), 613 part-time matriculated graduate/professional students (486 women). *Graduate faculty:* 56 full-time, 27 part-time/adjunct. *Computer facilities:* 175 computers available on campus for general student use. A campuswide network can be accessed from student residence rooms and from off campus. Internet access is available. *Library facilities:* Madonna University Library. *Graduate expenses:* Tuition: full-time $5,860; part-time $288 per semester hour. Required fees: $200; $50 per semester. One-time fee: $50. Tuition and fees vary according to course load and program.

General application contact: Sandra Kellums, Coordinator of Graduate Admissions, 734-432-5667.

Department of English
Dr. Andrew Domzalski, Director
Program in:
teaching English to speakers of other languages • MTESOL

Department of Psychology
Dr. Edythe Woods, Chairperson
Program in:
clinical psychology • MS

Program in Health Services
Sr. RoseMarie Kujawa, Dean
Program in:
health services • MS

Program in Hospice
Dr. Kelly Rhoades, Director
Program in:
hospice • MSH

Program in Nursing
Dr. Mildred Braunstein, Chairperson
Programs in:
adult health: chronic health conditions • MSN
adult nurse practitioner • MSN
nursing administration • MSN

Programs in Education
Dr. Robert Kimball, Dean
Programs in:
Catholic school leadership • MSA
educational leadership • MSA
learning disabilities • MAT
literacy education • MAT
teaching and learning • MAT

School of Business
Dr. Stuart Arends, Dean of Business School
Programs in:
business administration • MBA
international business • MSBA
leadership studies • MSBA
leadership studies in criminal justice • MSBA
quality and operations management • MSBA

■ MARYGROVE COLLEGE
Detroit, MI 48221-2599
http://www.marygrove.edu/

Independent-religious, coed, primarily women, comprehensive institution. *Computer facilities:* 115 computers available on campus for general student use. *General application contact:* Director of Graduate Studies, 313-864-8000 Ext. 445.

Graduate Division
Programs in:
educational administration • MA
human resources management • MA
pastoral ministry • MA

Division of Education
Programs in:
art of teaching • MAT
early childhood education • M Ed
education of the emotionally impaired • M Ed
modern language translation • M Ed
reading education • M Ed
special education • M Ed

■ MICHIGAN STATE UNIVERSITY
East Lansing, MI 48824
http://www.msu.edu/

State-supported, coed, university. CGS member. *Enrollment:* 5,719 full-time matriculated graduate/professional students (3,040 women), 3,305 part-time matriculated graduate/professional students (1,983 women). *Graduate faculty:* 1,977 full-time (525 women). *Computer facilities:* 2,000 computers available on campus for general student use. A campuswide network can be accessed from student residence rooms and from off campus. Internet access and online class registration are available. *Library facilities:* Main Library plus 14 others. *Graduate expenses:* Tuition, state resident: part-time $237 per credit hour. Tuition, nonresident: part-time $480 per credit hour. Required fees: $246 per semester. Tuition and fees vary according to course load, degree level and program. *General application contact:* Dr. Karen Klomparens, Dean of the Graduate School, 517-355-3220.

Find an in-depth description at www.petersons.com/graduate.

College of Human Medicine
Dr. Glenn C. Davis, Dean
Programs in:
anatomy • MS
anthropology • MA
biochemistry • MS, PhD
epidemiology • MS
human medicine • MD, MA, MS, PhD
human pathology • MS, PhD
microbiology • MS, PhD
pharmacology/toxicology • MS, PhD
physiology • MS, PhD
psychology • MA
sociology • MA
surgery • MS
zoology • MS

College of Osteopathic Medicine
Programs in:
anatomy • MS, PhD
biochemistry • MS, PhD
microbiology • PhD
osteopathic medicine • DO, MS, PhD
pathology • MS, PhD
pharmacology/toxicology • MS, PhD
physiology • MS, PhD

College of Veterinary Medicine
Dr. Lonnie J. King, Dean
Programs in:
large animal clinical sciences • MS, PhD
microbiology • MS, PhD
pathology • MS, PhD
pharmacology/toxicology • MS, PhD
small animal clinical sciences • MS
veterinary medicine • DVM, MS, PhD

Graduate School
Dr. Karen Klomparens, Dean of the Graduate School

College of Agriculture and Natural Resources
Dr. William Taylor, Acting Dean
Programs in:
agricultural and extension education • MS, PhD
agricultural economics • MS, PhD
agricultural economics—environmental toxicology • PhD
agricultural economics—urban studies • MS, PhD
agricultural engineering • MS, PhD
agricultural technology and systems management • MS, PhD
agriculture and natural resources • MS, PhD
animal science • MS, PhD
animal science-environmental toxicology • PhD
biosystems engineering • MS, PhD
building construction management • MS
crop and soil science • MS, PhD
crop and soil science-environmental toxicology • PhD
fisheries and wildlife • MS, PhD
forestry • MS, PhD
forestry-urban studies • MS, PhD
horticulture • MS, PhD
packaging • MS, PhD
park, recreation and tourism resources • MS, PhD
park, recreation and tourism resources-urban studies • MS, PhD
plant breeding and genetics-crop and soil sciences • MS, PhD
plant breeding and genetics-forestry • MS, PhD
plant breeding and genetics-horticulture • MS, PhD

Michigan State University (continued)
recreation • PhD
resource development • MS, PhD
resource development—environmental toxicology • PhD
resource development-urban studies • MS, PhD

College of Arts and Letters
Dr. Wendy Wilkins, Dean
Programs in:
adult language learning • MA
American studies • PhD
applied music • M Mus, DMA, PhD
art education • MA
arts and letters • M Mus, MA, MFA, DMA, PhD
ceramics • MFA
comparative literature • MA
conducting • M Mus
creative writing • MA
critical studies • MA
English • MA, PhD
English and American literature • MA
French • MA
French language and literature • PhD
German • MA, PhD
German language and literature • PhD
German studies • MA, PhD
graphic design • MFA
health and humanities • MA
history • MA, PhD
history of art • MA
history-secondary school teaching • MA
history-urban studies • MA, PhD
linguistics • MA, PhD
literature in English • MA
music composition • M Mus, DMA, PhD
music education • M Mus, PhD
music theory • M Mus, PhD
music therapy • M Mus
music, performance and conducting • DMA
musicology • MA, PhD
painting • MFA
performance • M Mus
philosophy • MA, PhD
piano • M Mus
piano pedagogy • M Mus
printmaking • MFA
Russian • MA
Russian language and literature • PhD
sculpture • MFA
secondary school/community college teaching • MA
Spanish • MA
Spanish language and literature • PhD
studio art • MA, MFA
teaching English in secondary school • MA
teaching of English to speakers of other languages • MA
theatre • MA, MFA, PhD

College of Communication Arts and Sciences
Dr. James Spaniolo, Dean
Programs in:
advertising • MA
audiology and speech sciences • MA, PhD
audiology and speech sciences-urban studies • PhD
communication • MA, PhD
communication arts and sciences • MA, PhD
communication-urban studies • MA
health communication • MA
journalism • MA
mass media • PhD
public relations • MA
telecommunication • MA
telecommunication-urban studies • MA

College of Education
Dr. Carole Ames, Dean
Programs in:
educational system design • Ed S
adult and continuing education • MA, Ed D, PhD, Ed S
college and university administration • MA, PhD
counseling • MA, Ed D, Ed S
counseling psychology • MA, PhD
counselor education • PhD
curriculum and teaching • MA
curriculum, teaching and education policy • PhD, Ed S
curriculum, teaching, and education policy • Ed D
education • MA, MS, Ed D, PhD, Ed S
educational psychology • MA, Ed D, PhD
educational system development • MA, Ed D
educational technology and instructional design • MA
educational technology and system design • MA
health and physical education • Ed D, PhD
health education and human performance • MA, PhD
higher education • Ed D, Ed S
higher, adult and lifelong education • PhD
K–12 educational administration • MA, PhD, Ed S
K-12 education administration • Ed D
kinesiology • MS, PhD
kinesiology-urban studies • MS
literacy instruction • MA
measurement and quantitative methods • PhD
measurement, evaluation and research design • MA, Ed D, PhD
physical education and exercise science • Ed D, PhD
physical education and exercise science-urban studies • MS
physical education and exercises science • MA
physical education-urban studies • MS
reading instruction • MA
rehabilitation counseling • MA
rehabilitation counseling and school counseling • PhD
school psychology • PhD, Ed S
special education • MA, Ed D, PhD
student affairs administration • MA

College of Engineering
Dr. Janie Fouke, Dean
Programs in:
chemical engineering • MS, PhD
civil engineering • MS, PhD
civil engineering-environmental toxicology • PhD
civil engineering-urban studies • MS
computer science • MS, PhD
electrical and computer engineering • MS, PhD
engineering • MS, PhD
engineering mechanics • MS, PhD
environmental engineering • MS, PhD
environmental engineering-environmental toxicology • PhD
materials science and engineering • MS, PhD
mechanical engineering • MS, PhD
mechanics • PhD
metallurgy • MS, PhD

College of Human Ecology
Dr. Julia R. Miller, Dean
Programs in:
apparel and textiles • MA
child development • MA
clothing and textiles • MA
community service-urban studies • MS
community services • MS
family and child ecology • PhD
family consumer sciences education • MA
family ecology • PhD
family economics and management • MA
family studies • MA
food science • MS, PhD
home economics education • MA
human design and management • PhD
human ecology • MA, MS, PhD
human nutrition • MS, PhD
human nutrition-environmental toxicology • PhD
interior design and facilities management • MA
interior design and human environment • MA
marriage and family therapy • MA
merchandising management • MS

College of Natural Science
Dr. George E. Leroi, Dean
Programs in:
- analytical chemistry • PhD
- applied mathematics • MS, PhD
- applied statistics • MS
- astrophysics and astronomy • MS, PhD
- beam physics • PhD
- biochemistry • PhD
- biochemistry and molecular biology • MS, PhD
- biochemistry-environmental toxicology • PhD
- biological sciences • MAT, MS
- botany and plant pathology • MS, PhD
- botany-environmental toxicology • PhD
- cell and molecular biology • PhD
- cellular and molecular biology • PhD
- chemical physics • MS, PhD
- chemistry • MS, PhD
- chemistry-environmental toxicology • PhD
- clinical laboratory science • MS
- computational chemistry • MS
- computational mathematics • MS
- computational statistics • MS
- entomology • MS, PhD
- entomology-environmental toxicology • PhD
- entomology-urban studies • MS, PhD
- environmental geosciences • MS, PhD
- environmental geosciences-environmental toxicology • PhD
- environmental toxicology • PhD
- genetics • PhD
- genetics-environmental toxicology • PhD
- geological sciences • MA, MS, PhD
- geology • MAT, PhD
- horticulture • PhD
- industrial mathematics • MS
- inorganic chemistry • MS, PhD
- mathematics • MA, MAT, MS, PhD
- mathematics education • PhD
- microbiology • PhD
- natural science • MA, MAT, MS, PhD
- neuroscience • PhD
- operations research-statistics • MS
- organic chemistry • MS, PhD
- physical science • MAT, MS
- physics • MAT, MS, PhD
- statistics • MA, MS, PhD
- zoology • MS, PhD
- zoology-environmental toxicology • PhD

College of Nursing
Dr. Marilyn Rothert, Dean
Program in:
- nursing • MSN, PhD

College of Social Science
Dr. Gary Manson, Acting Dean
Programs in:
- administration and program evaluation • MSW
- administration and program evaluation-urban studies • MSW
- anthropology • MA, PhD
- applied developmental science • MA, PhD
- clinical social work • MSW
- clinical social work-urban studies • MSW
- cricimal justice-urban studies • MS
- criminal justice • MS, PhD
- geography • MA, MS, PhD
- geography-urban studies • MA
- industrial relations and human resources • PhD
- infant studies • MA, PhD
- interdisciplinary social science/social work • PhD
- labor relations and human resources • MLRHR
- labor relations and human resources-urban studies • MLRHR
- neuroscience-psychology • MA, PhD
- organizational and community practice • MSW
- political science • MA, PhD
- political science-urban studies • PhD
- program evaluation-urban studies • MSW
- psychology • MA, PhD
- psychology-urban studies • MA, PhD
- public administration • MPA
- public administration-urban studies • MPA
- social science • MA
- social science-criminal justice • PhD
- social science-global application • MA
- social science-labor relations and human resources • PhD
- social science-social work • PhD
- social science-urban and regional planning • PhD
- sociology • MA, PhD
- sociology-urban studies • MA, PhD
- urban and regional planning • MURP
- urban planning • MUP

Eli Broad Graduate School of Management
Dr. Donald Bowersox, Acting Dean
Programs in:
- accounting • PhD
- business administration and research • MBA
- business information systems • MBA
- business management • MS
- business management of manufacturing • MS
- economics • MA, PhD
- entrepreneurship • MBA
- finance • MBA, PhD
- food service management • MS
- hospitality business • MBA
- hotel, restaurant, and institution management • MBA
- human resources management • MBA
- leadership and change management • MBA
- logistics • PhD
- management • MA, MBA, MS, PhD
- management policy and strategy • PhD
- marketing • MBA, PhD
- operations and sourcing management • PhD
- organizational behavior-personnel • PhD
- production and operations management • PhD
- professional accounting • MBA, MS
- supply chain management • MBA

Institute for Environmental Toxicology
Dr. Lawrence J. Fischer, Director
Program in:
- environmental toxicology • PhD

Urban Affairs Programs
Programs in:
- administration and program evaluation-urban studies • MSW
- audiology and speech sciences-urban studies • PhD
- civil engineering-urban studies • MS
- clinical social work-urban studies • MSW
- communication-urban studies • MA
- entomology-urban studies • MS, PhD
- environmental engineering-urban studies • MS
- forestry-urban studies • MS, PhD
- geography-urban studies • MA
- history-urban studies • MA, PhD
- labor relations and human resources-urban studies • MLRHR
- park, recreation and tourism resources-urban studies • MS, PhD
- physical education and exercise science-urban studies • MS
- political science-urban studies • PhD
- psychology-urban studies • PhD
- public administration-urban studies • MPA
- resource development-urban studies • MS, PhD
- sociology-urban studies • PhD
- telecommunication-urban studies • MA
- urban studies • MA, MLRHR, MPA, MS, MSW, PhD

■ MICHIGAN TECHNOLOGICAL UNIVERSITY

Houghton, MI 49931-1295
http://www.mtu.edu/

State-supported, coed, university. CGS member. *Enrollment:* 542 full-time matriculated graduate/professional students (168 women), 128 part-time matriculated graduate/professional students (40 women). *Graduate faculty:* 303 full-time (60 women), 16 part-time/adjunct (5 women). *Computer facilities:* 1,235 computers available on campus for general student use. A campuswide network can be accessed from student residence rooms and from off campus. Internet access and online class registration are available. *Library facilities:* J. R. Van Pelt Library. *Graduate expenses:* Tuition, state resident: full-time $4,872. Tuition, nonresident: full-time $10,008. Required fees: $136. Tuition and fees vary according to course load. *General application contact:* Dr. Marilyn J. Urion, Assistant Dean of the Graduate School, 906-487-2327.

Find an in-depth description at www.petersons.com/graduate.

Graduate School
Dr. Marilyn J. Urion, Assistant Dean of the Graduate School

College of Engineering
Dr. Robert O. Warrington, Dean
Programs in:
- chemical engineering • MS, PhD
- civil engineering • ME, MS, PhD
- computational science and engineering • PhD
- electrical engineering • ME, MS, PhD
- engineering • ME, MS, PhD
- engineering mechanics • MS
- engineering, general • ME
- environmental engineering • ME, MS, PhD
- environmental engineering science • MS
- geological engineering • MS, PhD
- geology • MS, PhD
- geophysics • MS
- geotechnical engineering • PhD
- materials science and engineering • MS, PhD
- mechanical engineering • MS, PhD
- mechanical engineering-engineering mechanics • PhD
- mining engineering • MS, PhD
- sensing and signal processing • PhD
- structural engineering • PhD

College of Sciences and Arts
Dr. Maximilian J. Seel, Dean
Programs in:
- biological sciences • MS, PhD
- chemistry • MS, PhD
- computer science • MS
- environmental policy • MS
- industrial archaeology • MS
- mathemataics • MS
- mathematical sciences • PhD
- physics • MS, PhD
- rhetoric and technical communication • MS, PhD
- sciences and arts • MS, PhD

School of Business and Economics
Dr. R. Eugene Klippel, Dean
Programs in:
- business administration • MS
- business and economics • MS
- mineral economics • MS
- operations management • MS

School of Forestry and Wood Products
Dr. Glenn D. Mroz, Interim Dean
Programs in:
- forest science • PhD
- forestry • MS

■ NORTHERN MICHIGAN UNIVERSITY

Marquette, MI 49855-5301
http://www.nmu.edu/

State-supported, coed, comprehensive institution. CGS member. *Computer facilities:* 450 computers available on campus for general student use. A campuswide network can be accessed from student residence rooms and from off campus. Internet access and online class registration are available. *Library facilities:* Lydia Olson Library plus 1 other. *General application contact:* Interim Dean of Graduate Studies, 906-227-2300.

College of Graduate Studies

College of Arts and Sciences
Programs in:
- administrative services • MA
- arts and sciences • MA, MFA, MPA, MS
- biology • MS
- chemistry • MS
- creative writing • MFA
- English • MA
- mathematics education • MS
- public administration • MPA
- science education • MS

College of Behavioral Sciences and Human Services
Programs in:
- administration and supervision • MA Ed, Ed S
- behavioral sciences and human services • MA Ed, MS, Ed S
- elementary education • MA Ed
- exercise science • MS
- secondary education • MA Ed
- special education • MA Ed

College of Nursing and Allied Health Science
Programs in:
- communication disorders • MA
- nursing • MSN
- nursing and allied health science • MA, MSN

■ OAKLAND UNIVERSITY

Rochester, MI 48309-4401
http://www.oakland.edu/

State-supported, coed, university. CGS member. *Enrollment:* 862 full-time matriculated graduate/professional students (563 women), 2,371 part-time matriculated graduate/professional students (1,520 women). *Graduate faculty:* 426 full-time, 71 part-time/adjunct. *Computer facilities:* 640 computers available on campus for general student use. A campuswide network can be accessed from student residence rooms and from off campus. *Library facilities:* Kresge Library plus 1 other. *Graduate expenses:* Tuition, state resident: part-time $223 per credit. Tuition, nonresident: part-time $488 per credit. Required fees: $124 per term. *General application contact:* Christina J. Grabowski, Associate Director of Graduate Study and Lifelong Learning, 248-370-3167.

Find an in-depth description at www.petersons.com/graduate.

Graduate Study and Lifelong Learning
Christina J. Grabowski, Associate Director of Graduate Study and Lifelong Learning

College of Arts and Sciences
Dr. David J. Downing, Dean
Programs in:
- applied mathematical science • PhD
- applied statistics • MS, PhD
- arts and sciences • MA, MM, MPA, MS, PhD, Certificate
- biological sciences • MA, MS
- cellular biology of aging • MS
- chemistry • MS, PhD
- English • MA
- health and environmental chemistry • PhD

history • MA
industrial applied mathematics • MS
linguistics • MA
mathematics • MA
medical physics • PhD
music • MM
physics • MS
public administration • MPA
statistical methods • Certificate

School of Business Administration
Dr. John Gardner, Dean
Programs in:
accounting • M Acc
business administration • MBA, Certificate

School of Education and Human Services
Dr. Mary L. Otto, Dean
Programs in:
counseling • MA, PhD, Certificate
curriculum, instruction and leadership • M Ed, MAT, PhD, Certificate
early childhood education • M Ed, PhD, Certificate
education and human services • M Ed, MA, MAT, MTD, PhD, Certificate, Ed S
educational specialist • Ed S
microcomputer applications in education • Certificate
reading • MAT, PhD, Certificate
special education • M Ed, Certificate
training and development • MTD

School of Engineering and Computer Science
Dr. Bhushan Bhatt, Acting Dean
Programs in:
computer science • MS
electrical and computer engineering • MS
engineering and computer science • MS, PhD
engineering management • MS
mechanical engineering • MS
software engineering • MS
systems engineering • MS, PhD

School of Health Sciences
Dr. Ronald E. Olson, Dean
Programs in:
exercise science • MS
orthopedic manual physical therapy • Certificate
pediatric rehabilitation • Certificate
physical therapy • MPT, MS, Certificate

School of Nursing
Dr. Kathleen Emrich, Interim Dean
Programs in:
adult health • MSN
family nurse practitioner • MSN, Certificate
nurse anesthetist • MSN
nursing • MSN, Certificate

■ SAGINAW VALLEY STATE UNIVERSITY
University Center, MI 48710
http://www.svsu.edu/

State-supported, coed, comprehensive institution. *Enrollment:* 75 full-time matriculated graduate/professional students (47 women), 1,488 part-time matriculated graduate/professional students (1,075 women). *Graduate faculty:* 63 full-time (22 women), 31 part-time/adjunct (17 women). *Computer facilities:* 408 computers available on campus for general student use. A campuswide network can be accessed from off campus. Internet access is available. *Library facilities:* Zahnow Library. *Graduate expenses:* Full-time $4,168; part-time $174 per credit hour. Tuition, nonresident: full-time $8,218; part-time $342 per credit hour. Required fees: $255; $10 per credit hour. Tuition and fees vary according to program. *General application contact:* Wynn P. McDonald, Director, Graduate Admissions, 517-249-1696.

College of Arts and Behavioral Sciences
Dr. Donald Bachand, Dean
Programs in:
arts and behavioral sciences • MA
communication and multimedia • MA
organizational leadership and administration • MA

College of Business and Management
Dr. Paul J. Uselding, Dean
Program in:
business and management • MBA

College of Education
Dr. Ken Wahl, Interim Dean
Programs in:
chief business officers • M Ed
early childhood education • MAT
education • M Ed, MAT, Ed S
education leadership • Ed S
educational administration and supervision • M Ed
elementary classroom teaching • MAT
learning and behavioral disorders • MAT
middle school • MAT
middle school classroom teaching • MAT
principalship • M Ed
reading • MAT
secondary classroom teaching • MAT
secondary school • MAT
superintendency • M Ed

College of Nursing
Dr. Cheryl Easley, Dean
Programs in:
client care management • MSN
clinical nurse specialist • MSN
nurse practitioner • MSN
nursing • MSN
nursing education • MSN

College of Science, Engineering, and Technology
Dr. Thomas Kullgren, Dean
Program in:
technological processes • MS

■ SIENA HEIGHTS UNIVERSITY
Adrian, MI 49221-1796
http://www.sienahts.edu

Independent-religious, coed, comprehensive institution. *Computer facilities:* 75 computers available on campus for general student use. A campuswide network can be accessed from student residence rooms and from off campus. Internet access is available. *General application contact:* Director, Graduate Studies, 517-264-7665.

Graduate Studies
Programs in:
agency counseling • MA
curriculum and instruction • MA
early childhood education • MA
elementary education • MA
elementary education/reading • MA
human resource development • MA
middle school education • MA
Montessori education • MA
school counseling • MA
secondary education • MA
secondary education/reading • MA

■ SPRING ARBOR UNIVERSITY
Spring Arbor, MI 49283-9799
http://www.arbor.edu/

Independent-religious, coed, comprehensive institution. *Enrollment:* 245 full-time matriculated graduate/professional students (153 women), 179 part-time matriculated graduate/professional students (121 women). *Graduate faculty:* 11 full-time (3 women), 82 part-time/adjunct (30 women). *Computer facilities:* 85 computers available on campus for general student use. Internet access is available. *Library facilities:* Hugh A. White Library plus 1 other. *Graduate expenses:* Tuition: full-time

Spring Arbor University (continued)
$3,518; part-time $289 per credit hour. *General application contact:* Admissions Representative, 517-750-6536.

School of Adult Studies
Natalie Gianetti, Dean of Adult Studies
Program in:
organizational management • MAOM

School of Business and Management
Dr. Richard Wallace, Dean
Program in:
business and management • MBA

School of Education
Dr. David Hamilton, Dean
Program in:
education • MAE

■ UNIVERSITY OF DETROIT MERCY

Detroit, MI 48219-0900
http://www.udmercy.edu/

Independent-religious, coed, university. *Computer facilities:* 250 computers available on campus for general student use. A campuswide network can be accessed from student residence rooms and from off campus. Internet access is available. *Library facilities:* McNichols Campus Library plus 3 others. *General application contact:* Dean, Enrollment Management, 313-993-1245.

College of Business Administration
Programs in:
business administration • MBA, MS
computer information systems • MS

College of Education and Human Services
Programs in:
addiction studies • Certificate
counseling • MA
criminal justice studies • MA, MS
curriculum and instruction • MA
early childhood education • MA
education and human services • MA, MS, Certificate, Ed S
educational administration • MA, Ed S
emotionally impaired • MA
learning disabilities • MA
security administration • MS
special education • MA

College of Engineering and Science
Programs in:
automotive engineering • DE
biology • MS
chemical engineering • ME, DE
civil and environmental engineering • ME, DE
computer science • MSCS
economic aspects of chemistry • MSEC
electrical engineering • ME, DE
elementary mathematics education • MATM
engineering and science • M Eng Mgt, MA, MATM, ME, MS, MSCS, MSEC, DE, PhD
engineering management • M Eng Mgt
junior high mathematics education • MATM
macromolecular chemistry • MS, PhD
manufacturing engineering • ME, DE
mathematics • MA
mechanical engineering • M Eng Mgt, ME, DE
polymer engineering • ME
secondary mathematics education • MATM

College of Health Professions
Programs in:
health care education • MS
health professions • MS
health services administration • MS
nurse anesthesiology • MS
physician assistant • MS

College of Liberal Arts
Programs in:
clinical psychology • MA, PhD
economics • MA
industrial/organizational psychology • MA
international politics and economics • MA
liberal arts • MA, MPA, PhD, Spec
liberal studies • MA
political science • MA
public administration • MPA
religious studies • MA
school psychology • MA, Spec

School of Dentistry
Programs in:
dentistry • DDS, MS, Certificate
endodontics • MS, Certificate
general practice residency • MS, Certificate
orthodontics • MS, Certificate

School of Law
Program in:
law • JD

■ UNIVERSITY OF MICHIGAN

Ann Arbor, MI 48109
http://www.umich.edu/

State-supported, coed, university. CGS member. *Computer facilities:* A campuswide network can be accessed from student residence rooms and from off campus. *Library facilities:* University Library plus 20 others. *General application contact:* Admissions Office, 734-764-8129.

College of Pharmacy
Programs in:
medicinal chemistry • MS, PhD
pharmaceutical chemistry (computational) • MS, PhD
pharmaceutics • MS, PhD
pharmacy • Pharm D, MS, PhD
pharmacy administration • MS, PhD

Horace H. Rackham School of Graduate Studies
Earl Lewis, Dean of the Graduate School and Vice Provost for Academic Affairs-Graduate Studies
Programs in:
American culture • AM, PhD
biophysics • PhD
education and psychology • PhD
English and education • PhD
medical and biological illustration • MFA
medicinal chemistry • PhD
modern Middle Eastern and North African studies • AM
neuroscience • PhD

College of Engineering
Programs in:
aerospace engineering • M Eng, MS, MSE, PhD, Aerospace E
applied mechanics • PhD
applied physics • PhD
atmospheric and space sciences • MS, PhD
atmospheric, oceanic and space sciences • MS, PhD
automotive engineering • M Eng
biomedical engineering • MS, PhD
chemical engineering • MSE, PhD, Ch E
civil engineering • MSE, PhD, CE
computer science and engineering • MS, MSE, PhD
concurrent marine design • M Eng
construction engineering and management • MSE
electrical engineering • MS, PhD
electrical science and engineering • MS, MSE, PhD
engineering • M Eng, MS, MSE, D Eng, PhD, Aerospace E,

App ME, CE, Certificate, Ch E, EE, IOE, Mar Eng, Nav Arch, Nuc E
- environmental engineering • MSE, PhD
- financial engineering • MS
- industrial and operations engineering • MS, MSE, PhD, IOE
- macromolecular science and engineering • MS, PhD
- manufacturing • M Eng, D Eng
- materials science and engineering • MS, PhD
- mechanical engineering • MSE, PhD
- naval architecture and marine engineering • MS, MSE, PhD, Mar Eng, Nav Arch
- nuclear engineering • Nuc E
- nuclear engineering and radiological sciences • MSE, PhD
- nuclear science • MS, PhD
- oceanography: physical • MS, PhD
- remote sensing and geoinformation • M Eng
- space and planetary physics • PhD
- space systems • M Eng
- systems science and engineering • MS, MSE, PhD

College of Literature, Science, and the Arts
Programs in:
- analytical chemistry • PhD
- ancient Israel/Hebrew Bible • AM, PhD
- anthropology • AM, PhD
- anthropology and history • PhD
- applied economics • AM
- applied social research • AM
- applied statistics • AM
- Arabic • AM, PhD
- Armenian • AM, PhD
- astronomy • MS, PhD
- biology • MS, PhD
- biopsychology • PhD
- Buddhist studies • AM, PhD
- chemical biology • PhD
- Chinese literature • AM, PhD
- Chinese studies • AM
- classical art and archaeology • PhD
- classical studies • PhD
- clinical psychology • PhD
- cognition and perception • PhD
- comparative literature • PhD
- creative writing • MFA
- Czech • AM, PhD
- developmental psychology • PhD
- early Christian studies • AM, PhD
- ecology and evolutionary biology • MS, PhD
- economics • AM, PhD
- English and education • PhD
- English and women's studies • PhD
- English language and literature • PhD
- film and video studies • Certificate
- French • PhD
- geology • MS, PhD
- German • AM, PhD
- Greek • AM
- Hebrew • AM, PhD
- history • PhD
- history and women's studies • PhD
- history of art • PhD
- inorganic chemistry • PhD
- Islamic studies • AM, PhD
- Japanese literature • AM, PhD
- Japanese studies • AM
- Latin • AM
- linguistics • PhD
- literature, science, and the arts • AM, MAT, MFA, MS, PhD, Certificate
- mass communication • PhD
- mathematics • AM, MS, PhD
- Mesopotamian and ancient Near Eastern studies • AM, PhD
- mineralogy • MS, PhD
- molecular, cellular, and developmental biology • MS, PhD
- oceanography: marine geology and geochemistry • MS, PhD
- organic chemistry • PhD
- organizational psychology • PhD
- Persian • AM, PhD
- personality psychology • PhD
- philosophy • AM, PhD
- physical chemistry • PhD
- physics • MS, PhD
- plant biology • MS
- Polish • AM, PhD
- political science • AM, PhD
- psychology and women's studies • PhD
- Romance linguistics • PhD
- Russian • AM, PhD
- Russian and East European studies • AM, Certificate
- Serbo-Croatian • AM, PhD
- Slavic linguistics • AM, PhD
- social psychology • PhD
- social work and economics • PhD
- social work and political science • PhD
- social work and sociology • PhD
- sociology • PhD
- South Asian studies • AM
- Southeast Asian studies • AM
- Spanish • PhD
- statistics • AM, PhD
- teaching Latin • MAT
- teaching of Arabic as a foreign Language • AM
- Turkish • AM, PhD
- Ukrainian • AM, PhD
- women's studies • Certificate

Division of Kinesiology
Dr. Beverly D. Ulrich, Dean
Program in:
- kinesiology • AM, MS, PhD, Certificate

Gerald R. Ford School of Public Policy
Program in:
- public policy • MPA, MPP, PhD

School of Art and Design
Bryan Rogers, Dean
Programs in:
- art and design • AM, MFA
- biomedical visualization • MFA

School of Education
Karen Wixson, Dean
Programs in:
- academic affairs and student development • PhD
- community college administration • AM
- curriculum development • AM
- early childhood education • AM, PhD
- education • AM, MS, PhD
- educational administration and policy • PhD
- educational foundation, administration, policy, and research methods • AM
- educational foundations and policy • PhD
- educational technology • AM, MS, PhD
- elementary education • AM, MS, PhD
- higher education • AM
- individually designed concentration • PhD
- literacy and English education • AM
- literacy, language, and culture • PhD
- mathematics education • AM, MS, PhD
- organizational behavior and management • PhD
- public policy • PhD
- public policy in postsecondary education • AM
- research, evaluation, and assessment • PhD
- science education • AM, MS, PhD
- secondary education • AM, MS, PhD
- social studies education • AM
- special education • PhD
- student development, support, and academic affairs • AM
- teacher education • PhD

School of Information
Programs in:
- archives and records management • MS
- human-computer interaction • MS
- information • PhD
- information economics, management and policy • MS
- library and information services • MS

School of Nursing
Dr. Ada Sue Hinshaw, Dean
Programs in:
- administration of nursing and patient care services • MS
- adult acute care nurse practitioner • MS

University of Michigan (continued)
adult primary care/adult nurse practitioner • MS
community care/home care • MS
community health nursing • MS
family nurse practitioner • MS
gerontology nurse practitioner • MS
gerontology nursing • MS
infant, child, adolescent health nurse practitioner • MS
medical-surgical nursing • MS
nurse midwifery • MS
nursing • MS, PhD, Certificate
nursing business and health services administration • MS
occupational health nursing • MS
parent-child nursing • MS
psychiatric mental health nurse practitioner • MS
psychiatric mental health nursing • MS

Law School
Jeffrey S. Lehman, Dean
Programs in:
comparative law • MCL
law • JD, LL M, SJD

Medical School
Dr. Allen S. Lichter, Dean
Programs in:
biological chemistry • PhD
biomedical sciences • MS, PhD
cell and developmental biology • PhD
cellular and molecular biology • PhD
human genetics • MS, PhD
immunology • PhD
medicine • MD, MS, PhD
microbiology and immunology • PhD
pathology • PhD
pharmacology • PhD
physiology • PhD

School of Business Administration
Programs in:
business • M Acc, MBA, PhD
business administration • M Acc, MBA, PhD

School of Dentistry
Program in:
dentistry • DDS, MS, PhD, Certificate

School of Music
Karen C. Wolff, Dean
Programs in:
composition • AM, A Mus D
composition and theory • PhD
conducting • A Mus D
design • MFA
modern dance performance and choreography • MFA
music • AM, MFA, MM, A Mus D, PhD
music education • PhD
musicology • AM, PhD
performance • A Mus D
theatre • PhD
theory • AM, PhD

School of Natural Resources and Environment
Dr. Barry Rabe, Interim Dean
Programs in:
industrial ecology • Certificate
landscape architecture • MLA, PhD
natural resources and environment • PhD
resource ecology and management • MS, PhD
resource policy and behavior • MS, PhD
spatial analysis • Certificate

School of Public Health
Noreen M. Clark, Dean
Programs in:
biostatistics • MPH, MS, PhD
clinical research design and statistical analysis • MS
dental public health • MPH
environmental health • MPH, MS, Dr PH, PhD
epidemiologic science • PhD
epidemiology • MPH, Dr PH
health behavior and health education • MPH, PhD
health management and policy • MHSA, MPH
health services organization and policy • PhD
hospital and molecular epidemiology • MPH
human nutrition • MPH, MS
industrial hygiene • MS, PhD
international health • MPH
occupational health • MPH, MS, PhD
occupational medicine • MPH
public health • MHSA, MPH, MS, Dr PH, PhD
toxicology • MPH, MS, PhD

School of Social Work
Programs in:
social work • MSW, PhD
social work and social science • PhD

Taubman College of Architecture and Urban Planning
Robert Beckley, Dean
Programs in:
architecture • M Arch, M Sc, PhD
architecture and urban planning • M Arch, M Sc, MUD, MUP, PhD, Certificate
gaming/simulation studies • Certificate
urban design • MUD
urban planning • MUP
urban, technological, and environmental planning • PhD

■ UNIVERSITY OF MICHIGAN–DEARBORN

Dearborn, MI 48128-1491
http://www.umd.umich.edu/

State-supported, coed, comprehensive institution. *Enrollment:* 77 full-time matriculated graduate/professional students (24 women), 1,713 part-time matriculated graduate/professional students (692 women). *Graduate faculty:* 247 full-time (80 women), 187 part-time/adjunct (64 women). *Computer facilities:* 350 computers available on campus for general student use. A campuswide network can be accessed from off campus. Internet access is available. *Library facilities:* Mardigian Library. *Graduate expenses:* Tuition, state resident: part-time $275 per credit hour. Tuition, nonresident: part-time $756 per credit hour. Required fees: $82 per course. *General application contact:* Vivian J. Ladd, Graduate Coordinator, 313-593-1494.

Find an in-depth description at www.petersons.com/graduate.

College of Arts, Sciences, and Letters
Dr. Paul Wong, Dean
Programs in:
applied and computational mathematics • MS
arts, sciences, and letters • MA, MS
environmental science • MS
liberal studies • MA

College of Engineering and Computer Science
Dr. Subrata Sengupta, Dean
Programs in:
automotive systems engineering • MSE
computer and information science • MS
computer engineering • MSE
electrical engineering • MSE
engineering • MS, MSE, D Eng
engineering management • MS
industrial and systems engineering • MSE
information systems and technology • MS
manufacturing systems engineering • MSE, D Eng
mechanical engineering • MSE
software engineering • MS

School of Education
Dr. John Poster, Dean
Programs in:
- adult instruction and performance technology • MA
- education • MA
- public administration • MPA
- special education • M Ed
- teaching • MA

School of Management
Dr. Gary Waissi, Dean
Program in:
- management • MBA, MSA, MSF

■ UNIVERSITY OF MICHIGAN–FLINT

Flint, MI 48502-1950
http://www.flint.umich.edu/

State-supported, coed, comprehensive institution. *Enrollment:* 97 full-time matriculated graduate/professional students (51 women), 433 part-time matriculated graduate/professional students (229 women). *Computer facilities:* 160 computers available on campus for general student use. A campuswide network can be accessed from off campus. Internet access and online class registration are available. *Library facilities:* Frances Willson Thompson Library. *Graduate expenses:* Full-time $6,290; part-time $394 per credit. Required fees: $204; $84 per semester. Full-time tuition and fees vary according to program. Part-time tuition and fees vary according to course load. *General application contact:* Ann Briggs, Administrative Associate, 810-762-3171.

Graduate Programs
Dr. Beverly J. Schmoll, Dean of Graduate Programs and Research
Programs in:
- American culture • MLS
- public administration • MPA

School of Education and Human Services
Dr. Marian Kugler, Interim Dean
Programs in:
- early childhood education • MA
- education • M Ed

School of Health Professions and Studies
Programs in:
- anesthesia • MSA
- health education • MS
- health professions and studies • MPT, MS, MSA, MSN
- nursing • MSN
- physical therapy • MPT

School of Management
Dr. Fred E. Williams, Dean
Program in:
- management • MBA

■ WAYNE STATE UNIVERSITY

Detroit, MI 48202
http://www.wayne.edu/

State-supported, coed, university. CGS member. *Enrollment:* 11,455 matriculated graduate/professional students. *Graduate faculty:* 1,103. *Computer facilities:* 1,000 computers available on campus for general student use. A campuswide network can be accessed from student residence rooms and from off campus. Internet access and online class registration are available. *Library facilities:* David Adamany Undergraduate Library plus 6 others. *Graduate expenses:* Tuition, state resident: part-time $208 per credit hour. Tuition, nonresident: part-time $459 per credit hour. Required fees: $18 per credit hour. *General application contact:* Michael Wood, Associate Director, 313-577-3596.

Graduate School
Dr. Hilary Ratner, Interim Dean
Programs in:
- alcohol and drug abuse studies • Certificate
- archives administration • Certificate
- developmental disabilities • Certificate
- gerontology • Certificate
- infant mental health • Certificate
- interdisciplinary studies • PhD
- library and information science • MLIS, Spec
- molecular and cellular toxicology • MS, PhD

College of Education
Dr. Paula Wood, Interim Dean
Programs in:
- counseling • M Ed, MA, Ed D, PhD, Ed S
- curriculum and instruction • Ed D, PhD, Ed S
- education • M Ed, MA, MAT, Ed D, PhD, Ed S
- educational evaluation and research • M Ed, Ed D, PhD
- educational leadership • M Ed
- educational psychology • M Ed, PhD, Ed S
- elementary education • M Ed, MAT
- general administration and supervision • Ed D, PhD, Ed S
- health education • M Ed
- higher education • Ed D, PhD
- instructional technology • M Ed, Ed D, PhD, Ed S
- marriage and family psychology • MA
- physical education • M Ed
- reading • Ed S
- reading education • Ed D
- recreation and park services • MA
- school psychology • MA
- science • Ed S
- secondary education • M Ed, MAT
- social studies • Ed S
- special education • M Ed, Ed D, PhD, Ed S
- sports administration • MA
- vocational rehabilitation counseling • MA, Ed S

College of Engineering
Dr. Ralph Kummler, Interim Dean
Programs in:
- biomedical engineering • MS, PhD
- chemical engineering • MS, PhD
- civil and environmental engineering • MS, PhD
- computer engineering • MS, PhD
- electrical engineering • MS, PhD
- electronics and computer control systems • MS
- engineering • MS, PhD, Certificate
- engineering management • MS
- engineering technology • MS
- environmental auditing • Certificate
- hazardous materials management on public lands • Certificate
- hazardous waste • MS, Certificate
- hazardous waste control • Certificate
- hazardous waste management • MS
- industrial engineering • MS, PhD
- manufacturing engineering • MS
- materials science and engineering • MS, PhD, Certificate
- mechanical engineering • MS, PhD
- operations research • MS
- polymer engineering • Certificate

College of Fine, Performing and Communication Arts
Linda Moore, Dean
Programs in:
- art • MA, MFA
- art history • MA
- choral conducting • MM
- communication studies • MA, PhD
- composition • MM
- design and merchandising • MA
- fine, performing and communication arts • MA, MFA, MM, MS, PhD, Certificate, PMC
- museology • PMC
- music • MA
- music education • MM
- orchestral studies • Certificate
- performance • MM
- public relations and organizational communication • MA
- radio-TV-film • MA, PhD
- speech communication • MA, PhD
- theatre • MA, MFA, PhD
- theory • MM

Wayne State University (continued)

College of Liberal Arts
Lawrence Scaff, Dean
Programs in:
anthropology • MA, PhD
archival administration • Certificate
classics • MA
comparative literature • MA
criminal justice • MPA
economics • MA, PhD
English • MA, PhD
French • MA
German • MA
history • MA, PhD
interdisciplinary studies • PhD
Italian • MA
language learning • MA
liberal arts • MA, MPA, MS, PhD, Certificate
linguistics • MA
modern languages • PhD
Near Eastern studies • MA
philosophy • MA, PhD
political science • MA, PhD
public administration • MPA
sociology • MA, PhD
Spanish • MA

College of Lifelong Learning
Dr. Paula Wood, Interim Dean
Programs in:
interdisciplinary studies • MIS
lifelong learning • MIS

College of Nursing
Dr. Barbara Redman, Dean
Programs in:
adult acute care nursing • MSN
adult primary care nursing • MSN
advanced practice nursing with women, neonates and children • MSN
child/adolescent psychiatric nursing • MSN
community health nursing • MSN
nursing • MSN, PhD, Certificate
nursing education • Certificate
psychiatric mental health nurse practitioner • MSN
transcultural nursing • Certificate

College of Pharmacy and Allied Health Professions
Beverly Schmoll, Dean
Programs in:
allied health professions • MS, MSPT, Certificate
industrial toxicology • Certificate
medical technology • MS
nurse anesthesia • MS
occupational health sciences • MS
occupational therapy • MS
ocupational safety • Certificate
pediatric anesthesia • Certificate
pharmaceutical sciences • MS, PhD
pharmacy • Pharm D, MS, PhD
pharmacy and allied health professions • Pharm D, MS, MSPT, PhD, Certificate
pharmacy practice • Pharm D, MS
physical therapy • MSPT
physician assistant • MS

College of Science
Robert Thomas, Dean
Programs in:
applied mathematics • MA, PhD
audiology • MS, Au D
biological sciences • MS, PhD
chemistry • MA, MS, PhD
clinical psychology • PhD
cognitive psychology • PhD
computer science • MA, MS, PhD
developmental psychology • PhD
electronics and computer control systems • MS
geology • MS
human development • MA
industrial/organizational psychology • PhD
mathematics • MA, PhD
molecular biotechnology • MS
nutrition and food science • MA, MS, PhD
physics • MA, MS, PhD
psychology • MA, PhD
science • MA, MS, Au D, PhD, Certificate
social psychology • PhD
speech language pathology • PhD
speech-language pathology • MA
statistics • MA, PhD

College of Urban, Labor and Metropolitan Affairs
Alma Young, Interim Dean
Programs in:
dispute resolution • MADR, Certificate
economic development • Certificate
geography • MA
industrial relations • MAIR
urban planning • MUP
urban, labor and metropolitan affairs • MA, MADR, MAIR, MUP, Certificate

Law School
Joan Mahoney, Dean
Program in:
law • JD, LL M

School of Business Administration
Dr. Harvey Kahalas, Dean
Programs in:
business administration • MBA
taxation • MS

School of Social Work
Phyllis Vroom, Interim Dean
Programs in:
social work • MSW
social work practice with families and couples • Certificate

School of Medicine
Dr. John D. Crissman, Dean
Program in:
medicine • MD, MS, PhD, Certificate

Graduate Programs in Medicine
Dr. Kenneth C. Palmer, Assistant Dean
Programs in:
anatomy and cell biology • MS, PhD
basic medical science • MS
biochemistry • MS, PhD
cancer biology • PhD
cellular and clinical neurobiology • PhD
community health • MS
community health services • Certificate
immunology and microbiology • MS, PhD
medical physics • PhD
medical research • MS
medicine • MS, PhD, Certificate
molecular biology and genetics • MS, PhD
pathology • PhD
pharmacology • MS, PhD
physical medicine and rehabilitation • MS
physiology • MS, PhD
radiological physics • MS

■ WESTERN MICHIGAN UNIVERSITY

Kalamazoo, MI 49008-5202
http://www.wmich.edu/

State-supported, coed, university. CGS member. *Graduate faculty:* 907 full-time (325 women), 128 part-time/adjunct. *Computer facilities:* 2,000 computers available on campus for general student use. A campuswide network can be accessed from student residence rooms and from off campus. *Library facilities:* Waldo Library plus 4 others. *Graduate expenses:* Tuition, state resident: full-time $3,999; part-time $167 per credit hour. Tuition, nonresident: full-time $9,594; part-time $400 per credit hour. Required fees: $602. *General application contact:* Paula J. Boodt, Coordinator, Graduate Admissions and Recruitment, 616-387-2000.

Find an in-depth description at www.petersons.com/graduate.

Graduate College
Dr. Donald E. Thompson, Dean
Programs in:
fine arts • MA, MFA, MM
graphic design • MFA
music • MA, MM
textile design • MA, MFA

College of Arts and Sciences
Dr. Elise B. Jorgens, Dean
Programs in:
- anthropology • MA
- applied behavior analysis • MA, PhD
- applied economics • PhD
- applied mathematics • MS
- arts and sciences • MA, MDA, MFA, MPA, MS, DPA, PhD, Ed S
- biological sciences • MS, PhD
- biostatistics • MS
- chemistry • MA, PhD
- clinical psychology • MA, PhD
- comparative religion • MA, PhD
- computational mathematics • MS
- computer science • MS, PhD
- creative writing • MFA
- development administration • MDA
- earth science • MS
- economics • MA
- English • MA, PhD
- experimental analysis of behavior • PhD
- experimental psychology • MA
- geography • MA
- geology • MS, PhD
- graph theory and computer science • PhD
- history • MA, PhD
- industrial/organizational psychology • MA
- mathematics • MA, PhD
- mathematics education • MA, PhD
- medieval studies • MA
- organizational communication • MA
- philosophy • MA
- physics • MA, PhD
- political science • MA, PhD
- professional writing • MA
- public affairs and administration • MPA, DPA
- school psychology • PhD, Ed S
- science studies • MA, PhD
- sociology • MA, PhD
- Spanish • MA
- statistics • MS, PhD

College of Education
Dr. David A. England, Dean
Programs in:
- administration • MA
- athletic training • MA
- career and technical education • MA
- coaching and sports studies • MA
- counseling psychology • PhD
- counselor education • MA, Ed D, PhD
- counselor education and counseling psychology • MA, PhD
- counselor psychology • MA
- early childhood education • MA
- education • MA, Ed D, PhD, Ed S
- education and professional development • MA
- educational leadership • MA, Ed D, PhD, Ed S
- educational studies • MA, Ed D
- elementary education • MA
- exercise science • MA
- family and consumer sciences • MA
- middle school education • MA
- motor development • MA
- physical education • MA
- reading • MA
- special education for handicapped children • MA

College of Engineering and Applied Sciences
Dr. Daniel M. Litynski, Dean
Programs in:
- computer engineering • MSE
- construction management • MS
- electrical engineering • MSE
- engineering and applied sciences • MS, MSE, PhD
- engineering management • MS
- industrial engineering • MSE
- manufacturing science • MS
- materials science and engineering • MS
- mechanical engineering • MSE, PhD
- operations research • MS
- paper, imaging, and chemical engineering • MS

College of Health and Human Services
Dr. Janet Pisaneschi, Dean
Programs in:
- audiology • MA
- blind rehabilitation • MA
- health and human services • MA, MS, MSW
- occupational therapy • MS
- physician assistant • MS
- social work • MSW
- speech pathology • MA

Haworth College of Business
Dr. James Schmotter, Dean
Programs in:
- accountancy • MSA
- business • MBA, MSA
- business administration • MBA

Minnesota

■ AUGSBURG COLLEGE

Minneapolis, MN 55454-1351
http://www.augsburg.edu/

Independent-religious, coed, comprehensive institution. *Enrollment:* 68 full-time matriculated graduate/professional students (62 women), 59 part-time matriculated graduate/professional students (53 women). *Graduate faculty:* 14 full-time (12 women), 11 part-time/adjunct (7 women). *Computer facilities:* 224 computers available on campus for general student use. A campuswide network can be accessed from student residence rooms and from off campus. Internet access and online class registration are available. *Library facilities:* James G. Lindell Library. *Graduate expenses:* Tuition: full-time $7,944; part-time $331 per credit. *General application contact:* Terry Cook, Coordinator, 612-330-1787.

Program in Leadership
Dr. Norma Noonan, Director
Program in:
- leadership • MA

Program in Social Work
Dr. Edward Skarnulis, Director
Program in:
- social work • MSW

Program in Transcultural Community Health Nursing
Dr. Bev Nilsson, Director
Program in:
- transcultural community health nursing • MA

■ BEMIDJI STATE UNIVERSITY

Bemidji, MN 56601-2699
http://www.bemidjistate.edu/

State-supported, coed, comprehensive institution. *Enrollment:* 36 full-time matriculated graduate/professional students (24 women), 204 part-time matriculated graduate/professional students (145 women). *Graduate faculty:* 62 part-time/adjunct (22 women). *Computer facilities:* 400 computers available on campus for general student use. A campuswide network can be accessed from student residence rooms and from off campus. Internet access and online class registration are available. *Library facilities:* A. C. Clark Library. *Graduate expenses:* Tuition, state resident: full-time $2,954; part-time $107 per credit. Tuition, nonresident: full-time $6,266; part-time $210 per credit. Required fees: $621; $107 per credit. *General application contact:* Dr. David J. Larkin, Dean, 218-755-3732.

Graduate Studies

College of Professional Studies
Programs in:
- curriculum and instruction • MS
- industrial education • MS
- physical education • MS
- professional studies • MS
- school administration • MS
- special education • MS

Bemidji State University (continued)

College of Social and Natural Sciences

Programs in:
- biology • MA
- environmental studies • MS
- mathematics • MS
- science • MS
- social and natural sciences • MA, MS

Division of Arts and Letters

Programs in:
- arts and letters • MA, MS
- English • MA, MS

■ BETHEL COLLEGE

St. Paul, MN 55112-6999

http://www.bethel.edu/

Independent-religious, coed, comprehensive institution. *Enrollment:* 288 full-time matriculated graduate/professional students (212 women). *Graduate faculty:* 38 full-time (18 women), 14 part-time/adjunct (7 women). *Computer facilities:* 367 computers available on campus for general student use. A campuswide network can be accessed from student residence rooms and from off campus. Internet access is available. *Library facilities:* Bethel College Library plus 1 other. *Graduate expenses:* Tuition: part-time $290 per credit. One-time fee: $100 part-time. Tuition and fees vary according to degree level and program. *General application contact:* Margaret Washenberger, Senior Admissions Coordinator, 651-635-8000.

Center for Graduate and Continuing Studies

Dr. Dennis R. Morrow, Dean

Programs in:
- anthropology and sociology • MA
- communication • MA
- education • M Ed, MAT
- music • MA
- nursing • MA
- organizational studies • MA
- psychology • MA

■ COLLEGE OF ST. CATHERINE

St. Paul, MN 55105-1789

http://www.stkate.edu/

Independent-religious, women only, comprehensive institution. *Enrollment:* 563 full-time matriculated graduate/professional students (499 women), 369 part-time matriculated graduate/professional students (334 women). *Graduate faculty:* 93 full-time (74 women). *Computer facilities:* 350 computers available on campus for general student use. A campuswide network can be accessed from student residence rooms and from off campus. Internet access, transcript are available. *Library facilities:* St. Catherine Library plus 2 others. *Graduate expenses:* Tuition: full-time $16,320; part-time $510 per credit. Required fees: $122. Tuition and fees vary according to program. *General application contact:* 651-690-6505.

Find an in-depth description at www.petersons.com/graduate.

Graduate Program

Dr. Mary Margaret Smith, Academic Dean

Programs in:
- education • MA
- library and information science • MA
- nursing • MA
- occupational therapy • MA
- organizational leadership • MA
- physical therapy • MPT
- social work • MSW
- theology • MA

■ THE COLLEGE OF ST. SCHOLASTICA

Duluth, MN 55811-4199

http://www.css.edu/

Independent-religious, coed, comprehensive institution. *Enrollment:* 232 full-time matriculated graduate/professional students (177 women), 323 part-time matriculated graduate/professional students (212 women). *Graduate faculty:* 38 full-time (20 women), 31 part-time/adjunct (27 women). *Computer facilities:* 160 computers available on campus for general student use. A campuswide network can be accessed from student residence rooms and from off campus. Internet access is available. *Library facilities:* College of St. Scholastica Library plus 1 other. *Graduate expenses:* Tuition: part-time $536 per credit. Tuition and fees vary according to course load and program. *General application contact:* Debra Bekkering, Graduate Administrative Assistant, 218-723-6285.

Graduate Studies

Dr. Rachel Applegate, Director

Programs in:
- education • M Ed
- educational media and technology • M Ed
- exercise physiology • MA
- health information management • MA
- management • MA
- nursing • MA
- occupational therapy • MA
- physical therapy • MA

■ HAMLINE UNIVERSITY

St. Paul, MN 55104-1284

http://www.hamline.edu/

Independent-religious, coed, comprehensive institution. *Enrollment:* 120 full-time matriculated graduate/professional students, 643 part-time matriculated graduate/professional students. *Graduate faculty:* 159. *Computer facilities:* 326 computers available on campus for general student use. A campuswide network can be accessed from student residence rooms and from off campus. Internet access and online class registration are available. *Library facilities:* Bush Library plus 1 other. *Graduate expenses:* Tuition: full-time $4,200; part-time $1,050 per course. One-time fee: $150. Tuition and fees vary according to course load, degree level and program. *General application contact:* 651-523-2900.

Graduate Liberal Studies Program

Mary Francóis Rockcastle, Director

Program in:
- liberal studies • MALS, MFA

Graduate School of Education

Deirde Kramer, Interim Dean

Program in:
- education • MA Ed, MAESL, MAT, Ed D

Graduate School of Public Administration and Management

Dr. Jane McPeak, Dean

Programs in:
- management • MAM
- nonprofit management • MANM
- public administration • MAPA

School of Law

Edwin J. Butterfoss, Dean

Program in:
- law • JD, LL M

■ MAYO GRADUATE SCHOOL

Rochester, MN 55905

http://www.mayo.edu/mgs/gs.html

Independent, coed, graduate-only institution. *Graduate faculty:* 327 full-time (47 women). *Computer facilities:* A campuswide network can be accessed from off campus. Internet access is available. *Library facilities:* Plummer Library plus 7 others. *Graduate expenses:* Tuition: full-time $17,900. *General application contact:* Melissa L. Berg, Admissions Coordinator, 507-538-1160.

Graduate Programs in Biomedical Sciences
Dr. Paul J. Leibson, Dean
Programs in:
- biochemistry • PhD
- biomedical engineering • PhD
- biomedical sciences • PhD
- immunology • PhD
- molecular biology • PhD
- molecular neuroscience • PhD
- neuroscience • PhD
- pharmacology • PhD
- tumor biology • PhD

■ METROPOLITAN STATE UNIVERSITY
St. Paul, MN 55106-5000
http://www.metrostate.edu

State-supported, coed, comprehensive institution. *Enrollment:* 75 full-time matriculated graduate/professional students (50 women), 500 part-time matriculated graduate/professional students (200 women). *Graduate faculty:* 24 full-time (9 women), 83 part-time/adjunct (31 women). *Computer facilities:* 150 computers available on campus for general student use. A campuswide network can be accessed from off campus. Internet access is available. *Graduate expenses:* Tuition, state resident: full-time $1,160; part-time $145 per credit. Tuition, nonresident: part-time $209 per credit. $1,673 full-time. Required fees: $6 per credit. *General application contact:* Gloria B. Marcus, Recruiter/Admissions Adviser, 612-373-2724.

College of Arts and Sciences
Program in:
- technical communication • MS

College of Management
Robert Kramarczuk, Graduate Director
Programs in:
- finance • MBA
- human resource management • MBA
- information management • MMIS
- international business • MBA
- law enforcement • MPNA
- management information systems • MBA
- marketing • MBA
- nonprofit management • MPNA
- organizational studies • MBA
- public administration • MPNA
- purchasing management • MBA
- systems management • MMIS

School of Nursing
Marilyn Loen, Interim Dean
Program in:
- nursing • MSN

■ MINNESOTA STATE UNIVERSITY, MANKATO
Mankato, MN 56001
http://www.mnsu.edu

State-supported, coed, comprehensive institution. CGS member. *Enrollment:* 1,677 matriculated graduate/professional students (1,073 women). *Graduate faculty:* 405 full-time (150 women), 120 part-time/adjunct (58 women). *Computer facilities:* 525 computers available on campus for general student use. A campuswide network can be accessed from student residence rooms and from off campus. Internet access and online class registration are available. *Library facilities:* Memorial Library. *Graduate expenses:* Tuition, state resident: part-time $158 per credit hour. Tuition, nonresident: part-time $237 per credit hour. Required fees: $21 per credit. *General application contact:* Joni Roberts, Admissions Coordinator, 507-389-5244.

College of Graduate Studies
Dr. Anthony J. Filipovitch, Chairperson
Program in:
- multidisciplinary studies • MS

College of Allied Health and Nursing
Dr. K. Heath, Interim Dean
Programs in:
- allied health and nursing • MA, MS, MSN, MT, SP
- communication disorders • MS
- community health • MS
- family consumer science and interior design • MS, MT
- family nursing • MSN
- health science • MS, MT
- human performance • MA, MS, MT, SP
- managed care • MSN
- rehabilitation counseling • MS

College of Arts and Humanities
Dr. Jane F. Earley, Dean
Programs in:
- art education • MS
- arts and humanities • MA, MAT, MFA, MM, MS, MT
- creative writing • MFA
- English • MA, MS
- French • MAT, MS
- German • MAT
- music • MM, MT
- Spanish • MAT, MS
- speech communication • MA, MS, MT
- studio art • MA
- teaching art • MAT, MT
- teaching English • MS, MT
- theatre arts • MA, MFA

College of Education
Dr. Joanne Brandt, Interim Dean
Programs in:
- bilingual/bicultural education • MS
- computer services administration • MS
- counseling and student personnel • MS
- curriculum and instruction • MAT, MT
- early childhood education • MS
- early education for exceptional children • MS
- education • MA, MAT, MS, MT, Certificate, SP
- education of the gifted and talented • MS
- education technology • MS
- educational administration • Certificate
- educational leadership • MS, Certificate, SP
- elementary education • MS, SP
- elementary school administration • MS, SP
- emotional disturbance • MS
- experiential education • MS
- general educational administration • MS
- higher education administration • MS
- learning disabilities • MS
- library media education • MS, SP
- mental retardation • MS
- reading consultant • MS
- secondary administration • MS, SP
- secondary teaching • MA, MS, SP
- severely handicapped • MS
- vocational-technical administration • MS

College of Science, Engineering and Technology
Dr. John Frey, Dean
Programs in:
- biology • MS
- chemistry • MA, MS
- computer science • MS
- computers • MS
- ecology • MS
- economic and political systems • MS

Minnesota State University, Mankato (continued)

- electrical engineering and electronic engineering technology • MSE
- environmental science • MS
- human ecosystems • MS
- manufacturing • MS
- mathematics • MA, MS
- mathematics: computer science • MS
- mechanical engineering • MS
- physical science • MS
- physics and astronomy • MS, MT
- science, engineering and technology • MA, MS, MSE, MT
- statistics • MS
- teaching mathematics • MT
- technology • MS

College of Social and Behavioral Sciences
Dr. Susan Coultrap-McQuin, Acting Dean
Programs in:

- anthropology • MS
- clinical psychology • MA
- geography • MA, MS, MT
- gerontology • MS
- history • MA, MS
- industrial psychology • MA
- political science • MA, MS, MT
- psychology • MT
- public administration • MAPA
- social and behavioral sciences • MA, MAPA, MS, MT
- social studies • MS
- sociology • MA, MT
- sociology: corrections • MS
- teaching history • MS, MT
- urban and regional studies • MA
- women's studies • MS

■ MINNESOTA STATE UNIVERSITY MOORHEAD
Moorhead, MN 56563-0002
http://www.mnstate.edu/

State-supported, coed, comprehensive institution. *Graduate faculty:* 126. *Computer facilities:* 450 computers available on campus for general student use. A campuswide network can be accessed from student residence rooms and from off campus. Internet access and online class registration are available. *Library facilities:* Livingston Lord Library. *Graduate expenses:* Tuition, state resident: full-time $3,310. Tuition, nonresident: full-time $5,246. *General application contact:* Karla Wenger, Graduate Studies Office Manager, 218-236-2344.

Graduate Studies
Director of Graduate Studies
Programs in:

- counseling and student affairs • MS
- creative writing • MFA
- curriculum and instruction • MS
- educational administration • MS, Ed S
- liberal studies • MLA
- music • MS
- music education • MS
- public and human services administration • MS
- reading • MS
- school psychology • MS, Spec
- special education • MS
- speech pathology and audiology • MS

■ ST. CLOUD STATE UNIVERSITY
St. Cloud, MN 56301-4498
http://www.stcloudstate.edu/

State-supported, coed, comprehensive institution. CGS member. *Enrollment:* 410 full-time matriculated graduate/professional students (247 women), 546 part-time matriculated graduate/professional students (360 women). *Graduate faculty:* 338 full-time (113 women), 67 part-time/adjunct (31 women). *Computer facilities:* 1,045 computers available on campus for general student use. A campuswide network can be accessed from student residence rooms and from off campus. Online class registration is available. *Library facilities:* Miller Learning Center. *Graduate expenses:* Tuition, state resident: part-time $149 per credit. Tuition, nonresident: part-time $225 per credit. *General application contact:* Dr. Dennis Nunes, Dean of Graduate Studies, 320-255-2113.

School of Graduate Studies
Dr. Dennis Nunes, Dean

College of Education
Dr. Joane McKay, Dean
Programs in:

- administration of special education • Spt
- behavior analysis • MS
- child and family studies • MS
- community counseling • MS
- counseling • MS
- educable mentally handicapped • MS
- education • MS, Spt
- educational administration and leadership • MS, Spt
- elementary education • MS
- emotionally disturbed • MS
- exercise science • MS
- gifted and talented • MS
- information media • MS
- junior high/middle school education • MS
- learning disabled • MS
- physical education • MS
- reading • MS
- rehabilitation counseling • MS
- school counseling • MS
- secondary education • MS
- social responsibility • MS
- special education • MS
- sports management • MS
- trainable mentally retarded • MS

College of Fine Arts and Humanities
Dr. Roland Specht-Jarvis, Dean
Programs in:

- art • MA
- communication disorders • MS
- conducting and literature • MM
- English • MA, MS
- fine arts and humanities • MA, MM, MS
- mass communication • MS
- music education • MM
- piano pedagogy • MM
- teaching English as a second language • MA

College of Science and Engineering
Dr. A. I. Musah, Dean
Programs in:

- biological sciences • MA, MS
- computer science • MS
- environmental and technological studies • MS
- mathematics • MS
- science and engineering • MA, MS

College of Social Sciences
Dr. Richard Lewis, Dean
Programs in:

- applied economics • MS
- criminal justice • MS
- geography • MS
- gerontology • MS
- history • MA, MS
- public and nonprofit institutions • MS
- social sciences • MA, MS

G.R. Herberger College of Business
Dr. Michael Pesch, Graduate Coordinator
Programs in:

- accounting • MS
- business • MBA, MS
- finance • MBA
- marketing • MBA

■ SAINT MARY'S UNIVERSITY OF MINNESOTA
Winona, MN 55987-1399
http://www.smumn.edu/

Independent-religious, coed, comprehensive institution. *Computer facilities:* 356 computers available on campus for general student use. A campuswide network can be accessed from student residence rooms and from off campus. Internet access is available. *Library facilities:* Fitzgerald Library. *General application contact:* Vice President, Graduate Programs, 612-874-9877.

Graduate School
Programs in:
- arts administration • MA
- business • MS
- counseling and psychological services • MA
- criminal justice • MS
- developmental disabilities • MA
- education • MA
- educational administration • MA
- educational leadership • Ed D
- human and health services administration • MA
- human development • MA
- management • MA
- natural resources • MS
- nurse anesthesia • MS
- philanthropy and development • MA
- public administration • MS
- telecommunications • MS

Institute of Pastoral Ministries
Program in:
- pastoral ministries • MA, Certificate

■ UNIVERSITY OF MINNESOTA, DULUTH

Duluth, MN 55812-2496
http://www.d.umn.edu/

State-supported, coed, comprehensive institution. *Enrollment:* 377 full-time matriculated graduate/professional students (241 women), 166 part-time matriculated graduate/professional students (93 women). *Graduate faculty:* 221 full-time (60 women), 63 part-time/adjunct (23 women). *Computer facilities:* 525 computers available on campus for general student use. A campuswide network can be accessed from student residence rooms and from off campus. Internet access and online class registration are available. *Library facilities:* University of Minnesota Duluth Library plus 1 other. *Graduate expenses:* Tuition, state resident: full-time $5,317; part-time $443 per credit. Tuition, nonresident: full-time $8,706; part-time $870 per credit. Required fees: $350. Tuition and fees vary according to course load and program. *General application contact:* Dr. Stephen C. Hedman, Associate Graduate Dean, 218-726-7523.

Graduate School
Dr. Stephen C. Hedman, Associate Graduate Dean
Program in:
- toxicology • MS, PhD

College of Education and Human Service Professions
Dr. Paul Deputy, Dean
Programs in:
- communication sciences and disorders • MA
- community counseling • MA
- education and human service professions • MA, MSW
- school counseling • MA
- social work • MSW

College of Liberal Arts
Dr. Linda Krug, Dean
Programs in:
- English • MA
- liberal arts • MA, MLS
- sociology/anthropology • MLS

College of Science and Engineering
Dr. James Riehl, Dean
Programs in:
- applied and computational mathematics • MS
- biology • MS
- chemistry • MS
- computer science • MS
- engineering management • MS
- environmental health and safety • MEHS
- geological sciences • MS
- physics • MS
- science and engineering • MA, MEHS, MS

School of Business and Economics
Kjell Knudsen, Dean
Programs in:
- business administration • MBA
- business and economics • MBA

School of Fine Arts
Dr. W. Robert Bucker, Dean
Programs in:
- fine arts • MFA, MM
- graphic design • MFA
- music education • MM
- performance • MM

School of Medicine
Dr. Richard J. Ziegler, Dean
Programs in:
- anatomy and cell biology • MS, PhD
- biochemistry and molecular biology • MS, PhD
- medical microbiology and immunology • MS, PhD
- medicine • MD, MS, PhD
- pharmacology • MS, PhD
- physiology • MS, PhD

■ UNIVERSITY OF MINNESOTA, TWIN CITIES CAMPUS

Minneapolis, MN 55455-0213
http://www.umn.edu/tc/

State-supported, coed, university. CGS member. *Enrollment:* 7,694 matriculated graduate/professional students (3,989 women). *Graduate faculty:* 2,700. *Computer facilities:* A campuswide network can be accessed from student residence rooms and from off campus. E-mail available. *Library facilities:* Wilson Library plus 17 others. *Graduate expenses:* Full-time $2,659; part-time $443 per credit. Tuition, nonresident: full-time $5,222; part-time $871 per credit. Required fees: $238. *General application contact:* Dr. Christine Maziar, Vice President for Research and Dean of the Graduate School, 612-625-3394.

Carlson School of Management
Dr. David Kidwell, Dean
Programs in:
- accounting • MBA, PhD
- business taxation • MBT
- e-business • MBA
- entrepreneurship • MBA
- finance • MBA, PhD
- healthcare management • MBA
- human resources and industrial relations • MA, PhD
- information and decision sciences • MBA, PhD
- international business • MBA
- management • EMBA, MA, MBA, MBT, MHA, MS, MSMOT, PhD
- marketing and logistics management • MBA, PhD
- operations and management science • MBA, PhD
- strategic management and organization • MBA, PhD
- supply chain management • MBA

College of Pharmacy
Programs in:
- medicinal chemistry • MS, PhD
- pharmaceutics • MS, PhD
- pharmacy • Pharm D, MS, PhD
- social and administrative pharmacy • MS, PhD

College of Veterinary Medicine
Dr. Jeffrey Klausner, Interim Dean
Programs in:
- molecular veterinary biosciences • MS, PhD
- veterinary medicine • MS, PhD

Graduate School
Dr. Christine Maziar, Vice President for Research and Dean

University of Minnesota, Twin Cities Campus (continued)
Programs in:
- biophysical sciences and medical physics • MS, PhD
- genetic counseling • MS
- health informatics • MS, PhD
- molecular, cellular, developmental biology and genetics • PhD
- neuroscience • MS, PhD
- pharmacology • MS, PhD
- scientific computation • MS, PhD

College of Agricultural, Food, and Environmental Sciences
Dr. Charles C. Muscoplat, Dean
Programs in:
- agricultural and applied economics • MS, PhD
- agricultural, food, and environmental sciences • MA, MBAE, MS, MSBAE, PhD
- animal science • MS, PhD
- applied plant sciences • MS, PhD
- biosystems and agricultural engineering • MBAE, MSBAE, PhD
- entomology • MS, PhD
- food science • MS, PhD
- horticultural science • MA, MS, PhD
- microbial ecology • MS, PhD
- nutrition • MS, PhD
- plant pathology • MS, PhD
- rhetoric and scientific and technical communication • MA, PhD
- scientific and technical communication • MS
- soil, water, and climate • MS, PhD

College of Architecture and Landscape Architecture
Programs in:
- architecture • M Arch
- architecture and landscape architecture • M Arch, MLA, MS
- landscape architecture • MLA, MS

College of Biological Sciences
Dr. Robert Elde, Dean
Programs in:
- biological science • MBS
- biological sciences • MBS, MS, PhD
- ecology, animal behavior, and evolution • MS, PhD
- plant biology • MS, PhD

College of Education and Human Development
Programs in:
- adult education • M Ed, MA, Ed D, PhD, Certificate
- agricultural education • M Ed, MA, Ed D, PhD
- applied kinesiology • M Ed
- art education • M Ed, MA, PhD
- business and marketing education • M Ed, MA, Ed D, PhD
- child psychology • MA, PhD
- Chinese • M Ed
- comparative and international development education • MA, PhD
- counseling • Ed S
- counseling and student personnel psychology • MA, PhD
- curriculum studies • MA, PhD
- early childhood education • M Ed
- earth science • M Ed
- education and human development • M Ed, MA, Ed D, PhD, Certificate, Ed S
- educational administration • MA, Ed D, PhD, Ed S
- educational policy and administration • MA, PhD
- educational psychology • MA, PhD, Ed S
- elementary administration • Ed S
- elementary education • M Ed, MA
- elementary special education • M Ed
- English • M Ed
- English as a second language • M Ed
- English education • MA
- evaluation studies • MA, PhD
- extension education • MA, Ed D, PhD
- family education • M Ed, MA, Ed D, PhD
- French • M Ed
- German • M Ed
- Hebrew • M Ed
- higher education • MA, PhD
- human resource development • M Ed, MA, Ed D, PhD, Certificate
- industrial education • M Ed, MA, Ed D, PhD
- instructional systems • MA, PhD
- international vocational education • M Ed, MA, Ed D, PhD
- Japanese • M Ed
- kinesiology • MA, PhD
- life sciences • M Ed
- mathematics • M Ed
- mathematics education • MA, PhD
- middle school science • M Ed
- physical education • M Ed
- psychological foundations of education • MA, PhD
- recreation, park, and leisure studies • M Ed, MA, PhD
- school psychological services • Ed S
- school psychology • MA, PhD
- school work • Certificate
- science • M Ed
- science education • MA, PhD
- second languages and cultures • M Ed, MA, PhD
- secondary administration • Ed S
- social studies • M Ed
- social studies education • MA, PhD
- Spanish • M Ed
- special education • M Ed, MA, PhD, Ed S
- special education administration • Ed S
- teacher leadership • M Ed
- teaching • M Ed
- vocational education • M Ed, MA
- vocational education administration • M Ed
- vocational special needs • M Ed, MA
- work, community, and family education • M Ed, MA, Ed D, PhD
- youth development leadership • M Ed

College of Human Ecology
Programs in:
- design, housing, and apparel • MA, MFA, MS, PhD
- family social science • MA, PhD
- human ecology • MA, MFA, MS, MSW, PhD
- social work • MSW, PhD

College of Liberal Arts
Programs in:
- American studies • PhD
- ancient and medieval art and archaeology • MA, PhD
- anthropology • MA, PhD
- art • MFA
- art history • MA, PhD
- audiology • MA, PhD
- biological psychopathology • PhD
- classics • MA, PhD
- clinical psychology • PhD
- cognitive and biological psychology • PhD
- comparative literature • MA, PhD
- comparative studies in discourse and society • MA, PhD
- counseling psychology • PhD
- design technology • MFA
- differential psychology/behavior genetics • PhD
- directing • MFA
- East Asian studies • MA
- economics • PhD
- English • MA, MFA, PhD
- French • MA, PhD
- geographic information science • MGIS
- geography • MA, PhD
- Germanic studies: German and Scandanavian • PhD
- Germanic studies: German track • MA, PhD
- Germanic studies: medieval • MA, PhD
- Germanic studies: Scnadanavian track • MA
- Germanic studies: teaching German • MA
- Greek • MA, PhD
- hearing science • PhD
- Hispanic and Luso-Brazilian literatures and linguistics • PhD
- Hispanic linguistics • MA
- history • MA, PhD
- industrial/organizational psychology • PhD
- Italian • MA
- Latin • MA, PhD

liberal arts • MA, MFA, MGIS, MM, MS, DMA, PhD
linguistics • MA, PhD
mass communication • MA, PhD
music • MA, MM, DMA, PhD
personality research • PhD
philosophy • MA, PhD
political science • MA, PhD
Portuguese • MA
psychometric methods • MA, PhD
Russian area studies • MA
school psychology • PhD
social psychology • PhD
sociology • MA, PhD
Spanish • MA
speech science • PhD
speech-communication • MA, PhD
speech-language pathology • MA, PhD
statistics • MS, PhD
theater arts and dance • PhD

College of Natural Resources
Dr. Alfred Sullivan, Dean
Programs in:
conservation biology • MS, PhD
fisheries • MS, PhD
forestry • MF, MS, PhD
natural resources • MF, MS, PhD
wildlife conservation • MS, PhD

Hubert H. Humphrey Institute of Public Affairs
Dr. John Brandl, Dean
Programs in:
advanced policy analysis methods • MPP
economic and community development • MPP
economic development • MURP
environmental and ecological planning • MURP
foreign policy • MPP
housing, social planning, and community development • MURP
land use and human settlements • MURP
landscape and urban design • MURP
planning process design and implementation • MURP
public affairs • MPA, MPP, MS, MURP, PhD/MPP
public and nonprofit leadership and management • MPP
science, technology, and environmental policy • MS
social policy • MPP
transportation planning • MURP
women and public policy • MPP

Institute of Technology
Programs in:
aerospace engineering • M Aero E, MS, PhD
astronomy • MS, PhD
astrophysics • MS, PhD
biomedical engineering • MS, PhD
chemical engineering • M Ch E, MS Ch E, PhD
chemistry • MS, PhD
civil engineering • MCE, MS, PhD
computer and information sciences • MCIS, MS, PhD
computer engineering • M Comp E, MS
electrical and computer engineering • MEE, MSEE, PhD
geological engineering • M Geo E, MS, PhD
geology • MS, PhD
geophysics • MS, PhD
history of science and technology • MA, PhD
industrial engineering • MSIE, PhD
infrastructure systems engineering • MS
management of technology • MSMOT
manufacturing systems • MS
materials science and engineering • M Mat SE, MS Mat SE, PhD
mathematics • MS, PhD
mechanical engineering • MSME, PhD
mechanics • MS, PhD
physics • MS, PhD
software engineering • MS
technology • M Aero E, M Ch E, M Comp E, M Geo E, M Mat SE, MA, MCE, MCIS, MEE, MS, MS Ch E, MS Mat SE, MSEE, MSIE, MSME, MSMOT, PhD

School of Nursing
Sandra Edwardson, Dean
Programs in:
adolescent nursing • MS
adult health clinical nurse specialist • MS
advanced clinical specialist in child and family nursing • MS
advanced clinical specialist in gerontology • MS
family nurse practitioner • MS
gerontology nurse practitioner • MS
midwifery • MS
nursing • MS, PhD
nursing education • MS
nursing management • MS
oncology nursing • MS
pediatric nurse practitioner • MS
psychiatric mental health clinical nurse specialist • MS
public health nursing • MS
school nursing • MS

Law School
E. Thomas Sullivan, Dean
Program in:
law • JD, LL M

Medical School
Alfred F. Michael, Dean
Program in:
medicine • MD, MA, MS, PhD

Graduate Programs in Medicine
Programs in:
biochemistry, molecular biology and biophysics • PhD
cellular and integrative physiology • MS, PhD
clinical laboratory sciences • MS
experimental surgery • MS
history of medicine • MA, PhD
medicine • MA, MS, PhD
microbial engineering • MS
microbiology, immunology and cancer biology • PhD
otolaryngology • MS, PhD
physical medicine and rehabilitation • MS, PhD
physical therapy • MS
rehabilitation science • PhD
surgery • MS, PhD

School of Dentistry
Dr. Peter J. Polverini, Dean
Programs in:
dentistry • DDS, MS, PhD
endodontics • MS
oral biology • MS, PhD
oral health services for older adults • MS
orthodontics • MS
pediatric dentistry • MS
periodontology • MS
prosthodontics • MS
temporal mandibular joint • MS

School of Public Health
Dr. Mark Becker, Dean
Programs in:
biostatistics • MPH, MS, PhD
clinical research • MS
community health education • MPH
environmental and occupational epidemiology • MPH, MS, PhD
environmental chemistry • MS, PhD
environmental health policy • MPH, MS, PhD
environmental microbiology • MPH, MS, PhD
environmental toxicology • MPH, MS, PhD
epidemiology • MPH, PhD
health services research, policy, and administration • MS, PhD
industrial hygiene • MPH, MS, PhD
maternal and child health • MPH
occupational health nursing • MPH, MS, PhD
occupational medicine • MPH
public health • MPH, MS, PhD
public health administration • MPH
public health nutrition • MPH

■ UNIVERSITY OF ST. THOMAS
St. Paul, MN 55105-1096
http://www.stthomas.edu/

Independent-religious, coed, university. *Enrollment:* 655 full-time matriculated

University of St. Thomas (continued)
graduate/professional students (352 women), 4,509 part-time matriculated graduate/professional students (2,260 women). *Graduate faculty:* 367 full-time (132 women), 411 part-time/adjunct (146 women). *Computer facilities:* 843 computers available on campus for general student use. A campuswide network can be accessed from student residence rooms and from off campus. Internet access and online class registration are available. *Library facilities:* O'Shaughnessy-Frey Library plus 2 others. *Graduate expenses:* Tuition: part-time $405 per credit hour. *General application contact:* Dr. Miriam Williams, Associate Vice President for Academic Affairs, 651-962-4435.

Find an in-depth description at www.petersons.com/graduate.

Graduate Studies
Dr. Ralph Pearson, Vice President for Academic Affairs
Programs in:
- Catholic studies • MA
- professional psychology • MA, Psy D
- social work • MSW

Graduate School of Applied Science and Engineering
Programs in:
- applied science and engineering • MMSE, MS, MSDD, MSS, Certificate
- manufacturing systems engineering • MMSE, MS, Certificate
- software • MS, MSDD, MSS, Certificate

Graduate School of Arts and Sciences
Academic Dean
Programs in:
- art history • MA
- arts and sciences • MA
- English • MA
- music education • MA

Graduate School of Business
Dr. Jeanne Buckeye, Interim Dean
Programs in:
- accounting • MBA, Certificate
- business • MBA, MBC, MIM, MS, Certificate
- business administration • MBA, Certificate
- business communication • MBC
- business writing • Certificate
- electronic commerce • MBA
- environmental management • MBA
- finance • MBA
- financial services management • MBA
- franchise management • MBA, Certificate
- government contracts • MBA, Certificate
- health care management • MBA, Certificate
- human resource management • MBA, Certificate
- human resource management—development • Certificate
- human resource management—organizational development • Certificate
- human resource management—training • Certificate
- human resource management–compensation • Certificate
- human resource management–employee benefits • Certificate
- human resource management–generalist • Certificate
- human resource management–law • Certificate
- industrial management (software systems • Certificate
- information management • MBA
- insurance and risk management • MBA
- internal communication • Certificate
- international finance • MIM, Certificate
- international human resource management • Certificate
- international human resources • MIM, Certificate
- international managerial communication • MIM, Certificate
- international marketing • MIM, Certificate
- management • MBA
- management communication • Certificate
- manufacturing systems • MBA, MIM, Certificate
- marketing • MBA
- marketing communication • Certificate
- medical group management • MBA
- nonprofit management • MBA, Certificate
- public relations • Certificate
- real estate • MBA
- real estate appraisal • MS, Certificate
- self-designed • MIM
- software systems • MIM
- sports and entertainment management • MBA
- survey of professional communication • Certificate
- venture management • MBA, Certificate

St. Paul Seminary School of Divinity
Dr. Victor Klimoski, Dean
Programs in:
- Catholic studies • MA
- divinity • M Div, MA, D Min
- ministry • D Min
- pastoral studies • MA
- religious education • MA
- theology • MA

School of Education
Dr. Miriam Williams, Associate Vice President for Academic Affairs
Programs in:
- curriculum and instruction • MA, Ed D, Ed S
- education • MA, Ed D, Certificate, Ed S
- educational leadership and administration • MA, Ed D, Certificate, Ed S
- learning and human development technology • MA, Ed D, Certificate
- reading and language technology • Certificate
- special education • MA
- teaching • MA

■ WALDEN UNIVERSITY
Minneapolis, MN 55401
http://www.waldenu.edu/

Proprietary, coed, graduate-only institution. CGS member. *Graduate faculty:* 7 full-time (1 woman), 199 part-time/adjunct (69 women). *Library facilities:* Indiana University Bloomington. *Graduate expenses:* Tuition: part-time $235 per credit. Part-time tuition and fees vary according to program. *General application contact:* Rita Sawyer, Associate Director Recruitment, 800-444-6795.

Find an in-depth description at www.petersons.com/graduate.

Graduate Programs
Dr. J. Kent Morrison, President
Programs in:
- administration/management • PhD
- education • PhD
- educational change and technology innovation • MS
- health services • PhD
- human services • PhD
- professional psychology • MS, PhD

■ WINONA STATE UNIVERSITY
Winona, MN 55987-5838
http://www.winona.msus.edu/

State-supported, coed, comprehensive institution. *Enrollment:* 114 full-time matriculated graduate/professional students (89 women), 258 part-time matriculated graduate/professional students (181 women). *Graduate faculty:* 66 full-time (36 women). *Computer facilities:* 1,400 computers available on campus for general student use. A campuswide network can be accessed from student residence rooms and from off campus. Internet access is available.

Library facilities: Maxwell Library. *Graduate expenses:* Tuition, state resident: part-time $145 per credit hour. Tuition, nonresident: part-time $229 per credit hour. Required fees: $20 per credit hour. *General application contact:* Dr. Pauline Christensen, Director of Graduate Studies, 507-457-5088.

Graduate Studies
Dr. Pauline Christensen, Director

College of Education
Dr. Carol Anderson, Dean
Programs in:
- counselor education • MS
- education • MS
- elementary school administration • MS
- general school administration • MS
- learning disabilities • MS
- mild to moderate mentally handicapped • MS
- secondary school administration • MS
- special education • MS

College of Liberal Arts
Dr. Peter Henderson, Dean
Programs in:
- English • MA, MS
- liberal arts • MA, MS

College of Nursing
Dr. Timothy Gaspar, Graduate Director
Program in:
- nursing • MS

Mississippi

■ ALCORN STATE UNIVERSITY

Alcorn State, MS 39096-7500
http://www.alcorn.edu/

State-supported, coed, comprehensive institution. CGS member. *Enrollment:* 202 full-time matriculated graduate/professional students (125 women), 336 part-time matriculated graduate/professional students (245 women). *Graduate faculty:* 64 full-time (21 women), 12 part-time/adjunct (4 women). *Computer facilities:* 400 computers available on campus for general student use. A campuswide network can be accessed from student residence rooms and from off campus. Online class registration is available. *Library facilities:* John Dewey Boyd Library. *Graduate expenses:* Tuition: full-time $2,570; part-time $120 per semester hour. Required fees: $24 per semester. *General application contact:* Lula Russell, Administrative Assistant to the Dean, School of Graduate Studies, 601-877-6122.

School of Graduate Studies
Dr. Irene Harris Johnson, Interim Dean
Program in:
- business • MBA

School of Agriculture and Applied Science
Napoleon Moses, Interim Dean
Programs in:
- agricultural economics • MS Ag
- agronomy • MS Ag
- animal science • MS Ag

School of Arts and Sciences
Dr. Bernard Cotton, Interim Dean
Programs in:
- arts and sciences • MS
- biology • MS
- computer and information sciences • MS

School of Business
Dr. John Gill, Dean
Program in:
- business • MBA

School of Psychology and Education
Dr. Josephine M. Posey, Dean
Programs in:
- agricultural education • MS Ed
- elementary education • MS Ed, Ed S
- guidance and counseling • MS Ed
- industrial education • MS Ed
- secondary education • MS Ed
- special education • MS Ed

School of Nursing
Dr. Frances C. Henderson, Dean
Program in:
- rural nursing • MSN

■ DELTA STATE UNIVERSITY

Cleveland, MS 38733-0001
http://www.deltast.edu/

State-supported, coed, comprehensive institution. *Enrollment:* 170 full-time matriculated graduate/professional students (97 women), 279 part-time matriculated graduate/professional students (196 women). *Graduate faculty:* 128 full-time (40 women), 33 part-time/adjunct (14 women). *Computer facilities:* 268 computers available on campus for general student use. A campuswide network can be accessed from student residence rooms and from off campus. Internet access and online class registration, e-mail are available. *Library facilities:* W. B. Roberts Library plus 1 other. *Graduate expenses:* Tuition, state resident: full-time $2,696; part-time $125 per hour. Tuition, nonresident: full-time $6,412; part-time $332 per hour. *General application contact:* Debbie Heslep, Coordinator of Admissions, 662-846-4018.

Graduate Programs
Dr. William F. McArthur, Vice President for Academic Affairs

College of Arts and Sciences
Dr. Richard S. Myers, Dean
Programs in:
- arts and sciences • M Ed, MM Ed, MSCD, MSCJ, MSNS, MSW
- biological sciences • MSNS
- community development • MSCD
- criminal justice • MSCJ
- English education • M Ed
- history education • M Ed
- mathematics education • M Ed
- music education • MM Ed
- social science education • M Ed
- social work • MSW

College of Business
Dr. William Stewart, Dean
Programs in:
- accounting and Computer Information Systems • MPA
- business • MBA, MCA, MPA
- commercial aviation • MCA
- management and marketing and office administration • MBA

College of Education
Dr. Everett Caston, Dean
Programs in:
- administration • M Ed
- administration and supervision • M Ed, Ed S
- education • M Ed, Ed D, Ed S
- elementary education • M Ed, Ed S
- elementary principalship • M Ed
- elementary supervision • M Ed
- guidance and counseling • M Ed
- physical education and recreation • M Ed
- professional studies • Ed D
- secondary principalship • M Ed
- secondary supervision • M Ed
- special education • M Ed

School of Nursing
Dr. Maureen Propst, Dean
Program in:
- nursing • MSN

■ JACKSON STATE UNIVERSITY

Jackson, MS 39217
http://www.jsums.edu/

State-supported, coed, university. CGS member. *Computer facilities:* A campuswide network can be accessed from off campus. Internet access is available. *Library facilities:* H. T. Sampson Library plus 1 other. *General application contact:* Dean of the Graduate School, 601-968-2455.

Find an in-depth description at www.petersons.com/graduate.

Graduate School

School of Allied Health
Program in:
allied health • MS

School of Business
Programs in:
accounting • MPA
business • M Bus Ed, MBA, MPA, MSSM, PhD
business administration • MBA
business education • M Bus Ed
systems management • MSSM

School of Education
Programs in:
community and agency counseling • MS
early childhood education • MS Ed, Ed D
education • MS, MS Ed, Ed D, PhD, Ed S
education administration • Ed S
educational administration • MS Ed, PhD
elementary education • MS Ed, Ed S
guidance and counseling • MS, MS Ed, Ed S
health, physical education and recreation • MS Ed
rehabilitative counseling service • MS Ed
secondary education • MS Ed, Ed S
special education • MS Ed, Ed S

School of Liberal Arts
Programs in:
clinical psychology • PhD
criminology and justice service • MA
English • MA
history • MA
liberal arts • MA, MAT, MM Ed, MPPA, MS, PhD
mass communications • MS
music education • MM Ed
political science • MA
public policy and administration • MPPA, PhD
sociology • MA
teaching English • MAT
urban and regional planning • MS

School of Science and Technology
Programs in:
biology education • MST
chemistry • MS, PhD
computer science • MS
environmental science • MS, PhD
hazardous materials management • MS
industrial arts education • MS Ed
mathematics • MS
mathematics education • MST
science and technology • MS, MS Ed, MST, PhD
science education • MST

School of Social Work
Program in:
social work • MSW, PhD

■ MISSISSIPPI COLLEGE

Clinton, MS 39058

Independent-religious, coed, comprehensive institution. *Enrollment:* 459 full-time matriculated graduate/professional students (217 women), 424 part-time matriculated graduate/professional students (296 women). *Graduate faculty:* 85 full-time (21 women), 24 part-time/adjunct (4 women). *Computer facilities:* 160 computers available on campus for general student use. A campuswide network can be accessed from student residence rooms and from off campus. *Library facilities:* Leland Speed Library plus 1 other. *Graduate expenses:* Tuition: part-time $924 per course. Required fees: $109 per semester. *General application contact:* Dr. Debbie C. Norris, Adviser, 601-925-3260.

Graduate School

Dr. Debbie C. Norris, Adviser

College of Arts and Sciences
Dr. Ron Howard, Dean
Programs in:
administration of justice • MSS
applied music performance • MM
art • MA, MFA
arts and sciences • M Ed, MA, MCS, MFA, MLS, MM, MS, MSC, MSS, MSS
biology • MCS
chemistry • MCS
communication • MSC
computer science • MS
conducting • MM
counseling psychology • MS
English • M Ed, MA
history • M Ed, MA, MSS
liberal studies • MLS
mathematics • MCS, MS
music education • MM
political science • MSS
psychology • MS
psychometry • M Ed
social sciences • M Ed, MSS
sociology • MSS
theory and composition • MM
vocal pedagogy • MM

School of Business Administration
Dr. Marcelo Eduardo, Dean
Programs in:
accounting • MBA
business administration • MBA
health services administration • MHSA

School of Education
Dr. Don Locke, Dean
Programs in:
art education • M Ed
biology education • M Ed
business education • M Ed
computer science education • M Ed
counseling psychology • MCP
education • M Ed, MCP, Ed S
educational leadership • M Ed
elementary education • M Ed
guidance and counseling • M Ed, Ed S
mathematics education • M Ed
sciences education • M Ed
secondary education • M Ed

School of Law
Sid L. Moller, Dean
Program in:
law • JD

■ MISSISSIPPI STATE UNIVERSITY

Mississippi State, MS 39762
http://www.msstate.edu/

State-supported, coed, university. CGS member. *Enrollment:* 1,748 full-time matriculated graduate/professional students (805 women), 1,506 part-time matriculated graduate/professional students (867 women). *Graduate faculty:* 934 full-time (273 women), 122 part-time/adjunct (67 women). *Computer facilities:* 2,000 computers available on campus for general student use. A campuswide network can be accessed from student residence rooms and from off campus. Internet access and online class registration are available. *Library facilities:* Mitchell Memorial Library plus 2 others. *Graduate expenses:* Tuition, state resident: full-time $3,117; part-time $173 per credit hour. Tuition, nonresident: full-time $7,065; part-time $393 per credit hour. Part-time tuition and fees vary according to course load and program. *General application contact:* Jerry B. Inmon, Director of Admissions, 662-325-2224.

College of Agriculture and Life Sciences
Dr. Charles Lee, Dean and Vice President
Programs in:
agribusiness management • MABM
agricultural pest management • MS
agriculture and extension education • MS
agriculture and life sciences • MABM, MLA, MS, Ed D, PhD, Ed S
agronomy • MS, PhD
animal physiology • MS, PhD
applied economics • PhD
biochemistry • MS
entomology • MS, PhD
food science and technology • MS, PhD
genetics • MS
horticulture • MS, PhD
landscape architecture • MLA
molecular biology • PhD
nutrition • MS, PhD
plant pathology • MS, PhD
poultry science • MS
weed science • MS, PhD

College of Arts and Sciences
Dr. Frank E. Saal, Dean
Programs in:
arts and sciences • MA, MFA, MPPA, MS, PhD
biological sciences • MS, PhD
chemistry • MS, PhD
clinical psychology • MS
cognitive science • PhD
electronic visualization • MFA
engineering physics • PhD
English • MA
experimental psychology • MS
French • MA
French/German • MA
geosciences • MS
German • MA
history • MA, PhD
mathematical sciences • PhD
mathematics • MS
physics • MS
political science • MA
public policy and administration • MPPA, PhD
sociology • MS, PhD
Spanish • MA
Spanish/French • MA
Spanish/German • MA
statistics • MS

College of Business and Industry
Dr. Sara A. Freedman, Dean
Programs in:
business administration • MBA, PhD
business and industry • MA, MBA, MPA, MSBA, MSIS, MTX, PhD
economics • MA
finance • MSBA
information systems • MSIS
project management • MBA

School of Accountancy
Dr. Dan P. Hollingsworth, Director
Program in:
accountancy • MPA, MTX

College of Education
Dr. William H. Graves, Dean
Programs in:
counselor education • MS, PhD, Ed S
curriculum and instruction • PhD
education • MS, MSIT, Ed D, PhD, Ed S
educational leadership • PhD
educational psychology • MS, PhD, Ed S
elementary education • MS, Ed D, PhD, Ed S
exercise science • MS
health education/health promotion • MS
instructional technology • MSIT
physical education • MS
school administration • MS, Ed S
secondary education • MS, Ed D, PhD, Ed S
special education • MS, Ed S
sports administration • MS
teaching/coaching • MS
technology • MS, Ed D, PhD, Ed S

College of Engineering
Dr. A. Wayne Bennett, Dean
Programs in:
aerospace engineering • MS
biological engineering • MS
biomedical engineering • MS, PhD
civil engineering • MS, PhD
computational engineering • MS, PhD
computer engineering • MS, PhD
computer science • MS, PhD
electrical engineering • MS, PhD
engineering • PhD
engineering mechanics • MS
industrial engineering • MS, PhD
mechanical engineering • MS, PhD

David C. Swalm School of Chemical Engineering
Dr. Donald Hill, Head
Program in:
chemical engineering • MS

College of Forest Resources
Dr. G. Sam Foster, Head
Programs in:
forest products • MS
forest resources • PhD
forestry • MS, PhD
wildlife ecology science • MS

College of Veterinary Medicine
Dr. John U. Thomson, Dean
Programs in:
environmental toxicology • PhD
veterinary medical science • MS, PhD
veterinary medicine • DVM, MS, PhD

School of Architecture
John M. McRae, Dean
Program in:
architecture • MS

■ MISSISSIPPI UNIVERSITY FOR WOMEN

Columbus, MS 39701-9998
http://www.muw.edu/

State-supported, coed, comprehensive institution. *Enrollment:* 81 matriculated graduate/professional students. *Graduate faculty:* 30 full-time (25 women), 3 part-time/adjunct (2 women). *Computer facilities:* 250 computers available on campus for general student use. A campuswide network can be accessed from student residence rooms and from off campus. Internet access, various software packages are available. *Library facilities:* John Clayton Fant Memorial Library. *Graduate expenses:* Tuition: full-time $2,656; part-time $148 per credit hour. Tuition and fees vary according to program. *General application contact:* Dr. Barbara Moore, Director, Graduate School, 601-329-7150.

Graduate School
Dr. Barbara Moore, Director

Division of Education and Human Sciences
Dr. Hal Jenkins, Division Head
Programs in:
gifted studies • M Ed
instructional management • M Ed
speech/language pathology • MS

Division of Health and Kinesiology
Dr. Jo Edna Spearman, Head
Program in:
health education • MS

Division of Nursing
Dr. Sheila Adams, Head
Program in:
nursing • MSN, Certificate

■ UNIVERSITY OF MISSISSIPPI

Oxford, University, MS 38677
http://www.olemiss.edu/

State-supported, coed, university. CGS member. *Enrollment:* 1,563 full-time matriculated graduate/professional students (718 women), 457 part-time matriculated graduate/professional

University of Mississippi (continued)
students (292 women). *Graduate faculty:* 505 full-time (98 women). *Computer facilities:* 3,500 computers available on campus for general student use. A campuswide network can be accessed from student residence rooms and from off campus. *Library facilities:* J. D. Williams Library plus 3 others. *Graduate expenses:* Tuition, state resident: full-time $3,153; part-time $175 per semester hour. Tuition, nonresident: full-time $7,106; part-time $395 per semester hour. $7,930 full-time. *General application contact:* Dr. Donald R. Cole, Associate Dean of Graduate School, 662-915-7474.

Graduate School
Dr. Maurice Eftink, Acting Dean

College of Liberal Arts
Dr. Glenn Hopkins, Dean
Programs in:
- anthropology • MA
- art education • MA
- art history • MA
- biology • MS, PhD
- chemistry • MS, DA, PhD
- classics • MA
- clinical psychology • PhD
- communicative disorders • MS
- English • MA, DA, PhD
- experimental psychology • PhD
- fine arts • MFA
- French • MA
- German • MA
- history • MA, PhD
- journalism • MA
- liberal arts • MA, MFA, MM, MS, MSS, DA, PhD
- mathematics • MA, MS, PhD
- music • MM, DA
- philosophy • MA
- physics • MA, MS, PhD
- political science • MA, PhD
- psychology • MA
- sociology • MA, MSS
- Southern studies • MA
- Spanish • MA
- theatre arts • MFA

School of Accountancy
Dr. James W. Davis, Dean
Programs in:
- accountancy • M Acc, PhD
- taxation accounting • M Tax

School of Business Administration
Dr. N. Keith Womer, Dean
Programs in:
- business administration • MBA
- economics • MA, PhD
- systems management • MS

School of Education
Dr. James Chambless, Acting Dean
Programs in:
- curriculum and instruction • M Ed, Ed D, Ed S
- education • PhD
- educational leadership • PhD
- educational leadership and educational psychology • M Ed, MA, Ed D, Ed S
- educational psychology • PhD
- exercise science • MA, MS
- exercise science and leisure management • PhD
- higher education/student personnel • M Ed, MA
- leisure management • MA
- secondary education • MA
- wellness • MS

School of Engineering
Dr. Kai-Fong Lee, Dean
Program in:
- engineering science • MS, PhD

School of Pharmacy
Dr. Barbara G. Wells, Dean
Programs in:
- medicinal chemistry • MS, PhD
- pharmaceutics • MS, PhD
- pharmacognosy • MS, PhD
- pharmacology • MS, PhD
- pharmacy • Pharm D, MS, PhD
- pharmacy administration • MS, PhD
- toxicology • PhD

School of Law
Dr. Samuel Davis, Dean
Program in:
- law • JD

■ UNIVERSITY OF SOUTHERN MISSISSIPPI
Hattiesburg, MS 39406
http://www.usm.edu/

State-supported, coed, university. CGS member. *Enrollment:* 1,242 full-time matriculated graduate/professional students (712 women), 1,124 part-time matriculated graduate/professional students (768 women). *Graduate faculty:* 654 full-time (262 women), 108 part-time/adjunct (30 women). *Computer facilities:* 600 computers available on campus for general student use. Internet access is available. *Library facilities:* Cook Memorial Library plus 4 others. *Graduate expenses:* Tuition, state resident: full-time $2,970; part-time $143 per semester hour. Tuition, nonresident: full-time $6,898; part-time $361 per semester hour. *General application contact:* Dr. Susan Siltanen, Director of Graduate Admissions, 601-266-5137.

Graduate School
Dr. Donald Cotten, Interim Dean

College of Business Administration
Dr. William Gunther, Dean
Programs in:
- business administration • MBA
- professional accountancy • MPA

College of Education and Psychology
Dr. Carl R. Martray, Dean
Programs in:
- adult education • M Ed, Ed D, PhD, Ed S
- alternative secondary teacher education • MAT
- business technology education • MS
- early childhood education • M Ed, Ed S
- education and psychology • M Ed, MA, MAT, MATL, MS, Ed D, PhD, Ed S
- education of the gifted • M Ed, Ed D, PhD, Ed S
- educational administration • M Ed, Ed D, PhD, Ed S
- elementary education • M Ed, Ed D, PhD, Ed S
- instructional technology • MS
- psychology • M Ed, MA, MS, PhD, Ed S
- reading • M Ed, MS, Ed S
- secondary education • M Ed, MS, Ed D, PhD, Ed S
- special education • M Ed, Ed D, PhD, Ed S
- technical occupational education • MS

College of Health and Human Sciences
Dr. Jane Boudreaux, Dean
Programs in:
- early intervention • MS
- family and consumer studies • MS
- health and human sciences • MPH, MS, MSW, Ed D, PhD
- health education • MPH
- health policy/administration • MPH
- human nutrition • MS
- human performance • MS, Ed D, PhD
- institution management • MS
- marriage and family therapy • MS
- nutrition and food systems • PhD
- occupational/environmental health • MPH
- public health nutrition • MPH
- recreation • MS
- social work • MSW
- sport administration • MS

College of International and Continuing Education
Dr. Tim W. Hudson, Dean
Programs in:
- economic development • MS
- geography • MS

international and continuing education • MS, PhD
international development • PhD

College of Liberal Arts
Dr. Glenn T. Harper, Dean
Programs in:
administration of justice • PhD
anthropology • MA
communication • MA, MS, PhD
corrections • MA, MS
English • MA, PhD
foreign languages and literatures • MATL
history • MA, MS, PhD
juvenile justice • MA, MS
law enforcement • MA, MS
liberal arts • MA, MATL, MLIS, MS, PhD, SLS
library and information science • MLIS, SLS
philosophy • MA
political science • MA, MS
public relations • MS
speech and hearing sciences • MA, MS, PhD

College of Marine Sciences
Dr. D. Jay, Dean
Programs in:
hydrography • MS
marine science • MS, PhD
marine sciences • MS, PhD

College of Nursing
Dr. Gerry Cadenhead, Director
Programs in:
adult health nursing • MSN
community health nursing • MSN
ethics • PhD
family nurse practitioner • MSN
leadership • PhD
nursing service administration • MSN
policy analysis • PhD
psychiatric nursing • MSN

College of Science and Technology
Dr. Steve A. Doblin, Dean
Programs in:
analytical chemistry • MS, PhD
biochemistry • MS, PhD
computer science • MS
engineering technology • MS
environmental biology • MS, PhD
geology • MS
inorganic chemistry • MS, PhD
marine biology • MS, PhD
mathematics • MS
medical technology • MS
microbiology • MS, PhD
molecular biology • MS, PhD
organic chemistry • MS, PhD
physical chemistry • MS, PhD
physics and astronomy • MS
polymer science • MS, PhD
science and mathematics education • M Ed, MS, Ed D, PhD
science and technology • M Ed, MS, Ed D, PhD
scientific computing • PhD

College of the Arts
Dr. Peter Alexander, Dean
Programs in:
art education • MAE
arts • MAE, MFA, MM, MME, DMA, DME, PhD
church music • MM
conducting • MM
history and literature • MM
music education • MME, DME, PhD
performance • MM
performance and pedagogy • DMA
theatre and dance • MFA
theory and composition • MM
woodwind performance • MM

■ WILLIAM CAREY COLLEGE

Hattiesburg, MS 39401-5499
http://www.wmcarey.edu/

Independent-religious, coed, comprehensive institution. *Computer facilities:* 30 computers available on campus for general student use. Internet access is available. *Library facilities:* I. E. Rouse Library. *General application contact:* Dean, College of Education and Psychology, 601-582-6217.

Graduate School
Programs in:
counseling psychology • MS
industrial and organizational psychology • MS

School of Business
Dr. Hubert Keasler, Interim Dean
Program in:
business • MBA

School of Education
Dr. Bonnie Holder, Interim Dean
Programs in:
art education • M Ed
art of teaching • M Ed
educational leadership • M Ed
elementary education • M Ed
English education • M Ed
gifted education • M Ed
secondary education • M Ed
special education • M Ed
teaching • MA Ed

Missouri

■ AVILA COLLEGE

Kansas City, MO 64145-1698
http://www.avila.edu/

Independent-religious, coed, comprehensive institution. *Enrollment:* 29 full-time matriculated graduate/professional students (21 women), 135 part-time matriculated graduate/professional students (87 women). *Graduate faculty:* 14 full-time (8 women), 20 part-time/adjunct (12 women). *Computer facilities:* 68 computers available on campus for general student use. A campuswide network can be accessed from student residence rooms and from off campus. Internet access is available. *Library facilities:* Hooley Bundshu Library. *Graduate expenses:* Tuition: full-time $2,500; part-time $325 per credit hour. Required fees: $5 per semester. Part-time tuition and fees vary according to class time, course load and program. *General application contact:* Sr. Marie Joan Harris, Vice President for Academic Affairs, 816-501-3758.

Graduate Programs
Sr. Marie Joan Harris, Vice President for Academic Affairs
Programs in:
business and economics • MBA
counseling psychology • MS
education • MS
psychology • MS

■ CENTRAL MISSOURI STATE UNIVERSITY

Warrensburg, MO 64093
http://www.cmsu.edu/

State-supported, coed, comprehensive institution. CGS member. *Enrollment:* 209 full-time matriculated graduate/professional students (129 women), 1,856 part-time matriculated graduate/professional students (1,182 women). *Graduate faculty:* 286 full-time (85 women), 33 part-time/adjunct (15 women). *Computer facilities:* 1,007 computers available on campus for general student use. A campuswide network can be accessed from student residence rooms and from off campus. Internet access and online class registration are available. *Library facilities:* James C. Kirkpatrick Library. *Graduate expenses:* Tuition, state resident: full-time $3,840; part-time $160 per credit hour. Tuition,

Central Missouri State University (continued)
nonresident: full-time $7,632; part-time $318 per credit hour. Required fees: $160 per credit hour. *General application contact:* Dr. Novella Perrin, Dean of Graduate Studies/Assistant Vice-President for Academic Affairs, 660-543-4092.

Find an in-depth description at www.petersons.com/graduate.

School of Graduate Studies
Dr. Novella Perrin, Dean of Graduate Studies/Assistant Vice President for Academic Affairs
Programs in:
- human services/learning resources • Ed S
- library science and information services • MS

College of Applied Sciences and Technology
Dr. Art Rosser, Dean
Programs in:
- agricultural technology • MS
- applied sciences and technology • MS, MSE, PhD, Ed S
- aviation safety • MS
- human services/industrial arts and technology • Ed S
- human services/public services • Ed S
- industrial hygiene • MS
- industrial management • MS
- industrial safety management • MS
- industrial technology • MS
- industrial, vocational, and technical education • MS
- K–12 education/industrial arts and technology • MSE
- occupational safety management • MS
- public services administration • MS
- rural and family nursing • MS
- safety management • MS
- secondary education/safety education • MSE
- security • MS
- technology management • PhD
- transportation safety • MS

College of Arts and Sciences
Dr. Robert Schwartz, Dean
Programs in:
- applied mathematics • MS
- art • MA
- art education • MSE
- arts and sciences • MA, MS, MSE
- biology • MS
- communication • MA
- English • MA
- English education • MSE
- history • MA
- mathematics • MS
- mathematics education • MSE
- music • MA
- social studies • MSE
- speech communication • MA, MSE
- teaching English as a second language • MA, MSE
- theatre • MA

College of Education and Human Services
Dr. Jim Bowman, Dean
Programs in:
- administration • Ed S
- adult education • MSE
- criminal justice • MS
- curriculum and instruction • Ed S
- education and human services • MA, MS, MSE, Ed D, Ed S
- education technology • MSE
- education, administration and higher education • MSE
- education, administration and higher education • MS, Ed S
- educational leadership • Ed D
- elementary education • MSE
- human services • Ed S
- human services-public services • Ed S
- human services/guidance and counseling • Ed S
- K–12 education • MSE
- physical education/exercise and sports science • MS
- psychology • MS
- reading • MSE
- school administration • MSE
- school counseling • MS
- secondary education • MSE
- social gerontology • MS
- sociology • MA
- special education • MSE, Ed S
- special education/human services • Ed S
- speech pathology and audiology • MS
- student personnel administration • MS

Harmon College of Business Administration
Dr. George Wilson, Interim Dean
Programs in:
- business administration • MA, MBA, MS
- economics • MA
- information technology • MS

■ DRURY UNIVERSITY
Springfield, MO 65802-3791
http://www.drury.edu/

Independent, coed, comprehensive institution. *Enrollment:* 43 full-time matriculated graduate/professional students (28 women), 255 part-time matriculated graduate/professional students (176 women). *Graduate faculty:* 12 full-time (7 women), 13 part-time/adjunct (8 women). *Computer facilities:* 205 computers available on campus for general student use. A campuswide network can be accessed from student residence rooms and from off campus. Internet access and online class registration, digital imaging lab are available. *Library facilities:* F. W. Olin Library plus 1 other. *Graduate expenses:* Tuition: part-time $204 per credit hour. Tuition and fees vary according to program. *General application contact:* Dr. Terry Hudson, Director of Teacher Education, 417-873-7271.

Breech School of Business Administration
Dr. Tom Zimmerer, Director
Programs in:
- business administration • MBA
- business and international management • MBA

Graduate Programs in Education
Dr. Daniel R. Beach, Director
Programs in:
- elementary education • M Ed
- gifted education • M Ed
- human services • M Ed
- middle school teaching • M Ed
- physical education • M Ed
- secondary education • M Ed

Program in Communication
Dr. Lynn Hinds, Graduate Director Communication
Program in:
- communication • MA

Program in Criminology/Criminal Justice
Programs in:
- criminal justice • MS
- criminology • MA

■ FONTBONNE COLLEGE
St. Louis, MO 63105-3098
http://www.fontbonne.edu/

Independent-religious, coed, comprehensive institution. *Enrollment:* 371 full-time matriculated graduate/professional students (231 women), 309 part-time matriculated graduate/professional students (231 women). *Graduate faculty:* 20 full-time (11 women), 105 part-time/adjunct (46 women). *Computer facilities:* 50 computers available on campus for general student use. A campuswide network can be accessed from student residence rooms and from off campus. Internet access and online class registration are available. *Library facilities:* Fontbonne Library. *Graduate expenses:* Tuition: full-time $6,768; part-time $376 per credit hour. Required fees: $170. *General application contact:* Peggy Musen, Associate Dean of Enrollment Management and Director of Admissions, 314-889-1400.

Graduate Programs
Dr. Judith Meyer, Vice President and Dean for Academic Affairs
Programs in:
art • MA
business administration • MBA
computer education • MS
early intervention in deaf education • MA
education • MA
fine arts • MFA
management • MM
speech language pathology • MS
taxation • MST

■ LINCOLN UNIVERSITY
Jefferson City, MO 65102
http://www.lincolnu.edu/

State-supported, coed, comprehensive institution. *Enrollment:* 22 full-time matriculated graduate/professional students (17 women), 135 part-time matriculated graduate/professional students (99 women). *Graduate faculty:* 2 full-time (0 women), 39 part-time/adjunct (11 women). *Computer facilities:* 175 computers available on campus for general student use. A campuswide network can be accessed from off campus. Internet access is available. *Library facilities:* Inman Page Library. *Graduate expenses:* Tuition, state resident: part-time $128 per credit hour. Tuition, nonresident: part-time $256 per credit hour. Required fees: $5 per credit hour. $20 per semester. Tuition and fees vary according to course load and program. *General application contact:* Nathan H. Cook, Vice President for Academic Affairs and Dean of Graduate Studies, 573-681-5074.

Graduate School
Nathan H. Cook, Vice President for Academic Affairs and Dean of Graduate Studies
Programs in:
education • M Ed
elementary and secondary teaching • M Ed
guidance and counseling • M Ed
school administration and supervision • M Ed

College of Arts and Sciences
Dr. Douglas Nancarrow, Dean
Programs in:
arts and sciences • MA
history • MA
sociology • MA
sociology/criminal justice • MA

College of Business and Professional Studies
Wayne Linhardt, Head
Program in:
business • MBA

College of Education
Patrick Henry, Dean
Programs in:
education • M Ed
elementary and secondary teaching • M Ed
guidance and counseling • M Ed
school administration and supervision • M Ed

■ LINDENWOOD UNIVERSITY
St. Charles, MO 63301-1695
http://www.lindenwood.edu/

Independent-religious, coed, comprehensive institution. *Computer facilities:* 160 computers available on campus for general student use. A campuswide network can be accessed. *Library facilities:* Butler Library. *General application contact:* Director of Graduate Admissions, 314-949-4933.

Graduate Programs
Programs in:
administration • MSA
business administration • MBA
corporate communication • MS
counseling psychology • MA
education • MA
gerontology • MA
health management • MS
human resource management • MS
human service agency management • MS
management • MSA
marketing • MSA
mass communication • MS
theatre arts • MA, MFA

■ MARYVILLE UNIVERSITY OF SAINT LOUIS
St. Louis, MO 63141-7299
http://www.maryville.edu/

Independent, coed, comprehensive institution. *Enrollment:* 90 full-time matriculated graduate/professional students (56 women), 392 part-time matriculated graduate/professional students (286 women). *Graduate faculty:* 56 full-time (42 women), 36 part-time/adjunct (18 women). *Computer facilities:* 260 computers available on campus for general student use. A campuswide network can be accessed from student residence rooms and from off campus. Internet access, e-mail, specialized software are available. *Library facilities:* Maryville University Library. *Graduate expenses:* Tuition: full-time $12,880; part-time $386 per credit hour. Required fees: $120; $30 per semester. *General application contact:* Director of Graduate Studies, 314-529-9300.

The John E. Simon School of Business
Dr. Pamela Horwitz, Dean
Programs in:
accountancy • MBA, PGC
business studies • PGC
e-business • MBA, PGC
information systems • MBA, PGC
international business • MBA, PGC
management • MBA, PGC
marketing • MBA, PGC

School of Education
Dr. Kathe Rasch, Dean
Programs in:
art education • MA Ed
early childhood education • MA Ed
elementary education • MA Ed
environmental education • MA Ed
gifted education • MA Ed
middle grades education • MA Ed
secondary education • MA Ed

School of Health Professions
Dr. Lance Carluccio, Director
Programs in:
health professions • MA, MOT, MPT, MSN
nursing • MSN
occupational therapy • MOT
physical therapy • MPT
rehabilitation counseling • MA

■ NORTHWEST MISSOURI STATE UNIVERSITY
Maryville, MO 64468-6001
http://www.nwmissouri.edu/

State-supported, coed, comprehensive institution. *Enrollment:* 133 full-time matriculated graduate/professional students (74 women), 741 part-time matriculated graduate/professional students (554 women). *Graduate faculty:* 165 full-time (55 women). *Computer facilities:* 2,450 computers available on campus for general student use. A campuswide network can be accessed from student residence rooms and from off campus. Internet access is available. *Library facilities:* B. D. Owens Library plus

Northwest Missouri State University (continued)

1 other. *Graduate expenses:* Tuition, state resident: full-time $2,479; part-time $138. Tuition, nonresident: full-time $4,176; part-time $232. Tuition and fees vary according to course level and course load. *General application contact:* Dr. Frances Shipley, Dean of Graduate School, 660-562-1145.

Graduate School
Dr. Frances Shipley, Dean

College of Arts and Sciences
Dr. C. Taylor Barnes, Dean
Programs in:
- agriculture • MS
- arts and sciences • MA, MS, MS Ed
- biology • MS
- English • MA
- English with speech emphasis • MA
- history • MA
- teaching agriculture • MS Ed
- teaching English with speech emphasis • MS Ed
- teaching history • MS Ed
- teaching mathematics • MS Ed
- teaching music • MS Ed

College of Education and Human Services
Dr. Max Ruhl, Dean
Programs in:
- counseling psychology • MS
- early childhood education • MS Ed
- education and human services • MS, MS Ed, Ed S
- educational leadership • MS Ed, Ed S
- educational leadership: elementary • MS Ed
- educational leadership: secondary • MS Ed
- elementary education • MS Ed
- elementary principalship • Ed S
- guidance and counseling • MS Ed
- health and physical education • MS Ed
- learning disabilities: elementary • MS Ed
- learning disabilities: elementary/secondary • MS Ed
- learning disabilities: secondary • MS Ed
- learning disabled and mentally handicapped • MS Ed
- mentally handicapped: elementary • MS Ed
- mentally handicapped: elementary/secondary • MS Ed
- mentally handicapped: secondary • MS Ed
- middle school education • MS Ed
- reading education • MS Ed
- science education • MS Ed
- secondary education • MS Ed
- secondary individualized prescribed programs • MS Ed
- secondary principalship • Ed S
- superintendency • Ed S
- teaching secondary • MS Ed

College of Professional and Applied Studies
Dr. Ron DeYoung, Dean
Programs in:
- accounting • MBA
- agricultural economics • MBA
- business administration • MBA
- educational uses of computer • MS Ed
- management information systems • MBA
- professional and applied studies • MBA, MS, MS Ed
- school computer studies • MS
- teaching instructional technology • MS Ed

■ PARK UNIVERSITY
Parkville, MO 64152-3795
http://www.park.edu/

Independent, coed, comprehensive institution. *Enrollment:* 140 full-time matriculated graduate/professional students, 85 part-time matriculated graduate/professional students. *Graduate faculty:* 13 full-time (5 women), 17 part-time/adjunct (7 women). *Computer facilities:* 116 computers available on campus for general student use. A campuswide network can be accessed from student residence rooms. Internet access and online class registration are available. *Library facilities:* McAfee Memorial Library. *Graduate expenses:* Tuition: part-time $225 per credit hour. *General application contact:* Erik Bergrud, Graduate Administrator, 816-421-1125.

Graduate School of Public Affairs
Dr. Jerzy Hauptmann, Dean
Program in:
- public affairs • MPA

Program in Business Administration
Dr. Nicolas Koudou, Director
Program in:
- business administration • MBA

Program in Education
Dr. Patricia Hutchens McClelland, Director of Education
Program in:
- education • M Ed

■ ROCKHURST UNIVERSITY
Kansas City, MO 64110-2561
http://www.rockhurst.edu/

Independent-religious, coed, comprehensive institution. CGS member. *Enrollment:* 240 full-time matriculated graduate/professional students (166 women), 453 part-time matriculated graduate/professional students (187 women). *Graduate faculty:* 46 full-time (20 women), 21 part-time/adjunct (10 women). *Computer facilities:* 500 computers available on campus for general student use. A campuswide network can be accessed from student residence rooms and from off campus. Internet access is available. *Library facilities:* Greenlease Library. *Graduate expenses:* Tuition: part-time $375 per semester hour. Tuition and fees vary according to program. *General application contact:* Director of Graduate Recruitment, 816-501-4100.

College of Arts and Sciences
Dr. William Haefele, Dean
Programs in:
- arts and sciences • MIHE, MOT, MPT, MS
- communication sciences and disorders • MS
- occupational therapy education • MOT
- physical therapy • MPT

Division of Behavioral and Social Sciences
Dr. Marilyn Carroll, Head
Program in:
- behavioral and social sciences • MIHE

Division of Humanities and Fine Arts
Dr. Joseph Cirincione, Head
Program in:
- integrated humanities and education • MIHE

School of Management
Dr. W. Earl Walker, Dean
Program in:
- management • MBA

■ SAINT LOUIS UNIVERSITY
St. Louis, MO 63103-2097
http://imagine.slu.edu/

Independent-religious, coed, university. CGS member. *Enrollment:* 2,293 full-time matriculated graduate/professional students (1,215 women), 1,733 part-time matriculated graduate/professional students (1,112 women). *Graduate faculty:* 1,150 full-time (378 women), 1,653 part-time/adjunct (456 women). *Computer facilities:* 6,500 computers available on campus for general student use. A campuswide network can be accessed from student residence rooms and from off campus. Internet access and online class registration are available. *Library facilities:* Pius XII Memorial Library plus 3 others. *Graduate expenses:* Tuition: part-time $600 per credit hour. *General application contact:* Dr. Marcia Buresch, Assistant Dean of the Graduate School, 314-977-2240.

Find an in-depth description at www.petersons.com/graduate.

Graduate School
Dr. Donald G. Brennan, Dean
Program in:
aerospace and mechanical engineering • MS, MS (R)

Center for Health Care Ethics
Dr. Gerard Magill, Executive Director
Program in:
health care ethics • PhD

College of Arts and Sciences
Dr. Shirley Dowdy, Dean
Programs in:
American studies • MA, MA (R), PhD
applied experimental psychology • MS (R), PhD
arts and sciences • M Pr Met, MA, MA (R), MS, MS (R), Ed D, PhD, Ed S
atmospheric science • M Pr Met, MS (R), PhD
biology • MS, MS (R), PhD
chemistry • MS, MS (R)

College of Public Service
Dr. James Gilsinian, Director
Program in:
communication sciences and disorders • MA, MA (R)

School of Allied Health Professions
Joan Hrubetz, Interim Director
Programs in:
allied health professions • MMS, MOT, MS, MSPT
medical dietetics • MS
nutrition and physical performance • MS
occupational therapy • MOT
physical therapy • MSPT
physician assistant • MMS

School of Nursing
Dr. John Hrubetz, Dean
Programs in:
nursing • MSN, MSN (R), PhD, Certificate

School of Public Health
Dr. Richard S. Kurz, Dean
Programs in:
community health • MPH
health administration • MHA
health services research • PhD
public health • MHA, MPH, PhD

John Cook School of Business
Dr. Neil E. Seitz, Dean
Programs in:
accounting • M Acct, MBA, PhD
business administration • MBA, PhD
business and administration • EMIB, M Acct, M Dec S, M Fin, M Mgt, MBA, MIB, MMIS, PhD
decision sciences • M Dec S, MBA, PhD
economics • MBA, PhD
finance • M Fin, MBA, PhD
information systems management • MBA
management • M Mgt, MBA, PhD
management information systems • MMIS
marketing • MBA, PhD

Boeing Institute of International Business
Dr. Seung H. Kim, Director
Programs in:
executive international business • EMIB
international business • MIB

School of Law
Jeffrey E. Lewis, Dean
Program in:
law • JD, LL M

School of Medicine
Dr. Patricia L. Monteleone, Dean
Programs in:
medicine • MD, MS (R), PhD

Graduate Programs in Biomedical Sciences
Dr. Willis K. Samson, Director
Programs in:
anatomy • MS (R), PhD
biochemistry and molecular biology • PhD
biomedical sciences • MS (R), PhD
cell and molecular biology • PhD
molecular microbiology and immunology • PhD
neurobiology • PhD
pathology • MS (R), PhD
pharmacological and physiological science • MS (R), PhD

School of Social Service
Dr. Susan Tebb, Dean
Program in:
social service • MSW

■ SOUTHEAST MISSOURI STATE UNIVERSITY

Cape Girardeau, MO 63701-4799

http://www.semo.edu/

State-supported, coed, comprehensive institution. CGS member. *Enrollment:* 220 full-time matriculated graduate/professional students (151 women), 971 part-time matriculated graduate/professional students (726 women). *Graduate faculty:* 223 full-time (78 women). *Computer facilities:* 650 computers available on campus for general student use. A campuswide network can be accessed from student residence rooms and from off campus. Internet access and online class registration are available. *Library facilities:* Kent Library. *Graduate expenses:* Tuition, state resident: full-time $1,549; part-time $129 per credit hour. Tuition, nonresident: full-time $2,808; part-time $234 per credit hour. Part-time tuition and fees vary according to degree level. *General application contact:* Dr. Phil Parette, Interim Dean of the School of Graduate Studies and Research, 573-651-2192.

School of Graduate Studies and Research
Dr. Phil Parette, Interim Dean
Programs in:
art education • MA
athletic administration • MSA
biology • MNS
business education • MA
chemistry • MNS
communication disorders • MA
community counseling • MA
criminal justice administration • MSA
educational administration • MA, Ed D, Ed S
educational studies • MA
educational technology • MA
elementary education • MA
English • MA
exceptional child education • MA
geosciences • MNS
guidance and counseling • MA
health fitness administration • MSA

Southeast Missouri State University (continued)

history • MA
home economics • MA
human services administration • MSA
mathematics • MNS
middle level education • MA
music education • MME
nursing • MSN
public administration • MSA
science education • MNS
social studies • MA
teaching English to speakers of other languages • MA

College of Business
Kenneth Heischmidt, Director
Program in:
business • MBA

■ SOUTHWEST BAPTIST UNIVERSITY

Bolivar, MO 65613-2597

http://www.sbuniv.edu/

Independent-religious, coed, comprehensive institution. *Enrollment:* 879 matriculated graduate/professional students. *Graduate faculty:* 10 full-time (3 women), 53 part-time/adjunct. *Computer facilities:* 130 computers available on campus for general student use. A campuswide network can be accessed from off campus. Internet access is available. *Library facilities:* Harriett K. Hutchens Library. *Graduate expenses:* Tuition: full-time $17,000; part-time $130 per credit hour. *General application contact:* Dr. Gordon Dutile, Provost, 417-328-1601.

Graduate Studies
Dr. Gordon Dutile, Provost

College of Business and Computer Science
Dr. David Whitlock, Dean
Programs in:
administration • MS
business • MS

College of Science and Mathematics
Dr. Gary Gray, Dean
Programs in:
physical therapy • MSPT
science and mathematics • MSPT

Lewis E. Schollian College of Education and Social Sciences
Dr. John Wheeler, Dean
Programs in:
education • MS
education and social sciences • MS
educational administration • MS

■ SOUTHWEST MISSOURI STATE UNIVERSITY

Springfield, MO 65804-0094

http://www.smsu.edu/

State-supported, coed, comprehensive institution. CGS member. *Enrollment:* 854 full-time matriculated graduate/professional students (478 women), 2,150 part-time matriculated graduate/professional students (1,474 women). *Computer facilities:* 3,500 computers available on campus for general student use. A campuswide network can be accessed from student residence rooms and from off campus. *Library facilities:* Meyer Library plus 3 others. *Graduate expenses:* Tuition, state resident: full-time $2,178; part-time $121 per credit. Tuition, nonresident: full-time $4,356; part-time $242 per credit. Required fees: $95 per credit. *General application contact:* Frank A. Einhellig, Associate Vice President for Academic Affairs and Dean, 417-836-5335.

Find an in-depth description at www.petersons.com/graduate.

Graduate College
Frank A. Einhellig, Associate Vice President for Academic Affairs and Dean
Program in:
administrative studies • MS

College of Arts and Letters
Dr. David O. Belcher, Dean
Programs in:
arts and letters • MA, MM, MS Ed
classics • MS Ed
communication and mass media • MA, MS Ed
English • MA, MS Ed
French • MS Ed
German • MS Ed
music • MM, MS Ed
Spanish • MS Ed
theatre • MA

College of Business Administration
Dr. Ronald Bottin, Dean
Programs in:
accountancy • M Acc
business administration • M Acc, MBA, MHA, MS, MS Ed
computer information systems • MS
health administration • MHA

College of Education
Dr. David L. Hough, Acting Dean
Programs in:
education • MS, MS Ed, Ed S
education administration • MS Ed, Ed S
elementary education • MS Ed
guidance and counseling • MS
reading and special education • MS Ed
secondary education • MS Ed

College of Health and Human Services
Dr. Cynthia Pemberton, Dean
Programs in:
cell and molecular biology • MS
communication sciences and disorders • MS
consumer and family studies • MS Ed
health and human services • MPH, MPT, MS, MS Ed, MSN, MSW
health promotion and wellness management • MS
health, physical education, and recreation • MS Ed
nurse anesthesia • MS
nursing • MSN
physical therapy • MPT
physician assistant studies • MS
psychology • MS, MS Ed
public health • MPH
social work • MSW

College of Humanities and Public Affairs
Dr. Denny Pilant, Acting Dean
Programs in:
defense and strategic studies • MS
economics • MS Ed
history • MA, MS Ed
humanities and public affairs • MA, MIAA, MPA, MS, MS Ed
international affairs and administration • MIAA
public administration • MPA
religious studies • MS

College of Natural and Applied Sciences
Dr. Lawrence E. Banks, Dean
Programs in:
agriculture • MS, MS Ed
biology • MS
biology education • MS
chemistry • MS
fruit science • MS
materials science • MS
mathematics • MS
natural and applied sciences • MNAS, MS, MS Ed
plant science • MS
resource planning • MS
technology • MS Ed

■ TRUMAN STATE UNIVERSITY

Kirksville, MO 63501-4221

http://www.truman.edu/

State-supported, coed, comprehensive institution. CGS member. *Enrollment:* 146 full-time matriculated graduate/

professional students (98 women), 27 part-time matriculated graduate/professional students (21 women). *Graduate faculty:* 140 full-time (41 women). *Computer facilities:* 769 computers available on campus for general student use. A campuswide network can be accessed from student residence rooms and from off campus. Internet access is available. *Library facilities:* Pickler Memorial Library plus 1 other. *Graduate expenses:* Tuition, state resident: full-time $2,205; part-time $169 per credit. Tuition, nonresident: full-time $4,014; part-time $305 per credit. *General application contact:* Crista Chappell, Graduate Office Secretary, 660-785-4109.

Find an in-depth description at www.petersons.com/graduate.

Graduate School
Dr. Maria DiStefano, Dean of Graduate Studies

Division of Business and Accountancy
Dr. Jeffrey Romine, Coordinator
Program in:
accounting • M Ac

Division of Education
Dr. Sam Minner, Head
Program in:
education • MAE

Division of Fine Arts
Robert Jones, Head
Program in:
music • MA

Division of Human Potential and Performance
Program in:
communication disorders • MA

Division of Language and Literature
Dr. Heinz Woehlk, Head
Program in:
English • MA

Division of Mathematics and Computer Science
Dr. Lanny Morley, Head
Program in:
mathematics • MA

Division of Science
Dr. Scott Ellis, Head
Program in:
biology • MS

Division of Social Science
Dr. Seymour Patterson, Head
Programs in:
counseling • MA
history • MA

■ UNIVERSITY OF MISSOURI–COLUMBIA
Columbia, MO 65211
http://www.missouri.edu/

State-supported, coed, university. CGS member. *Enrollment:* 3,332 full-time matriculated graduate/professional students (1,724 women), 1,919 part-time matriculated graduate/professional students (989 women). *Graduate faculty:* 1,453 full-time (396 women), 47 part-time/adjunct (20 women). *Computer facilities:* 1,150 computers available on campus for general student use. A campuswide network can be accessed from student residence rooms and from off campus. Internet access and online class registration, telephone registration are available. *Library facilities:* Ellis Library plus 11 others. *Graduate expenses:* Tuition: full-time $4,689. Required fees: $300. *General application contact:* Stephanie White-Thorn, Admissions, 573-882-3292.

College of Veterinary Medicine
Dr. Joe Kornegay, Dean
Programs in:
laboratory animal medicine • MS
pathobiology • MS, PhD
veterinary biomedical sciences • MS
veterinary clinical sciences • MS
veterinary medicine • MS

Graduate School
Dr. Suzanne Ortega, Dean
Programs in:
dispute resolution • LL M
health services management • MHA

College of Agriculture
Dr. Thomas T. Payne, Dean
Programs in:
agricultural economics • MS, PhD
agriculture • MS, PhD
agronomy • MS, PhD
animal sciences • MS, PhD
entomology • MS, PhD
food science • MS, PhD
foods and food systems management • MS
horticulture • MS, PhD
human nutrition • MS
nutrition • MS, PhD
plant pathology • MS, PhD
rural sociology • MS, PhD

College of Arts and Sciences
Dr. Richard Schwartz, Dean
Programs in:
analytical chemistry • MS, PhD
anthropology • MA, PhD
applied mathematics • MS
art • MFA
art history and archaeology • MA, PhD
arts and sciences • MA, MFA, MM, MS, MST, PhD
biological sciences • MA, PhD
classical studies • MA, PhD
communication • MA, PhD
economics • MA, PhD
English • MA, PhD
French • MA, PhD
genetics • PhD
geography • MA
geological sciences • MS, PhD
German • MA
history • MA, PhD
inorganic chemistry • MS, PhD
literature • MA
mathematics • MA, MST, PhD
music • MA, MM
organic chemistry • MS, PhD
philosophy • MA, PhD
physical chemistry • MS, PhD
physics • MS, PhD
political science • MA, PhD
psychology • MA, MS, PhD
religious studies • MA
sociology • MA, PhD
Spanish • MA, PhD
statistics • MA, PhD
teaching • MA
theatre • MA, PhD

College of Business
Dr. Bruce Walker, Dean
Programs in:
accountancy • M Acc, PhD
business • MBA, PhD
business and public administration • M Acc, MBA, MPA, PhD

College of Education
Dr. Richard Andrews, Dean
Programs in:
curriculum and instruction • M Ed, MA, Ed D, PhD, Ed S
education • M Ed, MA, Ed D, PhD, Ed S
education administration • M Ed, MA, Ed D, PhD, Ed S
educational and counseling psychology • M Ed, MA, PhD, Ed S
higher and adult education • M Ed, MA, Ed D, PhD, Ed S
library science • MA
practical arts and vocational technical education • M Ed, Ed D, PhD, Ed S
special education • M Ed, MA, Ed D, PhD, Ed S

College of Engineering
Dr. James Thompson, Dean
Programs in:
agricultural engineering • MS
biological engineering • MS, PhD
chemical engineering • MS, PhD

University of Missouri–Columbia (continued)

civil engineering • MS, PhD
computer engineering and computer science • MS, PhD
electrical engineering • MS, PhD
engineering • MS, PhD
environmental engineering • MS, PhD
geotechnical engineering • MS, PhD
industrial and manufacturing systems engineering • MS, PhD
mechanical and aerospace engineering • MS, PhD
nuclear engineering • MS, PhD
structural engineering • MS, PhD
transportation and highway engineering • MS
water resources • MS, PhD

College of Human Environmental Science
Dr. Bea Smith, Dean
Programs in:
consumer and family economics • MS
environmental design • MA, MS
exercise physiology • PhD
exercise science • MA
food science • MS, PhD
foods and food systems management • MS
human development and family studies • MA, MS, PhD
human environmental science • MA, MS, PhD
human nutrition • MS
textiles and apparel management • MA, MS

School of Public Affairs
Lisa Zanetti, Director of Graduate Studies
Program in:
public affairs • MPA

School of Journalism
Dr. Esther Thorson, Director of Graduate Studies
Program in:
journalism • MA, PhD

School of Natural Resources
Dr. A. R. Vogt, Director
Programs in:
fisheries and wildlife • MS, PhD
forestry • MS, PhD
natural resources • MS, PhD
parks, recreation and tourism • MS
soil and atmospheric sciences • MS, PhD

School of Social Work
Dr. Michael Kelly, Director of Graduate Studies
Program in:
social work • MSW

Sinclair School of Nursing
Dr. Rose Porter, Associate Dean
Program in:
nursing • MS, PhD

School of Law
Timothy J. Heinsz, Dean
Program in:
law • JD, LL M

School of Medicine
Dr. William Crist, Dean
Programs in:
biochemistry • MS, PhD
family and community medicine • MSPH
medicine • MD, MA, MHS, MPT, MS, MSPH, PhD
molecular microbiology and immunology • MS, PhD
pharmacology • MS, PhD
physiology • MS, PhD

School of Health Professions
Dr. Gordon Brown, Director
Programs in:
communication science and disorders • MHS
health professions • MHS, MPT
physical therapy • MPT

■ UNIVERSITY OF MISSOURI–KANSAS CITY
Kansas City, MO 64110-2499
http://www.umkc.edu/

State-supported, coed, university. CGS member. *Enrollment:* 2,310 full-time matriculated graduate/professional students (1,190 women), 2,297 part-time matriculated graduate/professional students (1,456 women). *Graduate faculty:* 478. *Computer facilities:* 400 computers available on campus for general student use. A campuswide network can be accessed from student residence rooms and from off campus. Internet access and online class registration are available. *Library facilities:* Miller-Nichols Library plus 3 others. *Graduate expenses:* Tuition, state resident: part-time $173 per credit hour. Tuition, nonresident: part-time $521 per credit hour. Required fees: $22 per credit hour. $30 per semester. *General application contact:* Mel Tyler, Director of Admissions, 816-235-1111.

Find an in-depth description at www.petersons.com/graduate.

College of Arts and Sciences
Dr. James R. Durig, Dean
Programs in:
acting • MFA
analytical chemistry • MS, PhD
art history • MA, PhD
arts and sciences • MA, MFA, MS, PhD
communication studies • MA
community psychology • PhD
criminal justice and criminology • MS
design technology • MFA
economics • MA, PhD
English • MA, PhD
geosciences • PhD
history • MA, PhD
inorganic chemistry • MS, PhD
liberal studies • MA
mathematics and statistics • MA, MS, PhD
organic chemistry • MS, PhD
physical chemistry • MS, PhD
physics • MS, PhD
political science • MA, PhD
polymer chemistry • MS, PhD
psychology • MA, PhD
Romance languages and literatures • MA
social work • MS
sociology • MA, PhD
studio art • MA
theatre • MA
urban environmental geology • MS

Conservatory of Music
Dr. Terry L. Applebaum, Dean
Programs in:
composition • MM, DMA
conducting • MM, DMA
music • MA
music education • MME, PhD
music history and literature • MM
music theory • MM
performance • MM, DMA

School of Biological Sciences
Dr. Marino Martinez-Carrion, Dean
Programs in:
biology • MA
cell biology and biophysics • PhD
cellular and molecular biology • MS, PhD
molecular biology and biochemistry • PhD

School of Business and Public Administration
Dr. Alfred N. Page, Dean
Programs in:
accounting • MS
business administration • MBA
business and public administration • MBA, MPA, MS, PhD

L. P. Cookingham Institute of Public Affairs
Dr. Robert Herman, Director
Program in:
public affairs • MPA, PhD

School of Dentistry
Dr. Michael Reed, Dean
Programs in:
advanced education in dentistry • Graduate Dental Certificate
dental hygiene education • MS
dental specialties • Graduate Dental Certificate
dentistry • DDS, MS, PhD, Graduate Dental Certificate
diagnostic sciences • Graduate Dental Certificate
oral and maxillofacial surgery • Graduate Dental Certificate
oral biology • MS, PhD
orthodontics and dentofacial orthopedics • Graduate Dental Certificate
pediatric dentistry • Graduate Dental Certificate
periodontics • Graduate Dental Certificate
prosthodontics • Graduate Dental Certificate

School of Education
Dr. Joan Gallos, Dean
Programs in:
counseling and guidance • MA, Ed S
counseling psychology • PhD
curriculum and instruction • Ed S
education • PhD
education research and psychology • MA
elementary education • MA
reading education • MA, Ed S
secondary education • MA
special education • MA
urban leadership and policy studies • MA, PhD, Ed S

School of Graduate Studies
Dr. Ronald MacQuarrie, Vice Provost/Dean
Program in:
interdisciplinary studies • PhD

School of Interdisciplinary Computing and Engineering
Dr. Mary Lou Hines, Interim Dean
Programs in:
computer networking • MS, PhD
software engineering • MS
telecommunications networking • MS, PhD

School of Law
Dr. Burnele Powell, Dean
Programs in:
general • LL M
law • JD, LL M
taxation • LL M

School of Medicine
Dr. Michael Friedland, MD, Interim Dean
Program in:
medicine • MD

School of Nursing
Dr. Nancy Mills, Dean
Programs in:
adult clinical nurse specialist • MSN
family nurse practitioner • MSN
neonatal nurse practitioner • MSN
nurse administrator • MSN
nurse educator • MSN
nursing • PhD
pediatric nurse practitioner • MSN

School of Pharmacy
Dr. Robert W. Piepho, Dean
Programs in:
pharmaceutical sciences • MS
pharmacy • Pharm D, MS

■ UNIVERSITY OF MISSOURI–ROLLA

Rolla, MO 65409-0910
http://www.umr.edu/

State-supported, coed, university. *Enrollment:* 621 full-time matriculated graduate/professional students (112 women), 232 part-time matriculated graduate/professional students (44 women). *Graduate faculty:* 238 full-time (13 women), 4 part-time/adjunct (0 women). *Computer facilities:* 800 computers available on campus for general student use. A campuswide network can be accessed from student residence rooms and from off campus. Internet access and online class registration are available. *Library facilities:* Curtis Laws Wilson Library. *Graduate expenses:* Tuition, state resident: full-time $4,298; part-time $179 per hour. Tuition, nonresident: full-time $12,929; part-time $539 per hour. Tuition and fees vary according to campus/location, program and student level. *General application contact:* Julie Sibley, Admissions Representative, 573-341-4315.

Graduate School
Dr. Y. T. Shah, Provost

College of Arts and Sciences
Dr. Russell Buhite, Dean
Programs in:
applied mathematics • MS
arts and sciences • MS, MST, PhD
chemistry • MS, PhD
chemistry education • MST
computer science • MS, PhD
mathematics • MST, PhD
mathematics education • MST
physics • MS, PhD

School of Engineering
Dr. O. Robert Mitchell, Dean
Programs in:
aerospace engineering • MS, PhD
chemical engineering • MS, PhD
civil engineering • MS, PhD
computer engineering • MS, DE, PhD
construction engineering • MS, DE, PhD
electrical engineering • MS, DE, PhD
engineering • M Eng, MS, DE, PhD
engineering management • MS, PhD
engineering mechanics • MS, PhD
environmental engineering • MS
fluid mechanics • MS, DE, PhD
geotechnical engineering • MS, DE, PhD
hydrology and hydraulic engineering • MS, DE, PhD
manufacturing engineering • M Eng, MS
mechanical engineering • MS, DE, PhD
sanitary engineering and environmental health • MS, DE, PhD
structural analysis and design • MS, DE, PhD
structural materials • MS
structural methods • DE, PhD
systems engineering • MS

School of Mines and Metallurgy
Dr. Lee W. Saperstein, Dean
Programs in:
ceramic engineering • MS, PhD
geochemistry • MS, PhD
geological engineering • MS, DE, PhD
geology • MS, PhD
geophysics • MS, PhD
groundwater and environmental geology • MS, PhD
metallurgical engineering • MS, PhD
mines and metallurgy • MS, DE, PhD
mining engineering • MS, DE, PhD
nuclear engineering • MS, DE, PhD
petroleum engineering • MS, DE, PhD

■ UNIVERSITY OF MISSOURI–ST. LOUIS

St. Louis, MO 63121-4499
http://www.umsl.edu/

State-supported, coed, university. CGS member. *Enrollment:* 443 full-time matriculated graduate/professional students (270 women), 1,910 part-time matriculated graduate/professional students (1,325 women). *Graduate faculty:* 402. *Computer facilities:* 750 computers available on campus for general student use. A campuswide

University of Missouri–St. Louis (continued)

network can be accessed from student residence rooms and from off campus. Internet access is available. *Library facilities:* Thomas Jefferson Library plus 2 others. *Graduate expenses:* Tuition, state resident: full-time $4,157; part-time $173 per credit hour. Tuition, nonresident: full-time $13,544; part-time $521 per credit hour. Required fees: $784; $33 per credit. *General application contact:* Graduate Admissions, 314-516-5458.

Find an in-depth description at www.petersons.com/graduate.

Graduate School
Dr. Douglas Wartzok, Associate Vice Chancellor for Research and Dean
Programs in:
gerontological social work • Certificate
gerontology • MS, Certificate
health policy • MPPA
nonprofit organization management • MPPA
nonprofit organization management and leadership • Certificate
public policy analysis • MPPA
public policy processes • MPPA
public sector human resources management • MPPA

College of Arts and Sciences
Dr. David Young, Dean
Programs in:
advanced social perspective • MA
American literature • MA
American politics • MA
applied mathematics • MA, PhD
applied physics • MS
arts and sciences • MA, MFA, MME, MS, MSW, PhD, Certificate
astrophysics • MS
biology • MS, PhD
biotechnology • Certificate
chemistry • MS, PhD
clinical psychology • PhD
clinical psychology respecialization • Certificate
community conflict intervention • MA
comparative politics • MA
computer science • MS
creative writing • MFA
criminology and criminal justice • MA, PhD
English • MA
English literature • MA
experimental psychology • PhD
general economics • MA
general psychology • MA
historical agencies • MA
industrial/organizational • PhD
international politics • MA
international studies • Certificate
linguistics • MA
managerial economics • Certificate
museum studies • MA, Certificate
music education • MME
philosophy • MA
physics • PhD
political process and behavior • MA
political science • PhD
program design and evaluation research • MA
public administration and public policy • MA
social policy planning and administration • MA
social work • MSW
telecommunications science • Certificate
tropical biology and conservation • Certificate
urban and regional politics • MA
women's and gender studies • Certificate

College of Business Administration
Dr. Thomas Eyssell, Director of Graduate Studies
Programs in:
accounting • MBA
business administration • Certificate
corporate accounting • M Acc
electronic commerce • Certificate
finance • MBA
human resource management • Certificate
information resources management • Certificate
management • MBA
management information systems • Certificate
marketing • MBA
marketing management • Certificate
public sector accounting • M Acc
quantitative management science • MBA
taxation • M Acc, Certificate
telecommunications management • Certificate

College of Nursing
Dr. Connie Koch, Associate Dean
Program in:
nursing • MSN, PhD

School of Education
Dr. Kathleen Haywood, Director of Graduate Studies
Programs in:
adult education • M Ed, Ed D, PhD
community education • M Ed
counseling • Ed D, PhD
curriculum and instruction • M Ed, Ed D, PhD
early childhood special education • M Ed
education • M Ed, Ed D, PhD
educational psychology, research, and evaluation • M Ed, Ed D, PhD
elementary administration • M Ed
elementary reading • M Ed, Ed D, PhD
elementary school counseling • M Ed
emotionally disturbed education • M Ed
general counseling • M Ed
higher education administration • Ed D, PhD
learning disabilities • M Ed
mentally retarded education • M Ed
reading • M Ed, Ed D, PhD
secondary administration • M Ed
secondary school counseling • M Ed

School of Optometry
Programs in:
optometry • OD, MS, PhD
physiological optics • MS, PhD

■ WASHINGTON UNIVERSITY IN ST. LOUIS
St. Louis, MO 63130-4899
http://www.wustl.edu/

Independent, coed, university. CGS member. *Enrollment:* 4,293 full-time matriculated graduate/professional students (2,191 women), 1,231 part-time matriculated graduate/professional students (485 women). *Graduate faculty:* 2,065 full-time (571 women), 520 part-time/adjunct (221 women). *Computer facilities:* 2,500 computers available on campus for general student use. A campuswide network can be accessed from student residence rooms and from off campus. Internet access and online class registration, e-mail are available. *Library facilities:* John M. Olin Library plus 13 others. *Graduate expenses:* Tuition: full-time $24,500. *General application contact:* 314-935-6880.

Find an in-depth description at www.petersons.com/graduate.

George Warren Brown School of Social Work
Dr. Shanti K. Khinduka, Dean and George Warren Brown Distinguished Professor of Social Work
Program in:
social work • MSW, PhD

Graduate School of Arts and Sciences
Robert E. Thach, Dean
Programs in:
American history • MA, PhD
anthropology • MA, PhD
art history • MA, PhD
arts and sciences • MA, MA Ed, MAT, MFAW, MM, MS, PhD, Certificate

Asian history • MA, PhD
Asian language • MA
Asian studies • MA
audiology • MS
British history • MA, PhD
chemistry • MA, PhD
Chinese • MA, PhD
Chinese and comparative literature • PhD
classical archaeology • MA, PhD
classics • MA, MAT
clinical psychology • PhD
comparative literature • MA, PhD
deaf education • MS
early childhood education • MA Ed
earth and planetary sciences • MA
East Asian studies • MA
economics • MA, PhD
educational research • PhD
elementary education • MA Ed
English and American literature • MA, PhD
environmental science • MA
European history • MA, PhD
European studies • MA
French • MA, PhD
general experimental psychology • MA, PhD
geochemistry • PhD
geology • MA, PhD
geophysics • PhD
Germanic languages and literature • MA, PhD
history • PhD
Islamic and Near Eastern studies • MA
Japanese • MA, PhD
Japanese and comparative literature • PhD
Jewish studies • MA
Latin American history • MA, PhD
mathematics • MA, PhD
mathematics education • MAT
Middle Eastern history • MA, PhD
movement science • PhD
music • MA, MM, PhD
performing arts • MA
philosophy • MA, PhD
philosophy/neuroscience/psychology • PhD
physics • MA, PhD
planetary sciences • PhD
political economy and public policy • MA
political science • MA, PhD
Romance languages • MA, PhD
secondary education • MA Ed, MAT
social psychology • MA, PhD
Spanish • MA, PhD
speech and hearing sciences • MA, PhD
statistics • MA, PhD
writing • MFAW

Division of Biology and Biomedical Sciences
Programs in:
biochemistry • PhD
bioorganic chemistry • PhD
computational biology • PhD
developmental biology • PhD
ecology • PhD
environmental biology • PhD
evolutionary and population biology • PhD
evolutionary biology • PhD
genetics • PhD
immunology • PhD
molecular biophysics • PhD
molecular cell biology • PhD
molecular genetics • PhD
molecular microbiology and microbial pathogenesis • PhD
neurosciences • PhD
plant biology • PhD

John M. Olin School of Business
Stuart I. Greenbaum, Dean
Programs in:
business • PhD
business administration • MBA
health services management • EMBA
manufacturing management • EMBA

School of Architecture
Programs in:
architecture • M Arch, MAUD
urban design • MAUD

School of Art
Jeff Pike, Dean
Programs in:
ceramics • MFA
painting • MFA
photography • MFA
printmaking/drawing • MFA
sculpture • MFA

School of Engineering and Applied Science
Programs in:
biomedical engineering • MS, D Sc
engineering and applied science • MA, MCE, MCE, MCM, MS, MSCE, MSE, MSEE, MSEE, D Sc

Sever Institute of Technology
Programs in:
chemical engineering • MS, D Sc
civil engineering • MSCE
computer science • MS, D Sc
construction engineering • MCE
construction management • MCM
control engineering • MCE
electrical engineering • MSEE, D Sc
engineering and policy • MA, MS, D Sc
environmental engineering • MS, D Sc
materials science and engineering • MS
materials science engineering • D Sc
mechanical engineering • MS, D Sc
structural engineering • MSE, D Sc
systems science and mathematics • MS, D Sc
systems science and mathematics and economics • D Sc
technology • MA, MCE, MCE, MCM, MS, MSCE, MSE, MSEE, MSEE, D Sc
transportation and urban systems engineering • D Sc

School of Law
Program in:
law • JD, LL M, MJS, JSD

School of Medicine
Dr. William A. Peck, Dean
Programs in:
health administration • MHA
medicine • MD, MA, MHA, MHS, MSOT, DPT, PhD, PPDPT
movement science • PhD
occupational therapy • MSOT
physical therapy • MHS, DPT, PhD, PPDPT

■ WEBSTER UNIVERSITY
St. Louis, MO 63119-3194
http://www.webster.edu/

Independent, coed, comprehensive institution. *Enrollment:* 3,526 full-time matriculated graduate/professional students (1,945 women), 8,679 part-time matriculated graduate/professional students (4,577 women). *Graduate faculty:* 76 full-time (32 women), 1,115 part-time/adjunct (228 women). *Computer facilities:* 185 computers available on campus for general student use. A campuswide network can be accessed. Internet access and online class registration are available. *Library facilities:* Eden-Webster Library. *Graduate expenses:* Tuition: full-time $6,894; part-time $383 per credit hour. *General application contact:* Dr. Beth Russell, Director of Evening Student Admissions, 314-968-7100.

College of Arts and Sciences
Dr. Janice I. Hooper, Acting Dean
Programs in:
arts and sciences • MA, MS, MSN, Certificate
counseling • MA
environmental management • MS
family systems nursing • MSN
gerontology • MA
international relations • MA
legal studies • MA
nurse anesthesia • MS
paralegal studies • Certificate

Webster University (continued)

College of Fine Arts
Peter Sargent, Dean
Programs in:
art • MA, MFA
arts management and leadership • MFA
church music • MM
composition • MM
conducting • MM
fine arts • MA, MFA, MM
jazz studies • MM
music education • MM
performance • MM
piano • MM

School of Business and Technology
Dr. Benjamin Ola Akande, Dean
Programs in:
business • MA, MBA
business and technology • MA, MBA, MS, DM, Certificate
computer distributed systems • Certificate
computer resources and information management • MA, MBA
computer science • MS
computer science/distributed systems • MS
finance • MA, MBA
health care management • MA
health services management • MA, MBA
human resources development • MA, MBA
human resources management • MA
international business • MA, MBA
management • MA, MBA
marketing • MA, MBA
procurement and acquisitions management • MA, MBA
public administration • MA
real estate management • MA, MBA
security management • MA, MBA
space systems management • MA, MBA, MS
telecommunications management • MA, MBA

School of Communications
Debra Carpenter, Dean
Program in:
media communication • MA

School of Education
Dr. Judith Walker DeFelix, Dean
Programs in:
communications • MAT
early childhood education • MAT
education • MAT
education technology • MAT
mathematics education • MAT
multidisciplinary studies • MAT
science education • MAT
social science education • MAT
special education • MAT

■ WILLIAM WOODS UNIVERSITY

Fulton, MO 65251-1098
http://www.williamwoods.edu/

Independent-religious, coed, comprehensive institution. *Enrollment:* 466 full-time matriculated graduate/professional students (278 women), 2 part-time matriculated graduate/professional students (both women). *Graduate faculty:* 14 full-time (6 women), 52 part-time/adjunct (21 women). *Computer facilities:* 105 computers available on campus for general student use. A campuswide network can be accessed from student residence rooms. Internet access is available. *Library facilities:* Dulany Library. *Graduate expenses:* Tuition: full-time $6,360. One-time fee: $25 full-time. Full-time tuition and fees vary according to program. *General application contact:* Barbara Danuser, Recruitment Representative, 800-995-3199.

College of Graduate and Adult Studies
Dr. Betty R. Tutt, Associate Provost
Programs in:
accounting • MBA
administration • M Ed
curriculum and instruction • M Ed
equestrian education • M Ed
health management • MBA

Montana

■ MONTANA STATE UNIVERSITY–BILLINGS

Billings, MT 59101-9984
http://www.msubillings.edu/

State-supported, coed, comprehensive institution. *Computer facilities:* 450 computers available on campus for general student use. A campuswide network can be accessed from student residence rooms and from off campus. Internet access and online class registration, on-line degree programs are available. *Library facilities:* Montana State University-Billings Library. *General application contact:* Director of Graduate Studies and Research, 406-657-2238.

College of Arts and Sciences
Programs in:
arts and sciences • MS
psychology • MS
public relations • MS

College of Business
Programs in:
business • MSIPC
information processing and communications • MSIPC

College of Education and Human Services
Programs in:
community counseling • MS, MS Sp Ed
early childhood education • M Ed
education and human services • M Ed, MS, MS Sp Ed, MSRC
educational technology • M Ed
emotionally disturbed • MS Sp Ed
general curriculum • M Ed
interdisciplinary studies • M Ed
mental retardation • MS Sp Ed
reading • M Ed
rehabilitation counseling • MSRC
school counseling • M Ed
secondary education • M Ed
special education • MS Sp Ed
special education generalist • MS Sp Ed
sport management • MS

College of Professional Studies and Lifelong Learning
Programs in:
health administration • MHA
professional studies and lifelong learning • MHA

■ MONTANA STATE UNIVERSITY–BOZEMAN

Bozeman, MT 59717
http://www.montana.edu/

State-supported, coed, university. CGS member. *Enrollment:* 475 full-time matriculated graduate/professional students (207 women), 463 part-time matriculated graduate/professional students (219 women). *Computer facilities:* 850 computers available on campus for general student use. A campuswide network can be accessed from student residence rooms and from off campus. Internet access and online class registration, e-mail are available. *Library facilities:* Renne Library plus 1 other. *Graduate expenses:* Tuition, state resident: full-time $3,533. Tuition, nonresident: full-time $9,530. $9,680 full-time. Tuition and fees vary according to course load and program. *General application contact:* Dr. Bruce McLeod, Dean, 406-994-4145.

College of Graduate Studies
Dr. Bruce McLeod, Dean

College of Agriculture
Dr. Sharron Quisenberry, Dean
Programs in:
- agriculture • MS, PhD
- animal and range science • MS
- applied economics • MS
- entomology • MS
- land rehabilitation • MS
- land resources and environmental sciences • MS, PhD
- plant pathology • MS
- plant science • MS, PhD
- veterinary molecular biology • MS, PhD

College of Arts and Architecture
Jerry Bancroft, Dean
Programs in:
- architecture • M Arch
- art • MFA
- arts and architecture • M Arch, MFA
- science and natural history filmmaking • MFA

College of Business
Dr. Richard J. Semenik, Dean
Program in:
- professional accountancy • MP Ac

College of Education, Health, and Human Development
Dr. Greg Weisenstein, Dean
Programs in:
- education • M Ed, Ed D, Ed S
- education, health, and human development • M Ed, MS, Ed D, Ed S
- health and human development • MS
- science education • MS

College of Engineering
Dr. Robert Marley, Interim Dean
Programs in:
- chemical engineering • MS
- civil engineering • MS
- computer science • MS
- construction engineering management • MCEM
- electrical engineering • MS
- engineering • PhD
- environmental engineering • MS
- industrial and management engineering • MS
- land rehabilitation • MS
- mechanical engineering • MS
- project engineering and management • MPEM

College of Letters and Science
Dr. James McMillan, Dean
Programs in:
- applied psychology • MS
- biochemistry • MS, PhD
- biological science • MS
- biological sciences • MS, PhD
- chemistry • MS, PhD
- earth sciences • MS
- English • MA
- fish and wildlife biology • PhD
- fish and wildlife management • MS
- history • MA
- land rehabilitation • MS
- letters and science • MA, MPA, MS, PhD
- mathematics • MS, PhD
- microbiology • MS, PhD
- Native American studies • MA
- physics • MS, PhD
- public administration • MPA
- statistics • MS, PhD

College of Nursing
Dr. Lea Acord, Dean
Program in:
- nursing • MN

■ MONTANA STATE UNIVERSITY–NORTHERN

Havre, MT 59501-7751
http://www.msun.edu/

State-supported, coed, comprehensive institution. *Enrollment:* 21 full-time matriculated graduate/professional students (15 women), 71 part-time matriculated graduate/professional students (49 women). *Graduate faculty:* 5 full-time (2 women), 9 part-time/adjunct (3 women). *Computer facilities:* 140 computers available on campus for general student use. A campuswide network can be accessed from student residence rooms and from off campus. Internet access and online class registration are available. *Library facilities:* VandeBogart Libraries. *Graduate expenses:* Full-time $3,195; part-time $89 per credit. Tuition, nonresident: full-time $8,360; part-time $232 per credit. Tuition and fees vary according to course load, degree level and program. *General application contact:* Dr. Darlene Sellers, Interim Dean, College of Education and Graduate Programs, 406-265-3745.

College of Education and Graduate Programs
Dr. Darlene Sellers, Interim Dean, College of Education and Graduate Programs
Programs in:
- counselor education • M Ed
- elementary education • M Ed
- general science • M Ed
- learning development • M Ed
- vocational education • M Ed

■ UNIVERSITY OF GREAT FALLS

Great Falls, MT 59405
http://www.ugf.edu/

Independent-religious, coed, comprehensive institution. *Computer facilities:* 75 computers available on campus for general student use. A campuswide network can be accessed. Internet access is available. *Library facilities:* University of Great Falls Library. *General application contact:* Dean of Graduate Studies Division, 406-791-5337.

Graduate Studies Division
Programs in:
- chemical dependent services • MHS
- counseling psychology • MSC
- criminal justice administration • MSCJA
- curriculum and instruction • MAT
- elementary administration • ME
- elementary education • MAT
- family services • MHS
- guidance and counseling • ME
- information systems • MIS
- liberal studies • MALS
- marriage and family counseling • MSC
- secondary education • MAT

■ THE UNIVERSITY OF MONTANA–MISSOULA

Missoula, MT 59812-0002
http://www.umt.edu/

State-supported, coed, university. CGS member. *Enrollment:* 678 full-time matriculated graduate/professional students (337 women), 549 part-time matriculated graduate/professional students (304 women). *Graduate faculty:* 539 full-time (180 women), 109 part-time/adjunct (51 women). *Computer facilities:* 545 computers available on campus for general student use. A campuswide network can be accessed from student residence rooms and from off campus. Internet access and online class registration are available. *Library facilities:* Maureen and Mike Mansfield Library plus 2 others. *Graduate expenses:* Tuition, state resident: full-time $948; part-time $105 per credit. Tuition, nonresident: full-time $3,112; part-time $240 per credit. *General application contact:* Dr. David A. Strobel, Dean, 406-243-2572.

Find an in-depth description at www.petersons.com/graduate.

The University of Montana–Missoula (continued)

Graduate School
Dr. David A. Strobel, Dean
Programs in:
individual interdisciplinary programs • PhD
interdisciplinary studies • MIS

College of Arts and Sciences
Dr. Thomas Storch, Dean
Programs in:
animal behavior • PhD
arts and sciences • MA, MFA, MPA, MS, MST, PhD, Ed S
chemistry • MS, PhD
chemistry teaching • MST
clinical psychology • PhD
communication studies • MA
computer science • MS
creative writing • MFA
criminology • MA
cultural heritage • MA
developmental psychology • PhD
economics • MA
English literature • MA
English teaching • MA
environmental studies • MS
experimental psychology • PhD
fiction • MFA
French • MA
geography • MA
geology • MS, PhD
German • MA
history • MA
linguistics • MA
mathematics • MA, PhD
non-fiction • MFA
poetry • MFA
political science • MA
public administration • MPA
rural and environmental change • MA
school psychology • MA, Ed S
Spanish • MA
teaching ethics • MA

Division of Biological Sciences
Dr. Don Christian, Associate Dean
Programs in:
biochemistry and microbiology • MS, PhD
biological sciences • MS, PhD
organismal biology and ecology • MS, PhD

School of Education
Dr. Don Robson, Dean
Programs in:
counselor education • M Ed, MA, Ed D, Ed S
curriculum and instruction • M Ed, MA, Ed D
education • M Ed, MA, MS, Ed D, Ed S
exercise and performance psychology • MS
exercise science • MS
health promotion • MS
school administration and supervision • M Ed, Ed S

School of Fine Arts
Dr. Shirley Howell, Dean
Programs in:
fine arts • MA, MFA
music • MM

School of Forestry
Dr. Perry Brown, Dean
Programs in:
ecosystem management • MEM
fish and wildlife biology • PhD
forestry • MEM, MS, PhD
recreation management • MS
resource conservation • MS
wildlife biology • MS

School of Journalism
Dr. Jerry Brown, Dean
Program in:
journalism • MA

School of Pharmacy and Allied Health Sciences
Dr. David Forbes, Dean
Programs in:
pharmaceutical sciences • MS
pharmacology • PhD
pharmacy and allied health sciences • MS, PhD
physical therapy • MS

School of Business Administration
Dr. Larry Gianchetta, Dean
Programs in:
accounting and finance • M Acct
business • MBA
business administration • M Acct, MBA

School of Law
E. Edwin Eck, Dean
Program in:
law • JD

Nebraska

■ BELLEVUE UNIVERSITY

Bellevue, NE 68005-3098
http://www.bellevue.edu/

Independent, coed, comprehensive institution. *Enrollment:* 418 full-time matriculated graduate/professional students (187 women), 212 part-time matriculated graduate/professional students (92 women). *Graduate faculty:* 28 full-time (11 women), 36 part-time/adjunct (10 women). *Computer facilities:* 377 computers available on campus for general student use. A campuswide network can be accessed from off campus. Internet access and online class registration are available. *Library facilities:* Freeman/Lozier Library plus 1 other. *Graduate expenses:* Tuition: full-time $4,680; part-time $260 per credit hour. Required fees: $35 per term. One-time fee: $50. Full-time tuition and fees vary according to campus/location. *General application contact:* Elizabeth A. Wall, Director of Marketing and Enrollment, 402-293-3702.

Graduate School
Dr. Jon B. Kayne, Vice President for Academic Affairs
Programs in:
business • MBA
computer information systems • MS
health care administration • MS
human services • MS
leadership • MA
management • MA

■ CHADRON STATE COLLEGE

Chadron, NE 69337
http://www.csc.edu/

State-supported, coed, comprehensive institution. *Enrollment:* 38 full-time matriculated graduate/professional students (21 women), 317 part-time matriculated graduate/professional students (235 women). *Graduate faculty:* 76 full-time (17 women). *Computer facilities:* 200 computers available on campus for general student use. A campuswide network can be accessed from student residence rooms and from off campus. Internet access and online class registration are available. *Library facilities:* Reta King Library. *Graduate expenses:* Tuition, state resident: part-time $83 per hour. Tuition, nonresident: part-time $165 per hour. Required fees: $15 per semester. *General application contact:* Dr. Thomas P. Colgate, Dean, School of Education and Graduate Studies, 308-432-6330.

School of Education and Graduate Studies
Dr. Thomas P. Colgate, Dean, School of Education and Graduate Studies
Programs in:
business • MA Ed
business and economics • MBA
counseling • MA Ed
educational administration • MS Ed, Sp Ed

elementary education • MS Ed
history • MA Ed
language and literature • MA Ed
secondary administration • MS Ed
secondary education • MS Ed

■ CONCORDIA UNIVERSITY

Seward, NE 68434-1599
http://www.cune.edu/

Independent-religious, coed, comprehensive institution. *Enrollment:* 276 part-time matriculated graduate/professional students (145 women). *Graduate faculty:* 36 full-time (10 women). *Computer facilities:* 75 computers available on campus for general student use. A campuswide network can be accessed from student residence rooms and from off campus. *Library facilities:* Link Library. *Graduate expenses:* Tuition: part-time $150 per credit hour. *General application contact:* Dr. Len Bassett, Dean of Graduate Studies, 402-643-7464.

Graduate Programs in Education

Dr. Len Bassett, Dean of Graduate Studies
Programs in:
early childhood education • M Ed
education • M Ed, MPE, MS
educational administration • M Ed
elementary education • M Ed
family life • MS
parish education • MPE
reading education • M Ed

■ CREIGHTON UNIVERSITY

Omaha, NE 68178-0001
http://www.creighton.edu/

Independent-religious, coed, university. CGS member. *Enrollment:* 2,139 full-time matriculated graduate/professional students (1,094 women), 333 part-time matriculated graduate/professional students (176 women). *Computer facilities:* A campuswide network can be accessed from student residence rooms and from off campus. Internet access and online class registration, on-line grade information are available. *Library facilities:* Reinert Alumni Memorial Library plus 2 others. *Graduate expenses:* Tuition: part-time $447 per credit. *General application contact:* Dr. Barbara J. Braden, Dean, Graduate School, 402-280-2870.

Graduate School

Dr. Barbara J. Braden, Dean

College of Arts and Sciences
Dr. Patricia Fleming, Interim Dean
Programs in:
arts and sciences • MA, MCS, MLS, MS
atmospheric sciences • MS
Christian spirituality • MA
computer sciences • MCS
educational administration • MS
guidance and counseling • MS
international relations • MA
liberal studies • MLS
mathematics and statistics • MS
ministry • MA
physics • MS
theology • MA

Eugene C. Eppley College of Business Administration
Dr. Robert Pitts, Dean
Programs in:
business administration • MBA
electronic commerce • MS
information technology • MS
management • MS

School of Dentistry

Program in:
dentistry • DDS

School of Law

Patrick J. Borchers, Dean
Program in:
law • JD

School of Medicine

Dr. M. Roy Wilson, Dean
Programs in:
biomedical sciences • MS, PhD
medical microbiology and immunology • MS, PhD
medicine • MD, MS, PhD
pharmaceutical sciences • MS
pharmacology • MS, PhD

School of Nursing

Dr. Edeth K. Kitchens, Dean
Program in:
nursing • MS

School of Pharmacy and Allied Health Professions

Dr. Sidney J. Stohs, Dean
Programs in:
occupational therapy • OTD
pharmaceutical sciences • MS
pharmacy • Pharm D
pharmacy and allied health • Pharm D, MS, DPT, OTD
physical therapy • DPT

■ DOANE COLLEGE

Crete, NE 68333-2430
http://www.doane.edu/

Independent-religious, coed, comprehensive institution. *Enrollment:* 197 full-time matriculated graduate/professional students, 421 part-time matriculated graduate/professional students. *Graduate faculty:* 4 full-time (2 women), 51 part-time/adjunct (29 women). *Computer facilities:* 200 computers available on campus for general student use. A campuswide network can be accessed from student residence rooms and from off campus. Internet access and online class registration are available. *Library facilities:* Perkins Library. *Graduate expenses:* Tuition: part-time $135 per credit. Tuition and fees vary according to program. *General application contact:* Lyn Forester, Dean of Graduate Studies in Education, 402-464-1223.

Program in Counseling

Thomas Gilligan, Dean
Program in:
counseling • MAC

Program in Education

Dr. Marilyn Kent Byrne, Co-Dean
Programs in:
curriculum and instruction • M Ed
educational leadership • M Ed

Program in Management

Frederic D. Brown, Acting Dean
Program in:
management • MAM

■ PERU STATE COLLEGE

Peru, NE 68421
http://www.peru.edu/

State-supported, coed, comprehensive institution. *Computer facilities:* 120 computers available on campus for general student use. A campuswide network can be accessed from student residence rooms. Internet access is available. *Library facilities:* Peru State College Library. *General application contact:* Division Chair, 402-872-2244.

Graduate Studies

Program in:
education • MS Ed

■ UNIVERSITY OF NEBRASKA AT KEARNEY

Kearney, NE 68849-0001

State-supported, coed, comprehensive institution. CGS member. *Enrollment:* 140 full-time matriculated graduate/professional students (101 women), 445 part-time matriculated graduate/professional students (296 women).

University of Nebraska at Kearney (continued)

Graduate faculty: 90 full-time (33 women). *Computer facilities:* 277 computers available on campus for general student use. A campuswide network can be accessed from student residence rooms and from off campus. Internet access and online class registration, online grade reports are available. *Library facilities:* Calvin T. Ryan Library. *Graduate expenses:* Tuition, state resident: full-time $1,665; part-time $93 per credit hour. Tuition, nonresident: full-time $3,150; part-time $175 per credit hour. Required fees: $15 per credit hour. One-time fee: $30. Tuition and fees vary according to course load and reciprocity agreements. *General application contact:* Dr. Kenneth Nikels, Graduate Dean, 308-865-8500.

College of Graduate Study
Dr. Kenneth Nikels, Dean

College of Business and Technology
Dr. Kathleen Smith, Dean
Programs in:
- business administration • MBA
- business and technology • MBA

College of Education
Dr. Marilyn Hadley, Dean
Programs in:
- adapted physical education • MA Ed
- counseling • MS Ed, Ed S
- curriculum and instruction • MS Ed
- early childhood education • MA Ed
- early childhood special education • MA Ed
- education • MA Ed, MS Ed, Ed S
- education of behaviorally disordered • MA Ed
- education of the gifted and talented • MA Ed
- educational administration • MA Ed, Ed S
- elementary education • MA Ed
- exercise science • MA Ed
- instructional technology • MS Ed
- master teacher • MA Ed
- middle school education • MA Ed
- mild/moderate handicapped • MA Ed
- reading education • MA Ed
- school psychology • Ed S
- special education • MA Ed
- specific learning disabilities • MA Ed
- speech pathology • MS Ed
- supervisor of educational media • MA Ed

College of Fine Arts and Humanities
Dr. Rodney Miller, Dean
Programs in:
- art education • MA Ed
- English • MA
- fine arts and humanities • MA, MA Ed
- French • MA Ed
- German • MA Ed
- music education • MA Ed
- Spanish • MA Ed

College of Natural and Social Sciences
Dr. Michael Schuyler, Dean
Programs in:
- biology • MS
- history • MA
- natural and social sciences • MA, MS, MS Ed
- science education • MS Ed

■ UNIVERSITY OF NEBRASKA AT OMAHA

Omaha, NE 68182
http://www.unomaha.edu/

State-supported, coed, university. CGS member. *Enrollment:* 578 full-time matriculated graduate/professional students (348 women), 1,609 part-time matriculated graduate/professional students (998 women). *Graduate faculty:* 308 full-time (65 women), 9 part-time/adjunct (1 woman). *Computer facilities:* 64 computers available on campus for general student use. A campuswide network can be accessed from student residence rooms and from off campus. Internet access and online class registration are available. *Library facilities:* University Library. *Graduate expenses:* Tuition, state resident: part-time $105 per course. Tuition, nonresident: part-time $252 per course. Required fees: $12 per credit hour. One-time fee: $56 part-time. *General application contact:* Penny Harmoney, Manager, Graduate Studies, 402-554-2341.

Graduate Studies and Research
Dr. Shelton E. Hendricks, Associate Vice Chancellor for Research and Dean

College of Arts and Sciences
Dr. John Flocken, Dean
Programs in:
- arts and sciences • MA, MAT, MS, PhD, Ed S
- biology • MA, MS
- communication • MA
- developmental psychobiology • PhD
- English • MA
- experimental child psychology • PhD
- geography • MA
- history • MA
- industrial/organizational psychology • MS, PhD
- mathematics • MA, MAT, MS
- political science • MA, MS
- psychology • MA
- school psychology • MS, Ed S
- sociology • MA

College of Business Administration
Dr. Stan Hille, Dean
Programs in:
- accounting • M Acc
- business administration • EMBA, M Acc, MA, MBA, MIB, MS
- economics • MA, MS

College of Education
Dr. John Christensen, Acting Dean
Programs in:
- behavioral disorders • MS
- community counseling • MA, MS
- counseling gerontology • MA, MS
- education • MA, MS, Ed D, Ed S
- educational administration and supervision • MS, Ed D, Ed S
- elementary education • MA, MS
- health, physical education, and recreation • MA, MS
- mental retardation • MA
- reading education • MA, MS
- resource teaching and learning disabilities • MS
- school counseling-elementary • MA, MS
- school counseling-secondary • MA, MS
- secondary education • MA, MS
- speech-language pathology • MA, MS
- student affairs practice in higher education • MA, MS
- teaching the hearing impaired • MS
- teaching the mentally retarded • MS

College of Fine Arts
Dr. Karen White, Dean
Programs in:
- dramatic arts • MA
- fine arts • MA, MM
- music • MM

College of Information Science and Technology
Dr. David Hinton, Dean
Programs in:
- computer science • MA, MS
- information science and technology • MA, MS
- management information systems • MS

College of Public Affairs and Community Service
Dr. Burton J. Reed, Chairperson
Programs in:
- criminal justice • MA, MS, PhD
- gerontology • MA, Certificate
- public administration • MPA, PhD

public affairs and community service • MA, MPA, MS, MSW, PhD, Certificate
social work • MSW

■ UNIVERSITY OF NEBRASKA–LINCOLN

Lincoln, NE 68588
http://www.unl.edu/

State-supported, coed, university. CGS member. *Enrollment:* 2,146 full-time matriculated graduate/professional students (1,001 women), 1,292 part-time matriculated graduate/professional students (667 women). *Graduate faculty:* 860 full-time (181 women), 43 part-time/adjunct (7 women). *Computer facilities:* 500 computers available on campus for general student use. A campuswide network can be accessed from student residence rooms and from off campus. Internet access is available. *Library facilities:* Love Memorial Library plus 10 others. *Graduate expenses:* Tuition, state resident: part-time $122 per credit hour. Tuition, nonresident: part-time $301 per credit hour. Required fees: $5 per credit hour. $15 per semester. One-time fee: $10 part-time. *General application contact:* Dr. Merlin P. Lawson, Dean of Graduate Studies, 402-472-2875.

Find an in-depth description at www.petersons.com/graduate.

College of Law
Steven Willborn, Dean
Programs in:
law • JD, MLS
legal studies • MLS

Graduate College
Dr. Merlin P. Lawson, Dean of Graduate Studies
Programs in:
museum studies • MA, MS
survey research and methodology • MS
toxicology • MS, PhD

College of Agricultural Sciences and Natural Resources
Dr. Steven S. Waller, Interim Dean
Programs in:
agricultural economics • MS, PhD
agricultural leadership, education and communication • MS
agricultural sciences and natural resources • M Ag, MA, MS, PhD
agriculture • M Ag
agronomy • MS, PhD
animal science • MS, PhD
biochemistry • MS, PhD
biological sciences • MA, MS, PhD
biometry • MS
entomology • MS, PhD
food science and technology • MS, PhD
horticulture • MS
horticulture and forestry • PhD
mechanized systems management • MS
natural resource sciences • MS
nutrition • MS, PhD
veterinary and biomedical sciences • MS, PhD

College of Architecture
Wayne Drummond, Dean
Programs in:
architecture • M Arch, MS
community and regional planning • MCRP, MS/MCRP

College of Arts and Sciences
Dr. Richard Hoffman, Dean
Programs in:
analytical chemistry • PhD
anthropology • MA
arts and sciences • M Sc T, MA, MAT, MS, PhD
astronomy • MS, PhD
chemistry • MS
classics • MA
communication studies and theatre arts • PhD
communications studies • MA
computer engineering • MS, PhD
computer science • MS, PhD
English • MA, PhD
French • MA, PhD
geography • MA, PhD
geosciences • MS, PhD
German • MA, PhD
history • MA, PhD
inorganic chemistry • PhD
mathematics and statistics • M Sc T, MA, MAT, MS, PhD
organic chemistry • PhD
philosophy • MA, PhD
physical chemistry • PhD
physics • MS, PhD
political science • MA, PhD
psychology • MA, PhD
sociology • MA, PhD
software engineering • MS
Spanish • MA, PhD

College of Business Administration
Dr. Cynthia H. Milligan, Dean
Programs in:
accountancy • PhD
actuarial science • MS
business • MA, MBA, PhD
business administration • MA, MBA, MPA, MS, PhD
economics • MA, PhD
finance • MA, PhD
management • MA, PhD
marketing • MA, PhD

College of Engineering and Technology
Dr. James L. Hendrix, Dean
Programs in:
agricultural and biological systems engineering • MS
agricultural science • MS
chemical engineering • MS
civil engineering • MS
electrical engineering • MS
engineering • PhD
engineering and technology • M Eng, MS, MS/MCRP, PhD
engineering mechanics • MS
environmental engineering • MS
industrial and management systems engineering • MS
manufacturing systems engineering • MS
mechanical engineering • MS

College of Fine and Performing Arts
Dr. Giacomo Oliva, Dean
Programs in:
art and art history • MFA
fine and performing arts • MFA, MM, DMA
music • MM, DMA
theatre arts and dance • MFA

College of Human Resources and Family Sciences
Dr. Marjorie J. Kostelnik, Dean
Programs in:
family and consumer sciences • MS
human resources and family sciences • PhD
nutritional science and dietetics • MS
textiles, clothing, and design • MA, MS

College of Journalism and Mass Communications
Dr. Will Norton, Dean
Program in:
journalism and mass communications • MA

Teachers College
Dr. James P. O'Hanlon, Dean
Programs in:
administration, curriculum and instruction • Ed D, PhD
community and human resources • Ed D, PhD
curriculum and instruction • M Ed, MA, MST, Ed S
education • M Ed, MA, MPE, MS, MST, Ed D, PhD, Certificate, Ed S
educational administration • M Ed, MA, Ed D, Certificate
educational psychology • MA, Ed S
health, physical education, and recreation • M Ed, MPE
psychological and cultural studies • Ed D, PhD
special education • M Ed, MA

University of Nebraska–Lincoln (continued)

special education and communication disorders • Ed S
speech-language pathology and audiology • MS

■ WAYNE STATE COLLEGE

Wayne, NE 68787
http://www.wsc.edu/

State-supported, coed, comprehensive institution. CGS member. *Computer facilities:* 200 computers available on campus for general student use. A campuswide network can be accessed. *Library facilities:* U. S. Conn Library plus 1 other. *General application contact:* Dean of Graduate Studies, 402-375-7232.

Graduate School

Division of Business
Program in:
business • MBA

Division of Education
Programs in:
alternative education • MSE
art education • MSE
business education • MSE
communication arts education • MSE
consumer science education • MSE
counselor education • MSE
curriculum and instruction • MSE
education • MSE, Ed S
education technology • MSE
educational administration • Ed S
elementary administration • MSE
elementary education • MSE
English as a second language • MSE
health and physical education/health • MSE
health and physical education/pedagogy • MSE
industrial technology education • MSE
mathematics education • MSE
music education • MSE
science education • MSE
secondary administration • MSE
social science education • MSE
special education • MSE

Division of Fine Arts
Program in:
art education • MSE

Division of Humanities
Programs in:
communication arts • MSE
English education • MSE

Division of Mathematics and Science
Programs in:
mathematics education • MSE
science education • MSE

Division of Physical Education
Programs in:
coaching • MSE
exercise science • MSE
health education • MSE
sport administration/management • MSE

Division of Social Sciences
Programs in:
history • MSE
social science • MSE

Nevada

■ UNIVERSITY OF NEVADA, LAS VEGAS

Las Vegas, NV 89154-9900
http://www.unlv.edu/

State-supported, coed, university. CGS member. *Enrollment:* 1,019 full-time matriculated graduate/professional students (604 women), 1,551 part-time matriculated graduate/professional students (977 women). *Graduate faculty:* 819 full-time (241 women). *Computer facilities:* 1,100 computers available on campus for general student use. A campuswide network can be accessed from student residence rooms and from off campus. Internet access and online class registration are available. *Library facilities:* James R. Dickinson Library. *Graduate expenses:* Tuition, state resident: part-time $100 per credit. Tuition, nonresident: full-time $6,980; part-time $205 per credit. Required fees: $62; $4 per credit. $62 per semester. *General application contact:* Dr. Paul Ferguson, Dean, Graduate College, 702-895-4391.

Find an in-depth description at www.petersons.com/graduate.

Graduate College

Dr. Paul Ferguson, Dean, Graduate College

College of Business
Dr. Richard Flaherty, Dean
Programs in:
accounting • MS
business • MA, MBA, MS
business administration • MBA
economics • MA

College of Education
Dr. Gene Hall, Dean
Programs in:
assessment and evaluation techniques for the exceptional • Ed D
education • M Ed, MA, MS, Ed D, PhD, Ed S
educational administration • M Ed, Ed D, Ed S
educational computing and technology • M Ed, MS
educational psychology • M Ed, MS
emotional disturbance • Ed D
English/language arts • M Ed, MS
general elementary curriculum • M Ed, MS
general secondary education • M Ed, MS
general special education • Ed D
health promotion • M Ed
instructional and curricular studies • Ed D, PhD, Ed S
language and literacy education • M Ed, MS
learning disabilities • Ed D
library science and audiovisual education • M Ed, MS
mathematics education • M Ed, MS
mental retardation • Ed D
middle school education • M Ed, MS
postsecondary education • M Ed, MS
school psychology • Ed S
special education • M Ed, MA, MS, Ed S
teaching English as a second language • M Ed, MS
vocational education • M Ed, MS

College of Fine Arts
Dr. Jeffrey Koep, Dean
Programs in:
acting • MA
architecture • M Arch
art • MFA
composition/theory • MM
dance • MM
design and technical • MA
directing • MA
fine arts • M Arch, MA, MFA, MM
music education • MM
performance • MM
playwriting • MA
theatre arts • MFA

College of Health Sciences
Dr. Carolyn Sabo, Dean
Programs in:
acute and chronic health problems • MS
exercise physiology • MS
family nurse practitioner • MS
health physics • MS
health sciences • MS
kinesiology • MS
physical therapy • MS
terminal illness • MS

College of Liberal Arts
Dr. James Frey, Dean
Programs in:
amelioration and social policy • MA

anthropology • MA, PhD
counseling • MA
creative writing • MFA
English • PhD
English and American literature • MA
ethics and policy studies • MA
French • MA
general psychology • MA
history • MA, PhD
language studies • MA
liberal arts • MA, MFA, PhD
political science • MA
preclinical • MA
psychology • PhD
sociology • PhD
Spanish • MA
theoretical • MA
writing • MA

College of Science
Dr. Peter Starkweather, Interim Chair
Programs in:
applied mathematics • MS
biological sciences • MS
environmental analytical chemistry • MS
environmental biology • PhD
general chemistry • MS
geoscience • MS, PhD
mathematics • MS
physics • MS, PhD
pure mathematics • MS
science • MA, MS, PhD
statistics • MS
water resources management • MS

Greenspun College of Urban Affairs
Dr. Martha Watson, Dean
Programs in:
community agency counseling • MS
criminal justice • MS
environmental sciences • MS
marriage and family counseling • MS
mass communications • MA
public administration • MPA
rehabilitation counseling • MS
social work • MSW
urban affairs • MA, MPA, MS, MSW

Howard R. Hughes College of Engineering
Dr. Ron Sack, Dean
Programs in:
civil and environmental engineering • MSE, PhD
computer science • MS, PhD
electrical and computer engineering • MSE, PhD
engineering • MS, MSE, PhD
mechanical engineering • MSE, PhD

William F. Harrah College of Hotel Administration
Dr. Stuart Mann, Dean
Programs in:
hospitality administration • MHA, PhD
hotel administration • MS
leisure studies • MS

William S. Boyd School of Law
Program in:
law • JD

■ UNIVERSITY OF NEVADA, RENO

Reno, NV 89557
http://www.unr.edu/

State-supported, coed, university. CGS member. *Computer facilities:* 150 computers available on campus for general student use. A campuswide network can be accessed from student residence rooms and from off campus. *Library facilities:* Getchell Library plus 5 others. *General application contact:* Admissions and Registrar Specialist, 775-784-6869.

Graduate School

Programs in:
biochemistry • MS, PhD
cell and molecular biology • MS, PhD
ecology, evolution, and conservation biology • PhD
hydrogeology • MS, PhD
hydrology • MS, PhD
judicial studies • MJS
land use planning • MS

Center for Environmental Sciences and Engineering
Programs in:
atmospheric sciences • MS, PhD
environmental sciences and health • MS, PhD

M. C. Fleischmann College of Agriculture
Programs in:
agriculture • MS, PhD
animal science • MS
environmental and natural resource science • MS
resource and applied economics • MS

College of Arts and Science
Programs in:
anthropology • MA, PhD
arts and science • MA, MATE, MATM, MM, MPA, MS, PhD
Basque studies • PhD
biology • MS
chemical physics • PhD
chemistry • MS, PhD
English • MA, MATE, PhD
French • MA
geography • MS
German • MA
history • MA, PhD
mathematics • MS
music • MA, MM
philosophy • MA
physics • MS, PhD
political science • MA, PhD
psychology • MA, PhD
public administration • MPA
social psychology • PhD
sociology • MA
Spanish • MA
speech communication • MA
teaching English as a second language • MA
teaching mathematics • MATM

College of Business Administration
Programs in:
accounting and computer information systems • M Acc
business administration • M Acc, MA, MBA, MS
economics • MA, MS

College of Education
Programs in:
counseling and educational psychology • M Ed, MA, MS, Ed D, PhD, Ed S
curriculum and instruction • Ed D, PhD, Ed S
education • M Ed, MA, MS, Ed D, PhD, Ed S
educational leadership • M Ed, MA, MS, Ed D, PhD, Ed S
elementary education • M Ed, MA, MS
secondary education • M Ed, MA, MS
special education • M Ed, MA, MS

College of Engineering
Programs in:
chemical engineering • MS, PhD
civil engineering • MS, PhD
computer engineering • MS, PhD
computer science • MS
electrical engineering • MS, PhD
engineering • MS, PhD
mechanical engineering • MS, PhD

College of Human and Community Sciences
Programs in:
human and community sciences • MS, MSW
human development and family studies • MS
nursing • MS
nutrition • MS
physical education • MS
social work • MSW

Donald W. Reynolds School of Journalism
Program in:
journalism • MA

Mackay School of Mines
Programs in:
geochemistry • MS, PhD
geological engineering • MS, Geol E
geology • MS, PhD

University of Nevada, Reno (continued)
geophysics • MS, PhD
metallurgical engineering • MS, PhD, Met E
mines • MS, PhD, EM, Geol E, Met E
mining engineering • MS, EM

School of Medicine
Program in:
medicine • MD, MS, PhD

Graduate Programs in Medicine
Programs in:
biomedical engineering • MS, PhD
cellular and molecular pharmacology and physiology • MS, PhD
medicine • MS, PhD
speech pathology • PhD
speech pathology and audiology • MS

New Hampshire

■ ANTIOCH NEW ENGLAND GRADUATE SCHOOL

Keene, NH 03431-3516
http://www.antiochne.edu/

Independent, coed, graduate-only institution. *Graduate faculty:* 36 full-time (17 women), 89 part-time/adjunct (49 women). *Computer facilities:* 12 computers available on campus for general student use. A campuswide network can be accessed. Internet access, e-mail, intranet services are available. *Library facilities:* Antioch New England Graduate School Library. *Graduate expenses:* Tuition: full-time $14,400. *General application contact:* Robbie P. Hertneky, Director of Admissions, 603-357-6265 Ext. 287.

Find an in-depth description at www.petersons.com/graduate.

Graduate School
James H. Craiglow, President
Programs in:
clinical psychology • Psy D
conservation biology • MS
counseling psychology • MA
dance/movement therapy • M Ed, MA
education by design • M Ed
educational administration and supervision • M Ed
elementary early childhood education • M Ed
environmental education • MS
environmental studies • MS, PhD
experienced educators • M Ed
human services administration • MHSA
integrated learning • M Ed
interdisciplinary studies • MA
management • MS
marriage and family therapy • MA
professional development • M Ed
resource management and administration • MS
science and environmental education • M Ed
substance abuse counseling • M Ed
substance abuse/addictions counseling • M Ed, MA
teacher certification in biology (7th-12th grade) • MS
teacher certification in general science (5th-9th grade) • MS
Waldorf teacher training • M Ed

■ DARTMOUTH COLLEGE

Hanover, NH 03755
http://www.dartmouth.edu/

Independent, coed, university. CGS member. *Enrollment:* 1,287 full-time matriculated graduate/professional students (520 women), 71 part-time matriculated graduate/professional students (44 women). *Graduate faculty:* 336 full-time (108 women), 716 part-time/adjunct. *Computer facilities:* 12,000 computers available on campus for general student use. A campuswide network can be accessed from student residence rooms and from off campus. Internet access and online class registration are available. *Library facilities:* Baker-Berry Library plus 10 others. *Graduate expenses:* Tuition: full-time $25,497. *General application contact:* Gary L. Hutchins, Assistant Dean of Graduate Studies, 603-646-2107.

Find an in-depth description at www.petersons.com/graduate.

Dartmouth Medical School
Program in:
medicine • MD

School of Arts and Sciences
Dr. Roger D. Sloboda, Dean
Programs in:
arts and sciences • AM, MALS, MS, PhD
biochemistry • PhD
biology • PhD
chemistry • PhD
cognitive neuroscience • PhD
comparative literature • AM
computer science • MS, PhD
earth sciences • MS, PhD
electro-acoustic music • AM
evaluative clinical sciences • MS, PhD
genetics • PhD
liberal studies • MALS
mathematics • PhD
pharmacology and toxicology • PhD
physics and astronomy • MS, PhD
physiology • PhD
psychology • PhD

Thayer School of Engineering
Dr. Lewis M. Duncan, Dean
Programs in:
biomedical engineering • MS, PhD
biotechnology and biochemical engineering • MS, PhD
computer engineering • MS, PhD
electrical engineering • MS, PhD
engineering • MEM, MS, PhD
engineering management • MEM
environmental engineering • MS, PhD
materials sciences and engineering • MS, PhD
mechanical engineering • MS, PhD

Tuck School of Business at Dartmouth
Paul Danos, Dean
Program in:
business • MBA

■ KEENE STATE COLLEGE

Keene, NH 03435
http://www.keene.edu/

State-supported, coed, comprehensive institution. *Enrollment:* 29 full-time matriculated graduate/professional students (18 women), 74 part-time matriculated graduate/professional students (54 women). *Graduate faculty:* 21 full-time, 15 part-time/adjunct. *Computer facilities:* 285 computers available on campus for general student use. A campuswide network can be accessed from student residence rooms and from off campus. Internet access, e-mail, personal web pages are available. *Library facilities:* Mason Library. *Graduate expenses:* Tuition, state resident: full-time $4,060; part-time $190 per credit. Tuition, nonresident: full-time $9,370; part-time $225 per credit. Required fees: $1,244; $28 per credit. *General application contact:* Peggy Richmond, Assistant Director of Admissions, 603-358-2276.

Division of Graduate and Professional Studies
Dr. David Hill, Acting Dean
Programs in:
- curriculum and instruction • M Ed
- educational administration • M Ed
- educational leadership • PMC
- school counselor • M Ed, PMC
- special education • M Ed, PMC

■ NOTRE DAME COLLEGE
Manchester, NH 03104-2299
http://www.notredame.edu/

Independent-religious, coed, comprehensive institution. *Computer facilities:* 22 computers available on campus for general student use. Internet access is available. *Library facilities:* Harvey Library. *General application contact:* Director, Office of Graduate Admissions and Continuing Education, 603-669-4298 Ext. 171.

■ PLYMOUTH STATE COLLEGE
Plymouth, NH 03264-1595
http://www.plymouth.edu/

State-supported, coed, comprehensive institution. *Enrollment:* 60 full-time matriculated graduate/professional students (47 women), 183 part-time matriculated graduate/professional students (135 women). *Graduate faculty:* 100 full-time (48 women), 101 part-time/adjunct (53 women). *Computer facilities:* 500 computers available on campus for general student use. A campuswide network can be accessed from student residence rooms and from off campus. Internet access and online class registration are available. *Library facilities:* Lamson Library. *Graduate expenses:* Tuition, state resident: part-time $247 per credit. Tuition, nonresident: part-time $272 per credit. Required fees: $15 per credit. *General application contact:* Maryann Szabadics, Administrative Secretary, 603-535-2636.

Graduate Studies
Programs in:
- athletic training • M Ed
- business • MBA
- counselor education • M Ed
- educational leadership • M Ed
- elementary and secondary education • M Ed
- elementary education (teacher certification K–8) • M Ed
- elementary education (teacher certification N–3) • M Ed
- English education • M Ed
- health education • M Ed
- mathematics education • M Ed
- reading and writing specialist • M Ed
- secondary education (teacher certification 7–12, K–12, 5–8) • M Ed

■ RIVIER COLLEGE
Nashua, NH 03060-5086
http://www.rivier.edu/

Independent-religious, coed, comprehensive institution. *Enrollment:* 125 full-time matriculated graduate/professional students (89 women), 478 part-time matriculated graduate/professional students (341 women). *Graduate faculty:* 28 full-time (16 women), 43 part-time/adjunct (20 women). *Computer facilities:* 93 computers available on campus for general student use. A campuswide network can be accessed from student residence rooms and from off campus. *Library facilities:* Regina Library plus 1 other. *Graduate expenses:* Tuition: part-time $324 per credit. *General application contact:* Ann McCormick, Director of Graduate Admissions, 603-897-8229.

Find an in-depth description at www.petersons.com/graduate.

School of Graduate Studies
Dr. Albert Johnson, Dean
Programs in:
- arts and sciences • M Ed, MA, MAT, MBA, MS, CAGS
- business administration • MBA
- computer information systems • MS
- computer science • MS
- counseling and psychotherapy • MA
- counselor education • M Ed
- early childhood education • M Ed
- educational administration • M Ed
- elementary education • M Ed
- English • MA, MAT
- French • MAT
- general education • M Ed
- health care administration • MBA
- human resources management • MS
- information science • MS
- learning disabilities • M Ed
- modern languages • MAT
- nursing and health sciences • MS
- professional development • MS
- reading • M Ed
- secondary education • M Ed
- Spanish • MAT
- writing and literature • MA

■ UNIVERSITY OF NEW HAMPSHIRE
Durham, NH 03824
http://www.unh.edu/

State-supported, coed, university. CGS member. *Enrollment:* 914 full-time matriculated graduate/professional students (528 women), 1,164 part-time matriculated graduate/professional students (670 women). *Graduate faculty:* 602 full-time. *Computer facilities:* 380 computers available on campus for general student use. A campuswide network can be accessed from student residence rooms and from off campus. Internet access and online class registration are available. *Library facilities:* Dimond Library plus 4 others. *Graduate expenses:* Full-time $6,070; part-time $337 per credit. Tuition, state resident: full-time $9,105; part-time $505 per credit. Tuition, nonresident: full-time $15,140; part-time $618 per credit. Required fees: $253 per semester. *General application contact:* Graduate Admissions Office, 603-862-3000.

Find an in-depth description at www.petersons.com/graduate.

Graduate School
Dr. Harry J. Richards, Associate Dean
Programs in:
- college teaching • MST
- environmental education • MS

College of Engineering and Physical Sciences
Dr. Arthur Greenberg, Dean
Programs in:
- applied mathematics • MS
- chemical engineering • MS, PhD
- chemistry • MS, MST, PhD
- civil engineering • MS, PhD
- computer science • MS, PhD
- earth sciences • MS, PhD
- electrical engineering • MS, PhD
- engineering and physical sciences • MS, MST, PhD
- hydrology • MS
- materials science • MS
- mathematics • MS, MST, PhD
- mathematics education • PhD
- mechanical engineering • MS, PhD
- ocean engineering • MS, PhD
- ocean mapping • MS
- physics • MS, PhD
- statistics • MS
- systems design and engineering • PhD

College of Liberal Arts
Dr. Marilyn Hoskin, Dean
Programs in:

University of New Hampshire (continued)
- adult and occupational education • MAOE
- counseling • M Ed, MA
- early childhood education • M Ed
- education • PhD
- educational administration • M Ed, CAGS
- elementary education • M Ed, MAT
- English • PhD
- English education • MST
- history • MA, PhD
- language and linguistics • MA
- liberal arts • M Ed, MA, MALS, MAOE, MAT, MFA, MPA, MS, MST, PhD, CAGS
- liberal studies • MALS
- literacy and schooling • PhD
- literature • MA
- museum studies • MA
- music education • MA
- music history • MA
- painting • MFA
- political science • MA
- psychology • PhD
- public administration • MPA
- reading • M Ed
- secondary education • M Ed, MAT
- sociology • MA, PhD
- Spanish • MA
- special education • M Ed
- teacher leadership • M Ed
- writing • MA

College of Life Sciences and Agriculture
Dr. Andrew Rosenberg, Dean
Programs in:
- animal and nutritional science • PhD
- animal and nutritional sciences • MS, PhD
- animal science • MS
- biochemistry and molecular biology • MS, PhD
- environmental conservation • MS
- forestry • MS
- genetics • MS, PhD
- life sciences and agriculture • MS, PhD
- microbiology • MS, PhD
- natural resources • MS, PhD
- nutritional sciences • MS
- plant biology • MS, PhD
- resource administration • MS
- resource economics • MS
- soil science • MS
- water resources management • MS
- wildlife • MS
- zoology • MS, PhD

School of Health and Human Services
Dr. James McCarthy, Dean
Programs in:
- communication sciences and disorders • MS, MST
- family studies • MS
- health and human services • MHA, MS, MST, MSW
- health management and policy • MHA
- kinesiology • MS
- marriage and family therapy • MS
- nursing • MS
- occupational therapy • MS
- social work • MSW

Whittemore School of Business and Economics
Dr. Steve Bolander, Dean
Programs in:
- accounting • MS
- business administration • MBA
- business and economics • MA, MBA, MS, PhD
- economics • MA, PhD

New Jersey

■ THE COLLEGE OF NEW JERSEY
Ewing, NJ 08628
http://www.tcnj.edu/

State-supported, coed, comprehensive institution. CGS member. *Enrollment:* 97 full-time matriculated graduate/professional students (85 women), 599 part-time matriculated graduate/professional students (491 women). *Graduate faculty:* 41 full-time, 12 part-time/adjunct. *Computer facilities:* 800 computers available on campus for general student use. A campuswide network can be accessed from student residence rooms and from off campus. Internet access and online class registration are available. *Library facilities:* Roscoe L. West Library. *Graduate expenses:* Tuition, state resident: full-time $5,777. Tuition, nonresident: full-time $8,086. Required fees: $710. *General application contact:* Frank Cooper, Director, Office of Graduate Studies, 609-771-2300.

Find an in-depth description at www.petersons.com/graduate.

Graduate Division
Dr. Suzanne Pasch, Dean

School of Arts and Sciences
Dr. Carlos Alvez, Associate Dean
Programs in:
- arts and sciences • MA
- English • MA

School of Education
Dr. Suzanne Pasch, Dean
Programs in:
- alcohol and chemical dependency counseling • Certificate
- audiology • MA
- community counseling • MA
- developmental reading • M Ed
- education • M Ed, MA, MAT, MS, Certificate, Ed S
- educational leadership • M Ed
- educational technology • MS
- elementary education • M Ed, MAT
- elementary teaching • MAT
- English as a second language • M Ed, Certificate
- health • MAT
- health and physical education • M Ed
- health education • M Ed, MAT
- instructional computing coordinator • Certificate
- marriage and family therapy • Ed S
- physical education • M Ed
- school counseling • MA
- secondary education • MAT
- special education • M Ed, MAT
- special education with learning disabilities • M Ed
- speech pathology • MA
- teaching English as a second language • Certificate

School of Nursing
Dr. Laurie N. Sherwen, Dean
Program in:
- nursing • MSN

■ FAIRLEIGH DICKINSON UNIVERSITY, FLORHAM-MADISON CAMPUS
Madison, NJ 07940-1099
http://www.fdu.edu/

Independent, coed, comprehensive institution. *Enrollment:* 143 full-time matriculated graduate/professional students (89 women), 589 part-time matriculated graduate/professional students (346 women). *Graduate faculty:* 62 full-time (7 women), 84 part-time/adjunct (12 women). *Computer facilities:* 300 computers available on campus for general student use. A campuswide network can be accessed from student residence rooms and from off campus. *Library facilities:* Friendship Library plus 1 other. *Graduate expenses:* Tuition: full-time $10,746; part-time $597 per credit. Required fees: $280. One-time fee: $130 part-time. *General application contact:* Susan St. Onge, Associate Director of Adult and Graduate Admissions, 973-443-8905.

Find an in-depth description at www.petersons.com/graduate.

Maxwell Becton College of Arts and Sciences
Dr. Barbara Salmore, Dean
Programs in:
- applied social and community psychology • MA
- arts and sciences • MA, MS
- biology • MS
- chemistry • MS
- clinical counseling • MA
- corporate and organizational communication • MA
- general experimental psychology • MA
- industrial/organizational psychology • MA
- organizational behavior • MA

New College of General and Continuing Studies
Kenneth T. Verhkens, Dean

School of Hotel, Restaurant and Tourism Management
Richard Wisch, Director
Program in:
- hospitality management studies • MS

Samuel J. Silberman College of Business Administration
Dr. Paul Lerman, Dean
Programs in:
- accounting • MS
- accounting for non-accountants • MBA
- business administration • MBA, MS
- entrepreneurial studies • MBA
- finance • MBA
- global management • MBA
- human resource management • MBA
- industrial and operations management • MBA
- information systems • MBA
- international business • MBA
- management • MBA
- management for executives • MBA
- management for health systems executives • MBA
- marketing • MBA
- pharmaceutical-chemical studies • MBA
- taxation • MS

George Rothman Institute of Entrepreneurial Studies
Leo Rogers, Director
Program in:
- entrepreneurial studies • MBA

■ FAIRLEIGH DICKINSON UNIVERSITY, TEANECK–HACKENSACK CAMPUS

Teaneck, NJ 07666-1914

http://www.fdu.edu/

Independent, coed, comprehensive institution. *Enrollment:* 593 full-time matriculated graduate/professional students (255 women), 1,150 part-time matriculated graduate/professional students (708 women). *Graduate faculty:* 148 full-time, 185 part-time/adjunct. *Computer facilities:* 210 computers available on campus for general student use. A campuswide network can be accessed from student residence rooms and from off campus. *Library facilities:* Weiner Library plus 2 others. *Graduate expenses:* Tuition: full-time $10,746; part-time $597 per credit. Required fees: $280. One-time fee: $130 part-time. Full-time tuition and fees vary according to degree level. *General application contact:* Andrew G. Nelson, Director of Adult and Graduate Admissions, 800-338-8803.

Find an in-depth description at www.petersons.com/graduate.

New College of General and Continuing Studies
Kenneth T. Vehrkeus, Dean

Public Administration Institutite
Dr. William Roberts, Director
Programs in:
- administrative science • MAS
- public administration • MPA

School of Hotel, Restaurant and Tourism Management
Richard Wisch, Director
Programs in:
- hospitality management • MS
- hospitality management studies • MS

Samuel J. Silberman College of Business Administration
Dr. Paul Lerman, Dean
Programs in:
- accounting • MS
- accounting for non-accountants • MBA
- business administration • MBA, MS
- entrepreneurial studies • MBA
- finance • MBA
- global management • MBA
- human resource management • MBA
- industrial and operations management • MBA
- information systems • MBA
- international business • MBA
- management • MBA
- management for executives • MBA
- management for health systems executives • MBA
- marketing • MBA
- pharmaceutical-chemical studies • MBA
- quantitative business analysis • MBA
- taxation • MS

George Rothman Institute of Entrepreneurial Studies
Leo Rogers, Director
Program in:
- entrepreneurial studies • MBA

University College: Arts, Sciences, and Professional Studies
Prof. Michael B. Sperling, Acting Dean
Programs in:
- arts, sciences, and professional studies • MA, MAS, MAT, MPA, MS, MSEE, MSN, PhD, Psy D
- systems science • MS

Henry P. Becton School of Nursing and Allied Health
Dr. minerva Guttman, Director
Programs in:
- medical technology • MS
- nursing • MSN

Peter Sammartino School of Education
Dr. Eloise Forster, Director
Programs in:
- education • MA, MAT
- education for certified teachers • MA
- educational leadership • MA
- learning disabilities • MA
- multilingual education • MA
- teaching • MAT

School of Communication Arts
Dr. Duane Edwards, Director
Program in:
- English and comparative literature • MA

School of Computer Science and Information Systems
Gertrude Levine, Director
Programs in:
- computer science • MS
- e-commerce • MS
- management information systems • MS

School of Engineering and Engineering Technology
Dr. Alfredo Tan, Director
Program in:
- electrical engineering • MSEE

School of Natural Sciences
Irwin R. Isquith, Director
Programs in:
- biology • MS
- science • MA

Fairleigh Dickinson University, Teaneck–Hackensack Campus (continued)

School of Political and International Studies
Prof. Faramarz Fatemi, Director
Programs in:
history • MA
international studies • MA
political science • MA

School of Psychology
Dr. Christopher Capuano, Director
Programs in:
clinical psychology • MA, PhD
general-theoretical psychology • MA
school psychology • MA, Psy D

■ GEORGIAN COURT COLLEGE

Lakewood, NJ 08701-2697
http://www.georgian.edu/

Independent-religious, women only, comprehensive institution. *Enrollment:* 54 full-time matriculated graduate/professional students (43 women), 439 part-time matriculated graduate/professional students (357 women). *Graduate faculty:* 9 full-time (5 women), 31 part-time/adjunct (16 women). *Computer facilities:* 131 computers available on campus for general student use. A campuswide network can be accessed from student residence rooms. Internet access, intranet are available. *Library facilities:* Georgian Court College Library. *Graduate expenses:* Tuition: full-time $7,092; part-time $394 per credit. Required fees: $350; $70 per year. Tuition and fees vary according to course load. *General application contact:* Marjorie Cooke, Dean of Admissions and Enrollment Services, 732-364-2200 Ext. 760.

Graduate School
Dr. Rita J. Carney, Vice President for Academic and Student Affairs
Programs in:
administration, supervision and curriculum planning (management specialization) • MA
administration, supervision, and curriculum planning • MA
biology • MS
business administration • MBA
counseling psychology • MA
instructional technology • MA
mathematics • MA
reading specialization • MA
special education • MA
teaching certificate • MA
theology • MA

■ KEAN UNIVERSITY

Union, NJ 07083
http://www.kean.edu/

State-supported, coed, comprehensive institution. CGS member. *Computer facilities:* 600 computers available on campus for general student use. A campuswide network can be accessed from student residence rooms and from off campus. Internet access and online class registration are available. *Library facilities:* Nancy Thompson Library plus 1 other. *General application contact:* Director of Graduate Admissions, 908-527-2665.

Find an in-depth description at www.petersons.com/graduate.

School of Business, Government, and Technology
Programs in:
business, government, and technology • MPA, MSMSA
health services administration • MPA
management systems analysis • MSMSA
public administration • MPA

School of Education
Programs in:
administration in early childhood and family studies • MA
advanced curriculum and teaching • MA
alcohol and drug abuse counseling • MA
bilingual education • Certificate
bilingual/bicultural education • MA
business and industry counseling • MA, PMC
classroom instruction • MA
community/agency counseling • MA
counselor education • MA, PMC
developmental disabilities • MA
earth science • MA
education • MA, Certificate, PMC
education for family living • MA
educational administration • MA, Certificate
emotionally disturbed and socially maladjusted • MA
English as a second language • Certificate
instruction and curriculum • MA, Certificate
learning disabilities • MA
mathematics/science/computer education • MA
pre-school handicapped • MA
reading specialization • MA
school counseling • MA
special education • MA
speech pathology • MA
teaching • MA
teaching English as a second language • MA
teaching of reading • Certificate

School of Liberal Arts
Programs in:
behavioral sciences • MA
business and industry counseling • PMC
educational psychology • MA
fine arts education • MA
liberal arts • MA, MSW, Diploma, PMC
liberal studies • MA
marriage and family therapy • Diploma
school psychology • Diploma
social work • MSW

School of Natural Sciences, Mathematics, and Nursing
Programs in:
computing, statistics and mathematics • MS
mathematics education • MA
natural sciences, mathematics, and nursing • MA, MS, MSN
nursing • MSN
occupational therapy • MS

■ MONMOUTH UNIVERSITY

West Long Branch, NJ 07764-1898
http://www.monmouth.edu/

Independent, coed, comprehensive institution. *Enrollment:* 355 full-time matriculated graduate/professional students (245 women), 1,087 part-time matriculated graduate/professional students (694 women). *Graduate faculty:* 56 full-time (18 women), 40 part-time/adjunct (17 women). *Computer facilities:* 400 computers available on campus for general student use. A campuswide network can be accessed from student residence rooms and from off campus. *Library facilities:* Murry and Leonie Guggenheim Memorial Library. *Graduate expenses:* Tuition: full-time $8,982; part-time $499 per credit. Required fees: $568; $142 per semester. *General application contact:* Charles Dresser, Director, Office of Graduate Admissions, 732-571-3452.

Find an in-depth description at www.petersons.com/graduate.

Graduate School
Dr. Datta V. Naik, Dean
Programs in:
community and international development • MSW
computer science • MS
corporate and public communication • MA

criminal justice administration • MA, Certificate
history • MA
human resources communication • Certificate
liberal arts • MA
media studies • Certificate
practice with families and children • MSW
professional counseling • PMC
psychological counseling • MA
public relations • Certificate
software development • Certificate
software engineering • MS, Certificate

The Marjorie K. Unterberg School of Nursing and Health Studies
Dr. Janet Mahoney, Director
Programs in:
advanced practice nursing • MSN, Certificate
nursing • MSN
school nursing • Certificate
substance awareness coordinator • Certificate

School of Business Administration
Dr. Catherine Bianchi, Dean
Programs in:
accounting • MBA
business administration • MBA
health care management • MBA
healthcare management • Certificate

School of Education
Dr. Bernice Willis, Dean
Programs in:
educational counseling • MS Ed
elementary education • MAT
learning disabilities-teacher consultant • Certificate
principal studies • MS Ed
reading specialist • MS Ed, Certificate
special education • MS Ed
supervisor • Certificate
teacher of the handicapped • Certificate

■ MONTCLAIR STATE UNIVERSITY
Upper Montclair, NJ 07043-1624
http://www.montclair.edu/

State-supported, coed, comprehensive institution. CGS member. *Enrollment:* 497 full-time matriculated graduate/professional students (358 women), 1,652 part-time matriculated graduate/professional students (1,338 women). *Graduate faculty:* 395 full-time, 392 part-time/adjunct. *Computer facilities:* 650 computers available on campus for general student use. A campuswide network can be accessed from student residence rooms and from off campus. Internet access is available. *Library facilities:* Sprague Library. *Graduate expenses:* Tuition, state resident: part-time $237 per credit. Tuition, nonresident: part-time $325 per credit. Required fees: $29 per credit. One-time fee: $35 part-time. Tuition and fees vary according to course load, degree level and program. *General application contact:* Dr. Carla M. Narrett, Dean of the Graduate School, 973-655-5147.

Find an in-depth description at www.petersons.com/graduate.

The School of Graduate, Professional and Continuing Education
Dr. Carla M. Narrett, Dean of the Graduate School

College of Education and Human Services
Dr. Ada Beth Cutler, Dean
Programs in:
administration and supervision • MA
art • MAT
biological science • MAT
business education • MAT
coaching and sports administration • MA
counseling and guidance • MA
critical thinking • M Ed
curriculum and teaching • M Ed, MA, MAT, Ed D
early childhood education • MAT
early childhood special education • MA
earth science • MAT
education • M Ed, Ed D
education and human services • M Ed, MA, MAT, Ed D
educator/trainer • MA
English • MAT
exercise science • MA
family life education • MA
family relations/child development • MA
French • MAT
health and physical education • MAT
health education • MA, MAT
home economics • MAT
home economics education • MA
home management/consumer economics • MA
human services • MA
industrial arts • MAT
learning disabilities • MA
mathematics • MAT
mathematics education • Ed D
music • MAT
nutrition education • MA
philosophy for children • M Ed, Ed D
physical education • MA, MAT
physical science • MAT
reading • MA
social studies • MAT
Spanish • MAT
teacher of ESL • MAT
teacher of handicapped • MAT
teaching • MAT
teaching and administration of physical education • MA
teaching middle school philosophy • MAT
technology education • MA

College of Humanities and Social Sciences
Dr. Richard Gigliotti, Dean
Programs in:
anthropology • MA
applied linguistics • MA
applied sociology • MA
child advocacy • Certificate
child/adolescent clinical psychology • MA
clinical psychology for Spanish/English bilinguals • MA
dispute resolution • MA
economics • MA
educational psychology • MA
English • MA
French • MA
history • MA
humanities and social sciences • MA, Certificate
industrial and organizational psychology • MA
law office management and technology • MA
legal studies • MA
paralegal • Certificate
practical anthropology • MA
psychology • MA
Spanish • MA
speech/language pathology • MA

College of Science and Mathematics
Dr. Robert Prezant, Dean
Programs in:
applied mathematics • MS
applied statistics • MS
biology science education • MS
chemistry • MS
computer science • MS
environmental studies • MS
geoscience • MS, Certificate
informatics • MS
mathematics • MS
mathematics education • MS
molecular biology • Certificate
object oriented computing • Certificate
pure and applied mathematics • MS
science and mathematics • MS, Certificate
statistics • MS
water resource management • Certificate

School of Business
Dr. Alan Oppenheim, Dean
Programs in:

Montclair State University (continued)
accounting • MBA
business • MA, MBA
business economics • MBA
business education • MA
economics • MA
finance • MBA
international business • MBA
management • MBA
management information systems • MBA
marketing • MBA
social science • MA

School of the Arts
Dr. Geoffrey Newman, Dean
Programs in:
art history • MA
arts • MA, MFA
communication arts • MA
music education • MA
music therapy • MA
performance • MA
studio arts • MA, MFA
theatre • MA
theory/composition • MA

■ NEW JERSEY CITY UNIVERSITY
Jersey City, NJ 07305-1597
http://www.njcu.edu/core.htm

State-supported, coed, comprehensive institution. *Enrollment:* 55 full-time matriculated graduate/professional students (39 women), 1,236 part-time matriculated graduate/professional students (921 women). *Graduate faculty:* 51 full-time (19 women), 10 part-time/adjunct (4 women). *Computer facilities:* 1,400 computers available on campus for general student use. *Library facilities:* Congressman Frank J. Guarini Library. *Graduate expenses:* Tuition, state resident: part-time $253 per credit. Tuition, nonresident: part-time $414 per credit. *General application contact:* Dr. Peter J. Donnelly, Director of Graduate Studies and Special Programs, 201-200-3409.

Graduate Studies
Dr. Peter J. Donnelly, Director

College of Arts and Sciences
Dr. Ansley W. Lamar, Dean
Programs in:
art • MA
art education • MA
arts and sciences • MA, PD
counseling • MA
educational psychology • MA, PD
mathematics education • MA
music education • MA
school psychology • PD

College of Education
Dr. Yiping Wan, Dean
Programs in:
administration, curriculum and instruction • MA
basics and urban studies • MA
bilingual/bicultural education and English as a second language • MA
early childhood education • MA
education • MA
educational technology • MA
literary education • MA
special education • MA
urban education • MA

College of Professional Studies
Dr. Sandra Bloomberg, Dean
Programs in:
accounting • MS
community health education • MS
criminal justice • MS
health administration • MS
holistic medicine • MS
professional studies • MA, MS, Certificate
urban medicine • MS

■ NEW JERSEY INSTITUTE OF TECHNOLOGY
Newark, NJ 07102-1982
http://www.njit.edu/

State-supported, coed, university. CGS member. *Enrollment:* 1,220 full-time matriculated graduate/professional students (357 women), 1,963 part-time matriculated graduate/professional students (531 women). *Graduate faculty:* 404 full-time (72 women), 223 part-time/adjunct (52 women). *Computer facilities:* 4,500 computers available on campus for general student use. A campuswide network can be accessed from student residence rooms and from off campus. *Library facilities:* Van Houten Library plus 1 other. *Graduate expenses:* Tuition, state resident: part-time $406 per credit. Tuition, nonresident: part-time $558 per credit. Required fees: $41 per credit. $76 per semester. *General application contact:* Kathy Kelly, Director of Admissions, 973-596-3300.

Office of Graduate Studies
Dr. Ron Kane, Dean of Graduate Studies
Programs in:
applied chemistry • MS, PhD
applied mathematics • MS
applied physics • MS, PhD
applied science • MS
bioinformatics • MS, PhD
biology • MS, PhD
biomedical engineering • MS
chemical engineering • MS, PhD, Engineer
chemistry • PhD
civil engineering • MS, PhD, Engineer
computational biology • MS
computer and information science • PhD
computer engineering • MS
computer science • MS
electrical engineering • MS, PhD, Engineer
engineering management • MS
engineering science • MS
environmental engineering • MS, PhD
environmental policy studies • MS
environmental science • MS, PhD
history • MA, MAT
history of technology, environment and medicine • MA
industrial engineering • MS, PhD
information systems • MS
materials science and engineering • MS, PhD
mathematical science • PhD
mechanical engineering • MS, PhD, Engineer
occupational safety and health engineering • MS
power engineering • MS
professional and technical communication • MS
telecommunications • MS
transportation • MS, PhD

School of Architecture
Urs Gauchat, Dean
Programs in:
architectural studies • MS
architecture • M Arch
infrastructure planning • MIP

School of Management
Mark Sommers, Acting Dean
Programs in:
e-commerce • MBA
management • MS, PhD
management information systems • MBA
management of technology • MBA
manufacturing • MBA
transportation • MBA

■ PRINCETON UNIVERSITY
Princeton, NJ 08544-1019
http://www.princeton.edu/

Independent, coed, university. CGS member. *Computer facilities:* 500 computers available on campus for general student use. A campuswide network can be accessed from student residence rooms and from off campus. *Library facilities:* Harvey S. Firestone Memorial

Library plus 22 others. *General application contact:* Director of Graduate Admission, 609-258-3034.

Graduate School

Programs in:
- African-American studies • PhD
- ancient history • PhD
- ancient Near Eastern studies • PhD
- anthropology • PhD
- applied and computational mathematics • PhD
- archaeology • PhD
- astrophysical sciences • PhD
- atmospheric and oceanic sciences • PhD
- biology • PhD
- cell biology • PhD
- chemistry • PhD
- Chinese and Japanese art and archaeology • PhD
- classical archaeology • PhD
- classical philosophy • PhD
- community college history teaching • PhD
- comparative literature • PhD
- composition • PhD
- demography • PhD, Certificate
- demography and public affairs • PhD
- developmental biology • PhD
- East Asian civilizations • PhD
- East Asian studies • PhD
- economics • PhD
- economics and demography • PhD
- English • PhD
- environmental engineering and water resources • PhD
- French • PhD
- geological and geophysical sciences • PhD
- Germanic languages and literatures • PhD
- history • PhD
- history of science • PhD
- history, archaeology and religions of the ancient world • PhD
- industrial chemistry • MS
- Islamic studies • PhD
- Latin American studies • PhD
- mathematical physics • PhD
- mathematics • PhD
- modern Near Eastern studies • MA
- molecular biology • PhD
- molecular biophysics • PhD
- musicology • PhD
- neuroscience • PhD
- philosophy • PhD
- physics • PhD
- physics and chemical physics • PhD
- plasma physics • PhD
- political philosophy • PhD
- politics • PhD
- polymer sciences and materials • MSE, PhD
- psychology • PhD
- religion • PhD
- Slavic languages and literatures • PhD
- sociology • PhD
- sociology and demography • PhD
- Spanish • PhD

School of Architecture

Program in:
- architecture • M Arch, PhD

School of Engineering and Applied Science

Programs in:
- applied and computational mathematics • PhD
- applied physics • M Eng, MSE, PhD
- chemical engineering • M Eng, MSE, PhD
- computational methods • M Eng, MSE
- computer engineering • PhD
- computer science • M Eng, MSE, PhD
- dynamics and control systems • M Eng, MSE, PhD
- electrical engineering • M Eng
- electronic materials and devices • PhD
- energy and environmental policy • M Eng, MSE, PhD
- energy conversion, propulsion, and combustion • M Eng, MSE, PhD
- engineering and applied science • M Eng, MSE, PhD
- environmental engineering and water resources • PhD
- financial engineering • M Eng
- flight science and technology • M Eng, MSE, PhD
- fluid mechanics • M Eng, MSE, PhD
- information sciences and systems • PhD
- mechanics, materials, and structures • M Eng, MSE, PhD
- operations research and financial engineering • MSE, PhD
- optoelectronics • PhD
- plasma science and technology • MSE, PhD
- polymer sciences and materials • MSE, PhD
- statistics and operations research • MSE, PhD
- transportation systems • MSE, PhD

Woodrow Wilson School of Public and International Affairs

Programs in:
- public affairs • MPA, MPA-URP, PhD
- public affairs and urban and regional planning • MPA-URP, PhD
- public and international affairs • MPA, MPA-URP, MPP, PhD

■ RIDER UNIVERSITY

Lawrenceville, NJ 08648-3001
http://www.rider.edu/

Independent, coed, comprehensive institution. *Enrollment:* 209 full-time matriculated graduate/professional students (136 women), 887 part-time matriculated graduate/professional students (590 women). *Graduate faculty:* 75 full-time, 63 part-time/adjunct. *Computer facilities:* 403 computers available on campus for general student use. A campuswide network can be accessed from student residence rooms and from off campus. Internet access is available. *Library facilities:* Franklin F. Moore Library plus 1 other. *Graduate expenses:* Tuition: part-time $470 per credit. Required fees: $15 per course. *General application contact:* Dr. John H. Carpenter, Dean, Continuing Studies, 609-896-5036.

College of Business Administration

Thomas Charles Kelly, Associate Dean

Programs in:
- accountancy • M Acc
- business administration • M Acc, MBA

School of Graduate Education and Human Services

Dr. Jesse DeEsch, Assistant Dean

Programs in:
- business education • Certificate
- counseling services • MA, Ed S
- curriculum, instruction and supervision • MA
- educational administration • MA
- elementary education • Certificate
- English education • Certificate
- foreign language education • Certificate
- graduate education and human services • MA, Certificate, Ed S
- human services administration • MA
- mathematics education • Certificate
- reading/language arts • MA
- science education • Certificate
- social studies education • Certificate

Westminster Choir College of Rider University

Dr. James Goldsworthy, Associate Dean

Programs in:
- choral conducting • MM
- composition • MM
- music education • MM, MME
- organ performance • MM
- piano accompanying and coaching • MM

Rider University (continued)
piano pedagogy and performance • MM
sacred music • MM
vocal pedagogy and performance • MM

■ ROWAN UNIVERSITY

Glassboro, NJ 08028-1701
http://www.rowan.edu/

State-supported, coed, comprehensive institution. CGS member. *Enrollment:* 155 full-time matriculated graduate/ professional students (109 women), 570 part-time matriculated graduate/ professional students (437 women). *Graduate faculty:* 84 full-time (30 women), 20 part-time/adjunct (5 women). *Computer facilities:* 350 computers available on campus for general student use. A campuswide network can be accessed from student residence rooms and from off campus. Internet access is available. *Library facilities:* Keith and Shirley Campbell Library plus 2 others. *Graduate expenses:* Tuition, state resident: full-time $7,315; part-time $311 per credit. Tuition, nonresident: full-time $11,227; part-time $474 per credit. Required fees: $36 per credit. *General application contact:* Dr. Jay Kuder, Dean, Graduate Studies, 856-256-4050.

Find an in-depth description at www.petersons.com/graduate.

Graduate Studies
Dr. Jay Kuder, Dean
Programs in:
fine and performing arts • MA, MM
music • MM
theatre • MA

College of Business
Dr. Edward Schoen, Dean
Programs in:
business • MBA
business administration • MBA

College of Communication
Dr. Antoinette Libro, Dean
Programs in:
college writing • MA
public relations • MA

College of Education
Dr. Burton Siseo, Dean
Programs in:
administration and supervision in health and physical education or athletics • MA
art education • MA
biological science education • MA
education • MA, MST, Ed D, Ed S
educational leadership • Ed D
elementary education • MA, MST
higher education administration • MA
learning disabilities • MA
mathematics education • MA
music education • MA
physical science education • MA
reading education • MA
school administration • MA
school administration-business administration • MA
school and public librarianship • MA
school psychology • MA, Ed S
science education • MA
special education • MA, MST
student personnel services • MA
subject matter teaching • MA
supervision and curriculum development • MA
teaching-secondary • MST

College of Engineering
Dr. James Tracey, Dean
Program in:
engineering • MS

College of Fine and Performing Arts
Dr. Donald Gephardt, Dean
Programs in:
fine and performing arts • MA, MM
music • MM
theatre • MA

College of Liberal Arts and Sciences
Dr. Jay Harper, Dean
Programs in:
applied psychology • MA
environmental education • MA
liberal arts and sciences • MA
mathematics • MA

■ RUTGERS, THE STATE UNIVERSITY OF NEW JERSEY, CAMDEN

Camden, NJ 08102-1401
http://camden-www.rutgers.edu/

State-supported, coed, university. *Enrollment:* 722 full-time matriculated graduate/ professional students (352 women), 599 part-time matriculated graduate/ professional students (298 women). *Graduate faculty:* 230 full-time (74 women), 146 part-time/adjunct (56 women). *Computer facilities:* 184 computers available on campus for general student use. A campuswide network can be accessed from student residence rooms and from off campus. Internet access, online grade reports are available. *Library facilities:* Paul Robeson Library plus 2 others. *Graduate expenses:* Tuition, state resident: full-time $7,116; part-time $293 per credit. Tuition, nonresident: full-time $10,434; part-time $433 per credit. Required fees: $993; $431 per term. *General application contact:* Dr. Deborah B. Bowles, Director of Admissions, 856-225-6056.

Find an in-depth description at www.petersons.com/graduate.

Graduate School
Dr. Margaret Marsh, Dean
Programs in:
American and public history • MA
biology • MS, MST
chemistry • MS
English • MA
health care management and policy • MPA
international public service and development • MPA
liberal studies • MA
mathematics • MS
physical therapy • MPT
public management • MPA

School of Business
Program in:
business • M Ac, MBA

School of Law
Rayman L. Solomon, Dean
Program in:
law • JD

■ RUTGERS, THE STATE UNIVERSITY OF NEW JERSEY, NEWARK

Newark, NJ 07102
http://info.rutgers.edu/newark/

State-supported, coed, university. CGS member. *Enrollment:* 1,211 full-time matriculated graduate/professional students (540 women), 1,952 part-time matriculated graduate/professional students (883 women). *Graduate faculty:* 415 full-time (151 women), 205 part-time/adjunct (93 women). *Computer facilities:* 708 computers available on campus for general student use. A campuswide network can be accessed from student residence rooms and from off campus. Internet access, online grade reports are available. *Library facilities:* John Cotton Dana Library plus 4 others. *Graduate expenses:* Tuition, state resident: full-time $7,116; part-time $293 per credit. Tuition, nonresident: full-time $10,434; part-time $433 per credit. Required fees: $859; $295 per term. *General application contact:* Bruce C. Neimeyer, Director of Admissions, 973-353-5205.

Find an in-depth description at www.petersons.com/graduate.

Graduate School
Dr. Gary Roth, Associate Dean
Programs in:
accounting • PhD
accounting information systems • PhD
American political system • MA
analytical chemistry • MS, PhD
applied physics • MS, PhD
biochemistry • MS, PhD
biology • MS, PhD
cognitive science • PhD
computer information systems • PhD
criminal justice • PhD
English • MA
environmental geology • MS
finance • PhD
health care administration • MPA
history • MA, MAT
human resources administration • MPA
information technology • PhD
inorganic chemistry • MS, PhD
integrated neuroscience • PhD
international business • PhD
international relations • MA
jazz history and research • MA
liberal studies • MALS
management science • PhD
marketing • PhD
mathematical sciences • PhD
organic chemistry • MS, PhD
organization management • PhD
perception • PhD
physical chemistry • MS, PhD
psychobiology • PhD
public administration • PhD
public management • MPA
public policy analysis • MPA
social cognition • PhD
urban systems and issues • MPA

Center for Global Change and Governance
Prof. Richard Langhorne, Director
Programs in:
global studies • MA
international studies • MS

College of Nursing
Dr. Joanne Stevenson, Program Director
Programs in:
nursing • MS
nursing research • PhD

School of Criminal Justice
Dr. Leslie Kennedy, Director
Program in:
criminal justice • MA, PhD

Graduate School of Management
Dr. Howard Tuckman, Dean, Faculty of Management
Programs in:
finance and economics • MBA
international business • MBA
management • M Accy, MBA, MQF, PhD
management science/computer information systems • MBA
marketing • MBA
organization management • MBA
professional accounting • MBA

School of Law
Stuart L. Deutsch, Dean
Program in:
law • JD

■ RUTGERS, THE STATE UNIVERSITY OF NEW JERSEY, NEW BRUNSWICK

New Brunswick, NJ 08901-1281
http://www.rutgers.edu/

State-supported, coed, university. CGS member. *Enrollment:* 2,786 full-time matriculated graduate/professional students (1,594 women), 3,244 part-time matriculated graduate/professional students (1,986 women). *Graduate faculty:* 1,843 full-time (579 women), 669 part-time/adjunct (325 women). *Computer facilities:* 1,450 computers available on campus for general student use. A campuswide network can be accessed from student residence rooms and from off campus. Internet access, online grade reports are available. *Library facilities:* Archibald S. Alexander Library plus 14 others. *Graduate expenses:* Tuition, state resident: full-time $7,116; part-time $293 per credit. Tuition, nonresident: full-time $10,434; part-time $433 per credit. Required fees: $876; $284 per term. *General application contact:* Dr. Donald J. Taylor, Director of Graduate Admissions, 732-932-7711.

College of Pharmacy
Dr. Joseph Barone, Director
Program in:
pharmacy • Pharm D

Edward J. Bloustein School of Planning and Public Policy
James W. Hughes, Dean
Programs in:
planning and public policy • MBA/MCRS, MCRP, MCRS, MPAP, MPH, MPP, Dr PH, PhD
public health • MPH, Dr PH, PhD
public policy • MPAP, MPP
urban planning and policy development • MBA/MCRS, MCRP, MCRS, PhD

Graduate School
Dr. Richard Falk, Dean of the Graduate School
Programs in:
agricultural economics • MS
air resources • MS, PhD
American political institutions • PhD
analytical chemistry • MS, PhD
anthropology • MA, PhD
applied mathematics • MS, PhD
applied microbiology • MS, PhD
aquatic biology • MS, PhD
aquatic chemistry • MS, PhD
art history • MA, PhD
astrophysics • MS, PhD
biochemistry • MS, PhD
biological chemistry • PhD
biomedical engineering • MS, PhD
biopsychology and behavioral neuroscience • PhD
bioresource engineering • MS
cell biology • MS, PhD
cellular and molecular pharmacology • PhD
ceramic and materials science and engineering • MS, PhD
chemical and biochemical engineering • MS, PhD
chemistry and physics of aerosol and hydrosol systems • MS, PhD
chemistry education • MST
civil and environmental engineering • MS, PhD
classics • MA, MAT, PhD
clinical microbiology • MS, PhD
clinical psychology • PhD
cognitive psychology • PhD
communication and information studies • PhD
communications and solid-state electronics • MS, PhD
comparative literature • PhD
comparative politics • PhD
composition • MA, PhD
computational fluid dynamics • MS, PhD
computational molecular biology • PhD
computer engineering • MS, PhD
computer science • MS, PhD
condensed matter physics • MS, PhD
control systems • MS, PhD
design and dynamics • MS, PhD
developmental biology • MS, PhD
digital signal processing • MS, PhD
diplomatic history • PhD
direct intervention in interpersonal situations • PhD
early American history • PhD
early modern European history • PhD
ecology and evolution • MS, PhD
economics • MA, PhD
educational policy • PhD
educational psychology • PhD

Rutgers, The State University of New Jersey, New Brunswick (continued)

elementary particle physics • MS, PhD
endocrine control of growth and metabolism • MS, PhD
entomology • MS, PhD
environmental chemistry • MS, PhD
environmental microbiology • MS, PhD
environmental toxicology • MS, PhD
exposure assessment • PhD
fluid mechanics • MS, PhD
food science • M Phil, MS, PhD
French • MA, PhD
French studies • MAT
geography • MA, MS, PhD
geological sciences • MS, PhD
German • PhD
global/comparative history • PhD
heat transfer • MS, PhD
history • PhD
history of technology, medicine, and science • PhD
horticulture • MS, PhD
immunology • MS, PhD
industrial and systems engineering • MS, PhD
industrial pharmacy • MS, PhD
industrial relations and human resources • MA, PhD
industrial-occupational toxicology • MS, PhD
inorganic chemistry • MS, PhD
interdisciplinary developmental psychology • PhD
interdisciplinary health psychology • PhD
intermediate energy nuclear physics • MS, PhD
international relations • PhD
Italian • MA
Italian history • PhD
Italian literature and literary criticism • MA, PhD
language, literature and civilization • MAT
Latin American history • PhD
linguistics • PhD.
literacy education • PhD
literature • MA, PhD
literatures in English • PhD
manufacturing systems • MS
mathematics • MS, PhD
mathematics education • PhD
mechanics • MS, PhD
medicinal chemistry • MS, PhD
medieval history • PhD
microbial biochemistry • MS, PhD
modern American history • PhD
modern British history • PhD
modern European history • PhD
molecular and cell biology • PhD
molecular biology • MS, PhD
molecular biology and biochemistry • MS, PhD
molecular genetics • MS, PhD
museum studies • MA
music history • MA, PhD
nuclear physics • MS, PhD
nutrition of ruminant and nonruminant animals • MS, PhD
nutritional sciences • MS, PhD
nutritional toxicology • MS, PhD
oceanography • MS, PhD
operations research • PhD
organic chemistry • MS, PhD
pathology • MS, PhD
pharmaceutical chemistry • MS, PhD
pharmaceutical toxicology • MS, PhD
pharmaceutics • MS, PhD
philosophy • PhD
physical chemistry • MS, PhD
physical metallurgy • MS, PhD
physics • MST
physiology and neurobiology • PhD
plant ecology • MS, PhD
plant genetics • PhD
plant physiology • MS, PhD
political and cultural history • PhD
political economy • PhD
political theory • PhD
polymer science • MS, PhD
production and management • MS
public law • PhD
quality and productivity management • MS
quality and reliability engineering • MS
reproductive endocrinology and neuroendocrinology • MS, PhD
social policy analysis and administration • PhD
social psychology • PhD
social work • PhD
sociology • MA, PhD
solid mechanics • MS, PhD
Spanish • MA, MAT, PhD
Spanish-American literature • MA, PhD
statistics • MS, PhD
structure and plant groups • MS, PhD
theoretical physics • MS, PhD
translation • MA
virology • MS, PhD
water and wastewater treatment • MS, PhD
water resources • MS, PhD
women and politics • PhD
women's history • PhD
women's studies • MA

Eagleton Institute of Politics
Program in:
politics • MS

Graduate School of Applied and Professional Psychology
Programs in:
applied and professional psychology • Psy M, Psy D
clinical psychology • Psy M, Psy D
organizational psychology • Psy M, Psy D
school psychology • Psy M, Psy D

Graduate School of Education
Dr. Louise Cherry Wilkinson, Dean
Programs in:
adult and continuing education • Ed M, Ed D
counseling psychology • Ed M
early childhood/elementary education • Ed M, Ed D
education • Ed M, Ed D, PhD, Ed S
education administration • Ed M
educational administration and supervision • Ed M, Ed D, Ed S
educational statistics and measurement • Ed M
English as a second language education • Ed M, Ed D
English education • Ed M
language education • Ed M, Ed D
learning cognition and development • Ed M
literacy education • Ed M, Ed D
mathematics education • Ed M, Ed D
reading education • Ed M
school business administration • Ed M
science education • Ed M, Ed D
social and philosophical foundations of education • Ed M, Ed D, Ed S
social studies education • Ed M, Ed D, Ed S
special education • Ed M
vocational-technical education • Ed M, Ed D, Ed S

Mason Gross School of the Arts
George B. Stauffer, Dean
Programs in:
acting • MFA
arts • MFA, MM, DMA, AD
design • MFA
directing • MFA
music • MM, DMA, AD
playwriting • MFA
visual arts • MFA

Programs in Engineering
Program in:
engineering • MS, PhD

School of Communication, Information and Library Studies
Dr. Friedrich W. Gustav, Dean
Programs in:
communication and information studies • MCIS
library and information science • MLS

School of Management and Labor Relations
Dr. John F. Burton, Dean
Programs in:
human resource management • MHRM

labor and employment relations • MLER
management and labor relations • MHRM, MLER, PhD

School of Social Work
Program in:
social work • MSW, PhD

■ SAINT PETER'S COLLEGE

Jersey City, NJ 07306-5997
http://www.spc.edu/

Independent-religious, coed, comprehensive institution. *Enrollment:* 90 full-time matriculated graduate/professional students (55 women), 505 part-time matriculated graduate/professional students (288 women). *Graduate faculty:* 25 full-time (4 women), 27 part-time/adjunct (5 women). *Computer facilities:* 150 computers available on campus for general student use. A campuswide network can be accessed from student residence rooms and from off campus. Internet access is available. *Library facilities:* Theresa and Edward O'Toole Library plus 1 other. *Graduate expenses:* Tuition: full-time $13,392; part-time $558 per credit. *General application contact:* Barbara A. Bertsch, Graduate Admissions Counselor, 201-915-9220.

Find an in-depth description at www.petersons.com/graduate.

Graduate Programs in Education
Dr. Joseph McLaughlin, Director
Programs in:
administration and supervision • MA
elementary teacher • Certificate
reading specialist • MA
supervisor of instruction • Certificate
teaching • MA, Certificate
urban education • MA

MBA Programs
Daniel Gerger, Administrative Coordinator
Programs in:
finance • MBA
international business • MBA
management • MBA
management information systems • MBA
marketing • MBA

Nursing Program
Dr. Marylou Yam, Director
Program in:
nursing • MSN

Program in Accountancy
Daniel Gerger, Administrative Coordinator
Program in:
accountancy • MS, Certificate

■ SETON HALL UNIVERSITY

South Orange, NJ 07079-2697
http://www.shu.edu/

Independent-religious, coed, university. CGS member. *Enrollment:* 1,492 full-time matriculated graduate/professional students (786 women), 2,428 part-time matriculated graduate/professional students (1,331 women). *Graduate faculty:* 381 full-time (158 women), 433 part-time/adjunct (178 women). *Computer facilities:* 500 computers available on campus for general student use. A campuswide network can be accessed from student residence rooms and from off campus. Internet access and online class registration are available. *Library facilities:* Walsh Library plus 1 other. *Graduate expenses:* Tuition: full-time $10,818; part-time $601 per credit. Required fees: $185 per semester. Tuition and fees vary according to course load, campus/location, program and student's religious affiliation.

Find an in-depth description at www.petersons.com/graduate.

College of Arts and Sciences
Programs in:
analytical chemistry • MS, PhD
arts and sciences • MA, MHA, MPA, MS, PhD
Asian studies • MA
biochemistry • MS, PhD
biology • MS
chemistry • MS
corporate and public communication • MA
English • MA
French • MA
inorganic chemistry • MS, PhD
Jewish-Christian studies • MA
microbiology • MS
museum professions • MA
organic chemistry • MS, PhD
physical chemistry • MS, PhD
Spanish • MA

Center for Public Service
Programs in:
arts administration • MPA
criminal justice • MPA
health policy and management • MPA
healthcare administration • MHA
management of nonprofit organizations • MPA
public service administration and policy • MPA
religious organization management • MPA

College of Education and Human Services
Dr. Richard Oghibene, Acting Dean
Programs in:
bilingual education • MA, Ed S
Catholic school leadership • MA
Catholic school teaching EPICS • MA
counseling psychology • PhD
counselor preparation • MA
education and human services • MA, MS, Ed D, Exec Ed D, PhD, Ed S
education media specialist • MA
elementary education • MA
English as a second language • MA
higher education administration • PhD
human resource training and development • MA
instructional design • MA, Ed S
K–12 administration and supervision • Ed D, Exec Ed D, Ed S
marriage and family counseling • MS, PhD, Ed S
professional development • MA, Ed S
psychological studies • MA
school psychology • Ed S
secondary education • MA

College of Nursing
Dr. Phyllis Hansell, Dean
Programs in:
acute care nurse practitioner • MSN
adult nurse practitioner • MSN
advanced practice in acute care nursing • MSN
advanced practice in primary health care • MSN
gerontological nurse practitioner • MSN
nursing • MA, MSN
nursing administration • MSN
nursing case management • MSN
nursing education • MA
pediatric nurse practitioner • MSN
school nurse practitioner • MSN
women's health nurse practitioner • MSN

Immaculate Conception Seminary School of Theology
Rev. Msgr. Robert F. Coleman, Rector/Dean
Programs in:
pastoral ministry • M Div, MA
theology • MA, Certificate

Seton Hall University (continued)

School of Diplomacy and International Relations
Clay Constantinou, Dean
Program in:
diplomacy and international relations • MA

School of Graduate Medical Education
Dr. John A. Paterson, Dean
Programs in:
athletic training • MS
health sciences • MS, PhD
medical education • MS, PhD, Sc D
occupational therapy • MS
physician assistant • MS
speech-language pathology • MS

School of Law
Patrick E. Hobbs, Dean
Program in:
law • JD, LL M, MSJ

Stillman School of Business
Dr. Karen Boroff, Dean
Programs in:
accounting • MS
business • MBA, MS, Certificate, Post-Graduate Certificate
international business • MS, Certificate
professional accounting • MS
taxation • MS, Post-Graduate Certificate

Center for Graduate Studies
Dr. Richard Hunter, Dean of Graduate Studies
Programs in:
accounting • MBA
business • Certificate
environmental affairs • MBA
finance • MBA
financial institutions • MBA
information systems • MBA
management • MBA
marketing • MBA
pharmaceutical operations • MBA
sports management • MBA, Post-Graduate Certificate

■ STEVENS INSTITUTE OF TECHNOLOGY

Hoboken, NJ 07030
http://www.stevens-tech.edu/

Independent, coed, university. *Enrollment:* 395 full-time matriculated graduate/professional students (88 women), 2,175 part-time matriculated graduate/professional students (631 women). *Graduate faculty:* 104 full-time (8 women), 80 part-time/adjunct (9 women). *Computer facilities:* 1,700 computers available on campus for general student use. A campuswide network can be accessed from student residence rooms and from off campus. Internet access and online class registration, online grade and account information are available. *Library facilities:* S. C. Williams Library. *Graduate expenses:* Tuition: part-time $726 per credit. *General application contact:* Dr. Charles L. Suffel, Dean of the Graduate School, 201-216-5234.

Find an in-depth description at www.petersons.com/graduate.

Graduate School
Dr. Charles L. Suffel, Dean
Program in:
interdisciplinary sciences and engineering • M Eng, MS, PhD

Charles V. Schaefer Jr. School of Engineering
Dr. Bernard Gallois, Dean
Programs in:
advanced manufacturing • Certificate
air pollution technology • Certificate
analysis of polymer processing methods • Certificate
biochemical engineering • M Eng, PhD, Engr
building energy systems • Certificate
civil engineering • M Eng, PhD, Certificate, Engr
coastal and ocean engineering • M Eng, PhD, Engr
computational methods in fluid mechanics and heat transfer • Certificate
computer and communications security • Certificate
computer and information engineering • M Eng, PhD, Engr
computer architecture and digital system design • M Eng, PhD, Engr
computer engineering • M Eng, PhD, Certificate, Engr
concurrent design management • M Eng
concurrent engineering • PhD, Certificate
construction accounting/estimating • Certificate
construction engineering • M Eng, PhD, Certificate, Engr
construction law/disputes • Certificate
construction management • MS
construction/quality management • Certificate
controls in aerospace and robotics • Certificate
design and production management • MS, Certificate
digital systems and VLSI design • Certificate
electrical engineering • M Eng, MS, PhD, Certificate, Engr
engineering • M Eng, MS, PhD, Certificate, Engr
environmental compatibility in engineering • Certificate
environmental engineering • M Eng, PhD, Certificate
environmental process • M Eng, PhD, Certificate
finite-element analysis • Certificate
fundamentals of modern chemical engineering • Certificate
geotechnical engineering • Certificate
geotechnical/geoenvironmental engineering • M Eng, PhD, Engr
groundwater and soil pollution control • M Eng, PhD, Certificate
image and signal processing • M Eng, PhD, Engr
information networks • Certificate
inland and coastal environmental hydrodynamics • M Eng, PhD, Certificate
integrated production design • Certificate
maritime systems • M Eng
materials engineering • M Eng, PhD
materials science • MS, PhD
mechanical engineering • M Eng, PhD, Engr
mechanism design • Certificate
ocean engineering • M Eng, PhD
polymer engineering • M Eng, PhD, Engr
polymer processing • Certificate
power generation • Certificate
process control • M Eng, PhD, Engr
process engineering • M Eng, PhD, Certificate, Engr
robotics and automation • M Eng, PhD, Engr
robotics and control • Certificate
robotics/control/instrumentation • M Eng, PhD, Engr
satellite communications engineering • Certificate
signal and image processing • M Eng, PhD, Engr
software engineering • M Eng, PhD, Engr
stress analysis and design • Certificate
structural analysis of materials • Certificate
structures • M Eng, PhD, Engr
surface modification of materials • Certificate
telecommunications engineering • M Eng, PhD, Engr
telecommunications management • MS, PhD, Certificate
vibration and noise control • Certificate
water quality • Certificate

School of Applied Sciences and Liberal Arts
Dr. Erich Kunhardt, Dean
Programs in:
- advanced programming: theory, design and verification • Certificate
- algebra • PhD
- analysis • PhD
- applied mathematics • MS, PhD
- applied optics • Certificate
- applied sciences and liberal arts • M Eng, MS, PhD, Certificate
- applied statistics • MS, Certificate
- artificial intelligence and robotics • MS, PhD
- chemistry • MS, PhD, Certificate
- computer and information systems • MS, PhD
- computer architecture and digital system design • MS, PhD
- database systems • Certificate
- elements of computer science • Certificate
- engineering physics • M Eng
- information systems • MS, Certificate
- mathematics • MS, PhD
- network and graph theory • Certificate
- physics • MS, PhD
- software design • MS, PhD
- software engineering • Certificate
- surface physics • Certificate
- theoretical computer science • MS, PhD, Certificate
- wireless communications • Certificate

Wesley J. Howe School of Technology Management
Dr. Jerry Hultin, Dean
Programs in:
- computer science • MS
- construction management • MS
- design and production management • MS, Certificate
- e-commerce • MS, Certificate
- general management • MS
- information management • MS, PhD, Certificate
- management planning • MS
- network planning and evaluation • MS, PhD
- project management • MS, PhD, Certificate
- technology applications in science education • Certificate
- technology management • EMTM, MIM, MS, MTM, PhD, Certificate
- technology management marketing • MS, PhD
- telecommunications management • MS, Certificate

■ THOMAS EDISON STATE COLLEGE

Trenton, NJ 08608-1176
http://www.tesc.edu/

State-supported, coed, comprehensive institution. *Enrollment:* 162 part-time matriculated graduate/professional students (72 women). *Graduate faculty:* 45 part-time/adjunct (13 women). *Computer facilities:* A campuswide network can be accessed from off campus. Internet access and online class registration are available. *Graduate expenses:* Tuition, state resident: part-time $298 per semester hour. *General application contact:* Gregg Dye, Coordinator of Graduate Advisement, 609-984-1168.

Find an in-depth description at www.petersons.com/graduate.

Graduate Studies
Dr. Sonja Eveslage, Dean of Graduate Studies/Associate Vice President of New Program Development
Programs in:
- leadership • MSM
- liberal studies • MAPS
- management • MSM
- project management • MSM

■ WILLIAM PATERSON UNIVERSITY OF NEW JERSEY

Wayne, NJ 07470-8420
http://www.wpunj.edu/

State-supported, coed, comprehensive institution. CGS member. *Enrollment:* 213 full-time matriculated graduate/professional students (158 women), 670 part-time matriculated graduate/professional students (539 women). *Computer facilities:* 150 computers available on campus for general student use. A campuswide network can be accessed from student residence rooms. *Library facilities:* Sarah Byrd Askew Library. *Graduate expenses:* Tuition, state resident: part-time $278 per credit. Tuition, nonresident: part-time $394 per credit. *General application contact:* Danielle Liautaud Watkins, Graduate Admissions Counselor, 973-720-3579.

Find an in-depth description at www.petersons.com/graduate.

College of Business
Cho-Kin Leung, Interim Dean
Program in:
- business • MBA

College of Education
Leslie Agard-Jones, Dean
Programs in:
- counseling • M Ed
- counseling services • M Ed
- education • M Ed, MAT
- elementary education • M Ed, MAT
- reading • M Ed
- special education • M Ed

College of Science and Health
Dr. Eswar Phadia, Dean
Programs in:
- biotechnology • MS
- general biology • MA
- limnology and terrestrial ecology • MA
- molecular biology • MA
- nursing • MSN
- physiology • MA
- science and health • MA, MS, MSN
- speech pathology • MS

College of the Arts and Communication
Ofelia Garcia, Dean
Programs in:
- arts and communication • MA, MM
- media studies • MA
- music • MM
- visual arts • MA

College of the Humanities and Social Sciences
Dr. Isabel Tirado, Dean
Programs in:
- applied clinical psychology • MA
- English • MA
- history • MA
- humanities and social sciences • MA
- sociology • MA

New Mexico

■ COLLEGE OF SANTA FE

Santa Fe, NM 87505-7634
http://www.csf.edu

Independent, coed, comprehensive institution. *Computer facilities:* 60 computers available on campus for general student use. A campuswide network can be accessed from student residence rooms and from off campus. *Library facilities:* Fogelson Library Center. *General application contact:* Assistant Dean for Academic Services, 505-473-6177.

Department of Business Administration
Program in:
- business administration • MBA

College of Santa Fe (continued)

Department of Education

Programs in:

- at-risk youth • MA
- bilingual/multicultural education • MA
- classroom teaching • MA
- community counseling • MA
- educational administration • MA
- leadership • MA
- multicultural special education • MA
- school counseling • MA

■ COLLEGE OF THE SOUTHWEST

Hobbs, NM 88240-9129

http://www.csw.edu/

Independent, coed, comprehensive institution. *Enrollment:* 53 full-time matriculated graduate/professional students (41 women), 58 part-time matriculated graduate/professional students (45 women). *Graduate faculty:* 4 full-time (all women), 11 part-time/adjunct (4 women). *Computer facilities:* 20 computers available on campus for general student use. *Library facilities:* Scarborough Memorial Library plus 1 other. *Graduate expenses:* Tuition: full-time $3,792; part-time $158 per hour. Required fees: $95 per credit hour. One-time fee: $50. *General application contact:* Charlotte Smith, Director of Admissions, 505-392-6561 Ext. 1012.

School of Education and Professional Studies

Dr. Elizabeth Posey, Dean

Programs in:

- curriculum and instruction • MS
- educational administration • MS
- educational counseling • MS
- educational diagnostian • MS

■ EASTERN NEW MEXICO UNIVERSITY

Portales, NM 88130

http://www.enmu.edu/

State-supported, coed, comprehensive institution. CGS member. *Enrollment:* 23 full-time matriculated graduate/professional students (16 women), 320 part-time matriculated graduate/professional students (225 women). *Graduate faculty:* 89 full-time (38 women), 13 part-time/adjunct (3 women). *Computer facilities:* 266 computers available on campus for general student use. A campuswide network can be accessed from student residence rooms and from off campus. Internet access and online class registration are available. *Library facilities:* Golden Library. *Graduate expenses:* Tuition, state resident: full-time $1,608; part-time $67 per credit. Tuition, nonresident: full-time $6,786; part-time $283 per credit. Required fees: $23 per credit. *General application contact:* Dr. Phillip Shelley, Dean, Graduate School, 505-562-2147.

Find an in-depth description at www.petersons.com/graduate.

Graduate School

Dr. Phillip Shelley, Dean

College of Business

Dr. Gerry Huybregts, Dean

Program in:

- business • MBA

College of Education and Technology

Dr. Kenneth Moore, Dean

Programs in:

- counseling • MA
- education • M Ed
- education and technology • M Ed, M Sp Ed, MA, MS
- physical education • MS
- school guidance • M Ed
- special education • M Sp Ed

College of Fine Arts

Dr. David Gerig, Interim Dean

Program in:

- fine arts • MM

College of Liberal Arts and Sciences

Dr. Thurman Elder, Dean

Programs in:

- anthropology • MA
- biology • MS
- chemistry • MS
- communication • MA
- English • MA
- liberal arts and sciences • MA, MS
- mathematical sciences • MA
- psychology and sociology • MA
- speech pathology and audiology • MS

■ NEW MEXICO HIGHLANDS UNIVERSITY

Las Vegas, NM 87701

http://www.nmhu.edu/

State-supported, coed, comprehensive institution. CGS member. *Enrollment:* 278 full-time matriculated graduate/professional students (194 women), 314 part-time matriculated graduate/professional students (202 women). *Graduate faculty:* 112 full-time (47 women), 15 part-time/adjunct (9 women). *Computer facilities:* 500 computers available on campus for general student use. A campuswide network can be accessed from student residence rooms and from off campus. Internet access and online class registration are available. *Library facilities:* Donnelly Library. *Graduate expenses:* Tuition, state resident: full-time $2,130; part-time $89 per credit hour. Tuition, nonresident: full-time $8,777; part-time $89 per credit hour. *General application contact:* Dr. Glen W. Davidson, Provost, 505-454-3311.

Graduate Studies

Dr. Glen W. Davidson, Provost

College of Arts and Sciences

Dr. Tomas Salazar, Dean

Programs in:

- administration • MA
- anthropology • MA
- applied chemistry • MS
- applied sociology • MA
- arts and sciences • MA, MS
- biology • MS
- cognitive science • MA, MS
- computer graphics • MA, MS
- design studies • MA
- digital audio and video production • MA
- English • MA
- environmental science and management • MS
- Hispanic language and literature • MA
- historical and cross-cultural perspective • MA
- history and political science • MA
- multimedia systems • MS
- networking technology • MA, MS
- political and governmental processes • MA
- psychology • MS

School of Business

Dr. Margaret Young, Dean

Program in:

- business • MBA

School of Education

Dr. James Abreu, Dean

Programs in:

- curriculum and instruction • MA
- education administration • MA
- guidance and counseling • MA
- human performance and sport • MA
- special education • MA

School of Social Work

Dr. Alfredo Garcia, Dean

Program in:

- social work • MSW

■ NEW MEXICO INSTITUTE OF MINING AND TECHNOLOGY

Socorro, NM 87801

http://www.nmt.edu/

State-supported, coed, university. *Enrollment:* 232 full-time matriculated graduate/

professional students (71 women), 58 part-time matriculated graduate/professional students (30 women). *Graduate faculty:* 29 full-time (2 women), 7 part-time/adjunct (0 women). *Computer facilities:* 225 computers available on campus for general student use. A campuswide network can be accessed from student residence rooms and from off campus. Internet access is available. *Library facilities:* New Mexico Tech Library plus 1 other. *Graduate expenses:* Tuition, state resident: full-time $1,802; part-time $101 per credit. Tuition, nonresident: full-time $7,432; part-time $413 per credit. Required fees: $795; $25 per credit. $100 per term. *General application contact:* Dr. David B. Johnson, Dean of Graduate Studies, 505-835-5513.

Find an in-depth description at www.petersons.com/graduate.

Graduate Studies
Dr. David B. Johnson, Dean
Programs in:
- astrophysics • MS, PhD
- atmospheric physics • MS, PhD
- biochemistry • MS
- biology • MS
- chemistry • MS
- computer science • MS, PhD
- engineering science in mechanics • MS
- environmental chemistry • PhD
- environmental engineering • MS
- explosives technology and atmospheric chemistry • PhD
- geochemistry • MS, PhD
- geology • MS, PhD
- geology and geochemistry • MS, PhD
- geophysics • MS, PhD
- hydrology • MS, PhD
- instrumentation • MS
- material engineering • MS, PhD
- mathematical physics • PhD
- mathematics • MS
- mineral engineering • MS
- operations research • MS
- petroleum engineering • MS, PhD
- science teaching • MST

■ NEW MEXICO STATE UNIVERSITY

Las Cruces, NM 88003-8001
http://www.nmsu.edu/

State-supported, coed, university. CGS member. *Enrollment:* 1,251 full-time matriculated graduate/professional students (586 women), 932 part-time matriculated graduate/professional students (531 women). *Graduate faculty:* 566 full-time (190 women). *Computer facilities:* 500 computers available on campus for general student use. A campuswide network can be accessed from student residence rooms and from off campus. Internet access and online class registration are available. *Library facilities:* New Library plus 1 other. *Graduate expenses:* Tuition, state resident: part-time $125 per credit. Tuition, nonresident: part-time $392 per credit. *General application contact:* Christine Marlow, Associate Dean of the Graduate School, 505-646-5746.

Graduate School
Dr. Timothy J. Pettibone, Dean
Programs in:
- interdisciplinary studies • MA, MS, PhD
- molecular biology • MS, PhD

College of Agriculture and Home Economics
Dr. Jerry Schickedanz, Dean
Programs in:
- agricultural economics • MS
- agriculture and extension education • MA
- agriculture and home economics • M Ag, MA, MS, PhD
- animal science • M Ag, MS, PhD
- economics • MA
- entomology, plant pathology and weed science • MS
- family and consumer sciences • MS
- general agronomy • MS, PhD
- horticulture • MS
- range science • M Ag, MS, PhD
- wildlife science • MS

College of Arts and Sciences
Dr. E. Rene Casillas, Dean
Programs in:
- anthropology • MA
- art • MA, MFA
- arts and sciences • MA, MAG, MCJ, MFA, MM, MPA, MS, PhD
- astronomy • MS, PhD
- biology • MS, PhD
- chemistry and biochemistry • MS, PhD
- communication studies • MA
- computer science • MS, PhD
- creative writing • MFA
- criminal justice • MCJ
- English • MA, PhD
- geography • MAG
- geological sciences • MS
- government • MA, MPA
- history • MA
- mathematical sciences • MS, PhD
- music • MM
- physics • MS, PhD
- psychology • MA, PhD
- sociology • MA
- Spanish • MA

College of Business Administration and Economics
Dr. Danny Arnold, Dean
Programs in:
- accounting and business computer systems • M Acct
- business administration • MBA
- business administration and economics • M Acct, MA, MBA, MS, PhD
- economics • MA, MBA, MS
- experimental statistics • MS
- management • PhD
- marketing • PhD

College of Education
Dr. Robert Moulton, Dean
Programs in:
- counseling and guidance • MA, Ed S
- counseling psychology • PhD
- curriculum and instruction • MAT, Ed D, PhD, Ed S
- education • MA, MAT, Ed D, PhD, Ed S
- educational administration • MA, PhD, Ed S
- educational management and development • Ed D
- general education • MA
- reading • Ed S
- special education/communication disorders • MA

College of Engineering
Dr. Jay B. Jordan, Dean
Programs in:
- chemical engineering • MS Ch E, PhD
- civil engineering • MSCE, PhD
- electrical and computer engineering • MSEE, PhD
- engineering • MS Ch E, MS Env E, MSCE, MSEE, MSIE, MSME, PhD
- environmental engineering • MS Env E
- industrial engineering • MSIE, PhD
- mechanical engineering • MSME, PhD

College of Health and Social Services
Dr. Jeffrey Brandon, Dean
Programs in:
- health and social services • MPH, MSN, MSW
- health science • MPH
- nursing • MSN
- social work • MSW

■ UNIVERSITY OF NEW MEXICO

Albuquerque, NM 87131-2039
http://www.unm.edu/

State-supported, coed, university. CGS member. *Enrollment:* 3,418 full-time matriculated graduate/professional students (1,879 women), 1,873 part-time

University of New Mexico (continued)
matriculated graduate/professional students (1,099 women). *Graduate faculty:* 1,403 full-time (510 women), 543 part-time/adjunct (259 women). *Computer facilities:* 382 computers available on campus for general student use. A campuswide network can be accessed from student residence rooms and from off campus. Internet access and online class registration are available. *Library facilities:* Zimmerman Library plus 7 others. *Graduate expenses:* Tuition, state resident: part-time $105 per credit hour. Tuition, nonresident: part-time $429 per credit hour. Required fees: $24 per credit hour. Tuition and fees vary according to course load, degree level, program and reciprocity agreements. *General application contact:* Dr. Kenneth Frandsen, Interim Dean of the Graduate School, 505-277-2711.

Find an in-depth description at www.petersons.com/graduate.

Graduate School

Dr. Kenneth Frandsen, Interim Dean of the Graduate School
Programs in:
- biochemistry and molecular biology • MS, PhD
- cell biology and physiology • MS, PhD
- molecular genetics and microbiology • MS, PhD
- neuroscience • MS, PhD
- occupational therapy • MOT
- pathology • MS, PhD
- pharmaceutical sciences • MS, PhD
- pharmacy administration • MS, PhD
- physical therapy • MPT
- public health • MPH
- toxicology • MS, PhD
- water resources • MWR

College of Arts and Sciences

Dr. Fritz Allen, Interim Dean
Programs in:
- American studies • MA, PhD
- anthropology • MA, MS, PhD
- arts and sciences • MA, MS, PhD
- biology • MS, PhD
- chemistry • MS, PhD
- clinical psychology • MS, PhD
- communication • MA, PhD
- comparative literature and cultural studies • MA
- earth and planetary sciences • MS, PhD
- economics • MA, PhD
- English • MA, PhD
- French • MA
- French studies • PhD
- geography • MS
- German studies • MA
- history • MA, PhD
- Latin American studies • MA, PhD
- linguistics • MA, PhD
- mathematics • MS, PhD
- optical sciences • PhD
- philosophy • MA, PhD
- physics • MS, PhD
- political science • MA, PhD
- Portuguese • MA
- psychology • MS, PhD
- sociology • MA, PhD
- Spanish • MA
- Spanish and Portuguese • PhD
- speech and hearing sciences • MS
- statistics • MS, PhD

College of Education

Dr. Viola E. Florez Tighe, Dean
Programs in:
- administration and supervision • Ed D
- art education • MA
- counselor education • MA, PhD
- education • MA, MS, Ed D, PhD, Ed S
- educational administration • MA, Ed S
- educational linguistics • Ed D, PhD
- educational psychology • MA, PhD
- educational thought and sociocultural studies • Ed D, PhD
- elementary education • MA
- family studies • MA, PhD
- health education • MS
- health, physical education and recreation • Ed D, PhD
- multicultural teacher and childhood education • Ed D, PhD
- nutrition • MS
- organizational learning and instructional technologies • MA, Ed D, PhD, Ed S
- physical education • MS
- recreation • Ed S
- secondary education • MA
- special education • MA, Ed D, PhD, Ed S

College of Fine Arts

Dr. Thomas A. Dodson, Dean
Programs in:
- art history • MA, PhD
- fine arts • M Mu, MA, MFA, PhD
- music • M Mu
- studio arts • MFA
- theatre and dance • MA

College of Nursing

Dr. Sandra Ferketich, Dean
Programs in:
- administration of nursing • MSN, Certificate
- advanced nurse practice • Certificate
- advanced nursing practice • MSN
- community health nursing • MSN
- primary care nursing • MSN

Robert O. Anderson Graduate School of Management

Dr. Howard L. Smith, Dean
Programs in:
- accounting • M Acc, MBA
- business administration • EMBA
- financial management • MBA
- financial, international and technology management • MBA
- general management • MBA
- human resources management • MBA
- international management • MBA
- international management in Latin America • MBA
- management information systems • MBA
- management of technology • MBA
- marketing management • MBA
- marketing, information and decision sciences • MBA
- operations and management science • MBA
- organizational studies • MBA
- policy and planning • MBA
- tax accounting • MBA

School of Architecture and Planning

Dr. Roger Schluntz, Dean
Programs in:
- architecture • M Arch
- architecture and planning • M Arch, MCRP, MLA
- community and regional planning • MCRP
- landscape architecture • MLA

School of Engineering

Joseph Cecchi, Interim Dean
Programs in:
- chemical engineering • MS, PhD
- civil engineering • MS
- computer science • MS, PhD
- electrical engineering • MS
- engineering • PhD
- hazardous waste engineering • MEHWE
- manufacturing engineering • MEME, MS
- mechanical engineering • MS
- nuclear engineering • MS, PhD
- optical sciences • PhD

School of Public Administration

Dr. T. Zane Reeves, Director
Program in:
- public administration • MPA

Health Sciences Center

Program in:
- health sciences • MD, Pharm D, MOT, MPH, MPT, MS, MSN, PhD, Certificate

College of Pharmacy

Dr. William Hadley, Dean
Program in:
- pharmacy • Pharm D, MS, PhD

School of Medicine
Program in:
medicine • MD, MOT, MPH, MPT, MS, PhD

School of Law
Robert J. Desiderio, Dean
Program in:
law • JD

■ WESTERN NEW MEXICO UNIVERSITY

Silver City, NM 88062-0680
http://www.wnmu.edu/

State-supported, coed, comprehensive institution. *Enrollment:* 61 full-time matriculated graduate/professional students (40 women), 307 part-time matriculated graduate/professional students (200 women). *Graduate faculty:* 42 full-time (24 women), 7 part-time/adjunct (2 women). *Computer facilities:* 85 computers available on campus for general student use. Internet access is available. *Library facilities:* Miller Library plus 2 others. *Graduate expenses:* Part-time $67 per credit hour. Tuition, state resident: full-time $1,062. Tuition, nonresident: full-time $3,634. Tuition and fees vary according to course load and campus/location. *General application contact:* Betsy Miller, Assistant Director of Admissions, 505-538-6106.

Graduate Division
Dr. Faye N. Vowell, Dean
Program in:
business • MBA

School of Education
Dr. Jerry Harmon, Dean
Programs in:
counselor education • MA
elementary education • MAT
reading • MAT
school administration • MA
secondary education • MAT
special education • MAT

New York

■ ADELPHI UNIVERSITY

Garden City, NY 11530
http://www.adelphi.edu/

Independent, coed, university. CGS member. *Enrollment:* 663 full-time matriculated graduate/professional students (552 women), 2,190 part-time matriculated graduate/professional students (1,731 women). *Computer facilities:* 450 computers available on campus for general student use. A campuswide network can be accessed from student residence rooms. Internet access is available. *Library facilities:* Swirbul Library plus 1 other. *Graduate expenses:* Tuition: full-time $12,480; part-time $520 per credit. Required fees: $500. One-time fee: $400 part-time. Tuition and fees vary according to course load, degree level and program. *General application contact:* Ernie Shepelsky, Associate Director of Admissions, 516-877-3050.

Find an in-depth description at www.petersons.com/graduate.

Derner Institute of Advanced Psychological Studies
Dr. Louis Primavera, Dean
Programs in:
clinical psychology • PhD, Post-Doctoral Certificate
general psychology • MA

Graduate School of Arts and Sciences
Gail Insler, Dean
Programs in:
art and art history • MA
arts and sciences • MA, MS, DA
biology • MS
English • MA
mathematics and computer science • MS, DA
physics • MS

School of Business
Dr. Anthony F. Libertella, Dean
Programs in:
administrative sciences • MBA
business • MBA, MS, Certificate
finance • MS
human resource management • Certificate
management for non-business majors • Certificate
management for women • Certificate

School of Education
Dr. Elaine Sands, Dean
Programs in:
bilingual education • MA, MS
communication sciences and disorders • MS, DA
education • MA, MS, DA, Certificate
educational leadership and technology • MA, Certificate
elementary education • MA, Certificate
health studies • MA, Certificate
physical education and human performance science • MA, Certificate
reading • MS, Certificate
secondary education • MA
special education • MS, Certificate
teaching English to speakers of other languages • MA, Certificate

School of Nursing
Dr. Kathleen Bond, Acting Dean
Program in:
nursing • MS, Certificate

School of Social Work
Dr. Brooke Spiro, Acting Dean
Programs in:
social welfare • DSW
social work • MSW

■ ALFRED UNIVERSITY

Alfred, NY 14802-1205
http://www.alfred.edu/

Independent, coed, university. CGS member. *Enrollment:* 189 full-time matriculated graduate/professional students (98 women), 159 part-time matriculated graduate/professional students (105 women). *Graduate faculty:* 130. *Computer facilities:* 390 computers available on campus for general student use. A campuswide network can be accessed from student residence rooms and from off campus. Internet access is available. *Library facilities:* Herrick Memorial Library plus 1 other. *Graduate expenses:* Tuition: full-time $22,444. Required fees: $660. One-time fee: $110 part-time. Full-time tuition and fees vary according to program. *General application contact:* Cathleen R. Johnson, Coordinator of Graduate Admissions, 607-871-2141.

Find an in-depth description at www.petersons.com/graduate.

Graduate School
Dr. Susan Strong, Acting Provost and Director of Graduate Studies
Programs in:
community services administration • MPS
electrical engineering • MS
mechanical engineering • MS
school psychology • MA, Psy D, CAS

College of Business
Lori Hollenbeck, Director of MBA Program
Program in:
business • MBA

Division of Education
Dr. Katherine D. Wiesendanger, Chair
Programs in:

Alfred University (continued)
counseling • MS Ed
elementary education • MS Ed
literacy teacher • MS Ed
secondary education • MS Ed

New York State College of Ceramics
Dr. Susan Strong, Acting Provost and Director of Graduate Studies
Programs in:
biomedical materials engineering science • MS
ceramic engineering • MS
ceramics • MFA, PhD
electronic integrated arts • MFA
glass art • MFA
glass science • MS, PhD
materials science • MS
sculpture • MFA

■ BERNARD M. BARUCH COLLEGE OF THE CITY UNIVERSITY OF NEW YORK

New York, NY 10010-5585
http://www.baruch.cuny.edu/

State and locally supported, coed, comprehensive institution. *Enrollment:* 996 full-time matriculated graduate/professional students (501 women), 1,621 part-time matriculated graduate/professional students (776 women). *Graduate faculty:* 453 full-time (152 women), 390 part-time/adjunct (141 women). *Computer facilities:* 1,500 computers available on campus for general student use. A campuswide network can be accessed from off campus. Internet access is available. *Library facilities:* The William and Anita Newman Library plus 1 other. *Graduate expenses:* Tuition, state resident: full-time $4,995; part-time $185 per credit. Tuition, nonresident: full-time $8,640; part-time $320 per credit. Required fees: $26 per semester. *General application contact:* Michael S. Wynne, Office of Graduate Admissions, 212-802-2330.

School of Public Affairs
Stan Altman, Dean
Programs in:
educational administration and supervision • MS Ed
higher education administration • MS Ed
public administration • MPA
public affairs • MPA, MS Ed

Weissman School of Arts and Sciences
Dennis Slavin, Acting Dean
Programs in:
arts and sciences • MA
business journalism • MA
corporate communication • MA

Zicklin School of Business
Sidney Lirtzman, Vice President and Dean
Programs in:
accounting • MBA, MS, PhD
business • EMBA, EMSF, MBA, MS, PhD, Certificate
business administration • EMBA
computer information systems • MBA, MS
economics • MBA
finance • EMSF, MBA, MS, PhD
general business • MBA
general management and policy • MBA
health care administration • MBA
human resources management • MBA
industrial and organizational psychology • MBA, MS, PhD, Certificate
industrial and service management • MBA
international business • MBA
management planning systems • PhD
management science • MBA
marketing • MBA, MS, PhD
operations research • MBA, MS
organization and policy studies • PhD
organizational behavior • MBA
statistics • MBA, MS
taxation • MBA, MS

■ BROOKLYN COLLEGE OF THE CITY UNIVERSITY OF NEW YORK

Brooklyn, NY 11210-2889
http://www.brooklyn.cuny.edu/

State and locally supported, coed, comprehensive institution. *Enrollment:* 329 full-time matriculated graduate/professional students (226 women), 2,889 part-time matriculated graduate/professional students (2,051 women). *Computer facilities:* 600 computers available on campus for general student use. A campuswide network can be accessed from off campus. Internet access and online class registration are available. *Library facilities:* Brooklyn College Library plus 1 other. *Graduate expenses:* Tuition, state resident: full-time $4,350; part-time $185 per credit. Tuition, nonresident: full-time $7,600; part-time $30 per credit. Required fees: $185; $93 per semester. $65 per semester. *General application contact:* Michael Lovaglio, Acting Assistant Director of Graduate Admissions, 718-951-5914.

Find an in-depth description at www.petersons.com/graduate.

Division of Graduate Studies
Dr. Richard Pizer, Dean
Programs in:
accounting • MA
acting • MFA
applied biology • MA
applied chemistry • MA
applied geology • MA
applied physics • MA
art • PhD
art history • MA
audiology • MS
biology • MA, PhD
chemistry • MA, PhD
community health • MA, MPH, MS
computer and information science • MA, PhD
computer science and health science • MS
creative writing • MFA
criticism • MA
design and technical production • MFA
directing • MFA
dramaturgy • MFA
drawing and painting • MFA
economics • MA
economics and computer and information science • MPS
English • MA, PhD
exercise science and rehabilitation • MS
experimental psychology • MA
fiction • MFA
geology • MA, PhD
health care management • MA, MPH
health care policy and administration • MA, MPH
history • MA, PhD
industrial and organizational psychology • MA
information systems • MS
Judaic studies • MA
liberal studies • MA
management and programming • MS
mathematics • MA, PhD
nutrition • MS
nutrition sciences • MS
pathology • MS
performing arts management • MFA
photography • MFA
physical education • MS, MS Ed
physics • MA, PhD
playwriting • MFA
poetry • MFA
political science • MA, PhD

political science, urban policy and administration • MA
printmaking • MFA
psychology • PhD
sculpture • MFA
secondary mathematics education • MA
sociology • MA, PhD
Spanish • MA
speech • MS Ed, PhD
speech-language pathology and audiology • MS
television and radio • MS
television production • MFA
thanatology • MA
theater history • MA

Conservatory of Music
Dr. Nancy Hager, Chairperson
Programs in:
composition • MM
music • PhD
music education • MA
musicology • MA
performance • MM
performance practice • MA

School of Education
Dr. Deborah Shanley, Dean
Programs in:
art education • MS Ed
art teacher • MA
bilingual education • MS Ed
bilingual special education • MS Ed
biology teacher • MA
chemistry teacher • MA
children with emotional handicaps • MS Ed
children with neuropsychological learning disabilities • MS Ed
children with retarded mental development • MS Ed
early childhood education • MS Ed
education • MA, MS Ed, CAS
education of speech and hearing handicapped • MS Ed
elementary education teacher • MS Ed
elementary mathematics education • MS Ed
English teacher • MA
general science teacher • MA
guidance and counseling • MS Ed, CAS
health and nutrition sciences: health teacher • MS Ed
home economics education • MS Ed
humanities education • MS Ed
liberal arts • MS Ed
mathematics teacher • MA
music education • MS Ed
music teacher • MS Ed
physical education teacher • MS Ed
physics teacher • MA
school administration and supervision • CAS
school psychology • MS Ed, CAS
school psychology-bilingual • CAS
science and environmental education • MS Ed
social science education • MS Ed
social studies teacher • MA
Spanish teacher • MA
speech teacher • MA
teaching reading • MS Ed

■ CANISIUS COLLEGE
Buffalo, NY 14208-1098
http://www.canisius.edu/

Independent-religious, coed, comprehensive institution. *Enrollment:* 619 full-time matriculated graduate/professional students (406 women), 802 part-time matriculated graduate/professional students (439 women). *Graduate faculty:* 74 full-time (18 women), 96 part-time/adjunct (28 women). *Computer facilities:* 208 computers available on campus for general student use. A campuswide network can be accessed from student residence rooms and from off campus. Internet access and online class registration are available. *Library facilities:* Andrew L. Bouwhuis Library plus 1 other. *Graduate expenses:* Tuition: part-time $458 per credit hour. Required fees: $10 per credit hour. Tuition and fees vary according to program. *General application contact:* Dr. Herbert J. Nelson, Vice President for Academic Affairs, 716-888-2120 Ext. 109.

Graduate Division
Dr. Herbert J. Nelson, Vice President for Academic Affairs

College of Arts and Sciences
Dr. James P. McDermott, Dean
Programs in:
arts and sciences • MS
organizational communication and development • MS

Richard J. Wehle School of Business
Laura McEwen, Director, Graduate Business Programs
Programs in:
business • MBA, MBAPA, MTM
business administration • MBA, MBAPA
professional accounting • MBAPA
telecommunications management • MTM

School of Education and Human Services
Dr. Keith R. Burich, Dean
Programs in:
college student personnel administration • MS
counselor education • MS, CAS
education and human services • MS, MS Ed, CAS, SAS
educational administration and supervision • MS, SAS
physical education • MS
reading • MS Ed
secondary education • MS
special education—preparation of teachers of the deaf • MS
sport administration • MS
teacher education • MS Ed

■ CITY COLLEGE OF THE CITY UNIVERSITY OF NEW YORK
New York, NY 10031-9198
http://www.ccny.cuny.edu/

State and locally supported, coed, university. *Enrollment:* 230 full-time matriculated graduate/professional students (103 women), 1,463 part-time matriculated graduate/professional students (807 women). *Graduate faculty:* 482 full-time (142 women), 328 part-time/adjunct (126 women). *Computer facilities:* 3,000 computers available on campus for general student use. A campuswide network can be accessed from off campus. Internet access is available. *Library facilities:* Morris Raphael Cohen Library plus 3 others. *Graduate expenses:* Tuition, state resident: full-time $4,350; part-time $185 per credit. Tuition, nonresident: full-time $7,600; part-time $320 per credit. Required fees: $20 per semester. *General application contact:* 212-650-6977.

Find an in-depth description at www.petersons.com/graduate.

Graduate School
Joseph Barba, Assistant Provost for Graduate Studies and Research

College of Liberal Arts and Science
Programs in:
advertising design • MFA
applied urban anthropology • MA
art history • MA
art history and museum studies • MA
biochemistry • MA, PhD
biology • MA, PhD
ceramic design • MFA
chemistry • MA, PhD
clinical psychology • PhD
creative writing • MA
earth and environmental science • PhD
earth systems science • MA
economics • MA
English and American literature • MA

City College of the City University of New York (continued)

experimental cognition • PhD
fine arts • MFA
general psychology • MA
history • MA
humanities and arts • MA, MFA
international relations • MA
language and literacy • MA
liberal arts and science • MA, MFA, MS, PhD
mathematics • MA
media arts production • MFA
museum studies • MA
music • MA
painting • MFA
physics • MA, PhD
printmaking • MFA
science • MA, PhD
sculpture • MFA
social science • MA, MS, PhD
sociology • MA
Spanish • MA
wood and metal design • MFA

School of Architecture and Environmental Studies
Lance Brown, Chair
Programs in:
architecture • PD
urban design • MUP

School of Education
Alfred Posamentier, Interim Dean
Programs in:
bilingual education • MS
early childhood education • MS
education • MA, MS, MS Ed, AC
educational administration • MS, AC
elementary education • MS
environmental education • MA
reading • MS, AC
secondary science education • MA
special education • MS

School of Engineering
Dr. Muntaz G. Kassir, Associate Dean for Graduate Studies
Programs in:
chemical engineering • ME, MS, PhD
civil engineering • ME, MS, PhD
computer sciences • MS, PhD
electrical engineering • ME, MS, PhD
engineering • ME, MS, PhD
mechanical engineering • ME, MS, PhD

■ CITY UNIVERSITY OF NEW YORK SCHOOL OF LAW AT QUEENS COLLEGE

Flushing, NY 11367-1358
http://www.law.cuny.edu/

State and locally supported, coed, graduate-only institution. *Computer facilities:* 200 computers available on campus for general student use. A campuswide network can be accessed from off campus. Internet access is available. *Library facilities:* City University of New York School of Law Library. *General application contact:* Director of Admissions, 718-340-4210.

Professional Program

Program in:
law • JD

■ CLARKSON UNIVERSITY

Potsdam, NY 13699
http://www.clarkson.edu/

Independent, coed, university. CGS member. *Enrollment:* 315 full-time matriculated graduate/professional students (103 women), 23 part-time matriculated graduate/professional students (9 women). *Graduate faculty:* 158 full-time (29 women), 21 part-time/adjunct (9 women). *Computer facilities:* 250 computers available on campus for general student use. A campuswide network can be accessed from student residence rooms and from off campus. Internet access is available. *Library facilities:* Andrew S. Schuler Educational Resources Center. *Graduate expenses:* Tuition: part-time $713 per credit hour. Required fees: $215. *General application contact:* Dr. Anthony G. Collins, Vice-President for Academic Affairs, 315-268-6445.

Graduate School

Dr. Anthony G. Collins, Vice-President for Academic Affairs
Programs in:
basic science • MS
computer science • MS
engineering and management • MS
engineering and manufacturing management • MS
health science • MS
information technology • MS
physical therapy • MS

Center for Health Science
Dr. Samuel B. Feitelberg, Associate Dean of Health Sciences
Programs in:
basic science • MS
health science • MS
physical therapy • MS

School of Business
Dr. Timothy F. Sugrue, Dean
Programs in:
business • MBA, MS
business administration • MBA
human resource management • MS
management information systems • MS
manufacturing management • MS

School of Engineering
Dr. Norbert L. Ackermann, Dean
Programs in:
chemical engineering • ME, MS, PhD
civil and environmental engineering • PhD
civil engineering • ME, MS
computer engineering • ME, MS
electrical and computer engineering • PhD
electrical engineering • ME, MS
engineering • ME, MS, PhD
engineering science • MS, PhD
mechanical engineering • ME, MS, PhD

School of Science
Dr. Anthony G. Collins, Vice-President for Academic Affairs
Programs in:
analytical chemistry • MS, PhD
computer science • MS
inorganic chemistry • MS, PhD
mathematics • MS, PhD
organic chemistry • MS, PhD
physical chemistry • MS, PhD
physics • MS, PhD
science • MS, PhD

■ COLLEGE OF MOUNT SAINT VINCENT

Riverdale, NY 10471-1093
http://www.cmsv.edu/

Independent, coed, comprehensive institution. *Computer facilities:* 150 computers available on campus for general student use. A campuswide network can be accessed from student residence rooms and from off campus. E-mail available. *Library facilities:* Elizabeth Seton Library. *General application contact:* Director of Transfer and Graduate Admissions, 718-405-3267.

Find an in-depth description at www.petersons.com/graduate.

Division of Nursing

Dr. Susan Apold, Chairperson
Programs in:
adult nurse practitioner • MSN, PMC
clinical nurse specialist • MSN
family nurse practitioner • MSN, PMC
nursing administration • MSN
nursing for the adult and aged • MSN

Program in Allied Health
Dr. Rita Scher Dytell, Director
Programs in:
- allied health studies • MS
- counseling • Certificate
- health care management • Certificate
- health care systems and policies • Certificate

Program in Education
Programs in:
- instructional technology and global perspectives • MS Ed, Certificate
- middle level education • MS Ed, Certificate
- multicultural studies • MS Ed, Certificate
- urban and multicultural education • MS Ed, Certificate

■ THE COLLEGE OF NEW ROCHELLE

New Rochelle, NY 10805-2308
http://cnr.edu/

Independent, coed, primarily women, comprehensive institution. CGS member. *Enrollment:* 118 full-time matriculated graduate/professional students (104 women), 829 part-time matriculated graduate/professional students (722 women). *Graduate faculty:* 19 full-time (10 women), 66 part-time/adjunct (52 women). *Computer facilities:* 120 computers available on campus for general student use. A campuswide network can be accessed from off campus. Internet access and online class registration are available. *Library facilities:* Gill Library plus 1 other. *Graduate expenses:* Tuition: full-time $8,550; part-time $356 per credit. *General application contact:* Ann Fitzpatrick, Associate Dean of the Graduate School, 914-654-5389.

Find an in-depth description at www.petersons.com/graduate.

Graduate School
Dr. Laura S. Ellis, Dean
Programs in:
- acute care nurse practitioner • MS, Certificate
- art education • MA
- art museum education • Certificate
- art therapy • MS
- clinical specialist in holistic nursing • MS, Certificate
- communication studies • MS, Certificate
- family nurse practitioner • MS, Certificate
- fine art • MS
- graphic art • MS
- nursing and health care management • MS
- nursing education • Certificate
- studio art • MS

Division of Education
Dr. John J. Koster, Division Head
Programs in:
- bilingual education • Certificate
- elementary education/early childhood education • MS Ed
- gifted education • MS Ed, Certificate
- reading • MS Ed
- reading/special education • MS Ed
- school administration and supervision • MS Ed, Certificate, PD
- special education • MS Ed
- speech-language pathology • MS
- teaching English as a second language • MS Ed, Certificate

Division of Human Services
Head
Programs in:
- career development • MS, Certificate
- community-school psychology • MS
- gerontology • MS, Certificate
- guidance and counseling • MS
- thanatology • Certificate

■ THE COLLEGE OF SAINT ROSE

Albany, NY 12203-1419
http://www.strose.edu/

Independent, coed, comprehensive institution. CGS member. *Enrollment:* 273 full-time matriculated graduate/professional students (212 women), 1,229 part-time matriculated graduate/professional students (904 women). *Graduate faculty:* 110 full-time (65 women), 53 part-time/adjunct (32 women). *Computer facilities:* 322 computers available on campus for general student use. A campuswide network can be accessed from student residence rooms and from off campus. Internet access and online class registration are available. *Library facilities:* Neil Hellman Library plus 1 other. *Graduate expenses:* Tuition: full-time $8,712. Required fees: $330. *General application contact:* Anne Tully, Dean of Graduate and Adult and Continuing Education Admissions, 518-454-5136.

Find an in-depth description at www.petersons.com/graduate.

Graduate Studies
Dr. William Lowe, Vice President of Academic Affairs

School of Arts and Humanities
Programs in:
- art education • MS Ed
- arts and humanities • MA, MS Ed
- English • MA
- history/political science • MA
- music • MA
- music education • MS Ed
- public communications • MA

School of Business
Dr. Severin C. Carlson, Dean
Programs in:
- accounting • MS
- business • MBA, MS, Certificate
- business administration • MBA
- not-for-profit management • Certificate

School of Education
Dr. Crystal J. Gips, Dean
Programs in:
- applied technology • Certificate
- applied technology education • Certificate
- college student personnel • MS Ed
- communication disorders • MS Ed
- community counseling • MS Ed
- counseling • MS Ed
- early childhood education • MS Ed
- education • MS Ed, Certificate
- educational administration and supervision • MS Ed, Certificate
- educational computing • Certificate
- educational psychology • MS Ed
- elementary education • MS Ed
- reading • MS Ed
- school counseling • MS Ed
- school psychology • MS Ed, Certificate
- secondary education • MS Ed
- special education • MS Ed
- teacher education • MS Ed, Certificate

School of Mathematics and Sciences
Dr. David Amey, Dean
Programs in:
- computer information systems • MS
- mathematics and sciences • MS

■ COLLEGE OF STATEN ISLAND OF THE CITY UNIVERSITY OF NEW YORK

Staten Island, NY 10314-6600
http://www.csi.cuny.edu/

State and locally supported, coed, comprehensive institution. *Enrollment:* 104 full-time matriculated graduate/professional students (70 women), 1,265 part-time matriculated graduate/professional students (1,029 women). *Graduate faculty:* 79 full-time (36 women), 10 part-time/adjunct (7 women). *Computer facilities:* 120 computers available on campus for general student use.

College of Staten Island of the City University of New York (continued)
A campuswide network can be accessed from off campus. Internet access is available. *Library facilities:* College of Staten Island Library. *Graduate expenses:* Tuition, state resident: full-time $4,350; part-time $185 per credit. Tuition, nonresident: full-time $7,600; part-time $320 per credit. Required fees: $32 per semester. *General application contact:* Mary Beth Reilly, Director of Admissions, 718-982-2010.

Find an in-depth description at www.petersons.com/graduate.

Graduate Programs

Dr. Mirella Affron, Senior Vice President for Academic Affairs and Provost
Programs in:
- adult health nursing • MS
- biology • MS
- cinema studies • MA
- computer science • MS, PhD
- educational supervision and administration • 6th Year Certificate
- elementary education • MS Ed
- English • MA
- environmental science • MS
- history • MA
- liberal studies • MA
- physical therapy • MS
- polymer chemistry • PhD
- secondary education • MS Ed
- special education • MS Ed

Center for Developmental Neuroscience and Developmental Disabilities
Dr. Ekkehart Trenkner, Deputy Director
Programs in:
- biology • PhD
- learning processes • PhD
- neuroscience • PhD
- psychology • PhD

■ COLUMBIA UNIVERSITY

New York, NY 10027
http://www.columbia.edu/

Independent, coed, university. CGS member. *Graduate faculty:* 2,870 full-time (942 women), 803 part-time/adjunct (324 women). *Graduate expenses:* Tuition: full-time $27,528.

Find an in-depth description at www.petersons.com/graduate.

College of Physicians and Surgeons

Programs in:
- medicine • MD, M Phil, MA, MS, DN Sc, PhD, Adv C
- occupational therapy (professional) • MS
- occupational therapy administration or education (post-professional) • MS
- physical therapy • MS

Graduate School of Arts and Sciences at the College of Physicians and Surgeons
Programs in:
- anatomy • M Phil, MA, PhD
- anatomy and cell biology • PhD
- biochemistry and molecular biophysics • M Phil, PhD
- biomedical sciences • M Phil, MA, PhD
- biophysics • PhD
- cellular, molecular and biophysical studies • M Phil, MA, PhD
- genetics • M Phil, MA, PhD
- medical informatics • M Phil, MA, PhD
- medicine • M Phil, MA, PhD
- neurobiology and behavior • M Phil, PhD
- pathobiology • M Phil, MA, PhD
- pharmacology • M Phil, MA, PhD
- pharmacology-toxicology • M Phil, MA, PhD
- physiology and cellular biophysics • M Phil, MA, PhD

Institute of Human Nutrition
Dr. Richard Deckelbaum, Director
Program in:
- nutrition • M Phil, MA, MS, PhD

Fu Foundation School of Engineering and Applied Science

Zvi Galil, Dean
Programs in:
- applied physics • MS, PhD
- applied physics and applied mathematics • Eng Sc D
- biomedical engineering • MS, Eng Sc D
- chemical engineering • MS, Eng Sc D, PhD, Engr
- civil engineering • MS, Eng Sc D, PhD, Engr
- computer science • MS, PhD, CSE
- earth resources engineering • MS, PhD
- electrical engineering • MS, Eng Sc D, PhD, EE
- engineering and applied science • ME, MS, Eng Sc D, PhD, CSE, EE, EM, Engr, Met E
- financial engineering • MS
- industrial engineering • MS, Eng Sc D, PhD, Engr
- materials science and engineering • MS, Eng Sc D, PhD
- mechanical engineering • ME, MS, Eng Sc D, PhD
- mechanics • MS, Eng Sc D, PhD, Engr
- medical physics • MS
- minerals engineering and materials science • Eng Sc D, PhD, Engr
- operations research • MS, Eng Sc D, PhD
- solid state science and engineering • MS, Eng Sc D, PhD
- telecommunications • MS

Graduate School of Architecture, Planning, and Preservation

Bernard Tschumi, Dean
Programs in:
- advanced architectural design • MS
- architecture • M Arch, PhD
- architecture and urban design • MS
- architecture, planning, and preservation • M Arch, MS, PhD
- historic preservation • MS
- real estate development • MS
- urban planning • MS, PhD

Graduate School of Arts and Sciences

Programs in:
- African-American studies • MA
- American studies • MA
- arts and sciences • M Phil, MA, MS, DMA, PhD, Certificate
- conservation biology • Certificate
- East Asian regional studies • MA
- East Asian studies • MA
- ecology and evolutionary biology • PhD
- environmental policy • Certificate
- French cultural studies • MA
- human rights studies • MA
- Islamic culture studies • MA
- Jewish studies • MA
- medieval studies • MA
- modern European studies • MA
- quantitative methods in the social sciences • MA
- Russian, Eurasian and East European regional studies • MA
- South Asian studies • MA
- theatre • M Phil, MA, PhD
- Yiddish studies • MA

Division of Humanities
Programs in:
- archaeology • M Phil, MA, PhD
- art history and archaeology • M Phil, MA, PhD
- classics • M Phil, MA, PhD
- comparative literature • M Phil, MA, PhD
- East Asian languages and cultures • M Phil, MA, PhD
- English literature • M Phil, MA, PhD
- French and Romance philology • M Phil, PhD
- Germanic languages • M Phil, MA, PhD

Hebrew language and literature • M Phil, MA, PhD
humanities • M Phil, MA, DMA, PhD
Italian • M Phil, MA, PhD
Jewish studies • M Phil, MA, PhD
literature-writing • M Phil, MA, PhD
Middle Eastern languages and cultures • M Phil, MA, PhD
modern art • MA
music • M Phil, MA, DMA, PhD
Oriental studies • M Phil, MA, PhD
philosophy • M Phil, MA, PhD
religion • M Phil, MA, PhD
Romance languages • MA
Russian literature • M Phil, MA, PhD
Slavic languages • M Phil, MA, PhD
Spanish and Portuguese • M Phil, MA, PhD

Division of Natural Sciences
Programs in:
astronomy • M Phil, MA, PhD
atmospheric and planetary science • M Phil, PhD
biological sciences • M Phil, MA, PhD
chemical physics • M Phil, PhD
epidemiology • M Phil, MA, PhD
experimental psychology • M Phil, MA, PhD
geochemistry • M Phil, MA, PhD
geodetic sciences • M Phil, MA, PhD
geophysics • M Phil, MA, PhD
inorganic chemistry • M Phil, MS, PhD
mathematics • M Phil, MA, PhD
natural sciences • M Phil, MA, MS, PhD
oceanography • M Phil, MA, PhD
organic chemistry • M Phil, MS, PhD
philosophical foundations of physics • MA
physics • M Phil, PhD
psychobiology • M Phil, MA, PhD
social psychology • M Phil, MA, PhD
statistics • M Phil, MA, PhD

Division of Social Sciences
Programs in:
American history • M Phil, MA, PhD
anthropology • M Phil, MA, PhD
economics • M Phil, MA, PhD
history • M Phil, MA, PhD
political science • M Phil, MA, PhD
social sciences • M Phil, MA, PhD
sociology • M Phil, MA, PhD

Graduate School of Business
Prof. Meyer Feldberg, Dean
Programs in:
accounting • MBA
business • PhD
business administration • EMBA, MBA
entrepreneurship • MBA
finance and economics • MBA
human resource management • MBA
international business • MBA
management • MBA
management science • MBA
marketing • MBA
media, entertainment and communications • MBA
operations management • MBA
public and nonprofit management • MBA
real estate • MBA

Graduate School of Journalism
Program in:
journalism • MS

Joseph L. Mailman School of Public Health
Programs in:
biostatistics • MPH, MS, Dr PH, PhD
environmental health sciences • MPH, Dr PH, PhD
epidemiology • MPH, MS, Dr PH, PhD
health policy and management • Exec MPH, MPH, Dr PH
population and family health • MPH
public health • MPH, Dr PH
sociomedical sciences • MPH, Dr PH, PhD

School of Dental and Oral Surgery
Programs in:
clinical specialty • MA
dental and oral surgery • DDS, MA, MS

School of International and Public Affairs
Dr. Lisa Anderson, Dean
Programs in:
earth systems science, policy and management • MPA
international affairs • MIA
international and public affairs • MIA, MPA, Certificate
public policy and administration • MPA

East Asian Institute
Dr. Madeleine Zelin, Director
Program in:
Asian studies • Certificate

Harriman Institute
Dr. Mark L. von Hagen, Director

Institute for the Study of Europe
Dr. John Micgiel, Director
Program in:
Europe • Certificate

Institute of African Studies
Prof. Mahmood Mamdani, Director
Program in:
African studies • Certificate

Institute of Latin American and Iberian Studies
Dr. Douglas Chalmers, Director
Program in:
Latin American and Iberian studies • Certificate

Institute on East Central Europe
Dr. John Micgiel, Director
Program in:
East Central Europe • Certificate

Middle East Institute
Dr. Gary Sick, Director
Program in:
Middle East studies • Certificate

Southern Asian Institute
Dr. Giauri Viswanathan, Director
Program in:
Southern Asian studies • Certificate

School of Law
David W. Leebron, Dean of Faculty of Law
Program in:
law • JD, LL M, JSD

School of Nursing
Programs in:
acute care nurse practitioner • MS, Adv C
adult nurse practitioner • MS, Adv C
family nurse practitioner • MS, Adv C
geriatric nurse practitioner • MS, Adv C
HIV nursing • MS, Adv C
neonatal nurse practitioner • MS, Adv C
nurse anesthesia • MS, Adv C
nurse midwifery • MS
nursing • MS, DN Sc, Adv C
nursing science • DN Sc
oncology nursing • MS, Adv C
pediatric nurse practitioner • MS, Adv C
psychiatric-community mental health nursing • MS, Adv C
women's health nurse practitioner • MS, Adv C

School of Social Work
Program in:
social work • MSSW, PhD

School of the Arts
Bruce Ferguson, Dean
Programs in:
arts • MFA, DMA, PhD
digital media • MFA
directing • MFA

Columbia University (continued)
- drawing • MFA
- fiction • MFA
- history/theory • MFA
- installation • MFA
- mixed media • MFA
- nonfiction • MFA
- painting • MFA
- photography • MFA
- poetry • MFA
- printmaking • MFA
- producing • MFA
- screen writing • MFA
- sculpture • MFA

Oscar Hammerstein Center for Theatre Studies
Kristin Linklater, Chair
Programs in:
- acting • MFA
- directing • MFA
- drama and theater arts • PhD
- dramaturgy • MFA
- playwriting • MFA
- theater management • MFA

■ CORNELL UNIVERSITY

Ithaca, NY 14853-0001
http://www.cornell.edu/

Independent, coed, university. CGS member. *Enrollment:* 5,405 full-time matriculated graduate/professional students (2,259 women). *Graduate faculty:* 1,448 full-time (317 women), 72 part-time/adjunct (15 women). *Computer facilities:* 700 computers available on campus for general student use. A campuswide network can be accessed from student residence rooms and from off campus. Internet access is available. *Library facilities:* Olin Library plus 17 others. *Graduate expenses:* Tuition: full-time $24,760. Required fees: $50. Full-time tuition and fees vary according to program. *General application contact:* Graduate School Application Requests, Caldwell Hall, 607-255-4884.

Find an in-depth description at www.petersons.com/graduate.

Graduate School
Dr. Walter Cohen, Dean
Programs in:
- acarology • MS, PhD
- advanced composites and structures • M Eng
- advanced materials processing • M Eng, MS, PhD
- aerospace engineering • M Eng, MS, PhD
- African history • MA, PhD
- African studies • MPS
- African-American literature • PhD
- African-American studies • MPS
- agricultural economics • MPS, MS, PhD
- agricultural education • MAT
- agriculture and life sciences • M Eng, MAT, MFS, MLA, MPS, MS, PhD
- agronomy • MPS, MS, PhD
- algorithms • M Eng, PhD
- American art • PhD
- American history • MA, PhD
- American literature after 1865 • PhD
- American literature to 1865 • PhD
- American politics • PhD
- American studies • PhD
- analytical chemistry • PhD
- ancient art and archaeology • PhD
- ancient history • MA, PhD
- ancient Near Eastern studies • MA, PhD
- ancient philosophy • PhD
- animal breeding • MS, PhD
- animal cytology • PhD
- animal genetics • MS, PhD
- animal nutrition • MPS, MS, PhD
- animal science • MPS, MS, PhD
- apiculture • MS, PhD
- apparel design • MA, MPS
- applied economics • PhD
- applied entomology • MS, PhD
- applied logic and automated reasoning • M Eng, PhD
- applied mathematics • PhD
- applied mathematics and computational methods • M Eng, MS, PhD
- applied physics • PhD
- applied probability and statistics • PhD
- applied research in human-environment relations • MS
- applied statistics • MPS
- aquatic entomology • MS, PhD
- aquatic science • MPS, MS, PhD
- Arabic and Islamic studies • MA, PhD
- archaeological anthropology • PhD
- artificial intelligence • M Eng, PhD
- arts and sciences • MA, MFA, MPA, MPS, MS, DMA, PhD
- Asian religions • MA, PhD
- astronomy • PhD
- astrophysics • PhD
- atmospheric sciences • MPS, MS, PhD
- baroque art • PhD
- behavioral biology • PhD
- behavioral physiology • MS, PhD
- biblical studies • MA, PhD
- bio-organic chemistry • PhD
- biochemical engineering • M Eng, MS, PhD
- biochemistry • PhD
- biological anthropology • PhD
- biological control • MS, PhD
- biological engineering • M Eng, MPS, MS, PhD
- biology • MAT
- biomechanical engineering • M Eng, MS, PhD
- biomedical engineering • MS, PhD
- biometry • MS, PhD
- biophysical chemistry • PhD
- biophysics • PhD
- biopsychology • PhD
- cardiovascular and respiratory physiology • MS, PhD
- cell biology • PhD
- cellular and molecular medicine • MS, PhD
- cellular and molecular toxicology • MS, PhD
- cellular immunology • MS, PhD
- chemical physics • PhD
- chemical reaction engineering • M Eng, MS, PhD
- chemistry • MAT
- Chinese philology • MA, PhD
- classical and statistical thermodynamics • M Eng, MS, PhD
- classical archaeology • PhD
- classical Chinese literature • MA, PhD
- classical Japanese literature • MA, PhD
- collective bargaining, labor law and labor history • MILR, MPS, MS, PhD
- colonial and postcolonial literature • PhD
- combustion • M Eng, MS, PhD
- communication • MPS, MS, PhD
- communication research methods • MS, PhD
- community and regional sociology • MPS, PhD
- community development process • MPS
- community nutrition • MPS, MS, PhD
- comparative and functional anatomy • PhD
- comparative literature • PhD
- comparative politics • PhD
- composition • DMA
- computer engineering • M Eng, PhD
- computer graphics • M Eng, PhD
- computer science • M Eng, PhD
- computer vision • M Eng, PhD
- concurrency and distributed computing • M Eng, PhD
- controlled environment horticulture • MPS, MS, PhD
- creative writing • MFA
- cultural studies • PhD
- curriculum and instruction • MPS, MS, PhD
- dairy science • MPS, MS, PhD
- decision theory • MS, PhD
- development policy • MPS
- developmental and reproductive biology • MS

developmental and reproductive biology • PhD
developmental biology • PhD
developmental psychology • PhD
drama and the theatre • PhD
dramatic literature • PhD
dynamics and space mechanics • MS, PhD
early modern European history • MA, PhD
earth science • MAT
East Asian studies • MA
ecological and environmental plant pathology • MPS, MS, PhD
ecology • PhD
econometrics • MS, PhD
econometrics and economic statistics • PhD
economic and social statistics • MILR, MPS, MS, PhD
economic development • MPS
economic development and planning • PhD
economic geology • M Eng, MS, PhD
economic theory • PhD
economy and society • MA, PhD
ecotoxicology and environmental chemistry • MS, PhD
electrical engineering • M Eng, PhD
electrical systems • M Eng, PhD
electrophysics • M Eng, PhD
endocrinology • MS, PhD
energy • M Eng, MPS, MS, PhD
energy and power systems • M Eng, MS, PhD
engineering • M Eng, MPS, MS, PhD
engineering geology • M Eng, MS, PhD
engineering physics • M Eng, PhD
engineering statistics • MS, PhD
English history • MA, PhD
English poetry • PhD
English Renaissance to 1660 • PhD
enivronmental information science • MS
environmental and comparative physiology • MS, PhD
environmental archaeology • MA
environmental economics • MPS, MS
environmental engineering • M Eng, MPS, MS, PhD
environmental fluid mechanics and hydrology • M Eng, MS, PhD
environmental geophysics • M Eng, MS, PhD
environmental information science • MPS, PhD
environmental management • MPS
environmental systems engineering • M Eng, MS, PhD
evolutionary biology • PhD
experimental design • MS, PhD
experimental physics • MS, PhD
extension, and adult education • MPS, MS, PhD
facilities planning and management • MS
fiber science • MS, PhD
field crop science • MPS, MS, PhD
fishery science • MPS, MS, PhD
floriculture crop production • MPS, MS, PhD
fluid dynamics, rheology and biorheology • M Eng, MS, PhD
fluid mechanics • M Eng, MS, PhD
food chemistry • MPS, MS, PhD
food engineering • MPS, MS, PhD
food microbiology • MPS, MS, PhD
food processing engineering • M Eng, MPS, MS, PhD
food processing waste technology • MPS, MS, PhD
food science • MFS, MPS, MS, PhD
forest science • MPS, MS, PhD
French history • MA, PhD
French linguistics • PhD
French literature • PhD
gastrointestinal and metabolic physiology • MS, PhD
gender and life course • MA, PhD
general geology • M Eng, MS, PhD
general linguistics • MA, PhD
general psychology • PhD
general space sciences • PhD
genetics • PhD
geobiology • M Eng, MS, PhD
geochemistry and isotope geology • M Eng, MS, PhD
geohydrology • M Eng, MS, PhD
geomorphology • M Eng, MS, PhD
geophysics • M Eng, MS, PhD
geotechnical engineering • M Eng, MS, PhD
geotectonics • M Eng, MS, PhD
German area studies • MA, PhD
German history • MA, PhD
German intellectual history • MA, PhD
Germanic linguistics • MA, PhD
Germanic literature • MA, PhD
Greek and Latin language and linguistics • PhD
Greek language and literature • PhD
heat and mass transfer • M Eng, MS, PhD
heat transfer • M Eng, MS, PhD
Hebrew and Judaic studies • MA, PhD
Hispanic literature • PhD
historical archaeology • MA
history and philosophy of science and technology • MA, PhD
history of science • MA, PhD
horticultural physiology • MS, PhD
horticulture physiology • MPS
hospitality management • MMH
hotel administration • MS, PhD
housing and design • MS
human development and family studies • PhD
human ecology • MA, MPS, MS, PhD
human experimental psychology • PhD
human factors and ergonomics • MS
human nutrition • MPS, MS, PhD
human resource studies • MILR, MPS, MS, PhD
human-environment relations • MS
immunochemistry • MS, PhD
immunogenetics • MS, PhD
immunopathology • MS, PhD
industrial organization and control • PhD
infection and immunity • MS, PhD
infectious diseases • MS, PhD
information organization and retrieval • M Eng, PhD
infrared astronomy • PhD
inorganic chemistry • PhD
insect behavior • MS, PhD
insect biochemistry • MS, PhD
insect ecology • MS, PhD
insect genetics • MS, PhD
insect morphology • MS, PhD
insect pathology • MS, PhD
insect physiology • MS, PhD
insect systematics • MS, PhD
insect toxicology and insecticide chemistry • MS, PhD
integrated pest management • MS, PhD
interior design • MA
international agriculture • M Eng, MPS, MS, PhD
international agriculture and developmentr • MPS
international and comparative labor • MILR, MPS, MS, PhD
international communication • MS, PhD
international economics • PhD
international food science • MPS, MS, PhD
international nutrition • MPS, MS, PhD
international planning • MPS
international population • MPS
international relations • PhD
Italian linguistics • PhD
Italian literature • PhD
kinetics and catalysis • M Eng, MS, PhD
Korean literature • MA, PhD
labor economics • MILR, MPS, MS, PhD
landscape architecture • MLA
landscape horticulture • MPS, MS, PhD
Latin American archaeology • MA
Latin American history • MA, PhD
Latin language and literature • PhD
lesbian, bisexual, and gay literature studies • PhD
literary criticism and theory • PhD
local government organizations and operation • MPS

Cornell University (continued)
local roads • M Eng, MPS, MS, PhD
machine systems • M Eng, MPS, MS, PhD
manufacturing systems engineering • PhD
material chemistry • PhD
materials and manufacturing engineering • M Eng, MS, PhD
materials engineering • M Eng, PhD
materials science • M Eng, PhD
mathematical programming • PhD
mathematical statistics • MS, PhD
mathematics • MAT, MS
mechanical systems and design • M Eng, MS, PhD
mechanics of materials • MS, PhD
medical and veterinary entomology • MS, PhD
medieval archaeology • MA, PhD
medieval art • PhD
medieval Chinese history • MA, PhD
medieval history • MA, PhD
medieval literature • PhD
medieval music • PhD
medieval philology and linguistics • PhD
medieval philosophy • PhD
Mediterranean and Near Eastern archaeology • MA
membrane and epithelial physiology • MS, PhD
microbiology • PhD
mineralogy • M Eng, MS, PhD
modern art • PhD
modern Chinese history • MA, PhD
modern Chinese literature • MA, PhD
modern European history • MA, PhD
modern Japanese history • MA, PhD
modern Japanese literature • MA, PhD
molecular and cell biology • PhD
molecular and cellular physiology • MS, PhD
molecular biology • PhD
molecular plant pathology • MPS, MS, PhD
monetary and macroeconomics • PhD
multiphase flows • M Eng, MS, PhD
musicology • PhD
mycology • MPS, MS, PhD
neural and sensory physiology • MS, PhD
neurobiology • PhD
nineteenth century • PhD
nuclear engineering • M Eng, MS, PhD
nuclear science • MS, PhD
nursery crop production • MPS, MS, PhD
nutrition of horticultural crops • MPS, MS, PhD
nutritional and food toxicology • MS, PhD
nutritional biochemistry • MPS, MS, PhD
Old and Middle English • PhD
operating systems • M Eng, PhD
operations research and industrial engineering • M Eng
organic chemistry • PhD
organizational behavior • MILR, MPS, MS, PhD
organizations • MA, PhD
paleobotany • PhD
paleontology • M Eng, MS, PhD
parallel computing • M Eng, PhD
performance practice • DMA
personality and social psychology • PhD
petroleum geology • M Eng, MS, PhD
petrology • M Eng, MS, PhD
pharmacology • MS
philosophy • PhD
physical chemistry • PhD
physics • MAT, MS, PhD
physiology of reproduction • MPS, MS, PhD
planetary geology • M Eng, MS, PhD
planetary studies • PhD
plant breeding • MPS, MS, PhD
plant cell biology • PhD
plant disease epidemiology • MPS, MS, PhD
plant ecology • PhD
plant genetics • MPS, MS, PhD
plant materials and horticultural taxonomy • MPS, MS, PhD
plant molecular biology • PhD
plant morphology, anatomy and biomechanics • PhD
plant pathology • MPS, MS, PhD
plant physiology • PhD
plant propagation • MPS, MS, PhD
plant protection • MPS
political sociology/social movements • MA, PhD
political thought • PhD
polymer chemistry • PhD
polymer science • MS, PhD
polymers • M Eng, MS, PhD
pomology • MPS, MS, PhD
population and development • MPS, PhD
population medicine and epidemiogyical sciences • PhD
Precambrian geology • M Eng, MS, PhD
premodern Islamic history • MA, PhD
premodern Japanese history • MA, PhD
probability • MS, PhD
program development and planning • MPS
programming environments • M Eng, PhD
programming languages and methodology • M Eng, PhD
prose fiction • PhD
public affairs • MPA
public finance • PhD
public policy • MPA
Quaternary geology • M Eng, MS, PhD
racial and ethnic relations • MA, PhD
radio astronomy • PhD
radiophysics • PhD
remote sensing • M Eng, MS, PhD
Renaissance art • PhD
Renaissance history • MA, PhD
reproductive physiology • MS, PhD
resource economics • MPS, MS, PhD
resource policy and management • MPS, MS, PhD
Restoration and eighteenth century • PhD
robotics • M Eng, PhD
rock mechanics • M Eng, MS, PhD
Romance linguistics • PhD
rural and environmental sociology • MPS, PhD
Russian history • MA, PhD
sampling • MS, PhD
science and environmental communication • MS, PhD
science and technology policy • MPS
scientific computing • M Eng, PhD
sedimentology • MS, PhD
sedimetology • M Eng
seismology • M Eng, MS, PhD
sensory evaluation • MPS, MS, PhD
social networks • MA, PhD
social psychology • MA, PhD
social psychology of communication • MS, PhD
social statistics • MS, PhD
social stratification • MA, PhD
social studies of science and technology • MA, PhD
sociocultural anthropology • PhD
soil and water engineering • M Eng, MPS, MS, PhD
soil science • MPS, MS, PhD
solid mechanics • MS, PhD
South Asian studies • MA
Southeast Asian art • PhD
Southeast Asian history • MA, PhD
Southeast Asian studies • MA
Spanish linguistics • PhD
state, economy, and society • MPS, PhD
statistical computing • MS, PhD
stochastic processes • MS, PhD
Stone Age archaeology • MA
stratigraphy • M Eng, MS, PhD
structural and functional biology • PhD
structural engineering • M Eng, MS, PhD
structural geology • M Eng, MS, PhD
structures and environment • M Eng, MPS, MS, PhD

surface science • M Eng, MS, PhD
systematic botany • PhD
textile science • MS, PhD
theatre history • PhD
theatre theory and aesthetics • PhD
theoretical astrophysics • PhD
theoretical chemistry • PhD
theoretical physics • MS, PhD
theory and criticism • PhD
theory of computation • M Eng, PhD
transportation engineering • M Eng, MS, PhD
turfgrass science • MPS, MS, PhD
twentieth century • PhD
urban horticulture • MPS, MS, PhD
uses and effects of communication • MS, PhD
vegetable crops • MPS, MS, PhD
veterinary medicine • MS, PhD
veterinary physiology • MS
virology • MS
water resource systems • M Eng, MS, PhD
weed science • MPS, MS, PhD
wildlife science • MPS, MS, PhD
women's literature • PhD

Field of Environmental Management
Program in:
environmental management • MPS

Graduate Field in the Law School
Director of Graduate Studies
Program in:
law • LL M, JSD

Graduate Field of Management
Director of Graduate Studies
Programs in:
accounting • PhD
behavioral decision theory • PhD
finance • PhD
managerial economics • PhD
marketing • PhD
organizational behavior • PhD
production and operations management • PhD

Graduate Fields of Architecture, Art and Planning
Dr. Porus Olpadwala, Interim Dean
Programs in:
architectural design • M Arch
architectural science • MS
architecture, art and planning • M Arch, MA, MFA, MLA, MPSRE, MRP, MS, PhD
city and regional planning • MRP, PhD
computer graphics • MS
creative visual arts • MFA
environmental studies • MA, MS, PhD
historic preservation planning • MA
history of architecture • MA, PhD
history of urban development • MA, PhD
international spatial problems • MA, MS, PhD
location theory • MA, MS, PhD
multiregional economic analysis • MA, MS, PhD
peace science • MA, MS, PhD
planning methods • MA, MS, PhD
planning theory and systems analysis • MRP, PhD
real estate • MPSRE
regional science • MRP, PhD
urban and regional economics • MA, MS, PhD
urban and regional theory • MRP, PhD
urban design • M Arch
urban planning history • MRP, PhD

Law School
Lee E. Teitelbaum, Dean
Program in:
law • JD, LL M

Professional Field of the Johnson Graduate School of Management
Robert J. Swieringa, Dean
Program in:
management • MBA

Professional School of Veterinary Medicine
Dr. Donald F. Smith, Dean
Program in:
veterinary medicine • DVM

■ DOWLING COLLEGE

Oakdale, NY 11769-1999
http://www.dowling.edu/

Independent, coed, comprehensive institution. *Enrollment:* 770 full-time matriculated graduate/professional students (478 women), 2,161 part-time matriculated graduate/professional students (1,498 women). *Graduate faculty:* 198 full-time (68 women), 1,646 part-time/adjunct (716 women). *Computer facilities:* 118 computers available on campus for general student use. A campuswide network can be accessed. Internet access and online class registration are available. *Library facilities:* Dowling College Library. *Graduate expenses:* Tuition: full-time $5,940; part-time $495 per credit. Required fees: $740; $246 per semester. *General application contact:* Ronnie Lee MacDonald, Director of Student Recruitment and Enrollment Services, 516-244-3030.

Graduate Programs in Education
Programs in:
computers in education • PD
educational administration • Ed D, PD
elementary education • MS Ed
reading • MS Ed
reading/special education • MS Ed
school administration and supervision • PD
school district administration • PD
secondary education • MS Ed
special education • MS Ed

School of Business
Ward Deutschman, Associate Provost
Programs in:
aviation management • MBA, Certificate
banking and finance • MBA, Certificate
general management • MBA
public management • MBA, Certificate
total quality management • MBA, Certificate

■ FORDHAM UNIVERSITY

New York, NY 10458
http://www.fordham.edu/

Independent-religious, coed, university. CGS member. *Computer facilities:* 617 computers available on campus for general student use. A campuswide network can be accessed from student residence rooms and from off campus. Internet access and online class registration are available. *Library facilities:* Walsh Library plus 3 others. *General application contact:* Assistant Dean, 718-817-4420.

Find an in-depth description at www.petersons.com/graduate.

Graduate School of Arts and Sciences
Programs in:
arts and sciences • MA, MS, PhD, CIF
biblical studies • MA, PhD
biological sciences • MS, PhD
classical Greek and Latin literature • MA
classical Greek literature • MA
classical Latin literature • MA
classical philology • PhD
clinical psychology • PhD
computer science • MS
criminology • MA
developmental psychology • PhD
economics • MA, PhD
English language and literature • MA, PhD
historical theology • MA, PhD

Fordham University (continued)
- history • MA, PhD
- humanities and sciences • MA
- international political economy and development • MA, CIF
- medieval Latin • PhD
- medieval studies • MA
- philosophical resources • MA
- philosophy • MA, PhD
- political science • MA, PhD
- psychometrics • PhD
- public communications • MA
- sociology • MA, PhD
- systematics • MA, PhD

Graduate School of Business
Dr. Ernest J. Scalberg, Dean
Programs in:
- accounting • MBA
- communications and media management • MBA
- finance • MBA
- information and communication systems • MBA
- management systems • MBA
- marketing • MBA
- taxation • MS

Graduate School of Education
Dr. Regis Bernhardt, Dean
Program in:
- education • MAT, MS, MSE, MST, Ed D, PhD, Adv C

Division of Administration, Policy, and Urban Education
Dr. Barbara Jackson, Chairperson
Programs in:
- administration and supervision • MSE, Adv C
- administration and supervision for church leaders • PhD
- educational administration and supervision • Ed D, PhD
- human resource program administration • MS

Division of Curriculum and Teaching
Dr. Terry Cicchelli, Chairperson
Programs in:
- adult education • MS, MSE
- bilingual teacher education • MSE
- curriculum and teaching • MSE
- early childhood education • MSE
- elementary education • MST
- language, literacy, and learning • PhD
- reading education • MSE, Adv C
- secondary education • MAT, MSE
- special education • MSE, Adv C
- teaching English as a second language • MSE

Division of Psychological and Educational Services
Dr. Giselle Esquivel, Chairman
Programs in:
- counseling and personnel services • MSE, Adv C
- counseling psychology • PhD
- educational psychology • MSE, PhD
- school psychology • PhD
- urban and urban bilingual school psychology • Adv C

Graduate School of Religion and Religious Education
Rev. Vincent M. Novak, SJ, Dean
Programs in:
- pastoral counseling and spiritual care • MA
- religious education • PD
- religious studies • MA, MS, PD
- spiritual direction • Certificate

Graduate School of Social Service
Program in:
- social service • MSW, PhD

School of Law
John Feerick, Dean
Programs in:
- banking, corporate and finance law • LL M
- international business and trade law • LL M
- law • JD

■ HOFSTRA UNIVERSITY
Hempstead, NY 11549
http://www.hofstra.edu/

Independent, coed, university. CGS member. *Enrollment:* 1,319 full-time matriculated graduate/professional students (669 women), 2,479 part-time matriculated graduate/professional students (1,762 women). *Graduate faculty:* 206 full-time (87 women), 146 part-time/adjunct (74 women). *Computer facilities:* 600 computers available on campus for general student use. A campuswide network can be accessed from student residence rooms. Internet access is available. *Library facilities:* Axinn Library plus 1 other. *Graduate expenses:* Tuition: full-time $11,880; part-time $495 per credit hour. Required fees: $882; $112 per semester. *General application contact:* Mary Beth Carey, Vice President of Enrollment Services.

Find an in-depth description at www.petersons.com/graduate.

College of Liberal Arts and Sciences
Dr. Bernard J. Firestone, Dean
Program in:
- liberal arts and sciences • MA, MS, PhD, Psy D, Post-Doctoral Certificate

Division of Humanities
Programs in:
- applied linguistics • MA
- audiology and speech-language pathology • MA
- bilingualism • MA
- English • MA
- English and creative writing • MA
- humanities • MA
- speech-language pathology • MA

Division of Natural Sciences, Mathematics, Engineering, and Computer Science
Programs in:
- applied mathematics • MA, MS
- biology • MA, MS
- computer science • MA, MS
- human cytogenetics • MS
- natural sciences, mathematics, engineering, and computer science • MA, MS

Division of Social Sciences
Programs in:
- clinical and school psychology • MA, PhD, Post-Doctoral Certificate
- industrial/organizational psychology • MA
- school-community psychology • MS, Psy D
- social sciences • MA, MS, PhD, Psy D, Post-Doctoral Certificate

Frank G. Zarb School of Business
Dr. Ralph Polimeni, Dean of Academics
Programs in:
- accounting • MBA, MS
- accounting information systems • MS
- business • Exec MBA, MBA, MS
- business computer information systems/quantitative methods • MBA
- computer information systems • MS
- finance • MBA, MS
- human resource management • MS
- international business • MBA
- management • MBA
- marketing • MBA, MS
- marketing research • MS
- taxation • MBA, MS

New College
David C. Christman, Dean
Program in:
- interdisciplinary studies • MA

School of Education and Allied Human Services
James Johnson, Dean
Programs in:
- art • MS Ed
- art education • MA, MS Ed

art therapy and special education • MA
bilingual education • MS Ed
biology • MS Ed
biology education • MA
business • MS Ed
business and distributive education • MA
chemistry • MA, MS Ed
consultation in special education • CAS
counseling • MS Ed, CAS, Professional Diploma
creative arts therapy • MA
deaf education • CAS
early childhood education • MA
early childhood special education • MS Ed, CAS
education and allied human services • MA, MPS, MS, MS Ed, Mus Doc, Ed D, PhD, CAS, Certificate, PD, Professional Diploma
educational administration • MS Ed, Mus Doc, Ed D, CAS
elementary and early childhood education • MA, MS Ed
elementary education • MA, MS Ed
emotional disturbance • MS Ed
English • MA, MS Ed
family therapy • Certificate
foundations of education • MS Ed, CAS
foundations of education and elementary education • CAS
French • MA, MS Ed
geology • MA, MS Ed
German • MA, MS Ed
gerontology • MS, CAS
health administration • MA
health education • MS Ed
learning disability • MS Ed
marriage and family therapy • MA, CAS, Certificate, Professional Diploma
mathematics • MA, MS Ed
mathematics, science, and technology in elementary education • MA
mental retardation • MS Ed
music • MS Ed
music education • MA, MS Ed
physical disability • MS Ed
physical education • MS
physics • MA, MS Ed
postsecondary transition specialist • CAS
program evaluation • MS Ed
reading • MA, MS Ed, Mus Doc, Ed D, PhD, CAS
rehabilitation administration • Professional Diploma
rehabilitation counseling • MS Ed, Professional Diploma
Russian • MA, MS Ed
secondary education • MA, MS Ed
sex counseling • CAS
social studies • MA
Spanish • MA, MS Ed
special education • MA, MPS, MS Ed, Mus Doc, CAS
special education and reading • Mus Doc
special education assessment and diagnosis • CAS
teaching English as a second language • MS Ed
teaching of writing • MA, CAS

School of Law
Dr. Stuart Rabinowitz, Dean
Programs in:
American legal studies • LL M
international law • LL M
law • JD

■ HUNTER COLLEGE OF THE CITY UNIVERSITY OF NEW YORK

New York, NY 10021-5085
http://www.hunter.cuny.edu/

State and locally supported, coed, comprehensive institution. *Computer facilities:* 600 computers available on campus for general student use. A campuswide network can be accessed. Internet access is available. *Library facilities:* Hunter College Library. *General application contact:* Director of Admissions, 212-772-4490.

Find an in-depth description at www.petersons.com/graduate.

Graduate School
Programs in:
biochemistry • MA
biological sciences • MA, PhD
physics • MA, PhD

Hunter-Bellevue School of Nursing
Dr. Diane Rendon, Director
Programs in:
adult nurse practitioner • MS
community health nursing • MS
gerontological nurse practitioner • MS
maternal child-health nursing • MS
medical/surgical nursing • MS
nursing • MS, AC
pediatric nurse practitioner • MS, AC
psychiatric nursing • MS

School of Arts and Sciences
Dr. Ann H. Cohen, Dean
Programs in:
analytical geography • MA
anthropology • MA
applied and evaluative psychology • MA
applied mathematics • MA
art history • MA
arts and sciences • MA, MFA, MS, MSSR, MUP, PhD
biopsychology and comparative psychology • MA
communications and mass culture • MA
computer science • PhD
creative writing • MFA
economics • MA
English and American literature • MA
English education • MA
environmental and social issues • MA
fine arts • MFA
French • MA
French education • MA
geographic information systems • MA
history • MA
Italian • MA
Italian education • MA
mathematics for secondary education • MA
music • MA
music education • MA
pure mathematics • MA
Russian area studies • MA
social research • MS
social, cognitive, and developmental psychology • MA
sociology • MSSR
Spanish • MA
Spanish education • MA
studio art • MFA
teaching Latin • MA
theater • MA
urban affairs • MS
urban planning • MUP

School of Education
Cortland Lee, Dean
Programs in:
bilingual education • MS
biology education • MA
blind or visually impaired • MS Ed
chemistry education • MA
corrective reading (K–12) • MS Ed
deaf or hard of hearing • MS Ed
early childhood education • MS
earth science • MA
education • MA, MS, MS Ed, AC
educational supervision and administration • AC
elementary education • MS
English education • MA
French education • MA
Italian education • MA
literacy • MS
mathematics education • MA
music education • MA
physics education • MA
rehabilitation counseling • MS Ed
school counselor • MS Ed

Hunter College of the City University of New York (continued)

severe/multiple disabilities • MS Ed
social studies education • MA
Spanish education • MA
special education • MS Ed
teaching English as a second language • MA

School of Health Sciences
Programs in:
audiology • MS
community health education • MPH
environmental and occupational health • MPH
environmental and occupational health sciences • MS
health sciences • MPH, MPT, MS
physical therapy • MPT
public heatlh nutrition • MPH
speech language pathology • MS
teacher of speech and hearing handicapped • MS
urban public health • MPH, MS

School of Social Work
Bogart R. Leashore, Dean
Program in:
social work • MSW, DSW

■ IONA COLLEGE

New Rochelle, NY 10801-1890

http://www.iona.edu/

Independent-religious, coed, comprehensive institution. *Enrollment:* 65 full-time matriculated graduate/professional students (40 women), 982 part-time matriculated graduate/professional students (599 women). *Graduate faculty:* 66 full-time (19 women), 52 part-time/adjunct (15 women). *Computer facilities:* 425 computers available on campus for general student use. A campuswide network can be accessed from student residence rooms and from off campus. Internet access is available. *Library facilities:* Ryan Library plus 1 other. *Graduate expenses:* Tuition: part-time $515 per credit. *General application contact:* Thomas Delahunt, Vice Provost, 914-633-2461.

Find an in-depth description at www.petersons.com/graduate.

Hagan School of Business
Dr. Nicholas J. Beutell, Dean
Programs in:
business • MBA, PMC
financial management • MBA, PMC
human resource management • MBA, PMC
information and decision technology management • MBA, PMC
international business • PMC
management • MBA, PMC
marketing • MBA, PMC

School of Arts and Science
Dr. Warren Rosenberg, Dean, School of A&S
Programs in:
arts and science • MA, MS, MS Ed, MST, Certificate, PMC
biology education • MS Ed, MST
business education • MST
communication • PMC
computer science • MS
criminal justice • MS
educational administration • MS Ed
educational technology • MS, Certificate
English • MA
English education • MS Ed, MST
family counseling • MS, Certificate
health service administration • MS, Certificate
history • MA
journalism • MS
mathematics education • MS Ed, MST
multicultural education • MS Ed
pastoral counseling • MS
psychology • MA
school counseling • MA
school psychologist • MA
science • MS Ed
social studies education • MS Ed, MST
Spanish • MA
Spanish education • MS Ed, MST
teaching elementary education • MST
telecommunications • MS, Certificate

■ ITHACA COLLEGE

Ithaca, NY 14850-7020

http://www.ithaca.edu/

Independent, coed, comprehensive institution. CGS member. *Enrollment:* 228 full-time matriculated graduate/professional students (177 women), 20 part-time matriculated graduate/professional students (16 women). *Graduate faculty:* 109 full-time (45 women), 4 part-time/adjunct (2 women). *Computer facilities:* 584 computers available on campus for general student use. A campuswide network can be accessed from student residence rooms and from off campus. Internet access and online class registration are available. *Library facilities:* Ithaca College Library. *Graduate expenses:* Tuition: full-time $14,400; part-time $600 per credit. *General application contact:* Dr. Garry Brodhead, Associate Provost and Dean of Graduate Studies, 607-274-3527.

Find an in-depth description at www.petersons.com/graduate.

Graduate Studies
Dr. Garry Brodhead, Associate Provost and Dean
Programs in:
business • MBA
management • MBA

Roy H. Park School of Communications
Dr. Thomas W. Bohn, Dean
Program in:
communications • MS

School of Business
Dr. Robert Ullrich, Dean
Programs in:
business • MBA
management • MBA

School of Health Sciences and Human Performance
Dr. Richard Miller, Dean
Programs in:
exercise and sport sciences • MS
health sciences and human performance • MS
occupational therapy • MS
physical therapy • MS
speech pathology • MS
teacher of the speech and hearing handicapped • MS

School of Music
Dr. Arthur Ostrander, Dean
Programs in:
composition • MM
conducting • MM
music • MM, MS
music education • MM, MS
music theory • MM
performance • MM
strings, woodwinds, or brasses • MM
Suzuki pedagogy • MM

■ LEHMAN COLLEGE OF THE CITY UNIVERSITY OF NEW YORK

Bronx, NY 10468-1589

http://www.lehman.cuny.edu/

State and locally supported, coed, comprehensive institution. *Enrollment:* 83 full-time matriculated graduate/professional students (59 women), 1,624 part-time matriculated graduate/professional students (1,234 women). *Graduate faculty:* 110 full-time, 36 part-time/adjunct. *Computer facilities:* 600 computers available on campus for general student use. Internet access is available. *Library facilities:* Lehman College Library plus 1 other. *Graduate expenses:* Tuition, state resident: full-time $4,350; part-time $185 per credit. Tuition, nonresident: full-time $7,600; part-time $320 per credit. Required fees: $120; $40 per semester. *General application contact:* Roland Valaz, Deputy Director of Admissions and Recruitment, 718-960-8856.

Division of Arts and Humanities
Marlene Gottlieb, Acting Dean
Programs in:
art • MA, MFA
arts and humanities • MA, MAT, MFA
English • MA
history • MA
music • MAT
Spanish • MA
speech-language pathology and audiology • MA

Division of Education
James V. Bruni, Dean
Programs in:
bilingual special education • MS Ed
business education • MS Ed
early childhood education • MS Ed
early special education • MS Ed
education • MA, MS Ed
elementary education • MS Ed
emotional handicaps • MS Ed
English education • MS Ed
guidance and counseling • MS Ed
learning disabilities • MS Ed
mathematics 7–12 • MS Ed
mental retardation • MS Ed
reading teacher • MS Ed
science education • MS Ed
social studies 7–12 • MA
special education • MS Ed
teaching English to speakers of other languages • MS Ed

Division of Natural and Social Sciences
Joseph Rachlin, Dean
Programs in:
accounting • MS
adult health nursing • MS
approved preprofessional practice • MS
biology • MA
clinical nutrition • MS
community nutrition • MS
computer science • MS
health education and promotion • MA
health N–12 teacher • MS Ed
mathematics • MA
natural and social sciences • MA, MS, MS Ed, PhD
nursing of old adults • MS
nutrition • MS
parent-child nursing • MS
pediatric nurse practitioner • MS
plant sciences • PhD
recreation • MA, MS Ed
recreation education • MA, MS Ed

■ LE MOYNE COLLEGE
Syracuse, NY 13214-1399
http://www.lemoyne.edu/

Independent-religious, coed, comprehensive institution. *Enrollment:* 34 full-time matriculated graduate/professional students (25 women), 416 part-time matriculated graduate/professional students (244 women). *Graduate faculty:* 33 full-time (13 women), 29 part-time/adjunct (16 women). *Computer facilities:* 225 computers available on campus for general student use. A campuswide network can be accessed from student residence rooms and from off campus. Internet access is available. *Library facilities:* Noreen Reale Falcone Library. *Graduate expenses:* Tuition: full-time $7,182; part-time $399 per credit hour. Tuition and fees vary according to program.

Department of Business
Dr. Wally Elmer, Director of MBA Program
Program in:
business • MBA

Department of Education
Dr. Robert P. Anderson, Chair, Education Department and Director of Graduate Education
Program in:
education • MS Ed, MST

■ LONG ISLAND UNIVERSITY, BROOKLYN CAMPUS
Brooklyn, NY 11201-8423
http://www.liu.edu/

Independent, coed, university. *Computer facilities:* 345 computers available on campus for general student use. A campuswide network can be accessed from student residence rooms and from off campus. *Library facilities:* Selena Library. *General application contact:* Associate Director of Admissions, 718-488-1011.

Arnold and Marie Schwartz College of Pharmacy and Health Sciences
Dr. Stephen M. Gross, Dean
Programs in:
cosmetic science • MS
drug information and communication • MS
drug regulatory affairs • MS
industrial pharmacy • MS
pharmaceutical and health care marketing administration • MS
pharmaceutics • PhD
pharmaceutics and industrial pharmacy • MS, PhD
pharmacology/toxicology • MS
pharmacology/toxicology/medicinal chemistry • MS
pharmacy • Pharm D, MS, PhD
pharmacy and health sciences • MS, PhD
pharmacy practice • MS
social and administrative sciences • MS

Richard L. Conolly College of Liberal Arts and Sciences
Programs in:
arts and sciences • MA, MS, PhD, Certificate
biology • MS
chemistry • MS
clinical psychology • PhD
economics • MA
English literature • MA
history • MS
political science • MA
professional and creative writing • MA
psychology • MA
speech-language pathology • MS
teaching of writing • MA
United Nations studies • Certificate
urban studies • MA

School of Business, Public Administration and Information Sciences
Programs in:
accounting • MS
business administration • MBA
business and public administration • MBA, MPA, MS
computer science • MS
human resources management • MS
public administration • MPA
taxation • MS

School of Education
Programs in:
bilingual education • MS Ed
computers in education • MS
counseling and development • MS, MS Ed, Certificate
education • MS, MS Ed, Certificate
elementary education • MS Ed
leadership and policy • MS

Long Island University, Brooklyn Campus (continued)
- mathematics education • MS Ed
- reading • MS Ed
- school psychology • MS Ed
- secondary education • MS Ed
- special education • MS Ed
- teaching English to speakers of other languages • MS Ed

School of Health Professions
Programs in:
- adapted physical education • MS
- athletic training and sports sciences • MS
- community mental health • MS
- exercise physiology • MS
- family health • MS
- health management • MS
- health professions • MS
- health sciences • MS
- physical therapy • MS

School of Nursing
Programs in:
- adult nurse practitioner • MS, Certificate
- nurse executive • MS
- nursing • MS, Certificate

■ LONG ISLAND UNIVERSITY, C.W. POST CAMPUS

Brookville, NY 11548-1300

http://www.cwpost.liunet.edu/cwis/cwp/post.html

Independent, coed, comprehensive institution. *Enrollment:* 933 full-time matriculated graduate/professional students (664 women), 1,537 part-time matriculated graduate/professional students (861 women). *Graduate faculty:* 307. *Computer facilities:* 357 computers available on campus for general student use. A campuswide network can be accessed from student residence rooms and from off campus. Internet access is available. *Library facilities:* B. Davis Schwartz Memorial Library. *Graduate expenses:* Tuition: full-time $12,600; part-time $525 per credit. Required fees: $100; $30 per term. One-time fee: $30. Full-time tuition and fees vary according to course load and program. *General application contact:* Beth Carson, Associate Director of Graduate Admissions, 516-299-2719.

Find an in-depth description at www.petersons.com/graduate.

College of Liberal Arts and Sciences
Dr. Paul Sherwin, Dean
Programs in:
- applied mathematics • MS
- biology • MS
- biology secondary education • MS
- clinical psychology • Psy D
- computer science education • MS
- English • MA
- English secondary education • MS
- environmental management • MS
- environmental science • MS
- French secondary education • MS
- general experimental psychology • MA
- history • MA
- information systems • MS
- interdisciplinary studies • MA, MS
- Italian secondary education • MS
- liberal arts and sciences • MA, MS, PhD, Psy D
- management engineering • MS
- mathematics for secondary school teachers • MS
- political science/international studies • MA
- social studies • MS
- social studies secondary education • MS
- Spanish • MA

College of Management
Dr. Robert J. Sanator, Dean
Program in:
- management • MBA, MPA, MS, Certificate

School of Business
Robert Bell, MBA Program Director
Programs in:
- business administration • Certificate
- chain management • MBA
- finance • MBA, Certificate
- general business administration • MBA
- human resource management • Certificate
- international business • MBA, Certificate
- logistical supply chain • Certificate
- logistics and supply • MBA
- management • MBA, Certificate
- management information systems • MBA, Certificate
- marketing • MBA, Certificate

School of Professional Accountancy
Dr. Lawrence P. Kalbers, Director
Programs in:
- accountancy/information system • MS
- accounting • MS
- taxation • MS

School of Public Service
Peter B. Volgyes, Chairperson, Department of Health Care and Public Administration
Programs in:
- fraud examination • MS
- gerontology • Certificate
- health care administration • MPA
- health care administration/ gerontology • MPA
- public administration • MPA
- public service • MPA, MS, Certificate
- security administration • MS

Palmer School of Library and Information Science
Dr. Michael E. D. Koening, Dean
Programs in:
- archives • Certificate
- information studies • PhD
- library and information science • MS
- records management • Certificate
- schooll library media specialist • MS

School of Education
Dr. Jeffrey Kane, Dean
Programs in:
- adolescence • MS
- art education • MS
- bilingual education • MS
- biology education • MS
- childhood • MS
- college student development counseling • MS
- computers in education • MS
- early childhood/literacy • MS
- earth science education • MS
- education • MA, MS, MS Ed, PD
- English education • MS
- French education • MS
- Italian education • MS
- literacy • MS
- marriage and family therapy • PD
- mathematics education • MS
- mental health counseling • MS
- music education • MS
- reading • MS Ed
- school administration and supervision • MS Ed
- school business administration • PD
- school counseling • MS
- school district administration • PD
- social studies • MS
- Spanish education • MS
- special education • MS Ed, PD
- speech-language pathology • MA

School of Health Professions
Dr. Theodora T. Grauer, Dean
Programs in:
- advanced practical nursing • MS
- cardiovascular perfusion • MS, Certificate
- clinical laboratory management • MS, Certificate
- dietetic internship • Certificate
- family nurse practitioner • MS, Certificate
- health professions • MS, Certificate
- hematology • MS

immunology • MS
medical biology • MS
medical chemistry • MS
microbiology • MS
nutrition • MS

School of Visual and Performing Arts
Lynn Croton, Dean
Programs in:
art • MA
art education • MS
clinical art therapy • MA
fine art and design • MFA
interactive multimedia arts • MA
music • MA
music education • MS
theatre • MA
visual and performing arts • MA, MFA, MS

■ MANHATTAN COLLEGE

Riverdale, NY 10471
http://www.manhattan.edu/

Independent-religious, coed, comprehensive institution. *Enrollment:* 253 matriculated graduate/professional students. *Graduate faculty:* 67. *Computer facilities:* 375 computers available on campus for general student use. A campuswide network can be accessed from student residence rooms and from off campus. Internet access is available. *Library facilities:* Cardinal Hayes Library plus 1 other. *Graduate expenses:* Tuition: full-time $17,770; part-time $435 per credit. *General application contact:* Dr. Weldon Jackson, Provost, 718-862-7303.

Find an in-depth description at www.petersons.com/graduate.

Graduate Division
Dr. Weldon Jackson, Provost

School of Education
Dr. Elizabeth Kosky, Director, Graduate Education Programs
Programs in:
administration and supervision • MS Ed, Diploma
counseling • MA, Diploma
special education • MS Ed, Diploma

School of Engineering
Dr. Richard H. Heist, Dean
Programs in:
chemical engineering • MS
civil engineering • MS
computer engineering • MS
electrical engineering • MS
environmental engineering • ME, MS
mechanical engineering • MS

School of Science
Dr. Edward B. Brown, Dean
Program in:
biotechnology • MS

■ MANHATTANVILLE COLLEGE

Purchase, NY 10577-2132
http://www.mville.edu/

Independent, coed, comprehensive institution. *Enrollment:* 144 full-time matriculated graduate/professional students (124 women), 717 part-time matriculated graduate/professional students (610 women). *Graduate faculty:* 38 full-time (17 women), 78 part-time/adjunct (50 women). *Computer facilities:* 83 computers available on campus for general student use. A campuswide network can be accessed from student residence rooms and from off campus. Internet access is available. *Library facilities:* Manhattanville College Library plus 1 other. *Graduate expenses:* Tuition: part-time $435 per credit. Required fees: $35 per semester. Tuition and fees vary according to program. *General application contact:* Barry Ward, Vice President of Enrollment and Student Development, 914-323-5153.

Find an in-depth description at www.petersons.com/graduate.

Graduate Programs
Dr. Luis A. Losada, Provost and Dean of Faculty
Programs in:
leadership and strategic management • MS
liberal studies • MA
management communications • MS
organization management and human resources development • MS
writing • MA

School of Education
Dr. Sylvia Blake, Dean
Programs in:
art education • MAT
education • MAT, MPS
elementary education • MAT
elementary education and special education • MPS
English • MAT
languages • MAT
mathematics • MAT
music education • MAT
reading and writing • MPS
science • MAT
secondary and special education • MPS
social studies • MAT
special education • MPS
special education and reading • MPS
teaching English as a second language • MPS

■ MARIST COLLEGE

Poughkeepsie, NY 12601-1387
http://www.marist.edu/

Independent, coed, comprehensive institution. *Enrollment:* 137 full-time matriculated graduate/professional students (76 women), 648 part-time matriculated graduate/professional students (324 women). *Graduate faculty:* 33 full-time (11 women), 30 part-time/adjunct (14 women). *Computer facilities:* 450 computers available on campus for general student use. A campuswide network can be accessed from student residence rooms and from off campus. Internet access is available. *Library facilities:* Marist College Library. *Graduate expenses:* Tuition: full-time $4,158; part-time $462 per credit. Required fees: $30 per semester. *General application contact:* Dr. H. Griffin Walling, Dean of Graduate and Continuing Education, 845-575-3530.

Graduate Programs
Dr. Artin Arslanian, Academic Vice President

School of Computer Science and Mathematics
Dr. Onkar Sharma, Dran
Program in:
computer science • MS

School of Management
Dr. Gordon Badovick, Dean
Programs in:
business administration • MBA, PGC
management • MBA, MPA, Certificate, PGC
public administration • MPA, Certificate

School of Social/Behavioral Sciences
Margaret Calista, Dean
Programs in:
counseling/community psychology • MA
education psychology • MA
school psychology • MA, Adv C

■ MERCY COLLEGE

Dobbs Ferry, NY 10522-1189
http://www.mercynet.edu/

Independent, coed, comprehensive institution. *Computer facilities:* 138 computers available on campus for general student use. A campuswide network can be

Mercy College (continued)
accessed from off campus. Internet access is available. *Library facilities:* Mercy College Library. *General application contact:* Vice President of Enrollment Management, 914-674-7600.

Department of Education
Programs in:
- administration and supervision • MS, PD
- education • MS
- reading • MS
- teaching English to speakers of other languages • MS

Division of Business and Accounting
Programs in:
- banking • MS
- direct marketing • MS
- finance • MBA
- human resource management • MS
- international business • MBA
- internet business systems • MS
- management • MBA
- marketing • MBA
- organizational leadership • MS
- securities • MS

Program in Human Resource Management
Program in:
- human resource management • MS

■ MOLLOY COLLEGE
Rockville Centre, NY 11571-5002

Independent, coed, comprehensive institution. *Enrollment:* 2 full-time matriculated graduate/professional students (both women), 207 part-time matriculated graduate/professional students (202 women). *Graduate faculty:* 17 full-time (15 women), 8 part-time/adjunct (7 women). *Computer facilities:* 246 computers available on campus for general student use. A campuswide network can be accessed. Internet access is available. *Library facilities:* James Edward Tobin Library. *Graduate expenses:* Tuition: part-time $494 per credit. Required fees: $195 per semester. One-time fee: $55 part-time. *General application contact:* Dr. Carol A. Clifford, Director, Graduate Program, 516-256-2218.

Department of Nursing
Dr. Carol A. Clifford, Director, Graduate Program
Programs in:
- adult nurse practitioner • MSN, Advanced Certificate
- clinical nurse specialist: adult health • MSN, Advanced Certificate
- family nurse practitioner • MSN, Advanced Certificate
- nurse practitioner psychiatry • MSN, Advanced Certificate
- nursing • MSN
- nursing administration • Advanced Certificate
- nursing administration with informatics • MSN
- nursing education • MSN, Advanced Certificate
- pediatric nurse practitioner • MSN, Advanced Certificate

■ MOUNT SAINT MARY COLLEGE
Newburgh, NY 12550-3494
http://www.msmc.edu/

Independent, coed, comprehensive institution. *Enrollment:* 16 full-time matriculated graduate/professional students (11 women), 393 part-time matriculated graduate/professional students (313 women). *Graduate faculty:* 15 full-time (10 women), 20 part-time/adjunct (16 women). *Computer facilities:* 150 computers available on campus for general student use. A campuswide network can be accessed from student residence rooms and from off campus. Internet access, intranet are available. *Library facilities:* Curtin Memorial Library plus 1 other. *Graduate expenses:* Tuition: full-time $9,720; part-time $405 per credit hour. One-time fee: $30 full-time. *General application contact:* Graduate Coordinator, 845-561-0800.

Division of Business
Dr. James Griesemer, Coordinator
Program in:
- business • MBA

Division of Education
Dr. Lucy DiPaola, Coordinator
Programs in:
- elementary education • MS Ed
- elementary/special education • MS Ed
- secondary education • MS Ed
- special education • MS Ed

Division of Nursing
Sr. Leona DeBoer, Coordinator
Programs in:
- adult nurse practitioner • MS
- clinical nurse specialist-adult health • MS

■ NAZARETH COLLEGE OF ROCHESTER
Rochester, NY 14618-3790
http://www.naz.edu/

Independent, coed, comprehensive institution. *Enrollment:* 118 full-time matriculated graduate/professional students (110 women), 992 part-time matriculated graduate/professional students (803 women). *Graduate faculty:* 41 full-time (22 women), 77 part-time/adjunct (39 women). *Computer facilities:* 190 computers available on campus for general student use. A campuswide network can be accessed from student residence rooms and from off campus. Internet access is available. *Library facilities:* Lorette Wilmot Library. *Graduate expenses:* Tuition: part-time $456 per credit hour. *General application contact:* Dr. Kay F. Marshman, Dean, 716-389-2815.

Graduate Studies
Dr. Kay F. Marshman, Dean
Programs in:
- art education • MS Ed
- art therapy • MS
- business education • MS Ed
- computer education • MS Ed
- early childhood education • MS Ed
- elementary education • MS Ed
- general secondary education • MS Ed
- gerontological nurse practitioner • MS
- literacy education • MS Ed
- management • MS
- music education • MS Ed
- social work • MSW
- special education • MS Ed
- speech pathology • MS
- teaching English to speakers of other languages • MS Ed

■ NEW SCHOOL UNIVERSITY
New York, NY 10011-8603
http://www.newschool.edu/

Independent, coed, university. *Graduate faculty:* 95 full-time (32 women), 347 part-time/adjunct (155 women). *Graduate expenses:* Tuition: full-time $22,090; part-time $782 per credit. Required fees: $380 per semester. Tuition and fees vary according to program. *General application contact:* Emily Johnson, Information Contact, 877-5AVE-321.

Find an in-depth description at www.petersons.com/graduate.

Actors Studio Drama School
James Lipton, Dean
Programs in:
acting • MFA
directing • MFA
playwriting • MFA

Graduate Faculty of Political and Social Science
Dr. Kenneth Prewitt, Dean
Programs in:
anthropology • MA, DS Sc, PhD
clinical psychology • PhD
economics • MA, DS Sc, PhD
general psychology • MA, PhD
historical studies • MA, PhD
liberal studies • MA
philosophy • MA, DS Sc, PhD
political and social science • MA, MS Sc, DS Sc, PhD
political science • MA, DS Sc, PhD
psychoanalytic studies • MS Sc
sociology • MA, DS Sc, PhD

New School
Ann Louise Shapiro, Dean
Programs in:
communication theory • MA
creative writing • MFA
global management, trade, and finance • MA, MS
international development • MA, MS
international media and communication • MA, MS
international politics and diplomacy • MA, MS
media studies • MA
service, civic, and non-profit management • MA, MS
teacher education • MST

Parsons School of Design
H. Randolph Swearer, Dean
Programs in:
architecture • M Arch
design • M Arch, MA, MFA, MS Ed
design and technology • MFA
history of decorative arts • MA
lighting design • MFA
painting • MFA
sculpture • MFA

Robert J. Milano Graduate School of Management and Urban Policy
Dr. Edward J. Blakely, Dan
Programs in:
career planning and development • Adv C
health services management and policy • MS
human resources management • MS
management and urban policy • MS, PhD, Adv C
medical group practice management • Adv C
nonprofit management • MS
organization development • Adv C
organizational change management • MS
public and urban policy • PhD
training and development • Adv C
urban policy analysis and management • MS

■ NEW YORK INSTITUTE OF TECHNOLOGY
Old Westbury, NY 11568-8000
http://www.nyit.edu/

Independent, coed, comprehensive institution. CGS member. *Enrollment:* 1,825 full-time matriculated graduate/professional students (860 women), 1,850 part-time matriculated graduate/professional students (915 women). *Graduate faculty:* 251 full-time (76 women), 521 part-time/adjunct (188 women). *Computer facilities:* 634 computers available on campus for general student use. A campuswide network can be accessed from student residence rooms and from off campus. Internet access, e-mail are available. *Library facilities:* George and Gertrude Wisser Memorial Library plus 4 others. *Graduate expenses:* Tuition: part-time $525 per credit. Required fees: $60 per semester. One-time fee: $135 part-time. *General application contact:* Jacquelyn Nealon, Dean of Admissions and Financial Aid, 516-686-7925.

Find an in-depth description at www.petersons.com/graduate.

Graduate Division
Vice President for Academic Affairs

School of Allied Health and Life Sciences
Dr. Barbara Ross-Lee, Dean
Programs in:
allied health and life sciences • MPS, MS
clinical nutrition • MS
human relations • MPS
occupational therapy • MS
physical therapy • MS

School of Architecture
Judith DiMaio, Interim Dean
Program in:
urban and regional design • M Arch

School of Arts, Sciences, and Communication
Dr. Robert C. Vogt, Dean
Programs in:
arts, sciences, and communication • MA
communication arts • MA

School of Education and Professional Services
Dr. Helen Greene, Dean
Programs in:
computers in education • Certificate
distance learning • Certificate
district leadership and technology • Advanced Diploma
education and professional services • MS, Advanced Diploma, Certificate
elementary education • MS
instructional technology • MS
mental health counseling • MS
multimedia • Certificate
school leadership and technology • Advanced Diploma

School of Engineering and Technology
Dr. Heskia Heskiaoff, Dean
Programs in:
computer science • MS
electrical engineering and computer engineering • MS
energy management • MS
energy technology • Certificate
engineering and technology • MS, Certificate
environmental management • Certificate
environmental technology • MS
facilities management • Certificate

School of Management
Dr. David R. Decker, Dean
Programs in:
accounting • Certificate
business administration • MBA
e-commerce • MBA, Certificate
finance • Certificate
health administration • MBA, Certificate
human resources administration • Advanced Certificate
human resources management and labor relations • MS
international business • Certificate
labor relations • Advanced Certificate
management • MBA, MS, Advanced Certificate, Certificate
management of information systems • Certificate
marketing • Certificate

New York College of Osteopathic Medicine
Dr. Stanley Schiowitz, Dean
Program in:
osteopathic medicine • DO

■ NEW YORK UNIVERSITY
New York, NY 10012-1019
http://www.nyu.edu/

Independent, coed, university. CGS member. *Enrollment:* 10,012 full-time matriculated graduate/professional

New York University (continued)
students (5,632 women), 7,919 part-time matriculated graduate/professional students (4,665 women). *Graduate faculty:* 2,647 full-time (950 women), 2,244 part-time/adjunct. *Computer facilities:* 1,400 computers available on campus for general student use. A campuswide network can be accessed from student residence rooms and from off campus. Internet access and online class registration are available. *Library facilities:* Elmer H. Bobst Library plus 11 others. *Graduate expenses:* Tuition: full-time $18,600; part-time $775 per credit. Required fees: $1,173; $36 per credit. Tuition and fees vary according to course load and program. *General application contact:* New York University Information, 212-998-1212.

Find an in-depth description at www.petersons.com/graduate.

College of Dentistry
Dr. Michael C. Alfano, Dean
Programs in:
- dentistry • DDS, MS, Advanced Certificate
- endodontics • Advanced Certificate
- general dentistry • Advanced Certificate
- oral and maxillofacial surgery • Advanced Certificate
- orthodontics • Advanced Certificate
- pediatric dentistry • Advanced Certificate
- periodontics • Advanced Certificate
- prosthodontics • Advanced Certificate
- prosthodontics (implantology) • Advanced Certificate

Gallatin School of Individualized Study
Dr. E. Frances White, Dean
Program in:
- individualized study • MA

Graduate School of Arts and Science
Catharine R. Stimpson, Dean
Programs in:
- Africana studies • MA
- American studies • MA, PhD
- anthropology • M Phil
- anthropology and French studies • PhD
- applied economic analysis • Advanced Certificate
- applied recombinant DNA technology • MS
- archaeological anthropology • MA, PhD
- archival management and historical editing • Advanced Certificate
- arts and science • M Phil, MA, MFA, MS, PhD, Advanced Certificate, Diploma
- biochemistry • MS, PhD
- biomaterials • MS
- biomedical journalism • MA
- biomedical reporting • MS
- business and economic reporting/journalism • Advanced Certificate
- cell biology • MS, PhD
- chemistry • MS, PhD
- classics • MA, PhD
- clinical psychology • PhD
- cognition and perception • PhD
- community psychology • PhD
- comparative literature • MA, PhD
- computers in biological research • MS
- creative writing • MFA
- cultural anthropology • MA, PhD
- culture and media • M Phil, MA, PhD
- early music performance • Advanced Certificate
- economics • MA, PhD
- English and American literature • MA, PhD
- environmental biology • PhD
- ethnomusicology • MA, PhD
- French studies and politics • PhD
- French studies and sociology • PhD
- French studies/history • PhD
- French studies/journalism • MA
- general biology • MS
- general psychology • MA
- Germanic languages and literatures • MA, PhD
- Hebrew and Judaic studies • MA, PhD
- Hebrew and Judaic studies/history • PhD
- Hebrew and Judaic studies/museum studies • MA
- Hellenic studies • MA, PhD
- history • MA, PhD
- humanities and social thought • MA
- industrial/organizational psychology • MA, PhD
- international politics and international business • MA
- Italian • MA, PhD
- Italian studies • MA
- journalism • MA
- journalism (cultural reporting and criticism) • MA
- Latin American and Caribbean studies/journalism • MA
- linguistic anthropology • MA, PhD
- linguistics • MA, PhD
- microbiology • MS, PhD
- Middle Eastern studies/history • PhD
- museum studies • Advanced Certificate
- museum studies and Africana studies • MA
- museum studies and Hebrew and Judaic studies • MA
- museum studies and Latin American and Caribbean studies • MA
- music (theory, composition and musicology) • MA, PhD
- Near Eastern studies/journalism • MA
- neural sciences and physiology • PhD
- oral biology • MS
- parasitology • PhD
- pathology • MS, PhD
- pharmacology • PhD
- philosophy • MA, PhD
- physical anthropology • MA, PhD
- physics • MS, PhD
- physiology • MS, PhD
- politics • MA, PhD
- politics (Near Eastern studies) • PhD
- population and evolutionary biology • PhD
- Portuguese • MA, PhD
- psychoanalysis • Advanced Certificate
- public history • MA, Advanced Certificate
- religion • Advanced Certificate
- religious studies • MA
- Romance languages and literatures • MA
- Russian literature • MA
- science and environmental reporting • Advanced Certificate
- science and environmental reporting/journalism • MA
- Slavic literature • MA
- social theory • Advanced Certificate
- social/personality psychology • PhD
- sociology • MA, PhD
- Spanish • MA, PhD
- urban anthropology • MA, PhD
- women's history • MA
- world history • MA

Center for European Studies
Martin Schain, Director
Program in:
- European studies • MA

Center for French Civilization and Culture
Thomas Bishop, Director
Programs in:
- French • PhD
- French civilization and culture • MA, PhD, Advanced Certificate
- French language and civilization • MA
- French literature • MA
- French Studies • PhD
- French studies • MA, PhD, Advanced Certificate

French studies and anthropology • PhD
French studies and history • PhD
French studies and journalism • MA
French studies and politics • PhD
French studies and sociology • PhD
Romance languages and literatures • MA

Center for Latin American and Caribbean Studies
Christopher Mitchell, Director
Programs in:
Latin American and Caribbean studies • MA
Latin American and Caribbean studies/journalism • MA
Latin American and Caribbean studies/museum studies • MA

Center for Neural Science
Daniel Sanes, Chairman
Program in:
neural science • PhD

Courant Institute of Mathematical Sciences
Edmund Schonberg, Director
Programs in:
atmosphere-ocean science and mathematics • PhD
computer science • MS, PhD
information systems • MS
mathematics • MS, PhD
mathematics and statistics/operations research • MS
mathematics in finance • MS
scientific computing • MS

Hagop Kevorkian Center for Near Eastern Studies
Zachary Lockman, Director
Programs in:
Middle Eastern studies • MA, PhD
Middle Eastern studies/history • PhD
Near Eastern studies • MA
Near Eastern studies/journalism • MA
Near Eastern studies/museum studies • MA

Institute for Law and Society
Christine Harrington, Director
Program in:
law and society • PhD

Institute of Fine Arts
James McCredie, Chair
Programs in:
classical art and archaeology • PhD
history of art and archaeology • MA, PhD
Near Eastern art and archaeology • PhD

Nelson Institute of Environmental Medicine
Dr. Max Costa, Director
Program in:
environmental health sciences • MS, PhD

Leonard N. Stern School of Business
George Daly, Dean
Programs in:
accounting • MBA, PhD, APC
business • MBA, MS, PhD, APC
economics • MBA, PhD, APC
executive finance • MBA
executive general management • MBA
finance • MBA, PhD
information systems • MBA, MS, PhD, APC
international business • MBA, PhD, APC
management • MBA, PhD, APC
marketing • MBA, PhD, APC
operations management • MBA
statistics and operations research • MBA, MS, PhD, APC

Robert F. Wagner Graduate School of Public Service
Dr. Jo Ivey Boufford, Dean
Programs in:
public and nonprofit management and policy • MPA
advanced management practice for clinicians • MS
advanced management program for clinicians • MS
developmental administration • Advanced Certificate
financial management • MPA
financial management and public finance • MPA, Advanced Certificate
health policy analysis • MPA
health services management • MPA
housing • Advanced Certificate
human resources management • Advanced Certificate
international administration • Advanced Certificate
management • MS
management for public and nonprofit organizations • MPA, Advanced Certificate
public administration • PhD
public and nonprofit management and policy • Advanced Certificate
public economics • Advanced Certificate
public policy analysis • MPA, Advanced Certificate
public service • MPA, MS, MUP, PhD, Advanced Certificate
quantitative analysis and computer applications • Advanced Certificate
quantitative analysis and computer applications for policy and planning • Advanced Certificate
urban planning • MUP
urban public policy • Advanced Certificate

School of Continuing and Professional Studies
Dr. David F. Finney, Dean
Programs in:
continuing and professional studies • MS, Advanced Certificate
information technology • Advanced Certificate

Center for Direct and Interactive Marketing
Lynda Confessore, Associate Director
Program in:
direct marketing communications • MS

Center for Hospitality, Tourism and Travel Administration
Dr. Lalia Rach, Associate Dean
Programs in:
customer service management • Advanced Certificate
hospitality industry studies • MS, Advanced Certificate
tourism and travel management • MS

Center for Publishing
Robert E. Baensch, Director
Programs in:
book publishing • MS
electronic publishing • MS
magazine publishing • MS

Real Estate Institute
D. Kenneth Patton, Associate Dean
Program in:
real estate • MS

The Virtual College
Howard Deckelbaum, Director, Information Technologies Institute
Program in:
management and systems • MS

School of Education
Dr. Ann Marcus, Dean
Programs in:
administration and management of technology and industry oriented programs • MA, Ed D, PhD, Advanced Certificate
applied psychology • MA, PhD, Psy D, Advanced Certificate
art education • MA, Ed D, PhD
art therapy • MA
arts and humanities education • MA, PhD
bilingual education • MA, PhD
bilingual special education • MA

New York University (continued)
business education • MA, Ed D, PhD, Advanced Certificate
community health education • MPH, Ed D, PhD
costume studies • MA
counseling and guidance • MA, PhD, Advanced Certificate
counseling psychology • PhD
counselor education • MA, PhD, Advanced Certificate
dance education • MA, Ed D, PhD
deafness rehabilitation • MA
drama therapy • MA
early childhood and elementary education • MA, PhD, Advanced Certificate
early childhood special education • MA
education • MA, MFA, MM, MPH, MS, DA, DPT, Ed D, PhD, Psy D, Advanced Certificate
educational administration and supervision • MA, Ed D, PhD, Advanced Certificate
educational communication and technology • MA, Ed D, PhD, Advanced Certificate
educational sociology • MA, PhD
educational theater • Advanced Certificate
educational theatre • MA, Ed D, PhD
English education • MA, PhD, Advanced Certificate
environmental art • MA
environmental conservation education • MA
folk art studies • MA
food and food management • MA, PhD
food management • MA
food studies • MA
food, nutrition, and dietetics • MS, PhD
for-profit sector • MA
foreign language education • MA, Advanced Certificate
general applied psychology • MA
graphic communications management and technology • MA, Ed D, PhD, Advanced Certificate
health education • MA, MPH, Ed D, PhD, Advanced Certificate
higher education • MA, Ed D, PhD
history of education • MA, PhD
human sexuality education • MA, Ed D, PhD
international education • MA, PhD
mathematics education • MA, PhD
measurement and evaluation • MA
media ecology • MA, PhD
multilingual/multicultural studies • MA, PhD, Advanced Certificate
music education • MA, Ed D, PhD, Advanced Certificate
music entertainment professions • MA
music performance and composition • MA, PhD
music technology • MM
music therapy • MA, DA
occupational therapy • PhD
pathokinesiology • MA
performing arts administration • MA
philosophy of education • MA, PhD
physical therapists • MA
physical therapists: developmental disabilities • MA
physical therapy • DPT, PhD
post-professional occupational therapy • MA
practicing physical therapist • DPT
professional child/school psychology • Psy D
professional occupational therapy • MA
professional program in health education • Advanced Certificate
psychological development • PhD
psychological foundations of reading • MA, PhD
public health nutrition • MPH
recreation and leisure studies • MA, PhD, Advanced Certificate
rehabilitation counseling • MA, PhD
school and college health education • MA, Ed D, PhD
school business administration • Advanced Certificate
school psychologist • Advanced Certificate
school psychology • PhD
science education • MA
social studies • MA
social studies education • MA
special education • MA, Advanced Certificate
special education learning consultant • Advanced Certificate
speech communication • MA, Advanced Certificate
speech-language pathology and audiology • MA, PhD
student personnel administration in higher education • MA
studio art • MA, MFA
studio art and environmental art • MA, MFA
teachers of business subjects in higher education • MA, Ed D, PhD
teaching English to speakers of other languages • MA, PhD, Advanced Certificate
visual arts administration • MA
visual culture • MA

Division of Nursing
Diane McGivern, Chairperson
Programs in:
adult acute care nurse practitioner • MA
adult primary care nurse practitioner • MA
advanced practice nursing: adult acute care • Advanced Certificate
advanced practice nursing: geriatrics • MA, Advanced Certificate
advanced practice nursing: mental health • MA, Advanced Certificate
advanced practice nursing: pediatrics • Advanced Certificate
advanced practice nursing: pediatrics/children with special needs • MA
holistic nursing • MA, Advanced Certificate
nurse midwifery • MA, Advanced Certificate
nursing • MA, PhD, Advanced Certificate
nursing administration • MA
nursing informatics • MA
palliative care • MA, Advanced Certificate
teaching of nursing • MA

School of Law
John Sexton, Dean
Program in:
law • JD, LL M, JSD

School of Medicine
Dr. Robert M. Glickman, Dean
Programs in:
biochemistry
cell biology
environmental health sciences
medicine • MD, PhD
microbiology
parasitology
pathology
pharmacology

Sackler Institute of Graduate Biomedical Sciences
Dr. Joel D. Oppenheim, Associate Dean for Graduate Studies
Programs in:
biochemistry • PhD
biomedical sciences • PhD
cell biology • PhD
immunology • PhD
medical and molecular parasitology • PhD
microbiology • PhD
molecular oncology • PhD
neuroscience • PhD
pathology • PhD
pharmacology • PhD
physiology • PhD

Shirley M. Ehrenkranz School of Social Work
Thomas Meenaghan, Dean
Program in:
social work • MSW, PhD

Tisch School of the Arts
Mary Schmidt Campbell, Dean
Programs in:

acting • MFA
arts • MA, MFA, MPS, PhD
cinema studies • MA, PhD
dance • MFA
design • MFA
dramatic writing • MFA
film and television • MFA
musical theatre writing • MFA
performance studies • MA, PhD
telecommunications • MPS

■ NIAGARA UNIVERSITY

Niagara Falls, Niagara University, NY 14109
http://www.niagara.edu/

Independent-religious, coed, comprehensive institution. *Enrollment:* 373 full-time matriculated graduate/professional students (248 women), 300 part-time matriculated graduate/professional students (201 women). *Graduate faculty:* 27 full-time (10 women), 24 part-time/adjunct (11 women). *Computer facilities:* 150 computers available on campus for general student use. A campuswide network can be accessed from student residence rooms. *Library facilities:* Our Lady of Angels Library. *Graduate expenses:* Tuition: part-time $470 per credit. Part-time tuition and fees vary according to program. *General application contact:* Fred Heuer, Assistant Director of Admissions, 716-286-8719.

Find an in-depth description at www.petersons.com/graduate.

Graduate Division of Arts and Sciences

Dr. Nancy McGlen, Director
Programs in:
arts and sciences • MS
criminal justice administration • MS

Graduate Division of Business Administration

Dr. Philip Scherer, Director
Programs in:
business • MBA
commerce • MBA

Graduate Division of Education

Dr. Debra A. Colley, Dean
Programs in:
administration and supervision • MS Ed, PD
biology • MAT
elementary education • MS Ed
foundations and teaching • MA, MS Ed
inclusive education • MS Ed
literacy instruction • MS Ed
mental health counseling • MS Ed
school counseling • MS Ed, PD
secondary education • MS Ed
teacher education • MS Ed

Graduate Division of Nursing

Dr. Dolores Bower, Dean
Program in:
family nurse practitioner • MS

■ PACE UNIVERSITY, NEW YORK CITY CAMPUS

New York, NY 10038
http://www.pace.edu/

Independent, coed, university. CGS member. *Enrollment:* 724 full-time matriculated graduate/professional students (378 women), 1,224 part-time matriculated graduate/professional students (556 women). *Graduate faculty:* 156 full-time, 141 part-time/adjunct. *Computer facilities:* 155 computers available on campus for general student use. A campuswide network can be accessed from student residence rooms and from off campus. *Library facilities:* Henry Birnbaum Library plus 3 others. *Graduate expenses:* Tuition: full-time $14,400; part-time $600 per credit. Tuition and fees vary according to course load and program. *General application contact:* Richard Alvarez, Director of Admissions, 212-346-1652.

Find an in-depth description at www.petersons.com/graduate.

Dyson College of Arts and Sciences

Dr. Gail Dinter-Gottlieb, Dean
Programs in:
arts and sciences • MA, MS, MS Ed, Psy D
psychology • MA
publishing • MS
school-clinical child psychology • Psy D
school-community psychology • MS Ed, Psy D

Lienhard School of Nursing

Dr. Harriet Feldman, Dean
Program in:
nursing • MS, Advanced Certificate

Lubin School of Business

Dr. Arthur Centonze, Dean
Programs in:
banking and finance • MBA
business • MBA, MS, DPS, APC
corporate economic planning • MBA
corporate financial management • MBA
economics • MS
financial economics • MBA
financial management • MBA
health systems management • MBA
information systems • MBA
international business • MBA
international economics • MBA
investment management • MBA, MS
management • MBA
management science • MBA
managerial accounting • MBA
marketing management • MBA
marketing research • MBA
operations management • MBA
professional studies • DPS
public accounting • MBA, MS
taxation • MBA, MS

School of Computer Science and Information Systems

Dr. Susan Merritt, Dean
Programs in:
computer communications and networks • Certificate
computer science • MS
computing studies • DPS
information systems • MS
object-oriented programming • Certificate
telecommunications • MS, Certificate

School of Education

Dr. Janet McDonald, Dean
Programs in:
administration and supervision • MS Ed
curriculum and instruction • MS
education • MST
school business management • Certificate

■ PACE UNIVERSITY, PLEASANTVILLE/BRIARCLIFF CAMPUS

Pleasantville, NY 10570
http://www.pace.edu/

Independent, coed, comprehensive institution. *Enrollment:* 34 full-time matriculated graduate/professional students (32 women), 99 part-time matriculated graduate/professional students (89 women). *Graduate faculty:* 6 full-time (all women), 5 part-time/adjunct (4 women). *Computer facilities:* 128 computers available on campus for general student use. A campuswide network can be accessed from student residence rooms and from off campus. *Library facilities:* Mortola Library plus 3 others. *Graduate expenses:* Tuition: full-time $12,600; part-time $525 per credit. Tuition and fees vary according

Pace University, Pleasantville/Briarcliff Campus (continued)
to course load and program. *General application contact:* Joanna Broda, Director of Admissions, 914-422-4283.

Lienhard School of Nursing
Dr. Harriet Feldman, Dean
Program in:
nursing • MS, Advanced Certificate

■ PACE UNIVERSITY, WHITE PLAINS CAMPUS

White Plains, NY 10603

http://www.pace.edu/

Independent, coed, graduate-only institution. *Graduate faculty:* 77 full-time, 83 part-time/adjunct. *Computer facilities:* 68 computers available on campus for general student use. A campuswide network can be accessed. Internet access is available. *Graduate expenses:* Tuition: full-time $14,400; part-time $600 per credit. *General application contact:* Joanna Broda, Director of Admissions, 914-422-4283.

Dyson College of Arts and Sciences
Gail Dinter-Gottlieb, Dean
Programs in:
arts and sciences • MPA, MS
counseling-substance abuse • MS
environmental science • MS
government management • MPA
health care administration • MPA
nonprofit management • MPA

Lubin School of Business
Dr. Arthur Centonze, Dean
Programs in:
banking and finance • MBA
business • MBA, MS, APC
corporate economic planning • MBA
corporate financial management • MBA
economics • MS
financial economics • MBA
financial management • MBA
health systems management • MBA
information systems • MBA
international business • MBA
international economics • MBA
investment management • MBA, MS
management • MBA
management science • MBA, MS
managerial accounting • MBA
marketing management • MBA
marketing research • MBA
operations management • MBA
public accounting • MBA, MS
taxation • MBA, MS

School of Computer Science and Information Systems
Dr. Susan Merritt, Dean
Programs in:
computer communications and networks • Certificate
computer science • MS
computing studies • DPS
information systems • MS
object-oriented programming • Certificate
telecommunications • MS, Certificate

School of Education
Dr. Janet McDonald, Dean
Programs in:
administration and supervision • MS Ed
curriculum and instruction • MS
education • MST
school business management • Certificate

School of Law
David S. Cohen, Dean
Programs in:
comparative legal studies • LL M
environmental law • LL M, SJD
law • JD

■ PLATTSBURGH STATE UNIVERSITY OF NEW YORK

Plattsburgh, NY 12901-2681

http://www.plattsburgh.edu/

State-supported, coed, comprehensive institution. *Computer facilities:* 366 computers available on campus for general student use. A campuswide network can be accessed from student residence rooms and from off campus. Internet access and online class registration are available. *Library facilities:* Feinberg Library. *General application contact:* Director of Graduate Admissions, 518-564-2040.

Center for Lifelong Learning
Program in:
liberal studies • MA

Faculty of Arts and Science
Programs in:
arts and science • MA, CAS
school psychology • MA, CAS

Faculty of Professional Studies
Programs in:
college/agency counseling • MS
professional studies • MA, MS, MS Ed, MST, CAS
school counseling • MS Ed
school counselor • CAS
speech-language pathology • MA

Center for Educational Studies and Services
Programs in:
biology 7-12 • MST
chemistry • MS Ed, MST
curriculum and instruction • MS Ed
earth sciences 7-12 • MST
educational studies and services • MS Ed, MST, CAS
elementary education • MST
elementary education Pre K-6 • MS Ed
English 7-12 • MS Ed, MST
English 7-9 • MS Ed, MST
English Pre K-6 • MS Ed, MST
French 7-12 • MST
general science 7-9 • MS Ed, MST
general science Pre K-6 • MS Ed
general science Pre-K • MST
mathematics 7-12 • MST
mathematics 7-9 • MS Ed, MST
mathematics Pre K-6 • MS Ed, MST
physics 7-12 • MST
reading teacher • MS Ed
school administrator and supervisor • CAS
social studies 7-12 • MS Ed, MST
social studies 7-9 • MS Ed, MST
social studies Pre K-6 • MS Ed, MST
Spanish 7-12 • MST
special education • MS Ed

■ POLYTECHNIC UNIVERSITY, BROOKLYN CAMPUS

Brooklyn, NY 11201-2990

http://www.poly.edu/

Independent, coed, university. CGS member. *Enrollment:* 415 full-time matriculated graduate/professional students (98 women), 522 part-time matriculated graduate/professional students (120 women). *Graduate faculty:* 178 full-time (34 women), 134 part-time/adjunct (33 women). *Computer facilities:* 350 computers available on campus for general student use. A campuswide network can be accessed from off campus. Internet access is available. *Library facilities:* Bern Dibner Library. *Graduate expenses:* Tuition: full-time $14,065; part-time $725 per credit. Required fees: $135 per term. Tuition and fees vary according to course load. *General application contact:* John S. Kerge, Dean of Admissions, 718-260-3200.

Department of Applied Mathematics
Dr. Erwin Lutwak, Head
Program in:
mathematics • MS, PhD

Department of Chemical Engineering, Chemistry and Materials Science
Dr. Kalle Levon, Head
Programs in:
chemical engineering • MS, PhD
chemistry • MS, PhD
materials chemistry • PhD
polymer science and engineering • MS

Department of Civil and Environmental Engineering
Dr. John Falcocchio, Head
Programs in:
civil engineering • MS, PhD
environmental engineering • MS
environmental health science • MS
transportation management • MS
transportation planning and engineering • MS

Department of Computer and Information Science
Dr. Stuart Steele, Head
Programs in:
computer science • MS, PhD
information systems engineering • MS

Department of Electrical Engineering
Dr. David Goodman, Head
Programs in:
computer engineering • MS
electrical engineering • MS, PhD
electrophysics • MS
systems engineering • MS
telecommunication networks • MS

Department of Humanities and Social Sciences
Dr. Harold Sjursen, Head
Programs in:
environment behavior studies • MS
history of science • MS
specialized journalism • MS

Department of Management
Mel Horwitch, Head
Programs in:
financial engineering • MS
management • MS
management of technology • MS
operations management • MS
organizational behavior • MS
telecommunications and information management • MS

Department of Mechanical, Aerospace and Manufacturing Engineering
Dr. Said Nourbaksh, Head
Programs in:
aeronautics and astronautics • MS
industrial engineering • MS
manufacturing engineering • MS
materials science • MS
mechanical engineering • MS, PhD

Program in Physics
Dr. Edward Wolf, Head
Program in:
physics • MS, PhD

■ POLYTECHNIC UNIVERSITY, WESTCHESTER GRADUATE CENTER

Hawthorne, NY 10532-1507
http://west.poly.edu/~www/

Independent, coed, graduate-only institution. *Graduate faculty:* 178 full-time (34 women), 134 part-time/adjunct (33 women). *Computer facilities:* 30 computers available on campus for general student use. A campuswide network can be accessed from off campus. Internet access is available. *Graduate expenses:* Tuition: full-time $14,065; part-time $725 per credit. Required fees: $135 per term. Tuition and fees vary according to course load. *General application contact:* John S. Kerge, Dean of Admission, 718-260-3200.

Graduate Programs
LaVerne Clark, Director of Campus Operations
Programs in:
chemical engineering • MS
chemistry • MS
civil engineering • MS, PhD
computer engineering • MS
computer science • MS, PhD
electrical engineering • MS, PhD
electrophysics • MS
environmental engineering • MS
industrial engineering • MS
information systems engineering • MS
manufacturing engineering • MS
materials science • MS
systems engineering • MS
telecommunication networks • MS
transportation management • MS

Division of Management
Mel Horwitch, Dean
Programs in:
financial engineering • MS
management • MS
operations management • MS
organizational behavior • MS

■ PRATT INSTITUTE

Brooklyn, NY 11205-3899
http://www.pratt.edu/

Independent, coed, comprehensive institution. *Enrollment:* 715 full-time matriculated graduate/professional students (474 women), 562 part-time matriculated graduate/professional students (402 women). *Graduate faculty:* 46 full-time (14 women), 220 part-time/adjunct (95 women). *Computer facilities:* 250 computers available on campus for general student use. A campuswide network can be accessed from student residence rooms and from off campus. Internet access and online class registration are available. *Library facilities:* Pratt Institute Library. *Graduate expenses:* Tuition: full-time $18,000; part-time $750 per credit. Required fees: $530; $135 per term. *General application contact:* Stephanie Patton, Director of Graduate Admissions, 718-636-3669.

School of Architecture
Thomas Hanrahan, Dean
Programs in:
architecture • M Arch, MS, MSCRP, MSUD, MSUESM
city and regional planning • MSCRP
facilities management • MS
urban design • MSUD
urban environmental systems management • MSUESM

School of Art and Design
Frank Lind, Dean
Programs in:
art and design • MFA, MID, MPS, MS
art and design education • MS
art history • MS
art therapy and creativity development • MPS
art therapy-special education • MPS
arts and cultural management • MPS
ceramics • MFA
communications design • MS
computer graphics design and interactive media • MFA
dance therapy • MPS
design management • MPS
industrial design • MID
interior design • MS
metals • MFA
new forms • MFA
package design • MS
painting • MFA
photography • MFA
printmaking • MFA
sculpture • MFA
theory and criticism • MS

School of Information and Library Science
Anne Woodsworth, Acting Dean
Program in:
information and library science • MS, Adv C

■ PURCHASE COLLEGE, STATE UNIVERSITY OF NEW YORK

Purchase, NY 10577-1400
http://www.purchase.edu/

State-supported, coed, comprehensive institution. *Enrollment:* 127 full-time matriculated graduate/professional students (68 women), 10 part-time matriculated graduate/professional students (8 women). *Graduate faculty:* 3 full-time (2 women), 7 part-time/adjunct (4 women). *Computer facilities:* 350 computers available on campus for general student use. A campuswide network can be accessed from student residence rooms and from off campus. Internet access, e-mail are available. *Library facilities:* Purchase College Library. *Graduate expenses:* Full-time $5,100; part-time $213 per credit. Tuition, nonresident: full-time $8,416; part-time $351 per credit. *General application contact:* Barbara Washington, Counselor, 914-251-6310.

Conservatory of Dance

Carol Walker, Dean
Programs in:
- choreography • MFA
- performance and pedagogy • MFA

Conservatory of Music

Karl Kramer, Dean
Programs in:
- composition • MFA
- instrumental • MFA
- voice • MFA

Conservatory of Theatre Arts and Film

Israel Hicks, Dean
Programs in:
- theatre design • MFA
- theatre technology • MFA

Division of Humanities

Gari LaGuardia, Head
Program in:
- art history • MA

School of Art and Design

Kenneth Strickland, Dean
Program in:
- art and design • MFA

■ QUEENS COLLEGE OF THE CITY UNIVERSITY OF NEW YORK

Flushing, NY 11367-1597
http://www.qc.edu/

State and locally supported, coed, comprehensive institution. CGS member. *Computer facilities:* 500 computers available on campus for general student use. A campuswide network can be accessed from off campus. Internet access is available. *Library facilities:* Benjamin S. Rosenthal Library plus 1 other. *General application contact:* Director of Graduate Admissions, 718-997-5200.

Find an in-depth description at www.petersons.com/graduate.

Division of Graduate Studies

Arts Division
Programs in:
- applied linguistics • MA
- art history • MA
- arts • MA, MFA, MS Ed
- creative writing • MA
- English language and literature • MA
- fine arts • MFA
- French • MA
- Italian • MA
- media studies • MA
- music • MA
- Spanish • MA
- speech pathology • MA
- teaching English to speakers of other languages • MS Ed

Division of Education
Programs in:
- administration and supervision • AC
- art • MS Ed
- bilingual education • MS Ed
- biology • MS Ed, AC
- chemistry • MS Ed, AC
- counselor education • MS Ed
- earth sciences • MS Ed, AC
- education • MS Ed, AC
- elementary education • MS Ed, AC
- English • MS Ed, AC
- French • MS Ed, AC
- Italian • MS Ed, AC
- mathematics • MS Ed, AC
- music • MS Ed, AC
- physics • MS Ed, AC
- reading • MS Ed
- school psychology • MS Ed, AC
- social studies • MS Ed, AC
- Spanish • MS Ed, AC
- special education • MS Ed

Mathematics and Natural Sciences Division
Programs in:
- biochemistry • MA
- biology • MA
- chemistry • MA
- clinical behavioral applications in mental health settings • MA
- computer science • MA
- earth and environmental science • MA
- home economics • MS Ed
- mathematics • MA
- mathematics and natural sciences • MA, MS Ed
- physical education and exercise sciences • MS Ed
- physics • MA
- psychology • MA

Social Science Division
Programs in:
- accounting • MS
- history • MA
- liberal studies • MALS
- library and information studies • MLS, AC
- social science • MA, MALS, MASS, MLS, MS, AC
- social sciences • MASS
- sociology • MA
- urban studies • MA

■ RENSSELAER POLYTECHNIC INSTITUTE

Troy, NY 12180-3590
http://www.rpi.edu/

Independent, coed, university. CGS member. *Enrollment:* 1,500 full-time matriculated graduate/professional students (436 women), 996 part-time matriculated graduate/professional students (239 women). *Graduate faculty:* 370 full-time (58 women), 17 part-time/adjunct (5 women). *Computer facilities:* 500 computers available on campus for general student use. A campuswide network can be accessed from student residence rooms and from off campus. Internet access and online class registration are available. *Library facilities:* Folsom Library plus 1 other. *Graduate expenses:* Tuition: full-time $21,000; part-time $700 per credit. Required fees: $1,205; $400 per year. *General application contact:* Teresa C. Duffy, Dean of Enrollment Management, 518-276-6216.

Find an in-depth description at www.petersons.com/graduate.

Graduate School

Dr. William Jennings, Acting Dean

Lally School of Management and Technology
Dr. Joseph G. Ecker, Dean
Programs in:

e-business • MBA, MS
environmental management and policy • MBA, MS
financial technology • MBA, MS
management • PhD
management and technology • MBA, MS, PhD
management information systems • MBA, MS
product development and management • MBA, MS
production and operations research • MBA, MS
technological entrepreneurship • MBA, MS

School of Architecture
Prof. Peter Parsons, Director, Graduate Programs in Architecture
Programs in:
architecture • M Arch
building conservation • MS
building sciences • MS
infomatics and architecture • MS
lighting • MS

School of Engineering
Dr. William A. Baeslack, Acting Dean
Programs in:
aeronautical engineering • M Eng, MS, D Eng, PhD
biomedical engineering • M Eng, MS, D Eng, PhD
ceramics and glass science • M Eng, MS, D Eng, PhD
chemical engineering • M Eng, MS, D Eng, PhD
composites • M Eng, MS, D Eng, PhD
computer and systems engineering • M Eng, MS, D Eng, PhD
decision sciences and engineering systems • PhD
electric power engineering • M Eng, MS, D Eng, PhD
electrical engineering • M Eng, MS, D Eng, PhD
electronic materials • M Eng, MS, D Eng, PhD
engineering • M Eng, MS, D Eng, PhD
engineering physics • M Eng, MS, D Eng, PhD
engineering science • MS, PhD
environmental engineering • M Eng, MS, D Eng, PhD
geotechnical engineering • M Eng, MS, D Eng, PhD
industrial and management engineering • M Eng, MS, PhD
manufacturing systems engineering • M Eng, MS, PhD
mechanical engineering • M Eng, MS, D Eng, PhD
mechanics • M Eng, MS, PhD
mechanics of composite materials and structures • M Eng, MS, D Eng, PhD
metallurgy • M Eng, MS, D Eng, PhD
nuclear engineering • M Eng, MS, D Eng, PhD
nuclear engineering and science • PhD
operations research and statistics • M Eng, MS, PhD
polymers • M Eng, MS, D Eng, PhD
structural engineering • M Eng, MS, D Eng, PhD
transportation engineering • M Eng, MS, D Eng, PhD

School of Humanities and Social Sciences
Dr. Faye Duchin, Dean
Programs in:
communication and rhetoric • MS, PhD
ecological economics • PhD
ecological economics, values, and policy • MS
economics • MS
electronic arts • MFA
human factors • MS
humanities and social sciences • MFA, MS, PhD
industrial-organizational psychology • MS
philosophy • MS
psychology • MS
science and technology studies • MS, PhD
technical communication • MS

School of Science
Dr. Sandra Nierzwicki-Bauer, Chair
Programs in:
analytical chemistry • MS, PhD
applied mathematics • MS
applied science • MS
biochemistry • MS, PhD
bioinformatics • MS
biophysics • MS, PhD
cell biology • MS, PhD
computer science • MS, PhD
developmental biology • MS, PhD
environmental chemistry • MS, PhD
geochemistry • MS, PhD
geology • MS, PhD
geophysics • MS, PhD
hydrogeology • MS
information technology • MS
inorganic chemistry • MS, PhD
mathematics • MS, PhD
microbiology • MS, PhD
molecular biology • MS, PhD
multidisciplinary science • PhD
natural sciences • MS
organic chemistry • MS, PhD
petrology • MS, PhD
physical chemistry • MS, PhD
physics • MS, PhD
planetary geology • MS, PhD
plant science • MS, PhD
polymer chemistry • MS, PhD
science • MS, PhD
tectonics • MS, PhD

■ ROBERTS WESLEYAN COLLEGE

Rochester, NY 14624-1997
http://www.roberts.edu/

Independent-religious, coed, comprehensive institution. *Computer facilities:* 160 computers available on campus for general student use. A campuswide network can be accessed from student residence rooms and from off campus. *Library facilities:* Ora A. Sprague Library. *General application contact:* Admissions Secretary, Office Manager for Adult and Graduate Education, 716-594-6600.

Division of Business and Management
Programs in:
business and management • MS
organizational management • MS

Division of Social Work and Social Sciences
Programs in:
child and family services • MSW
physical and mental health services • MSW

Division of Teacher Education
Program in:
teacher education • M Ed, Advanced Certificate

■ ROCHESTER INSTITUTE OF TECHNOLOGY

Rochester, NY 14623-5698
http://www.rit.edu/

Independent, coed, comprehensive institution. CGS member. *Enrollment:* 846 full-time matriculated graduate/professional students (340 women), 1,159 part-time matriculated graduate/professional students (418 women). *Computer facilities:* 2,500 computers available on campus for general student use. A campuswide network can be accessed from student residence rooms and from off campus. Internet access and online class registration, student account information are available. *Library facilities:* Wallace Memorial Library. *Graduate expenses:* Tuition: full-time $20,142; part-time $565 per credit hour. Required fees: $153; $24 per quarter. *General application contact:* Diane Ellison, Director, Graduate Enrollment Services, 716-475-7284.

Find an in-depth description at www.petersons.com/graduate.

Rochester Institute of Technology (continued)

Graduate Enrollment Services
Diane Ellison, Director, Graduate Enrollment Services
Programs in:
applied computer studies • AC
computer science • MS
computing and information sciences • MS, AC
information technology • MS
interactive multimedia development • AC
software development and management • MS
telecommunications software technology • MS

College of Applied Science and Technology
Dr. Wiley McKinzie, Dean
Programs in:
applied science and technology • MS, AC
computer integrated manufacturing • MS
cross-disciplinary professional studies • MS
environmental management • MS
health systems administration • MS
health systems-finance • AC
hospitality-tourism management • MS
human resources development • MS
instructional technology • MS
integrated health systems • AC
multidisciplinary studies • MS, AC
packaging science • MS
service management • MS

College of Business
Dr. Thomas D. Hopkins, Dean
Programs in:
accounting • MBA, MS
business • Exec MBA, MBA, MS
business administration • MBA
executive business administration • Exec MBA
finance • MS
international business • MS
manufacturing management and leadership • MS

College of Engineering
Dr. Harvey Palmer, Dean
Programs in:
applied statistics • MS
computer engineering • MS
electrical engineering • MSEE
engineering • ME, MS, MSEE, MSME, AC
engineering management • ME
industrial engineering • ME
manufacturing engineering • ME
mechanical engineering • MSME
microelectronic engineering • ME, MS
statistical quality • AC
systems engineering • ME

College of Imaging Arts and Sciences
Dr. Joan Stone, Dean
Programs in:
art education • MST
computer graphics design • MFA
crafts • MFA, MST
fine arts • MFA, MST
graphic arts publishing • MS
graphic arts systems • MS
graphic design • MFA, MST
imaging arts • MFA
imaging arts and sciences • MFA, MS, MST
industrial design • MFA, MST
interior design • MFA, MST
medical illustration • MFA
painting • MFA, MST
printing technology • MS
printmaking • MFA, MST

College of Liberal Arts
Dr. Andrew Moore, Dean
Programs in:
liberal arts • MS, AC
school psychology • MS, AC
school psychology and deafness • AC

College of Science
Dr. Ian Gatley, Dean
Programs in:
chemistry • MS
clinical chemistry • MS
color science • MS
imaging science • MS, PhD
industrial and applied mathematics • MS
materials science and engineering • MS
science • MS, PhD

Golisano College of Computing and Information Sciences
Walter Wolf, Interim Dean
Programs in:
applied computer studies • AC
computer science • MS
computing and information sciences • MS, AC
information technology • MS
interactive multimedia development • AC
software development and management • MS
telecommunications software technology • MS

National Technical Institute for the Deaf
Dr. Alan Hurwitz, Dean
Program in:
secondary education • MS

■ THE ROCKEFELLER UNIVERSITY
New York, NY 10021-6399
http://www.rockefeller.edu/

Independent, coed, graduate-only institution. CGS member. *Graduate faculty:* 225 full-time (60 women), 179 part-time/adjunct (41 women). *Computer facilities:* 18 computers available on campus for general student use. A campuswide network can be accessed from student residence rooms and from off campus. Internet access is available. *Library facilities:* Rockefeller University Library. *General application contact:* Dr. Sidney Strickland, Dean of Graduate Studies, 212-327-8086.

Program in Biomedical Sciences
Dr. Sidney Strickland, Dean of Graduate Studies
Program in:
biomedical sciences • PhD

■ SAGE GRADUATE SCHOOL
Troy, NY 12180-4115
http://www.sage.edu/

Independent, coed, graduate-only institution. *Graduate faculty:* 37 full-time (25 women), 32 part-time/adjunct (13 women). *Computer facilities:* 244 computers available on campus for general student use. A campuswide network can be accessed from student residence rooms and from off campus. Internet access is available. *Library facilities:* James Wheelock Clark Library plus 1 other. *Graduate expenses:* Tuition: full-time $7,200; part-time $400 per credit hour. Required fees: $100. *General application contact:* Melissa M. Robertson, Associate Director of Admissions, 518-244-6878.

Find an in-depth description at www.petersons.com/graduate.

Graduate School
Dr. Connell G. Frazer, Dean
Program in:
physical therapy • MS

Division of Education
Dr. Kathleen Gormley, Chair
Programs in:
biology • MAT
elementary education • MS Ed
English • MAT
guidance and counseling • MS, PMC
health education • MS
mathematics • MAT
nutrition and dietetics • MS
reading • MS Ed
reading/special education • MS Ed
social studies • MAT
special education • MS Ed
teaching • MAT

Division of Management, Communications and Legal Studies
Dr. Michael Hall, Director
Programs in:
communications • MBA, MS
finance • MBA
gerontology • MS
health education • MS
human resources management • MBA
human services administration • MS
management • MS
management, communications and legal studies • MBA, MS
marketing • MBA
nutrition and dietetics • MS
public management • MS

Division of Nursing
Dr. Glenda Kelman, Director
Programs in:
adult health • MS
adult nurse practitioner • MS
community health nursing • MS
family nurse practitioner • MS
gerontological nurse practitioner • MS
nursing • PMC
psychiatric–mental health nurse practitioner • MS
psychology mental health • MS

Division of Physical Therapy
Marjane Selleck, Director
Program in:
physical therapy • MS

Division of Psychology
Dr. Patricia O'Connor, Director
Programs in:
chemical dependence • MA
chemical dependence counseling • MA
child care and children's services • MA
community counseling • MA
community health • MA
community psychology • MA
forensic psychology • MA
general psychology • MA
psychology • MA
visual art therapy • MA

■ ST. BONAVENTURE UNIVERSITY

St. Bonaventure, NY 14778-2284
http://www.sbu.edu/

Independent-religious, coed, comprehensive institution. CGS member. *Enrollment:* 276 full-time matriculated graduate/professional students (191 women), 322 part-time matriculated graduate/professional students (201 women). *Graduate faculty:* 65 full-time (17 women), 28 part-time/adjunct (9 women). *Computer facilities:* 200 computers available on campus for general student use. A campuswide network can be accessed from student residence rooms and from off campus. Internet access and online class registration are available. *Library facilities:* Friedsam Library. *Graduate expenses:* Tuition: part-time $490 per credit hour. *General application contact:* Dr. David E. Cook, Dean of Graduate Studies, 716-375-2224.

School of Graduate Studies
Dr. David E. Cook, Dean

School of Arts and Sciences
Dr. James White, Dean
Programs in:
arts and sciences • MA
English • MA
history • MA
psychology • MA

School of Business
Dr. Michael J. Fischer, Dean
Programs in:
accounting • Adv C
accounting and finance • MBA
finance • Adv C
management • Adv C
management and marketing • MBA
marketing • Adv C

School of Education
Dr. Carol Anne Pierson, Dean
Programs in:
advanced instructional processes • MS Ed
counseling education • Adv C
counseling education-agency • MS, MS Ed
counseling education-school • MS, MS Ed
education • MS, MS Ed, Adv C
educational administration, supervision, and curriculum • MS Ed, Adv C
reading • MS Ed
secondary education • MS Ed
special education • MS Ed

School of Franciscan Studies
Sr. Margaret Carney, OSF, Dean
Program in:
Franciscan studies • MA, Adv C

■ ST. JOHN FISHER COLLEGE

Rochester, NY 14618-3597
http://www.sjfc.edu/

Independent-religious, coed, comprehensive institution. *Enrollment:* 66 full-time matriculated graduate/professional students (47 women), 381 part-time matriculated graduate/professional students (246 women). *Graduate faculty:* 50. *Computer facilities:* 133 computers available on campus for general student use. A campuswide network can be accessed from student residence rooms and from off campus. Internet access and online class registration are available. *Library facilities:* Charles V. Lavery Library plus 1 other. *Graduate expenses:* Tuition: part-time $440 per credit hour. *General application contact:* Dr. Kathleen A. Powers, Dean, School of Adult and Graduate Education, 716-385-8161.

School of Adult and Graduate Education
Dr. Kathleen A. Powers, Dean
Programs in:
childhood and adolescence • MS Ed
educational administration • MS Ed
family nurse practitioner • Certificate
human resources development • MS
human service administration • MS
international studies • MS
management • MBA
mathematics/science/technology education • MS
nursing • MS
reading • MS
special education • MS
taxation • MS

■ ST. JOHN'S UNIVERSITY

Jamaica, NY 11439
http://www.stjohns.edu/

Independent-religious, coed, university. CGS member. *Enrollment:* 1,371 full-time matriculated graduate/professional students (758 women), 2,542 part-time matriculated graduate/professional students (1,598 women). *Graduate faculty:* 535 full-time (167 women), 599 part-time/adjunct (246 women). *Computer facilities:* 950 computers available on campus for general student use. A campuswide network can be accessed from student residence rooms and from off campus. Internet access and online class registration, various software packages are available. *Library facilities:* St. John's University Library plus 2 others. *Graduate expenses:* Tuition: full-time $13,920; part-time $580 per credit. Required fees: $150; $75 per term. Tuition and fees vary according to class time, course load, degree level, program and student level. *General application contact:* Patricia G. Armstrong, Director, Office of Admission, 718-990-2000.

Find an in-depth description at www.petersons.com/graduate.

St. John's University (continued)

College of Liberal Arts and Sciences
Dr. Jeffrey Fagen, Acting Dean
Programs in:
- algebra • MA
- analysis • MA
- applied mathematics • MA
- arts and sciences • M Div, MA, MLS, MS, DA, PhD, Psy D, APC, Adv C
- biological sciences • MS, PhD
- chemistry • MS
- clinical psychology • MA, PhD
- clinical psychology-child • MA, PhD
- clinical psychology-general • MA, PhD
- computer science • MA
- drug information specialist • MLS, Adv C
- English • MA, DA
- general experimental psychology • MA
- geometry-topology • MA
- government and politics • MA
- government information specialist • MA, Adv C
- history • MA
- international law and diplomacy • Adv C
- library and information science • MLS, Adv C
- logic and foundations • MA
- modern world history • DA
- pastoral ministry • Adv C
- priestly studies • M Div
- probability and statistics • MA
- school psychology • MS, Psy D
- sociology • MA
- Spanish • MA
- speech pathology and audiology • MA
- theology • MA

Institute of Asian Studies
Dr. John Lin, Director
Programs in:
- Asian and African cultural studies • Adv C
- Asian studies • Adv C
- Chinese studies • MA, Adv C
- East Asian culture studies • Adv C
- East Asian studies • MA

College of Pharmacy and Allied Health Professions
Dr. Robert Mangione, Dean
Programs in:
- clinical pharmacy • MS
- cosmetic sciences • MS
- drug information specialist • Pharm D, MS, PhD
- industrial pharmacy • MS, PhD
- medical technology • MS
- medicinal chemistry • MS, PhD
- pharmaceutical • MS
- pharmaceutical sciences • MS, PhD
- pharmacology • MS, PhD
- pharmacotherapeutics • MS
- pharmacy • Pharm D, MS, PhD
- pharmacy administration • MS
- pharmacy and allied health professions • Pharm D, MS, PhD
- toxicology • MS, PhD

The Peter J. Tobin College of Business
Peter J. Tobin, Dean
Programs in:
- accounting • MBA, MS, Adv C
- business • MBA, MS, Adv C
- computer information systems and decision sciences • MBA, Adv C
- economics • MBA, Adv C
- finance • MBA, Adv C
- international business • MBA
- management • MBA, Adv C
- marketing • MBA, Adv C
- taxation • MBA, Adv C

School of Education and Human Services
Dr. Jerrold Ross, Dean
Programs in:
- administration and supervision • MS Ed, Ed D, PD
- bilingual school counseling • MS Ed
- bilingual special education • MS Ed, PD
- bilingual/multicultural education/teaching English to speakers of other languages • MS Ed
- education and human services • MS Ed, Ed D, PD
- elementary education • MS Ed
- instructional leadership • Ed D, PD
- reading special education • MS Ed
- reading specialist • MS Ed, PD
- rehabilitation counseling • MS Ed, PD
- school counseling • MS Ed, PD
- secondary education • MS Ed
- special education • MS Ed, PD
- special education/bilingual special education/reading special education • MS Ed, PD
- student development practice in higher education • MS Ed, PD

School of Law
Joseph W. Bellacosa, Dean
Programs in:
- bankruptcy • LL M
- law • JD

■ ST. THOMAS AQUINAS COLLEGE

Sparkill, NY 10976
http://www.stac.edu/

Independent, coed, comprehensive institution. *Enrollment:* 20 full-time matriculated graduate/professional students, 238 part-time matriculated graduate/professional students. *Graduate faculty:* 13 full-time (5 women), 16 part-time/adjunct (5 women). *Computer facilities:* 200 computers available on campus for general student use. A campuswide network can be accessed from student residence rooms and from off campus. Internet access is available. *Library facilities:* Lougheed Library plus 1 other. *Graduate expenses:* Tuition: part-time $430 per credit. *General application contact:* Tracey Howard-Ubelhoer, Director of Admissions, 845-398-4102.

Division of Business Administration
Barbara Donn, Chairperson
Programs in:
- finance • MBA
- management • MBA
- marketing • MBA

Division of Teacher Education
Dr. Meenakshi Gajria, Chairperson
Programs in:
- advanced study of education • Certificate
- elementary education • MS Ed
- reading • MS Ed, PMC
- secondary education • MS Ed
- special education • MS Ed, PMC

■ STATE UNIVERSITY OF NEW YORK AT ALBANY

Albany, NY 12222-0001
http://www.albany.edu/

State-supported, coed, university. CGS member. *Enrollment:* 2,265 full-time matriculated graduate/professional students (1,336 women), 1,838 part-time matriculated graduate/professional students (1,151 women). *Graduate faculty:* 558 full-time, 328 part-time/adjunct. *Computer facilities:* 500 computers available on campus for general student use. A campuswide network can be accessed from student residence rooms and from off campus. *Library facilities:* University Library plus 2 others. *Graduate expenses:* Tuition, state resident: full-time $5,100; part-time $213 per credit hour. Tuition, nonresident: full-time $8,416; part-time $351 per credit hour. Required fees: $880; $35 per credit hour. *General application contact:* Jeffrey Collins, Director, Graduate Admissions, 518-442-3980.

Find an in-depth description at www.petersons.com/graduate.

College of Arts and Sciences
V. Mark Durand, Interim Dean
Programs in:
African studies • MA
Afro-American studies • MA
anthropology • MA, PhD
art • MA, MFA
arts and sciences • MA, MFA, MRP, MS, DA, PhD, Certificate
atmospheric science • MS, PhD
biodiversity, conservation, and policy • MS
biopsychology • PhD
chemistry • MS, PhD
classics • MA
clinical psychology • PhD
communication • MA
computer science • MS, PhD
demography • Certificate
ecology, evolution, and behavior • MS, PhD
economics • MA, PhD, Certificate
English • MA, PhD
French • MA, PhD
general/experimental psychology • PhD
geographic information systems and spatial analysis • Certificate
geography • MA, Certificate
geology • MS, PhD
history • MA, PhD
humanistic studies • DA
industrial/organizational psychology • PhD
Italian • MA
Latin American and Caribbean studies • MA, Certificate
liberal studies • MA
mathematics • PhD
molecular, cellular, developmental, and neural biology • MS, PhD
philosophy • MA, PhD
physics • MS, PhD
psychology • MA
public history • Certificate
regional planning • MRP
Russian • MA, Certificate
Russian translation • Certificate
secondary teaching • MA
social/personality psychology • PhD
sociology • MA, PhD
sociology and communication • PhD
Spanish • MA, PhD
statistics • MA
theatre • MA
urban policy • Certificate
women's studies • MA

Nelson A. Rockefeller College of Public Affairs and Policy
Dr. Frank J. Thompson, Dean
Programs in:
administrative behavior • PhD
comparative and development administration • MPA, PhD
human resources • MPA
legislative administration • MPA
planning and policy analysis • CAS
policy analysis • MPA
political science • MA, PhD
program analysis and evaluation • PhD
public affairs and policy • MA
public finance • MPA, PhD
public management • MPA, PhD

School of Business
Richard Highfield, Dean
Programs in:
accounting • MS
business • MBA, MS, PhD
finance • MBA
human resource systems • MBA
management science and information systems • MBA
marketing • MBA
organizational studies • PhD
taxation • MS

School of Criminal Justice
James Acker, Dean
Program in:
criminal justice • MA, PhD

School of Education
Ralph W. Harbison, Interim Dean
Programs in:
counseling psychology • MS, PhD, CAS
curriculum and instruction • MS, Ed D, CAS
curriculum planning and development • MA
education • MA, MS, Ed D, PhD, Psy D, CAS
educational administration • MS, PhD, CAS
educational communications • MS, CAS
educational psychology • Ed D
educational psychology and statistics • MS
measurements and evaluation • Ed D
reading • MS, Ed D, CAS
rehabilitation counseling • MS
school counselor • CAS
school psychology • Psy D, CAS
special education • MS
statistics and research design • Ed D

School of Information Science and Policy
Philip Eppard, Dean
Programs in:
information science • MS, PhD
information science and policy • CAS
library science • MLS

School of Public Health
Dr. Jeryl Mumpower, Interim Dean
Programs in:
biochemistry, molecular biology, and genetics • MS, PhD
biometry and statistics • MS, PhD
cell and molecular structure • MS, PhD
environmental and occupational health • MS, PhD
environmental chemistry • MS, PhD
epidemiology • MS, PhD
health policy and management • MS
immunobiology and immunochemistry • MS, PhD
molecular pathogenesis • MS, PhD
neuroscience • MS, PhD
public health • MPH, MS, Dr PH, PhD
toxicology • MS, PhD

School of Social Welfare
Katharine Briar-Lawson, Dean
Program in:
social welfare • MSW, PhD

■ STATE UNIVERSITY OF NEW YORK AT BINGHAMTON

Binghamton, NY 13902-6000
http://www.binghamton.edu/

State-supported, coed, university. CGS member. *Enrollment:* 1,385 full-time matriculated graduate/professional students (638 women), 892 part-time matriculated graduate/professional students (459 women). *Graduate faculty:* 510 full-time (157 women), 293 part-time/adjunct (131 women). *Computer facilities:* 5,300 computers available on campus for general student use. A campuswide network can be accessed from student residence rooms and from off campus. Internet access and online class registration are available. *Library facilities:* Glenn G. Bartle Library plus 1 other. *Graduate expenses:* Tuition, state resident: full-time $5,100; part-time $213 per credit. Tuition, nonresident: full-time $8,416; part-time $351 per credit. Required fees: $754. *General application contact:* David E. Payne, Interim Dean of the Graduate School, 607-777-2070.

Find an in-depth description at www.petersons.com/graduate.

Graduate School
Programs in:
public administration • MPA

State University of New York at Binghamton (continued)

School of Arts and Sciences
Dr. Jean-Pierre Mileur, Dean
Programs in:
- analytical chemistry • PhD
- anthropology • MA, PhD
- applied physics • MS
- art history • MA, PhD
- arts and sciences • MA, MM, MS, PhD, Certificate
- behavioral neuroscience • MA, PhD
- biological sciences • MA, PhD
- chemistry • MA, MS
- clinical psychology • MA, PhD
- cognitive and behavioral science • MA, PhD
- comparative literature • MA, PhD
- computer science • MA, PhD
- economics • MA, PhD
- economics and finance • MA, PhD
- English • MA, PhD
- French • MA
- geography • MA
- geological sciences • MA, PhD
- history • MA, PhD
- inorganic chemistry • PhD
- Italian • MA
- music • MA, MM
- organic chemistry • PhD
- philosophy • MA, PhD
- physical chemistry • PhD
- physics • MA, MS
- political science • MA, PhD
- probability and statistics • MA, PhD
- public policy • MA, PhD
- sociology • MA, PhD
- Spanish • MA, Certificate
- theater • MA
- translation • Certificate
- translation research and instruction • Certificate

School of Education and Human Development
Dr. Ernest Rose, Dean
Programs in:
- biology education • MAT, MS Ed, MST
- early childhood and elementary education • MS Ed
- earth science education • MAT, MS Ed, MST
- education and human development • MASS, MAT, MS Ed, MST, Ed D
- educational theory and practice • Ed D
- English education • MAT, MS Ed, MST
- French education • MAT, MST
- mathematical sciences education • MAT, MS Ed, MST
- physics • MAT, MS Ed, MST
- reading education • MS Ed
- social science • MASS
- social studies • MAT, MS Ed, MST
- Spanish education • MAT, MST
- special education • MS Ed

School of Management
Dr. Glenn Pittman, Dean
Programs in:
- accounting • MS, PhD
- arts administration • MBA Arts
- business administration • MBA, PhD
- health care professional executive • MBA
- management • MBA, MBA Arts, MS, PhD

School of Nursing
Dr. Mary Collins, Dean
Program in:
- nursing • MS, PhD, Certificate

Thomas J. Watson School of Engineering and Applied Science
Dr. Lyle D. Feisel, Dean
Programs in:
- computer science • M Eng, MS, PhD
- electrical engineering • M Eng, MS, PhD
- engineering and applied science • M Eng, MS, MSAT, PhD
- mechanical engineering • M Eng, MS, PhD
- systems science and industrial engineering • M Eng, MS, MSAT, PhD

■ STATE UNIVERSITY OF NEW YORK AT NEW PALTZ

New Paltz, NY 12561
http://www.newpaltz.edu/

State-supported, coed, comprehensive institution. *Enrollment:* 349 full-time matriculated graduate/professional students (240 women), 1,310 part-time matriculated graduate/professional students (910 women). *Graduate faculty:* 116 full-time, 90 part-time/adjunct. *Computer facilities:* 600 computers available on campus for general student use. A campuswide network can be accessed from student residence rooms and from off campus. Internet access and online class registration, e-mail are available. *Library facilities:* Sojourner Truth Library. *Graduate expenses:* Tuition, state resident: full-time $5,100; part-time $213 per credit. Tuition, nonresident: full-time $8,416; part-time $351 per credit. *General application contact:* Dr. Phyllis Freeman, Adviser, 845-257-3470.

Graduate School
Dr. Phyllis Freeman, Adviser
Programs in:
- accounting • MBA
- finance • MBA
- international business • MBA
- marketing • MBA

Faculty of Education
Dr. Robert Michael, Dean
Programs in:
- early childhood education • MS Ed
- education • MAT, MPS, MS Ed, MST, CAS
- educational administration • MS Ed, CAS
- elementary education • MST
- English as a second language • MS Ed
- environmental education • MS Ed
- general education • MS Ed
- humanistic education • MPS
- reading • MS Ed
- secondary education • MAT, MS Ed
- special education • MS Ed

Faculty of Fine and Performing Arts
Dr. Patricia Phillips, Dean
Programs in:
- art education • MS
- ceramics • MA, MFA
- fine and performing arts • MA, MFA, MS
- metal • MA, MFA
- painting • MA, MFA
- photography • MA, MFA
- piano pedagogy • MA, MFA
- printmaking • MA, MFA
- sculpture • MA, MFA

Faculty of Liberal Arts and Sciences
Dr. Gerald Benjamin, Dean
Programs in:
- biology • MA, MAT, MS Ed
- communication disorders • MS Ed
- English • MA, MAT, MS Ed
- gerontological nursing • MS
- liberal arts and sciences • MA, MAT, MS, MS Ed
- psychology • MA
- sociology • MA

School of Physical Sciences and Engineering
Programs in:
- chemistry • MA, MAT, MS Ed
- computer science • MS
- electrical and computer engineering • MS
- engineering • MA, MAT, MS, MS Ed
- geological sciences • MA, MAT, MS Ed
- mathematics • MA, MAT, MS Ed
- physics • MS

■ STATE UNIVERSITY OF NEW YORK AT OSWEGO

Oswego, NY 13126
http://www.oswego.edu/

State-supported, coed, comprehensive institution. CGS member. *Enrollment:* 268 full-time matriculated graduate/professional students (173 women), 577 part-time matriculated graduate/

professional students (392 women). *Graduate faculty:* 75 full-time, 31 part-time/adjunct. *Computer facilities:* 600 computers available on campus for general student use. A campuswide network can be accessed from student residence rooms and from off campus. Internet access and online class registration are available. *Library facilities:* Penfield Library plus 1 other. *Graduate expenses:* Tuition, state resident: full-time $5,100; part-time $213 per credit. Tuition, nonresident: full-time $8,416; part-time $351 per credit. *General application contact:* Dr. Jack Y. Narayan, Dean of Graduate Studies, 315-312-3152.

Graduate Studies
Dr. Jack Y. Narayan, Dean

Division of Arts and Sciences
Dr. Sara Varhus, Dean
Programs in:
- art • MA
- arts and sciences • MA, MS
- chemistry • MS
- English • MA
- history • MA

School of Business
Dr. Lanny A. Karns, Dean
Programs in:
- business • MBA
- business administration • MBA

School of Education
Dr. Linda Markert, Dean
Programs in:
- art education • MAT
- counseling services • MS, CAS
- education • MAT, MS, MS Ed, CAS
- elementary education • MS Ed
- human services/counseling • MS
- instructional administration • MS Ed, CAS
- reading education • MS Ed
- school psychology • MS, CAS
- secondary education • MS Ed
- special education • MS Ed
- technology • MS Ed
- vocational-technical education • MS Ed

■ STATE UNIVERSITY OF NEW YORK COLLEGE AT BROCKPORT

Brockport, NY 14420-2997
http://www.brockport.edu/

State-supported, coed, comprehensive institution. *Enrollment:* 266 full-time matriculated graduate/professional students (186 women), 940 part-time matriculated graduate/professional students (596 women). *Graduate faculty:* 222. *Computer facilities:* 700 computers available on campus for general student use. A campuswide network can be accessed from student residence rooms and from off campus. Internet access is available. *Library facilities:* Drake Memorial Library. *Graduate expenses:* Tuition, state resident: full-time $5,100; part-time $213 per credit. Tuition, nonresident: full-time $8,416; part-time $351 per credit. Required fees: $537; $23 per credit. *General application contact:* Sue A. Smithson, Secretary—Graduate Admissions, 716-395-5465.

Find an in-depth description at www.petersons.com/graduate.

School of Arts and Performance
Sharon Vasquez, Dean
Programs in:
- arts and performance • MA, MFA, MS Ed
- communication • MA
- dance • MA, MFA
- physical education • MS Ed
- visual studies • MFA

School of Letters and Sciences
Dr. Michael Maggiotto, Dean
Programs in:
- biological sciences • MS
- computational science • MS
- English • MA
- history • MA
- letters and sciences • MA, MS
- liberal studies • MA
- mathematics • MA
- psychology • MA

School of Professions
Dr. Jospeh Mason, Dean
Programs in:
- bilingual education • MS Ed
- biology education • MS Ed
- chemistry education • MS Ed
- counselor education • MS Ed, CAS
- earth science education • MS Ed
- elementary education • MS Ed
- English education • MS Ed
- family nurse practitioner • MS, CAS
- health science • MS Ed
- mathematics education • MS Ed
- physics education • MS Ed
- public administration • MPA
- reading • MS Ed
- recreation and leisure studies • MS
- school administration and supervision • MS Ed, CAS
- school business administration • CAS
- school district administration • CAS
- secondary education • MS Ed
- social studies education • MS Ed
- social work • MSW

■ STATE UNIVERSITY OF NEW YORK COLLEGE AT BUFFALO

Buffalo, NY 14222-1095
http://www.buffalostate.edu/

State-supported, coed, comprehensive institution. CGS member. *Enrollment:* 382 full-time matriculated graduate/professional students (280 women), 1,631 part-time matriculated graduate/professional students (1,120 women). *Graduate faculty:* 185 full-time (67 women), 31 part-time/adjunct (14 women). *Computer facilities:* 900 computers available on campus for general student use. A campuswide network can be accessed from student residence rooms and from off campus. Internet access is available. *Library facilities:* E. H. Butler Library. *Graduate expenses:* Tuition, state resident: full-time $5,100; part-time $213 per credit hour. Tuition, nonresident: full-time $8,416; part-time $351 per credit hour. Required fees: $335; $14 per credit hour. *General application contact:* Graduate Studies and Research, 716-878-5601.

Graduate Studies and Research
Dr. Richard S. Podemski, Dean
Program in:
- multidisciplinary studies • MA, MS

Faculty of Applied Science and Education
Dr. Daniel King, Dean
Programs in:
- adult education • MS
- applied science and education • MPS, MS, MS Ed, CAS
- business and distributive education • MS Ed
- business education • MS Ed
- career and technical education • MS Ed
- creative studies • MS
- criminal justice • MS
- educational computing • MS Ed
- educational leadership and facilitation • CAS
- elementary and early secondary education • MS Ed
- elementary education • MS Ed
- English education • MS Ed
- general science education • MS Ed
- industrial technology • MS
- mathematics education • MS Ed
- reading • MPS, MS Ed
- social studies education • MS Ed
- special education • MS Ed
- speech language pathology • MS Ed
- student personnel administration • MS
- teaching bilingual exceptional individuals • MS Ed
- technology education • MS Ed

State University of New York College at Buffalo (continued)

Faculty of Arts and Humanities
Dr. Emile C. Netzhammer, Dean
Programs in:
- art conservation • CAS
- art education • MS Ed
- arts and humanities • MA, MS Ed, CAS
- conservation of historic works and art works • MA
- English • MA
- secondary education • MS Ed

Faculty of Natural and Social Sciences
Dr. Lawrence G. Flood, Dean
Programs in:
- applied economics • MA
- biology • MA
- chemistry • MA
- history • MA
- mathematics education • MS Ed
- natural and social sciences • MA, MS Ed
- secondary education • MS Ed

■ STATE UNIVERSITY OF NEW YORK COLLEGE AT CORTLAND

Cortland, NY 13045
http://www.cortland.edu/

State-supported, coed, comprehensive institution. *Enrollment:* 266 full-time matriculated graduate/professional students (166 women), 1,264 part-time matriculated graduate/professional students (873 women). *Graduate faculty:* 62. *Computer facilities:* 832 computers available on campus for general student use. A campuswide network can be accessed from student residence rooms and from off campus. *Library facilities:* Memorial Library. *Graduate expenses:* Tuition, state resident: full-time $5,100; part-time $213 per credit. Tuition, nonresident: full-time $8,416; part-time $351 per credit. *General application contact:* Mark Yacavone, Associate Director of Admissions, 607-753-4711.

Graduate Studies
Program in:
- American civilization and culture • CAS

Division of Arts and Sciences
Dr. John Ryder, Dean
Programs in:
- arts and sciences • MA, MAT, MS Ed
- biology • MAT, MS Ed
- chemistry • MAT, MS Ed
- earth science • MAT, MS Ed
- English • MA, MAT, MS Ed
- Englsih • MS Ed
- French • MS Ed
- history • MA, MS Ed
- mathematics • MAT, MS Ed
- physics • MAT, MS Ed
- social studies • MS Ed
- Spanish • MS Ed

Division of Professional Studies
Dr. Helen Giles-Gee, Dean
Programs in:
- childhood education • MST
- elementary education • MS Ed
- English education • MS Ed
- general science education • MS Ed
- health education • MS Ed
- mathematics education • MS Ed
- physical education • MS Ed
- professional studies • MS, MS Ed, MST, CAS
- reading • MS Ed
- recreation education • MS, MS Ed
- school administration and supervision • CAS
- school business administrator • CAS
- social studies education • MS Ed

■ STATE UNIVERSITY OF NEW YORK COLLEGE AT FREDONIA

Fredonia, NY 14063
http://www.fredonia.edu/

State-supported, coed, comprehensive institution. *Enrollment:* 85 full-time matriculated graduate/professional students (67 women), 263 part-time matriculated graduate/professional students (205 women). *Graduate faculty:* 35 full-time (11 women), 12 part-time/adjunct (9 women). *Computer facilities:* 500 computers available on campus for general student use. A campuswide network can be accessed from student residence rooms and from off campus. *Library facilities:* Reed Library. *Graduate expenses:* Tuition, state resident: full-time $3,400; part-time $213 per credit hour. Tuition, nonresident: full-time $8,300; part-time $351 per credit hour. Required fees: $825; $30 per credit hour. *General application contact:* J. Denis Bolton, Director of Graduate Admissions, 716-673-3251.

Graduate Studies
Dr. Leonard E. Faulk, Dean of Graduate Studies
Programs in:
- biology • MS, MS Ed
- chemistry • MS, MS Ed
- English • MA, MS Ed
- mathematics • MS Ed
- social sciences • MA, MS
- speech pathology and audiology • MS, MS Ed

School of Education
Dr. Julius Adams, Chair
Programs in:
- educational administration • CAS
- elementary education • MS Ed
- reading • MS Ed
- secondary education • MS Ed

School of Music
Dr. Peter Schoenbach, Director
Programs in:
- music • MM
- music education • MM

■ STATE UNIVERSITY OF NEW YORK COLLEGE AT GENESEO

Geneseo, NY 14454-1401
http://www.geneseo.edu/

State-supported, coed, comprehensive institution. *Enrollment:* 42 full-time matriculated graduate/professional students (39 women), 187 part-time matriculated graduate/professional students (157 women). *Graduate faculty:* 38 full-time (18 women), 20 part-time/adjunct (13 women). *Computer facilities:* 800 computers available on campus for general student use. A campuswide network can be accessed from student residence rooms and from off campus. Internet access and online class registration are available. *Library facilities:* Milne Library plus 1 other. *Graduate expenses:* Tuition, state resident: full-time $5,100; part-time $213 per credit. Tuition, nonresident: full-time $8,416; part-time $315 per credit. Required fees: $475; $475 per year. *General application contact:* Dr. Thomas Greenfield, Dean of the College, 716-245-5546.

Graduate Studies
Dr. Thomas Greenfield, Dean of the College
Program in:
- communicative disorders and sciences • MA

School of Education
Dr. Dennis Showers, Interim Head
Programs in:
- elementary education • MS Ed
- reading • MPS, MS Ed
- secondary education • MS Ed
- special education • MS Ed

■ STATE UNIVERSITY OF NEW YORK COLLEGE AT ONEONTA

Oneonta, NY 13820-4015
http://www.oneonta.edu/

State-supported, coed, comprehensive institution. CGS member. *Enrollment:* 36 full-time matriculated graduate/professional students (27 women), 163 part-time matriculated graduate/professional students (132 women). *Graduate faculty:* 144 part-time/adjunct. *Computer facilities:* 525 computers available on campus for general student use. A campuswide network can be accessed from student residence rooms and from off campus. Internet access and online class registration are available. *Library facilities:* Milne Library. *Graduate expenses:* Tuition, state resident: full-time $5,100; part-time $213 per credit. Tuition, nonresident: full-time $8,416; part-time $351 per credit. Required fees: $609; $12 per credit. *General application contact:* Dr. Carolyn Haessig, Director, 800-SUNY-123.

Graduate Studies
Dr. Carolyn Haessig, Director
Programs in:
- biology • MA
- earth science • MA
- history museum studies • MA

Division of Economics and Business
Dr. Wade Thomas, Chairperson
Program in:
- business economics • MS

Division of Education
Dr. Barbara Stoehr, Associate Dean
Programs in:
- community mental health • MS
- educational psychology • MS, MS Ed, CAS
- elementary and reading education • MS Ed
- elementary education • MS Ed
- marriage and family therapy • MS
- reading • MS Ed
- school counselor K-12 • MS Ed, CAS
- secondary education • MS Ed

■ STATE UNIVERSITY OF NEW YORK COLLEGE AT POTSDAM

Potsdam, NY 13676
http://www.potsdam.edu/

State-supported, coed, comprehensive institution. *Enrollment:* 287 full-time matriculated graduate/professional students (214 women), 282 part-time matriculated graduate/professional students (209 women). *Graduate faculty:* 48 full-time (11 women), 19 part-time/adjunct (7 women). *Computer facilities:* 400 computers available on campus for general student use. A campuswide network can be accessed from student residence rooms and from off campus. Internet access and online class registration, Appletalk network are available. *Library facilities:* F. W. Crumb Memorial Library plus 1 other. *Graduate expenses:* Part-time $213 per credit. Tuition, state resident: full-time $5,100. Tuition, nonresident: full-time $8,416; part-time $351 per credit. Required fees: $415; $17 per credit. *General application contact:* Dr. William Amoriell, Dean of Education and Graduate Studies, 315-267-2515.

Crane School of Music
Dr. Alan Solomon, Dean
Programs in:
- composition • MM
- history and literature • MM
- music education • MM
- music theory • MM
- performance • MM

School of Arts and Sciences
Dr. Galen K. Pletcher, Dean
Programs in:
- arts and sciences • MA
- English • MA
- mathematics • MA

School of Education
Dr. William Amoriell, Dean of Education and Graduate Studies
Programs in:
- education • MS Ed, MST
- educational technology • MS Ed
- elementary education • MS Ed, MST
- professional education • MS Ed
- reading education • MS Ed
- secondary education • MS Ed, MST
- special education • MS Ed

■ STATE UNIVERSITY OF NEW YORK COLLEGE OF ENVIRONMENTAL SCIENCE AND FORESTRY

Syracuse, NY 13210-2779
http://www.esf.edu/

State-supported, coed, university. *Enrollment:* 272 full-time matriculated graduate/professional students (135 women), 203 part-time matriculated graduate/professional students (66 women). *Graduate faculty:* 116 full-time (13 women), 5 part-time/adjunct (4 women). *Computer facilities:* 150 computers available on campus for general student use. A campuswide network can be accessed from student residence rooms and from off campus. Internet access and online class registration are available. *Library facilities:* F. Franklin Moon Library plus 1 other. *Graduate expenses:* Tuition, state resident: full-time $5,100. Tuition, nonresident: full-time $8,416. Required fees: $293. *General application contact:* Dr. Robert H. Frey, Dean, Instruction and Graduate Studies, 315-470-6599.

Find an in-depth description at www.petersons.com/graduate.

Faculty of Chemistry
Dr. John P. Hassett, Chairperson
Program in:
- environmental and forest chemistry • MS, PhD

Faculty of Environmental and Forest Biology
Dr. Neil H. Ringler, Chairperson
Program in:
- environmental and forest biology • MPS, MS, PhD

Faculty of Environmental and Resource Engineering
Dr. James M. Hassett, Chairperson
Program in:
- environmental and resource engineering • MPS, MS, PhD

Faculty of Environmental Science
Dr. Richard Smardon, Chairperson
Program in:
- environmental science • MPS, MS, PhD

Faculty of Forestry
Dr. William Bentley, Chair
Programs in:
- agronomy and soil sciences management • MPS, MS, PhD
- forest resources management • MPS, MS, PhD
- forestry • MPS, MS, PhD
- natural resources management • MPS, MS, PhD

Faculty of Landscape Architecture
Richard Hawks, Chairperson
Program in:
- landscape architecture • MLA, MS

■ STATE UNIVERSITY OF NEW YORK EMPIRE STATE COLLEGE

Saratoga Springs, NY 12866-4391

http://www.esc.edu/

State-supported, coed, comprehensive institution. *Enrollment:* 29 full-time matriculated graduate/professional students (19 women), 285 part-time matriculated graduate/professional students (181 women). *Graduate faculty:* 6 full-time (2 women), 109 part-time/adjunct (45 women). *Computer facilities:* 100 computers available on campus for general student use. A campuswide network can be accessed from off campus. Internet access and online class registration are available. *Graduate expenses:* Tuition, state resident: full-time $3,888; part-time $216 per credit hour. Tuition, nonresident: full-time $6,418; part-time $351 per credit hour. Required fees: $50 per term. Tuition and fees vary according to program. *General application contact:* Dr. Meredith Brown, Acting Director, 518-587-2100 Ext. 207.

Find an in-depth description at www.petersons.com/graduate.

Graduate Studies

Dean

Programs in:

- business administration • MBA
- business and policy studies • MA
- labor and policy studies • MA
- liberal studies • MA
- social policy • MA

■ STATE UNIVERSITY OF NEW YORK INSTITUTE OF TECHNOLOGY AT UTICA/ ROME

Utica, NY 13504-3050

http://www.sunyit.edu/

State-supported, coed, upper-level institution. *Enrollment:* 78 full-time matriculated graduate/professional students (36 women), 274 part-time matriculated graduate/professional students (155 women). *Graduate faculty:* 54 full-time (19 women), 7 part-time/adjunct (4 women). *Computer facilities:* 250 computers available on campus for general student use. A campuswide network can be accessed from student residence rooms and from off campus. Internet access and online class registration, various other software applications are available. *Library facilities:* SUNY Institute of Technology at Utica/Rome Library. *Graduate expenses:* Tuition, state resident: full-time $5,100; part-time $213 per credit hour. Tuition, nonresident: full-time $8,416; part-time $351 per credit hour. Required fees: $679; $21 per credit hour. *General application contact:* Marybeth Lyons, Director of Admissions, 315-792-7500.

Find an in-depth description at www.petersons.com/graduate.

School of Arts and Sciences

Dr. Daniel J. Murphy, Interim Dean of School of Arts and Sciences

Programs in:

- applied sociology • MS
- information design and technology • MS

School of Information Systems and Engineering Technology

Dr. Orlando Baiocchi, Dean

Programs in:

- advanced technology • MS
- computer and information science • MS
- telecommunications • MS

School of Management

Dr. Sanjay Varshney, Dean

Programs in:

- accountancy • MS
- business management • MS
- health services administration • MS

School of Nursing

Dr. Jeannine Muldoon, Dean

Programs in:

- adult nurse practitioner • MS, Certificate
- family nurse practitioner • MS, Certificate
- nursing administration • MS

■ STONY BROOK UNIVERSITY, STATE UNIVERSITY OF NEW YORK

Stony Brook, NY 11794

http://www.sunysb.edu/

State-supported, coed, university. CGS member. *Enrollment:* 2,939 full-time matriculated graduate/professional students (1,492 women), 2,705 part-time matriculated graduate/professional students (1,665 women). *Graduate faculty:* 1,132 full-time (311 women), 258 part-time/adjunct (100 women). *Computer facilities:* 500 computers available on campus for general student use. A campuswide network can be accessed from student residence rooms and from off campus. Internet access and online class registration are available. *Library facilities:* Frank Melville, Jr. Building Library plus 7 others. *General application contact:* Dr. Kent Marks, Director, Admissions and Records, 631-632-4723.

Find an in-depth description at www.petersons.com/graduate.

Graduate School

Dr. Lawrence B. Martin, Dean

College of Arts and Sciences

Dr. Bob Libermann, Interim Dean

Programs in:

- anthropology • MA, PhD
- art history and criticism • MA, PhD
- arts and sciences • MA, MAT, MFA, MM, MS, DA, DMA, PhD
- astronomy • MS, PhD
- biochemistry and molecular biology • PhD
- biochemistry and structural biology • PhD
- biological and biomedical sciences • PhD
- biopsychology • PhD
- cellular and developmental biology • PhD
- chemistry • MAT, MS, PhD
- clinical psychology • PhD
- dramaturgy • MFA
- earth and space science • MS, PhD
- earth and space sciences • MS, PhD
- earth science • MAT
- ecology and evolution • PhD
- economics • MA, PhD
- English • MA, PhD
- experimental psychology • PhD
- foreign languages • DA
- French • MA, MAT, DA
- genetics • PhD
- German • MA, MAT, DA
- Germanic languages and literatures • MA
- Hispanic languages and literature • MA, DA, PhD
- history • MA, MAT, PhD
- immunology and pathology • PhD
- Italian • MA, MAT, DA
- linguistics • MA, PhD
- mathematics • MA, PhD
- molecular and cellular biology • MA
- music • MA, PhD
- music history, theory and composition • MA, PhD
- music performance • MM, DMA
- neurobiology and behavior • PhD
- philosophy • MA, PhD
- physics • MA, MAT, MS, PhD
- political science • MA, PhD
- psychology • MA
- Romance languages and literatures • MA

Russian • MAT, DA
Slavic languages and literatures • MA
social/health psychology • PhD
sociology • MA, PhD
studio art • MFA
teaching English to speakers of other languages • MA, DA
theatre • MA

College of Engineering and Applied Sciences
Dr. Yacov Shamash, Dean
Programs in:
applied mathematics and statistics • MS, PhD
biomedical engineering • MS, PhD, Certificate
computer science • MS, PhD
electrical and computer engineering • MS, PhD
engineering and applied sciences • MBA, MS, PhD, Certificate
industrial management • Certificate
management and policy • MS
materials science and engineering • MS, PhD
mechanical engineering • MS, PhD
software engineering • Certificate
technological systems management • MS
technology management • MBA, MS

Institute for Terrestrial and Planetary Atmospheres
Marvin A. Geller, Director
Program in:
terrestrial and planetary atmospheres • PhD

Marine Sciences Research Center
Dr. Marvin A. Geller, Dean and Director
Programs in:
coastal oceanography • PhD
marine environmental sciences • MS
terrestrial and planetary atmospheres • PhD

Health Sciences Center
Dr. Norman H. Edelman, Dean and Vice President
Program in:
health sciences • DDS, MD, MS, MSW, PhD, Advanced Certificate, Certificate

School of Dental Medicine
Dr. Barry R. Rifkin, Dean
Programs in:
dental medicine • DDS
endodontics • Certificate
oral biology and pathology • PhD
orthodontics • Certificate
periodontics • Certificate

School of Health Technology and Management
Dr. Craig A. Lehmann, Dean
Programs in:
community health • Advanced Certificate
health care management • Advanced Certificate
health care policy and management • MS

School of Medicine
Dr. Norman H. Edelman, Dean and Vice President
Programs in:
anatomical sciences • PhD
medicine • MD, PhD
molecular and cellular pharmacology • PhD
molecular microbiology • PhD
physiology and biophysics • PhD

School of Nursing
Dr. Lenora J. McClean, Dean
Programs in:
adult health nurse practitioner • Certificate
adult health/primary care nursing • MS
child health nurse practitioner • Certificate
child health nursing • MS
family nurse practitioner • MS, Certificate
gerontological nursing • MS
mental health nurse practitioner • Certificate
mental health/psychiatric nursing • MS
neonatal nurse practitioner • Certificate
neonatal nursing • MS
nurse-midwifery • MS, Certificate
nursing • MS, Certificate
perinatal/women's health nurse practitioner • Certificate
perinatal/women's health nursing • MS

School of Social Welfare
Dr. Frances L. Brisbane, Dean
Programs in:
social welfare • PhD
social work • MSW

School of Professional Development and Continuing Studies
Dr. Paul J. Edelson, Dean
Programs in:
art and philosophy • Certificate
biology 7-12 • MAT
chemistry-grade 7-12 • MAT
coaching • Certificate
computer integrated engineering • Certificate
cultural studies • Certificate
earth science-grade 7-12 • MAT
educational computing • Certificate
English-grade 7-12 • MAT
environmental/occupational health and safety • Certificate
French-grade 7-12 • MAT
German-grade 7-12 • MAT
human resource management • Certificate
industrial management • Certificate
information systems management • Certificate
Italian-grade 7-12 • MAT
liberal studies • MA
Long Island regional studies • Certificate
oceanic science • Certificate
operation research • Certificate
physics-grade 7-12 • MAT
Russian-grade 7-12 • MAT
school administration and supervision • Certificate
school district administration • Certificate
social science and the professions • MPS
social studies 7-12 • MAT
waste management • Certificate
women's studies • Certificate

■ SYRACUSE UNIVERSITY
Syracuse, NY 13244-0003
http://www.syracuse.edu/

Independent, coed, university. CGS member. *Enrollment:* 2,392 full-time matriculated graduate/professional students (1,272 women), 2,022 part-time matriculated graduate/professional students (1,010 women). *Computer facilities:* 1,200 computers available on campus for general student use. A campuswide network can be accessed from student residence rooms and from off campus. Internet access and online class registration, online services, networked client and server computing are available. *Library facilities:* E. S. Bird Library plus 6 others. *Graduate expenses:* Tuition: part-time $613 per credit. Required fees: $203 per semester. *General application contact:* Dr. Howard Johnson, Dean of the Graduate School, 315-443-5012.

College of Law
Daan Braveman, Dean
Program in:
law • JD

Graduate School
Dr. Howard Johnson, Dean

Syracuse University (continued)
College of Arts and Sciences
Dr. Cathryn Newton, Dean
Programs in:
applied statistics • MS
art history • MA
arts and sciences • MA, MFA, MS, PhD, CAS
biology • MS, PhD
biophysics • PhD
chemistry • MS, PhD
classics • MA
clinical psychology • MA, MS, PhD
college science teaching • PhD
composition and cultural rhetoric • PhD
creative writing • MFA
English • PhD
experimental psychology • MA, MS, PhD
French language, literature and culture • MA
geology • MA, MS, PhD
hydrogeology • MS
linguistic studies • MA
literature and critical theory • MA
mathematics • MS, PhD
mathematics education • MS, PhD
philosophy • MA, PhD
physics • MS, PhD
psychology • MA, MS, PhD
religion • MA, PhD
school psychology • PhD
social psychology • PhD
Spanish language, literature and culture • MA
women's studies • CAS

College of Human Services and Health Professions
William Pollard, Dean
Programs in:
child and family studies • MA, MS, PhD
family mental health • MSW
gerontology • MSW
health care • MSW
human services and health professions • MA, MS, MSW, PhD
marriage and family therapy • MA, PhD
nursing • MS
nutrition science and food management • MA, MS, PhD
occupational social work • MSW

College of Visual and Performing Arts
Carole Brozozowski, Dean
Programs in:
advertising design • MFA
art and design • MA, MFA
art photography process • MFA
ceramics • MFA
cinema/drama • MFA
computer graphics • MFA
consumer studies • MA, MS
drama • MA, MFA
fashion design • MA
fiber structure interlocking • MFA
film-art/drama • MFA
illustration • MFA
metalsmithing • MFA
museum studies • MA
music composition • M Mus
organ • M Mus
painting • MFA
percussion • M Mus
piano • M Mus
printmaking • MFA
sculpture • MFA
speech communication • MA, MS
strings • M Mus
textile design • MS
theory • M Mus
video research • MFA
visual and performing arts • M Mus, MA, MFA, MS
voice • M Mus
wind instruments • M Mus

L. C. Smith College of Engineering and Computer Science
Dr. Edward Bogucz, Dean
Programs in:
aerospace engineering • MS, PhD
bioengineering • MS
chemical engineering • MS, PhD
civil engineering • MS, PhD
computer and information science • MS, PhD
computer engineering • MS, PhD, CE
computer science • MS
electrical engineering • MS, PhD, EE
engineering and computer science • MS, PhD, CE, EE
engineering management • MS
environmental engineering • MS
manufacturing engineering • MS
mechanical engineering • MS, PhD
neuroscience • MS, PhD
solid-state science and technology • MS, PhD
systems and information science • MS, PhD

Maxwell School of Citizenship and Public Affairs
John Palmer, Dean
Programs in:
anthropology • MA, PhD
citizenship and public affairs • MA, MPA, MS Sc, PhD, CAS
economics • MA, PhD
geography • MA, PhD
health services management and policy • CAS
history • MA, PhD
international relations • MA
political science • MA, PhD
public administration • MA, MPA, PhD
social sciences • MS Sc, PhD
sociology • MA, PhD

School of Architecture
Bruce Abbey, Dean
Program in:
architecture • M Arch

School of Education
Dr. Corinne Smith, Interim Dean
Programs in:
art education • MS, CAS
audiology and speech pathology • MS, PhD
counselor education • MS, Ed D, PhD, CAS
cultural foundations of education • MS, PhD, CAS
educating infants and young children with special needs • MS
education • M Mu, MS, Ed D, PhD, CAS
educational leadership • MS, Ed D, PhD, CAS
elementary education • MS, CAS
English education • MS, Ed D, PhD, CAS
exercise science • MS, CAS
higher education • MS, Ed D, PhD, CAS
instructional design, development, and evaluation • MS, Ed D, PhD, CAS
learning disabilities • MS
mathematics education • MS, Ed D, PhD, CAS
music education • M Mu, MS
reading and language arts • MS, Ed D, PhD, CAS
rehabilitation counseling • MS, Ed D, PhD
science education • MS, Ed D, PhD, CAS
social studies education • MS, CAS
special education (emotional disorders and severe disabilities) • MS, Ed D, PhD
teaching and curriculum • MS, Ed D, PhD, CAS

School of Information Studies
Dr. Raymond F. von Dran, Dean
Programs in:
information and library science • MLS, CAS
information management • MS
information resources management • MS
information transfer • PhD
telecommunications and network management • MS

School of Management
George Burman, Dean
Programs in:
accounting • PhD
business administration • MBA, PhD
finance • PhD
innovation management • PhD
management • MBA, MS, MS Acct, PhD

management information systems • PhD
marketing • PhD
operations management • PhD
organizational behavior • PhD
strategy • PhD

S. I. Newhouse School of Public Communications
David M. Rubin, Dean
Programs in:
advertising • MA
broadcast journalism • MS
communications management • MS
magazine, newspaper and online journalism • MA
mass communications • PhD
media • MA
media management • MS
new media • MS
photography • MS
public communications • MA, MS, PhD
public relations • MA, MS
television-radio-film • MA

■ TEACHERS COLLEGE, COLUMBIA UNIVERSITY

New York, NY 10027-6696
http://www.tc.columbia.edu/

Independent, coed, graduate-only institution. *Graduate faculty:* 134 full-time, 227 part-time/adjunct. *Computer facilities:* 169 computers available on campus for general student use. A campuswide network can be accessed from student residence rooms and from off campus. Internet access and online class registration are available. *Library facilities:* Milbank Memorial Library. *Graduate expenses:* Tuition: full-time $17,460. Required fees: $170 per semester. One-time fee: $340 full-time. *General application contact:* Christine Souders, Director of Admissions, 212-678-3710.

Graduate Faculty of Education
Arthur Levine, President
Programs in:
administration and supervision in special education • Ed M, MA, Ed D, PhD
adult education • MA, Ed D
anthropology • Ed M, MA, Ed D, PhD
applied educational psychology—school psychology • Ed M, MA, Ed D, PhD
applied linguistics • Ed M, MA, Ed D
applied physiology • Ed M, MA, MS, Ed D
art and art education • Ed M, MA, Ed D, Ed DCT
arts administration • MA
audiology • Ed M, MS, Ed D, PhD
behavioral disorders • MA, Ed D, PhD
bilingual and bicultural education • MA
blind and visual impairment • MA, Ed D
clinical psychology • MA, PhD
college teaching and academic leadership • Ed D
communications • Ed M, MA, Ed D
comparative and international education • Ed M, MA, Ed D, PhD
computing in education • MA
counseling psychology • Ed M, Ed D, PhD
curriculum and teaching • Ed M, MA, Ed D
curriculum and teaching in physical education • Ed M, MA, Ed D
dance and dance education • MA
developmental psychology • MA, Ed D, PhD
early childhood education • Ed M, MA, Ed D
early childhood special education • Ed M, MA
economics and education • Ed M, MA, Ed D, PhD
education • Ed M, MA, MS, Ed D, Ed DCT, PhD
educational administration • Ed M, MA, Ed D, PhD
educational media/instructional technology • Ed M, MA, Ed D
educational psychology-human cognition and learning • Ed M, MA, Ed D, PhD
elementary/childhood education, preservice • MA
giftedness • MA, Ed D
health education • MA, MS, Ed D
hearing impairment • MA, Ed D
higher education • Ed M, MA, Ed D, PhD
history and education • Ed M, MA, Ed D, PhD
inquiry in educational administration • Ed D
interdisciplinary studies • Ed M, MA, Ed D
international educational development • Ed M, MA, Ed D, PhD
learning disabilities • Ed M, MA, Ed D
mathematics education • Ed M, MA, MS, Ed D, Ed DCT, PhD
measurement, evaluation, and statistics • MA, MS, Ed D, PhD
mental retardation • MA, Ed D, PhD
motor learning • Ed M, MA, Ed D
music and music education • Ed M, MA, Ed D, Ed DCT
neuroscience and education • Ed M
nurse executive • Ed M, MA, Ed D
nursing, professional role • Ed M, MA, Ed D
nutrition and education • Ed M, MS, Ed D
nutrition education • Ed M, MS, Ed D
nutrition education and public health nutrition • Ed M, MS, Ed D
organizational psychology • MA, Ed D, PhD
philosophy and education • Ed M, MA, Ed D, PhD
physical disabilities • MA, Ed D, PhD
politics and education • Ed M, MA, Ed D, PhD
reading specialist • MA
reading/learning disability • Ed M
religion and education • Ed M, MA, Ed D
research in special education • Ed D
science education • Ed M, MA, MS, Ed D, Ed DCT, PhD
social and organizational psychology • MA, Ed D, PhD
social psychology • Ed D, PhD
social studies education • Ed M, MA, Ed D, PhD
sociology and education • Ed M, MA, Ed D, PhD
special education administration and supervision, instructional practice • Ed M, MA, Ed D
speech-language pathology • Ed M, MS, Ed D, PhD
student personnel administration • Ed M, MA, Ed D
teaching English to speakers of other languages • Ed M, MA, Ed D
teaching of English and English education • Ed M, MA, Ed D, PhD
teaching of Spanish • Ed M, MA, Ed D, Ed DCT, PhD

■ TOURO COLLEGE

New York, NY 10010
http://www.touro.edu/

Independent, coed, comprehensive institution. *Computer facilities:* 350 computers available on campus for general student use.

Barry Z. Levine School of Health Sciences
Programs in:
biomedical sciences • MS
health information management • Certificate
occupational therapy • MS
physical therapy • MS

Touro College (continued)

Jacob D. Fuchsberg Law Center

Programs in:
law • JD
U.S. law for foreign lawyers • LL M

School of Jewish Studies

Program in:
Jewish studies • MA

■ UNIVERSITY AT BUFFALO, THE STATE UNIVERSITY OF NEW YORK

Buffalo, NY 14260

http://www.buffalo.edu/

State-supported, coed, university. CGS member. *Enrollment:* 5,112 full-time matriculated graduate/professional students (2,466 women), 3,035 part-time matriculated graduate/professional students (1,647 women). *Graduate faculty:* 1,235 full-time (362 women), 714 part-time/adjunct (275 women). *Computer facilities:* 1,800 computers available on campus for general student use. A campuswide network can be accessed from student residence rooms and from off campus. Internet access and online class registration are available. *Library facilities:* Lockwood Library plus 7 others. *Graduate expenses:* Tuition, state resident: full-time $5,100; part-time $213 per credit hour. Tuition, nonresident: full-time $8,416; part-time $351 per credit hour. Required fees: $988; $77. *General application contact:* Katherine Gerstle Ferguson, Associate Vice Provost, 716-645-2992.

Find an in-depth description at www.petersons.com/graduate.

Graduate School

Dr. Myron A. Thompson, Interim Vice Provost for Graduate Education

Programs in:
biochemistry • PhD
biomedical sciences • MS, PhD
cellular and molecular biology • PhD
experimental pathology • PhD
immunology • PhD
molecular and cellular biophysics • MS, PhD
molecular pharmacology and cancer therapeutics • PhD
natural and biomedical sciences • MS

College of Arts and Sciences

Dr. Charles Stinger, Interim Dean

Programs in:
American studies • MA, PhD
anthropology • MA, PhD
art • MFA
art history • MA
arts and sciences • MA, MAH, MFA, MM, MS, Au D, PhD, Certificate
audiology • Au D
behavioral neuroscience • PhD
biological sciences • MA, MS, PhD
chemistry • MA, PhD
classics • MA, PhD
clinical psychology • PhD
cognitive psychology • PhD
communicative disorders and sciences • MA, PhD
comparative literature • MA, PhD
economics • MA, PhD
English • MA, PhD
financial economics • Certificate
French • MA, PhD
general psychology • MA
geographic information science • Certificate
geography • MA, PhD
geology • MA, PhD
German • MA
health services • Certificate
historical musicology and music theory • PhD
history • MA, PhD
humanities • MA
information and Internet economics • Certificate
international economics • Certificate
law and regulation • Certificate
linguistics • MA, PhD
mathematics • MA, PhD
media study • MAH, MFA
medicinal chemistry • MS
music composition • MA, PhD
music history • MA
music performance • MM
music theory • MA
natural science • MS
philosophy • MA, PhD
physics • MS, PhD
political science • MA, PhD
social sciences • MS
social-personality • PhD
sociology • MA, PhD
Spanish • MA, PhD
urban and regional economics • Certificate

Graduate School of Education

Dr. Thomas T. Frantz, Interim Dean

Programs in:
bilingual education • Ed M
biology • Ed M
chemistry • Ed M
counseling psychology • PhD
counselor education • PhD
Earth science • Ed M
education • Ed M, MA, MS, Ed D, PhD, Certificate
educational administration • Ed M, Ed D, PhD, Certificate
educational psychology • MA, PhD
elementary education • Ed M, Ed D, PhD
English • Ed M
English education • Ed D, PhD
foreign and second language education • Ed D, PhD
French • Ed M
general education • Ed M
German • Ed M
higher education • PhD
Italian • Ed M
Latin • Ed M
mathematics • Ed M
mathematics education • Ed D, PhD
music education • MA, Certificate
physics • Ed M
reading education • Ed D, PhD
reading teacher • Ed M
rehabilitation counseling • MS
Russian • Ed M
school administrator and supervisor • Certificate
school counseling • Ed M, Certificate
school psychology • MA
science education • Ed D, PhD
secondary education • Certificate
social foundations • PhD
social studies • Ed M
Spanish • Ed M
special education • PhD
teaching English to Speakers of Other Languages • Ed M

School of Architecture and Planning

Dr. Kenneth J. Levy, Interim Dean

Programs in:
architecture • M Arch
architecture and planning • M Arch, MUP
planning • MUP

School of Dental Medicine

Dr. Russell Nisengard, Interim Dean

Programs in:
advanced education in general dentistry • Certificate
biomaterials • MS
combined prosthodontics • Certificate
dental medicine • DDS, MS, PhD, Certificate
endodontics • Certificate
esthetic dentistry • Certificate
oral and maxillofacial pathology • Certificate
oral and maxillofacial surgery • Certificate
oral biology • PhD
oral sciences • MS
orthodontics • MS, Certificate
pediatric dentistry • Certificate
periodontics • Certificate

School of Engineering and Applied Sciences

Dr. Mark H. Karwan, Dean

Programs in:
aerospace engineering • M Eng, MS, PhD

chemical engineering • M Eng, MS, PhD
civil engineering • M Eng, MS, PhD
computer science • MS, PhD
electrical engineering • M Eng, MS, PhD
engineering and applied sciences • M Eng, MS, PhD
engineering science • MS
industrial engineering • M Eng, MS, PhD
mechanical engineering • M Eng, MS, PhD

School of Health Related Professions
Dr. Mark B. Kristal, Dean
Programs in:
exercise science • MS, PhD
health related professions • MS, DPT, PhD
medical technology • MS
nutrition • MS
occupational therapy • MS
physical therapy • DPT
rehabilitation science • PhD

School of Information Studies
Dr. Thomas Jacobson, Acting Dean
Programs in:
communication • MA, PhD
information studies • MA, MLS, PhD, Certificate
library and information studies • MLS, Certificate

School of Law
R. Nils Olsen, Dean
Program in:
law • JD, LL M

School of Management
Lewis Mandell, Dean
Programs in:
accounting • MS
management • MBA, PhD
management information systems • MS

School of Medicine and Biomedical Sciences
Dr. John R. Wright, Dean
Programs in:
biochemistry • MA, PhD
biophysical sciences • MS, PhD
epidemiology • MS
epidemiology and community health • PhD
medicine • MD
medicine and biomedical sciences • MD, MA, MPH, MS, PhD
microbiology • MA, PhD
pathology and anatomical sciences • MA, PhD
pharmacology and toxicology • MA, PhD
physiology • MA, PhD
public health • MPH

School of Nursing
Dr. Mecca S. Cranley, Dean
Programs in:
acute care nurse practitioner • MS, Certificate
adult health nursing • Certificate
adult health nursing-nurse practitioner • MS
case management nursing • Certificate
child health nursing • Certificate
child health nursing-nurse practitioner • MS
family nursing • Certificate
family nursing-nurse practitioner • MS
geriatric nurse practitioner • MS
maternal and women's health nursing • Certificate
maternal and women's health nursing-nurse practitioner • MS
nurse anesthetist • MS
nurse practitioner • Certificate
nursing • DNS
psychiatric – mental health nursing • Certificate

School of Pharmacy and Pharmaceutical Sciences
Dr. Wayne K. Anderson, Dean
Programs in:
pharmaceutical sciences • MS, PhD
pharmacy • Pharm D
pharmacy and pharmaceutical sciences • Pharm D, MS, PhD

School of Social Work
Dr. Lawrence Shulman, Dean
Program in:
social work • MSW, PhD

■ UNIVERSITY OF ROCHESTER

Rochester, NY 14627-0250
http://www.rochester.edu/

Independent, coed, university. CGS member. *Enrollment:* 2,456 full-time matriculated graduate/professional students (1,009 women), 1,218 part-time matriculated graduate/professional students (675 women). *Graduate faculty:* 1,985. *Computer facilities:* 260 computers available on campus for general student use. A campuswide network can be accessed from student residence rooms and from off campus. *Library facilities:* Rush Rhees Library plus 5 others. *Graduate expenses:* Tuition: part-time $723 per credit hour.

The College, Arts and Sciences
Thomas LeBlanc, Vice Provost and Dean
Programs in:
arts and sciences • MA, MS, PhD
brain and cognitive sciences • MS, PhD
cellular, molecular, and developmental biology • MS, PhD
chemistry • MS, PhD
clinical psychology • PhD
comparative literature • MA
computer science • MS, PhD
developmental psychology • PhD
ecology and evolutionary biology • MS, PhD
economics • MA, PhD
English literature • MA, PhD
French • MA
genetics • MS, PhD
geological sciences • MS, PhD
German • MA
history • MA, PhD
mathematics • MA, MS, PhD
philosophy • MA, PhD
physics • MA, MS, PhD
physics and astronomy • PhD
political science • MA, PhD
psychology • MA
social psychology • PhD
Spanish • MA
visual and cultural studies • MA, PhD

The College, School of Engineering and Applied Sciences
Kevin Parker, Dean
Programs in:
biomedical engineering • MS, PhD
chemical engineering • MS, PhD
electrical and computer engineering • MS, PhD
engineering and applied sciences • MS, PhD
materials science • MS, PhD
mechanical engineering • MS, PhD

Institute of Optics
Ian Walmsley, Interim Director
Program in:
optics • MS, PhD

Eastman School of Music
James Undercofler, Director
Programs in:
composition • MA, MM, DMA, PhD
conducting • MM, DMA
education • MA, PhD
jazz studies/contemporary media • MM
music education • MM, DMA
musicology • MA, PhD
pedagogy of music theory • MA
performance and literature • MM, DMA
piano accompanying and chamber music • MM, DMA
theory • MA, PhD

University of Rochester (continued)

Margaret Warner Graduate School of Education and Human Development
Raffaella Borasi, Acting Dean
Program in:
education and human development • MAT, MS, Ed D, PhD

School of Medicine and Dentistry
Dr. Edward Hundert, Dean
Programs in:
medicine • MD
medicine and dentistry • MD, MA, MPH, MS, PhD, Certificate

Graduate Programs in Medicine and Dentistry
Paul La Celle, Interim Senior Associate Dean
Programs in:
biochemistry • MS, PhD
biophysics • MS, PhD
genetics • MS, PhD
health services research and policy • PhD
marriage and family therapy • MS
medical statistics • MS
medicine and dentistry • MA, MPH, MS, PhD, Certificate
microbiology • MS, PhD
neurobiology and anatomy • MS, PhD
neuroscience • MS, PhD
oral biology • MS
pathology • MS, PhD
pharmacology • MS, PhD
physiology • MS, PhD
public health • MPH
statistics • MA, PhD
toxicology • MS, PhD

School of Nursing
Dr. Patricia Chiverton, Dean
Program in:
nursing • MS, PhD, Certificate

William E. Simon Graduate School of Business Administration
Charles Plosser, Dean
Program in:
business administration • MBA, MS, PhD

■ WAGNER COLLEGE

Staten Island, NY 10301-4495
http://www.wagner.edu/

Independent, coed, comprehensive institution. *Enrollment:* 190 full-time matriculated graduate/professional students (108 women), 200 part-time matriculated graduate/professional students (142 women). *Graduate faculty:* 27 full-time (13 women), 28 part-time/adjunct (15 women). *Computer facilities:* 150 computers available on campus for general student use. A campuswide network can be accessed from student residence rooms and from off campus. Internet access is available. *Library facilities:* August Horrmann Library. *Graduate expenses:* Tuition: part-time $650 per credit. *General application contact:* 718-390-3411.

Division of Graduate Studies
Dr. Constance Bradford Schuyler, Associate Provost and Dean
Programs in:
elementary education • MS Ed
family nurse practitioner • Certificate
finance • MBA
international business • MBA
management • Exec MBA, MBA
marketing • MBA
microbiology • MS
nursing • MS
secondary education • MS Ed
special education • MS Ed
teaching English to speakers of other languages • MS Ed

■ YESHIVA UNIVERSITY

New York, NY 10033-3201
http://www.yu.edu/

Independent, coed, university. CGS member. *Computer facilities:* 142 computers available on campus for general student use. Internet access is available. *Library facilities:* Mendel Gottesman Library plus 6 others. *General application contact:* Associate Director of Admissions, 212-960-5277.

Albert Einstein College of Medicine
Programs in:
medicine • MD, PhD

Sue Golding Graduate Division of Medical Sciences
Programs in:
anatomy • PhD
biochemistry • PhD
cell and developmental biology • PhD
cell biology • PhD
developmental and molecular biology • PhD
medical sciences • PhD
microbiology and immunology • PhD
molecular genetics • PhD
molecular pharmacology • PhD
neuroscience • PhD
pathology • PhD
physiology and biophysics • PhD

Azrieli Graduate School of Jewish Education and Administration
Dr. Yitzchak S. Handel, Director
Program in:
Jewish education and administration • MS, Ed D, Specialist

Benjamin N. Cardozo School of Law
Paul R. Verkuil, Dean
Programs in:
general law • LL M
intellectual property law • LL M
law • JD

Bernard Revel Graduate School of Jewish Studies
Dr. Arthur Hyman, Dean
Program in:
Jewish studies • MA, PhD

Ferkauf Graduate School of Psychology
Dr. Lawrence J. Siegel, Dean
Programs in:
clinical psychology • Psy D
developmental psychology • PhD
general psychology • MA
health psychology • PhD
psychology • MA, PhD, Psy D
school/clinical-child psychology • Psy D

Wurzweiler School of Social Work
Dr. Sheldon R. Gelman, Dean
Program in:
social work • MSW, PhD

North Carolina

■ APPALACHIAN STATE UNIVERSITY

Boone, NC 28608
http://www.appstate.edu/

State-supported, coed, comprehensive institution. CGS member. *Enrollment:* 601 full-time matriculated graduate/professional students (379 women), 514 part-time matriculated graduate/professional students (393 women). *Graduate faculty:* 437 full-time (128 women). *Computer facilities:* 500 computers available on campus for general student use. A campuswide network can be accessed from student residence rooms. Internet access is available. *Library facilities:* Carol Grotnes Belk Library plus 1 other. *Graduate expenses:* Tuition, state resident: full-time $1,152;

part-time $864 per year. Tuition, nonresident: full-time $8,422; part-time $6,316 per year. Required fees: $1,116; $626 per year. *General application contact:* Dr. E. D. Huntley, Senior Associate Dean for Graduate Studies, 828-262-2130.

Cratis D. Williams Graduate School
Dr. Judith E. Domer, Dean of Graduate Studies and Research

College of Arts and Sciences
Linda Bennett, Dean
Programs in:
- Appalachian studies • MA
- applied physics • MS
- arts and sciences • MA, MPA, MS, CAS
- biology • MA, MS
- clinical psychology • MA
- computer science • MS
- English • MA
- English education • MA
- general experimental psychology • MA
- geography • MA
- gerontology • MA
- health psychology • MA
- history • MA
- industrial and organizational psychology • MA
- mathematics • MA
- political science • MA
- public administration • MPA
- public history • MA
- romance languages • MA
- school psychology • MA, CAS
- social sciences • MA

College of Education
Dr. Charles Duke, Dean
Programs in:
- communication disorders • MA
- community counseling • MA
- curriculum specialist • MA
- early childhood education • MA
- education • MA, MLS, MSA, Ed D, Ed S
- educational leadership • Ed D
- educational media • MA, Ed S
- elementary education • MA
- higher education • MA, Ed S
- instructional technology • MA, Ed S
- library science • MA, MLS, Ed S
- marriage and family therapy • MA
- reading education • MA
- school administration • MSA
- school counseling • MA, Ed S
- secondary education • MA
- special education • MA
- speech pathology • MA
- student development • Ed S

College of Fine and Applied Arts
Dr. Ming Land, Dean
Programs in:
- exercise science • MS
- family and consumer sciences • MA
- fine and applied arts • MA, MS
- industrial education • MA
- industrial technology • MA
- master teacher • MA
- physical education • MA
- sport management • MA
- sports management • MA

John A. Walker College of Business
Dr. Kenneth Peacock, Dean
Programs in:
- accounting • MS
- business • MBA, MS
- business administration • MBA

School of Music
Dr. William Harbinson, Dean
Programs in:
- music • MM
- music education • MM

■ CAMPBELL UNIVERSITY
Buies Creek, NC 27506
http://www.campbell.edu/

Independent-religious, coed, university. *Enrollment:* 840 full-time matriculated graduate/professional students (494 women), 446 part-time matriculated graduate/professional students (279 women). *Graduate faculty:* 99 full-time (30 women), 49 part-time/adjunct (19 women). *Computer facilities:* 250 computers available on campus for general student use. A campuswide network can be accessed. Internet access is available. *Library facilities:* Carrie Rich Memorial Library plus 3 others. *Graduate expenses:* Tuition: full-time $14,770. Required fees: $1,619. *General application contact:* James S. Farthing, Director of Graduate Admissions, 910-893-1200 Ext. 1318.

Graduate and Professional Programs
Dr. M. Dwaine Greene, Vice President for Academic Affairs and Provost

Divinity School
Dr. Michael Glenn Cogdill, Dean
Programs in:
- Christian education • MA
- divinity • M Div

Lundy-Fetterman School of Business
Dr. Christian Ziakhan, Dean
Program in:
- business • MBA

Norman Adrian Wiggins School of Law
Willis Whichard, Dean
Program in:
- law • JD

School of Education
Dr. Karen P. Nery, Dean
Programs in:
- administration • MSA
- community counseling • MA
- elementary education • M Ed
- English education • M Ed
- interdisciplinary studies • M Ed
- mathematics education • M Ed
- middle grades education • M Ed
- physical education • M Ed
- school counseling • M Ed
- secondary education • M Ed
- social science education • M Ed

School of Pharmacy
Dr. Ronald W. Maddox, Dean
Programs in:
- clinical research • MS
- pharmaceutical science • MS
- pharmacy • Pharm D

■ DUKE UNIVERSITY
Durham, NC 27708-0586
http://www.duke.edu/

Independent-religious, coed, university. CGS member. *Enrollment:* 5,096 full-time matriculated graduate/professional students (2,261 women), 340 part-time matriculated graduate/professional students (246 women). *Graduate faculty:* 3,466. *Computer facilities:* 600 computers available on campus for general student use. A campuswide network can be accessed from student residence rooms and from off campus. Internet access and online class registration are available. *Library facilities:* Perkins Library plus 11 others. *Graduate expenses:* Tuition: full-time $19,000. Required fees: $3,300. *General application contact:* Bertie S. Belvin, Associate Dean for Academic Services, 919-684-3913.

Find an in-depth description at www.petersons.com/graduate.

Divinity School
Dr. L. Gregory Jones, Dean
Program in:
- theology • M Div, MCM, MTS, Th M

Fuqua School of Business
Douglas Breeden, Dean
Programs in:
- business • CCMBA, GEMBA, MBA, WEMBA, PhD
- health sector management • MBA

Duke University (continued)

Graduate School
Lewis M. Siegel, Dean
Programs in:
- art and art history • PhD
- biological chemistry • Certificate
- biological psychology • PhD
- biology • PhD
- business administration • PhD
- cell biology • PhD
- cellular and molecular biology • PhD
- chemistry • PhD
- classical studies • PhD
- clinical psychology • PhD
- cognitive psychology • PhD
- computer science • MS, PhD
- crystallography of macromolecules • PhD
- developmental psychology • PhD
- East Asian studies • AM, Certificate
- ecology • PhD, Certificate
- economics • AM, PhD
- English • PhD
- enzyme mechanisms • PhD
- experimental psychology • PhD
- French • PhD
- genetics • PhD
- geology • MS, PhD
- German studies • PhD
- gross anatomy and physical anthropology • PhD
- health psychology • PhD
- history • PhD
- human social development • PhD
- humanities • AM
- immunology • PhD
- Latin American studies • PhD
- liberal studies • AM
- lipid biochemistry • PhD
- literature • PhD
- mathematics • PhD
- medieval and Renaissance studies • Certificate
- membrane structure and function • PhD
- microbiology • PhD
- molecular biophysics • Certificate
- molecular cancer biology • PhD
- molecular genetics • PhD
- music composition • AM, PhD
- musicology • AM, PhD
- natural resource economics/policy • AM, PhD
- natural resource science/ecology • AM, PhD
- natural resource systems science • AM, PhD
- neuroanatomy • PhD
- neurobiology • PhD
- neurochemistry • PhD
- nucleic acid structure and function • PhD
- pathology • PhD
- performance practice • AM, PhD
- pharmacology and cancer biology • PhD
- philosophy • PhD
- physical anthropology • PhD
- physics • PhD
- physiology and cellular biophysics • PhD
- political science • AM, PhD
- protein structure and function • PhD
- religion • MA, PhD
- Slavic languages and literatures • AM, PhD
- social/cultural anthropology • PhD
- sociology • AM, PhD
- Spanish • PhD
- teaching • MAT
- toxicology • Certificate
- women's studies • Certificate

Center for Demographic Studies
Dr. Ken Manton, Director
Program in:
- demographic studies • PhD

Center for International Development Research
Dr. Francis Lethem, Director of Graduate Studies
Program in:
- international development policy • MA

Institute of Statistics and Decision Sciences
Valen Johnson, Director of Graduate Studies
Program in:
- statistics and decision sciences • PhD

School of Engineering
Dr. Kristina M. Johnson, Dean
Programs in:
- biomedical engineering • MS, PhD
- civil and environmental engineering • MS, PhD
- electrical and computer engineering • MS, PhD
- engineering • MEM, MS, PhD
- engineering management • MEM
- environmental engineering • MS, PhD
- materials science • MS, PhD
- mechanical engineering • MS, PhD

Terry Sanford Institute of Public Policy
Helen F. Ladd, Director of Graduate Studies
Program in:
- public policy • MPP

Nicholas School of the Environment
Dr. William Schlesinger, Dean
Programs in:
- coastal environmental management • MEM
- environmental science and policy • PhD
- environmental toxicology, chemistry, and risk assessment • MEM
- forest resource management • MF
- resource ecology • MEM
- resource economics and policy • MEM
- water and air resources • MEM

School of Law
Katharine T. Bartlett, Dean
Program in:
- law • JD, LL M, MLS, SJD

School of Medicine
Dr. Russel E. Kaufman, Vice Dean for Education and Academic Affairs
Programs in:
- clinical research • MHS
- medicine • MD, MHS, MS
- pathologists' assistant • MHS
- physical therapy • MS
- physician assistant • MHS

School of Nursing
Dr. Mary T. Champagne, Dean
Programs in:
- adult acute care • Certificate
- adult cardiovascular • Certificate
- adult oncology/HIV • Certificate
- adult primary care • Certificate
- clinical nurse specialist • MSN
- clinical research management • MSN, Certificate
- family • Certificate
- gerontology • Certificate
- health and nursing ministries • MSN, Certificate
- health systems leadership and outcomes • MSN, Certificate
- leadership in community based long term care • MSN, Certificate
- neonatal • Certificate
- nurse anesthetist • MSN, Certificate
- nurse practitioner • MSN
- nursing informatics • Certificate
- nursing ministries • MSN, Certificate
- pediatric • Certificate
- pediatric acute care • Certificate

■ EAST CAROLINA UNIVERSITY

Greenville, NC 27858-4353
http://www.ecu.edu/

State-supported, coed, university. CGS member. *Enrollment:* 1,518 full-time matriculated graduate/professional students (924 women), 1,276 part-time matriculated graduate/professional students (790 women). *Graduate faculty:* 526 full-time (131 women), 4 part-time/adjunct (0 women). *Computer facilities:* 1,465 computers available on campus for general student use. A campuswide network can be accessed from student residence rooms and from off campus. Internet access and online class registration are available. *Library facilities:* Joyner Library plus 1 other. *Graduate expenses:* Tuition, state resident: full-time $1,238; part-time $155 per semester. Tuition, nonresident: full-time $9,100; part-time $1,138 per semester. Required fees: $1,062; $132 per semester. *General application contact:* Dr. Paul D. Tschetter, Senior Associate Dean of the Graduate School, 252-328-6012.

Find an in-depth description at www.petersons.com/graduate.

Brody School of Medicine
Dr. Peter Kragel, Interim Dean
Programs in:
- anatomy and cell biology • PhD
- biochemistry • PhD
- interdisciplinary biological sciences • PhD
- medicine • MD, PhD
- microbiology and immunology • PhD
- pharmacology • PhD
- physiology • PhD

Graduate School
Dr. Thomas L. Feldbush, Vice Chancellor for Research and Graduate Studies
Programs in:
- coastal resource management • PhD
- computer science • MS
- computer science and communication • MS

College of Arts and Sciences
Dr. Keats Sparrow, Dean
Programs in:
- American history • MA, MA Ed
- anthropology • MA
- applied and biomedical physics • MS
- applied mathematics • MA
- applied resource economics • MS
- arts and sciences • MA, MA Ed, MPA, MS, PhD
- biology • MS
- chemistry • MS
- clinical psychology • MA
- English • MA, MA Ed
- European history • MA, MA Ed
- general psychology • MA
- geography • MA
- geology • MS
- international studies • MA
- maritime history • MA
- mathematics • MA, MA Ed
- medical physics • MS
- molecular biology/biotechnology • MS
- public administration • MPA
- school psychology • MA
- sociology • MA

School of Allied Health Sciences
Dr. Stephen Thomas, Interim Dean
Programs in:
- allied health sciences • MPT, MS, MSOT, PhD
- communication sciences and disorders • PhD
- occupational therapy • MSOT
- physical therapy • MPT
- rehabilitation studies • MS
- speech, language and auditory pathology • MS
- substance abuse • MS
- vocational evaluation • MS

School of Art
Jackie Leebrick, Director of Graduate Studies
Program in:
- art • MA, MA Ed, MFA

School of Business
Dr. Rick Niswander, Director of Graduate Studies
Program in:
- business • MBA, MSA

School of Education
Dr. Marilyn Sheerer, Dean
Programs in:
- adult education • MA Ed
- counselor education • MS, Ed S
- education • MA, MA Ed, MLS, MS, MSA, Ed D, CAS, Ed S
- educational administration and supervision • Ed S
- educational leadership • Ed D
- elementary education • MA Ed
- higher education administration • Ed D
- information technologies • MS
- instruction technology specialist • MA Ed
- learning disabilities • MA Ed
- library science • MLS, CAS
- mental retardation • MA Ed
- middle grade education • MA Ed
- school administration • MSA
- science education • MA, MA Ed
- severe and profound disabilities • MA Ed
- supervision • MA Ed
- vocation education • MA Ed

School of Health and Human Performance
Dr. Glen Gilbert, Dean
Programs in:
- bioenergetics • PhD
- exercise and sport science • MA, MA Ed
- health and human performance • MA, MA Ed, MS, PhD
- health education • MA, MA Ed
- recreation and leisure services administration • MS
- therapeutic recreation administration • MS

School of Human Environmental Sciences
Dr. Karla Hughes, Dean
Programs in:
- child development and family relations • MS
- human environmental sciences • MS
- marriage and family therapy • MS
- nutrition • MS

School of Industry and Technology
Dr. Ruben M. Desmond, Dean
Programs in:
- environment health • MS
- industrial technology • MS
- industry and technology • MS, MSEH
- occupational safety • MS

School of Music
Dr. Rodney Schmidt, Director of Graduate Studies
Programs in:
- music education • MM
- music therapy • MM
- performance • MM
- theory and composition • MM

School of Nursing
Dr. Phyllis Turner, Director of Graduate Studies
Program in:
- nursing • MSN

School of Social Work and Criminal Justice Studies
Dr. Linner Griffin, Interim Dean
Programs in:
- criminal justice studies • MA
- social work • MSW
- social work and criminal justice studies • MA, MSW

■ ELON UNIVERSITY
Elon College, NC 27244
http://www.elon.edu/

Independent-religious, coed, comprehensive institution. *Enrollment:* 114 full-time matriculated graduate/professional students (75 women), 124 part-time matriculated graduate/professional students (69 women). *Graduate faculty:* 39 full-time (19 women), 11 part-time/adjunct (8 women). *Computer facilities:* 500 computers available on campus for general student use. A campuswide network can be accessed from student residence rooms and from off campus. Internet access, e-mail are available. *Library facilities:* Carol Grotnes Belk. *Graduate expenses:* Tuition: part-time $291 per hour. *General application contact:* Greg L. Zaiser, Director of Graduate Admissions, 800-334-8448 Ext. 3.

Elon University (continued)

Program in Business Administration
Dr. Kevin J. O'Mara, Chair
Program in:
business administration • MBA

Program in Education
Dr. Judith B. Howard, Director
Programs in:
elementary education • M Ed
special education • M Ed

Program in Physical Therapy
Dr. Elizabeth A. Rogers, Director
Program in:
physical therapy • MPT

■ FAYETTEVILLE STATE UNIVERSITY

Fayetteville, NC 28301-4298
http://www.uncfsu.edu/

State-supported, coed, comprehensive institution. CGS member. *Computer facilities:* 300 computers available on campus for general student use. A campuswide network can be accessed from student residence rooms and from off campus. Internet access is available. *Library facilities:* Charles W. Chestnut Library. *General application contact:* Director of the Graduate Center, 910-486-1498.

Graduate School
Programs in:
biology • MAT, MS
business administration • MBA
education • Ed D
educational leadership and secondary education • MA Ed
elementary education • MA Ed
English • MA
history • MA, MAT
mathematics • MAT, MS
middle grades education • MA Ed
political science • MA, MAT
psychology • MA
sociology • MAT
special education • MA Ed

■ GARDNER-WEBB UNIVERSITY

Boiling Springs, NC 28017
http://www.gardner-webb.edu/

Independent-religious, coed, comprehensive institution. *Enrollment:* 63 full-time matriculated graduate/professional students (17 women), 674 part-time matriculated graduate/professional students (392 women). *Graduate faculty:* 51 full-time (20 women), 14 part-time/adjunct (5 women). *Computer facilities:* 150 computers available on campus for general student use. A campuswide network can be accessed from student residence rooms and from off campus. Internet access and online class registration are available. *Library facilities:* Dover Memorial Library. *Graduate expenses:* Tuition: part-time $200 per semester hour. *General application contact:* Dr. Darlene J. Gravett, Dean, Graduate School, 704-406-4723.

Graduate School
Dr. Darlene J. Gravett, Dean
Programs in:
elementary education • MA
English • MA
English education • MA
mental health counseling • MA
middle grades education • MA
physical education • MA
school administration • MA
school counseling • MA

Graduate School of Business
Dr. Anthony Negbenebor, Director
Program in:
business • M Acc, MBA

M. Christopher White School of Divinity
Dr. R. Wayne Stacy, Dean
Programs in:
Christian education • M Div
church music • M Div
missiology • M Div
pastoral care and counseling • M Div
pastoral ministry • M Div

■ MEREDITH COLLEGE

Raleigh, NC 27607-5298
http://www.meredith.edu/

Independent, women only, comprehensive institution. CGS member. *Enrollment:* 70 full-time matriculated graduate/professional students (all women), 61 part-time matriculated graduate/professional students (54 women). *Graduate faculty:* 17 full-time (10 women), 3 part-time/adjunct (1 woman). *Computer facilities:* 150 computers available on campus for general student use. A campuswide network can be accessed from student residence rooms. Internet access is available. *Library facilities:* Carlyle Campbell Library plus 1 other. *Graduate expenses:* Tuition: part-time $310 per credit hour. Required fees: $25 per credit hour. Tuition and fees vary according to program. *General application contact:* Deborah Horvitz, Dean, John E. Weems Graduate School, 919-760-8423.

John E. Weems Graduate School
Deborah Horvitz, Head
Programs in:
education • M Ed
music • MM

School of Business
Sidney Adkins, Dean
Program in:
business administration • MBA

■ NORTH CAROLINA AGRICULTURAL AND TECHNICAL STATE UNIVERSITY

Greensboro, NC 27411
http://www.ncat.edu/

State-supported, coed, university. CGS member. *Enrollment:* 385 full-time matriculated graduate/professional students (200 women), 513 part-time matriculated graduate/professional students (306 women). *Graduate faculty:* 466 full-time (176 women), 134 part-time/adjunct (71 women). *Computer facilities:* 250 computers available on campus for general student use. A campuswide network can be accessed from off campus. Internet access and online class registration are available. *Library facilities:* F. D. Bluford Library plus 1 other. *Graduate expenses:* Tuition, state resident: full-time $1,015; part-time $128 per credit hour. Tuition, nonresident: full-time $4,650; part-time $1,037 per credit hour. *General application contact:* Dr. Kenneth Murray, Interim Dean of the Graduate School, 336-334-7920.

Graduate School
Dr. Kenneth Murray, Interim Dean of the Graduate School

College of Arts and Sciences
Dr. Phillip Carey, Dean
Programs in:
art education • MS
arts and sciences • MA, MS, MSW
biology • MS
chemistry • MS
English • MA
English and Afro-American literature • MA
history education • MS
mathematics education • MS
social science education • MS
sociology and social work • MSW

College of Engineering
Dr. Joseph Monroe, Chairperson
Programs in:

architectural, agricultural and environmental engineering • MSAE, MSCE, MSE
chemical engineering • MSE
computer science • MSCS
electrical engineering • MSEE, PhD
engineering • MSAE, MSCE, MSCS, MSE, MSEE, MSIE, MSME, PhD
industrial and systems engineering • MSIE, PhD
mechanical engineering • MSME, PhD

School of Agriculture and Environmental and Allied Sciences
Dr. Alton Thompson, Chairperson
Programs in:
agricultural economics • MS
agricultural education • MS
agriculture and environmental and allied sciences • MS
food and nutrition • MS
plant science • MS

School of Education
Dr. Lelia L. Vickers, Dean
Programs in:
adult education • MS
biology education • MS
chemistry education • MS
early childhood education • MS
education • MS
educational administration • MS
educational media • MS
elementary education • MS
English education • MS
guidance and counseling • MS
health and physical education • MS
history education • MS
human resources • MS
intermediate education • MS
reading • MS
social science education • MS

School of Technology
Dr. Elazer Barnette, Dean
Programs in:
industrial arts education • MS
industrial technology • MS, MSIT
safety and driver education • MS
technology • MS, MSIT
technology education • MS
vocational-industrial education • MS

■ NORTH CAROLINA CENTRAL UNIVERSITY

Durham, NC 27707-3129
http://www.nccu.edu/

State-supported, coed, comprehensive institution. CGS member. *Enrollment:* 584 full-time matriculated graduate/professional students (371 women), 567 part-time matriculated graduate/professional students (422 women). *Graduate faculty:* 215 full-time (100 women), 84 part-time/adjunct (36 women). *Computer facilities:* 400 computers available on campus for general student use. *Library facilities:* Shepherd Library plus 1 other. *Graduate expenses:* Tuition, state resident: full-time $1,022. Tuition, nonresident: full-time $8,590. Required fees: $811. *General application contact:* Dr. Walter Harris, Vice Chancellor for Academic Affairs and Provost, 919-560-6230.

Division of Academic Affairs
Dr. Walter Harris

College of Arts and Sciences
Dr. Bernice D. Johnson, Dean
Programs in:
arts and sciences • MA, MPA, MS
biology • MS
chemistry • MS
criminal justice • MS
earth sciences • MS
English • MA
general physical education • MS
history • MA
human sciences • MS
mathematics • MS
psychology • MA
public administration • MPA
recreation administration • MS
sociology • MA
special physical education • MS
therapeutic recreation • MS

School of Business
Dr. H. James Williams, Dean
Program in:
business • MBA

School of Education
Dr. Sammie C. Parrish, Dean
Programs in:
agency counseling • MA
career counseling • MA
education • M Ed, MA
education of the emotionally handicapped • M Ed
education of the mentally handicapped • M Ed
educational leadership • MA
elementary education • M Ed, MA
instructional media • MA
school counseling • MA
speech pathology and audiology • M Ed

School of Law
Janice Mills, Dean
Program in:
law • JD, LL B

School of Library and Information Sciences
Dr. Benjamin F. Speller, Dean
Program in:
library and information sciences • MIS, MLS

■ NORTH CAROLINA STATE UNIVERSITY

Raleigh, NC 27695
http://www.ncsu.edu/

State-supported, coed, university. CGS member. *Computer facilities:* 4,600 computers available on campus for general student use. A campuswide network can be accessed from student residence rooms and from off campus. Internet access is available. *Library facilities:* D. H. Hill Library plus 4 others. *General application contact:* Graduate Admissions, 919-515-2871.

College of Veterinary Medicine
Programs in:
cell biology and morphology • MS, PhD
epidemiology and population medicine • MS, PhD
immunology • MS, PhD
microbiology and immunology • MS, PhD
pathology • MS, PhD
pharmacology • MS, PhD
specialized veterinary medicine • MS
veterinary medicine • DVM, MLS, MS, PhD

Graduate School
Programs in:
bioinformatics • MB, PhD
functional genomics • MFG, MS, PhD

College of Agriculture and Life Sciences
Programs in:
agricultural economics • M Econ, MS, PhD
agricultural education • MAEE, MS
agriculture and life sciences • M Ag, M Econ, M Ed, M Soc, M Tox, MA, MAEE, MAWB, MBAE, MLS, MS, MSA, Ed D, PhD
animal science • M Ag, MS, PhD
biochemistry • MS, PhD
biological and agricultural engineering • MBAE, MS, PhD
botany • MLS, MS, PhD
crop science • M Ag, MS, PhD
entomology • M Ag, MS, PhD
extension education • MAEE, MS
food science • M Ag, MS, PhD
genetics • MS, PhD
horticultural science • M Ag, MS, PhD
microbiology • MLS, MS, PhD
nutrition • MS, PhD
physiology • MLS, MS, PhD
plant pathology • M Ag, MLS, MS, PhD
poultry science • MS

North Carolina State University (continued)
- soil science • M Ag, MS, PhD
- toxicology • M Tox, MS, PhD
- zoology • MAWB, MLS, MS, PhD

College of Education and Psychology
Programs in:
- agency counseling • M Ed, MS
- agricultural education • M Ed, MS, CAGS
- counselor education • PhD, CAGS
- curriculum and instruction • M Ed, MS, Ed D
- education and psychology • M Ed, MS, MSA, Ed D, PhD, CAGS, Certificate
- educational administration and supervision • Ed D
- educational research and policy analysis • Ed D
- health occupations and teacher education • M Ed, MS
- health occupations education • M Ed, MS
- higher education administration • M Ed, MS, Ed D
- mathematics education • M Ed, MS, PhD
- middle years education • M Ed, MS
- occupational education • M Ed, MS, Ed D, CAGS
- psychology • MS, PhD
- school administration • MSA
- science education • M Ed, MS, PhD
- special education • M Ed, MS
- technology education • M Ed, MS, Ed D
- training and development • M Ed, MS

College of Engineering
Programs in:
- aerospace engineering • MS, PhD
- chemical engineering • M Ch E, MS, PhD
- civil engineering • MCE, MS, PhD
- computer engineering • MS, PhD
- computer networking • MS
- computer science • MC Sc, MS, PhD
- electrical engineering • MS, PhD
- engineering • M Ch E, M Eng, MBAE, MC Sc, MCE, MIE, MIMS, MME, MMSE, MNE, MOR, MS, MSIE, PhD, PD
- industrial engineering • MIE, MSIE, PhD
- integrated manufacturing systems engineering • MIMS
- materials science and engineering • MMSE, MS, PhD
- mechanical engineering • MME, MS, PhD
- nuclear engineering • MNE, MS, PhD
- operations research • MOR, MS, PhD

College of Humanities and Social Sciences
Programs in:
- English • MA
- history • MA
- humanities and social sciences • M Soc, MA, MAIS, MPA, MS, PhD
- international studies • MAIS
- liberal studies • MA
- organizational communication • MS
- public administration • MPA, PhD
- public history • MA
- rural sociology • MS
- sociology • M Soc, PhD
- technical communication • MS

College of Management
Programs in:
- accounting • MAC
- biotechnology • MS
- computer science • MS
- economics • M Econ, MA, PhD
- engineering • MS
- forest resources management • MS
- general business • MS
- management • MS
- management information systems • MS
- operations research • MS
- statistics • MS
- telecommunications systems engineering • MS
- textile management • MS
- total quality management • MS

College of Natural Resources
Programs in:
- fisheries and wildlife management • MS
- forestry • MF, MS, PhD
- geographic information systems • MS
- maintenance management • MRRA, MS
- natural resources • MF, MNR, MRRA, MS, MWPS, PhD
- recreation planning • MRRA, MS
- recreation resources administration/public administration • MRRA
- recreation/park management • MRRA, MS
- sports management • MRRA, MS
- travel and tourism management • MS
- wood and paper science • MS, MWPS, PhD

College of Physical and Mathematical Sciences
Programs in:
- applied mathematics • MS, PhD
- biomathematics • M Biomath, MS, PhD
- chemistry • MCH, MS, PhD
- ecology • PhD
- geology • MS, PhD
- geophysics • MS, PhD
- marine, earth, and atmospheric sciences • MS, PhD
- mathematics • MS, PhD
- meteorology • MS, PhD
- oceanography • MS, PhD
- physical and mathematical sciences • M Biomath, M Stat, MA, MCH, MS, PhD
- physics • MS, PhD
- statistics • M Stat, MS, PhD

College of Textiles
Programs in:
- fiber and polymer sciences • PhD
- textile chemistry • MS, MT
- textile engineering • MS
- textile management and technology • MT
- textile materials science • MS
- textile technology management • PhD
- textiles • MTE
- textiles/materials science • MT

School of Design
Programs in:
- architecture • M Arch
- design • M Arch, MGD, MID, MLA, PhD
- graphic design • MGD
- industrial design • MID
- landscape architecture • MLA

■ PFEIFFER UNIVERSITY

Misenheimer, NC 28109-0960
http://www.pfeiffer.edu/

Independent-religious, coed, comprehensive institution. *Computer facilities:* 64 computers available on campus for general student use. Internet access is available. *Library facilities:* Gustavus A. Pfeiffer Library. *General application contact:* Director of the MBA Program, 704-521-9116 Ext. 253.

Program in Business Administration
Programs in:
- business administration • MBA
- organizational management • MS

School of Religion and Christian Education
Program in:
- religion, philosophy, and Christian education • MACE

■ QUEENS COLLEGE

Charlotte, NC 28274-0002
http://www.queens.edu/

Independent-religious, coed, comprehensive institution. *Enrollment:* 75 full-time matriculated graduate/professional students (32 women), 253 part-time matriculated graduate/

professional students (136 women). *Graduate faculty:* 19 full-time (10 women), 9 part-time/adjunct (4 women). *Computer facilities:* 125 computers available on campus for general student use. A campuswide network can be accessed from student residence rooms. Internet access and online class registration are available. *Library facilities:* Everett Library plus 1 other. *Graduate expenses:* Tuition: part-time $310 per credit hour. Required fees: $40. Tuition and fees vary according to program. *General application contact:* Katie M. Wireman, Director of MBA Admissions, 704-337-2224.

College of Arts and Sciences
Dr. Norris Frederick, Head
Program in:
fine arts • MFA

Hayworth College
Dr. Darrel Miller, Dean
Programs in:
elementary education • MAT
organizational communications • MA

Division of Nursing
Dr. Joan McGill, Chair
Program in:
nursing management • MSN

McColl School of Business
Program in:
business • EMBA, MBA

■ THE UNIVERSITY OF NORTH CAROLINA AT CHAPEL HILL

Chapel Hill, NC 27599
http://www.unc.edu/

State-supported, coed, university. CGS member. *Enrollment:* 7,687 full-time matriculated graduate/professional students (4,264 women), 1,514 part-time matriculated graduate/professional students (988 women). *Graduate faculty:* 1,810 full-time (470 women), 613 part-time/adjunct (329 women). *Computer facilities:* 540 computers available on campus for general student use. A campuswide network can be accessed from student residence rooms and from off campus. Internet access and online class registration, on-line grade reports are available. *Library facilities:* Davis Library plus 14 others. *Graduate expenses:* Tuition, state resident: full-time $3,538. Tuition, nonresident: full-time $12,112. *General application contact:* Peggy O. Berryhill, Director of Admissions and Student Records, 919-962-1538.

Find an in-depth description at www.petersons.com/graduate.

Graduate School
Dr. Linda Dykstra, Dean
Programs in:
materials science • MS, PhD
public policy analysis • PhD
Russian and east European studies • MA
toxicology • MS, PhD

College of Arts and Sciences
Programs in:
acting • MFA
art history • MA, PhD
arts and sciences • MA, MFA, MPA, MRP, MS, MSRA, PhD, Certificate
athletic training • MA
biological psychology • PhD
botany • MA, MS, PhD
cell biology, development, and physiology • MA, MS, PhD
chemistry • MA, MS, PhD
city and regional planning • MRP
classical archaeology • MA, PhD
classics • MA, PhD
clinical psychology • PhD
cognitive psychology • PhD
communication studies • MA, PhD
comparative literature • MA, PhD
computer science • MS, PhD
costume technology • MFA
developmental psychology • PhD
ecology • MA, MS, PhD
ecology and behavior • MA, MS, PhD
economics • MS, PhD
English • MA, PhD
exercise physiology • MA
folklore • MA
French • MA, PhD
genetics and molecular biology • MA, MS, PhD
geography • MA, PhD
geological sciences • MS, PhD
Germanic languages • MA, PhD
history • MA, PhD
Italian • MA, PhD
Latin American studies • Certificate
linguistics • MA, PhD
marine sciences • MS, PhD
mathematics • MA, MS, PhD
morphology, systematics, and evolution • MA, MS, PhD
music • MA, PhD
operations research • MS, PhD
philosophy • MA, PhD
physics • MS, PhD
planning • PhD
Polish literature • PhD
political science • MA, PhD
Portuguese • MA, PhD
public administration • MPA
public policy analysis • PhD
quantitative psychology • PhD
recreation and leisure studies • MSRA
religious studies • MA, PhD
Romance languages • MA, PhD
Romance philology • MA, PhD
Russian literature • MA, PhD
Serbo-Croatian literature • PhD
Slavic linguistics • MA, PhD
social psychology • PhD
sociology • MA, PhD
Spanish • MA, PhD
sports administration • MA
statistics • MS, PhD
studio art • MFA
technical production • MFA
trans-Atlantic studies • MA

School of Education
Programs in:
culture, curriculum and change • PhD
curriculum and instruction • MA, Ed D
early childhood, family, and literacy studies • PhD
early intervention and family support • M Ed
education • M Ed, MA, MAT, MSA, Ed D, PhD
educational leadership • Ed D
educational psychology • M Ed, MA
elementary education • M Ed
English • MAT
French • MAT
German • MAT
Japanese • MAT
Latin • MAT
learning disabilities • M Ed
mathematics • MAT
music • MAT
psychological studies in education • PhD
school administration • MSA
school counseling • M Ed, MA
school psychology • M Ed, MA, PhD
science • MAT
secondary education • MAT
social studies/social science • MAT
Spanish • MAT
special education • M Ed, MA

School of Information and Library Science
Dr. Joanne Gard Marshall, Dean
Program in:
information and library science • MSIS, MSLS, PhD, CAS

School of Journalism and Mass Communication
Dr. Richard R. Cole, Dean
Program in:
mass communication • MA, PhD

The University of North Carolina at Chapel Hill (continued)

School of Public Health
Dr. William L. Roper, Dean
Programs in:
- air, radiation and industrial hygiene • MPH, MS, MSEE, MSPH, PhD
- aquatic and atmospheric sciences • MPH, MS, MSPH, PhD
- biostatistics • MPH, MS, Dr PH, PhD
- environmental engineering • MPH, MS, MSEE, MSPH, PhD
- environmental health sciences • MPH, MS, MSPH, PhD
- environmental management and policy • MPH, MS, MSPH, PhD
- epidemiology • MPH, MSPH, Dr PH, PhD
- health behavior and health education • MPH, Dr PH, PhD
- health care and prevention • MPH
- health policy and administration • MHA, MPH, MSPH, Dr PH, PhD
- leadership • MPH, Dr PH
- maternal and child health • MPH, MSPH, Dr PH, PhD
- nutrition • MPH, Dr PH, PhD
- nutritional biochemistry • MS
- occupational health nursing • MPH
- professional practice program • MPH
- public health • MHA, MPH, MS, MSEE, MSPH, Dr PH, PhD
- public health nursing • MPH

School of Social Work
Dr. Kim Strom-Gottfried, Interim Dean
Program in:
- social work • MSW, PhD

Kenan-Flagler Business School
Programs in:
- accounting • PhD
- business • MAC, MBA, PhD
- business administration • MBA, PhD
- business policy/strategy • PhD
- finance • PhD
- marketing • PhD
- operations management/quantitative methods • PhD
- organizational behavior • PhD

School of Dentistry
Programs in:
- dentistry • MS
- oral biology • PhD
- oral epidemiology • PhD

School of Law
Gene R. Nichol, Dean
Program in:
- law • JD

School of Medicine
Programs in:
- allied health sciences • MPT, MS, Au D, PhD
- biochemistry and biophysics • MS, PhD
- biomedical engineering • MS, PhD
- cell and developmental biology • PhD
- cell and molecular physiology • PhD
- experimental pathology • PhD
- genetics and molecular biology • MS, PhD
- human movement science • PhD
- immunology • MS, PhD
- medicine • MD, MPT, MS, Au D, PhD
- microbiology • MS, PhD
- microbiology and immunology • MS, PhD
- neurobiology • PhD
- occupational science • MS
- pathology and laboratory medicine • PhD
- pharmacology • PhD
- physical therapy • MPT
- rehabilitation psychology and counseling • MS
- speech and hearing sciences • MS, Au D, PhD

School of Nursing
Program in:
- nursing • MSN, PhD

School of Pharmacy
Program in:
- pharmacy • MS, PhD

■ THE UNIVERSITY OF NORTH CAROLINA AT CHARLOTTE

Charlotte, NC 28223-0001
http://www.uncc.edu/

State-supported, coed, university. CGS member. *Enrollment:* 738 full-time matriculated graduate/professional students (361 women), 1,334 part-time matriculated graduate/professional students (737 women). *Graduate faculty:* 484 full-time (152 women), 148 part-time/adjunct (48 women). *Computer facilities:* 750 computers available on campus for general student use. A campuswide network can be accessed from student residence rooms and from off campus. Internet access and online class registration are available. *Library facilities:* J. Murrey Atkins Library. *Graduate expenses:* Tuition, state resident: full-time $1,172; part-time $294 per year. Tuition, nonresident: full-time $8,442; part-time $2,110 per year. Required fees: $1,006; $266 per year. Tuition and fees vary according to course load. *General application contact:* Dr. Robert J. Mundt, Dean, 687-547-3366.

Graduate School
Dr. Robert J. Mundt, Dean
Program in:
- health administration • MHA

Belk College of Business Administration
Dr. Claude C. Lilly, Interim Dean
Programs in:
- accounting • M Acc
- business administration • M Acc, MBA, MS
- economics • MS

College of Architecture
Ken Lambla, Chair of Instruction
Program in:
- architecture • M Arch

College of Arts and Sciences
Dr. Schley R. Lyons, Dean
Programs in:
- applied mathematics • MS, PhD
- applied physics • MS
- applied statistics • MS
- arts and sciences • MA, MPA, MS, MSW, PhD
- biology • MA, MS, PhD
- chemistry • MS
- community/clinical psychology • MA
- criminal justice • MS
- English • MA
- English education • MA
- geography and earth sciences • MA
- gerontology • MA
- history • MA
- industrial/organizational psychology • MA
- liberal studies • MA
- mathematics • MA
- mathematics education • MA
- political science • MPA
- psychology • MA
- social work • MSW
- sociology • MA

College of Education
Dr. Mary Lynne Calhoun, Interim Dean
Programs in:
- child and family studies • M Ed
- community and school counseling • MA
- curriculum and supervision • M Ed
- education • M Ed, MA, MSA, Ed D, CAS
- educational administration • CAS
- educational leadership • Ed D
- elementary education • M Ed
- instructional systems technology • M Ed
- middle school and secondary education • M Ed

reading, language and literacy • M Ed
school administration • MSA
special education • M Ed
teaching English as a second language • M Ed

College of Information Technology
Dr. Mirsad Hadzikadic, Dean
Programs in:
computer science • MS
information technology • MS, PhD

College of Nursing and Health Professions
Dr. Sue M. Bishop, Dean
Programs in:
adult health nursing • MSN
family and community nursing • MSN
health promotion • MS
nursing and health professions • MS, MSN

The William States Lee College of Engineering
Dr. Robert E. Johnson, Interim Dean
Programs in:
civil engineering • MSCE
electrical and computer engineering • MSEE, PhD
engineering • ME, MS, MSCE, MSE, MSEE, MSME, PhD
engineering management • MS
mechanical engineering and engineering science • MS, MSME, PhD

■ THE UNIVERSITY OF NORTH CAROLINA AT GREENSBORO

Greensboro, NC 27412-5001
http://www.uncg.edu/

State-supported, coed, university. CGS member. *Enrollment:* 994 full-time matriculated graduate/professional students (700 women), 1,716 part-time matriculated graduate/professional students (1,183 women). *Graduate faculty:* 487 full-time (209 women), 38 part-time/adjunct (12 women). *Computer facilities:* 400 computers available on campus for general student use. A campuswide network can be accessed from student residence rooms and from off campus. Internet access and online class registration are available. *Library facilities:* Jackson Library plus 1 other. *Graduate expenses:* Tuition, state resident: full-time $515; part-time $172 per hour. Tuition, nonresident: full-time $3,685; part-time $1,229 per hour. *General application contact:* Dr. James Lynch, Director of Graduate Recruitment and Information Services, 336-334-4881.

Find an in-depth description at www.petersons.com/graduate.

Graduate School
Dr. Brad Bartel, Dean
Programs in:
genetic counseling • MS
gerontology • MS
liberal studies • MALS

College of Arts and Sciences
Walter Beale, Dean
Programs in:
art • M Ed
arts and sciences • M Ed, MA, MFA, MPA, MS, PhD, Certificate
biology • M Ed, MS
chemistry • M Ed, MS
clinical psychology • MA, PhD
cognitive psychology • MA, PhD
communication studies • M Ed, MA
computer science • MA
creative writing • MFA
developmental psychology • MA, PhD
drama • M Ed, MFA
English • M Ed, MA, PhD, Certificate
French • M Ed, MA
geography • MA
historic preservation • Certificate
history • M Ed, MA
Latin • M Ed
mathematical science • M Ed, MA
museum studies • Certificate
nonprofit management • Certificate
political science • MA
public affairs • MPA, Certificate
social psychology • MA, PhD
sociology • MA
Spanish • M Ed, MA
speech communication • M Ed, MA
studio arts • MFA
technical writing • Certificate
women's studies • Certificate

Joseph M. Bryan School of Business and Economics
James K. Weeks, Dean
Programs in:
accounting • MS
applied economics • MA
business administration • MBA, Certificate
business and economics • MA, MBA, MS, Certificate
information systems and operations management • MS
international business administration • Certificate

School of Education
Dr. David Armstrong, Dean
Programs in:
counseling and development • MS, MS/Ed S, Ed D, PhD
cross categorical • M Ed
curriculum and instruction • M Ed
curriculum and teaching • PhD
deaf education • M Ed, MA
education • M Ed, MA, MLIS, MS, MS/Ed S, MSA, Ed D, PhD, Ed S, PMC
educational leadership • Ed D, PhD, Ed S
educational research, measurement and evaluation • M Ed, PhD
gerontological counseling • PMC
higher education • M Ed, Ed S
interdisciplinary studies in preschool education • M Ed
library and information studies • MLIS
marriage and family counseling • PMC
school administration • MSA
school counseling • PMC
special education • M Ed
supervision • M Ed

School of Health and Human Performance
Robert Christina, Dean
Programs in:
dance • MA, MFA
exercise and sports science • M Ed, MS, Ed D, PhD
health and human performance • M Ed, MA, MFA, MPH, MS, Ed D, PhD
parks and recreation management • MS
public health education • MPH
speech pathology and audiology • MA

School of Human Environmental Sciences
Dr. Helen A. Shaw, Dean
Programs in:
housing and interior design • MS
human development and family studies • M Ed, MS, PhD
human environmental sciences • M Ed, MS, MSW, PhD
human nutrition • M Ed, MS, PhD
social work • MSW
textile products design and marketing • M Ed, MS, PhD

School of Music
Dr. James Prodan, Associate Dean
Programs in:
composition • MM
education • MM
music education • PhD
performance • MM, DMA

School of Nursing
Dr. Lynne Pearcey, Dean
Programs in:

The University of North Carolina at Greensboro (continued)

administration of nursing in health agencies • MSN
gerontological nurse practitioner • PMC
nurse anesthesia • MSN, PMC

■ THE UNIVERSITY OF NORTH CAROLINA AT PEMBROKE

Pembroke, NC 28372-1510
http://www.uncp.edu/

State-supported, coed, comprehensive institution. *Enrollment:* 25 full-time matriculated graduate/professional students (11 women), 344 part-time matriculated graduate/professional students (238 women). *Graduate faculty:* 27 full-time (9 women), 2 part-time/adjunct (1 woman). *Computer facilities:* 367 computers available on campus for general student use. A campuswide network can be accessed from student residence rooms and from off campus. Internet access is available. *Library facilities:* Sampson-Livermore Library. *Graduate expenses:* Tuition, state resident: full-time $1,022. Tuition, nonresident: full-time $8,292. Required fees: $686. Tuition and fees vary according to course load. *General application contact:* Dr. Kathleen C. Hilton, Dean, 910-521-6271.

Graduate Studies

Dr. Kathleen C. Hilton, Dean
Programs in:
art education • MA Ed
business administration • MBA
educational administration and supervision • MA Ed
elementary education • MA Ed
English education • MA
mathematics education • MA Ed
middle grades education • MA Ed
physical education • MA Ed
public management • MS
reading education • MA Ed
school administration • MSA
school counseling • MA
science education • MA Ed
service agency counseling • MA
social sciences education • MA Ed

■ THE UNIVERSITY OF NORTH CAROLINA AT WILMINGTON

Wilmington, NC 28403-3201
http://www.uncwil.edu/

State-supported, coed, comprehensive institution. CGS member. *Enrollment:* 213 full-time matriculated graduate/professional students (147 women), 414 part-time matriculated graduate/professional students (241 women). *Graduate faculty:* 127 full-time (52 women), 12 part-time/adjunct (3 women). *Computer facilities:* 778 computers available on campus for general student use. A campuswide network can be accessed from student residence rooms and from off campus. Internet access and online class registration are available. *Library facilities:* William M. Randall Library. *Graduate expenses:* Tuition, state resident: full-time $1,102. Tuition, nonresident: full-time $8,452. Required fees: $1,258. *General application contact:* Dr. Neil F. Hadley, Dean, Graduate School, 910-962-4117.

College of Arts and Sciences

Dr. JoAnn Seiple, Dean
Programs in:
arts and sciences • MA, MALS, MFA, MS
biology • MS
chemistry • MS
creative writing • MFA
English • MA
geology • MS
history • MA
liberal studies • MALS
marine biology • MS
mathematical sciences • MA, MS
psychology • MA

School of Business

Dr. Lawrence Clark, Dean
Programs in:
accountancy • MS
business • MBA, MS
business administration • MBA

School of Education

Dr. Cathy L. Barlow, Dean
Programs in:
education • M Ed, MAT
educational administration and supervision • M Ed
elementary education • M Ed
reading education • M Ed
secondary teacher education • M Ed
special education • M Ed
teaching • MAT

School of Nursing

Dr. Virginia W. Adams, Dean
Program in:
nursing • MSN

■ WAKE FOREST UNIVERSITY

Winston-Salem, NC 27109
http://www.wfu.edu/

Independent-religious, coed, university. CGS member. *Computer facilities:* 150 computers available on campus for general student use. A campuswide network can be accessed from student residence rooms and from off campus. Internet access and online class registration, personal computer are available. *Library facilities:* Z. Smith Reynolds Library plus 3 others. *General application contact:* Dean of the Graduate School, 336-758-5301.

Find an in-depth description at www.petersons.com/graduate.

Babcock Graduate School of Management

R. Charles Moyer, Dean
Programs in:
business administration • MBA
management • MBA

Graduate School

Programs in:
accountancy • MSA
analytical chemistry • MS, PhD
biology • MS, PhD
computer science • MS
English • MA
guidance and counseling • MA Ed
health and exercise science • MS
history • MA
inorganic chemistry • MS, PhD
liberal studies • MALS
mathematics • MA
organic chemistry • MS, PhD
pastoral counseling • MA
physical chemistry • MS, PhD
physics • MS, PhD
psychology • MA
religion • MA
secondary education • MA Ed
speech communication • MA

School of Law

Robert K. Walsh, Dean
Program in:
law • JD, LL M

School of Medicine

Program in:
medicine • MD, MS, PhD

Graduate Programs in Medicine

Programs in:
biochemistry • PhD
bioorganic and macromolecular structure • PhD
cancer biology • PhD

comparative medicine • MS
epidemiology • MS
health services research • MS
medical engineering • PhD
medical genetics • MS
medicine • MS, PhD
microbiology and immunology • PhD
molecular and cellular pathobiology • MS, PhD
molecular genetics • PhD
molecular medicine • PhD
neurobiology and anatomy • PhD
neuroscience • PhD
pharmacology • PhD
physiology • PhD

■ WARREN WILSON COLLEGE

Asheville, NC 28815-9000
http://www.warren-wilson.edu/

Independent-religious, coed, comprehensive institution. *Computer facilities:* 68 computers available on campus for general student use. A campuswide network can be accessed from student residence rooms and from off campus. Internet access, word processing, software are available. *Library facilities:* Pew Learning Center and Ellison Library. *General application contact:* Director, 828-298-3325 Ext. 380.

MFA Program for Writers
Program in:
creative writing • MFA

■ WESTERN CAROLINA UNIVERSITY

Cullowhee, NC 28723
http://www.wcu.edu/

State-supported, coed, comprehensive institution. CGS member. *Enrollment:* 367 full-time matriculated graduate/professional students (226 women), 634 part-time matriculated graduate/professional students (444 women). *Graduate faculty:* 300 full-time (107 women). *Computer facilities:* 351 computers available on campus for general student use. A campuswide network can be accessed from student residence rooms and from off campus. Internet access and online class registration, e-mail are available. *Library facilities:* Hunter Library. *Graduate expenses:* Tuition, state resident: full-time $982. Tuition, nonresident: full-time $8,252. Required fees: $1,126. *General application contact:* Kathleen Owen, Assistant to the Dean, 828-227-7398.

Find an in-depth description at www.petersons.com/graduate.

Graduate School
Dr. Abdul M. Turay, Dean

College of Applied Science
Dr. Dennis Depew, Dean
Programs in:
applied science • MAT, MHS, MPT, MS, MSN
family and consumer sciences • MAT
health sciences • MHS
industrial and engineering technology • MS
nursing • MSN
physical therapy • MPT

College of Arts and Sciences
Dr. Robert Vartabedian, Dean
Programs in:
American history • MA
art education • MAT
arts and sciences • MA, MA Ed, MAT, MPA, MS
biology • MA Ed, MAT, MS
chemistry and physics • MAT, MS
English • MA, MA Ed, MAT
mathematics and computer science • MA Ed, MAT, MS
music • MA
public affairs • MPA
social sciences • MAT
studio art • MA

College of Business
Dr. Ronald E. Shiffler, Dean
Programs in:
accountancy • M Ac
business administration • MBA
project management • MPM

College of Education and Allied Professions
Dr. A. Michael Dougherty, Dean
Programs in:
art education • MAT
behavioral disorders • MA Ed
biology • MAT
chemistry • MAT
clinical psychology • MA
communication disorders • MS
community college education • MA Ed
community counseling • MS
counseling • MA Ed, MS
education and allied professions • MA, MA Ed, MAT, MS, MSA, Ed D, Ed S
educational administration • MA Ed
educational leadership • Ed D, Ed S
educational supervision • MA Ed
elementary education • MA Ed
English • MAT
family and consumer sciences • MAT
general special education • MA Ed
human resource development • MS
learning disabilities • MA Ed
mathematics • MAT
mental retardation • MA Ed
middle grades education • MA Ed
physical education • MA Ed, MAT
reading • MAT
reading education • MAT
school administration • MSA
school counseling • MA Ed
school psychology • MA
secondary education • MAT
social sciences • MAT

North Dakota

■ MINOT STATE UNIVERSITY

Minot, ND 58707-0002
http://www.minotstateu.edu/

State-supported, coed, comprehensive institution. *Computer facilities:* 300 computers available on campus for general student use. A campuswide network can be accessed from student residence rooms and from off campus. Internet access and online class registration are available. *Library facilities:* Gordon B. Olson Library. *General application contact:* Dean of Graduate School, 800-777-0750 Ext. 3150.

Graduate School
Programs in:
audiology • MS
criminal justice • MS
education of the deaf • MS
elementary education • MS
English • MAT
learning disabilities • MS
management • MS
mathematics • MAT
music education • MME
psychology • Ed Sp
science • MAT
special education • MS
speech-language pathology • MS

■ NORTH DAKOTA STATE UNIVERSITY

Fargo, ND 58105
http://www.ndsu.edu/

State-supported, coed, university. CGS member. *Computer facilities:* 500 computers available on campus for general student use. A campuswide network can be accessed from student residence

North Dakota State University (continued)

rooms and from off campus. Internet access is available. *Library facilities:* North Dakota State University Library plus 3 others. *General application contact:* Interim Dean, 701-231-7033.

Find an in-depth description at www.petersons.com/graduate.

Graduate Studies and Research

Program in:
- natural resources management • MS

College of Agriculture

Programs in:
- agricultural economics • MS
- agriculture • MS, PhD
- animal science • MS, PhD
- cellular and molecular biology • PhD
- cereal science • MS, PhD
- crop and weed sciences • MS
- entomology • MS, PhD
- horticulture • MS
- microbiology • MS
- natural resources management • MS
- plant pathology • MS, PhD
- plant sciences • PhD
- range science • MS, PhD
- soil sciences • MS, PhD
- veterinary sciences • MS

College of Arts, Humanities and Social Sciences

Programs in:
- acting • MA
- directing • MA
- dramatic theory • MA
- English • MA, MS
- history • MA
- humanities and social sciences • MA, MS
- mass communication • MA, MS
- political science • MA, MS
- sociology • MA, MS
- speech communication • MA, MS
- technical direction and stage design • MA

College of Business Administration

Program in:
- business administration • MBA

College of Engineering and Architecture

Programs in:
- agricultural and biosystems engineering • MS
- civil engineering • MS
- electrical and computer engineering • MS
- engineering • PhD
- engineering and architecture • MS, PhD
- environmental engineering • MS
- industrial engineering and management • MS
- mechanical engineering and applied mechanics • MS
- natural resource management • MS

College of Human Development and Education

Programs in:
- agricultural education • M Ed, MS
- agricultural extension education • MS
- cellular and molecular biology • PhD
- child development and family science • MS
- counselor education • M Ed, MA, MS
- education • M Ed, MA, MS, Ed S
- educational administration • MS, Ed S
- family and consumer sciences education • M Ed, MS
- food and nutrition • MS
- human development and education • M Ed, MA, MS, PhD, Ed S
- pedagogy • M Ed, MS
- physical education and athletic administration • M Ed, MS

College of Pharmacy

Programs in:
- pharmaceutical sciences • MS, PhD
- pharmacy • MS, PhD

College of Science and Mathematics

Programs in:
- applied mathematics • MS, PhD
- biochemistry and molecular biology • MS, PhD
- botany • MS, PhD
- cellular and molecular biology • PhD
- chemistry • MS, PhD
- clinical psychology • MS
- computer science • MS, PhD
- general psychology • MS
- mathematics • MS, PhD
- natural resources management • MS
- operations research • MS
- physics • MS, PhD
- polymers and coatings • MS, PhD
- psychology • MS
- science and mathematics • MS, PhD
- statistics • MS, PhD
- zoology • MS, PhD

■ UNIVERSITY OF MARY

Bismarck, ND 58504-9652

http://www.umary.edu/

Independent-religious, coed, comprehensive institution. *Enrollment:* 233 full-time matriculated graduate/professional students (119 women), 423 part-time matriculated graduate/professional students (341 women). *Graduate faculty:* 19 full-time (13 women), 144 part-time/adjunct (67 women). *Computer facilities:* A campuswide network can be accessed. Internet access is available. *Library facilities:* University of Mary Library. *Graduate expenses:* Tuition: part-time $295 per credit hour. *General application contact:* Dr. Randy G. Krieg, Director of Graduate Studies, 701-255-7500 Ext. 386.

Department of Occupational Therapy

Stacie Lynn Iken, Director

Program in:
- occupational therapy • MS

Division of Nursing

Sr. Mariam Dietz, Chair

Programs in:
- family nurse practitioner • MSN
- nursing education • MSN

Program in Education

Dr. Ramona Klein, Director

Programs in:
- elementary education • MS
- elementary education administration • MS Ed
- higher education • MS Ed
- secondary education administration • MS Ed
- secondary teaching • MS Ed
- special education • MS

Program in Management

Marvin Borgelt, Chairperson

Program in:
- management • M Mgmt

Program in Physical Therapy

Michael Gary Parker, Program Director

Program in:
- physical therapy • MPT

■ UNIVERSITY OF NORTH DAKOTA

Grand Forks, ND 58202

http://www.und.edu/

State-supported, coed, university. CGS member. *Enrollment:* 1,067 full-time matriculated graduate/professional students (552 women), 572 part-time matriculated graduate/professional students (311 women). *Graduate faculty:* 387 full-time (115 women), 21 part-time/adjunct (6 women). *Computer facilities:* 951 computers available on campus for general student use. A campuswide network can be accessed from student residence rooms and from off campus. Internet access is available. *Library facilities:* Chester Fritz Library plus 2 others. *Graduate expenses:* Tuition, state resident: part-time $164 per credit. Tuition, nonresident: full-time $7,998; part-time $359 per credit. Tuition and fees vary according to program and reciprocity agreements. *General application contact:* Kristin A. Ellwanger, Admissions Officer, 701-777-2945.

Graduate School
Dr. Carl A. Fox, Interim Dean

College of Arts and Sciences
Dr. Albert J. Fivizzani, Dean
Programs in:
arts and sciences • M Ed, M Mus, MA, MFA, MS, DA, PhD
botany • MS, PhD
chemistry • MS, PhD
clinical psychology • PhD
communication • MA
ecology • MS, PhD
English • MA, PhD
entomology • MS, PhD
environmental biology • MS, PhD
experimental psychology • PhD
fisheries/wildlife • MS, PhD
genetics • MS, PhD
geography • M Ed, MA, MS
history • MA, DA
linguistics • MA
mathematics • M Ed, MS
music • M Mus
music education • M Mus
physics • MS, PhD
psychology • MA
sociology • MA
speech and hearing science • PhD
speech-language pathology • MS
theatre arts • MA
visual arts • MFA
zoology • MS, PhD

College of Business and Public Administration
Dr. Dennis J. Elbert, Dean
Programs in:
business administration • MBA
business and public administration • MBA, MPA, MS
industrial technology • MS
public administration • MPA

College of Education and Human Development
Dr. Dan R. Rice, Dean
Programs in:
counseling • MA
counseling psychology • PhD
early childhood education • MS
education and human development • M Ed, MA, MS, MSW, Ed D, PhD, Specialist
education/general studies • MS
educational leadership • M Ed, MS, Ed D, PhD, Specialist
elementary education • Ed D, PhD
instructional design and technology • M Ed, MS
kinesiology • MS
measurement and statistics • Ed D, PhD
reading education • M Ed, MS
secondary education • Ed D, PhD
social work • MSW
special education • Ed D, PhD

College of Nursing
Dr. Ginny W. Guido, Director
Program in:
nursing • MS

John D. Odegard School of Aerospace Sciences
Bruce A. Smith, Dean
Programs in:
atmospheric sciences • MS
aviation • MS
computer science • MS
space studies • MS

School of Engineering and Mines
Dr. Tom C. Owens, Chairperson
Programs in:
chemical engineering • M Engr, MS
civil engineering • M Engr
electrical engineering • M Engr, MS
energy engineering • PhD
engineering and mines • M Engr, MA, MS, PhD
geology • MA, MS, PhD
mechanical engineering • M Engr, MS
sanitary engineering • M Engr

School of Law
W. Jeremy Davis, Dean
Program in:
law • JD

School of Medicine
Dr. H. David Wilson, Dean
Programs in:
anatomy • MS, PhD
biochemistry • MS, PhD
clinical laboratory science • MS
medicine • MD, MPT, MS, PhD
microbiology and immunology • MS, PhD
pharmacology • MS, PhD
physical therapy • MPT
physiology • MS, PhD

Ohio

■ ANTIOCH UNIVERSITY MCGREGOR
Yellow Springs, OH 45387-1609
http://www.mcgregor.edu/

Independent, coed, upper-level institution. *Enrollment:* 68 full-time matriculated graduate/professional students (28 women), 307 part-time matriculated graduate/professional students (211 women). *Graduate faculty:* 13 full-time (9 women), 31 part-time/adjunct (12 women). *Computer facilities:* 49 computers available on campus for general student use. A campuswide network can be accessed from off campus. Internet access is available. *Library facilities:* Olive Kettering Library. *Graduate expenses:* Tuition: part-time $2,224 per quarter. *General application contact:* Ruth M. Paige, Associate Director of Admissions, 937-769-1825.

Find an in-depth description at www.petersons.com/graduate.

Graduate Programs
Dr. Steven Brzezinski, Academic Dean
Programs in:
conflict resolution • MA
educational leadership • M Ed
intercultural relations • MA
liberal and professional studies • MA
liberal studies • MA
management • MA

■ ASHLAND UNIVERSITY
Ashland, OH 44805-3702
http://www.ashland.edu/

Independent-religious, coed, comprehensive institution. CGS member. *Enrollment:* 936 full-time matriculated graduate/professional students (510 women), 1,305 part-time matriculated graduate/professional students (795 women). *Graduate faculty:* 92 full-time (36 women), 128 part-time/adjunct (43 women). *Computer facilities:* 90 computers available on campus for general student use. A campuswide network can be accessed from student residence rooms and from off campus. *Library facilities:* Ashland Library plus 2 others. *Graduate expenses:* Tuition: full-time $15,134. One-time fee: $100 full-time. Tuition and fees vary according to degree level and program. *General application contact:* Dr. Gene A. Telego, Associate Provost, 419-289-5751.

College of Business Administration and Economics
Dr. Paul A. Sears, Dean
Programs in:
business administration and economics • MBA
executive management • MBA

College of Education
Dr. John P. Sikula, Dean
Programs in:
administration • M Ed
business manager • M Ed

Ashland University (continued)
classroom instruction • M Ed
curriculum and instruction • M Ed
early childhood education • M Ed
early childhood intervention specialist • M Ed
economics education • M Ed
education • M Ed, Ed D
educational leadership • Ed D
intervention specialist-mild/moderate • M Ed
intervention specialist-moderate/intensive • M Ed
literacy • M Ed
school treasurer • M Ed
school treasurer or business manager • M Ed
sport education • M Ed
talent development education • M Ed
technology education • M Ed

Theological Seminary
Dr. Frederick J. Finks, President
Programs in:
biblical and theological studies • MA
Christian education • MACE
Christian ministry • MACM
ministry • D Min
ministry management • MAMM
pastoral counseling • MAPC
theological studies • MA
theology • M Div

■ BALDWIN-WALLACE COLLEGE
Berea, OH 44017-2088
http://www.bw.edu/

Independent-religious, coed, comprehensive institution. *Enrollment:* 211 full-time matriculated graduate/professional students (102 women), 482 part-time matriculated graduate/professional students (328 women). *Graduate faculty:* 41 full-time (22 women), 17 part-time/adjunct (10 women). *Computer facilities:* 386 computers available on campus for general student use. A campuswide network can be accessed from student residence rooms. Internet access is available. *Library facilities:* Ritter Library plus 2 others. *Graduate expenses:* Tuition: part-time $415 per credit. *General application contact:* Winifred W. Gerhardt, Director of Admission for the Evening and Weekend College, 440-826-2222.

Graduate Programs
Dr. MaryLou Higgerson, Academic Dean

Division of Business Administration
Dr. Peter Rea, Chairperson, Business Administration
Programs in:
accounting • MBA
executive management • MBA
health care executive management • MBA
international management • MBA
systems management • MBA

Division of Education
Dr. Patrick F. Cosiano, Chairperson and Director of MA Ed
Programs in:
educational technology • MA Ed
mild/moderate educational needs • MA Ed
pre-administration • MA Ed
reading • MA Ed

■ BOWLING GREEN STATE UNIVERSITY
Bowling Green, OH 43403
http://www.bgsu.edu/

State-supported, coed, university. CGS member. *Computer facilities:* 1,800 computers available on campus for general student use. A campuswide network can be accessed from student residence rooms and from off campus. Internet access and online class registration are available. *Library facilities:* Jerome Library plus 7 others. *General application contact:* Director of Graduate Admissions, 419-372-7713.

Find an in-depth description at www.petersons.com/graduate.

Graduate College
Program in:
interdisciplinary studies • MA, MS, PhD

College of Arts and Sciences
Programs in:
American culture studies • MA, MAT, PhD
applied biology • Specialist
applied philosophy • PhD
applied statistics • MS
art • MA
arts and sciences • MA, MAT, MFA, MPA, MS, PhD, Ed S, Specialist
biological sciences • MAT, MS, PhD
chemistry • MAT, MS
clinical psychology • MA, PhD
communication studies • MA, MAT, PhD
computer science • MS
creative writing • MFA
criminology/deviant behavior • MA, PhD
demography and population studies • MA, PhD
developmental psychology • MA, PhD
English • MA, PhD
experimental psychology • MA, PhD
family studies • MA, PhD
French • MA, MAT
French education • MAT
geology • MAT, MS
German • MA, MAT
history • MA, MAT, PhD
industrial/organizational psychology • MA, PhD
interpersonal communication • MA, PhD
mass communication • MA, MAT, PhD
mathematics • MA, MAT, PhD
mathematics supervision • Ed S
philosophy • MA
photochemical sciences • PhD
physics • MAT, MS
physics and astronomy • MAT
political science • MPA
popular culture • MA
public administration • MPA
quantitative psychology • MA, PhD
scientific and technical communication • MA
social psychology • MA, PhD
Spanish • MA, MAT
Spanish education • MAT
statistics • MA, MAT, PhD
studio art • MFA
teaching English as a second language • MA
theatre • MA, PhD

College of Business Administration
Programs in:
accountancy • M Acc
applied statistics • MS
business • MBA
business administration • M Acc, MA, MBA, MOD, MS
economics • MA
organization development • MOD

College of Education and Human Development
Programs in:
business education • M Ed
classroom technology • M Ed
college student personnel • MA
curriculum and teaching • M Ed
development kinesiology • M Ed
education and human development • M Ed, MA, MFCS, MRC, Ed D, PhD, Ed S
education and intervention services • M Ed, MA, MRC, Ed S
educational administration and supervision • M Ed, Ed S
food and nutrition • MFCS
guidance and counseling • M Ed, MA
higher education administration • PhD

human development and family studies • MFCS
leadership and policy studies • M Ed, MA, Ed D, PhD, Ed S
leadership studies • Ed D
mathematics supervision • Ed S
reading • M Ed, Ed S
recreation and leisure • M Ed
rehabilitation counseling • MRC
school psychology • M Ed
special education • M Ed
sport administration • M Ed

College of Health and Human Services
Programs in:
communication disorders • MS, PhD
health and human services • MPH, MS, PhD
public health • MPH

College of Musical Arts
Programs in:
composition • MM
music education • MM
music history • MM
music theory • MM
performance • MM

College of Technology
Programs in:
career and technology education • M Ed
manufacturing technology • MIT
technology • M Ed, MIT

■ CAPITAL UNIVERSITY
Columbus, OH 43209-2394
http://www.capital.edu/

Independent-religious, coed, comprehensive institution. *Computer facilities:* 100 computers available on campus for general student use. A campuswide network can be accessed from student residence rooms and from off campus. Internet access is available. *Library facilities:* Blackmore Library.

Law School
Steven C. Bahls, Dean
Programs in:
business • LL M
business and taxation • LL M
law • JD, LL M, MT
taxation • LL M

School of Management
Dr. William A. Raabe, Dean
Program in:
administration • MBA

School of Nursing
Dr. Elaine F. Haynes, Acting Dean and Professor
Programs in:
administration • MSN
family and community • MSN
interdisciplinary family focused health care across cultures • MSN
legal studies • MSN
occupational health • MSN
parish nursing • MSN
school health nursing • MSN
theological studies • MSN

■ CASE WESTERN RESERVE UNIVERSITY
Cleveland, OH 44106
http://www.cwru.edu/

Independent, coed, university. CGS member. *Computer facilities:* 100 computers available on campus for general student use. A campuswide network can be accessed from student residence rooms and from off campus. Internet access and online class registration, software library, CD-ROM databases are available. *Library facilities:* University Library plus 6 others. *General application contact:* Assistant Dean of Graduate Studies, 216-368-4390.

Find an in-depth description at www.petersons.com/graduate.

Frances Payne Bolton School of Nursing
Programs in:
acute care adult nurse practitioner • MSN
acute care pediatric nurse practitioner • MSN
adult practitioner • MSN
community health nursing • MSN
critical care nursing • MSN
family nurse practitioner • MSN
gerontological nurse practitioner • MSN
medical-surgical nursing • MSN
neonatal practitioner • MSN
nurse anesthesia • MSN
nurse midwifery • MSN
nurse practitioner • MSN
nursing • MSN, ND, PhD
oncology nursing • MSN
pediatric nurse practitioner • MSN
psychiatric-mental health nurse practitioner • MSN
women's health nurse practitioner • MSN

Mandel School of Applied Social Sciences
Dr. Darlyne Bailey, Dean
Programs in:
nonprofit organizations • MNO, CNM
social administration • MSSA
social welfare • PhD

School of Dentistry
Dr. Jerold S. Goldberg, Dean
Programs in:
advanced general dentistry • Certificate
dentistry • DDS, MSD, Certificate
endodontics • MSD
oral surgery • Certificate
orthodontics • MSD
pedodontics • Certificate
periodontics • MSD

School of Graduate Studies
Programs in:
acting • MFA
American studies • MA, PhD
analytical chemistry • MS, PhD
anthropology • MA, PhD
applied mathematics • MS, PhD
art education • MA
art history • MA, PhD
art history and museum studies • MA, PhD
astronomy • MS, PhD
bioethics • MA
biology • MS, PhD
clinical psychology • PhD
comparative literature • MA
contemporary dance • MFA
early music • D Mus A
English and American literature • MA, PhD
experimental psychology • PhD
French • MA, PhD
geological sciences • MS, PhD
gerontology • Certificate
history • MA, PhD
inorganic chemistry • MS, PhD
mathematics • MS, PhD
mental retardation • PhD
museum studies • MA
music • MA, PhD
music education • MA, PhD
nursing/anthropology • MA, PhD
organic chemistry • MS, PhD
physical chemistry • MS, PhD
physics • MS, PhD
political science • MA, PhD
sociology • PhD
speech-language pathology • MA, PhD
statistics • MS, PhD
theater • MFA

The Case School of Engineering
Dr. Robert F. Savinell, Interim Dean
Programs in:
aerospace engineering • MS, PhD
biomedical engineering • MS, PhD
ceramics and materials science • MS
chemical engineering • MS, PhD
civil engineering • MS, PhD

Case Western Reserve University (continued)

computer engineering • MS, PhD
computing and information science • MS, PhD
electrical engineering • MS, PhD
engineering • ME, MS, PhD
engineering mechanics • MS
fluid and thermal engineering sciences • MS
fluid and thermal engineering sciences • PhD
macromolecular science • MS, PhD
materials science and engineering • MS, PhD
mechanical engineering • MS, PhD
systems and control engineering • MS, PhD

School of Law
Gerald Korngold, Dean
Programs in:
law • JD
taxation • LL M
U.S. legal studies • LL M

School of Medicine
Dr. Nathan A. Berger, Dean
Programs in:
biomedical sciences • PhD
medicine • MD, MA, MPH, MS, PhD

Graduate Programs in Medicine
Programs in:
anesthesiology • MS
applied anatomy • MS
biochemical research • MS
biochemistry • MS, PhD
biological anthropology • MS, PhD
biophysics and bioengineering • PhD
biostatistics • MS, PhD
cell biology • MS, PhD
cell physiology • PhD
cellular biology • MS, PhD
developmental biology • PhD
dietetics • MS
environmental toxicology • MS, PhD
epidemiology • MS, PhD
exerscise physiology • MS
genetic counseling • MS
human, molecular, and developmental genetics and genomics • PhD
immunology • MS, PhD
medicine • MA, MPH, MS, PhD
microbiology • PhD
molecular biology • PhD
molecular toxicology • MS, PhD
neurobiology • PhD
neuroscience • PhD
nutrition • MS, PhD
pathology • MS, PhD
pharmacology • PhD
physiology • MS
physiology and biophysics • PhD
public health • MPH
public health nutrition • MS
systems physiology • PhD

Weatherhead School of Management
Programs in:
accountancy • M Acc, PhD
banking and finance • MBA, PhD
economics • MBA
information systems • MBA, MSM, PhD
labor and human resource policy • MBA, PhD
management • MS
management policy • MBA, PhD
marketing • MBA, PhD
operations research • PhD
organizational behavior and analysis • MBA, MS, PhD

Mandel Center for Nonprofit Organizations
Program in:
nonprofit organizations • MNO, CNM

■ CLEVELAND STATE UNIVERSITY
Cleveland, OH 44115
http://www.csuohio.edu/

State-supported, coed, university. CGS member. *Enrollment:* 945 full-time matriculated graduate/professional students (490 women), 2,571 part-time matriculated graduate/professional students (1,440 women). *Graduate faculty:* 440 full-time (125 women). *Computer facilities:* 600 computers available on campus for general student use. *Library facilities:* University Library plus 1 other. *Graduate expenses:* Tuition, state resident: full-time $5,484; part-time $229 per credit hour. Tuition, nonresident: full-time $10,824; part-time $451 per credit hour. $5,484 full-time. *General application contact:* Dr. William C. Bailey, Director of Graduate Admissions, 216-687-9370.

Find an in-depth description at www.petersons.com/graduate.

Cleveland-Marshall College of Law
Steven H. Steinglass, Dean
Program in:
law • JD, LL M

College of Graduate Studies
Dr. Mark A. Tumeo, Interim Dean

College of Arts and Sciences
Dr. Karen Steckol, Dean
Programs in:
analytical chemistry • MS, PhD
applied mathematics • MS
applied optics • MS
art history • MA
arts and sciences • MA, MACTM, MM, MS, MSW, PhD, Psy S
biological, geological, and environmental sciences • MS, PhD
clinical and counseling psychology • MA
clinical chemistry • MS, PhD
clinical/bioanalytical • PhD
communication • MACTM
composition • MM
condensed matter physics • MS
consumer/industrial research • MA
diversity management • MA
economics • MA
education and performance • MM
English • MA
history • MA
inorganic chemistry • MS
mathematics • MA
music history • MM
organic chemistry • MS
philosophy • MA
physical chemistry • MS
research psychology • MA
school psychology • Psy S
social work • MSW
sociology • MA
Spanish • MA
speech and hearing • MA
structural analysis • MS, PhD

College of Education
Dr. James McLoughlin, Dean
Programs in:
adult learning and development • M Ed
community health • M Ed
curriculum and instruction • M Ed
education • M Ed, PhD, Ed S
educational administration and supervision • M Ed, Ed S
educational research • M Ed
exercise science • M Ed
gifted education • M Ed
health education • M Ed
human performance • M Ed
pedagogy • M Ed
school and professional counseling • M Ed, Ed S
sport and exercise psychology • M Ed
sport management • M Ed
sport management/exercise science • M Ed
technology education • M Ed
urban education • PhD

Fenn College of Engineering
Dr. John H, Hemann, Interim Dean
Programs in:
applied biomedical engineering • D Eng
chemical engineering • MS, D Eng
civil engineering • MS, D Eng
electrical and computer engineering • MS, D Eng
engineering • D Eng
industrial engineering • MS
mechanical engineering • MS, D Eng

James J. Nance College of Business Administration
Dr. Rosemary P. Ramsey, Interim Dean
Programs in:
- accounting and financial information systems • MAC
- business administration • MBA, DBA
- health care administration • MBA
- labor relations and human resources • MLRHR
- management and organization analysis • MCIS
- public health • MPH
- systems programming • MCIS

Maxine Goodman Levin College of Urban Affairs
Dr. Dianne Rahm, Dean
Programs in:
- public administration • MPA, PhD
- urban affairs • MA, MAES, MPA, MS, MUPDD, PhD
- urban planning, design, and development • MUPDD
- urban studies • MA, MS, PhD

■ COLLEGE OF MOUNT ST. JOSEPH

Cincinnati, OH 45233-1670
http://www.msj.edu/

Independent-religious, coed, comprehensive institution. *Enrollment:* 27 full-time matriculated graduate/professional students (26 women), 135 part-time matriculated graduate/professional students (99 women). *Graduate faculty:* 20 full-time (13 women). *Computer facilities:* 227 computers available on campus for general student use. A campuswide network can be accessed from student residence rooms and from off campus. Internet access and online class registration, computer-aided instruction are available. *Library facilities:* Archbishop Alter Library. *Graduate expenses:* Tuition: full-time $13,500; part-time $345 per credit hour. Required fees: $75 per semester. Full-time tuition and fees vary according to program. *General application contact:* Peggy Minnich, Director of Admission, 513-244-4814.

Find an in-depth description at www.petersons.com/graduate.

Education Department
Dr. Clarissa Enio Rosas, Chair
Programs in:
- art • MA Ed
- education • MA Ed
- inclusive early childhood education • MA Ed
- professional development • MA Ed
- professional foundations • MA Ed
- reading • MA Ed
- special education • MA Ed

Interdisciplinary Program in Organizational Leadership
Dr. Lonnie Supnick, Director
Program in:
- organizational leadership • MS

Physical Therapy Department
Dr. Gene Kritzky, Chair, Health Science
Program in:
- physical therapy • MPT

Religious Studies Department
Dr. John Trokan, Chair
Programs in:
- religious studies • MA
- spiritual and pastoral care • MA

■ FRANCISCAN UNIVERSITY OF STEUBENVILLE

Steubenville, OH 43952-1763
http://www.franuniv.edu/

Independent-religious, coed, comprehensive institution. *Enrollment:* 163 full-time matriculated graduate/professional students (84 women), 290 part-time matriculated graduate/professional students (170 women). *Graduate faculty:* 8 full-time (2 women), 37 part-time/adjunct (5 women). *Computer facilities:* 126 computers available on campus for general student use. A campuswide network can be accessed. Internet access is available. *Library facilities:* John Paul II Library. *Graduate expenses:* Tuition: full-time $7,650; part-time $425 per credit. Required fees: $180; $10 per credit. Tuition and fees vary according to class time, course load and program. *General application contact:* Mark McGuire, Director of Graduate Enrollment, 800-783-6220.

Graduate Programs
Dr. Stephen Miletic, Dean of Faculty
Programs in:
- administration • MS Ed
- business • MBA
- counseling • MA
- nursing • MSN
- philosophy • MA
- teaching • MS Ed
- theology and Christian ministry • MA

■ HEIDELBERG COLLEGE

Tiffin, OH 44883-2462
http://www.heidelberg.edu/

Independent-religious, coed, comprehensive institution. *Computer facilities:* 125 computers available on campus for general student use. A campuswide network can be accessed from student residence rooms and from off campus. Internet access and online class registration are available. *Library facilities:* Beeghly Library plus 1 other. *General application contact:* Dean of Graduate Studies, 419-448-2288.

Graduate Programs
Programs in:
- business administration • MBA
- counseling • MA
- education • MA

■ JOHN CARROLL UNIVERSITY

University Heights, OH 44118-4581
http://www.jcu.edu/

Independent-religious, coed, comprehensive institution. CGS member. *Enrollment:* 187 full-time matriculated graduate/professional students (139 women), 606 part-time matriculated graduate/professional students (369 women). *Graduate faculty:* 133 full-time (40 women), 56 part-time/adjunct (32 women). *Computer facilities:* 210 computers available on campus for general student use. A campuswide network can be accessed from student residence rooms and from off campus. Internet access and online class registration are available. *Library facilities:* Grasselli Library. *Graduate expenses:* Tuition: part-time $498 per credit hour. Tuition and fees vary according to course level, course load and program. *General application contact:* Marsha K. Daley, Assistant Dean, Graduate School, 216-397-4284.

Graduate School
Dr. Mary E. Beadle, Dean
Programs in:
- administration • M Ed, MA
- biology • MA, MS
- chemistry • MS
- clinical counseling • Certificate
- communications management • MA
- community counseling • MA

John Carroll University (continued)
educational and school psychology • M Ed, MA
English • MA
history • MA
humanities • MA
mathematics • MA, MS
physics • MS
professional teacher education • M Ed, MA
religious studies • MA
school based elementary education • M Ed
school based secondary education • M Ed
school counseling • M Ed, MA

John M. and Mary Jo Boler School of Business
Dr. James M. Daley, Associate Dean
Program in:
business • MBA

■ KENT STATE UNIVERSITY

Kent, OH 44242-0001
http://www.kent.edu/

State-supported, coed, university. CGS member. *Enrollment:* 1,992 full-time matriculated graduate/professional students (1,227 women), 2,352 part-time matriculated graduate/professional students (1,665 women). *Graduate faculty:* 765. *Computer facilities:* 800 computers available on campus for general student use. A campuswide network can be accessed from student residence rooms and from off campus. Internet access is available. *Library facilities:* Kent Library plus 5 others. *Graduate expenses:* Tuition, state resident: full-time $2,811; part-time $306 per credit hour. Tuition, nonresident: full-time $5,399; part-time $542 per credit hour. *General application contact:* Division of Research and Graduate Studies, 330-672-2661.

College of Arts and Sciences

Dr. Daniele Finatello, Associate Dean
Programs in:
American politics • MA, PhD
analytical chemistry • MS, PhD
anthropology • MA
applied mathematics • MA, MS, PhD
arts and sciences • MA, MLS, MPA, MS, PhD
biochemistry • PhD
botany • MA, MS, PhD
chemical physics • MS, PhD
chemistry • MA, MS, PhD
clinical psychology • MA, PhD
comparative politics • MA
computer science • MA, MS, PhD
ecology • MS, PhD
English • MA, PhD
experimental psychology • MA, PhD
French • MA
geography • MA, PhD
geology • MS, PhD
German • MA
history • MA, PhD
inorganic chemistry • MS, PhD
international politics • PhD
international relations • MA
justice studies • MA
Latin • MA
liberal studies • MLS
organic chemistry • MS, PhD
philosophy • MA
physical chemistry • MS, PhD
physics • MA, MS, PhD
physiology • MS, PhD
political theory • MA, PhD
public administration • MPA
pure mathematics • MA, MS, PhD
sociology • MA, PhD
Spanish • MA
zoology • MA, PhD

College of Fine and Professional Arts

Dr. Timothy J. Chandler, Associate Dean
Program in:
fine and professional arts • M Arch, MA, MFA, MLS, MM, MPH, MS, PhD

Hugh A. Glauser School of Music
Dr. John M. Lee, Director
Programs in:
composition • MA
conducting • MM
ethnomusicology • MA, PhD
music education • MM, PhD
musicology • MA, PhD
performance • MM
piano pedagogy • MM
theory • MA
theory and composition • PhD

School of Architecture and Environmental Design
Conrad McWilliams, Director
Program in:
architecture • M Arch

School of Art
William Quinn, Director
Programs in:
art • MA, MFA
art education • MA
fiber arts • MA, MFA
visual communication design • MA, MFA

School of Communication Studies
Dr. Alan M. Rubin, Interim Director
Program in:
communication studies • MA, PhD

School of Exercise, Leisure and Sport
S. Harold Smith, Director
Programs in:
exercise physiology • PhD
physical education • MA

School of Family and Consumer Studies
Dr. Jeannie D. Sneed, Director
Programs in:
child and family relations • MA
nutrition • MS

School of Journalism and Mass Communication
Pamela J. Creedon, Director
Program in:
journalism and mass communication • MA

School of Library and Information Science
Dr. Richard E. Rubin, Director
Program in:
library and information science • MLS

School of Public Health
Dr. Amy Lee, Co-Director
Program in:
public health • MPH

School of Speech Pathology and Audiology
Dr. Peter B. Mueller, Director
Program in:
speech pathology and audiology • MA, PhD

School of Theatre and Dance
Dr. John R. Crawford, Director
Program in:
theatre • MA, MFA

College of Nursing

Dr. Davina Gosnell, Dean
Programs in:
clinical nursing • MSN
nursing administration • MSN
nursing education • MSN
parent-child nursing • MSN

Graduate School of Education

Dr. Joanne R. Schwartz, Dean
Programs in:
community counseling • M Ed, MA
counseling and human development services • PhD
cultural foundations • M Ed, MA, PhD
curriculum and instruction • M Ed, MA, PhD, Ed S
early childhood education • M Ed, MA, MAT
early childhood intervention • M Ed, MA
education • M Ed, MA, MAT, PhD, Ed S

educational administration • M Ed, MA, PhD, Ed S
educational foundations • M Ed, MA, PhD
educational psychology • M Ed, MA, PhD
elementary education • M Ed, MA
evaluation and measurement • M Ed, MA, PhD
gifted education • M Ed, MA
health and safety education • PhD
health education and promotion • PhD
hearing impaired education • M Ed, MA
higher education administration and student personnel • M Ed, MA, PhD, Ed S
instructional technology • M Ed, MA, PhD
K–12 leadership • M Ed, MA, PhD, Ed S
learning and development • M Ed, MA
middle childhood education • M Ed, MA
mild/moderate • M Ed, MA
moderate/intensive • M Ed, MA
reading • M Ed, MA
rehabilitation counseling • M Ed, MA, Ed S
school counseling • M Ed, MA
school psychology • M Ed, PhD, Ed S
secondary education • M Ed, MA, MAT
special education • M Ed, MA, PhD, Ed S
vocational and technical education • M Ed, MA, Ed S
vocational education • M Ed, MA, Ed S

Graduate School of Management
Dr. Frederick W. Schroath, Associate Dean
Programs in:
accounting • MS, PhD
business administration • MBA
economics • MA
finance • PhD
management • MA, MBA, MS, PhD
management systems • PhD
marketing • PhD

School of Biomedical Sciences
Programs in:
biological anthropology • PhD
biomedical sciences • MS, PhD
cellular and molecular biology • MS, PhD
neuroscience • MS, PhD
pharmacology • MS, PhD
physiology • MS, PhD

School of Technology
Dr. A. Raj Chowdhury, Dean
Program in:
technology • MA

■ LAKE ERIE COLLEGE
Painesville, OH 44077-3389
http://www.lec.edu/

Independent, coed, comprehensive institution. *Enrollment:* 255 part-time matriculated graduate/professional students (210 women). *Graduate faculty:* 11 full-time (4 women), 2 part-time/adjunct (1 woman). *Computer facilities:* A campuswide network can be accessed from student residence rooms and from off campus. Internet access is available. *Library facilities:* Lincoln Library plus 2 others. *Graduate expenses:* Tuition: part-time $385 per credit. *General application contact:* Admissions Office, 440-639-7879.

Division of Education
Dr. Carol Ramsay, Associate Dean of Teacher Education and Certification
Programs in:
education • MS Ed
effective teaching • MS Ed
reading • MS Ed

Division of Management Studies
Dr. Ronald A. Fullerton, Associate Dean
Programs in:
general management • MBA
management healthcare administration • MBA

■ MALONE COLLEGE
Canton, OH 44709-3897
http://www.malone.edu/

Independent-religious, coed, comprehensive institution. *Enrollment:* 11 full-time matriculated graduate/professional students (8 women), 191 part-time matriculated graduate/professional students (104 women). *Graduate faculty:* 21 full-time (6 women), 30 part-time/adjunct (12 women). *Computer facilities:* 145 computers available on campus for general student use. A campuswide network can be accessed from student residence rooms and from off campus. Internet access is available. *Library facilities:* Everett L. Cattell Library. *Graduate expenses:* Tuition: part-time $325 per semester hour. Part-time tuition and fees vary according to program. *General application contact:* Dan DePasquale, Director of Graduate Student Services, 330-471-8381.

Find an in-depth description at www.petersons.com/graduate.

Graduate School
Dr. Marietta Daulton, Interim Dean
Programs in:
business • MBA
Christian ministries • MA
community counseling • MA
curriculum and instruction • MA
curriculum, instruction, and professional development • MA
family and youth ministries • MA
instructional technology • MA
intervention specialist • MA
leadership in Christian church • MA
pastoral counseling • MA
reading • MA
school counseling • MA

■ MIAMI UNIVERSITY
Oxford, OH 45056
http://www.muohio.edu/

State-related, coed, university. CGS member. *Enrollment:* 997 full-time matriculated graduate/professional students (551 women), 231 part-time matriculated graduate/professional students (172 women). *Graduate faculty:* 623 full-time (188 women). *Computer facilities:* 1,000 computers available on campus for general student use. A campuswide network can be accessed from student residence rooms and from off campus. Internet access and online class registration are available. *Library facilities:* King Library plus 3 others. *Graduate expenses:* Tuition, state resident: full-time $5,506. Tuition, nonresident: full-time $9,026. Required fees: $1,100. Tuition and fees vary according to campus/location and program. *General application contact:* Dr. Robert C. Johnson, Associate Provost and Dean of the Graduate School, 513-529-4125.

Find an in-depth description at www.petersons.com/graduate.

Graduate School
Dr. Robert C. Johnson, Associate Provost and Dean

College of Arts and Sciences
Dr. John Skillings, Dean
Programs in:
analytical chemistry • MS, PhD
arts and sciences • M En S, MA, MAT, MGS, MS, MTSC, PhD
biochemistry • MS, PhD

Miami University (continued)
biological sciences • MAT
botany • MA, MS, PhD
chemical education • MS, PhD
chemistry • MS, PhD
clinical psychology • PhD
composition and rhetoric • MA, PhD
creative writing • MA
criticism • PhD
English and American literature and language • PhD
English education • MAT
experimental psychology • PhD
French • MA
geography • MA
geology • MA, MS, PhD
gerontology • MGS
history • MA
inorganic chemistry • MS, PhD
library theory • PhD
literature • MA, MAT, PhD
mass communication • MA
mathematics • MA, MAT, MS
mathematics/operations research • MS
microbiology • MS, PhD
organic chemistry • MS, PhD
philosophy • MA
physical chemistry • MS, PhD
physics • MS
political science • MA, MAT, PhD
religion • MA
social psychology • PhD
Spanish • MA
speech communication • MA
speech pathology and audiology • MS
statistics • MS
technical and scientific communication • MTSC
zoology • MA, MS, PhD

Institute of Environmental Sciences
Dr. Gene Willeke, Director
Program in:
environmental sciences • M En S

Richard T. Farmer School of Business Administration
Dr. Daniel Short, Dean
Programs in:
accountancy • M Acct
business administration • MBA
economics • MA
finance • MBA
general management • MBA
management information systems • MBA
marketing • MBA
quality and process improvement • MBA

School of Education and Allied Professions
Dr. Curtis Ellison, Acting Dean
Programs in:
adolescent education • MAT
child and family studies • MS
college student personnel services • MS
curriculum • MA, Ed D
curriculum and teacher leadership • M Ed
education and allied professions • M Ed, MA, MAT, MS, Ed D, PhD, Ed S
educational administration • Ed D, PhD
educational leadership • M Ed, MS, Ed D, PhD
educational psychology • M Ed
elementary education • M Ed, MAT
elementary mathematics education • M Ed
exercise science • MS
reading education • M Ed
school psychology • MS, Ed S
secondary education • M Ed, MAT
special education • M Ed, MA
sports studies • MS

School of Engineering and Applied Science
Dr. Marek Dollár, Chair
Programs in:
engineering and applied science • MS
paper science and engineering • MS
systems analysis • MS

School of Fine Arts
Pamela Fox, Dean
Programs in:
architecture • M Arch
art education • MA
fine arts • M Arch, MA, MFA, MM
music education • MM
music performance • MM
studio art • MFA
theatre • MA

■ THE OHIO STATE UNIVERSITY
Columbus, OH 43210
http://www.osu.edu/

State-supported, coed, university. CGS member. *Enrollment:* 8,684 full-time matriculated graduate/professional students (4,285 women), 4,045 part-time matriculated graduate/professional students (2,724 women). *Graduate faculty:* 2,882. *Computer facilities:* 1,000 computers available on campus for general student use. A campuswide network can be accessed from student residence rooms and from off campus. Internet access and online class registration are available. *Library facilities:* Main Library plus 12 others. *Graduate expenses:* Tuition, state resident: full-time $6,306; part-time $200 per credit hour. Tuition, nonresident: full-time $16,377; part-time $335 per credit hour. Tuition and fees vary according to course load, campus/location and program. *General application contact:* Marie Taris, Director, Graduate, International, and Professional Schools Admissions, 614-292-9444.

College of Dentistry
Henry W. Fields, Dean
Programs in:
dentistry • MS
oral biology • PhD

College of Law
Gregory H. Williams, Dean
Program in:
law • JD

College of Medicine and Public Health
Dr. Fred Sanfilippo, Dean and Vice President for Health Sciences
Programs in:
medicine • MD
medicine and public health • MD, MHA, MPH, MS, PhD
neuroscience • PhD

Graduate Programs in the Basic Medical Sciences
Dr. Susan L. Huntington, Vice Provost and Dean of the Graduate School
Programs in:
allied medicine • MS
anatomy • MS, PhD
basic medical sciences • MHA, MPH, MS, PhD
experimental pathobiology • MS, PhD
health administration • MHA, PhD
molecular virology, immunology and medical genetics • MS, PhD
pharmacology • MS, PhD
physiology and cell biology • PhD
public health • MPH, MS, PhD
toxicology • MS, PhD

College of Optometry
Dr. John Schoessler, Dean
Programs in:
optometry • OD, MS, PhD
vision science • MS, PhD

College of Pharmacy
Dr. John M. Cassady, Dean
Programs in:
hospital pharmacy • MS
medicinal chemistry and pharmacognosy • MS, PhD
pharmaceutical administration • MS, PhD
pharmaceutics • MS, PhD
pharmacology • MS, PhD
pharmacy • MS, PhD
pharmacy practice and administration • MS, PhD

Graduate School
Dr. Susan L. Huntington, Vice Provost for Graduate Studies and Dean
Program in:
Slavic and East European studies • MA

College of Biological Sciences
Richard W. Hall, Dean
Programs in:
biochemistry • MS, PhD
biological sciences • MS, PhD
biophysics • MS, PhD
cell and developmental biology • MS, PhD
entomology • MS, PhD
evolution, ecology, and organismal biology • MS, PhD
genetics • MS, PhD
microbiology • MS, PhD
molecular biology • MS, PhD
molecular, cellular and developmental biology • MS, PhD
plant biology • MS, PhD

College of Education
Dr. Donna Evans, Interim Dean
Programs in:
education • M Ed, MA, PhD, Certificate
educational administration • Certificate
educational policy and leadership • M Ed, MA, PhD
physical activity and educational services • M Ed, MA, PhD
teaching and learning • M Ed, MA, PhD

College of Engineering
Dr. James C. Williams, Dean
Programs in:
aeronautical and astronautical engineering • MS, PhD
architecture • M Arch, M Land Arch, MCRP, PhD
biomedical engineering • MS, PhD
chemical engineering • MS, PhD
city and regional planning • MCRP, PhD
civil engineering • MS, PhD
computer and information science • MS, PhD
electrical engineering • MS, PhD
engineering • M Arch, M Land Arch, MCRP, MS, PhD
engineering mechanics • MS, PhD
environmental science • MS, PhD
geodetic science and surveying • MS, PhD
industrial and systems engineering • MS, PhD
landscape architecture • M Land Arch
materials science and engineering • MS, PhD
mechanical engineering • MS, PhD
nuclear engineering • MS, PhD
welding engineering • MS, PhD

College of Food, Agricultural, and Environmental Sciences
Dr. Bobby D. Moser, Dean
Programs in:
agricultural economics and rural sociology • MS, PhD
agricultural education • MS, PhD
animal sciences • MS, PhD
food science and nutrition • MS, PhD
food, agricultural, and biological engineering • MS, PhD
food, agricultural, and environmental sciences • MS, PhD
horticulture and crop science • MS, PhD
natural resources • MS, PhD
plant pathology • MS, PhD
soil science • MS, PhD
vocational education • PhD

College of Human Ecology
David W. Andrews, Dean
Programs in:
family and consumer sciences education • M Ed, MS, PhD
family relations and human development • MS, PhD
family resource management • MS, PhD
food service management • MS, PhD
foods • MS, PhD
human ecology • M Ed, MS, PhD
nutrition • MS, PhD
textiles and clothing • MS, PhD

College of Humanities
Dr. Michael J. Hogan, Dean
Programs in:
African-American and African studies • MA
comparative studies • MA
East Asian languages and literatures • MA, PhD
English • MA, MFA, PhD
French and Italian • MA, PhD
Germanic languages and literatures • MA, PhD
Greek and Latin • MA, PhD
history • MA, PhD
humanities • MA, MFA, PhD, Certificate
Latin American studies • Certificate
linguistics • MA, PhD
Near Eastern languages and cultures • MA
philosophy • MA, PhD
Russian area studies • Certificate
Slavic and East European languages and literatures • MA, PhD
Spanish and Portuguese • MA, PhD
women's studies • MA

College of Mathematical and Physical Sciences
Dr. Robert Gold, Dean
Programs in:
astronomy • MS, PhD
biostatistics • PhD
chemical physics • MS, PhD
chemistry • MS, PhD
geological sciences • MS, PhD
mathematical and physical sciences • M Appl Stat, MA, MS, PhD
mathematics • MA, MS, PhD
physics • MS, PhD
statistics • M Appl Stat, MS, PhD

College of Nursing
Dr. Elizabeth R. Lenz, Dean
Program in:
nursing • MS, PhD

College of Social and Behavioral Sciences
Dr. Randall Ripley, Dean
Programs in:
anthropology • MA, PhD
atmospheric sciences • MS, PhD
clinical psychology • PhD
cognitive/experimental psychology • PhD
communication • PhD
counseling psychology • PhD
developmental psychology • PhD
economics • MA, PhD
geography • MA, PhD
journalism and communication • MA
Latin American studies • Certificate
mental retardation and developmental disabilities • PhD
political science • MA, PhD
psychobiology • PhD
public policy and management • MA, MPA, PhD
quantitative psychology • PhD
Russian area studies • Certificate
social and behavioral sciences • MA, MPA, MS, PhD, Certificate
social psychology • PhD
sociology • MA, PhD
speech and hearing science • MA, PhD

College of Social Work
Tony Tripodi, Dean
Program in:
social work • MSW, PhD

College of the Arts
Karen A. Bell, Interim Dean
Programs in:
art • MA, MFA
art education • MA, PhD
arts • M Mus, MA, MFA, DMA, PhD
arts policy and administration • MA
dance • MA, MFA
history of art • MA, PhD
industrial, interior, and visual communication design • MA, MFA
music • M Mus, MA, DMA, PhD
theatre • MA, MFA, PhD

The Ohio State University (continued)

Max M. Fisher College of Business
Joseph A. Alutto, Dean
Programs in:
- accounting and management information systems • M Acc, MA, PhD
- business • M Acc, MA, MBA, MLHR, PhD
- business administration • MA, MBA, PhD
- labor and human resources • MLHR, PhD

■ OHIO UNIVERSITY

Athens, OH 45701-2979
http://www.ohio.edu/

State-supported, coed, university. CGS member. *Enrollment:* 2,081 full-time matriculated graduate/professional students (973 women), 619 part-time matriculated graduate/professional students (321 women). *Graduate faculty:* 1,042 full-time (355 women), 661 part-time/adjunct (260 women). *Computer facilities:* 1,500 computers available on campus for general student use. A campuswide network can be accessed from student residence rooms and from off campus. *Library facilities:* Alden Library. *Graduate expenses:* Full-time $1,634; part-time $203 per credit. Tuition, nonresident: full-time $3,507; part-time $435 per credit. *General application contact:* Dr. Katherine Tadlock, Director, Graduate Student Services, 740-593-2800.

College of Osteopathic Medicine
Dr. Daniel J. Marazon, Interim Dean
Program in:
- osteopathic medicine • DO

Graduate Studies
Dr. Gary M. Schumacher, Associate Provost for Graduate Studies
Program in:
- interdisciplinary studies • MA, MS, PhD

Center for International Studies
Dr. Josep Rota, Director
Programs in:
- African studies • MA
- communications and development studies • MA
- development studies • MA
- international studies • MA
- Latin American studies • MA
- Southeast Asian studies • MA

College of Arts and Sciences
Dr. Leslie Flemming, Dean
Programs in:
- applied linguistics/TESOL • MA
- arts and sciences • MA, MPA, MS, MSS, MSW, PhD
- biological sciences • MS, PhD
- chemistry and biochemistry • MS, PhD
- clinical psychology • PhD
- economics • MA
- English language and literature • MA, PhD
- environmental and plant biology • MS, PhD
- environmental studies • MS
- experimental psychology • PhD
- French • MA
- geography • MA
- geological sciences • MS
- history • MA, PhD
- industrial and organizational psychology • PhD
- mathematics • MS, PhD
- microbiology • MS, PhD
- molecular and cellular biology • MS, PhD
- philosophy • MA
- physics • MS, PhD
- political science • MA
- public administration • MPA
- social sciences • MSS
- social work • MSW
- sociology • MA
- Spanish • MA
- zoology • MS, PhD

College of Business
Dr. Hugh Sherman, Assistant Dean
Programs in:
- business • EMBA, MBA, MSA
- business administration • EMBA, MBA, MSA

College of Communication
Dr. Kathy Krendl, Dean
Programs in:
- communication • MA, MS, PhD
- interpersonal communication • MA, PhD
- journalism • MS, PhD
- telecommunications • MA, PhD
- visual communication • MA

College of Education
Dr. James L. Heap, Dean
Programs in:
- adolescent to young adult education • M Ed
- college student personnel • M Ed
- community/agency counseling • M Ed
- computer education and technology • M Ed
- counselor education • PhD
- cultural studies • M Ed
- curriculum and instruction • M Ed, PhD
- education • M Ed, Ed D, PhD
- educational administration • M Ed, Ed D
- educational research and evaluation • M Ed, PhD
- elementary education • M Ed
- gifted and talented • M Ed
- higher education • M Ed, PhD
- instructional technology • PhD
- mathematics education • PhD
- middle child education • M Ed
- middle level education • PhD
- reading and language arts • PhD
- reading education • M Ed
- rehabilitation counseling • M Ed
- school counseling • M Ed
- secondary mathematics education • M Ed
- social studies education • PhD
- special education • M Ed, PhD
- supervision • PhD

College of Fine Arts
Dr. Raymond Tymas-Jones, Dean
Programs in:
- art education • MA
- art history • MFA
- art history/studio • MFA
- ceramics • MFA
- comparative arts • PhD
- conducting • MM
- film • MA, MFA
- fine arts • MA, MFA, MM, PhD
- history • MM
- literature • MM
- music education • MM
- painting • MFA
- performance • MM
- photography • MFA
- printmaking • MFA
- sculpture • MFA
- theater • MA, MFA
- theory • MM

College of Health and Human Services
Dr. Gary Neiman, Dean
Programs in:
- athletics training education • MS
- child development and family life • MSHCS
- coaching education • MS
- food and nutrition • MSHCS
- health and human services • MA, MBA, MHA, MPT, MS, MSA, MSHCS, MSP Ex, PhD
- health sciences • MHA
- physical education • MS
- physical education pedagogy • MS
- physical therapy • MPT
- physiology of exercise • MSP Ex
- recreation studies • MS
- speech pathology and audiology • MA, PhD
- sports administration • MBA, MSA
- sports physiology and adult fitness • MS

Russ College of Engineering and Technology
Dr. Jerrel Mitchell, Interim Dean
Programs in:
- chemical engineering • MS, PhD
- computer science • MS
- electrical engineering • MS, PhD
- engineering and technology • MS, PhD
- geotechnical and environmental engineering • MS, PhD
- industrial and manufacturing systems engineering • MS
- intelligent systems • PhD
- manufacturing engineering • MS
- materials processing • PhD
- mechanical engineering • MS, PhD
- water resources and structures • MS

■ THE UNION INSTITUTE
Cincinnati, OH 45206-1925
http://www.tui.edu/

Independent, coed, university. *Enrollment:* 1,122 full-time matriculated graduate/professional students (684 women). *Graduate faculty:* 62 full-time (28 women), 24 part-time/adjunct (8 women). *Computer facilities:* 18 computers available on campus for general student use. A campuswide network can be accessed from off campus. Internet access is available. *Graduate expenses:* Tuition: full-time $8,944. *General application contact:* Lisa Schrenger, Director of Admissions, 800-486-3116.

School of Interdisciplinary Arts and Sciences
Dr. Richard Genardi
Program in:
- interdisciplinary studies • PhD

School of Professional Psychology
Dr. Richard Genardi, Dean
Program in:
- clinical psychology • PhD

■ THE UNIVERSITY OF AKRON
Akron, OH 44325-0001
http://www.uakron.edu/

State-supported, coed, university. CGS member. *Enrollment:* 2,077 full-time matriculated graduate/professional students (1,019 women), 1,896 part-time matriculated graduate/professional students (1,155 women). *Graduate faculty:* 559 full-time (208 women), 149 part-time/adjunct (69 women). *Computer facilities:* 1,200 computers available on campus for general student use. A campuswide network can be accessed from student residence rooms and from off campus. Internet access and online class registration are available. *Library facilities:* Bierce Library plus 3 others. *Graduate expenses:* Tuition, state resident: full-time $6,004; part-time $189 per credit. $10,934 full-time. Required fees: $232; $9.7 per credit. *General application contact:* Dr. Lathardus Goggins, Associate Dean of the Graduate School, 330-972-7663.

Find an in-depth description at www.petersons.com/graduate.

Graduate School
Dr. George R. Newkome, Vice President for Research and Dean of the Graduate School

Buchtel College of Arts and Sciences
Dr. Roger Creel, Dean
Programs in:
- applied cognitive aging • MA, PhD
- applied mathematics • MS
- applied politics • MA
- arts and sciences • MA, MPA, MS, PhD
- biology • MS
- chemistry • MS, PhD
- computer science • MS
- counseling psychology • MA
- earth science • MS
- economics • MA
- English • MA
- geography • MS
- geology • MS
- geophysics • MS
- history • MA, PhD
- industrial/organizational psychology • MA, PhD
- labor and industrial relations • MA
- mathematics • MS
- physics • MS
- political science • MA
- psychology • MA, PhD
- public administration • MPA
- sociology • MA, PhD
- Spanish • MA
- statistics • MS
- urban planning • MA, PhD
- urban studies • MA, PhD
- urban studies and public affairs • PhD

College of Business Administration
Dr. Stephen F. Hallam, Dean
Programs in:
- accountancy • MS
- accounting • MBA
- business administration • MBA, MS, MT
- electronic business • MBA
- entrepreneurship • MBA
- finance • MBA
- international business • MBA
- management • MBA
- management of technology • MBA
- management-human resources • MS
- management-information systems • MS
- marketing • MBA
- quality management • MBA
- taxation • MT

College of Education
Dr. Elizabeth Stroble, Interim Dean
Programs in:
- administrative specialist • MA, MS
- athletic training/sports medicine • MA, MS
- classroom guidance for teachers • MA, MS
- community counseling • MA, MS
- counseling psychology • PhD
- education • MA, MS, Ed D, PhD
- educational administration • MA, MS, Ed D
- elementary education • MA, MS, PhD
- elementary education with certification • MS
- elementary school counseling • MA
- exercise physiology/adult fitness • MA, MS
- guidance and counseling • PhD
- higher education administration • MA, MS
- marriage and family therapy • MA, MS
- outdoor education • MA
- physical education K–12 • MS
- principalship • MA, MS
- school psychology • MS
- secondary education • MA, MS, PhD
- secondary education with certification • MS
- secondary school counseling • MA
- special education • MA, MS
- sports science/coaching • MA
- superintendent • MA, MS
- technical education • MS
- technical education teaching • MS
- technical education training • MS

College of Engineering
Dr. S. Graham Kelly, Interim Dean
Programs in:
- biomedical engineering • MS
- chemical engineering • MS, PhD
- civil engineering • MS, PhD
- electrical engineering • MS, PhD
- engineering • MS, PhD
- engineering (management specialization) • MS
- engineering (polymer specialization) • MS
- engineering-applied mathematics • PhD
- mechanical engineering • MS, PhD

The University of Akron (continued)

College of Fine and Applied Arts
Dr. Mark Auburn, Dean
Programs in:
arts administration • MA
audiology • MA
child development • MA
child life • MA
clothing, textiles and interiors • MA
communication • MA
composition • MM
family development • MA
fine and applied arts • MA, MM, MS
food science • MA
music education • MM
music history and literature • MM
music technology • MM
nutrition and dietetics • MS
performance • MM
social work • MS
speech-language pathology • MA
theatre arts • MA
theory • MM

College of Nursing
Dr. Cynthia F. Capers, Dean
Programs in:
nursing • MSN, PhD
public health • MPH

College of Polymer Science and Polymer Engineering
Dr. Frank Kelley, Dean
Programs in:
polymer engineering • MS, PhD
polymer science • MS, PhD

School of Law
Richard L. Aynes, Dean
Program in:
law • JD, JD/MSMHR

■ UNIVERSITY OF CINCINNATI

Cincinnati, OH 45221-0091
http://www.uc.edu/

State-supported, coed, university. CGS member. *Computer facilities:* 325 computers available on campus for general student use. A campuswide network can be accessed from student residence rooms and from off campus. *Library facilities:* Langsam Library plus 7 others. *General application contact:* Vice President and University Dean, 513-556-2872.

College of Law
Dr. Joseph P. Tomain, Dean
Program in:
law • JD

Division of Research and Advanced Studies
Program in:
interdisciplinary studies • PhD

College-Conservatory of Music
Programs in:
arts administration • MA
choral conducting • MM, DMA
composition • MM, DMA
directing • MFA
keyboard studies • MM, DMA, Diploma
music • MA, MFA, MM, DMA, DME, PhD, AD, Diploma
music education • MM, DME
music history • MM
music theory • MM, PhD
musicology • PhD
orchestral conducting • MM, DMA
performance • MM, DMA, AD
theater design and production • MFA
theater performance • MFA
wind conducting • MM, DMA

College of Allied Health Sciences
Programs in:
allied health sciences • M Ed, MA, MPT, MS, PhD
communication sciences and disorders • MA, PhD
genetic counseling • MS
nutrition science • M Ed
physical therapy • MPT

College of Business Administration
Programs in:
accounting • MBA, PhD
business administration • MBA, MS, PhD
finance • MBA, PhD
information systems • MBA, PhD
international business • MBA
management • MBA, PhD
marketing • MBA, PhD
operations management • MBA, PhD
quantitative analysis • MBA, MS, PhD
real estate • MBA

College of Design, Architecture, Art and Planning
Programs in:
architecture • MS Arch
art education • MA
art history • MA
community planning • MCP
design, architecture, art and planning • M Des, MA, MCP, MFA, MS, MS Arch
fashion design • M Des
fine arts • MFA
graphic design • M Des
health planning/administration • MS
industrial design • M Des
interior design • M Des
planning • MCP, MS

College of Education
Programs in:
community health • M Ed
counselor education • M Ed, Ed D, CAGS
criminal justice • MS, PhD
curriculum and instruction • M Ed, Ed D
early childhood education • M Ed
education • M Ed, MA, MS, Ed D, PhD, CAGS, Ed S
education administration • M Ed, Ed D, Ed S
educational foundations • M Ed, Ed D
educational studies • M Ed, Ed D, Ed S
elementary education • M Ed, Ed D
health promotion and education • M Ed
human services • M Ed, MA, Ed D, PhD, CAGS
reading/literacy • M Ed, Ed D
rehabilitation counseling • MA, CAGS
school psychology • M Ed, PhD
secondary education • M Ed
special education • M Ed, Ed D
teacher education • M Ed, Ed D

College of Engineering
Programs in:
aerospace engineering • MS, PhD
ceramic science and engineering • MS, PhD
chemical engineering • MS, PhD
civil engineering • MS, PhD
computer engineering • MS
computer science • MS
computer science and engineering • PhD
electrical engineering • MS, PhD
engineering • MS, PhD
engineering mechanics • MS, PhD
environmental engineering • MS, PhD
environmental sciences • MS, PhD
health physics • MS
industrial engineering • MS, PhD
materials science and engineering • MS, PhD
mechanical engineering • MS, PhD
metallurgical engineering • MS, PhD
nuclear engineering • MS, PhD
polymer science and engineering • MS, PhD
solid state electronics • MS

College of Medicine
Programs in:
anatomy • PhD
biophysics • MS, PhD
blood transfusion medicine • MS
cell and molecular biology • PhD
cell biology • PhD
cell biophysics • PhD
environmental and industrial hygiene • MS

environmental and occupational medicine • MS
environmental health • PhD
environmental hygiene science and engineering • MS, PhD
epidemiology and biostatistics • MS
medicine • MD, MS, D Sc, PhD
molecular and cellular pathophysiology • D Sc
molecular and developmental biology • MS, PhD
molecular genetics, biochemistry, microbiology and immunology • PhD
neurobiology • PhD
neuroscience • PhD
occupational safety • MS
pathology • PhD
pharmacology • PhD
physiology • MS, PhD
radiological sciences • MS
teratology • MS, PhD
toxicology • MS, PhD

College of Nursing
Dr. Andrea Lindell, Dean
Programs in:
adult health nursing • MSN
community health nursing • MSN
nurse anesthesia • MSN
nurse midwifery • MSN
nurse practitioner studies • MSN
nursing • PhD
nursing administration • MSN
occupational health • MSN
parent/child nursing • MSN
psychiatric nursing • MSN
woman's health • MSN

College of Pharmacy
Programs in:
pharmaceutical sciences • MS, PhD
pharmacy • Pharm D, MS, PhD
pharmacy practice • Pharm D

McMicken College of Arts and Sciences
Programs in:
analytical chemistry • MS, PhD
anthropology • MA
applied mathematics • MS, PhD
arts and sciences • MA, MALER, MAT, MPA, MS, PhD, Certificate
biochemistry • MS, PhD
biological sciences • MS, PhD
classics • MA, PhD
clinical psychology • PhD
communication • MA
economics • MA, PhD
English • MA, PhD
experimental psychology • MA, PhD
French • MA, PhD
geography • MA, PhD
geology • MS, PhD
Germanic languages and literature • MA, MAT, PhD
history • MA, MAT, PhD
inorganic chemistry • MS, PhD
labor and employment relations • MALER
mathematics education • MAT
organic chemistry • MS, PhD
philosophy • MA, PhD
physical chemistry • MS, PhD
physics • MS, PhD
political science • MA, PhD
polymer chemistry • MS, PhD
public affairs • MPA
pure mathematics • MS, PhD
social psychology • PhD
sociology • MA, PhD
Spanish • MA, PhD
statistics • MS, PhD
women's studies • MA, Certificate

School of Social Work
Program in:
social work • MSW

■ UNIVERSITY OF DAYTON

Dayton, OH 45469-1300
http://www.udayton.edu/

Independent-religious, coed, university. CGS member. *Enrollment:* 1,272 full-time matriculated graduate/professional students (587 women), 1,905 part-time matriculated graduate/professional students (1,242 women). *Graduate faculty:* 271 full-time, 410 part-time/adjunct. *Computer facilities:* 550 computers available on campus for general student use. A campuswide network can be accessed from student residence rooms and from off campus. Internet access and online class registration are available. *Library facilities:* Roesch Library plus 1 other. *Graduate expenses:* Tuition: part-time $438 per credit hour. *General application contact:* Nancy A. Wilson, Assistant to the Vice President for Graduate Studies and Research, 937-229-2390.

Find an in-depth description at www.petersons.com/graduate.

Graduate School

Dr. Gordon A. Sargent, Vice President for Graduate Studies and Research and Dean

College of Arts and Sciences
Dr. Paul J. Morman, Dean
Programs in:
applied mathematics • MS
arts and sciences • MA, MCS, MPA, MS, PhD
biology • MS, PhD
clinical psychology • MA
communication • MA
computer science • MCS
English • MA
general psychology • MA
human factors and research • MA
pastoral ministry • MA
public administration • MPA
theological studies • MA
theology • PhD

School of Business Administration
Dr. Sam Gould, Dean
Program in:
business administration • MBA

School of Education and Allied Professions
Dr. Thomas J. Lasley, Dean
Programs in:
adolescent/young adult • MS Ed
art education • MS Ed
college student personnel services • MS Ed
community counseling • MS Ed
early childhood education • MS Ed
education administration • MS Ed
education and allied professions • MS Ed, PhD, Ed S
educational leadership • PhD
exercise sports science • MS Ed
higher education administration • MS Ed
human development services • MS Ed
inclusive early childhood • MS Ed
interdisciplinary education • MS Ed
intervention specialist education, mild/moderate • MS Ed
literacy • MS Ed
middle childhood • MS Ed
physical education • MS Ed
school counseling • MS Ed
school psychology • MS Ed
teacher as child/with development specialist • MS Ed
teacher as leader • MS Ed
technology in education • MS Ed

School of Engineering
Dr. Blake Cherrington, Dean
Programs in:
aerospace engineering • MSAE, DE, PhD
chemical engineering • MS Ch E
electrical and computer engineering • MSEE, DE, PhD
electro-optics • MSEO, PhD
engineering • MS Ch E, MS Mat E, MSAE, MSCE, MSE, MSEE, MSEM, MSEM, MSEO, MSME, MSMS, DE, PhD
engineering management • MSEM
engineering mechanics • MSEM
environmental engineering • MSCE
management science • MSMS
materials engineering • MS Mat E, DE, PhD
mechanical engineering • MSME, DE, PhD
soil mechanics • MSCE
structural engineering • MSCE
transport engineering • MSCE

University of Dayton (continued)

School of Law
Francis J. Conte, Dean
Program in:
law • JD

■ THE UNIVERSITY OF FINDLAY

Findlay, OH 45840-3653

http://www.findlay.edu/

Independent-religious, coed, comprehensive institution. CGS member. *Enrollment:* 278 full-time matriculated graduate/professional students, 1,012 part-time matriculated graduate/professional students. *Graduate faculty:* 19 full-time, 15 part-time/adjunct. *Computer facilities:* 200 computers available on campus for general student use. A campuswide network can be accessed from student residence rooms and from off campus. Internet access is available. *Library facilities:* Shafer Library. *Graduate expenses:* Tuition: part-time $299 per semester hour. *General application contact:* Beth Stewart, Administrative Assistant, Graduate Programs, 419-424-4538.

Graduate Studies
Dr. James Riley, Associate Vice President for Academic Affairs
Programs in:
administration • MA Ed
early childhood • MA Ed
elementary education • MA Ed
professional studies • MA, MA Ed, MBA, MS, MSEM
special education • MA Ed
technology • MA Ed

College of Liberal Arts
Dr. Dale R. Brougher, Dean
Programs in:
bilingual and multicultural education • MA
liberal arts • MA
teaching English to speakers of other languages • MA

College of Science
Dr. Luke Bartolomeo, Dean
Programs in:
physical therapy • MS
science • MS, MSEM

MBA Program
Dr. Theodore C. Alex, Dean
Programs in:
financial management • MBA
human resource management • MBA
international management • MBA
management • MBA
marketing • MBA
public management • MBA

■ UNIVERSITY OF RIO GRANDE

Rio Grande, OH 45674

http://www.rio.edu/

Independent, coed, comprehensive institution. *Computer facilities:* 225 computers available on campus for general student use. A campuswide network can be accessed from student residence rooms and from off campus. Internet access is available. *Library facilities:* Jeanette Albiez Davis Library plus 2 others. *General application contact:* Director of Administration, 740-245-5353.

Graduate School
Program in:
classroom teaching • M Ed

■ UNIVERSITY OF TOLEDO

Toledo, OH 43606-3398

http://www.utoledo.edu/

State-supported, coed, university. CGS member. *Enrollment:* 1,064 full-time matriculated graduate/professional students (434 women), 1,883 part-time matriculated graduate/professional students (1,174 women). *Graduate faculty:* 408. *Computer facilities:* 1,700 computers available on campus for general student use. A campuswide network can be accessed from student residence rooms and from off campus. Internet access and online class registration, online transcripts, student account and grade information are available. *Library facilities:* Carlson Library plus 3 others. *Graduate expenses:* Tuition, state resident: full-time $2,906; part-time $242 per hour. Tuition, nonresident: full-time $6,281; part-time $282 per hour. *General application contact:* Dr. Richard A. Hudson, Interim Vice Provost for Graduate Education and Dean of the Graduate School, 419-530-1979.

Find an in-depth description at www.petersons.com/graduate.

College of Law
Phillip J. Closius, Dean
Program in:
law • JD

Graduate School
Dr. Richard A. Hudson, Interim Vice Provost for Graduate Education and Dean of the Graduate School

College of Arts and Sciences
Dr. David Stern, Chair
Programs in:
analytical chemistry • MES, MS, PhD
anthropology • MAE
applied mathematics • MS
arts and sciences • MA, MAE, MES, MLS, MM, MPA, MS, PhD
biological chemistry • MES, MS, PhD
biology • MES, MS, PhD
clinical psychology • PhD
economics • MA, MAE
English as a second language • MAE
English language and literature • MA, MAE
experimental psychology • MA, PhD
French • MA, MAE
geography • MA
geology • MS
German • MA, MAE
history • MA, MAE, PhD
inorganic chemistry • MES, MS, PhD
liberal studies • MLS
mathematics • MA, MES, PhD
music education • MM
organic chemistry • MES, MS, PhD
performance • MM
philosophy • MA
physical chemistry • MES, MS, PhD
physics • MES, MS, PhD
planning • MA
political science • MA
public administration • MPA
sociology • MA, MAE
Spanish • MA, MAE
statistics • MS

College of Business Administration
Dr. Gary Moore, MBA Director
Programs in:
accounting • MBA, MSA
business administration • EMBA, MBA, MS, MSA, PhD
decision sciences • MBA
finance • MBA
information systems • MBA
international business • MBA
management • MBA
manufacturing management • MS, PhD
marketing • MBA
operations management • MBA

College of Education and Allied Professions
Dr. Charlene Czerniak, Interim Dean
Programs in:
art education • ME
business education • ME, DE, PhD, Ed S
curriculum and instruction • ME, DE, PhD, Ed S
developmental, technological, and special area education • ME

early childhood education • DE, PhD, Ed S
education • MAE, ME, MES, DE, PhD, Ed S
education theory and social foundations • ME
educational administration and supervision • ME, Ed S
educational education and supervision • DE
educational media • DE, PhD, Ed S
educational psychology • ME, DE, PhD
educational research and measurement • DE, PhD
educational sociology • DE, PhD
elementary education • DE, PhD, Ed S
foundations of education • DE, PhD
higher education • ME, PhD
history of education • DE, PhD
philosophy of education • DE, PhD
secondary education • ME, DE, PhD, Ed S
special education • ME, DE, PhD, Ed S
vocational education • ME, Ed S

College of Engineering
Dr. Nagi Naganathan, Interim Dean
Programs in:
bioengineering • MS, PhD
chemical engineering • MS
civil engineering • MS
computer science • MS
electrical engineering • MS
engineering • MS, PhD
engineering sciences • PhD
industrial engineering • MS
mechanical engineering • MS

College of Health and Human Services
Dr. Jerome M. Sulivan, Dean
Programs in:
counseling • ME
exercise science • MS
guidance/counselor education • PhD
health education • DE, PhD
physical education • DE, PhD
public health • MES, MPH
recreation and leisure studies • ME
school psychology • ME, Ed S
speech language pathology • ME

College of Pharmacy
Dr. Wayne P. Hoss, Associate Dean Graduate Studies and Research
Programs in:
administrative pharmacy • MSPS
industrial pharmacy • MSPS
medicinal and biological chemistry • MS, PhD
pharmaceutical science • MSPS
pharmacology • MSPS
pharmacy • Pharm D, MS, MSPS, PhD

■ URSULINE COLLEGE
Pepper Pike, OH 44124-4398
http://www.ursuline.edu/

Independent-religious, coed, primarily women, comprehensive institution. *Enrollment:* 75 full-time matriculated graduate/professional students (63 women), 161 part-time matriculated graduate/professional students (128 women). *Graduate faculty:* 10 full-time (8 women), 15 part-time/adjunct (11 women). *Computer facilities:* 66 computers available on campus for general student use. A campuswide network can be accessed from student residence rooms. Internet access is available. *Library facilities:* Ralph M. Besse Library. *Graduate expenses:* Tuition: full-time $5,880; part-time $490 per credit hour. Tuition and fees vary according to course level, course load, program, reciprocity agreements and student's religious affiliation. *General application contact:* Dr. Catherine Hackney, Dean of Graduate Studies, 440-646-8119.

Graduate Studies
Dr. Catherine Hackney, Dean of Graduate Studies
Programs in:
art therapy • MA
education • MA
liberal studies • MALS
ministry • MA
non-public educational administration • MA
nursing • MSN

■ WALSH UNIVERSITY
North Canton, OH 44720-3396
http://www.walsh.edu/

Independent-religious, coed, comprehensive institution. *Enrollment:* 51 full-time matriculated graduate/professional students (37 women), 90 part-time matriculated graduate/professional students (65 women). *Graduate faculty:* 17 full-time (10 women), 7 part-time/adjunct (2 women). *Computer facilities:* 90 computers available on campus for general student use. A campuswide network can be accessed from student residence rooms and from off campus. *Library facilities:* Walsh University Library. *Graduate expenses:* Tuition: full-time $7,290; part-time $405 per credit hour. Required fees: $12 per credit hour. *General application contact:* Brett D. Freshour, Dean of Enrollment Management, 330-490-7286.

Graduate Programs
Dr. Nancy Blackford, Academic Dean
Programs in:
counseling and human development • MA
education • MA
management • MA
physical therapy • M Sc

■ WRIGHT STATE UNIVERSITY
Dayton, OH 45435
http://www.wright.edu/

State-supported, coed, university. CGS member. *Enrollment:* 1,556 full-time matriculated graduate/professional students (811 women), 1,946 part-time matriculated graduate/professional students (1,252 women). *Graduate faculty:* 749 full-time (232 women), 354 part-time/adjunct (195 women). *Computer facilities:* 450 computers available on campus for general student use. A campuswide network can be accessed from student residence rooms and from off campus. *Library facilities:* Paul Laurence Dunbar Library plus 2 others. *Graduate expenses:* Tuition, state resident: full-time $6,198; part-time $195 per quarter hour. Tuition, nonresident: full-time $10,794; part-time $337 per quarter hour. $10,950 full-time. Tuition and fees vary according to course load, degree level and program. *General application contact:* Gerald C. Malicki, Assistant Dean and Director of Graduate Admissions and Records, 937-775-2976.

Find an in-depth description at www.petersons.com/graduate.

School of Graduate Studies
Dr. Joseph F. Thomas, Dean and Associate Provost for Research
Program in:
interdisciplinary studies • MA, MS

College of Education and Human Services
Dr. Gregory R. Bernhardt, Dean
Programs in:
advanced curriculum and instruction • Ed S
advanced educational leadership • Ed S
business education • M Ed, MA
business, technology, and vocational education • M Ed, MA
chemical dependency • MRC
classroom teacher education • M Ed, MA

Wright State University (continued)

computer/technology education • M Ed, MA
counseling • M Ed, MA, MS
early childhood education • M Ed, MA
education and human services • M Ed, MA, MRC, MS, Ed S
educational administrative specialist: teacher leader • M Ed, MA
educational administrative specialist: vocational education administration • M Ed, MA
educational leadership • M Ed, MA
gifted educational needs • M Ed, MA
health, physical education, and recreation • M Ed, MA
higher education-adult education • Ed S
intervention specialist • M Ed, MA
library/media • M Ed, MA
mild to moderate educational needs • M Ed, MA
moderate to intensive educational needs • M Ed, MA
pupil personnel services • M Ed, MA
rehabilitation counseling • MRC
severe disabilities • MRC
student affairs in higher education-administration • M Ed, MA
superintendent • Ed S
vocational education • M Ed, MA

College of Engineering and Computer Science
Dr. James E. Brandeberry, Dean and Program Director
Programs in:
biomedical and human factors engineering • MSE
biomedical engineering • MSE
computer engineering • MSCE
computer science • MS
computer science and engineering • PhD
electrical engineering • MSE
engineering • PhD
engineering and computer science • MS, MSCE, MSE, PhD
human factors engineering • MSE
materials science and engineering • MSE
mechanical and materials engineering • MSE
mechanical engineering • MSE

College of Liberal Arts
Dr. Mary Ellen Mazey, Dean
Programs in:
composition and rhetoric • MA
criminal justice and social problems • MA
English • MA
history • MA
humanities • M Hum
international and comparative studies • MA
liberal arts • M Hum, M Mus, MA, MUA
literature • MA
music education • M Mus
teaching English to speakers of other languages • MA
urban administration • MUA

College of Nursing and Health
Dr. Patricia A. Martin, Dean
Programs in:
acute care nurse practitioner • MS
administration of nursing and health care systems • MS
adult health • MS
child and adolescent health • MS
community health • MS
family nurse practitioner • MS
nurse practitioner • MS
nursing and health • MS
school nurse • MS

College of Science and Mathematics
Dr. Roger K. Gilpin, Dean
Programs in:
anatomy • MS
applied mathematics • MS
applied statistics • MS
biochemistry and molecular biology • MS
biological sciences • MS
biomedical sciences • PhD
chemistry • MS
earth science education • MST
environmental geochemistry • MS
environmental geology • MS
environmental sciences • MS
geological sciences • MS
geophysics • MS
human factors and industrial/organizational psychology • MS, PhD
hydrogeology • MS
mathematics • MS
medical physics • MS
microbiology and immunology • MS
petroleum geology • MS
physics • MS
physics education • MST
physiology and biophysics • MS
science and mathematics • MS, MST, PhD

Raj Soin College of Business
Dr. Berkwood Farmer, Dean
Programs in:
accountancy • M Acc
business • M Acc, MBA, MS
business economics • MBA
e-commerce • MBA
finance • MBA
international business • MBA
logistics management • MBA
management • MBA
management information systems • MBA
marketing • MBA
operations management • MBA
project management • MBA
social and applied economics • MS

School of Medicine
Dr. Howard Part, Dean
Programs in:
aerospace medicine • MS
medicine • MD, MS, PhD
pharmacology and toxicology • MS

School of Professional Psychology
Dr. Leon D. VandeCreek, Dean
Program in:
clinical psychology • Psy D

■ XAVIER UNIVERSITY
Cincinnati, OH 45207
http://www.xu.edu/

Independent-religious, coed, comprehensive institution. *Enrollment:* 568 full-time matriculated graduate/professional students (347 women), 1,426 part-time matriculated graduate/professional students (746 women). *Graduate faculty:* 112 full-time (45 women), 96 part-time/adjunct (47 women). *Computer facilities:* 200 computers available on campus for general student use. A campuswide network can be accessed from student residence rooms and from off campus. Internet access is available. *Library facilities:* McDonald Library plus 1 other. *Graduate expenses:* Tuition: part-time $420 per credit hour. *General application contact:* John Cooper, Director of Graduate Services, 513-745-3357.

College of Arts and Sciences
Dr. Janice B. Walker, Dean
Programs in:
arts and sciences • MA
English • MA
humanities • MA
theology • MA

College of Social Sciences
Dr. Neil Heighberger, Dean
Programs in:
agency and community counseling • M Ed
art • M Ed
classics • M Ed
clinical psychology • Psy D
counseling • M Ed
criminal justice • MS
developmentally handicapped • M Ed
early childhood education of handicapped • M Ed
educational administration • M Ed
elementary education • M Ed
English • M Ed
experimental psychology • MA
gifted • M Ed

health services administration • MHSA
human resource development • M Ed
industrial/organizational psychology • MA
mathematics • M Ed
Montessori • M Ed
multicultural literature for children • M Ed
multiple handicapped • M Ed
music • M Ed
nursing administration • MSN
reading specialist • M Ed
school counseling • M Ed
secondary education • M Ed
severe behavior handicapped • M Ed
social sciences • M Ed, MA, MHSA, MS, MSN, Psy D, Certificate
special education • M Ed
specific learning disabilities • M Ed
sport administration • M Ed
theology • M Ed

Williams College of Business
Dr. Michael Webb, Dean
Programs in:
business • Exec MBA, MBA
business administration • Exec MBA, MBA

■ YOUNGSTOWN STATE UNIVERSITY

Youngstown, OH 44555-0001
http://www.ysu.edu/

State-supported, coed, comprehensive institution. CGS member. *Enrollment:* 206 full-time matriculated graduate/professional students (126 women), 962 part-time matriculated graduate/professional students (605 women). *Graduate faculty:* 246 full-time (71 women), 111 part-time/adjunct (49 women). *Computer facilities:* 1,250 computers available on campus for general student use. A campuswide network can be accessed from student residence rooms and from off campus. Internet access, online registration are available. *Library facilities:* Maag Library. *Graduate expenses:* Full-time $4,536; part-time $189 per semester hour. Tuition, state resident: full-time $6,816; part-time $284 per semester hour. Tuition, nonresident: full-time $9,216; part-time $384 per semester hour. Required fees: $78; $24 per semester. Tuition and fees vary according to reciprocity agreements. *General application contact:* Dr. Peter J. Kasvinsky, Dean of Graduate Studies, 330-742-3091.

Graduate School
Dr. Peter J. Kasvinsky, Dean of Graduate Studies

College of Arts and Sciences
Dr. Barbara Brothers, Dean
Programs in:
arts and sciences • MA, MS
biological sciences • MS
chemistry • MS
economics • MA
English • MA
history • MA
mathematics • MS

College of Education
Joseph Edwards, Interim Dean
Programs in:
counseling • MS Ed
early and middle childhood education • MS Ed
education • MS Ed, Ed D
educational administration • MS Ed
educational leadership • Ed D
gifted and talented education • MS Ed
secondary education • MS Ed
special education • MS Ed
teaching—elementary education • MS Ed
teaching—secondary reading • MS Ed

College of Fine and Performing Arts
Dr. George McCloud, Dean
Programs in:
fine and performing arts • MM
music education • MM
music history and literature • MM
music theory and composition • MM
performance • MM

College of Health and Human Services
Dr. John J. Yemma, Dean
Programs in:
criminal justice • MS
health and human services • MHHS
nursing • MSN
physical therapy • MPT

Warren P. Williamson Jr. College of Business Administration
Dr. Betty Jo Licata, Dean
Programs in:
accounting • MBA
business administration • EMBA, MBA
executive business administration • EMBA
finance • MBA
management • MBA
marketing • MBA

William Rayen College of Engineering
Dr. Charles A. Stevens, Dean
Programs in:
civil, chemical, and environmental engineering • MSE
electrical engineering • MSE
engineering • MSE
mechanical and industrial engineering • MSE

Oklahoma

■ CAMERON UNIVERSITY

Lawton, OK 73505-6377
http://www.cameron.edu/

State-supported, coed, comprehensive institution. CGS member. *Enrollment:* 159 full-time matriculated graduate/professional students (103 women), 331 part-time matriculated graduate/professional students (200 women). *Graduate faculty:* 49 full-time (24 women), 28 part-time/adjunct (12 women). *Computer facilities:* 350 computers available on campus for general student use. A campuswide network can be accessed. *Library facilities:* Cameron University Library. *Graduate expenses:* Tuition, state resident: full-time $1,506; part-time $837 per year. Tuition, nonresident: full-time $3,468; part-time $1,927 per year. *General application contact:* E. Suzanne Smeltzer, Graduate Admissions Coordinator, 580-581-2987.

School of Graduate Studies
Programs in:
behavioral sciences • MS
business • MBA
business administration • MBA
education • M Ed
education and behavioral sciences • M Ed, MAT, MS
teaching • MAT

School of Business
Programs in:
business • MBA
business administration • MBA

School of Education and Behavioral Sciences
Programs in:
behavioral sciences • MS
education • M Ed
education and behavioral sciences • M Ed, MAT, MS
teaching • MAT

■ EAST CENTRAL UNIVERSITY

Ada, OK 74820-6899
http://www.ecok.edu/

State-supported, coed, comprehensive institution. CGS member. *Computer facilities:* 40 computers available on campus for general student use. A campuswide network can be accessed. *Library facilities:* Linscheid Library. *General application contact:* Dean of the Graduate School, 405-332-8000 Ext. 709.

Graduate School

Programs in:
administration • MSHR
counseling • MSHR
criminal justice • MSHR
education • M Ed
psychology • MSPS
rehabilitation counseling • MSHR

■ NORTHEASTERN STATE UNIVERSITY

Tahlequah, OK 74464-2399
http://www.nsuok.edu/

State-supported, coed, comprehensive institution. *Enrollment:* 436 full-time matriculated graduate/professional students (280 women), 646 part-time matriculated graduate/professional students (431 women). *Graduate faculty:* 153 full-time (23 women), 10 part-time/adjunct (5 women). *Computer facilities:* 300 computers available on campus for general student use. A campuswide network can be accessed from student residence rooms and from off campus. Internet access is available. *Library facilities:* John Vaughn Library. *Graduate expenses:* Tuition, state resident: part-time $83 per credit hour. Tuition, nonresident: part-time $192 per credit hour. *General application contact:* Dr. Kenneth L. Collins, Dean of the Graduate College, 918-456-5511 Ext. 2093.

College of Optometry

Dr. George E. Foster, Dean
Program in:
optometry • OD

Graduate College

Dr. Kenneth L. Collins, Dean

College of Arts and Letters
Dr. Kathryn Robinson, Dean
Programs in:
arts and letters • MA
communication • MA

College of Behavioral and Social Sciences
Dr. Lyle Haskins, Dean
Programs in:
American studies • MA
behavioral and social sciences • M Ed, MA, MS
counseling psychology • MS
criminal justice • MS
school counseling • M Ed

College of Business and Industry
Dr. Penny Dotson, Dean
Programs in:
business administration • MBA
business and industry • MBA, MS
industrial management • MS

College of Education
Dr. Mark Clark, Dean
Programs in:
college teaching • MS
early childhood education • M Ed
education • M Ed, MS
health and human performance • MS
reading • M Ed
school administration • M Ed
special education • M Ed
special education/speech language pathology • M Ed
teaching • M Ed

■ NORTHWESTERN OKLAHOMA STATE UNIVERSITY

Alva, OK 73717-2799
http://www.nwalva.edu/

State-supported, coed, comprehensive institution. *Enrollment:* 37 full-time matriculated graduate/professional students (26 women), 153 part-time matriculated graduate/professional students (110 women). *Graduate faculty:* 50 full-time (22 women), 1 part-time/adjunct (0 women). *Computer facilities:* 100 computers available on campus for general student use. A campuswide network can be accessed. Internet access is available. *Library facilities:* J. W. Martin Library plus 1 other. *Graduate expenses:* Tuition, state resident: part-time $78 per credit hour. Tuition, nonresident: part-time $187 per credit hour. *General application contact:* Dr. Randy Smith, Dean of Graduate School, 580-327-8410.

School of Education, Psychology, and Health and Physical Education

Dr. James Bowen, Dean
Programs in:
behavioral sciences • MBS
education: non-certificate option • M Ed
elementary education • M Ed
guidance and counseling K–12 • M Ed
psychometry • M Ed
reading specialist • M Ed
secondary education • M Ed

■ OKLAHOMA CITY UNIVERSITY

Oklahoma City, OK 73106-1402
http://www.okcu.edu/

Independent-religious, coed, comprehensive institution. *Enrollment:* 1,382 full-time matriculated graduate/professional students (545 women), 597 part-time matriculated graduate/professional students (259 women). *Graduate faculty:* 127 full-time (41 women), 129 part-time/adjunct (45 women). *Computer facilities:* 264 computers available on campus for general student use. A campuswide network can be accessed from student residence rooms and from off campus. Internet access is available. *Library facilities:* Dulaney Browne Library plus 1 other. *Graduate expenses:* Tuition: full-time $9,960; part-time $415 per hour. *General application contact:* Stacy Messinger, Assistant Director of Admissions, 800-633-7242 Ext. 4.

Meinders School of Business

Dr. Bart Ward, Head
Programs in:
accounting • MSA
arts management • MBA
finance • MBA
health administration • MBA
information systems management • MBA
integrated marketing communications • MBA
international business • MBA
management • MBA
management and business sciences • MBA, MSA
marketing • MBA
public administration • MBA

Petree College of Arts and Sciences

Dr. Roberta Olson, Dean
Programs in:
art • MLA
arts and sciences • M Ed, MA, MCJA, MLA, MS
international studies • MLA
leadership management • MLA
literature • MLA
philosophy • MLA
writing • MLA

Division of Education
Dr. Sherry Sexton, Chair
Programs in:
curriculum and instruction • M Ed
early childhood education • M Ed
education • M Ed, MA
elementary education • M Ed
teaching English as a second language • MA

Division of Mathematics and Science
Dr. Molisa Derk, Program Director
Program in:
computer science • MS

Division of Social Sciences
Dr. Jody Horn, Director
Program in:
criminal justice administration • MCJA

Division of Theatre
Judith Palladino, Chairperson
Programs in:
costume design • MA
technical theatre • MA
theatre • MA
theatre for young audiences • MA

School of Law
Larry Hellman, Dean
Program in:
law • JD

School of Music
Mark Parker, Dean
Programs in:
music composition • MM
musical theatre • MM
opera performance • MM
performance • MM

School of Religion and Church Vocations
Dr. Donald Emler, Dean
Programs in:
church business management • MAR
religious education • M Rel
religious studies • MAR

■ OKLAHOMA STATE UNIVERSITY
Stillwater, OK 74078
http://www.okstate.edu/

State-supported, coed, university. CGS member. *Enrollment:* 1,791 full-time matriculated graduate/professional students (799 women), 2,212 part-time matriculated graduate/professional students (942 women). *Graduate faculty:* 941 full-time (268 women), 175 part-time/adjunct (73 women). *Computer facilities:* 2,000 computers available on campus for general student use. A campuswide network can be accessed from student residence rooms and from off campus. Internet access and online class registration are available. *Library facilities:* Edmon Low Library plus 4 others. *Graduate expenses:* Tuition, state resident: part-time $86 per credit. Tuition, nonresident: part-time $275 per credit. Required fees: $14 per semester. $21 per credit hour. One-time fee: $20 part-time. *General application contact:* Dr. Al Carlozzi, Interim Dean, 405-744-6368.

Find an in-depth description at www.petersons.com/graduate.

College of Veterinary Medicine
Dr. Joseph W. Alexander, Dean
Programs in:
veterinary biomedical sciences • MS, PhD
veterinary medicine • DVM, MS, PhD

Graduate College
Dr. Al Carlozzi, Interim Dean
Programs in:
biophotonics • MS, PhD
environmental sciences • MS, PhD
international studies • MS
natural and applied science • MS

College of Agricultural Sciences and Natural Resources
Dr. Samuel E. Curl, Dean
Programs in:
agricultural economics • M Ag, MS, PhD
agricultural education, communication and 4H • M Ag, MS, Ed D, PhD
agricultural sciences and natural resources • M Ag, M Bio E, MS, Ed D, PhD
agronomy • M Ag, MS, PhD
animal breeding • PhD
animal nutrition • PhD
animal sciences • M Ag, MS
biochemistry and molecular biology • MS, PhD
biosystems and agricultural engineering • M Bio E, MS, PhD
crop science • PhD
entomology • MS, PhD
food science • MS, PhD
forestry • M Ag, MS
horticulture and landscape architecture • M Ag, MS
plant pathology • M Ag, MS, PhD
plant science • PhD
soil science • PhD

College of Arts and Sciences
Dr. John M. Dobson, Dean
Programs in:
applied mathematics • MS
arts and sciences • MA, MM, MS, Ed D, PhD
botany • MS, PhD
chemistry • MS, PhD
clinical psychology • PhD
communications sciences and disorders • MA
computer education • Ed D
computer science • MS, PhD
corrections • MS
English • MA, PhD
experimental psychology • PhD
fire protection and safety • MS
general psychology • MS
geography • MS
geology • MS
history • MA, PhD
mass communication • MS, Ed D
mathematics • MS, Ed D, PhD
microbiology and molecular genetics • MS, PhD
music pedagogy • MM
philosophy • MA, PhD
physics • MS, PhD
political science • MA
sociology • MS, PhD
statistics • MS, PhD
theatre • MA
wildlife and fisheries ecology • MS, PhD
zoology • MS, PhD

College of Business Administration
Dr. James Lumpkin, Dean
Programs in:
accounting • MS, PhD
business administration • MBA, MS, PhD
economics and legal studies in business • MS, PhD
finance • MBA, PhD
management • MBA
management science and information systems • MBA
marketing • MBA
telecommunications management • MS

College of Education
Dr. Ann C. Candler-Lotven, Dean
Programs in:
applied behavioral studies • MS, Ed D, PhD
counseling and student personnel • MS, PhD
curriculum and educational leadership • MS, PhD
education • MS, Ed D, PhD, Ed S
educational administration • MS, Ed S
educational psychology • PhD
health • MS, Ed D
higher education • MS, Ed D
leisure sciences • MS, Ed D
physical education • MS, Ed D
physical education and leisure sciences • Ed D
technical education • MS, Ed D, Ed S
trade and industrial education • MS, Ed D, Ed S

Oklahoma State University (continued)

College of Engineering, Architecture and Technology
Dr. Karl N. Reid, Dean
Programs in:
- architectural engineering • M Arch E
- architecture • M Arch, M Arch E
- chemical engineering • M En, MS, PhD
- civil engineering • M En, MS, PhD
- electrical and computer engineering • M En, MS, PhD
- engineering, architecture and technology • M Arch, M Arch E, M Bio E, M En, M Gen E, MIE Mgmt, MS, PhD
- environmental engineering • M En, MS, PhD
- industrial engineering and management • M En, MIE Mgmt, MS, PhD
- manufacturing systems engineering • M En
- mechanical engineering • M En, MS, PhD

College of Human Environmental Sciences
Dr. Patricia Knaub, Dean
Programs in:
- design, housing and merchandising • MS, PhD
- family relations and child development • PhD
- hotel and restaurant administration • PhD
- human environmental sciences • MS, PhD
- nutritional sciences • PhD

■ ORAL ROBERTS UNIVERSITY
Tulsa, OK 74171-0001
http://www.oru.edu/

Independent-religious, coed, comprehensive institution. *Enrollment:* 287 full-time matriculated graduate/professional students (122 women), 523 part-time matriculated graduate/professional students (292 women). *Graduate faculty:* 29 full-time (5 women), 18 part-time/adjunct (4 women). *Computer facilities:* 253 computers available on campus for general student use. A campuswide network can be accessed from student residence rooms and from off campus. Internet access is available. *Library facilities:* John D. Messick Resources Center plus 1 other. *Graduate expenses:* Tuition: full-time $5,130; part-time $285 per credit. Required fees: $85 per semester. *General application contact:* 918-495-6236.

School of Business
Dr. David Dyson, Dean
Programs in:
- accounting • MBA
- finance • MBA
- human resource management • M Man
- international business • MBA
- management • MBA
- marketing • MBA
- nonprofit organization • M Man

School of Education
Dr. David Hand, Dean
Programs in:
- Christian school administration • Ed D
- Christian school administration (K-12) • MA Ed
- Christian school administration (post-secondary) • Ed D
- Christian school teaching • MA Ed
- curriculum and instruction • MA Ed
- early childhood education • MA Ed
- public school administration • MA Ed
- public school administration (K-12) • Ed D
- public school teaching • MA Ed
- teaching English as a second language • MA Ed

School of Theology and Missions
Dr. Thompson K. Mathew, Dean
Programs in:
- biblical literature • MA
- Christian counseling • MA
- Christian education • MA
- divinity • M Div
- missions • MA
- practical theology • MA
- theological/historical studies • MA
- theology • D Min

■ SOUTHEASTERN OKLAHOMA STATE UNIVERSITY
Durant, OK 74701-0609
http://www.sosu.edu/

State-supported, coed, comprehensive institution. *Enrollment:* 69 full-time matriculated graduate/professional students (43 women), 271 part-time matriculated graduate/professional students (169 women). *Graduate faculty:* 85 full-time (28 women), 2 part-time/adjunct (1 woman). *Computer facilities:* 118 computers available on campus for general student use. A campuswide network can be accessed. Internet access is available. *Library facilities:* Henry G. Bennett Memorial Library. *Graduate expenses:* Tuition, state resident: full-time $1,188; part-time $396 per semester. Tuition, nonresident: full-time $3,024; part-time $1,008 per semester. Required fees: $988; $494 per semester. *General application contact:* Teriki Hicks, Graduate Secretary, 580-745-2200.

Graduate School
Dr. Doug McMillan, Interim Dean

School of Arts and Sciences
Dr. C. W. Mangrum, Dean
Program in:
- technology • MT

School of Business
Dr. Buddy Gaster, Interim Dean
Program in:
- business • MBA, MS

School of Education
Dr. Doug McMillan, Interim Dean
Programs in:
- education • M Ed, MBS
- educational administration • M Ed
- educational instruction and leadership • M Ed
- educational technology • M Ed
- elementary education • M Ed
- guidance and counseling • MBS
- school counseling • M Ed
- secondary education • M Ed

■ SOUTHERN NAZARENE UNIVERSITY
Bethany, OK 73008
http://www.snu.edu/

Independent-religious, coed, comprehensive institution. *Computer facilities:* 55 computers available on campus for general student use. A campuswide network can be accessed from student residence rooms and from off campus. Internet access is available. *Library facilities:* R. T. Williams Learning Resources Center. *General application contact:* Dean of Graduate College, 405-491-6316.

Graduate College
Programs in:
- practical theology • M Min
- theology • MA

School of Business
Program in:
- business • MBA, MS Mgt

School of Education
Program in:
- education • MA

School of Psychology
Programs in:
- counseling psychology • MSCP
- marriage and family therapy • MA

■ SOUTHWESTERN OKLAHOMA STATE UNIVERSITY

Weatherford, OK 73096-3098
http://www.swosu.edu/

State-supported, coed, comprehensive institution. *Enrollment:* 307 full-time matriculated graduate/professional students (178 women), 296 part-time matriculated graduate/professional students (179 women). *Graduate faculty:* 131 full-time (36 women). *Computer facilities:* 270 computers available on campus for general student use. A campuswide network can be accessed from off campus. Internet access is available. *Library facilities:* Al Harris Library. *Graduate expenses:* Tuition, state resident: part-time $81 per credit hour. Required fees: $5 per credit hour. $15 per term. *General application contact:* Dr. Dan Dill, Associate Vice President for Academic Affairs and Dean of the Graduate School, 580-774-3769.

Graduate School

Dr. Dan Dill, Associate Vice President for Academic Affairs and Dean

School of Arts and Sciences
Dr. Vilas Prabhu, Dean
Programs in:
- arts and sciences • MM
- education • MM
- performance • MM

School of Business
Dr. Elizabeth Ferrell, Director
Program in:
- business • MBA

School of Education
Dr. Greg Moss, Dean
Programs in:
- agency counseling • M Ed
- art • M Ed
- early childhood education • M Ed
- education • M Ed
- educational administration • M Ed
- elementary education • M Ed
- English • M Ed
- health, physical education and recreation • M Ed
- mathematics • M Ed
- natural sciences • M Ed
- psychometry • M Ed
- school counseling • M Ed
- social sciences • M Ed
- special education • M Ed
- technology • M Ed

School of Pharmacy

Dr. David Bergman, Dean
Program in:
- pharmacy • Pharm D

■ UNIVERSITY OF CENTRAL OKLAHOMA

Edmond, OK 73034-5209
http://www.cwc.cc.wy.us/

State-supported, coed, comprehensive institution. CGS member. *Enrollment:* 328 full-time matriculated graduate/professional students (149 women), 1,428 part-time matriculated graduate/professional students (978 women). *Graduate faculty:* 325 full-time (143 women), 59 part-time/adjunct (22 women). *Computer facilities:* 250 computers available on campus for general student use. A campuswide network can be accessed from student residence rooms and from off campus. Internet access is available. *Library facilities:* Max Chambers Library. *Graduate expenses:* Tuition, state resident: full-time $1,188; part-time $66 per semester hour. Tuition, nonresident: full-time $1,962; part-time $109 per semester hour. Required fees: $297; $17 per semester hour. One-time fee: $15. *General application contact:* Dr. S. Narasinga Rao, Dean, College of Graduate Studies and Research, 405-974-3341.

College of Graduate Studies and Research

Dr. S. Narasinga Rao, Dean, College of Graduate Studies and Research
Programs in:
- arts, media, and design • MFA, MM
- design and interior design • MFA
- music education • MM
- performance • MM

College of Arts, Media, and Design
Dr. Christopher Markwood, Dean
Programs in:
- arts, media, and design • MFA, MM
- design and interior design • MFA
- music education • MM
- performance • MM

College of Business Administration
Dr. Thomas Boyt, Dean
Program in:
- business administration • MBA

College of Education
Dr. Judith Coe, Dean
Programs in:
- adult education • M Ed
- community services • M Ed
- counseling psychology • MS
- early childhood education • M Ed
- education • M Ed, MA, MS
- elementary education • M Ed
- family and child studies • MS
- family and consumer science education • MS
- general education • M Ed
- gerontology • M Ed
- guidance and counseling • M Ed
- instructional media • M Ed
- interior design • MS
- nutrition-food management • MS
- professional health occupations • M Ed
- psychology • MA
- reading • M Ed
- school administration • M Ed
- secondary education • M Ed
- special education • M Ed
- speech-language pathology • M Ed

College of Liberal Arts
Dr. T. H. Baughman, Dean
Programs in:
- composition skills • MA
- contemporary literature • MA
- creative writing • MA
- criminal justice management and administration • MA
- history • MA
- international affairs • MA
- liberal arts • MA
- museum studies • MA
- political science • MA
- social studies teaching • MA
- Southwestern studies • MA
- teaching English as a second language • MA
- traditional studies • MA
- urban affairs • MA

College of Mathematics and Science
Dr. William Caine, Dean
Programs in:
- applied mathematical sciences • MS
- biology • MS
- chemistry • MS
- industrial and applied physics • MS
- mathematics and science • MS

■ UNIVERSITY OF OKLAHOMA

Norman, OK 73019-0390
http://www.ou.edu/

State-supported, coed, university. CGS member. *Enrollment:* 2,781 full-time matriculated graduate/professional students (1,344 women), 3,308 part-time matriculated graduate/professional students (1,789 women). *Graduate faculty:* 813 full-time (209 women), 93 part-time/adjunct (28 women). *Computer facilities:* 600 computers available on campus for general student use. A campuswide network can be accessed from student residence rooms and from off campus. Internet access and online class registration are available. *Library facilities:* Bizzell Memorial Library plus 7 others. *Graduate expenses:* Full-time

University of Oklahoma (continued)
$2,064; part-time $86 per credit hour. Tuition, nonresident: full-time $6,588; part-time $275 per credit hour. Required fees: $560. *General application contact:* Patricia Lynch, Acting Director of Admissions, 405-325-2251.

Find an in-depth description at www.petersons.com/graduate.

College of Law
Dr. Andrew M. Coats, Dean
Program in:
law • JD

Graduate College
Lee William, Dean
Program in:
interdisciplinary studies • MA, MS, PhD

College of Architecture
Bob G. Fillpot, Dean
Programs in:
architecture • M Arch, MLA, MRCP, MS
construction science • MS
landscape architecture • MLA
regional and city planning • MRCP

College of Arts and Sciences
Dr. Paul B. Bell, Dean
Programs in:
advertising • MA
anthropology • MA, PhD
arts and sciences • M Nat Sci, MA, MHR, MLIS, MNS, MPA, MS, MSW, PhD, Certificate
astrophysics • MS, PhD
botany • M Nat Sci, MS, PhD
broadcasting and electronic media • MA
chemistry and biochemistry • MS, PhD
communication • MA, PhD
economics • MA, PhD
English • MA, PhD
French • MA, PhD
German • MA
health and exercise science • MS
history • MA, PhD
history of science • MA, PhD
human relations • MHR
library and information studies • MLIS, Certificate
mathematics • MA, MS, PhD
microbiology • M Nat Sci, MS, PhD
natural science • MNS
newspaper • MA
philosophy • MA, PhD
physics • MS, PhD
political science • MA, PhD
professional writing • MA
psychology • MS, PhD
public administration • MPA
public relations • MA
social work • MSW
sociology • MA, PhD
Spanish • MA, PhD
sport management • MS
zoology • M Nat Sci, MS, PhD

College of Education
Dr. Joan Karen Smith, Dean
Programs in:
adult and higher education • M Ed, PhD
community counseling • M Ed
counseling psychology • PhD
education • Certificate
educational administration, curriculum and supervision • PhD
educational administration, curriculum and supervision • M Ed, Ed D
historical, philosophical, and social foundations of education • M Ed, Ed D, PhD
instructional leadership and academic curriculum • M Ed, PhD
instructional psychology • M Ed, PhD
special education • M Ed, PhD

College of Engineering
Dr. Arthur Porter, Dean
Programs in:
aerospace engineering • MS, PhD
air • M Env Sc
chemical engineering • MS, PhD
civil engineering • MS, PhD
computer science • MS, PhD
electrical and computer engineering • MS, PhD
engineering • M Env Sc, MS, D Engr, PhD
engineering physics • MS, PhD
environmental engineering • MS
environmental science • M Env Sc, PhD
geotechnical engineering • MS
groundwater management • M Env Sc
hazardous solid waste • M Env Sc
industrial engineering • MS, PhD
mechanical engineering • MS, PhD
occupational safety and health • M Env Sc
petroleum and geological engineering • MS, PhD
process design • M Env Sc
structures • MS
transportation • MS
water quality resources • M Env Sc

College of Fine Arts
Marvin Lamb, Dean
Programs in:
art • MA, MFA
art history • MA
ceramics • MFA
choreography • MFA
drama • MA, MFA
film and video • MFA
fine arts • M Mus, M Mus Ed, MA, MFA, DMA, PhD
music • M Mus
music education • M Mus Ed, PhD
painting and drawing • MFA
performance and composition • DMA
photography • MFA
printmaking • MFA
sculpture • MFA
visual communications • MFA

College of Geosciences
Dr. John T. Snow, Dean
Programs in:
geography • MA, PhD
geology • MS, PhD
geology and geophysics • MS, PhD
geophysics • MS
geosciences • MA, MS, MS Metr, PhD
meteorology • MS Metr, PhD

College of Liberal Studies
Dr. George Henderson, Dean
Program in:
liberal studies • MLS

International Academic Programs
Dr. Gary B. Cohen, Director
Program in:
international studies • MA

Michael F. Price College of Business
Dr. Dennis Logue, Dean
Programs in:
accounting • M Acc
business administration • MBA, PhD
management information systems • MS

■ UNIVERSITY OF TULSA
Tulsa, OK 74104-3189
http://www.utulsa.edu/

Independent-religious, coed, university. CGS member. *Enrollment:* 833 full-time matriculated graduate/professional students (369 women), 451 part-time matriculated graduate/professional students (208 women). *Graduate faculty:* 217 full-time (55 women), 78 part-time/adjunct (26 women). *Computer facilities:* 718 computers available on campus for general student use. A campuswide network can be accessed from student residence rooms and from off campus. Internet access is available. *Library facilities:* McFarlin Library plus 1 other. *Graduate expenses:* Tuition: full-time $9,216; part-time $512 per credit. Required fees: $80. One-time fee: $80 part-time. Tuition and fees vary according to course load.

General application contact: Dr. Janet A. Haggerty, Dean of Research and Graduate Studies, 918-631-2336.

Find an in-depth description at www.petersons.com/graduate.

College of Law
Martin H. Belsky, Dean
Programs in:
- American Indian and indigenous law • LL M
- comparative and international law • LL M
- law • JD

Graduate School
Dr. Janet A. Haggerty, Dean of Research and Graduate Studies

College of Arts and Sciences
Dr. Thomas A. Horne, Dean
Programs in:
- anthropology • MA
- art • MA, MFA
- arts and sciences • MA, MFA, MSMSE, MTA, PhD
- clinical psychology • MA, PhD
- education • MA
- English language and literature • MA, PhD
- history • MA
- industrial/organizational psychology • MA, PhD
- math/science education • MSMSE
- speech-language pathology • MA
- teaching arts • MTA

College of Business Administration
Dr. W. Gale Sullenburger, Dean
Programs in:
- business administration • M Tax, MBA, METM, MISA, MS
- chemical engineering • METM
- computer science • METM
- corporate finance • MS
- electrical engineering • METM
- geological science • METM
- information systems and accounting • MISA
- international finance • MS
- investment and portfolio management • MS
- mathematics • METM
- mechanical engineering • METM
- petroleum engineering • METM
- risk management/financial engineering • MS
- taxation • M Tax

College of Engineering and Natural Sciences
Dr. Steve J. Bellovich, Dean
Programs in:
- biological sciences • MS, PhD
- chemical engineering • ME, MSE, PhD
- chemistry • MS
- computer science • MS, PhD
- electrical engineering • ME, MSE
- engineering and natural sciences • ME, METM, MS, MSE, PhD
- geosciences • MS, PhD
- mathematical sciences • MS
- mechanical engineering • ME, MSE, PhD
- petroleum engineering • ME, MSE, PhD

Oregon

■ CONCORDIA UNIVERSITY
Portland, OR 97211-6099
http://www.cu-portland.edu/

Independent-religious, coed, comprehensive institution. *Computer facilities:* 60 computers available on campus for general student use. A campuswide network can be accessed from student residence rooms and from off campus. Internet access is available. *Library facilities:* Concordia Library plus 1 other. *General application contact:* Director of Admissions, 503-280-8501.

College of Education
Programs in:
- curriculum and instruction (elementary) • M Ed
- educational administration • M Ed
- elementary education • MAT
- secondary education • MAT

■ EASTERN OREGON UNIVERSITY
La Grande, OR 97850-2899
http://www.eou.edu/

State-supported, coed, comprehensive institution. *Enrollment:* 66 full-time matriculated graduate/professional students (46 women), 118 part-time matriculated graduate/professional students (73 women). *Graduate faculty:* 12 full-time (6 women), 7 part-time/adjunct (3 women). *Computer facilities:* 125 computers available on campus for general student use. A campuswide network can be accessed from student residence rooms and from off campus. Internet access and online class registration are available. *Library facilities:* Pierce Library plus 1 other. *Graduate expenses:* Full-time $8,000; part-time $132 per credit hour. Required fees: $67 per year. *General application contact:* Dr. Kenneth M. Smith, Coordinator of Graduate Studies, 541-962-3772.

School of Education and Business
Dr. Michael Jaeger, Dean
Programs in:
- education and business • MTE
- elementary education • MTE
- secondary education • MTE

■ GEORGE FOX UNIVERSITY
Newberg, OR 97132-2697
http://www.georgefox.edu/

Independent-religious, coed, university. *Enrollment:* 300 full-time matriculated graduate/professional students (183 women), 627 part-time matriculated graduate/professional students (373 women). *Graduate faculty:* 51 full-time (14 women), 33 part-time/adjunct (20 women). *Computer facilities:* 1,300 computers available on campus for general student use. A campuswide network can be accessed from student residence rooms and from off campus. Internet access and online class registration are available. *Library facilities:* Murdock Learning Resource Center plus 1 other. *Graduate expenses:* Tuition: full-time $12,600. Tuition and fees vary according to class time and program. *General application contact:* Todd M. McCollum, Director of Admissions for Graduate and Professional Studies, 800-631-0921.

Find an in-depth description at www.petersons.com/graduate.

Graduate and Professional Studies
Dr. James Foster, Head
Programs in:
- business administration • MBA
- counseling • MA
- marriage and family therapy • MA
- organizational leadership • MAOL
- teacher education • M Ed, MAT, Ed D

George Fox Evangelical Seminary
Dr. Tom Johnson, Dean of George Fox Evangelical Seminary
Programs in:
- Christian education • MA
- divinity • M Div
- ministry • D Min
- theological studies • MA

George Fox University (continued)

Graduate School of Clinical Psychology
Dr. Leo Marmol, Director
Programs in:
clinical psychology • Psy D
psychology • MA

■ MARYLHURST UNIVERSITY

Marylhurst, OR 97036-0261

http://www.marylhurst.edu/

Independent-religious, coed, comprehensive institution. *Enrollment:* 43 full-time matriculated graduate/professional students (23 women), 181 part-time matriculated graduate/professional students (126 women). *Graduate faculty:* 6 full-time (4 women), 66 part-time/adjunct (35 women). *Computer facilities:* 40 computers available on campus for general student use. A campuswide network can be accessed. Internet access and online class registration are available. *Library facilities:* Shoen Library. *Graduate expenses:* Tuition: full-time $7,911. Required fees: $159. Tuition and fees vary according to course load and program. *General application contact:* Marilee King, Director, Enrollment Management, 503-699-6268 Ext. 4430.

Graduate Program in Applied Theology
Cecilia Ranger, Chair
Program in:
theology • MAAT

Graduate Program in Art Therapy
Christine Turner, Chair
Program in:
art therapy • MA

Graduate Program in Management
Burt Desmond, Head
Program in:
management • MBA

Program in Interdisciplinary Studies
Dr. Debrah B. Bokowski, Chair
Programs in:
gerontology • MA
human studies • MA
organizational communications • MA
spiritual traditions • MA

■ OREGON STATE UNIVERSITY

Corvallis, OR 97331

http://osu.orst.edu/

State-supported, coed, university. CGS member. *Enrollment:* 2,084 full-time matriculated graduate/professional students (1,018 women), 481 part-time matriculated graduate/professional students (255 women). *Graduate faculty:* 1,333 full-time (402 women), 555 part-time/adjunct (258 women). *Computer facilities:* 2,251 computers available on campus for general student use. A campuswide network can be accessed from student residence rooms and from off campus. *Library facilities:* Valley Library. *Graduate expenses:* Tuition, state resident: full-time $6,891; part-time $219 per credit. Tuition, nonresident: full-time $11,703; part-time $398 per credit. Required fees: $205 per credit. *General application contact:* Dr. Sally K. Francis, Dean of the Graduate School, Interim, 541-737-4881.

College of Veterinary Medicine
Dr. Howard Gelberg, Dean
Programs in:
comparative veterinary medicine • PhD
microbiology • MS
pathology • MS
toxicology • MS
veterinary medicine • DVM, MS, PhD

Graduate School
Dr. Sally K. Francis, Interim Dean
Programs in:
interdisciplinary studies • MAIS
plant physiology • MS, PhD

College of Agricultural Sciences
Dr. Thayne R. Dutson, Dean
Programs in:
agricultural and resource economics • M Agr, MAIS, MS, PhD
agricultural education • M Agr, MAIS, MAT, MS
agricultural sciences • M Ag, M Agr, MA, MAIS, MAT, MS, PhD
agriculture • M Agr
animal science • M Agr, MAIS, MS, PhD
crop science • M Agr, MAIS, MS, PhD
economics • MS, PhD
fisheries science • M Agr, MAIS, MS, PhD
food science and technology • M Agr, MAIS, MS, PhD
genetics • MA, MAIS, MS, PhD
horticulture • M Ag, MAIS, MS, PhD
poultry science • M Agr, MAIS, MS, PhD
rangeland resources • M Agr, MAIS, MS, PhD
soil science • M Agr, MAIS, MS, PhD
toxicology • MS, PhD
wildlife science • MAIS, MS, PhD

College of Business
Dr. Donald F. Parker, Dean
Program in:
business • MAIS, MBA, Certificate

College of Engineering
Ronald L. Adams, Dean
Programs in:
bioresource engineering • M Agr, MAIS, MS, PhD
chemical engineering • MAIS, MS, PhD
civil engineering • MAIS, MS, PhD
computer science • MA, MAIS, MS, PhD
electrical and computer engineering • MAIS, MS, PhD
engineering • M Agr, M Eng, M Oc E, MA, MAIS, MS, PhD
industrial engineering • MAIS, MS, PhD
manufacturing engineering • M Eng
materials science • MAIS, MS
mechanical engineering • MS, PhD
nuclear engineering • MS, PhD
ocean engineering • M Oc E
radiation health physics • MS, PhD

College of Forestry
Dr. Bart A. Thiegles, Associate Dean
Programs in:
economics • MS, PhD
forest engineering • MAIS, MF, MS, PhD
forest products • MAIS, MF, MS, PhD
forest resources • MAIS, MF, MS, PhD
forest science • MAIS, MF, MS, PhD
forestry • M Agr, MAIS, MF, MS, PhD
wood science and technology • MF, MS, PhD

College of Health and Human Performance
Dr. Jeffery A. McCubbin, Interim Dean
Programs in:
environmental health management • MAIS, MS
health • MS, PhD
health and human performance • MAIS, MAT, MPH, MS, PhD
health and safety administration • MAIS, MS
health education • MAIS, MAT, MS

human performance • MAIS, MS, PhD
movement studies for the disabled • MAIS, MS
physical education • MAT
public health • MPH

College of Home Economics and Education
Dr. Clara C. Pratt, Interim Dean
Programs in:
adult education • Ed M, MAIS
apparel, interiors, housing, and merchandising • MA, MAIS, MS, PhD
college student service administration • Ed M, MS
counseling • MS, PhD
education • Ed M, MAIS, MAT, MS, Ed D, PhD
elementary education • MAT
general education • Ed M, MAIS, MS, Ed D, PhD
gerontology • MAIS
home economics • MAIS, MS
home economics and education • Ed M, MA, MAIS, MAT, MS, Ed D, PhD
home economics education • MAT, MS
human development and family studies • MS, PhD
nutrition and food management • MAIS, MS, PhD
professional technical education • MAT
teaching • MAT

College of Liberal Arts
Dr. Kay F. Schaffer, Dean
Programs in:
anthropology • MAIS
applied anthropology • MA
economics • MA, MS, PhD
English • MA, MAIS
language arts education • MAT
liberal arts • MA, MAIS, MAT, MS, PhD
music education • MAT
scientific and technical communication • MA, MAIS, MS

College of Oceanic and Atmospheric Sciences
Mark R. Abbott, Dean
Programs in:
atmospheric sciences • MA, MS, PhD
geophysics • MA, MS, PhD
marine resource management • MA, MS
oceanography • MA, MS, PhD

College of Pharmacy
Dr. Wayne A. Kradjan, Dean
Program in:
pharmacy • Pharm D, MAIS, MS, PhD

College of Science
Dr. Sherman H. Bloomer, Interim Dean
Programs in:
advanced mathematics education • MAT
analytical chemistry • MS, PhD
applied statistics • MA, MS, PhD
biochemistry and biophysics • MA, MAIS, MS, PhD
biology education • MAT
biometry • MA, MS, PhD
chemistry • MA, MAIS
chemistry education • MAT
ecology • MA, MAIS, MS, PhD
entomology • M Agr, MA, MAIS, MS, PhD
environmental statistics • MA, MS, PhD
general science • MA, MS, PhD
genetics • MA, MAIS, MS, PhD
geography • MA, MAIS, MS, PhD
geology • MA, MAIS, MS, PhD
inorganic chemistry • MS, PhD
integrated science education • MAT
mathematical statistics • MA, MS, PhD
mathematics • MA, MAIS, MS, PhD
mathematics education • MA, MAT, MS, PhD
microbiology • M Agr, MA, MAIS, MS, PhD
molecular and cellular biology • MA, MAIS, MS, PhD
mycology • MA, MAIS, MS, PhD
nuclear and radiation chemistry • MS, PhD
operations research • MA, MAIS, MS
organic chemistry • MS, PhD
physical chemistry • MS, PhD
physics • MA, MS, PhD
physics education • MAT
plant pathology • MA, MAIS, MS, PhD
plant physiology • MA, MAIS, MS, PhD
science • M Agr, MA, MAIS, MAT, MS, PhD
science education • MA, MAT, MS, PhD
statistics • M Agr, MA, MS, PhD
structural botany • MA, MAIS, MS, PhD
systematics • MA, MAIS, MS, PhD
zoology • MA, MAIS, MS, PhD

■ PACIFIC UNIVERSITY

Forest Grove, OR 97116-1797

http://www.pacificu.edu/

Independent, coed, comprehensive institution. *Enrollment:* 847 full-time matriculated graduate/professional students (516 women), 145 part-time matriculated graduate/professional students (108 women). *Graduate faculty:* 76 full-time (40 women), 74 part-time/adjunct (35 women). *Computer facilities:* 150 computers available on campus for general student use. A campuswide network can be accessed from student residence rooms and from off campus. Internet access is available. *Library facilities:* Scott Memorial Library. *Graduate expenses:* Tuition: full-time $18,000. *General application contact:* Karen Dunston, Director of Admissions, 503-359-2218 Ext. 2321.

College of Optometry
Dr. Leland W. Carr, Dean
Programs in:
clinical optometry • MS
optometry • OD, M Ed, MS
visual function in learning • M Ed

School of Education
Dr. Willard Kniep, Dean
Programs in:
early childhood education • MAT
education • MAE
elementary education • MAT
high school education • MAT
middle school education • MAT

School of Occupational Therapy
Molly McEwen, Director
Program in:
occupational therapy • MOT

School of Physical Therapy
Dr. Daiva A. Banaitis, Director
Program in:
physical therapy • MSHS, MSPT

School of Physician Assistant Studies
Christine Legler, Director
Program in:
physician assistant studies • MS

School of Professional Psychology
Dr. Michel Hersen, Dean
Programs in:
clinical psychology • Psy D
counseling psychology • MA

■ PORTLAND STATE UNIVERSITY

Portland, OR 97207-0751

http://www.pdx.edu/

State-supported, coed, university. CGS member. *Enrollment:* 1,636 full-time matriculated graduate/professional students (1,049 women), 1,560 part-time matriculated graduate/professional students (888 women). *Graduate faculty:* 590 full-time (237 women), 332 part-time/adjunct (158 women). *Computer facilities:* 340 computers available on

Portland State University (continued)
campus for general student use. A campuswide network can be accessed from student residence rooms and from off campus. Internet access and online class registration are available. *Library facilities:* Branford P. Millar Library. *Graduate expenses:* Tuition, state resident: full-time $5,679; part-time $211 per credit. Required fees: $840; $18 per credit. One-time fee: $23 part-time. *General application contact:* Agnes A. Hoffman, Director of Admissions and Records, 503-725-3511.

Graduate Studies
William Feyerherm, Vice Provost for Research and Dean
Programs in:
- systems science/anthropology • PhD
- systems science/business administration • PhD
- systems science/civil engineering • PhD
- systems science/economics • PhD
- systems science/engineering management • PhD
- systems science/general • PhD
- systems science/mathematical sciences • PhD
- systems science/mechanical engineering • PhD
- systems science/psychology • PhD
- systems science/sociology • PhD

College of Engineering and Applied Science
Dr. Robert D. Dryden, Dean
Programs in:
- civil engineering • MS, PhD
- computer science • MS
- electrical and computer engineering • MS, PhD
- engineering and applied science • M Eng, ME, MS, PhD
- engineering and technology management • M Eng, MS, PhD
- manufacturing engineering • ME
- mechanical engineering • MS, PhD

College of Liberal Arts and Sciences
Dr. Marvin Kaiser, Dean
Programs in:
- anthropology • MA, PhD
- applied economics • MA, MS
- biology • MA, MS, PhD
- chemistry • MA, MS, PhD
- economics • PhD
- English • MA, MAT
- environmental management • MEM
- environmental sciences/biology • PhD
- environmental sciences/chemistry • PhD
- environmental sciences/civil engineering • PhD
- environmental sciences/economics • PhD
- environmental sciences/geography • PhD
- environmental sciences/geology • PhD
- environmental sciences/physics • PhD
- environmental studies • MS
- foreign literature and language • MA
- French • MA
- general arts and letters education • MAT, MST
- general economics • MA, MS
- general science education • MAT, MST
- general social science education • MAT, MST
- general speech communication • MA, MS
- geography • MA, MS, PhD
- geology • MA, MS, PhD
- German • MA
- history • MA
- liberal arts and sciences • MA, MAT, MEM, MS, MST, PhD
- mathematical sciences • MA, MAT, MS, MST, PhD
- mathematics education • PhD
- physics • MA, MS, PhD
- psychology • MA, MS, PhD
- science/geology • MAT, MST
- sociology • MA, MS, PhD
- Spanish • MA
- speech and hearing sciences • MA, MS
- teaching English to speakers of other languages • MA

College of Urban and Public Affairs
Dr. Nohad A. Toulan, Dean
Programs in:
- administration of justice • MS, PhD
- gerontology • Certificate
- government • MA, MAT, MPA, MPH, MS, MST, PhD
- health administration • MPA, MPH
- health administration and policy • MPH
- health education • MA, MS
- health education and health promotion • MPH
- political science • MA, MAT, MS, MST, PhD
- public administration • MPA
- public administration and policy • PhD
- urban and public affairs • MA, MAT, MPA, MPH, MS, MST, MURP, MUS, PhD, Certificate
- urban and regional planning • MURP, PhD
- urban studies • MUS, PhD
- urban studies and planning • MURP, MUS, PhD, Certificate
- urban studies: regional science • PhD

Graduate School of Social Work
Dr. James Ward, Dean
Programs in:
- social work • MSW
- social work and social research • PhD

School of Business Administration
Dr. Scott Dawson, Interim Dean
Programs in:
- business administration • MBA, MIM, MSFA, PhD
- financial analysis • MSFA
- international management • MIM

School of Education
Dr. Phyllis Edmundson, Dean
Programs in:
- counselor education • MA, MS
- early childhood education • MA, MS
- education • M Ed, MA, MS
- educational administration • MA, MS
- educational administration and leadership • MA, MS, Ed D
- educational leadership/educational administration • Ed D
- educational leadership/postsecondary adult and continuing education • Ed D
- educational leadership: curriculum and instruction • Ed D
- educational media/school librarianship • MA, MS
- elementary education • M Ed, MAT, MST
- postsecondary education • Ed D
- reading • MA, MS
- secondary education • M Ed, MAT, MST
- special education • MA, MS

School of Fine and Performing Arts
Dr. Robert Sylvester, Dean
Programs in:
- ceramics • MFA
- conducting • MM
- fine and performing arts • MA, MAT, MFA, MM, MST
- music education • MAT, MST
- painting • MFA
- performance • MM
- sculpture • MFA
- theater arts • MA

■ SOUTHERN OREGON UNIVERSITY

Ashland, OR 97520
http://www.sou.edu/

State-supported, coed, comprehensive institution. *Computer facilities:* 400 computers available on campus for general student use. A campuswide network can be accessed. *Library facilities:* Southern Oregon University Library. *General application contact:* Director of Admissions and Records, 541-552-6411.

Graduate Office

School of Arts and Letters
Programs in:
- arts and letters • MA, MS
- English • MA, MS
- music • MA, MS

School of Business
Program in:
- business • MA Ed, MIM, MS Ed

School of Sciences
Programs in:
- environmental education • MA, MS
- mathematics/computer science • MA, MS
- science • MA, MS

School of Social Science, Health and Physical Education
Programs in:
- applied psychology • MAP
- elementary education • MA Ed, MS Ed
- secondary education • MA Ed, MS Ed
- social science • MA, MS
- social science, health and physical education • MA, MA Ed, MAP, MAT, MS, MS Ed
- teaching • MAT

■ UNIVERSITY OF OREGON

Eugene, OR 97403

http://www.uoregon.edu/

State-supported, coed, university. CGS member. *Computer facilities:* 1,250 computers available on campus for general student use. A campuswide network can be accessed from student residence rooms and from off campus. Internet access and online class registration are available. *Library facilities:* Knight Library plus 5 others.

Graduate School
Program in:
- applied information management • MS

Charles H. Lundquist College of Business
Programs in:
- accounting • M Actg, PhD
- business • M Actg, MA, MBA, MHRIR, MS, PhD
- decision sciences • MA, MS, PhD
- finance • MA, MS, PhD
- human resources and industrial relations • MHRIR
- management • MA, MS, PhD
- management: general business • MBA
- marketing • MA, MS, PhD

College of Arts and Sciences
Programs in:
- anthropology • MA, MS, PhD
- arts and sciences • MA, MFA, MS, PhD
- Asian studies • MA
- biochemistry • MA, MS, PhD
- chemistry • MA, MS, PhD
- Chinese • MA, PhD
- classical civilization • MA
- classics • MA
- clinical psychology • PhD
- cognitive psychology • MA, MS, PhD
- comparative literature • MA, PhD
- computer and information science • MA, MS, PhD
- creative writing • MFA
- developmental psychology • MA, MS, PhD
- ecology and evolution • MA, MS, PhD
- economics • MA, MS, PhD
- English • MA, PhD
- environmental studies • MA, MS
- exercise and movement science • MS, PhD
- French • MA
- geography • MA, MS, PhD
- geological sciences • MA, MS, PhD
- Germanic languages and literatures • MA, PhD
- Greek • MA
- history • MA, PhD
- independent study: folklore • MA, MS
- international studies • MA
- Italian • MA
- Japanese • MA, PhD
- Latin • MA
- linguistics • MA, PhD
- marine biology • MA, MS, PhD
- mathematics • MA, MS, PhD
- molecular, cellular and genetic biology • PhD
- neuroscience and development • PhD
- philosophy • MA, PhD
- physics • MA, MS, PhD
- physiological psychology • MA, MS, PhD
- political science • MA, MS, PhD
- psychology • MA, MS, PhD
- Romance languages • MA, PhD
- Russian and East European Studies • MA
- social/personality psychology • MA, MS, PhD
- sociology • MA, MS, PhD
- Spanish • MA
- theater arts • MA, MFA, MS, PhD

College of Education
Programs in:
- communication disorders and sciences • MA, MS, PhD
- computer and education • PhD
- counseling psychology • M Ed, MA, MS, D Ed, PhD
- developmental disabilities • M Ed, MA, MS, D Ed, PhD
- early intervention • M Ed, MA, MS, PhD
- education • M Ed, MA, MS, D Ed, PhD
- educational administration • MS, D Ed
- educational policy and foundations • MS
- educational policy and management • M Ed, MA, MS, D Ed, PhD
- exceptional learner • M Ed, MA, MS, D Ed, PhD
- foundations and research • PhD
- higher education • MS
- management and leadership • PhD
- marriage and family therapy • MA
- organization and governance • PhD
- school psychology • M Ed, MA, MS, PhD
- special education • M Ed, MA, MS, D Ed, PhD

School of Architecture and Allied Arts
Programs in:
- architecture • M Arch
- architecture and allied arts • M Arch, MA, MCRP, MFA, MI Arch, MLA, MS, PhD
- art history • MA, PhD
- arts management • MA, MS
- community and regional planning • MCRP
- fine and applied arts • MFA
- historic preservation • MS
- interior architecture • MI Arch
- landscape architecture • MLA
- public affairs • MA, MS

School of Journalism and Communication
Program in:
- journalism • MA, MS, PhD

School of Music
Programs in:
- composition • M Mus, DMA, PhD
- conducting • M Mus
- dance • MA, MS
- jazz studies • M Mus
- music • MA
- music education • M Mus, DMA, PhD
- music history • PhD
- music theory • PhD
- performance • M Mus, DMA
- piano pedagogy • M Mus

School of Law
Rennard Strickland, Dean
Program in:
- law • JD

■ UNIVERSITY OF PORTLAND

Portland, OR 97203-5798

http://www.up.edu/

Independent-religious, coed, comprehensive institution. *Enrollment:* 114 full-time matriculated graduate/professional students (69 women), 248 part-time matriculated graduate/professional students (156 women). *Graduate faculty:* 84 full-time (26 women), 11 part-time/adjunct (5 women). *Computer facilities:* 200 computers available on campus for general student use. A campuswide network can be accessed from student residence rooms and from off campus. Internet access is available. *Library facilities:* Wilson M. Clark Library plus 1 other. *Graduate expenses:* Tuition: part-time $600 per semester hour. Required fees: $25 per semester hour. *General application contact:* Dr. Patricia L. Chadwick, Assistant to the Academic Vice President and Dean of the Graduate School, 503-943-7107.

Graduate School

Dr. Patricia L. Chadwick, Assistant to the Academic Vice President and Dean of the Graduate School

College of Arts and Sciences
Dr. Marlene Moore, Dean
Programs in:
- arts and sciences • MA, MFA, MS
- communication studies • MA
- drama • MFA
- management communication • MS
- music • MA
- pastoral ministry • MA

Dr. Robert B. Pamplin, Jr. School of Business
Program in:
- business • MBA

Multnomah School of Engineering
Dr. Zia Yamayee, Dean
Program in:
- engineering • MSCE, MSEE, MSME

School of Education
Dr. Maria Ciriello, OP, Dean
Programs in:
- early childhood education • M Ed, MA, MAT
- education • M Ed, MA, MAT
- religious education • M Ed, MA
- secondary education • M Ed, MA, MAT
- special education • M Ed, MA

School of Nursing
Dr. Terry Misener, Dean
Programs in:
- family nurse practitioner • Post Master's Certificate
- leadership in health care systems • Post Master's Certificate
- nursing • MS

■ WESTERN OREGON UNIVERSITY

Monmouth, OR 97361-1394

http://www.wou.edu/

State-supported, coed, comprehensive institution. *Enrollment:* 127 full-time matriculated graduate/professional students (72 women), 206 part-time matriculated graduate/professional students (150 women). *Graduate faculty:* 191 full-time (87 women), 25 part-time/adjunct (13 women). *Computer facilities:* 277 computers available on campus for general student use. A campuswide network can be accessed from student residence rooms and from off campus. Internet access is available. *Library facilities:* Wayne Lynn Hamersly Library. *Graduate expenses:* Tuition, state resident: full-time $4,509; part-time $167 per credit. Tuition, nonresident: full-time $8,550. Required fees: $56 per credit. *General application contact:* Alison Marshall, Director of Admissions, 503-838-8211.

Graduate Programs

Dr. Joseph W. Sendelbaugh, Director of Graduate Studies

College of Education
Dr. Meredith Brodsky, Dean
Programs in:
- bilingual education • MS Ed
- deaf education • MS Ed
- early childhood education • MS Ed
- education • MAT, MS Ed
- health • MS Ed
- humanities • MAT, MS Ed
- information technology • MS Ed
- initial licensure • MAT
- learning disabilities • MS Ed
- mathematics • MAT, MS Ed
- multihandicapped education • MS Ed
- rehabilitation counseling • MS Ed
- science • MAT, MS Ed
- social science • MAT, MS Ed
- teacher education • MAT, MS Ed

College of Liberal Arts and Sciences
Dr. James Chadney, Dean
Programs in:
- correctional administration • MA, MS
- liberal arts and sciences • MA, MS

Pennsylvania

■ ARCADIA UNIVERSITY

Glenside, PA 19038-3295

http://www.arcadia.edu

Independent-religious, coed, comprehensive institution. *Enrollment:* 275 full-time matriculated graduate/professional students (194 women), 839 part-time matriculated graduate/professional students (669 women). *Graduate faculty:* 71 full-time, 135 part-time/adjunct. *Computer facilities:* 110 computers available on campus for general student use. A campuswide network can be accessed from student residence rooms and from off campus. Internet access is available. *Library facilities:* Eugenia Fuller Atwood Library. *Graduate expenses:* Tuition: part-time $405 per credit. *General application contact:* 215-572-2910.

Find an in-depth description at www.petersons.com/graduate.

Graduate Studies

Maureen Guim, Interim Dean
Programs in:
- allied health • MA Ed, MSHE
- art education • M Ed, MA Ed
- biology education • MA Ed
- chemistry education • MA Ed
- child development • CAS
- computer education • M Ed, CAS
- computer education 7–12 • MA Ed
- counseling • MAC
- early childhood education • M Ed, CAS
- educational leadership • M Ed, CAS
- educational psychology • CAS
- elementary education • M Ed, CAS
- English • MAE
- English education • MA Ed
- environmental education • MA Ed, CAS
- fine arts, theater, and music • MAH
- genetic counseling • MSGC
- history education • MA Ed
- history, philosophy, and religion • MAH
- international peace and conflict management • MAIPCR
- language arts • M Ed, CAS
- literature and language • MAH
- mathematics education • M Ed, MA Ed, CAS
- music education • MA Ed
- physical therapy • DPT
- physician assistant studies • MSPAS
- public health • MSPH
- pupil personnel services • CAS
- reading • M Ed, CAS

school library science • M Ed
science education • M Ed, CAS
secondary education • M Ed, CAS
special education • M Ed, CAS
written communication • MA Ed

■ BLOOMSBURG UNIVERSITY OF PENNSYLVANIA

Bloomsburg, PA 17815-1905
http://www.bloomu.edu/

State-supported, coed, comprehensive institution. CGS member. *Enrollment:* 210 full-time matriculated graduate/professional students (154 women), 351 part-time matriculated graduate/professional students (244 women). *Graduate faculty:* 203 full-time (75 women), 1 part-time/adjunct (0 women). *Computer facilities:* 700 computers available on campus for general student use. A campuswide network can be accessed from student residence rooms and from off campus. Internet access and online class registration are available. *Library facilities:* Andruss Library. *Graduate expenses:* Tuition, state resident: full-time $4,138; part-time $230 per credit hour. Tuition, nonresident: full-time $7,008; part-time $778 per credit hour. *General application contact:* Carol Arnold, Secretary, 570-389-4015.

School of Graduate Studies
Dr. James F. Matta, Assistant Vice President and Dean of Graduate Studies and Research, Interim

College of Business
Dr. David Long, Dean
Programs in:
accounting • MS
business • M Ed, MBA, MS
business administration • MBA
business education • M Ed

College of Liberal Arts
Dr. Hsien-Tung Liu, Dean
Programs in:
art history • MA
arts and sciences • M Ed, MA, MS
biology • MS
biology education • M Ed
exercise science and adult fitness • MS
instructional technology • MS
studio art • MA

College of Professional Studies
Dr. Ann L. Lee, Dean
Programs in:
audiology • MS
curriculum and instruction • M Ed
early childhood education • MS
education • M Ed, MS
education of deaf/hard of hearing • MS
elementary education • M Ed
health sciences • MS, MSN
nursing • MSN
professional studies • M Ed, MS, MSN
reading • M Ed
special education • MS
speech language pathology • MS

■ CABRINI COLLEGE

Radnor, PA 19087-3698
http://www.cabrini.edu/

Independent-religious, coed, comprehensive institution. *Enrollment:* 47 full-time matriculated graduate/professional students (29 women), 358 part-time matriculated graduate/professional students (295 women). *Graduate faculty:* 2 full-time (1 woman), 27 part-time/adjunct (17 women). *Computer facilities:* 195 computers available on campus for general student use. A campuswide network can be accessed from student residence rooms. Internet access is available. *Library facilities:* Holy Spirit Library. *Graduate expenses:* Tuition: part-time $375 per credit. Required fees: $45 per semester. *General application contact:* Charles Spencer, 610-902-8552.

Graduate Education Programs
Dr. Dawn Middleton, Chairperson
Program in:
education • M Ed

■ CALIFORNIA UNIVERSITY OF PENNSYLVANIA

California, PA 15419-1394
http://www.cup.edu/

State-supported, coed, comprehensive institution. CGS member. *Enrollment:* 326 full-time matriculated graduate/professional students (205 women), 569 part-time matriculated graduate/professional students (379 women). *Graduate faculty:* 10 full-time (3 women), 93 part-time/adjunct (22 women). *Computer facilities:* 720 computers available on campus for general student use. A campuswide network can be accessed from student residence rooms and from off campus. Internet access is available. *Library facilities:* Manderino Library. *Graduate expenses:* Tuition, state resident: full-time $2,069; part-time $230 per semester. Tuition, nonresident: full-time $3,504; part-time $389 per semester. *General application contact:* Dr. Thomas G. Kinsey, Dean of Graduate Studies, 724-938-4187.

Find an in-depth description at www.petersons.com/graduate.

School of Graduate Studies
Dr. Thomas G. Kinsey, Dean

School of Education
Geraldine Jones, Acting Dean
Programs in:
athletic training • MS
communication disorders • MS
education • M Ed, MAT, MS, MSW
educational administration • M Ed
educational studies • MAT
elementary education • M Ed
guidance and counseling • M Ed, MS
mentally and/or physically handicapped education • M Ed
reading specialist • M Ed
reading specialist and reading supervision • M Ed
school psychology • MS
social work • MSW
technology education • M Ed

School of Liberal Arts
Dr. Richard Helldobler, Acting Dean
Programs in:
communication • MA
earth science • MS
geography • M Ed, MA
liberal arts • M Ed, MA, MS
social science • MA

School of Science and Technology
Dr. Leonard Colelli, Dean
Programs in:
biology • M Ed, MS
business administration • MS
computer science • M Ed
mathematics • M Ed
science and technology • M Ed, MS

■ CARLOW COLLEGE

Pittsburgh, PA 15213-3165
http://www.carlow.edu/

Independent-religious, coed, primarily women, comprehensive institution. *Enrollment:* 2 full-time matriculated graduate/professional students (both women), 278 part-time matriculated graduate/professional students (256 women). *Graduate faculty:* 14 full-time (12 women), 44 part-time/adjunct (33 women). *Computer facilities:* 660 computers available on campus for general student use. A campuswide network can be accessed from student residence rooms and from off campus. Internet access and online class registration, applications software, e-mail are available. *Library facilities:* Grace Library. *Graduate*

Carlow College (continued)
expenses: Tuition: part-time $427 per credit. Required fees: $25 per credit. *General application contact:* Maggie Golofski, Secretary, Graduate Studies, 412-578-8764.

Division of Education
Dr. Roberta Schomburg, Chair
Programs in:
- art education • M Ed
- early childhood education • M Ed
- early childhood supervision • M Ed
- educational leadership • M Ed

Division of Management
Dr. Mary Rothenberger, Chair
Program in:
- management and technology • MS

Division of Nursing
Dr. Mary Lou Bost, Acting Chair
Programs in:
- case management/leadership • Certificate
- home health advanced practice nursing • MSN, Certificate
- nursing case management/leadership • MSN
- nursing leadership • MSN

Division of Professional Leadership
Dr. M. Sandie Turner, Director
Programs in:
- health service education • MS
- nonprofit management • MS
- training and development • MS

■ CARNEGIE MELLON UNIVERSITY
Pittsburgh, PA 15213-3891
http://www.cmu.edu/

Independent, coed, university. CGS member. *Enrollment:* 2,507 full-time matriculated graduate/professional students (739 women), 783 part-time matriculated graduate/professional students (263 women). *Graduate faculty:* 1,078 full-time (264 women), 198 part-time/adjunct (90 women). *Computer facilities:* 450 computers available on campus for general student use. A campuswide network can be accessed from student residence rooms and from off campus. Internet access and online class registration are available. *Library facilities:* Hunt Library plus 2 others. *Graduate expenses:* Tuition: full-time $23,300; part-time $324 per unit. Required fees: $192.

Carnegie Institute of Technology
Dr. John L. Anderson, Dean
Programs in:
- bioengineering • MS, PhD
- biomedical engineering • MS, PhD
- chemical engineering • M Ch E, MS, PhD
- civil engineering • MS, PhD
- civil engineering and industrial management • MS
- civil engineering and robotics • PhD
- civil engineering/bioengineering • PhD
- civil engineering/engineering and public policy • MS, PhD
- colloids, polymers and surfaces • MS
- electrical and computer engineering • MS, PhD
- engineering and public policy • MS, PhD
- materials science and engineering • ME, MS, PhD
- mechanical engineering • ME, MS, PhD
- technology • M Ch E, ME, MS, PhD

Information Networking Institute
Dr. Pradeep K. Khosla, Head, Electrical and Computer Engineering
Program in:
- information networking • MS

College of Fine Arts
Dr. Martin Prekop, Dean
Programs in:
- art • MFA
- fine arts • M Des, M Sc, MAM, MET, MFA, MM, MSA, PhD

School of Architecture
Vivian Loftness, Head
Programs in:
- architecture • MSA
- building performance and diagnostics • M Sc, PhD
- computational design • M Sc, PhD

School of Design
Richard Buchanan, Head
Programs in:
- communication planning and design • M Des
- design theory • PhD
- interaction design • M Des, PhD
- new product development • PhD
- typography and information design • PhD

School of Drama
Peter Frisch, Head
Programs in:
- design • MFA
- directing • MFA
- dramatic writing • MFA
- performance technology and management • MFA

School of Music
Dr. Kenneth A. Keeling, Head
Programs in:
- composition • MM
- conducting • MM
- music education • MM
- performance • MM

College of Humanities and Social Sciences
Dr. John P. Lehoczky, Dean
Programs in:
- behavioral decision theory • PhD
- business • MAPW
- cognitive neuropsychology • PhD
- cognitive psychology • PhD
- communication planning and design • M Des
- computer-assisted language learning • MCALL
- design • MAPW
- developmental psychology • PhD
- English • MA
- history • MA, MS
- history and policy • MA, PhD
- humanities and social sciences • M Des, MA, MAPW, MCALL, MS, PhD
- literary and cultural theory • MA, PhD
- logic and computation • MS
- marketing • MAPW
- mathematical finance • PhD
- organization science • PhD
- philosophy • MA, MS
- policy • MAPW
- professional writing • MAPW
- pure and applied logic • PhD
- research • MAPW
- rhetoric • MA, PhD
- rhetorical theory • MAPW
- science writing • MAPW
- second language acquisition • PhD
- social and cultural history • PhD
- social and decision science • PhD
- social/personality psychology • PhD
- statistics • MS, PhD
- technical • MAPW

Center for Innovation in Learning
Dr. John R. Hayes, Director
Program in:
- instructional science • PhD

Graduate School of Industrial Administration
Dr. Douglas M. Dunn, Dean
Programs in:
- accounting • PhD
- algorithms, combinatorics, and optimization • MS, PhD
- business management and software engineering • MBMSE
- civil engineering and industrial management • MS
- computational finance • MSCF
- economics • MS, PhD

electronic commerce • MS
environmental engineering and management • MEEM
finance • PhD
financial economics • PhD
industrial administration • MBA, PhD
information systems • PhD
management of manufacturing and automation • MOM, PhD
manufacturing • MOM
marketing • PhD
mathematical finance • PhD
operations research • PhD
organizational behavior and theory • PhD
political economy • PhD
production and operations management • PhD
public policy and management • MS, MSED
software engineering and business management • MS

H. John Heinz III School of Public Policy and Management
Dr. Jeffrey Hunker, Dean
Programs in:
arts management • MAM
health care policy and management • MSHCPM
information systems management • MISM
medical management • MMM
public management • MPM
public policy analysis • PhD
public policy and management • MAM, MIS, MISM, MMM, MPM, MS, MSED, MSHCPM, PhD
sustainable economic development • MIS

Mellon College of Science
Dr. Richard D. McCullough, Dean
Programs in:
algorithms, combinatorics, and optimization • PhD
applied physics • PhD
biochemistry • PhD
biophysics • PhD
cell biology • PhD
chemical instrumentation • MS
chemistry • MS, PhD
colloids, polymers and surfaces • MS
computational biology • MS
developmental biology • PhD
genetics • PhD
mathematical finance • PhD
mathematical sciences • MS, DA, PhD
molecular biology • PhD
physics • MS, PhD
polymer science • MS
pure and applied logic • PhD
science • MS, DA, PhD

School of Computer Science
James Hiram Morris, Dean
Programs in:
algorithms, combinatorics, and optimization • PhD
computer science • PhD
entertainment technology • MET
human-computer interaction • MHCI, PhD
knowledge discovery and data mining • MS
pure and applied logic • PhD
software engineering • MSE, PhD

Language Technologies Institute
Jaime G. Carbonell, Director
Program in:
language technologies • MLT, PhD

Robotics Institute
Charles Thorpe, Director
Program in:
robotics • MS, PhD

■ CHESTNUT HILL COLLEGE
Philadelphia, PA 19118-2693
http://www.chc.edu/

Independent-religious, women only, comprehensive institution. *Enrollment:* 90 full-time matriculated graduate/professional students (73 women), 469 part-time matriculated graduate/professional students (383 women). *Graduate faculty:* 19 full-time (14 women), 63 part-time/adjunct (35 women). *Computer facilities:* 185 computers available on campus for general student use. Internet access, e-mail are available. *Library facilities:* Logue Library. *Graduate expenses:* Tuition: part-time $370 per credit. Required fees: $25 per semester. *General application contact:* JoAnn McVeigh, Administrative Assistant, 215-248-7161.

Find an in-depth description at www.petersons.com/graduate.

Graduate Division
Sr. Mary Anne Celenza, SSJ, Dean of the College for Women and Graduate Division
Programs in:
applied technology • MS
clinical psychology • MA, MS, Psy D
counseling psychology and human services • MA, MS
early childhood education • M Ed
educational leadership • M Ed
elementary education • M Ed
holistic spirituality • MA
holistic spirituality and spiritual direction • MA

■ CHEYNEY UNIVERSITY OF PENNSYLVANIA
Cheyney, PA 19319
http://www.cheyney.edu/

State-supported, coed, comprehensive institution. *Enrollment:* 47 full-time matriculated graduate/professional students (36 women), 317 part-time matriculated graduate/professional students (216 women). *Graduate faculty:* 4 full-time (2 women), 5 part-time/adjunct (1 woman). *Computer facilities:* 150 computers available on campus for general student use. A campuswide network can be accessed from student residence rooms and from off campus. Internet access and online class registration, various software packages are available. *Library facilities:* Leslie Pickney Hill Library plus 1 other. *Graduate expenses:* Tuition, state resident: full-time $4,138; part-time $230 per credit. Tuition, nonresident: full-time $7,008; part-time $389 per credit. Required fees: $380; $191 per year. *General application contact:* Dr. Wesley Pugh, Dean of Graduate Studies, 610-399-2400.

School of Education
Dr. Wesley Pugh, Dean of Graduate Studies
Programs in:
adult and continuing education • MS
early childhood education • Certificate
education • M Ed, MS, Certificate
educational administration and supervision • M Ed, Certificate
elementary education • M Ed
special education • M Ed, MS

■ CLARION UNIVERSITY OF PENNSYLVANIA
Clarion, PA 16214
http://www.clarion.edu/

State-supported, coed, comprehensive institution. CGS member. *Enrollment:* 177 full-time matriculated graduate/professional students (135 women), 204 part-time matriculated graduate/professional students (172 women). *Graduate faculty:* 124 full-time (50 women). *Computer facilities:* 400 computers available on campus for general student use. A campuswide network can be accessed from student residence rooms and from off campus. Internet access and online class registration are available. *Library facilities:* Carlson Library. *Graduate expenses:* Tuition, state resident: full-time $4,138; part-time $230

Clarion University of Pennsylvania (continued)
per credit. Tuition, nonresident: full-time $7,008; part-time $389 per credit. Required fees: $950; $83 per credit. *General application contact:* Dr. Brenda Dédé, Assistant Vice President for Academic Affairs, 814-393-2337.

Find an in-depth description at www.petersons.com/graduate.

College of Graduate Studies
Dr. Brenda Dédé, Assistant Vice President for Academic Affairs

College of Arts and Sciences
Dr. Stan Green, Dean
Programs in:
arts and sciences • M Ed, MA, MS
biology • MS
communication • MS
English • MA
mathematics • M Ed

College of Business Administration
Dr. James Pesek, Dean
Program in:
business administration • MBA

College of Education and Human Services
Dr. Gail Grejda, Graduate Coordinator
Programs in:
communication sciences and disorders • MS
education and human services • M Ed, MS, MSLS, CAS
elementary education • M Ed
library science • MSLS, CAS
reading • M Ed
science education • M Ed
special education • MS

School of Nursing
Dr. Mary Kavoosi, Director
Program in:
nursing • MSN

■ COLLEGE MISERICORDIA
Dallas, PA 18612-1098
http://www.miseri.edu/

Independent-religious, coed, comprehensive institution. *Enrollment:* 432 full-time matriculated graduate/professional students (356 women), 253 part-time matriculated graduate/professional students (198 women). *Graduate faculty:* 35 full-time (23 women), 30 part-time/adjunct (13 women). *Computer facilities:* 50 computers available on campus for general student use. A campuswide network can be accessed from student residence rooms and from off campus. Internet access is available. *Library facilities:* Mary Kintz Bevevina Library. *Graduate expenses:* Tuition: part-time $450 per credit. Part-time tuition and fees vary according to program. *General application contact:* Larree Brown, Coordinator of Part-Time Undergraduate and Graduate Programs, 570-674-6451.

Division of Health Sciences
Dr. Catherine Perry Wilkinson, Chair
Programs in:
health sciences • MSN, MSOT, MSPT
nursing • MSN
occupational therapy • MSOT
physical therapy • MSPT

Division of Professional Studies
Tom O'Neill, Director of Adult Education
Programs in:
education/curriculum • MS
organizational management • MS
professional studies • MS

■ DESALES UNIVERSITY
Center Valley, PA 18034-9568
http://www.desales.edu

Independent-religious, coed, comprehensive institution. *Computer facilities:* 270 computers available on campus for general student use. A campuswide network can be accessed from student residence rooms and from off campus. Internet access is available. *Library facilities:* Trexler Library. *General application contact:* Vice President for Academic Affairs and Director of Graduate Studies, 610-282-1100 Ext. 1342.

Graduate Division
Programs in:
biology • M Ed
business administration • MBA
chemistry • M Ed
clinical nurse specialist in adult and community health • MSN
computer education • M Ed
computer science • M Ed
computers in education for elementary teachers • M Ed
English • M Ed
family nurse practitioner • MSN
information systems • MSIS
mathematics • M Ed
nursing administration • MSN
physician assistant studies • MSPAS

■ DREXEL UNIVERSITY
Philadelphia, PA 19104-2875
http://www.drexel.edu/

Independent, coed, university. CGS member. *Enrollment:* 638 full-time matriculated graduate/professional students (294 women), 1,846 part-time matriculated graduate/professional students (736 women). *Graduate faculty:* 485 full-time (133 women), 426 part-time/adjunct (147 women). *Computer facilities:* 6,500 computers available on campus for general student use. A campuswide network can be accessed from student residence rooms and from off campus. Internet access and online class registration, campuswide wireless network are available. *Library facilities:* W. W. Hagerty Library. *Graduate expenses:* Tuition: part-time $534 per credit. Required fees: $75 per term. *General application contact:* Director of Graduate Admissions, 215-895-6700.

Find an in-depth description at www.petersons.com/graduate.

Graduate School
Dr. Richard Haracz, Associate Provost for Research and Graduate Studies

College of Arts and Sciences
Dr. Richard Rosen, Interim Dean
Programs in:
arts and sciences • MS, PhD
biological science • MS, PhD
chemistry • MS, PhD
clinical neuropsychology • MS, PhD
computer science • MS
food science • MS
mathematics • MS, PhD
nutrition and food sciences • MS, PhD
nutrition science • PhD
physics and atmospheric science • MS, PhD
science of instruction • MS
software engineering • MS
technical and science communication • MS

College of Business and Administration
Dr. Tom Hiudelzag, Associate Dean
Programs in:
accounting • MS
business administration • MBA, PhD, APC
business and administration • MBA, MS, PhD, APC
decision sciences • MS
finance • MS
marketing • MS
quantitative methods • MS
taxation • MS

College of Engineering
Dr. Selcuk Güçedil;eri, Dean
Programs in:
biochemical engineering • MS
chemical engineering • MS, PhD
civil engineering • MS, PhD

coputer engineering • MS
electrical and computer engineering • PhD
electrical engineering • MSEE
engineering • MS, MSEE, PhD
engineering geology • MS
engineering management • MS, PhD
manufacturing engineering • MS, PhD
materials engineering • MS, PhD
mechanical engineering and mechanics • MS, PhD
telecommunications engineering • MSEE

College of Information Science and Technology
Dr. Tom Childers, Associate Dean
Programs in:
information studies • PhD, CAS
information systems • MSIS
library and information science • MS

College of Media Arts and Design
Jonathan Estrin, Dean
Programs in:
arts administration • MS
design • MS
fashion design • MS
interior design • MS
media arts • MS
publication management • MS

School of Biomedical Engineering, Science and Health Systems
Dr. Banu Onaral, Director
Programs in:
biomedical engineering • MS, PhD
biomedical science • MS, PhD
biostatistics • MS
clinical/rehabilitation engineering • MS

School of Environmental Science, Engineering and Policy
Dr. Susan Kalham, Director
Programs in:
environmental engineering • MS, PhD
environmental science • MS, PhD

■ DUQUESNE UNIVERSITY
Pittsburgh, PA 15282-0001
http://www.duq.edu/

Independent-religious, coed, university. CGS member. *Enrollment:* 2,233 full-time matriculated graduate/professional students (1,298 women), 1,935 part-time matriculated graduate/professional students (1,129 women). *Computer facilities:* 650 computers available on campus for general student use. A campuswide network can be accessed from student residence rooms and from off campus. Internet access is available. *Library facilities:* Gumberg Library plus 1 other. *Graduate expenses:* Tuition: part-time $535 per credit. Required fees: $53 per credit. Part-time tuition and fees vary according to degree level and program. *General application contact:* Dr. Michael P. Weber, Provost and Academic Vice President, 412-396-6054.

Find an in-depth description at www.petersons.com/graduate.

Bayer School of Natural and Environmental Sciences
Dr. David Seybert, Acting Dean
Programs in:
biochemistry • MS, PhD
biology • MS
biology/environmental sciences • MS
chemistry • MS, PhD
environmental management • Certificate
environmental science • Certificate
environmental science and management • MS
natural and environmental sciences • MS, PhD, Certificate

Graduate School of Liberal Arts
Dr. Constance D. Ramirez, Dean
Programs in:
archival, museum, and editing studies • MA
clinical psychology • PhD
communication and rhetoric • MA, PhD
computational mathematics • MA
developmental psychology • MA, PhD
English • MA, PhD
general phenomenological psychology • MA
health care ethics • MA, DHCE, PhD
history • MA
liberal arts • M Phil, MA, MALS, MLLS, MS, DHCE, PhD, Certificate
liberal studies • M Phil, MALS, MLLS
multimedia technology • MS
pastoral ministry • MA
philosophy • MA, PhD
philosophy for theological studies • MA
religious education • MA
systematic theology • PhD
theology • MA

Graduate Center for Social and Public Policy
Dr. Michael Irwin, Head
Programs in:
conflict resolution and peace studies • Certificate
social and public policy • MA

John F. Donahue Graduate School of Business
James C. Stalder, Dean
Programs in:
business administration • MBA
information systems management • MS
taxation • MS

John G. Rangos, Sr. School of Health Sciences
Dr. Jerome L. Martin, Dean
Programs in:
health management systems • MHMS
occupational therapy • MOT
physical therapy • MPT
physician assistant • MPA
speech-language pathology • MSLP

Mary Pappert School of Music
Dr. Robert Shankovich, Graduate Chair
Programs in:
composition • MM
music education • MM
music performance • MM, AD
music theory • MM
sacred music • MM

School of Education
Dr. James Henderson, Dean
Programs in:
community counseling • MS Ed
counselor education • MS Ed, Ed D
counselor education and supervision • Ed D
early childhood education • MS Ed
education • MS Ed, Ed D, CAGS
educational leaders • Ed D
educational studies • MS Ed
elementary education • MS Ed
instructional leadership excellence • Ed D
instructional technology • MS Ed
marriage and family therapy • MS Ed
reading and language arts • MS Ed
school administration • MS Ed
school administration and supervision • MS Ed
school counseling • MS Ed
school psychology • MS Ed, CAGS
school supervision • MS Ed
secondary education • MS Ed
special education • MS Ed

School of Law
Program in:
law • JD

School of Nursing
Mary deChesnay, Dean
Programs in:
family nurse practitioner • MSN
nursing • MSN, PhD
nursing administration • MSN
nursing education • MSN

Duquesne University (continued)

School of Pharmacy
Dr. R. Pete Vanderveen, Dean
Programs in:
pharmacy • Pharm D, MS, PhD

Graduate School of Pharmaceutical Sciences
Dr. Aleem Gangjee, Director
Programs in:
medicinal chemistry • MS, PhD
pharmaceutical administration • MS
pharmaceutical chemistry • MS, PhD
pharmaceutics • MS, PhD
pharmacology/toxicology • MS, PhD

■ EASTERN COLLEGE

St. Davids, PA 19087-3696
http://www.eastern.edu/

Independent-religious, coed, comprehensive institution. *Computer facilities:* 60 computers available on campus for general student use. A campuswide network can be accessed from student residence rooms and from off campus. Internet access is available. *Library facilities:* Warner Library plus 1 other. *General application contact:* Director of Graduate Admissions, 610-341-5972.

Graduate Business Programs
Programs in:
business administration • MBA
economic development • MBA, MS
nonprofit management • MBA, MS

Graduate Education Programs
Programs in:
English as a second or foreign language • Certificate
multicultural education • M Ed
school health services • M Ed

Programs in Counseling
Programs in:
community/clinical counseling • MA
educational counseling • MA, MS
marriage and family • MA
school counseling • MA
school psychology • MS
student development • MA

■ EAST STROUDSBURG UNIVERSITY OF PENNSYLVANIA

East Stroudsburg, PA 18301-2999
http://www.esu.edu/

State-supported, coed, comprehensive institution. *Computer facilities:* 164 computers available on campus for general student use. A campuswide network can be accessed from off campus. Internet access is available. *Library facilities:* Kemp Library. *General application contact:* Dean of Graduate Studies and Continuing Education, 570-422-3536.

Find an in-depth description at www.petersons.com/graduate.

Graduate School

School of Arts and Sciences
Programs in:
arts and sciences • M Ed, MA, MS
biology • M Ed, MS
computer science • MS
general science • M Ed, MS
history • M Ed, MA
political science • M Ed, MA

School of Health Sciences and Human Performance
Programs in:
cardiac rehabilitation and exercise science • MS
community health education • MPH
health and physical education • M Ed
health education • MS
health sciences and human performance • M Ed, MPH, MS
physical education • MS
speech pathology and audiology • MS

School of Professional Studies
Programs in:
elementary education • M Ed
professional and secondary education • M Ed
professional studies • M Ed
reading • M Ed
special education • M Ed

■ EDINBORO UNIVERSITY OF PENNSYLVANIA

Edinboro, PA 16444
http://www.edinboro.edu/

State-supported, coed, comprehensive institution. *Enrollment:* 292 full-time matriculated graduate/professional students (220 women), 360 part-time matriculated graduate/professional students (253 women). *Graduate faculty:* 80 full-time (40 women), 3 part-time/adjunct (1 woman). *Computer facilities:* 700 computers available on campus for general student use. A campuswide network can be accessed from student residence rooms and from off campus. Internet access and online class registration, e-mail are available. *Library facilities:* Baron-Forness Library plus 1 other. *Graduate expenses:* Tuition, state resident: full-time $4,138; part-time $230 per credit hour. Tuition, nonresident: full-time $7,008; part-time $389 per credit hour. Required fees: $1,108; $57 per credit. *General application contact:* Dr. Terry L. Smith, Dean of Graduate Studies and Liberal Arts, 814-732-2856.

Graduate Studies
Dr. Terry L. Smith, Dean of Graduate Studies and Liberal Arts

School of Education
Programs in:
behavior management • Certificate
counseling • MA, Certificate
early childhood • M Ed
education • M Ed, MA, Certificate
educational psychology • M Ed
elementary education • M Ed
elementary education clinical • M Ed
elementary school administration • M Ed, Certificate
health and physical education • Certificate
language arts • M Ed
mathematics • M Ed
middle and secondary instruction • M Ed
reading • M Ed, Certificate
reading specialist • Certificate
school administration • M Ed, Certificate
school psychology • Certificate
science • M Ed
secondary school administration • M Ed, Certificate
social studies • M Ed
special education • M Ed

School of Liberal Arts
Dr. Terry L. Smith, Dean of Graduate Studies and Liberal Arts
Programs in:
art • MA
ceramics • MFA
clinical psychology • MA
communication studies • MA
jewelry • MFA
liberal arts • MA, MFA, MSW
painting • MFA
printmaking • MFA
sculpture • MFA
social sciences • MA
sociology, anthropology, and social work • MSW
speech-language pathology • MA

School of Science, Management and Technology
Dr. Eric Randall, Dean
Programs in:
biology • MS
family nurse practitioner • MSN
information technology • Certificate
mathematics and computer science • Certificate

public accounting • Certificate
science, management and technology • MS, MSN, Certificate

■ GANNON UNIVERSITY

Erie, PA 16541-0001
http://www.gannon.edu/

Independent-religious, coed, comprehensive institution. *Computer facilities:* 229 computers available on campus for general student use. A campuswide network can be accessed from student residence rooms and from off campus. Internet access is available. *Library facilities:* Nash Library plus 1 other. *General application contact:* Director of Admissions, 814-871-7240.

School of Graduate Studies

College of Humanities, Business, and Education
Programs in:
accounting • Certificate
business • MBA, Certificate
business administration • MBA, Certificate
counseling psychology • MS, PhD
curriculum and instruction • M Ed
early intervention • MS, Certificate
education • M Ed, MS, PhD, Certificate
educational computing technology • M Ed
English • M Ed, MA
finance • Certificate
gerontology • Certificate
human resources management • Certificate
humanities • M Ed, MA, MPA, MS, PhD, Certificate
humanities, business, and education • M Ed, MA, MBA, MPA, MS, PhD, Certificate
pastoral studies • MA, Certificate
public administration • MPA, Certificate
reading • M Ed, Certificate
secondary education • M Ed

College of Sciences, Engineering, and Health Sciences
Programs in:
administration • MSN
anesthesia • MSN
electrical engineering • MS
embedded software engineering • MS
engineering and computer science • MS
family nurse practitioner • MSN, Certificate
gerontology • MSN
health sciences • MOT, MPT, MS, Certificate
mechanical engineering • MS
medical-surgical nursing • MSN
natural sciences/environmental education • M Ed, Certificate
occupational therapy • MOT
physical therapy • MPT
physician assistant • MS
sciences • M Ed, Certificate
sciences, engineering, and health sciences • M Ed, MOT, MPT, MS, MSN, Certificate

■ GENEVA COLLEGE

Beaver Falls, PA 15010-3599
http://www.geneva.edu/

Independent-religious, coed, comprehensive institution. *Enrollment:* 205 full-time matriculated graduate/professional students (110 women), 82 part-time matriculated graduate/professional students (42 women). *Graduate faculty:* 21 full-time (7 women), 33 part-time/adjunct (6 women). *Computer facilities:* 150 computers available on campus for general student use. A campuswide network can be accessed from off campus. *Library facilities:* McCartney Library plus 5 others. *Graduate expenses:* Tuition: part-time $420 per credit hour. *General application contact:* Dr. Robin Ware, Director of Graduate Student Services, 724-847-6697.

Program in Business Administration

Dr. J. Randall Nutter, Chairperson
Program in:
business administration • MBA

Program in Counseling

Dr. Carol Luce, Director
Programs in:
marriage and family • MA
mental health • MA

Program in Higher Education

Dr. David S. Guthrie, Director
Programs in:
college teaching • MA
educational leadership • MA
student affairs administration • MA

Program in Organizational Leadership

Dr. James R. Dittbeth, Chair
Program in:
organizational leadership • MS

Program in Special Education

Dr. Jeff Wilson, Director
Program in:
special education • M Ed

■ GRATZ COLLEGE

Melrose Park, PA 19027
http://www.gratzcollege.edu/

Independent-religious, coed, comprehensive institution. *Enrollment:* 31 full-time matriculated graduate/professional students (24 women), 519 part-time matriculated graduate/professional students (411 women). *Graduate faculty:* 8 full-time (4 women), 57 part-time/adjunct (42 women). *Computer facilities:* 2 computers available on campus for general student use. A campuswide network can be accessed from off campus. *Library facilities:* Tuttleman Library. *Graduate expenses:* Tuition: full-time $9,470; part-time $1,335 per course. One-time fee: $50. *General application contact:* Adena E. Johnston, Director of Admissions, 215-635-7300 Ext. 140.

Find an in-depth description at www.petersons.com/graduate.

Graduate Programs

Dr. Jerome Kutnick, Dean for Academic Affairs
Programs in:
classical studies • MA
education • MA
Israel studies • Certificate
Jewish communal studies • MA, Certificate
Jewish education • MA, Certificate
Jewish music • MA, Certificate
Jewish studies • MA
Judaica librarianship • Certificate
modern studies • MA

■ GWYNEDD-MERCY COLLEGE

Gwynedd Valley, PA 19437-0901
http://www.gmc.edu/

Independent-religious, coed, comprehensive institution. *Enrollment:* 32 full-time matriculated graduate/professional students, 244 part-time matriculated graduate/professional students. *Graduate faculty:* 8 full-time (7 women), 35 part-time/adjunct (15 women). *Computer facilities:* 97 computers available on campus for general student use. A campuswide network can be accessed from student residence rooms and from off campus. Internet access is available. *Library facilities:* Lourdes Library plus 1 other. *Graduate expenses:* Tuition: part-time $325 per

Gwynedd-Mercy College (continued)
credit. *General application contact:* Dr. Ralph Hoffmann, Associate Vice President for Academic Affairs, 215-646-7300 Ext. 448.

Program in Nursing
Dr. Ann M. McGinn, Interim Dean
Programs in:
- gerontology • MSN
- nurse practitioner • MSN

School of Education
Dr. Lorraine Cavaliere, Dean
Programs in:
- educational administration • MS
- mental health counseling • MS
- reading • MS
- school counseling • MS
- teaching • MS

■ HOLY FAMILY COLLEGE

Philadelphia, PA 19114-2094
http://www.hfc.edu/

Independent-religious, coed, comprehensive institution. *Enrollment:* 73 full-time matriculated graduate/professional students (44 women), 663 part-time matriculated graduate/professional students (537 women). *Graduate faculty:* 16 full-time (10 women), 25 part-time/adjunct (14 women). *Computer facilities:* 148 computers available on campus for general student use. A campuswide network can be accessed. Internet access is available. *Library facilities:* Holy Family College Library plus 1 other. *Graduate expenses:* Tuition: part-time $350 per credit hour. Required fees: $85 per semester. *General application contact:* Dr. Antoinette M. Schiavo, Dean, Graduate Studies, 215-637-7700 Ext. 3230.

Graduate Studies
Dr. Antoinette M. Schiavo, Dean
Programs in:
- computer communications management • MS
- human resources management • MS

School of Business
Dr. Anthony DiPrimio, Dean
Programs in:
- computer communications management • MS
- human resources management • MS

School of Education
Dr. Leonard Soroka, Chair
Programs in:
- education • M Ed
- elementary education • M Ed
- reading specialist • M Ed
- secondary education • M Ed

School of Nursing
Sara Wuthnow, Graduate Coordinator
Program in:
- nursing • MSN

School of Social and Behavioral Sciences
Dr. Jane McGarrahan, Graduate Coordinator
Program in:
- counseling psychology • MS

■ IMMACULATA COLLEGE

Immaculata, PA 19345-0500
http://www.immaculata.edu/

Independent-religious, women only, comprehensive institution. *Enrollment:* 80 full-time matriculated graduate/professional students (64 women), 577 part-time matriculated graduate/professional students (456 women). *Graduate faculty:* 48. *Computer facilities:* 150 computers available on campus for general student use. A campuswide network can be accessed from student residence rooms and from off campus. Internet access is available. *Library facilities:* Gabriele Library. *Graduate expenses:* Tuition: part-time $375 per credit. Required fees: $40 per semester. *General application contact:* Sr. Ann M. Heath, Dean, 610-647-4400 Ext. 3211.

Find an in-depth description at www.petersons.com/graduate.

College of Graduate Studies
Sr. Ann M. Heath, Dean
Programs in:
- clinical psychology • Psy D
- counseling psychology • MA, Certificate
- cultural and linguistic diversity • MA
- educational leadership and administration • MA, Ed D
- elementary education • Certificate
- intermediate unit director • Certificate
- music therapy • MA
- nutrition education • MA
- nutrition education/approved pre-professional practice program • MA
- organization leadership • MA
- school principal • Certificate
- school psychology • Psy D
- school superintendent • Certificate
- seondary education • Certificate
- special education • Certificate

■ INDIANA UNIVERSITY OF PENNSYLVANIA

Indiana, PA 15705-1087
http://www.iup.edu/

State-supported, coed, university. CGS member. *Enrollment:* 853 full-time matriculated graduate/professional students (505 women), 822 part-time matriculated graduate/professional students (542 women). *Graduate faculty:* 367 full-time (141 women). *Computer facilities:* 3,200 computers available on campus for general student use. A campuswide network can be accessed from student residence rooms and from off campus. *Library facilities:* Stapleton Library. *Graduate expenses:* Tuition, state resident: full-time $4,138; part-time $230 per credit. Tuition, nonresident: full-time $7,008; part-time $389 per credit. Required fees: $128 per semester. *General application contact:* Donna Griffith, Assistant Dean, 724-357-2222.

Find an in-depth description at www.petersons.com/graduate.

Graduate School and Research
Dr. James C. Petersen, Dean
Programs in:
- applied mathematics • MS
- biology • MS
- chemistry • MA, MS
- elementary and middle school mathematics education • M Ed
- mathematics education • M Ed
- natural sciences and mathematics • M Ed, MA, MS, Psy D
- physics • MA, MS
- psychology • MA, Psy D

College of Education and Educational Technology
Dr. John Butzow, Dean
Programs in:
- administration and leadership studies • D Ed
- adult and community education • MA
- communications technology • MA
- community counseling • MA
- counselor education • M Ed
- curriculum and instruction • M Ed, D Ed
- early childhood education • M Ed
- education • M Ed, Certificate
- education and educational technology • M Ed, MA, MS, D Ed, Certificate
- education of exceptional persons • M Ed
- educational psychology • M Ed, Certificate
- literacy • M Ed

principal • Certificate
reading • M Ed
school psychology • D Ed
speech-language pathology • MS
student affairs in higher education • MA

College of Fine Arts
Michael Hood, Dean
Programs in:
art • MA, MFA
fine arts • MA, MFA
music • MA
music education • MA
music history and literature • MA
music theory and composition • MA
performance • MA

College of Health and Human Services
Dr. Carleen Zoni, Dean
Programs in:
aquatics administration and facilities management • MS
exercise science • MS
food and nutrition • MS
health and human services • MA, MS
industrial and labor relations • MA
nursing • MS
nursing and allied health • MS
safety sciences • MS
sport management • MS
sport science • MS

College of Humanities and Social Sciences
Dr. Brenda Carter, Dean
Programs in:
administration and leadership studies • PhD
composition and teaching English to speakers of other languages • MA, MAT, PhD
criminology • MA, PhD
generalist • MA
geography • MA, MS
history • MA
humanities and social sciences • MA, MAT, MS, PhD
literature • MA
literature and criticism • MA, PhD
public affairs • MA
rhetoric and linguistics • PhD
sociology • MA
teaching English • MAT
teaching English to speakers of other languages • MA

Eberly College of Business and Information Technology
Dr. Robert Camp, Dean
Programs in:
business • M Ed, MBA
business administration • MBA
business/workforce development • M Ed

■ KING'S COLLEGE
Wilkes-Barre, PA 18711-0801
http://www.kings.edu/

Independent-religious, coed, comprehensive institution. *Enrollment:* 27 full-time matriculated graduate/professional students (18 women), 116 part-time matriculated graduate/professional students (87 women). *Graduate faculty:* 13 full-time (7 women), 4 part-time/adjunct (3 women). *Computer facilities:* 273 computers available on campus for general student use. A campuswide network can be accessed from student residence rooms and from off campus. Internet access is available. *Library facilities:* D. Leonard Corgan Library. *Graduate expenses:* Tuition: full-time $19,950; part-time $490 per credit. Required fees: $700. *General application contact:* Dr. Elizabeth S. Lott, Director of Graduate Programs, 570-208-5991.

College of Arts and Sciences
Dr. William A. Shergalis, Dean
Programs in:
physician assistant studies • MSPAS
reading • M Ed

William G. McGowan School of Business
Russell Singer, Director
Programs in:
finance • MS
health care administration • MS

■ KUTZTOWN UNIVERSITY OF PENNSYLVANIA
Kutztown, PA 19530-0730
http://www.kutztown.edu/

State-supported, coed, comprehensive institution. CGS member. *Enrollment:* 176 full-time matriculated graduate/professional students (119 women), 834 part-time matriculated graduate/professional students (613 women). *Graduate faculty:* 54 full-time (15 women). *Computer facilities:* 650 computers available on campus for general student use. A campuswide network can be accessed from student residence rooms and from off campus. Internet access is available. *Library facilities:* Rohrbach Library. *Graduate expenses:* Tuition, state resident: part-time $230 per credit. Tuition, nonresident: part-time $389 per credit. Required fees: $37 per credit. *General application contact:* Sandra J. Hammann, Interim Dean of the Graduate School, 610-683-4200.

Find an in-depth description at www.petersons.com/graduate.

College of Graduate Studies and Extended Learning
Sandra J. Hammann, Interim Dean
Programs in:
agency counseling • MA
counselor education • M Ed
marital and family therapy • MA
student affairs in higher education • M Ed

College of Business
Theodore Hartz, Dean
Programs in:
business • MBA
business administration • MBA

College of Education
Dr. Eileen Shultz, Dean
Programs in:
biology • M Ed
curriculum and instruction • M Ed
early childhood education • Certificate
education • M Ed, MA, MLS, Certificate
elementary education • M Ed, Certificate
English • M Ed
library science • MLS, Certificate
mathematics • M Ed
reading • M Ed
secondary education • Certificate
social studies • M Ed
special education • Certificate

College of Liberal Arts and Sciences
Dr. Carl E. Brunner, Dean
Programs in:
computer and information science • MS
English • MA
liberal arts and sciences • MA, MPA, MS, Certificate
mathematics • MA
public administration • MPA
school nursing • Certificate
telecommunications • MS

College of Visual and Performing Arts
Dr. William Mowder, Dean
Programs in:
art education • M Ed, Certificate
visual and performing arts • M Ed, Certificate

■ LA ROCHE COLLEGE
Pittsburgh, PA 15237-5898
http://www.laroche.edu/

Independent-religious, coed, comprehensive institution. *Enrollment:* 72

La Roche College (continued)
full-time matriculated graduate/professional students (36 women), 176 part-time matriculated graduate/professional students (139 women). *Graduate faculty:* 9 full-time (5 women), 10 part-time/adjunct (5 women). *Computer facilities:* 95 computers available on campus for general student use. A campuswide network can be accessed from student residence rooms and from off campus. Internet access and online class registration are available. *Library facilities:* John J. Wright Library. *Graduate expenses:* Tuition: full-time $7,920; part-time $440 per credit. Required fees: $7 per credit. *General application contact:* Renee Kozlowski, Director of Admissions for Graduate and Continuing Education, 412-536-1265.

Graduate Studies
Dr. Ronald Gilardi, Vice President for Academic Affairs and Graduate Dean
Programs in:
- community health nursing • MSN
- critical care nursing • MSN
- family nurse practitioner • MSN
- gerontological nursing • MSN
- human resources management • MS
- nurse anesthesia • MS
- nursing management • MSN

■ LA SALLE UNIVERSITY
Philadelphia, PA 19141-1199
http://www.lasalle.edu/

Independent-religious, coed, comprehensive institution. *Enrollment:* 171 full-time matriculated graduate/professional students (96 women), 1,435 part-time matriculated graduate/professional students (844 women). *Graduate faculty:* 151. *Computer facilities:* 350 computers available on campus for general student use. A campuswide network can be accessed from student residence rooms and from off campus. Internet access and online class registration are available. *Library facilities:* Connelly Library. *Graduate expenses:* Tuition: part-time $269 per credit. Tuition and fees vary according to degree level and program. *General application contact:* Paul J. Reilly, Director of Marketing/Graduate Enrollment, 215-951-1946.

Business Administration Program
Joseph Y. Ugras, Associate Dean
Programs in:
- business administration • MBA, Certificate
- global management of technology • MS
- science and technology • EMBA

Program in Nursing
Dr. Zane R. Wolf, Dean
Programs in:
- adult health and illness, clinical nurse specialist • MSN
- clinical research • Certificate
- nurse anesthesia • MSN, Certificate
- nursing administration • MSN
- nursing education • Certificate
- nursing informatics • Certificate
- primary care of adults-nurse practitioner • MSN
- primary care of families-nurse practitioner • MSN, Certificate
- public health nursing • MSN
- school nurse • Certificate
- wound, ostomy, and continence nursing • MSN, Certificate

School of Arts and Sciences
Dr. Barbara C. Millard, Dean
Programs in:
- arts and sciences • MA, MS, Psy D
- bilingual/bicultural studies (Spanish) • MA
- Central and Eastern European studies • MA
- clinical geropsychology • Psy D
- clinical psychology • Psy D
- clinical-counseling psychology • MA
- computer information science • MS
- education • MA
- family psychology • Psy D
- information technology leadership • MS
- pastoral studies • MA
- professional communication • MA
- rehabilitation psychology • Psy D
- religion • MA
- theological studies • MA

■ LEBANON VALLEY COLLEGE
Annville, PA 17003-1400
http://www.lvc.edu/

Independent-religious, coed, comprehensive institution. *Enrollment:* 255 part-time matriculated graduate/professional students (108 women). *Graduate faculty:* 5 full-time (1 woman), 35 part-time/adjunct (9 women). *Computer facilities:* 194 computers available on campus for general student use. A campuswide network can be accessed from student residence rooms and from off campus. Internet access is available. *Library facilities:* Bishop Library. *Graduate expenses:* Tuition: part-time $399 per credit. *General application contact:* Cheryl L. Batdorf, Assistant Director, 717-867-6335.

Graduate Studies and Continuing Education
Barbara J. Denison, Associate Dean for Graduate and Continuing Education
Programs in:
- business administration • MBA
- science education • MSE

■ LEHIGH UNIVERSITY
Bethlehem, PA 18015-3094
http://www.lehigh.edu/

Independent, coed, university. CGS member. *Enrollment:* 575 full-time matriculated graduate/professional students (249 women), 1,212 part-time matriculated graduate/professional students (532 women). *Graduate faculty:* 391 full-time (76 women), 77 part-time/adjunct (33 women). *Computer facilities:* 516 computers available on campus for general student use. A campuswide network can be accessed from student residence rooms and from off campus. Internet access and online class registration are available. *Library facilities:* E. W. Fairchild-Martindale Library plus 1 other. *Graduate expenses:* Tuition: part-time $470 per credit hour.

Find an in-depth description at www.petersons.com/graduate.

College of Arts and Sciences
Dr. Bobb Carson, Dean
Programs in:
- applied mathematics • MS, PhD
- arts and sciences • MA, MS, DA, PhD
- behavioral and evolutionary bioscience • PhD
- behavioral neuroscience • PhD
- biochemistry • PhD
- biology • PhD
- chemistry • MS, DA, PhD
- earth and environmental sciences • MS, PhD
- English • MA, PhD
- experimental psychology • PhD
- history • MA, PhD
- mathematics • MS, PhD
- molecular biology • PhD
- physics • MS, PhD
- political science • MA
- sociology and anthropology • MA
- statistics • MS

College of Business and Economics
Kathleen A. Trexler, Associate Dean and Director

Programs in:
accounting and information analysis • MS
business • MBA, PhD
business administration • MBA
economics • MS, PhD

College of Education
Dr. Raymond Bell, Interim Dean
Programs in:
counseling and human services • M Ed
counseling psychology • M Ed, PhD, Certificate
curriculum and instruction • Ed D
education • M Ed, MA, MS, Ed D, PhD, Certificate, Ed S
educational leadership • M Ed, Ed D, Certificate
educational technology • MS, Ed D
elementary education • M Ed, Ed D, Certificate
school counseling • M Ed, Certificate
school psychology • PhD, Certificate, Ed S
secondary education • M Ed, MA, Certificate
special education • M Ed, PhD, Certificate
teacher education • M Ed, MA, Ed D, Certificate

P.C. Rossin College of Engineering and Applied Science
Dr. Philip A. Blythe, Associate Dean
Programs in:
applied mathematics • MS, PhD
chemical engineering • M Eng, MS, PhD
civil and environmental engineering • M Eng, MS, PhD
computer engineering • MS
computer science • MS, PhD
electrical engineering • M Eng, MS, PhD
engineering and applied science • M Eng, MS, PhD
industrial engineering • M Eng, MS, PhD
management science • MS
manufacturing systems engineering • MS
materials science and engineering • M Eng, MS, PhD
mechanical engineering • M Eng, MS, PhD
mechanics • M Eng, MS, PhD
quality engineering • MS

Center for Polymer Science and Engineering
Dr. Mohamed S. El-Aasser, Director
Program in:
polymer science and engineering • MS, PhD

■ LINCOLN UNIVERSITY

Lincoln University, PA 19352
http://www.lincoln.edu/

State-related, coed, comprehensive institution. *Computer facilities:* 200 computers available on campus for general student use. A campuswide network can be accessed from student residence rooms and from off campus. Internet access is available. *Library facilities:* Langston Hughes Memorial Library. *General application contact:* Acting Director, Graduate Program in Human Services, 610-932-8300 Ext. 3360.

Graduate Program in Human Services
Program in:
human services • M Hum Svcs

■ LOCK HAVEN UNIVERSITY OF PENNSYLVANIA

Lock Haven, PA 17745-2390
http://www.lhup.edu/

State-supported, coed, comprehensive institution. *Enrollment:* 68 full-time matriculated graduate/professional students (41 women), 25 part-time matriculated graduate/professional students (16 women). *Graduate faculty:* 5 full-time (2 women), 22 part-time/adjunct (7 women). *Computer facilities:* 270 computers available on campus for general student use. A campuswide network can be accessed from student residence rooms and from off campus. *Library facilities:* Stevenson Library. *Graduate expenses:* Full-time $4,138. Tuition, state resident: part-time $230 per credit. Tuition, nonresident: full-time $7,008; part-time $389 per credit. $9,480 full-time. Required fees: $46 per credit. Full-time tuition and fees vary according to campus/location and program. Part-time tuition and fees vary according to course load. *General application contact:* Donna R. Bierly, Secretary,Enrollment Services Office, 570-893-2124.

Office of Graduate Studies
Dr. James K. Smalley, Director of Enrollment Services
Programs in:
curriculum and instruction • M Ed
liberal arts • MLA
physician assistant in rural primary care • MHS

■ MANSFIELD UNIVERSITY OF PENNSYLVANIA

Mansfield, PA 16933
http://www.mansfield.edu/

State-supported, coed, comprehensive institution. *Enrollment:* 63 full-time matriculated graduate/professional students (40 women), 160 part-time matriculated graduate/professional students (122 women). *Graduate faculty:* 35 part-time/adjunct (16 women). *Computer facilities:* 371 computers available on campus for general student use. A campuswide network can be accessed from student residence rooms and from off campus. Internet access is available. *Library facilities:* North Hill Library. *Graduate expenses:* Tuition, state resident: full-time $4,138; part-time $230 per credit. Tuition, nonresident: full-time $7,008; part-time $389 per credit. Required fees: $412; $23 per credit. *General application contact:* Dr. J. Dennis Murray, Interim Associate Provost, 570-662-4807.

Graduate Studies
Dr. Joseph Murphy, Chairperson
Programs in:
art/communications • M Ed
elementary education • M Ed
music • MM
school library and information technologies • MS
secondary education • MS

■ MARYWOOD UNIVERSITY

Scranton, PA 18509-1598
http://www.marywood.edu/

Independent-religious, coed, comprehensive institution. *Enrollment:* 432 full-time matriculated graduate/professional students (352 women), 838 part-time matriculated graduate/professional students (653 women). *Graduate faculty:* 96 full-time (54 women), 92 part-time/adjunct (48 women). *Computer facilities:* 350 computers available on campus for general student use. A campuswide network can be accessed from student residence rooms and from off campus. Internet access and online class registration are available. *Library facilities:* Learning Resources Center. *Graduate expenses:* Tuition: part-time $499 per credit. *General application contact:* Deborah M. Flynn, Coordinator of Admissions, 570-340-6002.

Find an in-depth description at www.petersons.com/graduate.

Marywood University (continued)

Graduate School of Arts and Sciences
Dr. Lois King Draina, Chairperson
Programs in:
art education • MA
art therapy • MA
arts and sciences • M Ed, MA, MAT, MBA, MFA, MHSA, MPA, MS, PhD, Psy D
church music • MA
communication arts • MA
counseling • MA
counselor education-elementary • MS
counselor education-secondary • MS
criminal justice • MS
early childhood intervention • MS
education • M Ed
elementary education • MAT, MS
finance and investments • MBA
general management • MBA
health services administration • MHSA
human development • PhD
instructional technology • MS
management information systems • MBA, MS
music education • MA
musicology • MA
nursing • MS
nutrition and dietetics • MS
psychology • MA
psychology and counseling • Psy D
public administration • MPA
reading education • MS
school leadership • MS
special education • MS
special education administration and supervision • MS
speech language pathology • MS
studio art • MA
visual arts • MFA

School of Nursing
Dr. MaryAlice Golden, Chairperson
Program in:
nursing • MS

Graduate School of Social Work
Dr. William Whitaker, Dean
Program in:
social work • MSW

■ MCP HAHNEMANN UNIVERSITY

Philadelphia, PA 19102-1192
http://www.mcphu.edu/

Independent, coed, university. *Enrollment:* 1,837 matriculated graduate/professional students. *Graduate faculty:* 1,092. *Computer facilities:* 130 computers available on campus for general student use. A campuswide network can be accessed from student residence rooms and from off campus. *Library facilities:* University Library plus 4 others. *Graduate expenses:* Tuition: full-time $30,020. Full-time tuition and fees vary according to degree level and program. *General application contact:* Paula Greenberg, Director of Admissions and Recruitment, 215-762-8288.

College of Nursing and Health Professions
Dr. Gloria Donnelly, Dean
Programs in:
advanced physician assistant studies • MHS
art therapy • MA
clinical psychology • MA, MS
couples and family therapy • PhD
dance/movement therapy • MA
emergency and public safety service • MS
family therapy • MFT
forensic psychology • PhD
hand/upper quarter rehabilitation • MHS, MS, PhD
health psychology • PhD
law-psychology • PhD
movement science • MHS, MS, PhD
music therapy • MA
neuropsychology • PhD
nurse anesthesia • MSN
nursing • MSN
nursing and health professions • MA, MFT, MHS, MPT, MS, MSN, DPT, PhD, Certificate
orthopedics • MHS, MS, PhD
pediatrics • MHS, MS, PhD
physical therapy • MPT, DPT, Certificate
public health nursing • MSN

School of Medicine
Dr. Warren E. Ross, Dean
Program in:
medicine • MD, MBS, MLAS, MMS, MS, PhD, Certificate

Biomedical Graduate Programs
Dr. Abdul S. Rao, Senior Associate Dean for Research and Biomedical Graduate Studies
Programs in:
biochemistry • MS, PhD
biomedical sciences • MBS, MLAS, MMS, PhD, Certificate
laboratory animal science • MLAS
medical science • MBS, MMS, Certificate
microbiology and immunology • MS, PhD
molecular and cell biology • MS, PhD
molecular and human genetics • MS, PhD
molecular pathobiology • PhD
neuroscience • PhD
pharmacology and physiology • MS, PhD
radiation • MS
radiation biology • MS
radiation physics • PhD
radiation science • PhD
radiopharmaceutical science • MS, PhD

School of Public Health
Dr. Robert Valdez, Dean
Program in:
public health • MPH

■ MILLERSVILLE UNIVERSITY OF PENNSYLVANIA

Millersville, PA 17551-0302
http://www.millersville.edu/

State-supported, coed, comprehensive institution. CGS member. *Enrollment:* 138 full-time matriculated graduate/professional students (78 women), 562 part-time matriculated graduate/professional students (415 women). *Graduate faculty:* 205 full-time (89 women), 67 part-time/adjunct (32 women). *Computer facilities:* 425 computers available on campus for general student use. A campuswide network can be accessed from student residence rooms and from off campus. *Library facilities:* Helen A. Ganser Library. *Graduate expenses:* Tuition, state resident: full-time $4,138; part-time $230 per credit. Tuition, nonresident: full-time $7,008; part-time $389 per credit. Required fees: $1,012; $42 per credit. *General application contact:* Dr. Duncan M. Perry, Dean of Graduate Studies and Extended Programs, 717-872-3030.

Find an in-depth description at www.petersons.com/graduate.

Graduate School
Dr. Duncan M. Perry, Dean of Graduate Studies and Extended Programs

School of Education
Dr. Bennett Berhow, Dean
Programs in:
athletic coaching • M Ed
athletic management • M Ed
clinical psychology • MS
education • M Ed, MS
elementary education • M Ed
gifted education • M Ed
industrial arts/technology education • M Ed
leadership for teaching and learning • M Ed
psychology • MS

reading education • M Ed
reading/language arts education • M Ed
school counseling • M Ed
school psychology • MS
special education • M Ed
sport management • M Ed

School of Humanities and Social Sciences
Dr. Samuel Casselberry, Dean
Programs in:
art education • M Ed
English • MA
English education • M Ed
French • M Ed, MA
German • M Ed, MA
history • MA
humanities and social sciences • M Ed, MA
Spanish • M Ed, MA

School of Science and Mathematics
Dr. Edward C. Shane, Dean
Programs in:
biology • MS
mathematics • M Ed
nursing • MSN
science and mathematics • M Ed, MS, MSN

■ THE PENNSYLVANIA STATE UNIVERSITY AT ERIE, THE BEHREND COLLEGE

Erie, PA 16563
http://www.psu.edu/

State-related, coed, comprehensive institution. *Enrollment:* 10 full-time matriculated graduate/professional students (4 women), 166 part-time matriculated graduate/professional students (50 women). *Computer facilities:* 448 computers available on campus for general student use. A campuswide network can be accessed from student residence rooms and from off campus. Internet access and online class registration are available. *Graduate expenses:* Tuition, state resident: part-time $358 per credit. Tuition, nonresident: part-time $557 per credit. *General application contact:* Jack Burke, Interim Dean and Provost, 814-898-6160.

Graduate Center
John M. Lilley, Dean and Provost
Programs in:
business administration • MBA
manufacturing systems engineering • M Eng

■ THE PENNSYLVANIA STATE UNIVERSITY GREAT VALLEY CAMPUS

Malvern, PA 19355-1488
http://www.gv.psu.edu/

State-related, coed, graduate-only institution. *Graduate faculty:* 37 full-time (13 women), 78 part-time/adjunct (16 women). *Graduate expenses:* Tuition, state resident: full-time $6,886; part-time $291 per credit. Tuition, nonresident: part-time $641 per credit. *General application contact:* Dr. William Milheim, Acting Campus Executive Officer and Associate Dean, 610-648-3379.

Graduate Studies and Continuing Education
Dr. William Milheim, Acting Campus Executive Officer and Associate Dean
Program in:
health care administration • MBA

College of Education
Dr. Martin Sharp, Interim Division Head
Programs in:
curriculum and instruction • M Ed
instructional systems • M Ed, MS
special education • M Ed, MS

School of Graduate Professional Studies
Programs in:
graduate professional studies • M Eng, MS, MSE
information science • MS
software engineering • MSE
systems engineering • M Eng

■ THE PENNSYLVANIA STATE UNIVERSITY HARRISBURG CAMPUS OF THE CAPITAL COLLEGE

Middletown, PA 17057-4898
http://www.psu.edu/

State-related, coed, comprehensive institution. *Enrollment:* 132 full-time matriculated graduate/professional students (74 women), 1,015 part-time matriculated graduate/professional students (584 women). *Computer facilities:* 132 computers available on campus for general student use. A campuswide network can be accessed from student residence rooms and from off campus. Internet access and online class registration are available. *Graduate expenses:* Tuition, state resident: full-time $7,314; part-time $348 per credit. Tuition, nonresident: full-time $14,980; part-time $615 per credit. Required fees: $322; $161 per semester. *General application contact:* Dr. Madlyn L. Hanes, Provost and Dean, 717-948-6105.

Find an in-depth description at www.petersons.com/graduate.

Graduate Center
Dr. Madlyn L. Hanes, Provost and Dean

School of Behavioral Sciences and Education
Dr. William A. Henk, Director
Programs in:
adult education • D Ed
applied psychology • MA
behavioral sciences and education • M Ed, MA, D Ed
community psychology and social change • MA
health education • M Ed
teaching and curriculum • M Ed
training and development • M Ed

School of Business Administration
Dr. Mukund S. Kulkarni, Director
Programs in:
business administration • MBA, MSIS
information systems • MSIS

School of Humanities
Dr. William J. Mahar, Coordinator
Programs in:
American studies • MA
humanities • MA

School of Public Affairs
Dr. Steven A. Peterson, Director
Programs in:
health administration • MHA
public administration • MPA, PhD

School of Science, Engineering and Technology
Dr. William Welsh, Director
Programs in:
computer science • MS
electrical engineering • M Eng
engineering science • M Eng
environmental pollution control • M Eng, MEPC, MS

■ THE PENNSYLVANIA STATE UNIVERSITY UNIVERSITY PARK CAMPUS

State College, University Park, PA 16802-1503
http://www.psu.edu/

State-related, coed, university. CGS member. *Enrollment:* 4,249 full-time matriculated graduate/professional students (1,769 women), 1,914 part-time

The Pennsylvania State University University Park Campus (continued)
matriculated graduate/professional students (924 women). *Computer facilities:* 3,589 computers available on campus for general student use. A campuswide network can be accessed from student residence rooms and from off campus. Internet access and online class registration are available. *Library facilities:* Pattee Library plus 7 others. *Graduate expenses:* Tuition, state resident: full-time $7,484; part-time $316 per credit. Tuition, nonresident: full-time $14,980; part-time $624 per credit. Required fees: $111 per semester. *General application contact:* Dr. Graham Spanier, President, 814-865-1795.

Find an in-depth description at www.petersons.com/graduate.

Graduate School

Dr. Eva J. Pell, Vice President, Research and Dean
Programs in:
acoustics • M Eng, MS, PhD
bioengineering • MS, PhD
biotechnology • MS
ecology • MS, PhD
environmental pollution control • M Eng, MEPC, MS
genetics • MS, PhD
human nutrition • M Ed
information sciences and technology • PhD
integrative biosciences • MS, PhD
mass communications • PhD
materials • MS, PhD
nutrition • M Ed, MS, PhD
physiology • MS, PhD
plant physiology • MS, PhD
quality and manufacturing management • MMM

College of Agricultural Sciences
Dr. Robert D. Steele, Dean
Programs in:
agricultural and extension education • M Ed, MS, D Ed, PhD
agricultural economics • M Agr, MS, PhD
agricultural economics and demography • MS, PhD
agricultural sciences • M Agr, M Ed, MFR, MS, D Ed, PhD
agronomy • M Agr, MS, PhD
animal science • M Agr, MS, PhD
community and economic development • MS
entomology • M Agr, MS, PhD
food science • MS, PhD
forest resources • M Agr, MFR, MS, PhD
horticulture • M Agr, MS, PhD
pathobiology • MS, PhD
plant pathology • M Agr, MS, PhD
rural sociology • M Agr, MS, PhD
soil science • M Agr, MS, PhD
wildlife and fisheries sciences • M Agr, MFR, MS, PhD
youth and family education • M Ed

College of Arts and Architecture
Richard W. Durst, Dean
Programs in:
architecture • MS
art • MA, MFA
art education • M Ed, MS, D Ed, PhD
art history • MA, PhD
arts and architecture • M Ed, M Mus, MA, MFA, MLA, MME, MS, D Ed, PhD
ceramics • MFA
composition/theory • M Mus
conducting • M Mus
drawing/painting • MFA
graphic design • MFA
landscape architecture • MLA
metals • MFA
music and music education • M Ed, M Mus, MA, MME, PhD
music education • M Ed, MME, PhD
music theory and history • MA
musicology • MA
performance • M Mus
photography • MFA
piano pedagogy and performance • M Mus
printmaking • MFA
sculpture • MFA
theatre arts • MFA
voice performance and pedagogy • M Mus

College of Communications
Dr. Douglas Anderson, Dean
Programs in:
communications • MA, PhD
mass communications • PhD
media studies • MA
telecommunications studies • MA

College of Earth and Mineral Sciences
Dr. John A. Dutton, Dean
Programs in:
ceramic science • MS, PhD
earth and mineral sciences • M Eng, MS, PhD
fuel science • MS, PhD
geo-environmental engineering • MS, PhD
geochemistry • MS, PhD
geography • MS, PhD
geology • MS, PhD
geophysics • MS, PhD
metals science and engineering • MS, PhD
meteorology • MS, PhD
mineral economics • MS, PhD
mineral engineering management • M Eng
mineral processing • MS, PhD
mining engineering • M Eng, MS, PhD
petroleum and natural gas engineering • MS, PhD
polymer science • MS, PhD

College of Education
Dr. David Monk, Dean
Programs in:
adult education • M Ed, D Ed
bilingual education • M Ed, MS, D Ed, PhD
counseling psychology • PhD
counselor education • M Ed, MS, D Ed
early childhood education • M Ed, MS, D Ed, PhD
education • M Ed, MA, MS, D Ed, PhD
educational administration • M Ed, MS, D Ed, PhD
educational psychology • MS, PhD
educational theory and policy • MA, PhD
elementary counseling • M Ed, MS
elementary education • M Ed, MS, D Ed, PhD
higher education • M Ed, D Ed, PhD
instructional systems • M Ed, MS, D Ed, PhD
language arts and reading • M Ed, MS, D Ed, PhD
school psychology • M Ed, MS, PhD
science education • M Ed, MS, D Ed, PhD
social studies education • MS, D Ed, PhD
special education • M Ed, MS, PhD
supervisor and curriculum development • M Ed, MS, D Ed, PhD
workforce education and development • M Ed, MS, D Ed, PhD

College of Engineering
Dr. David N. Wormley, Dean
Programs in:
aerospace engineering • M Eng, MS, PhD
agricultural engineering • MS, PhD
architectural engineering • M Eng, MAE, MS, PhD
chemical engineering • MS, PhD
civil engineering • M Eng, MS, PhD
computer science and engineering • M Eng, MS, PhD
electrical engineering • M Eng, MS, PhD
engineering • M Eng, MAE, MS, PhD
engineering mechanics • M Eng, MS
engineering science • MS
engineering science and mechanics • PhD

environmental engineering • M Eng, MS, PhD
industrial engineering • M Eng, MS, PhD
manufacturing engineering • M Eng
mechanical engineering • M Eng, MS, PhD
nuclear engineering • M Eng, MS, PhD
structural engineering • M Eng, MS, PhD
transportation and highway engineering • M Eng, MS, PhD
water resources engineering • M Eng, MS, PhD

College of Health and Human Development
Dr. Raymond Coward, Dean
Programs in:
biobehavioral health • MS, PhD
communication disorders • M Ed, MS, PhD
health and human development • M Ed, MHA, MHRIM, MS, PhD
health policy and administration • MHA, MS, PhD
hotel, restaurant, and institutional management • MHRIM, MS, PhD
hotel, restaurant, and recreation management • M Ed, MHRIM, MS, PhD
human development and family studies • MS, PhD
kinesiology • MS, PhD
leisure studies • M Ed, MS, PhD
nursing • MS, PhD

College of Liberal Arts
Dr. Susan Welch, Dean
Programs in:
anthropology • MA, PhD
classical American philosophy • MA, PhD
clinical psychology • MS, PhD
cognitive psychology • MS, PhD
comparative literature • MA, PhD
contemporary European philosophy • MA, PhD
crime, law, and justice • MA, PhD
developmental psychology • MS, PhD
economics • MA, PhD
English • M Ed, MA, MFA, PhD
French • MA, PhD
German • M Ed, MA, PhD
history • M Ed, MA, PhD
history of philosophy • MA, PhD
industrial relations and human resources • MS
industrial/organizational psychology • MS, PhD
liberal arts • M Ed, MA, MFA, MS, PhD
political science • MA, PhD
psychobiology • MS, PhD
Russian and comparative literature • MA
social psychology • MS, PhD
sociology • MA, PhD
Spanish • M Ed, MA, PhD
speech communication • MA, PhD
teaching English as a second language • MA

Eberly College of Science
Dr. Daniel Larson, Dean
Programs in:
astronomy and astrophysics • MS, PhD
biochemistry, microbiology, and molecular biology • MS, PhD
biology • MS, PhD
cell and developmental biology • PhD
chemistry • MS, PhD
mathematics • M Ed, MA, D Ed, PhD
molecular evolutionary biology • MS, PhD
physics • M Ed, MS, D Ed, PhD
science • M Ed, MA, MS, D Ed, PhD
statistics • MA, MS, PhD

The Mary Jean and Frank P. Smeal College of Business Administration
Dr. Judy Olian, Dean
Programs in:
accounting • MS, PhD
business administration • MBA, MS, PhD
business logistics • MS
finance • MS
finance/insurance and real estate • PhD
insurance • MS
management and organization • PhD
management science and information systems • MS
management science/operations/logistics • PhD
marketing • MS
marketing and distribution • PhD
real estate • MS

School of Information Sciences and Technology
Dr. James Thomas, Dean
Program in:
information sciences and technology • PhD

■ PHILADELPHIA UNIVERSITY
Philadelphia, PA 19144-5497
http://www.philau.edu/

Independent, coed, comprehensive institution. *Enrollment:* 130 full-time matriculated graduate/professional students (92 women), 377 part-time matriculated graduate/professional students (261 women). *Graduate faculty:* 23 full-time (9 women), 57 part-time/adjunct (22 women). *Computer facilities:* 400 computers available on campus for general student use. A campuswide network can be accessed from student residence rooms and from off campus. Internet access, on-line registration for advanced workshops and seminars are available. *Library facilities:* Paul J. Gutman Library. *Graduate expenses:* Tuition: full-time $8,946. *General application contact:* William H. Firman, Director of Graduate Admissions, 215-951-2943.

School of Business
Dr. Elmore Alexander, Dean
Programs in:
accounting • MBA
business • MBA, MS
business administration • MBA
finance • MBA
health care management • MBA
international business • MBA
marketing • MBA
taxation • MS

School of Science and Health
Dr. William Brendley, Dean
Programs in:
instructional technology • MS
midwifery • MS
occupational therapy • MS
physician assistant studies • MS
science and health • MS

School of Textiles and Materials Science
Dr. David Brookstein, Dean of School of Textiles and Materials Technology
Programs in:
fashion-apparel studies • MS
textile design • MS
textile engineering • MS
textiles and materials science • MS

■ POINT PARK COLLEGE
Pittsburgh, PA 15222-1984
http://www.ppc.edu/

Independent, coed, comprehensive institution. *Enrollment:* 163 full-time matriculated graduate/professional students (87 women), 122 part-time matriculated graduate/professional students (70 women). *Graduate faculty:* 14 full-time, 38 part-time/adjunct. *Computer facilities:* 200 computers available on campus for general student use. A campuswide network can be accessed from student residence rooms and from off campus. Internet access is available. *Library facilities:* The Library Center. *Graduate expenses:* Tuition: full-time $7,700; part-time $385 per credit. Required fees: $200; $10 per credit.

Point Park College (continued)
General application contact: Kathryn B. Ballas, Director, Accelerated and Graduate Enrollment, 412-392-3812.

Department of Business
Kathryn B. Ballas, Director, Accelerated and Graduate Enrollment
Programs in:
accelerated business administration • MBA
international business administration • MBA

Department of Education and Community Services
Dr. Vincenne R. Beltran, Chair
Program in:
curriculum and instruction • MA

Department of Journalism and Mass Communications
Helen Fallon, Chair
Program in:
journalism and mass communications • MA

■ ROBERT MORRIS COLLEGE

Moon Township, PA 15108-1189
http://www.robert-morris.edu/

Independent, coed, comprehensive institution. *Enrollment:* 846 part-time matriculated graduate/professional students (387 women). *Graduate faculty:* 25 full-time (3 women), 28 part-time/adjunct (6 women). *Computer facilities:* 300 computers available on campus for general student use. A campuswide network can be accessed from off campus. Internet access and online class registration are available. *Library facilities:* Robert Morris College Library. *Graduate expenses:* Tuition: part-time $370 per credit. Required fees: $17 per credit. *General application contact:* Kellie Laurenzi, Director of Enrollment Services, 800-762-0097.

Find an in-depth description at www.petersons.com/graduate.

Graduate Studies
Dr. William J. Katip, Vice President for Academic and Student Affairs
Programs in:
accounting • MS
business • MBA, MS
business education • MS
communications and information systems • MS
finance • MS
information systems and communications • D Sc
information systems management • MS
instructional leadership • MS
Internet information systems • MS
marketing • MS
sport management • MS
taxation • MS

School of Business
Dr. Richard W. Stolz, Dean
Program in:
business • MBA, MS

School of Communications and Information Systems
Dr. Frederick G. Kohun, Associate Dean
Programs in:
communications and information systems • MS
information systems and communications • D Sc
information systems management • MS
Internet information systems • MS

■ SAINT FRANCIS UNIVERSITY

Loretto, PA 15940-0600
http://www.sfcpa.edu/

Independent-religious, coed, comprehensive institution. *Enrollment:* 175 full-time matriculated graduate/professional students (120 women), 402 part-time matriculated graduate/professional students (219 women). *Graduate faculty:* 31 full-time (15 women), 35 part-time/adjunct (9 women). *Computer facilities:* 60 computers available on campus for general student use. A campuswide network can be accessed from student residence rooms. *Library facilities:* Pasquerella Library. *Graduate expenses:* Tuition: part-time $473 per credit. Tuition and fees vary according to program. *General application contact:* Dr. Peter Raymond Skoner, Assistant Vice President for Academic Affairs, 814-472-3085.

Business Administration Program
Program in:
business administration • MBA

Department of Physical Therapy
Program in:
physical therapy • MPT

Department of Physician Assistant Sciences
Albert Simon, Chair
Program in:
physician assistant sciences • MPAS

Graduate School of Human Resource Management and Industrial Relations
Dr. Philip Benham, Director
Program in:
human resource management and industrial relations • MA

Medical Science Program
Dr. William Duryea, Director
Program in:
medical science • MMS

Occupational Therapy Program
Program in:
occupational therapy • MOT

Program in Education
Dr. Elizabeth Gensante, Department Chair
Program in:
leadership • M Ed

■ SAINT JOSEPH'S UNIVERSITY

Philadelphia, PA 19131-1395
http://www.sju.edu/

Independent-religious, coed, comprehensive institution. *Enrollment:* 368 full-time matriculated graduate/professional students (194 women), 2,076 part-time matriculated graduate/professional students (1,291 women). *Graduate faculty:* 89 full-time (34 women). *Computer facilities:* 180 computers available on campus for general student use. A campuswide network can be accessed from student residence rooms and from off campus. Internet access and online class registration are available. *Library facilities:* Francis A. Drexel Library plus 1 other. *Graduate expenses:* Tuition: part-time $610 per credit. *General application contact:* Dr. Robert H. Palestini, Graduate Programs Office, 610-660-1289.

Find an in-depth description at www.petersons.com/graduate.

College of Arts and Sciences
Programs in:
arts and sciences • MA, MS, Ed D, Certificate
biology • MA, MS
chemistry • MS

chemistry education • MS
computer science • MS
criminal justice • MS
education • MS, Certificate
educational leadership • Ed D
gerontological services • MS
health administration • MS
health education • MS
mathematics education • MS
nurse anesthesia • MS
professional education • MS
psychology • MS
reading • MS
secondary education • MS
special education • MS
training and development • MS

Erivan K. Haub School of Business
Dr. Joseph DiAngelo, Dean
Programs in:
accounting • MBA
business • MBA, MS
business administration • MBA
finance • MBA
financial services • MS
food marketing • MS
general business • MBA
health and medical services administration • MBA
human resource management • MS
information systems • MBA
international business • MBA
international marketing • MBA
management • MBA
marketing • MBA
pharmaceutical marketing • MBA

■ SHIPPENSBURG UNIVERSITY OF PENNSYLVANIA
Shippensburg, PA 17257-2299
http://www.ship.edu/

State-supported, coed, comprehensive institution. CGS member. *Enrollment:* 181 full-time matriculated graduate/professional students (112 women), 602 part-time matriculated graduate/professional students (373 women). *Graduate faculty:* 116 full-time (42 women), 22 part-time/adjunct (14 women). *Computer facilities:* 527 computers available on campus for general student use. A campuswide network can be accessed from student residence rooms and from off campus. Internet access, personal Web pages are available. *Library facilities:* Ezra Lehman Memorial Library plus 1 other. *Graduate expenses:* Tuition, state resident: full-time $4,138; part-time $230 per credit hour. Tuition, nonresident: full-time $7,008; part-time $389 per credit hour. Required fees: $714. *General application contact:* Renee Payne, Associate Dean of Graduate Admissions, 717-477-1231.

Find an in-depth description at www.petersons.com/graduate.

School of Graduate Studies and Research
Dr. James G. Coolsen, Dean of Graduate Studies and Associate Provost

College of Arts and Sciences
Dr. Janet Gross, Dean
Programs in:
arts and sciences • M Ed, MPA, MS
biology • M Ed, MS
communication studies • MS
computer science • MS
geoenvironmental studies • MS
information systems • MS
psychology • MS
public administration • MPA

College of Education and Human Services
Dr. Robert B. Bartos, Dean
Programs in:
administration of justice • MS
computer education • M Ed
counseling • MS
education and human services • M Ed, MS, Certificate
elementary education • M Ed
elementary school administration • M Ed
guidance and counseling • M Ed
reading • M Ed
secondary school administration • M Ed
special education • M Ed

■ SLIPPERY ROCK UNIVERSITY OF PENNSYLVANIA
Slippery Rock, PA 16057
http://www.sru.edu/

State-supported, coed, comprehensive institution. *Enrollment:* 323 full-time matriculated graduate/professional students (212 women), 335 part-time matriculated graduate/professional students (246 women). *Graduate faculty:* 65 full-time (30 women). *Computer facilities:* 545 computers available on campus for general student use. A campuswide network can be accessed from student residence rooms and from off campus. Internet access and online class registration are available. *Library facilities:* Bailey Library. *Graduate expenses:* Tuition, state resident: full-time $4,138; part-time $230 per credit. Tuition, nonresident: full-time $7,008; part-time $389 per credit. Required fees: $1,152; $61 per credit. Tuition and fees vary according to course load. *General application contact:* Dr. Duncan M. Sargent, Director of Graduate Studies, 724-738-2051 Ext. 2116.

Find an in-depth description at www.petersons.com/graduate.

Graduate School
Dr. Duncan M. Sargent, Director of Graduate Studies

College of Arts and Sciences
Dr. Charles Zuzak, Dean
Programs in:
arts and sciences • MA
English • MA
history • MA

College of Education
Dr. C. Jay Hertzog, Dean
Programs in:
addiction counseling • MA
child and adolescent counseling • MA
community counseling • MA
early childhood education • M Ed
education • M Ed, MA
elementary guidance and counseling • M Ed
math/science • M Ed
reading • M Ed
secondary education in math/science • M Ed
secondary guidance and counseling • M Ed
special education • M Ed
student personnel • MA

College of Health and Human Services
Dr. Leona Parascenzo, Acting Dean
Programs in:
environmental education • M Ed
health and human services • M Ed, MS, MSN, DPT
nursing • MSN
physical education • M Ed, MS
physical therapy • DPT
resource management • MS
sustainable systems • MS

College of Information Science and Business Administration
Dr. Frank V. Mastrianna, Dean
Programs in:
accounting • MS
information science and business administration • MS

■ TEMPLE UNIVERSITY
Philadelphia, PA 19122-6096
http://www.temple.edu/

State-related, coed, university. CGS member. *Enrollment:* 4,974 full-time matriculated graduate/professional students (2,501 women), 3,863 part-time

Temple University (continued)
matriculated graduate/professional students (2,152 women). *Graduate faculty:* 1,177 full-time (349 women). *Computer facilities:* 2,000 computers available on campus for general student use. A campuswide network can be accessed from student residence rooms and from off campus. Internet access and online class registration, student account and grade information are available. *Library facilities:* Paley Library plus 11 others. *Graduate expenses:* Tuition, state resident: full-time $6,336; part-time $352 per credit. Tuition, nonresident: full-time $8,712; part-time $484 per credit. Required fees: $300. Full-time tuition and fees vary according to course load and program. *General application contact:* Dr. Sheryl Ruzek, Acting Dean, 215-204-1380.

Find an in-depth description at www.petersons.com/graduate.

Graduate School

Dr. Sheryl Ruzek, Acting Dean

College of Education
Dr. Trevor Sewell, Dean
Programs in:
- adult and organizational development • Ed M
- counseling psychology • Ed M, PhD
- early childhood education and elementary education • MS
- education • Ed M, MS, Ed D, PhD
- educational administration • Ed M, Ed D
- educational psychology • Ed M, PhD
- kinesiology • PhD
- math/science education • Ed D
- physical education • Ed M
- reading and language education • MS, Ed D
- school psychology • Ed M, PhD
- secondary education • MS
- special education • MS
- urban education • Ed M, Ed D
- vocational education • MS

College of Liberal Arts
Dr. Morris Vogel, Acting Dean
Programs in:
- African-American studies • MA, PhD
- anthropology • MA, PhD
- clinical psychology • PhD
- cognitive psychology • PhD
- creative writing • MA
- criminal justice • MA, PhD
- developmental psychology • PhD
- English • MA, PhD
- experimental psychology • PhD
- geography • MA
- history • MA, PhD
- liberal arts • MA, MLA, PhD
- philosophy • MA, PhD
- political science • MA, PhD
- religion • MA, PhD
- social and organizational psychology • PhD
- sociology • MA, PhD
- Spanish • MA, PhD
- urban studies • MA

College of Science and Technology
Dr. Chris Platsoucas, Dean
Programs in:
- applied and computational mathematics • MA, PhD
- biology • MA, PhD
- chemistry • MA, PhD
- civil and environmental engineering • MSE
- computer and information sciences • MS, PhD
- electrical and computer engineering • MSE
- engineering • PhD
- environmental health • MS
- environmental health sciences • MS
- geology • MA
- mechanical engineering • MSE
- physics • MA, PhD
- pure mathematics • MA, PhD
- science and technology • MA, MS, MSE, PhD

Esther Boyer College of Music
Dr. Jeffrey Cornelius, Dean
Programs in:
- composition • MM, DMA
- dance • M Ed, MFA, PhD
- music • M Ed, MFA, MM, MMT, DMA, PhD
- music education • MM, PhD
- music history • MM
- music performance • MM, DMA
- music theory • MM
- music therapy • MMT, PhD

Fox School of Business and Management
Dr. M. Moshe Porat, Dean
Programs in:
- accounting • MBA, MS, PhD
- actuarial science • MS
- business administration • MBA
- business and management • EMBA, IMBA, MA, MBA, MS, PhD
- e-business • MBA, MS
- economics • MA, PhD
- executive business administration • EMBA
- finance • MBA, MS, PhD
- general and strategic management • MBA, PhD
- health-care financial management • MS
- health-care management • MBA
- healthcare management • MBA, MS
- human resource administration • MBA, MS, PhD
- international business • PhD
- international business administration • MBA
- management information systems • MBA, MS
- marketing • MBA, MS, PhD
- risk management and insurance • MBA
- risk, insurance, and health-care management • PhD
- statistics • MS, PhD

School of Communications and Theater
Dr. Priscilla Murphy, Associate Dean
Programs in:
- acting • MFA
- broadcasting, telecommunications and mass media • MA
- communications and theater • MA, MFA, MJ, PhD
- design • MFA
- film and media arts • MFA
- journalism • MJ
- mass media and communication • PhD

School of Social Administration
Dr. Linda M. Mauro, Associate Dean
Programs in:
- community health education • MPH
- health studies • PhD
- public health • MPH
- school health education • Ed M
- social administration • Ed M, MPH, MSW, PhD
- social work • MSW
- therapeutic recreation • Ed M

School of Tourism and Hospitality Management
Dr. Elizabeth Barber, Interim Head
Programs in:
- sport and recreation administration • Ed M
- tourism and hospitality management • Ed M, MTHM

Tyler School of Art
Rochelle Toner, Dean
Programs in:
- art • M Ed, MA, MFA, PhD
- art education • M Ed
- art history • MA, PhD
- ceramics • MFA
- fibers • MFA
- glass • MFA
- metalworking • MFA
- painting/drawing • MFA
- photography • MFA
- printmaking • MFA
- sculpture • MFA
- visual design • MFA

Health Sciences Center

Program in:
- health sciences • DMD, DPM, MD, Pharm D, MA, MPT, MS, MSN, PhD, Certificate

College of Allied Health Professions
Donna Weiss, Assistant Dean
Programs in:
allied health professions • MA, MPT, MS, MSN, PhD
applied communication • MA
communication sciences • PhD
linguistics • MA
nursing • MSN
occupational therapy • MS
physical therapy • MPT, MS, PhD
speech, language, and hearing • MA

School of Dentistry
Thomas E. Rams, Associate Dean for Advanced Education
Programs in:
advanced education in general dentistry • Certificate
dentistry • DMD, MS, Certificate
endodontology • Certificate
oral and maxillofacial surgery • Certificate
oral biology • MS
orthodontics • Certificate
periodontology • Certificate
prosthodontics • Certificate

School of Medicine
Dr. Leon Malmud, Dean
Programs in:
anatomy and cell biology • PhD
biochemistry • MS, PhD
medicine • MD, MS, PhD
microbiology and immunology • MS, PhD
molecular biology and genetics • PhD
pathology and laboratory medicine • PhD
pharmacology • MS, PhD
physiology • MS, PhD

School of Pharmacy
Dr. Cherng-Ju Kim, Director of Graduate Studies and Research
Programs in:
medicinal and pharmaceutical chemistry • MS, PhD
pharmaceutics • MS, PhD
pharmacy • Pharm D, MS, PhD
quality assurance/regulatory affairs • MS

School of Podiatric Medicine
Dr. John A. Mattiacci, Dean
Program in:
podiatric medicine • DPM

James E. Beasley School of Law
Robert J. Reinstein, Dean
Programs in:
law • JD
taxation • LL M
transnational law • LL M
trial advocacy • LL M

■ UNIVERSITY OF PENNSYLVANIA
Philadelphia, PA 19104
http://www.upenn.edu/

Independent, coed, university. CGS member. *Enrollment:* 8,254 full-time matriculated graduate/professional students (3,999 women), 1,638 part-time matriculated graduate/professional students (821 women). *Graduate faculty:* 2,251 full-time (549 women), 4,082 part-time/adjunct (1,467 women). *Computer facilities:* 1,000 computers available on campus for general student use. A campuswide network can be accessed from student residence rooms and from off campus. Internet access and online class registration are available. *Library facilities:* Van Pelt-Dietrich Library plus 13 others. *Graduate expenses:* Tuition: full-time $25,750. Required fees: $1,612. *General application contact:* Patricia Rea, Admissions Assistant, 215-898-5720.

Find an in-depth description at www.petersons.com/graduate.

Annenberg School for Communication
Dr. Kathleen Hall Jamieson, Dean
Program in:
communication • MAC, PhD

Fels Center of Government
Dr. John J. Mulhern, Administrator
Program in:
government • MGA

Graduate School of Education
Dr. Susan Fuhrman, Dean
Programs in:
counseling psychology • MS Ed
early childhood education • MS Ed
education • MS Ed, Ed D, PhD
education, culture, and society • MS Ed, Ed D, PhD
educational leadership • MS Ed, Ed D, PhD
educational linguistics • PhD
educational policy and leadership • MS Ed, Ed D, PhD
elementary education • MS Ed
higher education • MS Ed, Ed D, PhD
human development • MS Ed, PhD
human sexuality education • MS Ed, Ed D, PhD
intercultural communication • MS Ed
language in education • MS Ed, Ed D, PhD
policy research, evaluation, and measurement • MS Ed, PhD
psychological services • MS Ed
reading, writing, and literacy • MS Ed, Ed D, PhD
school, community, and clinical child psychology • PhD
secondary education • MS Ed
teaching English to speakers of other languages • MS Ed

Graduate School of Fine Arts
Gary Hack, Dean
Programs in:
architecture • M Arch
city and regional planning • MCP, PhD, Certificate
conservation and heritage management • Certificate
fine arts • M Arch, MCP, MFA, MLA, MS, PhD, Certificate
historic conservation • Certificate
historic preservation • MS
landscape architecture and regional planning • MLA
landscape studies • Certificate
real estate design and development • Certificate
urban design • Certificate

Law School
Michael A. Fitts, Dean
Program in:
law • JD, LL CM, LL M, SJD

School of Arts and Sciences
Dr. Joseph Farrell, Associate Dean for Graduate Students
Programs in:
American civilization • AM, PhD
ancient history • AM, PhD
anthropology • AM, MS, PhD
art and archaeology of the Mediterranean world • AM, PhD
arts and sciences • AM, MA, MBA, MS, PhD
Asian and Middle Eastern studies • AM, PhD
cell, molecular, and developmental biology • PhD
chemistry • MS, PhD
classical studies • AM, PhD
comparative literature • AM, PhD
demography • AM, PhD
ecology and population biology • PhD
economics • AM, PhD
English • AM, PhD
folklore and folklife • AM, PhD
French • AM, PhD
geology • MS, PhD
Germanic languages • AM, PhD
history • AM, PhD
history and sociology of science • AM, PhD
history of art • AM, PhD
international studies • MA
Italian • AM, PhD

University of Pennsylvania (continued)
linguistics • AM, PhD
literary theory • AM, PhD
mathematics • AM, PhD
music • AM, PhD
neurobiology/physiology and behavior • PhD
organizational dynamics • MS
philosophy • AM, PhD
physics • PhD
plant science • PhD
political science • AM, PhD
psychology • PhD
religious studies • PhD
sociology • AM, PhD
South Asian regional studies • AM, PhD
Spanish • AM, PhD

Joseph H. Lauder Institute of Management and International Studies
Dr. Richard J. Herring, Director
Program in:
international studies • MA

School of Dental Medicine
Dr. Raymond Fonseca, Dean
Program in:
dental medicine • DMD

School of Engineering and Applied Science
Eduardo D. Glandt, Interim Dean
Programs in:
applied mechanics • MSE, PhD
bioengineering • MSE, PhD
biotechnology • MS
chemical engineering • MSE, PhD
computer and information science • MCIT, MSE, PhD
electrical engineering • MSE, PhD
engineering and applied science • MCIT, MS, MSE, PhD
environmental resources engineering • MSE
environmental/resources engineering • PhD
management of technology • MSE
materials science and engineering • MSE, PhD
mechanical engineering • MSE, PhD
systems engineering • MSE, PhD
technology and public policy • MSE, PhD
telecommunications and networking • MSE
transportation • MSE, PhD

School of Medicine
Dr. Arthur K. Asbury, Interim Dean
Program in:
medicine • MD, MS, MSCE, PhD

Biomedical Graduate Studies
Dr. Michael E. Selzer, Director
Programs in:
biochemistry and molecular biophysics • PhD
biomedical studies • MS, PhD
biostatistics • MS, PhD
cell biology and physiology • PhD
cell growth and cancer • PhD
cell structure and function • PhD
developmental biology • PhD
gene therapy • PhD
genetics and gene regulation • PhD
immunology • PhD
microbiology and virology • PhD
neuroscience • PhD
parasitology • PhD
pharmacology • PhD

Center for Clinical Epidemiology and Biostatistics
Dr. Brian L. Strom, Chair
Programs in:
clinical epidemiology • MSCE
epidemiology • PhD

School of Nursing
Dr. Joyce Thompson, Associate Dean and Director of Graduate Studies
Programs in:
acute care nurse practitioner • MSN
administration/consulting • MSN
adult and special populations • MSN
adult oncology advanced practice nurse • MSN
adult/gerontological nurse practitioner • MSN
child and family • MSN
family health nurse practitioner • MSN, Certificate
geropsychiatrics • MSN
health care of women nurse practitioner • MSN
health leadership • MSN
neonatal nurse practitioner • MSN
nurse midwifery • MSN
nursing • MSN, PhD, Certificate
nursing and health care administration • MSN, PhD
pediatric acute/chronic care nurse practitioner • MSN
pediatric critical care nurse practitioner • MSN
pediatric nurse practitioner • MSN
pediatric oncology nurse practitioner • MSN
perinatal advanced practice nurse specialist • MSN
primary care • MSN

School of Social Work
Ira M. Schwartz, Dean
Programs in:
social welfare • PhD
social work • MSW, PhD

School of Veterinary Medicine
Dr. Alan M. Kelly, Dean
Program in:
veterinary medicine • VMD

Wharton School
Dr. Patrick T. Harker, Chairman
Programs in:
accounting • PhD
business • Exec MBA, MA, MBA, MS, PhD
business administration • MBA
business and public policy • PhD
executive business administration • Exec MBA
finance • PhD
health care systems • PhD
insurance and risk management • PhD
legal studies • MBA
management • PhD
marketing • PhD
operations and information management • MBA, MS, PhD
operations and information management operations research • PhD
real estate • PhD
statistics • PhD

■ UNIVERSITY OF PITTSBURGH

Pittsburgh, PA 15260
http://www.pitt.edu/

State-related, coed, university. CGS member. *Enrollment:* 5,908 full-time matriculated graduate/professional students (2,997 women), 2,997 part-time matriculated graduate/professional students (1,731 women). *Graduate faculty:* 3,053 full-time (998 women), 659 part-time/adjunct (323 women). *Computer facilities:* 600 computers available on campus for general student use. A campuswide network can be accessed from student residence rooms and from off campus. Internet access and online class registration, on-line class listings are available. *Library facilities:* Hillman Library plus 26 others. *Graduate expenses:* Tuition, state resident: full-time $8,754; part-time $359 per credit. Tuition, nonresident: full-time $18,026; part-time $742 per credit. Required fees: $480.

Find an in-depth description at www.petersons.com/graduate.

Center for Neuroscience
Dr. H. Richard Koerber, Co-Director
Programs in:
neurobiology • PhD
neuroscience • PhD

Faculty of Arts and Sciences
Dr. Steven Husted, Associate Dean, Graduate Studies and Research

Programs in:
anthropology • MA, PhD
applied mathematics • MA, MS
applied statistics • MA, MS
arts and sciences • MA, MFA, MS, PhD, Certificate
astronomy • MS, PhD
bioethics • MA
chemistry • MS, PhD
classics • MA, PhD
communication • MA, PhD
computer science • MS, PhD
East Asian studies • MA
ecology and evolution • MS, PhD
English • MA, MFA, PhD
French • MA, PhD
geology and planetary science • MS, PhD
Germanic languages and literatures • MA, PhD
Hispanic languages and literatures • MA, PhD
history • MA, PhD
history and philosophy of science • MA, PhD
history of art and architecture • MA, PhD
intelligent systems • MS, PhD
Italian • MA
linguistics • MA, PhD
mathematics • MA, MS, PhD
molecular biophysics • PhD
molecular, cellular, and developmental biology • PhD
music • MA, PhD
performance pedagogy • MFA
philosophy • MA, PhD
physics • MS, PhD
political science • MA, PhD
psychology • MS, PhD
religion • PhD
religious studies • MA
Slavic languages and literatures • MA, PhD
sociology • MA, PhD
statistics • MA, MS, PhD
teaching English as another language • MA, Certificate
theatre and performance studies • MA, PhD
women's studies • Certificate

Center for Latin American Studies
Billie R. DeWalt, Director
Program in:
Latin American studies • Certificate

Department of Economics
Jean-Frances Richard, Department Chair
Program in:
economics • MA, PhD

Graduate School of Public and International Affairs
Dr. Carolyn Ban, Dean
Programs in:
criminal justice • MPPM
development planning • MPPM
environmental management and policy • MPPM
international development • MPPM
international political economy • MPPM
international security studies • MPPM
management of non profit organizations • MPPM
metropolitan management and regional development • MPPM
personnel and labor relations • MPPM
policy analysis and evaluation • MPPM
policy research and analysis • MPA, MSW/MPA
public and international affairs • MPA, MPH/MPIA, MPIA, MPPM, MSW/MPA, MSW/MPIA, PhD
public and urban affairs • MPA, MSW/MPA
public management and policy • MPA
urban and regional affairs • MPA, MSW/MPA

Division of International Development
Dr. Louis Picard, Director, International Development Division
Program in:
economic and social development • MPIA

Division of Public and Urban Affairs
Dr. Stephen Farber, Director, Public and Urban Affairs Division
Programs in:
policy research and analysis • MPA, MSW/MPA
public and urban affairs • MPA, MSW/MPA
public management and policy • MPA
urban and regional affairs • MPA, MSW/MPA

Doctoral Program in Public and International Affairs
Programs in:
development studies • PhD
foreign and security policy • PhD
international political economy • PhD
public administration • PhD
public policy • PhD

International Affairs Division
Dr. Martin Staniland, Director, International Affairs Division
Programs in:
global political economy • MPIA
security and intelligence studies • MPIA

Graduate School of Public Health
Dr. Herbert S. Rosenkranz, Interim Dean
Programs in:
behavioral and community health services • MPH
biostatistics • MPH, MS, Dr PH, PhD
environmental and occupational health • MPH, MS, PhD
epidemiology • MPH, MS, Dr PH, PhD
genetic counseling • MS
health administration • MHA
health services administration • Dr PH
human genetics • MS, PhD
infectious diseases and microbiology • MPH, MS, Dr PH, PhD
occupational medicine • MPH
public health • MHA, MHPE, MPH, MS, Dr PH, PhD, Certificate
radiation health • Certificate

Joseph M. Katz Graduate School of Business
Dr. Frederick W. Winter, Dean
Programs in:
business • EMBA, MBA, MHA, MS, PhD
business administration • MBA, PhD
international business • MBA
international business administration • MBA
management of information systems • MS

School of Dental Medicine
Dr. Thomas W. Braun, Dean
Programs in:
anesthesiology • Certificate
dental medicine • DMD, MDS, MS, Certificate
endodontics • MS, Certificate
maxillofacial prosthodontics • Certificate
orthodontics • Certificate
pediatric dentistry • MDS, Certificate
periodontics • MDS, Certificate
prosthodontics • MDS, Certificate

School of Education
Dr. Alan Lesgold, Dean
Programs in:
child development • MS
cognitive studies • PhD
deaf and hard of hearing • M Ed
developmental movement • MS, PhD
early childhood education • M Ed
early education of disabled students • M Ed

University of Pittsburgh (continued)
education • M Ed, MA, MAT, MHPE, MS, Ed D, PhD
education of students with mental and physical disabilities • M Ed
education of the visually impaired • M Ed
educational and developmental psychology • PhD
educational leadership development • M Ed, Ed D
elementary education • M Ed, MAT
English/communications education • M Ed, MAT, Ed D, PhD
exercise physiology • MS, PhD
foreign languages education • M Ed, MA, MAT, Ed D, PhD
general special education • M Ed
health promotion and education • MHPE
higher education • M Ed, Ed D
international development education • MA, PhD
international developmental education • M Ed
mathematics education • M Ed, MAT, Ed D
reading education • M Ed, Ed D, PhD
research methodology • M Ed, MA, PhD
school leadership development • M Ed, Ed D
science education • M Ed, MAT, MS, Ed D, PhD
secondary education • M Ed, MA, MAT, MS, Ed D, PhD
social and comparative analysis • M Ed, MA, PhD
social studies education • M Ed, MAT, Ed D, PhD
social, philosophical, and historical foundations of education • M Ed, MA, PhD
special education • M Ed, Ed D, PhD

School of Engineering
Dr. Gerald D. Holder, Dean
Programs in:
bioengineering • MSBENG, PhD
chemical engineering • MS Ch E, PhD
civil and environmental engineering • MSCEE, PhD
electrical engineering • MSEE, PhD
engineering • MS Ch E, MS Met E, MSBENG, MSCEE, MSEE, MSIE, MSME, MSMSE, MSMfSE, MSPE, PhD, Certificate
industrial engineering • MSIE, PhD
manufacturing systems engineering • MSMfSE
materials science and engineering • MSMSE, PhD
mechanical engineering • MSME, PhD
metallurgical engineering • MS Met E, PhD
petroleum engineering • MSPE

School of Health and Rehabilitation Sciences
Dr. Clifford Brubaker, Dean
Programs in:
communication science and disorders • MA, MS, PhD
health and rehabilitation sciences • MS
physical therapy • MPT
rehabilitation engineering • Certificate
rehabilitation science • PhD
rehabilitation sciences • PhD
rehabilitation technology • Certificate
rehabilitation technology service delivery • Certificate
sports medicine • MS

School of Information Sciences
Programs in:
information science • MSIS, PhD, Certificate
information sciences • MLIS, MSIS, MST, PhD, Certificate
library and information science • MLIS, PhD, Certificate
telecommunications • MST, Certificate

School of Law
David J. Herring, Dean
Programs in:
business law • MSL
constitutional law • MSL
criminal justice • MSL
dispute resolution • MSL
education law • MSL
elder and estate planning law • MSL
employment and labor law • MSL
environment and real estate law • MSL
family law • MSL
general law and jurisprudence • MSL
health law • MSL
intellectual property and cyber law • MSL
international and comparative law • MSL
law • JD, LL M, MSL, Certificate
personal injury and civil litigation • MSL
regulatory law • MSL
self-designed • MSL

School of Medicine
Dr. Arthur S. Levine, Dean
Programs in:
biochemistry and molecular genetics • MS, PhD
biomedical sciences • PhD
cell biology and molecular physiology • MS, PhD
cellular and molecular pathology • MS, PhD
immunology • MS, PhD
medicine • MD, MS, PhD
molecular pharmacology • PhD
molecular virology and microbiology • MS, PhD
neurobiology • MS, PhD

School of Nursing
Dr. Ellen B. Rudy, Dean
Programs in:
acute and tertiary care • MSN
administration • MSN
anesthesia nursing • MSN
health and community systems • MSN
health promotion and development • MSN
informatics • MSN
nursing • MSN, PhD
nursing education • MSN
research • MSN

School of Pharmacy
Dr. Randy P. Juhl, Dean
Programs in:
pharmaceutical sciences • MS, PhD
pharmacy • Pharm D, MS, PhD

School of Social Work
Dr. David E. Epperson, Dean
Programs in:
employee assistance • Certificate
employee assistance programs • Certificate
family and marital therapy • Certificate
gerontology • Certificate
social work • MSW, PhD, Certificate

■ THE UNIVERSITY OF SCRANTON
Scranton, PA 18510
http://www.scranton.edu/

Independent-religious, coed, comprehensive institution. CGS member. *Enrollment:* 219 full-time matriculated graduate/professional students (140 women), 384 part-time matriculated graduate/professional students (240 women). *Graduate faculty:* 137 full-time (46 women), 34 part-time/adjunct (14 women). *Computer facilities:* 777 computers available on campus for general student use. A campuswide network can be accessed from student residence rooms and from off campus. Internet access and online class registration are available. *Library facilities:* Harry and Jeanette Weinberg Memorial Library plus 1 other. *Graduate expenses:* Tuition: part-time $515 per semester hour. Required fees: $25 per term. Tuition and fees vary according to program. *General application contact:* James L. Goonan, Director of Admissions, 570-941-6304.

Find an in-depth description at www.petersons.com/graduate.

Graduate School

Dr. Rose Sebastianelli, Acting Dean
Programs in:

- accounting • MBA
- adult health nursing • MS
- biochemistry • MA, MS
- chemistry • MA, MS
- clinical chemistry • MA, MS
- community counseling • MS
- early childhood education • MS
- educational administration • MS
- elementary education • MS
- elementary school administration • MS
- English • MA
- family nurse practitioner • MS
- finance • MBA
- general business administration • MBA
- health administration • MHA
- history • MA
- human resources • MS
- human resources administration • MS
- human resources development • MS
- international business • MBA
- marketing • MBA
- nurse anesthesia • MS
- organizational leadership • MS
- personnel/labor • MBA
- reading education • MS
- rehabilitation counseling • MS
- school counseling • MS
- secondary education • MS
- secondary school administration • MS
- software engineering • MS
- theology • MA

■ VILLANOVA UNIVERSITY

Villanova, PA 19085-1699
http://www.villanova.edu/

Independent-religious, coed, comprehensive institution. CGS member. *Enrollment:* 1,218 full-time matriculated graduate/professional students (577 women), 1,459 part-time matriculated graduate/professional students (887 women). *Computer facilities:* 800 computers available on campus for general student use. A campuswide network can be accessed from student residence rooms and from off campus. Internet access and online class registration are available. *Library facilities:* Falvey Library plus 2 others. *Graduate expenses:* Tuition: part-time $445 per credit. *General application contact:* Dr. Gerald Long, Dean, Graduate School of Liberal Arts and Sciences, 610-519-7090.

Find an in-depth description at www.petersons.com/graduate.

College of Commerce and Finance

Dr. Thomas F. Monahan, Dean
Programs in:

- accounting and professional consultancy • M Ac
- business administration • MBA
- commerce and finance • EMBA, LL M in Tax, M Ac, MBA, MT
- executive business administration • EMBA

College of Engineering

Programs in:

- chemical engineering • M Ch E
- civil engineering • MCE
- computer engineering • MSCE
- electrical engineering • MSEE
- engineering • M Ch E, MCE, MME, MSCE, MSEE, MSTE, MSWREE, Certificate
- manufacturing • Certificate
- mechanical engineering • MME
- transportation engineering • MSTE
- virtual manufacturing • Certificate
- water resources and environmental engineering • MSWREE

College of Nursing

Dr. Claire Manfredi, Graduate Director
Programs in:

- adult nurse practitioner • MSN, Post Master's Certificate
- clinical case management • MSN, Post Master's Certificate
- geriatric nurse practitioner • MSN, Post Master's Certificate
- health care administration • MSN
- nurse anesthetist • MSN, Post Master's Certificate
- nursing education • MSN, Post Master's Certificate
- pediatric nurse practitioner • MSN, Post Master's Certificate

Graduate School of Liberal Arts and Sciences

Dr. Gerald Long, Dean
Programs in:

- applied statistics • MS
- biology • MA, MS
- chemistry • MS
- classical studies • MA
- community counseling • MS
- computing sciences • MS
- counseling and human relations • MS
- criminal justice administration • MS
- educational leadership • MA
- elementary school counseling • MS
- elementary teacher education • MA
- English • MA
- history • MA
- human resource development • MS
- Latin • MA
- liberal arts and sciences • MA, MPA, MS, PhD
- liberal studies • MA
- mathematical sciences • MA
- philosophy • MA, PhD
- political science • MA, MPA
- psychology • MS
- public administration • MPA
- secondary administration • MS
- secondary school counseling • MS
- secondary teacher education • MA
- Spanish • MA
- theatre • MA
- theology • MA

School of Law

Mark A. Sargent, Dean
Programs in:

- law • JD, LL M in Tax, MT
- taxation • LL M in Tax, MT

■ WAYNESBURG COLLEGE

Waynesburg, PA 15370-1222
http://www.waynesburg.edu/

Independent-religious, coed, comprehensive institution. *Computer facilities:* 150 computers available on campus for general student use. A campuswide network can be accessed from student residence rooms and from off campus. Internet access is available. *Library facilities:* Waynesburg College Library. *General application contact:* Director, 412-854-3600.

Graduate and Professional Studies

Program in:

- business administration • MBA

■ WEST CHESTER UNIVERSITY OF PENNSYLVANIA

West Chester, PA 19383
http://www.wcupa.edu/

State-supported, coed, comprehensive institution. CGS member. *Enrollment:* 337 full-time matriculated graduate/professional students (254 women), 1,196 part-time matriculated graduate/professional students (814 women). *Graduate faculty:* 232. *Computer facilities:* 1,000 computers available on campus for general student use. A campuswide network can be accessed from student residence rooms and from off campus.

West Chester University of Pennsylvania (continued)
Internet access and online class registration are available. *Library facilities:* Francis Harvey Green Library plus 1 other. *Graduate expenses:* Tuition, state resident: full-time $4,167; part-time $230 per credit. Tuition, nonresident: full-time $7,008; part-time $389 per credit. Required fees: $718; $41 per credit. *General application contact:* Dr. Gopal Sankaran, Interim Dean, 610-436-2943.

Find an in-depth description at www.petersons.com/graduate.

Graduate Studies
Dr. Gopal Sankaran, Interim Dean

College of Arts and Sciences
Dr. Jennie Skerl, Dean
Programs in:
- arts and sciences • M Ed, MA, MS, MSA, Certificate
- biology • MS
- chemistry • M Ed, MS
- clinical chemistry • MS
- clinical psychology • MA
- communication studies • MA
- computer science • MS, Certificate
- English • MA
- French • M Ed, MA
- general psychology • MA
- gerentology • Certificate
- German • M Ed
- history • M Ed, MA
- industrial organizational psychology • MA
- Latin • M Ed
- long term care • MSA
- mathematics • MA
- philosophy • MA
- physical science • MA
- Spanish • M Ed, MA
- teaching English as a second language • MA

School of Business and Public Affairs
Dr. Christopher Fiorentino, Dean
Programs in:
- business and public affairs • MA, MBA, MS, MSA, MSW
- criminal justice • MS
- economics/finance • MBA
- executive business administration • MBA
- general business • MBA
- geography • MA
- health services • MSA
- human research management • MSA
- individualized • MSA
- leadership for women • MSA
- long-term care • MSA
- management • MBA
- public administration • MSA
- regional planning • MSA
- social work • MSW
- sport and athletic administration • MSA
- sport and athletic training • MSA
- technology and electronic commerce • MBA
- training and development • MSA

School of Education
Dr. Tony Johnson, Dean
Programs in:
- counseling and educational psychology • M Ed, MS
- early childhood and special education • M Ed
- educational research • MS
- elementary education • M Ed
- elementary school counseling • M Ed
- higher education counseling • MS
- literacy • M Ed
- professional and secondary education • M Ed, MS
- reading • M Ed
- secondary education • M Ed
- secondary school counseling • M Ed
- special education • M Ed
- teaching and learning with technology • Certificate

School of Health Sciences
Dr. Donald E. Barr, Dean
Programs in:
- communicative disorders • MA
- driver education • Certificate
- environmental health • MS
- exercise and sport physiology • MS
- gerontology • MS
- health sciences • M Ed, MA, MS, MSA, MSN, Certificate
- health services • MSA
- nursing • MSN
- nursing education • MSN
- physical education • MS
- public health • MS
- safety • Certificate
- school health • M Ed
- sport and athletic administration • MSA

School of Music
Dr. Timothy Blair, Dean
Programs in:
- accompanying • MM
- composition • MM
- music • MA, MM
- music education • MM
- music history • MA
- music theory • MM
- performance • MM
- piano pedagogy • MM

■ WIDENER UNIVERSITY
Chester, PA 19013-5792
http://www.widener.edu/

Independent, coed, comprehensive institution. CGS member. *Computer facilities:* 310 computers available on campus for general student use. A campuswide network can be accessed from student residence rooms and from off campus. Internet access is available. *Library facilities:* Wolfgram Memorial Library. *General application contact:* Assistant Provost for Graduate Studies, 610-499-4351.

Find an in-depth description at www.petersons.com/graduate.

College of Arts and Sciences
Programs in:
- arts and sciences • MA, MPA
- criminal justice • MA
- liberal studies • MA
- public administration • MPA

School of Business Administration
Programs in:
- accounting information systems • MS
- business administration • MBA, MHA, MHR, MS
- health and medical services administration • MBA, MHA
- human resource management • MHR, MS
- taxation • MS

School of Engineering
Programs in:
- chemical engineering • ME
- civil engineering • ME
- computer and software engineering • ME
- electrical/telecommunication engineering • ME
- engineering • ME
- engineering management • ME
- mechanical engineering • ME

School of Human Service Professions
Program in:
- human service professions • M Ed, MS, MSW, Ed D, Psy D

Center for Education
Programs in:
- adult education • M Ed
- counseling in higher education • M Ed
- counselor education • M Ed
- early childhood education • M Ed
- educational foundations • M Ed
- educational leadership • M Ed
- educational psychology • M Ed
- elementary education • M Ed
- English and language arts • M Ed
- health education • M Ed
- higher education leadership • Ed D
- home and school visitor • M Ed
- human sexuality • M Ed
- mathematics education • M Ed
- middle school education • M Ed
- principalship • M Ed
- reading and language arts • Ed D

reading education • M Ed
school administration • Ed D
science education • M Ed
social studies education • M Ed
special education • M Ed
technology education • M Ed

Center for Social Work Education
Program in:
social work education • MSW

Institute for Graduate Clinical Psychology
Programs in:
clinical psychology • Psy D

Institute for Physical Therapy Education
Program in:
physical therapy education • MS

School of Law at Wilmington
Douglas E. Ray, Dean
Programs in:
corporate law and finance • LL M
health law • LL M, MJ, D Law
juridical science • SJD
law • JD

School of Nursing
Program in:
nursing • MSN, DN Sc, PMC

Widener University School of Law
Douglas E. Ray, Dean
Program in:
law • JD

■ WILKES UNIVERSITY

Wilkes-Barre, PA 18766-0002
http://www.wilkes.edu/

Independent, coed, comprehensive institution. *Enrollment:* 295 full-time matriculated graduate/professional students (192 women), 1,513 part-time matriculated graduate/professional students (1,062 women). *Graduate faculty:* 113 full-time, 114 part-time/adjunct. *Computer facilities:* 700 computers available on campus for general student use. A campuswide network can be accessed from student residence rooms and from off campus. Internet access and online class registration are available. *Library facilities:* Eugene S. Farley Library. *Graduate expenses:* Tuition: full-time $13,656; part-time $569 per credit hour. Required fees: $312. Tuition and fees vary according to program. *General application contact:* Dr. Bonnie Bedford, Dean of Graduate Studies, 570-408-4600.

College of Arts, Sciences, and Professional Studies
Dr. Bonnie Bedford, Dean of Graduate Studies
Programs in:
accounting • MBA
arts, sciences, and professional studies • MBA, MS, MS Ed, MSEE, MSN
educational computing • MS Ed
educational development and strategies • MS Ed
educational leadership • MS Ed
electrical engineering • MSEE
elementary education • MS Ed
finance • MBA
health care • MBA
human resource management • MBA
international business • MBA
marketing • MBA
mathematics • MS, MS Ed
nursing • MSN
physics • MS Ed
secondary education • MS Ed

Nesbitt School of Pharmacy
Dr. Bernard Graham, Dean
Program in:
pharmacy • Pharm D

■ YORK COLLEGE OF PENNSYLVANIA

York, PA 17405-7199
http://www.ycp.edu/

Independent, coed, comprehensive institution. *Enrollment:* 72 full-time matriculated graduate/professional students (45 women), 178 part-time matriculated graduate/professional students (73 women). *Graduate faculty:* 17 full-time (3 women), 1 part-time/adjunct (0 women). *Computer facilities:* 250 computers available on campus for general student use. A campuswide network can be accessed from student residence rooms and from off campus. Internet access and online class registration are available. *Library facilities:* Schmidt Library plus 1 other. *Graduate expenses:* Tuition: part-time $308 per credit. Required fees: $80 per term. Full-time tuition and fees vary according to course load. *General application contact:* John F. Barbor, MBA Coordinator, 717-815-1491.

Department of Business Administration
John F. Barbor, MBA Coordinator
Programs in:
accounting/finance • MBA
general business • MBA
health care management • MBA
human resource management • MBA
information systems • MBA
management • MBA
marketing • MBA

Puerto Rico

■ BAYAMÓN CENTRAL UNIVERSITY

Bayamón, PR 00960-1725
http://www.ucb.edu.pr/

Independent-religious, coed, comprehensive institution. *Enrollment:* 206 full-time matriculated graduate/professional students (143 women), 122 part-time matriculated graduate/professional students (79 women). *Graduate faculty:* 1 (woman) full-time, 29 part-time/adjunct (17 women). *Computer facilities:* 130 computers available on campus for general student use. A campuswide network can be accessed. Internet access is available. *Library facilities:* BCU Library plus 1 other. *Graduate expenses:* Tuition: full-time $3,750; part-time $135 per credit. Required fees: $280; $140 per semester. *General application contact:* Christine Hernández, Director of Admissions, 787-786-3030 Ext. 2100.

Graduate Programs
Dr. Carmen Ortiz, Director
Programs in:
accounting • MBA
administration and supervision • MA Ed
biblical studies • MA
divinity • M Div
education of the autistic • MA Ed
elementary education (K–3) • MA Ed
elementary education (K–6) • MA Ed
general business • MBA
guidance and counseling • MA Ed
management • MBA
marketing • MBA
pastoral theology • MA
pre-elementary teacher • MA Ed
psychology • MA
religious studies • MA
special education • MA Ed
specific learning disabled • MA Ed
theological studies • MA
theology • MA

■ INTER AMERICAN UNIVERSITY OF PUERTO RICO, METROPOLITAN CAMPUS

San Juan, PR 00919-1293

http://metro.inter.edu/

Independent, coed, comprehensive institution. CGS member. *Computer facilities:* 400 computers available on campus for general student use. A campuswide network can be accessed from student residence rooms and from off campus. Internet access and online class registration are available. *Library facilities:* Centro de Acceso a la Informacion plus 1 other. *General application contact:* Graduate Coordinator, 787-250-1912.

Division of Science and Technology

Programs in:
- educational computing • MA
- medical technology • MS
- open information systems • MS

Graduate Programs

Division of Behavioral Science and Allied Professions

Programs in:
- criminal justice • MA
- psychology • MA
- social work • MA

Division of Education

Programs in:
- administration and supervision • MA
- education • Ed D
- elementary education • MA
- guidance and counseling • MA
- health and physical education • MA
- higher education • MA Ed
- occupational education • MA
- special education • MA Ed
- teaching of science • MA Ed
- vocational evaluation • MA

Faculty of Economics and Administrative Sciences

Programs in:
- accounting • MBA
- business and management development • PhD
- business education • MA
- finance • MBA
- human resources • MBA
- industrial management • MBA
- labor relations • MA
- marketing • MBA

School of Humanistic Studies

Programs in:
- humanistic studies • MA
- Spanish • MA
- teaching English as a second language • MA

School of Law

Program in:
- law • JD

School of Optometry

Program in:
- optometry • OD

■ INTER AMERICAN UNIVERSITY OF PUERTO RICO, SAN GERMÁN CAMPUS

San Germán, PR 00683-5008

http://www.sg.inter.edu/

Independent, coed, university. *Enrollment:* 324 full-time matriculated graduate/professional students, 563 part-time matriculated graduate/professional students. *Graduate faculty:* 39 full-time (18 women), 40 part-time/adjunct (15 women). *Computer facilities:* 520 computers available on campus for general student use. A campuswide network can be accessed. Internet access and online class registration are available. *Library facilities:* Juan Cancio Ortiz Library. *Graduate expenses:* Tuition: part-time $165 per credit. Required fees: $195 per term. Full-time tuition and fees vary according to degree level. *General application contact:* Dr. Waldemar Velez, Director of Graduate Program Center, 787-892-4300 Ext. 7358.

Graduate Programs

Dr. Waldemar Velez, Director of Graduate Program Center

Programs in:
- accounting • MBA
- administration of higher education institutions • MA
- art • MA
- business administration • MBA
- business education • MA
- curriculum and instruction • MA Ed
- educational administration • MA Ed
- environmental sciences • MS
- finance • MBA
- guidance and counseling • MA Ed
- health sciences • Certificate
- human resources • MBA
- industrial relations • MBA
- library science • MA
- management sciences • PhD
- marketing • MBA
- physical education and scientific analysis of human body movement • MA Ed
- psychology • MA, MS
- science education • MA
- special education • MS Ed
- teaching English as a second language • MA

■ PONTIFICAL CATHOLIC UNIVERSITY OF PUERTO RICO

Ponce, PR 00717-0777

http://www.pucpr.edu/

Independent-religious, coed, university. *Enrollment:* 850 full-time matriculated graduate/professional students (487 women), 1,067 part-time matriculated graduate/professional students (719 women). *Graduate faculty:* 60 full-time (29 women), 55 part-time/adjunct (19 women). *Computer facilities:* 419 computers available on campus for general student use. A campuswide network can be accessed from off campus. Internet access is available. *Library facilities:* Encarnacion Valdes Library plus 1 other. *Graduate expenses:* Tuition: full-time $2,700. Required fees: $360. Tuition and fees vary according to course load and degree level. *General application contact:* Ana O. Bonilla, Director of Admissions, 787-841-2000 Ext. 1000.

College of Arts and Humanities

Rev. Felix Lazaro, Chairperson

Programs in:
- arts and humanities • MA
- divinity • MA
- Hispanic studies • MA
- history • MA

College of Business Administration

Dr. Kenya Carrasquillo, Chairperson

Programs in:
- accounting • MBA
- business administration • PhD
- finance • MBA
- human resources • MBA
- merchandising • MBA
- office administration • MBA

College of Education

Dr. Myvian Zayas, Chairperson

Programs in:
- commercial education • MRE
- curriculum instruction • M Ed
- education • PhD
- education-general • MRE
- English as a second language • MRE
- religious education • MA Ed
- scholar psychology • MRE

College of Sciences

Carmen Velázquez, Dean

Programs in:
- chemistry • MS
- medical-surgical nursing • MS
- mental health and psychiatric nursing • MS
- obstetric nursing • MS
- sciences • MS

Institute of Graduate Studies in Behavioral Science and Community Affairs
Dr. Nilde Cordoline, Director
Programs in:
clinical psychology • MS
clinical social work • MSW
crimnology • MA
industrial psychology • MS
public administration • MA

School of Law
Charles Cuprill, Dean
Program in:
law • JD

■ UNIVERSIDAD DEL TURABO
Turabo, PR 00778-3030

Independent, coed, comprehensive institution. *Computer facilities:* A campuswide network can be accessed from off campus. Internet access is available. *General application contact:* Admissions Officer, 787-746-3009.

Graduate Programs
Programs in:
accounting • MBA
bilingual education • MA
criminal justice studies • MPA
education administration and supervision • MA
environmental studies • MES
human resources • MBA
human services administration • MPA
logistics and materials management • MBA
management • MBA
marketing • MBA
school libraries administration • MA
special education • MA
teaching English as a second language • MA

■ UNIVERSIDAD METROPOLITANA
Río Piedras, PR 00928-1150
http://umet_mie.suagm.edu/

Independent, coed, comprehensive institution. *Enrollment:* 389 full-time matriculated graduate/professional students (249 women), 365 part-time matriculated graduate/professional students (198 women). *Graduate faculty:* 13 full-time (8 women), 36 part-time/adjunct (11 women). *Computer facilities:* 50 computers available on campus for general student use. Internet access is available. *Graduate expenses:* Tuition: full-time $3,930; part-time $150 per credit. Required fees: $165 per term. Tuition and fees vary according to course load. *General application contact:* Gregorio Villegas, Director, 787-766-1717 Ext. 6416.

Graduate Programs in Education
Dr. Sonia Dávila, Dean
Programs in:
curriculum and teaching • MA
educational administration and supervision • MA
environmental education • MA
fitness management • MA
managing leisure services • MA
pre-school centers administration • MA
pre-school education • MA
special education • MA
teaching of physical education • MA

School of Business Administration
Prof. Pedro Hernández, Dean
Programs in:
accounting • MBA
management • MBA
marketing • MBA

School of Environmental Affairs
Dr. Alberto Rivera Renta, Head
Programs in:
conservation and management of natural resources • MEM
environmental affairs • MEM
environmental planning • MEM
environmental risk and assessment management • MEM

■ UNIVERSITY OF PUERTO RICO, MAYAGÜEZ CAMPUS
Mayagüez, PR 00681-9000
http://www.uprm.edu

Commonwealth-supported, coed, university. CGS member. *Computer facilities:* 1,066 computers available on campus for general student use. A campuswide network can be accessed from off campus. Internet access and online class registration are available. *Library facilities:* General Library plus 1 other. *General application contact:* Director of Graduate Studies, 787-265-3809.

Graduate Studies

College of Agricultural Sciences
Programs in:
agricultural economics • MS
agricultural education • MS
agricultural extension • MS
agricultural sciences • MS
animal industry • MS
crop protection • MS
crops • MS
food technology • MS
horticulture • MS
soils • MS

College of Arts and Sciences
Programs in:
applied mathematics • MS
arts and sciences • MA, MMS, MS, PhD
biological oceanography • MMS, PhD
biology • MS
chemical oceanography • MMS, PhD
chemistry • MS
computational sciences • MS
English • MA
geological oceanography • MMS, PhD
geology • MS
Hispanic studies • MA
physical oceanography • MMS, PhD
physics • MS
pure mathematics • MS
statistics • MS

College of Business Administration
Program in:
business administration • MBA

College of Engineering
Programs in:
chemical engineering • M Ch E, MS
civil engineering • MCE, MS, PhD
computer engineering • M Co E, MS
electrical engineering • MEE, MS
engineering • M Ch E, M Co E, MCE, MEE, MME, MMSE, MS, PhD
industrial engineering • MMSE
mechanical engineering • MME, MS

■ UNIVERSITY OF PUERTO RICO, RÍO PIEDRAS
San Juan, PR 00931
http://upracd.upr.clu.edu:9090/

Commonwealth-supported, coed, university. CGS member. *Enrollment:* 1,866 full-time matriculated graduate/professional students (1,088 women), 1,763 part-time matriculated graduate/professional students (1,309 women). *Computer facilities:* 170 computers available on campus for general student use. A campuswide network can be accessed from student residence rooms. *Library facilities:* Jose M. Lazaro Library plus 10 others. *Graduate expenses:* Tuition, commonwealth resident: full-time $1,200; part-time $70 per credit. $3,500 full-time. Required fees: $599; $599. *General application contact:* Cruz B. Valentin-Arbelo, Admission Office Director, 787-764-0000 Ext. 5653.

University of Puerto Rico, Río Piedras (continued)

College of Education
Dr. María A. Irizarry, Dean
Programs in:
- biology education • M Ed
- chemistry education • M Ed
- child education • M Ed
- curriculum and teaching • Ed D
- education • M Ed, Ed D
- educational research and evaluation • M Ed
- English education • M Ed
- guidance and counseling • M Ed, Ed D
- history education • M Ed
- home economics • M Ed
- mathematics education • M Ed
- physics education • M Ed
- school administration and supervision • M Ed, Ed D
- secondary education • M Ed
- Spanish education • M Ed
- special education • M Ed
- teaching English as a second language • M Ed

College of Humanities
Dr. José Luis Vega, Acting Dean
Programs in:
- comparative literature • MA
- English • MA
- Hispanic studies • MA, PhD
- history • MA, PhD
- humanities • MA, PhD, Certificate
- linguistics • MA
- philosophy • MA
- translation • MA, Certificate

College of Social Sciences
Dr. Ida de Jesús, Dean
Programs in:
- economics • MA
- psychology • MA, PhD
- social sciences • MA, MPA, MRC, MSW, PhD
- sociology • MA

Beatriz Lassalle Graduate School of Social Work
Dr. Norma Rodriguez, Acting Chairperson
Program in:
- social work • MSW

Graduate School of Rehabilitation Counseling
Dr. Hilda E. González, Interim Chairperson
Program in:
- rehabilitation counseling • MRC

School of Public Administration
Dr. Mario Negrón-Portillo, Chairperson
Program in:
- public administration • MPA

Faculty of Natural Sciences
Dr. Brad R. Weinner, Acting Dean
Programs in:
- applied physics • MS
- biology • MS, PhD
- chemistry • MS, PhD
- mathematics • MS
- natural sciences • MS, PhD
- physics • MS
- physics-chemical • PhD

Graduate School of Business Administration
Dr. Jorge Ayala, Coordinator
Program in:
- business administration • MBA, PhD

Graduate School of Librarianship
Dr. Consuelo Figuero-Alvarez, Director
Programs in:
- librarianship • Post-Graduate Certificate
- librarianship and information services • MLS

Graduate School of Planning
Dr. Elías R. R. Gutierrez, Director
Program in:
- planning • MP

School of Architecture
Dr. John B. Hertz, Dean
Program in:
- architecture • M Arch

School of Law
Antonio García-Padilla, Dean
Program in:
- law • JD

School of Public Communication
Dr. Eliseo Colón, Chairperson
Program in:
- public communication • MA

■ UNIVERSITY OF THE SACRED HEART
San Juan, PR 00914-0383
http://www.sagrado.edu/

Independent-religious, coed, comprehensive institution. *Enrollment:* 86 full-time matriculated graduate/professional students (69 women), 424 part-time matriculated graduate/professional students (277 women). *Graduate faculty:* 20 full-time (11 women), 15 part-time/adjunct (3 women). *Computer facilities:* 300 computers available on campus for general student use. A campuswide network can be accessed from off campus. *Library facilities:* Maria Teresa Guevara Library plus 1 other. *Graduate expenses:* Tuition: full-time $2,790; part-time $155 per credit. Required fees: $390. *General application contact:* Josué González, Coordinator of Admissions, 787-727-5500 Ext. 3237.

Graduate Programs
Dr. Cesar A. Rey, Dean, Academic and Student Affairs
Programs in:
- advertising • MA
- contemporary culture and means • MA
- human resource management • MBA
- instruction systems and education technology • M Ed
- journalism and mass communication • MA
- management information systems • MBA
- marketing • MBA
- medical technology • Certificate
- natural science • Certificate
- occupational health • MS
- public relations • MA
- taxation • MBA

Rhode Island

■ BROWN UNIVERSITY
Providence, RI 02912
http://www.brown.edu/

Independent, coed, university. CGS member. *Computer facilities:* 400 computers available on campus for general student use. A campuswide network can be accessed from student residence rooms and from off campus. Internet access and online class registration are available. *Library facilities:* John D. Rockefeller Library plus 6 others. *General application contact:* Admission Office, 401-863-2600.

Graduate School
Programs in:
- American civilization • AM, PhD
- anthropology • AM, PhD
- art history • AM, PhD
- biochemistry • PhD
- chemistry • Sc M, PhD
- classics • AM, PhD
- cognitive science • Sc M, PhD
- comparative literature • AM, PhD
- comparative study of development • AM
- computer science • Sc M, PhD
- economics • AM, PhD
- Egyptology • AM, PhD
- elementary education K–6 • MAT

English literature and language • AM, PhD
French studies • AM, PhD
geological sciences • MA, Sc M, PhD
German • AM, PhD
Hispanic studies • AM, PhD
history • AM, PhD
history of mathematics • AM, PhD
Italian studies • AM, PhD
Judaic studies • AM, PhD
linguistics • AM, PhD
mathematics • AM, Sc M, PhD
music • AM, PhD
old world archaeology and art • AM, PhD
philosophy • AM, PhD
physics • Sc M, PhD
political science • AM, PhD
population studies • PhD
psychology • AM, Sc M, PhD
religious studies • AM, PhD
Russian • AM, PhD
secondary biology • MAT
secondary English • MAT
secondary social studies • MAT
Slavic languages • AM, PhD
sociology • AM, PhD
theatre arts • AM
writing • MFA

Center for Environmental Studies
Harold Ward, Director
Program in:
environmental studies • AM

Center for Old World Archaeology and Art
Program in:
old world archaeology and art • AM, PhD

Center for Portuguese and Brazilian Studies
Programs in:
Brazilian studies • AM
Luso-Brazilian studies • PhD
Portuguese studies and bilingual education • AM

Division of Applied Mathematics
Program in:
applied mathematics • Sc M, PhD

Division of Biology and Medicine
Dr. Donald Marsh, Dean
Programs in:
artificial organs/biomaterials/cellular technology • MA, Sc M, PhD
biochemistry • M Med Sc, Sc M, PhD
biology • MA, PhD
biology and medicine • M Med Sc, MA, MS, Sc M, PhD
biostatistics • MS, PhD
cancer biology • PhD
cell biology • M Med Sc, Sc M, PhD
developmental biology • M Med Sc, Sc M, PhD
ecology and evolutionary biology • PhD
epidemiology • MS, PhD
health services research • MS, PhD
immunology • M Med Sc, Sc M, PhD
immunology and infection • PhD
medical science • PhD
molecular microbiology • M Med Sc, Sc M, PhD
molecular pharmacology and physiology • MA, Sc M, PhD
neuroscience • PhD
pathobiology • Sc M
toxicology and environmental pathology • PhD

Division of Engineering
Programs in:
aerospace engineering • Sc M, PhD
biomedical engineering • Sc M
electrical sciences • Sc M, PhD
fluid mechanics, thermodynamics, and chemical processes • Sc M, PhD
materials science • Sc M, PhD
mechanics of solids and structures • Sc M, PhD

Program in Medicine
Program in:
medicine • MD

■ JOHNSON & WALES UNIVERSITY
Providence, RI 02903-3703
http://www.jwu.edu/

Independent, coed, comprehensive institution. CGS member. *Computer facilities:* 340 computers available on campus for general student use. A campuswide network can be accessed from student residence rooms and from off campus. Internet access is available. *Library facilities:* Johnson & Wales University Library plus 2 others. *General application contact:* Director of Graduate Admissions, 401-598-1015.

Find an in-depth description at www.petersons.com/graduate.

The Alan Shawn Feinstein Graduate School
Programs in:
accounting • MBA
business administration • MAT
educational leadership • Ed D
food service • MAT
hospitality administration • MBA
international business • MBA
management • MBA

■ PROVIDENCE COLLEGE
Providence, RI 02918
http://www.providence.edu/

Independent-religious, coed, comprehensive institution. *Graduate faculty:* 33 full-time (13 women), 44 part-time/adjunct (15 women). *Computer facilities:* 150 computers available on campus for general student use. A campuswide network can be accessed from student residence rooms and from off campus. Internet access is available. *Library facilities:* Phillips Memorial Library. *Graduate expenses:* Tuition: part-time $215 per credit. *General application contact:* Dr. Thomas F. Flaherty, Dean, 401-865-2247.

Graduate School
Dr. Thomas F. Flaherty, Dean
Programs in:
administration • M Ed
biblical studies • MA
business administration • MBA
education literacy • M Ed
elementary administration • M Ed
guidance and counseling • M Ed
history • MA
mathematics • MAT
pastoral ministry • MA
religious education • MA
religious studies • MA
secondary administration • M Ed
special education • M Ed

■ RHODE ISLAND COLLEGE
Providence, RI 02908-1924
http://www.ric.edu/

State-supported, coed, comprehensive institution. CGS member. *Enrollment:* 259 full-time matriculated graduate/professional students (208 women), 525 part-time matriculated graduate/professional students (433 women). *Graduate faculty:* 222 full-time (68 women), 62 part-time/adjunct (34 women). *Computer facilities:* 350 computers available on campus for general student use. A campuswide network can be accessed from off campus. *Library facilities:* Adams Library. *Graduate expenses:* Tuition, state resident: full-time $3,024; part-time $168 per credit. Tuition, nonresident: full-time $6,030; part-time $335 per credit. Required fees: $322; $13 per credit. $42 per semester. Tuition and fees vary according to course level and program. *General application contact:* Dean of Graduate Studies, 401-456-8700.

Find an in-depth description at www.petersons.com/graduate.

Rhode Island College (continued)
School of Graduate Studies
Dean

Center for Management and Technology
Dr. James Schweikart, Director
Programs in:
- industrial technology • MS
- management and technology • MS

Faculty of Arts and Sciences
Dr. Richard R. Weiner, Dean
Programs in:
- art education • MAT
- art education and studio art • MA, MAT
- art studio • MA
- arts and sciences • MA, MAT, MFA, MM, CAGS
- biology • MA, MAT
- English • MA, MAT
- French • MA, MAT
- general science • MAT
- history • MA, MAT
- mathematics • MA, MAT, CAGS
- music • MM
- music education • MAT
- physical science • MAT
- psychology • MA
- Spanish • MAT
- theatre • MFA

Feinstein School of Education and Human Development
Dr. James a. Bucci, Dean
Programs in:
- agency counseling • MA
- bilingual/bicultural education • M Ed
- counselor education • M Ed, CAGS
- curriculum • CAGS
- early childhood education • M Ed
- education • PhD
- education and human development • M Ed, MA, MAT, MS, PhD, CAGS
- educational administration • M Ed, CAGS
- educational psychology • MA
- elementary education • M Ed, MAT
- English as a second language • M Ed
- health education • M Ed
- reading education • M Ed, CAGS
- school psychology • CAGS
- secondary education • M Ed
- special education • M Ed, CAGS
- teaching of the handicapped • M Ed, CAGS
- technology education • M Ed

School of Social Work
Dr. George Metrey, Dean
Program in:
- social work • MSW

■ SALVE REGINA UNIVERSITY

Newport, RI 02840-4192

http://www.salve.edu/

Independent-religious, coed, comprehensive institution. *Enrollment:* 47 full-time matriculated graduate/professional students (33 women), 379 part-time matriculated graduate/professional students (210 women). *Graduate faculty:* 12 full-time (5 women), 28 part-time/adjunct (7 women). *Computer facilities:* 163 computers available on campus for general student use. A campuswide network can be accessed from student residence rooms and from off campus. Internet access is available. *Library facilities:* McKillop Library. *Graduate expenses:* Tuition: full-time $5,400; part-time $300 per credit. *General application contact:* Laura E. McPhie-Oliveira, Dean of Enrollment Services, 401-847-6650 Ext. 2908.

Find an in-depth description at www.petersons.com/graduate.

Graduate School
Dr. Teresa I. Madonna, Dean of Graduate Studies
Programs in:
- administration of justice • MS
- biomedical technology/management • MS
- business administration • MBA, MS
- health services administration • MS
- holistic counseling • MA, CAGS
- human resources management • MA
- humanities • MA, PhD, CAGS
- international relations • MA

■ UNIVERSITY OF RHODE ISLAND

Kingston, RI 02881

http://www.uri.edu

State-supported, coed, university. CGS member. *Enrollment:* 1,377 full-time matriculated graduate/professional students (779 women), 2,338 part-time matriculated graduate/professional students (1,459 women). *Graduate faculty:* 672 full-time (230 women), 10 part-time/adjunct (6 women). *Computer facilities:* 552 computers available on campus for general student use. A campuswide network can be accessed from off campus. *Library facilities:* University Library plus 1 other. *Graduate expenses:* Tuition, state resident: full-time $3,636. Tuition, nonresident: full-time $10,390. Required fees: $40. *General application contact:* Harold D. Bibb, Associate Dean of the Graduate School, 401-874-2262.

Graduate School
Thomas J. Rockett, Vice Provost for Graduate Studies, Research and Outreach

College of Arts and Sciences
Stefen Rogers, Dean
Programs in:
- arts and sciences • MA, MM, MMA, MPA, MS, PhD, Certificate
- biochemistry • MS, PhD
- botany • MS, PhD
- chemistry • MS, PhD
- clinical psychology • PhD
- computer science and statistics • MS, PhD
- English • MA, PhD
- experimental psychology • PhD
- French • MA
- geology • MS
- history • MA
- international development studies • Certificate
- marine affairs • MA, MMA
- mathematics • MS, PhD
- microbiology • MS, PhD
- music • MM
- philosophy • MA
- physics • MS, PhD
- political science • MA
- public policy and administration • MPA
- school psychology • MS, PhD
- Spanish • MA
- zoology • MS, PhD

College of Business Administration
Dr. Sidney Stern, Dean
Programs in:
- accounting • MS
- applied mathematics • PhD
- finance • MBA
- international business • MBA
- international sports management • MBA
- management • MBA
- management science • MBA
- marketing • MBA

College of Continuing Education
Walter Crocker, Dean
Programs in:
- clinical laboratory sciences • MS
- continuing education • Exec MBA, MS

College of Engineering
Thomas Kim, Acting Dean
Programs in:
- chemical engineering • MS, PhD
- design/systems • MS, PhD
- electrical and computer engineering • MS, PhD

engineering • MS, PhD
environmental engineering • MS, PhD
fluid mechanics • MS, PhD
geotechnical engineering • MS, PhD
industrial engineering • MS
manufacturing engineering • MS
ocean engineering • MS, PhD
solid mechanics • MS, PhD
structural engineering • MS, PhD
thermal sciences • MS, PhD
transportation engineering • MS, PhD

College of Human Science and Services
Barbara Brittingham, Dean
Programs in:
adult education • MA
communicative disorders • MA, MS
elementary education • MA
guidance and counseling • MS
health • MS
home economics education • MS
human science and services • MA, MS
marriage and family therapy • MS
physical education • MS
physical therapy • MS
reading • MA
recreation • MS
secondary education • MA
textiles, fashion merchandising and design • MS

College of Nursing
Dr. Jean Miller, Dean
Programs in:
nursing • PhD
nursing service administration • MS
teaching of nursing • MS

College of Pharmacy
Louis Luzzi, Dean
Programs in:
medicinal chemistry • MS, PhD
pharmaceutics • MS, PhD
pharmacognosy • MS, PhD
pharmacology and toxicology • MS, PhD
pharmacy • Pharm D, MS, PhD
pharmacy administration • MS

College of the Environment and Life Sciences
Robert Miller, Dean
Programs in:
animal science • MS
community planning and area development • MCP
entomology • MS, PhD
environment and life sciences • MCP, MS, PhD
food and nutrition science • MS, PhD
food science and technology, nutrition and dietetics • MS, PhD
plant pathology • MS, PhD
plant pathology-entomology • MS, PhD
plant science • MS, PhD
resource economics and marine resources • MS, PhD

Graduate Library School
Director
Program in:
library science • MLIS

Graduate School of Oceanography
Dr. Robert Duce, Dean
Program in:
oceanography • MS, PhD

Labor Research Center
Dr. Charles T. Schmidt, Director
Program in:
labor and industrial relations • MS

South Carolina

■ CHARLESTON SOUTHERN UNIVERSITY

Charleston, SC 29423-8087
http://www.charlestonsouthern.edu/

Independent-religious, coed, comprehensive institution. *Enrollment:* 15 full-time matriculated graduate/professional students (7 women), 273 part-time matriculated graduate/professional students (184 women). *Graduate faculty:* 32 full-time (11 women), 10 part-time/adjunct (5 women). *Computer facilities:* 150 computers available on campus for general student use. A campuswide network can be accessed. Internet access is available. *Library facilities:* L. Mendel Rivers Library. *Graduate expenses:* Tuition: part-time $198 per credit hour. Required fees: $50. *General application contact:* Debbie Williamson, Executive Director of Enrollment Management, 804-863-7050.

Program in Business
Dr. Al Parish, MBA Director
Programs in:
accounting • MBA
finance • MBA
health care administration • MBA
information systems • MBA
organizational development • MBA

Program in Criminal Justice
Dr. Beth McConnell, Chair
Program in:
criminal justice • MSCJ

Programs in Education
Dr. Martha Watson, Graduate Director
Programs in:
administration and supervision • M Ed
elementary education • M Ed
English • MAT
science • MAT
secondary education • M Ed
social studies • MAT

■ THE CITADEL, THE MILITARY COLLEGE OF SOUTH CAROLINA

Charleston, SC 29409
http://www.citadel.edu

State-supported, coed, primarily men, comprehensive institution. *Enrollment:* 143 full-time matriculated graduate/professional students (92 women), 527 part-time matriculated graduate/professional students (300 women). *Graduate faculty:* 47 full-time (16 women), 17 part-time/adjunct (6 women). *Computer facilities:* 350 computers available on campus for general student use. A campuswide network can be accessed from student residence rooms and from off campus. Internet access and online class registration are available. *Library facilities:* Daniel Library. *Graduate expenses:* Tuition, state resident: part-time $140 per credit hour. Tuition, nonresident: part-time $280 per credit hour. *General application contact:* Dr. David H. Reilly, Dean, College of Graduate and Professional Studies, 843-953-7118.

College of Graduate and Professional Studies
Dr. David H. Reilly, Dean
Programs in:
biology education • MAE
business administration • MBA
educational administration • M Ed, Ed S
English • MA
guidance and counseling • M Ed
health and physical education • M Ed
history • MA
mathematics education • MAE
psychology • MA
reading • M Ed
school psychology • Ed S
secondary education • MAT
social studies education • MAE

■ CLEMSON UNIVERSITY

Clemson, SC 29634

http://www.clemson.edu/

State-supported, coed, university. CGS member. *Enrollment:* 1,747 full-time matriculated graduate/professional students (652 women), 1,051 part-time matriculated graduate/professional students (554 women). *Graduate faculty:* 912 full-time (194 women), 93 part-time/adjunct (46 women). *Computer facilities:* 1,000 computers available on campus for general student use. A campuswide network can be accessed from student residence rooms and from off campus. *Library facilities:* Robert Muldrow Cooper Library plus 1 other. *Graduate expenses:* Tuition, state resident: full-time $3,810; part-time $180 per credit. Tuition, nonresident: full-time $9,784; part-time $402 per credit. *General application contact:* Dr. Mark A. McKnew, Associate Dean of the Graduate School.

Graduate School

Dr. Bonnie Holaday, Dean

Program in:

policy studies • PhD, Certificate

College of Agriculture, Forestry and Life Sciences

Dr. William Wehrenberg, Dean

Programs in:

agricultural and applied economics • MS
agriculture, forestry and life sciences • M Ag Ed, MFR, MS, PhD
animal and food industries • MS
animal physiology • MS, PhD
applied economics • PhD
aquaculture, fisheries and wildlife • MS, PhD
biochemistry • MS, PhD
biology instruction and agricultural education • M Ag Ed
entomology • MS, PhD
environmental toxicology • MS, PhD
food technology • PhD
forest resources • MFR, MS, PhD
genetics • MS, PhD
horticulture • MS, PhD
microbiology • MS, PhD
plant and environmental studies • MS
zoology • MS, PhD

College of Architecture, Arts, and Humanities

Dr. Janice Schach, Dean

Programs in:

architecture • M Arch, MS
architecture, arts, and humanities • M Arch, MA, MCRP, MCSM, MFA, MFAC, MS
construction science and management • MCSM
English • MA
environmental planning • MCRP
fine arts in computing • MFAC
history • MA
land development planning • MCRP
professional communication • MA
visual arts • MFA

College of Business and Behavioral Science

Dr. Jerry Trapnell, Dean

Programs in:

accountancy • MP Acc
applied economics • PhD
applied psychology • MS
applied sociology • MS
business administration • MBA
business and behavioral science • M E!Com, MA, MBA, MP Acc, MPA, MS, PhD
economics • MA
electronic commerce • M E!Com
graphic communications • MS
human factors • MS
industrial management • MS, PhD
industrial/organizational psychology • PhD
management science • PhD
public administration • MPA

College of Engineering and Science

Dr. Thomas M. Keinath, Dean

Programs in:

applied and pure mathematics • MS, PhD
astronomy and astrophysics • MS, PhD
atmospheric physics • MS, PhD
bioengineering • MS, PhD
biophysics • MS, PhD
ceramic and materials engineering • MS, PhD
chemical engineering • MS, PhD
chemistry • MS, PhD
civil engineering • M Engr, MS, PhD
computational mathematics • MS, PhD
computer engineering • MS, PhD
computer science • MS, PhD
electrical engineering • M Engr, MS, PhD
engineering and science • M Engr, MS, PhD
engineering mechanics • MS, PhD
environmental engineering and science • M Engr, MS, PhD
hydrogeology • MS
industrial engineering • MS, PhD
management science • PhD
materials science and engineering • MS, PhD
mechanical engineering • M Engr, MS, PhD
operations research • MS, PhD
physics • MS, PhD
statistics • MS, PhD
textiles, fiber and polymer science • MS, PhD

College of Health, Education, and Human Development

Dr. Harold E. Cheatham, Dean

Programs in:

administration and supervision • M Ed, Ed S
counseling and guidance services • M Ed
curriculum and instruction • PhD
educational leadership • PhD
elementary education • M Ed
English • M Ed
health, education, and human development • M Ed, M In Ed, MHA, MHRD, MPRTM, MS, Ed D, PhD, Ed S
history and government • M Ed
human resource development • MHRD
industrial education • M In Ed
mathematics • M Ed
natural sciences • M Ed
nursing • MS
parks, recreation, and tourism management • MPRTM, MS, PhD
public health • MHA
reading • M Ed
secondary education • M Ed
special education • M Ed
vocational/technical education • Ed D

■ CONVERSE COLLEGE

Spartanburg, SC 29302-0006

http://www.converse.edu/

Independent, women only, comprehensive institution. *Enrollment:* 169 full-time matriculated graduate/professional students (142 women), 590 part-time matriculated graduate/professional students (511 women). *Graduate faculty:* 76 full-time (32 women), 11 part-time/adjunct (6 women). *Computer facilities:* 65 computers available on campus for general student use. A campuswide network can be accessed from student residence rooms and from off campus. Internet access is available. *Library facilities:* Mickel Library. *Graduate expenses:* Tuition: part-time $225 per credit hour. *General application contact:* Dr. Martha Thomas Lovett, Dean, 864-596-9082.

Carroll McDaniel Petrie School of Music

Programs in:

instrumental performance • MM
music education • MM
piano pedagogy • MM
vocal performance • MM

Department of Education
Programs in:
- administration and supervision • Ed S
- curriculum and instruction • Ed S
- economics • MLA
- education • Ed S
- elementary education • M Ed
- English • MLA
- gifted education • M Ed
- history • MLA
- leadership • M Ed
- liberal arts • MLA
- marriage and family therapy • Ed S
- political science • MLA
- secondary education • M Ed
- sociology • MLA
- special education • M Ed

■ FRANCIS MARION UNIVERSITY
Florence, SC 29501-0547
http://www.fmarion.edu/

State-supported, coed, comprehensive institution. *Enrollment:* 41 full-time matriculated graduate/professional students (32 women), 733 part-time matriculated graduate/professional students (606 women). *Graduate faculty:* 103 full-time (21 women). *Computer facilities:* 170 computers available on campus for general student use. A campuswide network can be accessed. *Library facilities:* James A. Rogers Library plus 1 other. *Graduate expenses:* Tuition, state resident: part-time $181 per credit hour. Tuition, nonresident: part-time $361 per credit hour. Required fees: $5 per credit hour. $45 per semester. *General application contact:* 843-661-1284.

Graduate Programs
Provost Office
Programs in:
- applied clinical psychology • MS
- applied community psychology • MS
- early childhood education • M Ed
- elementary education • M Ed
- learning disabilities • M Ed, MAT
- remediation education • M Ed
- school psychology • MS
- secondary education • M Ed
- substance abuse counseling • MS

School of Business
Dr. M. Barry O'Brien, Coordinator
Programs in:
- business • MBA
- health management • MBA

■ LANDER UNIVERSITY
Greenwood, SC 29649-2099
http://www.lander.edu/

State-supported, coed, comprehensive institution. *Enrollment:* 1 (woman) full-time matriculated graduate/professional student, 62 part-time matriculated graduate/professional students (57 women). *Graduate faculty:* 9 full-time (7 women). *Computer facilities:* 150 computers available on campus for general student use. A campuswide network can be accessed from student residence rooms and from off campus. Internet access and online class registration are available. *Library facilities:* Jackson Library. *Graduate expenses:* Tuition: full-time $3,888. *General application contact:* Dr. Phil Bennett, Dean, School of Education, 864-388-8225.

School of Education
Dr. Phil Bennett, Dean
Programs in:
- elementary education • M Ed
- teaching • MAT

■ SOUTH CAROLINA STATE UNIVERSITY
Orangeburg, SC 29117-0001
http://www.scsu.edu/

State-supported, coed, comprehensive institution. CGS member. *Computer facilities:* 300 computers available on campus for general student use. A campuswide network can be accessed. Internet access is available. *Library facilities:* Miller F. Whittaker Library plus 1 other. *General application contact:* Dean of the School of Graduate Studies, 803-536-7064.

School of Graduate Studies

School of Applied Professional Sciences
Programs in:
- applied professional sciences • MA, MS
- individual and family development • MS
- nutritional sciences • MS
- rehabilitation counseling • MA
- speech/language pathology • MA

School of Business
Programs in:
- agribusiness • MS
- agribusiness and economics • MS

School of Education
Programs in:
- early childhood and special education • M Ed
- early childhood education • MAT
- education • M Ed, MAT, Ed D, Ed S
- educational leadership • Ed D, Ed S
- elementary counselor education • M Ed
- elementary education • M Ed, MAT
- engineering • MAT
- general science • MAT
- mathematics • MAT
- secondary counselor education • M Ed
- secondary education • M Ed
- special education • M Ed
- speech pathology • MAT

■ SOUTHERN WESLEYAN UNIVERSITY
Central, SC 29630-1020
http://www.swu.edu/

Independent-religious, coed, comprehensive institution. *Enrollment:* 79 full-time matriculated graduate/professional students (34 women). *Graduate faculty:* 10 full-time (0 women), 8 part-time/adjunct (2 women). *Computer facilities:* 60 computers available on campus for general student use. A campuswide network can be accessed from student residence rooms and from off campus. Internet access is available. *Library facilities:* Rickman Library. *Graduate expenses:* Tuition: full-time $6,480. Required fees: $920. *General application contact:* Dr. Tom Griffin, Associate Academic Vice President, 864-639-2453 Ext. 401.

Program in Christian Ministries
Dr. Mari Gonlag, Director
Program in:
- Christian ministries • M Min

Program in Management
Dr. Tom Griffin, Vice President for Adult and Graduate Studies
Program in:
- management • MSM

■ UNIVERSITY OF SOUTH CAROLINA
Columbia, SC 29208
http://www.sc.edu/

State-supported, coed, university. CGS member. *Enrollment:* 3,519 full-time matriculated graduate/professional students (1,993 women), 3,778 part-time matriculated graduate/professional students (2,639 women). *Graduate faculty:* 1,387 full-time (406 women), 324

University of South Carolina (continued)
part-time/adjunct (139 women). *Computer facilities:* 11,000 computers available on campus for general student use. A campuswide network can be accessed from student residence rooms and from off campus. Internet access and online class registration are available. *Library facilities:* Thomas Cooper Library plus 7 others. *Graduate expenses:* Full-time $4,214; part-time $209 per hour. Tuition, nonresident: full-time $9,082; part-time $443 per hour. Tuition and fees vary according to program. *General application contact:* Dale Moore, Director of Graduate Admissions, 803-777-4243.

Find an in-depth description at www.petersons.com/graduate.

College of Pharmacy
Dr. Farid Sadik, Dean
Programs in:
- pharmaceutical sciences • MS, PhD
- pharmacy • Pharm D, MS, PhD

Graduate School
Dean
Program in:
- gerontology • Certificate

College of Criminal Justice
Cole Blease Graham, Dean
Program in:
- criminal justice • MCJ

College of Education
Dr. Les Sternberg, Dean
Programs in:
- community and occupational education • M Ed, MA, Ed D
- counseling education • PhD, Ed S
- curriculum and instruction • Ed D
- early childhood education • M Ed, MA, MAT, Ed D, PhD, Ed S
- education • IMA, M Ed, MA, MAT, MS, MT, Ed D, PhD, Certificate, Ed S
- educational administration • M Ed, MA, Ed D, PhD, Ed S
- educational psychology, research, foundations • M Ed, MA, PhD
- elementary education • M Ed, MA, MAT, Ed D, PhD, Ed S
- foundations in education • PhD
- health education administration • Ed D
- higher education leadership • Certificate
- instructional technology • M Ed
- physical education • IMA, MAT, MS, PhD
- reading education • M Ed, MA, Ed D, PhD, Ed S
- secondary education • IMA, M Ed, MA, MT, Ed D, PhD, Ed S
- special education • M Ed, MAT, PhD
- student personnel services • M Ed, MA
- teaching • Ed S

College of Engineering and Information Technology
Dr. Ralph E. White, Dean
Programs in:
- chemical engineering • ME, MS, PhD
- civil and environmental engineering • ME, MS, PhD
- computer engineering • ME, MS, PhD
- computer science • MS, PhD
- electrical engineering • ME, MS, PhD
- engineering and information technology • ME, MS, PhD
- mechanical engineering • ME, MS, PhD

College of Hospitality, Retail, and Sport Management
Dr. Pat G. Moody, Interim Dean
Programs in:
- hospitality • MHRTA
- hospitality, retail, and sport management • MHRTA

College of Journalism
Program in:
- journalism • MA, MMC, PhD

College of Liberal Arts
Dr. Gordon Smith, Associate Dean for Graduate Studies
Programs in:
- anthropology • MA
- archives • MA
- art education • IMA, MA, MAT
- art history • MA
- art studio • MA
- clinical/community psychology • PhD
- creative writing • MFA
- English • MA, PhD
- English education • MAT
- experimental psychology • MA, PhD
- French • IMA, MA, MAT
- French education • IMA, MAT
- geography • MA, MS, PhD
- geography education • IMA, MAT
- German • MA
- German education • IMA, MAT
- historic preservation • MA
- history • MA, PhD
- history education • IMA, MAT
- international studies • MA, PhD
- liberal arts • IMA, MA, MAT, MFA, MMA, MPA, MS, PhD, Certificate
- linguistics • MA, PhD
- media arts • MMA
- museum • MA
- museum management • Certificate
- philosophy • MA, PhD
- political science • MA, PhD
- public administration • MPA
- public history • MA, Certificate
- religious studies • MA
- school psychology • PhD
- sociology • MA, PhD
- Spanish • IMA, MA, MAT
- studio art • MFA
- teaching English as a foreign language • Certificate
- theater • IMA, MA, MAT, MFA
- women's studies • Certificate

College of Library and Information Science
Program in:
- library and information science • MLIS, Certificate, Specialist

College of Nursing
Dr. Mary Ann Parsons, Dean
Programs in:
- advanced practice nursing in clinical and psychiatric mental health • Certificate
- advanced practice nursing in primary care and women's health • Certificate
- clinical nursing • MSN
- community mental health and psychiatric health nursing • MSN
- health nursing • MSN
- nursing • ND
- nursing administration • MSN
- nursing science • PhD

College of Science and Mathematics
Dr. Gary Crawley, Dean
Programs in:
- applied statistics • CAS
- biology • MS, PhD
- biology education • IMA, MAT
- chemistry and biochemistry • IMA, MAT, MS, PhD
- ecology, evolution and organismal biology • MS, PhD
- geological sciences • MS, PhD
- marine science • MS, PhD
- mathematics • MA, MS, PhD
- mathematics education • M Math, MAT
- molecular, cellular, and developmental biology • MS, PhD
- physics and astronomy • IMA, MAT, MS, PhD
- science and mathematics • IMA, M Math, MA, MAT, MIS, MS, PhD, CAS
- statistics • MIS, MS, PhD

College of Social Work
Dr. Frank B. Raymond, Dean
Program in:
- social work • MSW, PhD

The Darla Moore School of Business
Joel A. Smith, Dean
Programs in:
accounting • M Acc
business administration • MBA, MS, PhD
economics • MA, PhD
human resources • MHR
international business • MIBS
international business administration • IMBA
taxation • M Tax

School of Music
Dr. Jămal J. Rossi, Dean
Programs in:
composition • MM, DMA
conducting • MM, DMA
jazz studies • MM
music education • MM Ed, PhD
music history • MM
music performance • Certificate
music theory • MM
opera theater • MM
performance • MM, DMA
piano pedagogy • MM, DMA

School of Public Health
Dr. Harris Pastides, Dean
Programs in:
alcohol and drug studies • Certificate
biostatistics • MPH, MSPH, Dr PH, PhD
communication sciences and disorders • MCD, MSP, PhD
environmental quality • MPH, MSPH, PhD
epidemiology • MPH, MSPH, Dr PH, PhD
exercise science • MS, DPT, PhD
general public health • MPH
hazardous materials management • MPH, MSPH, PhD
health administration • MHA, MPH, Dr PH, PhD
health education administration • Ed D
health promotion and education • MAT, MPH, MS, MSPH, Dr PH, PhD
industrial hygiene • MPH, MSPH, PhD
public health • MAT, MCD, MHA, MPH, MS, MSP, MSPH, DPT, Dr PH, Ed D, PhD, Certificate
school health education • Certificate

School of the Environment
Dr. Bruce C. Coull, Dean
Programs in:
earth and environmental resources management • MEERM
environment • MEERM

School of Law
John E. Montgomery, Dean
Program in:
law • JD

School of Medicine
Dr. Larry R. Faulkner, Dean
Programs in:
biomedical science • MBS, MNA, PhD
genetic counseling • MS
medicine • MD, MBS, MNA, MRC, MS, PhD
nurse anesthesia • MNA
rehabilitation counseling • MRC

■ WINTHROP UNIVERSITY

Rock Hill, SC 29733
http://www.winthrop.edu/

State-supported, coed, comprehensive institution. *Enrollment:* 256 full-time matriculated graduate/professional students (143 women), 389 part-time matriculated graduate/professional students (280 women). *Graduate faculty:* 162 full-time (52 women). *Computer facilities:* 250 computers available on campus for general student use. A campuswide network can be accessed from student residence rooms and from off campus. Internet access is available. *Library facilities:* Dacus Library. *Graduate expenses:* Tuition, state resident: full-time $4,132; part-time $173 per credit hour. Tuition, nonresident: full-time $7,458; part-time $312 per credit hour. Required fees: $10 per semester. *General application contact:* Sharon B. Johnson, Director of Graduate Studies, 800-411-7041.

College of Arts and Sciences
Dr. Thomas F. Moove, Director
Programs in:
arts and sciences • M Math, MA, MLA, MS, SSP
biology • MS
English • MA
history • MA
human nutrition • MS
liberal arts • MLA
mathematics • M Math
psychology • MS, SSP
Spanish • MA

College of Business Administration
Dr. Roger Weikle, Dean
Program in:
business administration • MBA

College of Education
Dr. Patricia Graham, Dean
Programs in:
agency counseling • M Ed
education • M Ed, MAT, MS, Ed S
educational leadership • M Ed
elementary education • M Ed
middle level education • M Ed
physical education • MS
reading education • M Ed
school counseling • M Ed
secondary education • M Ed, MAT
special education • M Ed

College of Visual and Performing Arts
Dr. Andrew Svedlow, Dean
Programs in:
art • MFA
art education • MA
conducting • MM
music education • MME
performance • MM
visual and performing arts • MA, MFA, MM, MME

South Dakota

■ MOUNT MARTY COLLEGE

Yankton, SD 57078-3724
http://www.mtmc.edu/

Independent-religious, coed, comprehensive institution. *Computer facilities:* 53 computers available on campus for general student use. A campuswide network can be accessed from student residence rooms. Internet access is available. *Library facilities:* Mount Marty College Library. *General application contact:* Director of Nurse Anesthesia Program, 605-357-9802.

Graduate Studies Division
Program in:
nursing anesthesia • MS

■ NORTHERN STATE UNIVERSITY

Aberdeen, SD 57401-7198
http://www.northern.edu/

State-supported, coed, comprehensive institution. *Enrollment:* 22 full-time matriculated graduate/professional students (12 women), 68 part-time matriculated graduate/professional students (45 women). *Graduate faculty:* 80 full-time (20 women). *Computer facilities:* 800 computers available on campus for general student use. A campuswide network can be accessed from student residence rooms and from off campus. Internet access and online class registration are available. *Library facilities:* Beulah Williams Library. *Graduate expenses:*

Northern State University (continued)
Tuition, state resident: full-time $2,267; part-time $97 per credit hour. Tuition, nonresident: full-time $6,490; part-time $279 per credit hour. Required fees: $1,240; $50. *General application contact:* Tammy K. Griffith, Senior Secretary, 605-626-2558.

Division of Graduate Studies in Education
Dr. Margaret J. Coxwell, Head
Programs in:
- education • MS Ed
- educational studies • MS Ed
- elementary classroom teaching • MS Ed
- elementary school administration • MS Ed
- guidance and counseling • MS Ed
- health, physical education, and coaching • MS Ed
- language and literacy • MS Ed
- secondary classroom teaching • MS Ed
- secondary school administration • MS Ed
- special education • MS Ed

■ SOUTH DAKOTA STATE UNIVERSITY
Brookings, SD 57007
http://www.sdstate.edu/

State-supported, coed, university. CGS member. *Computer facilities:* 278 computers available on campus for general student use. A campuswide network can be accessed from student residence rooms and from off campus. Internet access is available. *Library facilities:* H. M. Briggs Library. *General application contact:* Dean of the Graduate School, 605-688-4181.

Graduate School

College of Agriculture and Biological Sciences
Programs in:
- agriculture and biological sciences • MS, PhD
- agronomy • MS, PhD
- animal science • MS, PhD
- biological sciences • PhD
- biology • MS
- dairy science • MS, PhD
- economics • MS
- entomology • MS
- microbiology • MS
- plant pathology • MS
- rural sociology • MS, PhD
- wildlife and fisheries sciences • MS

College of Arts and Science
Programs in:
- analytical chemistry • MS, PhD
- arts and science • MA, MS, PhD
- biochemistry • MS, PhD
- chemistry • MS, PhD
- communication studies and theatre • MS
- English • MA
- geography • MS
- health, physical education and recreation • MS
- inorganic chemistry • MS, PhD
- journalism • MS
- organic chemistry • MS, PhD
- physical chemistry • MS, PhD

College of Education and Counseling
Programs in:
- counseling and human resource development • MS
- curriculum and instruction • M Ed
- education and counseling • M Ed, MS
- educational administration • M Ed

College of Engineering
Programs in:
- agricultural engineering • MS, PhD
- atmospheric, environmental, and water resources • PhD
- electrical engineering • MS
- engineering • MS
- industrial management • MS
- mathematics • MS
- mechanical engineering • MS
- physics • MS

College of Family and Consumer Sciences
Program in:
- family and consumer sciences • MS

College of Nursing
Program in:
- nursing • MS

College of Pharmacy
Programs in:
- pharmaceutical sciences • MS
- pharmacy • Pharm D, MS

■ UNIVERSITY OF SIOUX FALLS
Sioux Falls, SD 57105-1699
http://www.usiouxfalls.edu/

Independent-religious, coed, comprehensive institution. *Computer facilities:* 120 computers available on campus for general student use. A campuswide network can be accessed from student residence rooms and from off campus. Internet access is available. *Library facilities:* Norman B. Mears Library plus 1 other. *General application contact:* Director of Graduate Studies, 605-331-6710.

Program in Business Administration
Program in:
- business administration • MBA

Program in Education
Programs in:
- leadership • M Ed
- reading • M Ed
- technology • M Ed

■ UNIVERSITY OF SOUTH DAKOTA
Vermillion, SD 57069-2390
http://www.usd.edu/

State-supported, coed, university. *Enrollment:* 870 full-time matriculated graduate/professional students (482 women), 826 part-time matriculated graduate/professional students (470 women). *Graduate faculty:* 422 full-time, 41 part-time/adjunct. *Computer facilities:* 1,800 computers available on campus for general student use. A campuswide network can be accessed from student residence rooms and from off campus. Internet access is available. *Library facilities:* I. D. Weeks Library plus 2 others. *Graduate expenses:* Part-time $92 per credit. Tuition, nonresident: part-time $270 per credit. Required fees: $55 per credit. Full-time tuition and fees vary according to degree level and program. *General application contact:* Stephanie M. Bucklin, Administrative Assistant, 605-677-6287.

Find an in-depth description at www.petersons.com/graduate.

Graduate School
Dr. Royce C. Engstrom, Dean, Graduate School
Programs in:
- administrative studies • MS
- interdisciplinary studies • MA

College of Arts and Sciences
Dr. John Carlson, Dean
Programs in:
- arts and sciences • MA, MNS, MPA, MS, PhD
- audiology • MA
- biology • MA, MNS, MS, PhD
- chemistry • MA, MNS
- clinical psychology • MA, PhD
- computer science • MA
- English • MA, PhD
- history • MA
- mathematics • MA, MNS
- political science • MA
- psychology • MA, PhD
- public administration • MPA

sociology • MA
speech communication • MA
speech-language pathology • MA

College of Fine Arts
John A. Day, Acting Chair
Programs in:
art • MFA
fine arts • MA, MFA, MM
mass communications • MA
music • MM
theatre • MA, MFA

School of Business
Dr. Jerry Johnson, Dean
Programs in:
accounting • MP Acc
business • MBA, MP Acc
business administration • MBA

School of Education
Dr. Jeri Engelking, Dean
Programs in:
counseling and psychology in education • MA, Ed D, Ed S
curriculum and instruction • Ed D, Ed S
education • MA, MS, Ed D, PhD, Ed S
educational administration • MA, Ed D, Ed S
elementary education • MA
health, physical education and recreation • MA
secondary education • MA
special education • MA
technology for education and training • MS, Ed S

School of Law
Barry R. Vickrey, Dean
Program in:
law • JD

School of Medicine
Programs in:
cardiovascular research • MA, PhD
cellular and molecular biology • MA, PhD
medicine • MD, MA, MS, PhD
molecular microbiology and immunology • MA, PhD
neuroscience • MA, PhD
occupational therapy • MS
physical therapy • MS
physiology and pharmacology • MA, PhD

Tennessee

■ AUSTIN PEAY STATE UNIVERSITY
Clarksville, TN 37044-0001
http://www.apsu.edu/

State-supported, coed, comprehensive institution. CGS member. *Enrollment:* 176 full-time matriculated graduate/professional students (135 women), 287 part-time matriculated graduate/professional students (235 women). *Graduate faculty:* 58 full-time (30 women), 21 part-time/adjunct (5 women). *Computer facilities:* 411 computers available on campus for general student use. A campuswide network can be accessed from student residence rooms and from off campus. *Library facilities:* Felix G. Woodward Library. *Graduate expenses:* Tuition, state resident: full-time $3,593; part-time $157 per credit hour. Tuition, nonresident: full-time $9,221; part-time $400 per credit hour. Tuition and fees vary according to course load. *General application contact:* Dr. Parris Watts, Dean, College of Graduate Studies, 931-221-7414.

Graduate School
Dr. Parris Watts, Dean

College of Arts and Sciences
Richard Hogan, Dean
Programs in:
arts and sciences • M Mu, MA, MA Ed, MS
biology • MS
clinical psychology • MA
communication arts • MA
English • MA, MA Ed
guidance and counseling • MS
music • M Mu
music education • M Mu
psychological science • MA
school psychology • MA

College of Education
Dr. Sutton Flynt, Dean
Programs in:
administration and supervision • MA Ed, Ed S
counseling and guidance • Ed S
curriculum and instruction • MA Ed
education • MA, MA Ed, Ed S
elementary education • MA Ed, Ed S
reading • MA Ed
school psychology • Ed S
secondary education • Ed S
special education • MA

College of Human Services and Nursing
Dr. Lou Beasley, Dean
Programs in:
health and human performance • MA Ed, MS
human services and nursing • MA Ed, MS

■ BELMONT UNIVERSITY
Nashville, TN 37212-3757
http://www.belmont.edu/

Independent-religious, coed, comprehensive institution. *Enrollment:* 295 full-time matriculated graduate/professional students (213 women), 174 part-time matriculated graduate/professional students (95 women). *Graduate faculty:* 81 full-time (36 women), 18 part-time/adjunct (10 women). *Computer facilities:* 250 computers available on campus for general student use. A campuswide network can be accessed from student residence rooms and from off campus. Internet access and online class registration are available. *Library facilities:* Lila D. Bunch Library. *Graduate expenses:* Tuition: part-time $510 per credit hour. Tuition and fees vary according to course load and program. *General application contact:* Dr. Kathryn Baugher, Dean of Enrollment Services, 615-460-6785.

College of Arts and Sciences
Richard C. Fallis, Dean
Programs in:
arts and sciences • M Ed, MA
English • MA

School of Education
Dr. Trevor F. Hutchins, Associate Dean
Programs in:
childcare administration • M Ed
elementary education • M Ed
English • M Ed
secondary education • M Ed
sports administration • M Ed

College of Health Sciences
Dr. Debra B. Wollaber, Dean
Program in:
health sciences • MPT, MSN, MSOT, DPT

School of Nursing
Dr. Leslie J. Higgins, Director, Graduate Program
Program in:
nursing • MSN

School of Occupational Therapy
Dr. Scott Douglas McPhee, Associate Dean

Belmont University (continued)
Program in:
occupational therapy • MSOT

School of Physical Therapy
Dr. David G. Greathouse, Chairman
Program in:
physical therapy • MPT, DPT

College of Visual and Performing Arts
Cynthia R. Curtis, Dean
Program in:
visual and performing arts • MM

School of Music
Dr. Madeline S. Bridges, Director
Programs in:
church music • MM
music education • MM
pedagogy • MM
performance • MM

Jack C. Massey Graduate School of Business
Dr. James Clapper, Dean
Program in:
business • M Acc, MBA

■ CARSON-NEWMAN COLLEGE

Jefferson City, TN 37760
http://www.cn.edu/

Independent-religious, coed, comprehensive institution. *Enrollment:* 131 full-time matriculated graduate/professional students (102 women), 105 part-time matriculated graduate/professional students (89 women). *Graduate faculty:* 18 full-time (9 women), 7 part-time/adjunct (5 women). *Computer facilities:* 200 computers available on campus for general student use. A campuswide network can be accessed from student residence rooms and from off campus. Internet access is available. *Library facilities:* Stephens-Burnett Library plus 1 other. *Graduate expenses:* Tuition: part-time $200 per hour. *General application contact:* Jane W. McGill, Graduate Admissions and Services Adviser, 865-471-3460.

Graduate Program in Education
Dr. Margaret A. Hypes, Chair
Programs in:
curriculum and instruction • M Ed
elementary education • MAT
school counseling • M Ed
secondary education • MAT
teaching English as a second language • MATESL

■ CHRISTIAN BROTHERS UNIVERSITY

Memphis, TN 38104-5581
http://www.cbu.edu/

Independent-religious, coed, comprehensive institution. *Enrollment:* 254 full-time matriculated graduate/professional students (150 women), 211 part-time matriculated graduate/professional students (133 women). *Graduate faculty:* 22 full-time (8 women), 9 part-time/adjunct (3 women). *Computer facilities:* 300 computers available on campus for general student use. A campuswide network can be accessed from student residence rooms and from off campus. Internet access and online class registration, on-line class listings, e-mail, course assignments are available. *Library facilities:* Plough Memorial Library and Media Center. *Graduate expenses:* Tuition: full-time $10,000; part-time $375 per credit. Required fees: $50 per semester. *General application contact:* James T. Rhodes, Director, MBA Program, 901-321-3317.

Graduate Programs

School of Arts
Dr. Kristin Pruitt, Dean
Program in:
liberal arts • M Ed

School of Business
Dr. Thomas Dukes, Dean
Program in:
business • MBA

School of Engineering
Dr. Sinipong Malasri, Dean
Program in:
engineering • MEM

■ CUMBERLAND UNIVERSITY

Lebanon, TN 37087-3554
http://www.cumberland.edu/

Independent, coed, comprehensive institution. *Computer facilities:* 50 computers available on campus for general student use. A campuswide network can be accessed from student residence rooms and from off campus. Internet access is available. *Library facilities:* Doris and Harry Vise Library. *General application contact:* Director of Admissions, 615-444-2562 Ext. 1120.

Division of Graduate Studies
Programs in:
business administration • MBA
education • MAE
human relations management • MS
public service administration • MS

■ EAST TENNESSEE STATE UNIVERSITY

Johnson City, TN 37614
http://www.etsu.edu/

State-supported, coed, university. CGS member. *Enrollment:* 1,034 full-time matriculated graduate/professional students (640 women), 856 part-time matriculated graduate/professional students (523 women). *Graduate faculty:* 463 full-time (160 women), 54 part-time/adjunct (13 women). *Computer facilities:* 550 computers available on campus for general student use. A campuswide network can be accessed. Internet access and online class registration are available. *Library facilities:* Sherrod Library plus 2 others. *Graduate expenses:* Tuition, state resident: part-time $194 per hour. Tuition, nonresident: part-time $243 per hour. *General application contact:* Dr. Roberta Herrin, Associate Dean, 423-439-6146.

Find an in-depth description at www.petersons.com/graduate.

James H. Quillen College of Medicine
Dr. Ronald Franks, Vice President for Health Affairs, Dean
Programs in:
anatomy • MS, PhD
biochemistry • MS, PhD
biophysics • MS, PhD
medicine • MD, MS, PhD
microbiology • MS, PhD
pharmacology • MS, PhD
physiology • MS, PhD

School of Graduate Studies
Dr. Wesley Brown, Dean

College of Applied Science and Technology
Dr. Carroll Hyder, Interim Dean
Programs in:
applied science and technology • MS
clinical nutrition • MS
computer science • MS
information systems science • MS
software engineering • MS
technology • MS

College of Arts and Sciences
Dr. Don Johnson, Dean
Programs in:

art and design • MA, MFA
arts and sciences • M Mu Ed, MA, MFA, MS
biological sciences • MS
chemistry • MS
clinical psychology • MA
communication • MA
criminal justice and criminology • MA
English • MA
general psychology • MA
history • MA
mathematics • MS
music • M Mu Ed
sociology • MA

College of Business
Dr. Linda Garceau, Dean
Programs in:
accountancy • M Acc
business • M Acc, MBA, MCM, MPM, Certificate
business administration • MBA, Certificate
city management • MCM
community development • MPM
general administration • MPM
health care management • Certificate
municipal service management • MPM
urban and regional economic development • MPM
urban and regional planning • MPM

College of Education
Dr. Martha Collins, Dean
Programs in:
counseling • M Ed, MA
early childhood education • M Ed, MA
education • M Ed, MA, MAT, Ed D, Ed S
educational leadership • M Ed, Ed D, Ed S
educational media/educational technology • M Ed
elementary education • M Ed, MAT
physical education • M Ed, MA
reading and storytelling • MA
reading education • M Ed, MA
secondary education • M Ed, MAT
special education • M Ed, MA

College of Nursing
Dr. Joellen Edwards, Dean
Programs in:
advanced nursing practice • Post Master's Certificate
health care management • Certificate
nursing • MSN

College of Public and Allied Health
Dr. Wilsie Bishop, Dean
Programs in:
communicative disorders • MS
environmental health • MSEH
gerontology • Certificate
health care management • Certificate
physical therapy • MPT
public and allied health • MPH, MPT, MS, MSEH, Certificate
public health • MPH

Division of Cross-Disciplinary Studies
Dr. Rick E. Osborn, Associate Dean
Program in:
cross-disciplinary studies • MALS

■ FREED-HARDEMAN UNIVERSITY
Henderson, TN 38340-2399
http://www.fhu.edu/

Independent-religious, coed, comprehensive institution. *Enrollment:* 117 full-time matriculated graduate/professional students (79 women), 305 part-time matriculated graduate/professional students (198 women). *Graduate faculty:* 20 full-time (4 women), 8 part-time/adjunct (5 women). *Computer facilities:* 238 computers available on campus for general student use. A campuswide network can be accessed from student residence rooms and from off campus. Internet access is available. *Library facilities:* Loden-Daniel Library. *Graduate expenses:* Tuition: full-time $3,510; part-time $195 per semester hour. *General application contact:* Dr. W. Stephen Johnson, Director of Graduate Studies and Vice President for Academic Affairs, 731-989-6004.

Program in Counseling
Dr. Mike Cravens, Graduate Director
Program in:
counseling • MS

Program in Education
Dr. James Murphy, Graduate Director
Programs in:
curriculum and instruction • M Ed
school counseling • M Ed

School of Biblical Studies
Dr. Earl Edwards, Director of Graduate Studies
Programs in:
biblical studies • M Min, MA
ministry • M Min
New Testament • MA

■ LINCOLN MEMORIAL UNIVERSITY
Harrogate, TN 37752-1901
http://www.lmunet.edu/

Independent, coed, comprehensive institution. *Enrollment:* 570 full-time matriculated graduate/professional students (415 women), 256 part-time matriculated graduate/professional students (165 women). *Graduate faculty:* 9 full-time (4 women), 31 part-time/adjunct (17 women). *Computer facilities:* 150 computers available on campus for general student use. A campuswide network can be accessed from student residence rooms. Internet access is available. *Library facilities:* Carnegie Library. *Graduate expenses:* Tuition: full-time $5,220; part-time $290 per credit hour. Tuition and fees vary according to program. *General application contact:* Barbara McCune, Senior Assistant, Graduate Office, 423-869-6374.

Program in Business Administration
Dr. John Sellers, Dean
Program in:
business administration • MBA

Program in Education
Dr. Fred Bedelle, Dean, School of Graduate Studies
Programs in:
administration and supervision • M Ed, Ed S
counseling and guidance • M Ed
curriculum and instruction • M Ed, Ed S

■ LIPSCOMB UNIVERSITY
Nashville, TN 37204-3951
http://www.lipscomb.edu/

Independent-religious, coed, comprehensive institution. *Enrollment:* 73 full-time matriculated graduate/professional students (32 women), 165 part-time matriculated graduate/professional students (54 women). *Graduate faculty:* 23 full-time (2 women), 12 part-time/adjunct (2 women). *Computer facilities:* 232 computers available on campus for general student use. A campuswide network can be accessed from student residence rooms and from off campus. Internet access and online class registration are available. *Library facilities:* Beaman Library plus 1 other. *Graduate expenses:* Tuition: full-time $11,040; part-time $460 per semester hour. Tuition and fees vary according to course load and program. *General application contact:* Dr. Gary Holloway, Director of Graduate Bible Studies, 615-269-1000 Ext. 5761.

Lipscomb University (continued)

Graduate Program in Bible Studies
Dr. Gary Holloway, Director
Programs in:
biblical studies • MA, MAR
divinity • M Div

Graduate Studies in Education
Dr. Carolyn Tucker, Director
Program in:
education • M Ed

MBA Program
Dr. Perry G. Moore, Director
Program in:
business administration • MBA

■ MIDDLE TENNESSEE STATE UNIVERSITY

Murfreesboro, TN 37132
http://www.mtsu.edu/

State-supported, coed, university. CGS member. *Enrollment:* 227 full-time matriculated graduate/professional students (128 women), 1,477 part-time matriculated graduate/professional students (893 women). *Graduate faculty:* 390 full-time (142 women), 38 part-time/adjunct (9 women). *Computer facilities:* 2,200 computers available on campus for general student use. A campuswide network can be accessed from off campus. Internet access and online class registration are available. *Library facilities:* University Library. *Graduate expenses:* Tuition, state resident: full-time $2,984; part-time $156 per hour. Tuition, nonresident: full-time $8,612; part-time $400 per hour. Required fees: $11 per hour. One-time fee: $70 part-time. *General application contact:* Dr. Donald L. Curry, Dean of the College of Graduate Studies, 615-898-2840.

College of Graduate Studies
Dr. Donald L. Curry, Dean

College of Basic and Applied Sciences
Dr. E. Ray Phillips, Interim Dean
Programs in:
aerospace education • M Ed
airport/airline management • MS
asset management • MS
basic and applied sciences • M Ed, MS, MST, MVTE, DA
biology • MS, MST
chemistry • MS, DA
computer science • MS
engineering technology and industrial studies • MS, MVTE
mathematics • MS
mathematics education • MST
natural science • MS

College of Business
Dr. James E. Burton, Dean
Programs in:
accounting • MS
business • MA, MBA, MBE, MS, DA
business administration • MBA
business education • MBE
computer information systems • MS
economics • MA, DA
industrial relations • MA
information systems • MS

College of Education and Behavioral Science
Dr. Gloria Bonner, Dean
Programs in:
administration and supervision • M Ed
child development and family studies • MS
criminal justice administration • MCJ
curriculum and instruction • M Ed, Ed S
curriculum specialist • M Ed, Ed S
early childhood education • M Ed
education and behavioral science • M Ed, MA, MAT, MCJ, MS, DA, Ed S
elementary education • M Ed, Ed S
health, physical education, recreation and safety • MS, DA
industrial/organizational psychology • MA
middle school education • M Ed
nutrition and food science • MS
psychology • MA
reading • M Ed
school counseling • M Ed, Ed S
school psychology • Ed S
secondary education • M Ed, Ed S
special education • M Ed

College of Liberal Arts
Dr. John McDaniel, Dean
Programs in:
English • MA, DA
foreign languages and literatures • MAT
historic preservation • DA
history • MA, DA
liberal arts • MA, MAT, DA
music • MA
sociology • MA

College of Mass Communications
Dr. Deryl Leaming, Dean
Program in:
mass communications • MS

■ MILLIGAN COLLEGE

Milligan College, TN 37682
http://www.milligan.edu/

Independent-religious, coed, comprehensive institution. *Enrollment:* 80 full-time matriculated graduate/professional students (61 women), 36 part-time matriculated graduate/professional students (25 women). *Graduate faculty:* 7 full-time (4 women), 5 part-time/adjunct (2 women). *Computer facilities:* 79 computers available on campus for general student use. A campuswide network can be accessed from student residence rooms and from off campus. Internet access is available. *Library facilities:* P. H. Welshimer Memorial Library. *Graduate expenses:* Tuition: full-time $6,000; part-time $210 per credit hour. Required fees: $400. Tuition and fees vary according to course level and degree level. *General application contact:* Carrie Davidson, Director of Graduate Admissions, 423-461-8306.

Area of Teacher Education
Dr. Philip S. Roberson, Director
Program in:
teacher education • M Ed

Program in Occupational Therapy
Dr. Daniel Poff, Director
Program in:
occupational therapy • MSOT

■ TENNESSEE STATE UNIVERSITY

Nashville, TN 37209-1561
http://www.tnstate.edu/

State-supported, coed, comprehensive institution. CGS member. *Enrollment:* 477 full-time matriculated graduate/professional students (338 women), 803 part-time matriculated graduate/professional students (536 women). *Graduate faculty:* 208 full-time (62 women), 35 part-time/adjunct (15 women). *Computer facilities:* 320 computers available on campus for general student use. A campuswide network can be accessed from student residence rooms and from off campus. *Library facilities:* Martha M. Brown/Lois H. Daniel Library plus 1 other. *Graduate expenses:* Tuition, state resident: full-time $3,434; part-time $211 per credit hour. Tuition, nonresident: full-time $9,062; part-time $453 per credit hour. One-time fee: $90 full-time. *General application contact:* Dr. Helen Barrett, Dean of the Graduate School, 615-963-5901.

Graduate School
Dr. Helen Barrett, Dean

College of Arts and Sciences
Dr. William Lawson, Dean
Programs in:
arts and sciences • MA, MCJ, MS, PhD
biological sciences • MS, PhD
chemistry • MS
criminal justice • MCJ
English • MA
mathematics • MS
music education • MS

College of Business
Dr. Tilden J. Curry, Dean
Program in:
business • MBA

College of Education
Dr. Franklin Jones, Dean
Programs in:
counseling and guidance • MS
counseling psychology • PhD
curriculum and instruction • Ed D
curriculum planning • Ed D
education • M Ed, MA Ed, MS, Ed D, PhD
educational administration • M Ed, MA Ed, Ed D
elementary education • M Ed, MA Ed, Ed D
health, physical education and recreation • MA Ed
psychology • MS, PhD
school psychology • MS, PhD
special education • M Ed, MA Ed, Ed D

College of Engineering and Technology
Dr. Decatur B. Rogers, Dean
Program in:
engineering and technology • ME

Institute of Government
Dr. Ann-Marie Rizzo, Director
Program in:
public administration • MPA, PhD

School of Agriculture and Family Services
Dr. Troy Wakefield, Dean
Program in:
agriculture and family services • MS

School of Allied Health Professions
Dr. P. Burch-Sims, Interim Head
Program in:
allied health professions • M Ed

School of Nursing
Dr. Marion Anema, Dean
Program in:
nursing • MS

■ TENNESSEE TECHNOLOGICAL UNIVERSITY

Cookeville, TN 38505
http://www.tntech.edu/

State-supported, coed, university. CGS member. *Enrollment:* 350 full-time matriculated graduate/professional students (139 women), 866 part-time matriculated graduate/professional students (621 women). *Graduate faculty:* 341 full-time (62 women). *Computer facilities:* 407 computers available on campus for general student use. A campuswide network can be accessed from student residence rooms and from off campus. Internet access and online class registration are available. *Library facilities:* University Library. *Graduate expenses:* Tuition, state resident: full-time $3,430; part-time $174 per hour. Tuition, nonresident: full-time $9,058; part-time $419 per hour. *General application contact:* Dr. William P. Bonner, Interim Associate Vice President for Research and Graduate Studies, 931-372-3233.

Graduate School
Dr. William P. Bonner, Interim Associate Vice President for Research and Graduate Studies

College of Arts and Sciences
Dr. Jack Armistead, Dean
Programs in:
arts and sciences • MA, MS, PhD
chemistry • MS
English • MA
environmental biology • MS
environmental sciences • PhD
fish, game, and wildlife management • MS
mathematics • MS

College of Business Administration
Dr. Virginia Moore, Director
Program in:
business administration • MBA

College of Education
Dr. Darrell Garber, Dean
Programs in:
curriculum • MA, Ed S
early childhood education • MA, Ed S
education • MA, Certificate, Ed S
educational psychology • MA, Ed S
educational psychology and student personnel • MA, Ed S
elementary education • MA, Ed S
health and physical education • MA
instructional leadership • MA, Ed S
library science • MA
reading • MA, Ed S
secondary education • MA, Ed S
special education • MA, Ed S

College of Engineering
Dr. Glen Johnson, Dean
Programs in:
chemical engineering • MS, PhD
civil engineering • MS, PhD
electrical engineering • MS, PhD
engineering • MS, PhD
industrial engineering • MS, PhD
mechanical engineering • MS, PhD

■ TREVECCA NAZARENE UNIVERSITY

Nashville, TN 37210-2877
http://www.trevecca.edu/

Independent-religious, coed, comprehensive institution. *Enrollment:* 574 full-time matriculated graduate/professional students (387 women), 104 part-time matriculated graduate/professional students (70 women). *Graduate faculty:* 18 full-time (4 women), 41 part-time/adjunct (12 women). *Computer facilities:* 200 computers available on campus for general student use. A campuswide network can be accessed from student residence rooms and from off campus. Internet access is available. *Library facilities:* Mackey Library. *Graduate expenses:* Tuition: full-time $4,770; part-time $265 per credit. *General application contact:* Dr. Stephen Pusey, Vice President of Academic Affairs, 615-248-1258.

Graduate Division
Dr. Stephen Pusey, Vice President of Academic Affairs

Division of Natural and Applied Sciences
Dr. Mike Moredock, Division Chair
Programs in:
natural and applied sciences • MS
physician assistant • MS

Division of Social and Behavioral Sciences
Dr. Peter Wilson, Division Chair
Programs in:
counseling • MA
counseling psychology • MA
marriage and family therapy • MMFT
social and behavioral sciences • MA, MMFT

School of Business and Management
Dr. Jim Hiatt, Dean
Program in:
organizational management • MA

Trevecca Nazarene University (continued)

School of Education
Dr. Melvin Welch, Dean
Programs in:
- education • M Ed, MLI Sc, D Ed
- educational leadership • M Ed
- elementary education • M Ed
- instructional effectiveness • M Ed
- library and information science • MLI Sc
- professional practices • D Ed

School of Religion and Philosophy
Dr. Tim Green, Dean
Programs in:
- religion and philosophy • MA
- religious studies • MA

■ TUSCULUM COLLEGE
Greeneville, TN 37743-9997
http://www.tusculum.edu/

Independent-religious, coed, comprehensive institution. *Enrollment:* 304 full-time matriculated graduate/professional students (211 women). *Graduate faculty:* 28 full-time (13 women), 47 part-time/adjunct (16 women). *Computer facilities:* 60 computers available on campus for general student use. A campuswide network can be accessed from student residence rooms and from off campus. Internet access is available. *Library facilities:* Albert Columbus Tate Library plus 2 others. *Graduate expenses:* Tuition: full-time $5,635; part-time $250 per semester hour. Required fees: $75. *General application contact:* Tony Narkawicz, Dean, 423-693-1177 Ext. 330.

Graduate School
Dr. Suzanne T. Hine, Vice President for Graduate and Professional Studies
Programs in:
- adult education • MA Ed
- K–12 • MA Ed
- organizational management • MAOM

■ UNION UNIVERSITY
Jackson, TN 38305-3697
http://www.uu.edu/

Independent-religious, coed, comprehensive institution. *Enrollment:* 651 matriculated graduate/professional students. *Graduate faculty:* 71. *Computer facilities:* 236 computers available on campus for general student use. A campuswide network can be accessed from student residence rooms and from off campus. Internet access is available. *Library facilities:* Emma Waters Summar Library. *Graduate expenses:* Tuition: full-time $4,920. Required fees: $190. Full-time tuition and fees vary according to program. *General application contact:* Robbie Graves, Director of Enrollment Services, 731-661-5008.

McAfee School of Business Administration
Dr. Donald Lester, Dean
Program in:
- business administration • MBA

School of Education and Human Studies
Dr. Tom Rosebrough, Dean
Programs in:
- education • M Ed, MA Ed
- education administration generalist • Sp Ed
- educational supervision • Sp Ed

■ THE UNIVERSITY OF MEMPHIS
Memphis, TN 38152
http://www.memphis.edu/

State-supported, coed, university. CGS member. *Enrollment:* 2,236 full-time matriculated graduate/professional students (1,172 women), 2,637 part-time matriculated graduate/professional students (1,600 women). *Graduate faculty:* 552 full-time (135 women), 308 part-time/adjunct (141 women). *Computer facilities:* 2,000 computers available on campus for general student use. A campuswide network can be accessed from off campus. Internet access and online class registration are available. *Library facilities:* McWherter Library plus 6 others. *General application contact:* Dr. Dianne Horgan, Associate Dean of Graduate School, 901-678-2531.

Find an in-depth description at www.petersons.com/graduate.

Cecil C. Humphreys School of Law
Donald J. Polden, Dean
Program in:
- law • JD

Graduate School
Dr. Dianne Horgan, Associate Dean of Graduate School

College of Arts and Sciences
Programs in:
- anthropology • MA
- applied mathematics • MS
- applied statistics • PhD
- arts and sciences • MA, MCRP, MFA, MHA, MPA, MS, PhD
- biology • MS, PhD
- chemistry • MS, PhD
- city and regional planning • MCRP
- clinical psychology • PhD
- computer science • PhD
- computer sciences • MS
- creative writing • MFA
- criminology and criminal justice • MA
- earth sciences • PhD
- English • MA
- experimental psychology • PhD
- French • MA
- geography • MA, MS
- geology • MS
- geophysics • MS
- health administration • MHA
- health services administration • MPA
- history • MA, PhD
- human resources administration • MPA
- mathematics • MS, PhD
- non-profit administration • MPA
- philosophy • MA, PhD
- physics • MS
- political science • MA
- psychology • MS
- public administration • MPA
- school psychology • MA, PhD
- sociology • MA
- Spanish • MA
- statistics • MS, PhD
- urban affairs and public policy • MA, MCRP, MHA, MPA
- urban management and planning • MPA
- writing and language studies • PhD

College of Communication and Fine Arts
Programs in:
- applied music • M Mu
- art history • MA
- ceramics • MFA
- communication • MA
- communication and fine arts • M Mu, MA, MFA, DMA, PhD
- communication arts • PhD
- composition • DMA
- Egyptian art and archaeology • MA
- film and video production • MA
- general art history • MA
- general journalism • MA
- graphic design • MFA
- interior design • MFA
- journalism administration • MA
- music education • M Mu, DMA
- music history • M Mu
- music theory • M Mu
- musicology • PhD
- Orff-Schulwerk • M Mu
- painting • MFA
- performance • DMA
- piano pedagogy • M Mu
- printmaking/photography • MFA
- sacred music • M Mu, DMA

sculpture • MFA
Suzuki pedagogy-piano • M Mu
theatre • MFA

College of Education
Dr. John W. Schifani, Interim Dean
Programs in:
adult education • Ed D
clinical nutrition • MS
community education • Ed D
consumer science and education • MS
counseling and personnel services • MS, Ed D
counseling psychology • PhD
early childhood education • MAT, MS, Ed D
education • Ed S
educational leadership • Ed D
educational psychology and research • MS, Ed D, PhD
elementary education • MAT
exercise and sport science • MS
health promotion • MS
higher education • Ed D
instruction and curriculum • MS, Ed D
instruction design and technology • MS, Ed D
leadership • MS
policy studies • Ed D
reading • MS, Ed D
school administration and supervision • MS
secondary education • MAT
special education • MAT, MS, Ed D
sport and leisure commerce • MS

Fogelman College of Business and Economics
Dr. John J. Pepin, Dean
Programs in:
accounting • MBA, MS, PhD
accounting systems • MS
business and economics • MA, MBA, MS, PhD
economics • MBA, PhD
executive business administration • MBA
finance • PhD
finance, insurance, and real estate • MBA, MS
international business administration • MBA
management • MBA, MS, PhD
management information systems • MBA, MS
management information systems and decision sciences • PhD
management science • MBA
marketing • MBA, MS, PhD
real estate development • MS
taxation • MS

Herff College of Engineering
Programs in:
architectural technology • MS
automatic control systems • MS
biomedical engineering • MS, PhD
biomedical systems • MS
civil engineering • PhD
communications and propagation systems • MS
design and mechanical engineering • MS
electrical engineering • PhD
electronics engineering technology • MS
energy systems • MS
engineering • MS, PhD
engineering computer systems • MS
environmental engineering • MS
foundation engineering • MS
industrial and systems engineering • MS
manufacturing engineering technology • MS
mechanical engineering • PhD
mechanical systems • MS
power systems • MS
structural engineering • MS
transportation engineering • MS
water resources engineering • MS

School of Audiology and Speech-Language Pathology
Dr. Maurice Mendel, Dean
Program in:
audiology and speech-language pathology • MA, Au D, PhD

■ THE UNIVERSITY OF TENNESSEE
Knoxville, TN 37996
http://www.tennessee.edu/

State-supported, coed, university. CGS member. *Enrollment:* 3,923 full-time matriculated graduate/professional students (2,232 women), 1,723 part-time matriculated graduate/professional students (915 women). *Graduate faculty:* 1,254 full-time (356 women), 205 part-time/adjunct (108 women). *Computer facilities:* 1,000 computers available on campus for general student use. A campuswide network can be accessed from student residence rooms and from off campus. Internet access and online class registration are available. *Library facilities:* John C. Hodges Library plus 6 others. *Graduate expenses:* Tuition, state resident: full-time $3,454; part-time $192 per credit hour. Tuition, nonresident: full-time $9,796; part-time $545 per credit hour. Required fees: $275; $25 per credit hour. *General application contact:* Diana Lopez, Director of Graduate Admissions and Records, 865-974-3251.

Find an in-depth description at www.petersons.com/graduate.

College of Law
Karen R. Britton, Director of Admissions and Career Services
Program in:
law • JD

Graduate School
Dr. Anne Mayhew, Interim Dean of Graduate Studies
Programs in:
aviation systems • MS
comparative and experimental medicine • MS, PhD

College of Agricultural Sciences and Natural Resources
Dr. C. A. Speer, Dean
Programs in:
agribusiness • MS
agricultural economics • MS
agricultural education • MS
agricultural extension education • MS
agricultural sciences and natural resources • MS, PhD
animal anatomy • PhD
biosystems engineering • MS, PhD
biosystems engineering technology • MS
breeding • MS, PhD
crop physiology and ecology • MS, PhD
entomology • MS
floriculture • MS
food science and technology • MS, PhD
forestry • MS
landscape design • MS
management • MS, PhD
nutrition • MS, PhD
physiology • MS, PhD
plant breeding and genetics • MS, PhD
plant pathology • MS
public horticulture • MS
rural sociology • MS
soil science • MS, PhD
turfgrass • MS
wildlife and fisheries science • MS
woody ornamentals • MS

College of Architecture and Design
Marleen Davis, Dean
Program in:
architecture and design • M Arch

College of Arts and Sciences
Dr. Lorayne Lester, Dean
Programs in:
accompanying • MM
American history • PhD
analytical chemistry • MS, PhD
applied linguistics • PhD
applied mathematics • MS
archaeology • MA, PhD
arts and sciences • M Math, MA, MFA, MM, MPA, MS, MSP, PhD

The University of Tennessee (continued)

audiology • MA, PhD
behavior • MS, PhD
biochemistry and cellular and molecular biology • MS, PhD
biological anthropology • MA, PhD
botany • MS, PhD
ceramics • MFA
chemical physics • PhD
choral conducting • MM
clinical psychology • PhD
composition • MM
computer science • MS, PhD
costume design • MFA
criminology • MA, PhD
cultural anthropology • MA, PhD
drawing • MFA
ecology • MS, PhD
energy, environment, and resource policy • MA, PhD
English • MA, PhD
environmental chemistry • MS, PhD
environmental planning • MSP
European history • PhD
evolutionary biology • MS, PhD
experimental psychology • MA, PhD
French • MA, PhD
genome science and technology • MS, PhD
geography • MS, PhD
geology • MS, PhD
German • MA, PhD
graphic design • MFA
hearing science • PhD
history • MA
inorganic chemistry • MS, PhD
instrumental conducting • MM
inter-area studies • MFA
Italian • PhD
jazz • MM
land-use planning • MSP
lighting design • MFA
mathematical ecology • PhD
mathematics • M Math, MS, PhD
media arts • MFA
medical ethics • MA, PhD
microbiology • MS, PhD
modern foreign languages • PhD
music education • MM
music theory • MM
musicology • MM
organic chemistry • MS, PhD
painting • MFA
performance • MFA, MM
philosophy • MA, PhD
physical chemistry • MS, PhD
physics • MS, PhD
piano pedagogy and literature • MM
plant physiology and genetics • MS, PhD
political economy • MA, PhD
political science • MA, PhD
polymer chemistry • MS, PhD
Portuguese • PhD
printmaking • MFA
psychology • MA
public administration • MPA
real estate development planning • MSP
religious studies • MA
Russian • PhD
scene design • MFA
sculpture • MFA
Spanish • MA, PhD
speech and hearing science • PhD
speech and language pathology • PhD
speech and language science • PhD
speech pathology • MA
theatre technology • MFA
theoretical chemistry • PhD
transportation planning • MSP
watercolor • MFA
zooarchaeology • MA, PhD

College of Business Administration
Dr. Jan Williams, Interim Dean
Programs in:

accounting • M Acc, PhD
business administration • M Acc, MA, MBA, MS, PhD
economics • MA, PhD
finance • MBA, PhD
industrial statistics • MS
industrial/organizational psychology • PhD
logistics and transportation • MBA, PhD
management • PhD
management science • MS, PhD
marketing • MBA, PhD
operations management • MBA
professional business administration • MBA
statistics • MS, PhD
systems • M Acc
taxation • M Acc

College of Communications
Dr. Dwight Teeter, Dean
Programs in:

advertising • MS, PhD
broadcasting • MS, PhD
communications • MS, PhD
information sciences • PhD
journalism • MS, PhD
public relations • MS, PhD
speech communication • MS, PhD

College of Education
Dr. Glennon Rowell, Dean
Programs in:

adult education • MS
art education • MS
college student personnel • MS
counseling education • PhD
counseling psychology • PhD
cultural studies in education • PhD
curriculum • MS, Ed S
curriculum education research and evaluation • PhD
curriculum, educational research and evaluation • Ed D
early childhood education • PhD
early childhood special education • MS
education • MS, Ed D, PhD, Ed S
education of deaf and hard of hearing • MS
education psychology • PhD
educational administration and policy studies • Ed D, PhD
educational administration and supervision • MS, Ed S
educational psychology • Ed D
elementary education • MS, Ed S
elementary teaching • MS
English education • MS, Ed S
exercise science • MS, PhD
foreign language/ESL education • MS, Ed S
individual and collaborative learning • MS
industrial technology • PhD
instructional technology • MS, Ed D, Ed S
literacy, language education and ESL education • PhD
literacy, language education, and ESL education • Ed D
mathematics education • MS, Ed S
mental health counseling • MS
modified and comprehensive special education • MS
reading education • MS, Ed S
rehabilitation counseling • MS
school counseling • MS, Ed S
school psychology • PhD, Ed S
science education • MS, Ed S
secondary teaching • MS
social foundations • MS
social science education • MS, Ed S
socio-cultural foundations of sports and education • PhD
special education • Ed S
sport management • MS
sport studies • MS
teacher education • Ed D, PhD

College of Engineering
Dr. Jerry Stoneking, Dean
Programs in:

aerospace engineering • MS, PhD
applied artificial intelligence • MS
biomedical engineering • MS, PhD
chemical engineering • MS, PhD
civil engineering • MS, PhD
composite materials • MS, PhD
computational mechanics • MS, PhD
electrical engineering • MS, PhD
engineering • MS, PhD
engineering management • MS
engineering science • MS, PhD
environmental engineering • MS
fluid mechanics • MS, PhD
industrial engineering • PhD
manufacturing systems engineering • MS
materials science and engineering • MS, PhD
mechanical engineering • MS, PhD
nuclear engineering • MS, PhD

optical engineering • MS, PhD
polymer engineering • MS, PhD
product development and manufacturing • MS
solid mechanics • MS, PhD
traditional industrial engineering • MS

College of Human Ecology
Dr. James D. Moran, Dean
Programs in:
child and family studies • MS, PhD
community health • PhD
community health education • MPH
early childhood education • MS
gerontology • MPH
health planning/administration • MPH
health promotion and health education • MS
hospitality management • MS
human ecology • MPH, MS, PhD
human resource development • PhD
nutrition • MS
nutrition science • PhD
public health • MPH
recreation administration • MS
recreation, tourism, and hospitality management • MS
retail and consumer sciences • MS
retailing and consumer sciences • PhD
safety • MS
teacher licensure • MS
textile science • MS, PhD
textiles, retailing and consumer sciences • MS
therapeutic recreation • MS
tourism • MS
training and development • MS

College of Nursing
Dr. Joan L. Creasia, Dean
Program in:
nursing • MSN, PhD

College of Social Work
Dr. Karen Sowers, Dean
Programs in:
clinical social work practice • MSSW
social welfare management and community practice • MSSW
social work • PhD

College of Veterinary Medicine
Dr. Michael J. Blackwell, Dean
Program in:
veterinary medicine • DVM

School of Information Sciences
Dr. Elizabeth Aversa, Head
Program in:
information sciences • MS

■ THE UNIVERSITY OF TENNESSEE AT CHATTANOOGA
Chattanooga, TN 37403-2598
http://www.utc.edu/

State-supported, coed, comprehensive institution. CGS member. *Enrollment:* 416 full-time matriculated graduate/professional students (277 women), 821 part-time matriculated graduate/professional students (474 women). *Graduate faculty:* 119 full-time (42 women), 38 part-time/adjunct (18 women). *Computer facilities:* 300 computers available on campus for general student use. A campuswide network can be accessed from student residence rooms and from off campus. Internet access and online class registration are available. *Library facilities:* Lupton Library. *Graduate expenses:* Tuition, state resident: full-time $3,464; part-time $190 per hour. Tuition, nonresident: full-time $8,960; part-time $466 per hour. *General application contact:* Dr. Deborah E. Arfken, Dean of Graduate Studies, 423-755-1740.

Graduate Division
Dr. Deborah E. Arfken, Dean of Graduate Studies

College of Arts and Sciences
Dr. Herbert Burhenn, Dean
Programs in:
arts and sciences • MA, MM, MPA, MS
English • MA
environmental sciences • MS
industrial/organizational psychology • MS
music • MM
public administration • MPA
research psychology • MS
school psychology • MS

College of Business Administration
Dr. Richard P. Casavant, Dean
Programs in:
accountancy • M Acc
business administration • MBA
economics • MBA
finance • MBA
marketing • MBA
operations/production • MBA
organizational management • MBA

College of Education and Applied Professional Studies
Dr. Mary Tanner, Dean
Programs in:
athletic training • MS
curriculum and instruction • M Ed
early childhood education • M Ed
education and applied professional studies • M Ed, MS, Ed S
educational specialist • Ed S
elementary administration • M Ed
guidance and counseling • M Ed
reading • M Ed
secondary administration • M Ed
secondary education • M Ed
special education • M Ed

College of Engineering and Computer Sciences
Dr. Phil M. Kazemersky, Acting Dean
Programs in:
computer science • MS
engineering • MS
engineering management • MS

College of Health and Human Services
Dr. Galan Janeksela, Dean
Programs in:
administration • MSN
adult health • MSN
criminal justice • MSCJ
education • MSN
family nurse practitioner • MSN
health and human services • MSCJ, MSN, MSPT
nurse anesthesia • MSN
physical therapy • MSPT

■ THE UNIVERSITY OF TENNESSEE AT MARTIN
Martin, TN 38238-1000
http://www.utm.edu/

State-supported, coed, comprehensive institution. CGS member. *Enrollment:* 349 matriculated graduate/professional students (220 women). *Graduate faculty:* 114 full-time (31 women), 12 part-time/adjunct (8 women). *Computer facilities:* 185 computers available on campus for general student use. A campuswide network can be accessed from student residence rooms and from off campus. *Library facilities:* Paul Meek Library plus 1 other. *Graduate expenses:* Tuition, state resident: full-time $3,460; part-time $194 per semester hour. Tuition, nonresident: full-time $8,956; part-time $500 per semester hour. *General application contact:* Linda L. Arant, Administrative Secretary, 731-587-7012.

Graduate Studies
Dr. Victoria S. Seng, Interim Assistant Vice Chancellor and Dean

College of Agriculture and Applied Sciences
Dr. James Byford, Dean
Programs in:

The University of Tennessee at Martin (continued)

- agriculture and human environment • MSFCS
- child development and family relations • MSFCS
- food science and nutrition • MSFCS

College of Business and Public Affairs
Dr. Rhelda Barron, Dean
Programs in:
- accounting • M Ac
- business administration • M Ac, MBA

College of Education and Behavioral Sciences
Dr. B. C. DeSpain, Dean
Programs in:
- counseling • MS Ed
- education • MS Ed
- teaching • MS Ed

■ VANDERBILT UNIVERSITY

Nashville, TN 37240-1001
http://www.vanderbilt.edu/

Independent, coed, university. CGS member. *Enrollment:* 3,780 full-time matriculated graduate/professional students (1,810 women), 377 part-time matriculated graduate/professional students (242 women). *Graduate faculty:* 1,944 full-time, 1,472 part-time/adjunct. *Computer facilities:* 400 computers available on campus for general student use. A campuswide network can be accessed from student residence rooms and from off campus. Productivity and educational software available. *Library facilities:* Jean and Alexander Heard Library plus 7 others. *Graduate expenses:* Tuition: part-time $1,050 per hour. *General application contact:* Information Contact, 615-343-2727.

Divinity School
Dr. James Hudnut-Beumler, Dean
Program in:
- divinity • M Div, MTS

Graduate School
William P. Smith, Acting Dean
Programs in:
- anthropology • MA, PhD
- astronomy • MS
- biochemistry • MS, PhD
- biological sciences • MS, PhD
- biomedical informatics • MS, PhD
- biomedical sciences • PhD
- cancer biology • MS, PhD
- cell biology • MS, PhD
- cellular and molecular pathology • PhD
- chemistry • MA, MAT, MS, PhD
- classical studies • MA, MAT, PhD
- comparative literature • MA, PhD
- economics • MA, MAT, PhD
- educational leadership • MS, PhD
- English • MA, MAT, PhD
- fine arts • MA, MAT
- French • MA, MAT, PhD
- geology • MS
- German • MA, MAT, PhD
- hearing and speech sciences • MS, PhD
- history • MA, MAT, PhD
- Latin American studies • MA
- liberal arts and science • MLAS
- mathematics • MA, MAT, MS, PhD
- medical physics • MS
- microbiology and immunology • MS, PhD
- molecular physiology and biophysics • PhD
- neuroscience • PhD
- nursing science • PhD
- pharmacology • PhD
- philosophy • MA, PhD
- physics • MA, MAT, MS, PhD
- policy development and program evaluation • MS, PhD
- political science • MA, MAT, PhD
- Portuguese • MA
- psychology • MA, PhD
- psychology and human development • MS, PhD
- religion • MA, PhD
- sociology • MA, PhD
- Spanish • MA, MAT, PhD
- Spanish and Portuguese • PhD
- special education • MS, PhD
- teaching and learning • MS, PhD

Law School
Kent D. Syverud, Dean
Program in:
- law • JD, LL M

Owen Graduate School of Management
William G. Christie, Dean
Programs in:
- business administration • MBA
- executive business administration • MBA
- finance • PhD
- management • MBA, PhD
- marketing • PhD
- operations management • PhD
- organization studies • PhD

Peabody College
Dr. Camilla P. Benbow, Dean
Programs in:
- curriculum and instruction • M Ed
- early childhood education • M Ed, Ed D
- education • M Ed, Ed D
- elementary education • M Ed, Ed D
- English education • M Ed, Ed D
- general administrative leadership • Ed D
- higher education • M Ed, Ed D
- human development counseling • M Ed
- human resource development • M Ed, Ed D
- human, organizational and community development • M Ed
- language and literacy education • Ed D
- mathematics education • M Ed, Ed D
- organizational leadership • M Ed
- reading education • M Ed
- school administration • M Ed, Ed D
- science education • M Ed, Ed D
- secondary education • M Ed
- special education • M Ed
- technology and education • M Ed

School of Engineering
Dr. Kenneth F. Galloway, Dean
Programs in:
- biomedical engineering • M Eng, MS, PhD
- chemical engineering • M Eng, MS, PhD
- civil engineering • M Eng, MS, PhD
- computer science • M Eng, MS, PhD
- electrical engineering • M Eng, MS, PhD
- engineering • M Eng, MS, PhD
- environmental engineering • M Eng, MS, PhD
- management of technology • M Eng, MS, PhD
- materials science • M Eng, MS, PhD
- mechanical engineering • M Eng, MS, PhD

School of Medicine
Programs in:
- clinical investigation • MS
- medicine • MD, MPH, MS, PhD
- public health • MPH

School of Nursing
Programs in:
- adult acute care nurse practitioner • MSN
- adult/correctional health nurse practitioner • MSN
- family nurse practitioner • MSN
- gerontology nurse practitioner • MSN
- health systems management • MSN
- neonatal nurse practitioner • MSN
- nurse midwifery • MSN
- nursing science • PhD
- occupational health/adult health nurse practitioner • MSN
- pediatric nurse practitioner • MSN

psychiatric-mental health nurse practitioner • MSN
women's health nurse practitioner • MSN

Texas

■ ABILENE CHRISTIAN UNIVERSITY

Abilene, TX 79699-9100
http://www.acu.edu/

Independent-religious, coed, comprehensive institution. *Enrollment:* 268 full-time matriculated graduate/professional students (115 women), 257 part-time matriculated graduate/professional students (102 women). *Graduate faculty:* 9 full-time (0 women), 122 part-time/adjunct (30 women). *Computer facilities:* 650 computers available on campus for general student use. A campuswide network can be accessed from student residence rooms and from off campus. Internet access and online class registration are available. *Library facilities:* Brown Library. *Graduate expenses:* Tuition: full-time $8,328; part-time $347 per hour. Required fees: $500; $17 per hour. $5 per term. *General application contact:* Dr. Angela Brenton, Graduate Dean, 915-674-2354.

Graduate School
Dr. Angela Brenton, Graduate Dean
Program in:
organizational and human resource development • MS

College of Arts and Sciences
Dr. Colleen Durrington, Dean
Programs in:
arts and sciences • M Ed, MA, MLA, MS
clinical psychology • MS
communication sciences and disorders • MS
counseling psychology • MS
digital media • MS
educational diagnosis • M Ed
elementary teaching • M Ed
family studies • MS
general psychology • MS
gerontology • MS
history • MA
human communication • MA
liberal arts • MLA
literature • MA
reading specialist • M Ed
school administrator • M Ed
school counselor • M Ed
school psychology • MS
secondary teaching • M Ed
social services administration • MS
writing • MA

College of Biblical Studies
Dr. Jack Reese, Dean
Programs in:
biblical studies • MA
Christian ministry • MAR
divinity • M Div
history and theology • MA
marriage and family therapy • MMFT
ministry • D Min
missions • MA
New Testament • MA
Old Testament • MA

College of Business Administration
Bill Fowler, Department Chair
Program in:
business administration • M Acc

School of Nursing
Dr. Cecilia Tiller, Dean
Program in:
nursing • MSN

■ ANGELO STATE UNIVERSITY

San Angelo, TX 76909
http://www.angelo.edu/

State-supported, coed, comprehensive institution. CGS member. *Enrollment:* 109 full-time matriculated graduate/professional students (73 women), 302 part-time matriculated graduate/professional students (175 women). *Graduate faculty:* 109 full-time (37 women), 18 part-time/adjunct (3 women). *Computer facilities:* 325 computers available on campus for general student use. A campuswide network can be accessed from student residence rooms and from off campus. Internet access and online class registration are available. *Library facilities:* Portor Henderson Library plus 1 other. *Graduate expenses:* Tuition, state resident: full-time $1,043. Tuition, nonresident: full-time $3,623. *General application contact:* Jackie Droll, Coordinator of Graduate Admissions, 915-942-2169.

Find an in-depth description at www.petersons.com/graduate.

Graduate School
Dr. Carol Diminnie, Dean of Graduate School
Program in:
interdisciplinary studies • MA, MS

College of Business and Professional Studies
Dr. Robert K. Hegglund, Dean
Programs in:
accounting • MBA
business and professional studies • MBA, MS
kinesiology • MS
management • MBA

College of Liberal and Fine Arts
Dr. E. James Holland, Dean
Programs in:
communications • MA
English • MA
history • MA
international studies • MA
liberal and fine arts • MA, MPA, MS
psychology • MS
public administration • MPA

College of Sciences
Dr. David Loyd, Dean
Programs in:
animal science • MS
biology • MS
medical-surgical nursing • MSN
physical therapy • MPT
sciences • MPT, MS, MSN

School of Education
Dr. John J. Miazga, Dean of the School of Education
Programs in:
curriculum and instruction • MA
education • M Ed, MA
educational diagnostics • M Ed
guidance and counseling • M Ed
reading specialist • M Ed
school administration • M Ed

■ BAYLOR UNIVERSITY

Waco, TX 76798
http://www.baylor.edu/

Independent-religious, coed, university. CGS member. *Enrollment:* 1,470 full-time matriculated graduate/professional students (642 women), 429 part-time matriculated graduate/professional students (226 women). *Graduate faculty:* 350. *Computer facilities:* 1,300 computers available on campus for general student use. A campuswide network can be accessed from student residence rooms and from off campus. Internet access and online class registration are available. *Library facilities:* Moody Memorial Library plus 8 others. *Graduate expenses:* Tuition: full-time $6,390; part-time $355 per semester hour. Required fees: $652 per semester. *General application contact:* Suzanne Keener, Administrative Assistant, 254-710-6555.

Find an in-depth description at www.petersons.com/graduate.

Baylor University (continued)

George W. Truett Seminary
Dr. Paul W. Powell, Dean
Program in:
theology • M Div, D Min

Graduate School
Dr. Larry Lyon, Dean

Academy of Health Sciences
Col. Richard Shipley, Dean
Programs in:
health care administration • MHA
health sciences • MHA, MPT
physical therapy • MPT

College of Arts and Sciences
Dr. Wallace Daniel, Dean
Programs in:
American studies • MA
applied sociology • PhD
arts and sciences • MA, MCG, MES, MFA, MIJ, MPPA, MS, MSCP, MSCSD, MSG, MSL, MSW, PhD, Psy D
biology • MA, MS, PhD
chemistry • MS, PhD
clinical gerontology • MCG
clinical psychology • MSCP, Psy D
communication sciences and disorders • MA, MSCSD
communication studies • MA
directing • MFA
earth science • MA
English • MA, PhD
environmental biology • MS
environmental studies • MES, MS
geology • MS, PhD
gerontology • MSG
history • MA
international journalism • MIJ
international relations • MA
journalism • MA
limnology • MSL
mathematics • MS
museum studies • MA
neuroscience • MA, PhD
philosophy • MA
physics • MA, MS, PhD
political science • MA
public policy and administration • MPPA
religion • MA, PhD
social work • MCG, MSG, MSW
sociology • MA
Spanish • MA
theater arts • MA

Hankamer School of Business
Dr. Linda Livingstone, Director of Graduate Programs
Programs in:
accounting • M Acc, MT
business • M Acc, MA, MBA, MBAIM, MIM, MS, MS Eco, MSIS, MT
business administration • MBA
economics • MS Eco
information systems • MSIS
information systems management • MBA
international economics • MA, MS
international management • MBA, MBAIM, MIM

Institute of Biomedical Studies
Dr. Darden Powers, Director
Program in:
biomedical studies • MS, PhD

Institute of Statistics
Dr. Roger E. Kirk, Director
Program in:
statistics • MA, PhD

J. M. Dawson Institute of Church-State Studies
Dr. Derek H. Davis, Director
Program in:
church-state studies • MA, PhD

Louise Herrington School of Nursing of Baylor University
Dr. Phyllis S. Karns, Dean
Programs in:
family nurse practitioner • MSN
neonatal nurse practitioner • MSN
nursing administration and management • MSN

School of Education
Dr. Fred Curtis, Director of Graduate Studies
Programs in:
curriculum and instruction • MA, MS Ed, Ed D, Ed S
education • MA, MS Ed, Ed D, PhD, Ed S
educational administration • MS Ed, Ed D, Ed S
educational psychology • MA, MS Ed, PhD, Ed S
health, human performance and recreation • MS Ed

School of Engineering and Computer Science
Dr. Greg Speegle, Director of Graduate Studies
Program in:
computer science • MS

School of Music
Dr. Harry Elzinga, Director of Graduate Studies
Programs in:
church music • MM
composition • MM
conducting • MM
music education • MM
music history and literature • MM
music theory • MM
performance • MM
piano accompanying • MM
piano pedagogy and performance • MM

School of Law
Dr. Bradley J. B. Toben, Dean
Program in:
law • JD

■ DALLAS BAPTIST UNIVERSITY

Dallas, TX 75211-9299
http://www.dbu.edu/

Independent-religious, coed, comprehensive institution. *Enrollment:* 164 full-time matriculated graduate/professional students (107 women), 678 part-time matriculated graduate/professional students (414 women). *Graduate faculty:* 90 full-time (31 women), 66 part-time/adjunct (24 women). *Computer facilities:* 109 computers available on campus for general student use. A campuswide network can be accessed from student residence rooms and from off campus. Internet access is available. *Library facilities:* Vance Memorial Library. *Graduate expenses:* Tuition: full-time $5,670; part-time $315 per credit. *General application contact:* Sarah R. Brancaccio, Director of Graduate Programs, 214-333-5243.

College of Adult Education
Kerry Webb, Director
Programs in:
adult education • MLA
liberal arts • MLA

College of Business
Dr. Tinsop Park, Acting Dean
Programs in:
accounting • MBA
business • MA, MBA
conflict resolution management • MA
finance • MBA
general management • MA
human resource management • MA
international business • MBA
management • MBA
management information systems • MBA
marketing • MBA
technology and engineering management • MBA

College of Humanities and Social Sciences
Dr. Michael E. Williams, Dean
Programs in:
counseling • MA
humanities and social sciences • MA

Dorothy M. Bush College of Education
Dr. Mike Rosato, Dean
Programs in:
early childhood education • M Ed
education • M Ed, MAT
educational organization and administration • M Ed
elementary reading education • M Ed
general elementary education • M Ed
higher education • M Ed
reading specialist • M Ed
school counseling • M Ed
teaching • MAT

■ HARDIN-SIMMONS UNIVERSITY

Abilene, TX 79698-0001
http://www.hsutx.edu/

Independent-religious, coed, comprehensive institution. *Enrollment:* 159 full-time matriculated graduate/professional students (74 women), 191 part-time matriculated graduate/professional students (114 women). *Graduate faculty:* 80 full-time (21 women), 13 part-time/adjunct (1 woman). *Computer facilities:* 224 computers available on campus for general student use. A campuswide network can be accessed from student residence rooms and from off campus. Internet access is available. *Library facilities:* Richardson Library plus 1 other. *Graduate expenses:* Tuition: full-time $6,120; part-time $340 per credit. Required fees: $745. *General application contact:* Dr. Dan McAlexander, Dean of Graduate Studies, 915-670-1298.

Graduate School
Dr. Dan McAlexander, Dean of Graduate Studies
Programs in:
English • MA
environmental management • MS
family psychology • MA
history • MA
physical therapy • MPT

Irvin School of Education
Dr. Pam Williford, Dean
Programs in:
counseling and human development • M Ed
education • M Ed
gifted education • M Ed
reading specialist • M Ed
secondary physical education • M Ed
sports and recreation management • M Ed

Logsdon School of Theology
Dr. M. Vernon Davis, Dean
Programs in:
family ministry • MA
religion • MA
theology • M Div

School of Business
Dr. Jimmie Monhollan, Dean
Program in:
business • MBA

School of Music
Dr. Robert Brooks, Director
Programs in:
church music • MM
music education • MM
music performance • MM
theory-composition • MM

School of Nursing
Dr. Cecilia Tiller, Dean
Programs in:
advanced healthcare delivery • MSN
family nurse practitioner • MSN

■ HOUSTON BAPTIST UNIVERSITY

Houston, TX 77074-3298
http://www.hbu.edu/

Independent-religious, coed, comprehensive institution. *Enrollment:* 434 full-time matriculated graduate/professional students (307 women), 260 part-time matriculated graduate/professional students (70 women). *Graduate faculty:* 116 full-time, 85 part-time/adjunct. *Computer facilities:* 115 computers available on campus for general student use. A campuswide network can be accessed from off campus. *Library facilities:* Moody Library. *Graduate expenses:* Tuition: part-time $315 per credit hour. Required fees: $85 per quarter. $150 per quarter. *General application contact:* Ida Thompson, Director of Graduate Admissions.

College of Arts and Humanities
Dr. James Taylor, Dean
Programs in:
arts and humanities • MATS, MLA
liberal arts • MLA
theological studies • MATS

College of Business and Economics
Dr. Lynn Gillette, Dean
Programs in:
accountancy and information technology • MS Acct
accounting • MBA
business administration • MSM
business and economics • MBA, MS Acct, MSHRM, MSM, MSMCS
finance • MBA
human resource management • MBA
human resources management • MSHRM
information technology • MBA
international management • MBA
management, computing and systems • MSMCS

College of Education and Behavioral Sciences
Dr. Bill Borgers, Dean
Programs in:
bilingual education • M Ed
counselor education • M Ed
curriculum instruction • M Ed
education • M Ed
education and behavioral sciences • M Ed, MAP, MAPCP
educational administration • M Ed
educational diagnostician • M Ed
elementary education • M Ed
generic special education • M Ed
pastoral counseling and psychology • MAPCP
psychology • MAP
reading education • M Ed
secondary education • M Ed

College of Nursing
Dr. Nancy Yuill, Dean
Programs in:
congregational care nurse • MSN
family nurse practitioner • MSN
family nurse practitioner-congregational nurse • MSN
health administration • MSHA
nursing • MSHA, MSN

■ LAMAR UNIVERSITY

Beaumont, TX 77710
http://www.lamar.edu/

State-supported, coed, university. CGS member. *Enrollment:* 396 full-time matriculated graduate/professional students (150 women), 442 part-time matriculated graduate/professional students (280 women). *Graduate faculty:* 182 full-time (45 women), 20 part-time/adjunct (7 women). *Computer facilities:* 120 computers available on campus for general student use. A campuswide network can be accessed from student residence rooms and from off campus. *Library facilities:* Mary and John Gray Library. *Graduate expenses:* Full-time $594. Tuition, state resident: full-time $2,583; part-time $146 per hour. Tuition, nonresident: part-time $287 per hour.

Lamar University (continued)
Required fees: $196 per term. *General application contact:* Sandy Drane, Coordinator of Graduate Admissions, 409-880-8356.

Find an in-depth description at www.petersons.com/graduate.

College of Graduate Studies
Dr. James W. Westgate, Associate Vice President for Research and Dean

College of Arts and Sciences
Dr. Richard G. Marriott, Chair
Programs in:
- applied criminology • MS
- arts and sciences • MA, MPA, MS, MSN
- biology • MS
- chemistry • MS
- community/clinical psychology • MS
- English • MA
- history • MA
- industrial/organizational psychology • MS
- nursing administration • MSN
- public administration • MPA

College of Business
Dr. Robert A. Swerdlow, Associate Dean
Programs in:
- accounting • MBA
- information sstems • MBA
- management • MBA

College of Education and Human Development
Dr. R. Carl Westerfield, Dean
Programs in:
- counseling and development • M Ed, Certificate
- counselor • Certificate
- education administration • M Ed, Certificate
- education and human development • M Ed, MS, Certificate
- educational diagnostician • Certificate
- elementary education • M Ed, Certificate
- family and consumer sciences • MS
- kinesiology • MS
- mental retardation • Certificate
- principal • Certificate
- reading • Certificate
- secondary education • M Ed, Certificate
- special education • M Ed, Certificate
- superintendent • Certificate
- supervision • M Ed, Certificate

College of Engineering
Dr. Jack Hopper, Chair
Programs in:
- chemical engineering • ME, MES, DE
- civil engineering • ME, MES, DE
- computer science • MS
- electrical engineering • ME, MES, DE
- engineering • ME, MEM, MES, MS, DE
- engineering management • MEM
- environmental engineering • MS
- environmental studies • MS
- industrial engineering • ME, MES, DE
- mathematics • MS
- mechanical engineering • ME, MES, DE

College of Fine Arts and Communication
Dr. Russ A. Schultz, Dean
Programs in:
- art history • MA
- audiology • MS
- deaf education • MS, Ed D
- fine arts and communication • MA, MM, MM Ed, MS, Ed D
- music education • MM Ed
- music performance • MM
- photography • MA
- speech language pathology • MS
- studio art • MA
- theatre • MS
- visual design • MA

■ LETOURNEAU UNIVERSITY
Longview, TX 75607-7001
http://www.letu.edu/

Independent-religious, coed, comprehensive institution. *Enrollment:* 57 full-time matriculated graduate/professional students (22 women), 216 part-time matriculated graduate/professional students (108 women). *Graduate faculty:* 5 full-time, 53 part-time/adjunct. *Computer facilities:* 120 computers available on campus for general student use. A campuswide network can be accessed from student residence rooms and from off campus. *Library facilities:* Margaret Estes Resource Center. *Graduate expenses:* Tuition: full-time $7,860; part-time $365 per credit hour. Required fees: $250. *General application contact:* Dr. Herbert Tolbert, Director of Marketing and Enrollment Management, 903-233-3250.

Graduate and Professional Studies
Dr. Robert W. Hudson, Vice President of Graduate, and Professional Studies
Programs in:
- business administration • MBA
- health care • MBA

■ MIDWESTERN STATE UNIVERSITY
Wichita Falls, TX 76308
http://www.mwsu.edu/

State-supported, coed, comprehensive institution. *Enrollment:* 132 full-time matriculated graduate/professional students (70 women), 526 part-time matriculated graduate/professional students (327 women). *Graduate faculty:* 58 full-time (16 women), 12 part-time/adjunct (3 women). *Computer facilities:* 220 computers available on campus for general student use. A campuswide network can be accessed from student residence rooms and from off campus. *Library facilities:* Moffett Library. *Graduate expenses:* Tuition, state resident: full-time $1,754; part-time $40 per credit hour. Tuition, nonresident: full-time $5,624; part-time $255 per credit hour. Required fees: $765. Tuition and fees vary according to course load and program. *General application contact:* Darla Inglish, Assistant Registrar, 940-397-4321.

Graduate Studies
Dr. Jesse W. Rogers, Vice President for Academic Affairs

College of Business Administration
Dr. Yoshi Fukasawa, Dean
Programs in:
- business administration • MA, MBA
- public administration • MA

College of Education
Dr. Emerson Capps, Dean
Programs in:
- curriculum and instruction • M Ed
- education • M Ed, MA, MSK
- educational leadership • M Ed
- elementary education • M Ed
- general counseling • MA
- human resource development • MA
- kinesiology • MSK
- reading education • M Ed
- school counseling • M Ed
- special education • M Ed
- training and development • M Ed

College of Health and Human Services
Dr. Susan Sportsman, Dean
Programs in:
- family nurse practitioner • MSN
- health and human services • MA, MS, MSN
- nurse educator • MSN
- public administration • MA
- radiologic administration • MS
- radiologic education • MS

College of Liberal Arts
Dr. Michael Collins, Dean
Programs in:
English • MA
history • MA
liberal arts • MA
political science • MA
psychology • MA

College of Science and Mathematics
Dr. Norman Horner, Dean
Programs in:
biology • MS
computer science • MS
science • MS

■ OUR LADY OF THE LAKE UNIVERSITY OF SAN ANTONIO

San Antonio, TX 78207-4689
http://www.ollusa.edu/

Independent-religious, coed, comprehensive institution. *Enrollment:* 325 full-time matriculated graduate/professional students (240 women), 916 part-time matriculated graduate/professional students (620 women). *Graduate faculty:* 124 full-time (64 women), 157 part-time/adjunct (71 women). *Computer facilities:* 200 computers available on campus for general student use. A campuswide network can be accessed from off campus. *Library facilities:* Saint Florence Library plus 2 others. *Graduate expenses:* Tuition: full-time $9,840; part-time $410 per hour. Required fees: $258. *General application contact:* Michael Boatner, Acting Director of Admissions, 210-434-6711.

College of Arts and Sciences
Sr. Isabel Ball, Dean
Programs in:
English • MA
English communication arts • MA
language and literature • MA

School of Business
Dr. Lois Graff, Dean
Programs in:
general • MBA
health care management • MBA

School of Education and Clinical Studies
Dr. Jacquelyn Alexander, Dean
Programs in:
administration/supervision • M Ed
communication and learning disorders • MA
counseling psychology • MS, Psy D
curriculum and instruction • M Ed
human sciences • MA
human sciences and sociology • MA
leadership studies • PhD
learning resources • M Ed
psychology • MS, Psy D
school counseling • MS
school supervision • M Ed
sociology • MA
special education • MA

Worden School of Social Service
Dr. Morley Glicken, Dean
Program in:
social service • MSW

■ PRAIRIE VIEW A&M UNIVERSITY

Prairie View, TX 77446-0188
http://www.pvamu.edu/

State-supported, coed, comprehensive institution. *Enrollment:* 408 full-time matriculated graduate/professional students (291 women), 664 part-time matriculated graduate/professional students (480 women). *Graduate faculty:* 75 full-time (20 women), 18 part-time/adjunct (8 women). *Computer facilities:* 102 computers available on campus for general student use. *Library facilities:* John B. Coleman Library. *Graduate expenses:* Tuition: part-time $40 per semester hour. *General application contact:* Dr. William H. Parker, Dean of the Graduate School, 936-857-2315.

Graduate School
Dr. William H. Parker, Dean of the Graduate School

College of Agriculture and Human Sciences
Dr. Elizabeth Noel, Dean
Programs in:
agricultural economics • MS
animal sciences • MS
interdisciplinary human sciences • MS
marriage and family therapy • MS
soil science • MS

College of Arts and Sciences
Gerard Rambally, Dean
Programs in:
arts and sciences • MA, MS
biology • MS
chemistry • MS
English • MA
mathematics • MS
sociology • MA

College of Business
Dr. Lucille Pointer, Interim Dean
Program in:
general business administration • MBA

College of Education
Dr. M. Paul Mehta, Dean
Programs in:
counseling • MA, MS Ed
curriculum and instruction • M Ed, MS Ed
education • M Ed, MA, MA Ed, MS Ed
health education • MA Ed, MS Ed
physical education • MA Ed, MS Ed
school administration • M Ed, MS Ed
school supervision • M Ed, MS Ed
special education • M Ed, MS Ed

College of Engineering
Dr. Milton R. Bryant, Dean
Program in:
engineering • MS Engr

College of Nursing
Dr. Betty Adams, Dean
Program in:
nursing • MSN

School of Juvenile Justice and Psychology
Dr. Elaine Rodney, Dean
Program in:
juvenile justice • MSJJ, PhD

■ RICE UNIVERSITY

Houston, TX 77251-1892
http://www.rice.edu/

Independent, coed, university. CGS member. *Enrollment:* 1,587 full-time matriculated graduate/professional students (593 women), 56 part-time matriculated graduate/professional students (24 women). *Graduate faculty:* 434 full-time, 150 part-time/adjunct. *Computer facilities:* 600 computers available on campus for general student use. A campuswide network can be accessed from student residence rooms and from off campus. Internet access is available. *Library facilities:* Fondren Library. *Graduate expenses:* Tuition: full-time $16,700; part-time $930 per hour. Required fees: $400.

Graduate Programs

George R. Brown School of Engineering
C. Sidney Burrus, Dean of Engineering
Programs in:
bioengineering • MS, PhD
bioinformatics • MS
biostatistics • PhD
chemical engineering • M Ch E, MS, PhD

Rice University (continued)
circuits, controls, and communication systems • MS, PhD
civil engineering • MCE, MS, PhD
computational and applied mathematics • MA, MCAM, PhD
computational finance • PhD
computer science • MCS, MS, PhD
computer science and engineering • MS, PhD
electrical engineering • MEE
engineering • M Ch E, M Stat, MA, MCAM, MCE, MCS, MEE, MEE, MES, MME, MMS, MS, PhD
environmental engineering • MEE, MES, MS, PhD
environmental science • MEE, MES, MS, PhD
lasers, microwaves, and solid-state electronics • MS, PhD
materials science • MS, PhD
mechanical engineering • MME, MMS, MS, PhD
statistics • M Stat, MA, PhD

Jesse H. Jones Graduate School of Management
Program in:
business administration • MBA

School of Architecture
Lars Lerup, Dean
Programs in:
architecture • M Arch, D Arch
urban design • M Arch UD

School of Humanities
Gale Stokes, Interim Dean
Programs in:
education • MAT
English • MA, PhD
French studies • MA, PhD
history • MA, PhD
humanities • MA, MAT, PhD
linguistics • MA, PhD
philosophy • MA, PhD
religious studies • MA, PhD
Spanish • MA

School of Social Sciences
Robert M. Stein, Dean
Programs in:
anthropology • MA, PhD
economics • MA, PhD
industrial-organizational/social psychology • MA, PhD
political science • MA, PhD
psychology • MA, PhD
social sciences • MA, PhD

Shepherd School of Music
Dr. Michael Hammond, Dean
Programs in:
composition • MM, DMA
conducting • MM
history • MM
performance • MM, DMA
theory • MM

Wiess School of Natural Sciences
Dr. Kathleen S. Matthews, Dean of Natural Sciences
Programs in:
applied physics • MS, PhD
biochemistry and cell biology • MA, PhD
chemistry • MA
earth science • MA, PhD
ecology and evolutionary biology • MA, PhD
inorganic chemistry • PhD
mathematics • MA, PhD
natural sciences • MA, MS, PhD
organic chemistry • PhD
physical chemistry • PhD
physics • MA
physics and astronomy • MS, PhD

■ ST. EDWARD'S UNIVERSITY

Austin, TX 78704-6489
http://www.stedwards.edu/

Independent-religious, coed, comprehensive institution. *Enrollment:* 121 full-time matriculated graduate/professional students (60 women), 572 part-time matriculated graduate/professional students (309 women). *Graduate faculty:* 7 full-time (3 women), 38 part-time/adjunct (9 women). *Computer facilities:* 288 computers available on campus for general student use. A campuswide network can be accessed from student residence rooms and from off campus. Internet access and online class registration are available. *Library facilities:* Scarborough–Phillips Library. *Graduate expenses:* Tuition: full-time $7,236; part-time $402 per credit hour. *General application contact:* Andres Perez, Graduate Admissions Coordinator, 512-428-1061.

College of Professional and Graduate Studies
Dr. John Houghton, Vice President for Adult Programs
Programs in:
accounting • Certificate
administration • MAHS
business administration • MBA
conflict resolution • MAHS, Certificate
contract management • Certificate
counseling • MAHS
human resource management • MAHS
liberal arts • MLA
organizational leadership and ethics • MS
social and psychological services • MAHS
sports management • MAHS, Certificate

■ ST. MARY'S UNIVERSITY OF SAN ANTONIO

San Antonio, TX 78228-8507
http://www.stmarytx.edu/

Independent-religious, coed, comprehensive institution. *Computer facilities:* 100 computers available on campus for general student use. A campuswide network can be accessed from student residence rooms and from off campus. *Library facilities:* Academic Library plus 1 other. *General application contact:* Dean of the Graduate School, 210-436-3101.

Graduate School
Programs in:
Catholic school leadership • MA
clinical psychology • MA, MS
computer information systems • MS
correctional administration • MJA
counseling • PhD, Sp C
economics • MA
educational leadership • MA
electrical engineering • MS
electrical/computer engineering • MS
engineering administration • MS
engineering computer application • MS
history • MA
industrial engineering • MS
industrial psychology • MA, MS
international relations • MA
marriage and family relations • Certificate
marriage and family therapy • MA
mental health • MA
mental health and substance abuse counseling • Certificate
operations research • MS
pastoral administration • MA
police administration • MJA
political science • MA
public administration • MPA
reading • MA
speech communication • MA
substance abuse • MA
systems administration • MS
theology • MA

School of Business Administration
Program in:
business administration • MBA

School of Law
Robert William Piatt, Dean
Program in:
law • JD

■ SAM HOUSTON STATE UNIVERSITY

Huntsville, TX 77341

http://www.shsu.edu/

State-supported, coed, comprehensive institution. *Enrollment:* 305 full-time matriculated graduate/professional students (181 women), 879 part-time matriculated graduate/professional students (640 women). *Computer facilities:* 200 computers available on campus for general student use. A campuswide network can be accessed from off campus. Internet access is available. *Library facilities:* Newton Gresham Library. *Graduate expenses:* Tuition, state resident: full-time $1,152; part-time $384 per year. Tuition, nonresident: full-time $5,022; part-time $1,674 per year. Required fees: $644; $350 per year. *General application contact:* Dr. Brian Chapman, Dean, College of Arts and Sciences, 409-294-1401.

College of Arts and Sciences

Dr. Brian Chapman, Dean

Programs in:

- applied music and literature • MM
- art education • M Ed
- arts and sciences • M Ed, MA, MFA, MM, MS
- biological sciences • M Ed, MA, MS
- ceramics • MA, MFA
- chemistry • M Ed, MS
- computing science • M Ed, MS
- conducting • MM
- dance • MFA
- drawing • MA, MFA
- elementary • M Ed
- English • M Ed, MA
- history • MA
- instrumental • M Ed
- jewelry • MA
- Kodály pedagogy • MM
- Kodaly pedagogy • M Ed
- mathematics • M Ed, MA, MS
- music education • M Ed
- musicology • MM
- painting • MA, MFA
- performance • MM
- physics • MS
- political science • MA
- printmaking • MA, MFA
- sculpture • MA, MFA
- social research • MA
- sociology • MA
- statistics • MS
- studio art • MFA
- theory and composition • MM
- vocal • M Ed

College of Business Administration

Dr. R. Dean Lewis, Dean

Program in:

- business administration • MBA

College of Criminal Justice

Dr. Richard Ward, Dean

Program in:

- criminal justice • MA, MS, PhD

College of Education and Applied Science

Dr. Carl Harris, Dean

Programs in:

- agricultural business • MS
- agricultural education • M Ed
- agricultural mechanization • MS
- agriculture • MS
- bilingual education and English as a second language • Certificate
- clinical psychology • MA
- counseling • M Ed, MA
- curriculum and instruction • Ed D
- early childhood education • M Ed
- education and applied science • M Ed, MA, MLS, MS, Ed D, PhD, Certificate
- educational administration • M Ed, PhD
- elementary education • M Ed, Certificate
- forensic psychology • PhD
- health and kinesiology • M Ed, MA
- home economics • MA
- industrial education • M Ed, MA
- industrial technology • MA
- library science • MLS
- psychology • MA
- reading • M Ed
- school psychology • MA
- secondary education • M Ed, MA, Certificate
- special education • M Ed
- supervision • M Ed
- vocational education • M Ed, MS

■ SOUTHERN METHODIST UNIVERSITY

Dallas, TX 75275

Independent-religious, coed, university. CGS member. *Enrollment:* 1,716 full-time matriculated graduate/professional students (731 women), 2,114 part-time matriculated graduate/professional students (739 women). *Graduate faculty:* 528 full-time (155 women). *Computer facilities:* 409 computers available on campus for general student use. A campuswide network can be accessed from student residence rooms and from off campus. *Library facilities:* Central University Library plus 7 others. *Graduate expenses:* Tuition: part-time $323 per credit hour. Tuition and fees vary according to program. *General application contact:* Dr. U. Narayan Bhat, Dean of Research and Graduate Studies, 214-768-3268.

Find an in-depth description at www.petersons.com/graduate.

Dedman College

Dr. Jasper Neel, Dean

Programs in:

- anthropology • MA, PhD
- applied economics • MA
- applied geophysics • MS
- applied mathematics • MS
- archaeology • MA, PhD
- bilingual education • MBE
- biological sciences • MA, MS, PhD
- chemistry • MS
- clinical and counseling psychology • MA
- economics • MA, PhD
- English • MA
- exploration geophysics • MS
- geology • MS, PhD
- geophysics • MS, PhD
- history • MA, PhD
- Latin American studies • MA
- liberal arts • MBE, MLA
- mathematical sciences • PhD
- medical anthropology • MA, PhD
- medieval studies • MA
- physics • MS, PhD
- psychology • MA, PhD
- religious studies • MA, PhD
- statistical science • MS, PhD

Edwin L. Cox School of Business

Dr. Albert Neimi, Dean

Programs in:

- accounting • MSA
- business • Exec MBA, MBA, MSA

Meadows School of the Arts

Carole Brandt, Dean

Programs in:

- acting • MFA
- art history • MA
- arts • MA, MFA, MM, MMT, MSM
- choreographic theory and practice • MFA
- conducting • MM
- design • MFA
- directing • MFA
- music composition • MM
- music education • MM
- music history • MM
- music theory • MM
- music therapy • MMT
- performance • MM
- piano performance and pedagogy • MM
- sacred music • MSM
- studio art • MFA

Southern Methodist University (continued)

Center for Arts Administration
Dr. Gregory Poggi, Director
Program in:
• arts administration

Center for Communication Arts
Alan Albarran, Director
Program in:
communication arts • MA

Perkins School of Theology
Dr. Robin Lovin, Dean
Program in:
theology • M Div, MRE, MSM, MTS, D Min

School of Engineering
Dr. Stephen A. Szygenda, Dean
Programs in:
applied science • MS, PhD
civil engineering • MS
computer engineering • MS Cp E, PhD
computer science • MS, PhD
electrical engineering • MSEE, PhD
engineering • MS, MS Cp E, MSEE, MSEM, MSME, DE, PhD
engineering management • MSEM, DE
environmental engineering • MS
envrionmental systems management • MS
manufacturing systems management • MS
mechanical engineering • MSME, PhD
operations research • MS, PhD
software engineering • MS
systems engineering • MS
telecommunications • MS

School of Law
John B. Attanasio, Dean
Programs in:
comparative and international law • LL M
law • JD, LL M, SJD
taxation • LL M

■ SOUTHWEST TEXAS STATE UNIVERSITY

San Marcos, TX 78666
http://www.swt.edu/

State-supported, coed, comprehensive institution. CGS member. *Enrollment:* 1,002 full-time matriculated graduate/professional students (684 women), 2,009 part-time matriculated graduate/professional students (1,225 women). *Graduate faculty:* 256 full-time (106 women), 38 part-time/adjunct (15 women). *Computer facilities:* 731 computers available on campus for general student use. A campuswide network can be accessed from student residence rooms and from off campus. Internet access is available. *Library facilities:* Alkek Library. *Graduate expenses:* Tuition, state resident: full-time $720; part-time $80 per credit hour. Tuition, nonresident: full-time $4,590; part-time $510 per credit hour. Required fees: $1,490; $745 per semester. Full-time tuition and fees vary according to course load. *General application contact:* Dr. J. Michael Willoughby, Dean of the Graduate School, 512-245-2581.

Graduate School
Dr. J. Michael Willoughby, Dean
Programs in:
interdisciplinary studies in applied sociology • MAIS
interdisciplinary studies in criminal justice • MSIS
interdisciplinary studies in education administration and psychological services • MAIS
interdisciplinary studies in elementary mathematics, science, and technology • MSIS
interdisciplinary studies in health, physical education, and recreation • MAIS, MSIS
interdisciplinary studies in international studies • MA
interdisciplinary studies in liberal arts • MAIS
interdisciplinary studies in modern languages • MAIS
interdisciplinary studies in occupational education • MSIS
interdisciplinary studies in political science • MAIS
interdisciplinary studies in science • MSIS

College of Applied Arts and Technology
Dr. Jaime Chahin, Dean
Programs in:
agriculture education • M Ed
applied arts • M Ed, MS, MSCJ
criminal justice • MSCJ
family and child studies • MS

College of Business Administration
Dr. Denise Smart, Dean
Programs in:
accounting • M Acy
business administration • M Acy, MBA

College of Education
Dr. John Beck, Dean
Programs in:
counseling and guidance • M Ed, MA
developmental education • MA
education • M Ed, MA, MS, MSRLS
educational administration • M Ed, MA
elementary education • M Ed, MA
elementary education-bilingual/bicultural • M Ed, MA
health and physical education • MA
health education • M Ed
management of vocational/technical education • M Ed
physical education • M Ed
professional counseling • MA
reading education • M Ed
recreation and leisure services • MSRLS
school psychology • MA
secondary education • M Ed, MA
special education • M Ed
sports and leisure management • MS

College of Fine Arts and Communication
Dr. T. Richard Cheatham, Dean
Programs in:
fine arts and communication • MA, MM
mass communication • MA
music education • MM
music performance • MM
speech communication • MA
theatre arts • MA

College of Health Professions
Dr. Rumaldo Z. Juarez, Dean
Programs in:
allied health research • MSHP
communication disorders • MA, MSCD
health professions • MA, MHA, MSCD, MSHP, MSPT, MSW
healthcare administration • MHA
healthcare human resources • MSHP
physical therapy • MSPT
social work • MSW

College of Liberal Arts
Dr. Ann Marrie Ellis, Dean
Programs in:
applied geography • MAG
cartography/geographic information systems • MAG
creative writing • MFA
English • MA
environmental geography • PhD
environmental geography and geography education • PhD
geography • MAG
geography education • PhD
health psychology • MA
history • M Ed, MA
land/area studies • MAG
legal studies • MA
liberal arts • M Ed, MA, MAG, MAT, MFA, MPA, PhD
political science • M Ed, MA
political science education • M Ed
public administration • MPA

resource and environmental studies • MAG
sociology • MA
Spanish • MA, MAT
Spanish education • MAT
technical communication • MA

College of Science
Dr. Stanley C. Israel, Dean
Programs in:
aquatic biology • MS
biochemistry • MS
biology • M Ed, MA, MS
chemistry • M Ed, MA, MS
computer science • MA, MS
industrial technology • MST
mathematics • M Ed, MA, MS
physics • MA, MS
science • M Ed, MA, MS, MST
software engineering • MS

■ STEPHEN F. AUSTIN STATE UNIVERSITY

Nacogdoches, TX 75962

http://www.sfasu.edu/

State-supported, coed, comprehensive institution. *Enrollment:* 431 full-time matriculated graduate/professional students (255 women), 807 part-time matriculated graduate/professional students (525 women). *Graduate faculty:* 289 full-time, 75 part-time/adjunct. *Computer facilities:* 800 computers available on campus for general student use. A campuswide network can be accessed from student residence rooms and from off campus. Internet access and online class registration are available. *Library facilities:* Ralph W. Steen Library. *Graduate expenses:* Tuition, state resident: full-time $960; part-time $40 per hour. Tuition, nonresident: full-time $6,120; part-time $255 per hour. Required fees: $1,210; $55 per hour. Tuition and fees vary according to course load. *General application contact:* Dr. David Jeffrey, Associate Vice President for Graduate Studies and Research, 936-468-2807.

Graduate School
Dr. David Jeffrey, Associate Vice President for Graduate Studies and Research

College of Applied Arts and Science
Dr. James O. Standley, Dean
Programs in:
applied arts and science • MA, MIS, MSW
communication • MA
interdisciplinary studies • MIS
mass communication • MA
social work • MSW

College of Business
Dr. Marlin C. Young, Dean
Programs in:
business • MBA
computer science • MS
management and marketing • MBA
professional accountancy • MPAC

College of Education
Dr. Patsy Hallman, Interim Dean
Programs in:
agriculture • MS
counseling • MA
early childhood education • M Ed
education • M Ed, MA, MS, Ed D
educational leadership • Ed D
elementary education • M Ed
health education • M Ed
human sciences • MS
physical education • M Ed
school psychology • MA
secondary education • M Ed
special education • M Ed
speech pathology • MS

College of Fine Arts
Dr. Richard Berry, Interim Dean
Programs in:
art • MA
design • MFA
drawing • MFA
fine arts • MA, MFA, MM
music • MA, MM
painting • MFA
sculpture • MFA
theatre • MA

College of Forestry
Dr. Scott Beasley, Dean
Program in:
forestry • MF, MSF, PhD

College of Liberal Arts
Dr. Robert Szafran, Interim Dean
Programs in:
English • MA
history • MA
liberal arts • MA, MPA
psychology • MA
public administration • MPA

College of Sciences and Mathematics
Dr. Thomas Atchison, Dean
Programs in:
biology • MS
biotechnology • MS
chemistry • MS
environmental science • MS
geology • MS, MSNS
mathematics • MS
mathematics education • MS
physics • MS
sciences and mathematics • MS, MSNS
statistics • MS

■ SUL ROSS STATE UNIVERSITY

Alpine, TX 79832

http://www.sulross.edu/

State-supported, coed, comprehensive institution. *Computer facilities:* 200 computers available on campus for general student use. A campuswide network can be accessed from student residence rooms and from off campus. Internet access is available. *Library facilities:* Bryan Wildenthal Memorial Library. *General application contact:* Dean of Admissions and Records, 915-837-8050.

Division of Range Animal Science
Programs in:
animal science • M Ag, MS
range and wildlife management • M Ag, MS
range animal science • M Ag, MS

Rio Grande College of Sul Ross State University
Programs in:
business administration • MBA
teacher education • M Ed

School of Arts and Sciences
Programs in:
art education • M Ed
art history • M Ed
arts and sciences • M Ed, MA, MS
biology • MS
English • MA
geology and chemistry • MS
history • MA
political science • MA
psychology • MA
public administration • MA
studio art • M Ed

School of Professional Studies
Programs in:
bilingual education • M Ed
counseling • M Ed
criminal justice • MS
educational diagnostics • M Ed
elementary education • M Ed
industrial arts • M Ed
international trade • MBA
management • MBA
physical education • M Ed
professional studies • M Ed, MBA, MS
reading specialist • M Ed
school administration • M Ed
secondary education • M Ed
supervision • M Ed

■ TARLETON STATE UNIVERSITY

Stephenville, TX 76402
http://www.tarleton.edu/

State-supported, coed, comprehensive institution. *Enrollment:* 270 full-time matriculated graduate/professional students (154 women), 807 part-time matriculated graduate/professional students (506 women). *Graduate faculty:* 104 full-time (20 women). *Computer facilities:* 500 computers available on campus for general student use. A campuswide network can be accessed from off campus. Internet access and online class registration are available. *Library facilities:* Dick Smith Library plus 1 other. *Graduate expenses:* Tuition, state resident: full-time $1,776. Tuition, nonresident: full-time $6,672. Required fees: $623. *General application contact:* Dr. Linda M. Jones, Dean, 254-968-9104.

College of Graduate Studies
Dr. Linda M. Jones, Dean

College of Agriculture and Human Sciences
Dr. Jane Dennis, Acting Dean
Program in:
agriculture • MS

College of Business Administration
Dan Collins, Dean
Programs in:
business administration • MBA
computer and information systems • MS

College of Education
Dr. Joe Gillespie, Dean
Programs in:
counseling • M Ed
counseling and psychology • M Ed
counseling psychology • M Ed
curriculum and instruction • M Ed
education • M Ed, Certificate
educational administration • M Ed, Certificate
educational psychology • M Ed
health and physical education • M Ed, Certificate
reading • Certificate
secondary education • M Ed, Certificate
special education • Certificate

College of Sciences and Technology
Dr. Rueben Walter, Dean
Programs in:
arts and sciences • MA, MCJ, MS
biological sciences • MS
English and languages • MA
environmental science • MS
history • MA
mathematics • MA
political science • MA
social work, sociology, and criminal justice • MCJ

■ TEXAS A&M INTERNATIONAL UNIVERSITY

Laredo, TX 78041-1900
http://www.tamiu.edu/

State-supported, coed, comprehensive institution. *Computer facilities:* 200 computers available on campus for general student use. A campuswide network can be accessed from off campus. *Library facilities:* Sue and Radcliff Killam Library. *General application contact:* Director of Admissions, 210-326-2200.

Division of Graduate Studies

College of Arts and Humanities
Programs in:
arts and humanities • MA, MAIS, MSCJ
counseling psychology • MA
criminal justice • MAIS
English • MA, MAIS
history • MA, MAIS
mathematics • MAIS
political science • MA, MAIS
psychology • MAIS
public administration • MA
sociology • MA, MAIS
Spanish • MA, MAIS

College of Business Administration and Graduate School of International Trade and Business Administration
Programs in:
business administration • MBA
information systems • MSIS
international banking • MBA
international logistics • MSIL
international trade • MBA
professional accountancy • MP Acc

College of Education
Programs in:
administration • MS Ed
bilingual education • MS Ed
early childhood education • MS Ed
education • MS Ed
educational diagnostician • MS
elementary education • MS Ed
gifted and talented • MS Ed
guidance and counseling • MS Ed
reading • MS Ed
secondary education • MS Ed

■ TEXAS A&M UNIVERSITY

College Station, TX 77843
http://www.tamu.edu/

State-supported, coed, university. CGS member. *Computer facilities:* 1,500 computers available on campus for general student use. A campuswide network can be accessed from student residence rooms and from off campus. *Library facilities:* Sterling C. Evans Library plus 4 others. *General application contact:* 979-845-1044.

College of Agriculture and Life Sciences
Programs in:
agricultural chemistry • M Agr
agricultural economics • MAB, MS, PhD
agricultural education • M Agr, M Ed, MS, Ed D, PhD
agricultural engineering • M Agr, M Eng, MS, PhD
agriculture and life sciences • M Agr, M Ed, M Eng, MAB, MS, DE, Ed D, PhD
agronomy • M Agr, MS, PhD
animal breeding • MS, PhD
animal science • M Agr, MS, PhD
biochemistry • MS, PhD
biophysics • MS
dairy science • M Agr, MS
entomology • M Agr, MS, PhD
food science and technology • M Agr, MS, PhD
forest science • MS, PhD
genetics • MS, PhD
horticulture • PhD
horticulture and floriculture • M Agr, MS
molecular and environmental plant sciences • MS, PhD
natural resources development • M Agr
nutrition • MS, PhD
physiology of reproduction • MS, PhD
plant breeding • MS, PhD
plant pathology • MS, PhD
plant protection • M Agr
poultry science • M Agr, MS, PhD
range science • M Agr, MS, PhD
recreation and resources development • M Agr
recreation, park, and tourism sciences • MS, PhD
soil science • MS, PhD
wildlife and fisheries sciences • M Agr, MS, PhD

Faculty of Genetics
Program in:
genetics • MS, PhD

College of Architecture
Programs in:
- architectural design • M Arch
- architectural history and preservation • M Arch
- architecture • MS, PhD
- construction management • MS
- health facilities planning and design • M Arch
- interior architecture • M Arch
- landscape architecture • MLA
- management in architecture • M Arch
- urban and regional science • PhD
- urban planning • MUP
- visualization sciences • MS

College of Education
Programs in:
- bilingual education • M Ed, MS, PhD
- career development education • M Ed, MS, PhD
- counseling • MS
- counseling psychology • PhD
- curriculum development • M Ed, MS, Ed D, PhD
- education • M Ed, MS, Ed D, PhD
- educational administration • M Ed, MS, Ed D, PhD
- educational human resource development • MS, PhD
- educational technology • M Ed
- gifted and talented education • M Ed, MS
- health education • M Ed, MS, PhD
- intelligence, creativity, and giftedness • PhD
- kinesiology • M Ed, MS, Ed D, PhD
- learning, development, and instruction • M Ed, MS, PhD
- licensing specialist in school psychology • MS
- math/science • M Ed, MS, Ed D, PhD
- physical education • M Ed, Ed D
- reading • M Ed, MS, Ed D, PhD
- research, measurement and statistics • MS
- research, measurement, and statistics • M Ed, PhD
- school counseling • M Ed
- school psychology • PhD
- social foundation • M Ed, MS, Ed D, PhD
- special education • M Ed, PhD

College of Engineering
Programs in:
- aerospace engineering • M Eng, MS, PhD
- biomedical engineering • M Eng, MS, D Eng, PhD
- chemical engineering • M Eng, MS, PhD
- computer engineering • MCE, MS, PhD
- computer science • MCS, MS, PhD
- construction engineering and project management • M Eng, MS, D Eng, PhD
- electrical engineering • M Eng, MS, PhD
- engineering • M Eng, MCE, MCS, MS, D Eng, DE, PhD
- engineering mechanics • M Eng, MS, PhD
- environmental engineering • M Eng, MS, D Eng, PhD
- geotechnical engineering • M Eng, MS, D Eng, PhD
- health physics • MS
- health physics/radiological health • MS
- hydraulic engineering • M Eng, MS, PhD
- hydrology • M Eng, MS, PhD
- industrial engineering • M Eng, MS, PhD
- industrial hygiene • MS
- materials engineering • M Eng, MS, D Eng, PhD
- mechanical engineering • M Eng, MS, D Eng, PhD
- nuclear engineering • M Eng, MS, PhD
- ocean engineering • M Eng, MS, D Eng, PhD
- petroleum engineering • M Eng, MS, D Eng, PhD
- public works engineering and management • M Eng, MS, PhD
- safety engineering • MS
- structural engineering and structural mechanics • M Eng, MS, D Eng, PhD
- transportation engineering • M Eng, MS, D Eng, PhD
- water resources engineering • M Eng, MS, D Eng, PhD

College of Geosciences
Programs in:
- atmospheric sciences • MS, PhD
- geography • MS, PhD
- geology and geophysics • MS, PhD
- geosciences • MS, PhD
- oceanography • MS, PhD

College of Liberal Arts
Programs in:
- anthropology • MA, PhD
- clinical psychology • MS, PhD
- economics • MS, PhD
- English • MA, PhD
- general psychology • MS, PhD
- history • MA, PhD
- industrial/organizational psychology • MS, PhD
- liberal arts • MA, MPSA, MS, PhD, Certificate
- philosophy • MA
- political science • MA, PhD
- science and technology journalism • MS
- sociology • MS, PhD
- Spanish • MA
- speech communication • MA, PhD

George Bush School of Government and Public Service
Programs in:
- government and public service • MA, MPSA
- international affairs • MA

College of Science
Programs in:
- biology • MS, PhD
- botany • MS, PhD
- chemistry • MS, PhD
- mathematics • MS, PhD
- microbiology • MS, PhD
- molecular and cell biology • PhD
- physics • MS, PhD
- science • MS, PhD
- statistics • MS, PhD
- zoology • MS, PhD

College of Veterinary Medicine
Programs in:
- anatomy • MS, PhD
- epidemiology • MS
- genetics • MS, PhD
- physiology • MS, PhD
- toxicology • MS, PhD
- veterinary anatomy and public health • MS, PhD
- veterinary large animal medicine and surgery • MS
- veterinary medicine • DVM, MS, PhD
- veterinary microbiology • MS, PhD
- veterinary parasitology • MS
- veterinary pathology • MS, PhD
- veterinary physiology and pharmacology • MS, PhD
- veterinary public health • MS
- veterinary small animal medicine and surgery • MS

Intercollegiate Faculty in Nutrition
Program in:
- nutrition • MS, PhD

Interdisciplinary Faculty in Toxicology
Program in:
- toxicology • MS, PhD

Interdisciplinary Faculty of Biotechnology
Dr. Jorge Piedrahita, Head
Program in:
- Biotechnology • MBIOT

Texas A&M University (continued)
Lowry Mays Graduate School of Business
Dr. A. Benton Cocanougher, Dean
Programs in:
accounting • MS, PhD
business • EMBA, MBA, MLERE, MS, PhD
business administration • EMBA, MBA
finance • MS, PhD
human resource management • MSHRM
land economics and real estate • MLERE
management • MS, MSHRM, PhD
management information systems • MS, PhD
marketing • MS, PhD

■ TEXAS A&M UNIVERSITY–COMMERCE
Commerce, TX 75429-3011
http://www.tamu-commerce.edu/

State-supported, coed, university. CGS member. *Computer facilities:* 405 computers available on campus for general student use. A campuswide network can be accessed from student residence rooms and from off campus. Internet access and online class registration are available. *Library facilities:* Gee Library. *General application contact:* Graduate Admissions Adviser, 903-886-5167.

Find an in-depth description at www.petersons.com/graduate.

Graduate School

College of Arts and Sciences
Programs in:
agricultural education • M Ed, MS
agricultural sciences • M Ed, MS
art • MA, MS
art history • MA
arts and sciences • M Ed, MA, MFA, MM, MS, MSW, Ed D, PhD
biological and earth sciences • M Ed, MS
chemistry • M Ed, MS
college teaching of English • PhD
computer science • MS
English • MA, MS
fine arts • MFA
history • MA, MS
mathematics • MA, MS
music • MA, MS
music composition • MA, MM
music education • MA, MM, MS
music literature • MA
music performance • MA, MM
music theory • MA, MM
physics • M Ed, MS
social sciences • M Ed, MS
social work • MSW
sociology • MA, MS
Spanish • MA
studio art • MA
theatre • MA, MS

College of Business and Technology
Programs in:
business administration • MBA
business and technology • MA, MBA, MS
economics • MA, MS
industry and technology • MS

College of Education
Programs in:
counseling • M Ed, MS, Ed D
early childhood education • M Ed, MA, MS
education • M Ed, MA, MS, Ed D, PhD
educational administration • M Ed, MS, Ed D
educational psychology • PhD
elementary education • M Ed, MS
health and physical education • M Ed, MS
higher education • MS
learning technology and information systems • M Ed, MS
psychology • MA, MS
reading • M Ed, MA, MS
secondary education • M Ed, MA, MS
special education • M Ed, MA, MS
supervision of curriculum and instruction: elementary education • Ed D
supervision of curriculum and instruction: higher education • PhD
training and development • MS
vocational/technical education • M Ed, MA, MS

■ TEXAS A&M UNIVERSITY–CORPUS CHRISTI
Corpus Christi, TX 78412-5503
http://www.tamucc.edu/

State-supported, coed, comprehensive institution. *Computer facilities:* 300 computers available on campus for general student use. A campuswide network can be accessed from off campus. *Library facilities:* Mary and Jeff Bell Library. *General application contact:* Director of Admissions, 512-994-2624.

Graduate Programs

College of Arts and Humanities
Programs in:
English • MA
interdisciplinary studies • MA
liberal arts • MA, MPA
psychology • MA
public administration • MPA

College of Business Administration
Programs in:
accounting • M Acc
management • MBA

College of Education
Programs in:
curriculum and instruction • MS
educational administration • MS
educational administration and supervision • MS
educational leadership • Ed D
elementary education • MS
guidance and counseling • MS
occupational education • MS
secondary education • MS
special education • MS

College of Science and Technology
Programs in:
biology • MS
computer science • MS
environmental sciences • MS
mariculture • MS
mathematics • MS
nursing administration • MSN
science and technology • MS, MSN

■ TEXAS A&M UNIVERSITY–KINGSVILLE
Kingsville, TX 78363
http://www.tamuk.edu/

State-supported, coed, university. *Enrollment:* 360 full-time matriculated graduate/professional students (169 women), 763 part-time matriculated graduate/professional students (467 women). *Graduate faculty:* 120 full-time (21 women), 26 part-time/adjunct (7 women). *Computer facilities:* 600 computers available on campus for general student use. A campuswide network can be accessed from student residence rooms and from off campus. *Library facilities:* James C. Jernigan Library. *Graduate expenses:* Tuition, state resident: full-time $1,055. Tuition, nonresident: full-time $3,623. *General application contact:* Dr. Alberto M. Olivares, Dean, College of Graduate Studies, 361-593-2808.

Find an in-depth description at www.petersons.com/graduate.

College of Graduate Studies
Dr. Alberto M. Olivares, Dean

College of Agriculture and Home Economics
Dr. Charles DeYoung, Dean
Programs in:
agribusiness • MS
agricultural education • MS
agriculture and home economics • MS, PhD
animal sciences • MS
human sciences • MS
plant and soil sciences • MS
range and wildlife management • MS
wildlife science • PhD

College of Arts and Sciences
Dr. Mary Mattingly, Dean
Programs in:
applied geology • MS
art • MA, MS
arts and sciences • MA, MM, MS
biology • MS
chemistry • MS
communication sciences and disorders • MS
English • MA, MS
gerontology • MS
history and political science • MA, MS
mathematics • MS
music education • MM
psychology • MA, MS
sociology • MA, MS
Spanish • MA

College of Business Administration
Dr. Darvin Hoffman, Graduate Coordinator
Program in:
business administration • MBA, MS

College of Education
Dr. Fred Litton, Dean
Programs in:
adult education • M Ed
bilingual education • MA, MS, Ed D
early childhood education • M Ed
education • M Ed, MA, MS, Ed D, PhD
elementary education • MA, MS
English as a second language • M Ed
guidance and counseling • MA, MS
health and kinesiology • MA, MS
higher education administration • PhD
reading • MS
school administration • MA, MS, Ed D
secondary education • MA, MS
special education • M Ed
supervision • MA, MS

College of Engineering
Dr. Phil V. Compton, Dean
Programs in:
chemical engineering • ME, MS
civil engineering • ME, MS
computer science • MS
electrical engineering • ME, MS
engineering • ME, MS
environmental engineering • ME, MS
industrial engineering • ME, MS
mechanical engineering • ME, MS
natural gas engineering • ME, MS

■ TEXAS A&M UNIVERSITY–TEXARKANA
Texarkana, TX 75505-5518
http://www.tamut.edu/

State-supported, coed, upper-level institution. *Computer facilities:* 170 computers available on campus for general student use. A campuswide network can be accessed from off campus. Internet access and online class registration are available. *Library facilities:* John F. Moss Library plus 1 other. *General application contact:* Director of Admissions and Registrar, 903-223-3068.

Graduate School

Division of Arts and Sciences and Education
Programs in:
elementary education • M Ed, MA, MS
interdisciplinary studies • MA, MS
secondary education • M Ed, MA, MS
special education • M Ed, MA, MS

Division of Behavioral Sciences and Business Administration
Programs in:
business administration • MBA, MS
counseling psychology • MS

■ TEXAS CHRISTIAN UNIVERSITY
Fort Worth, TX 76129-0002
http://www.tcu.edu/

Independent-religious, coed, university. CGS member. *Enrollment:* 462 full-time matriculated graduate/professional students (215 women), 638 part-time matriculated graduate/professional students (374 women). *Graduate faculty:* 288. *Computer facilities:* 4,225 computers available on campus for general student use. A campuswide network can be accessed from student residence rooms and from off campus. Internet access and online class registration are available. *Library facilities:* Mary Couts Burnett Library. *Graduate expenses:* Tuition: part-time $420 per hour. Required fees: $65 per hour.

AddRan College of Humanities and Social Sciences
Dr. Mary Volcansek, Dean
Programs in:
economics • MA
English • MA, PhD
history • MA, PhD
humanities and social sciences • MA, PhD

Brite Divinity School
Dr. Leo Perdue, President
Programs in:
Biblical interpretation • PhD
Christian service • MACS
divinity • M Div
homiletics • D Min
pastoral theology and pastoral counseling • D Min, PhD
theological studies • MTS, CTS
theology • Th M

College of Communication
Dr. David Whillock, Interim Dean
Programs in:
communication • MA, MS
journalism • MS
mass communication • MS
media arts • MA
media studies • MS
speech communication • MS

College of Fine Arts
Dr. Scott Sullivan, Dean
Programs in:
art history • MA
ballet • MFA
ballet/modern dance • MFA
fine arts • M Mus, MA, MFA, MM Ed
modern dance • MFA
studio art • MFA

School of Music
Dr. Blaise Ferrandino, Director
Programs in:
conducting • M Mus
instrumental performance • M Mus
music education • MM Ed
musicology • M Mus
piano pedagogy • M Mus
theory/composition • M Mus
vocal performance • M Mus

College of Health and Human Services
Dr. Rhonda Keen-Payne, Dean
Programs in:
health and human services • MS
kinesiology and physical education • MS
speech-language pathology • MS

Texas Christian University (continued)

College of Science and Engineering
Dr. Michael McCracken, Dean
Programs in:
biology • MA, MS
chemistry • MA, MS, PhD
environmental sciences • MS
geology • MS
mathematics • MAT
physics • MA, MS, PhD
psychology • MA, MS, PhD
science and engineering • MA, MAT, MS, MSE, PhD
software engineering • MSE

Graduate Studies and Research
Dr. Don Coerver, Director
Program in:
liberal arts • MLA

M. J. Neeley School of Business
Dr. Bob Lusch, Dean
Programs in:
accounting • M Ac
business administration • MBA

School of Education
Dr. Sam Deitz, Dean
Programs in:
administration education • M Ed, Certificate
education • M Ed, MA, Certificate
educational counseling • MA
educational foundations • M Ed
elementary education • M Ed
secondary education • M Ed
special education • M Ed

■ TEXAS SOUTHERN UNIVERSITY
Houston, TX 77004-4584
http://www.tsu.edu/

State-supported, coed, university. CGS member. *Enrollment:* 731 full-time matriculated graduate/professional students (311 women), 1,032 part-time matriculated graduate/professional students (722 women). *Graduate faculty:* 158 full-time (56 women), 38 part-time/adjunct (13 women). *Computer facilities:* 410 computers available on campus for general student use. A campuswide network can be accessed. Internet access is available. *Library facilities:* Robert J. Terry Library plus 2 others. *Graduate expenses:* Tuition, state resident: full-time $1,188; part-time $50 per hour. Tuition, nonresident: full-time $4,644. Required fees: $900. Tuition and fees vary according to degree level. *General application contact:* Dr. Joseph Jones, Dean of the Graduate School, 713-313-7232.

Find an in-depth description at www.petersons.com/graduate.

College of Pharmacy and Health Sciences
Dr. Barbara Hayes, Dean
Program in:
pharmacy and health sciences • Pharm D

Graduate School
Dr. Joseph Jones, Dean
Programs in:
biology • MS
chemistry • MS
city planning • MCP
constructional technology • M Ed
educational technology • M Ed
English • MA, MS
environmental toxicology • MS, PhD
history • MA
human services and consumer sciences • MS
humanities, fine arts and social sciences • MA, MCP, MPA, MS
journalism • MA
mathematics • MA, MS
music • MA
public administration • MPA
science and technology • M Ed, MA, MS, PhD
sociology • MA
speech communications • MA
telecommunications • MA
transportation • MS

College of Education
Dr. Sybil A. Allman, Interim Dean
Programs in:
bilingual education • M Ed
business education • M Ed
counseling • M Ed, Ed D
counseling education • Ed D
curriculum, instruction, and urban education • Ed D
early childhood education • M Ed
education • M Ed, MS, Ed D
educational administration • M Ed, Ed D
elementary education • M Ed
health education • MS
higher education administration • Ed D
mid-management superintending • Ed D
physical education • MS
reading education • M Ed
research education and certification • Ed D
research education and education • Ed D
secondary education • M Ed
special education • M Ed

College of Humanities, Fine Arts and Social Sciences
Dr. Merline Pitre, Acting Dean
Programs in:
city planning • MCP
English • MA, MS
history • MA
human services and consumer sciences • MS
humanities, fine arts and social sciences • MA, MCP, MPA, MS
journalism • MA
music • MA
public administration • MPA
sociology • MA
speech communications • MA
telecommunications • MA

Jesse H. Jones School of Business
Dr. John H. Williams, Dean
Programs in:
business • MBA
business administration • MBA

School of Science and Technology
Dr. Daniel Davis, Dean
Programs in:
biology • MS
chemistry • MS
constructional technology • M Ed
educational technology • M Ed
environmental toxicology • MS, PhD
mathematics • MA, MS
science and technology • M Ed, MA, MS, PhD
transportation • MS

Thurgood Marshall School of Law
John C. Brittain, Dean
Program in:
law • JD

■ TEXAS TECH UNIVERSITY
Lubbock, TX 79409
http://www.ttu.edu/

State-supported, coed, university. CGS member. *Enrollment:* 2,088 full-time matriculated graduate/professional students (911 women), 1,301 part-time matriculated graduate/professional students (705 women). *Graduate faculty:* 740 full-time (188 women), 44 part-time/adjunct (11 women). *Computer facilities:* 2,000 computers available on campus for general student use. A campuswide network can be accessed from student residence rooms and from off campus. Internet access and online class registration are available. *Library facilities:* Texas Tech Library plus 3 others. *Graduate expenses:* Tuition, state resident: full-time $1,854; part-time $103 per credit hour. Tuition, nonresident: full-time $5,724;

part-time $318 per credit hour. Required fees: $535 per summer. Tuition and fees vary according to course level, course load and program. *General application contact:* Judith S. Toyama, Assistant Dean of Graduate Admissions and Recruitment, 806-742-2787.

Find an in-depth description at www.petersons.com/graduate.

Graduate School
Dr. Robert M. Sweazy, Interim Dean
Programs in:
- heritage management • MA
- interdisciplinary studies • MA, MS
- museum science • MA

College of Agricultural Sciences and Natural Resources
Dr. John R. Abernathy, Dean
Programs in:
- agricultural and applied economics • MS, PhD
- agricultural education • MS
- agricultural sciences and natural resources • M Agr, MLA, MS, PhD
- agriculture • M Agr
- agronomy • PhD
- animal science • MS, PhD
- crop science • MS
- entomology • MS
- fishery science • MS, PhD
- food technology • MS
- horticulture • MS
- landscape architecture • MLA
- range science • MS, PhD
- soil science • MS
- wildlife science • MS, PhD

College of Architecture
Dr. James E. White, Dean
Programs in:
- architecture • M Arch, MS, PhD
- land-use planning, management, and design • PhD

College of Arts and Sciences
Dr. Jane L. Winer, Dean
Programs in:
- anthropology • MA
- applied linguistics • MA
- applied physics • MS, PhD
- art • MFA
- art education • MAE
- arts and sciences • MA, MAE, MFA, MM, MM Ed, MME, MPA, MS, PhD
- atmospheric sciences • MS
- biology • MS, PhD
- chemistry • MS, PhD
- classical humanities • MA
- clinical psychology • PhD
- communication studies • MA
- counseling psychology • PhD
- economics • MA, PhD
- English • MA, PhD
- environmental toxicology • MA, PhD
- fine arts • MFA, PhD
- fine arts management • MA
- general experimental • MA, PhD
- geoscience • MS, PhD
- German • MA
- history • MA, PhD
- mass communications • MA
- mathematics • MA, MS, PhD
- microbiology • MS
- music education • MME
- music history and literature • MM
- music performance • MM
- music theory • MM
- philosophy • MA
- physical education • MS
- physics • MS, PhD
- political science • MA, PhD
- public administration • MPA
- Romance languages-French • MA
- Romance languages-Spanish • MA
- sociology • MA
- Spanish • PhD
- sports health • MS
- statistics • MS
- technical communication • MA
- technical communication and rhetoric • PhD
- theatre arts • MA, MFA
- zoology • MS, PhD

College of Education
Dr. Greg Bowes, Dean
Programs in:
- art education • Certificate
- bilingual education • M Ed
- counselor education • M Ed, Ed D, Certificate
- curriculum and instruction • M Ed, Ed D
- early childhood education • Certificate
- education • M Ed, Ed D, Certificate
- education diagnostician • Certificate
- educational leadership • M Ed, Ed D
- educational psychology • M Ed, Ed D
- elementary education • M Ed, Certificate
- higher education • M Ed, Ed D
- instructional technology • M Ed, Ed D
- language and literacy education • M Ed
- music education • Certificate
- physical education • Certificate
- principal • Certificate
- reading specialist • Certificate
- secondary education • M Ed, Certificate
- special education • M Ed, Ed D
- special education counselor • Certificate
- special education supervisor • Certificate
- superintendent • Certificate
- supervision • M Ed
- supervisor • Certificate

College of Engineering
Dr. William M. Marcy, Dean
Programs in:
- chemical engineering • MS Ch E, PhD
- civil engineering • MSCE, PhD
- computer science • MS, PhD
- electrical and computer engineering • MSEE, PhD
- engineering • M Engr, M Env E, MS, MS Ch E, MS Pet E, MSCE, MSEE, MSETM, MSIE, MSME, MSSEM, PhD
- environmental engineering • M Env E
- environmental technology and management • MSETM
- industrial engineering • MSIE, PhD
- mechanical engineering • MSME, PhD
- petroleum engineering • MS Pet E
- software engineering • MS
- systems and engineering management • MSSEM

College of Human Sciences
Linda Hoover, Interim Dean
Programs in:
- environmental design and consumer economics • MS, PhD
- family and consumer sciences education • MS, PhD
- food and nutrition • MS, PhD
- human development and family studies • MS, PhD
- human sciences • MS, PhD
- marriage and family therapy • MS, PhD
- restaurant, hotel, and institutional management • MS

Jerry S. Rawls College of Business Administration
Dr. R. Stephen Sears, Interim Dean
Programs in:
- design control accounting • MS Acct
- accounting • PhD
- assurance accounting • MS Acct
- audit/financial reporting • MS Acct
- banking • MSBA
- business administration • MBA, MS, MS Acct, MSA, MSBA, PhD, Certificate
- business statistics • MSBA, PhD
- controllership • MS Acct
- finance • MSBA, PhD
- health organization management • MBA, Certificate
- health organization management/controllership • MSA
- home health organization management • MS
- information systems • MS Acct
- management • PhD
- management information systems • MS, MSBA, PhD

Texas Tech University (continued)
- marketing and international business • MSBA, PhD
- operations management • PhD
- production management • MSBA, PhD
- taxation • MS Acct
- telecommunications • MSBA

School of Law
W. Frank Newton, Dean
Program in:
- law • JD

■ TEXAS WESLEYAN UNIVERSITY
Fort Worth, TX 76105-1536
http://www.txwesleyan.edu/

Independent-religious, coed, comprehensive institution. *Enrollment:* 540 full-time matriculated graduate/professional students (267 women), 578 part-time matriculated graduate/professional students (345 women). *Graduate faculty:* 37 full-time (11 women), 40 part-time/adjunct (13 women). *Computer facilities:* 65 computers available on campus for general student use. A campuswide network can be accessed. Internet access is available. *Library facilities:* Eunice and James L. West Library plus 1 other. *Graduate expenses:* Tuition: full-time $3,870; part-time $215 per credit hour. Required fees: $35 per credit hour. Tuition and fees vary according to program. *General application contact:* Terri Evans, Director of Transfer/Graduate Admissions, 817-531-4458.

Graduate Programs
Dr. Allen Henderson, Interim Provost
Programs in:
- business administration • MBA
- education • MA Ed, MAT, MS Ed
- nurse anesthesia • MHS, MSNA

School of Law
Richard L. Gershon, Dean
Program in:
- law • JD

■ TEXAS WOMAN'S UNIVERSITY
Denton, TX 76204
http://www.twu.edu/

State-supported, coed, primarily women, university. CGS member. *Enrollment:* 978 full-time matriculated graduate/professional students (846 women), 2,950 part-time matriculated graduate/professional students (2,579 women). *Computer facilities:* 332 computers available on campus for general student use. A campuswide network can be accessed from student residence rooms and from off campus. Internet access is available. *Library facilities:* Blagg-Huey Library. *Graduate expenses:* Tuition, state resident: full-time $1,728. Tuition, nonresident: full-time $5,562. Required fees: $596. Tuition and fees vary according to course load. *General application contact:* Dr. Michael H. Droge, Dean for Graduate Studies and Research, 940-898-3415.

Find an in-depth description at www.petersons.com/graduate.

Graduate School
Dr. Michael H. Droge, Dean for Graduate Studies and Research

College of Arts and Sciences
Dr. Richard Rodean, Interim Dean
Programs in:
- advertising design • MA
- applied music • MA
- art • MA
- art education • MA
- art history • MA
- arts and sciences • MA, MBA, MFA, MS, PhD
- biology • MS
- biology teaching • MS
- business administration • MBA
- ceramics • MA, MFA
- chemistry • MS
- chemistry teaching • MS
- counseling psychology • MA, PhD
- dance • MA, MFA, PhD
- drama • MA
- English • MA
- fashion and textiles • PhD
- fashion design • MA
- fashion merchandising • MS, PhD
- fibers • MA
- fibers and handmade paper • MFA
- general psychology • MA
- government • MA
- history • MA
- jewelry/metalsmithing • MA, MFA
- mathematics • MA, MS
- mathematics teaching • MS
- molecular biology • PhD
- music • MA
- music education • MA
- music pedagogy • MA
- music therapy • MA
- painting • MA, MFA
- photography • MA
- photography and typographic bookmaking • MFA
- rhetoric • PhD
- school psychology • MA, PhD
- science teaching • MS
- sculpture • MA, MFA
- sociology • MA, PhD
- textiles and apparel • MS
- women's studies • MA

College of Health Sciences
Dr. Jean Pyfer, Dean
Programs in:
- education of the deaf • MS
- exercise and sports nutrition • MS
- food science • MS
- health care administration • MHA
- health education • Ed D, PhD
- health sciences • MHA, MS, Ed D, PhD
- health studies • MS
- institutional administration • MS
- kinesiology • MS, PhD
- nutrition • MS, PhD
- speech-language pathology • MS

College of Nursing
Dr. Carolyn S. Gunning, Dean
Programs in:
- adult health nurse • MS
- adult health nurse practitioner • MS
- child health • MS
- community health nursing • MS
- family nurse practitioner • MS
- mental health nursing • MS
- nursing • PhD
- pediatric nurse practitioner • MS
- women's health nurse • MS
- women's health nurse practitioner • MS

College of Professional Education
Dr. Keith Swigger, Dean
Programs in:
- administration • M Ed, MA
- child development • MS, PhD
- counseling and development • M Ed, MS
- early childhood education • M Ed, MA, MS, Ed D
- family studies • MS, PhD
- family therapy • MS, PhD
- library science • MA, MLS, PhD
- professional education • M Ed, MA, MLS, MS, Ed D, PhD
- reading • M Ed, MA, Ed D, PhD
- special education • M Ed, MA, PhD
- supervision • M Ed, MA

School of Occupational Therapy
Dr. Sally Schultz, Interim Dean
Program in:
- occupational therapy • MA, MOT, PhD

School of Physical Therapy
Dr. Carolyn Rozier, Dean
Program in:
- physical therapy • MS, PhD

■ TRINITY UNIVERSITY
San Antonio, TX 78212-7200
http://www.trinity.edu/

Independent-religious, coed, comprehensive institution. CGS member. *Enrollment:* 108 full-time matriculated graduate/professional students (66 women), 107 part-time matriculated graduate/professional students (61 women). *Graduate faculty:* 22 full-time (10 women), 23 part-time/adjunct (9 women). *Computer facilities:* 100 computers available on campus for general student use. A campuswide network can be accessed from student residence rooms and from off campus. Internet access is available. *Library facilities:* Elizabeth Huth Coates Library. *Graduate expenses:* Tuition: full-time $8,214. *General application contact:* Dr. Mary E. Stefl, Dean, 210-999-7521.

Division of Behavioral and Administrative Studies
Dr. Mary E. Stefl, Dean
Programs in:
- accounting • MS
- behavioral and administrative studies • M Ed, MA, MAT, MS
- educational administration • M Ed
- health care administration • MS
- school psychology • MA
- teacher education • MAT

■ UNIVERSITY OF HOUSTON
Houston, TX 77204
http://www.uh.edu/

State-supported, coed, university. CGS member. *Enrollment:* 4,609 full-time matriculated graduate/professional students (2,331 women), 4,158 part-time matriculated graduate/professional students (2,372 women). *Graduate faculty:* 588 full-time (142 women), 337 part-time/adjunct (126 women). *Computer facilities:* 825 computers available on campus for general student use. A campuswide network can be accessed from student residence rooms and from off campus. Internet access and online class registration are available. *Library facilities:* M.D. Anderson Library plus 5 others. *Graduate expenses:* Tuition, state resident: full-time $1,440; part-time $80 per credit. Tuition, nonresident: full-time $5,274; part-time $293 per credit. Required fees: $1,234; $570 per semester. Tuition and fees vary according to course load, campus/location, program and reciprocity agreements. *General application contact:* Adrianna Higgins, Director of Admissions, 713-743-1010.

College of Architecture
Joseph Mashburn, Dean
Program in:
- architecture • M Arch

College of Education
Allen R. Warner, Dean
Programs in:
- allied health • M Ed, Ed D
- art education • M Ed
- bilingual education • M Ed
- counseling psychology • M Ed, PhD
- curriculum and instruction • Ed D
- early childhood education • M Ed
- education • M Ed, MS, Ed D, PhD
- education of the gifted • M Ed
- educational administration • M Ed, Ed D
- educational psychology • M Ed
- educational psychology and individual differences • PhD
- elementary education • M Ed
- exercise science • MS
- health education • M Ed
- higher education • M Ed
- historical, social, and cultural foundations of education • M Ed, Ed D
- mathematics education • M Ed
- physical education • M Ed, Ed D
- reading and language arts education • M Ed
- science education • M Ed
- second language education • M Ed
- secondary education • M Ed
- social studies education • M Ed
- special education • M Ed, Ed D
- teaching • M Ed

College of Liberal Arts and Social Sciences
Dr. Lois Zamora, Dean
Programs in:
- anthropology • MA
- applied English linguistics • MA
- clinical psychology • PhD
- economics • MA, PhD
- English and American literature • MA, PhD
- French • MA
- graphic communications • MFA
- history • MA, PhD
- industrial/organizational psychology • PhD
- interior design • MFA
- liberal arts and social sciences • MA, MFA, MM, DMA, PhD
- literature and creative writing • MA, MFA, PhD
- painting • MFA
- philosophy • MA
- photography • MFA
- political science • MA, PhD
- public history • MA
- sculpture • MFA
- social psychology • PhD
- sociology • MA
- Spanish • MA, PhD
- speech language pathology • MA

Moores School of Music
David Ashley White, Director
Programs in:
- accompanying • MM
- applied music • MM
- composition • MM, DMA
- conducting • DMA
- music education • MM, DMA
- music literature • MM
- music performance and pedagogy • MM
- music theory • MM
- performance • DMA

School of Communication
William Douglas, Director
Programs in:
- mass communication studies • MA
- public relations studies • MA
- speech communication • MA

School of Theatre
Sidney Berger, Director
Program in:
- theatre • MA, MFA

College of Natural Sciences and Mathematics
Dr. John L. Bear, Dean
Programs in:
- applied mathematics • MSAM
- biochemistry • MS, PhD
- biology • MS, PhD
- chemistry • MS, PhD
- computer science • MS, PhD
- geology • MS, PhD
- geophysics • MS, PhD
- mathematics • MSM, PhD
- natural sciences and mathematics • MS, MSAM, MSM, PhD
- physics • MS, PhD

College of Optometry
Jerald Strickland, Dean
Programs in:
- optometry • OD
- physiological optics/vision science • MS Phys Op, PhD

College of Pharmacy
Dr. M. F. Lokhandwala, Dean
Programs in:
- hospital pharmacy • MSPHR
- medical chemistry and pharmacology • MS
- pharmaceutics • MS, PhD
- pharmacology • MS, PhD
- pharmacy • Pharm D
- pharmacy administration • MSPHR

College of Technology
Bernard McIntyre, Dean
Programs in:
- construction management • MT
- manufacturing systems • MT
- microcomputer systems • MT
- occupational technology • MSOT

University of Houston (continued)

Conrad N. Hilton College of Hotel and Restaurant Management
Dr. Alan T. Stutts, Dean
Program in:
hotel and restaurant management • MHM

C. T. Bauer College of Business
Dr. Jerry Strawser, Dean
Programs in:
accountancy • MS Accy
accounting • PhD
business administration • MBA, MS, MS Accy, MS Admin, PhD
decision and information sciences • MBA, PhD
finance • MS, PhD
management • PhD
marketing and entrepreneurship • PhD

Cullen College of Engineering
Dr. Raymond W. Flumerfelt, Dean
Programs in:
aerospace engineering • MS, PhD
biomedical engineering • MS
chemical engineering • M Ch E, MS Ch E, PhD
civil and environmental engineering • MCE, MS Env E, MSCE, PhD
computer and systems engineering • MS, PhD
electrical and computer engineering • MEE, MSEE, PhD
engineering • M Ch E, MCE, MEE, MIE, MME, MS, MS Ch E, MS Env E, MSCE, MSEE, MSIE, MSME, PhD
environmental engineering • MS, PhD
industrial engineering • MIE, MSIE, PhD
materials engineering • MS, PhD
mechanical engineering • MME, MSME
petroleum engineering • MS

Graduate School of Social Work
Dr. Ira C. Colby, Dean
Program in:
social work • MSW, PhD

Law Center
Nancy B. Rapoport, Dean
Program in:
law • JD, LL M

■ UNIVERSITY OF HOUSTON–CLEAR LAKE
Houston, TX 77058-1098
http://www.cl.uh.edu/

State-supported, coed, upper-level institution. CGS member. *Enrollment:* 1,075 full-time matriculated graduate/professional students, 2,554 part-time matriculated graduate/professional students. *Graduate faculty:* 234. *Computer facilities:* 383 computers available on campus for general student use. A campuswide network can be accessed from off campus. Internet access and online class registration are available. *Library facilities:* Neumann Library. *Graduate expenses:* Tuition, state resident: full-time $3,482. Tuition, nonresident: full-time $7,686. Tuition and fees vary according to course load. *General application contact:* John F. Smith, Interim Executive Director of Enrollment Services, 281-283-2517.

Find an in-depth description at www.petersons.com/graduate.

School of Business and Public Administration
Dr. William Theodore Cummings, Dean
Programs in:
accounting • MS
administration of health services • MS
business administration • MBA
business and public administration • MA, MBA, MHA, MS
environmental management • MS
finance • MS
healthcare administration • MHA
human resource management • MA
public management • MA

School of Education
Dr. Dennis Spuck, Dean
Programs in:
counseling • MS
curriculum and instruction • MS
early childhood education • MS
education • MS
educational management • MS
instructional technology • MS
learning resources • MS
multicultural studies • MS
reading • MS

School of Human Sciences and Humanities
Dr. Spencer A. McWilliams, Dean
Programs in:
behavioral sciences • MA
clinical psychology • MA
cross-cultural studies • MA
family therapy • MA
fitness and human performance • MA
history • MA
human sciences and humanities • MA, MS
humanities • MA
literature • MA
school psychology • MA
studies of the future • MS

School of Natural and Applied Sciences
Dr. Charles McKay, Dean
Programs in:
biological sciences • MS
chemistry • MS
computer engineering • MS
computer information systems • MA
computer science • MS
environmental science • MS
mathematical sciences • MS
natural and applied sciences • MA, MS
physical science • MS
software engineering • MS
statistics • MS

■ UNIVERSITY OF HOUSTON–VICTORIA
Victoria, TX 77901-4450
http://www.vic.uh.edu/

State-supported, coed, upper-level institution. *Enrollment:* 125 full-time matriculated graduate/professional students (88 women), 725 part-time matriculated graduate/professional students (506 women). *Graduate faculty:* 45 full-time (19 women). *Computer facilities:* 150 computers available on campus for general student use. A campuswide network can be accessed from off campus. Internet access and online class registration are available. *Library facilities:* VC/UHV Library plus 1 other. *Graduate expenses:* Part-time $70 per credit hour. Tuition, state resident: full-time $1,260; part-time $255 per credit hour. Tuition, nonresident: full-time $4,590. Required fees: $900; $50 per credit hour. *General application contact:* Minnie Urbano, Enrollment Management and Recruitment Coordinator, 361-570-4135.

School of Arts and Sciences
Dr. Dan Jaeckle, Dean
Programs in:
arts and sciences • MA, MAIS
interdisciplinary studies • MAIS
psychology • MA

School of Business Administration
Charles Bullock, Dean
Program in:
business administration • MBA

School of Education
Dr. Diane Prince, Dean
Program in:
education • M Ed

■ UNIVERSITY OF MARY HARDIN-BAYLOR

Belton, TX 76513

http://www.umhb.edu/

Independent-religious, coed, comprehensive institution. *Enrollment:* 30 full-time matriculated graduate/professional students (22 women), 159 part-time matriculated graduate/professional students (113 women). *Graduate faculty:* 42 full-time (13 women), 4 part-time/adjunct (2 women). *Computer facilities:* 221 computers available on campus for general student use. A campuswide network can be accessed from student residence rooms. Internet access is available. *Library facilities:* Townsend Memorial Library. *Graduate expenses:* Tuition: full-time $5,760; part-time $320 per semester hour. Required fees: $360; $20 per semester hour. $180 per semester hour. One-time fee: $35 full-time. *General application contact:* Dr. Curtis Beaird, Vice President for Administrative and Academic Affairs, 254-295-4505.

Program in Health Services Management
Dr. Mary Anne Franklin, Chair
Program in:
- health services management • MHSM

School of Business
Dr. James King, Dean
Programs in:
- business • MBA, MSIS
- information systems • MSIS

School of Education
Dr. Clarence E. Ham, Dean
Programs in:
- educational administration • M Ed
- educational psychology • M Ed
- general studies • M Ed
- reading education • M Ed

School of Sciences and Humanities
Dr. Darrell G. Watson, Dean
Programs in:
- counseling • MA
- psychology • MA
- sciences and humanities • MA, MTS
- theological studies • MTS

■ UNIVERSITY OF NORTH TEXAS

Denton, TX 76203

http://www.unt.edu/

State-supported, coed, university. CGS member. *Enrollment:* 1,783 full-time matriculated graduate/professional students (993 women), 2,693 part-time matriculated graduate/professional students (1,647 women). *Graduate faculty:* 779 full-time (244 women), 320 part-time/adjunct (184 women). *Computer facilities:* 2,006 computers available on campus for general student use. A campuswide network can be accessed from student residence rooms and from off campus. *Library facilities:* Willis Library plus 4 others. *Graduate expenses:* Tuition, state resident: part-time $160 per hour. Tuition, nonresident: part-time $293 per hour. *General application contact:* Dr. C. Neal Tate, Dean, 940-565-2383.

Find an in-depth description at www.petersons.com/graduate.

Robert B. Toulouse School of Graduate Studies
Dr. C. Neal Tate, Dean
Programs in:
- information science • PhD
- interdisciplinary studies • MA, MS

College of Arts and Sciences
Dr. Warren Burggren, Dean
Programs in:
- arts and sciences • MA, MJ, MS, PhD
- biochemistry • MS, PhD
- biology • MA, MS, PhD
- chemistry • MS, PhD
- clinical psychology • PhD
- communication studies • MA, MS
- computer sciences • MA, MS, PhD
- counseling psychology • MA, MS, PhD
- drama • MA, MS
- economic research • MS
- economics • MA
- engineering technology • MS
- English • MA, PhD
- environmental science • MS, PhD
- experimental psychology • MA, MS, PhD
- French • MA
- geography • MS
- health psychology and behavioral medicine • PhD
- history • MA, MS, PhD
- industrial psychology • MA, MS
- journalism • MA, MJ
- labor and industrial relations • MS
- materials science • MS, PhD
- mathematics • MA, MS, PhD
- molecular biology • MA, MS, PhD
- philosophy and religion studies • MA
- physics • MA, MS, PhD
- political science • MA, MS, PhD
- psychology • MA, MS, PhD
- radio/television/film • MA, MS
- school psychology • MA, MS, PhD
- Spanish • MA
- speech-language pathology/audiology • MA, MS

College of Business Administration
Dr. Jared E. Hazleton, Dean
Programs in:
- accounting • MS, PhD
- administrative management • MBA
- banking • MBA, PhD
- business administration • MBA, MS, PhD
- finance • MBA, PhD
- information systems • MBA, PhD
- insurance • MBA
- management • MBA
- management science • MBA, PhD
- marketing • MBA, PhD
- organization theory and policy • PhD
- personnel and industrial relations • MBA, PhD
- production/operations management • MBA, PhD
- real estate • MBA

College of Education
Dr. Jean Keller, Dean
Programs in:
- applied technology and training development • M Ed, MS, Ed D, PhD, Certificate
- community health • MS
- computer education and cognitive systems • MS
- counseling and student services • M Ed, MS, PhD
- counselor education • M Ed, MS, PhD
- curriculum and instruction • Ed D, PhD
- development and family studies • MS
- early childhood education • M Ed, MS, PhD
- education • M Ed, MS, Ed D, PhD, Certificate
- educational administration • M Ed, Ed D, PhD
- educational research • PhD
- elementary education • M Ed, MS
- elementary school supervision • M Ed
- health promotion • MS
- higher education • Ed D, PhD
- kinesiology • MS
- reading • M Ed, MS, Ed D, PhD
- recreation and leisure studies • MS, Certificate
- school health • MS
- secondary education • M Ed, MS
- secondary school supervision • M Ed
- special education • M Ed, MS, PhD
- special subject supervision • M Ed
- vocational counselor • Certificate

College of Music
Dr. William V. May, Interim Dean
Programs in:
- composition • MM, DMA, PhD
- jazz studies • MM
- music • MA
- music education • MM, MME, PhD

University of North Texas (continued)
music theory • MM, PhD
musicology • MM, PhD
performance • MM, DMA

School of Community Service
Dr. David W. Hartman, Interim Dean
Programs in:
administration of aging organizations • MA, MS
administration of retirement facilities • MA, MS
aging • MA, MS, Certificate
applied economics • MS
behavior analysis • MS
community service • MA, MPA, MS, PhD, Certificate
public administration • MPA
rehabilitation counseling • MS
rehabilitation studies • MS
sociology • MA, MS, PhD
vocational evaluation • MS
work adjustment services • MS

School of Library and Information Sciences
Dr. Philip M. Turner, Dean
Programs in:
information science • MS, PhD
library science • MS

School of Merchandising and Hospitality Management
Dr. Judith C. Forney, Dean
Programs in:
hotel/restaurant management • MS
merchandising and fabric analytics • MS

School of Visual Arts
Dr. D. Jack Davis, Dean
Programs in:
art • PhD
art education • MA, MFA, PhD
art history • MA, MFA
ceramics • MFA
communication design • MFA
fashion design • MFA
fibers • MFA
interior design • MFA
metalsmithing and jewelry • MFA
painting and drawing • MFA
photography • MFA
printmaking • MFA
sculpture • MFA

■ UNIVERSITY OF ST. THOMAS
Houston, TX 77006-4696
http://www.stthom.edu/

Independent-religious, coed, comprehensive institution. *Enrollment:* 244 full-time matriculated graduate/professional students (104 women), 749 part-time matriculated graduate/professional students (445 women). *Graduate faculty:* 97 full-time (38 women), 72 part-time/adjunct (47 women). *Computer facilities:* 143 computers available on campus for general student use. A campuswide network can be accessed from student residence rooms and from off campus. Internet access is available. *Library facilities:* Doherty Library plus 1 other. *Graduate expenses:* Tuition: full-time $8,100; part-time $450 per credit. Required fees: $33; $11 per term. Tuition and fees vary according to program. *General application contact:* Elsie P. Biron, Dean of Admissions, 713-525-3505.

Cameron School of Business
Dr. Yhi-Min Ho, Dean
Program in:
business • MBA, MIB, MSA, MSIS

Center for Thomistic Studies
Dr. Daniel McInerny, Director
Program in:
philosophy • MA, PhD

Program in Liberal Arts
Dr. Janice Gordon-Kelter, Director
Program in:
liberal arts • MLA

School of Education
Dr. Ruth Strudler, Dean
Program in:
education • M Ed

School of Theology
Rev. Louis T. Brusatti, CM, Dean
Program in:
theology • M Div, MAPS, MAT

■ THE UNIVERSITY OF TEXAS AT ARLINGTON
Arlington, TX 76019
http://www.uta.edu/

State-supported, coed, university. CGS member. *Enrollment:* 2,022 full-time matriculated graduate/professional students (890 women), 2,952 part-time matriculated graduate/professional students (1,852 women). *Graduate faculty:* 411 full-time (98 women), 42 part-time/adjunct (10 women). *Computer facilities:* 700 computers available on campus for general student use. A campuswide network can be accessed from student residence rooms and from off campus. Online class registration is available. *Library facilities:* Central Library plus 2 others. *Graduate expenses:* Full-time $2,160. Tuition, nonresident: full-time $6,228. Required fees: $754. *General application contact:* Dr. H. Keith McDowell, Dean of Graduate Studies, 817-272-3186.

Find an in-depth description at www.petersons.com/graduate.

Graduate School
Dr. H. Keith McDowell, Dean of Graduate Studies
Programs in:
environmental science and engineering • MS, PhD
health care administration • MS
interdisciplinary studies • MA, MS
logistics • MS
management of technology • MS

College of Business Administration
Dr. Daniel D. Himarios, Dean
Programs in:
accounting • MBA, MP Acc, MS, PhD
business administration • PhD
business statistics • PhD
economics • MA
finance • MBA, PhD
information systems • MBA, MS, PhD
management • MBA, PhD
management sciences • MBA
marketing • MBA, PhD
marketing research • MS
personal and human resources management • MBA
real estate • MBA, MS
taxation • MS, PhD

College of Engineering
Dr. Bill D. Carroll, Dean
Programs in:
aerospace engineering • M Engr, MS, PhD
biomedical engineering • MS, PhD
civil and environmental engineering • M Engr, MS, PhD
computer science and engineering • M Engr, M Sw En, MCS, MS, PhD
electrical engineering • M Engr, MS, PhD
engineering • M Engr, M Sw En, MCS, MS, PhD
industrial engineering • M Engr, MS, PhD
materials science and engineering • MS, PhD
mechanical engineering • M Engr, MS, PhD

College of Liberal Arts
Dr. Richard Cole, Interim Dean
Programs in:
anthropology • MA
criminology and criminal justice • MA
English • MA
French • MA
German • MA

history • MA, PhD
humanities • MA, MAT
liberal arts • MA, MAT, MM, PhD
linguistics • MA, PhD
literature • PhD
political science • MA
rhetoric • PhD
sociology • MA
Spanish • MA

College of Science
Dr. Neal J. Smatresk, Dean
Programs in:
applied chemistry • PhD
biology • MS, PhD
chemistry • MS
experimental psychology • PhD
geology • MS
mathematical sciences • PhD
mathematics • MS
physics • MS
physics and applied physics • PhD
psychology • MS
science • MS, PhD

School of Architecture
Carroll Lee Wright, Interim Dean
Programs in:
architecture • M Arch, MLA
landscape architecture • MLA

School of Education
Dr. Jeanne M. Gerlach, Dean
Programs in:
curriculum and instruction • M Ed
educational administration • M Ed
teaching • M Ed T

School of Nursing
Dr. Elizabeth C. Poster, Dean
Programs in:
administration/supervision of nursing • MSN
nurse practitioner • MSN
teaching of nursing • MSN

School of Social Work
Dr. Santos H. Hernandez, Dean
Program in:
social work • MSSW, PhD

School of Urban and Public Affairs
Dr. Richard Cole, Interim Dean
Programs in:
city and regional planning • MCRP
public administration • MPA
urban and public administration • PhD
urban and public affairs • MA, MCRP, MPA, PhD

■ THE UNIVERSITY OF TEXAS AT AUSTIN

Austin, TX 78712-1111
http://www.utexas.edu/

State-supported, coed, university. CGS member. *Enrollment:* 11,834 matriculated graduate/professional students (5,556 women). *Graduate faculty:* 2,051 full-time (657 women), 857 part-time/adjunct (339 women). *Computer facilities:* 4,000 computers available on campus for general student use. A campuswide network can be accessed from student residence rooms and from off campus. Internet access, e-mail are available. *Library facilities:* Perry-Castañeda Library plus 18 others. *Graduate expenses:* Tuition, state resident: full-time $2,160. Tuition, nonresident: full-time $6,030. Required fees: $860. *General application contact:* Dr. William Paver, Director, Graduate and International Admissions Center, 512-475-7390.

College of Pharmacy
Dr. Steven W. Leslie, Dean
Program in:
pharmacy • Pharm D, MS Phr, PhD

Graduate School
Dr. Teresa A. Sullivan, Vice President and Dean
Programs in:
computational and applied mathematics • MA, PhD
Russian, East European and Eurasian studies • MA
science and technology commercialization • MS
writing • MFA

College of Business Administration
Robert G. May, Dean
Programs in:
accounting • MPA, PhD
business • MBA
business administration • MBA, MHRDL, MPA, PhD
finance • PhD
human resource development leadership • MHRDL
management • PhD
management sciences and information systems • PhD
marketing administration • PhD

College of Communication
Dr. Ellen Wartella, Dean
Programs in:
advertising • MA, PhD
communication • MA, MFA, PhD
communication sciences and disorders • MA, PhD
communication studies • MA, PhD
film/video production • MFA
journalism • MA, PhD
radio-television-film • MA, PhD

College of Education
Dr. Manuel J. Justiz, Dean
Programs in:
academic educational psychology • M Ed, MA
counseling education • M Ed
counseling psychology • PhD
curriculum and instruction • M Ed, MA, Ed D, PhD
education • M Ed, MA, MHRDL, Ed D, PhD
educational administration • M Ed, Ed D, PhD
foreign language education • MA, PhD
health education • M Ed, MA, Ed D, PhD
human development and education • PhD
kinesiology • M Ed, MA, Ed D, PhD
learning cognition and instruction • PhD
mathematics education • M Ed, MA, PhD
quantitative methods • PhD
school psychology • PhD
science education • M Ed, MA, PhD
special education • M Ed, MA, Ed D, PhD

College of Engineering
Dr. Ben G. Streetman, Dean
Programs in:
aerospace engineering • MSE, PhD
architectural engineering • MSE
biomedical engineering • MSE, PhD
chemical engineering • MSE, PhD
civil engineering • MSE, PhD
electrical and computer engineering • MSE, PhD
energy and mineral resources • MA, MS
engineering • MA, MS, MSE, PhD
engineering mechanics • MSE, PhD
environmental and water resources engineering • MSE
manufacturing systems engineering • MSE
materials science and engineering • MSE, PhD
mechanical engineering • MSE, PhD
operations research and industrial engineering • MSE, PhD
petroleum and geosystems engineering • MSE, PhD

College of Fine Arts
Robert Freeman, Dean
Programs in:
art education • MA
art history • MA, PhD
fine arts • M Music, MA, MFA, DMA, PhD
music • M Music, DMA, PhD
studio art • MFA
theatre • MA, MFA, PhD

College of Liberal Arts
Richard Lariviere, Dean
Programs in:
American studies • MA, PhD
Arabic studies • MA, PhD
archaeology • MA, PhD

The University of Texas at Austin (continued)
- Asian cultures and languages • MA, PhD
- Asian studies • MA, PhD
- classics • MA, PhD
- comparative literature • MA, PhD
- economics • MA, MS Econ, PhD
- English • MA, PhD
- folklore and public culture • MA, PhD
- French • MA, PhD
- geography • MA, PhD
- Germanic studies • MA, PhD
- government • MA, PhD
- Hebrew studies • MA, PhD
- Hispanic literature • MA, PhD
- history • MA, PhD
- Ibero-Romance philology and linguistics • MA, PhD
- Latin American studies • MA, PhD
- liberal arts • MA, MS Econ, PhD
- linguistic anthropology • MA, PhD
- linguistics • MA, PhD
- Luso-Brazilian literature • MA, PhD
- Middle Eastern studies • MA
- Persian studies • MA, PhD
- philosophy • MA, PhD
- physical anthropology • MA, PhD
- psychology • PhD
- Romance linguistics • MA, PhD
- Slavic languages and literatures • MA, PhD
- social anthropology • MA, PhD
- sociology • MA, PhD

College of Natural Sciences
Peter John, Graduate Adviser
Programs in:
- analytical chemistry • MA, PhD
- astronomy • MA, PhD
- biochemistry • MA, PhD
- biological sciences • MA, PhD
- cell and molecular biology • PhD
- cellular and molecular biology • PhD
- child development and family relations • MA, PhD
- computer sciences • MA, MSCS, PhD
- ecology, evolution and behavior • MA, PhD
- genetics and developmental biology • PhD
- geological sciences • MA, MS, PhD
- inorganic chemistry • MA, PhD
- marine science • MA, PhD
- mathematics • MA, PhD
- microbiology • MA, PhD
- microbiology and immunology • PhD
- natural sciences • MA, MS, MS Stat, MSCS, PhD
- nutrition • MA
- nutritional sciences • MA, PhD
- organic chemistry • MA, PhD
- physical chemistry • MA, PhD
- physics • MA, MS, PhD
- plant biology • MA, PhD
- statistics • MS Stat

Graduate School of Library and Information Science
Roberta I. Shaffer, Interim Dean
Program in:
- library and information science • MLIS, PhD

The Institute for Neuroscience
Dr. Creed W. Abell, Director
Program in:
- neuroscience • MA, PhD

Lyndon B. Johnson School of Public Affairs
Dr. Edwin Dorn, Dean
Programs in:
- public affairs • MP Aff
- public policy • PhD

School of Architecture
Lawrence Speck, Dean
Programs in:
- architecture • M Arch, MS Arch St, MSCRP, PhD
- community and regional planning • MSCRP, PhD

School of Nursing
Dr. Dolores Sands, Dean
Program in:
- nursing • MSN, PhD

School of Social Work
Dr. Barbara White, Dean
Program in:
- social work • MSSW, PhD

School of Law
William C. Powers, Dean
Program in:
- law • JD, LL M

■ THE UNIVERSITY OF TEXAS AT BROWNSVILLE
Brownsville, TX 78520-4991
http://www.utb.edu/

State-supported, coed, upper-level institution. CGS member. *Graduate faculty:* 131 full-time (48 women). *Computer facilities:* 580 computers available on campus for general student use. A campuswide network can be accessed from off campus. Internet access is available. *Library facilities:* Arnulfo L. Oliveira Library. *Graduate expenses:* Tuition, state resident: part-time $120 per credit. Tuition, nonresident: part-time $265 per credit. Required fees: $113 per semester. *General application contact:* Dr. John P. Ronnau, Dean, Graduate Studies, 956-544-8812.

Graduate Studies and Sponsored Programs
Dr. John P. Ronnau, Dean
Program in:
- health sciences • MSPHN

College of Liberal Arts
Dr. Farhat Iftekharuddin, Dean
Programs in:
- behavioral sciences • MAIS
- English • MA
- government • MAIS
- history • MAIS
- interdisciplinary studies • MAIS
- liberal arts • MA, MAIS
- Spanish • MA

College of Science, Mathematics and Technology
Dr. José G. Martin, Dean
Program in:
- biological sciences • MSIS

School of Business
Dr. Betsy V. Boze, Dean
Program in:
- business • MBA

School of Education
Dr. Sylvia C. Peña, Dean
Programs in:
- counseling and guidance • M Ed
- curriculum and instruction • M Ed
- early childhood education • M Ed
- educational administration • M Ed
- educational technology • M Ed
- elementary education/bilingual endorsement option • M Ed
- English as a second language • M Ed
- reading specialist • M Ed
- special education/educational diagnostician • M Ed
- supervision • M Ed

School of Health Sciences
Dr. Eldon Nelson, Dean
Program in:
- health sciences • MSPHN

■ THE UNIVERSITY OF TEXAS AT DALLAS
Richardson, TX 75083-0688
http://www.utdallas.edu/

State-supported, coed, university. CGS member. *Enrollment:* 1,454 full-time matriculated graduate/professional students (645 women), 1,684 part-time matriculated graduate/professional students (707 women). *Graduate faculty:* 275 full-time (54 women), 57 part-time/adjunct (27 women). *Computer facilities:* 428 computers available on campus for general student use. A campuswide network can be accessed from student residence rooms and from off campus.

Internet access and online class registration are available. *Library facilities:* Eugene McDermott Library plus 2 others. *Graduate expenses:* Tuition, state resident: full-time $1,920; part-time $80 per credit hour. Tuition, nonresident: full-time $7,080; part-time $295 per credit hour. Required fees: $2,183; $84 per credit hour. $138 per term. Tuition and fees vary according to course load and degree level.

Erik Jonsson School of Engineering and Computer Science
Dr. William P. Osborne, Dean
Programs in:
- computer science • MS, PhD
- electrical engineering • MSEE, PhD
- engineering and computer science • MS, MSEE, PhD
- microelectronics • MSEE
- telecommunications • MSEE

School of Arts and Humanities
Dr. Dennis M. Kratz, Dean
Program in:
- humanities • MA, MAT, PhD

School of General Studies
Dr. George Fair, Dean
Program in:
- interdisciplinary studies • MA

School of Human Development
Dr. Bert Moore, Dean
Programs in:
- applied cognition and neuroscience • MS
- audiology • Au D
- communications disorders • MS
- human development • MS, Au D, PhD
- human development and communication sciences • PhD
- human development and early childhood disorders • MS

School of Management
Dr. Hasan Pirkul, Dean
Programs in:
- accounting • MS
- business administration • EMBA, MBA
- international management studies • MA, PhD
- management • EMBA, MA, MBA, MS, PhD
- management and administrative sciences • MS
- management science • PhD

School of Natural Sciences and Mathematics
Dr. Richard Caldwell, Dean
Programs in:
- applied mathematics • MS, PhD
- biology • MS, PhD
- chemistry • MS
- engineering mathematics • MS
- geosciences • MS, PhD
- industrial chemistry • D Chem
- mathematical science • MS, PhD
- mathematics education • MAT
- molecular and cell biology • MS, PhD
- natural sciences and mathematics • MAT, MS, D Chem, PhD
- physics • MS, PhD
- science education • MAT
- statistics • MS, PhD

School of Social Sciences
Dr. Rita Mae Kelly, Dean
Programs in:
- applied economics • MS
- applied sociology • MA, MS
- geographic information sciences • MS
- political economy • PhD
- public affairs • MPA
- social sciences • MA, MPA, MS, PhD

■ THE UNIVERSITY OF TEXAS AT EL PASO
El Paso, TX 79968-0001
http://www.utep.edu/

State-supported, coed, university. CGS member. *Enrollment:* 222 full-time matriculated graduate/professional students (114 women), 2,047 part-time matriculated graduate/professional students (1,195 women). *Graduate faculty:* 536 full-time, 330 part-time/adjunct. *Computer facilities:* A campuswide network can be accessed from student residence rooms and from off campus. *Library facilities:* University Library. *Graduate expenses:* Tuition, state resident: part-time $74 per credit hour. Tuition, nonresident: part-time $289 per credit hour. Required fees: $22 per credit hour. $59 per term. *General application contact:* Dr. Charles H. Ambler, Associate Vice President for Graduate Studies, 915-747-5491 Ext. 7886.

Find an in-depth description at www.petersons.com/graduate.

Graduate School
Dr. Charles H. Ambler, Associate Vice President for Graduate Studies
Programs in:
- environmental science and engineering • PhD
- materials science and engineering • PhD

College of Business Administration
Dr. Frank Hoy, Dean
Programs in:
- accounting • MACY
- business administration • MACY, MBA, MS
- economics and finance • MS

College of Education
Dr. Arturo Pacheco, Dean
Programs in:
- education • M Ed, MA, Ed D
- educational leadership and foundations • M Ed, MA, Ed D
- educational psychology and special services • M Ed, MA
- teacher education • M Ed, MA

College of Engineering
Dr. Andrew H. Swift, Dean
Programs in:
- civil engineering • MS
- computer engineering • MS, PhD
- computer science • PhD
- electrical engineering • MS, PhD
- engineering • MEENE, MIT, MS, MSENE, PhD
- environmental engineering • MEENE, MSENE
- industrial engineering • MS
- manufacturing engineering • MS
- mechanical engineering • MS
- metallurgical engineering • MS

College of Health Sciences
Dr. John Conway, Dean
Programs in:
- adult health • MSN
- allied health • MPT, MS
- community health • MSN
- community health/family nurse practitioner • MSN
- health and physical education • MS
- health sciences • MPT, MS, MSN
- kinesiology and sports studies • MS
- nurse midwifery • MSN
- nursing administration • MSN
- parent-child nursing • MSN
- physical therapy • MPT
- psychiatric/mental health nursing • MSN
- speech language pathology • MS
- women's health care/nurse practitioner • MSN

College of Liberal Arts
Dr. Howard C. Daudistel, Dean
Programs in:
- art • MA
- border history • MA
- clinical psychology • MA
- communication • MA
- creative writing in English • MFA

The University of Texas at El Paso (continued)

creative writing in Spanish • MFA
English and American literature • MA
experimental psychology • MA
history • MA, PhD
liberal arts • MA, MAIS, MAT, MFA, MM, MPA, PhD
linguistics • MA
music education • MM
music performance • MM
political science • MA, MPA
professional writing and rhetoric • MA
psychology • PhD
sociology • MA
Spanish • MA
teaching English • MAT
theatre arts • MA

College of Science
Dr. Thomas E. Brady, Dean
Programs in:
biological sciences • MS, PhD
chemistry • MS
geological sciences • MS, PhD
geophysics • MS
interdisciplinary studies • MSIS
mathematical sciences • MAT, MS
physics • MS
science • MAT, MS, MSIS, PhD
statistics • MS

■ THE UNIVERSITY OF TEXAS AT SAN ANTONIO

San Antonio, TX 78249-0617
http://www.utsa.edu/

State-supported, coed, university. CGS member. *Enrollment:* 668 full-time matriculated graduate/professional students (343 women), 2,043 part-time matriculated graduate/professional students (1,263 women). *Graduate faculty:* 376 full-time (109 women), 60 part-time/adjunct (15 women). *Computer facilities:* 800 computers available on campus for general student use. A campuswide network can be accessed from student residence rooms and from off campus. Internet access and online class registration are available. *Library facilities:* John Peace Library plus 1 other. *Graduate expenses:* Part-time $126 per credit hour. Tuition, state resident: full-time $2,268; part-time $337 per credit hour. Tuition, nonresident: full-time $6,066. Required fees: $780. Tuition and fees vary according to course load and reciprocity agreements. *General application contact:* Sandra K. Speed, Interim Director of Admissions and Registrar, 210-458-4530.

College of Business
Dr. Bruce O. Bublitz, Dean
Programs in:
accounting • MP Acct
business administration • MBA
finance • MS
information technology • MSIT
management of technology • MSMOT
taxation • MT

College of Education and Human Development
Dr. Blandina Cardenas, Interim Director
Programs in:
bicultural studies • MA
bicultural-bilingual studies • MA
culture and languages • PhD
education • MA, Ed D
education and human development • MA, Ed D, PhD
teaching English as a second language • MA

College of Engineering
Dr. Dwight F. Henderson, Interim Dean
Programs in:
civil engineering • MSCE
electrical engineering • MSEE
engineering • MSCE, MSEE, MSME
mechanical engineering • MSME

College of Liberal and Fine Arts
Dr. Alan E. Craven, Dean
Programs in:
anthropology • MA
architecture and interior design • M Arch
art • MFA
art history • MA
English • MA
history • MA
liberal and fine arts • M Arch, MA, MFA, MM, MS
music • MM
political science • MA
psychology • MS
sociology • MS
Spanish • MA

College of Sciences
Dr. William H. Scouten, Dean
Programs in:
biology • MS, PhD
biology and biotechnology • MS
biotechnology • MS
chemistry • MS
computer science • MS, PhD
environmental sciences • MS
geology • MS
mathematics • MS
neurobiology • PhD
sciences • MS, PhD

College of Urban Professional Programs
Dr. Jesse T. Zapata, Vice Provost Downtown
Programs in:
justice policy • MA
urban professional programs • MA, MPA

Division of Criminal Justice
Dr. Patricia Harris, Director
Program in:
justice policy • MA

Division of Public Administration
Dr. Heywood T. Sanders, Director
Program in:
public administration • MPA

■ THE UNIVERSITY OF TEXAS AT TYLER

Tyler, TX 75799-0001
http://www.uttyler.edu/

State-supported, coed, comprehensive institution. *Enrollment:* 106 full-time matriculated graduate/professional students (69 women), 561 part-time matriculated graduate/professional students (345 women). *Graduate faculty:* 169 full-time (79 women), 73 part-time/adjunct (39 women). *Computer facilities:* 300 computers available on campus for general student use. A campuswide network can be accessed from student residence rooms and from off campus. Internet access is available. *Library facilities:* Robert Muntz Library. *Graduate expenses:* Tuition, state resident: part-time $247 per semester hour. Tuition, nonresident: part-time $380 per semester hour. *General application contact:* Carol A. Hodge, Office of Graduate Studies, 903-566-7142.

Graduate Studies
Graduate Coordinator

College of Business Administration
Dr. Jim Tarter, Dean
Programs in:
business administration • MBA
general management • MBA
health care track • MBA

College of Education and Psychology
Dr. J. Milford Clark, Dean
Programs in:
allied health/interdisciplinary studies • MS
art • MAT
biology • MAT
clinical exercise physiology • MS
clinical psychology • MS

computer science • MAT
curriculum and instruction • M Ed
early childhood education • M Ed, MA
education and psychology • M Ed, MA, MAT, MS, Certificate
educational administration • M Ed, Certificate
English • MAT
health and kinesiology • M Ed
history • MAT
interdisciplinary studies • MS
journalism • MAT
kinesiology • MS
kinesiology/interdisciplinary studies • MS
mathematics • MAT
music • MAT
political science • MAT
reading • M Ed, MA, Certificate
school counseling • MA, Certificate
secondary teaching • MAT
sociology • MAT
special education • M Ed, MA, Certificate
speech communication • MAT
technology • MS
theatre • MAT

College of Engineering
Dr. Leonard Hale, Dean
Program in:
engineering • M Engr

College of Liberal Arts
Dr. Donna Dickerson, Dean
Programs in:
art • MA
English • MA, MAT
history • MA, MAT
interdisciplinary studies • MA, MS
liberal arts • MA, MAT, MPA, MS
music • MA
political science • MA, MAT
public administration • MPA

College of Nursing
Dr. Linda Klotz, Dean
Program in:
nursing • MSN

College of Sciences and Mathematics
Dr. L. Lynn Sherrod, Dean
Programs in:
biology • MS
computer science • MS
interdisciplinary studies • MA, MS
mathematics • MA, MS
sciences and mathematics • MA, MS

■ THE UNIVERSITY OF TEXAS OF THE PERMIAN BASIN

Odessa, TX 79762-0001

http://www.utpb.edu/

State-supported, coed, comprehensive institution. *Computer facilities:* 130 computers available on campus for general student use. A campuswide network can be accessed from student residence rooms and from off campus. Internet access is available. *General application contact:* Director of Graduate Studies, 915-552-2530.

Graduate School

College of Arts and Sciences
Programs in:
applied behavioral analysis • MA
arts and sciences • MA, MS
biology • MS
clinical psychology • MA
criminal justice administration • MS
English • MA
geology • MS
history • MA
physical education • MA
psychology • MA

School of Business
Programs in:
accountancy • MPA
business • MBA, MPA
management • MBA

School of Education
Programs in:
counseling • MA
early childhood education • MA
education • MA
educational administration • MA
elementary education • MA
reading • MA
secondary education • MA
special education • MA
supervision • MA

■ THE UNIVERSITY OF TEXAS–PAN AMERICAN

Edinburg, TX 78539-2999

http://www.panam.edu/

State-supported, coed, comprehensive institution. CGS member. *Enrollment:* 346 full-time matriculated graduate/professional students (218 women), 1,226 part-time matriculated graduate/professional students (785 women). *Graduate faculty:* 137 full-time (40 women), 34 part-time/adjunct (9 women). *Computer facilities:* 500 computers available on campus for general student use. A campuswide network can be accessed from off campus. Internet access and online class registration are available. *Library facilities:* Learning Resource Library. *Graduate expenses:* Tuition, state resident: full-time $1,476; part-time $82 per semester hour. Tuition, nonresident: full-time $5,328; part-time $296 per semester hour. Required fees: $16 per semester hour. $19 per term. Tuition and fees vary according to course load and program. *General application contact:* David Zuniga, Director of Admissions and Records, 956-381-2206.

College of Arts and Humanities
Programs in:
arts and humanities • MA, MAIS, MFA, MSIS
English • MA, MAIS
English as a second language • MA
history • MA, MAIS
interdisciplinary studies • MAIS, MSIS
Spanish • MA
speech communication • MA
studio art • MFA
theatre • MA

College of Business Administration
Programs in:
business administration • MBA, MS, PhD
computer information systems • MS, PhD

College of Education
Programs in:
administration • M Ed
counseling and guidance • M Ed
early childhood education • M Ed
education • M Ed, MA, D Phil, Ed D
educational diagnostics • M Ed
educational psychology • D Phil
elementary bilingual education • M Ed
elementary education • M Ed
gifted and talented education • M Ed
kinesiology • M Ed
reading • M Ed
school psychology • MA
secondary education • M Ed
special education • M Ed
supervision • M Ed

College of Health Sciences and Human Services
Dr. Helen M. Castillo, Dean
Programs in:
adult health nursing • MSN
communication sciences and disorders • MA
family nurse practitioner • MSN
health sciences and human services • MA, MS, MSN, MSSW
rehabilitation counseling • MS
social work • MSSW

College of Science and Engineering
Programs in:
biology • MS
computer science • MS
mathematics • MS
science and engineering • MS

The University of Texas–Pan American (continued)

College of Social and Behavioral Sciences
Dean
Programs in:
criminal justice • MS
psychology • MA
public administration • MPA
social and behavioral sciences • MA, MPA, MS
sociology • MS

■ UNIVERSITY OF THE INCARNATE WORD

San Antonio, TX 78209-6397
http://www.uiw.edu/

Independent-religious, coed, comprehensive institution. *Enrollment:* 133 full-time matriculated graduate/professional students (67 women), 566 part-time matriculated graduate/professional students (392 women). *Graduate faculty:* 52 full-time (25 women), 24 part-time/adjunct (13 women). *Computer facilities:* 200 computers available on campus for general student use. A campuswide network can be accessed from student residence rooms and from off campus. Internet access and online class registration are available. *Library facilities:* J.E. and L.E. Mabee Library plus 1 other. *Graduate expenses:* Tuition: part-time $420 per hour. *General application contact:* Andrea Cyterski, Director of Admissions, 210-829-6005.

Find an in-depth description at www.petersons.com/graduate.

School of Graduate Studies and Research
Gilberto M. Hinojosa, Dean
Programs in:
graduate studies • M Ed, MA, MAA, MAMT, MBA, MS, MSN, PhD
multidisciplinary studies • MA

College of Education
Dr. Patricia Watkins, Dean
Programs in:
adult education • M Ed, MA
early childhood education • M Ed, MA
education • M Ed, MA
education of the hearing impaired • M Ed
educational diagnostics • M Ed, MA
elementary education • M Ed, MA
physical education • M Ed, MA
reading • M Ed, MA
reading specialist • M Ed, MA
secondary teaching • M Ed, MA
special education • M Ed, MA

College of Humanities, Arts, and Social Sciences
Dr. Donna Aronson, Dean
Programs in:
communication arts • MA
English • MA
humanities, arts, and social sciences • MA
religious studies • MA

School of Business and Applied Arts and Sciences
Dr. Patricia Burr, Dean
Programs in:
business administration • MBA
business and applied arts and sciences • MAA, MBA, PhD
general management • MAA
international administration • MAA
organization development • MAA
organizational leadership • PhD
sports management • MAA

School of Mathematics, Sciences, and Engineering
Dr. D. Reginald Traylor, Dean
Programs in:
biology • MA, MS
mathematics • MAMT, MS, PhD
mathematics, sciences, and engineering • MA, MAMT, MS, PhD

School of Nursing and Health Professions
Dr. Kathleen Light, Dean
Programs in:
nursing • MSN
nursing and health professions • MS, MSN
nutrition • MS

■ WAYLAND BAPTIST UNIVERSITY

Plainview, TX 79072-6998
http://www.wbu.edu/

Independent-religious, coed, comprehensive institution. *Enrollment:* 25 full-time matriculated graduate/professional students (9 women), 364 part-time matriculated graduate/professional students (159 women). *Graduate faculty:* 39 full-time (8 women), 16 part-time/adjunct (4 women). *Computer facilities:* 297 computers available on campus for general student use. A campuswide network can be accessed from student residence rooms and from off campus. Internet access is available. *Library facilities:* J.E. and L.E. Mabee Learning Resource Center. *Graduate expenses:* Tuition: full-time $4,680; part-time $260 per credit hour. Required fees: $40 per term. Tuition and fees vary according to course load and campus/location. *General application contact:* Dr. Glenn Saul, Vice President of Academic Services, 806-296-4574.

Graduate Programs
Dr. Glenn Saul, Vice President of Academic Services
Programs in:
business administration/management • MA, MBA
education • M Ed
religion • MA
science • MS

■ WEST TEXAS A&M UNIVERSITY

Canyon, TX 79016-0001
http://www.wtamu.edu/

State-supported, coed, comprehensive institution. *Enrollment:* 1,005 matriculated graduate/professional students. *Graduate faculty:* 115 full-time, 74 part-time/adjunct. *Computer facilities:* 800 computers available on campus for general student use. A campuswide network can be accessed from student residence rooms and from off campus. Internet access and online class registration are available. *Library facilities:* Cornette Library. *Graduate expenses:* Tuition, state resident: full-time $936. Tuition, nonresident: full-time $4,734. Required fees: $852. One-time fee: $10 full-time. *General application contact:* Dr. James R. Hallmark, Dean of the Graduate School, 806-651-2730.

Find an in-depth description at www.petersons.com/graduate.

College of Agriculture, Nursing, and Natural Sciences
Dr. James Clark, Dean
Programs in:
agricultural business and economics • MS
agriculture • MS
agriculture, nursing, and natural sciences • MS, MSN
animal science • MS
biology • MS
chemistry • MS
engineering technology • MS
environmental science • MS
mathematics • MS
nursing • MSN
plant science • MS

College of Education and Social Sciences
Dr. Ted Guffy, Dean
Programs in:

administration • M Ed
counseling education • M Ed
criminal justice • MA
curriculum and instruction • M Ed
education and social sciences • M Ed, MA, MS
educational diagnostician • M Ed
educational technology • M Ed
elementary education • M Ed
history • MA
political science • MA
professional counseling • MA
psychology • MA
reading • M Ed
secondary education • M Ed, MA
sports and exercise science • MS

College of Fine Arts and Humanities
Dr. Sue Park, Dean
Programs in:
art • MA
communication • MA
communication disorders • MS
English • MA
fine arts and humanities • MA, MFA, MM, MS
music • MA
performance • MM
studio art • MFA

Program in Interdisciplinary Studies
Dr. James R. Hallmark, Dean of the Graduate School
Program in:
interdisciplinary studies • MA, MS

T. Boone Pickens College of Business
Dr. John Cooley, Dean
Programs in:
accounting • MP Acc
business • MBA, MP Acc, MS
business administration • MBA
finance and economics • MS

Utah

■ BRIGHAM YOUNG UNIVERSITY

Provo, UT 84602-1001
http://www.byu.edu/

Independent-religious, coed, university. CGS member. *Enrollment:* 1,623 full-time matriculated graduate/professional students (531 women), 1,393 part-time matriculated graduate/professional students (560 women). *Graduate faculty:* 1,064 full-time (160 women), 141 part-time/adjunct (63 women). *Computer facilities:* 1,800 computers available on campus for general student use. A campuswide network can be accessed from student residence rooms and from off campus. Internet access and online class registration are available. *Library facilities:* Harold B. Lee Library plus 2 others. *Graduate expenses:* Tuition: full-time $3,860; part-time $214 per credit. *General application contact:* Adviser, 801-378-4541.

The David M. Kennedy Center for International and Area Studies
Dr. Donald B. Holsinger, Director
Programs in:
American studies • MA
ancient Near Eastern studies • MA
Asian studies • MA
international development • MA
international relations • MA

Graduate Studies
Bonnie Brinton, Dean

College of Biological and Agricultural Sciences
Dr. R. Kent Crookston, Dean
Programs in:
agronomy • MS
animal and veterinary sciences • MS
biological and agricultural sciences • MS, PhD
biological science education • MS
botany • MS, PhD
food science • MS
horticulture • MS
microbiology • MS, PhD
molecular biology • MS, PhD
nutrition • MS
range science • MS
wildlife and range resources • MS, PhD
zoology • MS, PhD

College of Engineering and Technology
Dr. Douglas M. Chabries, Dean
Programs in:
chemical engineering • MS
civil engineering • MS
electrical engineering • MS
engineering • PhD
engineering and technology • MS, PhD
engineering technology • MS
mechanical engineering • MS, PhD
technology teacher education • MS

College of Family, Home, and Social Sciences
Dr. Clayne L. Pope, Dean
Programs in:
anthropology • MA
clinical psychology • PhD
family, home, and social sciences • MA, MS, MSW, PhD
general psychology • MS
geography • MS
history • MA
marriage and family therapy • MS, PhD
marriage, family and human development • MS, PhD
psychology • PhD
social work • MSW
sociology • MS, PhD

College of Fine Arts and Communications
Dr. K. Newell Dayley, Dean
Programs in:
art education • MA
art history • MA
ceramics • MFA
child drama • MA
composition • MM
conducting • MM
fine arts and communications • MA, MFA, MM, PhD
mass communication • MA
music education • MA, MM
musicology • MA
painting-drawing • MFA
performance • MM
printmaking-drawing • MFA
sculpture • MFA
theatre design and technology • MFA
theatre history, theory, and criticism • MA

College of Health and Human Performance
Dr. Robert K. Conlee, Dean
Programs in:
athletic training • MS
curriculum and instruction in physical education • PhD
dance • MA
exercise physiology • MS
health and human performance • MA, MS, PhD
health promotion • MS
health promotion (physical medicine and rehabilitation) • PhD
sports pedagogy • MS
youth and family recreation • MS

College of Humanities
Dr. Van C. Gessel, Dean
Programs in:
Arabic • MA
Chinese • MA
comparative literature • MA
English • MA
Finnish • MA
French • MA
French studies • MA
general linguistics • MA
German • MA
German literature • MA

Brigham Young University (continued)
humanities • MA
Japanese • MA
Korean • MA
Portuguese • MA
Portuguese linguistics • MA
Portuguese literature • MA
Russian • MA
Scandinavian • MA
Spanish Latin literature • MA
Spanish linguistics • MA
Spanish literature • MA
Spanish teaching • MA
teaching English as a second language • MA, Certificate

College of Nursing
Dr. Elaine S. Marshall, Dean
Program in:
family nurse practitioner • MS

College of Physical and Mathematical Sciences
Earl M. Woolley, Dean
Programs in:
analytical chemistry • MS, PhD
applied statistics • MS
biochemistry • MS, PhD
computer science • MS, PhD
geology • MS
inorganic chemistry • MS, PhD
mathematics • MA, MS, PhD
organic chemistry • MS, PhD
physical and mathematical sciences • MA, MS, PhD
physical chemistry • MS, PhD
physics • MS, PhD
physics and astronomy • PhD

David O. McKay School of Education
Dr. Robert S. Patterson, Dean
Programs in:
audiology • MS
counseling and school psychology • MS
counseling psychology • PhD
education • M Ed, MA, MS, Ed D, PhD
educational leadership and foundations • M Ed, Ed D, PhD
instructional psychology and technology • MS, PhD
reading • Ed D
special education • MS
speech-language pathology • MS
teaching and learning • M Ed, MA

J. Reuben Clark Law School
Dr. Hansen Reese Hansen, Dean
Program in:
law • JD, LL M

Marriott School of Management
Dr. Ned C. Hill, Dean
Programs in:
accountancy and information systems • M Acc, MISM
business administration • MBA
executive business administration • MBA
management • M Acc, MBA, MISM, MOB, MPA
organizational behavior • MOB
public management • MPA

■ SOUTHERN UTAH UNIVERSITY
Cedar City, UT 84720-2498
http://www.suu.edu/

State-supported, coed, comprehensive institution. *Enrollment:* 67 full-time matriculated graduate/professional students (28 women), 167 part-time matriculated graduate/professional students (109 women). *Graduate faculty:* 26. *Computer facilities:* 300 computers available on campus for general student use. A campuswide network can be accessed from student residence rooms and from off campus. *Library facilities:* Southern Utah University Library. *Graduate expenses:* Tuition, state resident: full-time $1,768. Tuition, nonresident: full-time $6,586. Required fees: $454. Tuition and fees vary according to program. *General application contact:* Dr. D. Ray Reutzel, Provost, 435-586-7704.

College of Education
Dr. Paul Wilford, Director
Program in:
education • M Ed

School of Business
Carl Templin, Dean
Programs in:
accounting • M Acc
business • M Acc, MBA

■ UNIVERSITY OF UTAH
Salt Lake City, UT 84112-1107
http://www.utah.edu/

State-supported, coed, university. CGS member. *Enrollment:* 3,346 full-time matriculated graduate/professional students (1,484 women), 1,722 part-time matriculated graduate/professional students (828 women). *Graduate faculty:* 1,134 full-time (296 women), 23 part-time/adjunct (2 women). *Computer facilities:* 5,000 computers available on campus for general student use. A campuswide network can be accessed from student residence rooms and from off campus. Internet access and online class registration, on-line classes are available. *Library facilities:* Marriott Library plus 2 others. *Graduate expenses:* Tuition, state resident: full-time $1,871; part-time $147 per credit. Tuition, nonresident: full-time $6,603; part-time $520 per credit. Required fees: $477; $54 per credit. *General application contact:* Office of Admissions, 801-581-7281.

College of Law
Scott Matheson, Dean
Program in:
law • JD, LL M

College of Pharmacy
Programs in:
medicinal chemistry • MS, PhD
pharmaceutics and pharmaceutical chemistry • MS, PhD
pharmacology and toxicology • MS, PhD
pharmacy • Pharm D, MS, PhD
pharmacy practice • MS

Graduate School
Dr. David S. Chapman, Dean
Program in:
statistics • M Stat

College of Education
David J. Sperry, Dean
Programs in:
education • M Ed, M Stat, MA, MS, Ed D, PhD
education culture and society • M Ed, MA, MS, PhD
educational leadership and policy • M Ed, Ed D, PhD
educational psychology • M Ed, M Stat, MA, MS, PhD
special education • M Ed, MS, PhD
teaching and learning • M Ed, MA, MS, PhD

College of Engineering
Gerald B. Stringfellow, Dean
Programs in:
bioengineering • ME, MS, PhD
chemical and fuels engineering • M Phil, ME, MS, PhD
chemical engineering • M Phil, ME, MS, PhD
civil engineering • ME, MS, PhD
computer science • M Phil, MS, PhD
electrical engineering • M Phil, ME, MS, PhD, EE
engineering • M Phil, ME, MS, PhD, EE
environmental engineering • ME, MS, PhD
materials science and engineering • ME, MS, PhD
mechanical engineering • ME, MS, PhD
nuclear engineering • ME, MS, PhD

College of Fine Arts
Phyllis A. Haskell, Dean
Programs in:

art history • MA
ballet • MA, MFA
ceramics • MFA
drawing • MFA
film studies • MFA
fine arts • M Mus, MA, MFA, PhD
graphic design • MFA
illustration • MFA
modern dance • MA, MFA
music • M Mus, MA, PhD
painting • MFA
photography/digital imaging • MFA
printmaking • MFA
sculpture/intermedia • MFA
theatre • MFA, PhD

College of Health
Programs in:
audiology • MA, MS
exercise and sport science • MS, Ed D, PhD
foods and nutrition • MS
health • M Phil, MA, MOT, MPT, MS, Ed D, PhD
health promotion and education • M Phil, MS, Ed D, PhD
occupational therapy • MOT
parks, recreation, and tourism • M Phil, MS, Ed D, PhD
physical therapy • MPT
speech-language pathology • MA, MS
speech-language pathology and audiology • PhD

College of Humanities
Patricia L. Hanna, Dean
Programs in:
communication • M Phil, MA, MS, PhD
comparative literature • MA, PhD
creative writing • MFA
English • MA, PhD
French • MA, MAT
German • MA, MAT, PhD
history • MA, MS, PhD
humanities • M Phil, MA, MAT, MFA, MS, PhD
language pedagogy • MAT
linguistics • MA
Middle East studies • MA, PhD
philosophy • MA, MS, PhD
Spanish • MA, MAT, PhD

College of Mines and Earth Sciences
Programs in:
geological engineering • ME, MS, PhD
geology • MS, PhD
geophysics • MS, PhD
metallurgical engineering • ME, MS, PhD
meteorology • MS, PhD
mines and earth sciences • ME, MS, PhD
mining engineering • ME, MS, PhD

College of Nursing
Programs in:
gerontology • MS, Certificate
nursing • MS, PhD, Certificate

College of Science
Peter Stang, Dean
Programs in:
biology • M Phil
cell biology • PhD
chemical physics • PhD
chemistry • M Phil, MA, MS, PhD
ecology and evolutionary biology • MS, PhD
genetics • MS, PhD
mathematics • M Phil, M Stat, MA, MS, PhD
molecular biology • PhD
physics • MA, MS, PhD
science • M Phil, M Stat, MA, MS, PhD
science for secondary school teachers • MS
science teacher education • MS

College of Social and Behavioral Science
Programs in:
anthropology • MA, MS, PhD
economics • M Phil, M Stat, MA, MS, PhD
family and consumer studies • MS
geography • MA, MS, PhD
political science • MA, MS, PhD
psychology • M Stat, MA, MS, PhD
public administration • MPA, Certificate
social and behavioral science • M Phil, M Stat, MA, MPA, MS, PhD, Certificate

David Eccles School of Business
Jack Brittain, Dean
Programs in:
accounting • M Pr A, PhD
business • M Stat
business administration • MBA, PhD
finance • MS, PhD
management • PhD
marketing • PhD

Graduate School of Architecture
William C. Miller, Dean
Program in:
architecture • M Arch, MS

Graduate School of Social Work
Jannah H. Mather, Dean
Program in:
social work • MSW, PhD

School of Medicine
Programs in:
medicine • MD, M Phil, M Stat, MPH, MS, MSPH, PhD

Graduate Programs in Medicine
Programs in:
biochemistry • MS, PhD
biostatistics • M Stat
experimental pathology • PhD
human genetics • MS, PhD
medical informatics • MS, PhD
medical laboratory science • MS
medicine • M Phil, M Stat, MPH, MS, MSPH, PhD
neurology and anatomy • M Phil, MS, PhD
neuroscience • PhD
oncological sciences • MS, PhD
physiology • PhD
public health • MPH, MSPH

■ UTAH STATE UNIVERSITY
Logan, UT 84322
http://www.usu.edu/

State-supported, coed, university. CGS member. *Enrollment:* 961 full-time matriculated graduate/professional students (355 women), 1,147 part-time matriculated graduate/professional students (527 women). *Computer facilities:* 850 computers available on campus for general student use. A campuswide network can be accessed from student residence rooms and from off campus. Internet access and online class registration are available. *Library facilities:* Merrill Library plus 4 others. *Graduate expenses:* Tuition, state resident: full-time $1,553. Tuition, nonresident: full-time $5,436. $5,476 full-time. Required fees: $28 per credit. *General application contact:* Diana Thimmes, Admissions Officer, School of Graduate Studies, 435-797-1190.

School of Graduate Studies

College of Agriculture
Don Snyder, Interim Dean
Programs in:
agricultural systems technology • MS
agriculture • MA, MPSH, MS, PhD
animal science • MS, PhD
biometeorology • MS, PhD
bioveterinary science • MS, PhD
dairy science • MS
ecology • MS, PhD
plant science • MS, PhD
soil science • MS, PhD
toxicology • MS, PhD

College of Business
David B. Stephens, Dean
Programs in:
accountancy • M Acc
applied economics • MS
business • M Acc, MA, MBA, MS, MSS, Ed D, PhD
business administration • MBA
business education • MS
business information systems • MS
business information systems and education • Ed D

Utah State University (continued)
economics • MA, MS, PhD
education • PhD
human resource management • MSS

College of Education
Gerry Giordano, Dean
Programs in:
audiology • Ed S
business information systems and education • Ed D, PhD
clinical/counseling/school psychology • PhD
communication disorders and deaf education • M Ed
communicative disorders and deaf education • MA, MS
curriculum and instruction • Ed D, PhD
education • M Ed, MA, MRC, MS, Ed D, PhD, Ed S
elementary education • M Ed, MA, MS
health, physical education and recreation • M Ed, MS
instructional technology • M Ed, MS, PhD, Ed S
rehabilitation counselor education • MRC
research and evaluation • Ed D, PhD
research and evaluation methodology • PhD
school counseling • MS
school psychology • MS
secondary education • M Ed, MA, MS
special education • M Ed, MS, Ed D, PhD, Ed S

College of Engineering
A. Bruce Bishop, Dean
Programs in:
aerospace engineering • MS, PhD
biological and agricultural engineering • MS, PhD
civil and environmental engineering • ME, MS, PhD, CE
electrical engineering • ME, MS, PhD, EE
engineering • ME, MS, PhD, CE, EE
industrial technology • MS
irrigation engineering • MS, PhD
mechanical engineering • ME, MS, PhD

College of Family Life
Bonita W. Wyse, Dean
Programs in:
dietetic administration • MDA
family and human development • MS
family life • MDA, MFHD, MFMS, MS, PhD
food microbiology and safety • MFMS
human environments • MS
marriage and family therapy • MS
molecular biology • MS, PhD
nutrition and food sciences • MS, PhD

College of Humanities, Arts and Social Sciences
Ann Leffler, Interim Dean
Programs in:
advanced technical practice • MFA
American studies • MA, MS
art • MA, MFA
design • MFA
directing/performance • MFA
English • MA, MS
folklore • MA, MS
history • MA, MS, MSS
humanities, arts and social sciences • MA, MFA, MLA, MS, MSLT, MSS, PhD
journalism and communication • MA, MS
landscape architecture • MLA
political science • MA, MS
second language teaching • MSLT
sociology • MA, MS, MSS, PhD
theatre arts • MA, MFA
town and regional planning • MS

College of Natural Resources
Dr. F. E. Busby, Dean
Programs in:
ecology • MS, PhD
fisheries biology • MS, PhD
forestry • MS, PhD
geography • MA, MS
natural resources • MA, MNR, MS, PhD
range science • MS, PhD
recreation resources management • MS, PhD
science program • MS, PhD
wildlife biology • MS, PhD

College of Science
Don Fresinger, Interim Dean
Programs in:
applied statistics • MS
biochemistry • MS, PhD
biology • MS, PhD
chemistry • MS, PhD
computer science • MCS, MS
ecology • MS, PhD
geology • MS
mathematical sciences • PhD
mathematics • M Math, MS
physics • MS, PhD
science • M Math, MCS, MS, PhD

■ WEBER STATE UNIVERSITY

Ogden, UT 84408-1001

http://weber.edu/

State-supported, coed, comprehensive institution. *Enrollment:* 61 full-time matriculated graduate/professional students (22 women), 136 part-time matriculated graduate/professional students (93 women). *Graduate faculty:* 28 full-time (13 women), 8 part-time/adjunct (6 women). *Computer facilities:* 558 computers available on campus for general student use. A campuswide network can be accessed from student residence rooms and from off campus. Internet access and online class registration, Online Grades are available. *Library facilities:* Stewart Library plus 1 other. *Graduate expenses:* Tuition, state resident: full-time $1,596. Required fees: $424. Tuition and fees vary according to course load and program. *General application contact:* Christopher C. Rivera, Director of Admissions, 801-626-6046.

College of Education
Dr. David M. Greene, Dean
Programs in:
curriculum and instruction • M Ed
education • M Ed

John B. Goddard School of Business and Economics
Dr. Michael Vaughan, Dean
Programs in:
accountancy • MP Acc
business administration • MBA
business and economics • MBA, MP Acc

■ WESTMINSTER COLLEGE

Salt Lake City, UT 84105-3697

http://www.wcslc.edu/

Independent, coed, comprehensive institution. *Enrollment:* 149 full-time matriculated graduate/professional students (75 women), 376 part-time matriculated graduate/professional students (159 women). *Graduate faculty:* 27 full-time, 24 part-time/adjunct. *Computer facilities:* 238 computers available on campus for general student use. A campuswide network can be accessed from student residence rooms. Internet access and online class registration are available. *Library facilities:* Giovale Library plus 1 other. *Graduate expenses:* Tuition: full-time $9,720; part-time $540 per credit. Required fees: $200. *General application contact:* Philip J. Alletto, Vice President for Student Development and Enrollment Management, 801-832-2200.

The Bill and Vieve Gore School of Business
Dr. James Seidelman, Dean
Programs in:
business • MBA, Certificate
business administration • MBA, Certificate

St. Mark's-Westminster School of Nursing and Health Sciences
Dr. Marj Peck, Dean
Programs in:
nursing • MSN
nursing and health sciences • MSN

School of Arts and Sciences
Dr. Mary Jane Chase, Dean
Programs in:
arts and sciences • MPC
professional communication • MPC

School of Education
Dr. Janet Dynak, Dean
Program in:
education • M Ed

Vermont

■ CASTLETON STATE COLLEGE
Castleton, VT 05735
http://www.castleton.edu/

State-supported, coed, comprehensive institution. *Enrollment:* 36 full-time matriculated graduate/professional students (30 women), 89 part-time matriculated graduate/professional students (69 women). *Graduate faculty:* 15 full-time (11 women), 7 part-time/adjunct (4 women). *Computer facilities:* 215 computers available on campus for general student use. A campuswide network can be accessed from student residence rooms. Internet access is available. *Library facilities:* Calvin Coolidge Library. *Graduate expenses:* Tuition, state resident: full-time $4,236; part-time $177 per credit. Tuition, nonresident: full-time $9,924; part-time $414 per credit. Required fees: $664; $28 per credit. *General application contact:* Bill Allen, Dean of Enrollment, 802-468-1213.

Division of Graduate Studies
Ennis Duling, Director of Public Information
Programs in:
curriculum and instruction • MA Ed
educational leadership • MA Ed, CAGS
forensic psychology • MA
language arts and reading • MA Ed, CAGS
special education • MA Ed, CAGS

■ COLLEGE OF ST. JOSEPH
Rutland, VT 05701-3899
http://www.csj.edu/

Independent-religious, coed, comprehensive institution. *Enrollment:* 46 full-time matriculated graduate/professional students (31 women), 112 part-time matriculated graduate/professional students (87 women). *Graduate faculty:* 6 full-time (2 women), 17 part-time/adjunct (12 women). *Computer facilities:* 30 computers available on campus for general student use. A campuswide network can be accessed from student residence rooms. Internet access is available. *Library facilities:* St. Joseph Library plus 1 other. *Graduate expenses:* Tuition: full-time $8,630; part-time $235 per credit. Required fees: $100. *General application contact:* Steve Soba, Dean of Admissions, 802-773-5900 Ext. 206.

Graduate Program
Dr. Frank Miglorie, President

Division of Education
Dr. Stan Cianfarano, Chair
Programs in:
elementary education • M Ed
general education • M Ed
reading • M Ed
special education • M Ed

Division of Psychology and Human Services
Dr. Craig Knapp, Chair
Programs in:
clinical mental health counseling • MS
clinical psychology • MS
community counseling • MS
counseling psychology • MS
school guidance counseling • MS

■ GODDARD COLLEGE
Plainfield, VT 05667-9432
http://www.goddard.edu/

Independent, coed, comprehensive institution. *Computer facilities:* 27 computers available on campus for general student use. A campuswide network can be accessed from student residence rooms and from off campus. Internet access is available. *Library facilities:* Eliot Pratt Center. *General application contact:* Director of Admissions, 802-454-8311.

Graduate Programs
Programs in:
health arts and sciences • MA
individually designed liberal arts • MA
interdisciplinary arts • MFA
organizational development • MA
psychology and counseling • MA
social ecology • MA
teacher education • MA
writing • MFA

■ JOHNSON STATE COLLEGE
Johnson, VT 05656-9405
http://www.jsc.vsc.edu/

State-supported, coed, comprehensive institution. *Enrollment:* 27 full-time matriculated graduate/professional students (15 women), 135 part-time matriculated graduate/professional students (112 women). *Graduate faculty:* 15 full-time (9 women), 2 part-time/adjunct (both women). *Computer facilities:* 131 computers available on campus for general student use. A campuswide network can be accessed from student residence rooms and from off campus. Internet access is available. *Library facilities:* Library and Learning Center. *Graduate expenses:* Tuition, state resident: part-time $177 per credit. Tuition, nonresident: part-time $414 per credit. Required fees: $17 per credit. *General application contact:* Catherine H. Higley, Administrative Assistant, 802-635-2356 Ext. 1244.

Graduate Program in Education
Programs in:
curriculum and instruction • MA Ed
education of the gifted • MA Ed
reading education • MA Ed
special education • MA Ed

Program in Counseling
Program in:
counseling • MA

Program in Fine Arts
Programs in:
drawing • MFA
painting • MFA
sculpture • MFA

■ NORWICH UNIVERSITY
Northfield, VT 05663
http://www.norwich.edu/

Independent, coed, comprehensive institution. *Enrollment:* 537 full-time matriculated graduate/professional students (367 women), 19 part-time matriculated graduate/professional

Norwich University (continued)
students (3 women). *Graduate faculty:* 40 full-time (25 women), 100 part-time/adjunct (54 women). *Computer facilities:* 142 computers available on campus for general student use. A campuswide network can be accessed from student residence rooms and from off campus. Internet access is available. *Library facilities:* Kreitzberg Library. *Graduate expenses:* Tuition: full-time $9,416. Tuition and fees vary according to program. *General application contact:* Susan Bradt, Associate Director of Admissions, 800-336-6794.

Military Graduate Program
Dr. Fariborz L. Mokhtari, Director
Program in:
diplomacy and military science • MA

Program in Business Administration
Fred Snow, Director
Program in:
business administration • MBA

Vermont College
Dr. Richard Hansen, Vice President
Programs in:
art therapy • MA, CAS
education • M Ed, CAS
visual art • MFA, CAS
writing • MFA, CAS
writing for children • MFA, CAS

■ SAINT MICHAEL'S COLLEGE
Colchester, VT 05439
http://www.smcvt.edu/

Independent-religious, coed, comprehensive institution. *Graduate faculty:* 24 full-time (15 women), 137 part-time/adjunct (77 women). *Computer facilities:* 180 computers available on campus for general student use. A campuswide network can be accessed from student residence rooms and from off campus. Internet access is available. *Library facilities:* Durick Library. *General application contact:* Dee M. Goodrich, Dean of The Prevail School, 802-654-2223.

Graduate Programs
Dr. John P. Kenney, Dean
Programs in:
administration • M Ed, CAGS
administration and management • MSA, CAMS
adult education • CAGS
arts in education • CAGS
clinical psychology • MA
curriculum and instruction • M Ed, CAGS
information technology • CAGS
reading • M Ed
self designed • M Ed
special education • M Ed, CAGS
teaching English as a second language • MATESL, CAS
technology • M Ed
theology • MA, CAS, Certificate

■ SCHOOL FOR INTERNATIONAL TRAINING
Brattleboro, VT 05302-0676
http://www.sit.edu/

Independent, coed, graduate-only institution. *Graduate faculty:* 38 full-time (23 women), 19 part-time/adjunct (8 women). *Computer facilities:* 42 computers available on campus for general student use. A campuswide network can be accessed. Internet access is available. *Library facilities:* Donald B. Watt Library. *Graduate expenses:* Tuition: full-time $19,500. Required fees: $800. Full-time tuition and fees vary according to program. *General application contact:* Kim Noble, Admissions Assistant, 802-257-7751 Ext. 3267.

Find an in-depth description at www.petersons.com/graduate.

Graduate Programs
Jim Cramer, President
Programs in:
endorsement in bilingual-multicultural education • MAT
English for speakers of other languages • MAT
French • MAT
intercultural relations • MA
international and intercultural management • MIIM
international and intercultural service • MA
international education • MA
non-governmental organization leadership and management • MA, Postgraduate Diploma
organizational management • MS
Spanish • MAT
sustainable development • MA

■ UNIVERSITY OF VERMONT
Burlington, VT 05405
http://www.uvm.edu/

State-supported, coed, university. CGS member. *Enrollment:* 1,543 matriculated graduate/professional students (849 women). *Graduate faculty:* 702 full-time, 604 part-time/adjunct. *Computer facilities:* 685 computers available on campus for general student use. A campuswide network can be accessed from student residence rooms and from off campus. Internet access, e-mail, Web pages, on-line course support are available. *Library facilities:* Bailey-Howe Library plus 3 others. *Graduate expenses:* Tuition, state resident: part-time $321 per credit. Tuition, nonresident: part-time $802 per credit. *General application contact:* Ralph M. Swenson, Director of Admissions and Administration, 802-656-3160.

Find an in-depth description at www.petersons.com/graduate.

College of Medicine
Dr. John W. Frymoyer, Interim Dean
Programs in:
anatomy and neurobiology • PhD
biochemistry • MS, PhD
medicine • MD, MS, PhD
microbiology and molecular genetics • MS, PhD
molecular physiology and biophysics • MS, PhD
pathology • MS
pharmacology • MS, PhD

Graduate College
Dr. Anne Huot, Interim Dean
Program in:
cell and molecular biology • MS, PhD

College of Agriculture and Life Sciences
Dr. J. Bramley, Dean
Programs in:
agricultural biochemistry • MS, PhD
agriculture and life sciences • M Ext Ed, MAT, MS, MST, PhD
animal sciences • MS, PhD
biology • MST
botany • MAT, MS, PhD
community development and applied economics • M Ext Ed, MS
family and consumer sciences • MAT
field naturalist • MS
nutritional sciences • MS
plant and soil science • MS, PhD

College of Arts and Sciences
Dr. Joan Smith, Dean
Programs in:
arts and sciences • MA, MAT, MPA, MS, MST, PhD
biology • MS, PhD
biology education • MAT, MST
chemistry • MS, MST, PhD
chemistry education • MAT
clinical psychology • PhD
communication sciences • MS
engineering physics • MS

English • MA
English education • MAT
French • MA
French education • MAT
geography • MA, MAT
geology • MS
geology education • MAT, MST
German • MA
German education • MAT
Greek • MA
Greek and Latin • MAT
historic preservation • MS
history • MA
history education • MAT
Latin • MA
physical sciences • MST
physics • MAT, MS
political science • MA
psychology • PhD
public administration • MPA

College of Education and Social Services
Dr. Jill Tarule, Dean
Programs in:
counseling • MS
curriculum and instruction • M Ed
education and social services • M Ed, MS, MSW, Ed D
educational leadership • M Ed
educational leadership and policy studies • Ed D
educational studies • M Ed
higher education and student affairs administration • M Ed
interdisciplinary studies • M Ed
reading and language arts • M Ed
social work • MSW
special education • M Ed

College of Engineering and Mathematics
Dr. R. Jenkins, Dean
Programs in:
biomedical engineering • MS
biostatistics • MS
civil engineering • MS, PhD
computer science • MS
electrical engineering • MS, PhD
engineering and mathematics • MAT, MS, MST, PhD
materials science • MS, PhD
mathematics • MAT, MS, MST, PhD
mathematics education • MAT, MST
mechanical engineering • MS, PhD
statistics • MS

School of Allied Health Sciences
Dr. Betty Rambur, Dean
Programs in:
allied health sciences • MPT, MS
biomedical technologies • MS
physical therapy • MPT

School of Business Administration
Dr. Larry E. Shirland, Dean
Program in:
business administration • MBA

School of Natural Resources
Dr. D. DeHayes, Dean
Programs in:
forestry • MS
natural resources • MS, PhD
natural resources planning • MS, PhD
water resources • MS
wildlife and fisheries biology • MS

School of Nursing
Dr. Betty Rambur, Dean
Program in:
nursing • MS

Virgin Islands

■ UNIVERSITY OF THE VIRGIN ISLANDS

Charlotte Amalie, VI 00802-9990
http://www.uvi.edu/

Territory-supported, coed, comprehensive institution. *Enrollment:* 21 full-time matriculated graduate/professional students (15 women), 113 part-time matriculated graduate/professional students (99 women). *Graduate faculty:* 12 full-time (5 women), 2 part-time/adjunct (1 woman). *Computer facilities:* 100 computers available on campus for general student use. A campuswide network can be accessed from off campus. *Library facilities:* Ralph M. Paiewonsky Library. *Graduate expenses:* Part-time $228 per credit. Required fees: $130 per term. *General application contact:* Carolyn Cook, Director of Admissions and New Student Services, 340-693-1224.

Graduate Programs
Dr. Laverne Ragster, Senior Vice President and Provost
Program in:
public administration • MPA

Division of Business Administration
Dr. Solomon S. Kubuka, Chairperson
Program in:
business administration • MBA

Division of Education
Dr. Rita Howard, Chairperson
Program in:
education • MAE

Virginia

■ AVERETT UNIVERSITY

Danville, VA 24541-3692
http://www.averett.edu/

Independent-religious, coed, comprehensive institution. *Enrollment:* 101 full-time matriculated graduate/professional students (51 women), 488 part-time matriculated graduate/professional students (266 women). *Graduate faculty:* 14 full-time (6 women), 60 part-time/adjunct (12 women). *Computer facilities:* 100 computers available on campus for general student use. A campuswide network can be accessed. Internet access is available. *Library facilities:* Mary B. Blount Library. *Graduate expenses:* Tuition: part-time $353 per credit. Required fees: $300; $300 per year. *General application contact:* Katherine Pappas-Smith, Marketing Manager, 804-791-5844.

Division of Education
Dr. Pam Riedel, Chair
Programs in:
curriculum and instruction • M Ed
early childhood • M Ed
middle grades • M Ed
reading • M Ed
science • M Ed
special eduation • M Ed
teaching • MAT

Program in Business Administration
Dr. Peggy Wright, Dean
Program in:
business administration • MBA

■ THE COLLEGE OF WILLIAM AND MARY

Williamsburg, VA 23187-8795
http://www.wm.edu/

State-supported, coed, university. CGS member. *Enrollment:* 1,427 full-time matriculated graduate/professional students (681 women), 352 part-time matriculated graduate/professional students (173 women). *Graduate faculty:* 569 full-time (170 women), 149 part-time/adjunct (69 women). *Computer facilities:* 300 computers available on campus for general student use. A campuswide network can be accessed from student residence rooms and from off campus.

The College of William and Mary (continued)

Internet access is available. *Library facilities:* Swem Library plus 9 others. *Graduate expenses:* Tuition, state resident: full-time $3,063; part-time $170 per hour. Tuition, nonresident: full-time $14,235; part-time $525 per hour. Required fees: $2,385. Tuition and fees vary according to program. *General application contact:* Dr. Eugene Tracy, Dean of Research and Graduate Studies, 757-221-2467.

Find an in-depth description at www.petersons.com/graduate.

Faculty of Arts and Sciences
Dr. Eugene Tracy, Dean of Research and Graduate Studies
Programs in:
- American studies • MA, PhD
- anthropology • MA, PhD
- applied science • MS, PhD
- arts and sciences • MA, MPP, MS, PhD, Psy D
- biology • MA
- chemistry • MA, MS
- clinical psychology • Psy D
- computational operations research • MS
- computer science • MS, PhD
- general experimental psychology • MA
- history • MA, PhD
- physics • MA, MS, PhD
- public policy • MPP

School of Business
Dr. Lawrence Pulley, Dean
Programs in:
- accounting • M Acc
- business administration • MBA

School of Education
Dr. Virginia McLaughlin, Dean
Programs in:
- community and addictions counseling • M Ed
- community counseling • M Ed
- education • M Ed, MA Ed, Ed D, PhD, Ed S
- educational counseling • M Ed, Ed D, PhD
- educational leadership • M Ed
- educational policy, planning, and leadership • Ed D, PhD
- elementary education • MA Ed
- gifted education • MA Ed
- reading education • MA Ed
- school counseling • M Ed
- school psychology • M Ed, Ed S
- secondary education • MA Ed
- special education • MA Ed

School of Marine Science/ Virginia Institute of Marine Science
Dr. L. Donelson Wright, Dean and Director
Program in:
- marine science • MS, PhD

William & Mary Law School
W. Taylor Reveley, Dean
Program in:
- law • JD, LL M

■ GEORGE MASON UNIVERSITY
Fairfax, VA 22030-4444
http://www.gmu.edu/

State-supported, coed, university. CGS member. *Enrollment:* 1,822 full-time matriculated graduate/professional students (956 women), 4,936 part-time matriculated graduate/professional students (2,648 women). *Graduate faculty:* 916 full-time (327 women), 635 part-time/adjunct (310 women). *Computer facilities:* 1,500 computers available on campus for general student use. A campuswide network can be accessed from student residence rooms and from off campus. Internet access, telephone registration are available. *Library facilities:* Fenwick Library plus 1 other. *Graduate expenses:* Tuition, state resident: full-time $3,108; part-time $188 per credit hour. Tuition, nonresident: full-time $11,220; part-time $526 per credit hour. Required fees: $1,392. *General application contact:* Susan Swett, Director of Graduate Admissions, 703-993-2423.

Find an in-depth description at www.petersons.com/graduate.

College of Arts and Sciences
Danielle Struppa, Dean
Programs in:
- applied and engineering physics • MS
- arts and sciences • MA, MAIS, MFA, MPA, MS, PhD
- bioinformatics • MS
- biology • MS
- chemistry • MS
- clinical psychology • PhD
- creative writing • MFA
- cultural studies • PhD
- developmental psychology • PhD
- ecology, systematics and evolution • MS
- economics • MA, PhD
- English • MA
- English literature • MA
- environmental science and public policy • MS, PhD
- experimental neuropsychology • MA
- foreign languages • MA
- geography and cartographic sciences • MS
- history • MA
- human factors engineering psychology • MA, PhD
- industrial/organizational psychology • MA, PhD
- interdisciplinary studies • MAIS
- interpretive biology • MS
- liberal studies • MAIS
- life-span development psychology • MA
- linguistics • MA
- mathematics • MS
- molecular, microbial, and cellular biology • MS
- music • MA
- music education • MA
- organismal biology • MS
- professional writing and editing • MA
- public administration • MPA
- school psychology • MA
- sociology • MA
- teaching writing and literature • MA
- telecommunications • MA

College of Nursing and Health Science
Dr. Rita M. Carty, Dean
Programs in:
- advanced clinical nursing • MSN
- nurse practitioner • MSN
- nursing • MSN, PhD
- nursing administration • MSN

College of Visual and Performing Arts
William Reeder, Dean
Programs in:
- dance • MFA
- visual and performing arts • MA, MFA
- visual information technologies • MA

Graduate School of Education
Martin Ford, Acting Dean
Programs in:
- bilingual/multicultural/English as a second language education • M Ed
- counseling and development • M Ed
- early childhood education • M Ed
- education • M Ed, MA, MS, DA Ed, PhD
- education leadership • M Ed
- educational transformation • MA
- exercise science and health • MS
- instructional technology • M Ed
- middle education • M Ed
- reading • M Ed
- secondary education • M Ed
- special education • M Ed

The National Center for Community College Education
Program in:
- community college education • DA Ed

Institute for Conflict Analysis and Resolution
Dr. Sandra I. Cheldelin, Director
Program in:
conflict analysis and resolution • MS, PhD

School of Computational Sciences
Dr. W. Murray Black, Dean
Programs in:
computational sciences • MS
computational sciences and informatics • PhD
computational techniques and applications • Certificate

School of Information Technology and Engineering
Lloyd Griffiths, Dean
Programs in:
computer science • MS, PhD
electrical and computer engineering • PhD
electrical engineering • MS
information systems • MS
information technology and engineering • MS, PhD
operations research and management science • MS
software systems engineering • MS
statistical science • MS
systems engineering • MS

School of Law
Dr. Mark F. Grady, Dean
Program in:
law • JD

School of Management
Teresa Domzal, Dean
Programs in:
business administration • EMBA, MBA
management • EMBA, MBA, MS
technology management • MS

School of Public Policy
Dr. Kingsley Haynes, Director
Programs in:
enterprise engineering and policy • MS
international commerce and policy • MA
organizational learning • MSNPS
peace operations • MAIS
professional studies: organizational learning • MS
public policy • MA, MAIS, MS, MSNPS, PhD
regional economic development and technology • MAIS
transportation policy, operations and logistics • MSNPS

■ HAMPTON UNIVERSITY
Hampton, VA 23668
http://www.hamptonu.edu/

Independent, coed, comprehensive institution. CGS member. *Computer facilities:* 1,300 computers available on campus for general student use. A campuswide network can be accessed from student residence rooms and from off campus. Internet access is available. *Library facilities:* William R. and Norma B. Harvey Library. *General application contact:* Vice President for Research and Dean of Graduate College, 757-727-5310.

Find an in-depth description at www.petersons.com/graduate.

Graduate College
Programs in:
applied mathematics • MS
biological sciences • MA, MS
business • MBA
chemistry • MS
college student development • MA
communicative sciences and disorders • MA
community agency counseling • MA
computer science • MS
counseling • MA
elementary education • MA
museum studies • MA
nursing • MS
physical therapy • DPT
physics • MS, PhD
special education • MA
teaching • MT

■ JAMES MADISON UNIVERSITY
Harrisonburg, VA 22807
http://www.jmu.edu/

State-supported, coed, comprehensive institution. CGS member. *Enrollment:* 418 full-time matriculated graduate/professional students (261 women), 315 part-time matriculated graduate/professional students (163 women). *Graduate faculty:* 156 full-time (63 women), 30 part-time/adjunct (13 women). *Computer facilities:* 500 computers available on campus for general student use. A campuswide network can be accessed from student residence rooms and from off campus. Internet access and online class registration are available. *Library facilities:* Carrier Library plus 2 others. *Graduate expenses:* Tuition, state resident: full-time $3,312. Tuition, nonresident: full-time $10,224. *General application contact:* Dr. Dorothy A. Boyd-Rush, Dean of the Graduate School, 540-568-6131.

Find an in-depth description at www.petersons.com/graduate.

Graduate School
Dr. Dorothy A. Boyd-Rush, Dean

College of Arts and Letters
Dr. Richard F. Whitman, Dean
Programs in:
art education • MA
art history • MA
arts and letters • MA, MFA, MM, MPA, MS
ceramics • MFA
conducting • MM
drawing/painting • MFA
English • MA
history • MA
metal/jewelry • MFA
music education • MM
performance • MM
photography • MFA
printmaking • MFA
public administration • MPA
sculpture • MFA
studio art • MA
technical and scientific communication • MA, MS
theory-composition • MM
weaving/fibers • MFA

College of Business
Dr. Robert D. Reid, Dean
Programs in:
accounting • MS
business • MBA, MS
business administration • MBA

College of Education and Psychology
Dr. John W. Gilje, Interim Dean
Programs in:
counseling psychology • M Ed, MA, Ed S
early childhood education • M Ed
education • M Ed, MAT, MS Ed
education and psychology • M Ed, MA, MAT, MS, MS Ed, Psy D, Ed S
educational leadership • M Ed
general psychology • MA, Psy D
kinesiology and recreation studies • MS
middle school education • M Ed
reading education • M Ed
school psychology • MA, Ed S
secondary education • M Ed
special education • M Ed
vocational education • MS Ed

College of Integrated Science and Technology
Dr. A. Jerry Benson, Interim Dean
Programs in:

James Madison University (continued)
computer science • MS
health sciences • MS, MS Ed
hearing disorders • M Ed
integrated science and technology • M Ed, MS, MS Ed
speech pathology • MS

College of Science and Mathematics
Dr. David F. Brakke, Dean
Programs in:
biology • MS
science and mathematics • MS

■ LIBERTY UNIVERSITY
Lynchburg, VA 24502
http://www.liberty.edu/

Independent-religious, coed, comprehensive institution. *Enrollment:* 221 full-time matriculated graduate/professional students (67 women), 568 part-time matriculated graduate/professional students (252 women). *Graduate faculty:* 25 full-time (1 woman), 16 part-time/adjunct (3 women). *Computer facilities:* 245 computers available on campus for general student use. A campuswide network can be accessed from student residence rooms and from off campus. Internet access and online class registration are available. *Library facilities:* A. Pierre Guillermin Library plus 1 other. *Graduate expenses:* Tuition: full-time $1,050; part-time $225 per semester hour. Required fees: $500; $250 per year. Full-time tuition and fees vary according to program. *General application contact:* Dr. William E. Wegert, Coordinator of Graduate Admissions, 804-582-2175.

Find an in-depth description at www.petersons.com/graduate.

College of Arts and Science
Dr. Ronald E. Hawkins, Dean
Program in:
counseling • MA

Liberty Baptist Theological Seminary
Dr. Danny Lovett, Dean
Program in:
theology • M Div, MAR, MRE, Th M, D Min

School of Business and Government
Dr. Bruce K. Bell, Dean
Program in:
business and government • MBA

School of Education
Karen L. Parker, Dean
Programs in:
administration and supervision • M Ed
educational leadership • Ed D
elementary education • M Ed
reading specialist • M Ed
school counseling • M Ed
secondary education • M Ed
special education • M Ed

School of Religion
Dr. Elmer Towns, Dean
Program in:
religious studies • MA

■ LONGWOOD COLLEGE
Farmville, VA 23909-1800
http://www.lwc.edu/

State-supported, coed, comprehensive institution. *Enrollment:* 477 matriculated graduate/professional students (374 women). *Graduate faculty:* 69 part-time/adjunct. *Computer facilities:* 270 computers available on campus for general student use. A campuswide network can be accessed from student residence rooms and from off campus. Internet access is available. *Library facilities:* Longwood Library. *Graduate expenses:* Part-time $189 per credit hour. Tuition, nonresident: part-time $402 per credit hour. *General application contact:* Dr. Patricia Whitfield, Director of Graduate Studies, 804-395-2707.

Graduate Programs
Dr. Patricia Whitfield, Director of Graduate Studies
Programs in:
administration/supervision • MS
community and college counseling • MS
criminal justice • MS
curriculum and instruction specialist-elementary • MS
curriculum and instruction specialist-secondary • MS
English education and writing • MA
environmental studies • MS
guidance and counseling • MS
library science media specialist • MS
literature • MA
reading specialist • MS

■ LYNCHBURG COLLEGE
Lynchburg, VA 24501-3199
http://www.lynchburg.edu/

Independent-religious, coed, comprehensive institution. *Computer facilities:* 217 computers available on campus for general student use. A campuswide network can be accessed from student residence rooms. Internet access is available. *Library facilities:* Knight-Capron Library. *General application contact:* Academic Dean, 804-522-8232.

Graduate Studies

School of Business and Economics
Programs in:
administration • M Ad
business • MBA

School of Education and Human Development
Programs in:
agency counseling • M Ed
counseling • M Ed
curriculum and instruction • M Ed
curriculum and instruction: early childhood education • M Ed
curriculum and instruction: middle education • M Ed
early childhood education • M Ed
early childhood special education • M Ed
English education • M Ed
mental retardation • M Ed
middle school education • M Ed
reading • M Ed
school administration • M Ed
school counseling • M Ed
secondary education • M Ed
severely/profoundly handicapped education • M Ed
special education • M Ed
supervision • M Ed
teaching children with learning disabilities • M Ed
teaching the emotionally disturbed • M Ed

■ MARY BALDWIN COLLEGE
Staunton, VA 24401
http://www.mbc.edu/

Independent-religious, coed, primarily women, comprehensive institution. *Enrollment:* 26 full-time matriculated graduate/professional students (20 women), 37 part-time matriculated graduate/professional students (32 women). *Graduate faculty:* 1 (woman) full-time, 24 part-time/adjunct (11 women). *Computer facilities:* 175 computers available on campus for general student use. A campuswide network can be accessed from student residence rooms and from off campus. Internet access and online class registration are available. *Library facilities:* Grafton Library. *Graduate expenses:* Tuition: part-time $335 per semester hour. Required fees: $15 per semester hour. One-time fee: $50. *General application contact:* Dr. Carole Grove, Director, MAT Program, 540-887-7333.

Graduate Studies
Dr. Carole Grove, Director, MAT Program
Programs in:
elementary education • MAT
middle grades education • MAT

■ MARYMOUNT UNIVERSITY
Arlington, VA 22207-4299
http://www.marymount.edu/

Independent-religious, coed, comprehensive institution. *Enrollment:* 414 full-time matriculated graduate/professional students (317 women), 950 part-time matriculated graduate/professional students (639 women). *Graduate faculty:* 69 full-time (43 women), 52 part-time/adjunct (31 women). *Computer facilities:* 260 computers available on campus for general student use. A campuswide network can be accessed from off campus. On-line registration for graduate students available. *Library facilities:* Emerson C. Reinsch Library plus 1 other. *Graduate expenses:* Tuition: part-time $495 per credit. Required fees: $5 per credit. *General application contact:* Chris E. Domes, Vice President for Enrollment Management, 703-284-1500.

Find an in-depth description at www.petersons.com/graduate.

School of Arts and Sciences
Dr. Rosemary Hubbard, Dean
Programs in:
arts and sciences • MA, MS, Certificate
computer science • MS, Certificate
humanities • MA
interior design • MA
literature and language • MA

School of Business Administration
Dr. Robert Sigethy, Dean
Programs in:
business administration • MBA
business technologies • MS, Certificate
health care management • MS
human performance systems • MA
human resource management • MA
information management • MS
information resources management • Certificate
instructional design • Certificate
international business • Certificate
leading and managing change • Certificate
legal administration • MA
management studies • Certificate
organization development • MA, Certificate
organizational leadership and innovation • MS
paralegal studies • Certificate

School of Education and Human Services
Dr. Wayne Lesko, Dean
Programs in:
counseling psychology • MA, Certificate
education and human services • M Ed, MA, Certificate
elementary education • M Ed
English as a second language • M Ed
forensic psychology • MA
learning disabilities • M Ed
school counseling • MA
secondary education • M Ed

School of Health Professions
Dr. Catherine Connelly, Dean
Programs in:
critical care nursing • MSN, Certificate
family nurse practitioner • MSN, Certificate
health and nursing administration • MSN, Certificate
health professions • MS, MSN, MSPT, Certificate
health promotion management • MS
physical therapy • MSPT

■ NORFOLK STATE UNIVERSITY
Norfolk, VA 23504
http://www.nsu.edu/

State-supported, coed, comprehensive institution. CGS member. *Enrollment:* 241 full-time matriculated graduate/professional students (199 women), 166 part-time matriculated graduate/professional students (119 women). *Graduate faculty:* 68 full-time (22 women), 41 part-time/adjunct (20 women). *Computer facilities:* 512 computers available on campus for general student use. A campuswide network can be accessed from student residence rooms and from off campus. Internet access and online class registration are available. *Library facilities:* Lymon Beecher Brooks Library. *Graduate expenses:* Tuition, state resident: part-time $130 per credit hour. Tuition, nonresident: part-time $394 per credit hour. Required fees: $765; $61 per credit hour. *General application contact:* Dr. Ann Morris, Director, School of Graduate Studies, 757-823-8015.

Find an in-depth description at www.petersons.com/graduate.

School of Graduate Studies
Dr. Ann W. Morris, Dean

School of Education
Dr. Jean Braxton, Dean
Programs in:
early childhood education • MAT
education • MA, MAT
education of the gifted • MA
orthopedic education and education of the multiply handicapped and health impaired • MA
pre-elementary education • MA
principal preparation • MA
secondary education • MAT
urban education/administration • MA

School of Liberal Arts
Dr. Elsie Barnes, Dean
Programs in:
applied sociology • MS
arts and letters • MA, MFA, MM, MS, Psy D
broadcasting • MA
communication • MA
community/clinical psychology • MA
journalism • MA
music • MM
music education • MM
performance • MM
psychology • Psy D
theory and composition • MM
urban affairs • MA
visual studies • MA, MFA

School of Science and Technology
Dr. Sandra DeLoatch, Dean
Programs in:
health related professions and natural sciences • MS
materials science • MS

School of Social Work
Dr. Marvin Feit, Dean
Program in:
social work • MSW, DSW

■ OLD DOMINION UNIVERSITY
Norfolk, VA 23529
http://www.odu.edu/

State-supported, coed, university. CGS member. *Enrollment:* 1,306 full-time matriculated graduate/professional students (695 women), 2,101 part-time matriculated graduate/professional students (1,173 women). *Graduate faculty:* 607 full-time (203 women), 353

Old Dominion University (continued)
part-time/adjunct (198 women). *Computer facilities:* 790 computers available on campus for general student use. A campuswide network can be accessed from student residence rooms and from off campus. Internet access and online class registration, on-line courses are available. *Library facilities:* Douglas and Patricia Perry Library plus 2 others. *Graduate expenses:* Tuition, state resident: full-time $5,910; part-time $197 per credit hour. Tuition, nonresident: full-time $15,630; part-time $521 per credit hour. Required fees: $30 per semester. Tuition and fees vary according to campus/location. *General application contact:* Alice McAdory, Director of Admissions, 757-683-3685.

Find an in-depth description at www.petersons.com/graduate.

College of Arts and Letters
Dr. Janet Katz, Acting Dean
Programs in:
- applied linguistics • MA
- applied sociology • MA
- arts and letters • MA, MFA, PhD
- creative writing • MFA
- English • MA
- history • MA
- humanities • MA
- international studies • MA, PhD
- visual studies • MA, MFA

College of Business and Public Administration
Dr. Bruce Rubin, Graduate Program Director
Programs in:
- accounting • MS
- business administration • MBA, PhD
- business and public administration • MA, MBA, MPA, MS, MTX, MUS, PhD
- e-commerce systems • MS
- economics • MA
- policy analysis/program evaluation • MUS
- public administration • MPA
- public planning analysis • MUS
- taxation • MTX
- urban administration • MUS
- urban services/urban management • PhD

College of Engineering and Technology
Dr. William Swart, Dean
Programs in:
- aerospace engineering • ME, MS, PhD
- aerospace engineering mechanics • ME, MS, PhD
- civil engineering • ME, MS, PhD
- computer engineering • ME, MS
- design manufacturing • ME
- electrical engineering • ME, MS, PhD
- engineering and technology • ME, MEM, MS, PhD
- engineering management • MEM, MS, PhD
- engineering mechanics • ME, MS, PhD
- environmental engineering • ME, MS, PhD
- mechanical engineering • ME, MS, PhD
- modeling and simulation • ME, MS, PhD
- operations research/systems analysis • ME

College of Health Sciences
Dr. Cheryl T. Samuels, Dean
Programs in:
- community health professions • MS
- health sciences • MPH, MPT, MS, MSN, PhD, Certificate
- long-term care administration • Certificate
- nursing • MSN, Certificate
- physical therapy • MPT
- professional preparation • MS
- public health • MPH
- urban services/urban health services • PhD

Program in Dental Hygiene
Michele L. Darby, Graduate Program Director
Program in:
- dental hygiene • MS

College of Sciences
Dr. Thomas L. Isenhour, Dean
Programs in:
- analytical chemistry • MS
- biochemistry • MS
- biology • MS
- biomedical sciences • PhD
- clinical chemistry • MS
- clinical psychology • Psy D
- computational and applied mathematics • MS, PhD
- computer science • MS, PhD
- ecological sciences • PhD
- environmental chemistry • MS
- general psychology • MS
- geological sciences • MS
- industrial/organizational psychology • PhD
- oceanography • MS, PhD
- organic chemistry • MS
- physical chemistry • MS
- physics • MS, PhD
- sciences • MS, PhD, Psy D

Darden College of Education
Dr. William H. Graves, Dean
Programs in:
- biology • MS Ed
- business and industry training • MS
- chemistry • MS Ed
- community agency counseling • MS
- community college teaching • MS
- counseling • CAS
- early childhood education • MS Ed
- education • MS, MS Ed, PhD, CAS
- educational administration • CAS
- educational media • MS Ed
- educational training • MS Ed
- elementary education • MS Ed
- English • MS Ed
- higher education • MS Ed, CAS
- instructional technology • MS Ed
- library science • MS Ed
- mathematics • MS Ed
- middle and secondary teaching • MS
- middle school education • MS Ed
- occupational and technical studies • CAS
- physical education • MS Ed
- principal preparation • MS Ed
- reading • MS Ed
- school counseling • MS
- secondary education • MS Ed
- social studies • MS Ed
- special education • MS Ed
- speech-language pathology • MS Ed
- student development counseling in higher education • MS
- urban services/urban education concentration • PhD

■ RADFORD UNIVERSITY
Radford, VA 24142
http://www.radford.edu/

State-supported, coed, comprehensive institution. CGS member. *Enrollment:* 444 full-time matriculated graduate/professional students (313 women), 520 part-time matriculated graduate/professional students (388 women). *Graduate faculty:* 196 full-time (70 women), 11 part-time/adjunct (9 women). *Computer facilities:* 460 computers available on campus for general student use. A campuswide network can be accessed from student residence rooms and from off campus. Internet access is available. *Library facilities:* McConnell Library. *Graduate expenses:* Tuition, state resident: full-time $2,564; part-time $167 per credit hour. Tuition, nonresident: full-time $6,314; part-time $323 per credit hour. Required fees: $1,440. *General application contact:* Dr. Gary D. Ellerman, Interim Dean, 540-831-5431.

Find an in-depth description at www.petersons.com/graduate.

Graduate College
Dr. Gary D. Ellerman, Interim Dean

College of Arts and Sciences
Dr. Ivan B. Liss, Dean
Programs in:
arts and sciences • MA, MS, Ed S
clinical psychology • MA
corporate and professional communication • MS
counseling psychology • MA
criminal justice • MA, MS
engineering geosciences • MS
English • MA, MS
general psychology • MA, MS
industrial-organizational psychology • MA
school psychology • Ed S

College of Business and Economics
Dr. William A. Dempsey, Dean
Programs in:
business administration • MBA
business and economics • MBA, MS

College of Education and Human Development
Dr. R. Paul Sale, Dean
Programs in:
counselor education • MS
curriculum and instruction • MS
education and human development • MS, MSW
education of the emotionally disturbed • MS
educational leadership • MS
educational media • MS
learning disabilities • MS
mentally retarded • MS
reading • MS

College of Visual and Performing Arts
Dr. Joseph P. Scartelli, Dean
Programs in:
art • MFA
art education • MS
music • MA
music education • MS
visual and performing arts • MA, MFA, MS

Waldron College of Health and Human Services
Dr. Stephen L. Heater, Dean
Programs in:
communication science and disorders • MA, MS
health and human services • MA, MS, MSN, MSW
nursing • MS, MSN
social work • MSW

■ REGENT UNIVERSITY
Virginia Beach, VA 23464-9800
http://www.regent.edu/

Independent, coed, graduate-only institution. *Graduate faculty:* 90 full-time (17 women), 97 part-time/adjunct (47 women). *Computer facilities:* 78 computers available on campus for general student use. A campuswide network can be accessed. Internet access, Electronic Reference Center—University Library are available. *Library facilities:* University Library plus 1 other. *Graduate expenses:* Tuition: full-time $15,450; part-time $515 per credit hour. Tuition and fees vary according to course load, degree level and program. *General application contact:* Alice Souter-Jones, Director, Central Enrollment Management, 800-373-5504.

Find an in-depth description at www.petersons.com/graduate.

Graduate School
Dr. John E. Mulford, Acting Dean

Center for Leadership Studies
Dr. Kathaleen Reid-Martinez, Dean
Programs in:
leadership studies • Certificate
organizational leadership • MA, PhD
strategic leadership • DSL

College of Communication and the Arts
Dr. William J. Brown, Dean
Programs in:
communication • MA, PhD
communication and the arts • MA, MFA, PhD
fine arts • MFA
journalism • MA

Robertson School of Government
Dr. Kathaleen Reid-Martinez, Dean
Programs in:
public administration • MA
public management • MA
public policy • MA

School of Business
Programs in:
business administration • MBA
management • MA

School of Divinity
Dr. Vinson Synan, Dean
Programs in:
biblical studies • MA
ministry • D Min
missiology • M Div, MA
practical theology • M Div, MA

School of Education
Dr. Alan A. Arroyo, Dean
Program in:
education • M Ed, Ed D, CAGS

School of Law
Jeffrey Brauch, Dean
Programs in:
international taxation • LL M, MIT
law • JD

School of Psychology and Counseling
Dr. Rosemarie Hughes, Dean
Programs in:
counseling • MA
counseling psychology • Psy D

■ SHENANDOAH UNIVERSITY
Winchester, VA 22601-5195
http://www.su.edu/

Independent-religious, coed, comprehensive institution. *Enrollment:* 537 full-time matriculated graduate/professional students (388 women), 502 part-time matriculated graduate/professional students (325 women). *Graduate faculty:* 97 full-time (45 women), 45 part-time/adjunct (23 women). *Computer facilities:* 170 computers available on campus for general student use. A campuswide network can be accessed from student residence rooms and from off campus. Internet access and online class registration are available. *Library facilities:* Alson H. Smith Jr. Library plus 1 other. *Graduate expenses:* Tuition: part-time $500 per credit hour. Tuition and fees vary according to campus/location, program and reciprocity agreements. *General application contact:* Michael Carpenter, Director of Admissions, 540-665-4581.

Byrd School of Business
Stan Harrison, Dean
Programs in:
business administration • MBA
health care management • Certificate
information systems and computer technology • Certificate
public management • Certificate

Division of Nursing
Dr. Sheila Sparks, Interim Director
Program in:
nursing • MSN

Division of Occupational Therapy
Dr. Gretchen Stone, Director
Program in:
occupational therapy • MS

Division of Physical Therapy
Dr. Steven H. Tepper, Director
Program in:
physical therapy • MPT

School of Arts and Sciences
Dr. Catherine Tisinger, Dean
Programs in:

Shenandoah University (continued)
administration and leadership • D Ed
advanced professional teaching English to speakers of other languages • Certificate
business education • Certificate
computer education • MSC
computer studies for educators • Certificate
education • MSE
elementary education • Certificate
middle school education • Certificate
professional studies • Certificate
professional teaching English to speakers of other languages • Certificate
secondary education • Certificate

School of Pharmacy
Dr. Alan McKay, Dean
Program in:
pharmacy and non-traditional pharmacy • Pharm D

Shenandoah Conservatory
Dr. Charlotte A. Collins, Dean
Programs in:
arts administration • MS
church music • MM, Certificate
composition • MM
conducting • MM
dance accompanying • MM
dance choreography and performance • MFA
music education • MME, DMA
music therapy • MMT
pedagogy • MM
performance • MM, DMA
piano accompanying • MM

■ UNIVERSITY OF RICHMOND

Richmond, University of Richmond, VA 23173

http://www.richmond.edu/

Independent, coed, comprehensive institution. *Enrollment:* 505 full-time matriculated graduate/professional students (249 women), 263 part-time matriculated graduate/professional students (111 women). *Graduate faculty:* 172 full-time (43 women), 72 part-time/adjunct (26 women). *Computer facilities:* 500 computers available on campus for general student use. A campuswide network can be accessed from student residence rooms and from off campus. *Library facilities:* Boatwright Memorial Library plus 4 others. *Graduate expenses:* Tuition: full-time $20,240; part-time $350 per hour. Tuition and fees vary according to course load. *General application contact:* Dr. Dona J. Hickey, Director of the Graduate School, 804-289-8417.

Find an in-depth description at www.petersons.com/graduate.

The E. Claiborne Robins School of Business
Dr. Karen Newman, Dean
Programs in:
business • MBA
business administration • MBA

Graduate School
Dr. Barbara J. Griffin, Director
Programs in:
biology • MS
English • MA
history • MA
liberal arts • MLA
psychology • MA

School of Law
Dr. John R. Pagan, Dean
Program in:
law • JD

■ UNIVERSITY OF VIRGINIA

Charlottesville, VA 22903

http://www.virginia.edu/

State-supported, coed, university. CGS member. *Enrollment:* 5,168 full-time matriculated graduate/professional students (2,398 women), 445 part-time matriculated graduate/professional students (256 women). *Graduate faculty:* 1,918 full-time (512 women), 181 part-time/adjunct (80 women). *Computer facilities:* 1,859 computers available on campus for general student use. A campuswide network can be accessed from student residence rooms and from off campus. Internet access and online class registration are available. *Library facilities:* Alderman Library plus 14 others. *Graduate expenses:* Tuition, state resident: full-time $3,909. Tuition, nonresident: full-time $16,295. Required fees: $1,114. *General application contact:* Dean of Appropriate School, 804-924-0311.

College and Graduate School of Arts and Sciences
Stephen E. Plog, Associate Dean for Academic Programs
Programs in:
anthropology • MA, PhD
art history • MA, PhD
arts and sciences • MA, MAT, MFA, MS, PhD
Asian and Middle Eastern languages and cultures • MA
astronomy • MA, PhD
biochemistry • PhD
bioethics • MA
biological and physical sciences • MS
biology • MA, MS, PhD
biology education • MAT
biophysics • PhD
biotechnology • PhD
cell and molecular biology • PhD
cell biology • PhD
cell biology/anatomy • PhD
chemistry • MA, MS, PhD
chemistry education • MAT
classical art and archaeology • MA, PhD
classics • MA, MAT, PhD
clinical investigation • MS
clinical psychology • PhD
creative writing • MFA
drama • MFA
economics • MA, PhD
English • MA, MAT, PhD
environmental sciences • MA, MS, PhD
epidemiology • MS
foreign affairs • MA, PhD
French • MA, MAT, PhD
Germanic languages and literatures • MA, MAT, PhD
government • MA, MAT, PhD
health care informatics • MS
health care resource management • MS
health services research and outcomes evaluation • MS
history • MA, MAT, PhD
immunology • PhD
Italian • MA
linguistics • MA
mathematics • MA, MS, PhD
microbiology • PhD
molecular genetics • PhD
molecular physiology and biological physics • PhD
music • MA, MAT
neuroscience • PhD
pharmacology • PhD
philosophy • MA, PhD
physics • MA, MAT, MS, PhD
physiology • PhD
psychology • MA, PhD
religious studies • MA, PhD
Slavic languages and literatures • MA, PhD
sociology • MA, PhD
Spanish • MA, MAT, PhD
statistics • MS, PhD
surgery • MS
teaching Spanish • MAT

Curry School of Education
David W. Breneman, Dean
Programs in:
administration and supervision • M Ed, Ed D, Ed S

communication disorders • M Ed
counselor education • M Ed, Ed D, Ed S
curriculum and instruction • M Ed, Ed D, Ed S
education • M Ed, MT, Ed D, PhD, Ed S
educational policy studies • M Ed, Ed D
educational psychology • M Ed, Ed D, Ed S
health and physical education • M Ed, Ed D
higher education • Ed D, Ed S
special education • M Ed, Ed D, Ed S

Darden Graduate School of Business Administration
Edward A. Snyder, Dean
Program in:
business administration • MBA, DBA, PhD

McIntire School of Commerce
Robert S. Kemp, Director of Graduate Studies
Programs in:
accounting • MS
management information systems • MS

School of Architecture
Karen Van Lengen, Dean
Programs in:
architectural history • M Arch H, PhD
architecture • M Arch, M Arch H, M Land Arch, MP, PhD
landscape architecture • M Land Arch
urban and environmental planning • MP

School of Engineering and Applied Science
Richard W. Miksad, Dean
Programs in:
applied mechanics • MAM, MS
biomedical engineering • ME, MS, PhD
chemical engineering • ME, MS, PhD
computer science • MCS, MS, PhD
electrical and computer engineering • ME, MS, PhD
engineering and applied science • MAM, MCS, ME, MEP, MMSE, MS, PhD
engineering physics • MEP, MS, PhD
environmental engineering • ME, MS, PhD
materials science • MMSE, MS, PhD
mechanical and aerospace engineering • ME, MS, PhD
nuclear engineering • ME, MS, PhD
structural mechanics • ME, MS, PhD
systems engineering • ME, MS, PhD
transportation engineering and management • ME, MS, PhD
water resources • ME, MS, PhD

School of Law
John C. Jeffries, Dean
Program in:
law • JD, LL M, SJD

School of Medicine
Dr. Robert M. Carey, Dean
Program in:
medicine • MD

School of Nursing
B. Jeanette Lancaster, Dean
Program in:
nursing • MSN, PhD

■ VIRGINIA COMMONWEALTH UNIVERSITY
Richmond, VA 23284-9005
http://www.vcu.edu/

State-supported, coed, university. CGS member. *Enrollment:* 3,745 full-time matriculated graduate/professional students (2,327 women), 2,110 part-time matriculated graduate/professional students (1,356 women). *Computer facilities:* 900 computers available on campus for general student use. A campuswide network can be accessed from student residence rooms and from off campus. *Library facilities:* James Branch Cabell and Tompkins-McCaw Library. *Graduate expenses:* Tuition, state resident: full-time $4,112; part-time $228 per credit hour. Tuition, nonresident: full-time $12,185; part-time $677 per credit hour. Required fees: $1,142; $43 per credit hour. *General application contact:* Dr. Sherry T. Sandkam, Associate Dean, 804-828-6916.

Find an in-depth description at www.petersons.com/graduate.

Medical College of Virginia-Professional Programs
Dr. Hermes A. Kontos, Vice President for Health Sciences and Dean, School of Medicine
Program in:
medicine • DDS, MD, Pharm D, MPH, MS, PhD, CBHS

School of Dentistry
Dr. Ronald J. Hunt, Dean
Program in:
dentistry • DDS

School of Medicine
Dr. Hermes A. Kontos, Vice President for Health Sciences and Dean, School of Medicine
Program in:
medicine • MD, MPH, MS, PhD, CBHS

School of Pharmacy
Dr. Victor A. Yanchick, Dean
Program in:
pharmacy • Pharm D, MS, PhD

School of Graduate Studies
Dr. Jack L. Haar, Dean
Program in:
interdisciplinary studies • MIS

Center for Environmental Studies
Greg Garman, Director
Programs in:
environmental communication • MIS
environmental health • MIS
environmental policy • MIS
environmental sciences • MIS

Center for Public Policy
Dr. Robert D. Holsworth, Director
Program in:
public policy and administration • PhD

College of Humanities and Sciences
Dr. Stephen D. Gottfredson, Dean
Programs in:
account management • MS
account planning • MS
applied mathematics • MS
applied physics • MS
applied social research • CASR
art direction • MS
biology • MS
chemistry • MS, PhD
clinical psychology • PhD
computer science • MS
copywriting • MS
counseling psychology • PhD
creative writing • MFA
criminal justice • MS, CCJA
forensic science • MS
general psychology • PhD
history • MA
humanities and sciences • MA, MFA, MPA, MS, MURP, PhD, CASR, CCJA, CPM, CURP, Certificate
literature • MA
mass communications • MS
mathematics • MS
operations research • MS
physics • MS
political science and public administration • MPA
public management • CPM
sociology • MS
statistics • MS, Certificate
urban planning • MURP
urban revitalization • CURP
writing and rhetoric • MA

Virginia Commonwealth University (continued)

School of Allied Health Professions
Dr. Cecil B. Drain, Interim Dean
Programs in:
- advanced physical therapy • MS
- aging studies • CAS
- allied health professions • MHA, MS, MSHA, MSNA, MSOT, PhD, CAS, CPC
- anatomy and physical therapy • PhD
- clinical laboratory sciences • MS
- entry-level physical therapy • MS
- executive health administration • MSHA
- gerontology • MS
- health administration • MHA
- health services organization and research • PhD
- nurse anesthesia • MSNA
- occupational therapy • MS, MSOT
- patient counseling • MS, CPC
- physiology and physical therapy • PhD
- rehabilitation and counseling • MS
- rehabilitation counseling • CPC

School of Business
Dr. Michael Sesnowitz, Dean
Programs in:
- accountancy • MS, PhD
- accounting • M Acc, PhD
- business administration • MBA, PhD
- business administration and management • MBA, PhD
- decision sciences • MS
- economics • MA, MS
- finance, insurance, and real estate • MS
- human resources management and industrial relations • MS
- information systems • MS, PhD
- marketing and business law • MS
- real estate and urban land development • MS, Certificate
- tax • MS
- taxation • M Tax

School of Education
Dr. John S. Oehler, Dean
Programs in:
- administration and supervision • M Ed
- adult education and human resource development • M Ed
- counselor education • M Ed
- curriculum and instruction • M Ed
- early childhood • M Ed
- early education • MT
- education • M Ed, MS, MT, PhD, Certificate
- emotionally disturbed • M Ed, MT
- learning disabilities • M Ed
- mentally retarded • M Ed, MT
- middle education • MT
- physical education • MS
- reading • M Ed
- recreation, parks and tourism • MS
- secondary education • MT, Certificate
- severely/profoundly handicapped • M Ed
- special education • MT

School of Engineering
Dr. Robert J. Mattauch, Dean
Programs in:
- biomedical engineering • MS, PhD
- engineering • MS, PhD

School of Medicine Graduate Programs
Dr. Hermes A. Kontos, Vice President for Health Sciences and Dean, School of Medicine
Programs in:
- anatomy • MS, PhD, CBHS
- anatomy and physical therapy • PhD
- biochemistry • PhD
- biochemistry and molecular biophysics • MS, CBHS
- biostatistics • MS, PhD
- genetic counseling • MS
- human genetics • PhD, CBHS
- medicine • MPH, MS, PhD, CBHS
- microbiology • PhD
- microbiology and immunology • MS, CBHS
- molecular biology and genetics • PhD
- neurosciences • PhD
- pathology • MS, PhD
- pharmacology • PhD, CBHS
- pharmacology and toxicology • MS
- physiology • MS, PhD, CBHS
- preventive medicine • MPH

School of Nursing
Dr. Nancy F. Langston, Dean
Programs in:
- adult health nursing • MS
- child health nursing • MS
- family health nursing • MS
- health system • PhD
- immuno competence • PhD
- nurse practitioner • Certificate
- nursing administration • MS
- psychiatric-mental health nursing • MS
- risk and resilience • PhD
- women's health nursing • MS

School of Pharmacy Graduate Programs
Dr. Victor A. Yanchick, Dean
Programs in:
- pharmacy • Pharm D, MS, PhD
- pharmacy and pharmaceutics • Pharm D, MS, PhD

School of Social Work
Dr. Frank R. Baskind, Dean
Program in:
- social work • MSW, PhD

School of the Arts
Dr. Richard Toscan, Dean
Programs in:
- acting • MFA
- art education • MAE
- art history • MA, PhD
- arts • MA, MAE, MFA, MM, PhD
- ceramics • MFA
- composition • MM
- costume design • MFA
- directing • MFA
- education • MM
- fibers • MFA
- furniture design • MFA
- glassworking • MFA
- interior environment • MFA
- jewelry/metalworking • MFA
- painting • MFA
- pedagogy • MFA
- performance • MM
- photography—film • MFA
- printmaking • MFA
- scene design/technical theater • MFA
- sculpture • MFA
- visual communication • MFA

■ VIRGINIA POLYTECHNIC INSTITUTE AND STATE UNIVERSITY

Blacksburg, VA 24061
http://www.vt.edu/

State-supported, coed, university. CGS member. *Enrollment:* 3,875 full-time matriculated graduate/professional students (1,466 women), 2,272 part-time matriculated graduate/professional students (1,207 women). *Graduate faculty:* 1,514 full-time. *Computer facilities:* A campuswide network can be accessed from student residence rooms and from off campus. Internet access and online class registration are available. *Library facilities:* Newman Library plus 4 others. *Graduate expenses:* Tuition, state resident: full-time $4,221; part-time $235 per hour. Tuition, nonresident: full-time $7,101; part-time $395 per hour. Required fees: $848. Tuition and fees vary according to campus/location. *General application contact:* Graduate School Receptionist, 540-231-9563.

Graduate School
Dr. Joseph Merola, Acting Dean

College of Agriculture and Life Sciences
Programs in:
- agricultural and applied economics • MS, PhD
- agriculture and life sciences • MS, PhD

animal science • MS, PhD
Animal Science, Dairy • PhD
biochemistry • MS, PhD
cell and molecular biology • PhD
crop and soil environmental sciences • MS, PhD
Dairy Science • MS
entomology • MS, PhD
food science and technology • MS, PhD
genetics • PhD
horticulture • MS, PhD
plant pathology • MS, PhD
plant physiology • MS, PhD
poultry science • MS, PhD

College of Architecture and Urban Studies
Programs in:
architecture • M Arch, MS
architecture and urban studies • M Arch, MLA, MPA, MPIA, MS, MURP, PhD, CAGS
environmental design and planning • PhD
landscape architecture • MLA
public administration and policy • MPA, PhD, CAGS
public and international affairs • MPIA
urban and regional planning • MURP

College of Arts and Sciences
Programs in:
applied mathematics • MS, PhD
applied physics • MS
arts administration • MFA
arts and sciences • MA, MFA, MIS, MS, PhD
bio-behavioral sciences • PhD
botany • MS, PhD
botany and plant sciences • MS, PhD
chemistry • MS, PhD
clinical psychology • PhD
computer science • MS, PhD
costume design • MFA
developmental psychology • PhD
ecology and evolutionary biology • MS, PhD
economics • MA, PhD
English • MA
genetics and developmental biology • MS, PhD
geography • MS
geological sciences • MS, PhD
geophysics • MS, PhD
history • MA
industrial/organizational psychology • PhD
information systems • MIS
lighting design • MFA
mathematical physics • MS, PhD
microbiology • MS, PhD
philosophy • MA
physics • MS, PhD
political science • MA
property management • MFA
psychology • MS
pure mathematics • MS, PhD
scenic design • MFA
science and technology studies • MS, PhD
sociology • MS, PhD
stage management • MFA
statistics • MS, PhD
technical theatre • MFA
zoology • MS, PhD

College of Engineering
Programs in:
aerospace engineering • M Eng, MS, PhD
bio-process engineering • M Eng, MS, PhD
chemical engineering • MS, PhD
civil engineering • M Eng, MS, PhD
electrical and computer engineering • MS, PhD
engineering • M Eng, MEA, MS, PhD
engineering administration • MEA
engineering mechanics • M Eng, MS, PhD
environmental engineering • MS
environmental sciences and engineering • MS, PhD
food engineering • M Eng, MS, PhD
industrial engineering • M Eng, MS, PhD
land and water engineering • M Eng, MS, PhD
materials science and engineering • M Eng, MS, PhD
mechanical engineering • M Eng, MS, PhD
mining and minerals engineering • M Eng, MS, PhD
nonpoint source pollution control • M Eng, MS, PhD
ocean engineering • MS
operations research • M Eng, MS, PhD
systems engineering • M Eng, MS
watershed engineering • M Eng, MS, PhD
wood engineering • M Eng, MS, PhD

College of Human Resources and Education
Programs in:
administration and supervision of special education • Ed D, PhD, CAGS
adult and continuing education • MA Ed, MS Ed, Ed D, PhD, CAGS
adult development and aging • MS, PhD
adult learning and human resource development • MS, PhD
apparel business and economics • MS, PhD
apparel product design and analysis • MS, PhD
apparel quality analysis • MS, PhD
child development • MS, PhD
clinical exercise physiology • MS, PhD
community and international nutrition • MS, PhD
consumer studies • MS, PhD
curriculum and instruction • MA Ed, Ed D, PhD, Ed S
educational counseling • MA Ed, Ed D, PhD, CAGS
educational leadership • MA Ed, Ed D, PhD, CAGS
educational research and evaluation • PhD
family financial management • MS, PhD
family studies • MS, PhD
foods • MS, PhD
health and physical education • MS Ed
hospitality and tourism management • MS, PhD
household equipment • MS, PhD
housing • MS, PhD
human resources and education • MA Ed, MS, MS Ed, Ed D, PhD, CAGS, Ed S
interior design • MS, PhD
marriage and family therapy • MS, PhD
muscle physiology and biochemistry • MS, PhD
nutrition • MS, PhD
nutrition in sports and chronic disease • MS, PhD
resource management • MS, PhD
vocational-technical education • MS Ed, Ed D, PhD

College of Natural Resources
Programs in:
aquaculture • MS, PhD
conservation biology • MS, PhD
fisheries science • MS, PhD
forest biology • MF, MS, PhD
forest biometry • MF, MS, PhD
forest management/economics • MF, MS, PhD
forest products marketing • MF, MS, PhD
industrial forestry operations • MF, MS, PhD
natural resources • MF, MS, PhD
outdoor recreation • MF, MS, PhD
wildlife science • MS, PhD
wood science and engineering • MF, MS, PhD

Pamplin College of Business
Dr. Richard E. Sorensen, Dean
Programs in:
accounting and information systems • M Acct, PhD
business • M Acct, MBA, MS, PhD
business administration • MBA

Virginia Polytechnic Institute and State University (continued)

- business administration/finance • MS, PhD
- business administration/management • PhD
- business administration/management science • PhD
- business administration/marketing • MS, PhD

Virginia-Maryland Regional College of Veterinary Medicine
Programs in:

- veterinary medical sciences • MS, PhD
- veterinary medicine • DVM, MS, PhD

■ VIRGINIA STATE UNIVERSITY

Petersburg, VA 23806-0001
http://www.vsu.edu/

State-supported, coed, comprehensive institution. *Enrollment:* 52 full-time matriculated graduate/professional students (35 women), 828 part-time matriculated graduate/professional students (592 women). *Graduate faculty:* 44 full-time (11 women), 5 part-time/adjunct (0 women). *Computer facilities:* 491 computers available on campus for general student use. A campuswide network can be accessed. Internet access is available. *Library facilities:* Johnston Memorial Library. *Graduate expenses:* Tuition, state resident: full-time $2,352; part-time $108 per credit hour. Tuition, nonresident: full-time $8,294; part-time $367 per credit hour. Required fees: $30 per credit hour. *General application contact:* Dr. Wayne F. Virag, Dean, Graduate Studies, Research, and Outreach, 804-524-5985.

School of Graduate Studies, Research, and Outreach
Dr. Wayne F. Virag, Dean, Graduate Studies, Research, and Outreach
Program in:

- interdisciplinary studies • MIS

School of Agriculture, Science and Technology
Dr. Lorenza W. Lyons, Dean
Programs in:

- agriculture, science and technology • M Ed, MS, CAGS
- biology • MS
- mathematics • MS
- mathematics education • M Ed
- physics • MS
- psychology • MS
- vocational technical education • M Ed, MS, CAGS

School of Business
Dr. Sadie Gregory, Dean
Programs in:

- business • MA
- economics and finance • MA

School of Liberal Arts and Education
Dr. Leon Bey, Dean
Programs in:

- education • M Ed, MS
- educational administration and supervision • M Ed, MS
- English • MA
- guidance • M Ed, MS
- history • MA
- liberal arts and education • M Ed, MA, MS

Washington

■ ANTIOCH UNIVERSITY SEATTLE

Seattle, WA 98121-1814
http://www.antiochsea.edu/

Independent, coed, upper-level institution. *Enrollment:* 419 full-time matriculated graduate/professional students (304 women), 242 part-time matriculated graduate/professional students (178 women). *Graduate faculty:* 32 full-time, 39 part-time/adjunct. *Computer facilities:* 8 computers available on campus for general student use. *Library facilities:* Antioch Seattle Library. *Graduate expenses:* Tuition: full-time $3,375. Required fees: $90. Tuition and fees vary according to program. *General application contact:* Dianne Larsen, Director of Admissions and Enrollment Services, 206-441-5352 Ext. 5200.

Find an in-depth description at www.petersons.com/graduate.

Graduate Programs
Toni Murdock, President
Programs in:

- education • MA
- environment and community • MS
- individualized design • MA
- management • MS
- organizational systems renewal • MA
- psychology • MA

■ CENTRAL WASHINGTON UNIVERSITY

Ellensburg, WA 98926-7463
http://www.cwu.edu/

State-supported, coed, comprehensive institution. CGS member. *Enrollment:* 218 full-time matriculated graduate/professional students (131 women), 159 part-time matriculated graduate/professional students (96 women). *Graduate faculty:* 330 full-time (97 women). *Computer facilities:* 659 computers available on campus for general student use. A campuswide network can be accessed from student residence rooms and from off campus. Internet access is available. *Library facilities:* Central Washington University Library. *Graduate expenses:* Tuition, state resident: full-time $4,548. Tuition, nonresident: full-time $13,848. Required fees: $324. Tuition and fees vary according to course load. *General application contact:* Barbara Sisko, Office Assistant, Graduate Studies and Research, 509-963-3103.

Find an in-depth description at www.petersons.com/graduate.

Graduate Studies and Research
Dr. Richard S. Mack, Interim Associate Vice President for Graduate Studies, Research and Faculty
Program in:

- individual studies • M Ed, MA, MS

College of Arts and Humanities
Dr. Liahna Armstrong, Dean
Programs in:

- art • MA, MFA
- arts and humanities • MA, MFA, MM
- English • MA
- history • MA
- music • MM
- teaching English as a foreign language • MA
- teaching English as a second language • MA
- theatre production • MA

College of Education and Professional Studies
Dr. Rebecca Bowers, Dean
Programs in:

- apparel design • MS
- business and distributive education • M Ed
- curriculum and instruction • M Ed
- education and professional studies • M Ed, MS
- educational administration • M Ed
- elementary education • M Ed

engineering technology • MS
family and consumer sciences education • MS
family studies • MS
health, physical education and recreation • MS
nutrition • MS
reading education • M Ed
special education • M Ed

College of the Sciences
Dr. Barney Erickson, Interim Dean
Programs in:
biology • MS
chemistry • MS
counseling psychology • MS
experimental psychology • MS
geological sciences • MS
guidance and counseling • M Ed
mathematics • MAT
organizational development • MS
resource management • MS
school psychology • M Ed
sciences • M Ed, MAT, MS

■ CITY UNIVERSITY
Bellevue, WA 98005
http://www.cityu.edu/

Independent, coed, upper-level institution. *Enrollment:* 792 full-time matriculated graduate/professional students (480 women), 4,637 part-time matriculated graduate/professional students (2,298 women). *Graduate faculty:* 52 full-time, 1,043 part-time/adjunct. *Computer facilities:* 145 computers available on campus for general student use. A campuswide network can be accessed from off campus. Internet access is available. *Library facilities:* City University Library. *Graduate expenses:* Tuition: full-time $7,416; part-time $309 per credit. *General application contact:* 800-426-5596.

Find an in-depth description at www.petersons.com/graduate.

Graduate Division
Arthur C. Rogers, Executive Vice President and Academic Dean

Gordon Albright School of Education
Dr. Margaret M. Davis, Dean
Programs in:
completion-California • MIT
curriculum and instruction • M Ed
education technology • M Ed
educational leadership and principal certification • M Ed, Certificate
guidance and counseling • M Ed
reading and literacy • M Ed
teacher certification • Certificate
teacher credentialing-California • Certificate

School of Business and Management
Dr. Keith L. Smith, Dean
Programs in:
computer systems—individual • MS
C++ programming • Certificate
computer systems—C++ programming • MS
computer systems—web programming language • MS
e-commerce • MBA
executive accounting • MBA
financial management • MBA, Certificate
general management • MBA
human resource management • MBA
human resources management • Certificate
individualized study • MBA
information systems • MBA, Certificate
management • MA, Certificate
managerial leadership • MBA, Certificate
marketing • MBA, Certificate
personal financial planning • MBA, Certificate
project management • MBA, MS, Certificate
public administration • MPA, Certificate
web development • MS, Certificate
web programming language • Certificate

School of Human Services and Applied Behavioral Sciences
Deam
Programs in:
counseling psychology • MA
executive leadership • MA

■ EASTERN WASHINGTON UNIVERSITY
Cheney, WA 99004-2431
http://www.ewu.edu/

State-supported, coed, comprehensive institution. CGS member. *Enrollment:* 589 full-time matriculated graduate/professional students (410 women), 440 part-time matriculated graduate/professional students (278 women). *Graduate faculty:* 347. *Computer facilities:* 125 computers available on campus for general student use. A campuswide network can be accessed from student residence rooms and from off campus. Internet access, e-mail are available. *Library facilities:* John F. Kennedy Library plus 2 others. *Graduate expenses:* Tuition, state resident: part-time $144 per credit. Tuition, nonresident: part-time $428 per credit. Required fees: $4,485; $1,495 per quarter. *General application contact:* Dr. Larry Briggs, Director, Graduate Studies Office, 509-359-6297.

Find an in-depth description at www.petersons.com/graduate.

Graduate School
Dr. Ronald Dalla, Dean
Program in:
interdisciplinary studies • MA, MS

College of Business Administration
Dr. Dolores Martin, Dean
Programs in:
business administration • MBA, MPA, MURP
public administration • MPA
urban and regional planning • MURP

College of Education and Human Development
Dr. Foritz Erikson, Adviser
Programs in:
adult education • M Ed
college instruction • MA, MS
college instruction in physical education • MS
counseling psychology • MS
curriculum and instruction • M Ed
developing psychology • MS
early childhood education • M Ed
education and human development • M Ed, MA, MS
educational leadership (school principal) • M Ed
elementary teaching • M Ed
foundations of education • M Ed
literacy specialist • M Ed
physical education • MS
school counseling • MS
school library media administration • M Ed
school psychology • MS
science education • M Ed
social science education • M Ed
special education • M Ed
supervising • clinic teaching • M Ed

College of Letters and Social Sciences
Dr. Philip Castille, Dean
Programs in:
college instruction • MA
communications • MS
composition • MA
creative writing • MFA
English • MA
French education • M Ed
history • MA
instrumental/vocal performance • MA
letters and social sciences • M Ed, MA, MFA, MS, MSW
music education • MA
music history and literature • MA

Eastern Washington University (continued)
psychology • MS
school psychology • MS
social work and human services • MSW

College of Science, Mathematics and Technology
Dr. Ray Soltero, Dean
Programs in:
biology • MS
communication disorders • MS
computer science • M Ed, MS
geology • MS
mathematics • M Ed, MS
physical therapy • MPT
science, mathematics and technology • M Ed, MA, MPT, MS
technology • MA, MS

Intercollegiate Center for Nursing Education
Dr. Dorothy Detlor, Dean
Program in:
nursing education • MN

■ GONZAGA UNIVERSITY
Spokane, WA 99258
http://www.gonzaga.edu/

Independent-religious, coed, comprehensive institution. *Enrollment:* 1,146 full-time matriculated graduate/professional students (751 women). *Graduate faculty:* 154 full-time (34 women), 45 part-time/adjunct (15 women). *Computer facilities:* 340 computers available on campus for general student use. A campuswide network can be accessed from student residence rooms and from off campus. Internet access and online class registration are available. *Library facilities:* Ralph E. and Helen Higgins Foley Center plus 1 other. *Graduate expenses:* Tuition: full-time $8,370; part-time $465 per credit. Full-time tuition and fees vary according to course load. Part-time tuition and fees vary according to program. *General application contact:* Dr. Leonard Doohan, Dean of the Graduate School, 509-328-4220 Ext. 3546.

Graduate School
Dr. Leonard Doohan, Dean
Program in:
teaching english as a second language • MATESL

College of Arts and Sciences
Dean
Programs in:
arts and sciences • M Div, MA
pastoral ministry • MA
philosophy • MA
religious studies • M Div, MA
spirituality • MA

School of Business Administration
Dr. Clarence H. Barnes, Dean
Programs in:
accounting • M Acc
business administration • M Acc, MBA

School of Education
Dr. Corrine McGuigan, Dean
Programs in:
administration and curriculum • MAA
anesthesiology education • M Anesth Ed
counseling psychology • MAC, MAP
educational administration • MA Ed Ad
educational leadership • PhD
initial teaching • MIT
special education • MES
sports and athletic administration • MASPAA
teaching • MTA

School of Professional Studies
Dr. Richard Wolfe, Dean
Programs in:
nursing • MSN
organizational leadership • MOL
professional studies • MOL, MSN

School of Law
John E. Clute, Dean
Program in:
law • JD

■ HERITAGE COLLEGE
Toppenish, WA 98948-9599
http://www.heritage.edu/

Independent, coed, comprehensive institution. *Computer facilities:* 130 computers available on campus for general student use. A campuswide network can be accessed from student residence rooms and from off campus. Internet access is available. *Library facilities:* Library and Resource Center. *General application contact:* Dean, Education Division, 509-865-2244 Ext. 1306.

Graduate Programs in Education
Programs in:
bilingual education/ESL • M Ed
community and human resource development • M Ed
counseling • M Ed
early childhood education • M Ed
educational administration • M Ed
professional development • M Ed
special education • M Ed

■ PACIFIC LUTHERAN UNIVERSITY
Tacoma, WA 98447
http://www.plu.edu/

Independent-religious, coed, comprehensive institution. *Enrollment:* 136 full-time matriculated graduate/professional students (75 women), 84 part-time matriculated graduate/professional students (51 women). *Graduate faculty:* 38 full-time (18 women), 4 part-time/adjunct (2 women). *Computer facilities:* 200 computers available on campus for general student use. A campuswide network can be accessed from student residence rooms and from off campus. Internet access and online class registration are available. *Library facilities:* Mortvedt Library. *Graduate expenses:* Tuition: full-time $12,600; part-time $525 per credit. *General application contact:* Linda DuBay, Office of Admissions, 253-535-7151.

Find an in-depth description at www.petersons.com/graduate.

Division of Graduate Studies
Dr. Paul Menzel, Provost and Dean

Division of Social Sciences
Dr. David Huelsbeck, Chair
Programs in:
marriage and family therapy • MA
social sciences • MA

School of Business Administration and Management
Dr. Donald Bell, Dean
Program in:
business administration • MBA

School of Education
Dr. Lynn Beck, Dean
Programs in:
classroom language and literacy focus • MA
early childhood • MA
education • MA
education administration • MA
elementary education • MA
kindergarten through twelfth grade • MA
language and literacy • MA
school library media • MA
secondary education • MA
teaching • MA

School of Nursing
Dr. Terry Miller, Dean
Programs in:
client systems management • MSN
family nurse practitioner • MSN
gerontology • MSN

health care systems management • MSN
nursing • MSN
women's health care • MSN

■ SAINT MARTIN'S COLLEGE

Lacey, WA 98503-7500
http://www.stmartin.edu/

Independent-religious, coed, comprehensive institution. *Computer facilities:* 110 computers available on campus for general student use. A campuswide network can be accessed from student residence rooms and from off campus. Internet access is available. *Library facilities:* Saint Martin's College Library. *General application contact:* 360-438-4311.

Graduate Programs
Programs in:
business administration • MBA
classroom leadership • M Ed
computers in education • M Ed
counseling and community psychology • MAC
counseling and guidance • M Ed
economics and business administration • MBA
engineering management • M Eng Mgt
reading • M Ed
special education • M Ed
teaching • MIT

■ SEATTLE PACIFIC UNIVERSITY

Seattle, WA 98119-1997
http://www.spu.edu/

Independent-religious, coed, comprehensive institution. *Enrollment:* 157 full-time matriculated graduate/professional students (111 women), 500 part-time matriculated graduate/professional students (327 women). *Graduate faculty:* 51 full-time (10 women), 54 part-time/adjunct (25 women). *Computer facilities:* 150 computers available on campus for general student use. A campuswide network can be accessed from student residence rooms and from off campus. Internet access and online class registration are available. *Library facilities:* Seattle Pacific University Library. *Graduate expenses:* Tuition: part-time $282 per credit. Tuition and fees vary according to program. *General application contact:* Dr. Tom Trzyna, Dean of Graduate Studies, 206-281-2125.

Graduate School
Dr. Tom Trzyna, Associate Provost
Programs in:
clinical psychology • PhD
marriage and family therapy • MS

College of Arts and Sciences
Dr. Joyce Erickson, Dean
Programs in:
arts and sciences • MA, MS
physical education • MS
teaching English as a second language • MA

School of Business and Economics
Gary Karns, Associate Dean
Programs in:
business and economics • MBA
information systems management • MS

School of Education
Dr. Mark Pitts, Dean
Programs in:
education • M Ed, MAT, Ed D, Ed S
educational leadership • M Ed
reading/language arts education • M Ed
school counseling • M Ed
school psychology • Ed S
secondary teaching • MAT

School of Health Sciences
Dr. Lucille Kelley, Dean
Programs in:
leadership in advanced nursing practice • MSN
nurse practitioner • Certificate

School of Psychology, Family and Community
Dr. Nathan Brown, Chair
Programs in:
clinical psychology • PhD
marriage and family therapy • MS

■ SEATTLE UNIVERSITY

Seattle, WA 98122
http://www.seattleu.edu/

Independent-religious, coed, comprehensive institution. *Enrollment:* 351 full-time matriculated graduate/professional students (222 women), 1,261 part-time matriculated graduate/professional students (725 women). *Graduate faculty:* 119 full-time (59 women), 58 part-time/adjunct (34 women). *Computer facilities:* 401 computers available on campus for general student use. A campuswide network can be accessed from student residence rooms and from off campus. *Library facilities:* Lemieux Library plus 1 other. *Graduate expenses:* Tuition: full-time $10,233; part-time $379 per credit hour. Tuition and fees vary according to course load, degree level and program. *General application contact:* Janet Shandley, Associate Dean of Graduate Admissions, 206-296-5900.

Find an in-depth description at www.petersons.com/graduate.

Albers School of Business and Economics
Dr. Joseph Phillips, Dean
Programs in:
business administration • MBA, Certificate
business and economics • MBA, MIB, MPAC, MSF, Certificate
finance • MSF, Certificate
international business • MIB, Certificate
professional accounting • MPAC

College of Arts and Sciences
Dr. Wallace Loh, Dean
Programs in:
arts and sciences • MA Psych, MNPL, MPA
existential and phenomenological therapeutic psychology • MA Psych

Institute of Public Service
Dr. Russell Lidman, Director
Programs in:
public administration • MPA
public service • MNPL, MPA
social enterprise management and not-for-profit leadership • MNPL

School of Education
Dr. Sue Schmitt, Dean
Programs in:
adult education and training • M Ed, MA, Certificate
counseling • MA
curriculum and instruction • M Ed, MA, Certificate
education • M Ed, MA, MIT, Ed D, Certificate, Ed S
educational administration • M Ed, MA, Certificate, Ed S
educational diagnostics/school psychology • Ed S
educational leadership • Ed D
student development administration • M Ed, MA
teacher education • MIT
teaching English to speakers of other languages • M Ed, MA, Certificate

School of Law
Rudolph Hasl, Dean
Program in:
law • JD

School of Nursing
Dr. Mary Walker, Dean
Program in:
nursing • MSN, Certificate

Seattle University (continued)

School of Science and Engineering
Dr. George Simmons, Dean
Programs in:
science and engineering • MSE
software engineering • MSE

School of Theology and Ministry
Dr. Patrick Howell, SJ, Dean
Programs in:
divinity • M Div
pastoral studies • MAPS
theology and ministry • M Div, MAPS, MATS, Certificate
transforming spirituality • MATS, Certificate

■ UNIVERSITY OF WASHINGTON
Seattle, WA 98195
http://www.washington.edu/

State-supported, coed, university. CGS member. *Enrollment:* 8,087 full-time matriculated graduate/professional students (4,164 women), 2,481 part-time matriculated graduate/professional students (1,290 women). *Graduate faculty:* 8,078 full-time (4,164 women), 2,481 part-time/adjunct (1,290 women). *Computer facilities:* 285 computers available on campus for general student use. A campuswide network can be accessed from student residence rooms and from off campus. *Library facilities:* Suzzallo/Allen Library plus 21 others. *Graduate expenses:* Tuition, state resident: full-time $5,352; part-time $510 per quarter. Tuition, nonresident: full-time $13,890; part-time $323 per quarter. Required fees: $393; $36 per quarter. Tuition and fees vary according to course load and program. *General application contact:* Information Contact, 206-543-2100.

Graduate School
Marsha L. Landolt, Dean and Vice Provost
Programs in:
biology for teachers • MS
education • M Ed
global trade, transportation, and logistics • Certificate
K-8 education • Certificate
museology • MA
Near and Middle Eastern studies • PhD
preservation planning and design • Certificate
principalship • Certificate
quantitative ecology and resource management • MS, PhD
school administration • Certificate
urban design • Certificate

Business School
Program in:
business • MBA, MP Acc, PhD

College of Architecture and Urban Planning
Programs in:
architecture • M Arch
architecture and urban planning • M Arch, MLA, MS, MSCM, MUP, PhD, Certificate
construction management • MS, MSCM
historic preservation • Certificate
landscape architecture • MLA
lighting • Certificate
urban design • Certificate
urban design and planning • PhD
urban planning • MUP

College of Arts and Sciences
David C. Hodge, Dean
Programs in:
acting • MFA
anthropology • MA, PhD
applied mathematics • MS, PhD
art • MFA
art and design • MFA
art history • MA, PhD
arts and sciences • M Mus, MA, MAIS, MAT, MC, MFA, MM, MS, DMA, PhD
astronomy • MS, PhD
atmospheric sciences • MS, PhD
botany • MS, PhD
Central Asian studies • MAIS
chemistry • MS, PhD
China studies • MAIS
Chinese language and literature • MA, PhD
classics • MA, PhD
classics and philosophy • PhD
communication theory • PhD
communications • MA, MC, PhD
comparative literature • MA, PhD
comparative religion • MAIS
costume design • MFA
dance • MFA
directing • MFA
East European studies • MAIS
economics • MA, PhD
English • MA, MAT, MFA, PhD
English as a second language • MAT
French • MA, PhD
French and Italian studies • MA, PhD
genetics • PhD
geography • MA, PhD
geology • MS, PhD
geophysics • MS, PhD
German language and literature • MA
German literature and culture • PhD
Hispanic literacy and cultural studies • MA
history • PhD
international studies • MAIS
Italian • MA
Japan studies • MAIS
Japanese language and literature • MA, PhD
Korea studies • MAIS
Korean language and literature • MA, PhD
lighting design • MFA
linguistics • MA, PhD
mathematics • MA, MS, PhD
Middle Eastern studies • MAIS
music • M Mus, MA, MM, DMA, PhD
music education • MA, PhD
Near Eastern languages and civilization • MA
philosophy • MA, PhD
physics • MS, PhD
political science • MA, PhD
psychology • PhD
Romance languages and literature • PhD
Romance linguistics • MA, PhD
Russian literature • MA, PhD
Russian studies • MAIS
Russian, East European and Central Asian studies • MAIS
Scandinavian studies • MA, PhD
scene design • MFA
Slavic linguistics • MA, PhD
sociology • MA, PhD
South Asian language and literature • MA, PhD
South Asian studies • MAIS
Spanish and Portuguese • MA
speech and hearing sciences • MS, PhD
speech communication • MA, PhD
statistics • MS, PhD
theory and criticism • PhD
women studies • MA, PhD
zoology • PhD

College of Education
Dr. Patricia Wasley, Dean
Programs in:
curriculum and instruction • M Ed, Ed D, PhD
early childhood education • M Ed, Ed D, PhD
educational leadership and policy studies • M Ed, Ed D, PhD
educational psychology • M Ed, PhD
elementary special education • M Ed, Ed D, PhD
emotional and behavioral disabilities • M Ed
general special education • M Ed, Ed D, PhD
human development and cognition • M Ed, PhD
measurement and research • M Ed, PhD
school counseling • M Ed, PhD
school psychology • M Ed, PhD
severe disabilities • M Ed, Ed D, PhD
special education • M Ed, Ed D, PhD
teacher education • MIT

College of Engineering
Dr. Denice D. Denton, Dean
Programs in:
- aeronautics and astronautics • MAE, MSAA, PhD
- bioengineering • MS, MSE, PhD
- chemical engineering • MS Ch E, PhD
- computer science • MS, PhD
- electrical engineering • MSEE, PhD
- engineering • MAE, MS, MS Ch E, MSAA, MSCE, MSE, MSEE, MSIE, MSME, PhD
- environmental engineering • MS, MSCE, MSE, PhD
- hydraulic engineering • MSCE, MSE, PhD
- industrial engineering • MSIE, PhD
- inter-engineering specialization in materials science and engineering • MS
- materials science and engineering • MS, PhD
- mechanical engineering • MSE, MSME, PhD
- structural and geotechnical engineering and mechanics • MS, MSCE, MSE, PhD
- technical communication • MS
- transportation and construction engineering • MS, MSCE, MSE, PhD

College of Forest Resources
Dr. B. Bruce Bare, Dean
Programs in:
- forest economics • MS, PhD
- forest ecosystem analysis • MS, PhD
- forest engineering/forest hydrology • MS, PhD
- forest products marketing • MS, PhD
- forest soils • MS, PhD
- paper science and engineering • MS, PhD
- quantitative resource management • MS, PhD
- silviculture • MFR
- silviculture and forest protection • MS, PhD
- social sciences • MS, PhD
- urban horticulture • MFR, MS, PhD
- wildlife science • MS, PhD

College of Ocean and Fishery Sciences
Arthur R. M. Nowell, Dean
Programs in:
- aquatic and fishery sciences • MS, PhD
- biological oceanography • MS, PhD
- chemical oceanography • MS, PhD
- marine affairs • MMA
- marine geology and geophysics • MS, PhD
- ocean and fishery sciences • MMA, MS, PhD
- physical oceanography • MS, PhD

Daniel J. Evans School of Public Affairs
Program in:
- public affairs • MPA

The Information School
Michael B. Eisenberg, Director
Programs in:
- information science • PhD
- library and information services • MLIS

School of Nursing
Nancy F. Woods, Dean
Program in:
- nursing • MN, MS, PhD

School of Public Health and Community Medicine
Dr. Patricia W. Wahl, Dean
Programs in:
- biostatistics • MPH, MS, PhD
- epidemiology • MPH, MS, PhD
- genetic epidemiology • MS
- health services • MS, PhD
- health services administration and planning • MHA
- industrial hygiene • PhD
- industrial hygiene and safety • MS
- nutritional sciences • MPH, MS, PhD
- occupational medicine • MPH
- pathobiology • MS, PhD
- preventive medicine • MPH
- public health • MPH
- public health and community medicine • MHA, MPH, MS, PhD
- public health genetics • MPH, MS
- technology • MS
- toxicology • MS, PhD

School of Social Work
Nancy R. Hooyman, Dean
Program in:
- social work • MSW, PhD

School of Social Work, Tacoma Campus
Dr. Marcie M. Lazzari, Director
Program in:
- social work • MSW

School of Dentistry
Dr. Paul B. Robertson, Dean
Program in:
- dentistry • DDS, MS, MSD, PhD

School of Law
Roland L. Hjorth, Dean
Programs in:
- Asian law • LL M, PhD
- international environmental law • LL M
- law • JD
- law and marine affairs • LL M
- law of sustainable international development • LL M
- taxation • LL M

School of Medicine
Program in:
- medicine • MD, MOT, MPT, MS, MSE, PhD

Graduate Programs in Medicine
Programs in:
- biochemistry • PhD
- biological structure • PhD
- biomedical and health informatics • MS
- entry-level physical therapy • MPT
- immunology • PhD
- laboratory medicine • MS
- medicine • MOT, MPT, MS, MSE, PhD
- microbiology • PhD
- molecular and cellular biology • PhD
- molecular basis of disease • PhD
- molecular biotechnology • PhD
- neurobiology and behavior • PhD
- occupational therapy • MOT, MS
- pathology • MS
- pediatric physical therapy • MS
- pharmacology • MS, PhD
- physical therapy • MPT, MS
- physiology and biophysics • PhD
- rehabilitation medicine • MS

School of Pharmacy
Programs in:
- medicinal chemistry • PhD
- pharmaceutics • MS, PhD
- pharmacy • Pharm D, MS, PhD

■ WALLA WALLA COLLEGE
College Place, WA 99324-1198
http://www.wwc.edu/

Independent-religious, coed, comprehensive institution. *Enrollment:* 170 full-time matriculated graduate/professional students (135 women), 42 part-time matriculated graduate/professional students (27 women). *Graduate faculty:* 30 full-time (17 women), 13 part-time/adjunct (7 women). *Computer facilities:* 108 computers available on campus for general student use. A campuswide network can be accessed from student residence rooms and from off campus. Internet access and online class registration are available. *Library facilities:* Peterson Memorial Library plus 3 others. *Graduate expenses:* Tuition: full-time $14,859; part-time $381 per credit. *General application contact:* Dr. Joe G. Galusha, Dean of Graduate Studies, 509-527-2421.

Graduate School
Dr. Joe G. Galusha, Dean
Program in:
- biological science • MS

Walla Walla College (continued)

School of Education and Psychology
Dr. Steve Pawluk, Dean
Programs in:
counseling psychology • MA
curriculum and instruction • M Ed, MA
educational leadership • M Ed, MA, MAT
literacy instruction • M Ed, MA, MAT
professional practice • MAT
school counseling • M Ed, MA
special education • M Ed, MA, MAT
students at risk • M Ed, MA
teaching • MAT

School of Social Work
Dr. Wilma Hepker, Dean
Program in:
social work • MSW

■ WASHINGTON STATE UNIVERSITY

Pullman, WA 99164
http://www.wsu.edu/

State-supported, coed, university. CGS member. *Enrollment:* 2,283 full-time matriculated graduate/professional students (1,144 women), 1,218 part-time matriculated graduate/professional students (678 women). *Graduate faculty:* 721 full-time (160 women), 49 part-time/adjunct (13 women). *Computer facilities:* 10,000 computers available on campus for general student use. A campuswide network can be accessed from student residence rooms and from off campus. Internet access and online class registration are available. *Library facilities:* Holland Library plus 5 others. *Graduate expenses:* Tuition, state resident: part-time $283 per credit. Tuition, nonresident: part-time $693 per credit. *General application contact:* Dr. Steven R. Burkett, Associate Dean, Graduate School, 509-335-6424.

College of Veterinary Medicine
Dr. Warwick M. Bayly, Interim Dean
Programs in:
neuroscience • MS, PhD
veterinary clinical sciences • MS, PhD
veterinary comparative anatomy, pharmacology, and physiology • MS, PhD
veterinary medicine • DVM, MS, PhD
veterinary microbiology and pathology • MS, PhD
veterinary science • MS, PhD

Graduate School
Dr. Karen De Pauw, Dean

College of Agriculture and Home Economics
Dr. James Zuiches, Dean
Programs in:
agribusiness • MA
agricultural economics • MA, PhD
agriculture and home economics • MA, MLA, MS, PhD
animal sciences • MS, PhD
apparel, merchandising and textiles • MA
crop sciences • MS, PhD
entomology • MS, PhD
food science • MS, PhD
horticulture • MS, PhD
human development • MA
human nutrition • MS
interior design • MA
landscape architecture • MLA
natural resources sciences • MS, PhD
nutrition • PhD
plant pathology • MS, PhD
plant physiology • MS, PhD
soil sciences • MS, PhD

College of Business and Economics
Dr. Glenn Johnson, Interim
Programs in:
accounting and business law • M Acc
business administration • MBA, PhD
business and economics • M Acc, MA, MBA, MTM, PhD, Certificate
economics • MA, PhD
international business economics • Certificate
technology management • MTM

College of Education
Dr. Judy Mitchell, Dean
Programs in:
counseling psychology • MA, PhD
curriculum and instruction • Ed D, PhD
diverse languages • M Ed, MA
education • M Ed, MA, MAT, MIT, MS, Ed D, PhD
educational leadership • M Ed, MA, Ed D, PhD
elementary education • M Ed, MA, MIT
kinesiology • M Ed, MS
literacy • M Ed, MA
literacy education • PhD
math education • PhD
recreation and leisure studies • M Ed, MS
secondary education • M Ed, MA

College of Engineering and Architecture
Dr. Anjan Bose, Dean
Programs in:
architecture • MS
chemical engineering • MS, PhD
civil engineering • MS, PhD
computer science • MS, PhD
electrical engineering • MS, PhD
engineering and architecture • MS, PhD
environmental engineering • MS
materials science • MS, PhD
mechanical engineering • MS, PhD

College of Liberal Arts
Dr. Barbara Couture, Dean
Programs in:
American studies • MA, PhD
anthropology • MA, PhD
ceramics • MFA
clinical psychology • PhD
communications • MA
composition • MA
criminal justice • MA
drawing • MFA
electronic imaging • MFA
English • MA, PhD
history • MA, PhD
liberal arts • MA, MAT, MFA, MPA, MS, PhD
music • MA
painting • MFA
photography • MFA
political science • MA, PhD
print making • MFA
psychology • MS, PhD
public affairs • MPA
sculpture • MFA
sociology • MA, PhD
Spanish • MA
speech and hearing sciences • MA
teaching of English • MA
theater arts and drama • MA, MAT

College of Nursing
Dr. Dorothy Detlor, Dean
Program in:
nursing • M Nurs

College of Pharmacy
Dr. William Faffett, Interim Dean
Programs in:
health policy and administration • MHPA
pharmaceutical science • Pharm D
pharmacology and toxicology • MS, PhD
pharmacy • Pharm D, MHPA, MS, PhD

College of Sciences
Dr. Leon Radziemski, Dean
Programs in:
analytical chemistry • MS, PhD
biochemistry and biophysics • MS, PhD
biological systems • MS, PhD
biology • MS
botany • MS, PhD
chemical physics • PhD
environmental science • MS, PhD
genetics and cell biology • MS, PhD
geology • MS, PhD
inorganic chemistry • MS, PhD
material science • MS, PhD
materials science • PhD

materials science and engineering • MS
microbiology • MS, PhD
organic chemistry • MS, PhD
physical chemistry • MS, PhD
physics • MS, PhD
pure and applied mathematics • MS, DA, PhD
regional planning • MRP
sciences • MRP, MS, DA, PhD
zoology • MS, PhD

■ WESTERN WASHINGTON UNIVERSITY

Bellingham, WA 98225-5996
http://www.wwu.edu/

State-supported, coed, comprehensive institution. CGS member. *Enrollment:* 550 full-time matriculated graduate/professional students (331 women), 230 part-time matriculated graduate/professional students (159 women). *Graduate faculty:* 406. *Computer facilities:* 1,500 computers available on campus for general student use. A campuswide network can be accessed from student residence rooms and from off campus. Internet access and online class registration are available. *Library facilities:* Wilson Library plus 3 others. *Graduate expenses:* Tuition, state resident: full-time $1,604; part-time $151 per credit. Tuition, nonresident: full-time $4,703; part-time $461 per credit. *General application contact:* Graduate Office Admissions, 360-650-3170.

Graduate School
Dr. Moheb Ghali, Dean

College of Arts and Sciences
Dr. Ronald Kleinknecht, Interim Dean
Programs in:
anthropology • MA
arts and sciences • M Ed, MA, MS
biology • MS
chemistry • MS
communication sciences and disorders • MA
computer science • MS
English • MA
general psychology • MS
geology • MS
history • MA
human movement and performance • MS
mathematics • MS
mental health counseling • MS
physical education • M Ed
political science • MA
psychology • MS
school counseling • M Ed
science education • M Ed
sociology • MA
technology • M Ed

College of Business and Economics
Dr. Brian Burton, Graduate Program Adviser
Program in:
business and economics • MBA

College of Fine and Performing Arts
Dr. Bertil H. van Boer, Dean
Programs in:
art • M Ed
fine and performing arts • M Ed, M Mus, MA
music • M Mus
theatre • MA

Huxley College of Environmental Studies
Dr. Brad Smith, Dean
Programs in:
environmental science • MS
environmental studies • MS
geography • MS

Woodring College of Education
Dr. Marv Klein, Dean
Programs in:
adult education • M Ed
education • M Ed, MA, MIT
educational administration • M Ed
elementary education • M Ed
exceptional children • M Ed
rehabilitation counseling • MA
secondary education • M Ed, MIT
student personnel administration • M Ed

■ WHITWORTH COLLEGE

Spokane, WA 99251-0001
http://www.whitworth.edu/

Independent-religious, coed, comprehensive institution. *Enrollment:* 63 full-time matriculated graduate/professional students (39 women), 142 part-time matriculated graduate/professional students (105 women). *Graduate faculty:* 16 full-time, 55 part-time/adjunct. *Computer facilities:* 150 computers available on campus for general student use. A campuswide network can be accessed from student residence rooms and from off campus. *Library facilities:* Harriet Cheney Cowles Library. *Graduate expenses:* Tuition: full-time $14,600; part-time $275 per credit. Tuition and fees vary according to course load and program. *General application contact:* Fred Pfursich, Office of Admissions, 509-777-1000 Ext. 3212.

School of Education
Programs in:
education • M Ed, MA, MAT, MIT
education administration • M Ed
English as a second language • MAT
gifted and talented • MAT
guidance and counseling • M Ed
physical education and sport administration • MA
reading • MAT
school counselors • M Ed
social agency/church setting • M Ed
special education • MAT
teaching • MIT

School of Global Commerce and Management
Dr. Kyle B. Usrey, Dean
Program in:
international management • MIM

West Virginia

■ MARSHALL UNIVERSITY

Huntington, WV 25755
http://www.marshall.edu/

State-supported, coed, university. CGS member. *Enrollment:* 1,212 full-time matriculated graduate/professional students (740 women), 2,218 part-time matriculated graduate/professional students (1,477 women). *Graduate faculty:* 332 full-time, 109 part-time/adjunct. *Computer facilities:* 1,330 computers available on campus for general student use. A campuswide network can be accessed from student residence rooms and from off campus. Internet access and online class registration are available. *Library facilities:* John Deaver Drinko Library plus 2 others. *Graduate expenses:* Full-time $2,396; part-time $133 per credit. Tuition, state resident: full-time $5,008; part-time $426 per credit. Tuition, nonresident: full-time $7,670; part-time $278 per credit. Required fees: $488; $27 per credit. Tuition and fees vary according to campus/location and program. *General application contact:* Ken O'Neal, Assistant Vice President, Adult Student Services, 304-746-2500 Ext. 1907.

Find an in-depth description at www.petersons.com/graduate.

Graduate College
Dr. Leonard J. Deutsch, Dean

College of Education and Human Services
Dr. Larry Froehlich, Executive Dean
Programs in:

Marshall University (continued)
adult and technical education • MS
counseling • MA, Ed S
early childhood education • MA
education • MAT
education and human services • MA, MAT, MS, Ed S
education and professional development • MA, Ed S
elementary education • MA
exercise science • MS
exercise science, sports and recreation • MS
family and consumer sciences • MA
health and physical education • MS
human development and allied technology • MA, MS
leadership studies • MA, Ed S
reading education • MA, Ed S
school psychology • Ed S
secondary education • MA
special education • MA

College of Fine Arts
Dr. Donald Van Horn, Dean
Programs in:
art • MA
fine arts • MA
music • MA

College of Information, Technology and Engineering
Dr. James Hooper, Dean
Programs in:
engineering • MSE
environmental science • MS
environmental science and safety technology • MS
information systems • MS
information systems and technology management • MS
information, technology and engineering • MS, MSE
safety • MS
technology management • MS

College of Liberal Arts
Dr. Joan Mead, Dean
Programs in:
clinical psychology • MA
communication studies • MA
criminal justice • MS
English • MA
general psychology • MA
geography • MA, MS
history • MA
humanities • MA
industrial and organizational psychology • MA
liberal arts • MA, MS
political science • MA
sociology and anthropology • MA

College of Nursing and Health Professions
Dr. Lynne Welch, Dean
Programs in:
communication disorders • MA
nursing • MSN
nursing and health professions • MA, MSN

College of Science
Dr. Ralph Taylor, Dean
Programs in:
biological science • MA, MS
chemistry • MS
mathematics • MA, MS
physical science • MS
science • MA, MS

Lewis College of Business
Dr. Calvin Kent, Dean
Programs in:
business • MBA, MS
business administration • MBA
health care administration • MS
industrial and employee relations • MS
management • MBA, MS

School of Journalism and Mass Communications
Dr. Harold C. Shaver, Director
Program in:
journalism and mass communications • MAJ

Joan C. Edwards School of Medicine
Dr. Charles H. McKown, Dean and Vice President
Programs in:
biomedical sciences • MS, PhD
forensic science • MS
medicine • MD, MS, PhD

■ SALEM INTERNATIONAL UNIVERSITY

Salem, WV 26426-0500
http://www.salemiu.edu/

Independent, coed, comprehensive institution. *Enrollment:* 9 full-time matriculated graduate/professional students (6 women), 34 part-time matriculated graduate/professional students (24 women). *Graduate faculty:* 1 full-time (0 women), 11 part-time/adjunct (5 women). *Computer facilities:* 79 computers available on campus for general student use. A campuswide network can be accessed from off campus. *Library facilities:* Benedum Library. *Graduate expenses:* Tuition: full-time $10,000; part-time $170 per hour. Required fees: $5 per term. Full-time tuition and fees vary according to program. *General application contact:* Carolyn Sue Ritter, Director of Admissions, 304-782-5336.

Program in Bioscience
Dr. Patrick Lai, Director of Graduate Bioscience Program
Program in:
biotechnology/molecular biology • MS

Program in Education
Dr. Mary Harris John, Director of Graduate Program in Education
Programs in:
elementary education • MA
equestrian education • MA
secondary education • MA

■ WEST VIRGINIA UNIVERSITY

Morgantown, WV 26506
http://www.wvu.edu/

State-supported, coed, university. CGS member. *Enrollment:* 3,546 full-time matriculated graduate/professional students (1,709 women), 1,861 part-time matriculated graduate/professional students (1,216 women). *Graduate faculty:* 1,242 full-time (374 women), 406 part-time/adjunct (227 women). *Computer facilities:* 1,600 computers available on campus for general student use. A campuswide network can be accessed from student residence rooms and from off campus. Internet access is available. *Library facilities:* Wise Library plus 9 others. *Graduate expenses:* Tuition, state resident: full-time $3,004; part-time $167 per credit. Tuition, nonresident: full-time $8,640; part-time $480 per credit. *General application contact:* Information Contact, 800-344-WVU1.

College of Agriculture, Forestry and Consumer Sciences
Dr. Cameron R. Hackney, Dean
Programs in:
agricultural and resource economics • MS
agricultural biochemistry • PhD
agricultural education • MS
agricultural extension education • MS
agriculture, forestry and consumer sciences • M Agr, MS, MSF, MSFCS, PhD
agriculture, forestry, and consumer sciences • M Agr
agronomy • MS
animal and food sciences • PhD
animal and veterinary sciences • MS
animal breeding • MS, PhD
animal nutrition • PhD
animal physiology • PhD
animal sciences • MS
biochemical and molecular genetics • MS, PhD
breeding • MS

cytogenetics • MS, PhD
descriptive embryology • MS, PhD
developmental genetics • MS
entomology • MS
environmental microbiology • MS
experimental morphogenesis • MS
family and consumer sciences • MSFCS
food sciences • MS
forest resource science • PhD
forestry • MSF
horticulture • MS
human genetics • MS, PhD
immunogenetics • MS, PhD
life cycles of animals and plants • MS, PhD
molecular aspects of development • MS, PhD
mutagenesis • PhD
mutagenetics • MS
natural resource economics • PhD
nutrition • MS
oncology • MS, PhD
physiology • MS
plant and soil sciences • PhD
plant genetics • MS, PhD
plant pathology • MS
population and guantitative genetics • PhD
population and quantitative genetics • MS
production • MS
production management • PhD
recreation, parks and tourism resources • MS
regeneration • MS, PhD
reproductive physiology • MS, PhD
teaching vocational-agriculture • MS
teratology • MS, PhD
toxicology • MS, PhD
wildlife and fisheries resources • MS

College of Business and Economics
Dr. Lee Dahringer, Dean
Programs in:
accounting • MPA
business administration • MBA
business analysis • MA
business and economics • MA, MBA, MPA, MS, PhD
econometrics • PhD
industrial economics • PhD
industrial relations • MS
international economics • PhD
labor economics • PhD
mathematical economics • MA, PhD
monetary economics • PhD
public finance • PhD
public policy • MA
regional and urban economics • PhD
statistics and economics • MA

College of Creative Arts
Dr. Bernie Schultz, Dean
Programs in:
acting • MFA
art education • MA
art history • MA
ceramics • MFA
creative arts • MA, MFA, MM, DMA, PhD
graphic design • MFA
music composition • MM, DMA, PhD
music education • MM, DMA, PhD
music history • MM
music performance • MM, DMA, PhD
music theory • MM
painting • MFA
printmaking • MFA
sculpture • MFA
studio art • MA
theatre design/technology • MFA

College of Engineering and Mineral Resources
Dr. Eugene Cilento, Dean
Programs in:
aerospace engineering • MSAE, MSE, PhD
chemical engineering • MS Ch E, PhD
civil engineering • MSCE, MSE, PhD
computer engineering • PhD
computer science • MS, PhD
electrical engineering • MSE, MSEE, PhD
engineering • MSE
engineering and mineral resources • MS, MS Ch E, MS Min E, MSAE, MSCE, MSE, MSEE, MSEM, MSIE, MSME, MSPNGE, MSSE, PhD
industrial engineering • MSE, MSIE, PhD
mechanical engineering • MSE, MSME, PhD
mining engineering • MS Min E, PhD
occupational hygiene and occupational safety • MS
petroleum and natural gas engineering • MSPNGE, PhD
safety and environmental management • MS
safety management • MS
software engineering • MSSE

College of Human Resources and Education
Dr. William L. Deaton, Dean
Programs in:
behavioral disorders K-12 • MA
counseling • MA
counseling psychology • PhD
curriculum and instruction • Ed D
early intervention (preschool) • MA
educational leadership • MA, Ed D
educational psychology • MA, Ed D
elementary education • MA
gifted education 5-12 • MA
gifted education K-8 • MA
higher education administration • MA
higher education curriculum and teaching • MA
human resources and education • MA, MS, Ed D, PhD
information and communication systems • MA
instructional design and technology • MA
mentally impaired • MA
professional development • MA
public school administration • MA
reading • MA
rehabilitation counseling • MS
secondary education • MA
severe/profound handicaps • MA
special education • MA, Ed D
specific learning disabilities K-12 • MA
speech pathology and audiology • MS
technology and society • MA
technology education • MA, Ed D

College of Law
John W. Fisher, Dean
Program in:
law • JD

Eberly College of Arts and Sciences
Dr. M. Duane Nellis, Dean
Programs in:
African history • MA, PhD
African-American history • MA, PhD
American history • MA, PhD
American public policy and politics • MA
analytical chemistry • MS, PhD
animal behavior • MS
Appalachian/regional history • MA, PhD
applied mathematics • MS, PhD
applied physics • MS, PhD
applied social research • MA
arts and sciences • MA, MALS, MFA, MLS, MPA, MS, MSW, PhD
astrophysics • MS, PhD
behavior analysis • PhD
cellular and molecular biology • MS, PhD
chemical physics • MS, PhD
clinical psychology • MA, PhD
communication in instruction • MA
communication theory and research • MA
comparative literature • MA
condensed matter physics • MS, PhD
corporate and organizational communication • MA
creative writing • MFA
development psychology • PhD
discrete mathematics • PhD

West Virginia University (continued)
- East Asian history • MA, PhD
- elementary particle physics • MS, PhD
- energy and environmental resources • MA
- environmental plant biology • MS, PhD
- European history • MA, PhD
- French • MA
- geographic information systems • PhD
- geography • MA, PhD
- geography-regional development • PhD
- geology • MS, PhD
- geomorphology • MS, PhD
- geophysics • MS, PhD
- German • MA
- GIS/cartographic analysis • MA
- history of science and technology • MA, PhD
- hydrogeology • MS
- hydrology • PhD
- inorganic chemistry • MS, PhD
- interdisciplinary mathematics • MS
- international and comparative public policy and U.S. politics • MA
- Latin American history • MA
- legal studies • MLS
- liberal studies • MALS
- linguistics • MA
- literary/cultural studies • MA, PhD
- materials physics • MS, PhD
- mathematics for secondary education • MS
- organic chemistry • MS, PhD
- paleontology • MS, PhD
- petrology • MS, PhD
- physical chemistry • MS, PhD
- plant systematics • MS
- plasma physics • MS, PhD
- political science • PhD
- population genetics • MS
- public policy analysis • PhD
- pure mathematics • MS
- regional development and urban planning • MA
- solid state physics • MS, PhD
- Spanish • MA
- statistical physics • MS, PhD
- statistics • MS
- stratigraphy • MS, PhD
- structure • MS, PhD
- teaching English to speakers of other languages • MA
- theoretical chemistry • MS, PhD
- theoretical physics • MS, PhD
- writing • MA

School of Applied Social Science
Dr. David G. Williams, Chair
Programs in:
- aging and health care • MSW
- applied social science • MPA, MSW
- children and families • MSW
- mental health • MSW
- public administration • MPA

Perley Isaac Reed School of Journalism
Dr. Christine Martin, Dean
Program in:
- journalism • MSJ

School of Dentistry
Dr. James Koelbl, Dean
Programs in:
- basic science • MS
- dentistry • DDS, MS
- education/administration • MS
- endodontics • MS
- office management • MS
- orthodontics • MS
- prosthodontics • MS
- special patients • MS

School of Medicine
Dr. Robert M. D'Alessandri, Dean
Programs in:
- exercise physiology • MS, PhD
- medicine • MD, MOT, MPH, MPT, MS, PhD
- occupational therapy • MOT
- physical therapy • MPT

Graduate Programs in Health Sciences
Dr. George A. Hedge, Associate Dean/Graduate Coordinator
Programs in:
- autonomic pharmacology • MS, PhD
- biomedical pharmacology • MS, PhD
- cardiovascular physiology • MS, PhD
- cell physiology • MS, PhD
- chemotherapy • MS, PhD
- clinical chemistry • MS
- community health promotion • MS
- community health/preventative medicine • MPH
- developmental anatomy • MS
- developmental biology • MS
- endocrine pharmacology • MS, PhD
- endocrine physiology • MS, PhD
- energy transduction • MS
- enzymes and serum proteins • PhD
- enzymology • MS
- ernal physiology • PhD
- gene expression • MS, PhD
- genetics • MS, PhD
- gross anatomy • MS, PhD
- health sciences • MPH, MS, PhD
- hematology • MS
- hormonal regulation/metabolism • MS, PhD
- immunohematology • MS
- immunology • MS, PhD
- membrane biogenesis • MS, PhD
- microbiology • MS
- microscopic anatomy • MS, PhD
- molecular and developmental anatomy • PhD
- molecular virology • MS
- muscle physiology • MS, PhD
- mycology • PhD
- neural physiology • MS, PhD
- neuroanatomy • MS, PhD
- neuropharmacology • MS, PhD
- nucleic acids • MS, PhD
- nutritional oncology • PhD
- parasitology • MS, PhD
- pathogenic bacteriology • MS, PhD
- physiology • PhD
- protein chemistry • MS
- psysiology • MS
- renal physiology • MS
- respiratory physiology • MS
- secretory mechanisms • PhD
- toxicology • MS, PhD
- virology • MS, PhD

School of Nursing
Dr. E. Jane Martin, Dean
Programs in:
- nurse practitioner • Certificate
- nursing • MSN, DSN

School of Pharmacy
Dr. George R. Spratto, Dean
Programs in:
- administrative pharmacy • PhD
- behavioral pharmacy • MS, PhD
- biopharmaceutics/phamacokinetics • PhD
- biopharmaceutics/pharmacokinetics • MS
- clinical pharmacy • Pharm D
- industrial pharmacy • MS
- medicinal chemistry • MS, PhD
- pharmaceutical chemistry • MS, PhD
- pharmaceutics • MS, PhD
- pharmacology and toxicology • MS
- pharmacy • MS
- pharmacy administration • MS

School of Physical Education
Dr. Dana Brooks, Dean
Programs in:
- athletic coaching • MS
- athletic training • MS
- exercise physiology • Ed D
- physical education/teacher education • MS, Ed D
- sport management • MS
- sport psychology • MS, Ed D

■ WHEELING JESUIT UNIVERSITY

Wheeling, WV 26003-6295
http://www.wju.edu/

Independent-religious, coed, comprehensive institution. CGS member. *Enrollment:* 87 full-time matriculated graduate/professional students (46 women), 137 part-time matriculated graduate/professional students (85 women). *Graduate faculty:* 16 full-time (6 women), 9 part-time/adjunct (4 women). *Computer facilities:* 75 computers available on campus for general student use.

A campuswide network can be accessed from student residence rooms and from off campus. Internet access is available. *Library facilities:* Bishop Hodges Learning Center plus 1 other. *Graduate expenses:* Tuition: full-time $7,380; part-time $410 per credit hour. Required fees: $135; $55 per semester. One-time fee: $95 full-time. Full-time tuition and fees vary according to course load and program. *General application contact:* Tricia Lollini, Graduate Secretary, 304-243-2344.

Department of Business
Dr. Edward W. Younkins, Director
Programs in:
accounting • MS
business administration • MBA

Department of Nursing
Dr. Rose M. Kutlenias, Chair
Program in:
nursing • MSN

Department of Physical Therapy
Dr. Letha B. Zook, Director
Program in:
physical therapy • MSPT

Department of Theology
Dr. John L. McLaughlin, Director
Program in:
applied theology • MA

Teacher Preparation Program
Dr. H. Lawrence Jones, Director
Program in:
teacher preparation • MASMED

Wisconsin

■ CARDINAL STRITCH UNIVERSITY

Milwaukee, WI 53217-3985
http://www.stritch.edu/

Independent-religious, coed, comprehensive institution. *Enrollment:* 734 full-time matriculated graduate/professional students (380 women), 1,000 part-time matriculated graduate/professional students (713 women). *Graduate faculty:* 57 full-time (34 women), 212 part-time/adjunct (88 women). *Computer facilities:* 236 computers available on campus for general student use. A campuswide network can be accessed from student residence rooms and from off campus. Internet access is available. *Library facilities:* Cardinal Stritch University Library. *Graduate expenses:* Tuition: part-time $370 per credit. Required fees: $50 per semester. One-time fee: $20 part-time. Tuition and fees vary according to program. *General application contact:* Graduate Admissions, 414-410-4042.

College of Arts and Sciences
Dr. Dickson K. Smith, Associate Dean
Programs in:
arts and sciences • MA, ME
clinical psychology • MA
religious studies • MA
visual studies • MA

College of Business and Management
Dr. Arthur Wasserman, Dean
Programs in:
business administration • MBA
business and management • MBA, MS
financial services • MS
health care executives • MBA
health services administration • MS
management • MS

College of Education
Dr. Tia Bojar, Dean
Programs in:
computer science education • MS
education • MA, ME, MS, Ed D
educational computing • ME
educational leadership • MS
leadership • Ed D
professional development • ME
reading/language arts • MA
reading/learning disability • MA
special education • MA

College of Nursing
Zaiga G. P. Kalnins, RN, Dean
Program in:
nursing • MSN

■ CARTHAGE COLLEGE

Kenosha, WI 53140-1994
http://www.carthage.edu/

Independent-religious, coed, comprehensive institution. *Enrollment:* 141 part-time matriculated graduate/professional students (127 women). *Graduate faculty:* 3 full-time (2 women), 16 part-time/adjunct (11 women). *Computer facilities:* 200 computers available on campus for general student use. A campuswide network can be accessed from student residence rooms and from off campus. Internet access is available. *Library facilities:* Hedberg Library. *Graduate expenses:* Tuition: part-time $255 per credit. *General application contact:* Dr. Judith B. Schaumberg, Director of Graduate Programs, 262-551-5876.

Division of Teacher Education
Dr. Judith B. Schaumberg, Director of Graduate Programs
Programs in:
classroom guidance and counseling • M Ed
creative arts • M Ed
gifted and talented children • M Ed
language arts • M Ed
modern language • M Ed
natural sciences • M Ed
reading • M Ed, Certificate
social sciences • M Ed

■ CONCORDIA UNIVERSITY WISCONSIN

Mequon, WI 53097-2402
http://www.cuw.edu/

Independent-religious, coed, comprehensive institution. *Enrollment:* 410 full-time matriculated graduate/professional students (276 women), 341 part-time matriculated graduate/professional students (209 women). *Graduate faculty:* 13 full-time (5 women), 31 part-time/adjunct (17 women). *Computer facilities:* 100 computers available on campus for general student use. A campuswide network can be accessed from student residence rooms and from off campus. Internet access is available. *Library facilities:* Rinker Memorial Library. *Graduate expenses:* Tuition: full-time $14,700; part-time $325 per credit. Full-time tuition and fees vary according to program. *General application contact:* Dr. John F. Walther, Dean of Graduate Studies, 262-243-4285.

Graduate Studies, School of
Dr. John F. Walther, Dean
Programs in:
church administration • MBA
church music • MCM
counseling • MS Ed
curriculum and instruction • MS Ed
early childhood • MS Ed
educational administration • MS
family nurse practitioner • MSN
family studies • MS Ed
finance • MBA
geriatric nurse practitioner • MSN
health care administration • MBA
human resource management • MBA
international business • MBA
management • MBA
management information services • MBA

Concordia University Wisconsin (continued)

managerial communications • MBA
marketing • MBA
nurse educator • MSN
occupational therapy • MOT
physical therapy • MPT, MSPT
public administration • MBA
reading • MS Ed
risk management • MBA
student personnel administration • MSSPA

■ EDGEWOOD COLLEGE

Madison, WI 53711-1997
http://www.edgewood.edu/

Independent-religious, coed, comprehensive institution. *Enrollment:* 55 full-time matriculated graduate/professional students (39 women), 487 part-time matriculated graduate/professional students (328 women). *Graduate faculty:* 24 full-time (7 women), 24 part-time/adjunct (11 women). *Computer facilities:* 85 computers available on campus for general student use. A campuswide network can be accessed from student residence rooms and from off campus. Internet access is available. *Library facilities:* Oscar Rennebohm Library. *Graduate expenses:* Tuition: full-time $6,930; part-time $385 per credit hour. Required fees: $200; $200 per year. *General application contact:* Dr. Raymond Schultz, Associate Dean of Graduate Programs, 608-663-2377.

Program in Business
Dr. Gary Schroeder, Chair
Program in:
business • MBA

Program in Education
Dr. Joseph Schmiedicke, Chair
Programs in:
director of instruction • Certificate
director of special education and pupil services • Certificate
education • MA Ed
educational administration • MA
emotional disturbances • MA, Certificate
learning disabilities • MA, Certificate
learning disabilities and emotional disturbances • MA, Certificate
school business administration • Certificate
school principalship K-12 • Certificate

Program in Marriage and Family Therapy
Dr. Peter Fabian, Director
Program in:
marriage and family therapy • MS

Program in Nursing
Dr. Mary Kelly-Powell, Chair
Program in:
nursing • MS

Program in Religious Studies
Dr. Barbara B. Miller, Chairperson
Program in:
religious studies • MA

■ MARIAN COLLEGE OF FOND DU LAC

Fond du Lac, WI 54935-4699
http://www.mariancollege.edu/

Independent-religious, coed, comprehensive institution. *Enrollment:* 13 full-time matriculated graduate/professional students (8 women), 435 part-time matriculated graduate/professional students (280 women). *Graduate faculty:* 8 full-time (3 women), 40 part-time/adjunct (20 women). *Computer facilities:* 125 computers available on campus for general student use. A campuswide network can be accessed from student residence rooms. Internet access and online class registration are available. *Library facilities:* Cardinal Meyer Library. *Graduate expenses:* Tuition: part-time $285 per credit. *General application contact:* Dr. Donna Innes, Chair, Educational Studies, 920-923-7140.

Business Division
Dr. Richard M. Dienesch, Assistant Dean of Evening/Weekend Programs
Program in:
organizational leadership and quality • MS

Education Division
Dr. Donna Innes, Chair, Educational Studies
Programs in:
educational leadership • MA
teacher development • MA

■ MARQUETTE UNIVERSITY

Milwaukee, WI 53201-1881
http://www.marquette.edu/

Independent-religious, coed, university. CGS member. *Enrollment:* 869 full-time matriculated graduate/professional students (423 women), 1,403 part-time matriculated graduate/professional students (646 women). *Graduate faculty:* 519 full-time, 290 part-time/adjunct. *Computer facilities:* 600 computers available on campus for general student use. A campuswide network can be accessed from student residence rooms and from off campus. Internet access is available. *Library facilities:* Memorial Library plus 2 others. *Graduate expenses:* Tuition: full-time $17,080; part-time $385 per credit hour. *General application contact:* Rev. David A. Zampino, Manager, Graduate Inquiry Systems, 414-288-6302.

Find an in-depth description at www.petersons.com/graduate.

Graduate School
Dr. Lynn Miner, Interim Dean
Programs in:
interdisciplinary studies • PhD
physical therapy • MPT
physician assistant studies • MS

College of Arts and Sciences
Dr. Michael A. McKinney, Dean
Programs in:
algebra • PhD
American literature • PhD
analytical chemistry • MS, PhD
ancient philosophy • MA, PhD
arts and sciences • MA, MAT, MS, PhD
bio-mathematical modeling • PhD
bioanalytical chemistry • MS, PhD
biophysical chemistry • MS, PhD
British and American literature • MA
British empiricism and analytic philosophy • MA, PhD
British literature • PhD
cell biology • MS, PhD
chemical physics • MS, PhD
Christian philosophy • MA, PhD
clinical psychology • MS
computers • MS
developmental biology • MS, PhD
early modern European philosophy • MA, PhD
ecology • MS, PhD
endocrinology • MS, PhD
ethics • MA, PhD
European history • MA, PhD
evolutionary biology • MS, PhD
genetics • MS, PhD
German philosophy • MA, PhD
historical theology • MA, PhD
inorganic chemistry • MS, PhD
international affairs • MA
mathematics • MS
mathematics education • MS
medieval history • MA
medieval philosophy • MA, PhD
microbiology • MS, PhD
molecular biology • MS, PhD
muscle and exercise physiology • MS, PhD
neurobiology • MS, PhD
organic chemistry • MS, PhD
phenomenology and existentialism • MA, PhD
philosophy of religion • MA, PhD
physical chemistry • MS, PhD
political science • MA

psychology • PhD
religious studies • PhD
Renaissance and Reformation • MA
reproductive physiology • MS, PhD
social and applied philosophy • MA
Spanish • MA, MAT
statistics • MS
systematic theology • MA, PhD
theology • MA
theology and society • PhD
United States • MA, PhD

College of Business Administration
Dr. David Shrock, Dean
Programs in:
accounting • MSA
business administration • MBA, MSA, MSAE, MSHR
business economics • MSAE
financial economics • MSAE
human resources • MSHR
international economics • MSAE
public policy economics • MSAE

College of Communication
Dr. William R. Elliot, Dean
Programs in:
advertising • MA
broadcasting and electronic communication • MA
communication • MA
interpersonal communication • MA
journalism • MA
mass communication • MA
mass communications • MA
organizational communication • MA
public relations • MA
religious communications • MA
speech education • MA

College of Engineering
Dr. Douglas M. Green, Dean
Programs in:
bioinstrumentation/computers • MS, PhD
biomechanics/biomaterials • MS, PhD
computing • MS
construction and public works management • MS, PhD
electrical engineering • MS, PhD
engineering • MS, PhD
engineering management • MS
environmental/water resources engineering • MS, PhD
functional imaging • PhD
healthcare technologies management • MS
materials science and engineering • MS, PhD
mechanical engineering • MS, PhD
structural/geotechnical engineering • MS, PhD
systems physiology • MS, PhD
transportational planning and engineering • MS, PhD

College of Health Sciences
Programs in:
health sciences • MS
speech-language pathology • MS

College of Nursing
Dr. Madeline Wake, Dean
Programs in:
adult nurse practitioner • Certificate
advanced practice nursing • MSN
gerontological nurse practitioner • Certificate
neonatal nurse practitioner • Certificate
nurse-midwifery • Certificate
pediatric nurse practitioner • Certificate

School of Education
Dr. Mary P. Hoy, Dean
Program in:
education • MA, Ed D, PhD, Spec

Law School
Howard B. Eisenberg, Dean
Program in:
law • JD

School of Dentistry
Dr. William L. Lobb, Dean
Programs in:
advanced training in general dentistry • MS
dental biomaterials • MS
dentistry • DDS, MS
endodontics • MS
orthodontics • MS
prosthodontics • MS

■ MOUNT MARY COLLEGE
Milwaukee, WI 53222-4597
http://www.mtmary.edu/

Independent-religious, women only, comprehensive institution. *Enrollment:* 36 full-time matriculated graduate/ professional students (all women), 92 part-time matriculated graduate/ professional students (87 women). *Graduate faculty:* 6 full-time (all women), 16 part-time/adjunct (14 women). *Computer facilities:* 74 computers available on campus for general student use. A campuswide network can be accessed from student residence rooms and from off campus. Internet access is available. *Library facilities:* Haggerty Library. *Graduate expenses:* Tuition: full-time $6,840; part-time $380 per credit. Required fees: $150; $40 per semester. One-time fee: $35. *General application contact:* Marci Ocker, Associate Academic Dean for Graduate Programs, 414-256-1252.

Graduate Programs
Sr. Jane Forni, SSND, Vice President for Academics and Student Affairs
Programs in:
administrative dietetics • MS
art therapy • MS
clinical dietetics • MS
education • MA
gerontology • MA
nutrition education • MS
occupational therapy • MS
professional development • MA

■ SILVER LAKE COLLEGE
Manitowoc, WI 54220-9319
http://www.sl.edu/

Independent-religious, coed, comprehensive institution. *Enrollment:* 80 full-time matriculated graduate/ professional students (32 women), 222 part-time matriculated graduate/ professional students (165 women). *Graduate faculty:* 1 (woman) full-time, 30 part-time/adjunct (14 women). *Computer facilities:* 50 computers available on campus for general student use. A campuswide network can be accessed from off campus. Internet access is available. *Library facilities:* The Erma M. and Theodore M. Zigmunt Library. *Graduate expenses:* Tuition: full-time $6,508; part-time $270 per credit. *General application contact:* Lori Salm, Office Manager, Admissions, 920-686-6175.

Graduate Studies
Sr. Michaela Melko, OSF, Director
Programs in:
administrative leadership • MA
management and organizational behavior • MS
music education • MM Ed
teacher leadership • MA

■ UNIVERSITY OF WISCONSIN–EAU CLAIRE
Eau Claire, WI 54702-4004
http://www.uwec.edu/

State-supported, coed, comprehensive institution. CGS member. *Enrollment:* 98 full-time matriculated graduate/ professional students (70 women), 231 part-time matriculated graduate/ professional students (179 women). *Graduate faculty:* 369 full-time (120 women), 21 part-time/adjunct (13 women). *Computer facilities:* 925 computers available on campus for general student use. A campuswide network can be accessed from student residence rooms and from off campus. Internet

University of Wisconsin–Eau Claire (continued)
access and online class registration are available. *Library facilities:* William D. McIntyre Library plus 1 other. *Graduate expenses:* Tuition, state resident: full-time $4,186; part-time $233 per credit. Tuition, nonresident: full-time $13,130; part-time $730 per credit. Tuition and fees vary according to program and reciprocity agreements. *General application contact:* Robert Lopez, Director of Admissions, 715-836-5415.

Find an in-depth description at www.petersons.com/graduate.

College of Arts and Sciences
Dr. Ted Wendt, Dean
Programs in:
- arts and sciences • MA, MS, MSE, Ed S
- biology • MS
- English • MA
- history • MA
- school psychology • MSE, Ed S

College of Business
Dr. V. Thomas Dock, Dean
Programs in:
- business • MBA
- business administration • MBA

College of Professional Studies
Dr. Mark Clark, Dean
Program in:
- professional studies • MAT, MEPD, MS, MSE, MSN, MST

School of Education
Dr. Stephen Kurth, Associate Dean
Programs in:
- biology • MAT, MST
- education • MAT, MEPD, MSE, MST
- education and professional development • MEPD
- elementary education • MST
- English • MAT, MST
- history • MAT, MST
- mathematics • MAT, MST
- reading • MST
- special education • MSE

School of Human Sciences and Services
Dr. Carol Klun, Dean
Programs in:
- communicative disorders • MS
- environmental and public health • MS
- human sciences and services • MS

School of Nursing
Dr. Rita Kisting Sparks, Associate Dean, Interim
Program in:
- nursing • MSN

■ UNIVERSITY OF WISCONSIN–GREEN BAY

Green Bay, WI 54311-7001
http://www.uwgb.edu/

State-supported, coed, comprehensive institution. *Enrollment:* 29 full-time matriculated graduate/professional students (16 women), 145 part-time matriculated graduate/professional students (90 women). *Graduate faculty:* 44 full-time (15 women), 15 part-time/adjunct (7 women). *Computer facilities:* 550 computers available on campus for general student use. A campuswide network can be accessed from student residence rooms and from off campus. Internet access and online class registration, on-line degree progress are available. *Library facilities:* Cofrin Library. *Graduate expenses:* Tuition, state resident: full-time $3,756; part-time $209 per credit. Tuition, nonresident: full-time $12,700; part-time $706 per credit. Required fees: $712; $40 per credit. Tuition and fees vary according to reciprocity agreements. *General application contact:* Ronald D. Stieglitz, Associate Dean of Graduate Studies, 920-465-2123.

Find an in-depth description at www.petersons.com/graduate.

Graduate Studies
Ronald D. Stieglitz, Associate Dean
Programs in:
- administrative science • MS
- applied leadership for teaching and learning • MS Ed
- environmental science and policy • MS

■ UNIVERSITY OF WISCONSIN–LA CROSSE

La Crosse, WI 54601-3742
http://www.uwlax.edu/

State-supported, coed, comprehensive institution. CGS member. *Computer facilities:* 560 computers available on campus for general student use. A campuswide network can be accessed from student residence rooms and from off campus. *Library facilities:* Murphy Library. *General application contact:* 608-785-8939.

Find an in-depth description at www.petersons.com/graduate.

Graduate Studies

College of Business Administration
Program in:
- business administration • MBA

College of Health, Physical Education and Recreation
Programs in:
- adult fitness/cardiac rehabilitation • MS
- community health • MS
- community health education • MPH
- general pedagogy • MS
- general sports administration • MS
- health, physical education and recreation • MPH, MS
- human performance • MS
- recreation • MS
- school health • MS
- special adaptive physical education • MS

College of Liberal Studies
Programs in:
- liberal studies • MS Ed, CAGS
- school psychology • MS Ed, CAGS

College of Science and Allied Health
Programs in:
- biology • MS
- clinical microbiology • MS
- nurse anesthetist • MS
- physical therapy • MSPT
- science and allied health • MS, MSPT

School of Education
Programs in:
- college student development and administration • MS Ed
- education • MEPD, MS Ed
- elementary education • MEPD
- emotional disturbance • MS Ed
- K–12 • MEPD
- learning disabilities • MS Ed
- professional development • MEPD
- reading • MS Ed
- secondary education • MEPD

■ UNIVERSITY OF WISCONSIN–MADISON

Madison, WI 53706-1380
http://www.wisc.edu/

State-supported, coed, university. CGS member. *Enrollment:* 9,051 full-time matriculated graduate/professional students (4,348 women), 1,943 part-time matriculated graduate/professional students (969 women). *Graduate faculty:* 2,109 full-time (505 women), 22 part-time/adjunct (9 women). *Computer facilities:* 2,800 computers available on campus for general student use. A campuswide network can be accessed from student residence rooms and from off campus. Internet access is available. *Library facilities:* Memorial Library plus 40 others. *Graduate expenses:* Tuition, state resident: full-time $2,943; part-time $370 per credit. Tuition, nonresident: full-time $9,298; part-time $1,164 per credit.

Required fees: $33 per term. *General application contact:* Graduate Admissions, 608-262-2433.

Graduate School
Dr. Virginia Hinshaw, Dean
Programs in:
- biophysics • PhD
- cellular and molecular biology • PhD
- developmental biology • PhD
- endocrinology-reproductive physiology • MS, PhD
- engineering • PDD
- neuroscience • MS, PhD
- professional practice • ME
- technical Japanese • ME

College of Agricultural and Life Sciences
Elton D. Aberle, Dean
Programs in:
- agricultural and applied economics • MA, MS, PhD
- agricultural and life sciences • MA, MBA, MS, PhD
- agricultural journalism • MS
- agronomy • MS, PhD
- anatomy • MS, PhD
- animal sciences • MS, PhD
- bacteriology • MS
- biochemistry • MS, PhD
- biological systems engineering • MS, PhD
- biometry • MS
- cellular and molecular biology • MS, PhD
- comparative biosciences • MS, PhD
- dairy science • MS, PhD
- development • PhD
- entomology • MS, PhD
- environmental toxicology • MS, PhD
- family and consumer journalism • MS
- food science • MS, PhD
- forest science • MS, PhD
- forestry • PhD
- genetics • PhD
- horticulture • MS, PhD
- landscape architecture • MA, MS
- mass communication • PhD
- medical genetics • MS
- molecular and environmental toxicology • MS, PhD
- natural resources • MA, MS, PhD
- neurosciences • MS, PhD
- nutritional sciences • MS, PhD
- pharmacology • MS, PhD
- physiology • MS, PhD
- plant breeding and plant genetics • MS, PhD
- plant pathology • MS, PhD
- recreation resources management • MS
- soil science • MS, PhD
- wildlife ecology • MS, PhD

College of Engineering
Paul S. Peercy, Acting Director
Programs in:
- chemical engineering • MS, PhD
- civil and environmental engineering • MS, PhD
- electrical engineering • MS, PhD
- engineering • ME, MS, PhD, PDD
- engineering mechanics • MS, PhD
- environmental chemistry and technology • MS, PhD
- geological engineering • MS, PhD
- industrial engineering • MS, PhD
- limnology and marine science • MS, PhD
- manufacturing systems engineering • MS
- materials science • MS, PhD
- mechanical engineering • MS, PhD
- metallurgical engineering • MS, PhD
- nuclear engineering and engineering physics • MS, PhD
- polymers • ME

College of Letters and Science
Phillip R. Certain, Dean
Programs in:
- African languages and literature • MA, PhD
- Afro-American studies • MA
- anthropology • MA, MS, PhD
- applied English linguistics • MA
- art history • MA, PhD
- astronomy • PhD
- atmospheric and oceanic sciences • MS, PhD
- biological psychology • PhD
- botany • MS, PhD
- cartography and geographic information systems • MS
- chemistry • MS, PhD
- Chinese • MA, PhD
- choral • MM, DMA
- classics • MA, PhD
- clinical psychology • PhD
- cognitive and perceptual sciences • PhD
- communication arts • MA, PhD
- communicative disorders • MS, PhD
- comparative literature • MA, PhD
- composition • MM, DMA
- composition studies • PhD
- computer sciences • MS, PhD
- curriculum and instruction • PhD
- developmental psychology • PhD
- economics • PhD
- English language and linguistics • PhD
- ethnomusicology • MM, PhD
- family and consumer journalism • PhD
- French • MA, PhD
- French studies • MFS, Certificate
- geographic information systems • Certificate
- geography • MS, PhD
- geology • MS, PhD
- geophysics • MS, PhD
- German • MA, PhD
- Greek • MA
- Hebrew and Semitic studies • MA, PhD
- history • MA, PhD
- history of science • MA, PhD
- industrial relations • MA, MS, PhD
- instrumental • MM, DMA
- international public affairs • MPIA
- Italian • MA, PhD
- Japanese • MA, PhD
- journalism and mass communication • MA
- languages and cultures of Asia • MA, PhD
- Latin • MA
- Latin American, Caribbean and Iberian studies • MA
- letters and science • MA, MFA, MFS, MM, MPA, MPIA, MS, MSSW, DMA, PhD, Certificate
- library and information studies • MA, PhD, Certificate
- linguistics • MA, PhD
- literature • MA, PhD
- mass communication • PhD
- mathematics • MA, PhD
- music • MA, MM, DMA, PhD
- music education • MM
- musicology • MA, MM, PhD
- performance • MM, DMA
- philosophy • MA, PhD
- physics • MA, MS, PhD
- political science • MA, PhD
- Portuguese • MA, PhD
- psychology • PhD
- public affairs • MPA
- rural sociology • MS
- Scandinavian studies • MA, PhD
- Slavic languages and literature • MA, PhD
- social and personality psychology • PhD
- social welfare • PhD
- social work • MSSW
- sociology • MS, PhD
- Southeast Asian studies • MA
- Spanish • MA, PhD
- statistics • MS, PhD
- theatre and drama • MA, MFA, PhD
- theory • MA, MM, PhD
- urban and regional planning • MS, PhD
- zoology • MA, MS, PhD

Institute for Environmental Studies
Thomas M. Yuill, Director
Programs in:
- conservation biology and sustainable development • MS
- environmental monitoring • MS, PhD
- environmental studies • MS, PhD
- land resources • MS, PhD
- water resources management • MS

University of Wisconsin–Madison (continued)

School of Business
Dr. Andrew J. Policano, Dean
Programs in:
accounting • M Acc, MBA, MS, PhD
actuarial science • MS, PhD
agribusiness • MBA
arts administration • MA
business • M Acc, MA, MBA, MS, PhD
business administration • MBA
entrepreneurship • MBA
finance, investment, and banking • MBA, MS
general management • MBA
information systems analysis and design • MBA, MS
international business • MBA, MS
management and human resources • MBA, MS
manufacturing and technology management • MBA, MS
marketing • MBA
marketing research • MBA, MS
operations and information management • MBA, MS
real estate and urban land economics • MBA, MS
real estate appraisal and investment analysis • MS
risk management and insurance • MBA, MS, PhD
supply chain management • MBA, MS

School of Education
Programs in:
art • MA, MFA
art education • MA
chemistry education • MS
commercial arts education • MA
continuing and vocational education • MS, PhD
counseling • MS
counseling psychology • PhD
curriculum and instruction • MS, PhD
education • MA, MFA, MS, PhD
education and mathematics • MA
educational administration • MS, PhD
educational policy studies • MA, PhD
educational psychology • MS, PhD
English education • MA
French education • MA
geography education • MS
German education • MA
kinesiology • MS, PhD
Latin education • MA
music education • MS
physics education • MS
rehabilitation psychology • MA, MS, PhD
science education • MS
Spanish education • MA
special education • MA, MS, PhD
therapeutic science • MS

School of Human Ecology
Robin A. Douthitt, Dean
Programs in:
consumer behavior and family economics • MS, PhD
continuing and vocational education • MS, PhD
design • MS, PhD
family and consumer journalism • MS, PhD
human development and family studies • MS, PhD

Law School
Kenneth B. Davis, Dean
Programs in:
law • JD, LL M, MLI, SJD
legal institutions • MLI

Medical School
Dr. Philip M. Farrell, Dean
Programs in:
medicine • MD, MS, PhD

Graduate Programs in Medicine
Dr. Paul M. DeLuca, Associate Dean of Research and Graduate Studies
Programs in:
biomolecular chemistry • MS, PhD
genetics and medical genetics • MS, PhD
health physics • MS
medical physics • MS, PhD
microbiology • PhD
molecular and cellular pharmacology • PhD
neurophysiology • PhD
oncology • PhD
pathology and laboratory medicine • PhD
physiology • PhD
population health • MS, PhD

School of Nursing
Program in:
nursing • MS, PhD

School of Pharmacy
Programs in:
pharmaceutical sciences • MS, PhD
pharmacy • Pharm D, MS, PhD
social and administrative sciences in pharmacy • MS, PhD

School of Veterinary Medicine
Program in:
veterinary medicine • DVM, MS, PhD

■ UNIVERSITY OF WISCONSIN–MILWAUKEE
Milwaukee, WI 53201-0413
http://www.uwm.edu/

State-supported, coed, university. CGS member. *Enrollment:* 1,474 full-time matriculated graduate/professional students (851 women), 2,072 part-time matriculated graduate/professional students (1,236 women). *Graduate faculty:* 735 full-time (251 women). *Computer facilities:* 310 computers available on campus for general student use. A campuswide network can be accessed from off campus. *Library facilities:* Golda Meir Library. *Graduate expenses:* Tuition, state resident: full-time $5,722; part-time $497 per credit. Tuition, nonresident: full-time $17,678; part-time $1,245 per credit. Full-time tuition and fees vary according to program and reciprocity agreements. Part-time tuition and fees vary according to course load and program. *General application contact:* General Information Contact, 412-229-4982.

Graduate School
Wiliam R. Rayburn, Dean of the Graduate School and Associate Provost for Research

College of Engineering and Applied Science
Dr. William Gregory, Dean
Programs in:
computer science • MS, PhD
engineering • MS, PhD
engineering and applied science • MS, PhD

College of Letters and Sciences
Richard Meadows, Acting Dean
Programs in:
anthropology • MS, PhD
art history • MA
art museum studies • Certificate
biological sciences • MS, PhD
chemistry • MS, PhD
classics and Hebrew studies • MAFLL
clinical psychology • MS, PhD
communication • MA
comparative literature • MAFLL
economics • MA, PhD
English • MA, PhD
French and Italian • MAFLL
geography • MA, MS
geological sciences • MS, PhD
German • MAFLL
history • MA
human resources and labor relations • MHRLR
journalism and mass communication • MA
letters and sciences • MA, MAFLL, MHRLR, MILR, MPA, MS, PhD, Certificate
mathematics • MS, PhD
philosophy • MA
physics • MS, PhD
political science • MA, PhD

psychology • MS, PhD
public administration • MPA
Slavic studies • MAFLL
sociology • MA
Spanish • MAFLL
urban studies • MS, PhD

School of Allied Health Professions
Randall Lambrecht, Representative
Programs in:
allied health professions • MS
clinical laboratory science • MS
communication sciences and disorders • MS
human kinetics • MS
occupational therapy • MS

School of Architecture and Urban Planning
Robert Greenstreet, Dean
Programs in:
architecture • M Arch, PhD
architecture and urban planning • M Arch, MUP, PhD
urban planning • MUP

School of Business Administration
Sarah Sandin, Representative
Program in:
business administration • MBA, MS, PhD

School of Education
Dr. Mohammed Aman, Interim Dean
Programs in:
administrative leadership and supervision in education • MS
cultural foundations of education • MS
curriculum planning and instruction improvement • MS
early childhood education • MS
education • MS, PhD
educational psychology • MS
educational rehabilitation counseling • MS
elementary education • MS
exceptional education • MS
junior high/middle school education • MS
reading education • MS
secondary education • MS
teaching in an urban setting • MS
urban education • PhD

School of Information Studies
Wilfred Fong, Assistant Dean
Program in:
information studies • MLIS, CAS

School of Multidisciplinary Studies
Program in:
multidisciplinary studies • PhD

School of Nursing
Sue Dean-Baar, Representative
Program in:
nursing • MS, PhD

School of Social Welfare
James A. Blackburn, Dean
Programs in:
criminal justice • MS
social welfare • MS, MSW
social work • MSW

School of the Arts
Robert Greenstreet, Acting Dean
Programs in:
art • MA, MFA
art education • MA, MFA, MS
arts • MA, MFA, MM, MS
dance • MFA
film • MFA
music • MM
theatre • MFA

■ UNIVERSITY OF WISCONSIN–OSHKOSH
Oshkosh, WI 54901
http://www.uwosh.edu/

State-supported, coed, comprehensive institution. *Enrollment:* 190 full-time matriculated graduate/professional students (148 women), 1,012 part-time matriculated graduate/professional students (604 women). *Graduate faculty:* 265 full-time (83 women), 17 part-time/adjunct (7 women). *Computer facilities:* 475 computers available on campus for general student use. A campuswide network can be accessed from student residence rooms and from off campus. Internet access and online class registration are available. *Library facilities:* Forrest R. Polk Library. *Graduate expenses:* Tuition, state resident: full-time $4,186. Tuition, nonresident: full-time $13,130. Tuition and fees vary according to course load and program. *General application contact:* Gregory B. Wypiszynski, Coordinator of Graduate Studies, 920-424-1223.

Graduate School
Dr. Nancy Kaufman, Assistant Vice Chancellor

College of Business Administration
Dr. E. Alan Hartman, Dean
Programs in:
business administration • MBA, MS
information systems • MS

College of Education and Human Services
Dr. Carmen I. Coballes-Vega, Dean
Programs in:
counseling • MSE
curriculum and instruction • MSE
early childhood: exceptional education needs • MSE
education and human services • MS, MSE
educational leadership • MS
emotionally disturbed • MSE
learning disabilities • MSE
mental retardation • MSE
reading education • MSE

College of Letters and Science
Dr. Michael Zimmerman, Dean
Programs in:
biology • MS
English • MA
experimental psychology • MS
health care • MPA
industrial/organizational psychology • MS
letters and science • MA, MPA, MS
mathematics education • MS
physics • MS
public administration • MPA
speech and hearing science • MS

College of Nursing
Dr. Merritt Knox, Dean
Programs in:
family nurse practitioner • MSN
primary health care • MSN

■ UNIVERSITY OF WISCONSIN–PARKSIDE
Kenosha, WI 53141-2000
http://www.uwp.edu/

State-supported, coed, comprehensive institution. *Enrollment:* 14 full-time matriculated graduate/professional students (9 women), 135 part-time matriculated graduate/professional students (68 women). *Graduate faculty:* 28 full-time. *Computer facilities:* 180 computers available on campus for general student use. A campuswide network can be accessed from student residence rooms and from off campus. *Library facilities:* Library-Learning Center. *Graduate expenses:* Full-time $4,258; part-time $251 per credit. Tuition, nonresident: full-time $13,202; part-time $748 per credit. Required fees: $236; $27 per credit. Tuition and fees vary according to program. *General application contact:* Dr. Ronald Singer, Graduate Dean, 262-595-2266.

College of Arts and Sciences
Dr. Donald Cress, Dean
Programs in:
applied molecular biology • MAMB
arts and sciences • M Ed, MAMB
education • M Ed

University of Wisconsin–Parkside (continued)

School of Business and Technology
Dr. Marwan Wafa, Dean
Program in:
business and technology • MBA

■ UNIVERSITY OF WISCONSIN–PLATTEVILLE

Platteville, WI 53818-3099
http://www.uwplatt.edu/

State-supported, coed, comprehensive institution. *Enrollment:* 33 full-time matriculated graduate/professional students (23 women), 84 part-time matriculated graduate/professional students (58 women). *Graduate faculty:* 5 full-time (2 women), 90 part-time/adjunct (16 women). *Computer facilities:* 250 computers available on campus for general student use. A campuswide network can be accessed from student residence rooms and from off campus. Internet access is available. *Library facilities:* Karrmann Library. *Graduate expenses:* Tuition, state resident: full-time $4,438; part-time $246 per credit. Tuition, nonresident: full-time $13,919; part-time $773 per credit. Tuition and fees vary according to program. *General application contact:* Laurie Schuler, Admissions and Enrollment Management, 608-342-1125.

School of Graduate Studies
Dr. David P. Van Buren, Interim Dean
Programs in:
criminal justice • MS
engineering • ME
project management • MS

College of Business, Industry, Life Science, and Agriculture
Dr. Duane Ford, Dean
Programs in:
business, industry, life science, and agriculture • MS
industrial technology management • MS

College of Liberal Arts and Education
Dr. Sally Standiford, Director
Programs in:
adult education • MSE
counselor education • MSE
elementary education • MSE
liberal arts and education • MSE
middle school education • MSE
secondary education • MSE
vocational and technical education • MSE

Distance Learning Center
Dawn Drake, Executive Director
Programs in:
criminal justice • MS
engineering • ME
project management • MS

■ UNIVERSITY OF WISCONSIN–RIVER FALLS

River Falls, WI 54022-5001
http://www.uwrf.edu/

State-supported, coed, comprehensive institution. CGS member. *Enrollment:* 141 full-time matriculated graduate/professional students (99 women), 205 part-time matriculated graduate/professional students (158 women). *Graduate faculty:* 234 full-time (69 women), 5 part-time/adjunct. *Computer facilities:* 387 computers available on campus for general student use. A campuswide network can be accessed from student residence rooms and from off campus. Internet access and online class registration are available. *Library facilities:* Chalmer Davee Library. *Graduate expenses:* Tuition, state resident: full-time $2,454. Tuition and fees vary according to campus/location. *General application contact:* Julia Persico, Graduate Admissions, 715-425-3843.

School of Graduate and Professional Studies
Dr. Karen Viechnicki, Dean

College of Agriculture, Food, and Environmental Sciences
Gary E. Rohde, Dean
Programs in:
agricultural education • MS
agriculture, food, and environmental sciences • MS

College of Arts and Science
Gorden O. Hedahl, Dean
Programs in:
arts and science • MSE
language, literature, and communication education • MSE
mathematics education • MSE
science education • MSE
social science education • MSE

College of Education and Graduate Studies
Dr. Karen Viechnicki, Dean
Programs in:
communicative disorders • MS
counseling • MSE
education • MS, MSE
elementary education • MSE
reading • MSE
school psychology • MSE

■ UNIVERSITY OF WISCONSIN–STEVENS POINT

Stevens Point, WI 54481-3897
http://www.uwsp.edu/

State-supported, coed, comprehensive institution. *Enrollment:* 103 full-time matriculated graduate/professional students (80 women), 192 part-time matriculated graduate/professional students (137 women). *Graduate faculty:* 262 full-time (69 women), 18 part-time/adjunct (7 women). *Computer facilities:* 700 computers available on campus for general student use. A campuswide network can be accessed from student residence rooms and from off campus. Internet access is available. *Library facilities:* Learning Resources Center. *Graduate expenses:* Tuition, state resident: full-time $4,225; part-time $257 per credit. Tuition, nonresident: full-time $13,169; part-time $754 per credit. *General application contact:* David Eckholm, Director of Admissions, 715-346-2441.

College of Fine Arts and Communication
Gerard McKenna, Dean
Programs in:
fine arts and communication • MA, MM Ed
interpersonal communication • MA
mass communication • MA
music • MM Ed
organizational communication • MA
public relations • MA

College of Letters and Science
Justus Paul, Dean
Programs in:
business and economics • MBA
English • MST
history • MST
letters and science • MBA, MST

College of Natural Resources
Dr. Christina Thomas, Associate Dean
Program in:
natural resources • MS

College of Professional Studies
Joan North, Dean
Program in:
professional studies • MS, MSE

School of Communicative Disorders
Dr. Dennis Nash, Head
Program in:
communicative disorders • MS

School of Education
Dr. Leslie McClaine-Ruelle, Head
Programs in:
- education—general/reading • MSE
- educational administration • MSE
- elementary education • MSE
- guidance and counseling • MSE

School of Health Promotion and Human Development
John Munson, Associate Dean
Programs in:
- human and community resources • MS
- nutritional sciences • MS

■ UNIVERSITY OF WISCONSIN–STOUT
Menomonie, WI 54751
http://www.uwstout.edu/

State-supported, coed, comprehensive institution. *Enrollment:* 267 full-time matriculated graduate/professional students (178 women), 251 part-time matriculated graduate/professional students (152 women). *Graduate faculty:* 194 full-time (64 women). *Computer facilities:* 590 computers available on campus for general student use. A campuswide network can be accessed from student residence rooms and from off campus. Internet access and online class registration are available. *Library facilities:* Library Learning Center. *Graduate expenses:* Tuition, state resident: full-time $4,480. Tuition, nonresident: full-time $12,344. *General application contact:* Anne E. Johnson, Graduate Student Evaluator, 715-232-1322.

Graduate School
Julie Furst-Bowe, Associate Vice Chancellor

College of Human Development
Dr. John Wesolek, Dean
Programs in:
- applied psychology • MS
- counseling and psychological services • MS, Ed S
- education • MS
- food and nutritional sciences • MS
- home economics • MS
- hospitality and tourism • MS
- human development • MS, MS Ed, Ed S
- marriage and family therapy • MS
- school psychology • MS Ed, Ed S
- vocational rehabilitation • MS

College of Technology, Engineering, and Management
Dr. Bob Meyer, Dean
Programs in:
- industrial and vocational education • Ed S
- industrial/technology education • MS
- management technology • MS
- risk control • MS
- technology, engineering, and management • MS, Ed S
- training and development • MS
- vocational education • MS

■ UNIVERSITY OF WISCONSIN–SUPERIOR
Superior, WI 54880-4500
http://www.uwsuper.edu/

State-supported, coed, comprehensive institution. CGS member. *Enrollment:* 99 full-time matriculated graduate/professional students (67 women), 277 part-time matriculated graduate/professional students (176 women). *Graduate faculty:* 92 full-time (24 women), 27 part-time/adjunct (11 women). *Computer facilities:* 125 computers available on campus for general student use. A campuswide network can be accessed from student residence rooms and from off campus. Internet access and online class registration are available. *Library facilities:* Jim Dan Hill Library. *Graduate expenses:* Tuition, state resident: full-time $2,083; part-time $288 per credit. Tuition, nonresident: full-time $6,555; part-time $785 per credit. *General application contact:* Evelyn Hagfeldt, Program Assistant/Status Examiner, 715-394-8295.

Graduate Division
Dr. Rosemary Keefe, Dean of Facilities
Programs in:
- art education • MA
- art history • MA
- art therapy • MA
- community counseling • MSE
- educational administration • MSE, Ed S
- elementary school counseling • MSE
- emotionally disturbed learners • MSE
- human relations • MSE
- instruction • MSE
- learning disabilities • MSE
- mass communication • MA
- secondary school counseling • MSE
- special education • MSE
- speech communication • MA
- studio arts • MA
- teaching reading • MSE
- theater • MA

■ UNIVERSITY OF WISCONSIN–WHITEWATER
Whitewater, WI 53190-1790
http://www.uww.edu/

State-supported, coed, comprehensive institution. CGS member. *Enrollment:* 238 full-time matriculated graduate/professional students (162 women), 882 part-time matriculated graduate/professional students (570 women). *Graduate faculty:* 285. *Computer facilities:* 700 computers available on campus for general student use. A campuswide network can be accessed from student residence rooms and from off campus. *Library facilities:* Andersen Library. *Graduate expenses:* Tuition, state resident: full-time $4,215; part-time $234 per credit. Tuition, nonresident: full-time $13,159; part-time $73 per credit. One-time fee: $45. Tuition and fees vary according to course load and program. *General application contact:* Sally A. Lange, School of Graduate Studies, 262-472-1006.

School of Graduate Studies
Dr. Richard Lee, Dean

College of Arts and Communications
Dr. John Heyer, Dean
Programs in:
- arts and communications • MS
- corporate/public communication • MS
- mass communication • MS

College of Business and Economics
Dr. Joseph Domitrz, Dean
Programs in:
- accounting • MPA
- business administration • MBA
- business and economics • MBA, MPA, MS, MS Ed
- business education • MS
- management computer systems • MS
- school business management • MS Ed

College of Education
Dr. Jeffrey Barnett, Dean
Programs in:
- communicative disorders • MS
- counselor education • MS
- curriculum and instruction • MS
- education • MS, MS Ed
- educational administration • MS Ed
- reading • MS Ed
- safety • MS
- special education • MS Ed

College of Letters and Sciences
Dr. Howard Ross, Dean
Programs in:

University of Wisconsin–Whitewater (continued)

letters and sciences • MPA, MS Ed
public administration • MPA
school psychology • MS Ed

■ VITERBO UNIVERSITY

La Crosse, WI 54601-4797
http://www.viterbo.edu/

Independent-religious, coed, comprehensive institution. *Computer facilities:* 180 computers available on campus for general student use. A campuswide network can be accessed from student residence rooms and from off campus. Internet access, e-mail are available. *Library facilities:* Todd Wehr Memorial Library. *General application contact:* Director of Graduate Studies, 608-796-3090.

Graduate Program in Education

Program in:
education • MA

Graduate Program in Nursing

Bonnie Nesbitt, Director
Program in:
nursing • MSN

Wyoming

■ UNIVERSITY OF WYOMING

Laramie, WY 82071
http://www.uwyo.edu/

State-supported, coed, university. CGS member. *Enrollment:* 986 full-time matriculated graduate/professional students (466 women), 657 part-time matriculated graduate/professional students (360 women). *Graduate faculty:* 609 full-time (136 women), 60 part-time/adjunct (21 women). *Computer facilities:* 1,270 computers available on campus for general student use. A campuswide network can be accessed from student residence rooms and from off campus. Internet access and online class registration are available. *Library facilities:* Coe Library plus 7 others. *Graduate expenses:* Full-time $2,708. Tuition, state resident: part-time $150 per credit hour. Tuition, nonresident: full-time $7,790; part-time $433 per credit hour. Required fees: $409; $10 per credit hour. *General application contact:* Julie Houchin, Credentials Analyst/Advising Assistant, 307-766-2287.

Find an in-depth description at www.petersons.com/graduate.

College of Law

Jerry Parkinson, Dean
Program in:
law • JD

Graduate School

Dr. Stephen E. Williams, Dean

College of Agriculture

Steven Horn, Dean
Programs in:
agricultural and applied economics • MS
agriculture • MS, PhD
agronomy • MS, PhD
animal sciences • MS, PhD
entomology • MS, PhD
family and consumer sciences • MS
food science and human nutrition • MS
molecular biology • MS, PhD
pathobiology • MS
rangeland ecology and watershed management • MS, PhD
reproductive biology • MS, PhD

College of Arts and Sciences

Oliver Walter, Dean
Programs in:
American studies • MA
anthropology • MA
arts and sciences • MA, MAT, MFA, MM, MP, MPA, MS, MST, Pro MS, PhD
botany • MS, PhD
botany/water resources • MS
chemistry • MS, PhD
communication • MA
community and regional planning and natural resources • MP
computer science • MS, Pro MS, PhD
English • MA
French • MA
geography • MA, MP, MST
geography/water resources • MA
geology • MS, PhD
geophysics • MS, PhD
German • MA
history • MA, MAT
history and literature • MA
international studies • MA
mathematics • MA, MAT, MS, MST, PhD
mathematics/computer science • PhD
music education • MA
natural science • MS, MST
performance • MM
philosophy • MA
political science • MA
psychology • MA, MS, PhD
public administration • MPA
rural planning and natural resources • MP
sociology • MA
Spanish • MA
statistics • MS, PhD
theory and composition • MA
zoology and physiology • MS, PhD

College of Business

Dr. Kenyon Griffin, Interim Dean
Programs in:
accounting • MS
business • MBA, MS, PhD
business administration • MBA
economics • MS, PhD
finance • MS

College of Education

Dr. Charles Ksir, Dean
Programs in:
adult and postsecondary education • MA, Ed D, PhD
education • Ed S
education and curriculum and instruction • PhD
education curriculum and instruction • MA, Ed D, PhD
instructional technology • MS, Ed D, PhD
teaching and learning • MA

College of Engineering

Dr. Kynric Pell, Dean
Programs in:
atmospheric science • MS, PhD
chemical engineering • MS, PhD
civil engineering • MS, PhD
electrical engineering • MS, PhD
engineering • MS, PhD
environmental engineering • MS
mechanical engineering • MS, PhD
petroleum engineering • MS, PhD

College of Health Sciences

Dr. Robert O. Kelly, Dean
Programs in:
audiology • MS
health sciences • MS, MSW
nursing • MS
physical and health education • MS
social work • MSW
speech-language pathology • MS

School Index